Home Id 875 6993

D0607113

Geography and Development

FIFTH EDITION

Geography and Development

A World Regional Approach

Edited by

James S. Fisher

Florida Atlantic University

Prentice Hall
Englewood Cliffs, New Jersey 07632

Library of Congress Cataloging-in-Publication Data
Geography and development : a world regional
approach. — 5th ed. / edited by James S. Fisher.
   p. cm.
  Includes bibliographical references and index.
  ISBN 0-02-337941-3
  1. Economic development. 2. Economic
history. 3. Economic geography.
 4. Developing countries—Economic
conditions.
 I. Fisher, James S. (James Samuel)
 HD82.G39 1995
 330.9—dc20   94-23582
            CIP

Cover: Vietnam street scene: Tom Wagner/SABA;
antique map background: Westlight Map file.

Acquisitions Editor: Paul F. Corey
Production Editor: Mary Harlan
Copy Editor: Dan Duffee
Photo Researchers: Julie Tesser, Clare Maxwell
Cover Designer: Marianne Frasco
Production Buyer: Patricia A. Tonneman
Illustrations: Maryland CartoGraphics

This book was set in Garamond by Carlisle
Communications, Ltd., and was printed and bound by
Von Hoffmann Press, Inc. The cover was printed by
Von Hoffmann Press, Inc.

Printed in the United States of America

10 9 8 7 6 5 4 3 2 1

ISBN: 0-02-337941-3

Prentice-Hall International (UK) Limited, *London*
Prentice-Hall of Australia Pty. Limited, *Sydney*
Prentice-Hall of Canada, Inc., *Toronto*
Prentice-Hall Hispanoamericana, S. A., *Mexico*
Prentice-Hall of India Private Limited, *New Delhi*
Prentice-Hall of Japan, Inc., *Tokyo*
Simon & Schuster Asia Pte. Ltd., *Singapore*
Editora Prentice-Hall do Brasil, Ltda., *Rio de Janeiro*

Acknowledgments for figures and photographs appear
on pp. 705–707.

The Goode's Homolosine Equal-Area Projection base
maps in this text are used by permission of the
University of Chicago Committee on Geographic Studies.
Goode Base Map Series Copyright © The University of
Chicago.

Contributors

Leonard Berry
Florida Atlantic University

David L. Clawson
University of New Orleans

Louis De Vorsey, Jr.
University of Georgia

James S. Fisher
Florida Atlantic University

Douglas L. Johnson
Clark University

Clifton W. Pannell
University of Georgia

Roger L. Thiede
University of Wisconsin–Eau Claire

Jack F. Williams
Michigan State University

This political map reveals a highly compartmentalized world. The numerous political entities range in size from the vast area of Russia to minute but significant countries such as Singapore, Malta, and Grenada. The names of those political entities evoke images of different environments, peoples, cultures, and levels of well-being. However, the political boundaries that segregate more than 5 billion inhabitants do not clearly reflect the underlying geographic complexities of our world. Numerous other sets of boundaries could be imposed: boundaries that delineate multinational alliances, boundaries that classify economic and agricultural environments, boundaries that outline the world's myriad peoples, languages, and ideologies. Unraveling the complexities of our world requires intellectual attention to many questions relating to geography. This map and the chapters that follow are intended to start the student on a journey toward understanding our exciting and complex world.

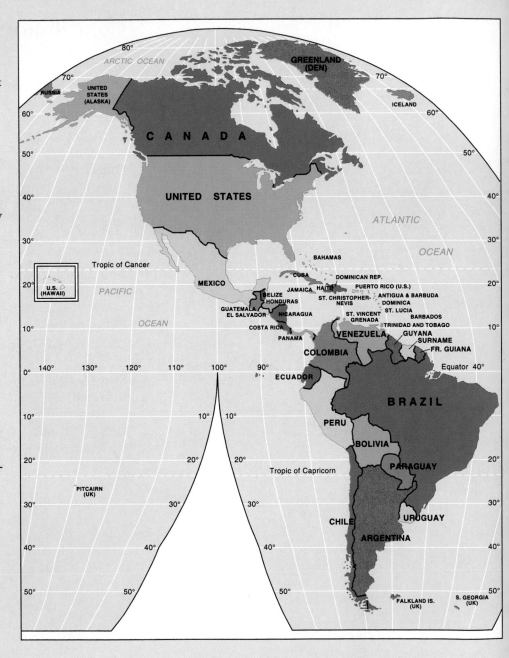

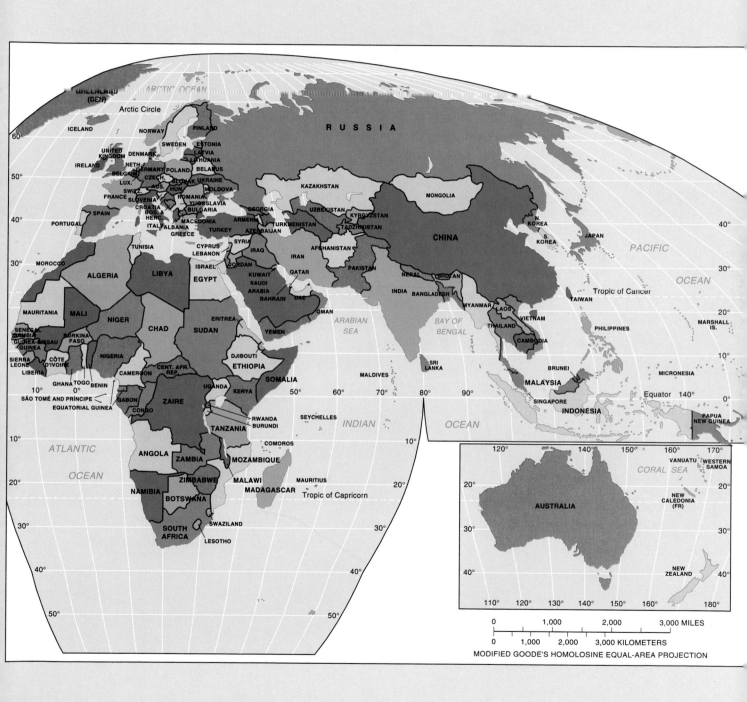

GREENLAND (DEN)

ARCTIC OCEAN

Arctic Circle

ICELAND

NORWAY FINLAND

SWEDEN ESTONIA
LATVIA
LITHUANIA
BELARUS

UNITED
KINGDOM DENMARK

IRELAND

NETH.
BELGIUM GERMANY POLAND
LUX. CZECH.
SWITZ. AUS. HUN. SLOVAK UKRAINE
FRANCE SLOVENIA ROMANIA MOLDOVA
CROATIA BOS.- YUGOSLAVIA
HERC. BULGARIA
SPAIN ITALY ALBANIA MACEDONIA
GREECE TURKEY

PORTUGAL

RUSSIA

60°

50°

40°

KAZAKHSTAN

MONGOLIA

GEORGIA
ARMENIA
AZERBAIJAN

UZBEKISTAN
KYRGYZSTAN
TURKMENISTAN TADZHIKISTAN

CHINA

N.
KOREA

JAPAN

S.
KOREA

PACIFIC

OCEAN

CYPRUS
LEBANON SYRIA
ISRAEL IRAQ
JORDAN

TUNISIA

MOROCCO

ALGERIA LIBYA EGYPT

30°

IRAN AFGHANISTAN

PAKISTAN

NEPAL BHUTAN

Tropic of Cancer

TAIWAN

KUWAIT
SAUDI QATAR
ARABIA
BAHRAIN UAE

INDIA BANGLADESH

MYANMAR LAOS
VIETNAM

40°

30°

MARSHALL
IS.

MAURITANIA MALI
NIGER

ERITREA
CHAD SUDAN

OMAN

YEMEN

ARABIAN
SEA

BAY OF
BENGAL

THAILAND

PHILIPPINES

CAMBODIA

20°

SENEGAL
GAMBIA
GUINEA-BISSAU BURKINA
GUINEA FASO
SIERRA NIGERIA
LEONE CÔTE
LIBERIA D'IVOIRE
GHANA TOGO BENIN
SÃO TOMÉ AND PRÍNCIPE CAMEROON
EQUATORIAL GUINEA GABON

CENT. AFR.
REP.

DJIBOUTI

ETHIOPIA

SOMALIA

MALDIVES

SRI
LANKA

BRUNEI

MALAYSIA

MICRONESIA

10°

CONGO ZAIRE

UGANDA
KENYA

Equator 140°

SINGAPORE

INDONESIA

0°

10°

TANZANIA

RWANDA
BURUNDI

SEYCHELLES

INDIAN

OCEAN

PAPUA
NEW GUINEA

ATLANTIC

ANGOLA ZAMBIA

COMOROS

MOZAMBIQUE

10°

OCEAN

NAMIBIA

ZIMBABWE
BOTSWANA

MALAWI
MADAGASCAR

MAURITIUS

Tropic of Capricorn

20°

SOUTH
AFRICA

SWAZILAND

LESOTHO

30°

40°

50°

120° 140° 150° 160° 170°

VANUATU WESTERN
SAMOA

CORAL SEA

20°

AUSTRALIA

NEW
CALEDONIA
(FR)

30°

110° 120° 130° 140° 150° 160°

NEW
ZEALAND

180°

40°

0 1,000 2,000 3,000 MILES

0 1,000 2,000 3,000 KILOMETERS

MODIFIED GOODE'S HOMOLOSINE EQUAL-AREA PROJECTION

Preface

Increasing development in faraway places is leading to a more interdependent world. Rapid advances in transportation, technology, and electronic communication are speeding up commercial, cultural, economic, and political interaction among countries and regions. One outgrowth of these changes is a global economy, which depends on the efficient exchange of raw materials and manufactured goods all over the world. Another consequence is the international impact of local politics. Because of political and economic linkages, unrest such as that in the Middle East affects Africa, Europe, the countries of the former Soviet Union, Japan, and the United States. In a sense, this movement toward global interdependence has made our world smaller and the study of it even more exciting. It certainly has underscored the need to study differences in physical and human geography from place to place.

College students are in a unique position to increase their understanding of the world and to use that knowledge to benefit themselves and others. Through the study of world regional geography, we begin to comprehend the issues involved in the pursuit of world peace, preservation of the environment, improved health, and higher levels of living. In fact, the Association of American Geographers, the National Geographic Society, and the National Council for Geographic Education have devoted significant resources and effort to improving geographic awareness. Even the U.S. Congress has cited geographic education as critical to our increasingly interdependent world.

This fifth edition of *Geography and Development: A World Regional Approach* is dedicated to college students who are seeking a better understanding of this complex and challenging world. It is written for both majors and nonmajors and does not require an extensive background in geography. We have retained the basic regional structure of the fourth edition, and our multiple-author approach permits each region to be discussed by one or two scholars who are experts in that area. Although our fields of expertise vary, we are united in our dedication to expanding geographical awareness. The differing perspectives on geography and development that emerge add strength to our overall presentation.

Geography and Development opens with four chapters that consider geography as a discipline, population and resources, physical and cultural elements of the environment, and the world condition as it relates to human development. Eight additional parts—twenty-four chapters—follow, organized within a regional framework. Within this regional framework students are introduced to basic geographical concepts and the essential geography and development of our world.

Although we encourage use of this text as an entity, its organization allows a variety of teaching strategies. As time requires, sections treating historical or environmental process, or specific regions, can be selectively emphasized or deleted. In a two-quarter or two-semester sequence, the book facilitates consideration along continental or regional divisions or along the lines of more developed–less developed countries. The suggested further readings at the end of each part can then be used to supplement the text; table and figure references can encourage students to pursue external data sources and analysis.

Geography and Development: A World Regional Approach contains numerous features that are designed to assist and stimulate students:

- More than one hundred full-color maps have been rendered by a professional cartographic studio, incorporating the latest boundary and name changes.

- Specially chosen color photographs, carefully integrated into the text, help communicate the personality of individual regions.
- Informative tables, graphs, and charts supplement textual material.
- Every chapter includes at least one boxed feature on a topic of special regional significance, such as population growth, environmental problems, food production, migration, manufacturing, or distinctive regional features.
- Each of the nine parts opens with a brief statement of intent and emphasis for the regions under consideration.
- Selected terms are presented in boldface type within the text and at the end of each chapter, and they are defined in a convenient glossary at the end of the book.
- Each part ends with a list of further readings for students who wish to deepen and broaden their understanding of particular topics.
- Appendix A provides information on map projections and scale. We are grateful to Phillip Muehrcke, professor of geography at the University of Wisconsin—Madison and former president of the American Cartographic Association, for his clear explanation of this complex subject.
- Appendix B includes a table of selected national statistics so that students can compare countries and regions.
- Measurements throughout the text are given in both English and metric equivalents. A convenient table of conversion factors is found in Appendix C.
- A study guide is available to help students assimilate concepts and information on regions under consideration.

For the instructor, a number of supplements are available—an instructor's manual, a computerized test bank, slides, and transparencies. (Please contact the publisher for more information.)

Our ultimate hope is that this book, in concert with teachers and other sources, will help students develop a better appreciation of the fascinating geography of our world. Indeed, that geography continues to change, for even as we go to press the people of the former Soviet Union and the Baltic states struggle to discern their approach to the organization of their space for the twenty-first century.

ACKNOWLEDGMENTS

The authors have been blessed with the help of several reviewers during the preparation of this fifth edition of *Geography and Development*. The suggestions and comments of these individuals have been indispensable. Two interesting features of their comments should be noted. First, many of their suggestions have addressed the needs of contemporary students who are seeking an understanding of our world. Second, the sometimes polar perspectives of the reviewers on regional problems in the Middle East, international trade, population growth and development, environmental degradation, cultural value systems, and other issue-laden topics have served to remind us of the variety of valid opinions on world problems and the consequent difficulty in solving them.

Neither original nor revised editions are accomplished by authors working in isolation. We owe thanks to numerous people for encouragement and tangible effort on behalf of our project. Specifically, we express gratitude for the team effort of Prentice Hall. Their staff was a constant and valuable source of support, encouragement, and occasional necessary nudging. Our regard for this team is enormous. Specific members include Paul Corey, Mary Harlan, Dan Duffee, and Julie Tesser.

Finally, to our families and students, we give thanks for your patience, endurance, and support.

James S. Fisher

Brief Contents

Contents

PART 3: Western Europe   185
Louis De Vorsey, Jr.

PART 8: The Middle East and North Africa   511
Douglas L. Johnson and Leonard Berry

PART 9: Monsoon Asia 555
Clifton W. Pannell

Geography and Development

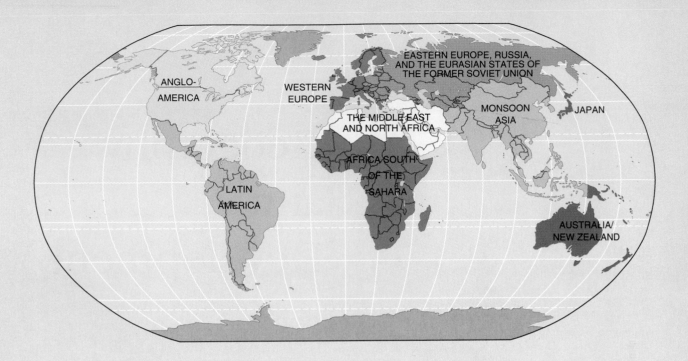

ANGLO-AMERICA

WESTERN EUROPE

EASTERN EUROPE, RUSSIA, AND THE EURASIAN STATES OF THE FORMER SOVIET UNION

MONSOON ASIA

JAPAN

THE MIDDLE EAST AND NORTH AFRICA

AFRICA SOUTH OF THE SAHARA

LATIN AMERICA

AUSTRALIA/ NEW ZEALAND

This book has been designed to provide an introduction to world geography by highlighting various geographical concepts. Its purpose is to acquaint the reader with the world in which we live and to organize that knowledge within a regional framework of economic development, broadly defined.

The word **development** is used in a variety of ways. Basically, it denotes a progressive change for the better. Economic development signifies a process of continual improvement in the quality of life, especially physical comfort and material wealth. As we shall see, economic development can be measured in several ways—by income, energy use, employment, and various other indicators. Such measures must be kept in proper perspective, however, for each may tell us little about other aspects of an area, a nation, or a people. For example, differences in income may simply reflect more basic differences in cultural goals and values.

An extended discussion of development is included in Chapter 1. In Chapter 2 we provide an overview of population and the concept of resources. Then in Chapter 3 we consider the natural environment, primarily from the standpoint of resources, and also attend to elements of culture, especially those that influence development. Finally, in Chapter 4 we use measures of economic well-being to define the more developed and less developed regions of the world. We also discuss the characteristics of such regions and present some theories of development. These chapters set the stage for further exploration of the more developed and less developed regions of the world.

PART 1

James S. Fisher

BASIC CONCEPTS AND IDEAS

1

Geography:
An Exciting
Discipline

Rice fields and limestone peaks at Guilin in south China.
The relationship between mankind and the physical
environment is one of the four traditions of geographical
scholarship.

James A. Michener, the noted American novelist, is a staunch supporter of the study of geography. He believes that his novels—including *Hawaii, Caravans, The Covenant, Centennial, Chesapeake, Poland, Texas* and *Caribbean*—enjoy great success because he fixes them firmly within a regional geographic context. Not surprisingly, he relies heavily on geographic works when he does research for his novels.

Geography, a branch of knowledge concerned with distributions over the earth, provides much more than an interesting context for good novels, however. Corporations use geographic principles and employ professional geographers to aid in locating new manufacturing plants and retail stores, because a good location can lower costs and increase profits. A commodities-trading firm may employ a geographer to monitor weather conditions in the Midwest in order to anticipate the volume of the coming harvest. Based on predicted supply figures, the company's brokers can then advise their clients to buy or sell animal and grain futures and stocks related to agriculture. Geography also provides an exciting perspective and methodology for understanding the character of our contemporary world. Analysis of the complex problems of world food supply, the environment, political antagonisms, or economic development is greatly facilitated by the application of geographic principles and techniques.

THE EVOLUTION OF GEOGRAPHY

These modern examples of geographic application illustrate only a fraction of the field's broad character and great utility. Geography has a rich and varied heritage. Its solid foundation rests on the works of ancient scholars, who recorded the physical and cultural characteristics of lands near and far. Although the study of geography apparently evolved in several civilizations, the Greeks made the most enduring contributions. In fact, the term *geography* comes to us from the Greek *geo* ("the earth") and *graphos* ("to write about or describe").

Contributions of the Greeks

The early Greeks studied formidable geographic problems. Herodotus, called by some the father of geography as well as the father of history, placed historic events in their geographic settings in his famous *Historia,* which he wrote in the mid–fifth century, B.C. He both described and explained the physical and human geography of his day. Aristotle (384–322 B.C.) discussed earth processes such as temperature, wind, alluvial deposition, and vulcanism in his *Meteorologica*. Both these scholars were concerned with explanations of the processes by which various events occur.

Herodotus and Aristotle were not unique, for other Greek scholars were concerned about the size and shape of the earth and its relationship to the rest of the cosmos. What methods, they wondered, could be used to show where places are in relation to one another and what people do in the various parts of the world? The Greeks did not answer all of their own questions, but they provided a perspective for seeking the answers.

Another Greek, Eratosthenes (276? –?196 B.C.), lived in Alexandria, Egypt, and, among other things, measured the earth's circumference. He had learned that on only one day of the year (the Northern Hemisphere's summer solstice) did the noon sun shine directly down a well near what is now the city of Aswan. On that special day Eratosthenes measured the noon sun's angle at Alexandria, some 500 miles (805 kilometers) north of Aswan, and found that there the sun's rays were not vertical but cast a shadow of 7.2° from a pole projecting straight up from the earth. Reasoning that the sun's rays are parallel to one another, he applied the geometric rule that when a straight line intersects two parallel lines, the alternate interior angles are equal. Therefore, he concluded, the distance between Aswan and Alexandria of 500 miles (805 kilometers) must be equal to a 7.2° arc of the earth's surface. With that information Eratosthenes then computed the value of a full circle's 360°, estimating the earth's circumference to be 25,200 miles (40,572 kilometers). Today we know that the circumference at the equator is quite close to that estimate: it is actually 24,901.5 miles (40,091.4 kilometers).

Eratosthenes and other Greeks recognized the need for maps to show the relationships between one place or region and another. They wanted a means of locating themselves on the earth and of describing their location to other people. To understand how challenging was their task, think of a mark on a smooth, uniform ball and then try to describe the position of the mark. Fortunately, the earth rotates around an axis that intersects the surface at two known points—the North Pole and the South Pole. With those points the Greek geographers established two reference lines: the equator halfway between the poles and another line extending from pole to pole. They then drew a grid of latitude and longitude lines from those geographic reference points, thereby permitting any point on earth to be located by just two numbers. The location of Washington, D.C., for example, is 38°50'N, 77°00'W.

The Greeks' next step was to use the geographic grid to construct a map whereby all or part of the earth could be reduced to a two-dimensional plane and the relative positions of places and regions could be established. The Greek geographers—indeed, all geographers down through the ages—were particularly fond of maps, and maps became the hallmark of geography.

Ptolemy (ca. A.D. 150), a Greek astronomer of Alexandria, was one of the early mapmakers. He designed a map of the world and then, using a coordinate system, compiled the location of 8,000 known places. This early work of the Greeks was not flawless, though. For instance, Christopher Columbus, accepting Ptolemy's view of the world, thought he had sailed to Asia when he had really reached the Americas.

Geography thrived during Greek and Roman times. New lands were discovered, and inventories of their resources and characteristics had great practical importance. One compiler was Strabo (63 B.C.?–? 24 A.D.), whose *Geographia* was a description of the known world. The accomplishments of Strabo, as well as Herodotus, Ptolemy, Hipparchus, and others, established geographers as leading figures of the times. Collectively, their most enduring contribution was the development of a scholarly approach that emphasized the importance of describing the world, viewing the world from a spatial perspective, and employing a holistic recognition of the interdependence of the elements of the world. Geography's position was one of acclaim until the Roman Empire began to decline.

The Middle Ages

Geography—indeed, all the sciences—stagnated and fell into disrepute in the West during Europe's Middle Ages, which lasted from about A.D. 500 to about 1500. A dogmatic Christianity based on literal interpretation of biblical passages replaced free intellectual inquiry. The advances in geographic knowledge that the Greeks had made were generally rejected. Even world maps became unreal distortions of the once-known world.

Concurrent with the Middle Ages in Europe was a golden period of Arabic civilization, and it was the Arabs who preserved much of the Greek and Roman geographic legacy. The Arabs, who themselves were formidable geographers, continued the tradition of mapmaking and recording data on maps. They also traveled widely and left copious notes of their journeys. Ibn-Batuta (1304–1368), for example, recorded his travels throughout the Arab portions of northern Africa and southern Asia and even beyond, into northern China. The Arabs also maintained interest in the physical earth and in the processes that had created differences between one place and another. Avicenna (980–1037), for example, was one of the first to understand some of the processes by which mountains are built and destroyed.

The geographic knowledge thus acquired by the Arabs was eventually diffused across the Mediterranean Sea to Spain and the great library at Toledo. Europeans also eventually rediscovered classical knowledge through the Crusades, through an interest in trade, and through Greek scholars who fled westward to escape the Turks during the fifteenth century.

The Renaissance and the Age of Discovery

The Renaissance and the Age of Discovery marked a resurgence of geography and other sciences. New routes to the Orient were needed, and a new era of the geographer-explorer began. Renaissance geographers were much like their forebears; they devised better maps, described the physical and cultural characteristics of foreign lands, and tried to understand the processes that created differences and similarities between one place and another. Explorers under the aegis of the world's first geographic institute, founded in 1418 by Prince Henry of Portugal, as well as such explorers as Christopher Columbus and Ferdinand Magellan, led in developing new routes to the outside world and acquiring new information about the world.

The revelations of those geographic voyages of discovery had a profound impact in Europe. By the sixteenth century, cartographers (i.e., mapmakers) were again producing more accurate renditions of the world image than those of the Middle Ages

(Figure 1–1). European scholars began to question age-old concepts in light of discoveries in other parts of the world. An age of scientific reasoning began, with experimentation and the testing of hypotheses. In the natural sciences new explanations were presented that challenged old ideas about the origin of continents and oceans, the formation of landforms, and the evolution of plants and animals.

After the early explorers came scientific travelers—students of natural history—who sought evidence of and explanation for the varied world around them. Among those was the great German geographer Alexander von Humboldt (1769–1859). Humboldt traveled widely in Europe and Latin America. His curiosity, careful observation, and broad background of study in botany, physics, chemistry, Greek, archaeology, and geology allowed him to synthesize information from a variety of fields into a coherent geographic composite. In his most celebrated work, *Kosmos* (1845–62), he attempted a comprehensive description of the earth.

Karl Ritter (1779–1859), a contemporary of Humboldt's, first studied geography as a basis for understanding history, but he eventually found that geography itself could provide an understanding of the human dimension of the world. His great work, *Die Erdkunde,* though never completed, included nineteen volumes on Africa and Asia. Ritter is generally recognized as having held the first chair of geography in Germany, at the University of Berlin in 1820.

By the middle of the nineteenth century geography was a respected discipline in European universities, and geographical societies served as meeting places for scholars of all disciplines who were interested in the world around them. From Europe the age of geography spread around the world.

In the United States, geography found a fertile environment. Because citizens were eager for knowledge about their country, especially the frontier regions, geographical literature was particularly popular. In 1852 the American Geographical Society was formed, followed by the National Geographic Society in 1888 and the Association of American Geographers in 1904. Geography as an academic field of study began to flower in the latter part of the nineteenth century, and in the subsequent hundred years it spread from a few centers to almost every major U.S. college and university.

Mainstream Western geographical thought can correctly be traced to the ancient Greeks, but other great centers of geographical thought existed as well. As already noted, Arab explorers and scholars served as a bridge from ancient to modern thought. Ancient China, too, was a major center of geographical scholarship and exploration, with Chinese travel books dating back to A.D. 1000. Although Chinese geography did not eclipse the work of Greek scholars during the classical period, it thrived from the fifth to the fifteenth centuries. During that millennium Chinese geographers traveled through southern Asia, the Mediterranean, and western Europe. They estab-

Figure 1-1
A world map (1571) by Flemish cartographer (mapmaker) Abraham Ortelius (1527-1598). By the late sixteenth century increased exploration was leading to more accurate renderings of world maps. By comparing this view of the east and west coasts of the Americas or the west coast of Africa with the South Pacific, we can see the effect of exploration.

lished human geography, completed regional studies inside and outside China, studied geomorphic processes, and wrote geographical encyclopedias.

Modern Geography

Modern geography has grown beyond a simple description of the earth. Today's geographers not only describe through words, maps, and statistics, but also attempt to explain why things are distributed over the earth as they are. Modern geography is best understood as the study of distributions and relationships among different distributions (e.g., the distribution of economic activities or per capita income) and the resultant regional character. Modern geography has improved our ability to explain the world by utilizing four traditional areas of study:

1. the way in which things are organized in area (spatial distribution)
2. the relationship between people and the land that supports them
3. regions, including analysis and explanation of why things are distributed as they are
4. the physical earth, perhaps the oldest of all geographic traditions.[1]

Interestingly, the focus of each of these traditions is evident in the work of the early Greek scholars. The **spatial tradition**, with its concern for distance, geometry, and movement, can be seen in the work of Ptolemy. The writings of Hippocrates were concerned with the relationship of human health to the surrounding environment, a theme common to the **man-land tradition**. Similarly, the **area studies tradition**, with its concern for the nature of places and for understanding the "where" of places, is evident in Strabo's *Geographia*. Lastly, the **earth science tradition**, as a study of the earth and its environments, is identifiable in the work of Aristotle and his students.

THE SUBDIVISIONS OF GEOGRAPHY

Geography has many subdivisions. The principal ones are:

1. physical geography
2. human geography
3. systematic geography
4. regional geography

Physical geography concerns the study of the environment from the viewpoint of distribution and process. For example, landform geographers, or ge-

omorphologists, are concerned with the location of terrain features and with the ways in which those features have acquired their shapes and forms. Geomorphologists might study the impact of stream deposition in a floodplain, the effect of wind erosion in a dry land, or the formation of coral reefs around a tropical island. Biogeographers are interested in the distribution of plants and animals, the ways organisms live together, the processes (both natural and people induced) that affect the biological earth, and the effect of changes on human life. Climatologists study the long-term characteristics of the atmosphere and any climatic differences created by temperature or energy and moisture conditions in various parts of the earth. Physical geography, which has blossomed in recent years, emphasizes the interdependence of people and the physical earth. Such contemporary problems as ozone depletion, acid rain, desertification, and rain forest removal are of particular interest.

Human geography concerns the study of various aspects of our occupancy of the earth. Urban geographers, for example, examine the location and structure of cities in an attempt to explain why urban areas are distributed as they are and to account for the pattern of distribution within cities. Urban geographers are interested in the process of urban growth and decline, in the types of activities carried on in cities, and in the movement of goods and people within urban settings. Cultural geographers examine the ways in which groups of people organize themselves; they study such cultural institutions as language and religion, as well as social and political structures. Economic geography involves the study of systems of livelihood, especially the distribution of related activities and explanations for such distribution. Economic geographers are concerned with analysis of natural and cultural resources and with their utilization.

Systematic, or topical, **geography** concerns the study of specific subjects. Historical geographers, for example, study past landscapes and the changes that have taken place. How did the people of the Great Plains organize themselves in 1870, as compared with their organization in 1920? What past characteristics have persisted, and what effect do they have on present-day distributional patterns? Michener used a concept of historical geography called sequential occupancy as the organizing theme of some of his novels. He described the geography of an area during different periods, gradually building an image of how it is organized today. Historical geography thus adds depth perception to time, facilitating an explanation of present patterns and their reasons for being. Systematic geographers normally study one aspect of the field—landforms, economic activities, or urban places, for example.

Regional geography involves the analysis of environmental and human patterns within a single area. A wide variety of facts are placed into a coherent form in order to explain how a region is organized and how it functions. A regional geographer, in essence, is an expert on a particular area of the world, applying systematic approaches to an understanding of that area (Figure 1–2). The regional approach provides the framework for this text.

All fields of geography, despite focusing on different sets of phenomena, share the geographic viewpoint; that is, all geographers analyze spatial arrangements (distributions) and search for explanations of the patterns and interrelationships among those and other phenomena. All geographers rely on maps as analytical tools, and many have added computers and remote-sensing techniques to aid in recording and analyzing data. The rapid growth in the use of computers has resulted in the burgeoning use of geographic information systems to analyze a wide range of geographical problems.

GEOGRAPHY AND OTHER DISCIPLINES

As a bridge between the social sciences and the physical sciences, geography possesses many characteristics similar to those of its sister fields. Yet geography is unique: its primary focus is spatial, which means that geographers look at the world from a distinctive point of view. For example, both botanists and geographers are interested in plants. But whereas botanists are concerned primarily with

Figure 1–2
A Himalayan mountain landscape in Nepal. This mountain landscape northwest of Kathmandu illustrates the harsh environments to which humankind has adapted. This fortified village lies in a deep gorge below the Annapurna (background). The study of earth environments is one of the four traditions in geographical scholarship.

plant growth, structure, propagation, and taxonomy, geographers analyze the distribution of plants—the processes of plant growth, interrelationships of plant groups, and the environmental factors (including human beings) that help or inhibit their survival.

As another example, economists are interested in the production, distribution, and consumption of goods and services. They study how people use resources to earn a livelihood, investigating such topics as the costs and benefits of resource allocation, the causes of changes in the economy, the impact of monetary policies, the workings of different economic systems, the problem of supply and demand, and business cycles and forecasting. Geography is also concerned with how people earn their livelihood, but geographers look at where the economic activity takes place and what reasons determine that location. Economic geography is concerned with the economic systems by which people sustain themselves, especially the spatial and environmental relationships that shape economic systems.

That same type of relationship exists between geography and other social and physical sciences, some of which are illustrated in Figure 1–3. Keep in mind that each discipline views the world from a different perspective, even though all fields of learning are linked. Because geography's linkages are extensive, it is a synthesizing, integrating field—synthesizing knowledge from many disciplines and integrating that knowledge into a geographical context. For instance, a geographer who studies the growing of wheat on the Great Plains or the Argentine pampas needs information on the climate, soils, and landforms of the region (the physical sciences), as well as knowledge of the farmers' cultural characteristics, the transport network, the costs of wheat farming (especially in relation to other economic opportunities), and a host of other socioeconomic factors (the social sciences).

Geography and history are both integrating disciplines. History, however, uses a **chronological** (time) framework, whereas geography's perspective is **chorologic** (place). Neither can be studied effectively with-

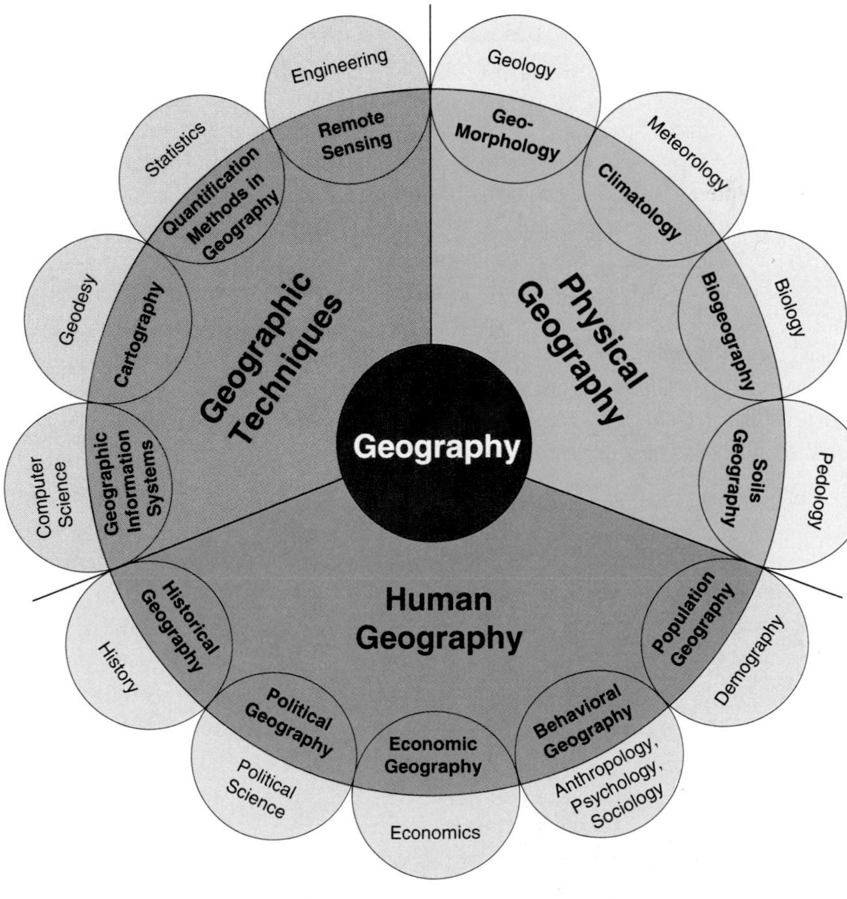

Figure 1-3
The scope of geography.
Geography is a synthesizing and integrating discipline. This diagram shows that geography interrelates with many fields of study, including the physical sciences, engineering, social sciences, and humanities.

out knowledge of the other. Isaiah Bowman, former president of Johns Hopkins University, said that "a man [or woman] is not educated who lacks a sense of time [history] and place [geography]."[2] By integrating information in a regional context, the geographer pulls together knowledge shared with a variety of disciplines into a single, all-encompassing, coherent picture.

CAREERS IN GEOGRAPHY

Modern geographers differ from their forebears in emphasizing explanation (Why is it there?) rather than description (Where is it?). That shift in emphasis has increased geographers' utility in solving many problems of our contemporary world. The result has been employment in roles such as market analysts, urban or regional planners, cartographers, and environmental analysts.

Education

Traditionally, many geographers have been employed as high school teachers or university professors. Yet evidence suggests that the geographic education provided American students is inadequate. Eighty-one percent of the respondents in a recent public poll believe that geography is an essential subject for high school students. No comparable survey exists for geography's role at the university level, but numerous educators and laypersons have decried the geographic ignorance of college students. Marion J. Levy, Jr., a sociologist at Princeton University, stated that "almost any test of geographical literacy would separate American students from students trained abroad, and the same may be said of the vast majority of American faculty members."[3] Bob Wedrich, a columnist for the *Chicago Tribune,* recently lamented the lack of geographic training at the college level:

> Based on the disquieting reports of geographic shortcomings, it is not unreasonable to suspect that some people still think the world is flat. But without classroom motivation, it is unlikely they ever will question what happens when the oceans splash over the edge.[4]

The 1987 Southern Governors Conference called for the teaching of geography as a required part of school curricula. The National Governors Conference echoed the same concern. In fact, a joint resolution of Congress declared the week of November 15, 1987, as National Geography Awareness Week, and during each ensuing year that observance of the value of geographic knowledge has been repeated. The original resolution speaks of the obvious need for geographic education and calls geographic instruction critical in our increasingly interdependent world:

> Whereas an ignorance of geography, foreign languages, and cultures places the United States at a disadvantage with other countries in matters of business, politics, and the environment;
>
> Whereas the United States is a nation of worldwide involvements and global influence, the responsibilities of which demand an understanding of the lands, languages, and cultures of the world; and
>
> Whereas national attention must be focused on the integral role that knowledge of world geography plays in preparing citizens of the United States for the future of an increasingly interdependent and interconnected world. . . .[5]

Specific examples of that interconnectedness come easily to mind. World economic interdependence is clear. Because the need is growing for products and materials that are not available in sufficient quantities within U.S. national borders, Americans are having to rely increasingly on foreign sources. For instance, much of the petroleum, nickel, bauxite, tin, and iron that we use comes from other countries (Figure 1–4).

In addition, Americans are affected by the political and social conditions in other countries. For example, in recent years large numbers of immigrants have entered the United States from Cuba, Haiti, Mexico, and Southeast Asia. Many of those immigrants have come because of adverse conditions in their home countries and because of perceived opportunities in this nation. The impact of such migration is great. A knowledge of our own geography and the geography of other countries that affect us may help us understand such events and establish policies to deal effectively with them.

International environmental concerns also reflect American connectedness with the rest of the world. As the world population grows and levels of living increase, pressure on our natural resources mounts. The interrelationships between humankind and the environment have been a traditional part of geography. Now, more than ever, it is critical for us to understand the environmental results of our actions and to find ways to reduce and avoid damage to the environment. Global warming of the environment is just one of many such concerns. Thus, the role of geographers as teachers must expand greatly as we become economically, politically, and environmentally more interdependent.

Figure 1-4
Beach line in Kuwait polluted by oil spill during the Persian Gulf War. Oil wealth has ensured the gulf states of economic and political significance in world affairs, as demonstrated by the war caused by Iraq's attempted annexation of Kuwait in 1990.

Business

Applied geography is another subdivision of the discipline. Geographers apply their perspective and skills in the business world in many ways. As mentioned earlier, many firms use geographers for location analysis. For example, the owners of a grocery store chain who decide to increase its retail outlets in a city want to know where new stores should be located. Should stores be opened in the central city or the suburbs? Selecting the appropriate location may involve a market analysis of potential customers, an analysis of traffic flow, and an assessment of any competitor's ability to attract the firm's potential customers. Perhaps the chain's owners want to establish an outlet at a location that will prove profitable at some future date, such as near a major highway interchange, rather than at the present point of maximum profit. The applied geographer must then study trends in neighborhood characteristics, including patterns of growth and decline, projected road construction, and a host of other variables. Similar techniques are used for the location of factories and services.

The work of Joseph A. Russell of the University of Illinois illustrates another way in which geography has been applied to business. The Ford Motor Company hired Russell as a consultant to demon-strate the valuable service a geographer could provide to the company. Russell decided to map the relative sales positions of Ford, General Motors, and Chrysler cars of comparable price. He placed the data on a United States map (by county) and found that the relative sales positions varied regionally; that is, in some parts of the country Chevrolet sold more than Ford, which sold more than Chrysler, but in other regions the relationships were different.

Ford officials were surprised that such sales data had never before been mapped, and their perusal of Russell's map led to many questions. Why, for instance, did the relative sales position show distinctive regional differences? What was Ford doing right to outsell its competitors in some areas? What was it doing wrong where its competitors had the advantage? Russell helped Ford answer the fundamental geographic questions—Where is it? and Why is it there?

Russell worked with Ford to assess the geographic influences that affect dealerships. By analyzing the location of dealerships in relation to traffic flow, he found that service and repair business in cities is increased if the dealership is located on the right side of the street for customers who are driving to work. He also discovered that such a location is further enhanced if public transportation facilities are nearby and if access to the garage is easy.

Other geographers who are employed in business may concentrate on area analysis. They might study the growth potential of a market area and assist in planning for industrial development, resource-use opportunities, travel and tourism industries, and transportation lines. Or they might utilize the skills of both the natural and the social sciences in assessing the impact of new construction, in order to avoid detrimental repercussions. Such studies are especially vital in determining environmental impacts.

Many geographers specialize in the study of foreign areas, and their knowledge of the cultural, human, and physical characteristics of those places can provide invaluable information on market opportunities, resources, location sites, and the problems of conducting business in such locations. Other geographers carry out specialized studies for businesses, such as weather forecasting for specific agricultural crops or analyzing the supply of specific labor skills. Still other geographers may serve as cartographers, travel agents, or consumer behaviorists, among many possibilities.

Government

Geographers hold numerous kinds of governmental positions. On a local level many are urban or regional planners, charged with facilitating orderly residential, business, and industrial growth.

On a national level geographers are employed in literally dozens of different types of positions. Many use cartographic skills or remote-sensing techniques to map and analyze numerous types of activities. A few serve the U.S. State Department as science or geographic attachés in the Office of the Geographer or as foreign service officers. Many others work as intelligence specialists or research analysts for various agencies or departments or for the U.S. Congress. Some are employed by scientific agencies, such as the National Science Foundation or the U.S. Geological Survey. Geographers also work for the Agency for International Development, where they assist foreign countries in initiating and carrying out such programs as resource analysis, regional development, urban reconstruction, and economic growth.

On an international level many geographers work on inventory analysis for socioeconomic development purposes. Agencies of the United Nations, the World Bank, and the Inter-American Development Bank employ geographers to measure natural and human resources in various parts of the world.

GEOGRAPHY AND DEVELOPMENT

An increasingly trite but accurate truism is that the world is getting smaller. Not only are we daily bombarded with news of such places as Iraq, Lebanon, India, China, El Salvador, Germany, Russia, the former Yugoslavia, and Japan, but events in those and other countries influence our daily lives. When the Organization of Petroleum Exporting Countries (OPEC) increased crude oil prices fivefold during the 1970s, we were quickly awakened to the degree of our reliance on other countries to supply our needs. A similar insight followed the Iraqi invasion and attempted annexation of Kuwait in 1990. A coffee crop failure in Brazil, the development of a new high-yielding variety of wheat, the discovery of a chemical process for making plastic, an outbreak of insect pests, and scores of other events all materially affect the way we live. As world population grows and standards of living improve, the level of international interdependence also increases. Consequently, we are forced to know something about the world in which we live in order to exert any influence on our fate.

The concern of this book is knowledge about economic achievement. A great disparity in material well-being exists among the world's societies. With a more intimate world brought about by better communication and transportation, knowledge of how others live is at our fingertips. Countries that are economically less fortunate often wish to emulate their materially richer neighbors but may be frustrated in their attempts by cultural, economic, and political constraints. The disparity in economic achievement is widening, and the social and political ramifications are manifold. The reasons for that disparity provide the focus and theme of this book.

Until recently, economic development was basically a Western concept. But Western ideas of materialism are spreading widely throughout the world, with other cultures accepting modern technology in order to support development. That penetration of Western ideas and technology into other cultures has often led to disruption and conflict, as illustrated by current tensions and strife in the Middle East. Not only are traditional economic patterns altered, but new modes of behavior and interpersonal relations are established. In addition, because few nations become completely Westernized, internal cultural and economic differences are often intensified. To appreciate the process of economic development, we must examine four factors that contribute to it: people, environment, culture, and history.

Figure 1–5
People watching solar-powered TV in Niger, Africa. As economic development and technological change have spread, traditional cultures can be dramatically impacted over a short time.

People

The first factor in economic development is people: their numbers, growth rates, and distribution. Improved sanitation and medical science have lowered death rates sharply and have caused a rate of population growth so great that it constitutes a population explosion. Wherever birthrates do not decrease to balance the lower death rates, economic advances and improved well-being may be difficult to achieve.

Environment

The natural environment of a country or region provides both the stage for development and the materials used in economic activities. Some environments are rich in resources that can be used for economic gain. For example, a well-watered alluvial plain coupled with a long growing season provides many opportunities for productive agriculture. Similarly, highly mineralized areas with easily extractable ores offer other means of live-lihood. Conversely, areas with steeply slop-ing land, thin soils, moisture deficiency, or few minerals provide relatively few opportunities for growing crops and thus present obstacles to development.

Culture

The way in which a society organizes itself in terms of beliefs, customs, and life-styles greatly influences both the direction and the degree of economic development. One feature of Western culture is materialism. The Protestant work ethic is an example of the American identification of material wealth as an index of success. Although not Western in tradition

or culture, Japan has a similar work ethic. Other cultures, however, do not place so high a priority on material advantages. (Figure 1–5).

The character of economic organization has a more direct influence on development. Some cultures (including certain Western cultures) have an economic structure that is ill designed to use modern technology effectively or a social and economic system so rigid that it constrains development of the human resource base. Other, more flexible systems are able to adapt to new ideas and to accept technology relatively easily.

History

That the past is a key to the present and a guidepost to the future is well demonstrated in the evolution of the world's various cultures and their economic activities. Economic development is not a short-term process. In most nations that are now undergoing rapid change or that have attained a high level of economic well-being, the necessary foundations or prerequisites for economic development were laid decades, even centuries, ago. For example, the cornerstones of Europe's Industrial Revolution, which began in the middle of the eighteenth century, were formed during the Renaissance, with beginnings in Roman and Greek times and even earlier. A more recent example is Taiwan, where many of the foundations for the island's remarkable growth were laid in the early part of this century.

TWO WORLDS

The theme of this text—development—supports our dividing the world into two broad types of regions (see the boxed feature Development). The more developed regions are: (1) Anglo-America, (2) Western Europe, (3) Eastern Europe, Russia, and the Eurasian states of the former Soviet Union, and (4) Japan and Australia/New Zealand. The less developed regions are: (1) Latin America, (2) Africa south of the Sahara, (3) the Middle East and North Africa, and (4) Monsoon Asia (South Asia, China and its neighbors, and Southeast Asia).

The More Developed World

Each subsequent unit of this book focuses on one region, including a historical perspective, an examination of the physical basis for development, and discussions of culture, economic structure, and present patterns, trends, and prospects of development. The emphasis, however, varies from region to region. The high standard of living in Anglo-America is viewed in light of the varied and bountiful physical resource base (Figure 1–6). Poverty pockets and cultural conflicts are also identified. The chapters on Western Europe have a greater accent on history, to explain the region's multiplicity of nation-states and its advanced technological attainments. The section on Eastern Europe, Russia, and the Eurasian states of the former Soviet Union contains an analysis of communist development theory and an appraisal of the failed drive for rapid economic growth in the old

Soviet bloc. The implications of political and economic reform in this region are examined on a local and regional level. Finally, Japanese growth, in spite of a poor natural endowment, is considered from the perspective of blended Western and local culture traits. Japan's status in the more developed world is unique.

The Less Developed World

After the units on the more developed regions, we turn our attention to the less developed world. Latin America is viewed from its base of cultural pluralism; we also focus on societal attitudes to the resources available and the region's rapid population growth. The African and Middle Eastern regions, truly diverse, have a recent history of colonialism, and the many newly independent nations still struggle for self-identity, which is expressed in different ways (Figure 1–7). The Arab-Israeli conflict and the oil-rich gulf states present other aspects of the development process. Finally, in Monsoon Asia (South Asia, China and its neighbors, and Southeast Asia) the emphasis is on the origin of different cultures and the relationship of economic organization to various cultural aspects. Special attention is given to the roles of the monsoon wind system and religion in South Asia and to the contrasts between traditional and communist China.

Figure 1-6
The central city of Vancouver, British Columbia, Canada, as viewed from Coal Harbor. Intense urbanization is a process that accompanies economic development.

DEVELOPMENT

Development is the process by which the political, social, and, especially, economic structures of a country are improved for the purpose of ensuring the well-being of its populace. The results of this process are highly varied when viewed from a global perspective. Extremely limited development is easy to spot: human productivity is low, labor is concentrated in agriculture, masses of people live in poverty, food supplies are inadequate, and health problems abound. The other extreme of development is easy to recognize, too: people are well fed, life expectancy is comparatively long, health is good, and wealth is abundant. Numerous other attributes can also be identified at the extremes of development. Not all countries, however, exhibit one extreme or the other. Most fall in between, along a continuum. Therefore, when we look at the level of development of a specific place, we see it in comparison with other places.

Development can be measured in many ways. One of the most common approaches is the measure of national productivity known as **gross national product (GNP)**. On the accompanying graph (Figure A) each red dot represents the per capita GNP of a country, creating a range of $100 to more than $33,000. Although countries are positioned all along the continuum, they are concentrated at the lower end of the scale. A few countries have achieved the middle range; even fewer are found at the upper end of the scale. Clearly, according to this one measure, the world has rich countries and poor countries.

Other terminology is also used to distinguish between those who are well off and those who are not. One common classification, based on economic systems and achievements, divides the globe into First World, Second World, and Third World countries. The First World, the well-off capitalist countries, comprises the United States and Canada, the countries of Western Europe, Japan, and Australia. The Second World, the comparatively well-off countries in process of transition from a centrally planned economy, comprises the countries of Eastern Europe, Russia, and the Eurasian states of the former Soviet Union. The Third World comprises the remaining and largely poorer countries of Latin America, Asia, and Africa. Obviously, some of the rich oil exporters do not fit easily into any of these three categories.

Another frequently used classification distinguishes among stages of development. Developed countries are identified as those that have achieved a high level of physical and material well-being (equivalent to the First and Second World countries). Countries with a low level of physical and material well-being are often referred to as developing, less developed, least developed, or underdeveloped. Other classifications exist, too—such as the haves and the have-nots or the advantaged and the disadvantaged.

Whatever the classification scheme, the essential point is that an easily recognizable difference exists among the world's countries: some are relatively well developed, some are less developed but are ambitiously pursuing development strategies, and some are relatively undeveloped.

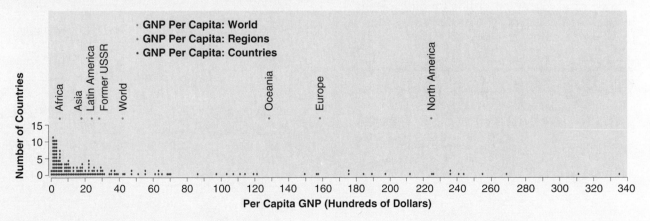

Figure A

Per capita GNP in dollars. Most countries of the world report a per capita income substantially below that of the relatively few rich countries.

Figure 1-7
A woman transporting harvested grain along the foot trail of a small village on the Transkei Coast of eastern South Africa. Poor regions often show a notable lack of infrastructure development. Area study, focusing on a particular area, is an important tradition in geographical scholarship.

SUMMARY
Patterns and Interactions

Geography's concern with spatial patterns and interactions within and between places provides a contemporary and analytic perspective with which we can come to understand the global, national, and local variations in economic development and its impact on the human condition. In addition, this examination of worldwide development will provide an excellent foundation for further study in many of the fields you as students may choose to pursue.

KEY TERMS

area studies tradition
chorologic
chronological

development
earth science tradition
geography

gross national product (GNP)
human geography
man-land tradition
physical geography

regional geography
spatial tradition
systematic geography

NOTES

1. William D. Pattison, "The Four Traditions of Geography," *Journal of Geography* 63 (May 1964): 211–216.

2. Quoted in Alfred H. Meyer and John H. Strietelmeyer, *Geography in World Society* (Philadelphia: Lippincott, 1963), 31.

3. Marion J. Levy, Jr., *New York Times,* 12 November 1961.

4. Bob Wedrich, *Chicago Tribune,* 6 November 1980.

5. U.S. Congress, joint resolution, *Geography Awareness Week,* 100th Congress, 1st session, 1987.

2

People and Resources

People

The Resource Concept

Clearing of land in the Amazon Basin. The clearing of tropical rain forests is sometimes the work of ranchers who want to expand large cattle operations; in other instances, peasants are attempting to establish small farms.

For most of humankind's existence, the world's population remained relatively small, but over the past hundred years it has increased so dramatically that the term **population explosion** is commonly used to describe the growth. A rapid and sustained increase in population may place a strain on the capacity of a society to fulfill the material needs and aspirations of its members. To counterbalance that increased demand, society's productive capacity must be expanded by the development of new resources and the accelerated exploitation of present resources (as can be seen in the chapter-opening photograph). But even if production capacity matches population growth, already-existent problems such as pollution, interpersonal and group rivalries, or scarcity of goods may become even more serious. In addition, new situations may challenge basic and traditional societal values and ways of life. The society itself may require drastic alteration.

PEOPLE

At the dawn of the **Agricultural Revolution**, some 7,000 to 10,000 years ago, the world's population probably numbered about 5 million (Figure 2–1). Plant cultivation and animal domestication, however, heralded a long and sustained period of population growth. Population clusters, at first confined to areas of agricultural innovation, later spread throughout the world, along with the diffusion of agriculture. In a few places, such as Australia, the diffusion process was delayed until the coming of European colonists. Today, only in polar zones, remote dry lands, and other harsh environments do small and dwindling numbers of people still live by the age-old occupations of hunting, fishing, and gathering.

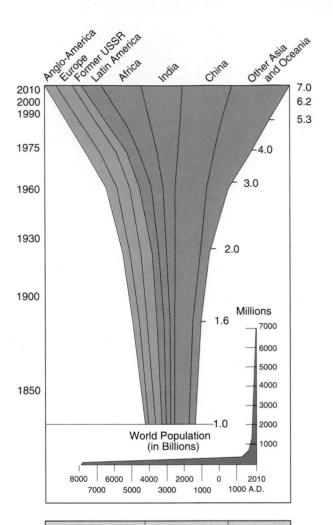

Figure 2–1
World population growth. For most of human history the world held relatively few people. In the last 400 years, however, the total number of people has expanded greatly and at an increasingly rapid rate. The term *population explosion* is often used to describe such rapid growth.

Region	Year 2010 Population (in Millions)	World Share
World	7,022	
Anglo-America	334	4.8%
Europe	519	7.3%
Former USSR	306	4.3%
Latin America	584	8.3%
Africa	1,078	15.4%
India	1,163	16.6%
China	1,376	19.6%
Other Asia and Oceania	1,660	23.7%

The Impact of the Agricultural Revolution

The Agricultural Revolution led to many fundamental changes. No longer did people depend on nature alone; domestic crops and animals far surpassed their wild cousins in utility. Thus, many more people could live close together at a higher level of existence. Villages grew, and a new social order was created to resolve the increasing conflicts brought about by more people living together.

Life was somewhat easier and more secure. Permanent homes, even substantial houses, replaced the crude huts or caves that had served as temporary lodgings. Many tools and other large and small luxuries were acquired—such as chairs, tables, and beds, which had previously been impractical because of the migratory way of life. Indeed, materialism may have had its true beginning with the development of agriculture. Possessions were able to be accumulated and passed on to new generations.

As production increased, a sense of security increased, too. Surpluses could be stored for an emergency. In addition, village life offered protection from hostile groups. Permanent fortifications and many defenders discouraged outside attempts to capture and control the agriculturists. Of course, defense was not always successful. For instance, after obtaining horses from the Spanish, the hunting and gathering Plains Indians of the United States were more than a match for the sedentary agricultural Indians along the eastern margin of the Great Plains. And long before that, the Romans had lost their agricultural tributary regions to more primitive northern and eastern tribes.

Increased population, production, and interpersonal contact created a need for group action and led to numerous secular leadership organizations. A political organization was established to settle disputes, govern, and provide leadership for collective action in warfare and in such public works as irrigation, drainage, and road building. The formation of a priestly class helped formalize religion. Religious leaders were frequently the holders of both philosophical and practical knowledge, often serving as medical men and weather forecasters. In the Mayan civilization of southern Mexico and Guatemala, for example, priests developed an agricultural calendar based on the progression of the sun, the planets, and the stars. It predicted the beginning of wet and dry seasons and told farmers when to prepare the land for planting to take full advantage of the seasonal rains. As increased production per worker yielded more than a family unit needed, a portion of the labor force was freed not only for government and religious activities but also for activities such as pottery making, metallurgy, and weaving.

From A.D. 1 to 1650

At the beginning of the Christian era, world population totaled little more than 260 million, of which about 250 million were in the Old World. Most of those people lived within three great empires: the Roman Empire, around the fringe of the Mediterranean Sea and northward into Europe; the Han dynasty of China, which extended into Southeast Asia; and the Mauryan Empire of northern India. In those empires the simpler political, economic, and social organizations of agricultural villages vied with the more complex, integrating structures of the empires and the newly created cities. Urbanism became a way of life.

Urban life meant specialization of labor; city dwellers became dependent on farmers for food and fiber. The cities, however, were the focal point of national life. The riches of the countryside and tribute from afar were concentrated in the cities, which like magnets drew people to their cores. Arts flourished, and education became available to those who could pay for it. The best lawyers and doctors practiced in the cities, where government employed increasing numbers of people to construct and maintain sewage lines, roads and streets, and irrigation systems. In all, the activities of those empire cities were not much different from those of a modern metropolis.

Empires and cities fostered regional specialization. Rather then simply producing what was needed, each part of the empire traded what it produced in surplus and received in turn what it did not produce or could produce only with difficulty. To be sure, regional specialization was not fully developed, but the concept was recognized and used. Rome, for example, exported Arretine pottery, wines and oils, metalware, glass, perfume, and gold. In return, Rome imported wheat from North Africa, cattle and hides from Sicily, metals and livestock from Spain, slaves and fur from Germany, and even rare spices and gems from India.

The people of the New World probably numbered only about 10 million at the beginning of the Christian era. The Agricultural Revolution, which was concentrated in Mesoamerica (Central Mexico to Honduras) and the Andes Mountains of Peru and Bolivia, did not affect the area as a whole.

By 1650 the world's population had grown to more than 500 million, despite interruptions of famine, plague, and warfare. Most of the growth was in and around the preexisting centers, with gradual expansion of the populace into areas that had been sparsely settled. Productive capacity expanded with improved technology and new resources. Urbanization became more pronounced, though agriculture remained the base of livelihood.

From 1650 to the Present

Since 1650 the world's population has increased more and more rapidly. It took 1,650 years for the population to double from 260 million to 500 million. By 1850, however, the population had doubled again to an estimated 1,175 million. Within the next 100 years the population doubled a third time, reaching 2 billion. By 1975 it had doubled again, to 4 billion. The world now has more than 5.5 billion people and will continue to experience a large increase in the foreseeable future. With the world population increasing at the rate of nearly 1 billion per decade, by the dawn of the twenty-first century it will exceed 6 billion and by 2025 will likely exceed 8.5 billion.

The Industrial Revolution

During the relatively short period from 1650 to the present, a second revolution, the **Industrial Revolution**, made an enormous impact on humankind, and that impact continues. Countless innovations have characterized the Industrial Revolution, ranging from the development of the steam engine to interplanetary flight. By the beginning of the nineteenth century the age of invention had arrived, and each new idea seemed to spawn many others. Relatively quickly, the muscle power of people and animals was replaced by inanimate power: the steam engine, the water turbine, and the internal combustion engine.

In the agricultural sector the use of the tractor and its attachments made farmers so productive in some parts of the world that only a small part of the labor force was needed to supply an abundance of food. Of course, other scientific advances—such as improved, higher-yielding seed and the application of fertilizers, herbicides, and insecticides—have also contributed substantially to that productivity.

The use of inanimate energy was fundamental to the development of modern transportation systems, which in turn facilitated the growth of cities. When combined with more raw materials from agriculture, mining, and forestry, those new energy sources also spurred industrialization. Especially since the eighteenth century, innovations in energy and manufacturing have made factory workers many times more productive. As a result, manufactured products have become relatively less expensive and more readily available. Craftsmen and small guilds have gradually given way to modern factories, where workers primarily tend machines. As the Industrial Revolution has brought about large-scale factory production, larger numbers of people have been drawn to the cities to work in the factories. Those cities, both small and large, have then become service, financial, educational, governmental, wholesale, and retail centers. Many cities have grown several times over (Table 2–1).

As the Industrial Revolution has continued and its effects have spread, urban growth has increased. The revolution, which began in Western Europe, moved quickly to Anglo-America and other areas where European colonists settled. It moved more slowly into Eastern Europe, the former Soviet Union, southern Europe, and Japan. Since the end of World War II, however, at least some aspects of the Industrial Revolution have had an effect almost everywhere.

Distribution and Density of Population

As Figure 2–2 shows, the world's **population distribution** (the arrangement of people) and **population density** (the number of people per unit area) show strong ties with the past. Three principal centers of dense population are readily apparent: the Indian subcontinent, eastern China and adjacent areas, and Europe. China and India represent old areas of large populations, stemming both from an early start in the Agricultural Revolution and from empire building. Today, at least half of the world's population lives in southern and eastern Asia, where agriculture

Table 2-1
The world's twenty largest urban agglomerations.

Agglomeration	Country or Area	Population (in millions)				Percentage of National Population in 1990
		1800	1900	1990	2000	
Tokyo/Yokohama	Japan	1.000	4.5	20.5	21.3	16.6
Mexico City	Mexico	.100	.3	19.4	24.3	21.9
New York	United States	.100	3.4	15.7	16.1	6.2
São Paulo	Brazil			18.4	23.6	12.0
Shanghai	China	.300	.9	12.6	14.7	1.1
Buenos Aires	Argentina	.040	.8	11.6	13.1	35.5
London	United Kingdom	.800	1.8	10.6	10.8	18.5
Calcutta	India	.600	.8	11.8	15.9	1.4
Rio de Janeiro	Brazil	.040	.8	11.1	13.0	7.2
Seoul	Republic of Korea			11.3	13.0	26.2
Los Angeles	United States			10.5	10.9	4.2
Osaka/Kobe	Japan	.350	1.3	10.5	11.2	8.5
Greater Bombay	India	.200	.8	11.1	15.4	1.3
Beijing	China	.700	1.0	9.7	11.5	0.9
Moscow	Russia	.300	1.0	9.4	10.1	6.3
Paris	France	.500	2.7	8.8	8.8	15.5
Tianjin	China	.600	.8	8.4	10.0	0.7
Cairo/Giza	Egypt	.300	.6	9.1	11.8	16.7
Jakarta	Indonesia			9.4	13.2	5.2
Milan	Italy	.170	.5	7.9	8.7	13.7

Sources: W.S. Woytinsky and E. S. Woytinsky, *World Population and Production: Trends and Outlook* (New York: Twentieth Century Fund, 1953); Bureau of the Census, *Statistical Abstract of the United States, 1993* (Washington, D.C.: Government Printing Office, 1993).

and village life remain important facets of society. Yet modern cities, with their service and manufacturing functions, are also present. The population density in India and China varies considerably, usually in association with the relative productivity of the land. **Physiologic density**, the number of people per square mile of arable land, is a useful expression of the density relationship in agricultural societies. On the coastal and river plains, where alluvial soils are rich and water is abundant, rural densities of 2,000 people per square mile (772 per square kilometer) are not uncommon. Away from well-watered lowlands, such as the Huang He or Yangtze valleys, densities diminish but may still be in the range of 250 to 750 people per square mile (97 to 290 per square kilometer).

Europe's high population density can be traced back to technological developments from the Middle East that were adopted by the Greeks and Romans and then expanded by the Industrial Revolution. Further increase in the European population has been readily associated with developments in technology. Many of the high-density areas in Western Europe are urban regions associated with coalfields or advantageous water transportation, indicating the importance of those assets in the Industrial Revolution (Figure 2–3, p. 28). Even though Europe's population density is high, it is significantly less than that of the Indian and Chinese areas. In addition, agricultural villages and agriculture itself are overshadowed in Europe by modern metropolises and manufacturing.

Secondary centers of high population density are more numerous worldwide. The northeast quadrant of the United States and the adjacent Canadian area are considered by some a principal cluster, though total population numbers are smaller than those of Europe and far less than those of East Asia.

Figure 2-2
World population distribution.
The world's population is unevenly distributed. Three
large areas of dense population are China, the Indian
subcontinent, and Europe.
Most of the sparsely populated areas have environmental impediments such as aridity or mountainous terrain.

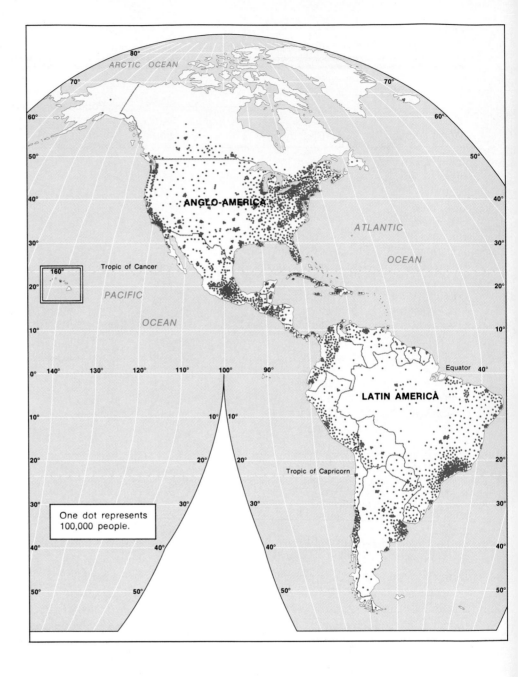

Nonetheless, in many respects—rate of urbanization
and employment, for instance—that region closely
resembles the European pattern. High densities also
occur in Africa along the Guinea Coast and the Nile
River and in the eastern highlands, but the total
number of people involved in each cluster is relatively small. Similarly, around major urban centers
of Latin America and in the old Aztec, Mayan, and
Inca realms, small but locally dense population cen-

ters are common. Other pockets of high density are
found in Asia, Java, the Malay Peninsula, and parts
of the Middle East.

Most of the rest of the world's land surface (80
percent) is more sparsely inhabited. Many of those
areas have serious environmental problems—cold-
ness, dryness, rugged terrain—that have kept them
from being made productive. The sparse population
of other areas, such as some of the humid tropics of

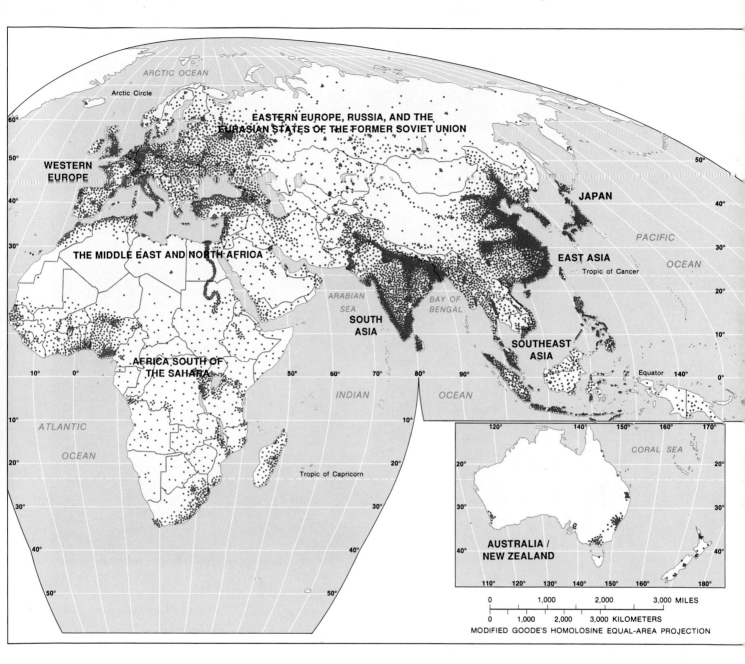

South America and Africa, are not so easy to explain, especially because similar environments in Asia are densely settled. It is tempting to relate population density to the broad physical patterns described in Chapter 3, and indeed some writers have done so. Yet a correlation between population and physical environment is an oversimplification. Technology and political organization are additional factors to be considered, as are other aspects of culture, such as desired family size and economic organization.

Models and Theories of Population Change

Overall, the **growth rate** for the world's population is 1.7 percent a year, but that growth is by no means uniform. One explanation of the varied growth pattern is the theory of **demographic transformation**, which is based on four population stages (Figure 2–4). Stage I postulates an agrarian society where **birthrates** and **death rates** are high, creating a stable or very slowly growing population. Productivity per

Figure 2-3
Overlooking the Rhine River in Basel, Switzerland. The Rhine and other rivers of Europe served as major transport arteries during Europe's development process. Spatial organization is one of the four traditions in geographical scholarship.

person is limited. Consequently, large families (or many births) are an asset, particularly since life expectancy is low and security depends on family members, including young children. Nonagricultural employment opportunities are few in this stage, and technology is stagnant or nearly so.

In Stage II the cultural custom of large families persists, and the birthrate remains high. The death rate, however, drops dramatically because of better sanitation and medical treatment and because of greater productivity. Productivity may increase in the agricultural sector, but more important is the advent of alternative economic activity resulting from industrialization. With industry come urbanization and labor specialization. The principal feature of Stage II is rapid population increase.

Numerous countries remained in Stage I until World War II. In the postwar years, however, death rates all over the world were greatly reduced. Several African countries moved into Stage II only in recent decades. We must remember that lower death rates, which have contributed to faster population growth, will decline even more in the future, so that even higher rates of population growth are likely. Ethiopia, Mali, and Sierra Leone provide illustrations of countries in precisely such a situation.

Stage III is characterized by continued urbanization, industrialization, and other economic trends begun in previous stages. Demographic conditions, however, show a significant change. The birthrate begins to drop rapidly, as small families become more prevalent. The shift toward small families may be related to the fact that children in an urban environment are generally economic liabilities rather than assets. In Stage III the population continues to grow, but at an ever-slowing pace.

Stage IV finds the population growth rate stable or increasing very slowly. Birthrates and death rates are low. The population is now urbanized, and birth control is in general use. Population density may be quite high. Countries such as Argentina and Chile may be considered to be in Stage III; the time of their complete transformation to Stage IV remains an open question. Virtually all of the countries in Western Europe are in Stage IV, as are the United States, Canada, and Japan, countries that exhibit a European style of industrialization and urbanization.

The difficulty of predicting exactly when a country will enter a particular stage is illustrated by the United States. Birthrates reached a very low level during the 1930s (comparable to current rates) but then accelerated sharply during the postwar years, creating growth conditions equivalent to those in Stage III. Birthrates are sociological phenomena that are strongly influenced by cultural value systems, unlike death rates, which can be reduced by control of disease, proper diet, and sanitation efforts.

The model of demographic transformation is based on analysis of Europe's experience with urbanization and industrialization. Other areas with different cultures may not follow the European example precisely (see the boxed feature Demographic Transition for Developed and Developing Countries). If the model is valid, however, population growth in many parts of the world will slow down as Stages III and IV are reached. Whether and when population growth will be reduced or stabilized is, of course, unknown (Figure 2–5). Meanwhile, the differences experienced in the rate of population growth, though seemingly minute, have enormous impacts on the absolute growth of population from region to region and on the utilization of resources (Table 2–2).

The **Malthusian theory** is another theory of population change that has received widespread attention and has numerous advocates. Thomas Malthus, an Englishman, first presented his theory in 1798, basing it on two premises:

1. Humans tend to reproduce prolifically, that is geometrically—2, 4, 8, 16, 32.
2. The capacity to produce food and fiber expands more slowly, that is, arithmetically—2, 3, 4, 5, 6.

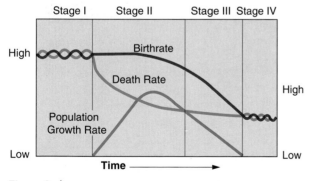

Figure 2–4
Model of demographic transformation. The demographic transformation model is based on the European experience. It may not represent what will happen elsewhere, especially in areas of non-European cultures. The model assumes an initial period of traditional rural life with high birthrates and death rates and no population growth. Then, with increased production and improved sanitation, the death rate declines, creating a condition of rapid population growth. As the population becomes more urbanized, the birthrate also declines until low birthrates and death rates finally prevail and the population no longer grows.

Table 2–2
Population doubling time by region.

Region	Population (in millions)	Growth Rate	Years to Double
Europe	506	.1	1025
North America	290	.7	98
Former Soviet Union	285[a]	.6	123
Oceania	28	1.2	57
Asia	3,322[b]	1.7	41
Latin America	470	2.0	35
Africa	700	2.9	24
World	5,607	1.6	43

Source: Population Reference Bureau, *World Population Data Sheet* (Washington, DC: 1994).

Note: The number of years required for population to double is based on the assumption that the current rate of increase will remain constant. The higher the growth rate, the more realistic is the projected doubling time.

[a]Data for the former Soviet Union are for mid-1993.

[b]Data for Asia are exclusive of countries formerly a part of the Soviet Union.

Figure 2–5
World population growth rates. There are great differences in population growth from one part of the world to another. Areas of the world that are highly urbanized and have advanced economies have low birthrates and death rates and consequently low rates of population growth. Areas that are less urbanized and less economically advanced have high birthrates, declining death rates, and moderately to rapidly growing populations. (From Population Reference Bureau, *World Population Data Sheet,* Washington, DC: 1994.)

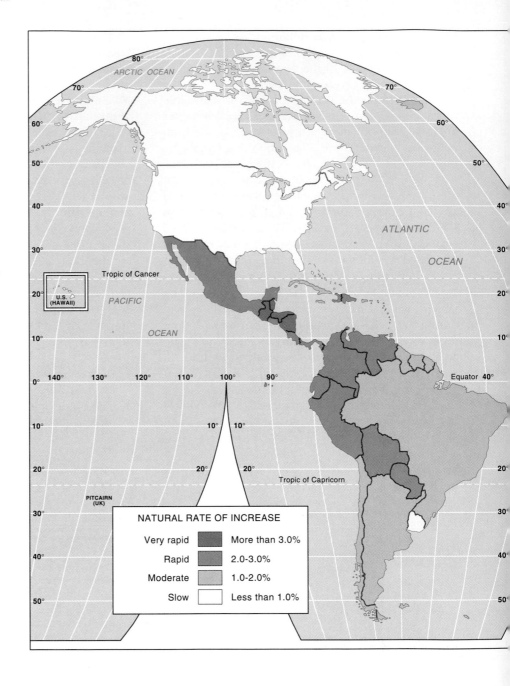

Thus, the population will exceed the food supply unless population growth is checked by society. If growth continues, surplus populations will be reduced by war, disease, and famine.

If we plot Malthus's idea on a graph, three stages of the relationship between population and production become apparent (Figure 2–6). In Stage I, human needs are not as great as production capacity. By Stage II, production capacity and increased hu-

man needs are roughly equal. In Stage III, population has grown to the point where its needs can no longer be met.

When Stage III occurs, the population dies off, and we cannot be sure what follows. One idea is that Stage III is simply a repetition of Stage II, with alternating periods of growth and die-off, represented by line (a) in Figure 2–6. Another idea is that the die-off is so great that Stage I is reproduced, as

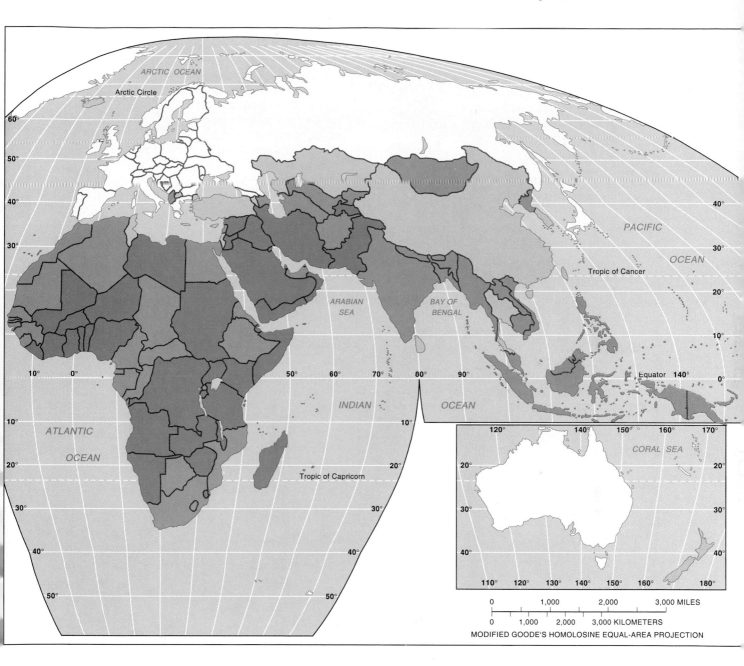

MODIFIED GOODE'S HOMOLOSINE EQUAL-AREA PROJECTION

represented by line (b). Malthus's theoretical die-off has not occurred, possibly because of the enormous increase in production associated with the Industrial Revolution. Malthus assumed that people would reject birth control on moral grounds, and he could not, of course, foresee the impact of the Industrial Revolution. For the past few decades, however, **neo-Malthusians** (present-day advocates of Malthus) have argued that the population/production crisis has merely been delayed and disaster may yet strike.

Karl Marx viewed the population question differently, considering the Malthusian perspective as simply a possible rationale for capitalist exploitation of the masses. According to Marxist theory, economic and social benefits can be enhanced only by increasing the labor force. So-called overpopulation and population pressure are seen as imperfections of a capitalistic economic system, not as an actual excess of people. Marx saw the underlying problem as the control of resources by that capitalistic system.

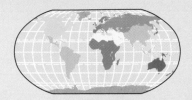

DEMOGRAPHIC TRANSITION FOR DEVELOPED AND DEVELOPING COUNTRIES

The demographic transition shown in Figure 2–4 is a model that illustrates well the experience to date of most European countries. The model in Figure A distinguishes between the experience of today's developed and developing countries. Several observations are appropriate.

The death rate in today's developed countries began a slow but significant decline during the late eighteenth and early nineteenth centuries and then accelerated that decline during the late nineteenth century. We should be aware of two important facts. First, the period of time required to lower the death rate was longer for developed than for developing countries. Second, by the time the death rate began its rapid decline in the developed countries, the birthrate had also begun its decline; the same is not true for today's developing countries. The result is that the developed countries overall never had the explosive growth rates of today's developing countries (rates of 1.75 to 2.50 percent a year versus 3 to 4 percent a year, respectively). In addition, the European countries had a safety valve in the form of migration opportunities, which are not readily available in today's high-growth countries. Another significant factor is that the death rate declined in the developed countries as a function of the need to discover, invent, and diffuse medical technology—a slow process. In today's world, reducing the death rate is less a matter of discovery or invention and much more a matter of diffusion of medical technology.

We should also understand that today's developed countries experienced a long Stage II and III of their demographic transformation, during which major economic development was occurring. By comparison, today's developing countries have been thrown into high growth rapidly (sometimes in a decade or two in response to a rapidly declining death rate). They have not experienced economic growth at a similar rate, but they are experiencing population growth rates in excess of anything known before. Furthermore, the base population to which those high growth rates are applied is larger: It includes more than 80 percent of the world's population. And the model for developing countries is open ended—we do not know how long their high-growth phase will continue. Given the diversity in culture, physical resources, and current level of economic and political organization of developing countries, we might want to consider the implications of such a population situation for the economic development process, regionally and in the world at large.

Figure A
The demographic transformation for developed and developing countries. Clearly, the demographic experience has not been the same for all countries. Striking differences are evident for developed and developing countries. (Adapted by permission from *The World Development Report 1982*, New York: Oxford University Press, 1982, p. 26.)

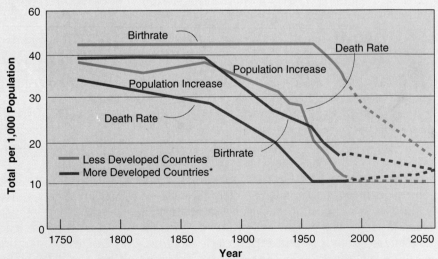

Rate of Population Increase = Birthrate - Death Rate

Note: These are crude birth- and death rates. The projected increase in death rate in developed countries after about 1980 reflects the rising proportion of older people in the population.

*Includes industrialized countries, the former Soviet Union, and Eastern Europe.

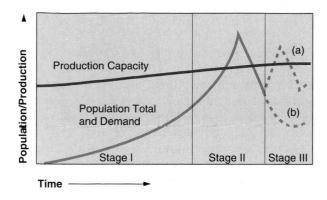

Figure 2-6
Malthusian theory. The Malthusian theory can be illustrated by a three-part diagram. In Stage I the needs of the population are less than production capacity. In Stage II, however, the increase in population is so great that need soon exceeds production capacity. For a while the population continues to grow by using surpluses accumulated from the past and overexploiting soil resources. Eventually, the pressure on the resource base is too great, and the population begins to die off. Stage III may be a continual repetition of Stage II (a) or a return to Stage I (b).

Communist nations still espouse Marx's view of population from an ideological standpoint, but some—China, for example—also actively encourage family planning. The Soviet Union's low birthrates resulted from economic and demographic pressures, and low birthrates continue in Russia today.

The Marxist idea that increasing population can lead to greater prosperity conflicts with Malthusian thought. Malthus painted a dark future for humankind without population controls. Marxists, in contrast, believe that population growth can lead to greater productivity if resources are adequately developed and distributed. Both theories suggest that the balance between population and resources, or productive capacity, is central to the development process.

Others also believe that population growth is beneficial. Ester Boserup, for example, has argued that the stress of increasing demand stimulates change in traditional agricultural systems.[1] Then, once the transformation is well under way, the rate of population growth declines in response to modernization. Boserup's thesis is an interesting contrast to the neo-Malthusian view of population growth.

All theories aside, the fact remains that the population of the world is large and that increasing numbers of people live in the poor world, or the developing nations (Figure 2–7). Figure 2–8 illustrates dramatically the changing population proportions and projects their continuation into the twenty-first century. Even now, famine, starvation, and disease are not uncommon, though they may be localized. Both the current suffering of individuals and the specter of what could occur on a more widespread scale require that we assess our potential to support the billions more to come.

THE RESOURCE CONCEPT

Some Definitions

The **resource concept** is built around three interacting components: resources, obstacles, and inert elements. A resource is anything that can be used to satisfy a need or a desire; it is a means to an end. An obstacle is anything that inhibits the attainment of a need or desire—the opposite of a resource. Inert elements in our surroundings neither help nor hinder that attainment.

If a man needs to walk from point A to point B, his legs are a resource that he can use to satisfy that need. If point B lies across a river and beyond some low hills, the river and the hills inhibit his walking and therefore are obstacles for him. If the man drives a car, the river becomes a formidable obstacle. Neither the hiker's doctorate in astrophysics nor the arable land across which he passes helps or hinders his walking; they are inert elements.

For the man's brother, a local farmer, resources may include seed and fertilizer. The river also becomes a resource for the farmer because he can use it for irrigation; it is no longer an obstacle. The hills may be obstacles to the farmer's plowing, but the minerals located in those hills may be the basic resource of a nearby miner.

Those simple examples suggest several points. First, resources are not just material objects. Knowledge is a resource: our farmer has to know when and how to tend crops. Skill and organization may also be resources, if they are necessary for the exploitation of the mineral deposit in our example. Other nonmaterial resources include inventiveness, good government, useful education, cooperation, and adequate social order.

Furthermore, material resources are not just natural resources. The farmer's and the miner's tools are culturally derived. Even the farmer's seeds and plants are culturally modified. In fact, most material items in the surroundings of an urban dweller are not natural but have been created by people—books, chairs, cars, bridges, and buildings, for instance.

In addition, elements in the environment may function as resources, obstacles, and/or inert elements all at the same time. The river is a resource to the farmer, an obstacle to the hiker, and an inert element to the miner.

Finally, resources are not static or finite. The farmer's tools were improved with the development of draft animals and, later, the tractor. Seed has continued to be improved by selective breeding. The miner's pick has probably been discarded in favor of power-driven equipment. Moreover, a given element may undergo frequent change in its volume as a resource, and other resources are constantly being created. A simple stick becomes a resource when used to poke, pry, or shake trees and bushes for food. With the discovery that the stick can also be used as a planting tool, its function as a resource is increased. In like manner, the rich coal deposits of western Pennsylvania were not resources before the Europeans arrived because the Indians of the area made no use of coal. The Agricultural Revolution and the Industrial Revolution are excellent examples of multiple-resource innovation.

Resources and Culture

Just like the hiker, the farmer, and the miner, diverse cultures have different resources. Each culture group has developed a set of customs, laws, and organizations that effectively structure the lives and attitudes of its members. Those cultural controls affect the way in which resources are viewed.

The few groups who still live by hunting, fishing, or gathering look at nature in terms of how many useful plants and animals it produces. They are not concerned about soil quality, growing season, or rainfall, even though those factors bear on natural production. Hunters, fishers, and gatherers probably do not even recognize the differences in clay deposits, some of which other groups use as raw materials for making bricks or pottery. But hunters, fishers, and gatherers do view as resources obsidian and other rock deposits from which they can fashion hunting, fishing, and cutting tools. Cultures that have metal instruments would consider such deposits to be of little significance. Similarly, various plants used for making mats and containers are seen as resources by hunters, fishers, and gatherers, whereas Western cultures may think of those same plants as weeds.

Perhaps even more important is the role that culture plays in directing economic activity, for resources are basically an economic concept. Some cultures, such as the Bedouin culture of the Middle East and several Asian cultures, are less materialistic

Figure 2-7
A small village in Tunisia. Settlements in the Sahara are restricted to oasis locations. The balance between population and the carrying capacity of the environment is precarious in such places.

than the American culture. Because the accumulation of wealth is not a primary goal for these peoples, their economic organization is structured to provide little more than basic needs. In other cultures social, political, and economic organization is such that large portions of the population have little or no opportunity to develop resources; cultural controls inhibit the application of technology and limit individual opportunity.

In almost all cultures certain economic activities are socially more acceptable than others. In other words, cultural attitudes tend to direct individuals to use different sets of resources. The Bedouin of the Arabian Desert are nomadic herders because their culture considers herding the highest possible occupation. The existence of large quantities of petroleum under the land means little to them; nor are they impressed by the possibility of becoming oasis agriculturists, even though water and good soil may

be available and the life of a farmer may be more secure. How different things are in the United States, where urban-oriented, white-collar employment is the goal of most Americans. Many of the students who go to college to prepare themselves for such jobs are responding to parental and peer pressure, a form of cultural control. Our population is so large and diverse, however, that a wide range of economic activities and opportunities exist.

Expansion of Resources. It is not difficult to comprehend that nonmaterial resources can be constantly created: new ideas and better organization have no limit. We can also see that material resources that can be replenished can be used confidently for years to come if wisely exploited. These, including trees, crops, animals, soils, and rivers, are known as **flow resources**, or renewable resources. What may be more difficult to understand is that

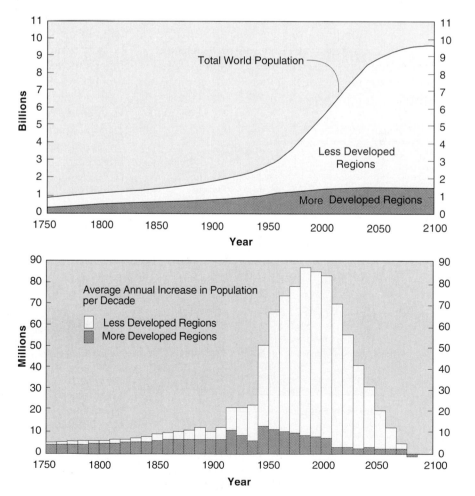

Figure 2-8
Population growth in developed and developing regions: 1750–2100. An increasingly large share of the world's population is found in developing regions, a situation that can be expected to continue well into the next century. (Adapted with permission from Thomas W. Merrick, with PRB staff, "World Population in Transition," *Population Bulletin* 41, no. 2, Washington, DC: Population Reference Bureau, April 1986, p. 4.)

fund resources, often called nonrenewable resources, can also be created. Examples of fund resources are such nonreusable minerals as coal or petroleum.

Our understanding of resources can also be enhanced by making a distinction between the total resources we believe to exist and proven reserves (Figure 2–9). Proven reserves are those materials actually available, given current prices and current technologies. Any review of U.S. resources (discussed in Chapter 5) would indicate that the reserves even of fund resources may increase or decrease on an annual basis.

Technological advances can result in the creation of fund resources in two major ways. First, a need may be found for a formerly unused mineral or element, many examples of which can be cited. For instance, the early phases of the Industrial Revolution led to the use of iron in conjunction with other metals to produce steel. In addition, many elements were inert until high-temperature technology created a need for them. Uranium had no use until atomic power was developed. And only in this century were techniques perfected for extracting nitrogen from the atmosphere, giving rise to an important segment of the fertilizer industry.

In the past 100 years a second, and perhaps more important, means of creating fund resources has been the inclusion of low-quality mineral deposits in the fund-resource base. Prior to the advent of mass transport and suitable processing equipment, only the richest mineral deposits could be mined economically. But those deposits represent only a small portion of the total amount of any mineral in the earth's crust (Figure 2–10). Once the technology became available to mine low-quality deposits, they, too, became resources. For example, today most of the world's copper is produced from ores containing less than 3 percent copper. And taconite, a low-quality ore previously considered worthless, has become the basis of continued exploitation in the famous Mesabi Range in northeastern Minnesota, following the depletion of its rich iron ores.

Fund resources can also be expanded by an increase in demand. If the demand for a particular item grows and higher prices are created, new resources are developed. Large quantities of petroleum in oil shales and tar sands have not been exploited because less-expensive oil is available from other sources. If petroleum prices rise again, extraction of these oil resources may become profitable.

In addition, technology has found several other ways to expand the agricultural resource base. For example, the amount of land that is arable has been increased by the use of improved seeds and mechanized cropping. Through seed selection and crossing (hybridization), new varieties of crops have been de-

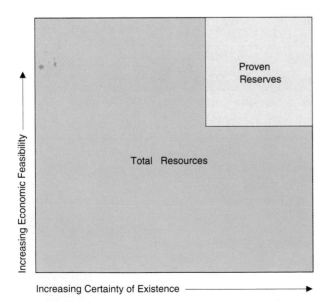

Figure 2–9
The distinction between proven reserves and total resources. Current technology and economic conditions limit our use of total resources to the proven reserves.

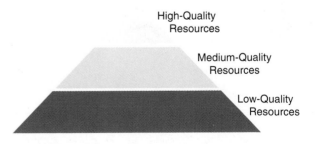

Figure 2–10
Resource pyramid. The pyramid concept applies to all types of resources: land, minerals, fish, people, crops. Most of the resources we use are of high quality. As technology improves or demand increases or depletion occurs, we use more medium- and low-quality resources, with the potential for negative environmental consequences.

veloped that are more tolerant of drought or that can mature in a shorter time. In the United States, corn can now be raised farther north and west than was feasible fifty years ago, and wheat is now grown in areas where only 15 inches (381 millimeters) of rain falls every year. Furthermore, mechanization of agriculture permits farmers to cultivate what was formerly nonarable land. By using power-driven equipment, one farmer can cultivate several hundred acres, thereby accumulating an adequate income even though each acre may yield only a small return. In the United States and Canada mechanized expansion of arable land is well developed. In other areas, such as China, similar land is little used despite the great need for it. The role of expanding knowledge and education in the creation and expansion of the resource base can hardly be overestimated.

Loss of Resources. Just as demand can create resources, a decrease in demand can reduce resources. Steel-cutting instruments have largely replaced the need for stone and obsidian tools; synthetic rubber has decreased the need for natural rubber. Similarly, artificial heating and our habits of living and working mainly indoors have decreased our need for heavy woolen clothing. Thus, the development of a new product often leads to the disuse of other products. Another version of this concept is illustrated when crop productivity increases without a significant change in demand, causing marginal producers to withdraw from that activity.

Resources can also be lost through use. Each drop of oil or gasoline burned and each morsel of wheat or corn eaten represent a decrease in resources. On the other hand, some resources are lost if they are not used. A tree that is allowed to decay means lost pulp or lumber, and unharvested crops are a lost resource, even though they may fertilize the soil and feed wild animals.

Unfortunately, resources are also destroyed by improper use. Poor farming techniques lead to erosion and soil depletion. And factories and cities may discharge harmful chemicals and sewage into rivers, destroying aquatic life and ruining water quality for those downstream. Finally, war destroys not only people—our most important resource—but also buildings, bridges, and other material resources.

Technocratic Theory

A number of authorities have observed the great technological advances made during the ongoing

Industrial Revolution and have derived what is often called the **technocratic theory.** That optimistic theory directly counters the concept formulated by Malthus (compare Figures 2–6 and 2–11). Technocrats accept the Malthusian population-growth curve but assume that productive capacity (i.e., use of resources) increases faster than population growth. To support their contention, technocrats point both to the expansion of the resource base during the past 400 years and to the increase in the standard of living within Western cultures. Technocrats believe that technology will continue to expand, supporting still greater populations.

Neo-Malthusians admit that the Industrial Revolution has postponed the day of disaster (Figure 2–12). They maintain, however, that the expansion of production capacity cannot continue indefinitely and that when population growth surpasses capacity, Malthus's prediction will be fulfilled. Neo-Malthusians suggest that in such areas as India, Bangladesh, and parts of Africa the notions of Malthus may yet be proven. For example, Bangladesh, which has 110 million people and is growing at 2.7 percent per year, will double its population again in twenty-five years or so. Since that

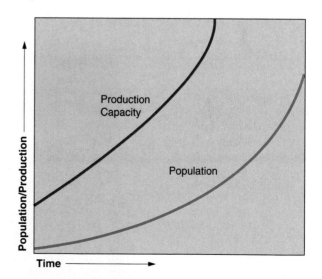

Figure 2-11
Technocratic theory. The technocratic theory assumes the same population curve as the Malthusian theory. What is different is the rate at which production capacity is assumed to grow. If production capacity increases faster than the population, higher standards of living are possible.

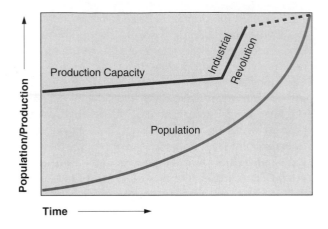

Figure 2–12
Neo-Malthusian theory. The neo-Malthusian theory is a recent refinement of classical Malthusian thought. It takes into account the great technological advances of the Industrial Revolution but argues that those rapid advances in productive capacity cannot be maintained.

large population occupies an area scarcely larger than many American states, the country may or may not be near the limits of its physiologic density (Figure 2–13).

We do not have a good sense of the world's **carrying capacity** for population, or the maximum number of people the world can support. Estimates range from less than 8 billion people to more than 40 billion. The resource demand of future populations is mind boggling if we assume that many countries will succeed in achieving their goals for economic development. We do not know the precise connections between population pressures and resource scarcities. But exponential growth of population and use of resources cannot continue indefinitely. Even now, masses of people—perhaps more than 1 billion—live in poverty, despite rising living standards for many others. Increasing population pressure may further exaggerate that economic and biologic inequality.

SUMMARY
Population Prospects

In all likelihood the world's population will continue to grow in the near future. By the year 2000 more than 6 billion people are expected to be living on the earth. By the year 2025 that number will top 8.5 billion if current growth rates are sustained. A few daring forecasters estimate a world population of 51 billion by the year 2100. Such long-range predictions, however, must be viewed with great caution.

Figure 2–13
The Bangladesh jute market. This heavily populated country is mainly dependent on agriculture or the processing of industrial raw materials such as jute. Countries overly dependent on agricultural production as a source of employment tend to exhibit low income levels.

Predictions of resource development are not easy to make because there is no way to determine what resources will be created. The Food and Agriculture Organization of the United Nations believes that the technology now exists to adequately feed and clothe the world's population for many decades. The problem is that the technology may not be available where it is most needed.

demographic
transformation

flow resources

fund resources

growth rate

Industrial Revolution

Malthusian theory

neo-Malthusian

physiologic density

population density

population distribution

population explosion

resource concept

technocratic theory

KEY TERMS

Agricultural Revolution

birthrate

carrying capacity

death rate

NOTES

1. Ester Bosrup, *The Conditions of Agricultural Growth* (Chicago: Aldine, 1968), 11–27.

3

Physical and Cultural Components of the Human Environment

Elements of the Physical Environment

Humanity and Culture

Social and Political Organization

Economic Activity

Agricultural village on one of Japan's small alluvial plains in southern Honshu. The mountainous terrain over much of Japan means that the Japanese must use intensively whatever agricultural land is available. The means by which people sustain themselves in different areas is dependent on the interaction of both cultural and physical environments.

41

In some parts of the world people live well; in other parts life is a constant struggle. Three principal factors affect the level of living in an area: the number of people and their rate of increase; the physical environment; and the political, educational, economic, and social systems in place. This chapter focuses on the physical environment and on the human cultural systems.

It must be recognized that society has an overriding economic concern: survival is based on some from of production, and production necessarily involves a relationship with the environment. The nature of that relationship depends on the skills and resources that a society accumulates and on the value system that motivates it. For example, the way people in the United States use a desert environment differs substantially from the way the Bushmen of Africa do.

Using the environment means modifying it, and modification can bring problems. Our recent experiences with water and air pollution and power problems sometimes encourage us to think that landscape modification and environmental problems are new phenomena, but that notion is inaccurate. Ancient inhabitants of the Middle East had culturally induced environmental problems; for example, the increased salinity of soils (high salt content), a result of irrigation practices, ultimately made many agricultural lands useless and contributed to the decline of some Mesopotamian civilizations.

Thus, **landscape modification** is as old as humankind. In fact, most, if not all, landscapes are not natural but are cultural, shaped and formed as societies have occupied and used the surface of the earth. Culture is a part of the environment, just as the physical world is, and recognizing that is essential to understanding the condition of the human race in various regions of the world.

ELEMENTS OF THE PHYSICAL ENVIRONMENT

The numerous elements of the physical environment—rocks, soils, landforms, climate, vegetation, animal life, minerals, and water—are interrelated. For instance, climate is partially responsible for variations in vegetative patterns, soil formations, and landforms; and organic matter from vegetation affects soil development. Environmental elements are all part of a large **ecosystem**, which often exists in a delicate balance. Recognizing the relationship among natural processes is vital, as is recognizing

that human beings interfere with those processes. The most active agent of environmental change on the surface of the earth is the human race.

Climate

Climate directly affects our efforts to produce food and industrial crops, and agricultural production in great quantities remains basic to the entire human race. All plants have specific requirements for optimum growth; some, such as rice, need substantial amounts of moisture, whereas others, such as wheat, are more tolerant of drought. Coffee requires a year-round growing season; it grows best in the tropics at elevations that provide cooler temperatures. Even though humans have modified the character of many plants, climatic differences ensure great geographic variation in crop cultivation.

The most important climatic elements are precipitation and temperature. Precipitation can be defined as moisture that has been removed from the atmosphere and then dropped onto the surface of the earth. Rainfall is the most common type of precipitation, but the solid forms—snow, sleet, and hail—are also significant. Melting snow has value as a source of water for streams or as soil moisture that can be used in later seasons. Sleet and hail are normally localized, but they can cause enormous damage and economic losses.

As the map of **average annual precipitation** shows, the rainy areas of the world can be found in the tropics and the middle latitudes (Figure 3-1). In the middle latitudes precipitation is particularly heavy on the western (windward) sides of continents. The eastern (leeward) sides of mid-latitude continents may be less rainy but may still receive sufficient precipitation to be considered humid regions, particularly if exposure to major water bodies is favorable. Notice in Figure 3–1 that the eastern United States and Canada as well as East Asia illustrate such a condition.

In contrast, the interiors of continents such as Asia or North America and the areas on leeward sides of mountains experience moisture deficiency. In addition, some subtropical areas—northern Africa, Australia, northern Chile and Peru, northwestern Mexico, and the southwestern United States—have only meager amounts of rain (Figure 3–2, p. 46). Subsiding air and divergent wind patterns, along with cold offshore waters, reduce the likelihood of precipitation in those areas.

The map of average annual precipitation is useful for analyzing the distribution of human activities. Areas of meager rainfall normally are not heavily populated (see Figure 2–2 for population distribution). Exceptions, such as the Nile Valley or southern California, require an exotic, or external, water supply. On the other hand, very high rainfall and high temperatures contribute to other environmental conditions that are difficult to overcome—namely, the infertile soils found in tropical regions.

Seasonal rainfall patterns are as important to land use as yearly rainfall totals. Most equatorial areas receive a significant amount of rainfall in every season. But tropical wet and dry regions have a distinct rainy season (i.e., summer) as well as an excessively dry season. Although temperatures in such regions are high enough for the growing season to be yearlong, that advantage is partly offset by the seasonality of the rainfall. Dry subtropical climates also experience distinct seasonal variations, except that summers are dry and winters have the maximum rainfall.

Variability of precipitation is the percentage of departure from the annual average, which is derived from a thirty- or fifty-year record of precipitation. The greatest variability is experienced in areas of minimal rainfall, where settlement is limited unless a special source of water is available. In contrast, transitional areas (e.g., steppes or savannas) between humid and dry regions are frequently important settlement zones with a significant production of staple foods (i.e., grains). Under normal conditions the Great Plains of the United States, the North China Plain, the Sahel (on the southern edge of the Sahara), and the Black Earth Region of Russia, Ukraine, and Kazakhstan typify such regions. Unfortunately, however, those and similar areas have experienced repeated droughts and overexploitation. Recently, for example, in the Sahel thousands died of starvation, emphasizing the danger of dependence on such transitional areas.

The human suffering associated with prolonged drought has encouraged the study of subhumid environments and the process by which their productivity is lessened. Deterioration of the ecosystem, especially of soils and vegetation, occurs as a result of both drought and human activities. Overpopulation, for instance, may encourage grazing or cultivation practices that have long-term detrimental effects on the environment—particularly during periods of recurring drought.

Temperature and Plant Growth.   Data on the annual amount, seasonality, and variability of rainfall reveal much about the utility of an environment. But the moisture actually available also depends on temperature conditions. High temperatures provide great potential for evaporation and plant transpiration, or a high **evapotranspiration rate**. An unfavorable relationship between precipitation and evapotranspiration means that not enough moisture is available for plant growth. Deserts represent the extreme cases of that moisture-temperature relationship.

Perhaps the most important aspect of temperature is the length of the **frost-free period**, which relates primarily to latitude but also to altitude and the location of large bodies of water. The modifying influence of water on temperature can be seen in marine locations: growing seasons are longer than would normally be expected at those latitudes. A comparison of northwestern Europe with similar latitudes in the Soviet Union or eastern North America offers an example (Figure 3–3, pp. 48–49).

Winter temperatures are significant, also. Many mid-latitude fruit trees require a specific dormancy period with temperatures below a certain level. Cold temperatures are necessary to ensure vernalization, the activation of a new flowering cycle.

In addition, the photoperiod (the length of the day, or the active period of photosynthesis) and the daily temperature range during the growing season affect plant growth. Some plants, such as barley, require a long daily photoperiod to flower or set seed; others, such as soybeans or rice, benefit from shorter photoperiods. Each plant variety has a specific range of daily low and high temperatures, called cardinal temperatures, within which plant growth can occur. Cardinal temperatures are known for most plants. The numerous varieties of wheat, for example, have cardinal temperatures that range from a low of 32° to 41°F (0° to 5°C) to a high of 87° to 98°F (31° to 37°C). Within that range the optimum temperatures for most varieties of wheat are between 77° and 88°F (25° and 31°C). Although less-than-optimum conditions do not mean that a particular crop cannot be cultivated, departures from the optimum reduce the efficiency with which that crop is produced. And efficiency, translated into cost per unit of production, is a major concern in commercial agriculture.

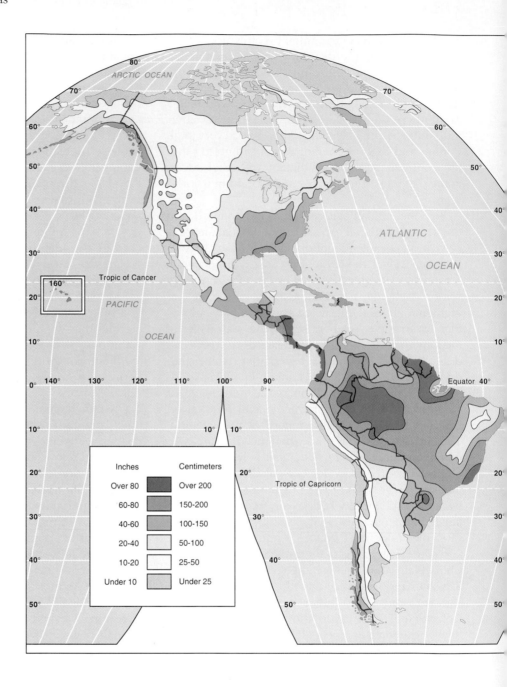

Figure 3–1
World mean annual precipitation. Precipitation varies greatly from one part of the world to another. Moreover, there is considerable variability in precipitation from one year to the next. Variability is usually greatest in areas of limited precipitation.

Climatic Classification. Climatic classification is based on both temperature and precipitation conditions (Table 3–1, p. 50). Although conditions may vary within a climatic region, a generalized classification system is useful for comparing the characteristics of different areas. Figure 3–3 shows the global distribution of climates and reveals a close relationship among latitude, continental position, and climate. The locational similarity of humid sub-

tropical climates in the United States, China, and Argentina is just one example.

The distinction between dry and humid climates is fundamental to classification, but no single specific precipitation limit can be used to separate the two. For example, areas are classified as desert or steppe if the potential for evaporation exceeds actual precipitation. In the mid-latitudes deserts normally receive less than 10 inches (254 millimeters)

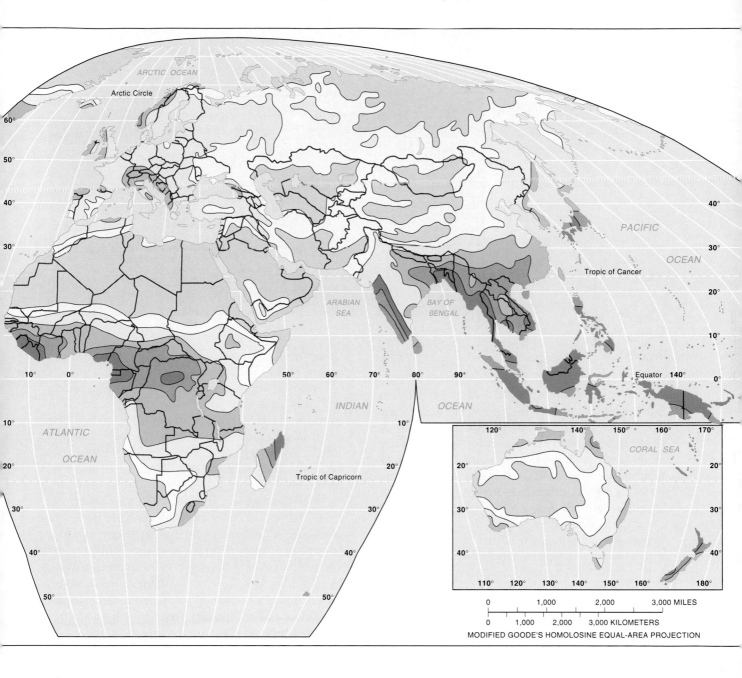

MODIFIED GOODE'S HOMOLOSINE EQUAL-AREA PROJECTION

of precipitation; steppes or semiarid regions receive between 10 and 20 inches (254 and 508 millimeters). For classification as a dry climate, however, the limits of precipitation are lower in the higher latitudes and higher in the lower latitudes. For instance, 25 inches (635 millimeters) of precipitation in the higher mid-latitudes may provide a humid climate and forest growth; that same amount in tropical areas may result in a semiarid, treeless environment.

Along with the other controls of climate—such as latitude, marine exposure, prevailing winds, and atmospheric pressure systems—elevation is another major factor. The highland climates shown on Figure 3–3 feature variable temperature and rainfall conditions according to specific elevation and position within mountains. Even though many mountainous areas are sparsely settled and provide a meager resource base for farmers, highland settlement is important in Latin America, East Africa, and Indonesia.

Figure 3-2
Fire burning in mountains north of Los Angeles in 1993. The dry summer subtropical landscape of grassland and shrub woodland is especially vulnerable to fire.

Vegetation

Vegetation patterns are closely associated with climate, as can be seen by using Figures 3–3 (pp. 48–49) and 3–4 (pp. 52–53) to compare world regions with similar locational attributes. For example, the Southeastern United States and Southeastern China exhibit clear similarities in both climatic and vegetational patterns. Less obvious on maps of this scale is the locational distinction between grasslands (herbaceous plants) and forests (woody plants). Grasslands in one form or another exist as part of mid-latitude prairies, Mediterranean woodland shrub vegetation, tropical savannas, steppes, and deserts; they are directly attributable to moisture deficiency, as found in climatic steppes and deserts, or extreme seasonal variation in precipitation, as found in dry summer subtropical and tropical wet and dry climates. A very cold climate (i.e., tundra) is also treeless, because the growing season is short or nonexistent and because subsoil is permanently frozen. The more humid climates are capable of supporting forest vegetation, which usually requires a minimum annual rainfall of 15 to 20 inches (381 to 508 millimeters), depending on evapotranspiration rates.

Natural vegetation is what would be expected in an area if vegetation succession were allowed to proceed over a long period without human interference. In earlier millennia natural vegetation permitted our ancestors to move easily across grass-covered plains and mingle with one another, whereas dense forests functioned as barriers, isolating culture groups and providing refuge for those who wanted to remain apart. The grasslands south of the Sahara represent one such cultural transition zone, with features of both African and Arab cultures. The equatorial rain forests of Central Africa, on the other hand, have always kept peoples apart, primarily because travel through them is difficult and the soils are poor.

Over the centuries humankind has greatly altered the world's natural vegetation. In fact, the phrase must be used quite carefully today, because few areas of truly natural vegetation remain; most vegetative cover is a reflection of human activity. In mid-latitude Asia, North America, and Europe, for example, increases in population and changes in agricultural technology have prompted the removal of broadleaf and mixed broadleaf and coniferous forests (see Figure 3–4) from vast areas so that field agriculture could expand (Figure 3–5, p. 54). High-latitude coniferous forests and tropical rain forests do still exist because they do not lend themselves to permanent settlement or to large-scale modern agriculture. But in countries like Brazil, rapid population growth, the need for space, and government economic policy have recently stimulated even rain-forest clearing. Some people view the expansion of Brazilian settlements in the Amazon rain forest with great hope—as a source of national pride and unity for Brazilians, a means of easing population pressure, and a source of new economic wealth. Others fear that these short-term gains may bring long-term damage to the forest, the soils, the streams, and the atmosphere. History is replete with examples in which short-term or immediate need has clouded our vision in matters of environmental stewardship.

Our attitudes toward natural vegetation have recently begun to change dramatically. Increasingly we are recognizing that vegetation is significant in many aspects of life and is related to other components of our environment, such as soil and air. Forest vegetation is becoming more critical as our numbers grow and as we consume ever-greater amounts of lumber and paper. Sustained-yield forestry—harvesting no more than the annual growth rate of trees can replace—is a more common practice as we realize that wasteful use results in greater resource problems. In addition, forests are valued for more than their wood. Not only do they represent an important botanical gene pool, but they also help to prevent erosion, which not only destroys land but also leads to the silting of rivers, streams, and reservoirs. Moreover, forests contribute to flood prevention by reducing water runoff. And in more affluent countries they are prized recreation areas.

Soils

In order to grow, plants need nutrients as well as moisture and energy from the sun. Nutrients are derived both from minerals in the earth and from humus, organic materials added to the soil by vegetation. The nutrients that soil contains depend on the kind of rock lying beneath it, the slope of the land, the vegetative cover, the microorganisms within the soil, and the soil's age. Three processes are particularly important in the formation of soil and greatly affect its supply of nutrients and therefore its fertility: laterization, podzolization, and calcification.

Laterization is a process by which infertile soils are formed in the tropics. The plentiful rainfall leaches the soil; that is, it dissolves the soluble minerals in the soil and carries them away. Unfortunately, the soluble minerals that are removed—calcium, phosphorous, potash, and nitrogen—are among the most important plant nutrients. Insoluble compounds of aluminum and iron remain, but those elements alone produce infertile soils. In addition, decomposed organic material,

which could provide nutrients, is minimal because rapid bacterial action is aided by the warm, moist conditions and by the microorganisms in the soil. After a few years of use, soils in areas of high rainfall and high temperature—the tropical and subtropical humid regions—show a marked decrease in fertility.

Podzolization occurs in high latitudes or in cold, humid climates where seasonal temperature variations are distinctive. In those locations normal leaching is less, either because rainfall is less or because the ground is frozen during part of the year. But poorly decomposed organic material, such as that from pine needles, combines with water to form weak, acidic solutions that remove aluminum and iron from the soil along with soluble minerals. What remains is a large amount of silica, which is low in fertility. Podzolization gives way to laterization nearer the tropics.

Calcification occurs on the drier margins of humid regions and in dry areas. In those locations reduced leaching, in response to limited precipitation, leads to greater accumulations of humus and calcium carbonate. Some soils formed under those conditions are very fertile but, paradoxically, often remain less productive because of the very moisture deficiency that favored their formation.

Residual soils are those that have formed where they are found. They reflect local environmental conditions and are strongly influenced by laterization, podzolization, or calcification. Some soils, however, are transported and thus have characteristics that bear little relationship to local environmental conditions. **Alluvium** is soil that is transported and deposited by water; **loess**, by wind. Alluvium and loess, along with soils formed from some volcanic materials, are exceptionally fertile. In humid areas they are often the most preferred for cultivation; but in excessively dry areas they may require great amounts of labor or capital for irrigation.

Humans have modified soils in many ways, sometimes improving inherently poor soils, sometimes repairing the damage done by depletion, erosion, or other forms of misuse. The addition of chemical or organic fertilizers can overcome the declining fertility that results from prolonged use. The addition of lime reduces acidity, which can be detrimental to many plants. Terraces can prevent erosion or help distribute irrigation water. Crops that place

Figure 3-3
Climatic regions of the world.
Climate is the long-term condition of the atmosphere. Although there are many elements of climate, most classifications use only the two most important: temperature (level and seasonality) and precipitation (amount and seasonality).

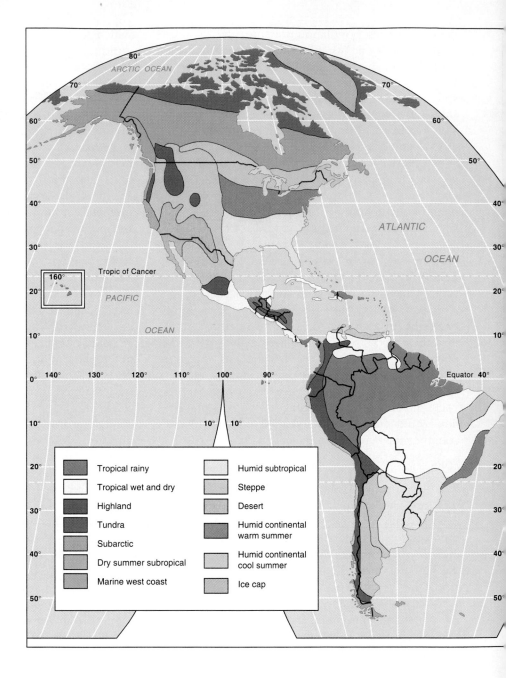

a serious drain on soil nutrients can be rotated with less-demanding plants or with leguminous plants, which have the capability of adding nitrogen. Fields themselves can be rotated, with some plots allowed to lie fallow, or rest, for several years between periods of cultivation so that fertility builds up again through natural processes. Farmers in many areas of the United States have even installed tile drains to remove excess moisture from poorly drained areas,

and other drainage techniques have been used in Asia and Europe with soils that otherwise would be unproductive.

Efforts to reduce soil destruction or improve fertility involve expenditures of labor and/or capital, but the long-term needs of society require that we accept the costs of maintaining the environment. Unfortunately, people are not always willing or able to bear such costs, particularly when short-

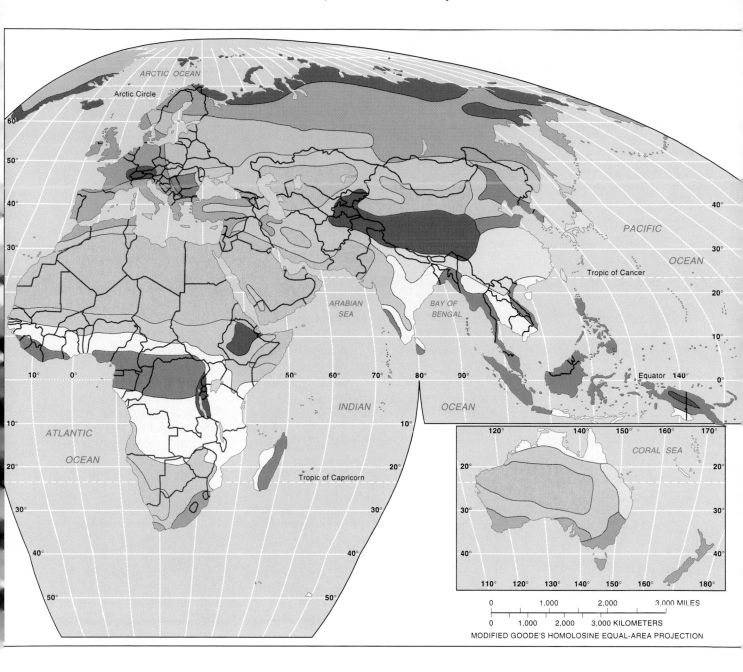

term profits or immediate survival is the main concern. An exploitive approach may lead to maximum return over a short period, but it often results in the rapid destruction of one of our most basic resources.

The experience of the United States illustrates the environmental damage and human hardship that can result from less-than-cautious use of resources. The years between 1910 and 1914 are often referred to as the golden years of American agriculture because of the high prices that farmers received for agricultural commodities. Indeed, prices continued to be favorable through World War I and into the 1920s. Those high prices and above-average rainfall encouraged farmers on the western margin of the Great Plains to convert their grassland into wheat fields. But then came several years of severe drought, which coincided

Table 3-1
Characteristics of world climate types.

Climate	Location, by Latitude (Continental Position, if Distinctive)	Temperature	Precipitation, in Inches Per Year (Millimeters Per Year)
Tropical rainy	Equatorial	Warm, range[a] less than 5° F; no winter	60+ (1,523+); no distinct dry season
Tropical wet and dry	5°–20°	Warm, range[a] 5°–15° F; no winter	25–60 (635-1,523); summer rainy, low-sun period dry
Steppe	Subtropics and middle latitudes (sheltered and interior continental positions)	Hot and cold seasons; dependent on latitude	Normally less than 20 (508), much less in middle latitudes
Desert	Subtropics and middle latitudes (sheltered and interior continental positions)	Hot and cold seasons; dependent on latitude	Normally less than 10 (254), much less in middle latitudes
Dry summer subtropical	30°–40° (western and subtropical coastal portions of continents)	Warm to hot summers; mild but distinct winters	20–30 (508–761); dry summer; maximum precipitation in winter
Humid subtropical	0°–40° (eastern and southeastern subtropical portions of continents)	Hot summers; mild but distinct winters	30–65 (761–1650); rainy throughout the year; occasional dry winter (Asia)
Marine west coast	40°–60° (west coasts of mid-latitude continents	Mild summers and mild winters	Highly variable, 20–100 (508–2,538); rainfall throughout the year; tendency to winter maximum
Humid continental (warm summer)	35°-45° (continental interiors and east coasts, Northern Hemisphere only)	Warm to hot summers; cold winters	20–45 (508–1,142); summer concentration; no distinct dry season
Humid continental (cool summer)	35°–45° (continental interiors and east coasts, Northern Hemisphere only)	Short, mild summers; severe winters	20–45 (508–1,142); summer concentration; no distinct dry season
Subarctic	46°–70° (Northern Hemisphere only)	Short, mild summers; long, severe winters	20–45 (508–1,142); summer concentration; no distinct dry season
Tundra	60° and poleward	Frost anytime; short growing season, vegetation limited	Limited moisture, 5–10 (127–635), except at exposed locations
Ice cap	Polar areas	Constant winter	Limited precipitation, but surface accumulation
Undifferentiated highland (see Figure 3–3)			

[a]The difference in temperature between the warmest months and the coldest months.

with the Depression of the 1930s. The unprotected cultivated lands were heavily damaged by wind erosion, and the farmers suffered terribly. Many of them moved away, abandoning their land. Banks failed, and whole towns were deserted.[1] That experience is not unlike the one currently taking place on the southern margin of the African Sahara (see the boxed feature Environmental Problems).

Landforms

The surface of the earth is usually divided into four categories of landforms:

1. plains, with little slope or local relief (i.e., few variations in elevation)
2. plateaus, or level land at high elevations
3. hills, with moderate to steep slopes and moderate local relief
4. mountains, with steep slopes and great local relief

Plains are the landform most widely used for settlement and production when other environmental characteristics permit. Large areas of land with little slope or relief are most suitable for agriculture, and humans have been agrarian beings for thousands of years. In addition, the ease of movement over plains, particularly those with grassland vegetation, has facilitated exchange with other societies. Not all exchange is peaceful, of course; the features of plains that contribute to their utility in peacetime can be handicaps in wartime. As shown by the rapid movement of mechanized armies across the plains of Europe during World War II, plains are easily overrun because they have few natural barriers to afford protection. Nonetheless, the great densities of population occur in areas where intensive agriculture is practiced or in regions where industrial and commercial activity is concentrated. Consequently, the early high-density agricultural populations were associated with plains. Those plains that exhibit limited settlement or utilization are less desirable for climatic reasons.

Hills and mountains offer quite a different habitat. In mountainous regions small basins and valleys become the focus of settlement and, because they are difficult to penetrate, may lead to the formation of distinct cultures. Although such areas do provide security from attack, they may also exhibit economic disparity in comparison with more favored regions.

Major differences and even conflicts between highland and lowland inhabitants are common and are a part of regional history in many areas of the world. Separatist movements are an expression of those differences, and isolated highland areas provide excellent bases for guerrilla armies. The mountain-dwelling Kurds of Iran and Iraq have been politically at odds with the governments of both those states; and in Myanmar the Karen of the Shan plateau have raised communist and indigenous insurrections against a government that is controlled by the lowland river-plain majority. Unifying a country that incorporates such contrasting environments and cultures remains difficult.

Minerals

Today's politically and economically powerful countries have built up their industrial structures by using huge amounts of **fossil fuels** (coal, petroleum, and natural gas) to process large quantities of minerals. Any country that wants to be considered a modern, industrialized nation must either possess such resources or acquire them. To date, neither nuclear energy nor hydroelectricity has surpassed fossil fuels in importance. Nuclear energy as yet contributes only minute quantities of power, and hydroelectricity generally has only local importance, providing a small portion of a nation's total power needs.

The use of petroleum and natural gas has increased rapidly in all industrialized areas since World War II, particularly in the United States. That trend has given those less developed countries with oil wealth a special importance in international politics, an importance far greater than their size or military strength could have provided. Although huge quantities of coal are available—especially in the United States, the Soviet Union, and China—petroleum is now being used as a substitute for coal because petroleum and natural gas are cleaner and contribute less to air pollution. Whether the increasing cost of petroleum will generate a reverse trend—that is, a move back to coal—is not yet clear.

Iron, aluminum, and copper are the most important metallic minerals used in industry. Others include chromium, copper, zinc, lead, gold, and silver. In addition, nonmetallic minerals such as nitrogen, calcium, potash, and phosphate are used for fertilizer. And salt, building stones, lime, sulfur,

Figure 3-4
World vegetation regions. The distribution of vegetation closely corresponds to climatic patterns. A map of vegetation can be used to determine an area's agricultural potential, since crops and natural vegetation use the same environmental elements for growth.

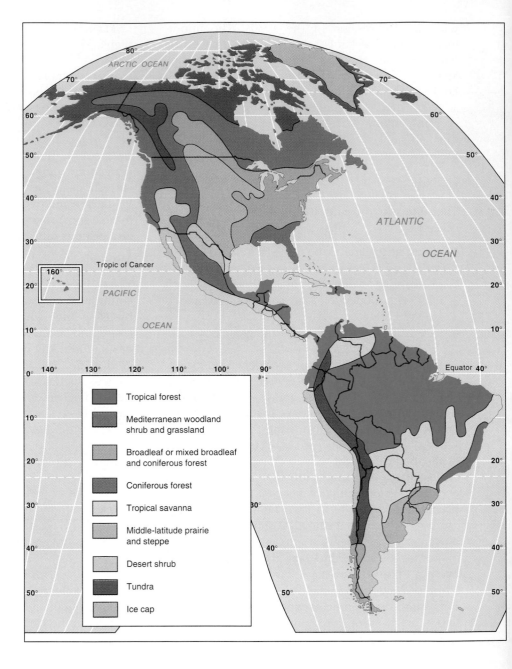

Tropical forest

Mediterranean woodland shrub and grassland

Broadleaf or mixed broadleaf and coniferous forest

Coniferous forest

Tropical savanna

Middle-latitude prairie and steppe

Desert shrub

Tundra

Ice cap

and sand are other commonly used nonmetallic minerals.

Future discoveries of significant mineral deposits in parts of the world that are currently nonproducing may greatly affect our evaluation of the industrial potential of such areas. At present, however, a crude balance of power exists between the United States and Russia. The power and position of those two nations in world society are based on their effective use of industrial and power resources. Western Europe is a close third but is somewhat more vulnerable because its supplies of petroleum are limited and it is politically fragmented. Japan is clearly vulnerable because its industrial structure depends heavily on imported resources. These centers of power could shift at any time in response to newly developed resources for industrial production.

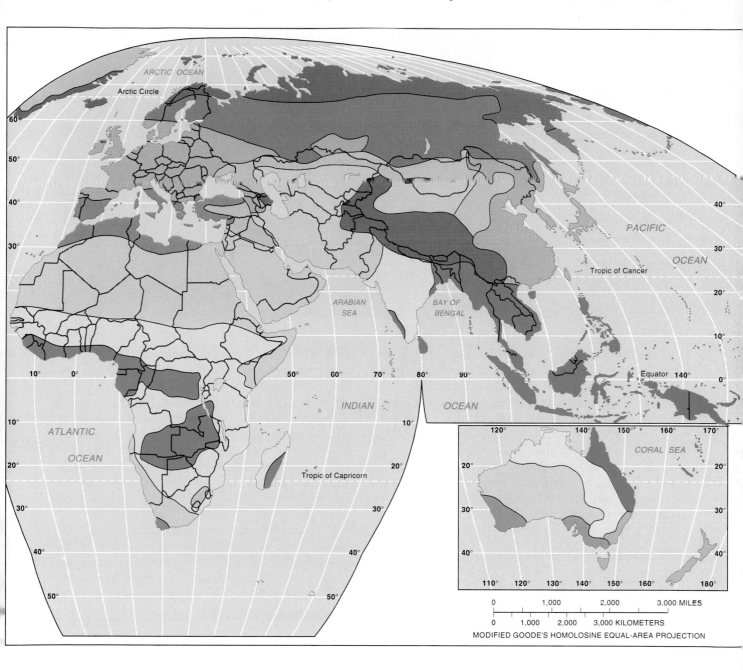

Use of the Environment

Three considerations are of the utmost importance in our use of the environment. First, our challenge is to avoid environmental deterioration at a time when increasing population and expanding expectations are placing ever-greater demands on it. The problems of human need, drought, famine, overgrazing, and environmental degradation in the Sahel illustrate the dangerous cycle. Nonuse is not the solution, nor is environmental destruction. What is necessary is intelligent use of the environment, which will be costly as well as elusive, complicated by the varied nature of the environment, about which we still have so much to learn.

Second, we must understand that the environment cannot be separated from the culture of the society that uses it, and societies differ. Motivations, attitudes,

Figure 3-5
Clear cuts and forest regrowth in the Olympia National Forest of Washington. Trees are a valuable resource for many products, but harvesting of forests also destroys wildlife habitats and may generate other environmental change, inevitably leading to conflicting notions about proper use of forests.

accumulated technology, and economic and political organization—all of those cultural considerations greatly affect the use of the environment.

Third, we must have long-range plans for using our physical environment. Our attitudes and immediate concerns seldom encourage us to formulate plans that consider the needs of humankind for more than two or three generations to come. Such a limited temporal perspective is not surprising, but it is ultimately unacceptable if the environment is to support humanity far into the future.

HUMANITY AND CULTURE

Humans are unique among living creatures: they can accumulate learned behavior and transmit it to successive generations. Those behavior patterns have helped to ensure sustenance and preserve the social order. With that accumulation of learned behavior, or culture, humans make decisions and create ways of life. Some behavior is based on **inherited culture**, a society's own earlier experiences; other actions are based on **diffused culture**, the experiences of other societies with which that one society has had contact. The entire set of elements that identifies a society's way of life—values, language, technology—also comprises its culture.

Another way of viewing culture is as a hierarchy of traits, complexes, and realms. A **culture trait** is the way a society deals with a single activity—for example, how people plant seeds. A **culture com-**

plex is a group of traits that are employed together in a more general activity, such as agricultural production (Figure 3–6). A **culture realm** is an area in which most of the population adheres to numerous culture complexes. Not all world regions have easily definable culture realms. Some have transition zones between realms, zones in which numerous distinct cultures have met and clashed. Even within a single political unit, cultural pluralism is frequently evident and adds to the difficulty of achieving national unity.

A **culture hearth** is a source area in which a culture complex has become so well established and advanced that its attributes are passed to future generations within and outside the immediate hearth area. No single hearth exists, as was once thought. Rather, several different hearths contribute to culture and become the basis for advancement over much larger areas.

Societies advance at uneven rates and along different paths. For example, the Bantu culture of western Africa advanced more rapidly than did that of the Bushmen or Hottentots of southern Africa. And the culture complexes of food production in China and Europe during the nineteenth century involved different traits. Cultural distinctiveness is not necessarily a difference in level of achievement; it may be merely a difference in kind.

The cumulative nature of cultural evolution, its dynamic quality, the unevenness with which it occurs, and its different orientations all contribute to funda-

Figure 3-6
A Portuguese woman drying sardines. Different cultures apply different technologies in the use of their resources.

mental and intriguing variations among the more than 5 billion people of our contemporary world.

The Growth of Culture

Most of the major human accomplishments have occurred during the past few thousand years, a short time span when measured against the 2 million years or so that hominids (the family of humanlike beings) have occupied the earth. By the end of the long Paleolithic period, or Old Stone Age, approximately 10,000 years ago, people had spread over most of the habitable portions of the earth, though low population densities were prevalent. Cultural accomplishments included the use of fire (perhaps the most significant achievement), the making of stone tools, and the construction of shelters. The Neolithic period, or New Stone Age, that followed marked the beginning of one of humankind's great developmental revolutions. Over a period of several thousand years the relationship between humankind

and the environment changed slowly but fundamentally, as new technologies were developed. Most people shifted from direct use of the environment through hunting, fishing, and gathering to indirect use through various systems of agriculture.

Early Primary Culture Hearths

The Middle East contained one of the world's foremost culture hearths (Figure 3–7). Known as the Fertile Crescent, the region actually consisted of several hearths that were close to one another. The earliest domestication of plants seems to have taken place in nearby hill lands; and by 10,000 years ago agricultural villages appeared in the Mesopotamian lowlands associated with the Tigris and Euphrates river valleys. From the fourth millennium B.C. on, civilizations, city-states, and empires flourished in that area. Among other major achievements, those civilizations codified laws, used metals, put the wheel to work, established mathematics, and

ENVIRONMENTAL PROBLEMS

The impact of world demand for greater space and increased productivity is evident in three major environmental problems: the desertification of the Sahel, the clearing of tropical rain forests in Brazil, and the creation of acid rain in the United States and Europe. Each problem exerts a different pressure on the environment, but each stems from human needs and wants.

The **Sahel** (meaning "border") is the semiarid southern margin of the African Sahara. It includes parts of Senegal and Mauritania in West Africa and extends eastward to Ethiopia across Mali, Burkina Faso, Niger, Chad, and the Sudan (see the political map preceding Part One). Rainfall is scant in the Sahel, but not too scant to prevent people from living there. The drier northern margin is used for grazing; the wetter southern margin, for grazing and cultivation. A dangerous combination of drought and increased population has caused the erosion and destruction of grazing land and cropland, sometimes to the point of rendering it useless. In some areas sand dunes have replaced once-productive land—hence, the term **desertification** (Figure A). Whether or not what we see as desertification is actually a longer-term ebb and flow of the desert margin is unclear.

Nevertheless, in areas like the Sahel, where technological advances in agriculture are limited, increased population pressure prompts the expansion of cultivation and grazing into marginal areas. Then, with the addition of recurring drought, the pressure on land resources becomes unbearable. The land deteriorates, food is in short supply, and people starve or migrate to other areas. The need for assistance is massive.

Brazil presents a different problem. It is a newly industrializing country (NIC) with the potential of becoming one of the world's industrial giants. Its development program includes the building of highways in the vast but sparsely populated Amazon Basin (40 percent of Brazil's area, 4 percent of its population). The Transamazonian Highway is intended to lead to the establishment of farms, to the building of power plants and industries, to forestry—and to Brazil's secure occupation of its national space. As a part of that development, widespread clearing of the Amazonian rain forests is taking place—an environmental disaster in the making, according to some ecologists. If too much rain forest is cut down, the climate may become warmer and drier and may destroy sensitive tropical soils. Thus, Brazil's challenge is to wisely incorporate that vast, vital, but ecologically delicate environmental realm into its aggressive program of national development.

A third environmental concern relates to the role of the United States as a major industrial producer. As such, the country is a massive consumer of coal-powered energy and a user of petroleum-based fuels for transportation. It is also a major processor of metals and a producer of chemical goods. A by-product of all that industrial activity in the United States, as in Europe, is **acid rain**. When fossil fuels are burned, particles of sulfur dioxide and nitrogen oxide that escape into the atmosphere combine with water vapor to form weak solutions of sulfuric acid and nitric acid. High-altitude winds then carry the acid solution across great distances, but sooner or later it falls to earth as rain, fog, or snow.

---

contributed several of the world's great religions—Zoroastrianism, Judaism, Christianity, and Islam.

Another of the world's great culture hearths developed in the Indus Valley (in present-day Pakistan), where a mature civilization existed by 2500 B.C. An exchange of ideas and materials with Mesopotamia began early and continued over a long period, from 3000 to 1000 B.C. Much of that exchange of culture was by way of ancient Persia (now Iran), and the two hearths may even have attracted migrant peoples from the same areas. The Indus Valley experienced repeated invasions and migrations of people from northwestern and central Asia, who brought an infusion of racial and cultural traits with each new invasion. The Indus and the adjacent Ganges Valley became the source area for

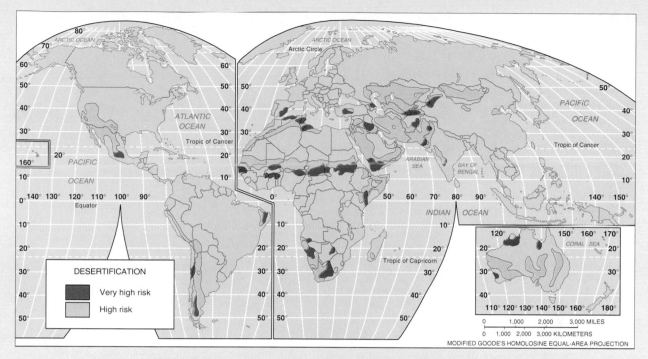

Figure A

Areas at risk of desertification. The margins of the earth's major dry realms are most at risk. In those regions the combination of human activities and marginal rainfall has the potential to create hazardous conditions for both people and environment. (From *World Resources 1987*, a report by the International Institute for Environment and Development and the World Resources Institute. Copyright© 1987 by the International Institute for Environment and Development and the World Resources Institute. Adapted by permission of Basic Books, Inc., Publishers, New York.)

Acid rain is produced in the high-density, urban-industrial regions of the United States and Europe. The "dump" areas, however, are often downwind and may be higher-altitude forests and lakes. In some parts of the United States and southeastern Canada, so much acid rain has fallen that trees are dying and lakes can no longer sustain fish. Europe's main dump area seems to be southern Norway. And in Siberia, Lake Baikal has been significantly impacted in a similar manner by the industrial development in Eurasia.

These examples show that environmental misuse can occur at any level of economic development; in other words, societies in all phases of development are vulnerable. If the populations of the future are to be served well, the world must find both the will and the way to reduce environmental destruction.

cultural traits that eventually spread throughout India. This particular culture hearth made significant contributions in literature, architecture, metalworking, and city planning. Philosophy also evolved and later contributed to Hinduism. The idea of living the sinless, good life may have been transferred to the Middle East, where it was incorporated into Judaism and later into Christianity.

The valley of the middle Yellow River, or Huang He, and its tributaries served as the hearth for the evolution of Chinese culture. China undoubtedly benefited also from contacts with other areas, despite the great distances and physical barriers separating it from other hearths. Wheat and oxen, part of the North China agricultural complex, may have had Middle Eastern origins. And the rice, pigs, poultry,

Figure 3-7

Early culture hearths of the world. Three major culture hearths are recognized as the principal contributors to modern societies throughout the world. From those hearths have spread plants and animals, ideas, religions, and other cultural characteristics. Minor hearths, although locally important, have not had much impact outside their source areas.

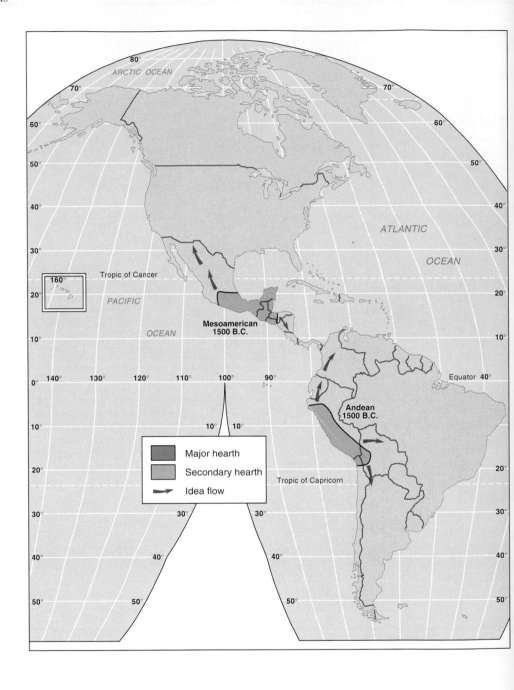

and water buffalo found in China originated in Southeast Asia. Nevertheless, the cultural achievements accumulated since early Neolithic times, as well as the distinctive Chinese traits maintained even after contact with other areas, clearly suggest that an original culture emanated from this hearth. Crop domestication, village settlement, distinctive architecture, early manufacturing, and metalworking were in evidence at the time of the Shang dy-

nasty (1700 B.C.). That Chinese culture eventually spread into South China and northeastward into Manchuria, Korea, and, later, Japan.

Each of the early primary culture hearths appears to have had independent accomplishments, yet each was also a recipient of ideas and commodities from other areas. Nonetheless, each hearth was able to maintain a distinct identity, which was transferred to succeeding generations or to invading or con-

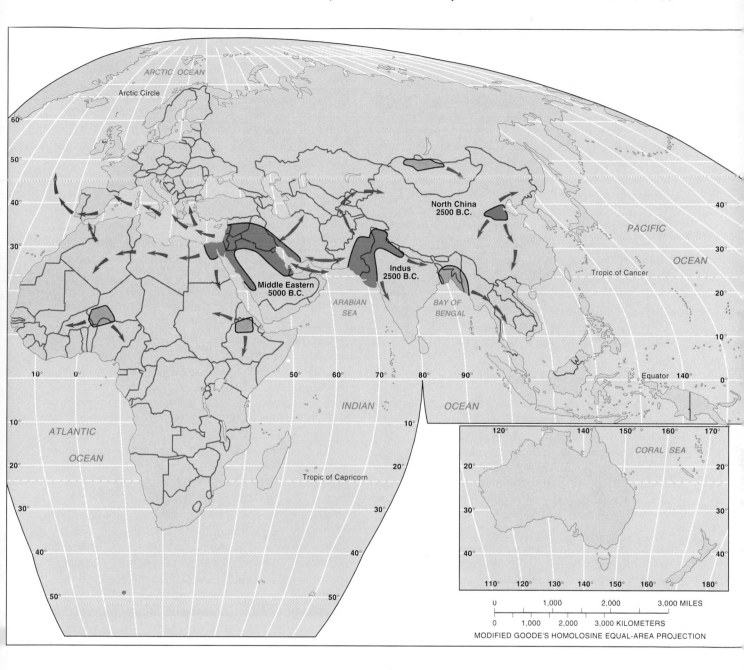

ARCTIC OCEAN

Arctic Circle

North China
2500 B.C.

Indus
2500 B.C.

Middle Eastern
5000 B.C.

PACIFIC

OCEAN

Tropic of Cancer

ARABIAN
SEA

BAY OF
BENGAL

ATLANTIC

OCEAN

INDIAN   OCEAN

Equator 140°

Tropic of Capricorn

CORAL SEA

0   1,000   2,000   3,000 MILES

0   1,000   2,000   3,000 KILOMETERS

MODIFIED GOODE'S HOMOLOSINE EQUAL-AREA PROJECTION

quered peoples who were eventually assimilated and acculturated.

Secondary Culture Hearths

Two areas in the Americas that began to develop around 1500 B.C. also served as culture hearths for major civilizations. The first appeared in northern Central America and southern Mexico (later becom-ing the Mayan civilization) and extended to central Mexico (later becoming the Aztec civilization). This large Mesoamerican region supported a sizable sedentary population and was characterized by cities, political-religious hierarchies, use of numeric systems, and domestication of maize, beans, and cotton.

The Middle Andean area of Peru and Bolivia was the site of the other American culture hearth, which gave rise to the Inca civilization. It advanced more slowly than its Middle American counterpart, but by the sixteenth century A.D. it had developed irrigation, worked metals, domesticated the white potato, established complex political and social system, set up a transportation network, and built an empire.

These culture hearths are considered secondary because the resulting civilizations never evolved into lasting culture realms. The Latin American culture realm as we now know it has mixed origins: indigenous American, European, and African.

Several other areas also functioned as secondary culture hearths. The Bantu language family seems to have had its source area in West Africa. The Ethiopian highlands were a secondary domestication center for wheat, millets, and sorghums. Central Asia was a domestication center for grains, too, and it was certainly a trade route along which ideas and commodities were exchanged among major civilizations, such as those of the Middle East and China.

Europe as a Culture Hearth

Europe was another major culture hearth, but it functioned quite differently. First, it flowered much later than the civilizations of the Middle East, southern and eastern Asia, and Latin America. Second, the Industrial Revolution associated with Europe affected virtually all parts of the earth. Many of our contemporary global problems have origins in the confrontation between modern European culture and the traditional systems found elsewhere. That confrontation did not necessarily represent a deliberate attempt to erase traditional ways of life. But the adjustments involved in transition to the European system have frequently been difficult.

Europe has a Mediterranean and Middle Eastern heritage. Technology (e.g., the wheel), plow agriculture, social concepts, and religions are of Middle Eastern origin, having spread through the Minoan (Crete-based), Greek, and Roman civilizations and into northern Europe. When Middle Eastern civilizations were ascending, Europe was a peripheral area, inhabited by "barbarians" who had not yet received or accepted the innovations of the Neolithic period. Rome had a civilizing influence on Western Europe through the introduction of order, roads, and sedentary agriculture and the establishment of towns as market centers. But barbarian invasions disrupted the Roman Empire, and

several centuries of limited progress followed, sometimes known as the Dark Ages (from the fall of the Roman Empire in A.D. 476 to approximately 1000). A long period of slow agricultural change then stimulated the Renaissance and, indirectly, the Industrial Revolution.

By the thirteenth century, agricultural and manufactured goods were commonly traded along the routes that crossed Europe. In addition, the Crusades (from the late eleventh century through the fourteenth century) led to new contacts and stimulated thought and learning. Between the fifteenth and the twentieth centuries, the Europeans extended their influence and culture around the world, spurred by internal competition and a new interest in science, exploration, and trade. They explored, traded, conquered, and claimed new territories in the name of their homelands. Modern European states emerged with the capability of extending their power over other areas, and many European people resettled in newly discovered lands in the Americas, southern Africa, Australia, and New Zealand.

Those activities have been aptly described as a **European explosion**. J. E. Spencer and W. L. Thomas argue that European explosion has stimulated a process of cultural convergence.[2] Their thesis is that isolated cultures are largely relics of the past, with assimilation or extinction as their not-so-different options. Spencer and Thomas see political organization, food production, industrialization using inanimate sources of power, and consumption as becoming more similar and predict that this blending of races and cultures will continue, with the technological aspects of European culture being the most readily accepted. Languages, religions, and attitudes adjust more slowly and frequently become sources of friction. **Acculturation**, the process by which a group takes on the cultural attributes of a more dominant society, does not occur painlessly.

This argument does not assert that the contributions of traditional cultures will be discarded or that they will totally disappear. Rather, large and viable culture complexes will be modified by cultural blending. Japan provides a good example of the way in which European traits can be accepted in modified form. In addition, the argument for convergence does not assert that **regional disparity** in economic, social, and biological conditions will cease. Indeed, the world continues to bear out the axiom that "the rich get richer and the poor get poorer." Acceptance of the European way of doing things means that particular areas will have great value because of their location and their material and human resources; other areas will not be so favored.

Special Elements of Culture

Language. Language gives a set of meaning to various sounds used in common by a number of people. It is the basic means by which culture is transferred from one generation to the next. Because of the relative isolation in which societies evolved, a great number of languages formed, frequently with common origins but without mutual intelligibility.

Linguistic differences can function as barriers to the exchange of ideas, the acceptance of common goals, and/or the achievement of national unity and allegiance. Most members of most societies are not bilingual and do not speak the language of a neighboring society if it is different from their own. Sometimes linguistic differences are overcome with a lingua franca, a language that is used throughout a wide area for commercial or political purposes by people with different native tongues. Swahili is the lingua franca of eastern Africa; English, of India; and Urdu, of Pakistan.

In many countries that acquired their independence after World War II, the political leadership has found national unity and stability difficult to achieve. Internal problems and conflict frequently stem, in part, from cultural differences, one of which is often linguistic variation. The situation in East Pakistan (now Bangladesh) and West Pakistan (now Pakistan) is a case in point. From 1947 to 1972 those two regions functioned as one political unit. Political leaders, seeking to promote a common culture and common goals, deemed a single national language necessary, even though several mother tongues were in use. Bengali, the language of East Pakistan, was derived centuries ago from Sanskrit; it provided East Pakistanis with a unifying cultural element. West Pakistan, on the other hand, encompassed a number of languages: Baluchi, Pashto, Punjabi, Sindhi, and Urdu, the lingua franca. That linguistic diversity was just one of the many problems that eventually led to the establishment of Bangladesh as a separate and independent state.

Pluralistic societies often lack a common language within a country, and that pluralism then frequently produces political instability or hinders develop-ment. Belgium and Switzerland are noteworthy because they have partially overcome the problem of linguistic pluralism. Others, such as Canada and the former Yugoslavia, have been less successful.

Religion. Religions have their origins in concern for comprehension and security, concerns that seem as old as humankind. Animism, the worship of natural objects believed to have souls or spirits, was among the earliest forms of religion. It includes rituals and sacrifices to appease or pacify spirits, but it usually lacks complex organization. Most animistic religions were probably localized; certainly, the few that have survived are found within small, isolated culture groups. The more important contemporary religions are codified, organized in hierarchical fashion, and institutionalized to ensure the transfer of basic principles and beliefs to other people, including following generations.

Modern religions can be classified as either ethnic or universalizing. Ethnic religions originate in a particular area and involve people with common customs, language, and social views. Examples of ethnic religions include Shintoism (in Japan), Judaism, and Hinduism (in India). Universalizing religions are those considered by their adherents to be appropriate—indeed, desirable—for all humankind. Buddhism, Christianity, and Islam all had ethnic origins but have become universal over the centuries, as they lost their association with a single ethnic group. Religions spread from one people to another through proselytizing, not only by missionaries but also by traders, migrants, and military personnel. Proselytizing is often considered a responsibility of those who practice a universalizing religion.

Religious ideology has had a great impact on civilization. Sacred structures contribute to the morphology, or form and structure, of rural and urban landscapes. In addition, religions have shaped many of the routine aspects of daily life. Centuries ago the spread of citrus-growing throughout Mediterranean lands was directly related to Jewish observances in which citrus was required for the Feast of Booths. Religious food restrictions also account for the absence of swine in the agricultural systems of Jewish and Muslim peoples in the Middle East. The Hindus' taboo on meat eating, a response to their respect for life, has produced the opposite effect: an overabundance of cattle that require space and feed while returning only limited material benefits (e.g., manure, milk, or draft power). In the United States the economic impact of religion is seen in taxation policies (e.g., organized churches are usually exempt from taxation), institutional ownership of land and resources, work taboos on specified days (e.g., the blue laws), and attitudes toward materialism and work.

One implied function of religion is the promotion of cultural norms, the results of which may be positive. Societies do benefit from the stability that cohesiveness and unity of purpose bring. Unfortunately, however, conflict also arises frequently from religion-based differences, evoking intolerance, suppression of minorities, or simply incompatibility among different peoples. Examples include the Crusades of the Middle Ages, in which Christians attempted to wrest the Holy Land from Islamic rule; the partition of the Indian subcontinent in 1947 in response to differences between Hindus and Muslims; and the warfare between Catholics and Protestants in Northern Ireland.

Political Ideology.   Political ideologies also have major implications for societal unity, stability, and the use of land and resources. Such ideologies need not be common to the majority of a population; people may be apathetic, or they may be unable to resist an imposed system of rules and decision making. In some instances, oligarchies, in which control is exercised by small groups, or dictators have made their particular philosophies basic to the functioning of their societies.

Most modern governments assume some responsibility for the well-being of the people in their states. Some socialist governments assume complete control over the allocation of resources, the investment of capital, and even the use of labor, thereby severely limiting individual decision making. In other societies governments assume responsibility for providing an environment in which individuals or corporations may own and decide on the use of resources.

National and economic development programs reflect the differences in political systems. The approach of socialistic governments, for example, is quite different from that of capitalistic countries, and those differences are treated in the chapters on Anglo-America, Russia, India, and China.

SOCIAL AND POLITICAL ORGANIZATION

Political organizations are control mechanisms that spring from the common bonds of a few families or of millions of people. The adoption of specified behavior patterns and institutions promotes those common bonds. The responsibilities of political organizations include resolution of conflicts between and within societies and control of the distribution, allocation, and use of resources. The ability to execute such functions in a satisfactory manner depends not only on those in authority and on the political system in place but also on the unity, support, or passivity of the people.

Bands and Tribes

The **band,** the simplest and once the most common political organization, has always existed. A band usually consists of no more than a few dozen people who occupy a loosely defined territory within which game, fish, insects, and vegetable matter are gathered. The community functions on a cooperative basis: no individual can direct group activity for long without voluntary cooperation, and no one has exclusive rights to resources or territory. Thus, groups of this sort are aptly called sharing societies. Probably no more than 100,000 members of sharing societies remain, scattered over remote and isolated parts of the earth (Figure 3–8). Contact between those societies and more advanced groups leads to the extinction of the bands. Of the few groups that have survived, the Bushmen of the Kalahari, the Motilón of Venezuela, and the Jívaro of Ecuador are examples.

Increases in population density and advances in technology (i.e., agricultural production) require a more specific allocation of resources and space. The community structure that evolves is based on kinship: elders or heads of extended families lead and direct the activities of the **tribe,** which may include hundreds, or even thousands, of people. Boundaries may be either vaguely or specifically defined, depending on external pressures, trespass by neighbors, or colonial imposition. The Ibo of Nigeria are an ethnically related group that was subdivided, prior to European penetration of Africa, into hundreds of patrilineal clans or lineages, each with a specific territory. Today, the Ibo are just one of many tribal groups that Nigeria must unify in its effort to build a modern state.

Territorial States

With an increase in population, size of territory needed, and economic specialization, a more formal organization becomes necessary. The focus of

Figure 3-8
A family unit belonging to the
Panare Indian tribe in the
Guiana Highland of Venezuela.
Small traditional societies reside
in the low-density tropical areas
of the world. A bow-and-spear
technology characterizes this
group.

power becomes more distinct, authority is channeled through a larger hierarchy, and society becomes more stratified. The importance of kinship as
a medium for organization disappears, and an identity emerges of a specific and defined territory, occupied by a people with a distinct bond to the area,
a definite sense of territory. A state is organized politically, if not economically, and controls the entire
territory and all of the people in it. Thus, it includes
territory, people, and an organizational system. In
this situation the territory is the state, and the people are the components; in lesser forms of political
organization the society is the state, and the territory
is of secondary importance in terms of identity.

City-states were among the earliest of states, but
conquests led to expansion and the formation of
empires. Preindustrial states emerged in the
Mesopotamian, Indus, and Nile valleys, in ancient
China, and probably in sub-Saharan Africa. The Inca
and Aztec civilizations of the Americas provide more
recent examples. But the difficulty of controlling diverse peoples with varied languages, religions, and
economies was frequently beyond the capabilities
of early governments. And traditional transportation systems, of course, further handicapped con-

trol. As a result, the disruption and breakup of such
states were frequent.

The evolution to modern states was a long, slow
process in Europe. During the later Middle Ages
the emergence of England, France, Norway, and
Russia, among other states, signified that local differences in language, religion, and feudal organization had been overcome sufficiently to permit
territories to be combined, but not on a continent-
wide basis.

Nation-States

The modern state is a product of the Industrial
Revolution. The increasing complexity of industrial
societies requires more complex organizations for
maintaining order, ensuring communication, providing protection, and promoting the common culture. The increased interaction and interdependence
of individuals lead to allegiance to the larger organization rather than to kin or individuals. Thus, nationalism is one of the results of industrialization
and urbanization, and that intense loyalty, long directed to a state organization occupying a specified
territory, leads to the formation of a **nation-state**.

The nation-state and its territory are occupied by a people with a high degree of cohesiveness, common goals, a culture that is transferred from generation to generation by a common language, and a loyalty to the larger political organization. Within the nation-state an emotional attachment is experienced that is not hindered by linguistic, ethnic, racial, or religious distinctions. Such conditions are most difficult to achieve, but Japan presents an excellent example, with its high level of national unity. The former Yugoslavia represented the other extreme, a multinational state consisting of several national groups. Although the nation-state may be desirable from the standpoint of achieving stability, few states exhibit complete national unity and allegiance.

Problems of State Development

Strong tribal tendencies and even remnant band societies still exist within the boundaries and organizational structure of modern states (Figure 3–9). The resulting internal confrontation between tribal loyalties and modern states is one of the basic problems of the developing world. That con-

flict, however, is not a sign of inherent backwardness but rather the natural outgrowth of imposing state organization on an already-existing political structure.

Africa provides numerous appropriate examples. When the new African states acquired their independence, they quickly became aware, sometimes by violent experience, of the difficulty in forging stable political units from a dual heritage. On the one hand were "Europeanization," modernization, and territorial definition from the colonial era; on the other, the indigenous heritage of a great variety of tribal groups with poorly defined territorial boundaries, linguistic differences, and variations in cultural achievement and acculturation under the Europeans. We should not have been surprised by the civil strife and secessionist attempts within Zaire during the 1960s or the Ibo attempt to secede from Nigeria and form Biafra, also during the 1960s. Chad, Uganda, and Angola face similar problems. And the Civil War in Liberia in the 1990s began largely as a struggle between opposing tribal groups: the Gio and Mano tribes overpowered the president and his troops from the Krahn and Mandingo tribes.

We must also guard against the notion that instability or divisiveness is characteristic only of recently independent and developing nations. Racial antagonism, for example, has been a problem in Malaysia, Uganda, Peru, and the United States. A strong culture group that extends control over a weaker group rarely makes social, economic, or political equality a priority. Instead, it may form a stratified society and impose a lower order or position on the weaker members, using physical traits as a method of identification. Sometimes the control group is formally aided by agencies and laws of the state, such as the policy of apartheid in South Africa. And when formerly subservient populations rule newly independent states, reverse discrimination may be the trend. Such a reversal of roles has been a stimulus for the migration of Asians out of East Africa in recent years.

Finally, the idea that a uniform religion ensures political stability should also be avoided. Religious unity did lead to the creation of Pakistan in 1947. But social and economic differences, combined with the physical fragmentation of the state's territory, ultimately led to the disintegration of Pakistan and the formation of Bangladesh in 1972.

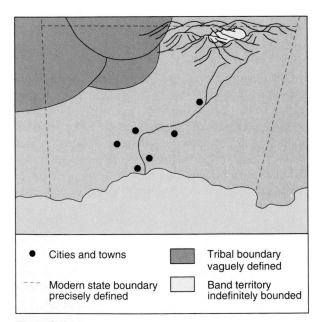

Cities and towns

- - - **Modern state boundary precisely defined**

Tribal boundary vaguely defined

Band territory indefinitely bounded

Figure 3–9

Contemporary political systems. Tribal and band identity weakens and disappears as the modern state develops and gains strength. But that process of modern state development may require a transition period of many generations before it is completed.

Multinational Alliances

The formation of a **multinational alliance** among states for the promotion of common goals is not a recent phenomenon. Military alliances have been the most common, usually with the objective of providing mutual aid and protection in the event of a military attack from a specified source. A contemporary example is the North Atlantic Treaty Organization (NATO), founded in 1949.

Alliances have also formed around other concerns, however. European countries that used to be competitive and independent are now trying interdependence and cooperation as a means of achieving progress. Their shared concern for the economic growth of Western Europe was the motivation for the European Economic Community (Common Market), a twelve-member alliance with a goal of economic integration. The assumption is that one large economic unit can be more effective than numerous small ones. Similarly, the Soviet Union and the Eastern European countries formed the Warsaw Pact, a military alliance, and the Council for Mutual Economic Assistance, an economic union, both of which served the common needs of member nations until events in the late 1980s changed the relationships of those countries. Canada, Mexico, and the United States formed a free trade union known as the North American Free Trade Agreement (NAFTA) in 1993, thought by some to be a possible forerunner to a larger western hemisphere trade union. Another alliance, the Organization of African Unity, was formed in 1963 to promote self-government and progress throughout Africa. Despite these linkages the underlying assumption remains untested: Are the national interests of individual countries best met through large coalitions or through separate arrangements?

ECONOMIC ACTIVITY

Economic activities are those in which human beings engage to acquire food and satisfy other wants. They are the most basic of all activities and are found wherever there are people. Economic activity is divided into four sectors. **Primary activity** involves the direct harvesting of the earth's resources. Fishing off the coast of Peru, pumping oil from wells in Libya, extracting iron ore from mines in Minnesota, and growing wheat in China are all examples of primary production. The commodities that result from those activities acquire value from the effort required in production and from consumer demand.

The processing of commodities is classified as a **secondary activity**. In this sector items are increased in value by having their forms changed to enhance their usefulness. Thus, a primary commodity such as cotton might be processed into fabric, and that fabric might be cut and assembled as apparel. Textile manufacturing and apparel manufacturing are both secondary activities.

An economic activity in which a service is performed is classified as a **tertiary activity** (Figure 3–10). Wholesaling and retailing are tertiary activities by which primary and secondary products are made available to consumers. Other tertiary activities include governmental, banking, educational, medical, and legal services, as well as journalism and the arts.

The service economy of highly developed countries has become so large and complex that a fourth sector of **quaternary activity** is sometimes included. Institutions and corporations that provide information are in the quaternary sector.

Transportation is a special kind of tertiary economic activity that is vital, in highly developed form, to modern commercial societies. An efficient transportation system reduces the significance of distance and greatly facilitates the exchange of resources and goods. A poorly developed transportation system, on the other hand, may reduce exchange and require self-sufficiency. The extent of transportation development in whatever form—automobiles, airplanes, trains, ships, or pipelines—reveals much about an area's economic organization and production system.

Every economic activity involves the creation of wealth. The value of primary commodities increases as they are transported to locations where they are needed (place utility). Value is also added by processing (form utility). Each move toward a market or each additional manufacturing stage adds more value to the items involved, though value does not increase equally with each step in the process. The primary sector does not usually produce great wealth for the society at large; most of the final value of a product comes from secondary and tertiary activities.

Figure 3–10
An early morning floating market outside Bangkok, Thailand. Food marketing systems are tertiary economic activities.

Economic Organization and Modernization

Numerous factors contribute to the specific manner in which economic activity is organized and accomplished. First, many facets of our physical world affect our decisions regarding economic activity. For example, moisture availability has major implications for crop selection. Second, the environment may be used in various ways, depending on what technology is available. Third, many other economic, social, and political conditions influence our decisions. For instance, location relative to existing markets may encourage or preclude some forms of production. Or long-established systems of land tenure may control that important resource. In addition, governments may aid economic production by ensuring the proper infrastructure (including credit systems, roads, and education) or may hinder it by suppressing reform efforts (e.g., the removal of trade restric-

tions or the promotion of agrarian reform). Traditions and attitudes also work as either positive or negative forces in the functioning of economies.

Two extremes of economic organization are recognized: the traditional system and the modern commercial system (Figure 3–11). In the **traditional subsistence economy** a family or small band undertakes both the production and the limited processing required for local consumption. Group members function as producers, processors, and consumers of their own commodities. Self-sufficiency and sharing are the distinctive features. Other than the Bushmen of Africa and the Campa of Peru, true subsistence societies are almost nonexistent today. Few people are so isolated that they do not engage in some kind of exchange, even if only occasionally.

No country has a pure subsistence economy. Even in a country that is less developed, some people engage in subsistence activities, some produce

Figure 3-11
Economic organization.
Evolution from a traditional society to a modern society requires several fundamental changes. Affected areas include the basis of exchange, settlement patterns, technology, utilization, energy development, and trade and production systems.

Traditional ◄─────────────────────────► Modern			
Subsistence	**Reciprocal**	**Peasant**	**Exchange**
Features Commodity sharing No urban foci Simple technology Animate power (muscle) Localized economy	Barter	Minor exchange for capital Village settlement pattern Mixed traditional and modern technologies Limited regional specialization	Commercial activity Major urban development Complex technology Inanimate power Regional specialization Regional trade
Production Systems Gathering Nomadic herding Shifting agriculture Labor-intensive subsistence agriculture			Commercial agriculture Commercial fishing Commercial grazing Commercial forestry Manufacturing and commerce

and exchange on a reciprocal or barter basis, and others are clearly in an exchange or money economy. Thus, real economies fall somewhere along a continuum between the extremes of a traditional subsistence economy and a **modern commercial economy**. Although the precise location of a given country on the continuum is difficult to pinpoint, certain economic characteristics indicate the level of modernization attained.

Employment by Sector. One indicator of modernization is the distribution of the labor force among the various sectors of economic activity. In traditionally oriented countries the majority of the labor force—as much as 80 percent in many African countries—is engaged in primary production, especially agriculture. Such a society generally has limited wealth; in other words, per capita gross national product for traditional economies is low, though exceptions such as oil-rich Kuwait do come to mind.

In modernized economies a high proportion of the labor force is employed in secondary and tertiary activities. The primary sector may involve less than 10 percent of the labor force when greater levels of industrialization and tertiary activity are reached. Such concentration in processing and services results in greater national income and influ-

ences both the distribution and the way of life of the population. Urbanization is an important corollary to economic development.

Per Capita Energy Consumption. In traditional societies production input is largely labor applied to land—that is, agriculture. Modernized societies substitute capital for labor: industry is automated and agriculture is mechanized. Such a shift to capital-intensive production is based on the use of inanimate power sources. Therefore, per capita energy consumption is a second good indicator of the extent of modernization.

Division of Labor and Regional Specialization. Division of labor reaches a high level in modern countries. It is evident at local levels, where members of a community perform a variety of tasks. With increased modernization it is also evident at the regional level. **Regional specialization** exists when areas produce goods for which they have a particular advantage or which are not produced elsewhere and then contribute their specialized production to the larger economic system. A third good indicator of modernization is when division of labor and regional specialization occur nationwide.

Regions that are engaged in specialized production illustrate the principle of comparative advantage. A comparative advantage may stem from climate, soils, labor, energy resources, capital and enterprise, transportation, institutional structure, or some combination of these factors. Whatever the advantage, the area gains by specializing in one product and trading for other commodities that it needs. Occasionally, an area produces goods for which it has no distinct advantage but may have the least disadvantage. Wheat production in the Great Plains of the United States illustrates this point. Wheat production becomes economically feasible in the Great Plains when other areas that could provide wheat more efficiently choose not to do so because alternative possibilities yield a higher return.

Urban Corelands.   The presence of a multiple-city coreland is a fourth indicator of modernization. Efficiency is increased and savings are realized when the secondary and tertiary activities that dominate modern society are close to each other; hence, the basis for cities. The United States and Canada, the European countries, Russia, and Japan all have **urban-industrial corelands.** Numerous neighboring cities with a high level of commercial and social interaction, a high population density, a high proportion of the nation's manufacturing output, and high standards of living characterize such corelands. Corelands also function as national educational, financial, political, and cultural centers. Less modernized countries often have only one major city, the "primate city," which functions as the coreland and attains a size disproportionate to other urban centers.

Urban-industrial corelands have peripheral economic regions, called extended hinterlands, that do not exhibit the features of a coreland but that do have clear functional ties to them. The extended hinterland may be located entirely within the country of the coreland, or it may include other regions of the world. In the United States the South long functioned as a hinterland for the U.S. coreland.

Trade Relationships

The traditional trade relationship between corelands and their outlying regions reveals the differences between core and periphery and is similar to the colonial trade relationship. Corelands are suppliers of manufactured goods. Both internal exchange and trade with other corelands of the world occur at high levels. Some manufactured goods flow to less industrialized hinterlands, but the volume is far smaller because of limited commercial market development. The

hinterlands, however, are suppliers of raw materials, mineral fuels, and food products for the corelands, which often cannot supply all of their high per capita needs. Figure 3–12 illustrates the trade relationship between rural areas that specialize in primary production and urban regions that specialize in secondary and tertiary activities. The relationship is the same, whether the exchange is domestic or international.

Such relationships often favor urban-industrial cores, and therein lies a problem. Because the value of primary goods does not generally increase as rapidly as that of secondary goods, the likelihood of regional income disparity is great. And if the exchange is between countries, balance-of-payment problems may result for the less developed regions.

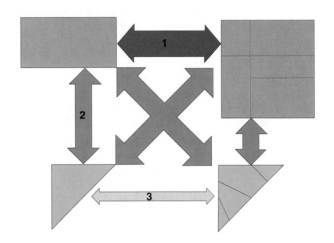

 Modernized country or blocks of countries with distinct urban-industrial corelands

 Traditional country or countries without multicity urban-industrial corelands

 Type 1. High volume; diversified trade; including primary and secondary goods

 Type 2. Moderate volume; primary goods (food, industrial raw materials, and mineral fuels) to urban corelands; reverse flow of secondary goods

 Type 3. Minimal or nonexistent trade

Figure 3-12
International trade flow types. Petroleum accounts for a large proportion of international trade. Petroleum flow is primarily from traditional countries to urban-industrial corelands.

Countries that supply primary goods to industrialized regions outside their own territory also face competition, price fluctuations, or political pressures over which they can exert little control. Furthermore, those countries often have only a few customers or depend heavily on two or three commodities for most of their exchange revenues. Thus, they face severe economic problems if trade is disrupted. The end result for many hinterland countries is a dependent relationship, which may handicap their efforts to develop internally.

More traditional countries often suffer from the problem of a **dual economy**. One part of the economy may concentrate on the commercial production of primary goods, many of which may flow to an external coreland. The other part of the economy may have a traditional structure, which may involve most of the population. Economic dualism is commonly reflected in distinct regional differences and in sharp differences between urban and rural areas. It is a form of **fragmented modernization**, which can contribute to internal social and political disunity.

Traditional trade relationships are changing, particularly in less advanced countries that have progressed to the point of establishing a manufacturing base. Newly industrializing countries—such as Brazil, Korea, and Taiwan—have become significant exporters of manufactured goods, sometimes with the encouragement of multinational corporations that are based in the corelands of the developed world. Such a shift adds even greater complexity to the global economy, in which international trade and investment are becoming increasingly important to a wider array of countries.

SUMMARY
A Complex but Critical Relationship

This chapter focuses on physical environments and the cultural systems by which people maintain their relationships with those environments. Carl O. Sauer has addressed several important points relative to this topic:

> Every human population, at all times, has needed to evaluate the economic potential of its inhabited area, to organize its life about its natural environment in terms of the skills available to it and the values which it accepted. In the cultural *mise en valeur* [exploitation] of the environment, a deformation of the pristine, or prehuman, landscape has been initiated that has increased with the length of occupation, growth in pop-

ulation, and addition of skills. Wherever men live, they have operated to alter the aspect of the earth, both animate and inanimate, be it to their boon or bane.[3]

In our upcoming study of various world regions we examine further the relationship of people and environment, and it should become evident that some peoples have attained a high level of well-being, whereas others experience deprivation and lack the basic necessities of life. We are not suggesting that all is well with modernized societies or that less-progressive countries should follow their lead. Although the latter are characterized by poverty, health problems, and regional disparities, the former have formidable problems, too. The high level of per capita consumption in modernized societies requires immense quantities of material and energy resources, so much that it is almost frightening to think of modern society as a model for the remainder of the world. And now space, quality of life, and suitable air and water are being demanded, just when life-styles are placing increased pressure on our total environment.

KEY TERMS

acculturation	frost-free period
acid rain	inherited culture
alluvium	landscape modification
average annual precipitation	laterization
	loess
band	modern commercial economy
calcification	
climate	multinational alliance
climatic classification	nation-state
cultural convergence	natural vegetation
culture complex	podzolization
culture hearth	primary activity
culture realm	quaternary activity
culture trait	regional disparity
desertification	regional specialization
diffused culture	Sahel
dual economy	secondary activity
ecosystem	tertiary activity
European explosion	traditional subsistence economy
evapotranspiration rate	
fossil fuels	tribe
fragmented modernization	urban-industrial coreland

NOTES

1. In the novel *Centennial* (New York: Random House, 1974) James A. Michener vividly describes the occupying of the western Great Plains and the problems that farmers faced when they attempted to use the land. John Steinbeck's novel *The Grapes of Wrath* (New York: Viking Press, 1939) portrays what happened to the farmers of the western Great Plains during the Depression and drought years of the 1930s.

2. J. E. Spencer and W. L. Thomas, *Introducing Cultural Geography* (New York: Wiley, 1973), 185–205.

3. Carl O. Sauer, "The Agency of Man on the Earth," in *Readings in Cultural Geography,* edited by Philip L. Wagner and Marvin W. Mikesell (Chicago: University of Chicago Press, 1962), 539.

4

More Developed and Less Developed Countries: An Overview

The Widening Gap

Measurements of Wealth

Characteristics of More Developed and Less Developed Regions

Theories of Development

Children playing in a rural schoolyard in the Philippines. Much of the world's population endures conditions far below the standards of the developed world.

Over the past 40 years the gap between more developed and less developed countries has increased, and the chances are good that it will widen even more. Statistical data can help us understand the dimensions of this disparity.

THE WIDENING GAP

Trends in Per Capita GNP

Since the end of World War II many countries have shown a significant increase in per capita gross national product (GNP), which is widely considered to be one of the best indicators of economic well-being.[1] In combination with other indicators—such as death rates, mortality rates, and dietary consumption—that increase in GNP would suggest considerable progress for those countries. Because of inflation, however, that gain has not always been real. Not only has it not resulted in greater purchasing power in all cases, but in some nations effective buying power has even decreased. Approximately 1 billion people—one-fifth of the world's population—remain in poverty, surviving by traditional economic systems in countries where the per capita GNP is less than $500 per year.

Figure 4–1 graphically demonstrates the increasing disparity between **more developed countries** and **less developed countries**. Ethiopia, which is representative of many African nations, has increased its per capita GNP by an average annual rate of less than 1 percent over the past twenty years. In fact, during the 1980s Ethiopia's GNP actually decreased somewhat. And India is only slightly better off, with an average increase of about 1.7 percent per year. For some of the world's poorest countries, even a 3 percent increase per year means only a few dollars more per person. In contrast, the United Kingdom, Australia, and the United States have enjoyed average yearly increases of 6 to 10 percent, which represent in absolute numbers gains of $600 to $1,000 per person. Such gains are almost startling in comparison with those of poorer nations.

This growing disparity is also evident when we compute a country's per capita GNP as a percentage of the per capita GNP of the United States (Table 4–1); the lower the percentage, the greater the existing **GNP gap**. We have used the United States as a base measure because of its image as a rich country, but we could just as well have used Japan or a wealthy European country. If we had used Japan's

GNP as the measure against which we compared other countries, the gap obviously would have been much greater. The countries included in Table 4–1 were selected to represent the various world regions and different development experiences.

When examining the data in the table, note that most countries in what is often considered as the well-off world decreased the gap between their GNP and that of the United States during the twenty-year period; that is, their percentage of the U.S. GNP increased from 1968 to 1988. Japan, most Western European countries, and Australia show that improved status. In fact, Japan and a few other countries now have a per capita GNP exceeding that of the United States. The notable exceptions in Europe are Poland, Hungary, Romania, the former Yugoslavia, and the countries of the former Soviet Union. Many countries of the less developed world, however, show an increasing gap or, at best, minuscule improvement. That group includes countries in Latin America and Asia as well as most of the countries in Africa.

Two types of countries that were once clearly in the less developed group show marked improvement in these statistics. The first type includes the rich oil exporters, with Saudi Arabia illustrating well the ability of such countries to narrow the gap. The second type includes the newly industrializing countries (NICs), represented in Table 4–1 by Brazil and South Korea. As mentioned earlier, the countries included in the table are only examples of varied development experiences, but we should remember the relative positions identified here (and in Figure A on page 80) as we examine other aspects of the disparity.

Trends in Agricultural Production

Part of the explanation for the widening gap between more developed and less developed countries lies in different levels of agricultural productivity. The trend in yields per unit of land area of the world's three principal cereal grains is demonstrated in Figure 4–2. Those three widely cultivated crops represent an important element in the diet of most of the world's people. Figure 4–2a suggests great variability in wheat yields, reflecting a variety of factors. In the United States and Australia production per areal unit is low because wheat is grown mainly in dry lands that are not well suited to high yields. But mechanization permits farmers to cultivate large

Figure 4-1
Per capita GNP in U.S. dollars for certain (a) more developed countries and (b) less developed countries. Most of the world's countries are experiencing an increase in their per capita GNPs. The real increase for more developed countries, however, is much greater than it is for less developed nations. (From Arthur S. Banks, comp., *Cross-Polity Time Series Data*, Cambridge, MA: MIT Press, 1971; and Population Reference Bureau, *World Population Data Sheet*, Washington, DC: 1983, 1990, 1993.)

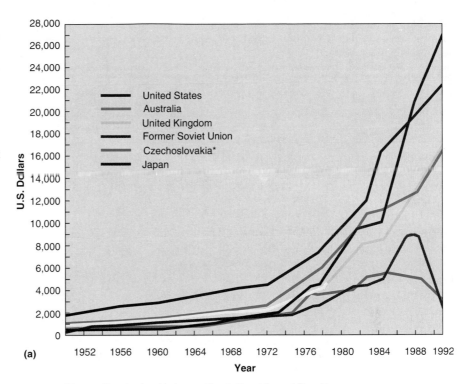

(a)

*Former Czechoslovakia is now Czech Republic and Slovakia

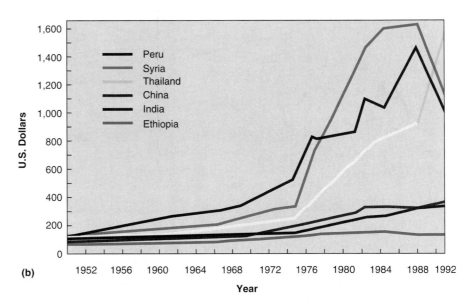

(b)

areas, so production is feasible even though yield per unit is low. In France and Hungary, wheat is raised under humid climatic conditions that favor high yields. In the less developed nations production is not mechanized, but wheat is generally grown in areas that are more humid than the wheat-growing regions of the United States or Australia.

The contrast between more developed and less developed countries is more striking when we look at the yields of maize (corn) or paddy rice (unhulled) per land unit. Yields have not changed much in some of the less developed nations since 1960. In the more developed nations, however, technological innovations have been more widely applied: seed has been improved, fertiliz-

Table 4–1
Gross national product (GNP) of selected countries, as a percentage of the United States' GNP (1968 and 1991).

	Per Capita GNP (in dollars)		Percent of U.S. GNP	
	1968	1991	1968	1991
North America				
United States	3,980	22,560	100.0	100.0
Africa				
Algeria	220	2,020	5.5	9.0
Ghana	170	400	4.3	2.0
Kenya	130	340	3.3	1.5
Central African Republic	120	390	3.0	2.0
Zimbabwe	220	620	5.5	2.75
Asia				
Saudi Arabia	360	7,070	9.1	31.3
India	100	330	2.5	1.7
Indonesia	100	610	2.5	2.7
China	90	370	2.3	1.6
South Korea	180	6,340	4.5	28.1
Japan	1,190	26,920	29.9	119.3
Europe				
Norway	2,000	24,160	50.3	107.1
Germany (former W. Germany only)	1,970	23,650	49.5	104.8
Poland	880	1,830	22.1	8.1
Hungary	980	2,690	24.6	11.9
Spain	730	12,460	18.4	55.2
Italy	1,230	18,580	30.9	82.4
Latin America				
Guatemala	320	930	8.1	4.1
Jamaica	460	1,380	11.6	6.1
Peru	380	1,020	9.5	4.5
Brazil	250	2,920	6.3	11.5
Argentina	820	2,780	20.6	13.0
Oceania				
Australia	2,070	16,590	52.0	73.5
USSR (former)	1,110	2,680	27.9	11.8

Source: Population Reference Bureau, *World Population Data Sheet* (Washington, DC: 1968, 1993).

ers and pesticides are used more extensively, and management techniques are better. Unfortunately, those improvements have not been applied as uniformly in the less developed nations. New varieties of maize and rice, for example, have made a significant impact in a few populous countries—but only a few (see the boxed feature The Green Revolution).

Figure 4–3 charts recent changes in per capita agricultural and food production. In some less developed nations per capita production has increased, which is no mean feat when we recall that the rate of population growth in less developed nations is two to three times the rate in most of the more developed nations. Despite the increase, however, long-term security is far from ensured. In the less developed countries most people are involved in producing food for local consumption. And even though we can be sure that population will continue to increase for years to

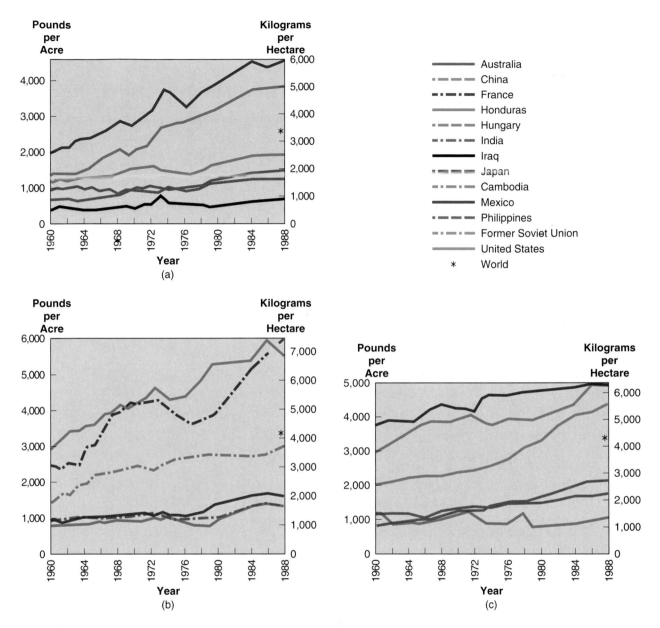

Figure 4-2
Yields of selected nations in major food grains: (a) wheat, (b) maize (corn), (c) paddy rice. The data points in these graphs were calculated with a three-year moving average, which lessens the effect of fluctuations in individual years and is useful in showing long-term trends. With that method the values for three consecutive years are totaled and divided by three, and the result is assigned to the middle year. (From *Production Yearbook,* New York: United Nations, 1991.)

come, we cannot be certain of the earth's carrying capacity or of our ability to continue to increase production. In addition, the gains achieved have been highly variable from place to place, as pointed out in

the boxed feature The Green Revolution. Most gains have resulted from progress in selected Asian regions, while Africa continues to lag in its struggle to attain higher food productivity per capita.

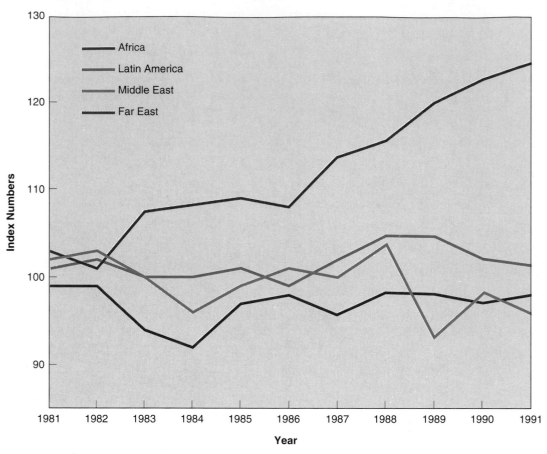

Figure 4-3

Per capita food production for selected regions. An index number relates the production of a specific year to that of the base period. If the index number is 110, it means that production (in this case, per capita production) is 10 percent greater than it was in the base period (in this case, 1979-1981). According to the data depicted here, per capita food production continues to lag in Africa and has actually declined in Latin America. (From *Production Yearbook*, New York: United Nations, 1991.)

Trends in Industrial Production

Another indicator of the widening gap between more developed and less developed countries is industrial production (Figure 4–4). Although data on manufacturing are not as complete as data on agriculture, we can draw some general conclusions.

Most of the less developed countries have a limited industrial sector: industry usually contributes less than 10 percent of the GNP. In the more developed world, however, manufacturing is very important, characteristically providing 15 to 25 percent of the GNP. For many years the relative growth rate of industrial production was about the same in less de-

veloped and more developed countries. But, as evident in Figure 4–5, the growth rate in recent years has been higher in less developed countries. Before we respond to that shift, however, we must be certain that we are interpreting it accurately. Much of the industrial progress of the less developed countries is concentrated in the small group of NICs that form the upper tier of developing countries. No specific definition exists for inclusion as an NIC, but the usual list includes Hong Kong, Singapore, the Republic of Korea (South Korea), and Taiwan in Asia. These are sometimes referred to as the "four tigers" of Asia because of their dramatic industrial and income growth. Other countries which may be

Figure 4-4
Industrial production for developed and developing countries.
Index values of industrial countries do not show a widening gap as clearly as do agricultural values. The reasons for this are: (1) industrial production in many developing countries is limited, so that large increases loom large relative to the base; (2) selected developing countries have been immensely successful in promoting industrial growth; and (3) many developed countries experience an economic restructuring in which industrial activity is of decreasing significance relative to other modern economic sectors. (From *Statistical Yearbook*, New York: United Nations, 1993.)

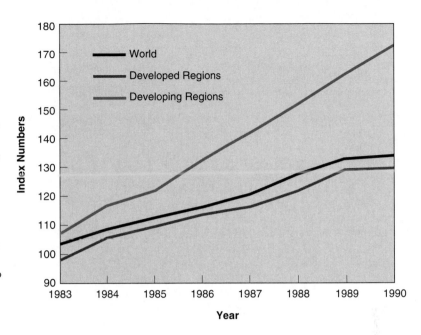

included are Brazil, Chile, and Mexico in Latin America and other Asian countries such as Indonesia, Thailand, and Malaysia. It should also be remembered that the absolute increase in production is higher in more developed countries because they have a much larger industrial base to begin with. Moreover, the industrialized countries of the world are experiencing an economic restructuring in which the tertiary sectors of their economies have become their growth sectors.

MEASUREMENTS OF WEALTH

Most authorities on economic development distinguish more developed from less developed countries by one or more of three measures: per capita GNP, per capita consumption of inanimate energy, and percentage of the labor force in primary activities. Of those measures, per capita GNP is the most widely used, but it must be used with caution. Per capita data are averages, obtained by dividing a total national value—in this case, wealth generated—by a total national population. In many of the poorer, less developed nations average values do not apply to large segments of the population because wealth is concentrated in the hands of a few. Per capita figures, therefore, are generally higher than the actual productivity of the majority of the people. In richer developed nations per capita values are more mean-

ingful because wealth is likely to be dispersed more evenly among the total populace.

A second caution concerns the fact that GNP values are only estimates, even with the best of accounting procedures. Thus, we should discount minor variations when we compare nations. Finally, per capita GNP values are so low in many of the poorer, less developed nations—Ethiopia, for example—that the survival of the vast majority of their people seems impossible. We must assume, therefore, that the actual per capita wealth generated is higher than is reported, or its nature is much different from that of the more developed nations.[2] Foodstuffs produced in a subsistence economy but not accounted for in a GNP estimate may account for some of the differential.

Per Capita GNP

We have already compared the per capita GNP of some more developed and less developed nations from a historical perspective (see Figure 4–1 and Table 4–1). When we turn to the current pattern of per capita GNP on a world scale (Figure 4–5), regional differences are striking. Areas of high per capita GNP (6,000 or more) include the United States and Canada, most of Europe, Israel, several of the major oil-exporting countries, Japan, Australia, and New Zealand. Russia and the other former states of the Soviet Union once were included but recent declines in GNP have eliminated them from

THE GREEN REVOLUTION

The success of some countries—namely, Bangladesh, India, Pakistan, Indonesia, the Philippines, and Mexico—in significantly improving the wheat, rice, maize, and sorghum yields in selected agricultural regions can be directly attributed to the **Green Revolution** (Figure A). That term encompasses a number of international research efforts that serve as models for cooperative efforts but also illustrate the difficulty of solving complex food problems.

The Green Revolution grew out of a joint research effort between Mexican and U.S. scientists during the 1940s, which established the Centro International de Majoramiento de Maize y Trigo (CIMMYT) in Mexico. Supported by the Mexican government and the Rockefeller Founda-

tion, those scientists first focused on wheat and maize. In 1960, with additional support from the Ford Foundation, a second international research center, the International Rice Research Institute (IRRI), was established in the Philippines. Now, several other international agricultural research centers exist, but none has been more successful than the CIMMYT and the IRRI.

The basic goal of those research efforts has been to improve food output and reduce hunger. Simply stated, they have developed high-yield varieties of grains (HYVs) in which fewer calories are stored in the stem and more in the grain, the part that is eaten. Success has not come easily, but increased food output has been significant, even if localized. Over many years, plant-breeding efforts by the research institutes have been repeated and expanded to develop seed varieties that would resist disease (rust) and pest and would be suited to many localized environments. Consideration has even been given to taste preferences.

The limited but important achievements of the Green Revolution illustrate several significant points. First, agricultural enterprise, even if largely subsistence, is part of a larger system composed of cultural, economic, and environmental elements. Changing one component of that sys-

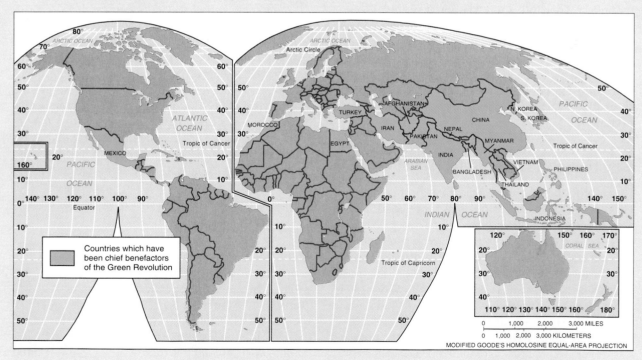

Figure A

Countries that have benefited most from Green Revolution technology. Though many populous countries have benefited, we can see the almost complete absence of benefit to any African countries. (Adapted by permission from Robert E. Huke, "The Green Revolution," *Journal of Geography* 84, November 1985, p. 248.)

tem may require or generate numerous additional changes. For example, HYVs have required additional irrigation, more fertilizers, better land preparation, and improved tending of crops. Some HYVs have also been more susceptible to disease problems. Consequently, the countries that adopted the seeds found it necessary to improve education, transportation, storage, and marketing procedures—all infrastructure considerations. And the farmers involved needed more capital and greater labor input.

A second point to remember is that rapid innovation and change may not benefit everyone. Some people find it impossible to adapt to new ways, so differences increase as development takes place. In the case of the HYVs, often the larger and better-off farmers adapted more easily, leading to the charge that the Green Revolution, though successful, contributed to greater disparity among farmers and even increased rural-to-urban migration, both of which are common phenomena in developing countries.

Third, targeting increased output signals a different approach to food problems, one that has been emerging in many parts of the world during the past several decades. In the nineteenth and early twentieth centuries, output was usually increased by expanding the amount of land in production. In the Green Revolution we are witnessing a much greater emphasis on improved technology and intensity of production, with greater input per areal unit expected to yield greater output.

Despite its attendant problems, the Green Revolution has helped millions of people produce more food and literally avoid starvation. Mexico and India have been very successful with wheat. India and Bangladesh have made important strides with rice, becoming at least temporarily self-sufficient in food grains. In addition, China is using hybrid sorghum, and the Philippines, Indonesia, Turkey, and Brazil are using HYVs. The graphs in Figure B illustrate the achievement of the state of Punjab, India, with wheat and rice. Again, however, success has required more than the adoption of new seed; it has meant an almost total transformation of the agricultural system.

The Green Revolution has not solved the world food problem. Although India is noted for its success, millions of Indians still lack the land, resources, or know-how to improve their productivity. As a matter of fact, India's per capita food output is estimated to be lower now than it was at the turn of the twentieth century. (But, of course, India's population has tripled since then.) In addition, millions of Africans continue to walk the food tightrope, and in many countries the urban poor suffer from hunger. Additional progress will require improved national research efforts and greater regional cooperation, which is not easily achieved.

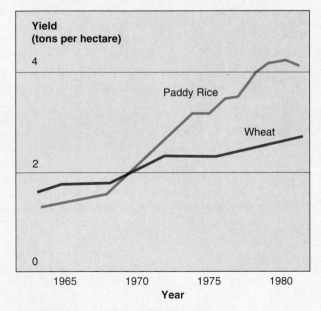

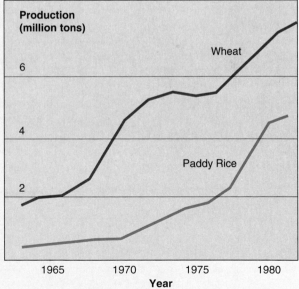

Figure B
Agricultural productivity increases in Punjab, India. The Green Revolution has been quite successful in Punjab, but achievement has been based on much more than HYV seed. Punjab's agricultural transformation included irrigation improvements, price incentives, road improvements, market development, and other infrastructural aid. The points plotted here are three-year moving averages. (Adapted by permission from *World Development Report 1982*, New York: Oxford University Press, 1982, p. 26.)

Figure 4-5

World per capita GNP. Per capita gross national product is considered the best single measure of economic well-being. High per capita GNPs are closely associated with areas of European culture and with oil-exporting countries. Israel and Japan also have high values. Low per capita GNPs are associated with southern, southeastern, and eastern Asia and much of Africa. (From Population Reference Bureau, *World Population Data Sheet*, Washington, DC: 1994.)

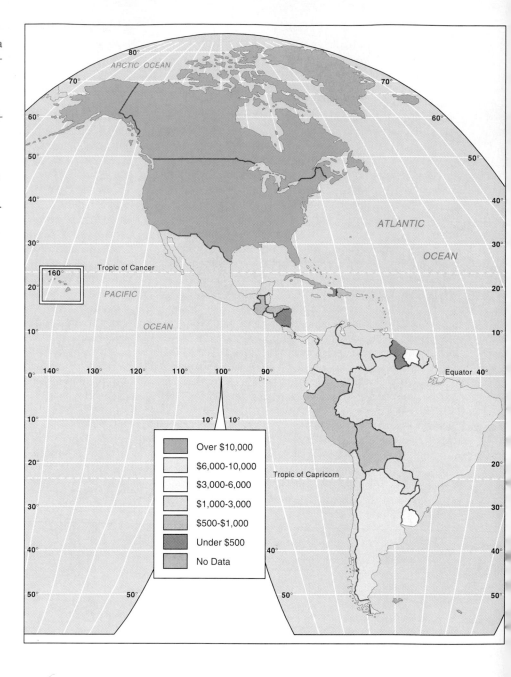

Legend:
- Over $10,000
- $6,000-10,000
- $3,000-6,000
- $1,000-3,000
- $500-$1,000
- Under $500
- No Data

the high-income group. Much of Latin America, parts of the Middle East, and Taiwan and Malaysia have per capita GNPs between $1,000 and $6,000. Countries with a per capita GNP of $500 to $1,000 are few, and they are widely dispersed throughout Latin America, Africa, and Asia. The poorest areas, with GNPs of less than $500, are in southern, southeastern, and eastern Asia and in southern and cen-

tral Africa, in addition to Haiti in Latin America. That group of countries suffers from persistent poverty. They have been identified by the United Nations as part of the growing dichotomy between developing countries that are progressing and those that are stagnating. They are continuously constrained by foreign debt, drought, population pressures, warfare, and ineffective economic and political systems.

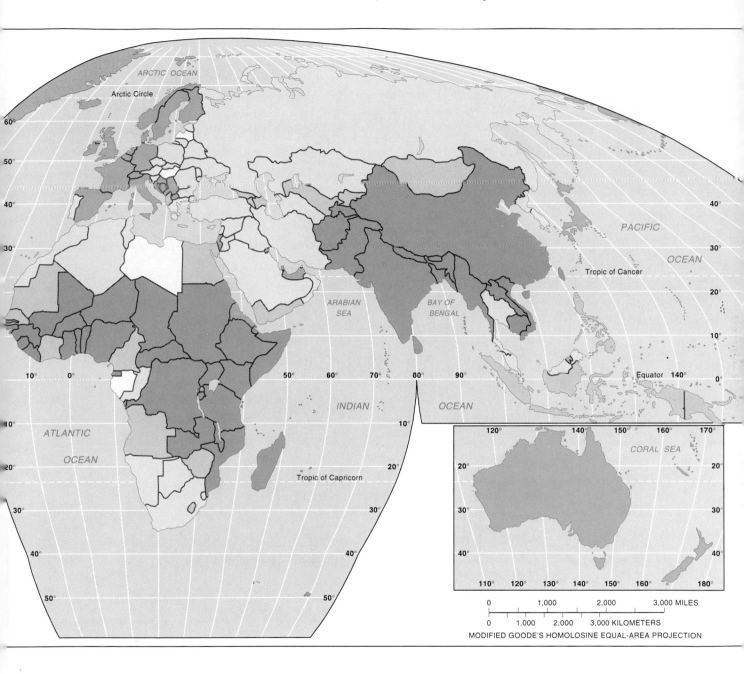

Per Capita Inanimate Energy Consumption

One of the characteristics of the Industrial Revolution has been a shift from animate power (human or beast) to inanimate energy—mineral fuels, hydroelectricity, and, more recently, nuclear power (Figure 4–6). The degree to which a country is able to supply inanimate energy from internal sources or to import it is an important indicator of applied modern technology and, consequently, of productivity. Just as per capita GNP measures productivity in terms of value, per capita inanimate energy use measures production in terms of power expended.

Thus, energy consumption is closely related to economic activity. Low per capita energy consumption is associated with subsistence and other non-mechanized agricultural economies; high per capita

Figure 4-6
A typical street scene in Jodhpur, India. Contrasting traditional and contemporary
transport technologies are often juxtaposed in developing areas.

energy use is associated with industrialized societies. Intermediate levels of energy use characterize regions that have both industrialized urban centers and more traditional nonmechanized rural areas. The distribution of per capita inanimate energy consumption is shown in Figure 4–7. The similarity of that distribution to the distribution of per capita GNP (see Figure 4–5) can be easily seen by comparing the two maps.

Percentage of the Labor Force in Primary Activities

Countries in which a large part of the labor force is engaged in primary activities do not produce much income and use relatively small amounts of power per capita. Conversely, countries with strong secondary and tertiary components usually have greater per capita GNPs and consume more energy.

Use of this indicator—percentage of the labor force in primary activities (mainly agriculture)—is based on those relationships.

Countries in which primary production is dominant offer limited opportunities for labor specialization, especially if the economy depends on subsistence agriculture, in which the vast majority of effort must be dedicated to meeting local food needs. In theory at least, labor specialization and production diversity are basic to economic growth. Thus, prospects for high levels of individual production are diminished if workers must not only grow the crops but also process, transport, and market them, in addition to providing their own housing, tools, and clothing.

Of all the primary activities, agriculture is by far the most important. Roughly 98 percent of the primary-sector labor force in the world is involved in agriculture; about 1 percent is engaged in hunting and fishing, and the other 1 percent, in mining. Consequently, a map showing the distribution of the labor force in agriculture (Figure 4–8) gives a good representation of the dominance of primary occupations. The broad pattern of that distribution is similar, in the inverse, to the distributions of per capita GNP and energy consumption.

Other Measures

Although GNP, energy use, and agricultural labor force are most often used to identify more developed and less developed countries, other measures are occasionally employed. Two that indicate quality of life are: life expectancy and food supply.

The life-expectancy measure would seem to be the ultimate indicator of development. Because some cultures are less materialistic than others, the standard measures of wealth may mask some important cultural attitudes of a society. All cultures, however, value the preservation of life. And at least in part, life expectancy is a measure of the end result of economic activity; it tells how well a system functions to provide life support, as well as death control through disease eradication and improved sanitation. A country whose inhabitants can expect a life span of only forty years has failed in its most important function. Figure 4–9, which shows the levels of life expectancy throughout the world, correlates generally with the maps we have examined in this chapter.

Two measures of food supply are also fundamental: (1) the number of calories available is an indicator of dietary quantity and (2) protein supply is an indicator of dietary quality. Adequate quantity is at least 2,400 available calories per person per day. Adequate protein supply is attained if at least 60 grams of protein are available per person per day. Figure 4–10 depicts the deficiency or inadequacy of caloric intake in large areas of the world. Those same areas are also commonly deficient in protein supply.

CHARACTERISTICS OF MORE DEVELOPED AND LESS DEVELOPED REGIONS

Combining the various measures of more developed and less developed countries into a single map permits us to identify some broad regional patterns (Figure 4–11). Such a map is, of course, highly generalized, so that some more developed nations—Israel, for example—are lumped with less developed

countries, and some less developed countries—such as Albania—are included in the more developed regions. Some countries are classified as more developed by all measures, and many are classified as less developed in all ways. A number of countries, however, fall among the more developed in some categories and among the less developed in others. At all points along the continuum from developed to undeveloped, countries are found in varying stages of transition to a more developed status.

The correlation is strong between more developed areas and populations of predominantly European origin. That finding, however, should not be interpreted as a cause-and-effect relationship; it is, instead, the outcome of a historical process. The fact is that industrialization and modernization began in Europe. Anglo-America by its very name implies European roots. Latin America, a less developed region, also has a European connection, but parts of it have been greatly influenced by Indian or African cultures as well. For example, Mexico, northern Central America, and Andean South America have large and viable Indian culture components. Wherever people of European tradition do form the dominant population (i.e., Argentina, Chile, Uruguay, and Venezuela), indicators tend toward the more developed end of the continuum. The populations of Australia and New Zealand are also European, leaving Japan the lone exception among the more developed regions, for it is truly non-European. In contrast, the less developed regions—Latin America, North Africa and the Middle East, Africa south of the Sahara, South Asia, Southeast Asia, and East Asia—have no common cultural background. In fact, diversity of population, culture, and history is the rule.

The More Developed World

We have already noted several characteristics of more developed countries: high per capita GNP and energy use; a small part of the labor force in primary activities and a consequent emphasis on secondary and tertiary occupations; a longer life expectancy; and a better and more abundant food supply. More developed countries also have a low rate of population growth. To a large degree those countries have attained Stage IV of the demographic transformation (discussed in Chapter 2). In addition, more developed countries share certain other economic and cultural characteristics.

Figure 4-7
World per capita consumption of inanimate energy, expressed in oil equivalents. Per capita energy consumption is a measure of development that indicates the use of technology. Because most forms of modern technology use large amounts of inanimate energy, countries that use small amounts of that type of energy must rely principally on human or animal power. (From *World Development Report 1992*, New York: Oxford University Press, 1992.)

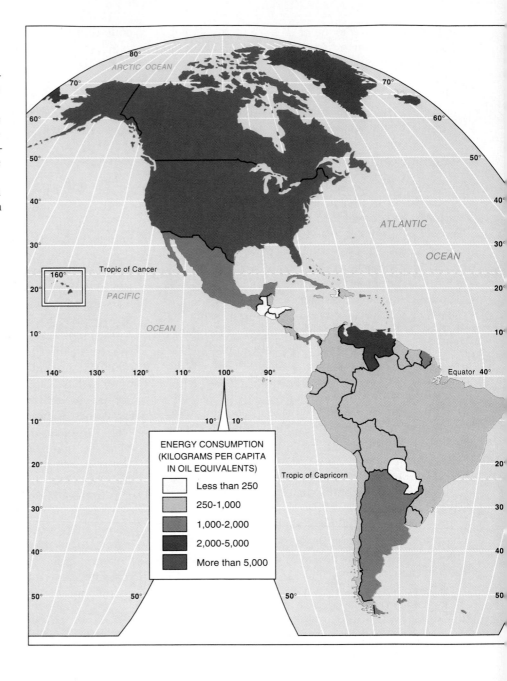

Economic Characteristics. The most basic economic characteristic of the more developed world is a widespread use of technology (Figure 4–12). In those regions the fruits of the Agricultural and Industrial Revolutions are widely applied, and new techniques are quickly adopted and diffused. New technologies mean new resources and the opportunity for still greater generation of wealth. Advanced technology also leads to increased labor productivity and the creation of an improved infrastructure, including roads, communications, energy and water supply, sewage disposal, credit institutions, and even schools, housing, and medical services. Those support facilities are necessary for accelerated economic activity and for specialization of production, which further enhances productivity.

The heavy dependence of the more developed countries on minerals further differentiates them

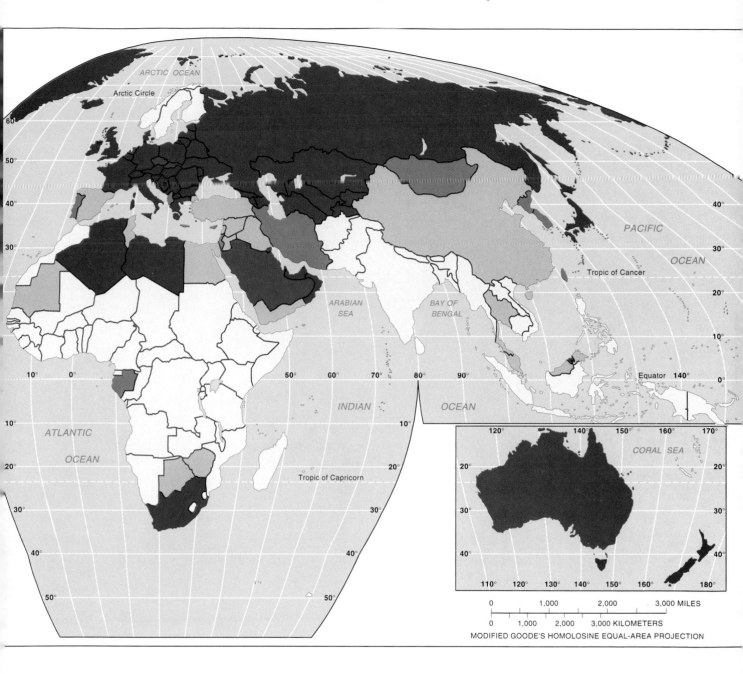

MODIFIED GOODE'S HOMOLOSINE EQUAL-AREA PROJECTION

from the less developed countries. Not only are we in an iron-and-steel age, but we are also in a fossil-fuel age, a cement age, a copper-and-aluminum age—the list is almost endless. To a greater and greater degree, more developed countries are importing those minerals from less developed countries and then exporting manufactured goods and, in some cases, food. That practice has led to trade surpluses for most of the more developed countries and trade deficits for many of the less developed countries because the price of raw materials (with the exception of petroleum) has increased more slowly than the price of manufactured goods. The more developed countries gain even more revenues by investing in less developed countries. That outside removal of wealth has encouraged some less developed countries to nationalize or restrict foreign investments.

Figure 4-8
World percent of the labor force in agriculture. The percentage of the labor force in agriculture shows the degree of economic diversity in a nation. If a large percentage of the population is engaged in agricultural pursuits, manufacturing and services are limited in their development. Conversely, if only a small percentage of the labor force is in agriculture, manufacturing and services are well staffed. (From *Production Yearbook*, New York: United Nations, 1991.)

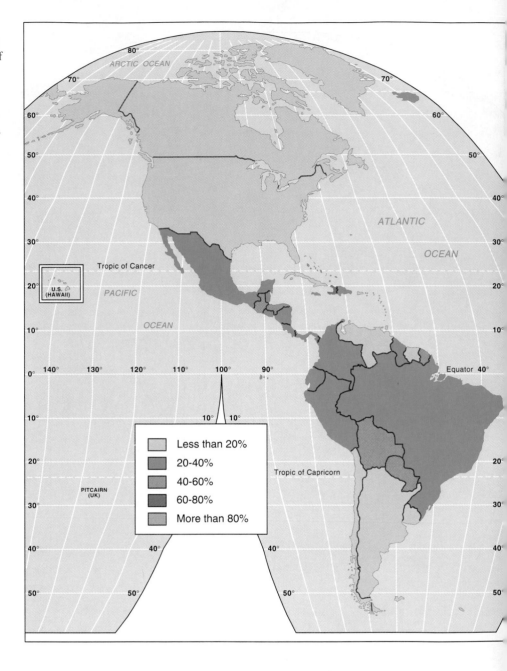

New technologies, high productivity, and a favorable trade balance result in higher personal and corporate incomes. Consequently, many individuals in more developed countries need to spend only a part of their income for food and shelter; other income can be used for services, products, and savings—where it stimulates further economic growth. For entrepreneurs (i.e., organizers who gather together labor, financing, and all those other things necessary to construct an effective economic activity), more developed countries offer numerous infrastructural advantages.

Cultural Characteristics.   The European heritage shared by many of the more developed countries is cultural. So are the attitudes and value systems that are reflected in economic performance. Followers of the Judeo-Christian ethic consider a commitment to

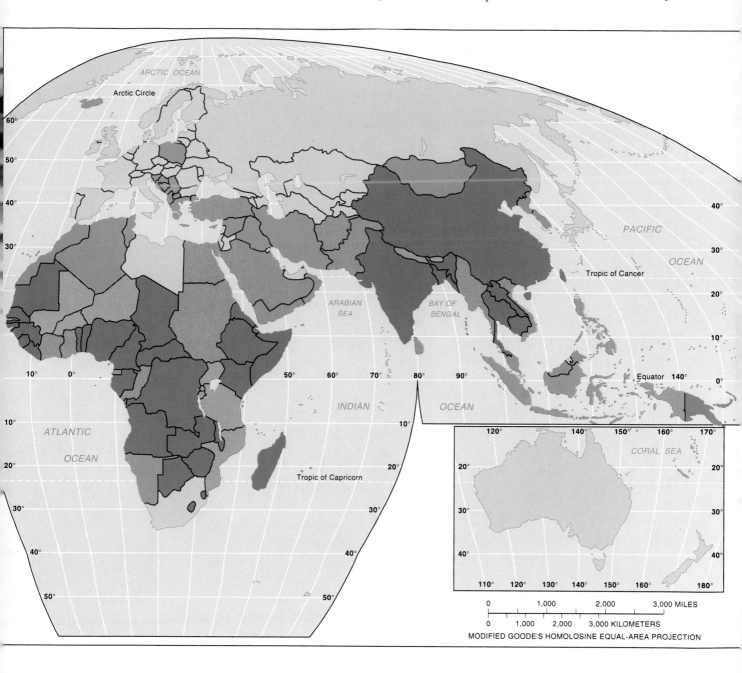

MODIFIED GOODE'S HOMOLOSINE EQUAL-AREA PROJECTION

productivity an important attribute; thus, an accumulation of material things becomes a representation of and a reward for work performance, and success and peer respect are measured largely by wealth. Japan's well-known cultural attitude toward work and success is similar to the European example, even though it is not based on a Judeo-Christian tradition.

Another cultural attribute of the more developed nations is the importance attached to education.

Education is enhanced by communications, and new ideas spread quickly. In addition, education is geared partly toward economic advancement: disciplines such as engineering, geography, economics, agronomy, and chemistry have obvious and direct applicability to resource development. An educated urban populace is an extremely important resource, for it more readily accepts change. And acceptance of change means that technology is more easily adopted,

Figure 4-9
World life expectancy at birth.
Life expectancy is a measure of
how well a nation is able to
care for its population. Long life
expectancy is closely associated
with the other indicators of
developed nations. (From
Population Reference Bureau,
World Population Data Sheet,
Washington, DC: 1994.)

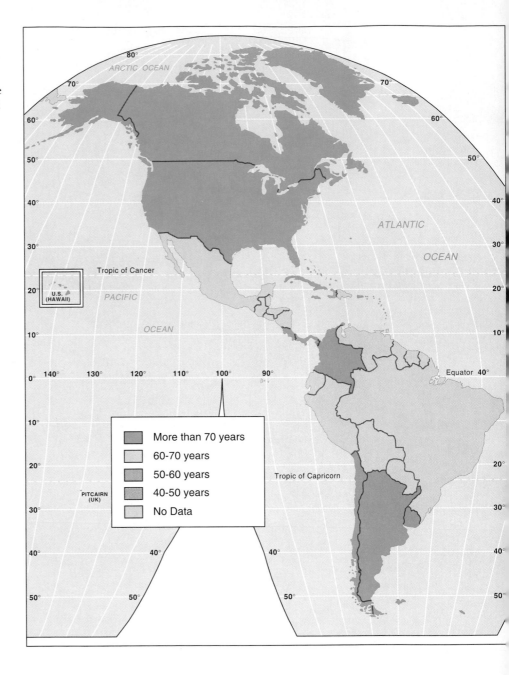

new products and services are welcomed, and the mobile population can more readily take advantage of opportunities in other areas of the country.

The Less Developed World

We have already learned that less developed nations are characterized by low per capita GNP and energy use, a high proportion of the labor force in primary pursuits, a comparatively short life span, and a diet often deficient in quantity and/or quality. In addition, less developed countries commonly display a variety of other characteristics.

Population Characteristics.   Less developed countries have a high rate of population growth, the result of a continuing high birthrate and a declining death rate (see Figure 2–6). As a consequence, the age structure of the population of a less developed country is

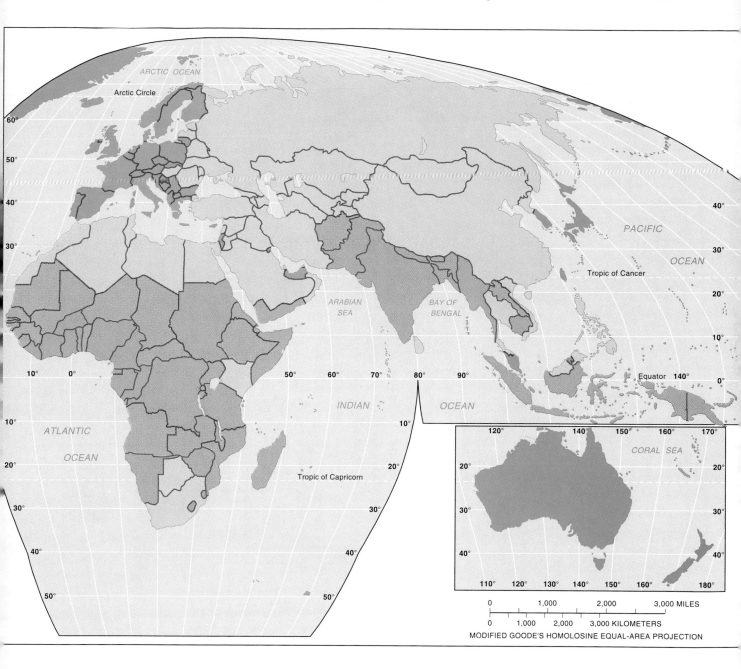

different from that of a more developed country. Figure 4–13 illustrates this difference graphically by means of **population pyramids**. In less developed countries a large segment of the population is outside the most productive age group: fully 40 percent of the population is less than fifteen years old. In a sense, then, per capita comparisons are unfair because all people are counted equally, yet in the less developed nations a smaller part (8 percent less) of the population is made up of mature laborers. A large youthful population also foretells continued rapid population growth and reduces the ability of women to engage in economic activities, because they are needed to tend the young.

The status of women in the diverse cultures of less developed countries often excludes them from

Figure 4-10
World daily per capita food supply. Food supply is a measure of well-being in the most basic sense. In various large areas of the world people have inadequate diets, as measured by caloric intake. (From *Production Yearbook*, New York: United Nations, 1991.)

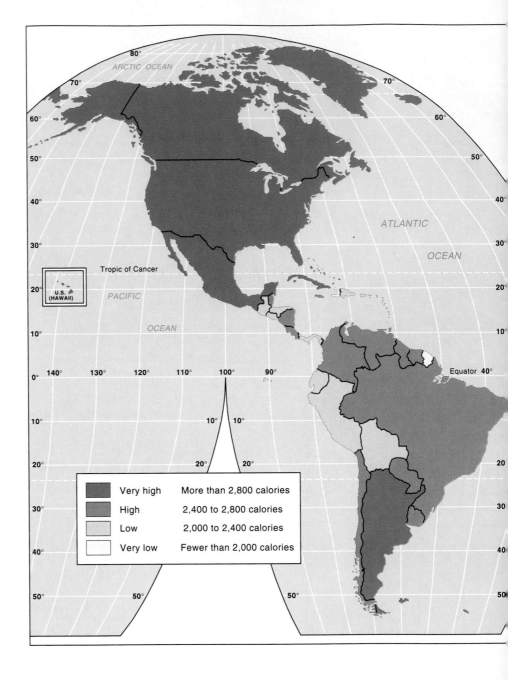

many occupations (see the boxed feature Female Labor Force Participation and Development). In the rural sector women may work with men in the fields during periods of peak labor requirement, but much of their time is spent in the home and in pursuit of fuel wood and water. While at home, women may engage in some craft industry, such as weaving for household use and for sale in the local market. In addition, many rural women in the less developed world play a pivotal role in marketing the family's surplus on a daily or weekly basis. In the cities women find employment as domestics, secretaries, or, more recently, industrial workers. For many illiterate women, however, those last two opportunities are not available.

Cultural Characteristics. The literacy rate in less developed countries is generally low. Most rural in-

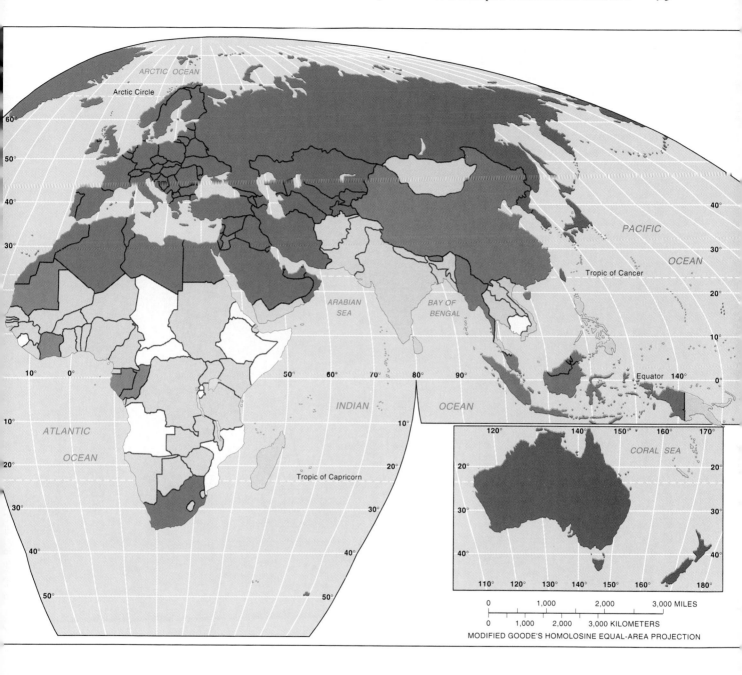

habitants cannot read or write or can do so only at minimal levels. Literacy is more prevalent in cities, but large numbers of urban poor still lack the ability to read effectively. That inability excludes a large mass of the population from learning new technologies and from engaging in more remunerative occupations. Unfortunately, despite some major campaigns to improve literacy, many countries have made little headway in this area.

Most of the cultures of the less developed world are also conservative and resistant to change, thereby presenting a fundamental paradox. Those cultures, by and large, wish to preserve their customs and mores, yet they want to partake of the material benefits that Western society enjoys. Clearly, economic development leads to cultural change, to the possible destruction of traditions, and to the acquisition of new behavior patterns. Sometimes the

Figure 4-11
More developed and less developed regions of the world. The preceding maps, which measure different aspects of development, have similar distributional patterns. This map generalizes those patterns, dividing the world into more developed and less developed regions.

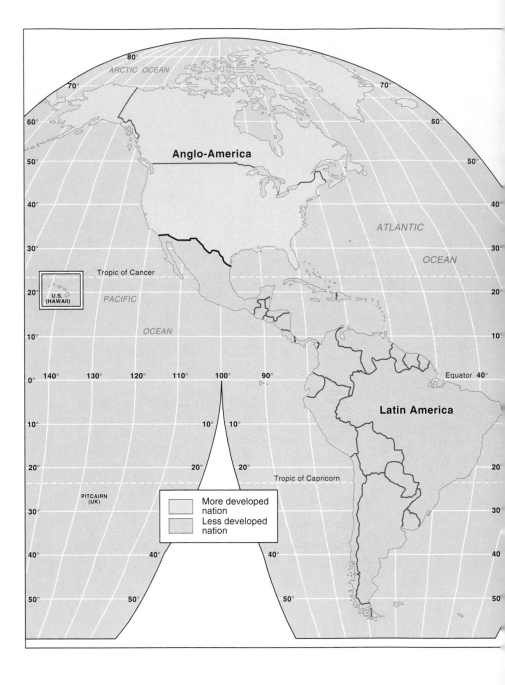

family loses part of its cohesiveness, villages become subservient to larger urban centers, labor specialization and regional specialization lead to commercialization of the economy, and loyalties to the local community give way to national allegiances. Those changes and others are inevitable when economic development occurs. Consequently, disruption is a characteristic of less developed countries, as old and new ways of life come into conflict.

Conflict between the old and new ways may also accentuate preexisting cultural differences. **Cultural pluralism** occurs when two or more ethnic groups exist within a single country, each having its own institutions, language, religion, life-style, and goals. In some places those ethnic groups live apart; in others they are intermingled. In either case, however, joint action for development is difficult if the differences among the groups are great or if mutual an-

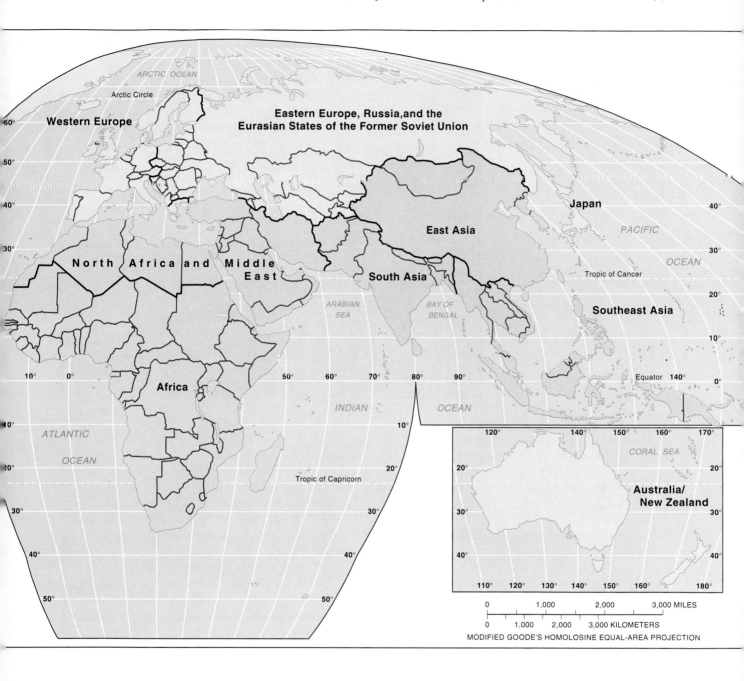

tagonism exists. In fact, opposing goals may lead to inaction, and any attempts to alter the status quo may cause conflict.

Numerous examples of unresolved or sharp differences are found in the less developed world. In various parts of Africa rural people cling to their traditional ways of life, while many city dwellers have adopted a Western economic system and cultural goals. In parts of southeastern Asia national unity is weak because life is oriented to the village and ethnic groups are diverse. In Latin America cultural pluralism is evident wherever the Indian population is large. Cultural pluralism does not preclude economic development, but it can create additional stress and obstacles to inter- and intraregional cooperation.

Figure 4-12
Women factory workers assembling instruments in Minsk, Belorussia. A well-developed manufacturing sector (secondary activity) is characteristic of economically developed countries.

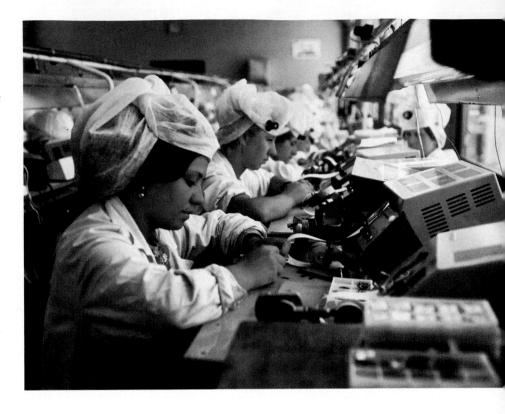

Economic Characteristics. Countries in the less developed world share many economic traits. Most have a dual economy, one part organized for domestic consumption and the other for export trade. All nations, of course, produce for both internal and external markets; in more developed nations, though farmers and factory workers produce the same items for both markets and rarely know whether they are consumed locally. In the less developed world, however, producers for the local market supply only that market, and different producers provide for the export trade. Domestic producers generally use antiquated techniques and are often subsistence-oriented. Export producers frequently have access to technological innovations and acquire the means to incorporate them. In fact, the export sector, which is fully within the market economy, has often obtained its investment capital from the more developed industrial corelands and must remain competitive with rivals. Domestic producers do not have the same incentives or capabilities.

Another characteristic of less developed countries is a primary reliance on flow (renewable) resources, principally those related to agriculture. That orientation does not necessarily mean that the peo-

ple live in ecological balance with their surroundings, however. In many regions increasing population pressures, coupled with static technology, have led to the exploitation of agricultural resources to a point that soil depletion and erosion have become serious problems. Of course, there are exceptions: in parts of China, where dense populations have lived for hundreds of years, agricultural resources have actually been improved.

Fund resources—for example, minerals—are important export commodities in many less developed countries, but they usually enter the domestic market in the form of finished goods imported from more developed nations. Such commodities earn few dollars as raw exports but are expensive when imported as finished goods. Thus, finished goods and food products are the main imports of less developed nations; raw materials and agricultural products are their principal exports.

Not surprisingly, poverty is widespread in the less developed world (Figure 4–14). The vast majority of the populace is in the lower class, with a smaller elite group controlling economic and political life. In most of the less develped countries the middle class is embryonic; in some it is growing as

Figure 4-13
Population pyramids for more developed and less developed countries. Population pyramids illustrate several demographic features. They show the distribution of the total population by age group and by gender. More developed countries are shown to have a greater proportion of their population in the most productive age group; less developed countries have a much greater potential for rapid population growth because a large part of the population is young. Thus, economic growth in less developed countries must be at a high level just to keep up with population growth. (From United Nations Population Division, *Population Bulletin*, no. 14, 1983.)

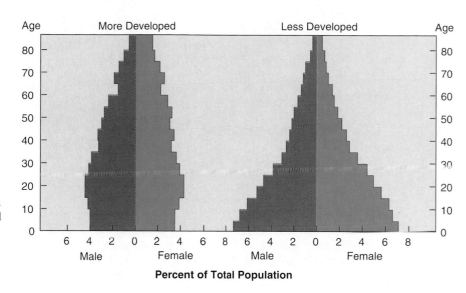

urbanization progresses. The limited income of the large bulk of the population results from several factors: low levels of productivity, a limited infrastructure, lack of applied technology, and social and economic structures that do not facilitate economic development. High levels of unemployment and widespread underemployment also contribute to the low-income pattern because few alternative occupations are open to most of the labor force. Accumulated wealth exists only in the hands of the upper class and is often unavailable for investment in new activities.

THEORIES OF DEVELOPMENT

Control Theories

A number of theories have been advanced to explain why some nations are more developed and others are less developed. No theory is accepted by everyone, and some theories are strongly opposed. One of the earliest theories was **environmental determinism**, which received considerable attention during the 1920s and 1930s but has been largely discredited since then. The most effective proponent of that theory was Ellsworth Huntington (1876-1947), who wrote or coauthored twenty-eight books, in-

cluding *The Pulse of Asia* and *Mainsprings of Civilization*. The premise of environmental determinism is that the physical environment controls or channels what people do. Mid-latitude climatic regions are said to be more stimulating for economic activity than polar or tropical climates are. Indeed, maps of economic development do show a majority of the more developed nations in mid-latitude locations and a majority of the less developed nations in the tropics. As an explanation for variations in well-being, however, environmental determinism is grossly inadequate.

Another control theory is **cultural determinism**. According to that theory, which is currently quite popular, a person's range of action is determined largely by culture. In other words, if the culture emphasizes a work ethic, most members of that society will work. Conversely, if the possession of worldly goods is not among a culture's priorities, economic performance measured in such terms will probably be low (Figure 4–15). Some previously cited examples illustrate continuing group support of economic activities that are not particularly productive: the Mayan maize culture, the Bedouin nomadic herding, and the adherence to subsistence-oriented village life and ethnic unity found among numerous groups in southeastern Asia.

FEMALE LABOR FORCE PARTICIPATION AND DEVELOPMENT

Development is not exclusively an economic process; rather, it requires and generates significant change in the social, demographic, and biologic dimensions of a society. Some of the affected dimensions include female participation in the labor force, female participation in agriculture, female literacy, infant mortality rates, primary school enrollment of children, and the incidence of selected diseases. Those additional measures of development, when examined carefully, reinforce the realization that women and children in developmentally lagging societies often bear disproportionately the burden of poverty, thereby ensuring a cycle of continuing poverty.

Figure A presents one of those measures—female participation in the labor force—an interesting measure that does not correlate directly with levels of development. Several factors contribute to the distribution pattern and thereby complicate interpretation. First, as with many forms of data, the method of reporting is not consistent from country to country, a reflection of data collection procedures as well as attitudinal bias regarding the value of work performed by women. For example, the map shows sharp distinctions in female labor in adjacent African countries, despite the high and increasing female participation in food production throughout sub-Saharan Africa. In that region males often migrate to cities in search of work and cash income, leaving the burden of food production, child care, and other domestic chores to women.

Another complicating factor is religious tradition, which may restrict female participation in the labor force. Indeed, the map shows the areas of least participation to be those where Islamic values are dominant.

A final complication is that developed and developing countries may exhibit similar participation rates under widely differing circumstances. Less developed countries, with the Islamic realm excepted, generally show a high percentage of economically active women engaged in agriculture. Indeed, their involvement is critical to the success of the food-producing system. Developed areas, on the other hand, which show moderate to high participation rates in Figure A, actually have low rates of female participation in agriculture. In fact, as development has progressed in Europe and North America, female participation in agriculture has decreased. During the latter half of the twentieth century, however, the percentage of women involved in other aspects of the labor force has increased dramatically, as a function of perceived need and changing social values. In the United States, for example, nearly 60 percent of women now participate in the labor force, but less than 1 percent of those women are employed in agriculture.

This hint at the complex relationship between culture and the development process suggests that the interpretation of many aspects of development must be specific to time, place, and culture.

We could easily combine those two control theories and conclude that harsh environments and cultural handicaps work together to ensure a vicious cycle of poverty. But such a simplistic view overlooks the fact that many people may be achieving at low levels merely because they have not had the opportunity to do otherwise.

Colonialism and Trade

Mercantilism is the philosophy that governed trade between most mother countries and their colonies after 1600. Under mercantilism the colonies supplied raw materials and foodstuffs needed by the mother country, and the mother country, in turn, used its colonies as a market for finished products and other surpluses. To ensure that the colonies did not compete with the mother country, they were prohibited from producing goods that the mother country had in abundance. Moreover, the colonies were permitted to trade only with the mother country. That arrangement obviously worked to the advantage of the mother country and severely limited the economic options of the colonies.

Colonialism in the traditional sense of the word is largely a thing of the past. In the years immediately after World War II, most colonial powers gave up, or were forced to give up, their possessions. Yet, many of the trade relationships and patterns of that era have been retained and are cited frequently as an explanation for the continuing uneven distribution of wealth. Many less developed countries, it is argued, suffer from economic dependence on the more developed regions of the world. The **depen-**

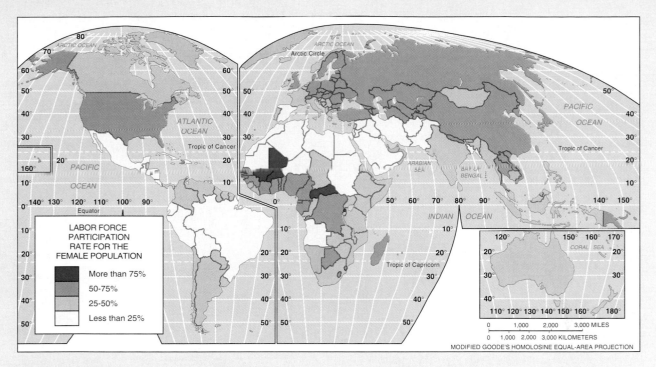

Figure A

Rates of female participation in the labor force. The variations evident are a reflection not only of real differences, but also of differences in value systems, which influence how countries report information on economic and social conditions. (Data from R. L. Sivard, *Women . . . A World Survey,* Washington, DC: World Priorities, 1985.)

dency theory traces the problem back to colonialism, which, by extension then, is responsible for today's underdevelopment. A more extreme form of that notion is the **imperialist theory**, in which the developed world is seen as deliberately controlling the less developed world.

Underdevelopment is not as simple as any one of those theories. The disadvantage of less developed countries in the traditional trade relationships cannot be denied. But some less developed countries were never totally controlled as colonies; others have been independent for many years. If we are to understand an individual country's place in today's interdependent world, we must examine its precolonial, colonial, and postcolonial experiences.

Circular Causation

Another economic concept know as **circular causation** results in either a downward or an upward spiral. An example of the downward spiral is a farm family that produces barely enough to feed itself. Because the family has little or no savings, it has nothing to fall back on if a minor crop failure reduces the harvest. Its members simply have less to eat, so they work less, produce less, and then have even less to eat. The upward spiral can also be illustrated by a farm family. Perhaps the family produces only enough to feed itself but, by good fortune, obtains some capital to buy fertilizer, which increases crop yields. As a result, the family eats better, works harder to produce more, and sells the

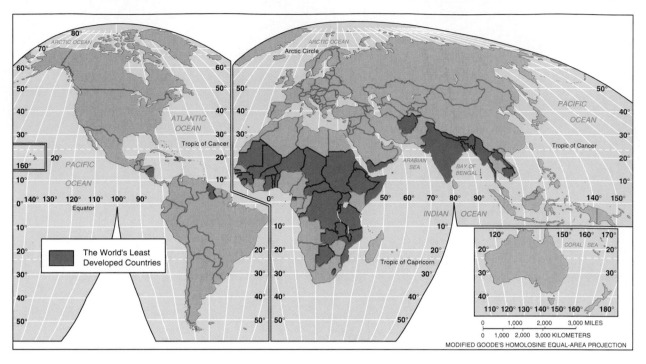

Figure 4-14
The world's least developed countries. Countries whose per capita GNP is usually less than $400 have been included among those countries officially designated by the United Nations as the least developed in the world. Many are landlocked, remote, and handicapped by difficult environments. Twenty-eight of these forty-two countries are within the African realm.

surplus, thus increasing its capacity to buy more fertilizer as well as improved seed. That theory is equally applicable to groups and nations.

Rostow's Stages

Walt Rostow compared historical economic data and came up with the idea that there are five **stages of economic growth**.[3] In the first stage we find traditional society. Most workers are in agriculture, have limited savings, and use age-old production methods. Indeed, all of the characteristics of a truly poor society are exhibited.

"Preconditions for takeoff" are established in the second stage, which may be initiated internally by the desire of the people for a higher standard of living or externally by forces that intrude into the region. In either case production increases, perhaps only slightly but enough to cause fundamental changes in attitudes, and individual and national goals are altered.

Takeoff occurs in the third stage, when new technologies and capital are applied and production is greatly increased. Manufacturing and tertiary activities become increasingly important and result in migration from rural areas to bustling urban agglomerations. Infrastructural facilities are improved and expanded, and political power is transferred from the landed aristocracy to an urban-based structure.

The fourth stage is the "drive to maturity," a continuation of the processes begun in the previous stage. Urbanization progresses, and manufacturing and service activities become increasingly important. The rural sector loses much of its population, but those who remain use mechanized equipment and modern technology to produce large quantities.

The final stage is high mass consumption. Personal incomes are high, and abundant goods and

Figure 4-15
New Guinea men carving out a canoe with primitive tools. Transport technology is a major part of the infrastructure affecting economic development, yet a wide range of transportation modes remains in use.

services are readily available. Individuals no longer worry about securing the basic necessities of life and can devote more of their energies to noneconomic pursuits.

It is difficult to place a specific country among Rostow's stages. Furthermore, in large countries different regions may exhibit different levels of development. Nevertheless, we can speculate on the positions of some countries within the model. For example, in the United States, citizens of European descent were never really in the first, or traditional, stage. The country was settled and developed by Europeans whose homelands already exhibited preconditions for takeoff. The United States approached takeoff by the 1840s, and by 1865 it be-

gan its drive to maturity, which was achieved, according to Rostow, by 1900. Even though development was achieved rapidly, great regional variations persisted.

The United States, Japan, Canada, Australia, and Germany are now in the stage of high mass consumption. Russia and most countries of Western Europe are in their drive to maturity. Countries in the takeoff stage include Mexico, Argentina, Brazil, and Venezuela in Latin America; Spain and Portugal in Europe; and South Korea in East Asia. Countries such as Kenya (in East Africa) and Nigeria (in West Africa) are displaying preconditions for takeoff, while countries in central Africa are still exhibiting the traits of traditional societies. No time frame can logically be specified for passage through any of the stages of the Rostow model.

The Lacostian View

The French geographer Lacoste has offered several cautions for any interpretation of developmental lag.[4] One is to avoid the view that population growth *per se* is causal to developmental lag. According to Lacoste, population growth may be a corollary to lag, along with poverty, but it is not causal. He further cautions against any view of external forces as the sole impetus for developmental lag. For example, although colonialism has contributed significantly to the problem of underdevelopment, he does not see it as the sole cause. Development problems may also stem from the unwillingness and/or inability of ruling elites to foster the political, social, and economic infrastructure essential to developmental progress. Lacoste points to their adoption of an "adulterated" capitalist system in conjunction with remnant feudal power relationships. Thus, the **Lacostian view** sees underdevelopment as the result of complex and interacting forces—of both internal and external origin.

The theories described here are presented in simplified form. Each may have some value in understanding a particular situation, but as a generally acceptable view of development theory each also has shortcomings. Indeed, of the foregoing notions, all implicitly attribute poverty and related problems to a lack of development. Another viewpoint, arising from the belief that development theory of the past forty years has failed to provide adequate explanation or solution to global problems—is that development itself, as practiced, has created scarcity and disparity.[5]

SUMMARY
An Unequal World

A wide range of more developed nations and less developed nations spans the globe. Many nations are undergoing economic development and are realizing progress, but for others the gap between the less developed and the more developed worlds is widening. The various indicators and theories discussed in this chapter will serve as useful measures of development as we examine specific regions and nations in the chapters to follow.

Two cautions are in order, however. First, our concept of development is Western in origin and may need to be reexamined before it can be applied to non-Western realms with goals and motivations quite different from ours. And second, the factors that restrain or enhance development are myriad and complex. Even though considerable emphasis is placed on the population equation, any explanation of developmental lag must look beyond a single issue.

KEY TERMS

circular causation	imperialist theory
cultural determinism	Lacostian view
cultural pluralism	less developed countries
dependency theory	mercantilism
environmental determinism	more developed countries
GNP gap	population pyramid
Green Revolution	stages of economic growth

NOTES

1. Gross national product is the total value of all goods and services produced and provided by one country during a given year. GNP estimates are subject to some error, particularly in nations with a significant part of the population engaged in subsistence activities. Such activities are often undervalued or are not reported.

2. GNP is often undervalued in less developed regions because part of the economy is not commercialized. Barbering is just one example. In more developed areas proceeds from the barber trade are figured into the GNP. In less developed areas, where barbering is done at home, no contribution to the GNP is acknowledged. In general, transactions in which money is not exchanged are not included in the GNP.

3. Walt W. Rostow, *The Stages of Economic Growth: A Non-Communist Manifesto*, 2d ed. (Cambridge: Cambridge University Press, 1971).

4. The several works of Lacoste are reviewed in H. A. Reitsma and J. M. G. Kleinpenning, *The Third World in Perspective* (Assen/Maastricht, Netherlands: Van Gorcum, 1989), 223–236.

5. Lakshman Yapa, "What Are Improved Seeds? An Epistemology of the Green Revolution," *Economic Geography* 69 (1993): 254–255.

FURTHER READINGS
Part One

Akinbode, Ade. "Population Explosion in Africa and Its Implications for Economic Development." *Journal of Geography* 76 (1977): 28–36. Examines the repercussions of rapid population growth on economic development in underdeveloped areas.

Boehm, Richard G. *Careers in Geography*. Princeton, NJ: Peterson's Guides, 1990. A description of professional opportunities for geographers, written for students.

Brown, Lester R. *The Twenty-Ninth Day: Accommodating Human Needs and Numbers to the Earth's Resources.* New York: Norton, 1978. A treatment of world ecological, economic, and social systems from an environmental perspective.

Brown, Lester, et al. *State of the World, 1994.* New York: Norton, 1994. One of an annual series by the World Watch Institute, with each volume containing a collection of papers treating contemporary world problems and issues such as environmental concerns, technological impacts, energy problems, and food supply.

Chang, Jen-Hu. "The Agricultural Potential of the Humid Tropics." *Geographical Review* 58 (1968): 333–361. A still-valuable exploration of problems inherent in the utilization of a specific environmental realm.

Chilcote, Ronald H. *Theories of Development and Underdevelopment.* Boulder, CO: Westview Press, 1984. A review of classical and contemporary interpretations of the process and causes of development and underdevelopment.

Cuff, David J. "The Economic Dimension of Demographic Transition." *Journal of Geography* 72 (1973): 11–16. A brief discussion of the relationship of demographic transformation stages to economic activity.

Dalton, George, ed. *Economic Development and Social Change.* Garden City, NY: Natural History Press, 1971. The impact of development from colonial times to the present, traced through case studies.

Detwyler, Thomas R., ed. *Man's Impact on Environment.* New York: McGraw-Hill, 1971. A look at how people modify the environment.

Economic Development and Cultural Change. A journal established to study the role of economic development as an agent of cultural change; contains numerous articles worthy of examination.

Espenshade, Edward B., Jr., ed. *Goode's World Atlas.* 19th ed. Chicago: Rand McNally, 1995. An excellent general reference atlas for use as a text supplement.

Fuson, Robert H. *A Geography of Geography.* Dubuque, IA: Brown, 1969. A history of the development of geography from its Middle Eastern origins to its role in the United States today.

Gaile, Gary L., and Cort J. Wilmott. *Geography in America.* Columbus, OH: Merrill, 1989. An excellent review of the entire range of subfields comprising contemporary American geography.

Geographic and Global Issues Quarterly. United States Department of State, Bureau of Intelligence and Research, Office of the Geographer. A quarterly publication providing updates from a geographic perspective on foreign policy topics, boundary and sovereignty disputes, migration and refugee flows, international political and economic issues; provides updates on the current status of nations.

Grossman, Larry. "Man-Environment Relationships in Anthropology and Geography." *Annals, Association of American Geographers* 67 (1977): 17–27. A good philosophical discussion of the man-environment relationship as examined by geographers since 1900, with lengthy and useful references.

Haggett, Peter. *The Geographer's Art.* Oxford: Basil Blackwell, 1990. An overview of the richness of geography as a discipline and its utility as a perspective for analysis by one of its foremost practitioners.

Jacobsen, Jodi. "Closing the Gender Gap in Development," pp. 61-79 in *State of the World: 1993,* edited by Lester R. Brown. New York: Norton, 1993. An overview of the problems of women of developing countries and their unequal burden in poverty.

Jackson, Robert M., ed. *Annual Editions: Global Issues 94/95.* Guilford, CT: Dushkin, 1994. An annual publication reprinting articles treating topics of contemporary concern to the developed and developing world; an excellent supplement to this text.

Johnston, R. J., and Peter J. Taylor, eds. *A World in Crisis? Geographical Perspective.* New York: Blackwell, 1986. A collection of papers treating contemporary problems from the geographic perspective.

McFalls, Joseph A., Jr. "Population: A Lively Introduction." *Population Bulletin* 96, no. 2 (1991). An introduction to the topic of population.

McKnight, Tom L. *Physical Geography: A Landscape Appreciation.* 3d ed. Englewood Cliffs, NJ: Prentice-Hall, 1990. An introductory textbook treating the entire spectrum of physical geography.

Meadows, Donella H., Dennis L. Meadows, Jorgen Randers, and William W. Behrens III. *The Limits of Growth: A Report for the Club of Rome's Project on the Predicament of Mankind.* New York: Universe Books, 1972. A sobering neo-Malthusian discussion of the race between population growth on the one hand and technology and pollution on the other.

Meadows, Donella H., Dennis L. Meadows, and Jorgen Randers. *Beyond the Limits*. Post Mills, VT: Chelsea Green, 1992. An update and contemporary extension of *Limits to Growth*.

National Council for Geographic Education. *Journal of Geography* 84 (November 1985). An entire issue examining population in relation to agricultural and more general development problems; provides excellent supplemental material for the regional discussions of Latin America, Eastern Europe and the (then) Soviet Union, Africa, and Anglo-America.

Pattison, William D. "The Four Traditions of Geography." *Journal of Geography* 63 (1964): 211–216. A discussion of the four traditions that have bound modern geography together.

Pitzl, Gerald, ed. *Annual Editions: Geography 94/95*. Gilford, CT: Dushkin, 1994. More than thirty reprinted articles treating contemporary themes in geography; an excellent supplement to this text because of its treatment of population, environment, and resources in relation to development.

The Professional Geographer 44 (February 1992). A special issue on the political geography of the post-cold war world.

Reitsma, H.A., and J. M. G. Kleinpenning. *The Third World in Perspective*. Assen/Maastricht, Netherlands: Van Gorcum, 1989. An excellent and extensive review of the concept of underdevelopment, including rural-agricultural and urban-industrial components; presents a good overview of related theory and case studies on Ethiopia, India, Cuba, and Taiwan.

Rostow, Walt W. *The Stages of Economic Growth: A Non-Communist Manifesto*. 2d ed. Cambridge: Cambridge University Press, 1971. An examination of economic development as a process and of the several stages through which a society must pass.

Selingson, Mitchell A., ed. *The Gap Between the Rich and the Poor*. Boulder, CO: Westview Press, 1984. A collection of twenty-nine papers defining the income and well-being gap, explaining it, summarizing empirical studies of it, and highlighting case studies by country.

Simon, Julian L. *The Ultimate Resource*. Princeton, NJ: Princeton University Press, 1981. A discussion of human resources as the ultimate resource for the solution of contemporary and future problems.

Smith, David M. *Where the Grass Is Greener: Living in an Unequal World*. Middlesex, England: Penguin Books, 1982. A review of the inequality among and within nations, treating measurement and pattern as well as causes and consequences.

Spencer, J. E., and W. L. Thomas. *Introducing Cultural Geography*. New York: Wiley, 1973. An introduction to cultural geography, written from a historical perspective.

Strahler, Alan H., and A. N. Strahler. *Modern Physical Geography*. 3d ed. New York: Wiley, 1992. An introductory textbook dealing with the entire spectrum of the physical environment.

Thomas, William L., ed. *Man's Role in Changing the Face of the Earth*. Chicago: University of Chicago Press, 1956. An old but classic work on the results of the man-environment relationship.

United Nations, Department of Economic Affairs. *Demographic Yearbook*. New York: United Nations, 1948–present. An annual compendium of useful population data, including total population, population growth rates, urban-rural ratios, births, deaths, life tables, and population movements.

United Nations, Department of Economic and Social Affairs. *Statistical Yearbook*. New York: United Nations, 1948–present. Annual statistics on a wide range of topics; particularly useful data on economic activities, including agriculture, forestry, fishing, mining, manufacturing, energy use, trade, transportation and communications, consumption of selected items, and national accounts.

United Nations, Food and Agriculture Organization. *Production Yearbook*. Rome: United Nations, 1946–present. An annual compendium of agricultural statistics, including area harvested, yields, and total production by country; also includes data on prices, pesticide and fertilizer consumption, and farm machinery.

Watts, Michael, and Peet, Richard, guest editors. "Environment and Development, Part I," *Economic Geography* 69 (1993): 227–327. A special issue devoted to environment and development with emphasis on the deficiencies of traditional development theory and practice and a much needed consideration of the social dimensions of development.

Wood, Harold A. "Toward a Geographical Concept of Development." *Geographical Review* 67 (1977): 462-468. Examines at local, regional, national, and multinational levels the major areas of concern in any development program—needs, territory, efficient transportation, environmental harmony, and quality of life.

The World Bank. *The World Development Report*. New York: The Oxford University Press. An excellent annual providing data updates and special reports on global economic development.

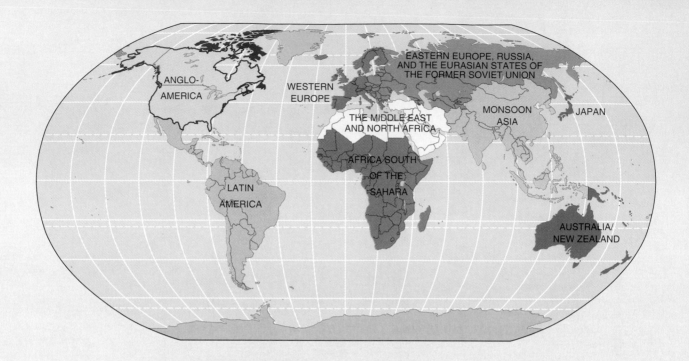

In the process of settlement and development both the United States and Canada have marshaled the rich resources of an enormous domain. As a result, the two nations, which together comprise Anglo-America, are two of the richest and most highly developed countries in the world.

In Chapter 5 we examine the generous resource endowment that has provided this varied and useful set of environments for development. Few peoples in the world have had the good fortune to have at their disposal such bountiful resources for agriculture, industry, and energy. Ironically, the economic systems in Anglo-America have become so large that massive importation of materials is required.

The settlement and development of Anglo-America was directed by people who came from other lands, places where the process of change and modernization was already under way. As development progressed, Native Americans were dispossessed, and captives from Africa were coerced into labor. The ongoing nature of Anglo-American development is evident in demographic change and the redistribution of population.

In Chapter 6 we emphasize the evolution of agricultural and industrial systems. The highly productive agricultural systems evolved on an abundant resource foundation, but not without cost to land and people. The industrialization of the United States and Canada occurred first in a concentrated coreland but now is dispersed and international. Indeed, the economic problems faced by these two countries reflect in large part the internationalization of economies on a worldwide scale and the rapid development that is occurring in various other parts of the world.

In Chapter 7 we caution that development *per se* does not preclude serious and complex problems. The chapter deals with income disparity; regional lag; difficulties experienced by minorities, such as blacks and Hispanics in the United States and the French in Canada; ethnic change; and relationships between the United States and Canada as economically interdependent neighbors. All three chapters are selective, emphasizing development as a continuous process that is not without inherent difficulties.

PART 2

James S. Fisher

ANGLO-AMERICA

5

Anglo-America: The Bases for Development

Physical Geography

Resources for Industrial Growth and Development

Early Settlement

Demographic Characteristics

Transportation and Development

The Chicago skyline looking south along the shore of Lake Michigan. Despite its interior location, Chicago serves as an international port and major industrial center.

Anglo-America consists of the United States and Canada, which together cover more than 14 percent of the world's land surface. The large size of the region implies that the two countries can marshal a great variety of resources to support their 286 million people, most of whom are clustered in the eastern United States and in the neighboring areas of Canada.

Anglo-America has attained a high level of economic and technical development. By virtue of its size, population, and social, political, and economic achievements—as well as the problems that go along with those achievements—Anglo-America serves as an excellent example of the development process. This chapter explores the bases for development in Anglo-America: physical geography, resources, settlement, demography, and transportation.

PHYSICAL GEOGRAPHY

The initially small populations that developed the United States and Canada had the advantage of an immensely rich environment. In fact, they and their successors have often used that environment as though it contained an endless supply of resources. The two countries, particularly the United States, now consume vast quantities of resources and by all indications will continue to do so. Although it would be foolish to think that Anglo-American attainments have been based solely on a rich and bountiful environment, it would be equally unrealistic not to recognize that land, water, minerals, and numerous other environmental features have provided great advantages for the complex and interacting processes of development.

Land Surface Regions

The physical geography of Anglo-America is highly varied, and that variation has affected the ways in which the land has been settled and used. Land surfaces have aided or inhibited agriculture, for example, and have functioned as both barriers to and routes for movement. A brief look at each of the nine land surface regions that comprise Anglo-America follows (Figure 5–1).

Coastal Plain. The Coastal Plain, which borders Anglo-America from Cape Cod to Texas, is of recent origin and is composed of sedimentary materials. No major topographic features inhibited travel or

settling, but some portions of the plain were given less attention for early settlement because of infertile soils or poor drainage. For example, Georgia's sandy pinelands, the Pine Barrens, are infertile; the Dismal Swamp, the Okefenokee Swamp, and the Everglades are typical of areas that are poorly drained. But the Coastal Plain has productive areas, too; the black-soil prairies of Texas and Alabama and the alluvial Mississippi Valley have some of the best soils in the South.

Appalachian Highlands. The Appalachian Highlands cover a vast area that extends from Newfoundland to Alabama. Though the highlands have a common geologic history, they contain a number of distinct regions with characteristic landforms, or **topographic regions**: the Piedmont, the Blue Ridge Mountains, the Ridge-and-Valley area, the Appalachian Plateau, and the New England section.

The Piedmont, a rolling upland plain, forms the eastern margin of the Appalachians from Pennsylvania south. The Blue Ridge Mountains are distinguished by their relative height; in their wider southern portion (in North Carolina, Tennessee, and Georgia) some peaks rise more than 6,000 feet (1,829 meters) above sea level.

The Ridge-and-Valley area, a strikingly crinkled landscape of long, parallel ridges and valleys, extends from New York to Alabama. The Great Valley, the most distinctive, runs all the way from northern New York to Alabama. The Hudson Valley, the Cumberland Valley, the Shenandoah Valley, the Valley of East Tennessee, and the Coosa in Alabama are some of the local names applied to parts of the Great Valley; the names are taken from some of the numerous rivers that provide drainage (Figure 5–2). Other valleys are neither as continuous nor as wide.

Despite the name Appalachian Plateau, this westernmost portion of the Appalachian Highlands has been severely eroded into hill lands and mountains, especially in West Virginia. Other areas, such as the Cumberland Mountains in Tennessee, retain features that are characteristic of plateaus.

The New England section is a northward extension of the Piedmont, Blue Ridge, and Ridge-and-Valley areas but differs from its counterparts in having been strongly impacted by glaciation. The New England section extends from the submerged

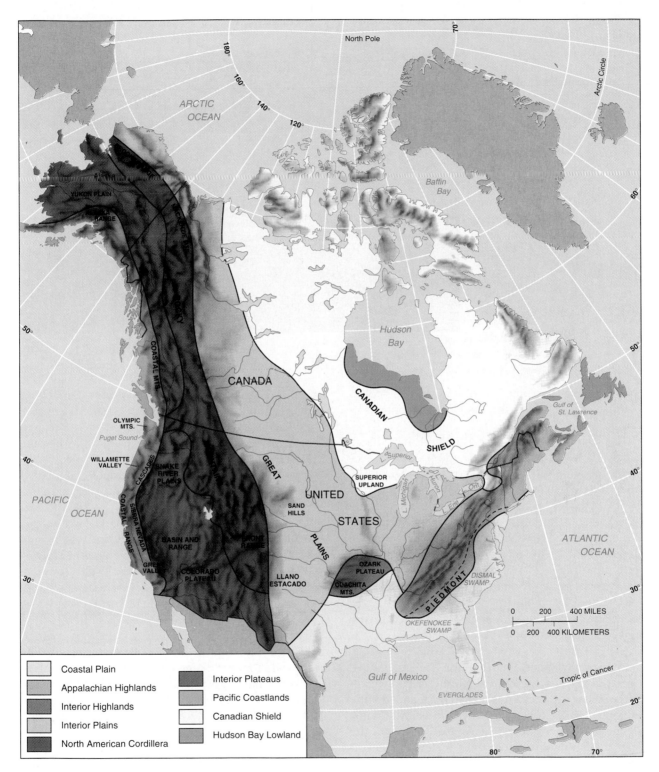

Figure 5–1
Land surface regions of Anglo-America. The physiographic diversity of Anglo-America—together with climate, vegetation, and soils—provides highly varied environmental realms and natural resources.

Figure 5-2
Apple orchards in the Shenandoah Valley. The Shenandoah, named after the river that formed the valley, is just one segment of the Great Valley, which extends from Alabama to New York.

coastal zone to the interior White Mountains or New Hampshire and Maine and the Green Mountains of Vermont.

The southern Appalachian Highlands have had a peculiar role in the evolution of the social and economic geography of the United States. The highlands lie close to all of the early European settlements, yet many parts have remained isolated and have lagged culturally. The physiographic character of the area has variously hindered population movement, influenced the direction in which settlers traveled, contributed to isolation, and functioned as a roadway for settlers. Some of the nation's finest coal resources exist within the Appalachian Highlands, yet the area has long had some of the most severe economic problems in the United States.

Interior Highlands. The Interior Highlands have a geologic history, structure, and physiography similar to those of the Appalachian Plateau and the Ridge-and-Valley regions. The Arkansas River Valley separates the northern Ozark Plateau from the Ouachita Mountains to the south. A similarity in culture and problems further links the southern Appalachians and the Interior Highlands.

Interior Plains. One of the largest continuous plains areas of the world, the Interior Plains extend from the Mackenzie Valley of northern Canada to central Kentucky and Tennessee in the southeast and Oklahoma and Texas in the southwest. Because much of the area north of the Ohio and Missouri rivers has experienced continental glaciation, glacial landscape features—such as moraines, till plains, former glacial lake beds, and disarranged drainage—are common.

Except for the western portion, known as the Great Plains, much of the Interior Plains is at low elevations. The eastern edge of the Great Plains is 2,000 feet (610 meters) above sea level. Elevation then gradually increases to the west, reaching 4,000 to 5,000 feet (1,219 to 1,524 meters) at the border of the Rocky Mountain system.

From a topographic standpoint the vast Interior Plains provide one of the most favorable settings in the world for agriculture. Great variations in climate, however, limit agricultural activity in the drier western and colder northern segments of the region.

North American Cordillera. Not long ago, geologically speaking, great mountain-building processes disturbed parts of western Anglo-America and formed the North American Cordillera, resulting in high elevations and a mixture of landforms. Portions of the Rocky Mountains, such as the Front Ranges of Colorado, consist of intrusions of material from deep within the earth that displaced and up-lifted the sedimentary layers of rock near the surface. The Canadian Rockies are formed of folded and faulted sedimentary materials. North and northwest of the Rockies are the Mackenzie, the Richardson, and the Brooks ranges. All together those ranges form a mountain system that extends from Alaska to the southwestern United States. Small settlements have been established in the many valleys and basins within the system.

Interior Plateaus.   West of the Rocky Mountains lie the Interior Plateaus. The essential character of this region is that of a level upland; elevations are usually in excess of 3,000 feet (914 meters). Notable exceptions, however, include Alaska's Yukon Plain and California's Death Valley, which is 282 feet (86 meters) below sea level.

The Colorado Plateau of Colorado and Arizona reveals the geologic history of the area. Many layers of sedimentary rock that now lie between 9,000 and 11,000 feet (2,743 and 3,353 meters) above sea level have been exposed by the Colorado River, which cut the Grand Canyon, providing spectacular evidence of the great depth of the underlying sedimentary rock. The Basin-and-Range segments of Utah, Nevada, and California are characterized by faulted mountain ranges that are half buried in alluvial debris. In the Columbia Plateau of eastern Washington, Oregon, and Idaho, formerly active volcanoes and fissure flows have deposited thick layers of lava; and through that lava the Snake River has cut a canyon that rivals the Grand Canyon in splendor.

Pacific Coastlands.   The Pacific Coastlands are a system of mountains and valleys extending from the Alaska Peninsula southward along the Canadian and U.S. coast to southern California. In the far north this region is formed by the Alaska Range and the Coastal Mountains of Canada. Along the western margin of the United States stand the Coastal Ranges, another chain of mountains with parallel ridges and valleys. The linear character of those ranges becomes less distinct in Oregon and is totally absent in the Olympic Mountains of Washington.

Several lowland areas separate the Coast Ranges from the Sierra Nevada and the Cascades. One of them is the Great Valley of California, a fertile alluvial trough that serves as one of the most productive agricultural regions of the United States. The Cascades and the Coast Ranges enclose the productive Willamette Valley and the Puget Sound Lowland.

The Coastal Mountains of Canada are discontinuous—they form islands off the Canadian coast—whereas the lowlands are submerged. The lowlands reappear only in Alaska, as basins south of the Alaskan and Aleutian ranges.

Canadian Shield.   Northern and northeastern Canada is covered by the huge Canadian Shield, which nearly encircles Hudson Bay and extends southward to the United States, forming the Superior Upland of Wisconsin, Minnesota, and Michigan. Continental glaciation has given the Canadian Shield a relatively smooth surface, as well as thin soils, stony surfaces, and areas with no soil at all. Lakes, marshes, bogs, and swamps are characteristic of many parts of the shield. Although its utility for agriculture is limited, the Canadian Shield has provided a wealth of furs, timber, and minerals.

Hudson Bay Lowland.   The Hudson Bay Lowland is a sedimentary region along the southern margin of the bay. This forested plain has only slight variation in elevation and, like the Canadian Shield, has experienced little development.

Climatic Regions

Anglo-America exhibits the variety of climates one would expect on a large continent that extends from subtropical to polar latitudes (see Figure 3–3). The eastern portion of the continent shows a strong latitudinal influence in the sequence of climates, ranging from humid subtropical, to humid continental (both warm summer and cool summer varieties), to subarctic, to polar. The most important differences among those climates are the shorter and cooler summers and the longer and more severe winters as one proceeds northward from the Gulf of Mexico. The interior West, which is remote from major moisture sources and sheltered from prevailing winds by major highlands, is dominated by dry climates (both desert and steppe).

Along the coast from California to Alaska is a West Coast sequence that also ranges from subtropical to high latitude: dry summer subtropical, to marine west coast, to subarctic, to polar climates. That sequence is similar to the one found in Western Europe, except that in Anglo-America the highlands are more effective in preventing the penetration of those humid climates into the interior.

Precipitation Patterns. Anglo-America has two **humid regions**, regions that receive precipitation in excess of the amount needed for evaporation and transpiration (Figure 5–3). One extends from the Atlantic as far north as Hudson Bay and southward to the Texas Gulf Coast. The general pattern in this region is one of decreasing precipitation with increasing distance from coastal areas. Although the southern Appalachians receive somewhat more rainfall than adjacent areas do, they are not an effective barrier to the moisture-laden winds from either the Atlantic Ocean or the Gulf of Mexico. Maritime air masses from those water bodies are the moisture source for areas far inland.

The second humid region covers a smaller area along the West Coast, from southern Alaska and the Aleutian Islands to California west of the Sierra Nevada. The great variations in precipitation are a reflection of elevation and exposure to rain-bearing winds. Locations at lower elevations in sheltered positions receive much less rainfall.

In between those two humid regions a region of low precipitation—less than 20 inches, or 508 millimeters, a year—extends from the Northwest Territories of Canada to the southwestern United States. In the far north it spreads from Greenland to Alaska, even though normally that area is not thought of as dry because its evapotranspiration rate is so low. The effect of the low precipitation rates is considerable, especially in the immense Interior Plains region, where agricultural potential is considerably reduced by the moisture deficiency over the Great Plains.

The distribution of precipitation is of major importance not only to agricultural activities but also to many functions of urban-industrial societies. Nonetheless, just because most of the people of Anglo-America live in areas where precipitation is plentiful does not preclude water problems, for those are precisely the areas where the greatest amounts of water are consumed. Indeed, one of the major difficulties with which people in the northeastern United States have to contend is an adequate and proper development of water resources for municipal, industrial, and recreational use—present and future—without an increase in pollution.

The water problems of the Southwest are different. A high proportion of the more limited water available is used for irrigation and therefore competes with urban-industrial water demand. The importance of water in meeting both areas of need is illustrated by the long history of legal disputes between Arizona and California and between the United States and Mexico over the rights to Colorado River water.

Both the Northeast and the Southwest illustrate the general principle that as a society proceeds from an underdeveloped to a highly developed condition, the transformation of the economic system greatly reshapes the demand for water. Certainly, water needs increase with population growth, both for direct consumption and for agriculture. Even more significant, however, is the growth of water needs associated with industrial expansion. Industrial societies utilize water in immense quantities as a solvent, waste carrier, and coolant. In the United States in recent years less than 10 percent of the water removed from surface sources (i.e., streams, rivers, or lakes) has been for domestic use. More than half has been for industrial use; the remainder, approximately 40 percent, has been used for irrigation.

Temperature Regimes. Because heat from the sun determines how much energy is available for converting nutrients and water into vegetable matter, temperature is a major factor in agriculture. The temperatures in Anglo-America show as much regional contrast as the precipitation does; accordingly, agriculture varies widely. In many parts of the southern United States, it is so warm that the **growing season**, the period of the year that crops can be grown without artificial heat, lasts more than 200 days, allowing for the cultivation of a great number of subtropical crops (e.g., cotton, peanuts, citrus, and even sugarcane). The length of the growing season decreases with higher latitude, leaving much of Canada and Alaska not at all suitable for agricultural production.

Temperature regimes also depend on altitude. The effect of higher altitude can particularly be seen in the western portion of the continent, where the more severe minimum-temperature regions occur in the Rocky Mountains. And in western Canada the highlands further detract from the utility of the Canadian environment for agriculture.

Large bodies of water affect temperature regimes, too. The marine influence is reflected in the long growing seasons associated with coastal zones, particularly the West Coast of the United States.

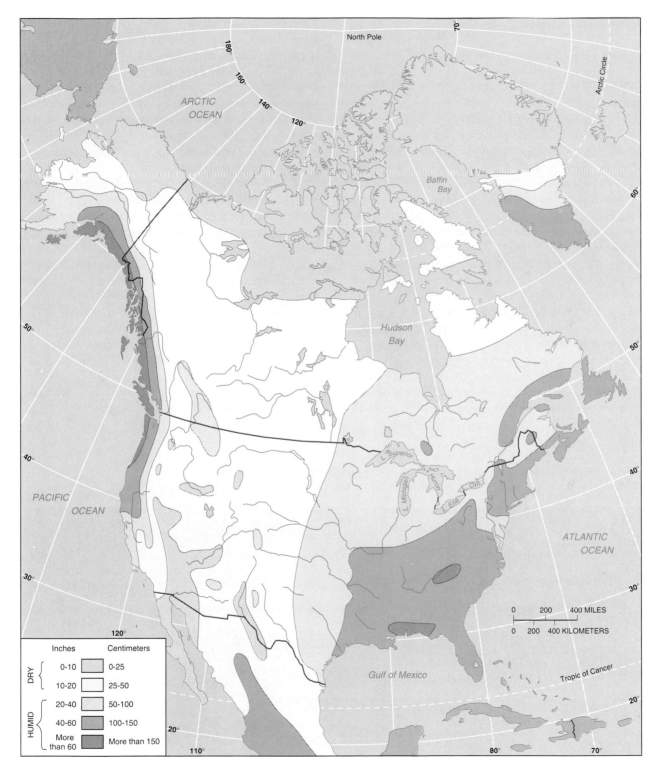

Figure 5-3
Annual precipitation in Anglo-America. A major humid region covers the eastern half of Anglo-America. A second, much smaller humid region is found along the western coast. Much of the western interior between the two humid regions is moisture deficient.

Vegetation Patterns

A narrow band of treeless tundra extends across the far northern portion of Anglo-America from Greenland to Alaska (Figure 5–4). This tundra pushes southward into the highland areas of Alaska and northwestern Canada (see Figure 3–4).

South of the tundra from Newfoundland to Alaska lies a vast expanse of evergreens—a **coniferous**, or **boreal**, **forest**—consisting chiefly of spruce, fir, and pine. That Anglo-American forest, like the similar taiga of the Soviet Union, is one of the largest forest expanses remaining in the world, even though the southern margins and the areas adjacent to waterways have been intensively exploited. In the humid eastern half of the continent the boreal forest gives way to a **deciduous forest**, one dominated by trees that lose their leaves, through a broad transitional zone of white and yellow birch, poplar, and maple (broadleaf species). Most of the northeastern United States was originally covered by a vast deciduous forest of oak, elm, hickory, beech, and maple; pines dominated in less fertile areas. That deciduous forest is perhaps the most modified region of vegetation in Anglo-America. Its very ex-

istence suggested to early European settlers that the climate and soil resources would be advantageous, once the trees were removed. The forest originally extended much farther south than is generally realized: the Piedmont used to be covered by immense hardwoods. They are gone now, replaced by pines through natural processes or by planting. Such reestablished forests have become part of the Anglo-American **cultural landscape**, the environment as modified by human habitation.

The grasslands of interior Anglo-America change from tall-grass areas on the eastern margin of the Great Plains to short-grass areas on the drier western margin. At the time of European settlement, the **prairies**, grassland areas with no forest vegetation, extended as far east as Ohio. Frequent "oak openings," forests interrupted by expanses of prairie, characterized the transition zone between the forest lands of the East and the grasslands of the West. That eastward extension of the prairies may have been caused by the repeated burning of the forests by Native Americans to improve their land or game habitat.

Although the presence of grasses instead of trees indicates moisture deficiency, the grasslands of in-

Figure 5-4
The treeless winter tundra near the Arctic Circle in Canada's Northwest Territory.
Daylight hours are short, and winter temperatures can reach –50°F (–46°C).

terior Anglo-America can be used for agriculture. Prairies are commonly associated with excellent soils, because the limited precipitation combines with rich organic matter to improve fertility. Of course, drought is always a risk; and even ranching is hazardous, for overgrazing has frequently damaged natural grasslands, which are then replaced by woody shrubs, such as sagebrush or mesquite.

Distribution of Soils

Since climate and vegetation are intricately involved in soil-forming processes, it is not surprising that the spatial distribution of fertile and infertile soils across Anglo-America corresponds with both climatic and vegetative patterns. Indeed, the interacton of those various components—and more—are what determines the agricultural productivity of an area. For example, the fertility of the soils—as well as the favorable topography, the moderate growing season, and the reliable rainfall—combine to make the area between central Ohio and Nebraska one of the world's most productive agricultural regions. The soils of the Great Plains of the United States and Canada are perhaps even more fertile, as measured by nutrient content, but they are less productive because of limited precipitation and recurring drought. Utilization of those soils requires farming systems that incorporate drought-resistant crops (e.g., wheat), grazing systems based on pasturage, or irrigation.

The soils of the South have been severely leached and require substantial amounts of fertilizer to remain productive. Many of the problems of Southern agriculture, though, are not inherent in the soils but are the result of farming methods. In the hilly Piedmont, for example, the planting of row crops year after year accelerated severe erosion, which contributed to the eventual abandonment of crop agriculture in many areas. In reality, the South is blessed with some exceptionally good soils—not only the black-soil belts of Texas and Alabama and the alluvial Mississippi Valley but also the limestone valleys of Appalachia.

Early settlers of Anglo-America had the understandable feeling that space was unlimited and that expansion could go on forever. Consequently, as in the Piedmont, soils suffered from poor farming techniques and became unproductive. In older areas of settlement east of the Appalachians, much land had cycled in and out of agricultural use by the time of

the Civil War. Elsewhere, large areas showed the damaging effects of soil erosion by the 1930s. Early destruction also resulted from overgrazing and from cropping land that was subject to drought. Almost no major agricultural region of the United States or Canada was immune.

Since the 1930s the Soil Conservation Service in the United States and comparable agencies in Canada have promoted both the removal of submarginal land from agriculture and the use of improved agricultural methods. It is important to recognize, however, that during most of the period since the 1930s, Anglo-American agricultural problems have been related to surplus production and low prices. From the standpoint of land needed for food production, population pressure has been low; thus, programs could be implemented that removed land from production or reduced the intensity of production without being detrimental to the larger economic system. Few areas of the world have been in such a position. Nonetheless, during the 1970s agricultural surpluses diminished in the United States, and farmland became more intensively used once again. Not surprisingly, soil erosion resurfaced as a major concern of those familiar with land-use problems.

RESOURCES FOR INDUSTRIAL GROWTH AND DEVELOPMENT

Energy and Power

As societies proceed through the various phases of industrial development, they become increasingly dependent on inanimate sources of power. That power can be purchased, certainly, but only at increasingly high prices and with potentially detrimental effects on a balance of payment. Thus, the limits of available power resources are an index of a nation's potential vulnerability.

Coal. Coal was the source of power for the industrial expansion of the United States. Even before World War II, however, coal's relative contribution to the energy supply was decreasing as supplies of petroleum and natural gas were developed. Both petroleum and natural gas are considered cleaner than coal and are preferred for heating and industrial use. Depending on the price and availability of those other energy resources, the production of coal has alternately decreased and increased. Coal now provides less than one-fourth of the nation's energy supply (Table 5–1).

The major coal-producing states are Kentucky, Wyoming, West Virginia, Pennsylvania, and Illinois (Figure 5–5). Large quantities of coal are available in the western states, but production is handicapped by the small local need and the great distances to major eastern markets. Nonetheless, coal from states such as Wyoming has the advantage of a lower sulfur content and can be extracted through lower-cost strip-mining techniques. Tremendous quantities of bituminous coal remain—enough to meet the energy needs of the United States for several hundred years. Unfortunately, however, the use of such coal is limited. Most coal is used in generating electrical power; the rest serves mainly as industrial fuel. Using coal for home heating or transportation would require costly conversion efforts and the application of new and expensive technology.

Canadian coal reserves are also large, but coal is less important as a source of power there (Table 5–1). Most of Canada's reserves are in two maritime provinces (New Brunswick and Nova Scotia) and two prairie provinces (Alberta and Saskatchewan), far from the major area of use (i.e., the urban-industrial regions of Ontario and Quebec). Consequently, Canadians find it more practical to import coal from the Appalachian region of the United States. Another result of the unfavorable location of Canadian coal is that Canada has placed a

correspondingly greater emphasis on petroleum (which costs less to transport) and water as power sources.

Coal is a prime example of the increasing effect that environmental concerns have on the feasibility of using various resources. Any effort to expand the use of coal as a source of power will be affected both by the restrictions and regulations placed on industries and individuals to control air quality and by concern for the scarred landscapes that result from open-pit coal mining (Figure 5–6). Thus, large-scale use of low-sulfur coal will be dependent on an economical means of removing sulfurous pollutants from high-sulfur coal or finding an acceptable way to use western coal.

Oil and Gas.   Petroleum and natural gas provide two-thirds of the power that is used in the United States (Table 5–1). Presently, the major regions of oil and natural gas production are in Texas, Alaska, Louisiana, California, and Oklahoma (Figure 5–7). Production in Alaska's North Slope has catapulted that state into prominence as a source of petroleum for domestic use.

The largest single use of petroleum (44 percent) is for automotive fuel. Approximately 26 percent is used as fuel oil; and the remaining 30 percent, as an industrial raw material (e.g., road oil or lubricants), in petrochemical industries (e.g., those that produce ammonia, carbon black, synthetic rubber, plastics, and synthetic fibers), and as industrial fuel.

The future of oil and gas in the energy picture of the United States and Canada is difficult to assess, one reason being that the United States is both a major producer and a major consumer. But unlike the U.S. production and consumption of coal, which have been almost equal until recently, the United States has produced approximately 12 percent of the world's petroleum for the past few years while accounting for nearly 26 percent of the world's demand, or about 6.0 billion barrels a year. And U.S. demand is sure to increase.

Oil imports currently account for nearly 43 percent of the oil consumed in the United States. Canada, though not one of the world's oil giants, does produce significant quantities of oil and natural gas in the prairie provinces of Alberta and Saskatchewan, and in recent years Canadian oil exports to the United States have become significant. The spatial pattern of production, exports, and imports by Canada illustrates vividly the impact of

Table 5-1
Power consumption in Anglo-America, by source.

Energy Source	Percent Contributed	
	United States (1990)	Canada (1989)
Coal	23.4	13.4
Petroleum	41.5	38.1
Natural gas	23.9	33.9
Water	3.6	11.6
Nuclear	7.6	3.0
Total	100.0	100.0

Sources: Bureau of the Census, *Statistical Abstract of the United States, 1993* (Washington, DC: Government Printing Office, 1993); and *Canada Yearbook, 1992* (Ottawa: Ministry of Supply and Services, 1991).

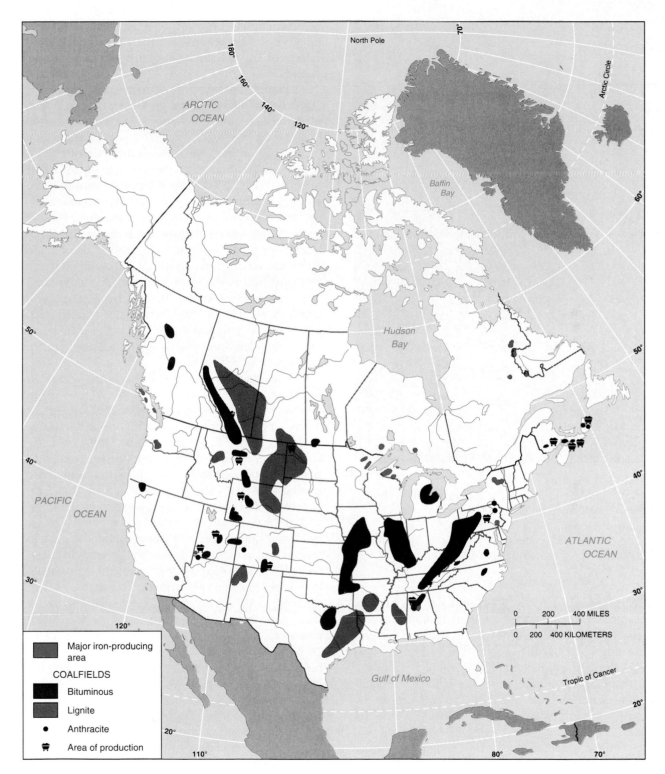

Figure 5–5
Coal and iron ore in Anglo-America. Major coalfields are found in many parts of
Anglo-America. The Appalachian fields were major contributors of power for the
United States industrial expansion during the late nineteenth century.

Figure 5-6
Strip mining coal in Montana with adjacent wheat field.
The industrial strength of developed countries has commonly depended on the use of mineral fuels and the processing of metals. The costs in terms of environmental degradation have frequently been high.

great size on a country of modest population. Despite the production and regional national export capacity of the western provinces, those in the east must import not only from western Canada but also from the adjacent United States (Figure 5–8).

Other major suppliers to the United States include Saudi Arabia, Mexico, Nigeria, Venezuela, and the United Kingdom. The extent to which the United States continues to rely on foreign oil will depend on price, which increased greatly during the 1970s, and on domestic and foreign availability as other countries also seek larger quantities of oil. The slight decrease in dependence on imported oil that occurred during the early 1980s seems to have

reversed upward, and no one really knows how much of the decrease was caused by conservation efforts or by repeated downturns in the national economy.

Evaluating the domestic oil reserves of the United States is difficult. The term **proven reserves** refers to oil that actual drilling has shown to be available and that can be removed at a given cost with existing technology. In the United States the ratio of proven reserves to production has been approximately 10:1 in recent years. That ratio does not mean that the country will run out of petroleum in nine years; it is merely a measure of our working inventory. Present estimates of proven and unproven reserves indicate that more than 500 billion barrels of oil remain, about half of which is currently recoverable. But that recovery rate is likely to increase, and continued new information on the Alaskan oil reserves will probably require upward adjustment of those figures. Thus, depending on the level of consumption and foreign importation, enough oil may be beneath the surface to last for some decades.

The most familiar source of petroleum is the vast reservoirs that lie beneath the land or the sea. But petroleum is also found in oil shales and in tar sands. The solid organic materials in the shale formations of Utah, Colorado, and Wyoming (i.e., the Green River formation) represent one of the world's largest deposits of hydrocarbons, with an immense energy potential. The contribution that those resources will make to the energy supply will be limited in the near future, but advances in technology or changes in the price of petroleum could change their role dramatically during the twenty-first century. The technology for extracting oil from shale does exist, but shale oil cannot compete in cost with other types of energy. Moreover, even if shale oil were economically feasible to use, enormous environmental problems would have to be overcome. To produce shale oil, vast quantities of rock have to be processed, and restoration policies for minimizing environmental destruction would be significant factors in any large-scale production. In addition, the process of extracting oil from shale requires a great deal of water, a rather scarce commodity in the Green River formation.

Tar sands along the Athabasca River in Alberta also contain enormous quantities of oil. Despite the unprecedented capital investment in new technologies required to tap that reserve, consortiums in-

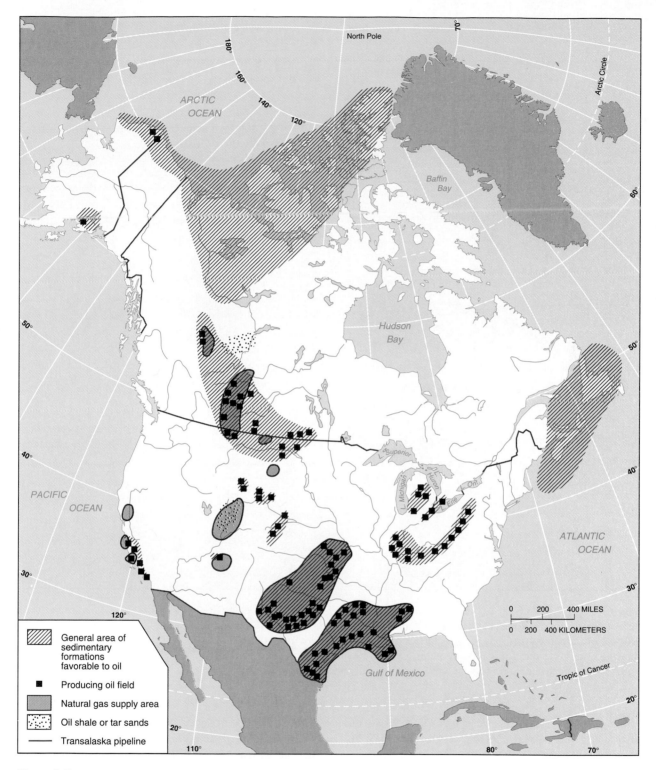

Figure 5-7
Petroleum and natural gas in Anglo-America. The United States and Canada have had the advantage of large oil and gas supplies. Nevertheless, the level of development, substitution of oil and gas for coal, and high per capita consumption have made the cost and availability of oil a significant issue, particularly for the United States. Power resources remain a long-term concern for many developed countries.

Legend (within map):

- General area of sedimentary formations favorable to oil
- Producing oil field
- Natural gas supply area
- Oil shale or tar sands
- Transalaska pipeline

Map labels: North Pole, ARCTIC OCEAN, Arctic Circle, Baffin Bay, Hudson Bay, PACIFIC OCEAN, ATLANTIC OCEAN, Gulf of Mexico, Tropic of Cancer, L. Superior, L. Michigan, L. Huron, L. Erie, L. Ont.

Scale: 0 200 400 MILES / 0 200 400 KILOMETERS

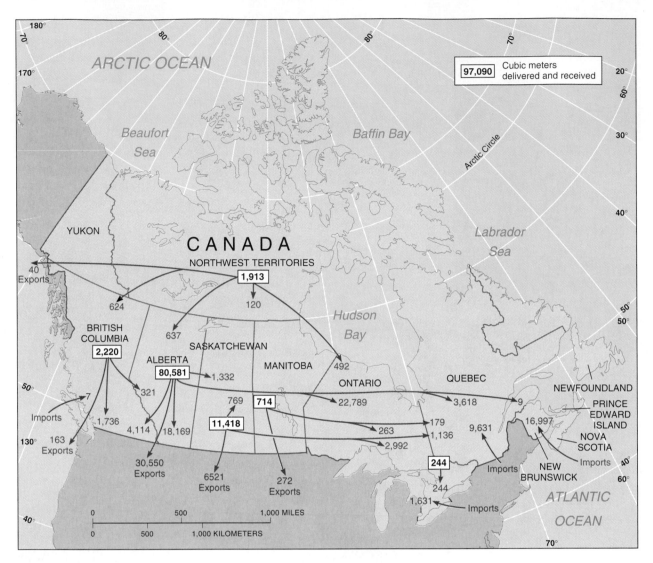

Figure 5-8
Oil movements within Canada and between Canada and the United States. The great
expanse of Canada means that in some instances Canadians find it more practical to
import energy resources for some provinces while the same energy resource is being exported elsewhere. Maps for natural gas and coal would reveal similar patterns.

volving numerous firms are developing those tar
sands, and the current modest production may increase significantly in the future.

Water.   Waterpower can also be used to gener-
ate electrical power (i.e., hydroelectricity).
Currently, it provides 70 percent of the electricity in
Canada but only 9.7 percent of that in the United
States. The reason for that striking difference is sim-
ple: Canada has a great deal of water and relatively

little coal. Waterpower has contributed directly to
the massive Canadian aluminum industry. Although
the use of water as a source of power is likely to increase somewhat in the United States and Canada,
the total percentage of power thus provided, electrical and other, will probably continue to decline.
The Columbia River Basin, the Tennessee River
Valley and southern Piedmont, and the St. Lawrence
Valley are all areas where waterpower generation is
proportionately high (Figure 5–9).

Nuclear. The use of nuclear power increased rapidly during the 1970s and the 1980s and now accounts for nearly 23 percent of U.S. electric utility generation. Whether nuclear power will become a major energy source in the future is uncertain, however. Much depends on continued advances in nuclear technology, the cost of alternative fuels, the need for and cost of foreign oil, and environmental concerns. Events such as those associated with Three Mile Island and Chernobyl encourage reassessment of continued expansion of nuclear power. Thus, the extent to which uranium and thorium will be used for energy purposes in the future is difficult to predict. Furthermore, the supply of uranium in the United States may not be enough to meet a large, long-term demand.

Metals

Iron Ore. Iron ore, complemented by coal, provided the foundation for industrial development in the nineteenth and early twentieth centuries. Today, the United States remains both a major producer (9 percent of the world total) and a major consumer (8 percent of the world total) of iron ore. Despite recent substitutions of aluminum, iron remains the metal that is consumed in greatest quantity.

More than 90 percent of the domestic iron consumed in the United States comes from the Lake Superior area, especially the great Mesabi Range (see Figure 5–5), which has been yielding riches since 1890. Other significant domestic sources include Michigan, Utah, and Missouri. The Adirondack Mountains of New York and the area around Birmingham, Alabama, are other locales of historic importance. Numerous iron ore deposits are also scattered throughout western states, notably Texas, Wyoming, and California, as well as the aforementioned Utah. Distance from major United States markets, however, dictates that those ores be used in the smaller steel centers of California and Utah.

During the 1940s high-grade ores (i.e., ores with an iron content of 60 percent or more) became less readily available in the United States, and the next two decades saw U.S. dependence on foreign ores grow. Today, about half of the ore imported into the United States comes from Canada, which, considering the size of its population, must be considered

Figure 5-9
The Grand Coulee Dam on the Columbia River in Washington. The dam is located at the northern extremity of the Interior Plateaus. The hydroelectric power generated by this facility has aided the growth of the aluminum industry in the Pacific Northwest.

one of the mineral-rich nations. Canadian ore is available in the Lake Superior district at Steep Rock Lake, Ontario; other major deposits have been developed in Labrador. In addition, high-grade ores are available from Brazil and Venezuela. Use of those higher-grade foreign ores has been made more feasible by the development and subsequent improvement of the St. Lawrence Seaway and the construction of large ore carriers, which have significantly cut transportation costs.

Almost half of the iron ore used in the United States during the 1970s came from foreign sources, but by the late 1980s foreign sources provided less than one-fourth and have subsequently decreased rapidly. One explanation for that decrease is that technological advancements now allow the use of ores such as taconite, a very hard rock with low iron content. Accordingly, the taconite industry has expanded rapidly in Minnesota and Michigan, partially in response to favorable tax concessions. In addition, recent declines in the U.S. steel industry have undoubtedly accounted for a major portion of the reduced dependence on foreign ores.

Aluminum.   During the past three decades aluminum has become an extremely useful and much sought-after metal. It is used extensively in the transportation and construction industries and for consumer products. Although aluminum is a common earth element, its occurrence in the form of bauxite, which can be used in manufacturing metal, is limited. Most of the world's aluminum ore reserves have been found in tropical, underdeveloped countries (e.g., Jamaica, Suriname, and Guyana in the Western Hemisphere) and in Australia. The United States produces, mostly in Arkansas, under 5 percent of the bauxite it needs, yet it consumes almost 25 percent of the world's processed aluminum. Canada, interestingly, is the world's third-ranking producer of finished aluminum and the number-one exporter, even though the Canadian industry is based totally on imported ores, as well as substantial local hydroelectric power. Greater aluminum independence for the United States will depend on improved technology that would make lower-grade domestic ores feasible to use.

EARLY SETTLEMENT

The Anglo-American environments have been used, and often misused, by numerous peoples with different cultural heritages and experiences. At the time of first European settlement, the aboriginal people occupying what we now call Anglo-America probably consisted of no more than 1,000,000 people scattered thinly over the territory now occupied by the United States and Canada. The indigenous or American Indian people are believed to have migrated from Asia, perhaps within the last 30,000 years. By 1900 nearly three centuries of European settlement had almost decimated this indigenous population. This decimation by warfare and disease meant that the indigenous population would have only modest cultural impact on contemporary Anglo-America. Indeed, today's population is less than .5 percent of the total Anglo-American population. Contemporary Anglo-America is a reflection of nearly four centuries of European, African, Latin American, and Asian migration and settling.

Early European exploration of the New World was carried out by the Spanish, the Portuguese, the French, and the English. The Spanish were the first to establish a permanent colony—St. Augustine, Florida, in 1565. Except in the southwestern United States, though, the Spanish were never able to establish a viable society from which their culture could diffuse inland. At least four other early European settlements did serve as source areas for **cultural imprints**, or identifiable traits of a culture, that have lasted to the present (Figure 5–10).

The first permanent European settlements from which distinctive American culture traits evolved were the English Jamestown colony, established in 1607, and the French settlement at Quebec, established in 1608. Soon afterward came the Plymouth colony, founded by the English in 1620, and Dutch settlements in New York, starting in 1625. Germans and Scandinavians also made their appearance, but the English cultural imprint was by far the most profound and lasting. The English came in great numbers and, over all, exercised the greatest control in the development process. Their dominance, however, should not keep us from recognizing the contributions to Anglo-American culture of Native American, African, and Asian peoples, as well as other Europeans (such as the French in Quebec).

From the time of those first European settlements, more than a century passed before the initial core areas were occupied effectively. Even during the early phase of settlement, however, distinct contrasts among the colonies began to emerge, and ultimately those differences contributed to significant regional variations within Anglo-America.

Figure 5–10
**Early European settlement areas
in Anglo-America.** Culture traits
evolved in these four areas and
were later diffused to other
parts of Anglo-America.

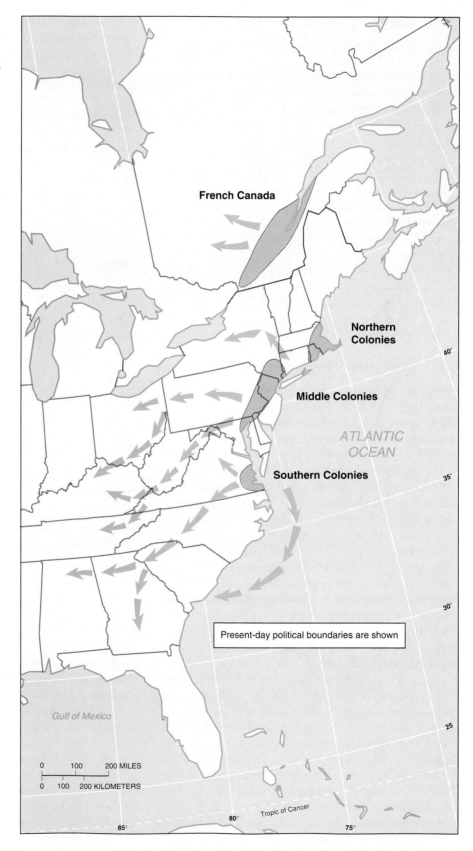

New England

Agricultural efforts were necessary to sustain the settlers in New England, but no special crop provided great wealth or formed the basis for trade, as tobacco did in the southern colonies. Instead, New Englanders accumulated wealth from their varied resources and trade. White pine provided lumber for shipbuilding and trade, and codfish from offshore banks proved to be another commodity that could be traded. Those resources became a source of capital, and the wealth generated by their exchange established commercialism early in the Northeast. By the late eighteenth century, capital was available for industrial growth, and nonagricultural pursuits were already a tradition. Waterpower potential in mechanical form—the waterwheel—was substantial, and the capacity existed for ocean shipping of raw materials and manufactured goods. Shortly after independence, the budding industries of New England began to exhibit a distinctive regional character.

The Southern Colonies

From the start the colonies in the South differed from those in New England. Tobacco became a commercial crop almost immediately; indigo, rice, and cotton were added later, as settlements were extended southward at various coastal points. Where commercialism was feasible, the **plantation** began to evolve—spatially, socially, and operationally—as a distinct agrarian system. Indentured and slave labor led to a distinction between labor and management, particularly when it was applied on a large scale. Thus emerged the commercial plantation, larger than family size, with divisions between labor and management, social distinctions, and attendant forms of organization and building layout. The emphasis was on one or two crops to be sold commercially. In contrast, many inland settlers, hampered by their lack of access to water, were subsistence farmers.

The plantation system was established from the Tidewater area of Virginia (the lower Chesapeake Bay area) to Maryland and southward from Virginia to Georgia at various coastal points. Inland from Tidewater and coastal agricultural colonies, and beyond easy water routes, were smaller, free-labor farms (run by yeoman farmers), particularly on the North Carolina and Virginia Piedmont. When an improved cotton gin became available after 1800, both the yeoman-farmer culture and the plantation culture spread throughout the lower South, but the plantation system generally prevailed in the choice areas for agricultural settlement.

Basic sectional differences appeared early in North America, as evidenced by differing attitudes toward **tariffs**, the duties or customs imposed on imports and exports. For commercially oriented Southerners, agriculture was their source of wealth. Because the markets for agricultural products were in Europe, Southern producers wanted no tariff system that might inhibit the movement of their goods. Northern industrial producers, on the other hand, sought tariffs to protect their young industries. Other differences arose over the socially stratified society that evolved in the South, along with the economic system based on slave labor.

The Middle Colonies

New York and Pennsylvania, together with portions of New Jersey and Maryland, made up a third early settlement core. It was not a transition zone, either in a cultural or an economic sense, but contrasted with both New England and the Southern colonies.

A variety of peoples settled the middle colonies: English, Dutch, Germans, Scotch-Irish, and Swedes. Neither the cash crops of the South nor the lumbering and fishing activities of New England were significant sources of income for them. Instead, the settlers from these middle colonies who moved southward into the Appalachians and westward along the Ohio Valley and on into the Midwest took with them a system of fattening hogs and cattle on Indian maize, now called corn. Those settlers also made tools, guns, and wagons; and they worked the deposits of iron ore that they found in eastern Pennsylvania.

The Lower St. Lawrence Valley

The English were also important settlers in Canada, but they were not the sole cultural influence, despite having dominated Canada since 1763. In fact, the United States also functioned as a source area for Canada, and the French spread themselves over vast areas as fur trappers, traders, and missionaries. But only in the lower St. Lawrence Valley, between Montreal and Quebec, did the French settle as farmers and make a lasting cultural imprint. Their descendants, though now more urbanized, still give a distinctive French character to the entire province of Quebec.

Southern Appalachia

Southern Appalachia, from Virginia and West Virginia southward (including the Blue Ridge Mountains and the Ridge-and-Valley region), functioned as a secondary settlement area. The region was settled during the early eighteenth century by descendants of the Scotch-Irish, Germans, and English who peopled the middle colonies. They moved southward along the Piedmont and the Appalachian valleys and westward to the plateaus of western Virginia, Kentucky, and eastern Tennessee. Those settlers carved out small subsistence farms as slaveless yeoman farmers, contributing traits that still distinguish southern Appalachia from the rest of the lower South: the area is characterized by small farms and a population that is almost totally white.

Yet another culture evolved in the more isolated portions of Appalachia, where remote coves and valleys were unaffected by improvements in transportation, except when transport was necessary to remove a special resource, such as lumber or coal. The relict status of the mountain culture can still be seen in its Elizabethan speech and music, use of distinctive suffixes attached to place names (such as cove, gap, or hollow), and mountaineer attitudes. Poverty and low levels of education have long been vexing problems.

By the middle of the nineteenth century the population of Appalachia had increased so much that out-migration became necessary. Southern Appalachia then functioned as a source area for the Interior Highlands of Arkansas and Missouri and for the hill country of central Texas.[1] The surplus population found refuge in areas that were somewhat similar to their home environment and provided isolation for a culture that the people were not eager to change.

DEMOGRAPHIC CHARACTERISTICS

The population of Anglo-America grew slowly in the seventeenth and eighteenth centuries, even in New England and the Chesapeake Bay area, where English interests and activity were most intense. In 1776 the United States included only about 3 million people, and Canada did not have that many people until almost a century later. The early size differential between the populations of the United States and Canada was established and maintained largely because of differences in **net migration**, or in-migration minus out-migration.

Population Growth in the United States

The rapid population growth experienced by the United States after 1800 was a response to high birthrates, declining mortality, and **immigration**, the movement of people into a country of which they are not native residents. Although exact figures are not available, birthrates and death rates in the early nineteenth century may have exceeded 5 percent and 2 percent per year, respectively. A century later (during the Depression of the 1930s) the birthrate had decreased to 1.8 percent per year, but it rose sharply after World War II, possibly to compensate for wartime delays in family growth and to respond to postwar economic prosperity. During the **baby boom** of 1946 to 1965, the birthrate reached a new high of 2.7 percent per year. But then came a **birth dearth**, as the birthrate dipped to a historic low of 1.46 percent per year during the mid-1970s. When the baby boomers themselves reached childbearing age, a very modest upturn took place, and by the early 1990s the birthrate was just slightly above 1.6 percent (Table 5–2). Because of the increased population, that rate represents nearly 4.1 million births per year, not so different from the 4.3 million at the peak of the baby boom.

The declining population growth rate of the past century has not been in exact correspondence with changes in birthrates. Reduced mortality rates have also had an effect. The decline in infant mortality and the extension of life expectancy beyond seventy years mean that more people are alive at any given time.

Immigration has been another important factor in the growth of the United States. More than 50 million people have immigrated to the United States since 1820. Those immigrants not only enlarged the population as they came but also increased the base for future growth. Legal immigration during the 1970s and much of the 1980s has been at the rate of about 600,000 persons a year and accounted for about 26 percent of the population growth during the 1980s. Recent rates have increased sharply, however, to nearly 1.8 million in the early 1990s. The precise extent of illegal immigration is not known but is considered to be substantial.

Even though the rate of population growth has declined from more than 3 percent per year in the

Table 5-2
Demographic features of Anglo-America, 1993.

	United States	Canada
Population	258,300,000	28,100,000
Birthrate (%)	1.6	1.5
Death rate (%)	0.9	0.7
Natural increase (%)	0.8	0.8
Legal immigration rate (%)	0.72[a]	0.4[b]
Emigration rate (%)	—[c]	0.4[b]

Sources: World Population Data Sheet (Washington, DC: Population Reference Bureau, 1993); Bureau of the Census, *Statistical Abstract of the United States, 1990* (Washington, DC: Government Printing Office,1990); and *Canada Yearbook, 1992* (Ottawa: Ministry of Supply and Services, 1992).

Note: Population growth rates are determined both by birthrate and death-rate differentials and by net immigration. As a result, and despite belief to the contrary, population growth in the United States averaged more than 1 percent per year during the 1980s. The discrepancy between this figure and that suggested by 1993 data is explained by the compounding effect of population growth and immigration.

[a]Value for 1991. This rate is now substantially higher than it was in the early 1980s as a result of the inclusion of persons granted residence under the legalization program of the Immigration Reform and Control Act of 1986.

[b] Figures calculated from data for the years 1981–1986.

[c]An accurate emigration rate for the United States is not known; however, it is estimated to be negligible in the national population equation. The emigration rate has historically been a significant factor in the Canadian population equation.

early nineteenth century to approximately 1 percent per year in the late 1980s, the increments in population are not small. By virtue of both the natural rate of increase and legal immigration, the United States continues to grow by more than 2 million people per year.

Population Growth in Canada

The Canadian demographic experience has been generally similar to that of the United States insofar as birthrates and mortality rates are concerned, but not in terms of immigration. Much of Canada is unfavorable for settlement, so it has attracted far fewer immigrants than the United States has. As a result, roughly a tenth as many people live in Canada as in the United States.

Canada grew mainly by natural increase between 1867, when the population numbered about 3.5 million, and 1900. But even its natural increase was limited somewhat because of a low fertility rate, a result of the migration of young Canadians to the United States. Net migration was negative during most of that early period, but after 1900 a large influx of immigrants arrived from Europe, raising fertility rates and slowing the decline of birthrates. Like the United States, Canada experienced a low birthrate during the Depression and a sharp rise after World War II, despite urbanization and industrialization. The Canadian baby boom was also followed by a decline in the birthrate during the late 1960s and early 1970s and now remains at about 1.5 percent.

Immigration to Canada has exceeded 9 million, but **emigration**—people leaving—is estimated at over 6 million. Many immigrants have returned to their countries of origin or have moved on to the United States. Positive net migration has aided Canadian population growth during only two periods: the first three decades of this century and the years after World War II. The greatest growth took place during the 1950s, the result of high birthrates, a larger population base, and positive net migration. An increase in immigration since 1988—to nearly 200,000 persons per year—has contributed to the growth of several provinces, but Ontario and British Columbia especially.

Low Population Growth and the Future

The United States, Canada, and some thirty other highly developed nations are experiencing historically low birthrates. In most of the rest of the world, however, birthrates are high and death rates are low.

Zero population growth, maintenance of a stable population, will probably not occur in the United States or Canada for some years, if ever. The U.S. Bureau of Census projects future population in several growth-series estimates. The lowest series projects zero growth by the year 2017. The more likely scenario is the middle series, with a projected population of 268 million in the year 2000 and 305 million in 2030. Thereafter, the total population of the United States, like that of any other country with rapidly reduced birthrates, will probably grow at a modest rate or will fluctuate positively or negatively around a base level. The present youthful population, however, even with lowered fertility rates, has the potential to create another small baby boom simply because of the large number of people involved.

Reduced birthrates affect the age structure of a population (Figure 5–11). By 2030 more than 21 percent of the U.S. population may be over the age of 65, and there will probably be fewer young people. That changing age structure has numerous economic and social implications, but experts disagree on whether the changes will prove troublesome. Will the proportionately smaller youthful population mean possible labor shortages, especially for particular industries? Will some industries experience dramatic market declines? Will educational institutions have an oversupply of facilities and personnel? Will the facilities required and the cost of caring for a disproportionately large older population place a disturbingly high tax and Social Security burden on the economically active population? Or will this new age structure allow an immense improvement and solid attack on some of the economic and social problems currently facing the United States?

Population Distribution

Most of the population of the United States lives east of the Mississippi River (Figure 5–12 and Table 5–3). The greatest concentrations are in the northeastern quadrant of the country, the area bounded by the Mississippi and Ohio rivers, the Atlantic Ocean, and the Great Lakes. Population densities are somewhat lower in the South, except in such growth areas as the Piedmont and southern Florida. Most of the West Coast population is clustered in lowland areas, such as the Los Angeles Basin, the Great Valley of California, the valleys of the Coastal Ranges in the vicinity of San Francisco and Oakland, and the Willamette Valley and Puget Sound Lowland. The remainder of the western United States is sparsely populated, particularly west of the 100th meridian. Exceptions include the higher population densities around such oases as Phoenix, Arizona, and Salt Lake City, Utah.

Given the harsh environments of the Canadian north, it is not surprising that most Canadians live

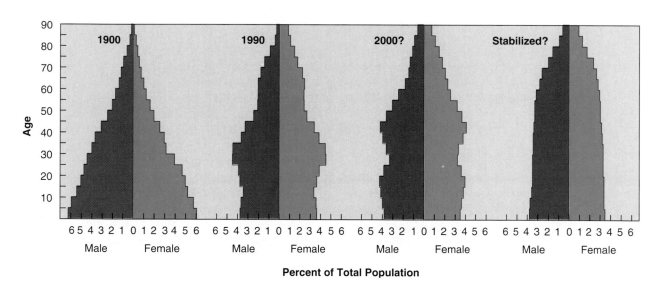

Figure 5–11
United States population pyramids. Population pyramids for the United States since 1900 exemplify the changing age and sex structure of a country that has gone through demographic transition. Predictions regarding future demographic conditions must be treated with caution, however. (Adapted from Charles F. Westoff, "The Population of the Developed Countries," *Scientific American* 231, 1974; and Bureau of the Census, *Statistical Abstract of the United States, 1990,* Washington, DC: Government Printing Office, 1990.)

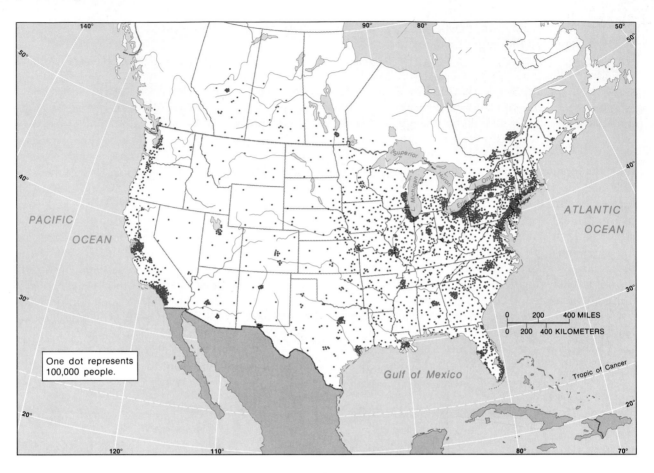

Figure 5-12
Distribution of Anglo-American population. The unevenness of population in the
United States and Canada reflects numerous influences, including natural environments, early settlement areas, levels of urban and industrial growth, and ongoing
redistribution (mobility).

within 200 miles (322 kilometers) of the United
States border. The prairie provinces provide the
only significant exception. If it were not for the interruption caused by the sparse population on the
barren Canadian Shield immediately north of Lake
Superior, the distribution might be described as a
long east-west ribbon, north of which lies most of
the vast, almost-empty Canadian space. More than
62 percent of Canada's population lives on the
Ontario Peninsula and in the St. Lawrence Valley of
southern Quebec (Figure 5–12). The maritime
provinces contain less than 9 percent of the population; the prairie provinces, about 17 percent (Table
5–4). The populous urban-industrial area of Ontario
(36 percent of the total population) has been expe-

riencing positive net migration and so, along with
British Columbia, exhibits a population growth rate
significantly above the national norm. Alberta experienced significant growth during the 1970s and
early 1980s in response to the development of petroleum resources, but more recently has experienced net outmigration. British Columbia is experiencing its higher growth as a result of both
international and interprovincial migration.

Population Redistribution

The distributional pattern of population in the United
States and Canada has always been quite dynamic.
Redistribution of the population began even before

Table 5-3
Population of the United States, by region and race, 1990 (in thousands).

	Total[a]	White	Black	American Indian, Eskimo, and Aleut	Asian and Pacific Islander	Hispanic Origin[b]
United States	248,710	199,686	29,986	1,959	7,274	22,354
Northeast	50,809	42,069	5,613	125	1,335	3,754
New England	13,207	12,033	628	33	232	568
Middle Atlantic	37,602	30,036	4,986	92	1,104	3,186
North Central	59,669	52,018	5,716	338	768	1,727
East North Central	42,009	35,764	4,817	150	573	1,438
West North Central	17,660	16,254	899	188	195	289
South	85,446	65,582	15,829	563	1,122	6,767
South Atlantic	43,567	33,391	8,924	172	631	2,133
East South Central	15,176	12,049	2,977	41	84	95
West South Central	26,703	20,142	3,929	350	407	4,539
West	52,786	40,017	2,828	933	4,048	10,106
Mountain	13,659	11,762	374	481	217	1,992
Pacific	39,127	28,255	2,454	453	3,831	8,114

Source: Bureau of the Census, *Statistical Abstract of the United States, 1993* (Washington, DC: Government Printing Office, 1993).
[a]Includes other races not shown separately.
[b]Persons of Hispanic origin may be of any race.
Note: Because these figures have been rounded, the sum of the subtotals may not equal the total.

the initial settlement of the more habitable parts of the United States and Canada was complete. The shift from an agrarian society to an industrial society started early in the nineteenth century and was the basis for major urban growth, particularly during the second half of the century. That growth has continued during the twentieth century but now is spurred more by the expansion of tertiary activities than by industrial growth. Nonetheless, **urbanization**, the agglomeration of people in cities, has been the dominant settlement process for more than a century.

The northeastern quarter of the United States led the country in urban growth for many years. In 1900 more than 50 percent of the northern population was classified as urban; now, urban population exceeds 80 percent in some northern states. Even many of the people classified as rural are such only in residence, since most rural dwellers today work in an urban setting. Other parts of the country—namely, the West Coast and the Southwest—have also become highly urbanized. The South and the Great Plains (including the Canadian segment) ur-

banized more slowly, as one would expect of areas with an agrarian orientation. In recent decades, however, urban growth in the South has been substantial as the region has shifted away from agriculture toward industry.

After World War II the people of the United States and Canada continued to concentrate in urban areas, with the most rapid population growth occurring in the larger metropolitan areas. Another significant movement, the shift of people from the larger central cities to the suburbs, meant that the amount of space occupied by urban areas was also increasing at that time.

More recent data suggest that the post-World War II era of rapid growth in the larger metropolitan areas may be ending. The share of total population classified as urban is now at about 75 percent. But many central cities have been losing population, as have many of the larger metropolitan areas, especially those located in the urban-industrial region adjacent to the Great Lakes. Furthermore, some nonmetropolitan regions, especially those near or adjacent to metropolitan areas, have been experiencing population growth rates that, even though modest, have exceeded those of metropolitan areas. In addition, the smaller metropolitan areas (those with fewer than 100,000 people) have grown at rates higher than those of the large centers. Nevertheless, the total share of population classified as rural continues to decline modestly.

This shift in growth from larger metropolitan to selected smaller metropolitan and nonmetropolitan areas may or may not herald a significant new pattern. It is important to note that the overall slowing of urban growth is not a consistent experience across the United States. The growth of both metropolitan and nonmetropolitan areas has slowed substantially in the Northeast and the Midwest but continues at or above the national norm in the South and the West.

Population growth patterns also show trends in interregional migration (see the boxed feature,

Population Mobility). Recent net migration has favored population growth in both the South and the West (Table 5–5). Specifically, growth has been strong in the Sun Belt—the Piedmont, the southern Ridge-and-Valley area, intermittent areas of the Gulf Coast from southern Florida to Texas, and the Far West and Southwest (Figure 5–13). At the same time population is declining in much of the Coastal Plain from Virginia to Texas, in the middle and lower Mississippi Valley, in the Great Plains from the Canadian border to central Texas, and in portions of the Mountain West. It is difficult to generalize about Appalachia: much of the region has lost population, but some of it has gained population—particularly the Piedmont and the Ridge-and-Valley areas just mentioned, as well as northwestern Georgia and northeastern Alabama. These continuing changes in the distribution of population indicate that Anglo-America has not yet evolved a mature settlement landscape (Figure 5–14).

TRANSPORTATION AND DEVELOPMENT

Development in nineteenth-century Anglo-America was rooted in the Industrial Revolution. The market expansion that coincided with that revolution stimulated the commercialization of agriculture, which prompted more and better transport systems and numerous technological inventions and improve-

Table 5-4

Population of Canada, by province or territory, 1990, and population increase, 1981-1990.

	Population (thousands)	Population Increase (%)
Canada	26,602	9.3
Maritime Provinces	4,562.7	7.8
Newfoundland	573	1.0
Prince Edward Island	130	6.4
Nova Scotia	894	5.5
New Brunswick	723	3.9
Quebec	6,769	5.1
Ontario	9,743	13.0
Prairie Provinces	2,321	3.9
Manitoba	1,091	6.4
Saskatchewan	995	3.2
Alberta	2,471	10.5
British Columbia	3,126	13.9
Yukon	26	12.5
Northwest Territories	53	17.7

Source: Canada Yearbook, 1992 (Ottawa: Ministry of Supply and Services, 1992).

Note: Newfoundland, Prince Edward Island, Nova Scotia, and New Brunswick are commonly referred to collectively as the maritime provinces. Manitoba, Saskatchewan, and Alberta are commonly referred to collectively as the prairie provinces.

Table 5-5

Interregional migration in the United States, 1986 to 1991 (in thousands).

	Northeast	Midwest	South	West
In-migration	2,005	4,040	6,879	4,119
Out-migration	3,807	4,311	5,237	3,688
Net migration	-1,801	-271	1,641	431
Movers from abroad	1,304	886	1,917	2,645
Net migration, Including movers from abroad	-497	615	3,558	3,076

Sources: Bureau of the Census, Geographical Mobility: March 1990 to March 1991 (Washington, DC: Government Printing Office); Current Population Reports: Population Characteristics, Geographical Mobility: March 1990 to March 1991 (Washington, DC: Government Printing Office, 1992), P20-463.

POPULATION MOBILITY

Geographical mobility is a long-standing and significant part of the American and Canadian experience. Among the many major population movements of the past century have been:(1) the east-west flow of settlers occupying national space, (2) immigration, (3) rural-to-urban migration, (4) black migration from the rural South to the cities of the North, (5) the post-World War II movement from central cities to suburbs, and (6) the prewar and postwar migration to West Coast states. Several of those movements have involved interregional migration. Figure A shows the net result of interregional migration from 1990 to 1991. Population flows normally include movement both into and out of a region, and the net result may have a significant impact on regional population dynamics, especially now that growth by natural increase has been reduced. It is notable that movement from abroad impacts significantly on the net population equation by region.

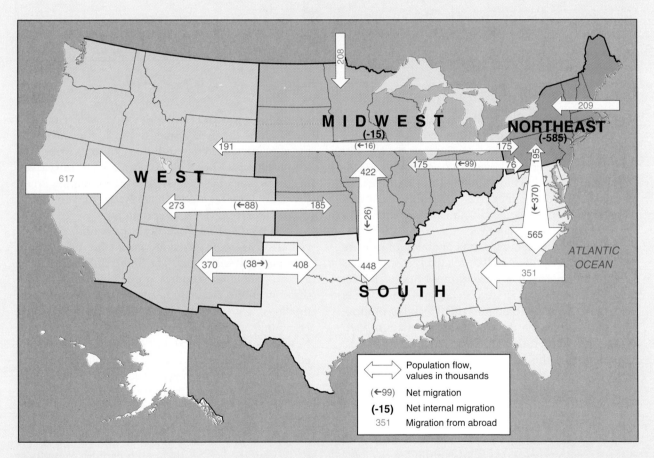

Figure A
Net interregional migration of population from 1990 to 1991. Each year more than 3 million people move among the four major regions of the United States. During recent years the flow has been greatest out of the Northeast and Midwest and into the South. (Adapted from the U.S. Department of Commerce, Bureau of the Census, *Geographical Mobility: March 1990 to March 1991*, Current Population Reports, Series P–20, no. 436.)

Figure 5-13
Population increase in the United States during the 1980s. Population shifts during the 1980s continued to favor the South Atlantic states and the southwestern states. California experienced the largest growth in the West, while Florida and Georgia posted the largest increases in the East.

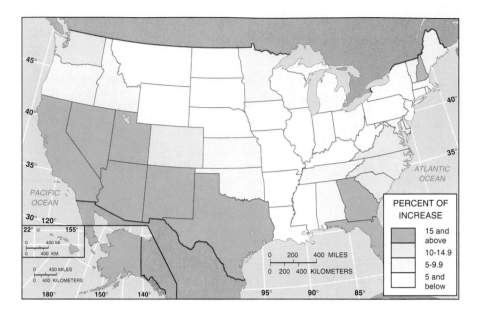

ments, which in turn had far-reaching effects. For example, Eli Whitney's cotton gin reduced the labor required for the removal of seeds from cotton, and much of the lower South was then settled as the cultivation of cotton became economically feasible. But nothing has had a greater effect on resource use and life-style than the changes in nineteenth- and twentieth-century transportation.

A transport system with the capability of moving great quantities of materials at relatively low cost has been essential to the utilization of industrial resources in both the United States and Canada. As costs have been lowered and the feasibility of moving goods has been increased, transportation technology has altered the significance of many places. For example, the great cost advantage of water transport had a profound effect on early settlement, both for those people inclined toward agriculture and for those with a commercial bent. And by the early nineteenth century, water transportation—by raft, barge, or sailing vessel—had increased even more in importance, particularly in the interior portions of Anglo-America.

Then, with the development of steam power, the utility of the Ohio-Mississippi and other river systems grew appreciably, prompting the completion of the Erie Canal in 1825 and the beginning of a canal-building era. The cost and time required for shipping goods from Buffalo to New York City via the Erie Canal and the Hudson River were reduced from $100 a ton and twenty days to $5 a ton and five days. Thus, the Erie Canal allowed efficiently produced agricultural commodities from beyond the Appalachians to be marketed in the East. Later, connecting canals on the Great Lakes complemented the Erie Canal and facilitated the movement of grains, forest products, and minerals.

As a result of improved transportation, commercial activities were extended far inland, drawing on new and rich resources. The value of New England as an agricultural resource area declined, and production there concentrated on specialized commodities. The vast new hinterland, by way of the Erie Canal and the Hudson River Valley, centered on New York (Figure 5–15) and gave that city a distinct edge over other eastern cities, particularly Boston.

The railroad era began even before the short canal boom ended. Although occasionally competitive with canals, railroads generally complemented water transportation and greatly increased the significance of the Great Lakes as an interior waterway. By the middle of the nineteenth century, new focal points had been identified. Rail networks focused on selected coastal ports—New York again—and also converged on interior ports, such as Chicago and St. Louis.

The rails connected farm, forest, and mineral-resource areas with ports and cities. Continued improvements in rail technology made long-haul transportation feasible and allowed raw materials

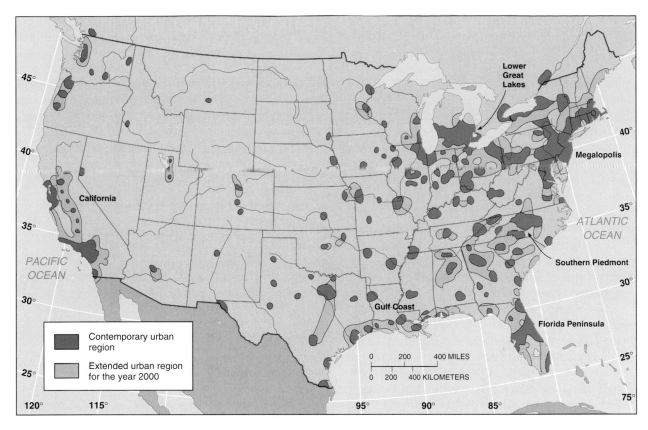

Figure 5–14
Urban regions of the United States in 1990 and 2000. The continued growth of metropolitan regions suggests further evolution of the urban system, not only in the Northeast but also along the margins of the Great Lakes and the West Coast.

Figure 5–15
The South Street seaport in New York City. New York's rise to urban prominence was related to its location at the mouth of the Hudson River and its excellent harbor.

to be concentrated at a few selected points. Railroads contributed to the opening of agricultural land in the West and the tapping of copper, lead, and zinc deposits in the Far West. Grains were moved to and from ports, coal was hauled to Great Lakes ports and inland cities, and iron ore went from Great Lakes ports to Pittsburgh and other inland cities.

By the late 1860s a major turning point was reached in the selective growth of urban-industrial centers. Transportation technology provided special focus on selected cities, most of which were located by water. As a result, during the next half century, massive urban and industrial growth proceeded in those selected cities, and major or national transportation routes were established among them. Some port facilities declined in importance, while a few became centers of attention.

Railroads are still important as long-haul freight carriers, but they have lost a large part of their function as a carrier of passengers and short-haul freight. Both automotive and air transport have captured passenger traffic, and the highway system has become extremely important in the movement of freight. Nonetheless, the national routes and flows established during the railroad era have been essentially maintained during the automotive and air era so that large, established centers have continued to grow (Figure 5–16).

The settled portions of the United States and Canada now contain intensive networks of paved roads. In the United States those range from paved county roads to the system of limited-access interstate highways. The present highway system does have a selective effect in localized areas but does not reroute national flows. Instead, the system aids in the integration of existing economic regions.

In recent decades international waterways have also received renewed attention. The completion of improvements in the St. Lawrence Seaway in 1959 extended the Great Lakes system from the western end of Lake Superior and the southern end of Lake Michigan to the Atlantic Ocean via the St. Lawrence and the New York State Barge Canal (formerly the Erie Canal). The Great Lakes are thus important not only as an internal waterway but also as an international water route connecting cities such as Toronto, Hamilton, Cleveland, Detroit, and Chicago with Europe. In addition, a canal-river system between Chicago and St. Louis connects the most important inland urban-industrial concentration in the United

States with the Mississippi and its numerous tributaries (see Figure 5–16). These waterways are used for massive movements of grain, coal, iron ore, and petrochemicals—that is, for bulk commodities. In effect, waterways surround the highly urbanized and industrialized northeastern United States and penetrate inland more than 2,000 miles (3,220 kilometers) along the southern border of Canada, giving the continental interiors of each country major transportation advantages.

SUMMARY
Resources for Anglo-American Development

The United States and Canada are large countries with great quantities of basic resources, but Anglo-America also has a large population that consumes materials at high per capita rates. The great resource base and the ability to use it have contributed to both a high material level of living and a primary power position in world society. Maintaining that position requires continued high consumption of resources.

The varied climatic and soil regions of Anglo-America allow diversified agricultural production of food and industrial raw materials. Not only are domestic needs met, but large quantities of agricultural commodities (e.g. wheat, soybeans, cotton) are normally available for export. Such exports significantly affect the balance-of-trade position of both the United States and Canada.

Anglo-America is also well endowed with industrial resources. Many decades of high-level consumption and higher levels of demand, however, have put increasingly strenuous pressure on those resources. The result has been an increase in dependence on foreign materials and fuel. Even if programs aimed at saving energy are successful, they will probably only slow the rate at which consumption increases.

The dependence of the United States on foreign sources for basic needs has been, to a substantial degree, economic. Technology or politics may decrease that dependence, but another possibility is that dependence on foreign areas may increase. Underdeveloped areas in the world are demonstrating a growing desire to control the production, processing, and price of their own resources—such as bauxite in Jamaica or oil in Venezuela—even when developed nations are the ultimate

Figure 5-16
Major rail routes and inland waterways of Anglo-America. Of great advantage to the
United States has been a system of natural waterways, coastal and interior, which
have been linked by rails and have contributed much to the economic integration of
a large and rich resource area.

consumers. Such a trend will mean higher prices for those resources. It may also provide the United States with an incentive for domestic exploration and development of the technology needed to use lower-grade domestic materials.

The Canadian situation is somewhat different. Canada is deficient in high-grade coal, except in the maritime provinces and British Columbia, but it can obtain U.S. coal for its industrial needs with relative ease and at low cost. In other respects Canada is rich in minerals. But the country must determine the degree of dependence its economy should place on primary production, with petroleum and metals a significant part of that effort. In addition, Canada must decide the extent to which the much smaller Canadian population should allow the neighboring industrial giant to draw on Canadian petroleum, gas, copper, iron ore, nickel, and other metals, as well as forest resources.

KEY TERMS

baby boom	immigration
birth dearth	net migration
coniferous (boreal) forest	plantation
cultural imprint	prairies
cultural landscape	proven reserves
deciduous forest	tariff
emigration	topographic regions
growing season	urbanization
humid regions	zero population growth

NOTES

1. Terry G. Jordan, "The Imprint of the Upper and Lower South on Mid-Nineteenth Century Texas," *Annals, Association of American Geographers* 57 (1967): 667–690.

6

Anglo-America: Economic Growth and Transformation

Anglo-American Agriculture

Anglo-American Manufacturing

Industrialization and Urbanization

Wheat fields in the rolling Palouse of eastern Washington. Wheat production is common not only here but also throughout the Great Plains of both Canada and the United States.

Commercial economic activity began in Anglo-America shortly after the first Europeans settled there. Wherever transportation was suitable—which usually meant having access to water—commercialism rapidly became the norm. Agricultural commodities, lumber, furs, and fish were produced or gathered for exchange. Thus, primary production and tertiary activities (i.e., trade) were important long before the settlement of North America was complete and before secondary manufacturing activities became significant. Agriculture quickly became the economic mainstay, and it remained so for more than two centuries.

Soon after the United States became independent, the growth of population, domestic markets, and transportation stimulated the beginning of manufacturing, which expanded particularly rapidly from 1860 until the end of World War II. During that time a complete change in economic emphasis was occurring. Today few Anglo-Americans are farmers: in the United States 3 percent of workers are employed in agriculture; in Canada only 3.4 percent (Table 6–1). The United States and Canada each have about 17 percent employed in manufacturing. Most of the remaining workers are engaged in the distribution of goods or the provision of services. Since the turn of the century and especially since World War II, the tertiary sector has become the dominant source of employment and the basis for continued urbanization. These employment changes illustrate the transformation of Anglo-America from an **agrarian**

society, one based on agriculture, to a highly developed **urban-industrial society**, one in which people live predominantly in urban settings and work in secondary or tertiary occupations.

ANGLO-AMERICAN AGRICULTURE

Availability of Agricultural Land

Anglo-American agriculture evolved in a large and rich environment. Of the total land area of the United States, approximately one-fifth is classified as cropland, though not all of it is cultivated in any given year. Pasture and rangelands, also part of the food-producing resource base, make up about 29 percent of the land area. In other words, the United States has almost 5 acres (2 hectares) per person for the production of agricultural goods, either foodstuffs or industrial raw materials. Obviously, such agricultural land resources are substantial, relative to the population.

Only 4.4 percent of the land in Canada is devoted to cropland and pasture, primarily because so much of the land lies in more northern latitudes. The Canadian population, however, is considerably smaller than that of the United States, so the ratio of agricultural land to people is much the same (4.6 acres, or 1.8 hectares, per person). And despite the small proportion of total land area used for agriculture, the export of primary commodities, which include farm products (wheat in particular), is important to the Canadian economy.

The figures cited here are based on the land actually used for production in recent years and do not include land that might be added by clearing forests or draining wetlands. In addition, in both countries there has been a decline in agricultural use of marginal areas that are not essential for food supply, areas settled during earlier expansion periods when agriculture was the dominant economic activity. Thus, much additional land not now being used for agriculture could be converted into cropland. For example, in the lower Mississippi Valley and the Southeast, 50 million acres (20 million hectares) are considered convertible from woodland and pasture to cropland.

Agricultural Regions

The largest expanse of highly productive land in Anglo-America is that part of the Interior Plains known as the Corn Belt (Figure 6–1). That region,

Table 6–1
Employment by economic sectors in Anglo-America (percentages).

Economic Sector	United States (1992)	Canada (1989)
Primary	3.9	5.7
Agriculture	3.0	3.4
Other primary	.9	2.3
Secondary	22.0	23.1
Manufacturing	17.1	17.0
Construction	4.9	6.1
Tertiary	74.1	71.2

Sources: Bureau of the Census, *Statistical Abstract of the United States, 1993* (Washington, DC: Government Printing Office, 1993); and *Canada Yearbook, 1992* (Ottawa: Ministry of Supply and Services, 1991).

which extends from central Ohio into Nebraska, is a vast area of moderately rolling-to-flat, glaciated plains, highly suited to mechanized agriculture. The outstanding climatic conditions are the reliable rainfall and a moderately long growing season. In addi-

tion, the soils are among the best in Anglo-America. Such a favorable combination of features provides a resource base that can be used for the production of a great variety of grains, forage crops, vegetables, and livestock.

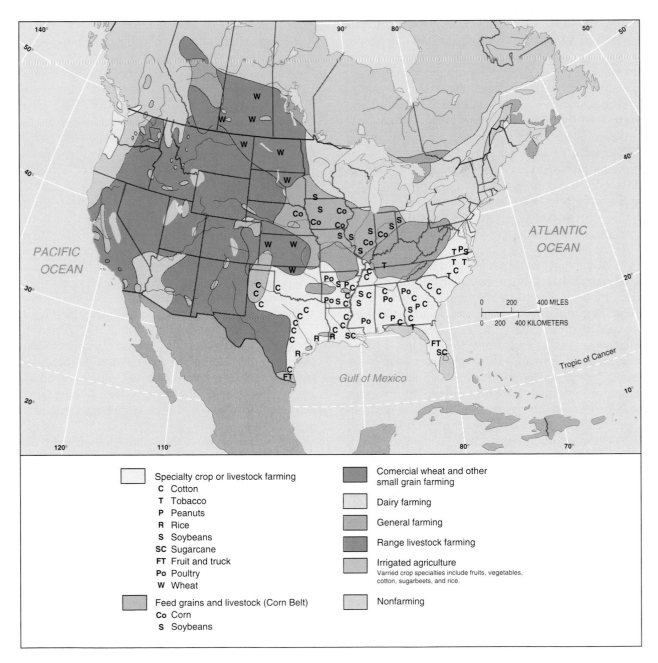

Figure 6–1
Agricultural regions of Anglo-America. A diversity of natural environments has contributed to the great variety in types of agricultural specialties possible in the United States and Canada.

Individual farmers in the Corn Belt, however, tend to specialize in one or two activities, and the single most important crop throughout the region is corn—hence, the name. Some corn is produced as a feed grain and marketed commercially. In other instances it is used to fatten cattle and hogs on the same farms where the grain is grown; such farms are referred to as feedlot farms. Other crops, such as soybeans and wheat, are also grown in this region, commonly on the same farms that produce corn for commercial markets. Other production systems in the area include dairying and vegetable growing.

The natural advantages of the Corn Belt are enhanced by the location of transportation routes and urban-industrial districts. Various parts of the region lie between or adjacent to the great inland waterways of the United States and Canada, and the area is laced with a dense network of railroads. Thus, a good transport system makes it easy for Corn Belt farmers to market their efficiently produced commodities in nearby eastern markets and even in far-distant nations.

Surrounding that superlative agricultural region are several others that are not quite as productive. A dairying and general-farming region extends from New England and Nova Scotia across Canada's Ontario Peninsula and the Great Lakes states to Minnesota. Much of the dairy region has a decided advantage because of its location next to one of the largest urban regions in the world. In addition, the humid, cool summers are favorable for forage crops and feed grains. To the north, though, the environment becomes harsh, the growing season short, and the soils thin and infertile. The Canadian section of this region is narrow in latitudinal extent and represents a transition to the nonagricultural northern lands.

The Northeast, where Anglo-American agriculture had its beginnings, does not provide such large expanses of favorable terrain and fertile soils. The topography of the region is generally hilly to mountainous, and the soils are thin and, in many places, infertile. Productive land—for example, the Connecticut Valley, the Hudson Valley, the limestone soil of Lancaster County in southeastern Pennsylvania—is the exception.

As better interior lands became accessible, northeastern farmers, wanting to make good use of their one great advantage—proximity to growing northeastern markets—found it necessary to specialize in the production of items that were needed in the nearby cities. Thus evolved both the vegetable and poultry production of New Jersey and the Delmarva Peninsula and the dairying of New England, New York, and Pennsylvania. Those commodities are of high value but require great capital input, are expensive to transport, and are sometimes perishable.

Although agriculture may be profitable in such a setting, it is also unstable. Closeness to urban centers can bring high taxes, pressure to relocate, and complaints from urban neighbors about farm odors and noises. Over the past several decades a great deal of farmland has been lost to rapidly expanding urban areas, but far more has been made idle or has been shifted to less intensive use (such as grazing or forestry) simply because farming has not been profitable.

The southern United States, from southern Maryland and Virginia to Texas, has varied and variable resources for agriculture (Figure 6–2). Large sections of hill land in the Appalachians, the Ozarks, and the South have slopes that are too steep for sustained use as cropland. When farming does take place in those locations, it is often quasi-subsistence. Other areas, such as the Piedmont, have been used for agriculture during favorable economic periods, such as when cotton prices were high, but the land has deteriorated with continued row-crop production. In addition, many coastal areas of swamp and **pine barrens**—sandy pine lands of the Southeast—are not at all suited to intensive agriculture.

Some subregions of the South, however, are exceptionally good agricultural areas because of their topography, soils, and subtropical environment. Such subregions include the limestone valley of Appalachia, the Nashville and Bluegrass basins, the alluvial Mississippi Valley, and the black-soil belts of Alabama and Texas. Farming in those areas is diverse, with many different specialties in different locations—tobacco, peanuts, rice, sugarcane, citrus, soybeans, poultry, and cattle, among others. Cotton, which used to be so important across much of the lower South, is now produced mainly in the western sector of the South—the Mississippi Valley (Tennessee, Arkansas, Mississippi, and Louisiana), the Coastal Plain of Texas, the lower Rio Grande Valley, and the high plains of Texas—and in the far western states of Arizona and California.

Figure 6-2
Tobacco field and barns in western North Carolina. Tobacco, intensively grown, remains a major crop in the Carolinas, Georgia, Virginia, Tennessee, and Kentucky, usually on small farms.

Farmers in the Great Plains of the United States and the prairie provinces of Canada (i.e., Alberta, Saskatchewan, and Manitoba) face recurrent **drought**, months or years of below-normal rainfall. Even normal rainfall sometimes results in water deficiencies. Wheat farming, frequently diversified to include livestock (usually cattle), is characteristic of the wetter parts of the plains states and provinces. The drier margins are given over almost exclusively to cattle raising. Areas such as the Sand Hills of Nebraska, which are stabilized sand dunes that do not hold moisture well, and the rolling Flint Hills of Kansas are devoted to specialized ranching.

Only where irrigation water is available in this region is the pattern of dry farming and ranching broken. Among the plains states Nebraska and Kansas have shown particularly great increases in irrigation. In addition, irrigation allows the high plains of Texas to function as one of the major cotton-producing regions of the United States. And eastern Colorado is able to produce sugar beets and corn for nearby livestock-finishing farms similar to those in Illinois and Iowa. The plains are food-surplus areas, and much of what is produced is transported elsewhere to meet domestic and international needs. The products of the Canadian Great Plains provide the greatest competition for United States farm output in the international marketplace.

The productivity of the plains states is somewhat hampered by dry conditions and distance from eastern markets, but areas farther west are downright handicapped. Most of the West, not suited to farming because of rugged terrain, aridity, or inaccessibility, is used extensively as grazing land. The exceptions to that generalization are extremely important, however. Aside from the Pacific Northwest (northern California, western Oregon, and Washington), agriculture, when it is carried on at all, is intensive at oasis locations. The valleys east of the Cascades, the Snake River plains, the Salt Lake oasis, and California's Imperial Valley, Los Angeles Basin, and Great Valley are some of the areas with highly productive agriculture. Farmers in those areas make use of fertile soils, level terrain, and national transport systems that allow them to market their products in the East, but they are utterly dependent on irrigation. These conditions have made California the most diversified and most productive agricultural area in either the United States or Canada (Figure 6–3).

The Pacific Northwest has a humid climate and is therefore less dependent on irrigation. The Puget Sound Lowland and the Willamette Valley contain a productive agricultural industry that includes dairy products, other livestock products, grains, orchard crops, and berries.

Commercialized Agriculture

The commercial emphasis of Anglo-American agriculture began early. Tobacco was the first successful venture, with rice, indigo, and cotton following as colonies were established southward along the Atlantic Coast. Even those early frontier farmers, who were generally subsistence oriented, produced items such as livestock, which could be driven to markets. Later, the urbanization and industrialization of Europe created larger markets, which stimulated the

Figure 6-3
Citrus groves along California's Pacific Coast Highway near Santa Cruz. Much of California's citrus and other orchard crop production has been displaced by massive urban growth during the post–World War II years.

expansion of commercial agriculture in various parts of the world, including Anglo-America. During the nineteenth century the expansion and improvement of rail transportation allowed Anglo-American settlers to participate in an expanding commercial system.

As a result of better transportation and more widespread settlement, land with greatly varying capabilities became accessible for many kinds of production, enabling the principle of **comparative advantage** to operate. That principle suggests that some locations are clearly better for the production of one or more items than other locations are; if transportation is adequate for commercial exchange, regional specialization will result. Thus, farmers who have an advantage in several forms of production will choose the form that provides the greatest return. They may concentrate on one or two crops or on some combination of crops and livestock. Farmers in areas with no advantage may concentrate on items that are ignored by others. In that way, areas specialize in limited types of production, either because of advantage or by default, and contribute their products to the larger economic system through exchange.

Continuing Adjustments in Agriculture

Despite a comparatively short history, Anglo-American agriculture has experienced many changes in response to numerous factors. Often, the adjust-

ments have also generated changes in spatial patterns. For example, lean cattle used to be driven from frontier areas to market areas in the East, where they were fattened before slaughter. Gradually, that system spread westward along the Ohio Valley and into the Midwest, which is an excellent area for the production of feed grains. Today, grain production and cattle fattening are specialized functions that occur almost exclusively in the Midwest and portions of the Great Plains. The East lost its comparative advantage.

Similarly, both rice and cotton production have undergone major spatial shifts. The coastal zone of South Carolina and Georgia was a major rice-producing region until the latter half of the nineteenth century. But the disruption resulting from the Civil War and from hurricanes—coupled with competition from newer lands in Louisiana, Arkansas, and California—led to the complete disappearance of rice on the southeastern coast. Likewise, cotton acreage has declined in older production areas of the Southeast—the victim of the boll weevil, government controls, soil erosion, and ineffective methods. Now, cotton production is concentrated in the better lands of the Mississippi Valley and westward.

Another factor prompting change was the early settling of farmers in locations that were not particularly well suited to agriculture. Some settled in the Appalachian hills, where the steep slopes were easily eroded. Others occupied the western edge of the Great Plains, where drought brought disaster. In the early nineteenth century agriculture retreated from the New England uplands and subsequently from many other areas. Through the years that process has often been repeated as some agricultural efforts have been withdrawn from marginal lands and concentrated on better lands. Even today land clearing for cropland expansion is continuing in the Mississippi Delta.

The agricultural labor force has undergone significant change, also. During the nineteenth century a substantial immigrant and native-born population was available as a labor force. Later, however, urban-industrial growth, combined with the availability of land to be owned, made farm labor for hire scarce in most regions other than the South. As a result, labor-saving devices, such as mechanical reapers, were developed in the nineteenth century. Eventually, the growing industrial capacity of Anglo-America created a varied supply of implements, by which agriculture could be fully mechanized.

The **mechanization** of agriculture has been a complex adjustment, involving more than just the substitution of capital for labor, although that in itself has often been difficult. Mechanization has frequently meant operational reorganization, larger capital expenditures, and a greater scale of production. In the adjustment process many people have found it impossible to make the necessary changes and have not survived as farmers (Figure 6–4). For those who can find other jobs, the move away from farming is not necessarily bad: a shift of inefficient and low-income farmers into other activities can benefit the larger economy. Not all farmers, however, have been able to find satisfactory alternatives, and large numbers of poor tenant farmers and farm laborers have migrated to the cities since the 1920s, ill prepared for city life, jobs, stress, and the urban discrimination that may affect both blacks and poor whites.

Agricultural Productivity

Anglo-American agriculture is extremely productive; the high degree of regional specialization enables the best resources to be used for many crops. By world standards the yields per land unit rank high for many commodities (see Figure 4–2).

U.S. productivity has increased greatly during the past three decades (Table 6–2). One of the reasons has been mechanization, which sometimes helps to

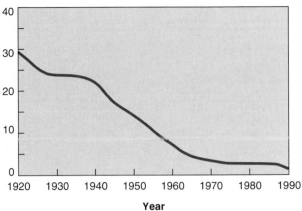

Percent

Figure 6–4

U.S. farm population as a percent of total population. The percentage of the U.S. population living on farms has continually decreased, a result of increased mechanization and other advances in farming methods as well as the growth of urban centers with their diversity of economic opportunities. (From Bureau of the Census, *Statistical Abstract of the United States, 1993,* Washington, DC: Government Printing Office, 1993.)

raise yields per unit of land, but more importantly has been increases in output per worker. With the aid of machinery, one person can do the work of many. Other significant causes of increased productivity are improved seed and plant varieties, more effective fertilizers, new pesticides, and chemicals to control disease and weeds. Currently, rapid progress is being made in developing hybrid wheats, which will probably result in a great increase in yield and production, similar to that which occurred with corn. In addition, genetic engineering can be expected to contribute further changes.

A Paradox: Productive Agriculture and Farm Problems

As is frequently true in times of rapid change and innovation, many adjustments are required of farmers who wish to participate in improved production methods. As noted earlier, many farm laborers who were no longer needed because of mechanization or farm reorganization have migrated to cities, particularly in the South, where the landless farm population was once large. Other farmers remain marginal producers with low incomes, usually in

Table 6–2
Agricultural productivity in the United States.

	Corn for Grain		Cotton		Wheat	
	Bushels per Acre	Hours Required per 100 Bushels	Pounds per Acre	Hours Required per 500=pound Bale	Bushels per Acre	Hours Required per 100 Bushels
1935–1939	26.1	108.0	226.0	209.0	13.2	67.0
1950–1959	39.4	34.0	296.0	107.0	17.3	27.0
1989–1992	118.7	3.0[a]	650.0	5.0[a]	36.5	7.0[a]

Sources: Bureau of the Census, *Statistical Abstract of the United States, 1974, 1988, 1993* (Washington, DC: Government Printing Office, 1974, 1988, 1993).

[a]Average hours 1982–1986.

Note: All figures are averages for the years indicated.

marginal farming areas. They contribute little to the national agricultural economy, for most agricultural output comes from the small number of farms that are large and capital intensive. Even if food demand increases, marginal farmers will not necessarily contribute more, because of their shortage of capital and land.

Farm problems are not restricted to marginal farmers, however. Most farmers are independent producers who are vulnerable to variations in weather and to fluctuating commodity prices on national and international markets. In addition, as American agriculture has become capital intensive, much of that capital has been borrowed, leaving farmers at even greater risk.

ANGLO-AMERICAN MANUFACTURING

Manufacturing activities are basic to the modern Anglo-American economies. In the United States almost 20 million people are now employed in manufacturing; in Canada nearly 1.6. Those individuals, as well as the great numbers of people required for the distribution of goods and the provision of services, form the basis for the extensive urbanization in Anglo-America.

The proportion of the total labor force employed in manufacturing has decreased as relatively faster growth has occurred in tertiary activities, a characteristic of developed societies. But manufacturing remains basic to the stability of the American economy. Approximately 19 percent of the income of the

United States is directly derived from manufacturing; but even more important is the great number of employment opportunities provided in the tertiary realm as goods are distributed to consumers and services are provided for manufacturers.

The Evolution of Manufacturing in the United States

Industry developed first in southeastern New England and the Middle Atlantic area from New York City to Philadelphia and Baltimore, two of the early American settlement cores. Before the railroad era began, access to water offered great transportation advantages, and industrial power was available in the form of mechanical waterpower. In addition, as capital was accumulated from other pursuits— such as lumbering, fishing, and ocean shipping— people who sought financial backing for new industrial activities were able to find entrepreneurs with both available capital and a venturesome spirit. Furthermore, New England had become an agricultural area out of necessity, even though its soils and slopes were not well suited to agriculture (see Chapter 5). Consequently, the surplus rural populations of New England, suffering from the economic competition of newly opened land in the interior, readily gave up farming for work in the textile mills, leather and shoe factories, and the machine-tool industry, all of which dominated New England industry by 1900. Shipbuilding, food processing, papermaking and printing, and ironworking were other early industries of the region.

The United States and Canada were largely settled by British and other European peoples whose homelands were already in economic transition. The traditional feudal society was decaying in Europe, and the concept of individual worth was emerging. In addition, capitalism was developing, as those with excess wealth diverted funds into new trade, transportation, power-supply, and manufacturing enterprises. Against this background the people who built Anglo-America were able to bring the United States to Rostow's takeoff stage by the 1840s and Canada by the 1890s (see Chapter 4).

With takeoff came an era of great industrial expansion, aided by railroads that made possible the movement of materials over great distances. The railroads themselves became a major market for steel, which was available from the 1850s on. By 1865 the United States was experiencing a drive to maturity, which would be achieved by 1900. During those years the improvements in the railroads, continued immigration, and an extremely favorable population-resource balance aided growth. At the same time the immense growth of industry, primarily in the northern states, was directly responsible for urbanization.

As railroads became the backbone of the transportation system and the dominant market for steel, specific northern locations took on new meaning and value. For example, eastward movement of goods from the interior by way of the Mohawk Valley and the Hudson River strengthened the focus on New York City. In addition, the agricultural goods that moved eastward to market stimulated domestic industry in the market area. The impact of the new and growing steel industries was more complex. As the bituminous coalfields of Appalachia and the iron ore deposits of the Mesabi Range increased in importance, the locations with utility became those between the coal and the iron ore: Pittsburgh, at the junction of the Monongahela and Allegheny rivers, and Cleveland, Erie, and Chicago, among others, on the Great Lakes. Railroads complemented the lakes by moving coal westward and northward to meet iron ore that was moving eastward by water. At the same time the areas between the Appalachians and the lakes and along the periphery of the lakes gained importance in the assembly of materials for production.

The South, remote from the new national transportation routes, continued to produce agricultural goods for external markets. The regional differences discussed in Chapter 5 had led the southern colonies to develop a commercial system that was financially and socially rewarding for a select few, who tended to invest their economic surplus in more land. Thus, to some extent, the South was like a colonial appendage. Manufacturing did exist in the antebellum and postbellum South, but it never achieved the rate of growth or the dominance that it did in the North. After the Civil War (1861–1865), when the weakness of southern industry was evident, other conditions made a reversal of the traditional economy even more difficult. And many southern leaders continued to advocate an agrarian philosophy even after the war.

Thus, regional variations were great by the 1930s, when the process of economic development was well into its maturity. The northeastern quarter of the United States had evolved as a major urban-industrial region, with numerous specialized urban-industrial districts interspersed among agricultural regions. The industrial coreland was an area of relatively high urbanization, high industrial output, high income, and immense internal exchange. The South was a region of low urbanization, limited industrial growth, and poverty for great numbers of whites and blacks in overpopulated rural areas.

Manufacturing in the Anglo-American Coreland

The Anglo-American manufacturing region is a large area in the northeastern United States and southeastern Canada that consists of numerous **urban-industrial districts**, within which distinct industrial specialties can be identified (Figure 6–5). Altogether, that coreland today contains just under 50 percent of the manufacturing capacity of the United States and Canada and the majority of the Anglo-American market. The complementary transportation system of water, roads, and railroads provides great advantages for both assembling materials and distributing finished products.

Measured by employment, southern New England is one of the most industrialized districts in the United States. The area's prominence is based on the nineteenth-century growth of its textile, leather-working, and machine-tool industries. In the twentieth century, however, the region has suffered some severe economic problems. Any area that depends on only a few products risks severe economic

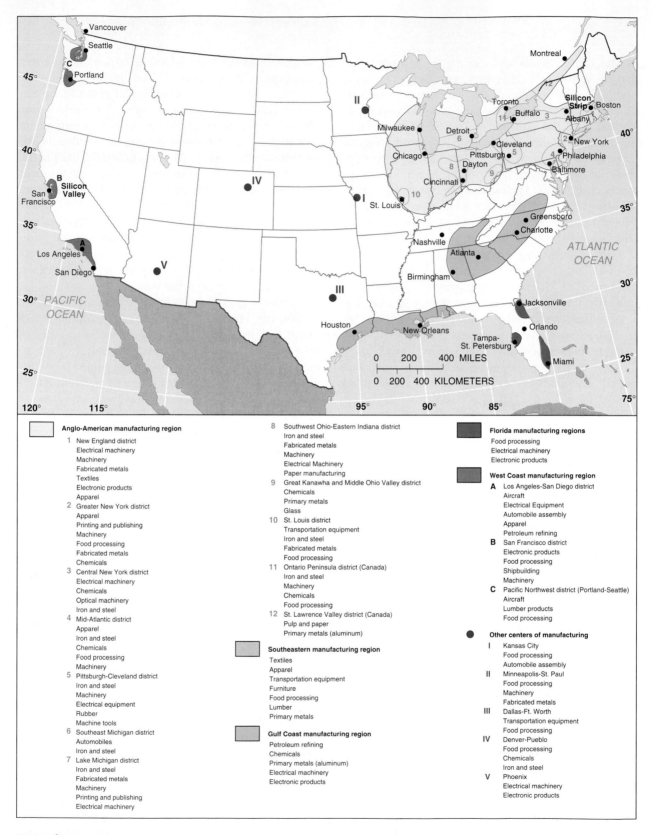

Figure 6–5

Manufacturing regions and urban-industrial districts of Anglo-America. Industrial regions and districts show as much variety in specialties as agriculture does. Industrial specialties reflect influences of markets, materials, labor, power, and historic forces.

consequences if the competition comes from more efficient producers. In addition, New England and the significance of its location changed with industrial maturity. Today, New England is a high tax area, has highly unionized labor markets, and relies on imported resources for power. Moreover, population increases farther west have adversely affected New England's location relative to national markets: eastern New England is now peripheral in some respects. And the area's once-dominant industries have moved to the South, where labor costs are lower. To compensate for that loss, New England is now emphasizing high-value products—such as electronic equipment, electrical machinery, firearms, machinery, and tools—that can withstand high transportation, power, and labor costs. The region's success in attracting service activities has also aided its transformation to a modern economy. All in all, the New England district illustrates how the industrial structure of a region can change, not always by conscious choice.

Metropolitan New York contains the largest manufacturing complex in the United States. The city's location at the mouth of the Hudson River, its function as the major port for the rich interior, and its own huge population have combined to generate and support almost 5.5 percent of all manufacturing in the United States. The tendency in that district is toward diversified manufacturing, including printing, publishing, machinery making, food processing, metal fabricating, and petroleum refining. A heavy concentration of garment manufacturing also characterizes industry in greater New York, along with a lack of primary metals processing. Inertia, immense capital investments, and linkages with other industries once ensured considerable locational stability for steel industries. But now all three manufacturing districts with prominent steel industries are undergoing major industrial change. The first of those districts includes Baltimore and Philadelphia, Bethlehem, and Harrisburg, Pennsylvania. A massive steel-producing capacity exists near all of those cities and supports shipbuilding (along the Delaware River and the Chesapeake Bay) and many other machinery industries. The steel industry has expanded there because of proximity to large eastern markets (i.e., other manufacturers of fabricated metals and machinery) and accessibility to external waterways. The importance of waterway accessibility has grown as dependence on foreign sources of iron ore has increased.

The second major steel district is a large triangle with points at Pittsburgh and Erie, Pennsylvania, and Toledo, Ohio. It is the oldest steel-producing center in the United States. Its **initial advantage**, early factors that propelled development, was derived from its location between the Appalachian coalfields and the Great Lakes. But the locational advantage of Pittsburgh and its steel-producing suburbs has diminished. Now, South American iron ore is shipped to East Coast works, and Canadian ore comes by way of the St. Lawrence Seaway and the Great Lakes. Thus, the eastern steel district (Baltimore-Philadelphia) is closer to both eastern markets and foreign ores; and Detroit and Chicago are more easily reached by Canadian ore and are closer to midwestern markets.

The third area lies around the southwestern shore of Lake Michigan. It includes Gary, Indiana; Chicago, Illinois; and Milwaukee, Wisconsin, which have a vast array of machinery-manufacturing plants that are supplied by the massive steelworks nearby. The steel industries of Chicago and Gary have benefited from a superb location: ore moving southeastward across the Great Lakes meets coal from Illinois, Indiana, Ohio, Kentucky, and West Virginia. By the late nineteenth century, Chicago had also become a major transportation center: railroads met and complemented freighters, making the southern Lake Michigan area an excellent site for assembling materials and distributing manufactured products. The St. Lawrence Seaway has simply given renewed importance to the location, for now Chicago and other inland cities can function as midcontinent ports from which ships can almost sail in a Great Circle route to Europe (a Great Circle route is the shortest distance between two points on the surface of the earth.)

Southern Michigan and neighboring parts of Indiana, Ohio, and Ontario are distinguished by their emphasis on automotive production, both parts and assembly. Those industries are linked not only to the Detroit steel industry but also to steel manufacturers in the Chicago area and along the shores of Lake Erie (cities such as Toledo, Lorain, and Cleveland, Ohio). The automotive industry serves as a huge market for major steel-producing districts on either side of the international border.

Major problems have jeopardized the vitality of manufacturing in the Anglo-American coreland since the 1970s. First, manufacturers of steel and au-

Figure 6-6

(Left) A modern American automobile assembly plant utilizing robotics; (right) idle steel milling facilities in Youngstown, Ohio. Manufacturing enterprises that survive do so by emphasizing capital-intensive technology and reduced labor requirements. The result is that while many industries survive, the residual labor force suffers from unemployment.

tomobiles have faced intense competition from foreign producers, whose labor costs are lower and whose equipment is more modern. The resulting economic and social stress has been felt throughout the industrial community because the steel and automotive industries are integrated into an entire complex of industries. Second, recurring national recessions and economic fluctuations have created economic environments in which it has been difficult for those industries to remain competitive. Third, social problems have plagued the coreland: questions of residential quality, social conflict, air and water pollution, and urban water supply, as well as the need to govern and integrate numerous adjoining political units.

All of those problems have resulted in the **restructuring** of industry—that is, shifts in emphasis and the spatial adjustment of manufacturing; some industries have grown and others have declined. Both the steel industry and the automobile industry

provide examples of manufacturing activities that are undergoing major changes. Both have undergone employment reductions due to reduced market shares (i.e., foreign competition) and attempts to modernize and economize production (Figure 6–6). And in the process both have been undergoing significant locational changes.

Regional changes in the manufacturing share of total employment have also been evident in the restructuring. Some regions have increased; others have decreased (Figure 6–7 and Table 6–3). Regional variations have become particularly notable during the 1970s and 1980s, as many of the states within the Anglo-American manufacturing region have experienced absolute declines in manufacturing employment (Figure 6–8). Even in areas of increased manufacturing employment, however, the contribution of manufacturing to total nonagricultural employment has decreased, providing further evidence of the overall shift to a service economy

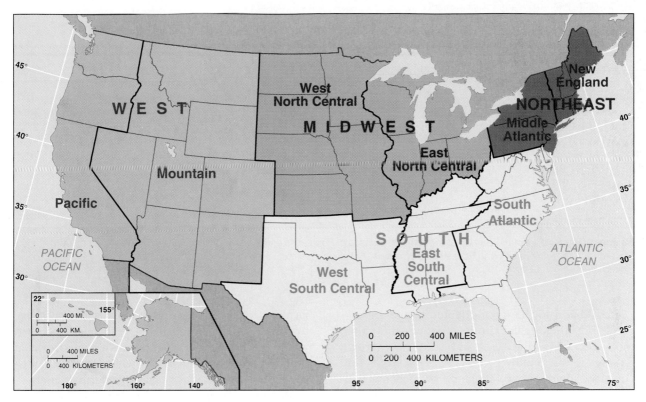

Figure 6–7
U.S. Bureau of Census divisions. The Bureau of the Census compiles social and eco-
nomic data at many levels, ranging from tracts to regions. The data provided in
Tables 6–3 and 6–4 are organized on a divisional level.

(Table 6–4). In every region the percentage of workers in the service sector of the economy has grown,
thereby accounting for much of the contemporary
metropolitan expansion.

The Southern Economic Revolution

The beginning of the economic revolution in the
South is difficult to pinpoint. It probably started in
the 1880s with the **New South** advocates, who believed that industrialization was necessary for the re-
vitalization of the region. Thus, the recent increase
in the southern (and western) share of manufacturing in the United States is really the continuation of
a process of industrial dispersion that has been under way for many decades.

The first major manufacturing activity to become
distinctly identified with the South was the textile industry, which had evolved as a dominant force in
the nineteenth-century industrial growth of New
England. By the early twentieth century, however,

the industrial maturity of New England was reflected
in high wages, unionization, costly fringe-benefit
programs, high power costs (imported coal), and
obsolete equipment and buildings. Thus, as old
New England textile plants closed, new ones were
established in the South.

Because the textile industry did not grow on a
nationwide basis after 1920, the regional shift
benefited one region at the expense of another.
Firms in the South found a major advantage in the
quantity of labor that was available at a relatively
low cost; the agrarian South had a surplus of landless rural people willing to switch from farming to
manufacturing. Other advantages were a better
location with respect to raw materials (cotton),
lower cost of power, and lower taxes. By 1930
more than half of the nation's textile industry was
located in the South. At present more than 90 percent of cotton, 75 percent of synthetic fiber, and
40 percent of woolen textiles are of southern
manufacture.

Table 6-3
Percentages of U.S. workers in manufacturing, by division.

Division	1899	1929	1954	1967	1977	1987	1992
New England	18.1	12.4	9.0	8.1	7.1	7.1	6.0
Middle Atlantic	34.1	29.0	26.6	22.6	18.7	15.8	13.7
East North Central	22.8	28.8	28.6	26.7	25.3	22.1	22.3
West North Central	5.6	5.4	6.0	6.2	6.6	7.0	7.6
South Atlantic	9.7	10.3	11.0	12.9	14.3	16.4	16.4
East South Central	3.8	4.3	4.5	5.7	6.7	6.9	7.9
West South Central	2.4	3.4	4.5	5.6	7.3	7.6	8.6
Mountain	0.9	1.2	1.1	1.6	2.4	3.2	3.5
Pacific	2.6	5.3	8.8	10.6	11.6	14.1	13.7

Sources: Various years of the Bureau of the Census, *Census of Population* and *Census of Manufacturers* (Washington, DC: Government Printing Office); and Bureau of the Census, *Statistical Abstract of the United States, 1993* (Washington, DC: Government Printing Office, 1993).

In addition to the labor-oriented textile and apparel industries, material-oriented pulp-and-paper, food-processing, and forest industries have grown rapidly in the South as well. And in Texas and Louisiana, petroleum-refining and petrochemical industries have contributed much to Gulf Coast industrial expansion. The overall economic transformation has now reached a stage where the South itself provides a significant regional market, which generates further industrial growth to respond to population growth and the needs of existing industry. The automotive industry is a good example: automobile assembly plants have been built in Louisville, Atlanta, and Dallas to serve regional markets. The transformation from an agrarian way of life to an urban one has brought higher incomes and new consumption patterns that have greatly increased the market importance of a formerly rural populace. Approximately 33 percent of the nation's manufacturing is now accomplished in the South.

Southern Manufacturing Regions

The Southeastern manufacturing region coincides with much of the southern Piedmont and the neighboring parts of Alabama (see Figure 6–5). That region—from Danville, Virginia, to Birmingham, Alabama—is characterized by light industry: textiles, apparel, food processing, and furniture. The chief attraction has undoubtedly been the availability of suitable labor at costs below industry wage scales elsewhere. As an industrial region, the Piedmont is quite unlike the core districts of the Anglo-American manufacturing region. Much of its industry is in small cities, towns, and—not infrequently—rural areas. And even where urbanization is occurring, it is a more dispersed form of urbanization than that which occurred in association with turn-of-the-century industrialization.

Birmingham and Atlanta are two major exceptions to the general pattern in the Southeastern region. The Birmingham-Gadsden, Alabama, area is known for its steel industry, which started because of a unique circumstance: coal, iron ore, and limestone are all available nearby. Long the major steel region of the South, that area is now experiencing a decline in production. Atlanta, much like Dallas–Fort Worth in Texas, is noted as a center for aircraft manufacture and automobile assembly; it is not typical of southern industrial centers but has grown because of its function as a regional center.

The Gulf Coast is another southern manufacturing region, a series of distinctly separate industrial nodes between Mobile, Alabama, and Corpus Christi, Texas. Petroleum, natural gas, salt, sulfur, and agricultural products provide the base for much of the region's industry and recent growth. Industrial activities include petroleum refining and production of petrochemicals and other chemicals; aluminum smelting and refining, using ores from Jamaica and Guyana and power from local natural gas; processing of sugar and rice; and steel manufacturing based on local and imported ores. The region's coastal location is a great advantage, for both importing raw materials and exporting finished products.

Figure 6-8
Manufacturing employment shifts between 1967 and 1991. The industrial coreland has experienced a decline in manufacturing employment as the South and West have expanded.

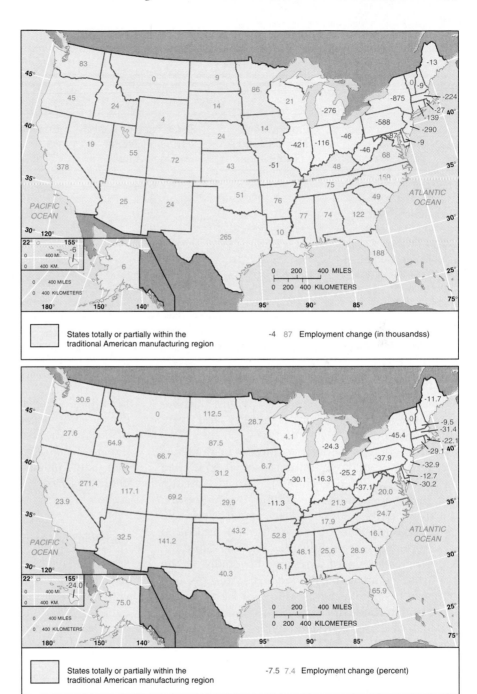

States totally or partially within the traditional American manufacturing region

-4   87   Employment change (in thousandss)

States totally or partially within the traditional American manufacturing region

-7.5   7.4   Employment change (percent)

In addition, there has been significant growth in manufacturing in central Florida. Especially important there are electronic products and electrical machinery. Those portions of the Coastal Plain falling outside these regions are not without industry. Pulp-and-paper industries and pine plywood industries have expanded greatly since World War II, mainly because the pine forests grow rapidly on the plain.

The Growth of Manufacturing on the West Coast

Approximately 14 percent of all manufacturing in the United States is carried out on the Pacific Coast, with the largest single concentration in the greater Los Angeles area. The productivity of California's agriculture and commercial fishing

Table 6-4
Manufacturing employment in relation to nonagricultural employment in the United
States, by division.

Division	1967		1987	
	Employment in Manufacturing (Thousands)	Percentage of Total Nonagricultural Employment	Employment in Manufacturing (Thousands)	Percentage of Total Nonagricultural Employment
New England	1,564	36.4	1,091	18.3
Middle Atlantic	4,325	32.2	2,491	15.3
East North Central	5,118	36.9	4,041	21.4
West North Central	1,226	24.3	1,373	16.7
South Atlantic	2,559	27.2	2,983	15.3
East South Central	1,130	32.0	1,432	22.5
West South Central	1,107	20.2	1,555	14.1
Mountain	321	13.7	626	10.3
Pacific	2,065	24.7	2,481	15.1

Sources: Bureau of the Census, *Statistical Abstract of the United States, 1974* (Washington, DC.: Government Printing Office, 1974); and Bureau of the Census, *Statistical Abstract of the United States, 1993* (Washington, DC: Government Printing Office, 1993).

stimulated the food-processing activities that became the state's first major industry and were dominant until the 1940s. World War II then generated the defense industries, aircraft manufacturing, and shipbuilding; and defense has continued to be a major employer in the Los Angeles area in the postwar decades. In addition, automobiles, electronic parts, petrochemicals, and apparel have achieved importance in California's **industrial structure**, the mix of industries that constitute the industrial makeup of a region. Especially in the Los Angeles area, the growing Hispanic population has become a major source of labor for the large apparel industry.

Much of California's early industrial growth was based on local material resources and rapidly growing local markets. Since the 1950s, however, industries that serve national markets have grown enormously. California, particularly southern California, has received large numbers of migrants from other parts of the United States. And industries, especially those in which material and power costs are not high, have followed the migrants.

Manufacturing efforts in the Pacific Northwest include food processing (dairy, fruit, vegetable, and fish products), forest-products industries, primary metals processing (aluminum), and aircraft factories (Figure 6–9). The emphasis is on the processing of local primary resources and the use of hydroelectric power

from the Columbia River system. The region's great distance from eastern markets and the smaller size of local markets have historically inhibited its growth. But the growing importance of the Pacific Rim should ultimately prove a major stimulus to the entire West Coast, including the Portland and Seattle areas.

Canadian Industrial Growth

Secondary activities are important in Canada as well. In fact, Canadian manufacturing is closely integrated with that of the United States, as indicated by both trade flows and the high level of U.S. investment in Canadian industry.

The takeoff period in Canadian economic development began in the 1890s and coincided with an immense boom in economic growth. The relatively late start—takeoff began in the United States in the 1840s—may have been caused by several factors: (1) the harsh physical environment attracted fewer immigrants; (2) political independence came later, so efforts to industrialize were less concerted until late in the nineteenth century; and (3) economic ties with the United States were limited until the country approached maturity, which then stimulated Canadian development.

Canadian industry and exports have been closely tied to the production and processing of staples: first,

Figure 6-9
Jet aircraft manufacturing at a Boeing Aircraft Company plant in Everett, Washington. Aircraft manufacturing is one of several manufacturing industries that have experienced highly cyclical employment.

fishing and furs; later, wheat, forest products, and metals. A maturing of the Canadian economy since World War II has reduced the dominance of primary commodities, particularly in Ontario, but that emphasis nevertheless remains an identifying feature of the Canadian economy. Wheat, primary metals (raw or partially processed), forest products, oil and its refined products, and tourism are still the major dollar earners.

Early twentieth-century growth in Canada was a response to markets and capital in the United States, and Canadians feared that their location would make them simply a supplier of materials for the United States—a kind of economic colony. Consequently, tariffs were adopted to encourage manufacturing and exportation, thereby ensuring that primary production and secondary processing would take place in Canada. Some Canadians have argued that the tariff policy has resulted in higher prices for the commodities they consume and, therefore, in a lower level of living. But tariffs have forced the use of Canadian resources, both human and material, by stimulating manufacturing at home, which has attracted an immense investment of capital in the Canadian economy by U.S. and other foreign companies. In 1987 the United States and Canada agreed to work toward a reduction of trade restraints. That beginning culminated in the North American Free Trade Agreement. Canada, Mexico, and the United States are now members of a single trade union intended to lead eventually

to totally free trade and greater trade between the member countries. Even now, Canada and the United States are each other's most important trading partner, a relationship not unlike that of the members of Europe's Common Market and an indication of the **economic integration**, or interrelatedness, already underway in North America. Success may eventually lead to consideration of a larger Western Hemispheric trade organization.

The Distribution of Canadian Manufacturing

The St. Lawrence Valley and the Ontario Peninsula form the industrial heart of Canada, producing 79 percent of the nation's output. The Canadian area adjoins the industrial core of the United States and may be thought of as its northern edge, specializing in the production and processing of materials from Canadian mines, forests, and farms.

Montreal is the site of approximately 13 percent of Canadian industry. In some ways it parallels New York City. In both are produced a variety of consumer items (chiefly foodstuffs, apparel, and books and magazines) intended for local and national markets. And both cities function as significant ports for international trade.

Outside Montreal the Canadian industrial structure is more specialized. The immense hydroelectric potential of Quebec is a major source of power for industries along the St. Lawrence River and has provided the basis for Canada's important production of aluminum. With bauxite shipped in from Jamaica and Guyana, the Saguenay and St. Maurice rivers, tributaries of the St. Lawrence, have powered aluminum refining and smelting at Alma, Arvida, Shawinigan Falls, and Beauharnois. And because Canada's production of aluminum far exceeds its consumption, it is a leading exporter. The aluminum industry illustrates Canada's role as a processor and supplier for other nations, using both national and international resources in that capacity. Other metal-processing industries located near production centers deal with copper and lead at Flin Flon and Noranda, nickel at Sudbury, and magnesium at Haleys.

The valleys of the St. Lawrence and its tributaries also represent Canada's major area of pulp-and-paper manufacturing, with the boreal forests providing the resource base. Canada is the world's leading supplier of newsprint, most of which is sent to the United States and Europe.

Beyond Montreal and its vicinity the most intense concentration of industry is found in the **golden horseshoe**, a district that extends from Toronto and Hamilton around the western end of Lake Ontario to St. Catharines. That district produces most of Canada's steel and a great variety of other industrial goods, such as automobile parts, assembled automobiles, electrical machinery, and agricultural implements. It is one of the most rapidly growing industrial districts in Canada, partly because more than 60 percent of Canada's market is found along the southern edges of Ontario and Quebec provinces, and industry appears to be increasingly market oriented.

Canada's high protective tariff has been another reason for the growth of industry in the golden horseshoe. The tariff was initially important when foreign capital, especially from the United States and Great Britain, was invested in industries that processed Canadian resources for foreign use. It has become even more important as a mature Canadian industry has sought to serve expanding Canadian markets. Foreign companies have found it necessary to locate in Canada to avoid tariffs; and they have tended to locate in larger Canadian industrial centers—Windsor, Hamilton, Toronto, and Montreal— or close to the city containing the parent U.S. firm. For example, many Detroit firms with subsidiary operations in Canada have located immediately across the river in Windsor.[1] Had the tariffs not been imposed, Canadian industry would probably be even more oriented to the processing of primary materials than it is.

INDUSTRIALIZATION AND URBANIZATION

The industrial growth of the United States and Canada during the late nineteenth century and the early twentieth century stimulated employment in tertiary activities. New industrial jobs have a **multiplier effect**, because they generate employment opportunities in the service activities that support the new workers. Thus, employment expands in wholesaling, retailing, education, government, the professions, and a host of other urban-oriented activities. The cumulative growth may generate even more new industry, research and development activity, and additional service activities because a larger market exists.

Secondary and tertiary activities are more economical when they are clustered in towns and cities. The growth of such activities, therefore, has been the basis for tremendous urban expansion. Manufacturing activities were probably the principal catalyst for urban growth until the 1920s, but in the past 60 years tertiary growth has become the major stimulus. During the 1970s and 1980s, in particular, net growth in employment has been entirely in the service sector. The United States and Canada have also experienced an enormous increase in information services, now called quaternary activities (see the boxed feature, Economic Restructuring).

The distribution of population reflects those shifts in employment. In 1900, when industrialization was well under way, the rural population of the United States was 46 million, or 60 percent of the total population. By the close of the 1980s the rural population had grown to 61 million but was only 24 percent of the total population. Furthermore, the vast majority of rural residents are nonfarmers who live in rural areas and small towns but work in urban areas. They send their children to school and shop in urban areas; in fact, they are urban in almost everything except residence. Less than 5 million people who live in rural parts of the United States are actually farmers. At the same time rural-to-urban migration and the natural increase of population in cities has swelled the urban population to almost 190 million in the United States and to 17 million in Canada.

ECONOMIC RESTRUCTURING

The term **postindustrial society** refers to the recent and extensive economic and social changes that have enveloped the United States and Canada. Those changes include the rapid growth of employment in traditional service activities and information services, along with a de-emphasis on manufacturing. Some people have even labeled that restructuring of employment as "deindustrialization."

Several points should be understood regarding the nature of this transformation. First, the post-1950s era is not the only time the economy of the United States has been rapidly restructured. As Table A reveals, the shift from employment in primary activities (largely agriculture) to employment in the secondary, tertiary, and quaternary sectors was extensive during the first half of this century, illustrating the classic transformation from an agrarian society to an industrial one. The second structural shift has occurred since 1950, especially since 1970, as the primary and secondary sectors have given way in relative and absolute terms to the tertiary and quaternary sectors. The first restructuring generated widespread rural-to-urban migration and massive urban growth. One impact of the second transformation has been selective urban growth and decline, as older industrial centers struggle to transform their economies and other cities thrive with the growth of services.

A second point to remember is that the emergence of a postindustrial economy does not mean that manufacturing will disappear. The growth and decline of industry will be selective in both the United States and Canada; but resources, huge markets, and modern technologies will ensure that manufacturing remains a significant component of the economy of Anglo-America.

Third, this continuing evolution of the Anglo-American economic system includes a **global interdependence**, or worldwide economic integration, in which international trade is fundamental to economic health. Indeed, manufacturing itself is developing a global structure through the expansion of **multinational corporations**, companies that operate in several countries.

Table A
Sectoral shifts in the United States labor force, 1910-1980.

	Economic Sector			
	Primary	Secondary	Tertiary	Quaternary
1910	31.1	36.3	17.7	14.9
1920	32.5	32.0	17.8	17.7
1930	20.4	35.3	19.8	24.5
1940	15.4	37.2	22.5	24.9
1950	11.9	38.3	19.0	30.8
1960	6.0	34.8	17.2	42.0
1970	3.1	28.6	21.9	46.4
1980	2.1	22.5	28.8	46.6

Source: Compiled from Daniel Bell, "The Social Framework of the Information Society," in M. L. Dertouzos and Joel Moses, eds., *The Computer Age: A Twenty-Year View* (Cambridge: MIT Press, 1979), 163-211.

Present and Future Regions

From the standpoint of population, both the United States and Canada consist of a number of urban regions, many of which adjoin each other and continue to intensify and increase. Figure 5–14 shows the present urban regions of the United States and those projected for the year 2000. Urban development is already so widespread in some areas as to justify use of the term **megalopolis**. Megalopolitan areas include numerous cities that are next to each other or are in such proximity that their boundaries are almost indistinguishable. The interaction among those high-density centers becomes so great that it is almost impossible to identify the individual cities, yet administratively they continue to function as separate entities.

Jean Gottmann first used the term **megalopolis** to describe the massive urban region between northern Virginia and southern New Hampshire.[2] The core of that northeastern megalopolis is composed of the cities of Washington, Baltimore, Philadelphia, New York, and Boston. Together with a host of nearby cities, they comprise a giant urban region with more than 40 million people. That megalopolis also contains massive industrial complexes with much of the nation's manufacturing capacity and the nation's most intense market concentration.

However, Gottmann's designation of the northeastern megalopolis as the "Main Street and crossroads of the nation" implies a functional significance for the region far beyond that of manufacturing.[3] Indeed, it is a center of political and corporate management and decision making. The ports—particularly New York City but also Boston, Philadelphia, Baltimore, and others—are the focal points of international and national trade, as well as the major termini of inland railroad and highway systems. Furthermore, the nation's most prestigious financial and educational centers are located in the region, which indeed functions as "downtown USA."

Even agriculture in and near the megalopolis has a distinctive character. Dairy products, vegetables, poultry, and other specialty items are produced in quantity for the nearby markets. Although production costs are high, transportation costs are low. Farmers in the area occupy land that is high in value because of its potential for urban use, not its inherent food-producing capacity. Thus, farmland, like recreational land, faces tremendous pressure from the spreading urban areas. High taxes and inflated offers from developers take their toll on the farms, even highly productive ones.

The eastern megalopolis may extend from southern Virginia to southern Maine by the year 2000. The projection for that year also shows a Great Lakes megalopolitan region connecting with the eastern megalopolis. The Great Lakes megalopolitan region is already well advanced and by 2000 may be a major part of a massive urban-industrial coreland that extends from Wisconsin and Illinois to the Atlantic Coast. A series of less intense but nonetheless distinct urban regions will extend along the Piedmont and into northern Georgia and northern Alabama. Florida, the Gulf Coast, and the rapidly growing California megalopolis between San Diego and San Francisco are other extended urban regions.

Some Urban Problems

All of those urban regions must deal with certain common problems, one of which is administration. A single city in a functional sense is subdivided into many independent political units; one government tries to provide services and maintain jurisdiction over the inner city, while numerous suburbs attempt the same in outlying areas. In addition, community administrative functions frequently overlap those provided by county governments. Thus, consolidation of services and government remains a major issue in urban regions, but planning and problem solving are complicated by differences between cities and suburbs. Economic, social, and racial segregation leave communities with unequal abilities to generate funds for the provision of services. That problem becomes particularly acute in central cities that have in-migration of poor whites, blacks, and in some cases Asians and out-migration of more prosperous whites and blacks. Consolidated urban political regions, or political boundaries that coincide with real cities, would provide a more equitable tax base. Not surprisingly, however, such an idea is often opposed. Among the few cities that have attempted such solutions are Nashville, Tennessee, and Jacksonville, Florida.

Population is only one aspect of urban growth; expanding land area is another. Cities and suburbs continue to absorb substantial amounts of land,

Figure 6–10
"Alphabet City" on the lower east side of New York. Inner city decay is a major problem for many large urban centers in the United States.

sometimes so rapidly that planning fails to prevent unsightly development and traffic congestion. At the same time, farmers find a new life-style, system of land use, and tax scale invading their domain, and many genuinely resent being squeezed out of some of the nation's best agricultural land. To protect good farmland, New Jersey, for example, has found it necessary to enact legislation to preserve its better agricultural lands.

Our seeming cultural predisposition to emphasize the new and to spread ourselves outward from old cities suggests that some urban problems may intensify. The **economic base**, or income-producing activities, of many **central cities**, the central business district and surrounding area, continues to weaken (Figure 6–10). Even some metropolitan areas are having similar problems. Many cities are losing population; yet areas next to them, smaller cities, and even remote rural areas are growing. Thus, we are experiencing the problems of growth and decline at the same time. Indeed, a major Anglo-American dilemma is whether to restore central cities or to neglect them benignly and thus allow the evolution of new urban forms and the dispersion of population and economic activity.

SUMMARY
Continued Growth and Transformation

This chapter has emphasized the role of agriculture and manufacturing in the development of the United States and Canada. Both of those fundamental economic activities have played an integral part in shaping the geography of Anglo-America, as is evident in the wealth created, the resources used, and the rural and urban landscapes. Even as these two economic sectors continue to evolve, however, we see their comparative importance diminish as economic restructuring emphasizes the growth of services. The result is a reshaping and expansion of the urban landscape, unemployment in some areas with growth in others, and a redistribution of population. At the same time many other changes are taking place in the United States and Canada. Indeed, their economic systems, like those of other countries, are becoming part of a global economy. These problems and contemporary changes confirm that economic development is an ongoing process.

KEY TERMS

agrarian society

central city

comparative advantage

drought

economic base

economic integration

global interdependence

golden horseshoe

industrial structure

initial advantage

mechanization

megalopolis

multinational corporation

multiplier effect

New South

pine barrens

postindustrial society

restructuring

urban-industrial district

urban-industrial society

NOTES

1. Michael Ray, "The Location of United States Manufacturing Subsidiaries in Canada," *Economic Geography* 47 (1971): 389–400.

2. Jean Gottmann, *Megalopolis: The Urbanized Northeastern Seaboard of the United States* (Cambridge: MIT Press, 1961).

3. Ibid., 7–9.

7

Anglo-America:
Problems in a
Developed Realm

Income Disparity and Regional Problems

African-Americans

Hispanic-Americans

Canadian Identity and Unity

Rural poverty in Louisiana. Both rural and urban poverty continue to be serious problems in many areas of the United States.

Even such developed and prosperous countries as the United States and Canada have significant and sometimes pressing problems. We have already discussed the complexities of supplying and consuming enormous quantities of resources. In addition, unbalanced economic growth, ineffective integration of various regions into a national economy, and the social, economic, and political situations of minority groups are other fundamental problems with which the United States and Canada must deal.

INCOME DISPARITY AND REGIONAL PROBLEMS

Large numbers of people in the United States and Canada have been unable to acquire the material benefits of the average resident of Anglo-America. Exactly how many poor people live in Anglo-America depends, of course, on exactly how poverty is defined. In general, **poverty** is a material deprivation that affects biologic and social well-being. About 14 percent of the United States population can be considered poor (Table 7–1). Slightly more than 32.7 percent of those 35.7 million people are black; in other words, according to the U.S. Bureau of the Census, one-third of the 30 million African-Americans live in poverty. Although that proportion is higher than the proportion of whites who live in poverty, the actual number of poor whites is more than double that of poor blacks—23.7 million in comparison with 10.2 million. Hispanics account for 6.2 million of those included in the white population.

At one time the poor in the United States were almost equally divided between metropolitan and nonmetropolitan areas. Currently, however, almost 72 percent of all poor people live in metropolitan areas, with most, but not all, of those persons being concentrated in central cities. Poor people often make up a smaller proportion of a metropolitan population than they do of a nonmetropolitan population, but the metropolitan poor are more intensely concentrated and frequently live in ghetto communities (Figure 7–1). Poor people in nonmetropolitan areas are generally scattered about and are therefore less visible, adding to their problems of employment and services.

Not surprisingly, the greatest concentrations of poor people live in the larger states of California, New York, Texas, Florida, Illinois, Pennsylvania, and Ohio. Numerous poor are also found throughout the southern Coastal Plain, from Virginia to Texas, and in the upland South, particularly the Appalachian Plateau and the Ozarks. Rural poverty is not limited to the South, though it is most widespread there. Areas of rural poverty can also be found in New England, the upper Great Lakes (i.e., Michigan, Wisconsin, and Minnesota), the northern Great Plains, and the Southwest.

Table 7-1
Poverty in the United States, by residence and race, 1991.

Residence	Percentage of Persons Below Poverty Level[a]			
	Total Population	White Population	Black Population	Hispanic[b]
United States	14.2	11.3	32.7	28.7
Northeast	12.2	10.0	28.1	36.3
North Central	13.2	9.9	37.7	23.5
South	16.0	11.7	33.6	26.1
West	14.3	13.5	24.0	28.8

Source: Bureau of the Census, *Statistical Abstract of the United States, 1993* (Washington, DC: Government Printing Office, 1993).

[a]"Poverty level" is indexed to the consumer price index and varies with size of family, number of children, and age of the householder. As least 11.5 percent of all families were living below the poverty level in 1991. The number of "persons" in poverty in 1991 constituted 14.2 percent of the United States population.

[b]Hispanics are defined as persons of Puerto Rican, Cuban, Central American, South American, or some other Spanish culture of origin, regardless of race.

It would be unwise to assign a simple, single cause or solution to a problem that exhibits such variation in social, economic, and physical settings. Certainly racial biases and cultural attitudes have created immense barriers for African-Americans, Mexican-Americans, Native Americans, and Appalachian whites in both rural and metropolitan areas. Not only have those biases had a direct effect on employment opportunities, but they have also contributed to unequal education and training.

Other factors, however, have also contributed to poverty. For example, in portions of Appalachia, agriculture has been the basic activity since the area was first settled. Elsewhere, agriculture has evolved into a profitable commercial enterprise, but isolated Appalachian farmers with small farms and poor land have not been able to adjust to modern ways. Like people in other areas, they have slipped into poverty as they failed to modernize—a major problem in any dynamic and changing society.

Another factor that has contributed to **income disparity**, significant differences in income between specified groups or regions, is an imbalance in the supply of and demand for workers with particular qualities and skills—a problem with spatial implications. For instance, in the nineteenth and twentieth centuries large parts of the South had relatively dense rural populations, where agriculture remained labor-intensive and agricultural workers rarely earned more than low or modest incomes. In other parts of the country, urban-industrial growth was rapid, and workers developed skills that provided them with higher incomes. The result is distinct regional variations in income, with greater proportions of the total southern population living in poverty (Figure 7–2).

Regional differences in income often prompt workers to migrate from poorer areas to richer ones. Unfortunately, many such migrants are inadequately prepared to achieve an urban life that is materially rewarding. Few of them can succeed when faced with little money or few skills with which to begin, life in crowded ghettos, and deep social biases.

The changing significance of places, the reduced need for specific kinds of resources, and the decline in particular kinds of economic activities have also contributed to unemployment and poverty. New England has experienced a decline in its once-dominant textile industry. Miners from Pennsylvania to Kentucky have seen their jobs disappear as mines were automated and the demand for coal failed to increase. Farmers in the South have witnessed a declining and changing agricultural scene with major implications for farm laborers, tenants, and owners. And the industrial restructuring currently in progress has left many urban factory workers without jobs because the demand for their particular skills has lessened.

The result of such changes is often pockets of economic problems, if not widespread poverty. Migration may concentrate poor people in cities, but many residual farmers, miners, and unwanted

Figure 7–1
The Watts district of Los Angeles.
Virtually any large American city reveals neighborhoods of extreme poverty.

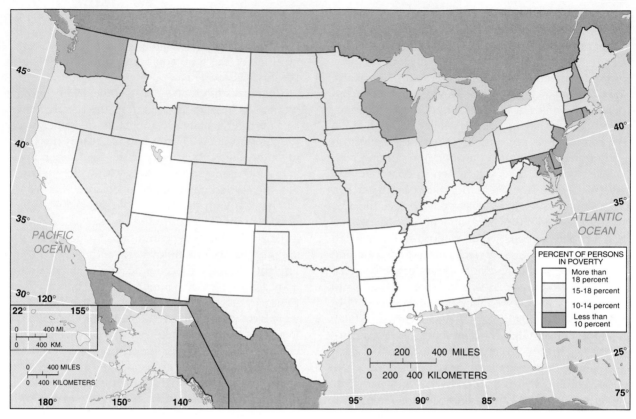

Figure 7–2
Poverty in the United States. The percent of total population in poverty varies
significantly by region and reflects differences in the development process over
many decades.

factory laborers—unable to adjust to a changing society—also exist in poverty. Any solution to poverty must address a wide variety of situations and circumstances.

Appalachia

Appalachia provides an excellent illustration of the problems of poverty and the approaches to solutions. For some people a mention of the region brings to mind beautiful mountain forests, rushing streams, isolated hollows, upper valleys with picturesque farmsteads, hillside orchards, and prosperous farms on valley floors favored with soils formed on limestone bedrock. Other people envision homespun mountain folk with little formal education, living a life of isolation and poverty. Indeed, by the 1960s the Appalachian region was one of several in the United States that lagged far behind the national norm.

The problems of Appalachia arose from its isolation and inability to participate in the modernization and commercialization of agriculture. The prosperity of the coal mining era was short-lived, and more wealth ended up in other regions than in Appalachia itself. After 1940, mining rapidly became automated and concentrated on fewer mines, leaving behind unemployed people and scarred landscapes. In much the same way, lumbering operations removed the wealth and beauty of an area in just a decade or two, severely affecting both the physical and the human ecology of the region. Soil erosion, the scars of strip-mining, flooding worsened by poor agricultural techniques, and the removal of forest vegetation from watersheds were all major problems even before the twentieth century. Appalachia has known poverty, low expectations, violence, and stagnation as a way of life for generations (Figure 7–2).

Appalachia consists of uplands that extend from the maritime provinces of Canada to central Georgia and Alabama, including several distinct physiographic regions (see Chapter 5). The area with the most severe economic and social problems is usually considered to be restricted to the Appalachian Plateau, the Ridge-and-Valley area, and the mountain areas south and west of the Mohawk and Hudson river valleys. But the hard-core problem area does not coincide exactly with the physiographic region. Figure 7–3 shows the **Appalachian corridor**, or problem area, as defined by the Appalachian Regional Commission.

The Appalachian Regional Commission administers the funds allocated under the Appalachian Regional Development Act of 1965, which provided for a concerted effort to eliminate poverty. The greatest emphasis thus far has been on highway development, to lessen isolation. And in truth, one reason that early subsistence farmers in the more remote sections of Appalachia could not adjust to commercial agriculture was their distance from markets. Similarly, although lumber and coal resources were harvested in Appalachia, the profitable markets were elsewhere, and transportation was developed only to the degree necessary to haul the products out of the region. Because outside companies controlled the resources, profits flowed to other regions, not to Appalachia.

Remember the concept of circular causation and growth (see Chapter 4). If advantages can initiate a process of circular causation, disadvantages can do the same, but in reverse. In Appalachia isolation, poverty, low education levels, and limited incentive have fed on one another and have led to further problems. Some believe that improvements in transportation will stop the cycle of poverty by stimulating economic growth; they argue that industry will locate near highways and that Appalachia's potential for recreation and tourism can then be exploited.

Other people view the problem differently. They believe that the interior of Appalachia is disadvantaged by both history and location, and they do not consider transportation development a panacea. Isolated Appalachian communities have only a small, scattered, unskilled or wrongly skilled labor supply and might easily become overindustrialized relative to their labor supply, even if low-wage, labor-intensive industry were involved. People with this view think that the greatest potential for growth

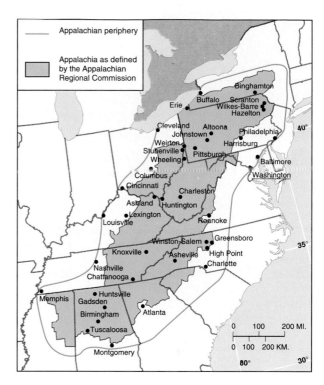

Figure 7–3
Appalachian region of the United States. The Appalachian region has long been an area of economic and social problems. It should be recognized, however, that such a region is not uniform; some portions are areas of growth and economic progress, even as other portions continue to lose population. One of the most persistent and severe problem areas has been the Kentucky and West Virginia portion, where the declining need for coal miners contributed major problems after World War II.

and economic improvement lies in the cities on the edges of the region, where interaction with other cities or population regions is more likely. Most of the urban growth centers in the area are, in fact, peripheral to the Appalachian corridor. The northern edge, in Pennsylvania and New York, is relatively prosperous. So is the peripheral Piedmont, between Virginia and Alabama. Highways may simply help some of the corridor people reach the more advantageous periphery and may not really change conditions within the corridor.

Despite all of the efforts expended on Appalachian development, the region continues to lag behind the national economy: per capita income in Appalachia is about 81 percent of the national level (see the boxed

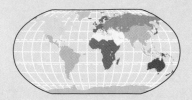

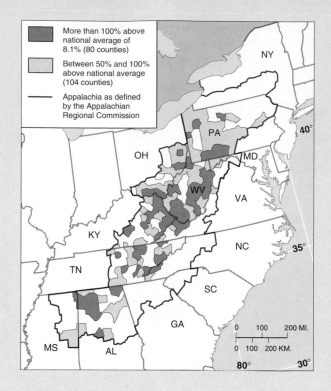

More than 100% above national average of 8.1% (80 counties)

Between 50% and 100% above national average (104 counties)

Appalachia as defined by the Appalachian Regional Commission

APPALACHIAN UNEMPLOYMENT

Measuring the economic well-being of a region is difficult. Per capita income, infant mortality, employment growth, level of urbanization, crime rates, and migration rates are only some of the numerous indicators that can be used to measure regional health. Figure A provides an additional measure: the percentage of the labor force unemployed. Unemployment can fluctuate substantially over short periods of time in response to cyclic economic conditions. It can also be persistent or chronic over long periods as a reflection of changes in the economic system or the inability of a region to participate effectively in a national economy.

Appalachian unemployment rates relative to the national norm are illustrated in Figure B. Rates are not only considerably higher in Appalachia than in many other regions, but are also spatially variable within the region. That variation may be related to the depressed economic condition of the region's coalfields and older industrial communities. But whatever the reason, 82 percent of the Appalachian counties experienced unemployment above the national average in 1983. In Appalachia, as elsewhere, such an employment situation has a major impact on other indicators of well-being.

Figure B
Appalachian areas with most severe unemployment (November 1983). Unemployment rates vary considerably from place to place, depending on short-term economic cycles. Some segments of Appalachia, however, have experienced chronic and persistent high unemployment over many years. (From *Appalachia, Journal of the Appalachian Regional Commission* 18, no. 3, March 1985, p. 82.)

Figure A
Percentage of the U.S. labor force unemployed in 1986. This map highlights some of the areas of persistent unemployment. The use of percentages, however, suppresses the severity of unemployment in selected large urban centers. (Adapted with permission from *Goode's World Atlas* © 1990 by Rand McNally R.L. 90–S–243.)

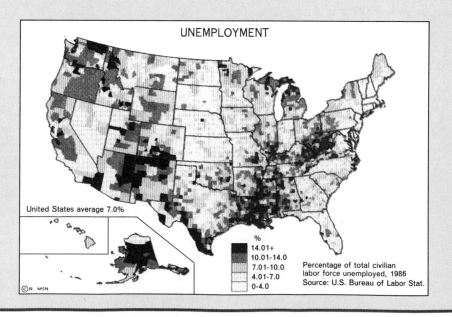

UNEMPLOYMENT

United States average 7.0%

%
14.01+
10.01-14.0
7.01-10.0
4.01-7.0
0-4.0

Percentage of total civilian labor force unemployed, 1986
Source: U.S. Bureau of Labor Stat.

feature, Appalachian Unemployment). Not surprisingly, the effectiveness of this type of regional planning effort is being debated, and some think that agencies like the Appalachian Regional Commission should be abolished.

Nevertheless, by 1980 the commission was able to cite substantial progress in improving conditions in Appalachia. In addition to more than 1,700 miles (2,737 kilometers) of highway improvements, manufacturing had increased, per capita income had risen modestly (though not to national norms), and health care had improved notably. Infant mortality was down from 27.9 deaths per 1,000 births in 1963 (not unlike the rates in some poor countries) to 11.4 in 1982. Out-migration had ceased in some areas, and reverse migration had led to population growth.

Unfortunately, some parts of Appalachia continue to struggle, and conditions may even have worsened as structural changes have occurred in the American economy. With manufacturing no longer a major growth sector, some industries, such as iron and steel, have experienced significant declines in employment. As a result, places such as West Virginia, which were heavily dependent on those industries, have suffered greatly as poverty has increased. As the U.S. economy shifts further away from industry toward services, the interior, or hardcore, segments of Appalachia may find their attempt to become industrialized a very difficult task.

Other Problem Areas

The numerous causes of poverty may operate independently or in concert—more often the latter—and may vary in their individual importance from one region to another. Appalachia is certainly not the only region to have difficulty achieving equality with the remainder of the nation. The Ozarks, the Four Corners (i.e., where Colorado, Utah, New Mexico, and Arizona meet), and parts of the Atlantic Coastal Plain have also experienced economic lag. In addition, the maritime provinces of Canada have long had income levels below the Canadian national norms. Harsh environments and remote locations have handicapped regional development there.

AFRICAN–AMERICANS

It is not unusual for political units to contain a number of subgroups distinguishable by race, ethnic and linguistic differences, or economic achievement. Nonetheless, such divisions can be major obstacles to unified political organization and social and economic satisfaction. The difficulty of integrating such groups into a larger society stems not only from outward cultural differences but also from basic human nature. The relationship between blacks and whites in the United States is an excellent illustration of that problem.

In the United States the initial patterns of black residence and black-white relationships were an outgrowth of the diffusion of the plantation system across the lower South. A small percentage of blacks, possibly one-seventh, were freedmen living outside the South or in southern urban areas, where slightly less rigid social pressures allowed them to be artisans. The rest of the black population formed the backbone of the plantation system.

The southern plantation was a land-based social and economic system, engaged in commercial production using slave labor on relatively large holdings. The original center for that system was Tidewater Virginia and neighboring parts of Maryland and North Carolina. As settlement proceeded southward, slavery accompanied commercial crops, such as rice and indigo, to the coastal cities of Wilmington, North Carolina; Charleston, South Carolina; and Savannah, Georgia. In the hill lands of the South and northward into the Middle Atlantic and New England colonies, slavery never became important and was eventually declared illegal. The emphasis in those areas was usually on less labor-intensive economic activities.

In the areas of the lower South that were considered best for agricultural production, the plantation became the basic system. The diffusion of that system went hand in hand with the diffusion of slave labor and thus established the initial pattern of black residence across the South. Predominantly black populations were found then only in selected areas, including a narrow coastal zone of islands and riverbanks in South Carolina and Georgia, the inner Coastal Plain, the outer Piedmont, the Mississippi Valley (i.e., Missouri, Tennessee, Arkansas, Mississippi, and Louisiana), the Tennessee Valley of northern Alabama, the black-soil belt of Alabama, and—by 1860—portions of Texas. The Nashville and Bluegrass basins also had some plantations and, therefore, some blacks. But the rest of the South—southern Appalachia, including the inner edge of the Piedmont;

the Ozarks; portions of the Gulf Coast; and lower Texas—either had no blacks or had only a few in proportion to the number of white yeoman farmers.

The distribution of blacks did not change immediately after the Civil War. The only thing about the freedmen that changed was that they were no longer slaves. They were still agricultural laborers with no land, no capital, and little training beyond their farming skills. They did not migrate in large numbers after the Civil War but stayed where they were and entered into a system of tenancy with white landowners. With few exceptions the rural parts of today's South with large numbers of African-Americans are the same areas in which the plantation system once flourished.

By 1900 the South had a large, landless tenant labor force of rural blacks. By World War I the great century of European immigration (1814–1914) had ended, and new European immigrants were no longer available as workers. As blacks took their places, opportunities for employment outside the South grew, and blacks moved in large numbers from rural to urban areas. Although this **black migration** slowed somewhat during the 1930s, when economic conditions were as bad in urban areas as they were in rural areas, the northward movement continued into the 1970s. Today, African-Americans live in urban areas of the North as well as urban and rural areas of the South (Figure 7–4). Interestingly, the proportion of blacks living in the South seems to have stabilized and hovers around 53 percent (Table 7–2); more blacks are now moving to the South than are leaving it.

Patterns of migration have implications that go far beyond mere redistribution of population. Many African-Americans have clearly improved their economic and social positions in urban areas (Figure 7–5), but the improvement has been a group achievement not easily won and not without failure for many individuals, as evidenced by the poverty-ridden central-city neighborhoods of many large American cities. Many migrants to the cities have been the better educated and more motivated representatives of rural areas; but, paradoxically, they have also lacked the skills needed to do well in urban areas. Racial and social biases have further added to the difficulty of obtaining suitable housing, proper education, and access to economic opportunity. Thus, many blacks have ended up in ghettos, with an unemployment rate that is consistently higher than it is for other segments of society. The seeming inability of the United States to fully absorb this large segment of its population into the national mainstream remains a major problem.

The residential pattern for urban blacks stems from their economic and social position: highly concentrated black neighborhoods appear in older residential areas, often vacated as economically progressive blacks and whites flee to the city's periphery or to suburban communities. That process has progressed so far that numerous cities have become more black than white. The strength of those

Figure 7–4
African-American population as a percentage of total population in the United States in 1980.
Use caution when interpreting maps based on percentages. Throughout the South, blacks are found in rural areas, as well as in urban centers. The black population in northern communities (approximately one-half of the U.S. black population) is located in the most populous urban areas. Those northern concentrations, therefore, appear underrepresented on the map. (Adapted with permission from *Goode's World Atlas* © 1990 by Rand McNally R.L. 90–S–243.)

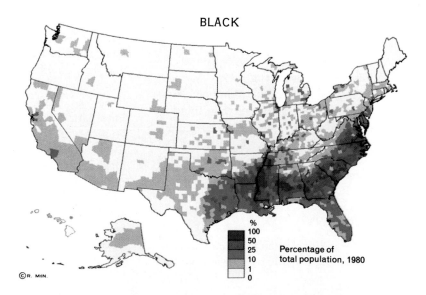

BLACK

%
100
50
25
10
1
0

Percentage of total population, 1980

Table 7-2
African-American population of the conterminous United States.

	Total (millions)	Regional Distribution (%)			
		Northeast	North Central	South	West
1900	8,834	4.4	5.6	89.7	0.3
1910	9,828	4.9	5.5	89.0	0.5
1920	10,463	6.5	7.6	85.2	0.8
1930	11,891	9.6	10.6	78.7	1.0
1940	12,886	10.6	11.0	77.0	1.3
1950	15,042	13.4	14.8	68.0	3.8
1960	18,860	16.1	18.3	60.0	5.7
1970	22,580	19.2	20.2	53.0	7.5
1980	26,505	18.3	20.1	53.0	8.5
1990	29,986	18.7	19.1	52.8	9.4

Sources: U.S. Bureau of the Census, Census of Population (Washington, DC: Government Printing Office, 1910–80); U.S. Bureau of the Census, Current Population Reports, Population Estimates and Projections, *Projections of the Population of States by Age, Sex, and Race: 1988 to 2010.* Series P-25, No. 1017; and Bureau of the Census, *Statistical Abstract of the United States, 1993* (Washington, DC: Government Printing Office, 1993).

Note: Because these figures have been rounded, the totals by year may not equal 100%.

black numbers is evident in the increasing number of black central-city mayors.

The 1954 ruling of the U.S. Supreme Court that official segregation of schools is unconstitutional is a landmark in black-white American history. But the process that led to a new social and economic position for African-Americans began long before 1954. An important part of that process was the demise of the southern agrarian system as it was structured during the nineteenth and early twentieth centuries. In its place was evolving an urban, industrial, and economically stronger South, complete with a rising black consciousness. Fortunately, urbanization has brought economic and educational gains and opportunities for many blacks. Their new status, hopes, and demands for participation in mainstream society could only have come with a break from the old system; and migration, whether to northern or southern cities, was symptomatic of that break.

HISPANIC-AMERICANS

Hispanics, persons in the United States from a Spanish culture, are the second largest minority in the United States; in 1990 they numbered about 22.3 million, whereas blacks numbered about 30 million

Figure 7-5
A Hispanic and several black police officers on patrol in Miami. Many members of minorities, especially black Americans, have migrated to urban centers during the past half century. Economic success has often been elusive, but opportunities for young professionals have created a significant black middle class.

(Table 7–3). The proportion of the U.S. population considered Hispanic increased from 4.5 percent in 1970 to 6.5 percent in 1980 and 9.0 percent in 1990. The absolute number of Hispanics increased by 36 percent between 1980 and 1988, with more than half of the increase due to immigration. The Hispanic population is expected to reach 30 million by 2010.

The majority (more than 60 percent) of the Hispanic population resides in the southwestern United States (Figure 7–6). Texas is 24 percent Hispanic; New Mexico, 35 percent; Arizona, 18 percent; and California, 23 percent. People with Spanish surnames almost completely dominate many smaller communities and even some sizable cities. In Texas, Corpus Christi is 49 percent Hispanic; San Antonio, 45 percent; and Brownsville, 77 percent.

The initial Hispanic infusion into what is now the southwestern United States resulted from the region's inclusion in the expanding Spanish Empire in the late sixteenth and seventeenth centuries. The general area in which this cultural infusion took place has become known as the **Hispanic-American borderland** (Figure 7–7). Thinly scattered Spanish settlements eventually extended from Texas to California, but the Spanish were unable to prevent a flood of Anglo-American settlement in the nineteenth century. The initial growth of those settlements diminished the proportion of the population that was Hispanic, but it did not erase the long-established cultural imprints. In the twentieth century,

legal immigration from neighboring Mexico has been considerable, and illegal immigration has been especially great since 1950. This migration rate, combined with a higher-than-the-national-average fertility rate among Hispanics, is contributing to a renewed increase in Hispanic influence in the borderland.

Several large metropolitan areas outside the Southwest borderland also have significant Hispanic populations (Figure 7–8). In New York and Chicago (13.8 percent and 10 percent Hispanic, respectively), those populations are largely of Puerto Rican descent, reflecting a major wave of migration to the mainland in the post-World War II years. During the 1970s and 1980s, however, people of Mexican descent have become the major source of Hispanic growth in many cities. In southern Florida the large Hispanic minority is Cuban, a result of the widespread migration of the middle class after the Cuban Revolution. Miami, for example, is 28 percent Hispanic.

Although significant numbers of Hispanics work as agricultural laborers, most are urban residents. Whether rural or urban, the Hispanics experience problems similar to those of African-Americans: low levels of income and education, limited economic opportunities, and substandard and crowded housing.

The Hispanic-American culture region is also the area that is occupied by almost half of the 1.9 million Native American Indians in the United States (Figure 7–9). Although the Indians of the Southwest

Table 7–3
Population by region, race, and Hispanic origin, 1990.

	Population (thousands)	Distribution by Region (%)			
		Northeast	Midwest	South	West
Total U.S.	248,710	20.4	24.0	34.4	21.2
White	199,686	21.1	26.0	32.8	20.0
Black	29,986	18.7	19.1	52.8	9.4
American Indian[a]	1,959	6.4	17.2	28.7	47.6
Asian or Pacific Islander	7,274	18.4	10.6	15.4	55.7
Other Races	9,805	17.0	8.5	24.0	50.6
Hispanic Origin[b]	22,354	16.8	7.7	30.3	45.2

Source: Bureau of the Census, *Statistical Abstract of the United States, 1993* (Washington, DC: Government Printing Office, 1993).

[a]American Indian, Eskimo, or Aleut.

[b]Persons of Hispanic origin may be of any race.

Figure 7-6
Hispanic population as a percentage of total population in the United States in 1980. The distribution of Hispanics exhibits two distinctive patterns. The concentration in the Southwest results from a long tradition of Spanish and Mexican influence. Concentrations in urban centers of the eastern United States result from post–World War II migrations of Puerto Ricans, Cubans, and Mexicans. (Adapted with permission from *Goode's World Atlas* © 1990 by Rand McNally R.L. 90–S–243.)

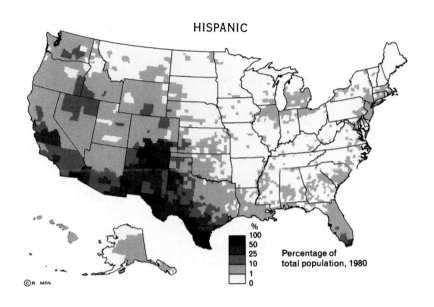

HISPANIC

%
100
50
25
10
1
0

Percentage of total population, 1980

©R. MEN.

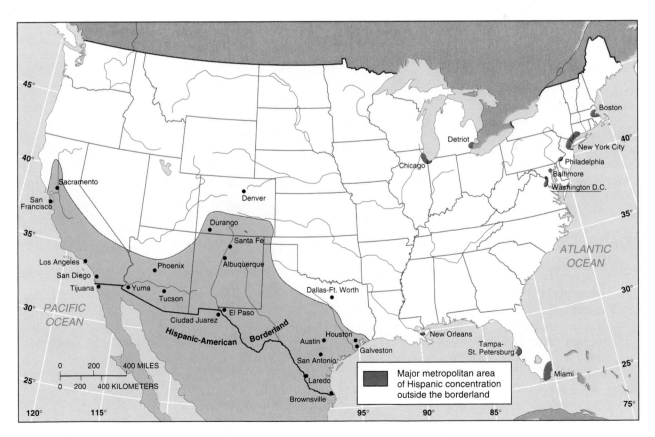

Figure 7-7
The Hispanic-American borderland. The region designated as the Hispanic-American borderland is an area where Hispanic influence is strong, as reflected in ethnicity, language, and many other dimensions of culture.

Figure 7-8
A Cuban-American street scene in the Little Havana area of Miami. Hispanic people have formed significant communities in many large American cities.

Figure 7-9
Native American Indian population as a percentage of total U.S. population in 1980. The distribution of the American Indian population is most strongly associated with the American West. (Adapted with permission from *Goode's World Atlas* © 1990 by Rand McNally R.L. 90–S–243.)

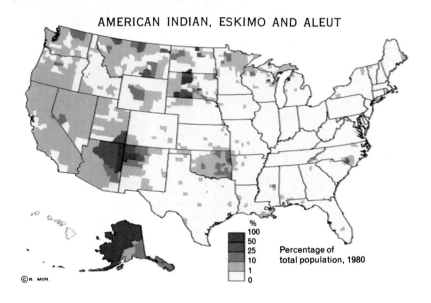

have maintained their tribal structure better than other Native Americans have, they, in particular, endure greater socioeconomic disparities than any other minority does (Figure 7–10).

Another rapidly growing segment of the United States includes various Asian peoples, whose numbers have greatly increased during the 1970s and 1980s in response to immigration (Figure 7–11). Growth has been particularly noteworthy in urban centers of the west. Obviously, the United States must effectively integrate those various groups into the economic mainstream or become an increasingly pluralistic society. Although Table 7–3 and Figures 4,

6, 9, and 11 reveal that the Asian peoples and other minorities are found throughout the United States, their spatial distribution is distinctive in each instance. The diversity associated with the total population is not similar in proportion by region.

CANADIAN IDENTITY AND UNITY

French Canada

Canada, too, is a pluralistic society. Consequently, national identity and unity are a major concern of Canadian political and community leaders. In fact,

Figure 7-10
A Pueblo Indian village near Taos, New Mexico. Despite a long heritage in North America, many American Indians continue to experience great socioeconomic disparity.

Canada was organized as a federation more than 100 years ago because the descendants of French settlers insisted that any system of union preserve the French identity and influence. A confederation of colonies was thus promoted with already-distinctive cultural differences—**French Canada** and **English Canada**.

The French settled first in the lower St. Lawrence Valley and later in Acadia, the area around the Bay of Fundy; but great numbers of French settlers did not follow those first settlers. And even though France held vast territories in Canada as fur-extracting areas, few French communities were established in the larger region. By 1763 the British had reduced French sovereignty in North America to such a point that French culture was retained only in the lower St. Lawrence Valley, where the British allowed French agriculturists to remain.

As the neighboring thirteen colonies came closer to revolution, many loyalists from the New England and Middle Atlantic colonies moved north to Canada. In fact, so many loyalists went to Nova Scotia and Newfoundland that a new colony, New

Brunswick, was created. Other loyalists settled inland, in Ontario. That rapid spread of people of British descent further weakened the position of the French, except along the lower St. Lawrence, where they remained firmly established.

Even to the present, French Canadians have maintained their identity and are intent on continuing to do so. Their distinctiveness is not only linguistic—although that, in itself, is enough to promote a separate cultural identity—but also religious. French Canadians are Roman Catholic, in contrast to the largely Protestant English Canadians. In other respects, however, the French of Canada have been stereotyped to a misleading degree, even by other Canadians. It is a misconception to characterize them as quaint, rural, agrarian, unchanging people with high birthrates. In truth, the province of Quebec, which is about 82 percent French, is 75 percent urban, part of industrial Canada, second only to Ontario in income, and clearly integrated into the nation's economic core. Quebec was once more agrarian and did have high population growth

Figure 7-11
Asian-American population as a percentage of total U.S. population in 1980. Asian peoples represent a rapidly increasing population segment in the Pacific Coast states. (Adapted with permission from *Goode's World Atlas* © 1990 by Rand McNally R.L. 90–S–243.)

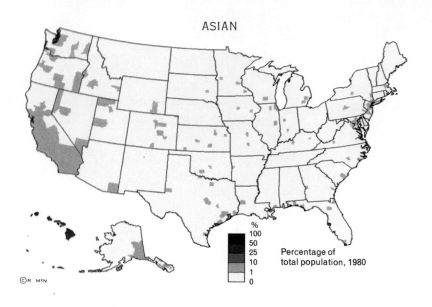

ASIAN

%
100
50
25
10
1
0

Percentage of total population, 1980

rates, which engendered some fear that French culture would overwhelm English culture. With modernization and an urban life-style, however, birthrates in Quebec have fallen below the national average. Some 70 percent of all French Canadians now live in urban areas, but their occupational structure has yet to match that of English Canadians. Even though French Canadians have a social hierarchy and political power, occupationally they remain overrepresented in the primary sector and in unskilled jobs.

Because both French and English are official languages, Canada must forge a national unit in a bilingual framework—no easy task. In addition, significant numbers of Poles, Dutch, Germans, and Italians have arrived during the twentieth century, sometimes to the consternation of the French, who often oppose immigration because it diminishes their numerical strength. Moreover, slightly more than 700,000 Canadians (3 percent) are at least partially of American Indian, Metis, or Inuit origin. The officially recognized or "status" Indians include 466,337 people with membership in nearly 600 bands (Figure 7–12). Nearly 60 percent live in rural Canada on reserves. And during the 1980s rather large numbers of Asians have also become part of the migration stream (see the boxed feature, Canadian Unity).

Canada and the United States

Canadian identity is further affected by Canada's proximity to the United States. Canada is one of the largest countries in the world, but all its vast area

contains only about 28 million people. It is rich in forest, water, and mineral resources, but its value for agricultural production is modest because so much of its environment is harsh. In light of Canada's available resources and its proximity to the industrialized United States, it is not surprising that major economic linkages have evolved between the two countries. Indeed, Canada and the United States have become the most important trading partners for each other, focusing much of that relationship on the removal and processing of Canada's special material resources. In addition, a high proportion—almost 40 percent—of Canadian industries are controlled by U.S. parent firms.

As mentioned earlier, Canada's fear of a colonial relationship generated its long-standing tariff policy. Paradoxically, the success of that policy has prompted concern over foreign influence and control, which has spurred efforts to "Canadianize" the economy, that is, to increase Canadian investment levels in Canada's economic activity. Nevertheless, Canadian control of some industries has continued to decrease. Economic prosperity in Canada remains significantly tied to prosperity in the United States, thereby contributing to the problem of Canadian identity. Political efforts to redirect trade relationships toward other areas might run counter to the normal economic relationships expected between two well-endowed neighboring countries. The North American Free Trade Agreement embodies recognition of the advantages that accrue from such proximity.

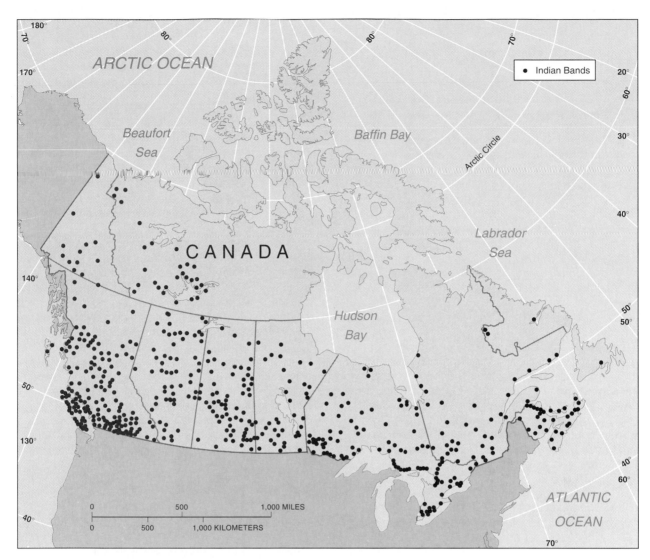

Figure 7-12
Indian bands in Canada. There are 598 Indian bands in Canada located on nearly
2,300 reserves and Crown lands. The more than 466,000 Indians who are accorded
"status" now account for 1.7 percent of the population, but are expected to increase
to 2.2 percent by the year 2000. A lower death rate, a high birthrate, and recent
amendments to the Indian Act account for a rapid increase in "status" Indians.

SUMMARY
Canada and the United States
in Retrospect

Both Canada and the United States are large and
have immense resources. Each has achieved a
high level of living for the majority of its populace and a powerful position in the world, and
each will certainly attempt to maintain that level
and position.

Out of the Anglo-American development experience has come a technology that can be of
great benefit to the remainder of the world. But
the resources of underdeveloped areas have fre-

CANADIAN UNITY

The achievement of Canadian unity seems increasingly difficult. Indeed, political separation and even violence have sometimes been promoted by extreme French nationalists. In 1980 a referendum in Quebec was supported by the Parti Quebecois to determine whether the provincial government should move toward separation from the remainder of Canada. The referendum failed, but 42 percent of all voters did vote in the affirmative, as did 52 percent of the French in Quebec. Thereafter, the notion of an independent Quebec seemed to diminish for a few years. More recent polls and events, however, suggest that a clear majority of Quebec's French still favor some form of separation.

In 1982 Canada attempted to strengthen its union by revising its constitution to include a bill of rights. The then-separatist government of Quebec refused to sign the new document, ostensibly because it would not permit Quebec to extend its cultural identity as a distinct society within the framework of a larger Canada. A later conference, held in 1987 at Meech Lake in Quebec, considered new proposals designed to overcome Quebec's objections. The results were a document referred to as the Meech Lake Accord, to be ratified by the ten provinces by June 23, 1990. Manitoba and Newfoundland ultimately refused to ratify, arguing that the accord gave Quebec freedom in language and culture that the other provinces did not have. That impasse left Canada facing the possibility of political disintegration. Quebec has demanded a national constitution which would grant even greater provincial autonomy. Some believe that disintegration will never occur; nevertheless, it is a recurring topic in national politics.

Obvious cultural differences would appear to underlie the debate between French and English Canadians. But even English Canada is not ethnically uniform. The maritime provinces are a unique mixture of French, German, English, Scotch, and Irish. In addition, more than 700,000 Canadians are at least partially of aboriginal origin—largely North American Indian, Metis, or Inuit. The natives are in the majority in the Northwest Territories and are significantly represented in the prairie provinces. Indeed, it was the special privileges granted to Quebec in the Meech Lake Accord but not to the aboriginal population of Manitoba that led Manitoba to oppose ratification.

The considerable economic diversity that permeates Canada also contributes to a sense of fragmentation. The maritime provinces present yet another example of North American regional disparity; they are poorer provinces dependent on fishing, farming, and mining (all primary activities), as well as subsidies from the central government. Quebec is an industrial province; but several of its major industries are owned by the government, and those privately owned are labor intensive, unionized, and unlikely to experience much growth. Ontario represents the Canadian heartland, with its strong commercial and industrial base. The prairie provinces are producers of wheat and cattle. However, the discovery of oil has produced a boom for Alberta, while Manitoba and Saskatchewan remain economically depressed. British Columbia is a western growth center known for its lumbering and trade, but it is far removed from much of the remainder of Canada in both distance and spirit.

Thus, Canada is a large and disparate country. Even its geography works against unity and cohesion. And when resources and development are added to the picture, the various regions seem even more distinct (Figure A). Indeed, achieving a greater sense of Canadian unity remains a monumental task.

---

quently been used to promote the welfare and economic expansion of the United States and Canada. As other countries develop and consume more of their own material resources, one important issue will be to determine how much the United States and Canada can—or should—gather from them.

The processes of immigration and settlement have affected the two neighbors differently. The larger population of the United States has aided in the accumulation of greater wealth through the processing and use of the nation's resources. The United States, however, is now consuming on such a scale that the cost and availability of basic goods may well encourage or require the limitation of growth, or even stabilization. On the other hand, the economic sluggishness of the Anglo-American economies during the early 1980s and again in the early 1990s and the problems of economically dying communities suggest that limiting growth may be difficult or unwise. For less populous Canada greater economic independence and

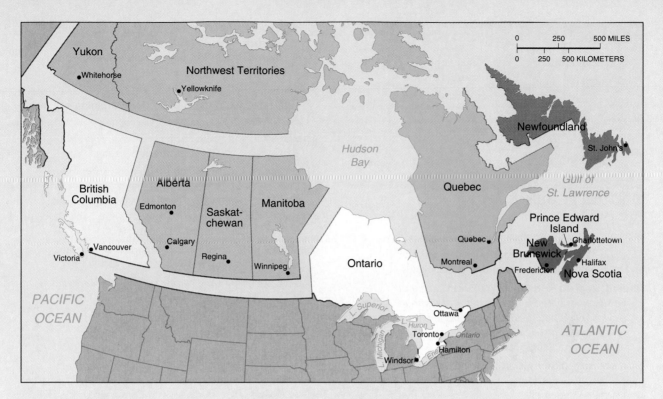

Figure A
The several Canadas. The attention given Quebec and its relationship to the remainder of Canada sometimes obscures the fact that numerous differences exist among the several regions of the vast Canadian territory.

internal industrial growth may require domestic population growth and expansion. The value of population growth for developing and using resources is even now reflected in Canadian immigration policies.

The internal problems of both countries include the need to integrate minority groups into the larger society. As the United States and Canada progressed, entire regions, as well as minority groups, lagged in the acquisition of wealth and position within the system. Effective means are now needed to incorporate the pockets of poverty and isolation into the larger economy.

American society will have to make other adjustments, too. North Americans are becoming even more urban, though the form of urban areas may differ from that of the past. The large urban formations—the megalopolitan regions discussed in Chapter 6—may require new approaches to government and planning. Certainly such highly integrated urban systems will necessitate a regional framework that extends far beyond the traditional political city.

KEY TERMS

Appalachian corridor

black migration

English Canada

French Canada

Hispanic

Hispanic-American
borderland

income disparity

poverty

FURTHER READINGS
Part Two

Annals, Association of American Geographers 62 (1972):155–374. A special issue devoted entirely to the regional geography of the United States.

Birdsall, Stephen S., and John W. Florin. *Regional Landscapes of the United States and Canada.* 4th ed. New York: Wiley, 1992. A basic regional textbook covering the physical, economic, and social aspects of the United States and Canada.

Blackbourne, Anthony, and Robert G. Putnam. *The Industrial Geography of Canada.* New York: St. Martin's Press, 1984.

Borchert, John R. "American Metropolitan Evolution." *Geographical Review* 57 (1967): 301–332. A classic work describing American metropolitan evolution in the context of changing transport technology.

Boswell, Thomas D., and Timothy C. Jones. "A Regionalization of Mexican Americans in the United States." *Geographical Review* 78 (1980): 88–98. A study defining the regions and the character of regions of Mexican-American inhabitance.

Brunn, Stanley D., and James O. Wheeler, eds. *The American Metropolitan System: Present and Future.* New York: Halsted Press, 1980. A collection of writings on the contemporary metropolitan system.

Bureau of the Census. *Statistical Abstract of the United States.* Washington, DC: Government Printing Office. A very useful annual publication with an enormous array of social, demographic, and economic data.

Bureau of Mines. *Mineral Facts and Problems.* Washington, DC: Government Printing Office. An annual publication with information on the resource position of Anglo-America.

Canada Yearbook. Ottawa: Dominion Bureau of Statistics. An annual publication of statistics with narratives on Canada's resources, history, institutions, and social and economic conditions.

Clark, David. *Post-Industrial America: A Geographical Perspective.* New York: Methuen, 1985. Describes the economic system evolving with the shift to a service economy.

Economic Geography 48 (1972): 1–134. A special issue entitled "Contributions to an Understanding of Black America."

Ehrlich, Paul, and Anne Ehrlich, eds. *The Population Explosion.* New York: Simon & Schuster, 1990.

Fisher, James S., and Ronald L. Mitchelson. "Forces of Change in the American Settlement Pattern." *Geographical Review* 71 (1981): 298–310. A discussion of the varied forces contributing to shifts in population and American settlement.

Fley, William H. "Metropolitan America: Beyond the Transition." *Population Bulletin* 45, no. 2 (1990).

Garreau, Joel. *The Nine Nations of North America.* Boston: Houghton Mifflin, 1981. A popular description of nine identifiable regions in North America, based on economic and social considerations.

Gober, Patricia. "Americans on the Move." *Population Bulletin* 48, no. 3 (1990).

Gottman, Jean. *Megalopolis: The Urbanized Northeastern Seaboard of the United States.* Cambridge, MA: MIT Press, 1961. A classic description of America's first megalopolitan region.

Gregor, Howard F. "The Large Industrialized American Crop Farm: A Mid-Latitude Plantation Variant." *Geographical Review* 60 (1970): 151–175.

Hart, John Fraser. *The Look of the Land.* Englewood Cliffs, NJ: Prentice-Hall, 1975. A good synthesis of the origins and character of the American landscape.

———. "Loss and Abandonment of Cleared Farmland in the Eastern United States." *Annals, Association of American Geographers* 58 (1968): 417–440.

Historical Atlas of Canada. Vol. I, *From the Beginning to 1800,* edited by R. Cole Harris. Vol. II, *The Land Transformed, 1800-1891,* edited by R. Louis Gentilcore. Vol. III, *Addressing the Twentieth Century,* edited by Donald Kerr and Deryck Holdsworth. Toronto: The University of Toronto Press, 1987, 1990, 1993. A scholarly three-volume work detailing the Canadian experience from initial settling to the contemporary.

Janelle, Donald G., ed. *Geographical Snapshots of North America.* New York: Guilford, 1992. Numerous short pieces on the physical, cultural, and economic geography of Anglo-America.

Kaplan, David H. "Population and Politics in a Plural Society: The Changing Geography of Canada's Linguistic Groups." *Annals of the Association of American Geographers* 84 (March 1994).

Lloyd, William J. "Understanding Late Nineteenth-Century American Cities." *Geographical Review* 71 (1981): 460–471.

Malcolm, Andrew H. *The Canadians.* New York: Time Books, 1985.

McHugh, Kevin E. "Black Migration Reversal in the United States." *Geographical Review* 77 (1987): 171–182. Details the reversal in black migratory streams during the 1970s and 1980s.

Meinig, Donald W. *The Shaping of America: A Geographical Perspective on 500 Years of History.* Vol. 1, *Atlantic America, 1492–1800.* New Haven: Yale University Press, 1986.

Mitchell, Robert D., and Paul A. Groves, eds. *North America: The Historical Geography of a Changing Continent.* Savage, MD: Rowman & Littlefield, 1987. A collection of papers on the historical aspect of North American development.

Morrill, Richard L., and Ernest H. Wolenberg. *The Geography of Poverty in the United States.* New York: McGraw-Hill, 1971.

Norton, William. *Explorations in the Understanding of Landscape: A Cultural Geography,* Westport, CT: Greenwood Press, 1989.

Nostrand, Richard L. "The Hispanic-American Borderland: Delimitation of an American Culture Region." *Annals, Association of American Geographers* 60 (1970): 638–661.

Noyelle, Thierry J., and Thomas M. Stanbeck. *The Economic Transformation of American Cities.* Totowa, NJ: Rowman & Allanheld, 1984. Treats the impact of the North American economic transformation on cities.

O'Hare, William P. "America's Minorities—The Demographics of Density." *Population Bulletin* 47, no. 4 (1992).

O'Hare, William P., Kelvin M. Pollard, Taynia L. Mann, and Mary M. Kent. "African Americans in the 1990s." Population Bulletin 46, no. 1 (1991).

Paterson, J. H. *North America: A Geography of Canada and the United States.* 8th ed. New York: Oxford University Press, 1989. A standard textbook on Canada and the United States, organized with a topical and regional framework.

Phillips, Phillip D., and Stanley D. Brunn. "Slow Growth: A New Epoch of American Metropolitan Evolution." *Geographical Review* 68 (1978): 274–292. A discussion of the likely impact of slow population growth on metropolitan evolution; a good companion piece to the Borchert article cited earlier.

Pred, Allan. "Industrialization, Initial Advantages, and American Metropolitan Growth." *Geographical Review* 55 (1965): 158–185. A good discussion of the basis for the location of early American urban-industrial centers.

Raitz, Karl B., et al. *Appalachia: A Regional Geography.* Boulder, CO: Westview Press, 1984.

Robinson, J. Lewis. *Concepts and Themes in the Regional Geography of Canada.* Vancouver: Talon Books, 1989. A geographic description of the six major regions of Canada.

Smith, Everett G., Jr. "America's Richest Farms and Ranches." *Annals, Association of American Geographers* 70 (1980): 528–541.

Smith, Neil, and Dennis Ward. "The Restructuring of Geographical Scale: Coalescence and Fragmentation of the Northern Core Region." *Economic Geography* 63 (1987): 160–182. An analysis of contemporary region shifts in manufacturing.

Turner, B. L., Robert W. Kates, and William C. Clark. *The Earth as Transformed by Human Action.* Cambridge, England: Cambridge University Press, 1990. A global view of the environmental modifications that have occurred over the past 300 years.

White, C. Langdon, Edwin J. Foscue, and Tom L. McKnight. *Regional Geography of Anglo-America.* 8th ed. Englewood Cliffs, NJ: Prentice-Hall, 1989. A standard textbook organized according to a regional framework.

Zelinsky, Wilbur. *The Cultural Geography of the United States.* Englewood Cliffs, NJ: Prentice-Hall, 1973. A short but excellent treatment.

———. "North America's Vernacular Regions." *Annals, Association of American Geographers* 70 (1980): 1–17

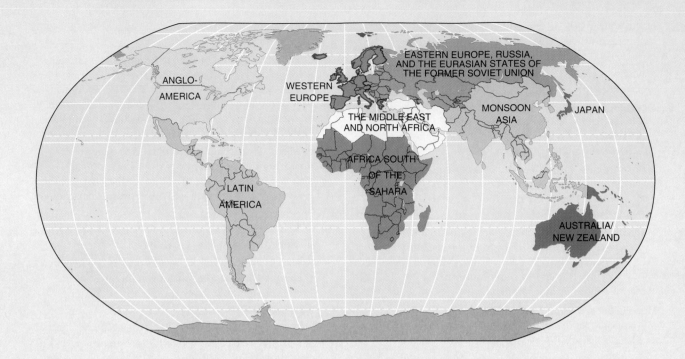

ANGLO-AMERICA

WESTERN EUROPE

EASTERN EUROPE, RUSSIA, AND THE EURASIAN STATES OF THE FORMER SOVIET UNION

MONSOON ASIA

JAPAN

THE MIDDLE EAST AND NORTH AFRICA

AFRICA SOUTH OF THE SAHARA

LATIN AMERICA

AUSTRALIA/ NEW ZEALAND

One thing that never fails to impress North American visitors to Europe is the way in which European life and landscapes incorporate elements of the past into the patterns of the present. Standing near the ancient Tower of London, built by William the Conqueror, the visitor can see ultramodern hydrofoils skimming along the Thames River, carrying commuters to their high-tech jobs in a world center of financial decision making. A few steps farther on, a colorful London tabloid newspaper (boasting the world's largest daily circulation) can be purchased at a newsstand built against the ruins of a Roman temple that dates back to the time of the Caesars. In the countryside the visitor can drive a luxuriously appointed, computer-monitored European "road machine" along roads that have been altered little since Roman engineers laid them out. Traces of relict fields established by Iron Age Celtic farmers lie next to modern, highly mechanized farms that are veritable food factories. Everywhere in Western Europe the landscape bears eloquent testimony that the present is but the past flowing into the future.

North Americans can learn much from the Western European heirs to such a long and rich heritage of cultural and economic development. Some observers suggest that the forces of modern economic development may be leading toward a world culture pattern that strongly resembles Western Europe's urban-industrialized culture, which began to take form two centuries ago. Right or wrong, that is a challenging notion.

Throughout a long cultural evolution, the peoples of Western Europe have created rich and varied landscapes. On one level those landscapes provide the fascinating visual panoramas that captivate visitors from other continents and countries. On another level those landscapes can be studied as metaphorical documents, for they reveal many things about the people who shaped them and gave them their distinctive character. How have Western Europeans utilized the unique physical attributes of their homelands? Those attributes are outlined and discussed in Chapter 8; the crucial question of how they have been utilized is addressed in Chapter 9. The facets of the European experience that are discussed here will help us understand the geographical consequences of development in our own country as well as the rest of the world.

In Chapter 10 we review the many individual countries and national economies that make up Western Europe today. It should quickly become clear that modern Western Europe is involved in an unprecedented economic, geographical, and political

PART 3

Louis De Vorsey, Jr.

WESTERN EUROPE

integration—an integration of historic political entities that promises to have a profound impact on people throughout the world. Western European affairs are the concern of all, particularly the people of North America and the rest of the developed world. Without the example of a successfully integrating Western Europe it is doubtful that the North American Free Trade Agreement would have been approved by Mexico, Canada, and the United States in 1993.

8

Western Europe: A Varied Home for Humanity

Western Europe:
Center of the Land Hemisphere

Maritime Orientation

The Continental Architecture
of Western Europe

The Climates of Western Europe

A night view of London with the Thames River and Westminster Bridge in the foreground. At the far end of the bridge is Big Ben; to the left are the Houses of Parliament, with Westminster Abbey located behind them. The contrast of modern and historic architecture is sharp. London serves as the seat of the world's oldest parliamentary government and the urban focal point of England's national culture. Urbanization is as pervasive in much of Western Europe as it is in North America.

Western Europe is home to over 390 million of the world's most productive and prosperous people (Figure 8–1). The many political units they inhabit cover an area much smaller than either the United States or Canada: only 3 percent of the earth's total land surface is occupied by Western Europe. In addition, many of the most populous and advanced countries of Western Europe are at the same latitude as the thinly populated northern portion of Canada. How have so many people managed to create such productive and comfortable life-styles in a relatively small and northerly region? The answer is not simple. But because of their high state of development, Western Europeans often appear closer to being the masters of their physical environment than do the people of any of the world's other major regions (see the boxed feature, The Eighth Wonder of the World).

WESTERN EUROPE: CENTER OF THE LAND HEMISPHERE

By moving far into space, astronauts and cosmonauts have been able to gain a unique view of our planet; they have seen and photographed it, one hemisphere at a time. If a photograph were taken from space directly above Germany—the *X* on the map of the world in Figure 8–2—it would reveal the most important hemisphere of all, the **Land Hemisphere**. This half of the earth's surface contains about 90 percent of the inhabited land area and about 94 percent of the total population and economic production of the world.

As a result of that central location in the Land Hemisphere, Western Europeans enjoy relatively easy contact with almost the entire habitable world and its resources. Their advantageous location began to have significance in the fifteenth century, when Europeans mastered the art and technology of distant oceanic navigation and when world sea-lanes to the New World, Africa, India, and East Asia began to function as circulation routes for people, materials, products, and ideas. Thus, the colonial empires of many Western European nations were partly a reflection of Europe's centrality and early technological prowess. Later, the advent of railroad technology opened up the vast continental interiors and enlarged the world network that focused on Western Europe.

Long-range aviation and high-speed oceanic commerce have further emphasized the tremendous significance of the centrality of Western Europe. And Western Europeans have consistently been in the forefront of commercial aviation. Count Ferdinand von Zeppelin of Germany organized the world's first commercial airline in 1910 with his famous airships, or zeppelins, as the lighter-than-air craft were known. By 1919 the first regular international air-mail service had been established between London and Paris. And in 1952 British Overseas Airways began the first regularly scheduled jet airliner service. Thus, it is not surprising that the British and French combined to develop the world's first supersonic commercial airliner, the sleek Concorde.

In addition, as the Arctic Ocean basin becomes increasingly important in world **geopolitics**—politics as rationalized by geography, economics, and ethnicity—the northeast and northwest passage sea routes are certain to be used more and more for world shipping. Those historic arctic sea-lanes to the north of Eurasia and North America represent significant shortcuts between Western Europe and the markets of Japan, China, and the west coast of North America. Soviet, U.S., and Canadian icebreakers are all able to reach the North Pole during the summer. Thus, it seems safe to predict that the centrality of Western Europe will become even more important as transportation technologies such as submersible oil tankers and cargo-carrying lighter-than-air craft are perfected in the years ahead.

MARITIME ORIENTATION

Western Europe, viewed from a continental perspective, forms a ragged Atlantic fringe on the vast Eurasian landmass. Its sheltered coasts and many harbors provided an almost perfect setting for the development of maritime economies as the Europeans extended their world trade and political linkages during the past five centuries. Because of its irregular and fragmented outline, Western Europe has a higher ratio of coastline to total land area than any of the world's other major regions has.

Only a small handful of the countries in Western Europe lack direct ocean access, and no part of Western Europe is far from the sea and its challenges. Seas, gulfs, and bays—including the Norwegian, North, Baltic, Mediterranean, Adriatic,

Figure 8-1
Countries and principal cities of Western Europe. Western Europe comprises many countries. Most are small in area, but some have large populations. The home of Western culture and the Industrial Revolution, this region plays a major role in world affairs.

THE EIGHTH WONDER OF THE WORLD

In the widely read text *A Geography of Europe*, Jean Gottmann writes, "Sweat has flowed freely to bring European landscapes to their present shape." In that single sentence Gottmann captures much of the essence of a major theme in the human geography of this important region of the world. For centuries the task of mastering Europe's natural environment was arduous and depended largely on human and animal muscle power. Peasants spent long hours plowing and fertilizing sterile soils to make them productive. Along the coastal fringes of the North Sea, countless generations struggled to drain land and keep it dry enough for cultivation. The vast oak forests that once covered much of the northern half of Europe presented yet another challenge. Hardy axmen gradually turned small clearings into open fields for the mixed farming system that eventually came to dominate this region.

The work of mastering the powerful environmental forces of Western Europe continues even today, with increasingly larger projects and increasingly more sophisticated techniques and equipment. An excellent example is found on the Thames River, which flows through London. A little downstream from the city the Thames Barrier, the world's largest movable flood barrier, is now operating to ensure that a catastrophic tidal surge—a huge surge of water forced upstream by the tide—will not flood the streets and subways of the heart of London. A brochure distributed at the well-equipped visitors' center next to the barrier proclaims it the eighth wonder of the world.

Indeed, London has been subject to tidal flooding for much of its long history. The *Anglo-Saxon Chronicle* contains an entry for 1089 describing a surge tide: "On the festival of St. Martin the sea flood sprung up to such a height and did so much harm as no man remembered that it ever did before." In 1236 an observer reported that "men did row with wherries in the midst of Whitehall's great palace." And over the centuries flood levels have risen; data from the eighteenth century onward indicate that flood depths have increased at the rate of about 2 feet (0.61 meters) per century.

The risk of floods has also increased (1) because the level of the sea is rising gradually all over the world, (2) because the continental plate on which England lies is tilting toward the southeast, and (3) because London is slowly sinking as the great weight of its buildings compresses and compacts the underlying clay soils. If a storm surge should coincide with a high tide, the risk of flooding is even greater, and this continuing threat cannot be predicted. To make matters worse, when the Thames estuary was dredged so that larger ships could enter it, the channel was unintentionally streamlined, and the upstream rush of the tidewaters was accelerated.

In 1953 a North Sea tidal surge caused by heavy storm winds created havoc in the Netherlands and also inundated much of the east coast of England. More than 300 Britons drowned, 100 of them along the lower reaches of the Thames. In the 1970s and early 1980s warning posters on London's subway platforms told people what to do during a flood alert and mapped those parts of the city that were in danger of flooding. The direct costs of such a flood, were it to occur in modern London, might well top $7 billion.

Officially put into operation in 1986, the barrier took more than a decade to construct. Planning even required the creation of an exact scale model of the Thames's 60-mile (97-kilometer) course from its estuary to the tidal limit upstream from London. The barrier consists of enormous movable steel gates set between concrete piers that house the machinery to raise and lower the gates. When the barrier is not in use, the floodgates lie in submerged precast concrete sills set in the bed of the river. The normal ebb and flow of the tide are not affected, and ships can pass right over the gates and between the piers. But if a tidal surge appears likely, the floodgates can be raised to form a temporary dam, or barrier, higher than the 1953 high-tide level. Thus, a safe and secure London, threatened by catastrophic floods just a few years ago, now boasts the eighth wonder of the world.

Ligurian, and Aegean seas, the Gulf of Bothnia, and the Bay of Biscay—provide Western Europeans with matchless opportunities for ocean-borne contacts and trade. No wonder flags of the Western European nations are commonplace in ports the world over.

THE CONTINENTAL ARCHITECTURE OF WESTERN EUROPE

The region's **continental architecture**—the arrangement of the many landforms, such as plains, uplands, and mountains—provides the physical framework, or

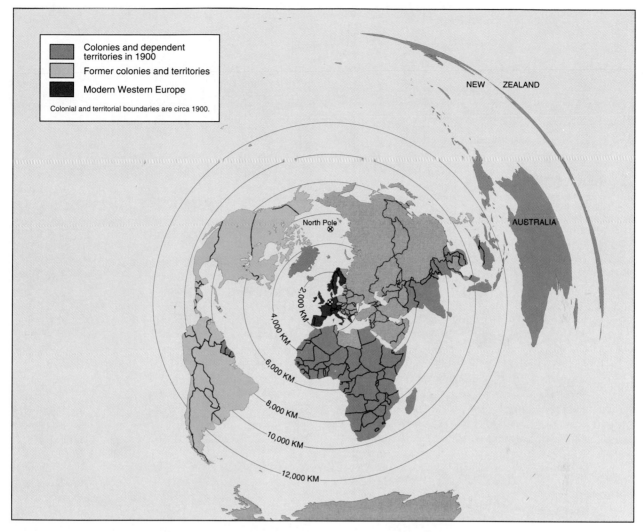

Figure 8-2
Western Europe, the center of the Land Hemisphere and a worldwide colonizer. The impact of Western European culture has been so great that the phrase "European explosion" is used to characterize the region's influence in many parts of the world. Western European countries used their colonies as sources of raw materials and as markets for mother-country products.

skeleton, on which Western Europeans have built their landscapes. At first glance the architecture of Europe might seem complicated and confusing (Figure 8–3). But extensive areas share certain landforms, a fact that helps explain the diverse human and economic patterns of modern Western Europe.

Western Europe occupies a portion of each of the four great physiographic subdivisions of Europe:

1. the Northwestern Highlands
2. the Great European Plain
3. the Central Uplands
4. the Alpine mountain system of southern Europe

The divisions follow a general west-to-east trend across Europe, which contrasts sharply with that of Anglo-America, where the major physiographic divisions are aligned from north to south.

That west-to-east orientation has had a profound influence on Western Europe's development. For example, it has allowed marine climatic influences to penetrate relatively easily into much

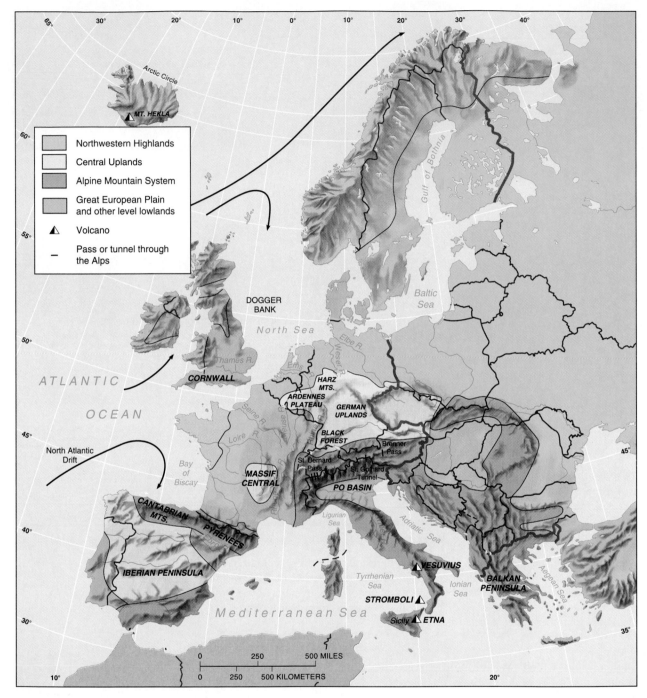

Figure 8-3
Selected physical features and physiographic regions of Western Europe. Most of
Western Europe's population lives in the fertile Great European Plain and other
lowland areas. Many of the region's minerals, however, are located in the Central
Uplands and the Northwestern Highlands. The Alpine Mountains are a hindrance
to north-south transport and serve as a climatic barrier.

of the region. If a lofty range of mountains, such as the Rockies, had crossed Europe from north to south, then penetration into the continent would have been severely limited, and Western Europe would have developed in a far different way. Or if the Alps and the Northwestern Highlands had formed a continuous barrier from the Mediterranean to the Arctic, Western Europe might today be part of the underdeveloped world. Such an alignment in the northerly latitudes of Western Europe would certainly have created a far more severe climate there, resulting in a greatly narrowed range of agricultural opportunities and extremely difficult transportation. Basic geographic patterns impact human economic development in a most significant way.

The Northwestern Highlands

The Northwestern Highlands include Iceland and Norway, much of Sweden, a large portion of the British Isles and Finland, and the Breton Peninsula in northwestern France. Generally speaking, the area is underlain by very hard and geologically ancient rocks. In a few areas, including Iceland, volcanic processes, or **volcanism**, are still actively building masses of igneous rock. Craggy, hilly uplands and windswept plateaus dominate the landscape in the Northwestern Highlands (Figure 8–4). Isolation and ruggedness, plus the cold climate and exposure to gale-force winds, often create many serious problems for the people of that region.

Several thousand years ago the climate in this part of the world was much colder than it is today. Annual snowfalls accumulated on highland surfaces and failed to melt in the cool summers. Gradually, the great thickness of the accumulating snowfields led to the formation of vast ice fields and glaciers. Those ponderous masses of ice flowed slowly but relentlessly from the higher elevations toward the sea, grinding and gouging the land over which they passed (Figure 8–5). As a result of this **glaciation**, many areas in the Northwestern Highlands have almost no soil and exist as vast stretches of barren rock that continue to defy human attempts to put them to productive use. Such landscapes go a long way toward explaining why many Icelanders, Norwegians, and other northern Europeans have traditionally turned to the sea and its resource potential in their search for a rewarding way of life. Of course, the location of some of the world's most

productive fishing grounds just off the coasts of those countries has also encouraged fishing rather than farming as a preferred way of life.

Other visible relics of the glacial heritage of the Northwestern Highlands are the vast areas of marshland and countless lakes that dot the landscapes of much of Ireland, Sweden, and Finland. Natural and manmade lakes serve as reservoirs for producing hydroelectricity, the region's chief source of power. Except for some United Kingdom coal, fossil fuels (i.e., petroleum and coal) are almost entirely absent from the geologically ancient Northwestern Highlands. Consequently, hydroelectric power installations have played a significant role in industrial development there (Figure 8–5). Norway and Sweden are among the world's leading producers of hydroelectricity.

Still other reminders of the glacial heritage are the deep **fjords** that characterize the coast of northwestern Europe. Those glacially excavated, now-flooded valleys allow the sea to penetrate deeply into the land. In Scotland and Norway the stark beauty of the fjords has become the basis for a thriving and profitable tourist trade.

Figure 8-4
A small cottage on a remnant lava field in Iceland, where volcanism remains a force. Windswept and hilly uplands characterize much of the Northwest Highlands, of which Iceland is a part.

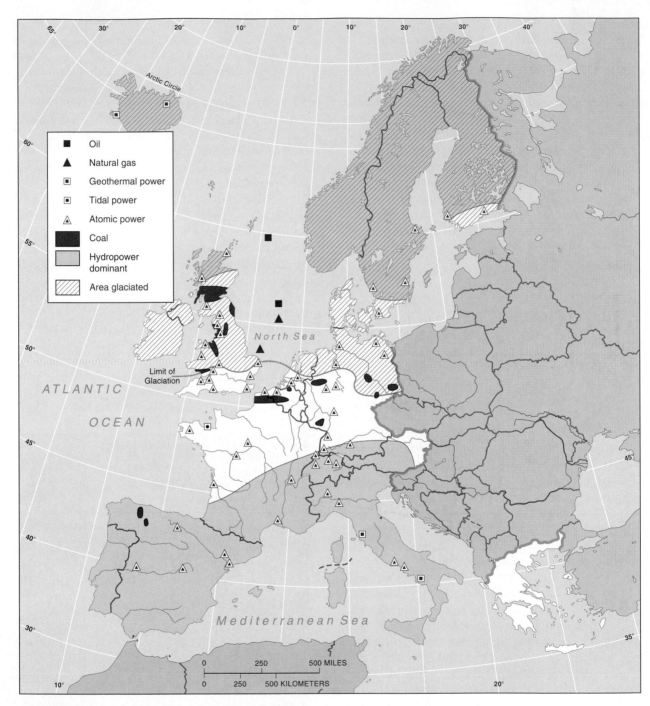

Figure 8–5
Energy sources in Western Europe. The glacial heritage of the Northwestern
Highlands presents limited economic opportunities, but glacial scouring has created
a landscape with hydroelectric power potential. In the United Kingdom and adjacent
northwestern Europe, thick and easily worked coal seams have provided the energy
source for modern manufacturing and urban life. But much of southern Europe is
coal deficient, relying largely on hydroelectric plants in the Alpine mountain system.
Throughout Western Europe atomic power is becoming increasingly important.

The agricultural potential of the Northwestern Highlands is severely limited by the rugged topography, thin and infertile soils, remoteness, and the excessively cloudy, wet, cool climate. Consequently, agriculture is largely restricted to grazing sheep and cattle. In more sheltered inland locations the grass cover is replaced by hardy coniferous forests, the westernmost extent of the great coniferous (or taiga) forest belt that girdles subarctic Eurasia from the North Sea to the Sea of Okhotsk (see Figure 3–4). In this region trees are grown as a crop to provide the raw materials for a host of forest-related industries, such as paper-and-pulp manufacturing, lumbering, and construction. Large segments of the national economies of Norway, Sweden, and Finland are based on such industries; in fact, Sweden and Finland consistently rank as Europe's first and second most important exporters of both lumber and wood pulp.

In addition, metallic minerals are found in some of the ancient rock masses of the highlands and frequently support important mining operations. By far the best known of such mining centers is north of the Arctic Circle near the Swedish cities of Kiruna and Gällivare. Those two ultramodern cities have been built to support the mining of one of the world's great deposits of high-grade iron ore. But such cities in the interior of the Northwestern Highlands are the exception rather than the rule; the region is one of Europe's most thinly settled areas. Little in the habitat of the Northwestern Highlands encourages people to settle there in large numbers. It is a land dominated largely by glaciers, rugged uplands, quiet crystal lakes, rushing rivers, and dark forests that yield their wealth only grudgingly to a small but hardy population.

The Great European Plain

South of the Northwestern Highlands, the Great European Plain stretches eastward from the Pyrenees Mountains to the Ural Mountains. In most places the plain is a broad, gently rolling lowland, but in Western Europe it narrows considerably and is interrupted by semienclosed bodies of water, such as the English Channel, the North Sea, and the Baltic Sea. Generally, the Great European Plain is underlain by geologically younger rocks, including many sedimentary layers. Most of those sedimentary rocks are relatively soft and weather more easily than the harder crystalline rocks of the adjacent highlands. The plain has a softer look, even where local folding and warping have thrust up ranges of hills. The hills are only moderately high, but they have considerable local importance because their soils and precipitation rates are different from those of the surrounding lowlands. On the whole, this region has presented a stimulating degree of challenge rather than impenetrable barriers (Figure 8–6). The area is also richly endowed with a wide range of resources and as a result is one of the world's most populous and highly developed regions.

Figure 8-6
Canal and street scene in Amsterdam. This great city, which rose to prominence during the seventeenth and eighteenth centuries, has long served as the cultural center of the Netherlands.

During glacial periods part of this region was covered by the continental ice sheets that flowed down from the Northwestern Highlands. Wherever the glaciers stopped advancing, they deposited great quantities of rock, sand, and soil. As a result, the topography, drainage, and soils in those areas are more varied and complex than they are in areas that the glaciers did not reach. Such differences contribute to the agricultural variety that marks much of the Great European Plain today.

As Figure 8–3 shows, the Great European Plain is bounded by seas to the north and high land to the south. Many large rivers—the Seine, the Rhine, the Elbe, the Ems, and the Weser—flow across the region in a northwesterly direction, providing the people of Western Europe with natural travel and trade routes. In fact, the Great European Plain itself has served as Europe's major west-to-east route. Today, the highways, railways, rivers, and canals of the Great European Plain are integrated into one of the world's most efficient transportation networks. Unlike the Great Plains of North America, the Great European Plain supports a closely woven productive web of urban and industrial activities.

Many of the world's greatest cities and industrial centers—Paris and Berlin, for example—have flourished in the Great European Plain. An important reason for the growth of some, like those in the Ruhr River valley, has been the proximity of coal deposits (Figure 8–5). As a fuel resource coal had only local significance for a very long time. Not until the middle decades of the eighteenth century did it become a factor that changed the lives of large numbers of Western Europeans. During that period the steam engine was perfected, and coke (a residue of coal) was used in blast furnaces to process iron ore in large quantities.

The agricultural potential of the Great European Plain in Western Europe is immense. In Denmark and the Netherlands, for example, almost 75 percent of the total land area is used for some form of agricultural activity. The range of crops is broad, also, including most of the temperate-climate foods and fibers known today. The generally mild, moist climate contributes to the agricultural potential; rainfall, though not heavy, is evenly distributed throughout all seasons of the year, and temperatures are moderate in summer and winter.

In terms of almost every factor needed to support intensive development, the Great European Plain of Western Europe is well endowed, which has al-
lowed modern, technologically advanced societies to emerge there in large degree. In that habitat, alert, inventive, and energetic populations have been able to create some of the world's richest and most varied ways of life.

The Central Uplands

The Central Uplands are an interrupted zone of hilly and rugged plateau surfaces that cross the central part of Europe, generally south of the Great European Plain. Composed of geologically ancient rocks, they resemble portions of the Appalachian Mountains of the United States. Like the Appalachians they tend to be rounded, only moderately high, and heavily forested.

Many of Europe's great rivers flow through the Central Uplands in deep valleys that make movement across the region difficult. Most of the area's transportation routes and important settlements are located in those valleys, which form the chief focus for life in the Central Uplands.

The Central Uplands are not as productive or as densely populated as the Great European Plain is, but they are important for their extensive and varied mineral deposits. Metalworking had an early start in the region, thanks to the coal found near the surface of the land where the river valleys passed from the Central Uplands to the Great European Plain. The Ruhr Valley, in Germany, is typical of that coal-producing zone and traditionally ranks among the world's greatest mining and industrial regions.

The Central Uplands are not particularly well suited to agricultural enterprises either; much of the upland terrain is rugged and steeply sloping. But the cooler temperatures and more abundant rainfall favor the growing of grass and other fodder crops for herds of grazing animals. And the densely populated industrial regions in and around the margins of the Central Uplands are ready markets for livestock products.

The Alpine Mountain System

The Alpine region, which stretches across the southern flank of Europe, is characterized by high mountains, rugged plateaus, and steeply sloping land. Parts of three major peninsulas—the Iberian, the Italian, and the Balkan—are included in this region, as are a number of Mediterranean islands.

Geologically, the lofty, folded Alps are relatively young and in many respects similar to the Rocky Mountains of the United States. Like the Rockies the Alps have many peaks that rise more than 10,000 feet (3,048 meters) above sea level; some top 15,000 feet (4,572 meters). Breaks in the Alpine system are few but extremely important. The passes, or lower portions of the mountains, have served as traditional focal points for routes connecting northern Europe with the Mediterranean Basin. Certain of the Alpine passes—such as the Brenner, St. Bernard, and St. Gotthard—have been among the most important routes of human movement in all history. Today, highway and railroad tunnels speed travelers under the passes in comfort during all seasons. And pipelines carry oil from ports on the Mediterranean Sea to the industrial regions of central Europe through the same historic Alpine passes that saw the march of Caesar's armies. People who live in the Alpine region are frequently reminded of the area's geological youth. Earthquakes, a symptom of tectonic activity, are common. Volcanic activity, too, is a sign of tectonic unrest and youthfulness. In the Italian province of Tuscany, volcanic hot springs and steam geysers are tapped to provide geothermal energy for industrial use.

Industrial activity in southern Europe is concentrated in such centers as Barcelona, Spain; Marseilles, France; Genoa, Turin, and Milan, Italy; and Athens, Greece. Those centers are located on coastal plains or in enclosed lowland basins within the Alpine region. Because coal and petroleum are largely lacking in this part of Europe, the rapidly flowing rivers of the Alps have been used extensively to produce hydroelectricity (see Figure 8–5).

High elevations, thin soils, and steep slopes severely limit agriculture in large areas of the Alpine region. In some places, however, agriculture flourishes. Vineyards, orchards, and olive groves lend a distinctive character to the agricultural landscapes along Europe's southern flank (Figure 8–7). And the proportion of people engaged in agriculture is far higher in this region of Western Europe than it is in the three regions to the north. For example, only about 2 percent of the labor force in the United Kingdom is employed in agriculture. In Greece, in contrast, about 24 percent of the labor force is engaged in farming. The Alpine region is quite different from the three other physiographic divisions that make up Western Europe. It is a region of tremendous challenge, frequent disappointment, and occasional disaster.

THE CLIMATES OF WESTERN EUROPE

The Alps can be viewed as a **climatic divide**. To the north, most of the heavily inhabited area enjoys an extremely temperate and moist marine climate; to the south, the area has a dramatically different dry summer subtropical climate (Figure 8–8). The marine climate in the north normally produces a lush, green landscape. Ireland's nickname, the Emerald Isle, emphasizes that characteristic regional greenness (Figure 8–9). South of the gleaming glaciers and snowfields that crown the towering Alps, the summer landscape changes rapidly to the browns and yellows of parched Mediterranean fields and the purple-gray of mountains.

When the ancient Romans left their Mediterranean homeland to conquer most of Western Europe, they found a strange and hostile world. It is easy to sympathize with Tacitus, who wrote in about A.D. 100: "The climate in Britain is disgusting from the frequency of rain and fog." He did find, however, that "the cold is never severe." Countless millions of vigorous and productive humans have flourished in each of Western Europe's climatic regions in the past, and they will continue to do so. One climate is not superior to the other; the two are simply very different and thus provide very different challenges and opportunities for the people who live in them.

Marine Climate

The marine climate owes its essential characteristics of moderate temperatures and abundant moisture to the Atlantic Ocean, which lies to the west of Europe. Water heats up and cools off more slowly than land does; consequently, it has a moderating influence on climate. In addition, the surface waters of the Atlantic are warmer than one might expect from their latitude, for they receive a great drift of warm, tropical water that is pushed in a clockwise direction by the prevailing winds of the Northern Hemisphere. That warm water forms the Gulf Stream along the coast of the United States from Florida to Maine. Off the Canadian provinces of Nova Scotia and Newfoundland, the Gulf Stream spreads out into a broad area of relatively warm water that drifts eastward—the **North Atlantic Drift**. Furthermore, Western Europe lies where the wind usually blows from the west, thereby bringing with it the moderating influence of the Atlantic. Thus, thanks to the North Atlantic Drift and prevailing westerly winds, northwestern Europe has mild,

Figure 8-7
Hillside vineyards near Montreux on Lake Geneva, Switzerland. Though landlocked within the geologically young and lofty Alps, Switzerland has created a stable and prosperous economy.

moist winters and cool, moist summers. The climate of Dublin typifies the conditions that prevail over much of maritime Western Europe north of the Alps (see Figure 8–8). Farther inland, winter temperatures are lower, and summer conditions are generally warmer and less cloudy.

Dry Summer Subtropical Climate

The southern margins of Europe share a climate that is common to the Mediterranean Basin and is thus often called the Mediterranean climate. It is characterized by clear, dry, hot summers and moderately moist, mild winters. A dry summer subtropical climate is also found in California, central Chile, southernmost Africa, and southern Australia.

The Mediterranean lies close to the 30th parallel of north latitude, which marks the approximate center of the belt of relatively high pressure known as the subtropical high. In summer this belt of desert-making high pressure shifts a few degrees to the north and covers the Mediterranean Basin. When it

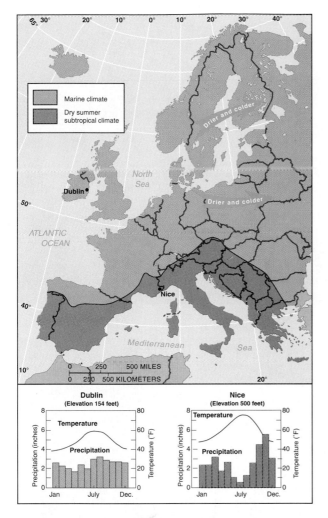

Figure 8-8
Climates of Western Europe. Climate and weather conditions in Western Europe vary markedly between the north, represented by Dublin, and the south, represented by Nice. The moderating influence of the ocean is felt especially in the north. In the south, rainfall is less, and the graphs show that both average rainfall and temperatures vary much more from season to season.

does, it brings the clear, sunny skies and dry air that are found over the Sahara to the south. In winter the subtropical high pressure belt shifts a few degrees to the south, and the Mediterranean Basin is once again influenced by the marine air masses and cyclonic disturbances of the prevailing westerly winds. Those air masses and storms bring cloudy skies, cooler temperatures, and the winter rains that are common to the region. The city of Nice is representative of this pattern of hot, dry conditions that char-

acterize Mediterranean summers (see Figure 8–8). Actually, Nice receives slightly more rain than Dublin does in an average year, but the seasonal drought during June, July, and August is a far more important factor for plant life in the area.

The result of this wet-dry climatic rhythm is seen in almost every aspect of the landscape in the southern part of the Alpine region of Europe. The summer drought is extremely hard on many plants that are common elsewhere in Europe. Thus, the natural vegetation of the Mediterranean Basin includes many plant species that resist excessive evaporation and loss of moisture. Some have thickened stems or bark, thorns, waxy coatings, small leaves, or hairy fibers. Succulent (i.e., water-storing) plants such as cactus also do very well there.

Human life is geared to the alternation of wet and dry seasons, too. Farmers plant and tend crops during winter and spring and harvest them in early summer. Fruit and other deep-rooted tree crops such as olives are well adapted and form an important part of the Mediterranean agricultural scene. In fact, olives are so representative of the region that their cultivation limits are taken by some as the limits of the dry summer subtropical climatic region. Wheat probably originated in the eastern Mediterranean Basin and remains the chief grain crop of the region. The moisture of the Mediterranean winter is ideal for the germination and growth of wheat; the aridity of the summer, for its maturation and harvest (Figure 8–10).

The reliably sunny summer weather of Mediterranean Europe has become one of the region's greatest economic assets. It is the basis of a flourishing tourist industry that provides a great deal of income. Hundreds of thousands of prosperous Western Europeans from the northern industrial centers enjoy their yearly vacations in the sun and blue waters of unpolluted stretches of Mediterranean coast.

SUMMARY
The Small but Habitable Continent

In this chapter we show how the location and physical geography of Western Europe are related to the region's rich and varied life-styles. On the whole, our view here has been continental rather than regional or local; such a perspective has not permitted us to deal directly with the effect of those various patterns and elements on individual

Figure 8-9
County Kerry and Ballinskellings Bay. The Emerald Isle is an apt nickname for the lush green landscapes of Ireland, which are produced by the marine climate.

Figure 8-10
Wheat harvesting south of Pamplona in Spain. The dry summer subtropical climate of much of the Mediterranean region discourages growing many of the crops common in more northern parts of Europe. Olives, grapes, and wheat, however, are very adaptable to the Mediterranean environment and are common elements in the agricultural systems of southern Europe.

Western Europeans. For an understanding of Western Europe and its position in our unfolding modern world, recognition of human responses is essential. In the introduction to the splendid book *Europe from the Air*, Salvador Madariaga, one of Europe's most respected humanists, writes that the continent has a "landscape of quality, not of quantity, rich in nuances and tensions, . . . where humanity has achieved clear definition not only in the individual but also in the nations . . ."[1] In the following chapters we investigate how the Western Europeans have molded and modified their portion of that "landscape of quality" in response to their own aspirations and assessment of its potential.

KEY TERMS

climatic divide	glaciation
continental architecture	Land Hemisphere
fjord	North Atlantic Drift
geopolitics	volcanism

NOTES

1. Salvador Madariaga, Introduction to *Europe from the Air*, by Emil Egli and Hans Richard Muller, translated from the German by E. Osers (London: Harrap, 1959), 47.

9

Western Europe: Landscapes of Development

European Culture

Language in Western Europe

The Trend Toward Unity

Population Patterns

Patterns of Industrialization

Patterns of Agriculture

The Pattern of Urbanization

Houses and vineyards of Burgundy viewed from the Côte d' Or. This region in eastern France, of which Dijon is the provincial capital, is the source of many of the best French wines.

Western Europe is a world culture hearth, a place from which fundamental changes in human life have flowed. Even though Europe flowered much later than did the other world culture hearths, it has spawned profound and far-reaching changes. It is ironic but important that, historically, prowess in the art of warfare gave Europeans their favorable edge. All too often the civilizing fruits of European culture were thrust on traditional societies at sword point or in the shadow of cannon barrels. Thus, perhaps it is not surprising that many of the world's most serious contemporary problems stem from the tensions generated as an exploding European culture, particularly its technology, confronts traditional non-European societies around the globe.

Terry Jordan has gone so far as to suggest that the world is in the process of being Europeanized in numerous, fundamental ways. In fact, European culture may one day be world culture, as regional differences give way to an increasing acceptance of the European way of life.[1]

EUROPEAN CULTURE

This diffusion of European ways, or **Europeanization**, is increasingly visible in the material and tangible aspects of human life, even in the farthest corners of the inhabited world. An acculturated Eskimo of the polar North who drives a bulldozer or operates a radar system now has more in common with American, Canadian, Danish, or Russian co-workers than with tradition-bound ancestors, who were hunters.

Similar statements could be written about the Bedouin of the oil-rich Old World deserts or about the Stone Age tribes of Latin America's rain forests—in fact, about primitive and traditional societies around the world. What is it about the Europeans and their culture that continues to make them such a potent force for world change? Many geographers and other scholars have sought to answer that question, and their attempts can help us understand Western Europe, one of the most influential of the world's developed regions.

Europeanness

Jordan has defined the European culture area as Old World areas in which the people:

1. are Caucasian
2. speak one of the related Indo-European languages
3. have a religious tradition of Christianity

To those three basic traits Jordan has added ten more that he finds necessary to form a detailed areal definition of present-day Europe:

1. a well-educated population
2. a healthy population
3. a well-fed population
4. birthrates and death rates far below world averages
5. an average annual national income per capita far above the world average
6. a predominantly urban population
7. an industrially oriented economy
8. a market-oriented agriculture
9. an excellent transportation system
10. a long history

Most of those ten additional traits are also important traits of all the developed or rich nations of the world. Using those traits to define European culture, or **Europeanness**, Jordan evaluated the countries of Europe, producing a map of their Europeanness similar to that in Figure 9–1. Interestingly, almost all of the countries with the highest degree of Europeanness are in Western Europe. If we accept Jordan's criteria, it follows that a country's degree of Europeanness is positively associated with modern technological development and widespread wealth for its citizens. According to this reasoning, Spain appears to be less European than Italy. As we might expect, however, many people would disagree with that conclusion. Europeanness appears to defy quantitative analysis; like beauty, Europeanness may reside in the eye of the beholder.

Political Fragmentation

The total area of Western Europe is only about one-third that of Canada, yet it is divided into eighteen fully autonomous and independent countries, plus five smaller units, or **microstates**: Andorra, Liechtenstein, Monaco, San Marino, and Vatican City. No wonder Western Europe appears to be politically fragmented!

In many ways those individual countries have served as cultural cradles for the various national groups in Western Europe. Until a little over a century ago, when steam power was put on wheels in the first rail transportation systems, the great majority of people spent their lives almost within walking distance of their birthplaces. Even modest ranges of

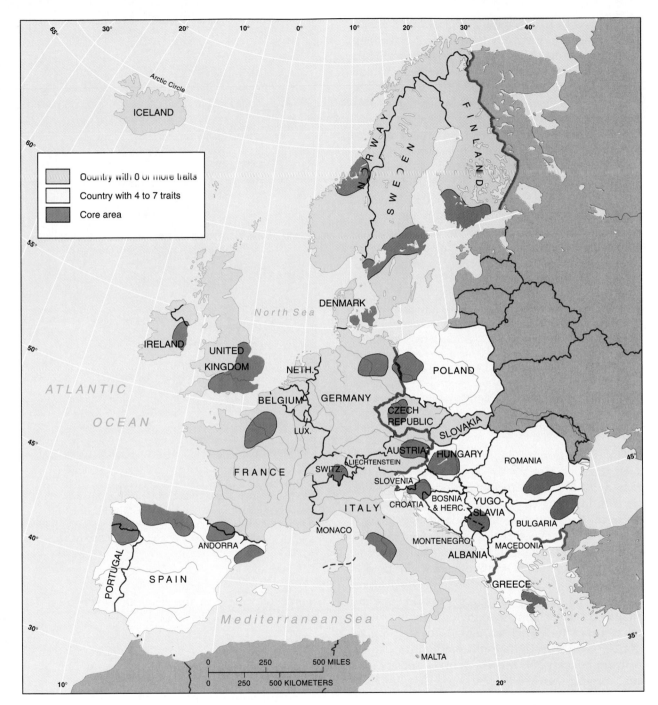

Figure 9–1

Traits of Europeanness and core areas. European cultural characteristics are most highly developed in Western Europe. Many of those traits, however, have been spread across the earth, and some authorities believe that other cultures will eventually be replaced by a modified European culture. Core areas have played an important role in the growth of many of Europe's modern states. (Adapted from J. G. Pounds and S. S. Ball, "Core-Areas and the Development of the European States System," *Annals, Association of American Geographers* 54, 1964, p. 24.)

hills helped to define natural regions, or compartments, where distinctive patterns of living, working, and speaking developed in relative isolation. Then, in the period before the Industrial Revolution, slow improvements in transportation and communication gradually brought many of those neighborhoodlike regions together to form larger groupings.

Over many years the larger groupings adopted patterns of living that became typical within particularly influential regions called **core areas** (see Figure 9–1). For example, the characteristically English way of life originated in southern England and gradually spread over much of the British Isles. Similarly, the French pattern of life and culture first developed in the fertile region drained by the Seine River and its tributaries. According to Norman J. G. Pounds and Sue S. Ball:

> A core-area must have considerable advantages in order to . . . perform [its] role. Simply put, it must have within itself the elements of viability. It must be able to defend itself against encroachment and conquest from neighboring core-areas, and it must have been capable at an early date of generating a surplus income above the subsistence level, necessary to equip armies and to play the role in contemporary power politics that territorial expansion necessarily predicts.[2]

The formation of nation-states as we know them today is a relatively recent development in human organization. In the period that followed the withdrawal of the Roman Empire from Western Europe, the major language groups evolved along several paths, which eventually led to the present linguistic and political patterns. Certain states, such as Portugal and Spain, unified early and led the Western Europeans to a position of world influence through exploration. Some, such as Germany, remained divided until just a little more than a century ago. Others, such as France, grew through the efforts of strong kings. Switzerland grew by the voluntary association of small regions—the Swiss cantons, or counties—into a confederation.

Whatever their eventual structures, the many countries of Western Europe represent the will and ambitions of their citizens. Without doubt the political fragmentation that has characterized Western Europe in the past several centuries has had a profound influence on the lives and activities of the millions of people in the culture area (Figure 9–2). Their differences have resulted in an exceptional

Figure 9–2
The Downtown Marketplace in Helsinki. Finland occupies a border location between Western Europe and Russia and therefore has pursued its international relationships with caution.

degree of variety in the ways in which local resources have been developed.

LANGUAGE IN WESTERN EUROPE

Language is one of the most vital elements in any culture. It is the vehicle of communication not only between the individuals and groups that make up a society but also between one generation or age and another. Many experts contend that language, of all the elements of culture, most distinguishes one people from another. And historically, it certainly has functioned that way in Western Europe.

The map of European languages illustrates the linguistic mosaic that characterizes Western Europe (Figure 9–3). In most of the area people speak languages that evolved from an ancestral tongue known as Indo-European. Most linguists believe that the roots of modern European languages began to form about 5,000 to 6,000 years ago, when the original Indo-European-speaking group began to split up and move west into Europe.

As a result of being relatively isolated, regionally detached groups served as cores within which the Indo-European language began to change. A Germanic core developed in the area of Denmark and southern Scandinavia. In the area north of the Carpathian Mountains of Eastern Europe, two Slavic cores came into being, one interior and one touching on the Baltic Sea. Thanks to the great power and extent of the Roman Empire, a small Romance-language core in Italy spread widely across Mediterranean Europe. Some languages, such as Greek, resisted replacement by Latin and survived in their core areas. Other languages, such as Celtic, did not fare as well. Celtic had developed in a core centered in the Rhine Valley and extending from Switzerland and Austria to the Low Countries (now the Benelux countries of Belgium, the Netherlands, and Luxembourg); today Celtic survives only in rugged refuge areas along the Atlantic fringe of Europe.

In addition to providing a rich commentary on the historic migrations of people into and across Western Europe, a map of European languages is indispensable to an understanding of current events. Many of the flash points of Western Europe—the places where political tensions often erupt into violence—have linguistic bases. In northern Spain, for example, Basque-speaking extremists belong to a violent group called Basque Homeland and Liberty, which uses terrorism to achieve its goal of independence for the Basque region. Political activities in Spain are impossible to comprehend without an appreciation of the Basque problem, a legacy from the repressive regime of the dictator Francisco Franco, who ruled from 1939 until 1975. Among other things, Franco outlawed the use of the Basque language.

In France, also, political affairs are deeply influenced by problems associated with regional linguistic minorities. In the north 700,000 Breton speakers occupy the western portion of Brittany. Flemish, a dialect of Dutch, is spoken by a much smaller group in the area near the Belgian border. And as Figure 9–3 shows, Basques live on both sides of the Pyrenees Mountains, thereby making about 750,000 of them citizens of France. Fortunately, the Basques in France have never suffered the repression their relatives in Spain have. In fact, in France both Basque and Breton groups have their own newspapers and literature. In addition to those dialects, Catalan, a dialect of Spanish, is the mother tongue of about 200,000 French citizens living near the Mediterranean end of the Pyrenees. And Corsica, the birthplace of Napoleon Bonaparte, has about 175,000 Italian speakers. There, too, terrorist bomb blasts occasionally emphasize the demands of a separatist movement. Finally, Alsatian, a dialect of German, is the mother tongue of thousands of French people in the historic Rhineland and eastern frontier zone.

Many other potential flash points exist in Western Europe, especially where linguistic and political boundaries do not coincide precisely. An area with strong ethnic and historical ties to one country but under the political rule of another is called an irredenta in political geography. A political policy directed toward the restoration of such areas to the ethnically related country is termed **irredentism**. In the past, great wars have been sparked by attempts to unite such political pockets with their "natural parent" countries. Although major warfare among the modern states of Western Europe is unlikely now, age-old linguistic friction and flash points have not totally lost their significance. If they are not handled carefully by majority governments, such tensions could slow or stop the trend toward greater European cooperation and unity.

THE TREND TOWARD UNITY

Since World War II the leaders and people of Western Europe have increasingly recognized the advantages of greater unity, particularly in such areas as economic development and military defense. If and when union does occur, the pattern of political fragmentation that has characterized Western Europe for so long may change drastically. Many observers believe that a truly unified political system—a **United States of Europe**—is already evolving. Many others are equally convinced that the roots of European nationalism reach deep and unity is more imaginary than real. In a memorable speech delivered at Zurich University in 1946, Britain's charismatic wartime leader, Winston Churchill, called for the creation of a:

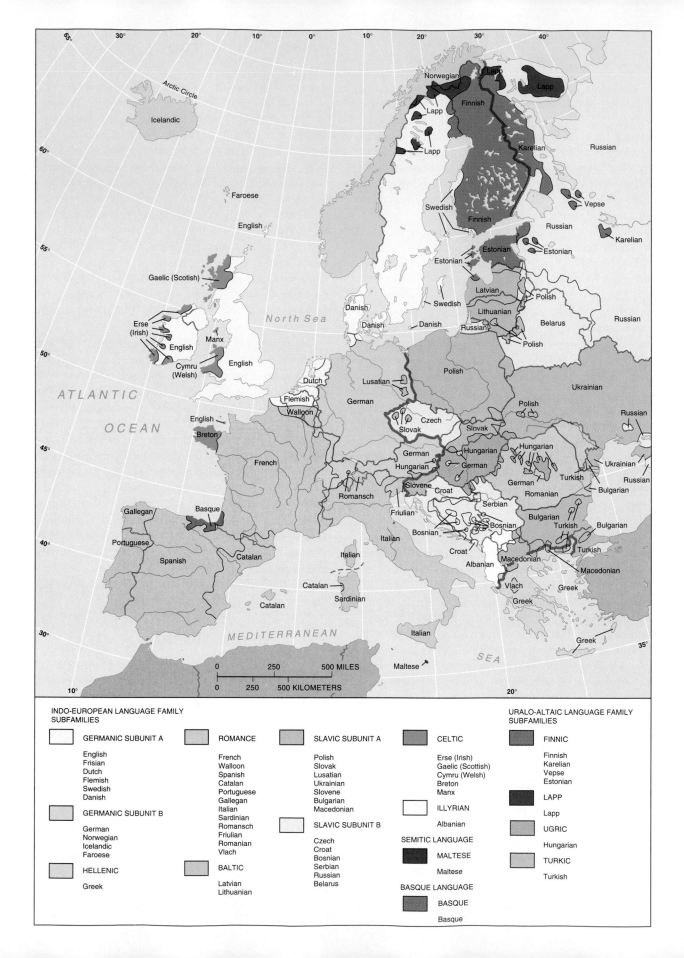

Figure 9-3
Languages of Europe. Few parts of the world exhibit the multiplicity of languages that marks Europe. Of particular importance in Western European affairs are the flash points, where political boundaries cut across language regions. In such places political tensions, built up among linguistic minorities, often explode in political extremism or violence.

> European Family . . . with a structure under which it can dwell in peace, in safety and in freedom. . . . We must build a kind of United States of Europe. In this way only will hundreds of millions of toilers be able to regain the simple joys and hopes which make life worth living.[3]

Churchill's was only one of countless voices that urged the unification of Europe in the dark days that followed the havoc of World War II. A sense of common misfortune developed into a resolve that Europe must never again experience the indiscriminate horror of modern warfare. Along with that resolve grew a conviction on the part of many European leaders that the traditional national frameworks of the European states were too narrow. Europe, many believed, must be revived in an economic framework of sufficiently large scale to allow it to compete with the world's superpowers, the United States and the Soviet Union.

Perhaps the most important force for unity was the highly successful European Coal and Steel Community (ECSC), which included France, West Germany, Italy, and the three Benelux states. The ECSC was organized to ensure, among other goals, that the full potential of the Ruhr coal supplies in West Germany and the Lorraine iron ore deposits in France would be realized as the vital steel industry of Western Europe was rebuilt. In other words, industrial and economic interdependence was replacing traditional rivalry. As a result, modern and efficient mills and mines brought benefits to the workers in both of those important industrial regions, and production and profits soared.

The European Communities

It was no coincidence that the members of ECSC would become the European Economic Community (EEC), or Common Market, which initiated the current drive for Western European unity. The obvious success of the ECSC in the 1950s was coupled with the long-standing tradition of a customs union among the Benelux countries. And in 1955 the governments of Belgium, Luxembourg, and the Netherlands urged the member states of the ECSC to take a new step along the road toward European integration. They stated that "the establishment of a united Europe must be sought through the development of common institutions, the progressive fusion of national economies, the creation of a large common market and the progressive harmonization of social policies."[4]

In an effort to further the positive achievements of the ECSC, the foreign ministers of the six member countries charged a committee headed by Paul-Henri Spaak of Belgium with looking into the possibilities for increased integration.

In 1956 the Spaak committee presented its report, which formed the basis for the negotiations that led to treaties establishing two additional European communities: the European Atomic Community (Euratom) and the European Economic Community (EEC, or Common Market). Both treaties were signed by the six countries in March, 1957, and became effective on January 1, 1958. As the term suggests, Euratom was organized to ensure an integrated approach to the development and use of nuclear energy in the community. Collectively those three legal entities—the European Coal and Steel Community (ECSC), the European Economic Community (EEC, or Common Market), and the European Atomic Energy Community (Euratom)—comprise the **European Community (EC)**.

In 1972 Norway, Denmark, Ireland, and the United Kingdom actively began to seek membership. The Norwegians ultimately voted against the move, but the others completed membership negotiations and became full-fledged European Community members in 1973 (see the boxed feature, Closing the Gap: The Eurotunnel).

The European Parliament

In 1979 the citizens of the nine countries of the European Community took part in the world's first truly international election when they voted for the members of the **European Parliament**. That body exercises democratic control over the executive and administrative institutions of the EC, and its creation

CLOSING THE GAP: THE EUROTUNNEL

This fortress built by Nature for herself
Against infection and the hand of war,
This happy breed of men, this little world,
This precious stone set in the silver sea,
Which serves it in the office of a wall,
Or as a moat defensive to a house,
Against the envy of less happier lands,
This blessed plot, this earth, this realm, this England.

William Shakespeare, *Richard II*

When Shakespeare wrote those immortal lines, the English Channel was in truth a defensive moat that had kept England safe from Europe's frequent broils and destructive wars for centuries. And thus it served succeeding generations, discouraging invasion schemes by Spanish kings, French emperors, and German führers.

In times of peace, however, the need to cross the often-stormy 20-mile (32.2-kilometer) stretch of water to reach the continent has been an inconvenience at best and a serious economic handicap at worst. Notorious for its fogs, the channel can be impassable for extended periods. Consequently, export orders that depend on tight delivery deadlines can be lost, and thousands of tourists can waste precious hours or days of their vacations waiting for cross-channel car ferries to resume fog-delayed service. In addition, as ocean-going shipping in the world's busiest sea-lane continues to increase, the potential for collisions between ferries and ships in the channel will soon reach unacceptable levels.

Especially after the United Kingdom joined the European Economic Community, British producers often found themselves at a disadvantage in competing with firms on the Continent; the British were penalized because the English Channel formed an obstacle in the flow of products to and from the continent. Continent-based producers felt the same disadvantage as they tried to market their products in Great Britain.

Not surprisingly, the centuries-old idea of a cross-channel bridge or tunnel came under increasingly serious discussion in the 1970s. Bridge advocates lost out because many people believed that a bridge would represent an unacceptable hazard for the increasing shipping in the channel. Thus, the way was open for tunnel advocates to promote the idea of what was popularly termed a "chunnel" between Great Britain and France.

Exhaustive engineering and feasibility studies resulted in a consensus to build a railroad tunnel under the English Channel, and construction of the Eurotunnel was begun. Motorists drive their cars onto specially designed shuttle trains in Folkstone, England, or Calais, France, and are whisked under the channel in approximately 35 minutes. The shuttles are brightly lit and well ventilated, and attendants provide information and assistance. Two locomotives, one at each end of the half-mile-long (0.8-kilometer) shuttle trains, reach speeds of up to 100 miles (161 kilometers) an hour during the journey. Commercial vehicles are accommodated on larger freight shuttles.

In 1983 existing air and surface cross-channel services carried 46 million passengers. By the year 2003 that number is expected to more than double, to 94 million. When the Eurotunnel links are completed, travelers will travel between London and Brussels in about 2 hours, 45 minutes, and between London and Paris in about 3 hours. Shakespeare's metaphorical moat will still be girding England's continental flank, but it will no longer serve as a serious barrier to the ongoing integration of Europe.

was not easy. During the 1960s bitter partisan political battles and even riots took place as the European Community countries moved from traditional and strongly nationalistic policies toward the ideal of economic and political unity. Nevertheless, as the 1970s opened, the economic success of the European unification was clear to all.

The European Parliament does not sit in continuous full session; many of its members are also elected representatives in the national parliaments of their home countries. Instead, the European Parliament is in session for one week every month, on average. And although those full sessions are important, they constitute only a small part of the parliament's work. As in the U.S. Congress, much of the work is accomplished in specialized standing committees and political party groups. Full sessions alternate between the European Parliament headquarters in Luxembourg and the Palace of Europe in Strasbourg, France. Much work is also conducted in Brussels, Belgium, where parliamentary committees hold their meetings.

Although the European Parliament does not enjoy all of the powers that the national parliaments of its member states enjoy, it is steadily increasing its role in managing the affairs of the community. In the normally crucial area of budget, for example, it has the last word on all community items that are classified as nonobligatory—in other words, about one-fourth of all funds appropriated. The parliament also has the power to reject the community's budget as a whole and thus force a new one to be drawn up and proposed.

Memories of the bitter 1960s have faded, and a new generation is experiencing the personal satisfaction of moving easily from one EC-member country to another with only a simple identification card, not a formal passport. For travel outside the EC, a distinctive European passport is used, which most member states have been issuing since 1985. This burgundy-red document is entitled "European Community" but also gives the name of the bearer's home country. After a long period of introduction, that symbol of European identity has become an important icon in furthering the ideal of a true United States of Europe.

From Community to Union

The most recent chapter in the story of Western Europe's trend toward unity was written late in 1993 with the implementation of the Treaty on European Union, which was first worked out at Maastricht in the Netherlands. With the adoption of the Maastricht treaty, changes in terminology regarding the EC and some of its institutions were found to be necessary. The umbrella term is now the **European Union (EU)**, replacing *European Community (EC)* in most contexts.

The treaty is based on four simple-sounding ambitions for the EU: (1) greater economic prosperity, (2) greater external ambition, (3) greater effectiveness, and (4) greater democracy. The ratification process resulted in a true public debate on the construction of an increasingly unified Europe, particularly its aims and methods. In that debate it became clear that many found the concept of a unified Europe and the bureaucracy that would result to be distant and troubling. The most urgent challenge

facing the new European Union is convincing citizens of its member states that it can help in coping with the complex problems of industrial and social transformation currently plaguing them. Western Europe's citizens generally agree that the European Community has brought them an end of bloody warfare within the EC's borders and a higher level of prosperity. The great question now is can the European Union aid in combatting the many modern scourges that begin with nationalistic and ethnic extremism and extend to unemployment, family breakdown and drug abuse? Whatever the future may bring, the European Union is certain to play a major role in shaping its direction, on both the world and local stage.

POPULATION PATTERNS

Although the pattern of population distribution in Western Europe is less familiar than the political pattern, it is even more important for an understanding of that highly developed region. Where people choose to live and center their activities results from a complex interaction of varied human and physical factors. It might even be argued that knowing where and how the people of any area live is central to understanding the area's physical geography and cultural history, as well as the people's way of life.

Environmental conditions always have a significant effect on the pattern of population. For example, the rather harsh environments of the Northwestern Highlands have not attracted the vast numbers of people that the richly endowed Great European Plain has. It is not that modern Western Europeans are merely pawns of their environments; quite the contrary, they are probably closer to being the masters of their environments than are the peoples of many other regions of the world. Nevertheless, most human decisions of a spatial nature necessarily reflect the physical environment to some extent.

Population Distribution

Although by world standards Western Europe is densely populated, its 390 million inhabitants are unevenly distributed within their homelands. As the map of population density shows, northern Europe and the Alps have sparse populations (Figure 9–4). In contrast, the Great European Plain, particularly near industrial areas, has a very high population den-

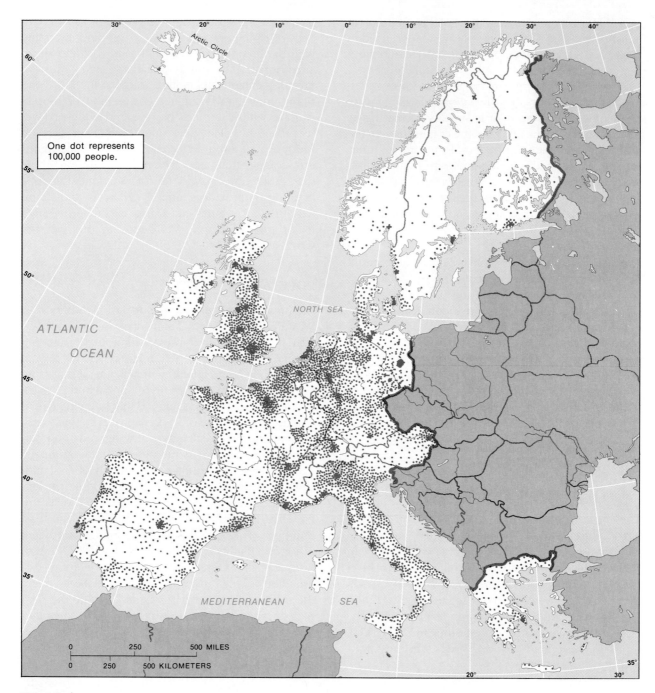

One dot represents
100,000 people.

Figure 9-4
Distribution of Europe's population. Western Europe is one of the world's most
densely populated regions. Unlike densely populated China and India, however,
Western Europe's population is primarily urban and enjoys a high level of living.

sity. Belgium and the Netherlands, two of Western Europe's most densely settled countries, lie in that plain. In addition, the Po Valley and neighboring parts of northern and central Italy are densely settled. So, too, are the areas that flank the Rhine River from Switzerland northward. Other densely populated areas include the central lowlands of Scotland, portions of central England, the London Basin, the Rhone-Saone corridor in southern France, and coastal Portugal and Spain. Such areas of dense, productive population help to form the economic and political muscle of Western Europe.

Population Change Through Time

The distribution of the population of Western Europe has changed significantly through time. At the beginning of the Christian era, about 2,000 years ago, the areas of densest population lay along the Mediterranean Sea (Table 9–1). There, in southern Spain, France, Italy, and Greece, the great classical empires of Greece and Rome developed flourishing agrarian economies and an urban focus. In those days most of Europe north of the Alps was thinly peopled.

Notice in Table 9–1 the lowered population totals during the first ten centuries of the Christian era. After the decline of the Roman Empire, with its well-integrated economic system, Europe suffered a long period of economic collapse, with famines, epidemics, and invasions of barbarians from the north and east. The toll in human life was enormous. In the 700s the great Islamic empire of the Middle East and North Africa conquered the Iberian Peninsula

Table 9-1
Estimated population of Western Europe, A.D. 1–2000 (selected years).

	Total Population (millions)	British Isles		France, Benelux		Iberia, Italy, Greece		Scandinavia, Finland, Iceland		Germany, Austria, Switzerland,	
		Population (millions)	% of Total	Population (millions)	% of Total	Population (millions)	% of Total	Population (millions)	% of Total	Population (millions)	% of Total
1	27.0	0.3	1.1	6.6	24.4	16.5	61.2	0.3	1.1	3.3	12.2
350	18.9	0.3	1.6	5.2	27.5	10.0	52.9	0.2	1.1	3.2	16.8
600	13.2	0.7	5.3	3.1	23.5	7.2	54.5	0.2	1.5	2.0	15.2
800	22.0	1.2	5.4	4.9	22.3	11.6	52.7	0.3	1.4	4.0	18.2
1000	25.9	1.5	5.8	6.1	23.6	14.1	54.4	0.4	1.5	3.8	14.7
1200	37.7	2.9	7.7	9.8	26.0	17.6	46.7	0.5	1.3	6.9	18.3
1340	57.3	5.6	9.8	18.9	33.0	21.0	36.6	0.6	1.0	11.2	19.5
1400	43.2	—	—	—	—	—	—	—	—	—	—
1500	43.1	3.9	9.0	16.2	37.6	15.1	35.0	0.6	1.4	7.3	16.9
1650	76.0	7.0	9.2	30.0	39.5	26.0	34.2	2.0	2.6	11.0	14.5
1700	80.3	7.9	9.8	27.2	33.9	26.0	32.4	4.5	5.6	14.7	18.3
1750	96.6	9.8	10.2	32.2	33.3	30.8	31.9	5.6	5.8	18.2	18.8
1820	132.3	21.0	15.9	35.7	27.0	42.0	31.7	6.3	4.8	27.3	20.6
1900	235.1	39.2	16.7	54.9	23.3	70.5	30.0	11.7	5.0	58.8	25.0
1930	280.0	50.0	17.8	60.0	21.4	80.0	28.6	15.0	5.4	75.0	26.8
1950	324.5	60.5	18.6	71.5	22.0	99.0	30.5	16.5	5.1	77.0	23.7
1990	377.0	60.9	16.0	81.6	21.6	117.6	31.0	23.1	6.1	93.8[a]	24.8
2000	383.0	62.5	16.3	83.8	21.6	117.7	30.5	23.3	6.0	93.8[a]	24.4

Source: Terry G. Jordan, *The European Culture Area: A Systematic Geography* (New York: Harper & Row, 1973); *World Population Data Sheet* (Washington, DC: Population Reference Bureau, 1990); and *Basic Statistics of the Community,* 29th ed. (Luxembourg: Statistical Office of the European Communities, 1992).

[a]1990 and 2000 totals include former East Germany.

and threatened to overrun Western Europe. The term **Dark Ages** is sometimes used to identify this period of Western European history.

The population gradually began to increase again as relative stability returned to Europe. By 1340 it had reached 57 million, more than double what it was at the beginning of the Christian era. In 1348, though, disaster struck in the form of the bubonic plague, known as the **Black Death**. In the next two years about one-fourth of all Europeans died of the plague—and considerably more in certain locations. For example, from 1348 to 1379 England's total population dropped from an estimated 5.7 million to 2 million, a decrease of more than 50 percent in the course of one lifetime. It is not at all surprising to find many people today using these 600-year-old statistics in debates about the spread of the viral infection known as AIDS. Many health workers predict that a similar disaster could result if action to stop its spread is not taken in all societies around the world.

Wars have also contributed to high death rates in Western Europe. The early barbarian invasions caused a net decline in total population, and the Hundred Years' War (1337–1453) added to the toll in the period following the first outbreaks of bubonic plague. Then between 1618 and 1648 the Thirty Years' War left another negative mark on overall population growth.

Demographic Transformation

With the Peace of Westphalia in 1648, Europe achieved relative peace and stability. At that time families were generally large, with an average of six to eight children sharing in the labor associated with their agricultural way of life. In addition, the Black Death had by then disappeared as a scourge. As a result, from 1650 to 1750 the population of Western Europe grew by 20 million, so that on the eve of the Industrial Revolution the total population was almost 100 million. The year 1750 also marks the point at which Western Europe began its demographic transformation (see Chapter 2). Figure 9-5 presents the actual population statistics for England and Wales in terms of the model of demographic transformation (compare Figure 2–4).

Stage I is characterized by rather static population growth; high death rates counterbalanced the high birthrates of the traditional agrarian way of life in early eighteenth-century England and Wales. At one

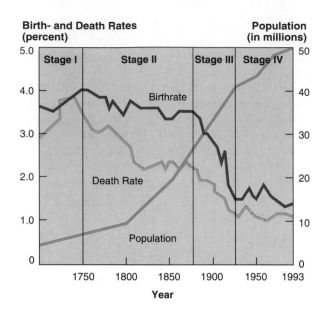

Figure 9-5

Demographic transformation of England and Wales. The model of demographic transformation appears in Figure 2–4; here we see a representation of what has actually happened in a particular location. Not surprisingly, the idea for a model of demographic transformation was based on an analysis of Western European birthrates and death rates.

point in the late 1730s the birthrate was about 3.9 percent, and the death rate was the same. As a result there was no natural increase in the population in that period. But by 1750 a clear trend of continuing high birthrates accompanied by sharply dropping death rates shows that England and Wales had entered Stage II of their demographic transformation, with a consequent acceleration of population growth. A huge surplus of births over deaths could have spelled disaster for the traditional agricultural society, but in Western Europe those changes coincided with the Industrial Revolution and the opening of overseas empires and other emigration opportunities. Thus, rather than disaster, the surplus provided the substance of Europe's most important export of all times—people. Western European explorers and colonizers, followed by emigrants, carried their culture to the far corners of the world and set in motion processes of change that remain ongoing today.

By 1880 the population of England and Wales had grown to approximately 26 million, and a noticeable decline in the birthrate had begun. The urban-industrial way of life had come of age, and attitudes toward family size were changing (Stage III). Children were no longer viewed as economic assets; child labor laws were enacted, and formal education became widespread. In addition, more women joined the work force and sought freedom from the burdens of numerous pregnancies and large families. The result was a shift toward smaller families, with a sharp drop in birthrates. At the same time growing affluence and improved medical knowledge and health care brought about an equally sharp decline in death rates. Those trends, which began in England and Wales, diffused across Europe from west to east until, by the 1930s, most of the nations of Europe were clearly in Stage IV of the demographic transformation.

PATTERNS OF INDUSTRIALIZATION

E. Willard Miller once observed that "the Industrial Revolution was largely a revolution in energy consumption, and coal predominated as the source of energy for mechanical power until after World War I."[5] With the advent of the coal-burning period in the nineteenth century, a pattern of industrial coalescence in the vicinity of easily worked coal deposits began in the United Kingdom and spread to the rest of Western Europe.

Locational Shifts in Industry

Over the centuries a coalescence and spatial shift took place in the iron and steel industry of southern Wales, which is just one of countless areas in Western Europe where such a shift has occurred (Figure 9–6). An impressively large charcoal-iron industry was flourishing in southern Wales in the mid-eighteenth century, but that industry had no relationship to the coal seams which underlay the region. In fact, the charcoal-iron industry of 1750 was so large that the supply of wood was growing short, and the industry was beginning to drift to the rugged and still-forested valleys of western Wales and the interior. In the map for 1750 that dispersed pattern can be seen quite clearly.

As is often the case, developments that were taking place some distance away from those shrinking woodlands of southern Wales were responsible for the spatial shift of ironworking sites that can be seen on the 1839 map. Those developments took place in Shropshire, the border county to the north, where

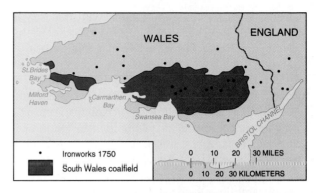

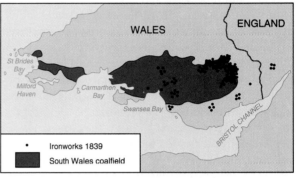

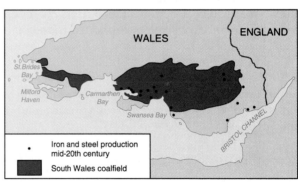

Figure 9-6
Industrial coalescence in southern Wales. The Industrial Revolution brought many changes to Western Europe. One change was the gradual coalescence of manufacturing activities around coalfields. The distributional pattern of iron and steel plants in southern Wales illustrates this historical coalescence and a more modern dispersal.

a Quaker ironmaster named Abraham Darby made an important technological breakthrough at blast furnaces he had built between 1755 and 1758. There, near Coalbrookdale on the upper Severn River, Darby produced pig iron that could be converted to tough bar iron with the plentiful coke of the area rather than with increasingly expensive charcoal.

Darby's successful experiments with coke as a blast-furnace fuel became a model for other iron-masters and led to the widespread adoption of the new technique. By the end of the eighteenth century almost no charcoal was being used in the blast furnaces of southern Wales. Thus, the occurrence of coal, iron ore, and limestone in proximity to one another became the crucial factor in the location of iron industry. In the 1839 map a distinct clustering of ironworks can be seen on the northeastern outcrop of the coalfield, near easily mined deposits of iron ore and limestone.

In modern times the Welsh iron and steel industry has become increasingly dependent on imported coal, iron ore, and scrap steel for its operations. That shift in which raw materials are used has resulted in a peripheral pattern, with most steelworks now being located near harbors. Such locational shifts have had a profound effect on both the people and the environment of Wales. There—as in many of Western Europe's older industrial regions—derelict buildings and mine-head works, spoil heaps, and serious subsidence, or land settling, often blight the landscape. In recent decades those problems have been compounded by world economic conditions, which often favor imported iron and steel over locally produced supplies. Thus, high unemployment rates are a major concern. So, too, are the many once-flourishing ports that have been outmoded by the shift to increasingly larger cargo carriers and tankers.

Recent Industrial Development

Coal has played a much less significant locational role in countries and regions that have become industrialized more recently. Italy and Sweden are among the best examples of industrialization in the absence of local supplies of coal. In both countries hydroelectricity, a more recently perfected energy source, has played a strong role in industrial location.

In Italy about three-quarters of all manufacturing takes place in the north, in the Po Valley. Within that region no single factor accounts for the industrial pattern. Most industrial materials must be brought into the area from outside, thus giving a distinct advantage to cities that are well served by transportation facilities. Often those are very old places, such as Turin and Milan, with rich cultural traditions. But

the availability of inexpensive hydroelectric power over wide areas means that there is more choice in the location of industries.

Similar conditions prevail in central Sweden, between Stockholm on the Baltic and Göteborg on the Atlantic. In that lake-studded area of Sweden, as on Italy's northern plain, a diversity of light industrial activities blends urban and rural landscapes with a greater degree of visual harmony than is usually found in the older and more concentrated, coalfield-oriented industrial belts of the United Kingdom, France, Belgium, and Germany (Figure 9–7).

Untapped sources of hydropower are bound to be developed rapidly wherever they exist in Europe. One reason is that coal-fired electricity-generating plants create problems of international air pollution and acid rain. Another reason is that inexpensive superconductors have been developed, which allow electricity to be transmitted from remote areas. Western Europeans can be expected to devise innovative programs to maximize their access to this source of power.

Tariffs and Boundaries as Locational Factors

Another set of locational factors that was traditionally important to Western European industrialization—tariff policies and international boundaries—now seems to be disappearing. High tariff walls, which were widespread in Western Europe before World War II, encouraged the development of a broad range of industries within each European country. Many of those industries had relatively inefficient plants that could not have competed with larger foreign producers. They were kept alive only through the protection of high tariffs, which forced the price of imported goods to higher levels than would otherwise have existed.

As a result of import duties and tariffs, a factory located near an international political boundary often suffered a distinct disadvantage because the boundary acted like a barrier to the distribution of products. The sizable addition to the cost of products at the border greatly lowered their competitive position in the market of the neighboring country. Also, fears of invasion or battle damage in times of conflict made border-zone locales less attractive.

Those problems are greatly minimized in present-day Western Europe. The EU member states now form one economic unit, having eliminated

PATTERNS OF AGRICULTURE

Despite Western Europe's high state of industrial development, agriculture remains the dominant form of land use, though cultural factors and physical environmental conditions have interacted to produce extremely varied patterns of agricultural activity. Three fairly distinctive types of agricultural systems can be identified: Mediterranean polyculture, dairy farming, and mixed livestock and crop farming. Each system dominates and characterizes the area in which it is located (Figure 9–8).

Mediterranean Polyculture

The region dominated by Mediterranean polyculture forms a fairly continuous ribbon along the Mediterranean coast. Agriculture in that area has an ancient heritage. Since very early times, wheat has been grown through the moist, mild winter season to provide a harvest in the spring. Several drought-resistant, deeply rooted vines and trees, particularly grape and olive, also characterize the Mediterranean landscapes, and have since classical times (Figure 9–9). In many respects the agricultural emphasis in the Mediterranean Basin resembles that of California, where a similar climatic condition prevails. Because most of the activity is extremely labor intensive, such countries as Portugal, Spain, Italy, and Greece show a relatively high proportion of their total labor force engaged in agricultural pursuits (Table 9–2).

Recent developments in the Mediterranean polyculture region have resulted from accelerating specialization and commercialization, in response to the huge market in the industrialized and urbanized countries to the north. Improved transportation facilities make it possible for Mediterranean growers to speed highly perishable fruits and early vegetables to the affluent markets of Britain, France, Benelux, Germany, and Scandinavia.

One notable trend has been the specialization of whole districts in one or a few crops. Within the French Mediterranean belt, for example, vast areas have been turned into a huge sea of vines, so dominant are the vineyards. Along the Mediterranean belt in coastal Spain, irrigated citrus orchards present a similar scene. Olive trees, too, dominate broad areas, lending a distinctive gray-green appearance to the landscape. In addition, early tomatoes are cultivated extensively for the northern

Figure 9-7
The BMW corporate headquarters in Munich, Germany.
Modern Munich is the center of a major industrial region located far from the coal deposits that accompanied northern Germany's industrial development.

barriers to the movement of raw materials, labor, capital, and finished goods. The other important international trade group in Western Europe, the **European Free Trade Association (EFTA)**, is similarly dedicated to removing artificial obstacles to commerce. Norway, Sweden, Finland, Iceland, Switzerland, and Austria make up the EFTA.

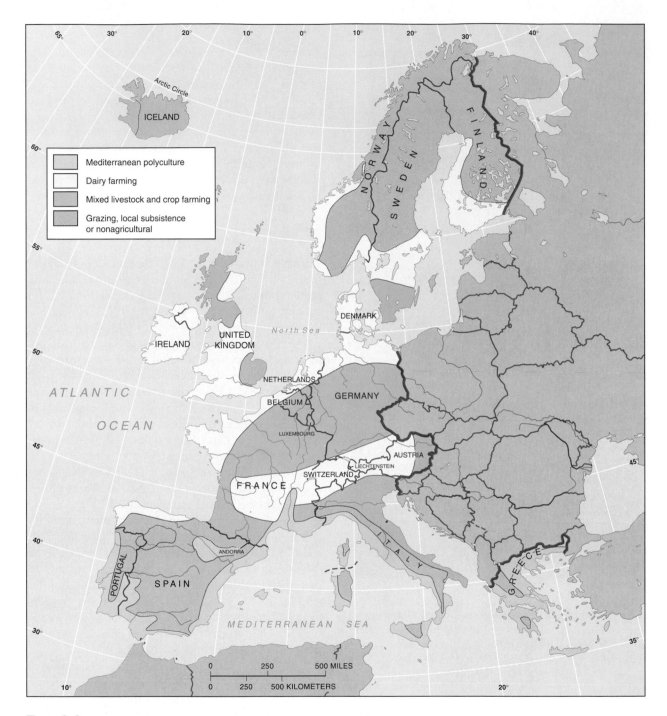

Figure 9-8
Agricultural regions of Western Europe. Although Western Europe is a center of industrialization, agriculture has always been an important activity. Today, most of Western Europe's agricultural activities are highly productive and intensive. Of necessity this map is highly generalized.

Figure 9-9
Agricultural landscape in Sicily, Italy. Tomatoes are shown in the foreground; vineyards and olive orchards appear in the background. Considerable labor intensity is required for Mediterranean crops.

European market, as are perishable melons, apricots, and table grapes. Tobacco, another labor-intensive crop, is also an important source of income, particularly in Italy and Greece.

Goats and sheep have traditionally provided the milk for the region's famous cheeses. In some mountainous areas large flocks are still maintained by small numbers of herders, who follow a seasonal herding rhythm called **transhumance**. Transhumance involves the grazing of animals in high mountain pastures during dry Mediterranean summers and in the lower areas during moist winters, when grass flourishes.

The future of Mediterranean agriculture appears bright, since the farmers enjoy a considerable advantage over other subtropical producers in the world. They are close to the rich and growing markets of urbanized northern Europe, and local industrialization promises to increase steadily, thereby providing growing markets within the region. But a history of deforestation and exploitive farming has resulted in serious soil-erosion prob-

lems. Fortunately, conservation measures, such as terracing and reforestation, are receiving strong support from government and private agencies.

Dairy Farming

As the map of Western European agriculture indicates, a considerable area to the north of the Mediterranean is devoted to dairy farming, which is usually linked to the rich urban populations of the Western world. The dairy belt stretches from the British Isles and the Breton Peninsula along the shores of the North and Baltic seas to Finland. A second large area of dairying has developed in the Alps of France, Switzerland, and Austria. Both dairy belts are located in some of the cloudiest and coolest portions of Western Europe, where many field crops often fail to mature or may suffer from fungus attacks, but where hay and a number of other fodder crops flourish. In the rugged Alpine terrain the steep, grass-clad slopes can be grazed carefully or cropped for hay with little or no danger of soil erosion.

Table 9–2
Distribution of Western European labor forces in 1990
(by percentage of national employment).

	Economic Sector		
	Agriculture	Industry	Services
Germany	3.4	39.8	56.8
France	6.1	29.9	64.0
Italy	9.0	32.4	58.6
Netherlands	4.6	26.3	69.1
Belgium	2.7	28.7	68.5
Luxembourg	3.2	30.7	66.1
United Kingdom	2.2	29.5	68.3
Ireland	15.0	28.7	56.3
Denmark	5.7	25.6	68.7
Greece	25.3	27.5	47.1
Spain	11.8	33.4	54.8
Portugal	17.8	34.9	47.4
Austria	7.9	36.8	55.3
Iceland	23.0	43.0	34.0
Norway	6.5	24.7	68.8
Sweden	3.3	29.2	67.5
Switzerland	5.6	35.0	59.5
Finland	8.4	31.0	60.6

Source: Basic Statistics of the Community, 29th ed.
(Luxembourg: Statistical Office of the European
Communities, 1992).

Note: Because of rounding, figures for each country may not
total 100 percent.

The long tradition of dairy farming in northern Europe is reflected in the fact that almost every major breed of dairy cattle originated there: the large brown Swiss from Schwyz Canton in central Switzerland; the popular Jersey and Guernsey breeds from the small islands in the English Channel, near the coast of France; and the Holstein from Schleswig-Holstein, in northern Germany. Colonists who traveled overseas in recent centuries carried those and other, less well-known breeds with them. Now, herds of distinctly northern European animals are a familiar sight in New Zealand and Australia, as well as in the United States and Canada.

Both the nature and intensity of dairying vary somewhat from region to region in northern Europe. Denmark, for example, has specialized in the production of butter, accounting for almost one-fifth of the butter in international trade. Skim milk, a by-product of butter production, is then used to fatten pigs, which in turn are utilized in the production of world-famous Danish ham and bacon. In the Netherlands much grazing takes place on land reclaimed from the sea, land where the water table is too high for the cultivation of many crops. The Dutch specialize in the production of cheese and condensed and powdered milk, much of which they export to markets throughout the world. In the United Kingdom much fluid milk is produced, but it is marketed locally for human consumption. Posters urging Britons to "Drinka Pinta Day" are familiar sights in England.

Because the most densely settled urban and industrial areas of Western Europe are so close at hand, dairy farming will in all likelihood continue to be a vital agricultural activity. Changes will probably occur as dairy farms become larger and as the mechanization and specialization of the industry increase.

Mixed Livestock and Crop Farming

Between the animal-dominated dairy farming belts in the north and the intensive crop specialization of the Mediterranean polyculture region lies a broad zone characterized by a mixed form of farming. Environmental conditions there facilitate a wide range of agricultural activities, and the resultant landscape is extremely mixed and varied (Figure 9–10). Diversity in the area is also promoted by political fragmentation, which has discouraged the evolution of vast regional belts of agricultural specialization such as those found in the United States, Canada, Russia, and Australia.

Mixed livestock and crop farming has evolved from the subsistence farming systems that developed during medieval times. Crops came to dominate any areas with fertile, easily tilled soils, such as the loess lands that stretch across northern France to central Germany. Livestock assumed significance in valley areas with heavy clay soils or in cool, moist uplands. Swine were particularly important among Germanic groups, who grazed them in herds in heavily forested areas. Soil fertility was maintained by rotating crops and spreading animal manure. In many respects the medieval farming scene was one that would have delighted modern ecology-conscious conservationists.

As population pressure increased in postmedieval Europe, however, that traditional approach to agriculture began to change somewhat. New high-

Figure 9-10
A rural scene near Devon, England. The massive urban population of Europe
provides major markets for the agricultural products of the North European Plain.

yielding crops, such as the white potato and maize
(corn), were introduced from the New World, and
each found an important niche in the agricultural
system of Western Europe. The potato was ideally
suited to the cool, moist conditions of the north, and
maize grew well in the sunnier conditions of the
midsouth.

In addition, a more striking change is currently
occurring in Western European mixed agriculture—
the rapidly declining importance of small farms
(Table 9–3). In highly developed countries such as
France, Belgium, and Germany, where mixed livestock and crop farming are widespread, there were
dramatic drops in the percentages of traditional,
small, family-operated farms between 1960 and
1987. As agriculture ceases to be a way of life for
many people, becoming instead a technologically
complex form of business enterprise, Western
Europeans will have many adjustments to make.

THE PATTERN OF URBANIZATION

Urbanized societies dominate the Western European
scene today (Figure 9–11). Such societies, in which
the majority of people live in towns and cities, result from a recent step in humanity's social evolution. Modern cities form large and dense agglomerations and involve their inhabitants in a degree of
human contact and social complexity never before
witnessed. Few people seem to comprehend fully
either the newness of such great urbanization or the
speed with which this process has taken place. As
Kingsley Davis wrote some thirty years ago:

> Before 1850 no society could be described as predom-
> inantly urbanized, and by 1900 only one—Great
> Britain—could be so regarded. Today, only 65 years
> later, all industrial nations are highly urbanized, and in
> the world as a whole the process of urbanization is ac-
> celerating rapidly.[6]

Cities as such are not new to Western Europe. But
what is new is the overwhelming influence of the
form and function of cities, which have become the
norm in modern Western European societies.

Early Cities

The city of the classical age was first introduced into
Europe by the ancient Greeks and Phoenicians as

221

they spread their commercially oriented civilizations around the Mediterranean Basin. Later, the Romans carried the urban form of life deep into Western Europe, founding new cities in their conquered provinces to the west, east, and north.

Table 9-3
Percentages of European Community farms under 25 acres (10 hectares) in size.

	1960	1975	1987
West Germany	72	55	47.0
France	56	36	29.9
Italy	89	86	74.8
Netherlands	54	47	43.3
Belgium	75	53	45.8
Luxembourg	40	32	28.8
United Kingdom	—	27	25.9
Ireland	49	38	31.3
Denmark	47	32	18.0
Greece	96	—	89.4
Spain	79	—	72.3
Portugal	—	—	87.5

Source: Basic Statistics of the Community, 29th ed. (Luxembourg: Statistical Office of the European Communities, 1992).

With the fall of the Roman Empire, Europe experienced a period of urban decline. Commerce fell off sharply, and the subsistence societies that arose in the wake of Roman withdrawal had little need for cities. Some commercial towns reverted completely to agricultural villages; others were abandoned and forgotten. A few with considerable religious or political significance survived the Dark Ages. By and large, though, the urban way of life ceased to be a dominant feature of the Western European scene until commercialism became important again.

After about the year 1000 many of the moribund Roman towns were revived to become centers of urban commercial activity once more. Many new towns were also established, both inside and outside the limits of the old empire. Often the new towns grew around a fortified preurban core, where a feudal lord or ecclesiastical authority ensured a degree of security and protection. As the towns grew, they sought and gained political autonomy, which was spelled out in formal charters.

Those medieval cores still exist in many Western European towns, and the narrow streets of the cores cause tremendous problems for automobile users. A study of 141 West German cities indicated that well over three-fourths of the total urban street mileage is too narrow for safe two-way traffic in any significant amount. In addition, in such areas as Florence

Figure 9-11
The Cathedral of Notre Dame in Paris, France. Paris, on the Seine River, serves as the cultural, commercial, and political center of France.

and Rome, Italy, and Athens, Greece, air pollution, primarily from automobile exhaust, is threatening priceless works of art and sculpture as well as ancient marble temples. Coping with the automobile is one of the major problems facing most Western European city authorities. The pressure to create parking lots and wider streets is growing, and pollution must be controlled.

Industrialization and Contemporary Urbanization

Industrialization brought the present pattern of urbanization to the people of Western Europe. In about 1800 only 10 percent of the people in England and Wales were living in cities of 100,000 or more. That proportion doubled to 20 percent in the next forty years and doubled again in another sixty years. By 1900 the British were an urbanized society, the first in the modern world.

The population of Western Europe as a whole is now increasing only slowly, though its urbanized population is growing rapidly. In five countries—Iceland, the United Kingdom, Belgium, the Netherlands, and Spain—nine out of ten citizens live in urban settings (Figure 9–12). Only Portugal, where only 30 percent of the population is urban, falls below the world average of 41 percent.

Unfortunately, much, if not most, of the urban expansion in Western Europe has taken a heavy toll on the environment. Since World War II careless and unenlightened planning and the hasty building of shoddy high-rise apartment buildings have scarred the urban fabric of cities all across the region. In addition to the spread of housing, offices, and factory buildings, expansion has spawned vast networks of roads, power lines, railroads, and other needed facilities. Unfortunately, the rapid urban sprawl has brought many social problems that can be linked to the breakup of neighborhoods and the degradation of the urban environment.

Western European political leaders, academics, and journalists are now aware of these problems, so it is not surprising to find concern for the quality of urban life high on public agendas. The period between March 1987 and March 1988 was proclaimed the European Year of the Environment, to give a truly international focus to increasingly serious environmental problems and

their solutions. In the words of a press release outlining the EC's commitment to the Year of the Environment:

> The environmental problems we know today have their origins in urban, industrial and agricultural development that has been over-intensive and often anarchic. Scarce resources have been wasted, and there has been an accumulation of pollution, nuisances and technological risks which threaten our health and surroundings.

Suburbanization

Much of the urbanization in contemporary Europe is actually **suburbanization**. Modern trends in urban living in Europe, as in other areas of the developed world, are bringing about decreasing population densities in central cities. As a result, ever-increasing amounts of rural and agricultural land are being converted to urban uses. In England and Wales, for example, only about 5 percent of the total land area was classified as urbanized in 1900; by 1972 fully 11 percent of the land was urban. This slow but inexorable process is changing Britain's famed "green and pleasant land" to an urbanized, paved landscape, much to the dismay of most Britons. In the Netherlands and West Germany the situation is even worse. By the year 2000 one-fourth of the Netherlands will be urbanized; the total for the former West Germany will be about 18 percent (Figure 9–13). Thus, the sprawling suburbs so common in Anglo-America are now increasingly obvious features in Western Europe, as more and more agricultural land disappears before the bulldozers' onslaught. In France urbanization is officially considered "the main problem in environment planning" nationally.

In their national planning to cope with the increasing urbanization of the Paris region, French officials have adopted a scheme to encourage growth in selected peripheral cities, designated as regional metropolises (Figure 9–14). Great effort is being put into equipping those cities with high-level facilities in research, higher education, medical care, government, culture, and communications, in an attempt to counterbalance the lure of Paris, France's principal city. Those cities are now functioning as full-scale regional metropolises (Figure 9–15).

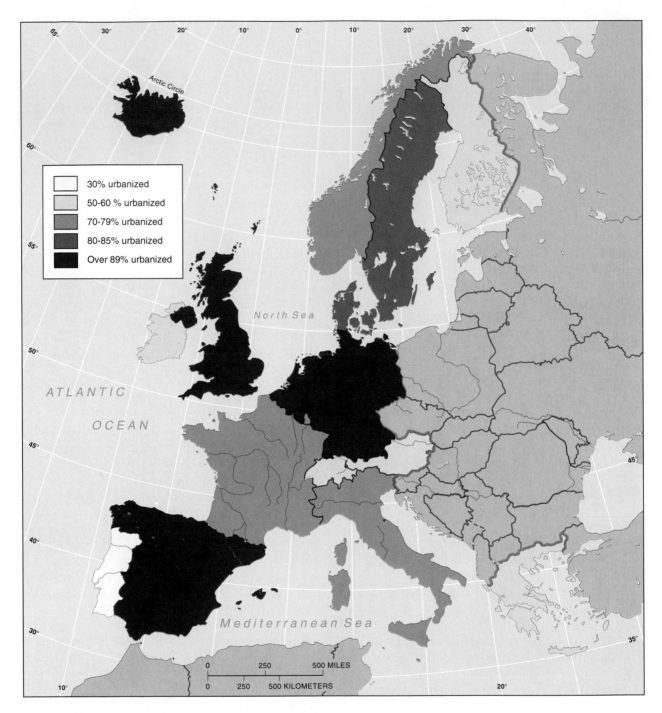

Figure 9-12
Western European urbanization. Western Europe is one of the world's most highly urbanized regions. This map reflects the percentages of the total population living in areas defined as urban.

Figure 9-13
Romerberg Square, also known as the International Building Center, in Frankfurt, Germany. Slightly northwest of the center of the picture is Old Town Hall (with the stairstepped roof line). Europe's continued urbanization and suburbanization often impact on historic cities and landscapes in less than desirable ways.

Figure 9-14
Regional metropolises of France and their spheres of influence. In an effort to diminish the population growth of Paris and to spread urban economic activities to other cities, French officials have devised a plan to encourage growth in selected regional centers. Those centers receive special aid to stimulate their growth. (From Service de Press et d'Information, *France, Town and Country Environment Planning,* New York: Ambassade de France, 1965.)

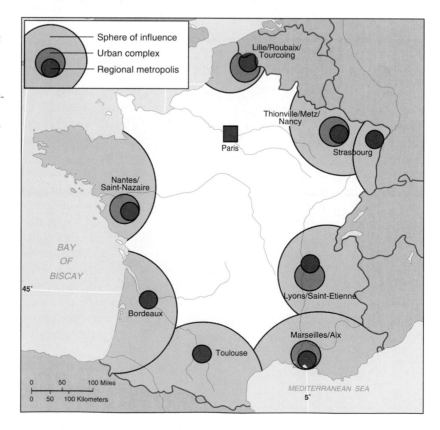

Figure 9-15
Regional growth in France to 1989. In this map population growth is given for the "spheres of influence" shown in Figure 9–14. Such growth gives an indication of the success or failure of the 1965 growth plan. Notable is the growth around Paris, which has been kept below the national average, whereas growth around Marseille has soared at almost three times that average. The old heavy industrial regions of the North and East are shown to remain as major challenges remaining almost immune to growth.

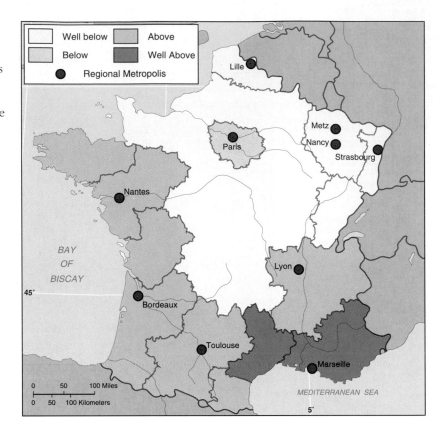

SUMMARY
A Developed Region's Movement Toward Unity

Some of the chief qualities that characterize the people of Western Europe are similar to the major socioeconomic traits used to define the developed countries of the world. Early technological and political achievements allowed the Europeans to reach out in the Age of Exploration and the centuries that followed. Their exploration led to economic exploitation, the planting of colonies, and the building of empires on all habitable continents.

The same technological and political achievements that favored the Western Europeans in their overseas accomplishments were important at home. Industrialization and urbanization, along with mechanized agriculture and a revolution in transportation technology, changed the face of the continent. The modern countries of Western Europe exhibit the history of their economic and social development in their landscapes.

Unbridled competition among the countries of Western Europe for control of area and resources led to warfare and destruction. In the twentieth century two devastating world wars erupted in a single lifetime. In the aftermath of World War II, it was almost universally recognized that far more could be gained through peaceful cooperation than through continued competition. Beginning with the European Coal and Steel Community and several other postwar cooperative organizations, the countries of Western Europe began moving toward the goal of economic and political integration. The momentum toward integration is real and increasing. There can be no doubt that a more integrated Western Europe will play an important role in shaping world affairs.

KEY TERMS

Black Death	Europeanization
core area	Europeanness
Dark Ages	irredentism
European Community (EC)	microstate
European Free Trade Association (EFTA)	suburbanization
	transhumance
European Parliament	United States of Europe
European Union (EU)	

NOTES

1. Terry G. Jordan, *The European Culture Area: A Systematic Geography* (New York: Harper & Row, 1973), 15.
2. Norman J. G. Pounds and Sue S. Ball, "Core-Areas and the Development of the European States System," *Annals, Association of American Geographers* 54 (1964): 24.
3. S. Patijn, *Landmarks in European Unity* (Leiden, Netherlands: Sijthoff, 1970), 29.
4. Ibid., 93.
5. E. Willard Miller, *A Geography of Manufacturing* (Englewood Cliffs, NJ: Prentice-Hall, 1962), 130.
6. Kingsley Davis, "The Urbanization of the Human Population," *Scientific American* 213 (September 1965): 41.

10

Western Europe: Multinational Groupings to Meet Modern Challenges

The European Union

The European Free Trade Association and European Economic Area

Celebrating on the Berlin Wall. The reunification of East and West Germany, symbolized by the dismantling of the Berlin Wall, was one of the dramatic and unexpected events of the 1990s.

Modern economic and political realities suggest that the countries of Western Europe fall into two groupings:

1. the twelve full members of the European Union (EU), sometimes known as the European Economic Community (EEC), European Community (EC), or the Common Market: Belgium, Denmark, Germany, France, Greece, Ireland, Italy, Luxembourg, the Netherlands, Portugal, Spain, and the United Kingdom.
2. the seven states of the European Free Trade Association (EFTA), several of which are in the process of becoming EU members: Austria, Finland, Iceland, Liechtenstein, Norway, Sweden, and Switzerland.

THE EUROPEAN UNION

The twelve member states that make up the European Union stretch from Portugal to Greece on the south and to Ireland, the United Kingdom, and Denmark on the north (Figure 10–1). Together those twelve countries form the world's richest market, and their total population of 350 million is larger than that of either the United States or the Soviet Union. The European Union is easily the world's biggest importer and exporter, accounting for more than one-third of all world trade and ranking second only to Canada as the largest trading partner of the United States. In recent years about one-fifth of all imports purchased by the EU have come from the United States, and about 19 percent of the EU's exports have gone to the U.S.

As for steel, the most basic industrial product, the EU countries produce considerably more than either the United States or Russia. They also lead the world in the production of several important agricultural commodities, such as hogs, wine, milk, butter, and cheese. In addition, three times more wheat is harvested in an average year in the European Union than in Canada. And the EU produces about 3 million more passenger cars than either the United States or Japan does in an average year. To help move their extraordinary volume of foreign trade, the EU countries support a merchant fleet more than four times as large as that of the United States. (Of course, much U.S. commerce is carried by U.S.-owned vessels registered in foreign countries, such as Liberia, so the real difference is somewhat less dramatic.) All of those statistics help us appreciate the tremendous significance of the European Union in these days of sharpening economic competition.

Since World War II, individual mobility and mass communications have provided young Europeans with many more shared experiences than ever before. Eurovision, an international television broadcasting organization, makes possible the transmission of important events to audiences throughout Western Europe simultaneously. Furthermore, most of the elements of modern popular culture cross boundaries with ease in today's Europe. People who live in the EU do not need passports to visit other member countries; and border-crossing formalities and requirements have been greatly lessened throughout Western Europe, making it simple for hordes of tourists to travel about and support an increasingly important tourist industry. In addition, most EU governments have joined in plans and programs for large-scale youth exchanges deliberately designed to help break down the psychological barriers created by the intense nationalism of the past. There is even an international public opinion poll within the European Union, to keep tabs on how the majority of people are feeling about various issues, including how to make decisions about environmental policies that will affect all EU countries (see the boxed feature, The Fouled Nest: Pollution and Unification).

Historians, geographers, and other EU academics are cooperating with this movement by producing school textbooks with European rather than nationalistic emphasis and interpretation. Schools in Brussels and Luxembourg have worked to develop truly European curricula and outlooks, and those efforts have led to the adoption of similar ideas in many other cities. To encourage pupils to approach their studies on a European rather than a national basis, a great deal of classroom time is devoted to reading and speaking other European languages.

Nonetheless, as we briefly review each EU country, keep in mind always that the roots of nationalism and individuality run deep in Western Europe. And an understanding of those roots is essential to an understanding of the role of Western Europe in today's world—and tomorrow's (Table 10–1).

Germany

Few Americans old enough to drive an automobile need to be reminded that Germany is a highly developed, industrialized country that ranks among the world's leading economic powers. Mercedes

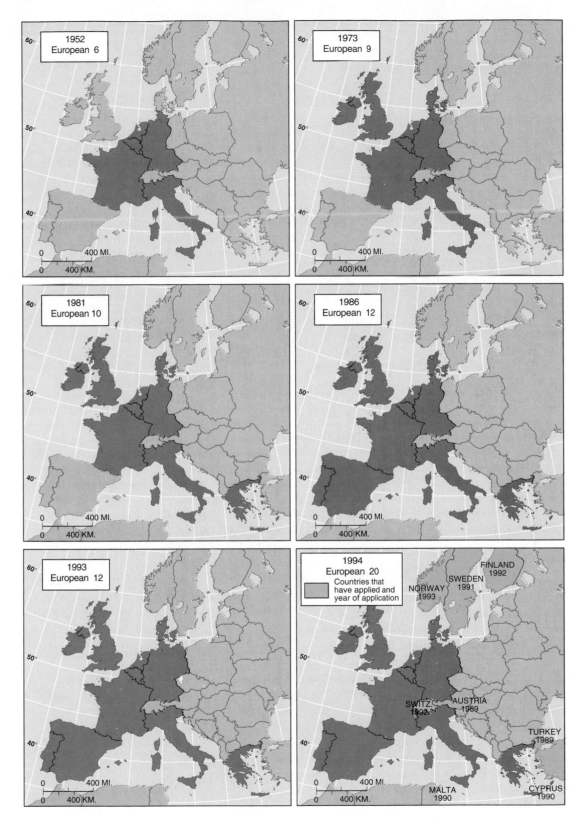

Figure 10-1

The growth of the European Union. In these six maps the territorial growth of the multinational group of countries known as the European Union is highlighted. In the 1990s several more states are scheduled for membership. The European Union will reach to Asia when Turkey and Cyprus are admitted to membership.

THE FOULED NEST
Pollution and Unification

Shortly before the Maastricht Summit (the meeting of heads of state that led to the Maastricht treaty), a public opinion survey found that over two-thirds (69 percent) of the Europeans responding agreed that EU environmental policies should be based on joint decision making. Support for the idea varied from a high of 83 percent in the centrally located Netherlands to a low of 52 percent in peripheral Ireland. As European Union leaders are quick to point out, pollution knows no frontiers! Air, water, and even soil pollution originating in one EU country can spread freely to its neighbors, even those outside the union.

Oil spills, ozone depletion, hazardous chemical waste, soil erosion, nuclear accidents, chemical fertilizer runoff, noxious emissions in the atmosphere—all are the results of poorly planned past and present economic development. As one expert emphasized, "Pollution is the measure of our failure to organize for a larger human presence in the biosphere." Although waste has always resulted from human activities, it did not exceed the earth's capacity to regenerate until the present age. Now, however, this capacity is stretched beyond its limits in many corners of Western Europe.

At their June, 1990, meeting in Dublin the heads of EU member states announced:

> We recognize our special responsibility for the environment, both to our own citizens and to the wider world. We undertake to intensify our efforts to protect and enhance the natural environment of the Union itself and the world of which it is a part. We intend that action by the Union and its Member States will be developed . . . on the principles of sustainable development and preventive and precautionary action. . . . The objective of such action must be to guarantee citizens the right to a clean and healthy environment. . . . The full achievement of this objective must be a shared responsibility.

But will the Western Europeans be willing or able to share the staggering cost of cleaning up the environment of their Eastern neighbors? Even Germany, an economic powerhouse, is being severely strained by the enormousness of the cleanup task that came with reunification. In Poland alone the cost of basic equipment needed to begin reducing the terrible air pollution caused by coal-fired power plants is estimated to be in excess of 60 billion U.S. dollars—which exceeds the whole of Poland's foreign debt by 20 billion dollars! In many areas of Eastern Europe people, especially children, are chronically ill due to environmental pollution, and life expectancy is falling. The unanswered question is whether the Western Europeans will be willing to assume the huge bill for the environmental cleanup that acceptance in the EU of countries such as Poland, Hungary, and the Czech Republic will bring?

Benz, BMW, Audi, and Porsche regularly set the high-tech standard of motoring excellence; and the Volkswagen, in one guise or another, remains a fixture on America's roads and highways more than four decades after its introduction.

After the Allied powers—chiefly the Soviet Union, Britain, the United States, and France—defeated Germany in World War II, the country was divided into occupation zones administered by the military authorities of the four chief allies. The original plan had been to treat Germany as a single unit for economic purposes. But differences between the Soviet Union and the Western Allies increased after the war; and in 1948 the Soviets ended their cooperation with the four-power governing arrangement of Germany and its former capital city, Berlin, which had also been divided. From then on, Berlin was cut off from the area under Allied control, for it was deep within the Soviet-controlled zone.

The differences between the Soviet Union and the United States and its allies crystallized into open hostilities just short of war, what became known as the **cold war**. As a result, two separate and distinctive political units were formed: the Federal Republic of Germany in the west and the Democratic Republic of Germany in the east. Winston Churchill had struck a prophetic note in a telegram he sent to President Truman in the spring of 1945:

> An iron curtain is drawn down upon their [the Russian] front. We do not know what is going on behind. There seems little doubt that the whole of the regions east of the line Lubeck-Trieste-Corfu will soon be completely in their hands. To this must be added the further enormous area conquered by the American armies between Eisenbach and Elbe, which will I suppose be occupied, when the Americans retreat, by the Russian Power.[1]

Table 10-1
Selected characteristics of major Western European countries.

	Total Area		Utilized Agricultural Areas (thousands of hectares)			Wooded Areas (thousands of hectares)	Total Labor Force (thousands)
	Square Miles (thousands)	Square Kilometers (thousands)	Arable Land	Permanent Crops	Permanent Grassland		
Germany	138	357	12,000	602	5,900	10,288	39,000
France	210	544	17,753	1,218	11,389	14,869	23,929
Italy	116	301	9,109	3,323	4,878	6,434	23,724
Netherlands	16	41	897	36	1,062	330	6,784
Belgium	12	31	766	15	626	617	4,091
Luxembourg	1	3	56	2	69	89	167
United Kingdom	94	244	6,589	57	11,785	2,297	28,133
Ireland	27	70	1,045	2	4,612	327	1,294
Denmark	17	43	2,571	11	217	493	2,889
Greece	51	132	2,925	1,027	1,789	5,755	3,967
Spain	195	505	15,560	4,900	6,650	12,511	15,021
Portugal	51	92	2,906	865	761	2,968	4,694
Austria	32	84	1,459	74	2,015	3,200	3,526
Norway	125	324	878	—	111	8,330	2,104
Sweden	174	405	2,853	—	558	28,020	4,577
Switzerland	16	41	391	21	1,609	1,052	3,583
Finland	130	337	2,453	—	123	23,222	2,545

Source: Basic Statistics of the Community, 29th ed. (Luxembourg: Statistical Office of the European Communities, 1992).

After Churchill again used the term **iron curtain** in a speech he delivered at Fulton, Missouri, in 1946, it became a household word. So, too, did *cold war.* Not until the 1970s did the tensions that so seriously divided Europe and the world for three decades begin to lessen (Figure 10–2).

The economy of West Germany made a recovery after World War II that can only be termed miraculous. Over the years the country experienced some periods of business recession, but high levels of employment and a stable currency were maintained more successfully in West Germany than in most other developed countries. During the first ten years of the European Community, the gross national product of West Germany grew at the impressive average annual rate of 6.6 percent.

This changed for the worse in the early 1990s, when the true costs of the unification with formerly communist East Germany began to be felt. Although West German leaders knew that the economy of East Germany was in a bad way when the Berlin

Wall came down, it took a few years for the enormity of the costs involved with integrating the two dissimilar social systems to become known. In part this was because the government of East Germany had consistently published grossly inflated favorable statistical reports on the state of their economy. One of the most serious problems that the unification-triggered economic slump created was Germany's shift from being a leading exporter of capital to a net borrower in world financial markets. Until that condition reverses Germany's economy will tend to slow rather than fuel the economic growth of Europe as a whole.

The steady productivity of the coal industry contributed to the early good health of West Germany's economy. Nevertheless, like all members of the EU, Germany is a net importer of energy; and its dependence on foreign energy sources, largely petroleum, remains at a high level (Table 10–2). Natural gas, which is being used in growing quantities, is imported from the nearby Netherlands; and agree-

Table 10-2
Dependence of EU countries on foreign energy sources (percentages of total supply).

	West Germany	France	Italy	Netherlands	Belgium	Luxembourg
1960	9.6	41.0	58.1	50.9	32.6	99.8
1961	12.8	43.7	62.8	49.6	35.8	99.4
1962	17.7	44.3	68.1	58.6	40.9	99.5
1963	22.4	52.6	70.2	63.2	49.4	99.7
1964	27.2	54.1	71.5	65.8	54.7	99.7
1965	32.6	55.0	73.5	62.8	59.3	99.3
1969	42.8	63.8	78.2	47.7	73.5	99.3
1970	47.9	71.0	81.8	42.3	81.8	99.2
1971	50.6	73.1	81.8	26.2	84.6	99.5
1973	54.8	78.0	83.0	6.3	86.4	99.6
1974	51.1	82.3	83.1	-9.1	91.2	99.4
1975	55.0	73.8	79.1	-24.8	84.7	99.5
1980	58.1	81.3	90.4	4.8	89.2	99.6
1981	51.5	70.1	85.0	5.2	77.7	99.2
1982	51.7	66.9	85.6	13.9	80.8	99.0
1983	51.1	61.5	80.5	7.0	73.9	98.7
1984	49.6	60.7	85.0	10.6	70.9	98.9
1985	50.2	57.2	83.9	5.2	71.3	99.0
1987	53.6	55.9	86.4	15.1	71.5	99.6
1988	52.7	54.6	81.9	27.0	73.0	98.2
1989	51.1	54.5	85.7	21.5	76.4	98.7
1990	53.4	55.8	85.7	22.7	76.2	99.4

Source: Basic Statistics of the Community, 29th ed. (Luxembourg: Statistical Office of the European Communities, 1992).
Note: Negative percentages indicate that the country was a net exporter of that much of its total energy supply.

ments have also been reached to purchase large amounts of natural gas from Russia. Table 10–3 shows how West Germany met its large energy requirements in 1990, just before reunification with East Germany.

The major industries of Germany are steel and iron, chemicals, machinery, electrical equipment, and automobiles. The industrial sector of the German economy uses approximately one-third of all the foreign oil that is imported; transportation, about one-fourth; and residential/commercial uses, approximately one-third. The remainder is consumed as a nonenergy raw material. Clearly, reliance on imported oil represents the most serious threat to the continued development of the German economy.

Another problem of great significance for Germany is large-scale migration since World War II. At war's end, the political boundaries of each central European country were redrawn, and more than 82,000 square miles of territory passed from German to Polish or Soviet administration. With that shift a human tide was set in motion: tens of thousands of Poles moved west to avoid Soviet control, and Germans moved west to escape control by Poland or to escape from the Soviet zone of occupation, which became East Germany. The hardships and misery of those displaced persons stimulated massive relief efforts by the United States and several other countries in the dark days that followed the Allied victory over Hitler's army.

During the 1950s West Germany absorbed several million Germans from the communist east, and its economy began to boom. In 1961, however, that westward flow of labor and talent was seriously slowed by the erection of the **Berlin Wall**, a physical barrier dividing the city. That wall prevented movement for nearly thirty years (see the boxed feature, The Wall Came Tumbling Down). Nonetheless, the

	United Kingdom	Ireland	Denmark	Greece	Spain	Portugal
1960						
1961						
1962						
1963	26.3	71.9	98.0			
1964						
1965						
1969	43.8	73.0	99.6			
1970	45.1	76.1	100.0	83.5		
1971	49.5	80.5	100.0	82.3		
1973	48.2	80.7	99.6	91.4		
1974	50.2	82.2	99.5	96.6		
1975	43.2	84.6	99.1	68.3		
1980	5.7	81.7	98.7	85.3		
1981	-6.4	72.5	95.6	77.6	81.3	91.1
1982	-11.3	65.0	89.2	67.1	70.1	91.9
1983	-17.8	61.9	85.6	65.4	68.8	89.8
1984	-11.3	57.3	85.1	64.5	63.2	93.4
1985	-15.1	54.0	79.6	64.5	60.6	90.0
1987	-15.5	64.7	65.2	63.3	63.3	94.1
1988	-9.0	66.2	59.6	63.8	64.3	88.5
1989	3.7	66.1	58.9	62.1	65.5	94.6
1990	3.4	70.4	50.2	64.2	66.8	96.4

robust economy was producing increased demands for labor, so West Germans began a systematic recruitment of foreign workers. First Italy was tapped, then Spain and Portugal. Ultimately, other Mediterranean countries, especially Yugoslavia and Turkey, supplied workers for West German factories and construction projects (Figure 10–3). By the early 1970s between 2 million and 3 million **guest workers**, as they were euphemistically termed, composed more than 10 percent of the West German work force. The majority of those workers were men, but before long many of them were joined by their families. And soon ghettolike conditions were appearing in West German industrial centers, where the foreign workers, often in the lowest-paid jobs, clustered with their families.

As the oil embargo of 1973 began to cause a slackening of industrial production and economic activity, the foreigners were among the first to lose their jobs.

Rather than return to their villages in Yugoslavia or Turkey, however, many opted to remain in the industrial centers where they had earlier been in demand. Needless to say, a wide range of problems emerged to vex West German industrial leaders, local and national government officials, and the out-of-work foreigners and their families. By 1980 the proportion of foreign workers had dropped to just under 8 percent, but their concentration in inner-city enclaves had not changed significantly.

Foreign workers and the problems associated with them are not unique to Germany (see Figure 10–3). In 1980 about 6.5 percent of all workers in the United Kingdom, 8.2 percent in Belgium, and 16.5 percent in Switzerland were foreigners. Without a doubt, the problem of integrating foreign workers and their families into the larger society around them stands as a major challenge for Western Europeans in the last years of the twentieth century.

Figure 10-2
Street scene in Rostock, formerly East Germany. The lagging technology, lower per capita incomes, and lack of personal and political freedom in East Germany created the unrest that ultimately resulted in the reunification of Germany.

The demographic realities of aging populations and shrinking birthrates, coupled with the unwillingness of most Western Europeans to do menial jobs or undertake hard physical labor, ensure that some foreign labor will be essential. Germany and several other West European countries are being severely challenged by the need to integrate their guest workers in a way that is fair to the newcomers without appearing to threaten the majority of workers.

France

Almost four-fifths the size of Texas, France is the largest Western European country and the linchpin of the European Community. France combines great natural wealth with a central location; and it is endowed with a wide variety of terrain, two-thirds of which is nearly level or gently rolling (Figure 10–4)

Without doubt France has exercised the strongest influence on the European Union to date. Somewhat unique among the major industrial countries of Western Europe, France boasts an important agricultural sector with substantial domestic resources of primary raw materials, a diversified and modern industrial plant, and a capable labor force. The gross national product of France usually ranks fifth in the world, and per capita GNP is equally impressive. Just under 10 percent of French exports are destined for sale in the United States.

France is amply provided with such raw materials as iron ore, bauxite, and uranium; and its hydroelectric power sources are well developed. As a result, France stands as one of Western Europe's major suppliers of metals and minerals and an important producer of iron ore and bauxite. In addition, it possesses large deposits of antimony, magnesium, pyrites, tungsten, and certain radioactive minerals.

In recent years France has emerged as a leader in the peaceful use of nuclear energy. It has been said, with some rhetorical exaggeration, that France has four reasons to succeed in using that controversial energy source: first, it has no oil; second, it has no coal; third, it has no gas; fourth, it has no choice.

Table 10-3
Energy sources as percentages of total energy consumption in EC countries, 1990.

	Petroleum	Coal and Lignite	Natural Gas	Nuclear Energy	Tidal, Hydro, and Geothermal Energy
West Germany	40.6	28.1	17.7	13.3	0.3
France	41.4	9.2	11.7	37.2	0.5
Italy	58.9	9.7	25.8	0.0	5.8
Netherlands	37	14.1	46.4	1.4	1.1
Belgium	38.7	21.6	17.4	22.2	0.1
Luxembourg	45.7	34.1	11.4	0.0	8.8
United Kingdom	38.6	30.3	22.3	7.8	1.0
Ireland	46.0	34.9	19.0	0.0	0.1
Denmark	49.1	35.9	10.6	0.0	4.4
Greece	59.3	38.2	0.5	0.0	2.0
Spain	53.6	22.2	5.8	16.0	2.4
Portugal	76.3	17.3	0.0	0.0	6.4

Source: Basic Statistics of the Community, 29th ed. (Luxembourg: Statistical Office of the European Communities, 1992).

When the 1973 oil crisis occurred, the French government opted for nuclear electric-generating plants. The national electric company was given the mandate of initiating a nuclear energy development program that could meet the country's needs by the 1990s. According to French experts, the price of imported oil would now have to be less than $5.00 a barrel in order for oil-fired plants to compete with nuclear generators. And there is little likelihood that the price of oil will ever again drop to that low figure.

When French nuclear experts are queried about the potential for an accident like the one at Chernobyl in Ukraine, which spread dangerous radioactivity over a vast area, they are quick to point out that their country's reactors are based on a different technology. Like most reactors in the United States, French plants are enclosed in a confinement building designed to contain any accidental release of radioactive material. At worst, they claim, accidents in France would be of the type experienced at Three Mile Island in Pennsylvania. The rest of the world hopes the French experts are correct.

Historically one of the world's leading manufacturing countries, France competes in all major branches of industrial activity. French aluminum and chemical industries rank among the largest in the world, as do the mechanical and electrical sectors. In addition, the French automobile industry produces more than 3 million vehicles a year. And the electronics, telecommunications, and aerospace indus-

tries have all contributed to the present high level of technological development that characterizes much of French industry. Military use of atomic energy, as well as certain civilian applications, has also achieved an impressive level of sophistication. In spite of increasing criticism from other countries in the South Pacific region, France maintains a nuclear weapons test facility on Mururoa atoll in French Polynesia.

In 1962 France joined with the United Kingdom to produce the first supersonic commercial jet air transport, the Concorde. And in 1965 France launched its first earth-orbiting satellite; it continues to pursue an active space research program, with rocket-launching facilities in French Guiana.

Italy

Compared with many other Western European countries, Italy has been poorly endowed by nature. Much of the country is unsuited for modern farming because of mountainous terrain or an unfavorably dry climate. In addition, it has no significant deposits of coal or iron ore, and most other important industrial mineral deposits are widely dispersed and of poor or indifferent quality. Deposits of natural gas, discovered in the Po Basin after World War II, are the country's most important mineral resource, but the gas supply is being rapidly depleted and does not constitute a long-term source of energy. As a result of such natural deficiencies, Italy must im-

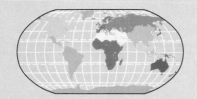

THE WALL CAME TUMBLING DOWN

The scenes of November 9, 1989, will not be soon forgotten by television viewers around the world. That day the Berlin Wall, hated symbol of the cold war and state brutality, came tumbling down. Berliners from both the East and West sectors of the long-divided center of German culture were televised dancing and joyously embracing against the backdrop of the graffiti-smeared broken wall, amidst sounds of sledge-hammer blows and popping champagne corks.

To many viewers, the joyous pictures seemed almost unreal. Only a few months before, the same television screens had shown the bloody suppression of peaceful student demonstrators by the Chinese army in Beijing's Tiananmen Square. Could it be possible that Soviet tanks and steel-helmeted East German border guards would not move to stamp out the revelers in Berlin in much the same way?

The answer to that question had been given the month before—in October, 1989—by Mikhail Gorbachev, president of the Soviet Union, when he gave explicit approval of the political reforms taking place in such Eastern European countries as Poland, Hungary, and Czechoslovakia. Seen in retrospect, one of Gorbachev's comments—"Life punishes those who come too late"—was particularly prophetic for Erich Honecker, East Germany's hard-line communist leader. Earlier that year Honecker had declared:

> Despite the vigorous stance of Herr Genscher [West German Foreign Minister] and Mr. Shultz [U.S. Secretary of State], the wall will remain as long as the conditions leading to its erection have not changed. It will still be standing in fifty and even one hundred years' time. . . .

Ironically, both Honecker and the wall were removed from service before the end of that same year.

Before it actually tumbled down, the wall had begun to crack—most noticeably when Hungary opened its borders with Austria in September, 1989. Within days more than 15,000 discontented—mostly young—citizens of East Germany "voted with their feet" by fleeing through Czechoslovakia, Hungary, and Austria to the West. Then, in October massive popular demonstrations began taking place in East Germany to protest the repressive nature of Honecker's communist successors. The demonstrators sang again "Deutschland Uber Alles," an old anthem of German unity that had been discredited by the Nazis. And in that same spirit West Germany's Chancellor Helmut Kohl welcomed the more than 50,000 East German refugees who had fled through Hungary, as well as the 62,000 who had come through Czechoslovakia.

With the end of the wall and the virtual collapse of East Germany's communist regime, it is not surprising that the move for German unity soon became a tide. On Sunday, July 1, 1990, a treaty on monetary, economic, and social union came into effect, and on October 3, 1990, total political union followed. It is too soon to say what the outcome of union will mean in the day-to-day lives of the German people, but it is clear that the unified German economy will rank with those of the world's productive superpowers.

---

port most raw materials for manufacturing. Other obstacles to development have included low levels of productivity in agriculture and in certain industrial sectors, as well as the need to upgrade the skill of much of the labor force.

The south of Italy, an area known as the **Mezzogiorno** (Land of the Midday Sun), is one of the major regions of underdevelopment in the European Union. It includes the Italian peninsula south of Rome and the islands of Sicily and Sardinia—an area approximately the size of Pennsylvania and Delaware. There a rugged landscape, poor soils, and a Mediterranean climate have had a most profound impact on the economy.

Only 15 percent of that area is considered level enough for cultivation; 50 percent is categorized as hilly, and the remainder is mountainous (Figure 10–5).

Unfortunately, the mountains of the Mezzogiorno are not high enough to ensure year-round snow accumulations. As a result, the rivers are dry for long periods of the year, flowing only during the moist Mediterranean winter season. Ironically, winter is also frequently a period of flooding, waterlogged fields, and serious soil erosion. Irrigation schemes are difficult and exceedingly expensive in the area.

Although it still lags, the Mezzogiorno is now making economic progress. The effects of mas-

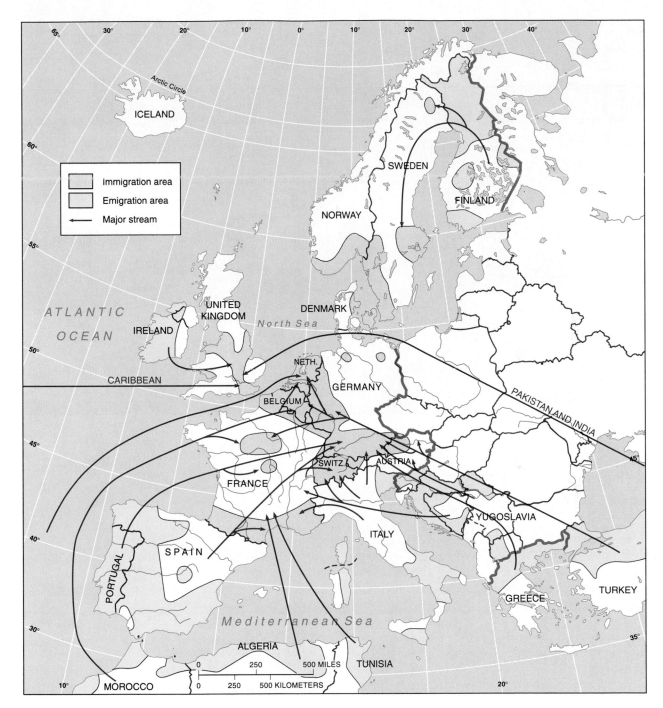

Figure 10-3
Guest worker flows. This map shows the principal source regions and destinations of Western Europe's major post-World War II influx of guest workers.

Figure 10-4
The harbor at Cannes, France, a major tourism center on the Mediterranean coast. The mild climate, scenic landscapes, and rich cultural heritage have made tourism a major economic activity throughout southern Europe.

sive post–World War II investments in regional agricultural-improvement schemes and industrial development are beginning to be felt. It will be a long time, however, before the Italian south begins to equal the north in terms of productivity and prosperity. And as a result, people are still leaving the area at a disturbing rate in search of a better life.

Conditions are considerably different in northern Italy. There the economy—more influenced by private enterprise—has flourished. The names of such corporate giants as Fiat and Olivetti have become household words in North America, where innumerable smaller Italian firms also find a ready and profitable market for their fashionable shoes and clothing. Despite a severe economic recession in 1971 and the relative stagnation of the early 1970s, Italy normally ranks about

seventh among the world's most important industrial powers.

Italy is even more dependent on foreign energy sources than is France (see Table 10–2). Especially disturbing for Italians is the overwhelmingly important role that oil plays in meeting their energy requirements (see Table 10–3).

The Netherlands

With 932 people per square mile (363 per square kilometer), the Netherlands is the most densely populated country in Western Europe—it is even more densely populated than Japan. For centuries the Dutch have been responding to that reality by energetically adding to their low-lying territory through land reclamation and drainage schemes. Dike building, which protected land that lay above the low-tide

240

level, appears to have begun about A.D. 1000 in the extensive tidal marshes of the southern Netherlands. Sluice gates in the dikes allowed surplus water to drain out of ditches at low tide but could be closed to keep out the incoming tidal flow. Nonetheless, the protected lands that resulted, known as **polders**, were still subject to periodic flooding when storms occurred during high tides. Not until windmills, and later steam-driven pumps, were perfected could the Dutch begin to create agriculturally productive polders in areas that lay below sea level (Figure 10–6).

Figure 10-5
Lemon and grape production along the rugged coast south of Naples, Italy. Although these and other crops are adaptable to the dry summer subtropical climate, much of peninsular Italy constitutes a poor agricultural resource. The southern portion, the Mezzogiorno, provides a classic example of regional lag in the development process.

In 1953 the Dutch suffered a severe disaster when storm winds of up to 100 miles (161 kilometers) an hour drove the waters of the Rhine-Maas-Schelde river system across farmlands and towns. An estimated 1,800 people died, and another 100,000 had to be evacuated. The flood damage was conservatively estimated at more than $500 million. To prevent a recurrence of such a flood, the Dutch constructed the immense Delta Project, which consists of four huge sea dikes, to control most of the mouths of the Rhine-Maas-Schelde distributary system.

Many observers of the Netherlands speak of the **Dutch miracle**—they are properly impressed that the Dutch have created almost 40 percent of their country by diking and draining polders. There, more than anywhere else in Europe, it is appropriate to speak of a human landscape. Today, productive agricultural enterprises flourish on much of the reclaimed land, and many new towns and industrial areas have been developed.

The Dutch economy is characterized by private enterprise, but the central government plays a strong role. A limited base of natural resources—primarily gas, oil, and coal—as well as the country's strategic location, has led to an economy unusually dependent on foreign trade. Industry is modernized and characteristically competitive, backed by a diligent and highly skilled labor force and a vigorous and adaptable business community. The Netherlands boasts that direct U.S. investment amounts to almost $600 per capita of Dutch population, well over twice the average for the European Union as a whole and higher than the per capita figure for any other European country.

Agriculture, though almost completely modernized and characterized by high crop yields, plays only a small role in the overall Dutch economy. As an industry, agriculture relies heavily on imports, particularly livestock feed. The livestock industry, in turn, accounts for about two-thirds of the total farm output. Expansion in this sector has been the result of the European Union's agricultural policy, which favors efficient producers; the Netherlands is the most efficient dairy and livestock producer.

In recent years economic sectors in the Netherlands have continued to show the kind of postindustrial shifts that characterize older developed societies throughout the rich world. The percentage of the labor force engaged in primary pursuits has dropped slightly, from 6.5 percent in 1974 to 4.7 percent in 1990. The manufacturing sector registered an even greater decline, from 34.7 percent in 1974 to 27.1 percent in 1990. Service, including government employment, rose from 58.9 to 68.2 percent in the same period.

Belgium

The kingdom of Belgium has long been at the geographical and cultural crossroads of Western Europe. Today, Belgians are sharply divided along ethnolinguistic lines: the **Walloons**, who speak French, live in the southern half of the country; the **Flemish**, who speak a dialect of Dutch, live in the northern half. The continued existence of Belgium as a unified state may well depend on how successful the central government is in allowing each national group to achieve the almost complete autonomy it is demanding.

Belgium emerged from World War II much less damaged than its neighbors. The immediate postwar era saw rapid reconstruction, liberalization of trade, and high economic growth rates. The pace slackened, however, until 1958, when the establishment of the European Community brought a new surge in the Belgian economy. Confidence in the opportunities that the Common Market provided for Belgian producers led to bold new investments in manufacturing plants and equipment.

Agriculture plays a relatively minor role in the current Belgian economy. In recent years agriculture has been responsible for less than 3 percent of the GNP, and it employs roughly the same percentage of the labor force. Livestock and poultry raising are the dominant agricultural activities, though traditional crops—sugar beets, potatoes, wheat, and barley—still form an important part of the rural scene.

With its crossroads location and its dense concentration of industry and population, Belgium has played an impressive role in international trade. The country's industries contribute $50 billion in exports and about 33 percent of the total GNP, with the iron and steel and metal-fabricating sectors leading the way. But because Belgium does not possess any significant stores of natural resources, it must import most raw materials, as well as fuel, machinery, transportation equipment, and about one-fourth of its food. The country's development and prosperity are largely the product of its highly skilled labor force and its managerial expertise.

Luxembourg

Closely linked in an economic union with Belgium for more than half a century, tiny Luxembourg is similar to its larger neighbor in many ways. After Germany violated the neutrality of both nations during World War I and World War II, both became staunch charter members of the **North Atlantic Treaty Organization (NATO)**, a military alliance of western nations founded in 1949. In addition, the government of each country is a constitutional monarchy. Luxembourg, however, has no king; rather, its executive power is in the hands of the hereditary grand duke and a cabinet. Internally, Luxembourg is

Figure 10-6
Farmstead and farmland on a polder in Zeeland Province of the Netherlands. A ship is visible in the channel behind the dike. Since much of the Netherlands is below sea level, reclamation of this northern segment of the Great European Plain has been an engineering marvel.

divided into 126 communes, each administered by an elected council, in a system closely patterned after that of Belgium.

A high level of industrialization provides the inhabitants of this Rhode Island-sized country with one of the highest per capita GNPs in the European Community. Despite large-scale attempts to diversify, Luxembourg's industrial scene is dominated by iron and steel, which accounts for about half of the country's total industrial production. In recent years steel output has declined to 4 million tons annually, still a real feat for a country of only 390,000 people.

Agriculture absorbs about 3 percent of the labor force, mostly in small-scale livestock raising and mixed farming. In addition, the vineyards of the Mosel Valley provide the raw material for a profitable wine industry, and Luxembourg's excellent dry white wines are exported widely.

A surprisingly large number of workers are engaged in Luxembourg's flourishing financial activities. The country has more than sixty large banks, making it one of the world's important financial centers, and trading in multinational corporate securities is significant. Favorable tax treatment by the government has encouraged many large holding companies to establish their headquarters in Luxembourg.

The United Kingdom

The terms *United Kingdom (UK)* and *Britain* are used synonymously to refer to the United Kingdom of Great Britain and Northern Ireland, which consists of England, Wales, Scotland, and Northern Ireland (sometimes called by its traditional name, **Ulster**). In the eighteenth century the island-based British gained mastery of the seas and established an empire scattered over all the continents. That empire was enlarged and reinforced in the nineteenth century, and Britain became the supreme world power. But changing world conditions, punctuated by two costly world wars, severely weakened Britain's position in the twentieth century. Many of the British colonies gained their political independence, and the old empire gave way to the Commonwealth of Nations, a loose political, cultural, and economic association of the United Kingdom and many of its former colonies. Of the 50 member countries in the Commonwealth, 44 are in the developing world.

When the European Community was formed, several Western European countries did not join initially, fearing a division between the countries that were in it and those that remained outside. Britain, in particular, was faced with several problems because of its long-standing connections with the Commonwealth. It tried to interest the original "inner six" EC countries in forming a European Industrial Free Trade Area (EIFTA). The six were suspicious of Britain's motives, however, fearing that EIFTA was just a device to sidetrack the development of the European Community. At that time the United Kingdom insisted on retaining its own national autonomy and Commonwealth economic preferences.

Seven countries—Austria, Denmark, Norway, Portugal, Sweden, Switzerland, and the United Kingdom—then formed the European Free Trade Association (EFTA), or "outer seven," during the 1960s. But Britain, with more than half of EFTA's total population and almost 60 percent of its total production, clearly dominated the organization.

By the mid-1960s it was becoming obvious that Britain's brightest economic prospects lay with the European Community, rather than with the Commonwealth and EFTA. Trade with the Commonwealth was declining, whereas trade with Western Europe was increasing (Table 10–4). Furthermore,

Table 10-4
Destinations of United Kingdom exports (percentage).

		Western Europe				
Year	Commonwealth	EEC	EFTA	Other	Total	United States
1958	38	14	11	2	27	9
1960	37	15	12	2	29	10
1965	28	19	14	4	37	10
1966	26	19	16	4	38	13

Source: Basic Statistics of the Community, 15th ed. (Luxembourg: Statistical Office of the European Communities, 1977).

once the European Community was crystallized, it would produce a formidable barrier to British imports. For example, German cars sold in France and French cars sold in Germany would not be subject to any import duty; British cars sold to European Community countries, in contrast, would be subject to their common external tariff. Also, it was obvious that Commonwealth countries were intent on rapidly developing their own industrial sectors and would no longer be considered ready markets for British goods. Therefore, in 1973 Britain and Denmark left EFTA and, with the Republic of Ireland, joined the European Community.

Leaders in both the UK and the European Community enthusiastically hailed Britain's entry. They saw it as a step that could greatly increase the security and stability of the European Community and the prosperity and quality of life of the peoples of Western Europe. Certainly, the present twelve nations of the European Union are a more diverse and impressive economic unit than were the original EC six.

The most notable feature of Britain's economy is the importance of industry, services, and trade. It ranks fourth in world trade behind the United States, West Germany, and Japan, taking about 6 percent and contributing more than 5 percent of the world's

Figure 10-7
North Sea oil and gas areas. The North Sea petroleum deposits now being developed are providing substantial supplies of energy to Western Europe. Dependable energy resources are especially critical to areas of industrial activity and to densely populated areas with high levels of living.

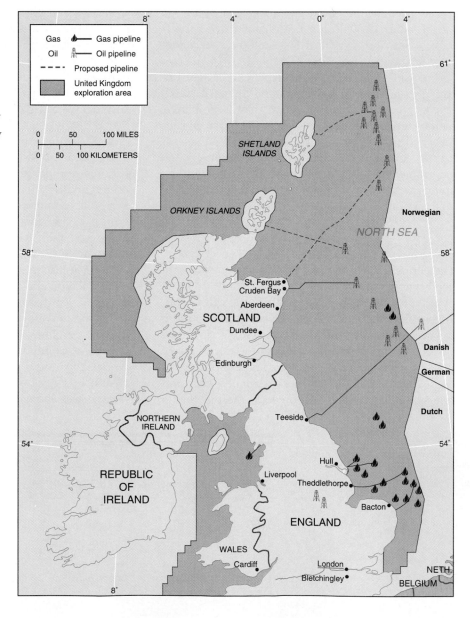

Figure 10–8
An oil rig being towed to Norway's Statfjord field in the North Sea. The huge deposits of petroleum and natural gas beneath the North Sea have been of great benefit to Britain and Norway and of lesser value to Germany, the Netherlands, and Denmark, in an otherwise oil-and-gas deficient Europe.

exports. In its share of invisible world trade (e.g., financial services, civil aviation, travel, and overseas investments), Britain ranks second, immediately behind the United States.

Britain has the oldest industrialized economy in the world. But coal, the paramount energy source for that early industrialization, declined in importance during the twentieth century, and an alarming reliance on imported petroleum developed. Then, during the mid-1960s huge deposits of petroleum and natural gas were discovered under the bed of the North Sea (Figure 10–7). By 1972 natural gas from the North Sea fields accounted for 88 percent of all gas available in the UK. More than half of all gas sold in Britain is for industrial and commercial uses; the remainder goes to domestic consumers.

Reliable sources of energy are imperative if Britain and other Western European countries are to maintain and improve their standards of living (Figure 10–8). The stakes are high; astronomical sums must be invested in exploration and production now as a guarantee that future economic development will be possible in Western Europe. The energy crunch brought about by the boycott of Arab petroleum-producing nations in 1973 and 1974 and the 1979 revolution in Iran have made this fact painfully clear. Britain was one of several Western

European participants who joined the U.S. in the Gulf War against Iraq in early 1991.

For Britain, the future outlook for energy production seems good. With the pumping of the first petroleum from the offshore Argyll field in 1975, Britain moved into the ranks of producing nations. Within five years Britain became self-sufficient in petroleum, and by the end of the decade it joined the list of important oil-exporting nations (see Table 10–2). Although speculation about the future is hazardous, an energy renaissance clearly has taken place in the world's senior developed country.

Ireland

The Republic of Ireland occupies about five-sixths of the island of Ireland, which was once entirely controlled by England. The island's northern portion encompasses the six counties that make up Northern Ireland, still an integral part of the United Kingdom. In recent years Northern Ireland, which is predominantly Protestant, has been embroiled in a bitter civil dispute that often erupts into bombings and street warfare. In contrast, the Republic of Ireland is about 94 percent Roman Catholic. Late in 1994, an uneasy peace began between the militant Irish unification group known as the Irish Republican Army (IRA) and the British Government.

English is the common language in Ireland, but the Irish form of the Celtic language of **Gaelic**, currently encouraged by the government of the Irish Republic, is spoken in some places; both English and Irish are official languages. After a century of decline, Irish is again showing signs of growth. For example, Irish-speaking schools have become popular in several urban areas, and highway directional signs are printed in both English and Irish.

The Republic of Ireland is notably lacking in most industrial natural resources. Until very recently, what industrial development it did have was oriented primarily toward the domestic market. Efforts have lately been to accelerate industrial development; therefore, the country's entry into the European Community was seen as a great boon.

Not surprisingly, agriculture remains a major factor in the national development schemes of the Republic of Ireland. But agricultural output has failed to keep pace with industrial growth in recent years, even though exports are still largely agricultural.

Although the Republic of Ireland's economic links with the United Kingdom are close, the country adheres scrupulously to a policy of political independence from its large and more affluent neighbor. In recent years Irish Republican troops have served with distinction in a number of United Nations peace-keeping operations around the globe. Nonetheless, the country remains outside NATO, and in 1969 the prime minister stated that the Irish international policy—like that of Sweden, Austria, and Switzerland—was neutrality. That position was reaffirmed when the Republic of Ireland joined the European Community in 1973.

Denmark

Long an agriculturally dominated economy, Denmark shifted its emphasis to industry in the early 1960s. In 1964 industrial exports outstripped agricultural sales for the first time, and in recent years industrial products have accounted for about 60 percent of Denmark's total export trade. More than one-fourth of all Danish workers are now engaged in industrial pursuits, and manufacturing contributes about 30 percent of the GNP.

Denmark is poorly endowed with fuel resources. Some low-grade iron ore is found in the south, but on the whole Denmark depends on imports for its principal industrial raw materials.

One of the reasons for the successful postwar development of the Danish economy has been its adaptability, which has resulted in a wide range of competitive and specialized products. Danes boast of being able to one-up their trading partners—selling fine smoking pipes in England, whiskey in Scotland, chewing gum in the United States. In addition, Europe's two largest breweries are located in Denmark, and Danish beer is sold widely throughout the world. Clearly, one of Denmark's important domestic raw materials is its skilled labor.

The most extensive use of Denmark's 16,633 square miles (43,043 square kilometers) of territory remains agricultural. And by far the largest portion of the agricultural land is cultivated for animal foodstuffs. Ninety percent of the farm gross income derives from animal production, chiefly butter, cheese, bacon, beef, veal, poultry, and eggs.

Greece

Greece, the ancient cradle of democracy and European culture, became the tenth member of the European Community on January 1, 1981. Along with Spain and Portugal, Greece had applied for membership in the 1970s, when all three southern European countries emerged from long dictatorships. To those requests for admission, the European Commission, the executive arm of the European Community, responded:

> When Greece, Portugal, and Spain, newly emerging as democratic States after a long period of dictatorship, asked to be admitted to the Community, they were making a commitment which is primarily a political one. Their choice is doubly significant, both reflecting the concern of these three new democracies for their own consolidation and protection against the return of dictatorship and constituting an act of faith in a United Europe, which demonstrates that the ideas inspiring the creation of the Community have lost none of their vigour or relevance.[2]

Thus, political concerns rather than economic factors were crucial to the EC membership of Greece, Spain, and Portugal.

The European Commission's focus on politics was probably good for Greece, because its level of economic development was lower than in other EC countries. For example, at that time only 8.4 percent of the EC labor force was engaged in agriculture, whereas well over one-third of all Greek workers were involved in agrarian activities. Nonetheless, Greece's location and long maritime tradition had given the nation an impressive strength in commerce. When Greece joined the European Community, its merchant fleet comprised almost 10 percent of the world's total. Thus, with the Greek fleet the European Community gained control of approximately 15,000 of the world's 70,000 large merchant ships.

Greece's fabled natural beauty and usually pleasant Mediterranean climate have combined with reasonable prices and good facilities to provide the country's chief source of foreign exchange—tourism. More than 10 million tourists visited Greece in 1992, bringing in the equivalent of $3 billion in foreign currency. Both the increased stability and the ease of travel that membership in the European Union guarantees should make tourism an even more important element in the Greek economy in the years ahead.

Spain

Spain, about equal in size to the states of Arizona and Utah combined, is a large country by European standards. Negotiations for Spain's entrance into the European Community began during the 1960s and culminated in full membership in the mid-1980s. With Portugal, Spain, France, Italy, and Greece as members, the present European Union is certainly the major force in the Mediterranean Basin. Such a presence surely has a profound impact on the countries of North Africa and the Middle East that share the shores of this great inland sea.

Spain's entry into the European Community became possible when long-time dictator Francisco Franco died in 1975 and Prince Juan Carlos de Borbón y Borbón assumed the position of king and chief of state. Political freedom was restored, and in 1977 Spain held its first elections since 1936. The Spanish Cortes, or parliament, has since proven itself an effective branch of government.

Along with its adoption of a democratic government, Spain has also experienced significant changes in its economy. The protective, centralized economic policies followed during Franco's dictatorship proved unworkable in the open society of the late 1970s, and competitive economic forces took their place. Although high energy costs and world economic uncertainties pose enormous problems, the outlook for Spain's economic growth is promising; and membership in the European Union ensures that the country's long-term development aspirations will more easily be achieved.

In recent years more than half of Spain's overall exports have gone to the countries of the European Union, and almost 40 percent of its imports have come from those countries. Traditionally, about two-thirds of Spain's agricultural exports have gone to the Common Market. Crops and products typical of the Mediterranean—such as citrus fruits, wine, fresh vegetables, soybean oil, olives, olive oil, and nuts—form a major part of those exports.

British control of **Gibraltar** is a frequent bone of contention between Britain and Spain. Gibraltar, a small mountainous peninsula in the south, commands one of the world's most strategically important sea-lanes, the Strait of Gibraltar, which connects the Atlantic Ocean and the Mediterranean Sea. Known as the Rock, Gibraltar was taken from Spain by the British during the War of Spanish Succession in 1704. Gibraltar is clearly a relic of colonialism and something of an embarrassment to the British. But the residents of Gibraltar, known as Gibraltarians, voted nearly unanimously in a 1967 referendum to retain their political ties to the United Kingdom. As Spain's economy and political climate improve, the position of the Gibraltarians may soften, and the Gibraltar question may become more amenable to a solution that is satisfactory to all three groups. Certainly Spain's membership in the European Union will help speed that solution.

Portugal

In size Portugal resembles the state of Indiana, but in population it is almost twice as large: Indiana has approximately 5.5 million citizens; Portugal, approximately 10 million. The northern portion of the country is rugged and mountainous, whereas the area south of the Tagus River is largely rolling plains. Thanks to the country's position fronting the Atlantic Ocean, most of Portugal has a more moist and temperate climate than is found in the Mediterranean Basin to the east. That combination of terrain and climate allows almost half of Portugal's total land area to be utilized for agricultural purposes, and almost 90 percent of that area is classified as arable land, on which crops, orchards, and vineyards can be developed. (Figure 10–9).

Figure 10-9
Vineyards in Upper Douro Valley of northern Portugal. Beautiful landscapes and a most pleasant climate characterize Portugal. Nevertheless, the country's 10 million people remain more dependent on agriculture than is typical of Western Europe and experience a comparatively low standard of living.

Although the percentage of the work force engaged in agriculture has declined in recent decades, from 42 percent in 1960 to 18 percent in 1991, Portugal still lags behind most other EU countries in this respect. Nonetheless, the industrial and service sectors have shown the increases that usually accompany economic development in the modern world. In 1960, for example, the industrial work force accounted for only 21 percent of the total, whereas today approximately one-third of the workers are employed in the industrial sector. And the shift into the service sector has been equally dramatic, with more than 48 percent of workers engaged in service functions in 1991.

Portugal is one of Europe's oldest countries; its modern roots go back to A.D. 1139, when Alfonso I became king. The present-day boundaries were drawn in 1249, after a long period devoted to expelling the Moors. During the Age of Discovery, Portuguese explorers pushed to almost every part of the world and laid the foundations for a great territorial empire in Africa, Asia, and South America (where they colonized Brazil). In the 1970s Portugal fought expensive wars in a futile effort to retain its African colonies in such places as Angola and Mozambique. The drain of those wars on the Portuguese economy was disastrous and ultimately led to the downfall of the dictatorial regime of Antonio Salazar, who had been in power since the 1930s. Recently, Portugal reached an agreement with the government of the People's Republic of China whereby Macao, a Portuguese colony for more than four centuries, will be returned to Chinese control in 1999, just two years after Britain returns nearby Hong Kong.

In 1974 Portuguese voters chose an assembly to draft a democratic constitution and thereby launched the country on its present path of representative parliamentary government. That accomplishment was crucial to the Portuguese in 1977, when their government sought entry into the European Community. In recommending the eventual acceptance of Portugal, the European Commission noted that democracy was an established fact there:

> The community cannot leave Portugal out of the process of European integration. . . . The resulting disappointment would be politically very grave and the source of serious difficulties. The accession of Portugal, which set its face firmly towards Europe almost as soon as its democracy was restored, can only strengthen the European ideal.

Portugal, with Spain, entered the European Community in 1986. Clearly, Portugal's long-term future and economic development will be closely tied to that of the expanded European Union.

THE EUROPEAN FREE TRADE ASSOCIATION AND EUROPEAN ECONOMIC AREA

The EFTA is composed of Austria, Finland, Iceland, Liechtenstein, Norway, Sweden, and Switzerland. The organization exists to encourage the free trade of industrial products among the seven countries involved. Specifically, in the words of the Stockholm Convention, which established the EFTA in January 1960, the EFTA's objectives are these:

> To promote . . . a sustained expansion of economic activity, full employment, increased productivity and the rational use of resources, financial stability and continuous improvement in living standards; To secure that trade between member states takes place in conditions of fair competition; To avoid significant disparity between member states in conditions of supply of raw materials produced within the area of the Association; and To contribute to the harmonious development and expansion of world trade and to the progressive removal of barriers to it.

The EFTA constitutes an important part of the economic integration that has been taking place in Western Europe since the end of World War II. Free-trade agreements between EU and EFTA countries have promoted a growth of trade for all concerned and the creation of a free-trade zone for industrial products throughout Western Europe. Four of the countries that make up the EFTA have applied for membership in the European Union, (see Figure 10–1). Austria completed its formal application in 1989, Sweden in 1991, and Finland and Switzerland in 1992. In October 1994 the Finnish people voted to join the EU in hopes of boosting their country's sagging economy.

On January 1, 1993, the seven EFTA nations joined the European Union in forming the world's biggest integrated market. Known as the **European Economic Area (EEA)**, it spreads from the Arctic to the Mediterranean. The citizens of EFTA countries and EU countries can enjoy all the economic benefits of a single European market. Such an arrangement makes good sense, since the two groups are each other's most important trading partner. In a way, membership in the EEA can be seen as a first step toward full membership in an expanding European Union.

Austria

The people of Austria speak German, and about 90 percent of them are Roman Catholic. Two small but significant ethnic minority groups exist: some 20,000 Slovenes, in the region known as Carinthia in south-central Austria; and some 25,000 Croatians in Burgenland, on the border with Hungary. These groups serve as reminders of the days before World War I when Austria was the center of the great Austro-Hungarian Empire, which controlled a vast multinational territory in Europe, including the former Yugoslavia.

Almost all of Austria's terrain is either hilly or mountainous. The Alps dominate the southern and western provinces and provide an important basis for the country's thriving tourist industry. As a result of the uneven terrain and historical factors, Austrian farms are small and fragmented, making farm products relatively expensive. Agriculture's share of the national economic output has declined steadily; it is now less than 5 percent of the gross domestic product.

Austria's most important trading partners are EU members, which take almost 60 percent of its exports. EFTA countries take about 27 percent. On the import side the EU accounts for more than 60 percent and the EFTA approximately 20 percent. In addition, trade with Eastern European countries is significant, with some 10 percent of Austrian exports going to Eastern Europe and about 10 percent of Austrian imports coming from that area.

Both geographically and economically, Austria is in a strategic position between the East and the West. After World War II, Austria was required to deliver goods worth more than $150 million, plus 10 million tons of petroleum, to the Soviet Union. In 1955, when Austria once more became a sovereign state, its parliament passed a law making the country neutral in international affairs. As a result, Austria actively pursues policies that are best described as bridge-building to the East, designed to increase contact with Eastern Europe and the countries of the former Soviet Union at all levels. In that way the Austrians believe they can make a contribution to the easing of East-West tensions far beyond what might otherwise be possible for a country with such a small population. When Austria's formal application for membership in the European Union is approved, it will be well poised to profit from trade between Eastern and Western Europe. In the summer of 1994, two-thirds of Austrians approved a referendum to join the EU.

Iceland

Iceland, an island country slightly smaller in area than the state of Kentucky, is located on an active volcanic summit east of Greenland and immediately south of the Arctic Circle. It was one of the most remote countries of Western Europe until the advent of modern air transportation. Iceland's population of almost 260,000 comprises a remarkably homogeneous group, descendants of Norwegian and Celtic peoples who first colonized the island late in the ninth century and early in the tenth. The modern Icelandic language is reputed to have changed relatively little since the twelfth century and thus is very close to the language spoken by the Vikings.

Thanks to the relatively warm waters of the North Atlantic Drift (see Figure 8–3), Iceland's lowland climate is surprisingly mild. Summers are damp and cool; winters are very windy, but temperatures are relatively mild. For example, Reykjavik, the capital, has an average temperature of 52°F (11°C) in July and 30°F (–1°C) in January.

Chief among the resources on which Icelanders have built their prosperous economy are fish, hydroelectricity, and geothermal energy. The main agricultural products are livestock, hay, fodder, and cheese. The work force numbers close to 113,000 and is almost entirely literate—Iceland boasts one of the highest literacy rates in the world. As might be expected, a fairly high percentage of the work force

is engaged in primary economic activities, especially agriculture and the all-important fisheries. About 30 percent of Iceland's exports go to the EU, and another 10 percent are purchased by EFTA partners. The United States is also a large customer, taking some 28 percent of Iceland's exports. More than three-fourths of all Icelandic exports are products of the country's highly developed fishing industry.

Iceland was occupied by British and American military forces during World War II, after which the country became a charter member of NATO. During the early 1950s, at the request of NATO, the United States and Iceland agreed that the United States should assume responsibility for Iceland's defense. Since then Iceland has been the only NATO country without its own military forces.

Norway

Like Iceland, Norway is a northern land. Almost one-third of its 1,100-mile (1,771-kilometer) length is north of the Arctic Circle; and even its southernmost point, at Lindesnes, reaches only as far south as 58°N, the approximate latitude of Juneau, Alaska. Roughly the size of New Mexico, which is large by European standards, Norway suffers from a lack of land suitable for agriculture. In fact, only 4 percent of Norway's total area of 125,181 square miles (324,219 square kilometers) is suitable for farming. About one-fourth of the country is forested, and an amazing 72 percent is classified as mountainous, with bogs, glaciers, and barren rock wastes (Figure 10–10).

Adding to the difficulty of developing such terrain is the character of Norway's coastline, which is marked by deep fjords, which are steep-sided valleys dug by glaciers and now flooded by the sea. Where Norway is narrowest, the fjords virtually cut the country into segments, and thus there is no continuous land route from the southern part of the country to the northern provinces. The far-flung towns and settlements of northern Norway can be reached only by airplane, ship, or—with difficulty—highway-ferry links.

Norway's chief natural resources are fish, timber, hydroelectric power, and —in recent years—oil and natural gas from the North Sea fields. Offshore oil was discovered in the 1960s, and development began in the 1970s. Thanks to the rapid rise in oil prices, Norway's economy has enjoyed a considerable boost from this new and technologically de-

Figure 10-10
The rugged Norwegian coast.
This area provides little land suitable for settlement or agriculture; it is characterized by numerous rugged islands, deep fjords, and barren rock surfaces.

manding industry. In 1991 about 48 percent of the value of all Norwegian exports came from oil and gas that were sold abroad. A policy of moderate production has been adopted to ensure that petroleum will remain an important part of the Norwegian economy for many decades.

Sweden

Sweden shares the Scandinavian peninsula with Norway and, like its neighbor, is a long and narrow country. If Sweden were superimposed on a map of the United States, it would spread from the southern tip of Florida to Washington, DC, a distance of slightly less than 1,000 miles (1,610 kilometers). Although Sweden lies at approximately the same latitude as Alaska, the warming influences of the North Atlantic Drift help to provide much of Sweden's southern half with a climate like that of New England. Winter days, however, are noticeably shorter: the sun sets at about 3:00 P.M. during Stockholm's midwinter weeks. Midsummer days are delightfully long.

Sweden's per capita GNP consistently ranks among the three or four highest in the world, higher than that of Canada. As might be expected, Sweden is basically an industrial country. Agriculture and forestry together contribute only about 5 percent of its annual GNP, and in recent years only about 4 percent of the work force has been employed in agri-

culture. Extensive forests, rich deposits of iron ore, and abundant hydroelectric power, along with a highly literate and well-trained population, are the basic resources on which Sweden has built a productive economy. As a leading trading nation, Sweden exports more than 50 percent of its industrial output. The chief markets for Sweden's wood products, iron ore, machinery, metals, bearings, ships, instruments, and automobiles are Norway, the United Kingdom, Denmark, and Finland.

An important social problem in Sweden is one that is beginning to concern many rich countries: the adjustments required as increasing numbers of citizens reach retirement and join the over-65 group. Life expectancy, a good measure of development, is more than 78 years in Sweden. Just what social institutions and programs will best suit the increasing ranks of senior citizens is a question that all developed countries will need to answer in the future. Without doubt, Sweden's solutions to the problem will be studied closely by leaders and planners in every country of the rich world.

Switzerland

In the heart of Western Europe and bounded by West Germany, Liechtenstein, Austria, Italy, and France, Switzerland has traditionally controlled the major routes between northern and southern Europe. The modern country of Switzerland traces its roots back to 1291, when three county-sized districts called **cantons** signed the Eternal Alliance, which bound them together in resistance to foreign rule. Through time other cantons joined the confederation; and in 1848 a federal constitution was adopted, partially modeled on the U.S. Constitution. Swiss neutrality was guaranteed by the great powers of Europe early in the nineteenth century, and today Switzerland remains a staunchly neutral country composed of several distinct ethnic groups.

Reflecting that ethnic diversity, Switzerland has four national languages. Romansch, derived from Latin, is spoken by a small Swiss minority that lives in the Alpine valleys of the southeast. Italian is the language of Ticino Canton in the south. The western cantons speak French. Finally, German is the language of approximately two-thirds of all Swiss. The highly developed urban-industrial core of the country is in the German-speaking region.

After World War II Switzerland was one of the few Western European countries whose economies were virtually unscathed. Since most industrial raw materials must be imported, the Swiss concentrate on those products containing high labor and skill inputs, such as watches and precision instruments. They also make specialized quality products like chemicals, pharmaceuticals, cheese, and chocolate, as well as items that do not lend themselves to mass production, such as power generators and turbines.

The small domestic market can consume only a limited portion of the industrial output, so Switzerland depends on the world economy for its prosperity. In combination with Switzerland's highly developed tourist industry, international banking, and the insurance and transportation industries, exports form the foundation for one of the world's highest standards of living. The countries of the European Union provide well over two-thirds of Switzerland's imports and buy half of the Swiss exports. Like the other EFTA members, Switzerland cannot escape a future closely tied to the fortunes of the European Union in the new European Economic Area.

Finland

The Finnish name for Finland is *Suomi*, or "land of marsh"—a good description of the heavily glaciated, lake-strewn landscape that comprises most of the country. Like neighboring Sweden and Norway, Finland is a northern land, with about one-third of its 724-mile (1,166-kilometer) length within the Arctic Circle. It shares lengthy land boundaries with Sweden and Norway in the north and Russia in the east.

Until 1809, when Finland was conquered by the Russians, it was closely associated with Sweden. Swedish is still an official language, and about 5 percent of the population of Finland speak it as their mother tongue. From 1809 until 1917 Finland was connected with the Russian Empire as a grand duchy. Then, taking advantage of the Bolshevik Revolution in Russia, the Finns declared their independence in 1917. During the tense period that preceded World War II, the Soviet Union requested that Finland surrender territory north of St. Petersburg and permit the Soviet navy to establish a base on the coast of the Gulf of Finland, in exchange for territory in eastern Karelia. The Finns refused. In late 1939 Soviet troops invaded Finnish territory, and the Soviet air force bombed several Finnish cities. After a number of battles the Finns were forced to accede to the demands of the Soviet Union.

Finland's territorial losses from World War II amounted to 17,800 square miles (46,102 square kilometers), roughly the area of Massachusetts and New Hampshire combined. But the entire population of those lost territories chose to move to Finland rather than become Soviet citizens. Not surprisingly, relocating and integrating those 400,000 displaced Finns was an enormous challenge. To experience a problem of comparable magnitude, the United States would have to lose 12 percent of its total area while accommodating a sudden influx of 16 million immigrants. In addition, the Soviet Union exacted a huge indemnity, which the Finns were forced to pay in ships, machinery, and other manufactured goods.

In the face of such monumental obstacles, the economy of Finland made a spectacular recovery in the postwar decades. Finland's future development and prosperity will depend on its continued ability to secure foreign markets for its exports in an increasingly competitive world. Its membership in the EU is one important means to that end.

SUMMARY
A United States of Europe?

What will Europe look like in the year 2000? Will it be a smoothly functioning confederation of twenty or more countries stretching from the Arctic to the Mediterranean and from the Atlantic to the borders of Romania, Ukraine, and Belarus? Will more than 370 million prosperous citizens and their businesses—no longer checked at a score of borders be using a common currency and be served at the international level by common institutions?

As the decade of the 1990s unfolds Europe appears to be closer than ever before to achieving these goals. Practically all of Western Europe is included in the memberships of the European Union (EU) or the European Free Trade Association (EFTA) and forms of the European Economic Area (EEA). Changes to the east occasioned by the breakup of the old Soviet Union have made it possible for the former Soviet "satellite" countries of Eastern Europe to adopt free-market economies and move toward the West in their political alignments. In December, 1991, for example, Czechoslovakia, Hungary, and Poland signed far-reaching formal trade and cooperation agreements with the European Union. In praising the EU for its adoption of the Maastricht treaty, U.S. President George Bush stressed that "a more united Europe offers the United States a more effective partner, prepared for larger responsibilities in helping the citizens of Central and Eastern Europe transform their societies." Developments such as these emanating from Western Europe hold the promise of change that will increasingly affect people around the world in the last decade of the current millennium.

KEY TERMS

Berlin Wall	guest workers
canton	iron curtain
cold war	Mezzogiorno
Dutch miracle	North Atlantic Treaty
European Economic	Organization (NATO)
Area (EEA)	polder
Flemish	Ulster
Gaelic	Walloons
Gibraltar	

NOTES

1. Winston Churchill, telegram to Harry S. Truman, 12 May 1945, Naval Aide Files—Box 7, Harry S. Truman Library, Independence, MO.
2. Commission of the European Communities, *The Second Enlargement of the European Community* (Luxembourg: Office for Official Publications of the European Community, 1979), 5.

FURTHER READINGS
Part Three

Beaujeu-Granier, J. *France*. New York: Longman, 1976. A noted geographer's examination of the diversity of the French landscape, with an analysis of the future of French regional planning.

Berger, John, and Jean Mohr (photographs). *A Seventh Man: Migrant Workers in Europe*. New York: Viking Press, 1975. An intensely subjective view of the problems of Europe's guest workers in the early 1970s, when the movement was at its height; forces the reader to think of the human beings behind the official statistics.

Burtenshaw, D., M. Bateman, and G. J. Ashworth. *The City in West Europe*. New York: John Wiley & Sons, 1981. An excellent review of the region's urban geography.

Chandler, T. J., and S. Gregory, eds. *The Climate of the British Isles*. London: Longman, 1976. An overview of climatological factors that incorporates the findings of broad research into a description of the climatic regimes of the British Isles.

Chapman, Keith. *North Sea Oil and Gas: A Geographical Perspective*. North Pomfret, VT: David & Charles, 1976. An informative assessment of the first decade of exploitation of the North Sea hydrocarbons.

Clout, H. *The Regional Problem in Western Europe*. London: Cambridge University Press, 1976. A slim volume that identifies some of the regional problems of Western Europe.

Commission of the European Communities. *Europeans and Their Holidays*. Washington, DC: Commission of the European Communities, Office of Press and Public Affairs, 1987. An offset copy of a report based on a survey of a large, representative sample of the adult populations of the twelve EC countries.

EFTA. *Bulletin*. A magazine-style periodical including informative but specialized articles; published in English, French, German, and Scandinavian versions by the EFTA Press and Information Service.

Findley, Allan, and **Paul White**. *West European Population Change*. Dover, NH: Croom Helm, 1986. A thorough exploration of the recent dynamics in Western Europe's population changes and the charting of a probable future for the region.

Hudson, Ray, David Rhind, and **Helen Mounsey**. *An Atlas of EEC Affairs*. New York: Methuen, 1984. A very informative source of information that extends far beyond maps alone and contains lengthy discussions on many aspects of the European Community.

Jones, Peter. "The Geography of Dutch Elm Disease in Britain." *Transactions, Institute of British Geographers* 6 (1981): 324–334. Tracing the spread of a new strain of Dutch elm disease, which has killed the vast majority of elms in southern Britain in the past twenty years and has thus destroyed an important and traditional component of many rural English landscapes.

Knox, Paul L. *The Geography of Western Europe: A Socio-Economic Survey*. Totowa, NJ: Barnes & Noble, 1984. A small text offering an excellent continuation of and elaboration on several of the themes introduced in these chapters.

Le Roy Ladurie, Emmanuel. *Times of Feast, Times of Famine: A History of Climate Since the Year 1000*. Translated by Barbara Bray. Garden City, NY: Doubleday, 1971. A fascinating reconstruction of climatic fluctuations in Europe and their effect on the human community

Mellor, Roy E. *The Two Germanies: A Modern Geography*. London: Harper & Row, 1978. A lucid and highly readable study contrasting the separate geographical developments of these now-reunified states, whose centrality on the continent makes an understanding of their problems essential.

Paxton, John. *A Dictionary of the European Communities*. New York: St. Martin's Press, 1982. A valuable tool for any detailed study of the EC.

Riley, R. C., and **G. J. Ashworth**. *Benelux: An Economic Geography of Belgium, the Netherlands, and Luxembourg*. New York: Holmes & Meier, 1975. An analysis of the economic transformation of the Benelux nations, with specific reference to the significance of governmental decisions in the process of regional development.

Salt, John, and **H. Clout, eds**. *Migration in Post-War Europe: Geographical Essays*. London: Oxford University Press, 1976. A discussion of the effects of the emerging patterns of migration in Europe, which remains the migratory continent par excellence.

Sloan, Stanley. *NATO's Future*. Washington, DC: National Defense University Press, 1985. A skillful attempt to assess NATO's role in a world of rapid technological and political change.

Sundquist, James L. *Dispersing Population: What America Can Learn from Europe*. Washington, DC: Brookings Institution, 1975. An analysis of the national population policies of five European nations in the hope that American planners will gain useful information from their collective experiences

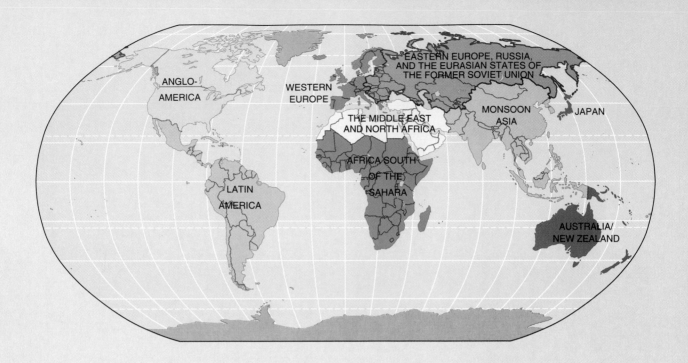

Eastern Europe and the European part of the former Soviet Union generally share with Western Europe the basic characteristics of a Christian tradition, a dominance of Indo-European languages, and Caucasian racial features. In contrast, the Asian countries of the old Russian and Soviet empires, including Siberia, evidence quite different religious traditions and languages, most notably Islam and the Turkic tongues, respectively. Yet Russian control of these Asian states during much of the nineteenth and twentieth centuries, as well as their continued association economically and politically with Russia, dictate their inclusion in a study of this region. Together, Eastern Europe, Russia, and the Eurasian states of the former Soviet Union demonstrate many distinctive characteristics that distinguish the region from Western Europe and justify its consideration as a distinct entity.

This region is one of great diversity. For example, Albania and the three Baltic states are small in both population and area, whereas Russia is the world's largest country in area and contains approximately 150 million people. Even Russia, with its majority European Russian population, is a country of many races and cultural traditions.

Underscoring the importance of the region is that Russia's economic, political, and military influ-

ence is felt by the whole world. Clearly, the critical role played by the Soviet Union in the recent past, the promise of a continued prominent place these countries will have in world affairs, and the dramatic and unsettling events unfolding throughout the whole region demand that we learn more about this realm.

For all intents and purposes, Eastern Europe became part of the Soviet sphere after the close of World War II. Soviet-style political and economic systems were instituted throughout Eastern Europe and remained intact for over four decades. During that time the Soviet Union was characterized by an ideology known as **Marxism**, or **communism**, which purports to have uncovered the laws of economic and social development. Marxist ideas developed in Western Europe, and there they became integrated into essentially democratic systems. The Soviet variant, however, with modifications by such communist leaders as Lenin, Stalin, and Gorbachev, evolved quite differently. In the Soviet model the central government controlled virtually all investment capital and operated through an extensive centralized planning system.

During the cold war that followed World War II, the Soviet Union and the West, with the leadership of the United States, fought ideological, economic, and, indirectly, military wars (e.g., Korea, Greece, and Vietnam), vying for the hearts and minds of the world's people. By means of direct military intervention, economic and military aid, covert action, propaganda, and training foreign leaders the Soviet Union helped establish communist dictatorships in Eastern Europe, China, Vietnam, Cuba, Ethiopia, and elsewhere. But economic breakdown within the Soviet Union, as well as discontent among those under Soviet control, forced the government, led by Soviet President Mikhail Gorbachev, to enact reforms. In 1990 the Communist party even renounced its monopolistic role in Soviet life, and the cold war appeared to be over.

In 1991 a failed coup attempt revealed deep unrest within the Soviet republics. The eventual outcome was the dissolution of the Soviet Union. Russia and the other fourteen republics became independent countries. Ten of the fifteen created the Commonwealth of Independent States (CIS). The CIS is a loose confederation of independent countries that is attempting to solve enormous economic and political problems. The name Soviet Union, or Union of Soviet Socialist Republics (USSR) refers to the area that comprised Russia and the other former Soviet republics prior to December 25, 1991. On that date, Soviet President Gorbachev resigned; Boris Yeltsin, president of the Russian Federation, assumed control of the nuclear arsenal on Russian territory; and the world's countries acknowledged Russia as the successor to the Soviet seat in the United Nations. Two of the other fourteen republics, Belarus and Ukraine, have had UN membership since the creation of that world body; the twelve other new countries quickly applied for memberships.

The removal of Soviet influence has allowed the people of Eastern Europe to seek their own approaches to development. In Chapter 11 we discuss the geographical bases of Eastern Europe and look at how its position between the West and the Soviet Union has affected its development. We also examine the cultural and environmental characteristics and consider the responses of the Eastern European countries to their political and economic needs. In Chapter 12 we deal with the physical, cultural, and population geography of Russia and the other countries of the former Soviet Union. In Chapter 13 we examine the economic geography of the region, the abandoned Soviet approach to development problems, and prospects for the future.

PART 4

Roger L. Thiede

EASTERN EUROPE, RUSSIA, AND THE EURASIAN STATES OF THE FORMER SOVIET UNION

11

Eastern Europe: The Land Between

Political Evolution

Physical Diversity

Cultural Diversity

Population

Levels of Economic Development

Recent Development Strategies

Agriculture

Industry

The Czech city of Prague in the Bohemian Basin. The former Czechoslovakia illustrates well the history of political instability in Eastern Europe. The kingdom of Bohemia, which disappeared as a political entity in 1620, reappeared as Czechoslovakia when the Czechs and Slovaks were united into a single country after World War I. The country was reconfigured again after World War II. But on January 1, 1993, Czechoslovakia ceased to exist, as the Czech Republic and the Slovak Republic became two independent political states.

259

In Eastern Europe 1989 was a year of revolutions. With the exception of Romania's, the revolutions were peaceful, and the results were startling. In August the first noncommunist to lead a government in Eastern Europe since 1948 came into power in Poland. At the same time East Germans began to leave their country by the thousands. In early October the Hungarian Communist party changed its name to the Socialist party and officially broke with communist doctrines of the past. In the midst of such change Soviet President Mikhail Gorbachev announced that his country had no political or moral right to intervene in the domestic affairs of Eastern Europe.

Countries continued to discard communism throughout the remainder of 1989 and into 1990. The Berlin Wall crumbled, after twenty-eight years as the major symbol of the division between East and West. A noncommunist government led East Germany into reunification with West Germany. The Bulgarian Communist party became the Socialist party. The Romanians overthrew and executed their dictator, Nicolae Ceaucescu, and the Romanian Communist party was renamed the National Salvation Front. Free or partially free elections were held throughout the region. In 1991 the republics that composed Yugoslavia declared their independence, and violent wars erupted there. Even in Albania a tight dictatorial control by the Communist party ended and free elections were held. Throughout all of Eastern Europe things were not at all as they had been.

POLITICAL EVOLUTION

For nearly half a century the countries of Eastern Europe, including the German Democratic Republic (East Germany), were dominated by the Soviet Union. Immediately after World War II, Soviet-trained communists had stepped into positions of leadership in those countries; and leftist groups, often with support from the Soviet army, had transformed them into **people's republics**, or **people's democracies**, with governments similar to the Soviet Union's. By 1948 Soviet-style institutions existed in all eight Eastern European countries, and an iron curtain had been drawn between East and West. Eastern Europe became a **buffer zone**, a group of weak countries separating the Soviet Union from Western Europe (Figure 11–1). Those countries,

though, were largely under Soviet influence and for that reason were known as satellites of the Soviet Union.

Throughout Eastern Europe the Communist party became the sole political party. Land, industries, banks, and all but the smallest commercial establishments were nationalized. Traditional religions came under close government supervision and control as the communist philosophy affected virtually every aspect of life.

A primary objective of all the new governments was economic reconstruction and industrial development. The ideological goal was to create a true communist society in which there was no private property and the people owned all the means of production; all people would "give according to their ability and take according to their need." According to the Soviet Marxist philosophy, there would be a specified transitional period of socialism, during which the remnants of the former economic, political, and social systems would be eliminated. Finally, the state would own all the means of production. Under guidance from the Soviet Union, the Communist parties of Eastern Europe were to direct those new **command economies**, or centrally controlled and planned economic systems.

Dissent soon appeared in Soviet-dominated Eastern Europe. When the communist-nationalist leader of Yugoslavia, Marshal Tito, became increasingly resistant to Soviet meddling in Yugoslav affairs, the Soviet leader Joseph Stalin responded by expelling Yugoslavia from the world communist movement. That action allowed Yugoslavia to follow an independent path of socialism, one that involved many economic and cultural contacts with the West. Later, in the 1950s, dissent took a different form in Albania. A process of de-Stalinization was occurring under Soviet leader Nikita Khrushchev; that is, many of the practices of the former leader were being revised or abandoned in the Soviet Union. This process led to Albania's withdrawal from the **Soviet bloc**, the group of countries that included the Soviet Union and its satellites, because its leaders continued to embrace Stalinist authoritarianism.

During the 1960s and 1970s the six remaining satellites—East Germany, Poland, Czechoslovakia, Hungary, Romania, and Bulgaria—were allowed to follow more distinctive and independent courses within the Soviet bloc. Leaders of the Soviet Union recognized that there were "different paths to

Figure 11-1
Nations and major cities of Eastern Europe. Eastern Europe has often been called a shatter zone because of the many ethnic groups that have sought sovereignty over its various parts. As a consequence the region has a history of political instability and conflict.

the building of communism." For example, Czechoslovakia, Hungary, and Bulgaria were eventually able to introduce economic reforms that the Soviet Union had considered too Western for implementation there.

In Poland the collectivization of agriculture came to an end, and many millions of Poles openly acknowledged the authority of the Catholic church, especially as it spoke through the voice of Pope John Paul II, the first pope of Polish origin. In 1984 Romania refused to join the Soviet-led boycott of the Summer Olympics and also spurned the Soviet Union in other, more critical matters.

Dissent continued to grow as the countries of Eastern Europe fell further and further behind the economic progress of the West. Food shortages, lim-

ited availability of consumer goods, low levels of productivity, economic inefficiency, massive environmental deterioration, and severe restrictions on human rights fostered the internal unrest that finally prompted revolts in the late 1980s. By the end of 1989 six of the eight Eastern European countries—East Germany, Poland, Hungary, Czechoslovakia, Romania, and Bulgaria—had overturned their governments. East Germany, freed from communist control, joined with West Germany to reestablish a united Germany. Soon even tightly controlled Albania rejected authoritarian communism. The Albanian Communist party subsequently began to lose its firm control, thousands of dissidents were allowed to leave the country, and the government began opening its doors to the West.

Yugoslavia, composed of several republics, fell apart completely: Slovenia and Croatia declared their independence, followed by similar declarations from Bosnia-Hercegovina, Montenegro, and Macedonia. Serbia, which claimed to represent the old Yugoslavia, formed a union with Montenegro, creating a new country that took the name of the old, Yugoslavia. Bitter civil wars broke out, at first between Serbia and Croatia and then among Bosnia, Croatia, and Serbia. Peace continues to be elusive in the old Yugoslavia.

Finally, in 1993 the country of Czechoslovakia dissolved. In a relatively peaceful divorce the two new countries were created: the Czech Republic and Slovakia.

In total, Eastern Europe now consists of twelve independent countries in an area which at the beginning of the 1990s contained only seven sovereign states.

The new political systems dominating most of those countries require a redefinition of the region. For a long period Soviet domination was the major distinguishing characteristic of the area; geographers, and as a consequence social scientists, journalists, and the general public thought of the region as Eastern Europe—an area pulled to the East by Soviet political and economic ideas and, in most cases, by Soviet military pressure. But after the revolutions of 1989–1990 it became more appropriate to think of the region as distinct from either West or East. In the areas north—that is, in Poland, the Czech Republic, Slovakia, and Hungary (historically known as Central Europe), as well as in northern Yugoslavia (Slovenia and Croatia)—cultural and historical links are more directly related to the West than to Russia and other Eurasian states. Only in the Balkans—in Romania, Bulgaria, Albania, and the rest of Yugoslavia (Serbia and Montenegro, Bosnia-Hercegovina, and Macedonia)—have Eastern cultural influences been dominant. And most Romanians consider themselves to be culturally more Western, because of the country's origin as a colony of the Roman Empire. As the old cold war tensions continue to lessen and lines of cooperation become clearer, Eastern Europe may function less as a buffer zone and more as a transition zone, blending the influences of both East and West.

In the remainder of this chapter, we look at other issues of concern in Eastern Europe—environmental, cultural, and economic. Despite its moderate size (one-third the area of Western Europe), Eastern Europe exhibits great physical and cultural diversity. In addition, we examine some of the outside pressures placed on Eastern Europe and look further at the dramatic changes occurring there.

PHYSICAL DIVERSITY

The landforms of the northern part of Eastern Europe contrast sharply with those of the central and southern parts (Figure 11–2). In the north is the low-lying Great European Plain, which is drained by the Elbe, the Vistula, and a number of other rivers. Most of Poland lies within this plain. The central and southern portions of Eastern Europe encompass regions of hills and mountains, separated by smaller fertile plains. Noteworthy are the low mountain ranges of the almost-circular Bohemian Massif, the crests of which form the western boundary of the Czech Republic. Enclosed within the massif lies the Bohemian Plain, the site of the Czech capital, Prague. The Carpathian Mountains, an extension of the Alps, follow part of the boundary between Poland and its two southern neighbors the Czech Republic and Slovakia and continue into central Romania. The Transylvanian Alps (once home to the historical Count Dracula) and the Balkan Mountains in Bulgaria are continuations of the Carpathians. Between them lies the Wallachian Plain, which, like the Hungarian Plain to the west, is a large natural grassland where soils are fertile and agriculture is productive. Both of those plains are drained by the Danube, the most important river in Eastern Europe, which rises in southern Germany and flows into the Black Sea. South of the Hungarian Plain is the rugged terrain of the Central Balkan Ranges and the Dinaric Alps, which cover most of the former Yugoslavia and all of Albania.

Studying the topography of an area is not merely an end in itself; it is also a means of understanding more significant features of human geography. For example, the complexity of the mountain ranges of the Balkan Peninsula—that stretch of land bounded by the Adriatic, Black, and Mediterranean seas—contributes to the diversity of the ethnic groups found there. It also complicates the construction of a well-integrated transportation network over much of the region. In the north, on the other hand, the easily traversed Great European Plain more readily exposes the Poles to conquerors from both east and west.

Figure 11-2
Land surface regions of Eastern Europe. In Eastern Europe most of the population lives in the plains, where most of the large cities are located and where much of the manufacturing occurs. Hills and mountains serve as sources of minerals, water, and wood and—especially in the south—areas of livestock raising. The mineral resources of the Bohemian Massif and the northern Carpathian Mountains are particularly important.

In terms of climate Eastern Europe may be viewed as a bridge between the west coast marine climate of northwestern Europe and the severe continental climates to the east (see Figure 3–3). The continental influence is felt most strongly in eastern Poland, which has the coldest winters as well as the longest periods of snow cover in Eastern Europe. Western Poland and the Czech Republic, in contrast, have a climate somewhat moderated by marine influences, with cooler summers and milder winters than found farther east.

The central and southern sections of Eastern Europe experience warmer summers and mild winters. The warm-to-hot summers and adequate precipitation of Hungary, northern Serbia, Croatia, Slovenia, Romania, and Bulgaria provide an ideal growing season for a wide variety of crops, such as wheat, tomatoes, and grapes. In addition, the Black Sea beaches of Bulgaria and Romania are crowded in the summer with tourists from both the East and the West. Once even more popular, however, were the resorts of coastal Croatia. Spectacular mountain scenery meets the blue waters of the Adriatic, and a dry summer subtropical, or Mediterranean, coastal climate provided a pleasant escape for northwestern Europeans before the civil wars of the 1990s erupted, destroying not only the tranquility but also many of the picturesque ancient villages and towns, such as Dubrovnik. The summers along the Croatian, Bosnian, and Montenegran coast, as in most of Albania, are hot and dry, and the winters are mild and wet. In the higher elevations of the Dinaric Alps, snow and cold temperatures bring a genuine winter season. In fact, the Bosnian city of Sarajevo, only about 100 miles from the Adriatic coast, was the site of the 1984 Winter Olympic games.

CULTURAL DIVERSITY

Eastern Europe is also a region of great cultural diversity. Political unity has been difficult to achieve in this part of the world, leaving the region always vulnerable to invaders from the west, east, and south. Eastern Europe has often been called the

180 YEARS OF BOUNDARY CHANGES IN THE SHATTER BELT

The expression *shatter belt* describes the political instability of a region. In this particular case, it describes the inability of Eastern Europe to resist the greater military and political power of its past and present neighbors, especially the Ottoman Empire, Germany, Austria, and the Soviet Union.

Cultural fragmentation has contributed to the weakness of Eastern Europe, at times creating a political vacuum that almost invites outside intervention. The patchwork of ethnic groups has also brought the conflict associated with irredentist policies. **Irredentism** refers to one country's claim of another country's territory on the grounds that members of the first country's ethnic group live in the second country and should be united with their national kin. The term is derived from the Italian word *irredenta,* which means "unredeemed" or "unfulfilled." As modern Italy was being formed in the late nineteenth century, the term was used to call for the acquisition of Italian-speaking areas that were not yet part of the new nation. In Eastern Europe the appeal to irredentism has been frequent—it has been used by Germans, Poles, Russians, Hungarians, Romanians, Bulgarians, and Serbians, among others. Consequently, throughout much of modern history the boundaries of Eastern European countries have changed periodically. Maps of the region between 1815 and 1994 provide ample evidence of continuous political change (Figure A).

The Eastern Europe of 1815 was dominated by four great powers: Prussia and Russia controlled the north; Austria, the center; and the Ottoman (Turkish) Empire, the south. During the next century the most notable changes occurred in the Balkan Peninsula, where Turkish power declined rapidly. The frequent changes in political boundaries that took place in the Balkans throughout the nineteenth and early twentieth centuries led to a new political-geographical term, **Balkanization**, meaning the breakup or fragmentation of a once-large political unit into numerous smaller ones. Parts of the old Ottoman Empire were absorbed by Austro-Hungary; other parts were made into new states, such as Romania and Bulgaria. In the north the German Empire was formed in 1871 by the consolidation of Prussia and other German states, while Russia increased its territory only slightly. The defeat of Germany and Austro-Hungary in

World War I signaled further political upheaval in Eastern Europe. The Austro-Hungarian Empire was dissolved, and three independent states—Austria, Czechoslovakia, and Hungary—were created in its stead. Other territories formerly held by the empire became parts of new or expanded independent countries. In addition, a new Poland was created from German, Russian, and Austrian lands; Romania gained lands from Hungary; and the new kingdom of Yugoslavia was formed by uniting Serbia with other southern Slavic territories.

In 1919 national independence reached new heights in Eastern Europe. The four powers (Russia, Britain, France, and the United States) that had earlier dictated the fate of Eastern Europe had either been removed from the scene or had been stripped of power. Russia remained, but chaos reigned in that country in the aftermath of the 1917 Bolshevik Revolution. Not only did

Figure A

Maps of Eastern Europe between 1815 and 1994. These maps show the principal changes in the region from the early nineteenth century to today.

1914

NORWAY

SWEDEN

North Sea

DENMARK

Baltic Sea

55°

RUSSIAN EMPIRE

GERMAN EMPIRE

AUSTRO-HUNGARIAN EMPIRE

ROMANIA

45°

Black Sea

ITALY

MONTENEGRO

SERBIA

BULGARIA

TURKEY

ALBANIA

Tyrrhenian Sea

40°

GREECE

Aegean Sea

0   100   200MI.

0   100   200 KM.

10°   20°   25°

1919

NORWAY   20°

SWEDEN

North Sea

DENMARK

Baltic Sea

55°

ESTONIA

LATVIA

LITHUANIA

GERMANY

USSR

POLAND

GERMANY

CZECHOSLOVAKIA

AUSTRIA   HUNGARY

ROMANIA   45°

Black Sea

ITALY

YUGOSLAVIA

BULGARIA

TURKEY

ALBANIA

Tyrrhenian Sea

40°

GREECE

Aegean Sea

0   100   200MI.

0   100   200 KM.

10°   20°   25°

1945

NORWAY   20°

SWEDEN

North Sea

DENMARK

Baltic Sea

55°

USSR

POLAND

EAST GERMANY

WEST GERMANY (FRG)

CZECHOSLOVAKIA

AUSTRIA   HUNGARY

ROMANIA   45°

Black Sea

Adriatic Sea

YUGOSLAVIA

BULGARIA

ITALY

TURKEY

ALBANIA

Tyrrhenian Sea

40°

GREECE

Aegean Sea

0   100   200MI.

0   100   200 KM.

10°   20°   25°

1994

NORWAY   20°

SWEDEN

RUSSIA

North Sea

DENMARK

Baltic Sea

55°

ESTONIA

LATVIA

LITHUANIA

RUSSIA

BELARUS

POLAND

GERMANY

CZECH REPUBLIC

SLOVAKIA

UKRAINE

AUSTRIA   HUNGARY

MOLDOVA

SLOVENIA

CROATIA

ROMANIA   45°

BOSNIA-HERCEGOVINA

SERBIA

Black Sea

ITALY

MONTENEGRO

YUGOSLAVIA

BULGARIA

ALBANIA

MACEDONIA

TURKEY

Tyrrhenian Sea

40°

GREECE

Aegean Sea

0   100   200MI.

0   100   200 KM.

10°   20°   25°

Russia lose territory to Romania and Poland, but its Baltic lands were also divided into the independent states of Estonia, Latvia, and Lithuania.

That surge of independence throughout Eastern Europe lasted fewer than twenty years. The Nazis, seeking revenge for the defeat of Germany in World War I, attempted to gain control of all of Europe. First with the threat of force and then by actual invasion, Germany began its temporary domination of Eastern Europe. The Soviet Union, initially an ally of Germany, annexed parts of Romania and Poland as well as the Baltic states. But Adolf Hitler's uncontrolled appetite for land and power soon ended that uneasy alliance, and the Germans invaded the Soviet Union. By 1945 the force of the Soviets in the east and the forces of the United States and Great Britain in the west brought about Germany's defeat, and once again boundaries were redrawn.

The Soviet Union, which emerged from World War II as the dominant force in Eastern Europe, turned the region into a vast buffer zone between itself and the West. Major boundary changes were drawn at the expense of Germany and to the advantage of the Soviet Union. The eastern Polish boundary was shifted westward, but Poland was compensated for lost land by the acquisition of German territory. The Oder and Neisse rivers became the new boundary between Polish and German lands. In addition, the German territory of East Prussia was divided between the Soviet Union and Poland, and the Soviets turned their occupation zone in Germany into the German Democratic Republic, or East Germany. The Soviets also acquired the eastern tip of Czechoslovakia, thereby gaining a strategic foothold in the Hungarian Plain. Finally, the Baltic states were reincorporated into the Soviet Union, and the part of Romania called Bessarabia (Moldova) was annexed by the Soviets.

The 1990s witnessed another change in the political map of Eastern Europe. The Soviet Union's decision not to use its troops to support Eastern European communist regimes—and its eventual breakup—awoke nationalistic, anticommunist, pro-market and pro-democratic forces in the East, giving rise not only to new governments but also new countries. East Germany was reunified with the Federal Republic of Germany, or West Germany. Yugoslavia was further Balkanized when its ethnic republics declared independence, followed by military struggles for land in Bosnia-Hercegovina and Croatia. Five sovereign countries came to occupy what was Yugoslavia, though continued fighting meant that the borders of Serbia, Bosnia, and Croatia were not yet final. Czechoslovakia in 1993 split into the countries of Slovakia and the Czech Republic. The Romanians have even gone so far as to press for reunification with their ethnic relatives in Moldova, a part of the former Soviet Union. Finally, the dissolution of the Soviet Union and the creation of fifteen new sovereign states in that area has significantly added to the uncertainty of the shatter belt.

shatter belt, because it has long been a region of great internal variety and conflict, beset by pressures from the outside that lead to frequent political divisions and boundary changes (see the boxed feature, 180 Years of Boundary Changes in the Shatter Belt).

Varieties of Language

All of the peoples of Eastern Europe, with the exception of the Hungarians and some small Turkish minorities, speak a language that belongs to the large and varied family of Indo-European languages. Nonetheless, the multiplicity of languages is a clear measure of the cultural diversity of Eastern Europe (Figure 11–3). The majority of Eastern Europeans speak one of the Slavic languages, which are divided into three subgroups: eastern, western, and southern. The eastern Slavic languages—Russian, Ukrainian, and Belarus—are spoken in the former Soviet Union. The western Slavic languages—Polish, Czech, and Slovak are the major ones—can be heard in the northern portion of Eastern Europe. Finally, the southern Slavic languages—Serbo-Croatian, Slovene, Macedonian, and Bulgarian—are spoken in the Balkans.

The main non-Slavic Indo-European languages of Eastern Europe include: Romanian, a Romance language related to Italian and French but with strong Slavic influences; Albanian, probably the oldest of the Indo-European tongues spoken in Europe; German, spoken in parts of Poland, the Czech Republic, Hungary, Romania, Slovenia, and Serbia; and Romany, the language of the ethnic group known as gypsies. Romany, interestingly, does not belong to the European branch of the Indo-European languages. Instead, it originated in India, from which the ancestors of the original gypsies migrated into Eastern Europe in the fourteenth century.

Eastern Europe also includes languages that are not classified as Indo-European, notably Hungarian

Figure 11-3
Language patterns in Eastern Europe. The large number of different languages in Eastern Europe illustrates the region's ethnic diversity. Cultural differences such as language and religion inhibit political stability and, consequently, economic development.

INDO-EUROPEAN FAMILY OF LANGUAGES

SLAVIC GROUP
Western Slavic languages
P   Polish
C   Czech
S   Slovak
L   Lusatian

South Slavic languages
Slovene
SC Serbo-Croatian
M   Montenegran
Macedonian
Bulgarian

Eastern Slavic languages
Ru Russian
Be Belorussian
U   Ukrainian

GERMANIC GROUP
G   German
Danish
Swedish

ROMANCE GROUP
R   Romanian
I   Italian

ILLYRIAN GROUP
A   Albanian

HELLENIC GROUP
Gr Greek

BALTIC GROUP
Latvian
Lithuanian

INDO ARYAN
GROUP
RY Romany
**URALIC FAMILY
OF LANGUAGES**
UGRIC GROUP

H   Hungarian
**ALTAIC FAMILY
OF LANGUAGES**
TURKISH GROUP

T   Turkish

(Bold letters on the map indicate where a significant minority of each language is found.)

(or **Magyar**) and Turkish. Turkish speakers, like the gypsies, are found largely in the southern Balkans, especially in Bulgaria, which has an ethnic Turkish minority of 800,000 people. During the 1980s the Bulgarian government embarked on a campaign to **Bulgarize** the Turks by forcing them to adopt Bulgarian last names. The Bulgarian government was intent on ridding itself of any reminders of those Turks who ruled Bulgaria for 500 years—even

claiming that scientific anthropological research proves that the Bulgarian brain is pure, uncontaminated by Turkish stock. Although the claim was preposterous, its implication was clear: there are no Turks in the country, only Bulgarians who speak Turkish. With the recent political changes in Bulgaria, however, the Turks have reappeared as a viable political force, reasserting their cultural identity and demanding their rights.

Small minorities of various language groups can be found in all of the Eastern European countries, though the political changes in the early 1990s have resulted in a map in which language and political borders correspond more closely than ever before. In all countries but one the political name also describes the dominant language. The exception is Bosnia-Hercegovina, where the predominant language is Serbo-Croatian. Croatia has a sizeable Serbian minority who are fighting for inclusion in Serbia. And the Serbian province of Kosovo is another ethnic trouble spot of the Balkans. There ethnic Albanians make up 90 percent of the population but have very little economic and political power. Increasingly they have demanded a greater political voice, which the Serbian government is reluctant to give. Many of the Kosovo Albanians see eventual unification with Albania as their ultimate political goal.

Patterns of Religious Heritage

Even greater complexity is added to the map of cultural diversity when traditional religious affiliations are considered. Although communist governments for decades imposed restrictions throughout Eastern Europe, religions continued to exist. Lately, with the collapse of communism, the role of religion in the life of Eastern Europeans has increased significantly. New religious ventures seem to arise weekly. Religious orders once banned and religious publications once censored have reappeared and are legal. Religious instruction has been reestablished in Polish schools, and the pope has visited Poland, Hungary, and other Catholic parts of Eastern Europe. In Slovakia, the Czech Republic, and Romania, the Catholic church can now appoint bishops without the approval of the government. And even in Albania, which once called itself "the world's only officially atheistic state," Islamic and Christian religious services are increasing in number and openness.

As in other parts of the world, East European religious traditions have played an important part in the formation of national characteristics. In the face of governmental persecution the churches assumed the role of protector of people and values, a role that provided unity and strength to antigovernment and anticommunist forces. But with the new freedom the churches face new problems. For example, of the many factors that contributed to the division

of Czechoslovakia was an increasing awareness of differing religious values: the generally conservative and traditional Catholic values of Slovakia clashed with the generally liberal and secular values of the Czech Republic, which contains a strong protestant minority. Another problem is that with the demise of authoritarian rule there has been a disturbing increase in anti-Semitic acts throughout the region. A major problem for Eastern European churches is how to withstand the secular influences entering the region with U.S. dollars, German marks, and the new capitalistic marketplace. In reaction to those forces, powerful religious institutions could threaten to stifle democratic trends in Eastern Europe. The 1990s and the early part of the next century will be a critical period for religion in Eastern Europe.

All three major branches of Christianity—Roman Catholicism, Protestantism, and Eastern Orthodoxy—can be found in this region of the world. Numerically, Eastern Europeans who profess religious beliefs are predominantly Roman Catholic; that group includes a majority of Poles, Czechs, Slovaks, Hungarians, Slovenes, and Croats (Figure 11–4). Protestant minorities are also found in the Czech Republic, Slovakia, Hungary, Romania, and Serbia.

The second largest religious group in the region is composed of Eastern Orthodox Christians. Orthodoxy is predominant among the Serbs, Montenegrans, Macedonians, Bulgars, and Romanians. Whereas Roman Catholicism was brought by missionaries from Rome, Orthodoxy came to Eastern Europe from Constantinople (now Istanbul), the seat of Eastern Christianity. In addition to religion, those Orthodox missionaries brought their alphabet and, consequently, a written language for the people they converted.

Today, that link between religion and written language continues in Eastern Europe. The language of the Orthodox-dominated Serbs, Macedonians, and Bulgars is written in the **Cyrillic alphabet**, as are the eastern Slavic languages. In contrast, the Roman Catholic cultural areas of Eastern Europe, as well as the Protestant areas (once Roman Catholic), use the Roman alphabet. An exception to the rule is the Romanians, who, though traditionally Orthodox in their faith, use a Roman alphabet derived from their pre-Christian Latin heritage. One result of this link between religion and written language is that the Serbs and the Croats speak the same language

Figure 11-4
A baroque Roman Catholic church in the Czech Republic.
Despite several decades of government restrictions, religion continues to be an important part of the cultural milieu in several Eastern European countries. Among the several religious traditions of Eastern Europe, Roman Catholicism is predominant.

Table 11-1
Population of Eastern European countries in 1994.

	Population (in millions)
Eastern Europe	123.0
Poland	38.6
Romania	22.7
Czech Republic	10.3
Hungary	10.3
Yugoslavia (Serbia and Montenegro)	10.5
Bulgaria	8.4
Slovakia	5.3
Croatia	4.8
Bosnia-Hercegovina	4.6
Albania	3.4
Macedonia	2.1
Slovenia	2.0

Source: Population Reference Bureau, *World Population Data Sheet* (Washington, DC: 1994).

represents a small minority in Bulgaria. The prime reason for the creation of the former Yugoslav republic of Bosnia-Hercegovina (often simply called Bosnia) was in fact the large population of Serbo-Croatian speaking Muslims, who are called Bosnians. At the beginning of the 1990s approximately 44 percent of the population in Bosnia was Muslim, with the remainder largely Eastern Orthodox Serbians and Roman Catholic Croatians. Finally, Judaism also has a presence in Eastern Europe, though the Jewish population is only a fraction of what it was before World War II and the Nazi drive to exterminate that group.

POPULATION

The total population of the twelve Eastern European countries is about 123 million, approximately half that of the United States (Table 11–1). The largest is Poland, with 38.6 million people, making it the sixth most populous country in Europe (following Germany, Italy, Britain, France, and Spain). In contrast, Slovenia and Macedonia, each with about 2 million people, are smaller than all of the countries of Western Europe except Luxembourg, Iceland, and Malta.

(Serbo-Croatian) but use different alphabets—the Orthodox Serbs use the Cyrillic alphabet; the Catholic Croats use the Roman alphabet. And related to religion and written language is cultural identification. The Serbians have traditionally looked toward Russia as their cultural mentor, whereas the Croats have always considered themselves more Western.

The Islamic heritage in Eastern Europe is prevalent in Albania and Bosnia-Hercegovina and also

Distribution

The distribution of the population throughout Eastern Europe is highly variable (Figure 11–5). The largest areas of high population density are found in the northwestern part of the Czech Republic and southernmost Poland. A smaller high-density zone surrounds Budapest, Hungary. Moderate population densities are found in much of the remaining Great European Plain, the Wallachian Plain, the Hungarian Plain, and adjoining areas in southern Slovakia, northeastern Serbia, and southeastern Romania. Lower population densities prevail in the Carpathians and the mountainous areas that cover much of Albania, Bulgaria, and the countries of the former Yugoslavia.

Population Growth

Much of World War II was fought on Eastern European soil. As a result of military and civilian losses and migration, the postwar population of the region was 10 percent less than the prewar population. During the early postwar years the population increased at generally high rates, except in East Germany; large numbers of East Germans migrated to the West until the Berlin Wall was built in 1961. During that postwar period the communist governments of Eastern Europe were following a Marxist theory of population growth, which holds that population growth is economically beneficial as long as the economic system has created an even distribution of resources. Some early postwar policies, such as subsidies to families and provision of day-care centers, definitely supported a high birthrate. But other government policies had opposite effects. For example, in response to a demand for women to join a growing labor force, the availability of abortions was greatly increased. That and other factors, such as the shortage of adequate housing and the need of families for the woman's income, helped to slow the birthrate. By the mid-1960s the governments of Czechoslovakia, Hungary, Romania, and

Figure 11–5
Eastern Europe's population.
Population distribution in Eastern Europe is quite un-even. Population density is higher in the north than in the south and higher in the plains than in the uplands.

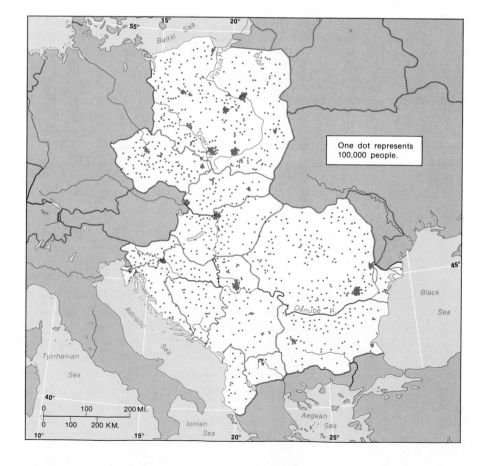

Bulgaria feared that dropping growth rates would lead to an inadequate supply of labor. In the Western industrial economies, zero population growth is seen as the ideal, but Eastern European countries are not as highly automated and mechanized as their Western neighbors and tend to rely more heavily on human labor resources. Therefore, population policies were modified in Eastern Europe to encourage an increase in the birthrate. The reform measures largely relied on improved social programs, such as increased subsidies for families, extended maternity leave, and improved social welfare programs.

The most severe policy in this regard was enacted by the communist government in Romania, where the Ceaucescu dictatorship used force to pursue its goal of 30 million people by the year 2000. Abortions and all contraceptive methods were outlawed, and security police were used to monitor pregnancies to be sure they reached term. The consequences of that policy were devastating. Many women who had complications arising from illegal abortions died rather than seek medical help and risk being sent to prison. In addition, Romania achieved the highest infant mortality rate in Europe, partly attributable to passive infanticide, or permitting a baby to die of starvation or medical neglect. And more than 14,000 unwanted children were living in squalid conditions in Romanian orphanages at the time the communist government was toppled.

The new government of Romania quickly legalized abortions and contraceptives, and many of the unwanted children were adopted by Western Europeans. But the status of birth control remains unclear throughout the entire region, particularly in the northern countries and especially in Poland, where religious beliefs play an important role in countering birth-control programs. Nonetheless, in most Eastern European countries, including Romania, population has continued to grow at an extremely slow rate.

Almost all of today's Eastern European countries fit into the last stage of the demographic transformation: low birthrates, low death rates, and low rates of natural increase (1 percent or less per year). As those countries make serious adjustments to a freer economy and become more developed and urban, their populations will probably continue to grow very slowly. A number of countries have already attained zero population growth; in fact, in

Bulgaria, Hungary, Romania, and Croatia the number of deaths slightly exceeds the number of births. Of course, the wars in the Balkans have tragically taken a tremendous number of lives.

Albania is the lone exception to this Eastern European pattern, because of its high birthrate (2.3 percent) and low death rate (0.6 percent). The result in an annual rate of population growth of 1.8 percent. That figure has been slowly declining during the last decade but is still comparable to the rate in many developing countries, such as Mexico (2.2 percent), Vietnam (2.3 percent), and India (1.9 percent) (see Appendix B).

Urban Populations

Eastern Europe is less urbanized than Western Europe, where the urban population averages more than 80 percent of the total population. In Eastern Europe the urban population averages only about 60 percent of the total, reflecting the greater predominance of agriculture as a way of life in Eastern Europe and the smaller role of industrial and service activities in the economy.

Levels of urbanization vary from country to country. The Czech Republic is one of the more urbanized states in Europe: more than 75 percent of its people live in cities. At the other end of the scale are Bosnia-Hercegovina and Albania, where respectively 34 percent and 36 percent of the people are urban. With the exception of Portugal, Bosnia is the least urbanized country in Europe. The level of urbanization in other Eastern European countries ranges from 67 percent in Bulgaria to 47 percent in the new Yugoslavia (Serbia and Montenegro).

Six Eastern European cities have a population of more than one million: Budapest, Bucharest, Warsaw, Prague, Belgrade, and Sofia. Except for Belgrade these cities—along with Tirane, Albania—are good examples of a primate city. **A primate city** is disproportionately large (generally, more than twice as large) when compared with other cities in the same country, and it dominates the economic, cultural, and political life of the country. Such cities tend to be found in less developed countries, where the scarcer capital and resources are usually more geographically concentrated.

Because the communist regimes of Eastern Europe placed a high priority on industrial growth, urban development proceeded briskly after World

War II. Existing cities were reconstructed and expanded, and several new industrial towns were built. The new towns include Nowa Huta (specializing in iron and steel) in Poland, Victoria (specializing in chemicals) in Romania, and Havirov (a mining center) near the city of Ostrava in the Czech Republic.

LEVELS OF ECONOMIC DEVELOPMENT

The emphasis on industrialization in Eastern Europe during the communist era led to concentration on heavy industry and the manufacture of producer goods (goods used in the production of other commodities) and on development of mineral resources and energy. Nonetheless, despite considerable progress in industrial production—and in agriculture as well—Eastern Europe is still less industrialized and has a poorer economic landscape than Western Europe. The Eastern European economy remains quite varied, however, especially in terms of three standard indicators—per capita GNP, per capita consumption of energy, and percent of the labor force in agriculture. The two supplementary measures—daily food supply and life expectancy—are more uniform throughout the region.

As the 1990s began, the economies of the entire region were in flux, facing serious problems as they attempted to establish free-market economies and trade relationships with Western Europe and the rest of the world. The impact of these transitions can be seen in a comparison of the 1989 and 1992 per capita GNP for Bulgaria, Hungary, Poland, and Romania; the drop for all four countries was significant (Table 11–2). There have been encouraging signs, however, that point to stabilizing conditions and increased production in Poland, Hungary, and the Czech Republic. but economic data is difficult to access for the new countries, particularly war-torn countries. By way of comparison, the 1992 per capita GNP for the United States was $23,120 and for Russia, $2,680.

In Eastern Europe, per capita energy consumption is relatively low and employment in agriculture is relatively high, when compared with the rates in Western Europe (Figure 11–6). Thus, most Eastern European countries should be considered transitional, or developing; they belong neither to the developed nor the undeveloped world but are working hard to develop modern free market economies. The Czech Republic, Slovenia, Hungary, and Poland

Table 11–2
GNP, 1989 and 1992 (in U.S. dollars).

	1989	1992	Percentage Change
Bulgaria	5,710	1,330	-79%
Hungary	6,110	3,010	-51%
Poland	4,570	1,960	-57%
Romania	3,445	1,090	-68%

have the best chances of success. In contrast, countries such as Albania, Macedonia, and Bosnia will likely find the road to economic betterment much more difficult.

RECENT DEVELOPMENT STRATEGIES

The Eastern European countries can be divided into three categories in terms of their progress in implementing economic development strategies for the 1990s. First are those countries where war has resulted in severe economic dislocations and prevented progress toward development; these include the new Yugoslavia (Serbia and Montenegro), Bosnia-Hercegovina, and Croatia. The second category includes Albania, Slovakia, Macedonia, Romania, and Bulgaria, all of which proclaim their support for dismantling the old communist economic structure and establishing market economies but have been slow to enact change due to internal political problems. Former communists play a strong role in these countries, particularly in Slovakia, Romania, and Bulgaria. The third category includes the Czech Republic, Poland, Hungary, and Slovenia; these four countries have gone the furthest in establishing a capitalistic market economy.

Serbia and Montenegro, Croatia, Bosnia-Hercegovina, and Macedonia

The old Yugoslavia abandoned the centralized planning model of the Soviet Union in the 1950s and replaced it with a more market-oriented economy, in which **workers' self-management councils** were responsible for operating state enterprises with direction from the government. From the mid-1960s to the mid-1970s Yugoslavia underwent a ma-

Figure 11-6
Rural landscape in the republic of Montenegro in southern Yugoslavia. The thin, stoney soils of upland regions such as this result in low incomes for many rural people. The contrast between rural and urban life remains sharp in much of Eastern Europe.

jor change in its internal economic processes; its six republics and two autonomous provinces assumed a greater role in decision making while the role of the federal government was sharply curtailed. Despite this restructuring, during the 1980s Yugoslavia suffered a slowdown in economic growth because of heavy foreign borrowing and difficulty in financing imports of raw materials, semifinished products, and other equipment and goods necessary for expansion.

The economic contrasts within the former Yugoslavia were as sharp as the country's ethnic divisions. Slovenia, the wealthiest republic, had a per capita GNP five times higher than that of the poorest area—the Kosovo Province. Not surprisingly, Slovenia and Croatia, the wealthiest areas with the greatest Western orientation, were the republics

most intent in freeing their economies and ending their responsibilities for support of the poorer areas. In 1991 both of those republics declared their independence from a Serbian-dominated Yugoslavia.

By the mid-1990s Serbia, Croatia, and Bosnia-Hercegovina were all in dire economic straits due to the vicious fighting that was widespread throughout those countries. Agricultural production had plummeted, industrial production had fallen, unemployment was high, and inflation was running rampant, especially in Serbia, where it was calculated in late 1993 at almost 2,000 percent a month—which would translate to an annual rate of 363 quadrillion percent!

Although Macedonia was not directly affected by the war plaguing most of the former Yugoslavia, this mountainous, rural area had severe problems that stemmed primarily from its failure to gain recognition by the world community due to Greek objections over use of the name *Macedonia*. To the Greeks, the name represents a vital part of Greek culture, for Macedonia was the home of one of its most famous historical figures, Alexander the Great. Greece has been adamant that the name not be "usurped" by the Slavic Macedonians. Also, there is concern among Greeks that Slavic Macedonia will make claims on lands in northern Greece that have long been called Macedonia.

Bulgaria, Romania, Albania, and Slovakia

Although former communists play important roles in all the Eastern European countries, their presence is most notable and controversial in these four countries. Many Bulgarians and Romanians, **in particular, believe that their p**resent leadership is still dominated by the old-line communist functionaries—called the ***nomenklatura*** throughout Eastern Europe—even though party names have changed from Communist to Socialist in Bulgaria and to the National Salvation Front in Romania. Bulgarian steps toward a market economy are still in the preliminary, discussion stage, whereas Romania actually took the first step in the summer of 1990 with the creation of the National Privatization Agency. **Privatization**, the transfer of state-owned industries and farms partially or completely to private control, has become a most important process in the Eastern Europe of the 1990s, and such a shift to the private sector represents an awesome task.

The cost of rebuilding and restructuring the economies of Bulgaria and, especially, Romania will be high. A recent study by the U.S. Central Intelligence Agency (CIA) foresees a decline in the living standard in both countries as attempts are made to make their economies more productive and more competitive with the West. Unemployment will likely increase as inefficient firms are closed, and prices will likely rise as producers lose their state subsidies. Bulgaria already has a large foreign debt that must be paid, and neither country can rely any longer on the old Soviet Union as a supplier of reasonably priced raw materials and a buyer of their often shoddily produced goods.

The economic situation in Slovakia is much more severe than in its former partner the Czech Republic. In late 1993 the inflation rate reached 20 percent, compared to an approximate 7 percent rate in the Czech Republic; and Slovak unemployment was approaching 20 percent, whereas Czech unemployment stood at 5 percent. Numerous political problems have further complicated the situation, making wise economic decisions few and far between. Adding to Slovakia's problems is a weak industrial base, one that once had a disproportionate share of the Soviet Bloc's arms industry, for which there is today no market.

Throughout recent history Albania has held the dubious distinction of having the poorest economy of all of Europe. Albania's decline in industrial production from 1990 to 1992—in excess of 60 percent—was the greatest in the region; for comparison, the figure for Poland was approximately 35 percent. Albanian farmland has been privatized, the government has been actively seeking foreign investors, and a severe rate of inflation has abated. But the country still lacks basic democratic principles, and it has a long way to go to reach even Eastern European levels of prosperity.

The Czech Republic, Poland, Hungary, and Slovenia

These four countries all have similar characteristics and similar problems, but with significant differences. The Czechs in many ways are in the best position to make the transition to a market economy. The Czech Republic is the only Eastern European country to have been industrialized before the communist occupation. Prior to World War II Czechoslovakia had a democratic tradition and ranked tenth in the world in per capita income. When the split occurred in 1993, the Czechs inherited the most industrialized section of the country, and the Slovaks the more agrarian section. The Czech Republic has a relatively low foreign debt, a skilled labor force, and a low inflation rate. With those advantages to build on, the government has been proceeding cautiously in its reforms. Its first step toward privatization was the sale of a thousand state-owned firms, which could be purchased by citizens using state-issued vouchers. In addition, the government has attempted to freeze the prices of all goods and make the Czech currency freely convertible to Western currencies. Through such measures, Czechs hope to make their enterprises more attractive to foreign investors.

Poland has carried on the swiftest and boldest economic reforms, principally because its failing economy needed rapid repair (Figure 11–7).

Figure 11-7
The shipyards of Gdansk on the Baltic shore of Poland. The Czech republic and
Poland are the more industrialized states of Eastern Europe.

Rampant inflation, an extreme shortage of consumer goods, and a burdensome foreign debt have all plagued Polish economic life. Reform measures have included the start of the largest sale of state property in Eastern Europe as well as the ending of price controls, which led to higher consumer prices but better-stocked stores. Unemployment has soared as enterprises have regained the right to fire unproductive workers. In addition, the cutback of state subsidies has forced inefficient firms to reduce their work force, thereby adding further to unemployment. A good example of the previous low productivity of Polish industry is the massive steel plant in Nowa Huta, which employed 28,000 workers to produce as much steel as Western European plants produce with half that number of workers.

Of these four Eastern European countries, Hungary had gone the furthest to reform its centrally controlled economy before the 1989 revolutions be-

gan; consequently, its reforms have not seemed so radical. The process of privatization is well underway in Hungary, aided significantly by General Electric's purchase of 50 percent of a Hungarian light-bulb company. In addition, a capitalist-style stock exchange has been established in Budapest, and price controls have been removed from three-fourths of Hungary's goods.

The greatest economic success story in Eastern Europe so far has been Slovenia, formerly a republic of old Yugoslavia. Bordering Austria, Italy, and Hungary on the north, Slovenia is removed from the hostilities facing its Croatian and Serbian neighbors. Furthermore, Slovenia has practically no minority problems or irredentist claims. Economically it is more involved in trade with its Western European neighbors and the Slovene currency is both stable and convertible with world currencies. According to *The Economist* magazine, the Slovene per capita

Gross Domestic Product (the total value of goods and services produced within the country) adjusted for purchasing power is almost $9,000, compared to about $7,000 for the Czech Republic, $6,700 for Hungary, $4,300 for Poland, $3,000 for Croatia, $3,000 for Serbia, and $850 for Albania.[1]

The Economic Future for Eastern Europe

All of the Eastern European countries are in the process of reorienting their trade toward the West, with the collapse of the **Council for Mutual Economic Assistance (CMEA, or Comecon).** That international organization was created by the Soviets to control and integrate trade within Soviet bloc countries, with Poland, Hungary, Czechoslovakia, Romania, and Bulgaria as full members and Yugoslavia as an associate member. CMEA trade contracts have been canceled, and Eastern European countries that once had a ready market for their products must look elsewhere. That task is extremely difficult because of worldwide industrial cutbacks and recessionary conditions, as well as the added problem of the relatively low quality of Eastern European products. In search of capital and markets Hungary, Poland, the former Czechoslovakia, Bulgaria, and Romania all became associate members of the European Community, And all have expressed their intention to seek full membership in the European Union as soon as they get their economies in shape. The year 2000 is the target date for EU membership for Hungary, Poland, the Czech Republic, Slovakia, and Slovenia.

AGRICULTURE

The various physical environments, historical legacies, and local reactions to Soviet policies have all contributed to the creation of a diverse agricultural landscape in Eastern Europe.

Types of Agricultural Production

The cooler northern section of Eastern Europe—Poland, Slovakia, and the Czech Republic—is a major grain-growing region, with wheat and rye the principal bread grains. In addition, emphasis on industrial crops, including sugar beets, oils, and fiber plants, has increased in the north. Potatoes, an important staple in the Eastern European diet, are grown throughout the region, though other vegeta-bles and fruits are more prominent near urban areas. Cattle and hogs constitute the principal livestock in the northern part of Eastern Europe, though a shortage of meat has long been a chronic problem. The area planted with fodder crops has increased but is still not adequate to meet the needs of the meat and dairy industries.

In the southern part of Eastern Europe the principal grain-growing regions are the Hungarian and Wallachian plains, followed by parts of Albania and Bulgaria, as well as parts of the former Yugoslavia. Wheat and corn are the most important grains, though lately emphasis has also been placed on the cultivation of industrial crops, most notably sugar beets. Bulgaria is Eastern Europe's major producer of cotton, tobacco, and vegetables. Bulgaria, Romania, and Hungary all export vegetables, both fresh and processed, principally to Russia and the northern section of Eastern Europe. The dry summer subtropical climate of Albania and the countries of the former Yugoslavia produces a variety of specialized crops such as citrus, olives, and vegetables. In addition, vineyards, primarily for wine grapes, are a significant feature of the dry summer zone of Croatia, Serbia, Albania, and parts of Romania and Bulgaria. Livestock production has encountered the same difficulties in this part of Eastern Europe as encountered in the north, largely because of an inadequate feed base, though the raising of sheep for both meat and wool is an important phase of the livestock industry.

Collectivization

At the end of World War II much of Eastern Europe suffered from chronic overpopulation in rural areas. In the northern and central sections of the region major problems included the existence of large estates and the shortage of good agricultural land for the peasants. In the Balkans agriculture generally occurred on small, highly fragmented farms and had achieved only a subsistence level. Numerous attempts at land reform were made throughout Eastern Europe before World War II. None could compare, however, with the drastic changes that were accomplished after the postwar communist regimes were established. Large estates were nationalized, and that land was redistributed among the peasants. The next step was the **collectivization** of agriculture: land was consolidated into large-scale units, either Soviet-style **state farms** or **collective**

farms. The central governments funded and directed the state farms; individual farmers were responsible for operating the collective (or communal) farms, within the framework of government directives.

The objectives of collectivization in Eastern Europe were the same as those in the Soviet Union. This form of agricultural organization was intended to make it easier for the government to control that important sector of the economy and thereby indirectly support industrial development programs. The communist governments expected the large-scale agricultural units to be more productive because of the greater mechanization and specialization of labor, and thus the amount of food available for the growing number of industrial workers was expected to increase.

The results of collectivization were mixed. Resistance to it was widespread, particularly in Poland and Yugoslavia, where most of the arable land remained in private hands. In the other countries it proved much more durable. All of Albania's farms were in the socialist sector (i.e., state farms and collective farms). In Czechoslovakia, Hungary, Romania, and Bulgaria the socialist sector controlled 84 to 92 percent of the agricultural land. Throughout Eastern Europe, however, low productivity, lack of capital, shortages of fertilizers and herbicides, and inadequate farm machinery all served to limit food production.

The General State of Agriculture

On the whole, agriculture plays a larger role in the economy of Eastern Europe than it does in Western Europe. One indicator is the percentage of the labor force employed in agricultural pursuits.[2] As expected, the lowest proportions of farm workers are encountered in the more industrialized and wealthier countries. But even in those countries the percentages of the working force employed in agriculture is relatively high. For example, in Hungary in 1991 11 percent were employed in agriculture, compared to less than 4 percent for Western Europe as a whole.

In many respects Hungary has been the most successful with its agricultural economy. The fertile soils of the Hungarian Plain are well equipped with machinery comparable to that in Western Europe, thereby helping to make Hungary a net exporter of farm products. In addition, in the period before communist control ended Hungary had gone the

furthest in allowing collectives to make their own decisions, even though poor financial incentives there and throughout the region discouraged the farm workers.

The Balkan countries—Romania, Bulgaria, the countries of the former Yugoslavia, and Albania—are more agricultural than the Eastern European countries in the north, with the possible exception of Poland. In Albania almost five out of every ten workers (47.7 percent) are engaged in agriculture. In the other Balkan countries, as well as in Poland, about 20 percent of the work force is involved in agriculture. During the communist era the majority of farms were in private hands in both Poland and Yugoslavia. The two countries were generally self-sufficient in food production, though during years of poor harvest some food had to be imported. The turmoil in Bosnia, Serbia, and Croatia that occurred after Yugoslavia broke apart has severely reduced production throughout the area. In contrast, Romania and Bulgaria are both net exporters of foodstuffs. Compared with pre–World War II agricultural production, the Balkan countries have made substantial gains. Nevertheless, both per capita and per area productivity in the Balkans remain among the lowest in Europe.

The Transition to a Market Economy

Unquestionably, the shift to a market economy will be more difficult in the agricultural sector of Eastern Europe than in the industrial and service sectors. Every one of the Eastern Europe countries has embarked on a program of privatizating agriculture; however, the problems are enormous, and progress has been slow. Agricultural production in 1992 was at least 10 percent below 1991 levels in almost all Eastern European countries. Conflicting claims to the land, inaccessibility to capital by farmers, and lack of entrepreneurial and other skills necessary for operating an independent farm are some of the obstacles that must be overcome. The state farm system could remain, perhaps privatized as factory-type establishments, but the collective farms pose a more complex challenge. The basic idea that the land of the collective farm should be returned to the peasants is accepted in all Eastern European countries, but the actual transfer is beset with complications. Who should receive the land? Only peasants whose families owned the land? What about the farm workers? And what about those landowners whose large estates were confiscated decades ago by the communists? What should be done about agricultural land that was converted to urban and industrial use? And who should own a collective farm's livestock, tools, and buildings?

Agriculture in Eastern Europe will certainly not be promoted by breaking the collective farms into small, inefficient farms worked by peasants with neither capital nor supplies. Such is the case in Bulgaria, where more than 90 percent of the land that has been privatized consists of tiny plots less than 2.47 acres (one hectare). The most sensible solution seems to be to retain the collective operation but give the peasants shares based on their labor and former ownership. Of course, there is always the possibility that a farmer would want the land to remain in one piece, especially if it had the potential to be sold for some nonagricultural use. Undoubtedly, it will take years to make this transition complete.

A free market economy also requires an end to state subsidies of the agricultural sector. In the past, communist subsidies traditionally kept food prices low, making it sometimes cheaper to feed livestock bread rather than grain. As subsidies on food are removed, prices will rise and consumption will drop, reducing the farmers' income and perhaps leading to violent demonstrations, such as those in Poland in the summer of 1990. Even more significant is the problem of supplies. If state subsidies are removed from the production of fertilizers, tools, and other farm supplies, farmers will find it increasingly difficult to pay the higher prices for those supplies. A dilemma thus exists: in order to achieve a free and rational market economy, the state-maintained collective economy must end; yet for the new class of farmers to buy seed, equipment, and other supplies, they must receive some form of subsidies on the order of those paid to their counterparts in Western Europe and the United States.

Overall, the peasants of Eastern Europe are not eager for the return of capitalism. For many a free market evokes memories of past hardships and forecasts a decline in present living standards. *The Economist* magazine analyzed the farmer's position clearly:

> From the Baltic to the Black Sea, the peasants are not interested in getting their land back.... Co-operative (collective) farm members, like peasants the world over, fear change and are happiest with the status quo.

For East European farmers the status quo is sitting on a tractor eight hours a day taking orders from a foreman....

The idea of taking back the ancestral six hectares—15 acres—often broken up into a dozen scattered strips, not only threatens the lucky owner with a traumatic change, but would also present some very practical difficulties. Capital would have to be borrowed, buildings to be erected, machinery purchased and, worst of all, risks taken. The few remaining workers who can remember the old days of ploughing with oxen and running a dairy herd of two cows do not wish to repeat the experience at the age of 65. The younger ones have only the stories of unceasing work for little reward to encourage them. Neither find the prospect attractive.[3]

INDUSTRY

The Resource Base

Eastern Europe is not well endowed with industrial resources (Figure 11–8). The region is deficient in energy resources, iron ore, and other minerals, and the few resources that do exist are unequally distributed. In addition, many of them are of inferior quality and are expensive to utilize. The only substantial deposit of high-quality coal is the Silesian-Moravian field. Most of that deposit lies in Poland, with a small part extending into the Czech Republic. As a result, Poland produces more coal than any other Eastern European country. A high-quality coalfield of secondary importance is found in the Czech Republic, and smaller deposits dot the region. For the former Yugoslav republics, coal was the most important energy source. Small deposits of high-quality hard coal are found in Bosnia, eastern Serbia, and northwestern Croatia. The Serbian province of Kosovo has Europe's largest lignite field. Low-quality coals, used both for the production of electricity and for domestic heating, are also widely scattered throughout Eastern Europe.

In addition, there is a shortage of oil and natural gas in Eastern Europe. Romania's Ploesti field has the oldest commercial oil well in the world. But the total reserves of Romania—including the Ploesti field, the newer Bacau field in the eastern part of the country, and other scattered small deposits—are expected to last only a few more years at present rates of production (Figure 11–9). Albania is now a small exporter of petroleum products. In the past, Yugoslavia supplied only a small proportion of its

Figure 11-8
Mineral resources and industrial districts of Eastern Europe.
Eastern Europe has two principal industrial districts: the Silesia-Moravia district of Poland and the Czech Republic and the Bohemian Basin in the Czech Republic. Both of those industrial centers are located on or near coal deposits and have access to other nearby minerals.

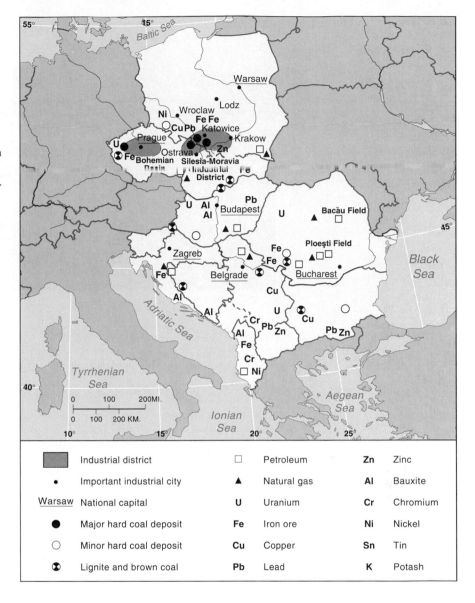

oil and gas needs from fields in Bosnia, and gas deposits in Croatia and in the Adriatic off the Montenegran coast. Most European countries, then, are dependent on imported petroleum and gas. Since oil and gas consumption is increasing throughout Eastern Europe, dependence on foreign sources, particularly Russia, will inevitably increase, but prices will also increase, thereby accentuating the problem of more money leaving these countries than coming in.

Hydroelectric potential is also limited in Eastern Europe, except for the countries of the Balkans. At present there is little developed hydroelectric power, and most plants are quite small. The potential for development is greatest in the countries of the former Yugoslavia, where extensive construction is currently under way to greatly increase electric output.

Because good-quality energy resources are so scarce, leaders in Eastern European countries have expressed considerable interest in nuclear power. At present, nuclear generation of electricity remains limited but is expected to increase. Uranium, the fuel for nuclear power, is mined in much of the region, though details of production are closely guarded secrets.

Figure 11-9
The Ploesti oil field in Romania, one of the world's oldest commercial oil fields. Eastern Europe is not well endowed with oil or natural gas. Even this field is not expected to serve as a major fuel source in the future.

Ferrous and nonferrous metals are also in short supply in Eastern Europe. Most critical is the limited amount of iron ore. Even Poland, which has the largest iron and steel industry in Eastern Europe, must rely on Ukraine and Russia for iron ore. A wide variety of ferrous and nonferrous ores are distributed throughout the territory of the former Yugoslavia, even though most of those metallic deposits are relatively small and production is limited. Europe's major mercury deposits are found in Slovenia; Bosnia-Hercegovina has bauxite and iron ore (80 percent of the former Yugoslavia's reserves); Serbia possesses copper, chromium, lead and zinc ores; and Macedonia contains chromium, manganese and uranium. In other Eastern European countries the most important metallic ores and metals include bauxite in Hungary and chromium in Albania. The most noteworthy of the region's nonmetallic minerals is sulfur; mined in Poland, this mineral provides a raw material for chemical industries.

The Location of Industrial Activity

Theoretically, according to Marxists, equal and balanced regional economic development throughout a country is possible only in a planned socialist society that has eliminated capitalism. Marxists contend that capitalism involves the exploitation of one person, group, or region by another, and therefore an uneven distribution of economic activity occurs. Consequently, Eastern European planners tried to stimulate the development of backward areas, such as eastern Poland and Slovakia. Those efforts to decentralize industrial activity met with some success; but the older, established centers continued to grow, and they still dominate the industrial geography of the region.

A large industrialized area extends from Western Europe across the northern part of Eastern Europe, including western Poland and the western Czech Republic. The concentration of industry is particularly great in the Silesian-Moravian district of Poland and the Czech Republic and the Czech Bohemian Basin (see Figure 11–8). The Silesian-Moravian district used to be Germany's second-largest heavy-industrial region. But after World War II Poland acquired most of Silesia, with a small section being given to Czechoslovakia. Now, Silesia is Poland's major heavy-industrial district because of the local coal resources. In addition to coal mining and the production of iron and steel, industry there includes the manufacture of agricultural machinery, machine tools, and various chemicals. The Czech section of Silesia is dominated by the city of Ostrava, the nation's iron and steel center.

The Bohemian Basin in the western Czech Republic is also an iron- and steel-producing district, in connection with small coal mines that are worked in the area. The Czech Republic's capital and largest city, Prague, is located within the basin and is the country's center of industrial production. The basin's diversified industries include important chemicals, foods, and machinery.

Manufacturing outside the principal industrial area occurs chiefly in the large cities. For example, such cities as Warsaw, Budapest, and Belgrade are major focal points of diverse industries. Other centers of production, generally smaller, are often associated with the location of a particular raw material (e.g., the chemical industries at Ploesti).

Pollution of the Environment

The Soviet model for economic development that was used in Eastern Europe was disastrous for the environment. Success was measured by the output of goods, usually with a limited investment and virtually no concern for any environmental degradation that might accompany a successful venture. Natural resources were usually wasted because the system underpriced their value. One example of such waste is the great amounts of water used in Poland, Hungary, the Czech Republic, Romania, and Bulgaria, where consumption rates are double those in Western Europe.

In addition, limited capital usually meant no money for environmental safety, and wastes, often toxic, were dumped into the nearest river or open patch of land. Two-thirds of Bulgaria's rivers became polluted. The Sava River, which flows through Slovenia, Croatia, Bosnia, and Serbia, contains no plant or animal life—and neither do 90 percent of Poland's rivers. Only 5 percent of Warsaw's sewage is treated; the rest is dumped into the Vistula River. And soil contamination in Poland is so rampant that a full 25 percent of the land is unfit to grow food safe for animal or human consumption. In fact, the Polish Academy of Sciences has named Poland the most polluted country in the world; one-third of its population is expected to suffer from some environmentally induced disease, such as cancer or respiratory illness.

Although unwise farming practices, such as the overuse of subsidized fertilizers, did contribute to the problem, industry bears the major responsibility for Eastern Europe's environmental pollution. The major source of air pollution is sulphur dioxide from the burning of low-grade coals and lignite. A Czech official has stated that levels of sulphur dioxide in Prague and Bohemia are twenty times the country's average. As a result, life expectancy in that part of the Czech Republic is eleven years less than it is in the rest of the country. In addition, acid rain is estimated to have damaged as much as 43 percent of the forests of Bulgaria, 48 percent of those in Poland, and 71 percent of those in Czech and Slovak lands.

Under one-party rule the communists were able to prevent such information from being publicly disclosed. But deteriorating conditions became increasingly intolerable, and the 1980s saw the rise of many environmental groups in Poland, Hungary, Czechoslovakia, Yugoslavia, and Bulgaria. Now that Eastern European governments are more open and most are freely elected, the main task is to halt the damage and begin the cleanup.

That task will not be easy; the problems are large, complex, and international. For example, the Danube is polluted by fertilizer runoff in Hungary and then flows through Yugoslavia, Bulgaria, and Romania; and the toxic air from Romanian chemical plants drifts over Bulgarian towns and villages. Workable policies must be formulated to fine polluters and close polluting plants that cannot be cleaned up. Fortunately, there are signs of increased international cooperation, but a lot of money is needed to build sewage treatment facilities, install desulphurization equipment, and create safe dumps for hazardous waste—all in a region where investment capital is already scarce. Solutions to these problems are likely to require Western capital.

SUMMARY
An Uncertain Future

The changes triggered by the momentous events of 1989 and 1990 continue to unfold, causing uncertainty in Eastern Europe and the world as a whole. The region that eventually emerges from all this chaos should be more diverse, more free, more affluent, and more Western. It will also experience increasing problems: intense nationalism and ethnic rivalries will continue to cause great unrest, especially in Croatia, Serbia, and Bosnia Hercegovina. Economic difficulties are widespread, and living standards will mostly worsen before they improve, though Slovenia, the Czech Republic, Poland, and Hungary are displaying some encouraging signs of economic improvement. Unemployment and rising prices plague the region, and these problems lead to greater political uncertainty as parties from right, left, and center vie for power. The process of democratization will be uneven. In Albania, the democratic process and a market economy have begun with the introduction of competing political parties and the privatization of agricultural land, but that country economically still lags far behind the rest of the region. Democratic progress is most likely in the Czech Republic, Poland, Hungary, and Slovenia, with prospects in Romania and Bulgaria looking dimmer. Throughout the region the privatization of the economy is fraught with complications, especially in rural areas. Again, the most likely areas of success will be Poland, Slovenia, the Czech Republic, and Hungary. Environmental issues will create greater concern as the full extent of the problems and the full cost of their solutions are revealed.

Much of Eastern Europe's future lies outside its borders. The success of democracy and a free-market economy in Russia are critical to the region; any return to an orthodox communist government in Russia would certainly affect the future of Eastern Europe. Many Western business leaders and academics, however, expect Germany to replace the former Soviet Union as the primary economic influence. The success of the European Union, as well as the growth of economic and political stability in the countries of Eastern Europe will help determine what role the region will play in the Europe of the future.

In looking to the future, it might be appropriate to recall the words of Willy Brandt, former mayor of West Berlin, when the Berlin Wall was opened: "This is a beautiful day after a long voyage, but we are only at a way station. We are not at the end of the way."[4] Perhaps in the near future all of Eastern Europe will be part of a single Europe and the labels Eastern Europe and Western Europe will be only arbitrary geographical descriptions.

KEY TERMS

Balkanization
buffer zone
Bulgarize
collective farm
collectivization
command economy
communism
Council for Mutual Economic Assistance (CMEA, or Comecon)
Cyrillic alphabet
irredentism
Magyar
Marxism
nomenklatura
people's democracies
people's republics
primate city
privatization
shatter belt
Soviet bloc
state farm
workers' self-management councils

NOTES

1. *The Economist* (June 26–July 2, 1993): 55.
2. Use of this indicator, the percentage of the labor force employed in agriculture, overemphasizes the contribution of agriculture to the economy. In terms of dollar value added to the GNP, Eastern European farmers are only one-third to one-half as productive as industrial workers are.
3. "No Yeoman They," *The Economist* 316, no. 7664 (21 July 1990): 16.
4. *New York Times,* 11 Nov. 1989, p. 6.

12

Russia and the Eurasian States of the Former Soviet Union: Land and People

Natural Regions

Landform Regions

Population

A night view of Moscow, focusing on the Church of St. Basil in Red Square. Moscow, the largest city in Russia, serves as the capital for the Russian Federation.

Russia and its newly independent neighbors, which together once made up the Soviet Union, cover a huge area (Figure 12–1). The western quarter of the region, considered a part of Europe, contains: the European section of Russia, the countries known as the Baltic states—Estonia, Latvia, and Lithuania—Belarus (formerly known as Belorussia), Ukraine, and Moldova (Moldavia). These last-named six countries all lie between Russia and Eastern Europe. Europe traditionally also includes the Caucasian peninsula; therefore, the countries known as the Transcaucasus states—Georgia, Armenia, and Azerbaidzhan—are considered part of Europe.

The remaining three-fourths of the former Soviet empire lies in Asia. Included in that vast area is Asian Russia—called Siberia—as well as the Central Asian republics of Kazakhstan, Uzbekistan, Turkmenistan (Turkmenia), Kyrgyzstan (Kirghizia), and Tadzhikistan.

This total area occupies one-sixth of the earth's land surface. It measures 6,000 miles (9,660 kilometers) from the Baltic Sea to the Bering Straits; and its maximum north-south extent is almost equal to the width of the United States—approximately 2,900 miles (4,669 kilometers). The area is two-and-a-half times as large as the United States, and it stretches across eleven time zones. Russia alone occupies slightly more than three-quarters of the territory of the former Soviet Union.

The image of the vastness of this European-Asian, or Eurasian, landmass evokes for many people an image of unlimited raw materials and vast tracts of virgin lands just waiting to be exploited. In reality, Russia and many countries of the former Soviet Union are well endowed with the raw materials, though not all the countries of the region share in this wealth. Furthermore, the mere presence of natural resources does not ensure the appropriate development of those resources. First of all, their exploitation requires large capital investments, which the governments may be unable to make. In addition, some of the resources that have been developed have not been developed wisely. The sheer magnitude of the environmental base encouraged waste during the Soviet era. In the case of Russia the remoteness of the deposits from consuming areas and the consequent high transportation costs add to the price of exploitation.

Other features of the physical environment also play a critical role in the economic development of these Eurasian states. Much of the land is considered inhospitable for settlement and unsuitable for agriculture because it is too cold, too wet, or too dry. Soviet planners suggested, discussed, and even undertook many schemes to change some of those negatives. Their ideas were as basic as irrigation systems and the draining of marshes, and as grand as planting extensive belts of trees to change the climate of the steppe and the semidesert. Some of their ideas were even grandiose and impractical, such as damming the Bering Straits to modify the climate of the Pacific coast. All developmental projects, however—whether large or small, practical or impractical—left their mark on the landscape of the developing societies. Unfortunately, under Soviet rule, corners were often cut to increase output, regardless of the effect on the environment or the amount of the total resource base wasted in the process (see the boxed feature Environmental Degradation in the Former Soviet Union).

NATURAL REGIONS

The magnitude of this Eurasian landmass and its high latitudinal location are important factors in the severe continental climates that dominate the country. The southernmost part of the region lies at approximately 35°N latitude—similar to that of Memphis, Tennessee. Moscow, however, is farther north than Edmonton, Canada; and more than 75 percent of the area lies north of the 49th parallel, which constitutes the northern boundary of much of the United States.

A useful device for studying the physical environment is the natural region (Figure 12–2). **Natural regions** are essentially vegetation zones with related general climatic and soil characteristics. The term can be misleading, though; large parts of the area have been altered by humankind and thus are not in a natural, or primordial, state.

Tundra

The northernmost natural region of Russia is tundra, a natural region also found in higher mountain elevations. This tundra covers approximately 13 percent of the Russian Republic. The mean temperature of the tundra's warmest month depends on location, but the average ranges between 50°F (10°C) and 32°F (0°C). The very short growing season and poor soils result in sparse vegetation, characterized by such hardy plants as reindeer moss, lichens, and shrubs. The tundra is treeless because of the limited heat received in the high latitudes, the high winds, and the presence of **permafrost**, permanently frozen ground that restricts root growth.

Needless to say, the tundra, with its bleak, cold climate, is the natural region that has been least affected by humans. No place, however, is completely safe from the impact of technology—contamination from the Chernobyl nuclear accident in Ukraine, some 1,300 miles (2,100 kilometers) away, is detected even in that remote area. The few who have penetrated that inhospitable region include people stationed at military posts, widely scattered indigenous tribes, hunters, trappers, and miners.

Forest Regions

Natural forest vegetation covers more than 41 percent of the Russian territory, all of Belarus and the Baltic states, and a small portion of northwestern Ukraine. The forests are divided into three subregions: the vast taiga of Russia; the mixed forest of the Baltics, Belarus, Ukraine, and European Russia; and the broadleaf forest of the Siberian (Russian) far east.

Taiga

The **taiga**, or coniferous forest, lies south of the tundra. It covers the northern half of European Russia as well as most of Siberia. Although coniferous forests cover most of the taiga, extensive swamps and meadows are interspersed among them in many places. The climate of the taiga is primarily subarctic; in fact, lower temperatures have been recorded in the taiga region than in the tundra. As the frigid air settles in the mountain valleys, the thermometer plummets; temperatures as low as −90°F (−68°C) have been recorded in Verkhoyansk in northeast Siberia. Indeed, that part of the world has recorded the lowest temperature on the globe outside Antarctica. Because taiga summers are short and cool, the growing season is generally less than a hundred days, and agriculture is very limited.

The dominant soils of the taiga, which are grayish in color, have been leached of many nutrients and are infertile, as well as highly acidic. Moreover, areas of permafrost cover virtually all of eastern Siberia except the extreme southeast; in western Siberia only the northern portion of the taiga is affected. In addition to retarding root growth, permafrost can contribute to excessive waterlogging of the topsoil in the summer. And waterlogging can make soil move sideways, causing havoc for rail-road lines, roads, pipelines, and even buildings if they are not firmly anchored in the frozen subsoil.

During the Soviet era nomadic native groups of the region turned to more sedentary forms of herding and some agricultural pursuits. The traditional wealth of the taiga—timber, fur-bearing animals, and precious metals—is still significant. But newly developed industrial resources, such as the oil and gas fields in northwestern Siberia, are growing in importance.

Mixed Forest and Broadleaf Forest

Between the taiga and the grasslands to the south lies a triangular-shaped region of mixed forest of coniferous and broadleaf trees. From north to south, deciduous trees displace the conifers more and more until they eventually take over completely. Belarus and the Baltic states are found within this natural region, as is a substantial part of central European Russia.

Temperatures and length of growing season increase toward the south of the region, but precipitation decreases; and the forest cover thins as open meadows increase. This mixed-forest region has been culturally modified more than any other in the region; centuries of settlement have resulted in the clearing of land for agriculture and cities. The longer growing season and the less acidic and more fertile soils make the mixed forest more suited to agriculture than the taiga is. A broadleaf forest is found in the southern part of far eastern Siberia. The region has cold, dry winters and hot, humid summers. The vegetation is mostly broad-leaved deciduous trees of Asiatic origin, with some conifers and open, grassy meadows.

Forest Steppe and Steppe

The Eurasian steppe natural region consists of two subregions: the forest steppe, a region of transition from the forested land to the north, and the treeless, grassy, true steppe. Moldova, Ukraine, southern European and western Siberian Russia, and northern Kazakhstan all fall within this natural region. A small region of steppe vegetation is also found in eastern Azerbaidzhan. The forest steppe is characterized by woods separated by extensive grasslands. In the true steppe, trees grow only in the river valleys, and grasslands stretch as far as the eye can see. In addition, the soils of the forest steppe are more leached than they are in the true steppe, where higher tem-

Figure 12–1
Russia and the Eurasian states of the former Soviet Union. These newly independent countries, which together once composed the Union of Soviet Socialist Republics, cover a huge area of the world. About a quarter of that area is considered part of Europe; the remaining two-thirds lies in Asia.

peratures and higher evaporation rates reduce the effectiveness of precipitation. Consequently, in the true steppe the buildup of humus and minerals in the topsoil is greater, producing rich, fertile soils, called **chernozems** ("black earth") in Russian.

The entire steppe region is important for agriculture. Conditions for farming are best in the forest steppe, where the soil is fertile and precipitation is generally sufficient and reliable. In the true steppe, arid conditions and the variability of precipitation increase the risk of drought.

Desert

South of the steppe, principally in the trans-Volga area (i.e., the southern lands east of the Volga River), aridity increases until true desert conditions exist. Southern Kazakhstan and the larger parts of Uzbekistan and Turkmenistan are included in this natural region. Precipitation is generally less than 10 inches (254 millimeters) a year, and very hot, dry conditions prevail in summer. Winters are cold. Vegetation consists mostly of grass and xerophytic plants, which can store moisture.

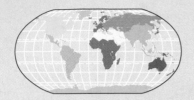

ENVIRONMENTAL DEGRADATION IN THE FORMER SOVIET UNION

The collapse of communism and the subsequent opening of society in the former Soviet Union has had two major impacts on environmental issues: (1) people here, as elsewhere, have become more acutely aware of the severity of their environmental problems, and (2) grass-roots movements, along with increased governmental and industrial concern, have led to more active policies and programs both to protect what is left and to repair the damage that has been done (Figure A).

Environmental issues were not totally absent in the Soviet Union of the past: articles criticizing waste and mismanagement were printed in the Soviet press as early as the 1960s. But the full effects of environmental degradation were never exposed. The first cause célèbre of the environmental movement was the conflict over the potential pollution of Lake Baikal from the industrial development on its shores. Lake Baikal not only is the world's largest lake in terms of volume (it contains more water than all of the Great Lakes of North America) but also is the world's deepest lake (it is approximately 1 mile from surface to bottom). More significantly, about 1450 of the 1800 species of plant and animal life in the lake are endemic to Baikal (i.e., they are found only in that lake). As a result of widespread publicity, two proposed wood-processing projects were canceled, and efforts were made to control pollution.

The turning point of the ecological movement in the Soviet Union, however, was undoubtedly the 1986 nuclear disaster at Chernobyl in Ukraine. Nuclear power development had always been kept under the tightest security, but that incident, because of the international impact of radiation pollution, caused an outcry in the West. Nonetheless, had a policy of openness not been operative in the Soviet Union at that time, it is doubtful that the Chernobyl disaster would have been so fully publicized.

What is known is that nuclear radiation leaked from the Chernobyl plant, causing several hundred deaths. In addition, radioactive contamination of the land and water forced evacuation of thousands of people, and an increased rate of cancer and genetic aberration has been detected in the area. The accident was a direct result of poor planning and inadequate construction, technology, and supervision. Soviet estimates placed the number of people living on contaminated land in Ukraine and Belarus at 3.7 million.

As a result of the tragedy, several nuclear projects were discontinued, and antinuclear activism developed in Russia, Ukraine, and Kazakhstan from groups such as the Green World and the Nevada Movement. Members of Green World have publicly demonstrated against nuclear power; for example, its members initiated a roadblock of another nuclear plant in Ukraine in 1990. The Nevada Movement used its branches in Semipalatinsk in Kazakhstan and Russian Novaya Zemlya in the Arctic to challenge nuclear testing at those sites.

A brief examination of two other environmental problems should indicate the enormous impact of Soviet development. The first involves the rapid shrinking of the Aral and Caspian seas in the southern dry lands of Kazakhstan and Uzbekistan. Since 1960 the Aral Sea has lost 40 percent of its volume, partly because of evaporation but largely because of the diversion of water from its two sources, the Amu-Dar'ya and the Syr-Dar'ya, into irrigation projects to make the desert productive (Figure B). As a result, the habitat of countless species of fish has been or is about to be destroyed, thereby devastating the local fishing industry. In addition, the loss of sea area is actually changing the climate, and the increased salinization of the land and the expansion of the desert threaten the health of the residents. Winds filled with sand, salts, and chemicals fill their lungs, causing an alarming increase in the incidence of cancer and respiratory disease. If the loss of water flowing into the Aral Sea is not controlled, the lake will continue to shrink, and conditions will worsen. Efforts are underway to stabilize the water level of the Aral Sea, but they are very expensive and may be too late.

Hydroelectric development and irrigation projects along the Volga have also resulted in a lower water level in the Caspian Sea. The consequences there are similar to those in the Aral Sea, and the solutions are equally complex. A recent plan to divert more water from the Volga with the construction of the Volga–Don II canal was halted, but new irrigation projects, which are often poorly constructed and result in the waste of thousands of cubic tons of water, are still projected.

The most grandiose of the solutions for the Aral and Caspian seas has been water diversion projects that would shift waters southward from Russian rivers in Siberia and northern Europe. Those projects, discussed for years, were finally rejected in 1986 because of their high cost and a variety of other concerns: (1) the fear of ecological consequences to the habitat of the fish in the northern rivers; (2) the reduction of fresh water flowing into the Arctic Ocean, which might affect the local climate; and (3) the flooding by new reservoirs that would destroy farmlands and dislocate industries, settlements, and historic sites. Increased conservation and smaller diversion projects may slow the death of the Aral and Caspian seas, but the outcome remains uncertain.

The second problem is the environmental change that has taken place in Siberia—the pollution of lakes and streams, the destruction of the fragile tundra surface, the flooding of millions of acres of land when enormous reservoirs were created for huge hydroelectric stations, and the contamination of air, land, and water. Many Siberians see

Figure A

A cement plant in Estonia. Heavy emphasis on agricultural and industrial development over several decades has led to numerous environmental problems, air pollution among them. Both the general public and the scientific community are becoming increasingly sensitive to those problems.

Figure B

Projected Aral Sea in 2040, if the loss of water intake is not controlled. (Reprinted by permission from M.I. Lvovich and I.D. Tsigelnaya, "Man-agement of the Water Balance of the Aral Sea," *Soviet Geography: Review and Translation* 20, no. 3, March 1979, p.148.)

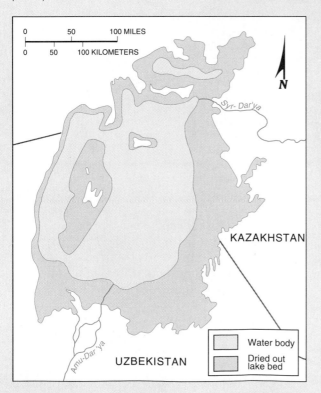

their land as merely a storehouse of natural resources, to be plundered for national and foreign development. This attitude has led to an increase in regional identification and to campaigns for greater independence.

Air pollution has become a severe problem in numerous areas of Siberia, partially because developers have tended to concentrate huge projects close to one another to create economies of scale. Climatic conditions called inversions then trap life-threatening pollutants over cities, particularly the city of Norilsk and others in the Kuznets Basin and the Kansk-Achinsk coal basin. Siberian smelters emit sulfurous pollutants at double the rate of North America's worst polluters, though the current emission rate at Norilsk is half what it was in 1984. Clearly, some progress is being made, but the tasks that remain seem almost overwhelming.

Overall, efforts to restore the Soviet environment have suffered from a lack of funds, equipment, and expertise. Solutions require establishing effective environmental law, imposing punitive fines to stop pollution, and establishing incentives to include environmental protection measures in all projects. Increased public activism and cooperation among the new countries are needed, as are Western capital and technology, since the Soviets were years behind the West in environmental matters. Unfortunately, the shift to market economies will emphasize economic growth first, with environmental concerns taking a back seat.

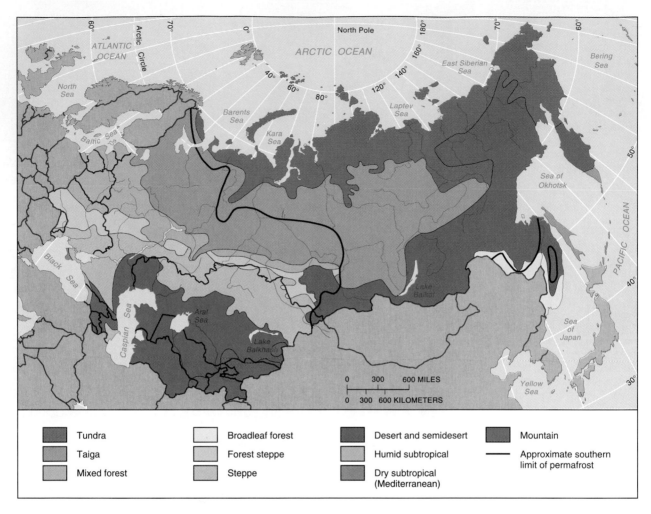

Figure 12-2
Natural regions of Russia and Eurasian states. Many different environments are found on this large land mass. That diversity provides an opportunity to grow many different types of crops, and the large area enhances the possibility of a varied mineral resource base. Much of the area, however, is at high latitudes and is little used.

In widely scattered oases and along the few rivers that flow through the desert, a rich plant life is supported on alluvial soils. The cultivation of crops is limited to areas watered by streams or irrigation projects. Large parts of the desert are used for grazing livestock.

The Subtropical South

Two small but important natural regions are the humid subtropical region along the east cost of the Black Sea (in Georgia and part of Russia) and the dry summer subtropical region along the southern coast of the Crimean Peninsula in Ukraine. The Crimean Mountains help to protect the narrow coastal region of the peninsula from the severe cold winds of the north. The mild climate and the moisture from the Black Sea contribute to a varied agriculture, including nuts, fruits, and vineyards. The Crimea is a famous resort area, where old palatial residences of the wealthy—including the czars' former palace at Livadia—were turned into hotels for Soviet workers and bureaucrats.

The humid subtropical region of the Black Sea coast is also a favorite vacation spot. In addition, Georgia is renowned for its specialized agriculture:

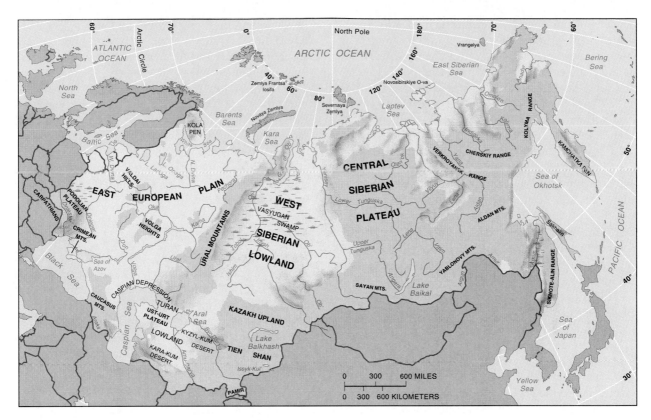

Figure 12-3
Landform regions of Russia and Eurasian states. The surface of this part of Eurasia is extremely varied. Most of the European part of the country is characterized by rolling plains with small, scattered uplands and mountain areas. In Siberia and Central Asia vast lowlands, uplands, and extensive mountain landscapes create a complex landform map, which, as it does in the European area, helps to shape the maps of population and economic geography.

tea and citrus fruits are the most important crops. The moisture-laden winds from the sea bring large amounts of precipitation, and the soils are quite fertile, able to support a luxuriant vegetation.

Mountain Areas

The climate, soils, and vegetation of the mountain areas are diverse, reflecting the location of the mountains, their local relief, and, most important, their altitude. Many valleys, foothills, and meadows of the mountain systems in the Central Asian countries of Kyrgyzstan, Tadzhikistan, and Uzbekistan, as well as the Transcaucasus states of Armenia, Georgia, and Azerbaidzhan, support relatively large populations on productive agricultural lands. Complex mountain systems also dominate in the

Russian far east and along the southern margins of Russian Siberia. As much as 30 percent of Russia is covered by these mountain regions.

LANDFORM REGIONS

European Section

In addition to the features of the natural regions—climate, soil, and vegetation—it is important to be familiar with the shape of the land—mountain ranges, hills, and level plains—to fully appreciate the potential of the land for development. The Baltic states, Belarus, Moldova, Ukraine, and most of the European part of Russia lie within the East European Plain (Figure 12–3). This plain covers a vast area from the Arctic Ocean to the Black Sea and from the Eastern European countries to the Ural Mountains.

The plain is drained by numerous rivers; the largest and most important for transport and hydroelectric development are the Volga and the Dnieper. Most of the plain is less than 650 feet (198 meters) above sea level and is quite flat, with extensive sections of low, rolling hills. On the Kola Peninsula in the north low mountains reach levels just above 3,900 feet (1,189 meters). There, and to the northwest on the lands adjoining Finland, repeated glaciation has left a landscape containing tens of thousands of lakes and small rivers. Mountains also border the plain in the south. The Carpathian Mountains briefly pass through Ukraine in the southwest. On the Crimean Peninsula short and relatively low mountain ranges, no higher than 5,068 feet (1,545 meters), help to protect the coastal resorts from the frigid northern air.

The Caucasus Mountains, which stretch from the Black Sea to the Caspian Sea, provide similar protection for the humid subtropical region of resorts and specialized agriculture at the eastern end of the Black Sea. The Caucasus are actually two ranges. The spectacular, snow-capped, northern Greater Caucasus are the higher. In that range is Mt. Elbrus, at 18,510 feet (5,642 meters) and the highest peak in all of Europe. The lower Lesser Caucasus are shared with Turkey and Iran. The East European Plain ends in the east at the Urals, a chain of ancient, greatly eroded, low mountains best known as the traditional boundary between Asia and Europe. The Urals are extremely important to the Russian economy, for they contain a multitude of ores for mining.

Siberia

Beginning immediately beyond the Urals, the immense West Siberian Lowland stretches eastward for more than 1,000 miles (1,610 kilometers). The lowland is so flat that from north to south, which is a distance of more than 1,200 miles (1,932 kilometers), elevation varies by no more than 400 feet (122 meters).

The Ob River and its tributaries drain most of the West Siberian Lowland. They flow slowly and broadly across that flat land into the Arctic Ocean. Spring thaws affect the upper, or southern, courses of the rivers first, while downstream the rivers are still frozen. As a result, thousands of cubic feet of water flood the land, contributing to the problems involved in developing and settling the region.

Two of the other great rivers of Siberia (and the world) are the Yenisey and the Lena. The Yenisey marks the boundary between the West Siberian Lowland and the Central Siberian Plateau. The Lena approximates the border between the Central Siberian Plateau and the complex mountain system that dominates most of eastern Siberia (Figure 12–4). The plateau is an upland, most of which is more than 1,600 feet (488 meters) above sea level. But rivers have cut deep gorges into the plateau, which help to give the area great potential for hydroelectric development. Superlatives are appropriate there: the Angara River, which drains the world's deepest lake, Lake Baikal, is dammed by two of the world's largest dams.

Kazakhstan and Central Asia

South of the West Siberian Lowland is the Kazakh Upland, a rough, hilly country. Large parts of western Kazakhstan and parts of Turkmenistan and Uzbekistan are included in the Turan Lowland. Toward the center of the lowland the Aral Sea is fed by two exotic rivers (i.e., rivers that flow through an arid environment), the Amu-Dar'ya and the Syr-Dar'ya, which originate in the mountains of Central Asia. Those mountains—which include the Pamirs and the Tian Shan—lie along borders with Iran, Afghanistan, and China and contain some of the highest mountain peaks in the world, with elevations in excess of 24,000 feet (7,400 meters).

POPULATION

The populations of the fifteen countries that once formed the Soviet Union vary greatly. Russia has a population of approximately 150 million people, making it the sixth most populous country in the world after China, India, the United States, Indonesia, and Brazil. At the other end of the scale, ten of the countries have populations of less than 10 million; Estonia, at only 1.5 million, is the smallest. Ukraine has about 52 million people, a bit smaller than the United Kingdom, France, and Italy, whereas Uzbekistan, Kazakhstan, and Belarus roughly approximate the populations of Romania, the Netherlands, and Greece, respectively (Table 12–1).

Formation of a Multinational State

The present state of Russia is slightly more than three-quarters the size of the former Russian and Soviet empires. These empires were created by the Russians during an 800-year-long process of growth that began with the small duchy of Muscovy. The princes of Moscow, the czars of Russia, and then the Soviet leaders were able to expand their territory by overcoming scores of different peoples along the borders. The Russian expansion through Siberia was similar to the westward expansion of the United States. The desire for furs, land, and minerals—especially gold—motivated a militarily superior Russia to overcome the many small, scattered indigenous tribes of the region and extend its empire to the Pacific Ocean.

The expansion of Russia into Central Asia, the Caucasus, and even parts of Europe is the Russian equivalent of the European colonialism that built world empires. But instead of crossing the seas to the Americas, Africa, or Asia—as Portugal, Great Britain, France, and other European states had to do—Russia simply extended its control over neighboring territories to create a large, contiguous empire. Unlike the other European powers, Russia was able to hold onto its colonial conquests, even after the communist revolution in 1917 and the formation of the Soviet Union, or the **Union of Soviet Socialist Republics (USSR)**, in 1922.

To minimize potential ethnic conflict among the more than 100 nationalities that were included within its borders, the Soviet Union not only used the all-pervasive power of the central state but also employed a government structure that allowed a few ethnic rights, depending in part on the group's size, culture, and economy. These rights included: the use of native languages in schools, courts, places of business, newspapers, and books; maintenance of ethnic customs (but with severe limitations on religious practices until recently); and, for fifty-three of the groups, a politically recognized territory. But the laws, customs, and acts of the ethnic groups could not conflict with the dictates of the central government.

That central government, which was essentially the same as the national Communist party, was controlled by the largest ethnic group in the country—the Russians. Although some of the customs and traditions of other ethnic groups were protected, **Russification**, a process of cultural and economic integration, continued for seven decades after the communist revolution. Russians migrated into other

Figure 12–4
Summer exploratory party crossing a tributary of the Lena River in Siberia. This vast region of frozen tundra, forest, and rich mineral resources includes more than two-thirds of Russia. Despite the problem of accessibility, this region served as an industrial frontier for the Soviet Union and holds great potential for Russia's development.

Table 12-1
The countries of the former Soviet Union.

| | | Area | | |
	Capital	Square Miles (in thousands)	Square Kilometers (in thousands)	Population, 1994 (in millions)
Russia	Moscow	6,593	17,075	147.8
Lithuania	Vilnius	25	65	3.7
Latvia	Riga	25	65	2.5
Estonia	Tallinn	17	45	1.5
Ukraine	Kiev	233	604	51.5
Belarus (Belorussia)	Minsk	80	208	10.3
Moldova (Moldavia)	Kishinev	14	34	4.4
Azerbaidzhan	Baku	33	87	7.4
Georgia	Tbilisi	27	70	5.5
Armenia	Yerevan	12	30	3.7
Kazakhstan	Alma-Ata	1,049	2,717	17.1
Turkmenistan (Turkmenia)	Ashkhabad	189	488	4.1
Uzbekistan	Tashkent	173	447	22.1
Kyrgyzstan (Kirghizia)	Bishkek	77	199	4.5
Tadzhikistan	Dushanbe	55	143	5.9

Source: USSR Central Statistical Committee, *Narodnoye, Khozyastvo SSSR za 70 let* (Moscow: Finansy i Statistika, 1987), 373; "The 1989 Census: A Preliminary Report," *Current Digest of the Soviet Press* 41, no. 17 (24 May 1989): 17; and Population Reference Bureau, *World Population Data Sheet* (Washington, DC: 1994).

ethnic areas and are now the major population group in many. In addition, Russian was a required language for all students throughout the Soviet Union.

Throughout the history of the USSR, the Soviets faced increasing difficulties from the multitude of ethnic groups, which vary widely in language, history, religious tradition, physical characteristics, and geographic distribution (Figure 12–5). The presence of different ethnic groups within a state is frequently a threat to the unity and the existence of the state. In the early 1990s—seventy-three years after the communist revolution, the Soviet Union could no longer contain these pressures and dissolved.

Ethnic Composition

The diverse ethnic composition of the region can be seen in the multitude of language groups (Figure 12–6). The eastern Slavs—Russians, Ukrainians, and Belorussians—speak languages that belong to the Indo-European family. That group is the largest in the former Soviet Eurasian realm, accounting for 70 percent of the region's population. Russians predominate in the central and northern European parts of Russia, as well as in Siberia and Kazakhstan. But they are also found throughout the other countries of the region and are important minority groups, especially in cities. The Ukrainians are the second most numerous group in the region; although the great majority of them are found in their own country, they, like the Russians, were widely diffused throughout the former Soviet Union. Other ethnic groups representing the Indo-European family of languages are found predominantly in the European part of the region, including Latvians and Lithuanians in the Baltic area, Armenians in the Caucasus, and Tadzhiks (an Iranian people) in Central Asia.

More than 50 million people in the region speak a language that belongs to the Altaic family of languages. That family includes languages spoken by the many Turkic groups, who have a predominantly

Largest Ethnic Group (% of total)	Second Largest Group (% of total)	Principal Religions
Russian (83)	Tatar (4)	Eastern Orthodox
Lithuanian (80)	Russian (9)	Roman Catholic
Latvian (54)	Russian (33)	Lutheran, Roman Catholic
Estonian (65)	Russian (28)	Lutheran
Ukrainian (74)	Russian (21)	Eastern Orthodox
Belorussian (79)	Russian (12)	Eastern Orthodox
Moldavian (64)	Ukrainian (14)	Eastern Orthodox
Azerbaidzhani (78)	Armenian (8)	Islam
Georgian (69)	Armenian (9)	Georgian Christian
Armenian (90)	Azerbaidzhani (8)	Armenian Christian
Russian (41)	Kazakh (36)	Islam, Eastern Orthodox
Turkmen (68)	Russian (13)	Islam
Uzbek (13)	Russian (11)	Islam
Kirghiz (48)	Russian (26)	Islam
Tadzhik (59)	Uzbek (23)	Islam

Islamic heritage. Those groups live principally in Central Asia, the middle Volga Valley, and the Caucasus. The Uralian family of languages has a relatively small representation (about 5 million speakers). It includes the Estonians and several groups of people in the northern European and western Siberian sections of Russia. The patchwork of nationalities found in this region—such as the Georgians in the Caucasus, the Mongols, the Koreans, and the indigenous tribes of Siberia—speak many other languages.

A variety of traditional religions, which have seen a resurgence since the downfall of communism, are also represented in this vast region. Among these belief systems are the Eastern Orthodox Christianity, Islam, Lutheranism, and Roman Catholicism. Jews formed the seventeenth-largest ethnic group in the Soviet Union in 1988. They were and are predominantly urban and live mostly in the western parts of the region. An attempt to establish a Soviet homeland for Jews in the Russian far east, the Jewish Autonomous District, was not successful in attracting the Jewish population. Less than 7 percent of the population in that district is Jewish.

Political Divisions and Divisiveness

The highest level of political territory in the former Soviet Union was the union republic. These republics in the early 1990s became the new countries of Eurasia. Rough guidelines for the formation of those republics included a population of more than 1 million, location on the periphery of the country, and a majority population of the ethnic group for which the republic was named, though Kazakhstan and Kyrgyzstan did not meet that final criterion. The former Soviet republics represented large ethnic groups; they did not, however, represent all the largest population groups. For example, Russians now make up the first or second largest ethnic group in the Baltic countries and in seven of the other former republics.

Thirty-eight other ethnic groups had administrative units of lesser status. The people of those units had various rights of language and custom but were subordinate to the laws of the republics in which they were located—and to the central government. Where there were no significant ethnic groups, the territory was divided into administrative districts.

Figure 12-5
Women at the marketplace in Samarkand, Uzbekistan. The women evidence the ethnic and racial features of Uzbeks, the majority people, whose language is of the Turkic group and whose religion is Islam. Russians are only 11 percent of this former republic of the USSR.

The vast majority of these smaller national groups are now found in Russia, and they have increasingly demanded greater separation from the Russian government.

In the 1980s Soviet President Mikhail Gorbachev proposed that the Soviet Union become a more open society in which people would be free to expose corruption and, by means of greater participation in the system—*demokratizatsiya*—make things right. His objective was to correct the disastrous economic conditions of the country. Little did he realize that he was opening a Pandora's box of resentment and discord that eventually helped destroy the very existence of the country. Numerous nationality movements and political parties, once kept underground, surfaced. Reports of discrimination and the maltreatment of minorities, particularly in the armed forces, became widespread.

Although the country's constitution stipulated that the Soviet Union was a federal state formed by a voluntary union of "equal **Soviet Socialist Republics**," in reality that union had been anything but voluntary. In fact, it had been formed by force. Nonetheless, the constitution bestowed on each republic the right of secession—even though none had ever been allowed to exercise that right.

Nationality groups, however, increasingly demonstrated against the central government, as well as against each other. Old ethnic hostilities reappeared,

including anti-Semitism and a bitter conflict between Armenians and Azerbaidzhans. And in thirteen of the fifteen former republics ethnic movements were aimed directly at Russians there. Within Russia itself there were widespread protests against the communist political system and calls for a revival of traditional Russian culture. All too often such frustrations were expressed violently. At least 408 people died in ethnic-related conflicts between the end of 1986 and the spring of 1990, and during that time 500,000 people became refugees from their homelands.[1]

As tensions mounted, Lithuania took the boldest step when it redeclared its independence, stating that its annexation by the Soviets in 1940 was illegal. Strong economic sanctions forced the Lithuanians to suspend their declaration of secession, but by the fall of 1991 all the republics had declared either their autonomy or independence. In 1991, just prior to the scheduled vote on a new Soviet constitution that would have given the republics greater power and a procedure for seceding from the union, a right-wing faction attempted to overthrow Mikhail Gorbachev. The failure of this coup led to the establishment of a new interim government, and the Baltic states of Lithuania, Latvia, and Estonia declared their independence. By the beginning of 1992, all the other former Soviet republics had achieved nationhood. On January 1, 1992, the hammer and sickle of the Soviet flag was lowered

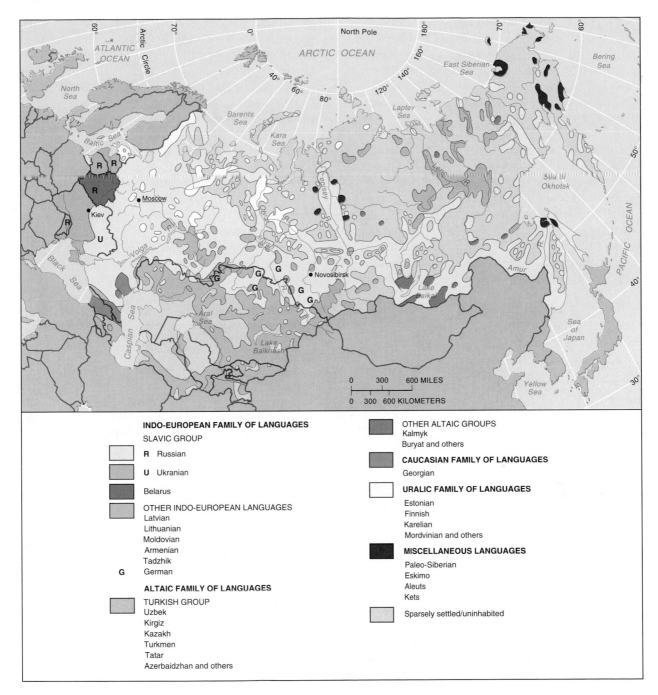

Figure 12-6
Major language groups of Russia and the Eurasian States of the former Soviet Union.
Society in the Soviet Union was often falsely characterized as monolithic. This map
of languages shows that there is considerable cultural diversity within the region.

for the last time and Gorbachev resigned as president. The Union of Soviet Socialist Republics officially passed into the history books as the countries of the world recognized the newly independent states of Eurasia.

Post-Independence Nationality Problems

The Soviet Union had been created through centuries of Russian and Soviet imperialistic expansion. As a consequence, an extreme ethnic diversity is present in virtually all corners of the region, proving a challenge to political and economic cooperation. Since the demise of the Soviet Union, some eighty border disputes have occurred, largely due to ethnic conflicts. Over 25 million Russians live outside of Russia, and a total of 60 million people live beyond the borders of their national republics. A most basic question is who should be citizens of these new countries; specifically, what to do with the large numbers of Russians who were settled outside of Russia during the communist era. In Estonia, the proportion of ethnic Russians grew from 8 percent before its annexation by the Soviet Union to 28 percent in 1993. In Latvia, ethnic Latvians constitute only slightly more than half of the population. Both countries have struggled to establish a basis for citizenship. Among the proposals considered are such requirements as being able to speak the native language (which most Russians cannot do) and residency prior to 1940.

Ethnic and border disputes have created serious problems, and there remains the possibility of even more hostilities. Twenty of the twenty-three repub-

Figure 12-7
Armenians in Karabakh in Azerbaidzhan. The Armenians represent a minority in Azerbaidzhan and would prefer a political affiliation with neighboring Armenia. The disunity and demands for independence within bordering republics strongly reflect the multinational character of the former Soviet Union.

lican borders of the former Soviet Union have been disputed. In Moldova ethnic Russians and Ukrainians, fearing Moldovan independence and possible union with Romania, declared their own "Dniester Republic." Much more serious, however, has been the war between Armenia and Azerbaidzhan over the Armenian-populated enclave of Nagorno-Karabakh, which lies within Azerbaidzhan (Figure 12–7).

The nationality question, however, does not stop at conflict between countries. In addition to the fifteen republics that composed the Soviet Union, many smaller ethnic groups were recognized and given their own designated territories. In Georgia two of these groups—the Southern Ossetians and the Abkhazy—declared their secession from the Georgian government, and armed conflict erupted. Most of the smaller ethnic groups, however, are found within Russia itself. Most of these ethnic

groups are located in the Russian Caucasus, the middle Volga River region, and Siberia. But non-Russians form a majority in only nine of these numerous ethnic territories. Altogether, the Russian government recognizes thirty-nine of these groups, of whom more than twenty have declared their independence from Russia (Figure 12–8). Thus, it is possible, though unlikely, that the fifteen new sovereign states of Eurasia may be joined by four, five, ten, or even twenty newly independent republics.

Many of the ethnic groups living within Russian borders are worried about their future in the new Russia. Although Russian leaders have promised them a greater role in government, most Russians are intent on keeping the republic "one and indivisible." Some of these ethnic groups—such as the Tatars, who live in the resource and industrial area of the middle Volga River—see total independence from Russia as the only solution.

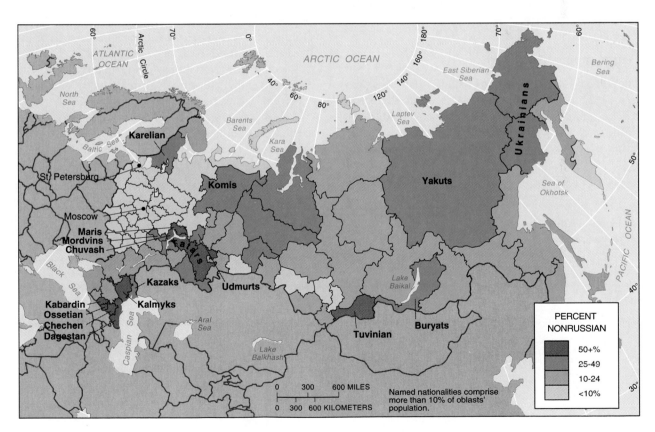

Figure 12–8
Percent of non-Russian ethnic groups in Russia. These ethnic groups, most of which are found in the Russian Caucasus, the middle Volga region, and Siberia, may prove problematic for the future of Russia. More than twenty have already declared their independence from Russian control.

Another primary concern is the region's more than 50 million Muslims, who may want to form a Pan-Islamic federation. Increased Muslim fundamentalism would significantly heighten tensions not only within the region itself but also in the Middle East and, hence, the entire world.

Clearly the political geography of Russia and the other states of the region is uncertain at this time. Although such events as the failed Russian coups of 1991 and 1993 point to a reduced likelihood of a return to centralized control in Russia, one can never dismiss the possibility of attempts to re-establish a new authoritarian Soviet Union. If the new countries of this region are going to proceed peacefully to develop a new economic and political order, they must overcome these national self-interests and hostilities. The alternative is violent hostilities that could make the fighting among Serbs, Croatians, and Bosnians look like a family squabble. The 1990s will be a decisive decade, not only for Eurasia but also for the whole world.

Demographic Characteristics

The Slavs, Baltic peoples, and other modern European culture groups have passed into that stage of demographic transformation in which birthrates, death rates, and natural growth rates are low. Other ethnic groups with a more traditional and agricultural way of life maintain higher birthrates, which, with low death rates, result in faster population growth. Thus, ethnic groups in Central Asia, the Caucasus, and Siberia have a higher rate of population growth than do the Slavs and other European groups.

Tadzikistan, Uzbekistan, Turkmenistan, Kyrgyzstan, and Azerbaidzhan have rates of natural increase equivalent to levels in Third World countries. In contrast, Latvia, Estonia, Ukraine, and Russia have seen a decline in their rates of natural increase (Table 12–2).

Between 1979 and 1989, the population of ethnic Russians grew by only 5.6 percent and ethnic Ukrainians by 4.2 percent, while the Tadzhiks, Turkmen, Uzbeks, and Kyrgyz registered gains of 45.5, 34.0, 34.0, and 32.8 percent, respectively (Table 12–3). Those differences in growth rates have quite naturally had an effect on the composition of the region's population. In 1959 the eastern Slavs comprised about 75 percent of the Soviet Union's population; in 1989 they made up 70 percent. During that same period the proportion of ethnic Russians declined from 55 to 51 percent.

Despite the variations in population growth among the diverse ethnic groups, in the seventy-four-year existence of the Soviet Union that country passed from a stage of high birthrates and high death rates to a stage of low birthrates and low death rates. The birthrate for the Russian Empire in

Table 12–2
Birthrates, death rates, and rates of natural increase.

	Birthrate (per 1000)	Death Rate (per 1000)	Rate of Natural Increase (annual %)
Latvia	12	13	−0.1
Estonia	10	14	−0.4
Ukraine	12	13	−0.2
Russia	11	12	−0.2
Belarus	12	11	0.1
Lithuania	14	11	0.3
Moldova	16	10	0.6
Georgia	17	9	0.8
Kazakhstan	20	8	1.2
Armenia	21	7	1.4
Azerbaidzhan	26	6	1.9
Kyrgyzstan	29	7	2.1
Turkmenistan	33	7	2.6
Uzbekistan	33	6	2.7
Tadzhikstan	35	6	2.9

Source: Population Reference Bureau, *World Population Data Sheet* (Washington, DC: 1994).

1913 was 4.5 percent; in 1990 it was 1.7 percent. The death rate for that same period went from 2.9 percent to 1.0 percent. The corresponding rates of natural increase went from 1.6 percent to 0.7 percent.

As birth and death rates declined, the number of years that citizens could expect to live increased. At the end of the nineteenth century life expectancy in European Russia was thirty-one years for men and thirty-three years for women. Modernization added greatly to the life span of the average citizen, even though life expectancy in the region remains much lower than it is in the United States. Today, a male child born in Russia can expect to live sixty-four years; in the United States, seventy-two years. The life expectancy for a Russian female is seventy-four years; for an American female, seventy-nine years. The current Russian figures represent no overall improvement from a high in the late 1970s. Alcoholism and inadequate health care are major factors in the relatively low life expectancy, especially for men. According to the World Health Organization, life expectancy in Russia is the lowest of all industrialized states.

One striking feature of the post–World War II population, particularly in the European part of the former Soviet Union, is the imbalance in male and female populations. Worldwide, a population of 95 to 99 males for every 100 females is considered normal; the Soviet Union in 1987 had 89 males for every 100 females. Yet that abnormal male-female ratio is primarily caused by the ratios among the older age groups, reflecting not only the longer life expectancy of women but also the toll that men, in particular, have paid for war, revolution, and the civil strife that accompanied collectivization of agriculture in the 1930s. As the population ages, that difference is slowly being reduced. In 1970 there were 18.9 million more women than men; by 1987 the difference was only 16.3 million (Figure 12–9). In less than two generations the ratio should be normal. A

Table 12-3
Percentage increase of republic national groups, 1979 to 1989.

Tadzhiks	45.5
Uzbeks	34.0
Turkmen	34.0
Kirghiz	32.8
Kazakhs	24.1
Azerbaijanis	24.0
Moldavians	13.0
Georgians	11.6
Armenians	11.5
Lithuanians	7.6
Belorussians	6.0
Russians	5.6
Ukrainians	4.2
Latvians	1.7
Estonians	0.7

Source: Bohdan Nahaylo and Victor Swoboda, *Soviet Disunion: A History of the Nationality Problem in the USSR,* New York: Free Press, 1990, p. 363.

Figure 12–9
Soviet population pyramid for 1987. In this pyramid the 40–44 age group reveals the low birthrates of the World War II period. The effects of war and of natural attrition are apparent in the older age groups, where the female population is significantly larger than the male population. (From USSR Central Statistical Committee, *Narodnoye Khozyaystro SSSR v1987g,* Moscow: Finansy i Statistika, 1988, p. 346.)

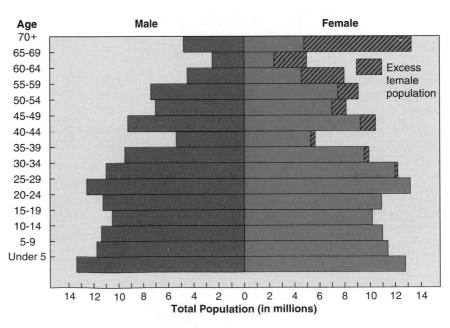

very practical ramification of the shortage of males has been the use of females in many occupations, including heavy labor.

The availability of labor—and hence the economy—has also been affected by variations in the birthrates. During World War II the birthrate dropped sharply, leading to severe labor shortages in the late 1950s and early 1960s. Later in the 1960s the number of young workers entering the labor force steadily increased; however, the reduced number of women born during the war years and entering their prime childbearing years during the 1960s led to lower birthrates again in the 1960s, which generated further labor shortages in the 1980s and 1990s. Between 1979 and 1989 the number of working-age men (age 16–59) and women (age 16–54) grew by only 4.6 percent, while the groups under and over the working age in-

creased by 11.9 percent and 20.5 percent, respectively.

Although the Soviet Union theoretically accepted the Marxist position that favored high population growth, it did not have a clearly defined pronatal policy, one that would encourage having children. Bachelors and childless couples paid an additional income tax, and awards and monetary stipends were given to mothers with four or more children. But those stipends were small and thus were not a real incentive for large families. In addition, the availability of government-provided contraceptive devices and abortions—together with numerous economic factors, such as the high proportion of women in the work force and the severe shortage of housing—encouraged small families.

Declining birthrates and prospective labor shortages stimulated government discussions of institut-

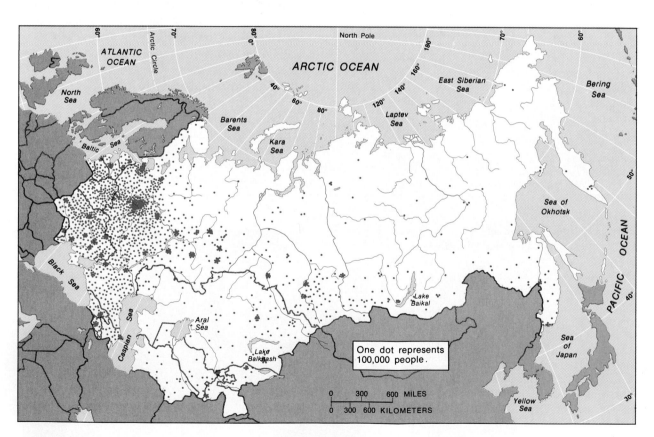

Figure 12–10
Distribution of Commonwealth and Baltic population. Population distribution in the regions is uneven. Most of the people live in the European west, leaving much of the north and east sparsely settled.

ing a more forceful pronatal policy, but the problem was not simple. In regions such as Kazakhstan, Central Asia, and the Caucasus, the growth rate needed to be reduced; in the urban, industrialized Slavic and Baltic regions, the population and labor supply was not growing fast enough. Encouraging population growth in some areas and discouraging it in others was tricky, especially in view of the many nationalities involved. No clear-cut natal policies have emerged as yet from the confusion which besets the new countries. Economic and political stability will have to be established before the demographic picture of the early twenty-first century can be seen.

Distribution of Population

The regional population is unevenly distributed (Figure 12–10). In the western Ukraine, rural population densities are higher than 250 per square mile (100 per square kilometer), whereas large tracts of Russian tundra and Asian deserts are virtually unpopulated. Almost three-fourths of the population lives in the European area, which constitutes only about one-fourth of the national area. Within that area most densities of at least twenty-five people per square mile (ten per square kilometer) occur south of the 60th parallel. The areas of highest population density are in the southwestern Ukraine, the lowlands of the Caucasus, and the vicinity of industrial regions and large cities, such as the eastern Ukraine, the Moscow area, and the middle Volga lands.

Outside the European section of the region, the heaviest population concentrations are found in the foothills and valleys of the Central Asian mountains, along principal rivers, and in irrigated areas. Scattered places with population densities exceeding twenty-five people per square mile (ten per square kilometer) are found in the southern portions of Siberia, where the Trans-Siberian Railway has contributed to agricultural and industrial development. Throughout most of the taiga, tundra, and desert natural regions, densities are two people or fewer per square mile (one per square kilometer).

Urbanization

Despite increasing industrialization and commercialization in czarist Russia, only 18 percent of the

population lived in cities in 1913. Not until the Soviet Union embarked on an all-out program of industrialization in the late 1920s did urban growth become significant. By 1940 the urban population had nearly doubled, to 33 percent of the total population. World War II temporarily slowed that pace, but by the early 1960s as many people lived in cities as in rural areas. Since 1913 the urban population has increased more than sixfold, while the rural population has declined by 33 million.

The urban population of the region's fifteen countries shows considerable variation. The highest levels of urbanization are found in the European part; the lowest in Central Asia. Nearly three-quarters of the Russians live in cities, and approximately 70 percent of Estonians, Belarussians, Latvians, and Lithuanians are urban dwellers. In contrast, only 31 percent of the Tadzhiks, 37 percent of the Kyrgyz, and 40 percent of the Uzbeks are found in cities and towns (Table 12–4).

The distribution of cities, just like that of the population as a whole, is uneven. Most of the large cities—those with a population of 100,000 or more—are in the European part (Figure 12–11). In

Table 12-4

Percent of population in Russia and the Eurasian states of the former Soviet Union that are urban dwellers.

	Urban Population (% of total)
Russia	73
Estonia	71
Latvia	70
Lithuania	69
Ukraine	68
Armenia	68
Belarus	67
Kazakhstan	58
Georgia	56
Azerbaidzhan	54
Moldova	48
Turkmenistan	45
Uzbekistan	40
Kyrgyzstan	37
Tadzhikstan	31

Source: Population Reference Bureau, *World Population Data Sheet* (Washington, DC: 1994).

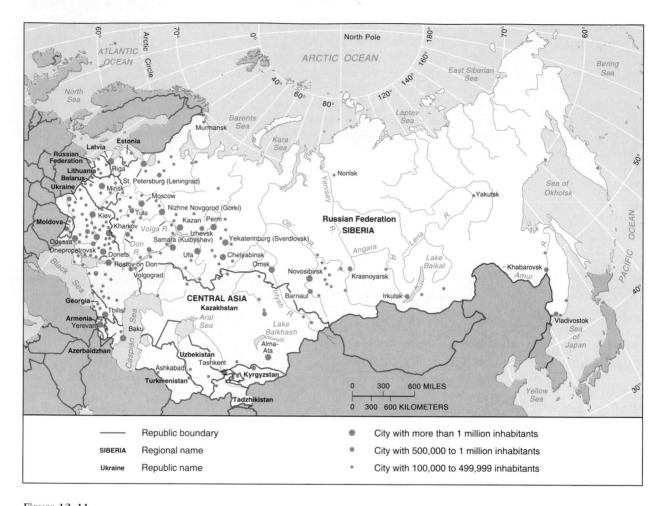

Figure 12-11
Selected cities with more than 100,000 inhabitants. Politically the former Soviet
Union is now divided into fifteen countries. Most of the area's major cities are found
in the western fourth of the country.

Russian Siberia, large cities are concentrated primarily in the southern part of the region, along or near the Trans-Siberian Railway. In the Eurasian states, there are twenty-two cities with a population of more than 1 million people. Two—Novosibirsk and Omsk—are in Siberian Russia. Another two—Tashkent, Uzbekistan, and Alma-Ata, Kazahstan—are in Central Asia. Four—Perm, Yekaterinburg, Chelyabinsk, and Ufa—are in the Russian Urals. The remaining fifteen lie on or west of the Volga River. Both population and urban patterns clearly suggest the dominant role of the western sections in the economic life of the area.

SUMMARY
A Vast Expanse

Not only is the territory occupied by Russia and the other fourteen countries of the former Soviet Union large, but it also has diverse environmental and human resources. Knowing the nature and distribution of those resources is vital to an understanding of the economic geography of the region. For example, the quality of soil, the length of the growing season, the availability of water, and the shape of the land all contribute to the character of agriculture, as do the cultures of the people.

Unfortunately, past Soviet developmental strategies have resulted in serious environmental disruption: wasted raw materials, a polluted atmosphere, and contaminated soil, lakes, and rivers. The mixed-forest and the steppe parts of the European quarter of the region contain the largest population, and those are the most densely settled parts. There is the original core area of the Slavic peoples: the Russians, Ukrainians, and Belarussians. There the Russian Empire began and expanded into the vast Siberian taiga and tundra, through the desert of Kazakhstan and Central Asia, and to the high mountains of the south. More than 100 different ethnic groups were eventually brought under Russian control.

Retaining effective control over that ethnic mosaic—with its diverse cultures and demographic patterns—was an ever-present task for the Soviet state. Tight central control (with a strong Russian flavor) was the approach for many years. But in the early 1990s it all began to unravel. National de-sires for freedom led to the breakup of the Soviet Union into fifteen separate countries. Only time will tell if and how the diverse nationalities of these countries and the scores of other ethnic peoples in the region will be able to work cooperatively to establish stability in this part of the world.

KEY TERMS

chernozem

Commonwealth of
  Independent States

demokratizatsiya

natural region

permafrost

Russification

Soviet Socialist
  Republic

taiga

Union of Soviet Socialist
  Republics (USSR)

NOTE

1. "Lashed by the Flags of Freedom," *Time,* 12 March 1990, p. 33.

LAISVE
RED ARMY GO
PATS
LAISVE, UŽ GYVYBĘ TU BRANGESNÉ !
1920 1939
LENIN STALIN

13

Russia and the Eurasian States of the Former Soviet Union: Economic Activity

The Soviet Approach

Planned Development

Soviet Economic Reforms

The Challenge of Development for the New Eurasian States

Industrial Resources

Industrial Regions

Agriculture

Protesting crowd in Vilnius, Lithuania. The signs reflect the frustrations of the Baltic people with the former Soviet Union, frustrations that led to Lithuania's independence in 1991.

In 1913 the Russian Empire celebrated the 300th anniversary of the Romanov dynasty. Amid the great pomp Czar Nicholas II, autocrat of all the Russians and numerous other peoples, seemed little concerned about the undercurrents of dissent that were spreading through his vast domain. Within only four years, however, his large empire was involved in a disastrous war and two revolutions, he was forced from the throne, and he and his family were sent to their deaths. The events that shaped the Russian Empire and led to its self-destruction are fascinating and involved. Certainly, the government—the czar and the bureaucracy—failed to understand the needs of the country and its people.

At the beginning of the twentieth century some 80 percent of the Russian people were peasants, with the vast majority of them having too little land to feed their families adequately. Most, deeply in debt, found it impossible to break the chains of poverty. Industry was growing rapidly: the 1890s are generally recognized by economic historians as the decade when Russia entered what Rostow called the takeoff stage of economic development. In other words, the 1890s were the beginning of Russia's Industrial Revolution. Russia was still overwhelmingly agricultural in 1913, but it was also the fifth-largest industrial country in the world in total industrial output (though only ninth in per capita production). Despite that status, the minority industrial workers were not much better off economically than the majority peasant population.

Time and again during the course of nineteenth and early twentieth century Russian history, movements, uprisings, and revolts occurred with demands for more freedom for the peoples of the empire. All were doomed to failure; the moribund autocracy was unyielding. World War I finally provided the stage on which the Russian state collapsed. The empire, technologically and militarily inferior—and rent with bureaucratic and political incompetence—could withstand neither the military defeats inflicted by the Central Powers nor the people's cries for "land, peace, and bread."

In February, 1917, the czar was forced to abdicate, and a group of Constitutional Democrats assumed control. Their government did not move decisively enough, however; Russia remained bogged down in war, and the people's demands went unheeded. Consequently, a small group of Marxists, called **Bolsheviks**, took advantage of the situation.[1]

With a very effective organization under the astute leadership of Vladimir Lenin, those Bolsheviks led a small group of soldiers and sailors in revolt, toppling the nine-month-old democratic government. Their revolt, known as the October Revolution, was the beginning of a bloody civil war that eventually led to a Bolshevik victory and the establishment of the Union of Soviet Socialist Republics in 1922.

THE SOVIET APPROACH

The word *soviet* means "council" in Russian. The new government was to consist of many soviets of workers, soldiers, and peasants under the leadership and control of a small group of elite members of the Communist party. Actually, throughout most of Soviet history that leadership has been more or less concentrated in the hands of one man—Lenin, Stalin, Khrushchev, Brezhnev, Gorbachev.

The Soviets contended that the key to their economic development lay in the application of the principles of social and economic development expounded by Karl Marx, a nineteenth-century German intellectual. Simply stated, that doctrine contends that capitalism is a natural stage in the development of societies. But the capitalist stage, like all previous stages, is doomed to destruction because a handful (i.e, the wealthy capitalists) exploits the many (i.e., the workers, or the proletariat) by underpaying them for their labor. A communist revolution occurs when those workers overthrow the capitalists and establish a society without exploitation, a communist society. According to the theory, the formerly exploited workers then own all the means of production and live in perfect harmony with one another. Ironically, the first successful communist revolution took place in Russia, a country where capitalism was not fully developed and, therefore, a country that was not ready for revolution, according to Marx. Bolshevik leaders did acknowledge Russia's situation but declared that the dictatorship of the Communist party would lead the backward country through economic development and eventually to communism. The country never reached that stage.

The most significant achievement of the Soviet Union during its first seventy years of existence was its rapid industrial development. In fact, industrialization progressed to the point that the Soviet Union emerged as a major world power, second only to the

United States. Soviet propaganda continued to identify two principal goals: (1) becoming the world's greatest economic power and (2) raising the Soviet standard of living to the highest level. Soviet leaders believed that, in the process, they would prove their system superior to any of the capitalist varieties.

PLANNED DEVELOPMENT

Behind the Soviet Union's industrialization was a command economy; that is, an economy in which virtually all investment income was controlled by the Communist party leadership and its government functionaries. The mammoth state planning agency, following party directives, worked out detailed plans for the economy, including annual production goals for more than 70,000 items and prices for 200,000 goods and services. Plans were devised for five-year periods and for each year within the period.

The complexities of those vast economic blueprints invariably led to numerous problems. Frequently, overoptimistic production goals had to be reduced. In addition, because the targets were usually expressed in quantity of production, the Soviet economy was faced with perennial problems of wasted resources, inefficient use of labor, and poor-quality goods.

Despite those and many other shortcomings, the Soviet Union achieved notable success in its overall economic growth. But that growth resulted largely from the development of heavy industry and from industries that were associated with the military. Sectors of the economy such as agriculture and light industry—notably, consumer goods—suffered from low rates of investment. Official Soviet statistics support a helpful comparison: if we assign a base value of 1 to each of three areas—producer goods, agricultural products, and consumer goods—in 1940, then by the late 1980s these values were, 3.5, 2.7, and 1.3, respectively. That performance of the consumer-goods industries can only be described as dismal (see the boxed feature The Soviet Consumer).

SOVIET ECONOMIC REFORMS

In spite of the official figures, which often showed economic success, the reality was that economic stagnation and decreasing growth rates in the 1970s and 1980s were leading to ever more disastrous economic conditions. The Soviet Union could not feed itself, its currency (the ruble) was valueless outside the country, military spending was consuming 20 to 25 percent of the national budget, store shelves were sparsely supplied when they were not empty, and people had to wait daily in long lines to get the necessities of life.

The government's refusal to loosen its hold on the economy finally gave way in the late 1980s with economic reforms previously unheard of in the Soviet Union. As the changes unfolded, President Mikhail Gorbachev made the Russian words *glasnost, demokratizatsiya,* and *perestroika* commonplace around the world. Through **glasnost** ("openness") problems were to be exposed. By means of *demokratizatsiya* ("democratization") more people—from workers to managers—were to play a bigger role in the economy. And with **perestroika** ("restructuring") institutional changes were to be made that would allow the market to have some say in determining prices. Soviet factories were expected to turn out better-quality products with a value that exceeded the cost of their production.

In the years following those dramatic changes, however, the economic situation failed to improve; in fact, it steadily got worse. One public opinion poll reported that 73 percent of those polled were partly or wholly dissatisfied with the way the government was handling the economy. The basic debate concerned whether the government should continue to perpetuate the communist system or should move vigorously toward a free-market economy. In mid-1990 a radical plan was presented to revolutionize the economic system in a period of 500 days. Central planning was to give way to economic autonomy for the republics, and the right of private ownership was to be expanded. Up to 70 percent of industry and 90 percent of construction and retail trade were to be out of state control. Gorbachev initially gave his support to the plan but then, late in the year, opted for more gradual reform. These reform measures never had an opportunity to be enacted, for within five months the Soviet Union ceased to exist.

THE CHALLENGE OF DEVELOPMENT FOR THE NEW EURASIAN STATES

Saving the region's economies is an enormous task that will not be accomplished quickly or cheaply. The movement toward a market economy has

THE SOVIET CONSUMER

The cornerstone of the communist philosophy is the ability of the state to provide the people with everything they need. But the Soviet system fell far, far short of meeting that goal. When the focus of economic development was on increasing coal and steel production, laying more railroad lines, and fulfilling similar basic industrial needs, the government had little difficulty in giving its citizens a basic diet, minimal clothes, and a roof over their heads. But as the demands of Soviet consumers grew, the government found it impossible to keep up.

A major goal of the Soviet Union was always to surpass the production levels of the West—a nearly impossible task as the living standards of the West continued to rise and become increasingly sophisticated. But the Soviet inability to match the availability of consumer goods in the West posed a real threat to that system, and it proved to be the principal factor that brought about the downfall of the system. As John Kenneth Galbraith said, "Of all the threats to planning in the Soviet System as it now exists, none quite rivals the impact of Western living standards—not those of Madison Avenue, to be sure, but those of the average middle-class household in Bremen, West Germany, or Worcester, Massachusetts."*

A tremendous contradiction existed in the Soviet Union. On the one hand, the society had enormous industrial capacity and spent billions on sophisticated space programs and high-tech military matériel. On the other hand, the people faced food shortages and had to wait patiently in long lines to buy even a pair of shoes. As Robert V. Daniel put it, the Soviet Union was a "paradox of industrial plenty in the midst of consumer poverty."[†] Furthermore, many of the consumer goods that were available were shoddy, so they tended not to work for long, if they worked at all. In 1986, a shocking 40 percent of the 28,056 fires reported in Moscow were caused by faulty television sets.[‡]

Some consumer prices in the Soviet Union were subsidized, which meant that prices were low and sometimes not changed for decades. Items such as a loaf of bread, a head of cabbage, or bus fare cost less than or the same in Moscow as they did in Washington, DC, in terms of the amount of work time required for the purchase (Table A). Other items, however, were far beyond the reach of the average Soviet citizen. Overall, a Soviet worker had to work three times as long as the average American worker even to attain such basics as weekly food needs. In addition, the Soviet citizen paid (in U.S. dollars) about $12,700 for a compact car and $1,100 for a color television set but made only an average of $318 a month. Consequently, a television set represented almost four months' work.

Abject poverty did not exist in the Soviet Union: no one was starving, naked, or living in the streets. The problem is that Soviet standards of consumption and material well-being fell far below those of the West. Medical care was free, but complaints about its quality were rampant. Housing was inexpensive—only a few dollars a month—but its quality and quantity were appalling. The Soviet government originally set the standard at 9 square meters of living space per capita; that

---

*John Kenneth Galbraith, "Can the Russians Reform? The Soviet Economy: Prospects for Change," *Harper's* (June 1987): 55.

[†]Paul Kennedy, "What Gorbachev Is Up Against," *Atlantic Monthly* 259, no. 6 (June 1987): 32.

[‡]*Time*, 27 July 1987, p. 32.

---

brought unemployment and higher prices, resulting initially in a lower standard of living for many. Certainly, such risks will be viewed differently by those who benefited most from the centrally controlled system and those who would gain the most from economic freedom. Currently, the level of economic well-being differs greatly from republic to republic. A good indicator of comparative living standards is per capita GNP. In 1992, the republics ranged from a high of $2,910 (U.S. dollars) in Belarus to a low of $480 in Tadzhikistan (Table 13–1). These figures indicate, for example, that the living standards in the Baltic countries are much higher than those in the less developed republics, such as Armenia and Tadzhikistan. Is it any wonder that the Baltic states early sought to gain their independence? They wanted to protect their material quality of life.

This vast territory almost two-and-one-half times the size of the United States—with a population of 290 million people, consisting of over 100 different ethnic groups of significant cultural diversity—has

is, each person was supposed to have a room approximately 10 feet by 10 feet to live in. By the late 1970s, however, the average living space was only 8.2 square meters, less even than that cramped legal minimum. In 1990, an estimated 20 percent of Soviet city dwellers lived in communal apartments, with one or more families occupying a single room of an apartment that was originally intended to house only one family in its entirety. In such arrangements all of the families shared the bathroom and the kitchen.

Improvements in Soviet living standards had failed to materialize in the first years of *perestroika*. By the summer of 1990, bread, the staple of the Russian diet, had disappeared from store shelves. A poll taken that same year indicated that 50 percent of the respondents felt that daily life was a little (28 percent) or a lot (22 percent) worse than it had been five years before. The Soviet system has been abandoned, but it will require serious adjustments of the region's economies, along with further consumer hardships, before life gets better.

Table A
A comparison of consumer costs in the former Soviet Union and the United States.

Item	Work Time Required	
	Moscow	Washington
One loaf of rye bread	11 min.	18 min.
One chicken	189 min.	18 min.
One grapefruit	112 min.	6 min.
One liter of milk	20 min.	4 min.
One liter of red wine	257 min.	37 min.
One head of cabbage	7 min.	7 min.
Three ounces of tea	36 min.	10 min.
A car wash	139 min.	40 min.
One bar of soap	17 min.	3 min.
Bus fare for two miles	3 min.	7 min.
An hour of babysitting	279 min.	44 min.
One first-class postage stamp	3 min.	2 min.
A man's haircut	34 min.	62 min.
One pair of jeans	56 hrs.	4 hrs.
One pair of men's shoes	37 hrs.	6 hrs.
A washing machine	177 hrs.	37 hrs.

Source: Radio Free Europe/Radio Liberty, as reported in the *New York Times,* 28 June 1987, sec. 4.

Note: The data were gathered in October 1986 and reflect the wages of an average industrial worker.

just discarded the rules that held it together for over seven decades. Now it must establish an entirely new, more democratic, free-market system, one that will allow all its citizens to partake of the prosperity, peace, security, and freedom that the old order promised but never delivered.

Enormous difficulties are inherent in the privatization of the state enterprises; the task has to be accomplished smoothly with least disruption to the economy. Economic wealth should be fairly distributed, yet the final outcome must lead to efficient and productive enterprises. In Russia, approximately 41 percent of all state enterprises had been removed from state control by the end of 1993, and the process was continuing at a rate of 3 to 4 percent of Russian industry moving into private hands per month. The largest number of these enterprises have been small establishments; almost all retail shops had been privatized by late 1993.

As more and more larger state enterprises are transferred from state control to private hands, many—as many as 35 to 40 percent of them, ac-

Table 13–1
Economic Resources of Russia and the Eurasian states of the former Soviet Union.

	Per Capita GNP, 1992 (in U.S. $)[a]	Major Resources	Principal Industrial Cities
Belarus	2,910	Peat, oil	Minsk
Estonia	2,750	Oil shale, peat, phosphorous	Tallinn
Russia	2,680	Oil, natural gas, coal, iron ore, hydroelectric power, gold, polymetallic ores, aluminum ore, timber, diamonds, platinum, fertile soils	Moscow, St. Petersburg, Nizhe Novgorod, Yekaterinburg, Novosibirsk, Perm, Chelyabinsk
Latvia	1,930	Peat	Riga
Kazakhstan	1,680	Coal, iron ore, copper, chrome, cobalt, fertile soils	Alma-Ata, Karaganda, Kustanay
Ukraine	1,670	Coal, oil, iron ore, manganese, natural gas, uranium, fertile soils	Kiev, Kharko, Dnepropetrovsk, Donetsk, Odessa
Lithuania	1,310	Peat	Vilnius
Turkmenistan	1,270	Oil, natural gas	Ashkhabad
Moldova	1,260		Kishinev
Azerbaidzhan	870	Oil, natural gas	Baku
Uzbekistan	860	Oil, natural gas, gold	Tashkent
Georgia	850	Manganese, coal, oil	Tbilisi
Kyrgyzstan	810	Oil, coal	Bishkek
Armenia	780	Aluminum ore	Yerevan
Tadzhikistan	480	Natural gas, hydroelectric power	Dushanbe

[a]*Source:* Population Reference Bureau, *World Population Data Sheet* (Washington, DC: 1994).

cording to some estimates—will not be able to continue functioning. It is not surprising, therefore, that the economies of Russia and the other new countries are in shambles. Agricultural production fell 30 percent for the entire region in 1991, and food shortages continued to run rampant throughout the former Soviet Union. Inflation sky-rocketed, reaching 1200 percent in Russia by the end of 1993; consumer prices almost tripled between 1990 and 1991. During the early 1990s Russia's gross national product fell by about 1 percent a month. Industrial production in Russia in early 1993 was only about 80 percent of production levels at the end of 1991. Conditions are similar throughout the region, and in some countries, such as Ukraine, conditions are even worse.

The major challenge to the republics is economic, but nationality differences—even hostility—and the problems of military security, including control of nuclear weapons, are also significant ob-

stacles to be conquered. The region stands at the beginning of a new era, one fraught with enormous problems, exacerbated by the geography of the region—its spatial economic, cultural, and environmental patterns.

The economic policies of the old communist government make solutions to the present problems especially difficult. First of all, the Soviet leaders were suspicious of every expression of national distinction. Consequently, the politicians and central planners adopted policies that discouraged republic self-sufficiency and encouraged interregional dependency. The former fifteen republics are therefore highly dependent on trade with the other republics for survival. For eleven of the fifteen republics, interrepublic trade accounted for 40 to 60 percent of their output: cotton from Uzbekistan supplied the textile mills of Russia; oil and natural gas from Siberia was transported throughout the Soviet Union; the Baltic states supplied 20 percent of all

Principal Manufactured Goods	Major Agricultural Products
Machinery, food, woodworking, electrical goods	Potatoes, dairy products, flax, beef, swine, wheat, rye
Machinery, electrical goods, agricultural machinery	Dairy products, swine, beef, potatoes, flax
Steel, machinery, metal working, textiles, chemicals, paper, food products, transport equipment, electronics, woodworking	Wheat, rye, potatoes, dairy products, beef, swine, corn, barley, oats
Machinery, transport equipment, electrical goods, chemicals	Dairy products, beef, potatoes, flax, sugar beets
Agricultural equipment, metal working, food, chemicals, steel	Wheat, beef, sheep, barley, sunflowers, cotton, rice
Steel, machinery, metal working, chemicals, food products, agricultural equipment	Wheat, sugar beets, corn, barley, beef, swine, sunflowers
Food, machinery, wood products, chemicals, ships	Dairy products, beef, swine, potatoes, flax, sugar beets
Construction materials, food, machinery	Cotton, sheep, rice, vineyards, nuts
Food, machinery, chemicals, leather	Wheat, corn, fruits, vegetables, vineyards, tobacco
Petrochemicals, food, machinery	Cotton, tea, subtropical fruits
Textiles, machinery, food	Cotton, sheep, rice, wheat, vineyards, nuts
Machinery, food, building materials, steel, chemicals	Tea, subtropical fruits, vineyards, tobacco
Food, machines, textiles	Cotton, fruits, sheep, vineyards, nuts, rice
Chemicals, food, machinery, light metallurgy	Vineyards, grains, fruits, vegetables, tobacco
Machinery, food, building materials	Fruits, sheep, nuts, vineyards, tobacco

Soviet consumer goods, and Baltic food products helped feed the citizens of Leningrad (now St. Petersburg); the major regions of heavy industry, including iron and steel, are in Russia and Ukraine; most of the tea consumed in this tea-thirsty part of the world is from Georgia. The list of interdependency goes on and on.

Further complicating the situation is that the central planners of the Soviet Union favored giant, large-scale production; consequently, numerous products are produced in only one factory. For example, all machinery for harvesting cotton, corn, and potatoes comes from single factories, each located in different republics. Therefore, the political system that evolves during this transitional period cannot interfere, at least for the near future, with trade between countries or economic chaos throughout the region will result. Even the countries of Latvia, Lithuania, and Estonia will profit from some type of economic confederation with the

countries of the new, but still ineffectual Commonwealth of Independent States. The **Commonwealth of Independent States (CIS)**, created in late 1992, includes Russia, Belarus, Moldova, Ukraine, Armenia, Kazakhstan, Uzbekistan, Turkmenistan, Kyrgyzstan, and Tadzhikistan. To facilitate trade, CIS countries will have to use a common currency, or at least currencies that are easily convertible from country to country.

Of all the countries, Russia and Ukraine have the best chance of success as separate economic and political entities. Ukraine, with a population of 52 million, is not only the agricultural heartland of the region but also possesses major industrial resources and manufacturers. Russia, with almost 150 million people living on 75 percent of the territory of the former Soviet Union, has extensive natural resources, including rich coal, oil, and natural gas deposits, as well as the largest industrial regions and good agricultural lands. In contrast, the remaining countries are relatively weak in industrial and agricultural resources.

This is especially true for the semi-arid, arid, and mountainous countries of Central Asia. In 1991 Germany's Deutsche Bank evaluated the wealth of the republics, measuring their potential for industrialization, agricultural production, and mineral resource output on a scale from 10 (good potential) to 0 (no potential). The results indicated the relative strength of Russia, Ukraine, Kazakhstan, and the Baltic states compared to the weaker potential for development in the Central Asian republics, Moldova, and Armenia (Figure 13–1).

The Baltics states demonstrated the highest potential for industrialization, with a score of 10. On that same measure, Ukraine, Russia, and Belarus scored 9, 8, and 8, respectively. Russia's greatest potential lies in its wealth of mineral resources. Kazakhstan and Ukraine also possess a high mineral

resource availability, whereas the Baltic states, Moldova, and Belarus have little or no mineral resources. But Moldova showed considerable agricultural potential, as did the Baltic states, and to a lesser degree, Russia and Georgia. In the Central Asia republics and the Caucasus (excluding Geor-gia), agricultural resources were indicated at the same relatively low levels as industrial potential. From those results, Ukraine, with the greatest agricultural potential, is in the strongest position for economic success, with Russia a close second.

For most of the new countries it will be necessary to maintain some economic cooperation, though the problems of doing so are enormous. Consider the variety of attitudes leaders in these countries could have toward the degree and speed of developing a free-market economy. It is improbable that all would agree on all aspects of the economic reforms proposed, and thus questions

Figure 13–1
The economic development potential. The fifteen former republics show great variation in their potential for economic growth. (Copyright © 1991 by the New York Times Company. Reprinted by permission.)

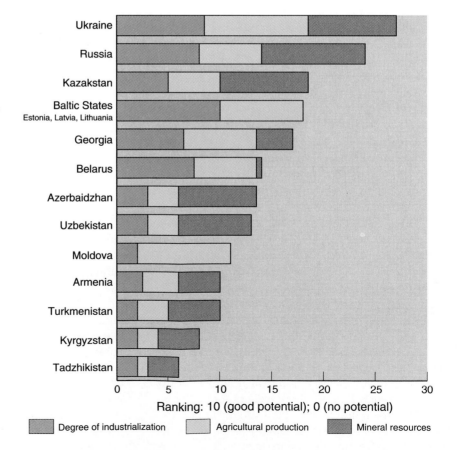

will arise about the degree of power a centralized body must have to coordinate reform, movement of trade, outside investment from abroad as well as from neighboring countries, and ownership of land, resources, and factories. These issues will take some time to resolve, and there always remains the possibility that parts, if not most, of the former Soviet Union will fall into utter chaos. Economic reforms will require drastic steps and further sacrifices by the people, raising doubts about whether a free-market economy, as well as democratic institutions, can be achieved in the near future.

INDUSTRIAL RESOURCES

The rich and diverse natural resources found throughout the region also play a part in the current struggle of the republics for greater independence. Not surprisingly, they want to control the resources within their borders. Such control of natural resources is an issue within Russia itself, where the numerous ethnic groups, such as the Tatars, are working for greater independence from the central government. Overall, this region ranks among the world's leaders in natural resources, though the resources are not equally shared by all of the fifteen new countries (see Table 13–1). In the Baltics, for example, industrial resources are virtually nonexistent.

Unfortunately, much of that great resource potential lies in remote areas, accessible to markets only at tremendous cost. Transportation may involve long and expensive hauls by railroad, or it may even be necessary to build transportation facilities to reach the sites of the deposits. In addition, many deposits are located in harsh environments, which makes attracting workers difficult. Nonetheless, those resources are a critical factor in future industrialization and economic development of the region.

Energy Sources

The most significant development in the Soviet fuel industry in recent decades was the growth of oil and gas production. Soviet petroleum production more than quadrupled between 1960 and 1990, and gas production increased tenfold. At the same time the output of coal grew by only 30 percent, and the harvesting of wood as a fuel declined by one-third.

Before its breakup, the Soviet Union was the world's largest producer of both petroleum and coal, and it challenged the United States as the leading supplier of natural gas.

Approximately one-half of the region's oil comes from Siberia, and virtually all of Siberian oil comes from the West Siberian fields (Figure 13–2). Most of the growth in Soviet petroleum production after the early 1970s came from those extensive deposits. But production has been hampered by the harshness of the environment, especially the permafrost, which complicates drilling and the laying of pipelines. The Soviet oil industry also suffered from antiquated equipment and poor management, which left it unable to increase production to take advantage of the higher world prices precipitated by the world oil crisis of 1990.

West Siberian oil moves by a growing pipeline network, which also serves Russia's second most important petroleum-producing area, the Volga-Urals fields. The pipeline network carries oil to eastern Siberia and to the major industrial and urban centers of Europe, the Baltics, Belarus, Ukraine, and European Russia. Recently discovered deposits along the upper reaches of the Lena River in eastern Siberia will also help to meet future petroleum needs. Most notable among the remaining oil-producing areas of the region are several fields in the Caspian Sea off the coast of Azerbaidzhan, as well as deposits in Ukraine, Kazakhstan, and northern European Russia (Figure 13–3).

Natural gas has become an increasingly important energy resource; estimates give the region as much as 40 percent of the world's reserves. The Soviet government placed a high priority on developing those reserves. With an increased output of natural gas, it would be possible to substitute gas for petroleum in heating, saving the scarcer oil for transportation and industrial uses. Expanded production would also mean more gas for export by pipeline to Eastern and Western Europe. Sales in the latter area are important, for they provide the Russians, in particular, with Western currency for the purchase of Western technology.

Several U.S. companies have expressed interest in the Siberian and Kazak fields and have proposed financial and technical assistance in exchange for gas. Japan has also indicated an interest in Siberian gas. But those deposits are especially important to Western Europe, where they are expected to ac-

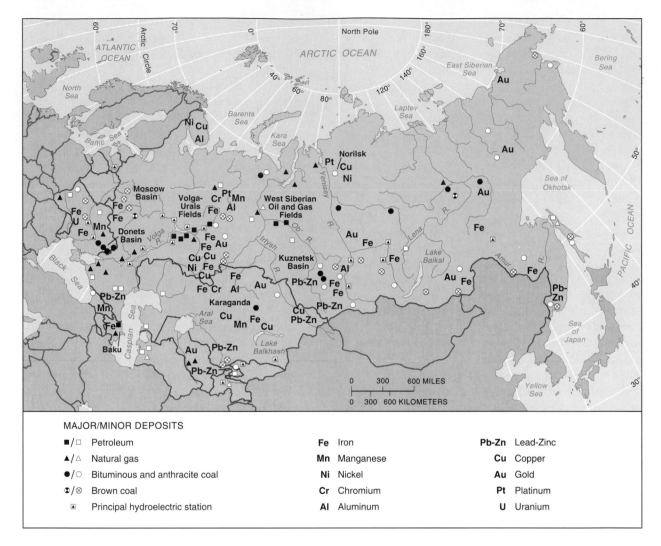

Figure 13–2

Natural resources. Russia, Ukraine, and Kazakhstan in particular are rich in minerals. High-quality coal is found in the Ukrainian Donets and Russian Kuznetsk basins and in the Kazakh Karaganda deposits. Oil and gas is produced in Azerbaidzhan and the Russian West Siberian and Volga-Urals fields. The Volga River provides hydroelectric power. Most of the area's metals are found in the west and along the southern fringe of the region.

count for as much as 40 percent of natural gas consumption in the near future. Approximately one-third of the region's natural gas comes from the West Siberian fields. Other fields are in Ukraine, Turkmenistan, and Uzbekistan, as well as in Russia's northern Caucasus and southern Ural mountains.

The Soviet Union was the leading producer of coal in the world, and its coal reserves (about one-third of the world's proven reserves) rank among the world's largest. At present rates of consumption, it is estimated that the region's coal will last for almost 8,000 years. More than 93 percent of those reserves are in Asia, the majority in Siberia. Coal production, however, is concentrated in western Russia and Ukraine, accounting for about 60 percent of the extracted coal. The Donets Basin, in Ukraine,

Figure 13-3
Old oil field in Azerbaidzhan.
The Baku oilfield near the
Caspian Sea was the major oil
supply area for the former
Soviet Union but has now been
surpassed in importance by the
West Siberian and Volga-Urals
fields in Russia.

produces on its own 35 percent of the total output. The Kuznetsk Basin is Russia's major source of coal, meeting local needs and shipping coal as far west as the Urals. Russian goals call for increased production of Siberian coal, as Ukrainian supplies become increasingly problematic.

The lower-grade fuels (peat and oil shale) are locally significant as energy sources for small thermal electric stations. With the increasing availability of natural gas and petroleum, however, those less-efficient fuels are losing their comparative cost advantages.

Most electricity in the region is generated by thermal stations that utilize peat, coal, oil, or gas. Although peat and coal are the most common fuels for thermal plants, their increased use will further pollute an already-polluted atmosphere. Currently, atomic power plants produce about 10 percent of the country's electrical energy; eventually, that figure could rise to 25 percent. But the 1986 disaster at the Chernobyl plant in Ukraine forced the Soviet government to radically cut back its plans for nuclear energy.

Only about 15 percent of all electricity generated comes from hydroelectric stations, in spite of the enormous hydroelectric potential, which is estimated at twice that of the United States. A major handicap for the country is location; about 70 percent of that potential lies within Siberia, far from the centers of demand. Consequently, the planners focused most of their attention on thermal and nuclear stations in the western part of the country.

Hydroelectric potential is more fully developed in the western areas, particularly in Russia along the Volga and its tributary, the Kama. The construction of hydroelectric stations and their necessary reservoirs has converted those rivers into a string of large lakes. The stations supply electricity to cities along the Volga, as well as to the Urals and the Moscow area. Since 1960 hydroelectric capacity has also been expanded in the Caucasus and Central Asian mountains.

Metallic Ores

An ample and diverse base of metallic resources complements the region's energy resources, though tungsten, tin, and aluminum resources, especially bauxite, are in short supply. Collectively the iron ore reserves of the region are the largest in the world, representing 40 percent of all known reserves. The most important of the producing iron ore deposits are in the west, in Russia and Ukraine, whereas the majority of the known reserves are in Siberia and Kazakhstan. Approximately 50 percent of the iron ore extracted in the former Soviet Union came from deposits in Ukraine, of which the Krivoi Rog fields were the most significant. Those ores continue to supply the region's largest concentration of ironworks and steelworks, found in Ukraine. Shipment to factories in western Russia and Eastern Europe is becoming increasingly difficult due to demands for higher prices and stable currencies. Russia's major areas of iron ore mining are the Urals and the Kursk deposits in European Russia.

A wide array of other mineral ores are located in this vast region. Important manganese and mercury deposits are in Ukraine. Kazakhstan has a wide range of industrial resources, including bauxite, tungsten, molybdenum, chromium, lead, and zinc, as well as one of the world's largest copper deposits, in addition to oil and coal. Mercury and gold are found in Uzbekistan, while tungsten, molybdenum, and gold are available in Turkmenistan. Russia, however, is the richest of the new Eurasian states in terms of industrial resources: the Urals hold a great range of mineral wealth, including gold, copper, and bauxite. The vastness of Siberia contains gold, tin, tungsten, copper, zinc, and platinum, while northwestern European Russia contains bauxite and nickel deposits.

INDUSTRIAL REGIONS

In the old Soviet command economy, planning for regional distribution and development of industries was a major task, compounded by the country's large area, the unequal distribution of natural resources, and the diversity of ethnic groups at different stages of economic development. From the start of the industrialization program, the Soviets attempted to disperse their industrial production beyond the limits of the European part of the country, for ideological as well as strategic reasons. The Soviet Union wanted to be able to withstand any attack from Western capitalist powers, which Josef Stalin, Soviet leader from the 1920s, believed to be imminent. Thus, the development of industrial production in the more militarily defensible areas—the eastern portions of the country—seemed advisable. And with much fanfare the Soviets embarked on expansion of the Urals industrial base and the development of the Kuznetsk metallurgical base in Siberia.

World War II was the greatest stimulus to increased industrial production in the eastern portion of the country. In reality, the Soviets did not have much choice, for German occupation controlled 40 percent of the population of the European USSR as well as the bulk of heavy industry (62 percent of the coal production and 58 percent of the steel produc-

tion). Consequently, between 1940 and 1943 industrial production increased 3.4 times in western Siberia. After World War II the western part of the Soviet Union was reconstructed and regained its dominant position in industrial production, though not quite at its prewar level.

Even though Soviet economic policies emphasized the balanced distribution of economic activities, those policies also stressed: (1) production that was close to raw materials and markets in order to minimize transportation costs, (2) development of specialized forms of production in areas best suited to them, and (3) creation within each region of adequate production to meet the basic needs of the people. Regional development seemed to favor increased industrial investment in the west, particularly in medium-sized cities in areas with large labor supplies. Siberian development is expected to continue, though the high cost of attracting and sustaining labor there means that development in Siberia will be more technological than labor intensive.

Soviet industrial policies overall favored the development of manufacturing in Russia. Of the six districts of prime industrial significance in the former Soviet Union five were located in Russia and one was in Ukraine (Figure 13–4). The Russian industrial districts are: (1) the Central industrial district, or simply the Center; (2) St. Petersburg; (3) the Mid-Volga Area; (4) the Urals; and (5) the Kuznetsk Basin. The Donets-Dnieper industrial district is in Ukraine.

The Center

The Center—which contains Moscow, Russia's most populous and largest industrial city—owes its industrial prominence to a number of factors, including a large market, an ample supply of labor both trained and unskilled, and excellent transportation to all parts of the country. In addition, electric lines from Volga hydropower stations and gas and oil pipelines from Ukraine, north Caucasus, the Volga-Urals fields, Central Asia, and western Siberia supply the Center with important sources of energy. All of those factors ensure the area's continued prominence in industrial production, though its share of total industrial output may slowly decline.

Despite its prominence, the industrial resource base of the Center is weak. Energy resources of brown coal and timber are inferior. Small iron ore deposits exist, as do phosphorus for fertilizer and some building materials. Nonetheless, textile manu-

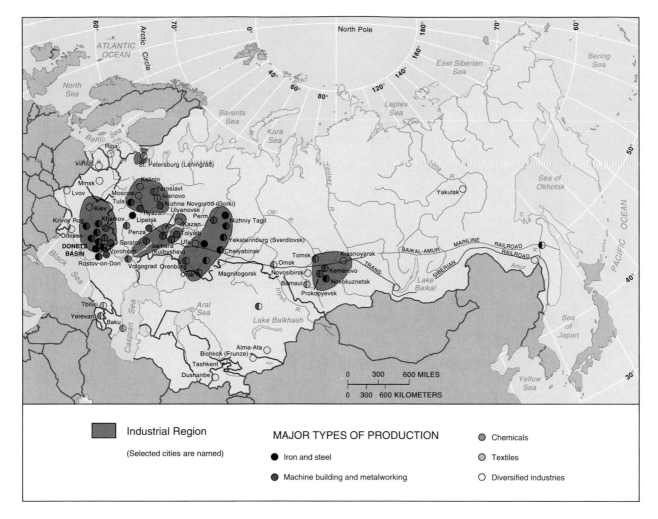

Figure 13-4

Industrial regions and selected cities. Industry in the region is concentrated in six regions. Except for the Moscow and St. Petersburg areas, those regions possess abundant local energy supplies. Soviet industry was oriented toward capital goods. In recent years production of consumer goods has increased.

facturing is significant. Around Moscow some 30 percent of all industrial workers are employed in the manufacture of linen, cotton, wool, and silk fabrics. Other major industries include metals, machine construction, engineering industries, chemicals, food processing, and woodworking.

St. Petersburg (Leningrad)

St. Petersburg, for decades called Leningrad, is the second largest city in Russia. It was long not only the principal port for Russia but also for the entire Soviet Union. Czar Peter the Great planned and built this imperial capital in the early eighteenth century as a symbol of the new Russia he was creating. It was the country's window to the West—Russia's most important contact point with a modernizing Western Europe.

Today, St. Petersburg occupies a position similar to that of Moscow: it lies in a region with a deficient resource base. Except for hydroelectric stations, local energy resources are limited to peat deposits and oil shales. St. Petersburg industries include machine tools, equipment for hydroelectric plants, and shipbuilding. The city's highly skilled work force is one of the best in Russia.

The Mid-Volga Area

The industrial strength of the mid-Volga industrial area rests primarily on its extensive energy resources. It not only contains one of the major petroleum-producing areas of Russia—the Volga-Urals fields—but also has important gas fields and surplus hydroelectric power generated by some of the country's largest dams. During World War II the area experienced rapid industrial and population growth. It was situated east of the battle lines but close enough to supply needed war matériel to the front. After the late 1950s, industrial production increased faster in the Volga area than in the Soviet Union as a whole.

In addition to its fuels and hydroelectric power, the mid-Volga area also has the advantage of being connected by the Volga River and its tributaries to large areas in the west. The Volga River system is the nation's major water route, carrying more than 60 percent of all freight transported by river. That accessibility by water, as well as rail and pipeline, has allowed the expansion of industrial activities as a whole. One major example is the large automotive plant built at Tolyatti as a joint venture with Fiat, an Italian firm. The plant was intended to produce 600,000 cars a year, 48 percent of Russia's total planned yearly automobile output.

The Urals

In terms of overall industrial production, the Urals rank third in the region, behind the Center and the Ukrainian industrial district. Industry in the Urals depends chiefly on the rich and varied local mineral deposits. In addition to an important iron and steel industry, the district is known for copper smelting and refining, zinc refining, the production of alumina, and the refining of aluminum. Yekaterinburg, a major railroad center, is the largest of the district's cities. Machine construction, especially for the mining industry, dominates the area, and ferrous metallurgy is also prominent.

Siberia

The Siberian manufacturing district lies between the Ob and the Yenisey rivers in western Siberia. The rich coal deposits of the Kuznetsk Basin and the area's hydroelectric power are major reasons for the industrial development there (Figure 13–5). The region includes a complex of metallurgical industries in the Kuznetsk Basin and in several cities outside the basin, including Novosibirsk, the largest city in all of Siberia. Novosibirsk, a major transportation center, is situated on the Trans-Siberian Railroad and the Ob River. It is also a major industrial city, producing metallurgical products, machines, foods, and textiles.

Figure 13–5
Apartment housing, industry, and a branch of the Trans-Siberian Railroad just east of Lake Baikal. The resource wealth of Siberia has led to considerable development, which is often rather bleak.

Siberia as a whole has great industrial potential, but high transportation costs, as well as high production costs and a shortage of workers, have slowed development. Nevertheless, even though recent governments have stressed renewing and modernizing existing industry in the west, Siberian development will not be neglected. Emphasis there will be on industries that use large amounts of energy, given the area's energy surplus. Also, more processing of Siberian minerals and lumber will be done where the resources are located in order to reduce transportation costs, and more effort will be made to develop those industries that will provide the specific goods Siberia needs.

An indication of willingness by the Soviets to invest in Siberia is the 1,990-mile-long (3,204-kilometer) Baikal-Amur Mainline (BAM) Railroad (see Figure 13–4). Completed in 1984, the BAM begins several hundred miles north of the Trans-Siberian Railroad, west of Lake Baikal, and runs to the Amur River in the far east (see Figure 13–6). Further expansion of Siberian railroads is on hold while Russia attempts to deal with the serious problem of restructuring its economy. Siberian development could be greatly assisted by Japanese technology and capital, but Japan has held back on its invest-

ment in the area until the Russians negotiate the return of some of the Kurile Islands, which were seized at the end of World War II.

Ukraine Industrial District

The Ukrainian industrial district was the principal heavy-manufacturing area of the Soviet Union. The availability of coal, iron ore, and ferroalloys continues to facilitate major iron and steel production, including heavy machine construction and a coal-based chemical industry. The largest concentration of cities within the industrial area is on the coalfields of Donets Basin.

The industrial resource base of Ukraine extends beyond its coal and iron ore. Energy resources are supplemented by gas fields to the north and by the gas and oil fields of the northern Caucasus. The base of raw materials also includes such minerals as salts, potash, mercury, and brown coal. Furthermore, the high productivity of agriculture within the district and throughout the southern steppes of European Russia has stimulated the development of extensive food-processing industries and the production of agricultural equipment.

Figure 13-6
The Trans-Siberian express.
Railroads have played a major role in the economic organization of this huge and resource-rich region. The rail system of Siberia will likely be expanded to facilitate development of the mineral resources of the area.

The two largest cities of Ukraine—Kiev and Kharkov—are on the northern margins of the manufacturing area. Kharkov is important in the production of heavy machinery; Kiev, the capital of Ukraine, is a diversified industrial city, producing machinery, textiles, and processed foods. To the southwest is the diversified industrial port of Odessa.

AGRICULTURE

Soviet agriculture never developed as well as Soviet industry did, partly because of the harsh environment and partly because economic policies placed more emphasis on industrial development. From the late 1920s to the early 1950s, agricultural output barely kept pace with population growth. From the 1950s to the late 1980s, however, the production of agricultural goods—both crops and livestock—grew almost three times as fast as the population.

Nonetheless, Soviet farm production still lagged behind that of the United States. For every American farm worker, the Soviet Union had eight. In another comparison, about 22 percent of the Soviet labor force was engaged in agriculture; in the United States that figure is about 2 percent. Furthermore, the area sown to crops was 73 percent greater in the Soviet Union than in the United States, yet Soviet crop production was only 80 percent as great as that of the United States. Overall, the average American farmer of the 1980s was ten times more productive than the average Soviet farmer. Thus, one Soviet agricultural worker grew enough food to feed eight fellow citizens; one U.S. farmer grew enough food to feed fifty-two Americans. Little has changed since the demise of the Soviet system.

Agriculture and Soviet Development

The decision in the late 1920s to embark on an all-out program of rapid industrialization necessitated the collectivization of agriculture. The major factors in the decision to collectivize were political as well as economic:

1. The peasant class represented a capitalist or latent capitalist element that was ideologically unacceptable to the regime.
2. It was more efficient to control the peasantry on large farms than in smaller units.
3. By forcing the peasants into large collectives, agricultural prices and wages could be controlled

at low levels, to allow capital to accumulate for industrial expansion.
4. Strict control would facilitate the flow of foodstuffs to the cities in order to feed the growing industrial labor force.
5. Large-scale units could be mechanized to increase agricultural productivity and to free labor for the growing industrial activities.

In response to this early collectivization, war raged in the countryside. A second Bolshevik revolution took place, and millions of people were killed. Livestock herds were decimated as peasants slaughtered their animals rather than surrender them to the new collectives. The Soviet economy was in chaos. By 1940, however, the power of the central government prevailed, and virtually all peasant households were part of the collective agricultural economy. The government had won.

Two forms of farm organization emerged: the collective farm and the state farm (see Chapter 11). A collective farm brought together a group of workers who were responsible for seeing that state production quotas were met (Figure 13–7). After the quotas were fulfilled and the needs of the collective farm were satisfied (i.e., capital for farm repairs, taxes, and seed for the next season), the remaining crop was divided among the workers as their share of the profit. The peasants were, therefore, residual claimants to the farm's production. In contrast, workers on a state farm were paid a set wage, and the total cost of the operation was underwritten by the state.

Needless to say, it cost the government more to operate the state farms than the collectives. The collective system was greatly favored by the Stalin regime, but efficiency suffered because of the government's fixed lower prices for agricultural products. Thus, the capital that accumulated to operate the collectives was insufficient and failed to provide work incentives. In addition, the state's investment in fertilizers, machinery, and other necessary technological improvements for the collectives was woefully inadequate. All of those factors contributed to stagnant agricultural production through the early 1950s and a hard life for farm workers, especially those on collectives.

The critical difference between survival and starvation was the private sector of Soviet agriculture—collective and state-farm workers and some industrial workers who were permitted to raise products

Figure 13-7
Soldiers from the Moscow Military Academy harvesting potatoes in 1991. Despite the
use of modern machinery on many farms, agriculture in many parts of the former
Soviet Union often remains labor intensive and lacking in modern technology. It has
not been unusual for labor to be conscripted to work during harvest seasons.

on plots of 0.5 to 1.25 acres (0.2 to 0.5 hectares). In
1953 such **private plots** took up only about 4 percent of the cultivated land in the Soviet Union but
produced 72 percent of the potatoes, 48 percent of
the vegetables, 52 percent of the meat, 67 percent of
the milk, and 84 percent of the eggs. The free-market sales of products from those private plots generated the majority of the income for collective farmers. At the close of the Soviet era the private plots
produce approximately 25 percent of all foodstuffs
and 30 percent of all meat and poultry on less than
3 percent of the region's farmland.

The Permanent Crisis

The ongoing nature of the agricultural problem in
the Soviet Union prompted some Western critics to
call it a **permanent crisis**. Even at the time of Stalin's
death the dire condition of agriculture forced his
successors to turn their attention to the needs of that
part of the economy. An expansion of cultivated
lands in the dry steppes east of the Volga region initially resulted in a significant increase in agricultural
production. That so-called virgin-and-idle-lands
program brought 116 million acres (46.4 million

hectares) of new land under cultivation, mostly in western Siberia and northern Kazakhstan. But because annual precipitation there ranges from 16 inches (406 millimeters) in the north to 9 inches (228 millimeters) in the south, those are marginal farming areas. Anticipated production levels were not attained; actual production varied from year to year. Nevertheless, the increased area devoted to wheat freed land in the moister European parts of the region for other crops.

In the 1960s and 1970s the Soviets adopted a more tolerant attitude toward private plots, further increased purchase prices from the collectives, and introduced a guaranteed minimum wage for collective farm workers. In addition, the prices of machinery and fertilizers were reduced, and the state recognized the right of collective farms to participate more in the planning procedure. The last half of the 1960s was marked by notable success in agricultural production: output increased by 23 percent from 1965 to 1971. In the 1980s, however, there were signs that the condition of agriculture was failing to improve further. The year 1983 was considered a good year in Soviet agriculture, but still the country was not self-sufficient in food. And despite increased wages the average collective farmer still made less per year than the average industrial worker or even the average state farm employee.

The need of the Soviet government to import large quantities of grain underscored the fact that Soviet agriculture was still beset by numerous problems, among them inadequate mechanical equipment and deficient storage and transportation facilities. By some estimates, during the 1990 harvest 2 million tons of grain were lost daily because of such inadequacies. The more productive young workers left the farms because of low salaries, restricted opportunities for advancement, and scarce amenities, which are more available in the cities. Furthermore, centralized decision making in the Soviet system contributed to interference by party bureaucrats and inefficient use of agricultural resources.

In 1950 Soviet agricultural output was about 60 percent of that of the United States. By the late 1980s farm production was 80 percent of American production, but it had to feed 40 million people more than did U.S. agriculture. From the early 1970s Soviet agricultural plans called for production levels equaling those of the United States. But the gap between the American farmer and the Soviet farmer remained great.

The failure of the collective system to adequately feed the Soviet population necessitated dramatic change. The trend since the late 1980s has been to encourage more private farmers; thus, in all the new countries of the region there are programs at various stages of implementation to establish private agricultural economies. Many so-called **cooperatives** have been organized in which small self-sufficient teams of farmers with a profit motive cooperate in producing and selling their products. In several countries, such as the Baltics and Ukraine, peasants now have the right to own and lease land and farm independently. That is a transition step toward genuine private farms; the final goal of free enterprise agriculture, however, is far from being accomplished.

In 1993 President Boris Yeltsin signed a decree that made it legal for the first time since 1917 for Russians to own land. Almost a third of the collective and state farms rejected state ownership and opted for a form of cooperative partnerships in the form of limited liability societies, where the workers assume responsibility of farm operations. In reality, though, the day-to-day operations of agriculture remain much the same as they did under the Soviets.

Full adjustment from collective to private production will be difficult in most of the Eurasian states. In the Baltic states the reemergence of private agriculture is well under way. But in other countries, such as Russia or Ukraine, that task will be far more arduous. The entrenched conservatism of the peasantry—the fear of change—has to be dealt with, as does a shortage of capital and knowledge required to be a successful farmer. Also, many collective and state farms functioned as companies, paying benefits such as child care and pensions to the peasants. If these farm enterprises are eliminated, who would assume the responsibility of providing these benefits, which the farmers and retirees expect? Such concerns are reflected in the following excerpts from an interview with a collective farm worker:

"Let's say I buy land," he mused, as he and a visitor toured the repair sheds that are his domain.

"What am I going to grow on it? Where am I going to sell my crop? What kind of equipment am I going to need? It would be very hard to get started.

"When my father was still alive he hoped one day to have his own land—maybe I would have gone into business with him. But now, you see, I'm a mechanic. I don't work the land. I'm 40 years old. . . .

"I'm used to the idea that I should not work for myself, but for the collective farm," he said. "I'd have to forget all my experience to remake myself into something else."[2]

A quick remedy to the permanent crisis is unlikely.

Agricultural Regions

Soviet agriculture suffered both from the institutional restraints of its organization and from physical environmental handicaps. Although the land area of the Soviet Union was two-and-a-half times as large as that of the United States, its area suitable for crop cultivation was only one-third greater; in other words, only about 11 percent of the region's territory is arable. Figure 13–8 shows generalized zones of agricultural use in the former Soviet Union. The areas with no agriculture or with widely scattered small farms clearly occupy the majority of the land. Areas that are too cool and that have poor soils cover the northern European part of Russia and virtually all of Siberia. In addition, the bulk of Central

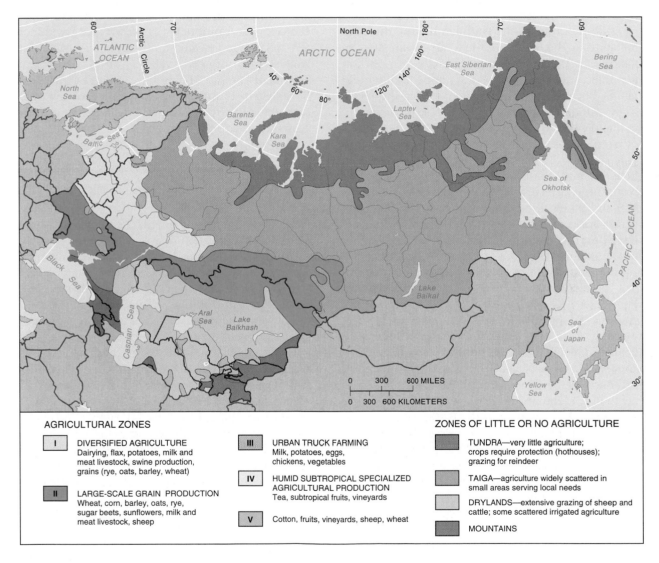

AGRICULTURAL ZONES

| I | DIVERSIFIED AGRICULTURE |
Dairying, flax, potatoes, milk and meat livestock, swine production, grains (rye, oats, barley, wheat)

| II | LARGE-SCALE GRAIN PRODUCTION |
Wheat, corn, barley, oats, rye, sugar beets, sunflowers, milk and meat livestock, sheep

| III | URBAN TRUCK FARMING |
Milk, potatoes, eggs, chickens, vegetables

| IV | HUMID SUBTROPICAL SPECIALIZED AGRICULTURAL PRODUCTION |
Tea, subtropical fruits, vineyards

| V | Cotton, fruits, vineyards, sheep, wheat |

ZONES OF LITTLE OR NO AGRICULTURE

TUNDRA—very little agriculture; crops require protection (hothouses); grazing for reindeer

TAIGA—agriculture widely scattered in small areas serving local needs

DRYLANDS—extensive grazing of sheep and cattle; some scattered irrigated agriculture

MOUNTAINS

Figure 13–8

Agricultural zones. Agriculture in the former Soviet Union was confined largely to the southwest quarter of the region. After World War II, attempts were made to expand the area of crop production into the dry lands east of the Caspian Sea and into western Siberia.

Asia is desert. Even in the agricultural zones of the territory, some parts are too cool, too moist, or too dry. In the United States such areas would be judged marginal for agriculture.

The agricultural zones lie mainly south of 60°N latitude in the European section, including Estonia, Latvia, Lithuania, Ukraine, Belarus, and western Russia. In Siberia, the agricultural zones are mostly south of the 57th parallel. The southern agricultural area is limited by high evapotranspiration rates. In Figure 13–8, Zones I and II represent the **fertile triangle**, or that part of the region with the greatest agricultural potential.

Zone I, bordering the southern limit of the taiga forest from the Baltic to the Urals, is an area of mixed agriculture. Dairying and swine production are major activities. Flax (for linen) and hardier grains, such as rye and oats, do well in the short, moist summers. Potatoes, long a staple of Slavic and Baltic diets, are a principal crop; and numerous other vegetables are also raised there. In the southern part of Zone I (southern Russia, southern Belarus, and northern Ukraine), the amount of cropped land increases. Grains (e.g., rye, oats, barley, and wheat), in addition to potatoes, flax, and hemp (for coarse cloth and rope), are characteristic. Dual-purpose cattle (i.e., for milk and meat) are raised extensively. The far eastern section of the zone in Russian Siberia has a product mix similar to that of the more southerly parts of the zone in Europe; it includes wheat, sugar beets, livestock, and rice.

Zone II is the country's principal large-scale grain-producing area. The northwestern parts of the zone cover most of Ukraine, Moldova, and adjoining parts of the Russian republic. Precipitation is generally adequate, and temperatures are higher and soils are better than in the Baltic states or most of Russia. Those factors have helped create a very important region of surplus food production, specializing in sugar beets, wheat, corn, barley, rye, oats, and potatoes. The semiarid southern and eastern sections of Zone II have fertile soils and are especially famous for the large-scale wheat farms that produce most of the country's grain. Winter wheat is grown largely in the European section, whereas spring wheat dominates in the east. Corn has become an increasingly important crop in the more humid west, and plantings have expanded into the drier steppes to the east. Sunflowers for oil are an-

other major crop, particularly in the western sections. A variety of grains and other crops (e.g., sugar beets, potatoes, flax, and barley), along with milk and meat livestock and sheep, round out the agriculture of the zone.

In addition to the zones surrounding urban areas (Zone III), where fruits, vegetables, eggs, milk, and chickens are produced for city dwellers, two zones are noted for their specialized crop production. One (Zone IV) is the trans-Caucasus, where citrus crops and tea thrive in the well-watered, protected western portion of the area, as well as in Georgia and a very limited part of Russia. In the drier eastern Georgian portion, tea is grown along with cotton and rice in irrigated regions. Zone V, which includes the irrigated valleys of Azerbaidzhan, Turkmenistan, Uzbekistan, Kyrgyzstan, and Kazakhstan, is the principal cotton-growing area. Rice, the staple food of Central Asia, is also a major crop in that zone.

SUMMARY
An Unknown Future

Rarely in a person's lifetime is there an opportunity to witness the creation of a new economic, political, and social system. The American Revolution, French Revolution, and Russian Revolution of 1917 started these countries on a path of building a new order from the ground up. The dismal failure of the developmental strategies of the communist system have given the inheritors of that legacy a chance to begin anew. It is far too early to tell what the outcome will be. Possibly, a rational system of truly free, independent, and economically secure states will evolve. Such a process will take considerable time. It will not be easy to find solutions to common problems and at the same time ensure the national integrity and independence of the individual countries. The task of overcoming economic, political, and nationalistic conflicts challenges possibilities of creating a truly viable and cooperative Commonwealth of of Independent States. More bloodshed could erupt in several areas of the old Soviet Union, and authoritarian regimes, such as the Georgian government that emerged in 1991, may appear. There remains the possibility that hardliners from the old system may attempt to reassert central control over all the states of the region. Russia, likewise, may affirm its role as "first among equals," pushing its interests over those of its neighbors. One bright spot is likely to be the Baltic states. With a strong agricultural and industrial potential and a well-educated, productive work force, a more European orientation, and the consequent interest that Western European countries (notably the Nordic states) and the United States have in this region, the promise that independence will prosper is greater. Western cooperation and aid in the form of private investment and government grants and loans will likewise be critical if the newly independent countries of Eurasia are going to work through their problems and develop into stable economic, political, and social states.

The Baltic states have a strong agricultural and industrial potential and will most likely expand their commercial ties with the West. The rest of the new countries, however, face many more problems. Their economies are in decline. Some Western critics question whether Russia, the principal successor to the Soviet Union, can any longer be considered a superpower. The USSR's early economic success was impressive; its strong emphasis on industrial and military development, its abundance of raw materials, and its use of Western technology enabled the country to achieve high levels of economic growth. But that progress was costly. Natural resources were wasted, and labor was not used efficiently. More importantly, personal liberty and material well-being were sacrificed for the state's development plans.

Past efforts to remedy the Soviet Union's economic difficulties focused largely on reducing waste and improving efficiency rather than making fundamental organizational changes. Those programs were a failure. It is too early to tell what kind of economic reforms will be enacted by the new governments, but they will most likely include cooperation between countries and free-market economies. The power of the Communist party has been drastically reduced or eliminated altogether in these countries, but government bureaucracies are still reluctant to accept the risks that come with a market economy.

The rich natural resource base of several countries of the region, notably Russia, Ukraine, and Kazakhstan, put them in an enviable position. Not only can they provide for their own economic growth, but they can also make the region an important supplier of raw materials for deficient industrial states and the Third World. To maximize that potential, however, they along with the Baltic states need Western technological and financial assistance. Expanding commercial relations with the United States and other industrialized Western nations are necessary, as is the convertibility of the ruble (and the other new national currencies that have been created) to gain purchasing power throughout the world.

Agriculture remains the major problem in the region's economy. Despite significant improvements in production in the 1980s, Soviet agriculture failed to provide the quantity and quality of foodstuffs promised by the government. Frequent crop failures required food to be imported. The establishment of an independent farming class with food prices reflecting the cost of production should eventually lessen agricultural problems.

In addition to its economic problems, the region is facing the serious threat of ethnic turmoil. Only the future will reveal if the new order of Eurasian countries will succeed in establishing democracy, free-market economies, and interstate cooperation, or if the forces of totalitarianism will re-emerge and ethnic hostilities will destroy any hope for peaceful development. The territory of the former Soviet Union is in a volatile state. Dramatic events there in the past few years have had a tremendous impact on the world; we will continue to view further developments with nervous anticipation.

KEY TERMS

Bolsheviks	*glasnost*
Commonwealth of Independent States (CIS)	*perestroika*
	permanent crisis
cooperatives	private plots
fertile triangle	*soviet*

NOTES

1. *Bolshevik* is the Russian word for "majority." In reality, that so-called majority was a minority composed of Russian Marxists.

2. *New York Times,* 22 August 1990, p. 10.

FURTHER READINGS
Part Four

Bater, James H. *The Soviet Scene: A Geographical Perspective*. London: Edward Arnold, 1989.

Berg, L. S. *Natural Regions of the USSR*. New York: Macmillan, 1950. The classic study of Soviet landscape zones by an eminent Soviet geographer.

Besemeres, John F. *Socialist Population Politics: The Political Implications of Demographic Trends in the USSR and Eastern Europe*. White Plains, NY: M. E. Sharpe, 1980. An examination of the Marxist view of population as well as a study of population policy and demographic trends and their impact on politics, ethnic relations, social issues, and foreign relations in Poland, Yugoslavia, and the Soviet Union of the 1980s.

Carcroft, James, ed. *The Soviet Union Today: An Interpretive Guide*. Chicago: Education Foundation for Nuclear Science, 1983. An examination of the Soviet environment, history, economy, politics, armed forces, society, culture, and technology, with contributions from twenty-six Soviet specialists.

Cole, J. P. *Geography of the Soviet Union*. Boston: Butterworth, 1984.

Demko, George, and Roland J. Fuchs, eds. *Geographical Studies on the Soviet Union: Essays in Honor of Chauncy D. Harris*. Department of Geography, Research Paper no. 211. Chicago: University of Chicago, 1984. Thirteen essays by eminent geographers who are specialists on the area; includes essays as diverse as "The Urban Network of Later Medieval Russia" and "The Development of Siberia: Regional Planning and Economic Society."

Fischer-Galati, Stephen, ed. *Eastern Europe in the 1980s*. Boulder, CO: Westview Press, 1981. A collection of articles by Eastern European experts, surveying recent industrial, agricultural, political, cultural, and educational developments.

Goldman, Marshall I. *USSR in Crisis: The Failure of an Economic System*. New York: Norton, 1983. Reviews the country's economic strategy for development and the reasons that the system had faltered by the 1980s.

Goldman, Minton F. *Commonwealth of Independent States and Central/Eastern Europe*. Guildford, CT: Dushkin, 1992.

Hoffman, Eva. *Exit into History: A Journey Through the New Eastern Europe*. New York: Viking, 1993.

Howe, G. Melvyn. *The Soviet Union: A Geographical Study*. 2d ed. Estover, Eng.: Macdonald & Evans, 1983.

Kaiser, Robert G. *Russia: The People and the Power*. New York: Atheneum, 1978.

Littlejohn, Gary. *A Sociology of the Soviet Union*. New York: St. Martin's Press, 1986. A Western view of Soviet society.

Lydolph, Paul E. *Geography of the USSR*. 3d ed. New York: Wiley, 1977. A discussion of the area's geography, organized according to the former Soviet Union's nineteen major economic regions.

_____. *Geography of the USSR: Topical Analysis*. Elkhart Lake, WI: Misty Valley, 1979. An excellent topical treatment of the area's geography, with an emphasis on economic aspects of the former Soviet Union; short updated supplements published irregularly.

Mellor, Roy E. H. *Eastern Europe: A Geography of the Comecon Countries*. New York: Columbia University Press, 1975.

Nagorski, Andrew. *Reluctant Farewell: An American Reporter's Candid Look Inside the Soviet Union*. New York: Henry Holt, 1987.

Nahaylo, Bohdan, and Victor Swoboda. *Soviet Disunion: A History of the Nationalities Problem in the U.S.S.R.* NewYork: The Free Press, 1990.

Parker, W. H. *A Historical Geography of Russia*. Chicago: Aldine, 1968. The historical geographical development of the Russian Empire and the Soviet state.

Pounds, Norman J. G. *Eastern Europe*. Chicago: Aldine, 1969.

Report on the USSR. New York: Radio Free Europe and Radio Liberty Research Institute on Current Soviet Affairs, 1988. Excellent and timely articles on economic, ethnic, political, and demographic developments at the end of the Soviet era.

Rodgers, Allan, ed. *The Soviet Far East: Geographical Perspectives on Development*. London: Routledge, 1990.

Smith, Alan H. *The Planned Economies of Eastern Europe*. New York: Holmes & Meier, 1983. A good book to begin one's study of the economies of the former Soviet bloc countries; explains the basis of the system, provides good historical background, and is easily read by noneconomists.

Smith, Hedrick. *The Russians*. New York: Ballantine Books, 1976. A highly readable and popular account of many aspects of life in the Soviet Union of the 1970s.

_____. *The New Russians*. New York: Random House, 1990. An update of the author's 1976 book examining the impact of recent changes on Russian life.

Soviet Geography: Review and Translation. Washington, DC: Winston, in cooperation with the American Geographical Society, 1961–present. Translations of Soviet articles on geography, research articles by Western scholars (primarily from the United States), and extensive notes on economic and geographic developments; an invaluable source for studying and teaching the area's geography.

The Soviet Union. 2d. ed. Washington, DC: Congressional Quarterly, 1986. An excellent reference book on the Soviet Union.

Symons, Leslie. *The Soviet Union: A Systematic Geography.* New York: Routledge, 1990.

U.S. Congress, Joint Economic Committee. *Soviet Economy in a Time of Change.* Washington, DC: Government Printing Office, 1979. A two-volume, comprehensive collection of scholarly articles on the past, present, and future performance of the Soviet economy.

Willis, David K. *Klass: How Russians Really Live.* New York: St. Martin's Press, 1985.

Yanowitch, Murray, ed. *The Social Structure of the USSR: Recent Studies.* Armonk, NY: M. E. Sharpe, 1986. A collection of studies by Soviet scholars; interesting for Western readers because it provides an opportunity to view social issues through Soviet eyes toward the end of the Soviet era.

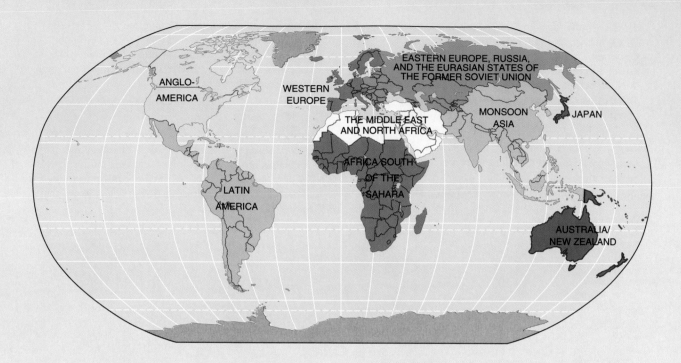

J apan, Australia, and New Zealand are the out-
liers of the so-called developed world. Far removed in distance from the major centers of
world power and wealth—North America and
Europe—Japan and Australia/New Zealand have
developed in completely different geographical
settings, in utterly different cultural environments,
and with different economic systems and problems from those of the major powers. Yet Japan in
the north and Australia and New Zealand in the
south share something very important: they are
the only truly developed nations in the western
Pacific.

Because of their isolation from North America
and Europe and their relatively small size (in both
area and population), textbook discussion of Japan
and Australia/New Zealand is often relegated to
subordinate parts of larger chapters, as if neither
really mattered that much in understanding world
patterns of resources and development. This text
obviously takes a different approach. Because of
Japan's enormous economic importance in the
world today, two chapters are devoted to that nation alone. Japan has achieved distinction for its extraordinary industrial productivity and its important
role in international trade and finance. Likewise,
though Australia and New Zealand account for a
tiny fraction of the world's people, their large collective land area and rich resources, among other
factors, warrant separate consideration. Both
Australia and New Zealand have achieved levels of
wealth in spite of limited industrialization.

Jack F. Williams

JAPAN AND AUSTRALIA/ NEW ZEALAND

CHAPTER 14
Japan: Physical and Human Resources

CHAPTER 15
Japan: The Economic Giant

CHAPTER 16
Australia and New Zealand: Isolation and Space

14

Japan:
Physical and Human
Resources

Resources: Compensating for Scarcity

Human Resources: The Hybrid Culture

Picking tea leaves in Japan. A manicured appearance is common in gardens and on small farms in Japan, where land for agriculture is scarce and the density of people per unit of arable land is extremely high. Mt. Fuji, a great volcanic peak southwest of Tokyo, is visible in the background.

Japan was the first non-Western country to be counted among the developed nations, the first to reach the fifth stage in Rostow's model (see Chapter 4). As the twentieth century approaches its close, Japan also is emerging as the leader of a group of **Pacific Rim** nations—composed primarily of South Korea, Taiwan, Hong Kong, and Singapore, but in the near future likely to be joined by Malaysia, Thailand, and at least coastal parts of China. Collectively these countries are developing rapidly as the world's third major economic center, to rival the two older centers of North America and Europe. Japan has unquestioned supremacy within that group in terms of economic development. It also has an unparalleled opportunity to lead Asia at a time when the sole remaining superpower, the United States, is finding its dominance of the world gradually slipping away.

Japan is clearly a wealthy nation, whatever standard is used. Its GNP is more than $3 trillion, second only to that of the United States; and per capita income exceeds $24,000, which is more than that of the United States. Japan is among the world's top producers of automobiles, iron and steel, electronics, transport equipment, and a variety of other industrial manufactures. As a result, Japanese products, as well as Japanese tourists and business representatives, have become ubiquitous. Any travel in Japan reveals the physical signs of affluence: a modern, thriving society with well-dressed, well-fed people.

Japan is a key member of important international financial and economic organizations, and many nations of Asia and other parts of the world depend on Japan for manufactured goods as well as investment capital. In fact, Japan has succeeded so well that unflattering expressions, such as **Japan, Inc.** and **economic imperialism**, have sometimes been directed at Japanese efforts by the rest of the world. Japan is without question an economic giant in world affairs today, playing a role far out of proportion to its population and resource base.

RESOURCES: COMPENSATING FOR SCARCITY

Japan might be used to disprove the old theory of environmental determinism (see Chapter 4); the Japanese have succeeded, seemingly, in spite of their natural environment and poor resource endowment. Yet a closer analysis reveals a more complex situation. The various elements that make up Japan's physical environment—location, size, topography, climate, soils, arable land, mineral resources—have had positive as well as negative effects on Japan's development. In short, the Japanese have tried to make the best possible use of what they have, and they have shopped in the rest of the world for what they lack.

Location and Insularity

Japan's unique role in East Asian civilization can be attributed in part to the nation's relative isolation off the east coast of Asia (Figure 14–1). The country consists of four main islands—Hokkaido, Honshu, Shikoku, and Kyushu—as well as many lesser islands. All together they form an arc about 1,400 miles (2,254 kilometers) long that reaches from about 31°N to 45°N latitude (Figure 14–2). The Japanese Ryukyu Islands, of which Okinawa is the most important, continue southward from Kyushu in another arc to almost 24°N latitude; the Ogasawara, or Bonin, Islands run southward below central Honshu (Figure 14–3).

The development experience and historical roles of Japan are sometimes compared with those of Great Britain, but in fact the differences are great. For one thing, Japan has been more isolated than Britain. Tsushima Strait, which separates Japan from the Korean peninsula, is 115 miles (185 kilometers) wide, whereas the Strait of Dover, between France and Great Britain, is only 21 miles (34 kilometers) wide. The impact of Japan's isolation has been significant. For example, Japan has had natural protection from invaders; unlike Britain, it has never been successfully invaded. In addition, that relative isolation has enabled Japan to decide which aspects of foreign, especially Chinese, culture it wished to adopt—voluntarily and selectively. The Japanese could then adapt those new elements to their own situation to create a truly unique and brilliant culture.

Both Britain and Japan are similar, however, in having attempted to overcome the resource limitations of their small national territories by building overseas empires. The Japanese Empire, acquired mostly by conquest between the late nineteenth century and the end of World War II, once stretched from Sakhalin in the north to the Dutch East Indies

Figure 14-1

Japan's location off the east coast of Asia. Japan is formed by an island arc 1,400 miles (2,254 kilometers) long. The inset map illustrates Japan's latitudinal position in comparison with that of the eastern United States.

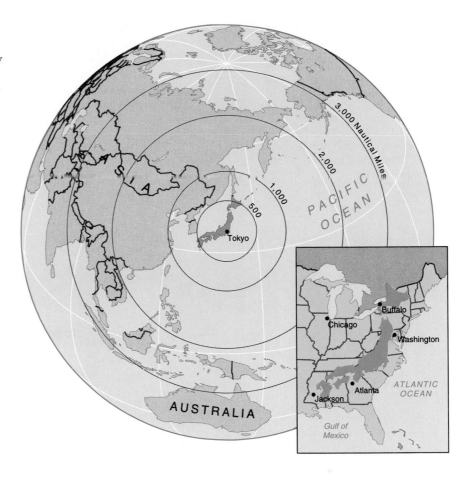

(Figure 14–3). Japan still claims the southern Kuril (Chishima) Islands northeast of Hokkaido, which were occupied by the Soviet Union near the end of the war.

A Temperate Land

Japan's long latitudinal sweep within the temperate zone, combined with its insularity, gives the country a beneficial climate, one that is roughly comparable to that of the East Coast of Anglo-America from New England to northern Florida (Figure 14–4). Japan's climate is influenced primarily by the monsoonal patterns of mainland Asia (see Chapter 24), but it is moderated by the surrounding seas and warm ocean currents. Thus, Japan has no real dry season, whereas Korea and North China, which are at the same latitude, frequently suffer from drought. Rainfall is sufficient throughout the year for crop growth; it ranges from about 40 inches (1,015 millimeters) a year on

Hokkaido and in the Inland Sea area to more than 100 inches (2,538 millimeters) a year in the wettest sections of the south. There is a general progression from long, cold winters and short, mild summers in Hokkaido to long, hot summers and short, mild winters in subtropical Kyushu. Likewise, the growing season ranges from around 150 days in Hokkaido to more than 260 days in Kyushu.

A significant dividing line in Japan runs roughly along the 37th parallel. South of the line, two crops in one growing season, or **double-cropping**, is possible—usually paddy rice in flooded fields during the summer and a dry crop in the winter. North of the line, the winters are usually too long to permit double-cropping. That division has been reflected in Japan's historical development: settlement north of the line, in northern Honshu and Hokkaido, came much later than it did in central and southern Japan. Even today, most of Japan's population lives south of 37°N latitude. The northern lands

Figure 14-2

Japan's coreland and selected cities. Japan is an island nation, often compared to the United Kingdom. In the past, Japan's insular location provided a natural barrier to outside forces; in the modern world it contributes to accessibility, since ocean transport is the least expensive way to move goods.

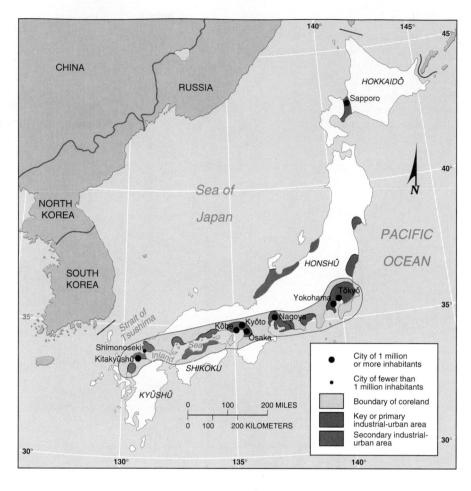

remain less densely populated and have larger farms, fewer cities, and less industry. Hokkaido is still a frontier region in Japan, with a much less developed appearance than that of the southern parts of the country.

A Crowded Land

Compared with the other great world powers, Japan is small—a mere 143,619 square miles (371,973 square kilometers), which is slightly smaller than California. In comparison with the nations of Western Europe, Japan is smaller than France but larger than Great Britain, Italy, or Germany. Japan's land problem stems from having too many people on too little land.

Compounding that problem is the rugged nature of Japan's terrain. Its islands are the summits of immense submarine ridges thrust up from the floor of the Pacific Ocean; the islands rise abruptly from the deep waters of the Pacific on the east and the Sea of

Japan on the west. The entire island chain is part of the unstable **orogenic** (mountain-making) **zone** that encircles the Pacific Ocean. As a result, Japan has hundreds of volcanoes (10 percent of the world's active volcanoes), and earthquakes are a serious natural hazard.

In such a geologic setting, low, level lands are in short supply. Only 25 percent of the total land area of Japan has slopes of less than 15 degrees. The other 75 percent of the land is too steep for cultivation and has little other utility for human occupancy. What level land does exist is found in narrow river valleys and alluvial coastal plains separated from one another by stretches of rugged hills. Thus, Japan's 124 million people are concentrated in a land area slightly smaller than the state of Indiana. The real population density per square mile of arable land is more than 5,800 (15,022 per square kilometer), one of the highest densities in the world (Figure 14–5). Even the density per unit of total land area, which comes to more than 840 (2,176 per

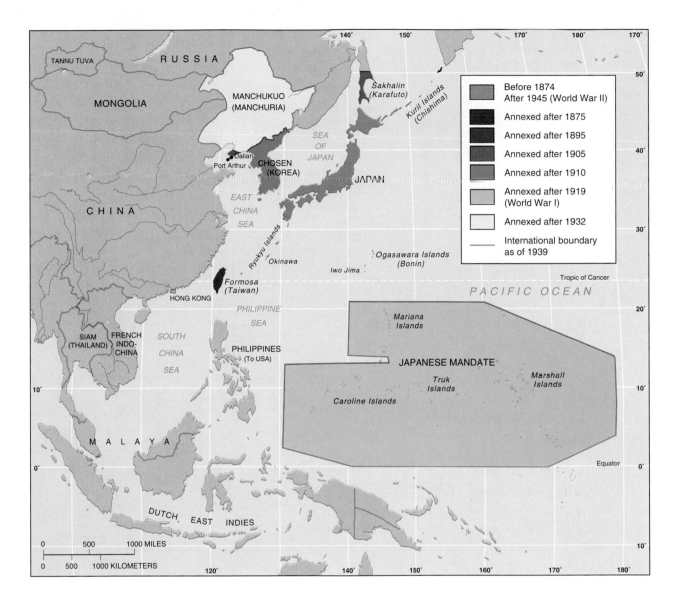

Figure 14-3
Japanese Empire before World War II. The empire included the Kuril Islands, Taiwan, Sakhalin, and Korea. Japan also established Manchuria as the Manchukuo Protectorate after 1931, though Japan had controlled Port Arthur since 1905 and thus had long exerted influence in that region of China. After World War I the Mariana Islands, Caroline Islands, Truk Islands, and Marshall Islands were mandated to Japan by the League of Nations. Prior to defeat in World War II, Japan also controlled much of North China and virtually all of Southeast Asia. (Adapted from *Teikoku's Complete Atlas of Japan*, Tokyo: Teikoku-Shoin, 1985, p. 8.)

square kilometer), is ten times higher than that of the United States. Japan is one of the most crowded nations in the world (Figure 14–6). The Japanese have been able to support such a dense population because they adopted from China, quite early in their history, an intensive form of irrigated agriculture, which is almost like gardening and produces high yields per land unit. They have also relied on large imports of food stuffs and agricultural products.

Figure 14-4

Climatic regions and frost-free days in Japan. Japan's climate is similar to that of the eastern United States, except that Japan experiences more moderate weather. The surrounding seas cause lower temperatures in the summer and warmer temperatures in the winter. Rainfall is more abundant also, and much of Japan enjoys a long growing season.

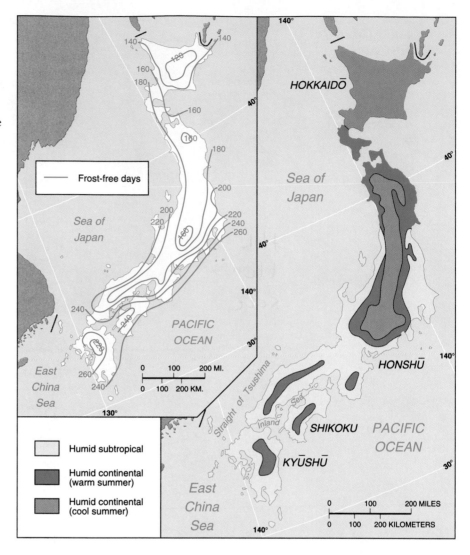

A Maritime Nation

The rugged coastline of Japan has countless bays and inlets, the most important of which is the great **Inland Sea**, which separates Honshu from Shikoku and Kyushu. In premodern times land communication was difficult in Japan, and the surrounding seas provided links among the islands and along the coast, as well as contact with the outside world. Most of Japan's population still lives close to the sea, which has always played an important role in Japan's national life.

Long ago, fishing became a major activity of the Japanese, and it remains one of the country's most important industries, stimulated by the shortage of land for livestock raising. Dependence on seafood was also a consequence of Buddhism, which early became the major religion of Japan. Today, the Japanese continue to obtain a major share of their dietary protein from fish and other sea products, much of which comes from **aquaculture**—the raising or growing of seafood products, such as shellfish and seaweed—along the coast. Over the years the fishing industry has become a global enterprise, with vessels roaming the four corners of the earth in search of seafood for Japan's large population. Japan is one of the few countries that still hunts whales, in spite of intense pressure from environmental and conservation groups around the world.

It is not surprising that the Japanese became significant shipbuilders early in their history. Then, with the coming of industrialization at the close of

Figure 14-5
Population distribution in Japan.
Population density in Japan is
extremely high, especially when
measured as physiological density, or as persons per unit of
arable land. Much of Japan's
land is mountainous and unusable for agriculture. The large
population, agricultural needs,
and massive urbanization provide great land-use pressures.

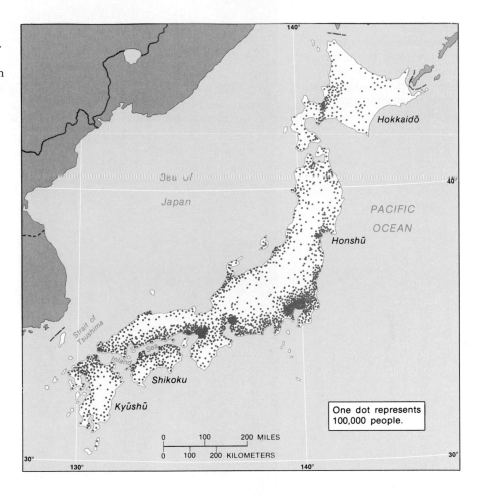

the nineteenth century, they intensified their efforts
even more. Their shortage of domestic raw materials was an added stimulus. As a result, Japan became one of the world's major maritime powers by
the time of World War I, a position it holds to this
day. In fact, in the post–World War II era Japan
surged ahead as the leading shipbuilder in the
world. Even though Japan's shipbuilding industry is
not as strong today because of competition from
other, lower-cost Asian producers (especially South
Korea), the Japanese merchant fleet remains one of
the world's largest. Access to the sea, for both fishing and transport of trade goods, remains vital to the
physical survival of Japan.

Agricultural Resources

Forests still cover more than 65 percent of Japan's land
area, one of the highest proportions of any of the
world's developed nations. Unlike the Chinese, who

have not been particularly conservation-minded
through most of their long history, the Japanese have
treated their forest lands with great care, in spite of
high population density and a demand for agricultural
land. Their motivation has stemmed partly from the
fact that the forests are found primarily on the steeper
slopes, which are unsuited to agriculture, and partly
from the importance of wood products in the
Japanese culture. Even today, the majority of the
Japanese prefer to live in detached wooden houses,
although economic necessity is forcing a growing proportion to live in apartment blocks. In addition, wood
and charcoal are important domestic fuels; and the
great relative importance of hydroelectric power, as
well as the need for abundant irrigation water for
growing paddy rice, has long encouraged the
Japanese to respect the role of forested watersheds.
Still, the demand for forest products far exceeds domestic production, and such products are among
Japan's major imports (see Chapter 15).

Figure 14-6
Pedestrian traffic on Ginza Street in Tokyo. The Tokyo metropolitan region contains nearly 29 million people, the largest urban concentration in the world.

Preservation of the forests has helped to protect Japan's valuable water resources, though the rivers are not without problems. Because of their shortness, steep gradients, and relatively small drainage basins, the rivers are subject to flash flooding and landslides after heavy rains. Such rains are often associated with **typhoons**, the Asian equivalent of hurricanes, which may strike Japan several times a year, particularly in late summer.

Within the limited areas suitable for agriculture, the most important resource is, of course, the soil. Japan's soils are not particularly good, partly because of their intensive use for so many centuries and partly because of the country's geologic and topographic character. The most important soils are the alluvial deposits on floodplains, deltas, and alluvial fans. These, the most productive soils, are used primarily for rice cultivation (Figure 14–7). Japan's high productivity in agriculture is directly dependent on large inputs of chemical and organic fertilizers, as well as very careful cultivation techniques.

Mineral Resources

Japan lost the resource lottery for minerals; the country is practically devoid of significant deposits. As a result, the Japanese have had to rely overwhelmingly on imported raw materials for

Figure 14-7
Transplanting rice seedlings on the alluvial coastal plain in Japan. Even though the Japanese farm population has diminished, agriculture still exhibits considerable labor intensity. Many of the Japanese farm part-time and also hold other jobs.

their industrial development. The country's present dependence on imports ranges from 100 percent for such metals as aluminum and nickel to 55 percent for zinc. In addition, Japan must import virtually all of its iron ore and petroleum, most of its coking coal, and almost all of its copper.

Among the important raw materials needed for industry, the country is self-sufficient only in limestone and sulfur.

Demand for all kinds of raw materials has mushroomed in the post–World War II period. Raw materials (interpreted in the broadest sense to include foodstuffs, minerals and metals, and fuels) now account for more than 50 percent of Japan's total imports; and they are the reason for more than 40 percent of Japanese investment overseas. Foreign trade thus assumes special importance for Japan, when compared with other major industrial countries such as the United States and Russia, which are far more self-sufficient. The desire to secure permanent sources of raw materials was one of the reasons for Japan's imperial expansion earlier in this century, and it remains a critical consideration.

Japan's energy resources clearly illustrate the country's dependence. Until the 1950s the primary energy source was coal. With subsequent expansion of the economy, however, the increased demand for energy came to be met mainly by petroleum (Figure 14–8). Since the two oil crises of the 1970s, conservation efforts have managed to reduce petroleum consumption by substituting other forms of energy. As a result, the total volume of imported crude oil declined in the mid-1980s, in spite of falling oil prices. Nonetheless, oil remains Japan's largest single import commodity, accounting for about 14 percent of its total imports. And Japan still spends ap-

proximately $30 billion a year for oil, thus remaining hostage to the volatile world oil economy. The bulk of Japan's oil is imported from Persian Gulf producers, with the United Arab Emirates and Saudi Arabia the dominant suppliers. About 74 percent of Japan's oil imports currently come from the Middle East, the remainder from Indonesia, Mexico, and increasingly China.

Coal remains Japan's second major source of energy, with most of it coming from Australia and the United States; and hydropower continues to provide about 5 percent of energy needs. The biggest gain, however, has been in nuclear power, which rose from almost nothing in the early 1970s to around 10 percent of Japan's total energy consumption by the end of the 1980s. In spite of opposition from some environmentalists, Japan remains committed to further expansion of nuclear energy, which accounted for more than one-fourth of electricity generation by the late 1980s and is projected to reach 60 percent by the year 2030. Japan has an extreme dependence on foreign supplies of natural resources, especially when compared to the United States, Germany, France, and the United Kingdom (Table 14–1 and Table 14–2).

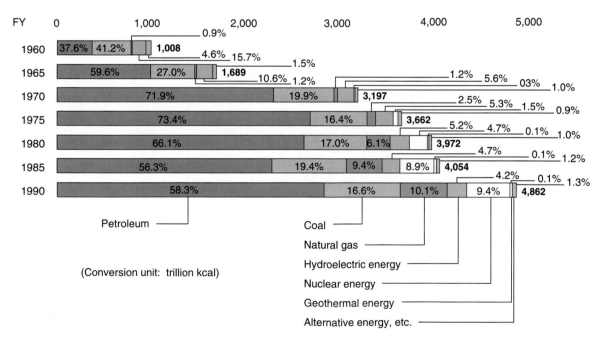

Figure 14–8
Japan's changing energy sources. Because Japan has few local energy resources, all of the petroleum and much of the coal it uses must be imported. Industry is the principal user of energy in Japan. (From *Statistical Handbook of Japan 1990*, Tokyo: Statistics Bureau, Management and Coordination Agency, p. 41.)

Table 14-1
Dependence of selected countries on imported natural resources in 1989.

	Percentage of Dependence[a]				
	Japan	United States	Germany	France	Great Britain
Energy[b]	84.5	17.5	51.3	53.4	3.3
Coal	92.1	−13.6[c]	−2.7[c]	55.5	10.8
Oil	99.6	43.5	92.5	95.2	−2.6[c]
Natural Gas	95.8	7.0	76.2	80.5	19.2
Iron Ore[d]	100.0	27.1	99.8	77.5	99.8
Copper	98.9	0.0	100.0	100.0	99.8
Lead	93.0	9.7	95.7	99.0	98.8
Zinc	82.9	69.8	84.6	90.8	97.0
Tin	100.0	99.7	100.0	100.0	0.0
Bauxite	100.0	71.3	97.9	62.8	84.4
Nickel	100.0	100.0	100.0	0.0	100.0

Source: OECD, Energy Balances of OECD Countries, 1980/1989; WBMS, World Metal Statistics, ILZSG, as reported in *Japan 1993: An International Comparison* (Tokyo: Japan Institute for Social and Economic Affairs), p. 65.

[a]The percentage of dependence is derived from the following formula:

$$\frac{\text{Import volume} - \text{Export volume}}{\text{Volume of domestic production} + \text{Import volume} - \text{Export volume}} \times 100$$

[b]Calculations included coal, coke, oil, natural gas, hydroelectric power, and nuclear-generated electricity, expressed in oil-equivalent terms.

[c]A negative value indicates a surplus of the percentage shown.

[d]Figures are for 1990.

Table 14-2
Largest suppliers of Japan's imported resources in 1990.

Value of Imported Resource (in millions of U.S. dollars)		Largest Suppliers (with percentages of total imported resource[a])		
		No. 1	No. 2	No. 3
Crude Oil	$31,584	United Arab Emirates (21.8)	Saudi Arabia (20.0)	Indonesia (12.6)
Wood	7,472	United States (39.3)	Malaysia (24.2)	Canada (15.0)
Coal	6,187	Australia (48.6)	Canada (21.7)	United States (12.3)
Iron Ore	3,374	Australia (39.0)	Brazil (26.5)	India (15.8)
Copper	2,441	Canada (27.1)	Philippines (11.3)	United States (11.2)
Pulp	1,922	United States (40.1)	Canada (36.1)	Brazil (7.2)

Source: Japan Tariff Association, Foreign Trade Almanac, 1991, as reported in *Japan 1993: An International Comparison* (Tokyo: Japan Institute for Social and Economic Affairs), p. 66.

[a]Calculated on the basis of value.

HUMAN RESOURCES: THE HYBRID CULTURE

No attempt to understand Japan would be complete without some examination of the nature of Japan's human resources, particularly from the perspective of ethnic composition, cultural development, and social characteristics. Much is made of the homogeneity of Japan's people; the Japanese themselves are fond of stressing that as one of their superior attributes (Figure 14–9). Certainly the Japanese are a far more homogeneous people than the pluralistic countries of Anglo-America, and that racial and cultural homogeneity has been a source of strength because it has helped to foster a sense of national identity, which has been critical to Japan's successful modernization in the past century.

Japan's homogeneity, however, is far from complete and has been achieved by forcing conformity on all who deviate from socially accepted norms. Japan does, indeed, have ethnic and cultural minorities (see the boxed feature The Outsiders: Minorities in Japan). More than 800,000 Koreans and some 250,000 Chinese live in Japan, largely as a legacy of the colonial era. A few thousand Ainu also remain, along with a much larger cultural minority— the *burakumin*, or social outcasts, who are a carry-over from Japan's feudal past. Those ethnic and cultural minorities still tend to be treated badly by the Japanese majority, and employment opportunities are often restricted to the most menial of tasks. Such basic **ethnocentrism**—the attitude that one's ethnic group is superior—is held to be a principal factor in the difficulties Japan sometimes has in foreign relations, particularly with nearby Asian neighbors such as Korea and China.

The Emergence of the Japanese

The distinctive linguistic and physical identity of the Japanese emerged some 2,000 years ago. The language of the Japanese is polysyllabic and highly inflected, similar to Korean and the Altaic languages of northern Asia. The written form of Japanese continues to use a large number of Chinese characters but is actually very different from Chinese. In fact, language was one of the factors that helped Japan preserve its cultural distinctiveness.

In physical form the Japanese are basically homogeneous today, though numerous racial strains have been blended into that ethnic group over a long period. Neolithic peoples with partially Mongoloid racial features inhabited the islands for several millennia—hunting, fishing, and gathering. But the primary racial infusion into the Japanese stock came from the **Mongoloid** peoples—the major Asian racial stock—who migrated from the mainland via the Korean peninsula, starting with the Han dynasty (206 B.C. to A.D. 220). The Ainu were also important in the creation of the modern Japanese. A proto-Caucasoid people who inhabited much of

Figure 14–9
Japanese family members in their small home. Many in Japan have adopted Western cultural ways, but differences between traditional and modern Japan often appear as generational features.

THE OUTSIDERS: MINORITIES IN JAPAN

Japan's human resources and culture are not as purely homogeneous as popular myth would suggest: ethnic and social minorities make up approximately 4 percent of the population, or roughly 5 million people. The ethnic minorities consist of Koreans, Chinese, Okinawans, Ainu, and foreign residents; the social minorities are composed of the *burakumin,* handicapped persons, and children of interracial ancestry.

The cultural homogeneity that Japan does have has been obtained through racism and discrimination against any deviants—ethnic or social—from the cultural/social mainstream, even against those who are physically impaired. The Japanese regard themselves as a unique people, with a culture and a history completely different from that of other races. They sometimes refer to themselves as the **Yamato people,** in reference to the Yamato Plain around Kyoto, where the Japanese culture and state developed in centuries past and from which the ancestry of the imperial family is derived. There is a strong current in Japanese society to preserve the purity of the majority, or Yamato, strain; anyone else is automatically an outsider and can never hope to be fully accepted in the mainstream. The 1947 constitution expressly prohibits discrimination in political, economic, or social relations because of race, creed, sex, social status, or family origin. But that United States–imposed provision has been unable to fundamentally alter many centuries-old attitudes and practices.

Among the ethnic minorities the Koreans are the largest group and the one that suffers most. Numbering more than 800,000, the Koreans first came to Japan during the colonial occupation (1910–1945), when thousands were forcibly brought or enticed to move to Japan as low-cost laborers. By the end of World War II some 2.5 million Koreans were living in Japan. Those who chose to remain after the war were deprived of citizenship when the Japanese government declared them aliens in the 1952 peace treaty with the United States.

Birth in Japan does not guarantee citizenship even today, and the government makes it very difficult for Koreans to obtain citizenship, although most of them have Japanese names, speak the language fluently, and have attempted to integrate into Japanese society. The Koreans remain mired at the lower end of the economic ladder, victims of social and economic discrimination. They are heavily concentrated in ghettos in the Kinki (Kyoto-Osaka) area and in places such as Saiwaku, a section of the industrial city of Kawasaki (south of Tokyo), where they struggle to make a living and to survive in a hostile environment.

The **Ainu** were among the earliest inhabitants of Japan. Racially different, they, too, were treated as aliens by the Yamato Japanese. The Ainu have been reduced by warfare, disease, and —since the turn of the century—a low birthrate. Fewer than 25,000 Ainu remain, almost all of whom live in a few parts of Hokkaido Island. The Ainu have been heavily assimilated into Japanese culture, but a few, like the American Indians, struggle to maintain some of their ethnic and cultural identity.

The **Okinawans,** in the Ryukyu Islands south of Kyushu, were not politically incorporated into Japan until early in the seventeenth century, even though they are of basically the same stock as the majority Japanese. Isolated from the main islands and speaking a variant form of Japanese, the Okinawans have been treated as second-class citizens ever since their incorporation—something like Japanese hillbillies. Their position is reflected in a lower standard of living, lower educational levels, and various forms of discrimination.

Even foreign residents in Japan, such as Filipinos and Thais, who are in Japan only temporarily as low-cost workers or in other capacities, suffer all sorts of restrictions and discrimination. Indeed, there is strong opposition to allowing large-scale labor migration to Japan, despite the fact that the labor force is shrinking as the population ages and the Japanese are displaying increasing disdain for low-wage menial labor. Foreigners within the country, including Americans, are—at best—tolerated as a necessity of Japan's global economy.

The largest and most abused social minority in Japan is the *burakumin.* They are physically indistinguishable from other Japanese; they have the same racial and cultural origins. However, somewhat like India's untouchables, Japan's *burakumin* have been discriminated against for centuries because of their past association with the slaughtering of animals and similar occupations. In Buddhism and Shintoism, the two major religions of Japan, those activities are regarded as polluting and defiling. Thus, a subclass of Japanese people has been branded forever as unfit for association with the "pure" majority. That discrimination was formalized and legalized during the **Edo period** (1600–1868), and it is still deeply entrenched in Japanese society despite government and private efforts to root it out.

Most of the *burakumin,* who number between 2 and 3 million, live in ghettos scattered throughout the country. Denied access to better-paying jobs, housing, and other benefits of Japan's economic miracle, they eke out a living at the bottom of the socioeconomic ladder. Many *burakumin* try to hide their origin and quietly integrate into the mainstream of society, but they are usually found out when background checks are made for marriage or employment.

Resistance by minorities through such actions as lawsuits, sometimes with the support of enlightened Japanese, is beginning to crack the system and bring a certain amount of improvement. But some people argue that discrimination will never disappear completely, given the cultural attitudes of the Japanese majority.

northern Japan, the Ainu are still found in small numbers on the island of Hokkaido. Their influence is believed to account for the fact that some Japanese today have more facial and body hair than do Koreans or Chinese. In addition, other traits may have been acquired from the peoples of Southeast Asia through diffusion along coastal southern China (Figure 14–10).

The Settling of Japan

Along with the Mongoloid peoples from the mainland came paddy-rice agriculture and the use of bronze and iron. Domesticated animals—such as horses, cattle, and pigs—also came via that route. During succeeding centuries the settlers gradually moved farther eastward along the margins of the Inland Sea. That area provided the optimum environment—in terms of climate, soil, fishing, and water transportation—for the development of Japan's culture hearth. By the eighth century the focus of political and cultural power was centered in the Yamato Plain, lowlands at the eastern end of the Inland Sea. Nara for a short time and then Kyoto for more than 1,000 years were the political capitals of Japan, which continued for several centuries to borrow from and adapt the Chinese civilization. Ultimately, the Japanese acquired much more than language from China: Confucian values, Buddhism, the emperor system (diluted to preserve the power of Japanese clans), city design, architecture, art, music, and more.

Figure 14-10

Origin and spread of Japanese culture. Many of Japan's cultural characteristics originated in China, but Japan's insular location ultimately fostered the development of a distinctive culture. The Japanese culture hearth first began to form along the Sea of Japan and the Strait of Tsushima; it then spread to the Inland Sea area, especially the Yamato Plain, and eventually northward to the Kanto Plain (Tokyo).

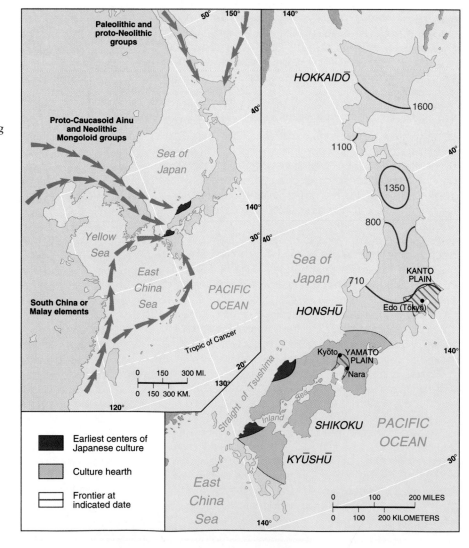

As the Japanese settlements moved northward through Honshu, they encountered the very different Ainu. The clash of cultures and the demand for land resulted in military struggles along the frontier similar to the clashes between European settlers and American Indians. Most of the Ainu retreated. As the Japanese reached northern Honshu in the ninth century, they found themselves in a forested environment with a much cooler climate and few directly usable land resources. Clearing the land for agriculture was difficult, and the shorter growing season prevented a high population density. Consequently, the development of Japan focused on the area south of about the 37th parallel.

During the **Tokugawa period** (1615–1868) the focus of power shifted further eastward to Tokyo (then called Edo) in the Kanto Plain. Today, Japan's core area remains in essentially the same region in which the nation's foundations were laid and in which its early growth took place. That core is a belt between approximately 34°N and 36°N latitude, extending from Tokyo on the east to Shimonoseki at the western end of Honshu and encompassing the Inland Sea. The major share of Japan's population, cities, industry, and modern economy are still concentrated in that zone (see Figure 14–2).

SUMMARY
Japanese Achievement in a Land of Scarcity

Japan is a very rich nation; indeed, it is the only non-Western country to have achieved such a high overall level of economic well-being. Deficient in good agricultural land, lacking in the minerals essential to industrial development, and acutely short of space, Japan nevertheless has produced a spectacular economy by honing its human resources into remarkable and efficient achievers.

The basic character of the Japanese has been shaped by a variety of forces over a long period of time. Homogeneity is one of the attributes of Japanese society that is regarded as a major contributor to the success of Japanese development. Within that homogeneity Confucianism and Buddhism have played important roles in instilling the virtues of self-denial, stressing the responsibilities and obligations of the individual within a clearly defined social hierarchy, and putting the interests of the group ahead of the wishes of the individual. Those social characteristics have helped to unify the nation behind its leaders, who can rely on the total commitment of the people to whatever goals are set forth. Although the unparalleled affluence of recent years is beginning to weaken some of those social characteristics, at least in the eyes of critics, the Japanese remain one of the most vigorous and purposeful societies in the world.

KEY TERMS

Ainu	Japan, Inc.
aquaculture	Mongoloid
burakumin	Okinawans
double-cropping	orogenic zone
economic imperialism	Pacific Rim
Edo period	Tokugawa period
ethnocentrism	typhoons
Inland Sea	Yamato people

15

Japan:
The Economic Giant

Fishing fleet in Nagasaki harbor in Kyushu. Japan's
scarcity of industrial resources requires that a great
volume of mineral fuels and other materials be imported.
The numerous natural harbors facilitate access to the sea.
Japan is also one of the world's major fishing nations.

It can be said of virtually every nation-state that understanding its present requires knowledge of its past. In the case of Japan the extraordinary nature of the country today is difficult to comprehend without some understanding of the roots of its seemingly enigmatic society and its powerful economic system. The birth of modern Japan is commonly associated with the **Meiji Restoration** in 1868, when a group of young Japanese revolutionaries overthrew the feudal Tokugawa rulers and embarked on one of the most dramatic and successful national transformations in modern history. Outwardly, Japan appears today to be the most Westernized nation in Asia, but inwardly it remains firmly rooted in its own cultural traditions.

In a manner of speaking, Japan has gone through **three transformations** since the Meiji Restoration. The first consisted of modernization and industrialization during the Meiji period (1868–1914) in the late nineteenth century, with a move to heavy industry and militarization that reached its peak with World War II. The second transformation was the reconstruction and return to international power in the postwar period. The third transformation, now in its formative stages, involves the search for new directions in a world of increasing competition and discontent with past strategies.

JAPAN'S FIRST TRANSFORMATION: RISING TO POWER

The Japanese experience illustrates the kind of cooperation and balance needed between government and people in the economic development of a nation. Nineteenth-century Japanese leaders recognized the military superiority of the West. They also saw with alarm how widespread foreign influence was in China because that country had failed to respond adequately to the challenge of the West. Japan's leaders were determined that a similar fate would not befall their country.

Accordingly, the Japanese adopted a pragmatic step-by-step approach and within a mere fifty years from the Meiji Restoration created a sound and modernized economy, achieving national security and international equality in the process. Their achievement was due in part to the government's provision of a proper environment for development. Feudal restrictions were removed from trade within the country and from individual activities. Sound currency, a banking system, reasonable taxation, and efficient government were provided. In addition, the government took a direct role in pioneering many industrial fields and encouraging businessmen to move into new and risky ventures. The government also helped fund many ventures, providing private entrepreneurs with aid and privileges. Active cooperation between government and big business worked well in Japan and during this period, and such cooperation continues to be a basic characteristic of the economy.

The role of the people was equally important in making the transformation a success, however. Thousands of individual Japanese responded to new economic opportunities, and in the long run their private initiative was the driving force behind Japan's economic modernization.

According to the Rostow model, Japan passed from the traditional-society stage to preconditions for takeoff at the beginning of the Meiji period and continued in that second stage through the remainder of the century, as the foundations for later growth were laid. A critical aspect of the process was the emphasis, during the first two decades of the Meiji period, on developing the traditional areas of the economy: agriculture, commerce, and cottage industry. There was no attempt to build modern industry immediately and directly on a weak local economy, as many developing nations in the postwar period have mistakenly tried to do.

The Growth of Industry and Empire

The modern industries that were deemed important by the Japanese government were those on which military power depended. Hence, the government led the way in developing shipbuilding, munitions, iron and steel, and modern communications. The first railroad was built between Tokyo and Yokohama in 1872. At the same time, as the need for importing raw materials grew, export industries were encouraged, particularly silk and textiles.

At the end of the nineteenth century, the country still had a small industrial base. In a quantitative sense Japan's takeoff period did not begin until after the Russo-Japanese War of 1905. Then industry blossomed. Between 1900 and the late 1930s the production of manufactured goods increased more than twelvefold. Export trade grew twentyfold in the same period, with manufactured goods accounting for most of the increase. The Japanese excelled at producing inexpensive light-industrial and consumer goods more cheaply than many other countries—an approach to production that has continued to serve the Japanese well. Foreign markets, however, played a less important role in that export strategy than is commonly believed. Japan's economic growth in the early twentieth century was largely self-generated.

Two decisive events that shaped the course of Japan's development in the twentieth century were its victories over China in 1895 and over Russia in 1905. Those two wars had a number of consequences. For one thing, they started Japan on a course of imperial conquest that ended in the disaster of World War II. That course was partly an imitation of the colonial practices of modern Western nations, but it was also partly a quest for secure sources of raw materials and markets for industrial goods. As a result of the two wars, Japan's territory was greatly expanded: it controlled Taiwan, Korea, and parts of China, including Manchuria (see Figure 14–3). By the end of World War I, Japan was a fully accepted imperial world power.

The Growth of Population and the Development of Agriculture

A significant change that accompanied the modernization of Japan after 1868 was an upsurge in population growth. During the latter half of Tokugawa rule, Japan's population had stabilized at about 33 million. Between 1868 and 1940, however, Japan provided a classic illustration of the interaction of economic and demographic factors; as industrialization and urbanization proceeded, both birthrates and death rates declined. Population began to increase at an average rate of only about 1.5 percent per year, but that rate was sufficient to more than double the population, to just over 73 million, by 1940.

At the close of the Tokugawa era in 1868, about four-fifths of the labor force was engaged in agriculture, forestry, or fishing. From that time to the present, the rural population has declined steadily in proportion to the urban population, even though it did not start declining in absolute terms until just before World War II. Today, agricultural workers constitute only about 10 percent of the total labor force.

Yet, even as the percentage of farmers was declining, production was increasing rapidly, right up

until World War I. Japanese agriculture at that time was characterized by more efficient irrigation, better crop strains, pest control, and, above all, the lavish application of fertilizers. As a result, the farmers succeeded in supplying all but a small part of the increased demand for rice that accompanied the population growth and the rise in per capita consumption. As Japan's population continued to expand, however, the country's ability to feed itself declined steadily, and reliance on the colonies of Taiwan and Korea increased.

After World War I the declining self-sufficiency in rice stimulated considerable spatial expansion in agriculture (Figure 15–1). Much of the agricultural land that is now farmed in northern Honshu and Hokkaido—including the terraced hillsides so common in those regions—was brought into cultivation at that time. Hokkaido farms, which often specialize in dairying and are ten times the national average in size, still reflect the reduced land pressure of that period. Nevertheless, the average Japanese farm remained extremely small, and productivity depended on heavy labor input on tiny, fragmented fields (Figure 15–2). In addition, many Japanese farmers did not even control their own land but functioned instead as tenant farmers. Not surprisingly, then, as industrialization progressed, the gap between urban and rural standards of living continued to increase. And as a result, there was a growing tendency for rural people to seek part-time employment in secondary economic activities; rice alone was not able to sustain an acceptable standard. Many farmers raised silkworms, and large numbers of rural people, especially young women, worked in silk mills.

During that time from World War I to the late 1930s, Japan was going through its drive-to-maturity stage of development; agriculture was receding in relative importance as secondary and tertiary activities were expanding dramatically. The transfer of workers from agriculture to industry, which was further hastened by the depression of the 1930s, kept industrial wages down. And those low wages, combined with technical improvements during the period, enabled Japanese industry to remain competitive in world markets. Textile and food-processing industries gradually gave way to heavy industry, especially as Japan militarized in the 1930s.

The war years, between 1937 and 1945, saw a reversal of sorts; since Japan's economy was geared to the war effort, personal consumption was met with

Figure 15–1
Land utilization in Japan. Nearly 75 percent of Japan is unusable for agriculture. Farms on Honshu, Shikoku, and Kyushu remain small and are intensively worked, with rice the dominant grain crop. Agriculture in less densely populated Hokkaido, a middle-latitude environment, is less intensive, and farms are commonly larger than they are in the remainder of Japan. Self-sufficiency in agriculture is steadily declining in Japan.

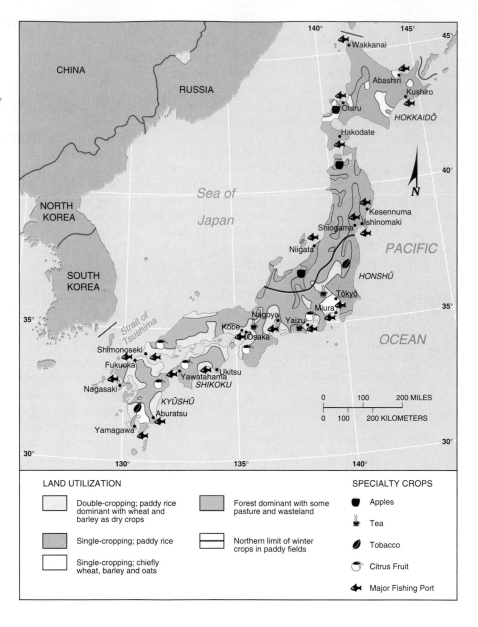

austerity and shortages. Japan's extreme vulnerability—its lack of domestic raw materials—doomed the nation to eventual defeat.

JAPAN'S SECOND TRANSFORMATION: RISING FROM THE ASHES OF WAR

When Japan surrendered in August, 1945, the nation was prostrate. Destruction from the war had been catastrophic, especially in urban and indus-

trial areas. Stripped of its empire, the nation consisted only of the main archipelago; and the future of the 72 million Japanese people seemed bleak indeed.

Within a decade, however, Japan was thriving. Most of the physical destruction of the war had been erased, and the nation was soon well on its way to regaining a position of economic might in Asia and the world. In a manner of speaking, Japan had gone through a compressed repetition of the

Figure 15–2
Combining of rice in Japan. Miniature mechanization is common in the form of small tillers, tractors, and threshers.

takeoff and drive-to-maturity stages. The war had been a costly mistake, but Japan quickly made up for lost time.

The postwar revival is attributable in substantial part to the resilient fiber of the Japanese people. War does not destroy the inherent qualities of a strong society, and Japan, like Germany in 1918 and 1945, still had a solid base of educated, technically proficient people. Its able administrators and entrepreneurs were eager to seize the reins and rebuild the nation, just as fast as the American occupation authorities would allow. At the same time the Cold War in the late 1940s and the victory in China of the communists in 1949 let the United States to return control of the government to the Japanese much faster than might otherwise have been the case. The United States needed a strong Japanese ally.

The Role of the United States

American assistance took several forms. Financial aid was especially critical immediately after the war. It consisted of billions of dollars in foodstuffs, military procurement orders during the Korean War (1950–1953), and other aid. Of even greater long-range benefit was the open-door policy for Japanese exports to the United States. By the early 1990s the United States was buying almost 30 percent of Japan's total exports. Another form of assistance was military protection, which enabled Japan to spend less than 1 percent of its annual GNP for defense. Also beneficial was American technology. With their own facilities nearly leveled by the war, the Japanese bought American technology at bargain prices and used it to revitalize their industry. Thus, they gained a competitive advantage over many

355

other countries, including the United States, whose plants and technology were much older and could not be replaced so easily.

The Development Strategy of the Japanese

The policies of the Japanese government and business community were probably even more important to Japan's revival than U.S. assistance was. Close cooperation between government and business continued, grew, and remains the pattern today. That cooperation was particularly important in financing the modernization process. Banking credit was backed by the government, which made heavy capital investment possible. The Japanese economy was geared to a high-growth-rate strategy that relied on large increases in productivity to provide surpluses to pay back capital debts. High rates of personal savings gave the banks more money to loan out, and since banks are more patient than stockholders, Japanese firms were able to concentrate on long-range strategies and research. Two-thirds of the capital requirements of the average Japanese company were met by loans from banks and only one-third by stock; the reverse is the system in the United States.

The Japanese strategy worked. The GNP grew at an average rate of almost 9 percent per year in the 1950s, more than 11 percent in the 1960s, and more than 10 percent in the 1970s. The maturing of the economy by the 1980s caused the growth rate to slow down to about 4 percent per year during that decade, but that rate was still higher than the growth rates in most industrialized countries. In fact, Japan passed the United States in per capita income (on a dollar basis) by the late 1980s.

To a far greater degree than has occurred in the United States, the Japanese government has guided the economy; yet Japan's system is far from a centrally planned, command-type economy, as in communist countries. Growth industries are selected and then supported with generous assistance of many kinds, including high depreciation allowances, inexpensive loans, subsidies, and low taxes. In addition, the results of research carried out in government laboratories are turned over to companies for commercial development.

As Japan's economy has grown, its industry has shifted to capital-intensive heavy industry. Textiles and food processing, which had dominated until the war years, shrank rapidly in importance after 1950.

At that time the government stimulus shifted to iron and steel, petrochemicals, machinery, automobiles and other transportation equipment, precision tools, and electronics. Heavy industry's share of total industrial production passed the 50 percent mark around 1965. In iron and steel alone Japan surpassed France, Great Britain, and West Germany in the early 1960s to become the world's third-largest steel-producing nation. It moved ahead of the United States in the early 1970s and was second only to the former Soviet Union in steel production in 1991, and it may now well be ahead of Russia in production (Figure 15–3). Japan remains the world's largest exporter of steel, a remarkable accomplishment for a country with almost no coal and iron ore resources of its own.

Although the Japanese government does all it can to help industries that have a potential for growth, it has little sympathy for industries that have lost their comparative advantage. The attitude is that uncompetitive industries should not be subsidized, so that resources can be directed toward more efficient enterprises. That transfer of resources from less efficient to more efficient sectors is an important ingredient of economic progress.

During the 1950s and 1960s, especially, Japan followed a protectionist policy by raising tariff barriers against foreign products. Foreign investment in Japan was also restricted. The rationale for that policy was that Japan's economy was too weak to withstand uncontrolled imports and foreign investment. By the mid-1970s, however, the tariff and foreign-investment barriers began to fall, and Japan is now a much more open country economically, though probably not open enough to satisfy foreign critics completely. Much of the frustration of foreign companies trying to do business in Japan stems from their difficulty in penetrating the complex marketing system, and that difficulty often stems from ignorance of the Japanese and their culture.

The *Zaibatsu*

Corporate structure has also played a key role in Japan's development. When any traditional country industrializes, it experiences a shortage of capital, skilled labor, and technical resources. To obtain rapid growth, resources must be concentrated. In the late nineteenth and early twentieth centuries the concentration of resources in Japan fell into private hands, and the *zaibatsu,* or financial cliques,

Figure 15-3
Crude steel production Japan.
Japan recently became the second-ranking steel producer worldwide after surpassing the United States. (From *Statistical Handbook of Japan 1990*, Tokyo: Statistics Bureau, Management and Coordination Agency, p. 82.)

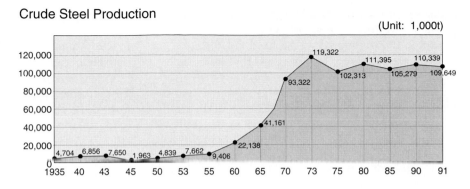

Crude Steel Production

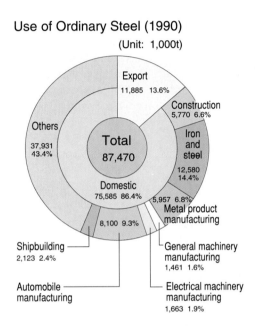

Use of Ordinary Steel (1990)

emerged out of the close relationship between government and business. The *zaibatsu* worked through vertical and horizontal integration of the economy; thus, a single *zaibatsu* may have controlled an entire operation, from obtaining raw materials to retailing the final product. The nearest equivalent in the West is a giant conglomerate or multinational corporation. By the 1920s the *zaibatsu*—particularly the big three of Mitsui, Mitsubishi, and Sumitomo—controlled a large part of the nation's economic power.

The *zaibatsu* were efficient and provided the entrepreneurial strength that led to modernization. Despite their monopolistic tendencies, *zaibatsu* prices stayed competitive because of the importance of foreign markets and raw materials. And even though much of the nation's wealth became concentrated in a few immensely rich and powerful families, enough profits filtered down to establish a substantial and growing Japanese middle class.

Efforts by the U.S. occupation authorities to break up the *zaibatsu* were not very successful. Many reemerged after the occupation and were joined by other giant corporations outside the *zaibatsu* system.

The Double Structure of the Economy

A peculiar double structure has long characterized Japan's economy. Basically, the structure consists of a handful of giant combines, thousands of tiny workshops, and relatively few medium-sized firms. That structure had fully emerged by the 1930s and was, in part, the result of a **split technology,** with the leaders of modern industry following Western technology and the owners of small shops staying rooted in the traditional ways of old Japan.

Because of large outlays for advanced techniques, the giant, modernized companies have succeeded in greatly increasing the productivity of their labor force over the years. The medium-sized and small firms have relatively little capital outlay and rely on cheap labor (e.g., women and part-time workers) to make their products competitive. Surprisingly, the relationship between the two levels of that economic hierarchy is close. The larger companies job out substantial parts of their production to the smaller firms to keep expenses down.

In the postwar period the rapid growth of large industries, accompanied by a sharply decreased rate of population growth, has caused the percentage of workers in small industries to decline. Nevertheless, even though the double structure of the economy is diminishing, about 70 percent of Japan's labor force is still employed by small and medium-sized firms; only about 30 percent works in the large firms.

Population Stabilization

In 1945 Japan faced the specter of becoming so densely populated that the quality of life would deteriorate seriously. To control population growth, the government passed the Eugenics Protection Law in 1948, legalizing abortion. In addition, efforts were made to spread birth-control practices, and public education stressed the advantages of small families. Other factors—including more years of education, later marriage, and the two-child family—also contributed to a steady decline in the rate of population growth.

Even though the total population of Japan now approaches 125 million, the annual growth rate has fallen to barely 0.3 percent, one of the lowest rates in the world. Accordingly, the age structure of Japan's population has changed significantly since 1950, with a sharp decline in the youthful age group and a large increase in the over-65 age group (Figure 15–4). The total population is expected to peak at approximately 136 million in about the year 2013.

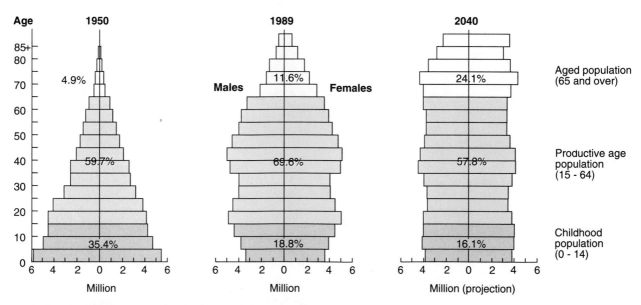

Figure 15-4
Japan's changing population structure. The percentage of Japan's population under fifteen years of age has been declining and will continue to do so for some time. The older population, in contrast, will continue to increase for many years, as it does in highly developed countries with low rates of population increase and low death rates. (From *Statistical Handbook of Japan 1990,* Tokyo: Statistics Bureau, Management and Coordination Agency, p. 19.)

The Growth of Cities and Industry

One of the most dramatic developments of the postwar era, and one with profound consequences for Japan, has been the rapid increase in urbanization. In 1950 there were 6.2 million farm households, almost the same number that existed during the early Meiji period. By the early 1990s that number had declined to less than 4 million. Farm population as a percentage of the total population declined from 85 percent early in the Meiji period to about 50 percent in 1945 and barely 14 percent in the late 1980s. Urban population, in turn, increased. As late as 1960 the urban population accounted for less than half of the population; today that figure is around 80 percent. Thus, Japan's transformation to a predominantly urbanized nation has taken place relatively recently.

A striking characteristic of the urbanization in Japan is the concentration of that urban population in a small portion of the country, in cities scattered through the core area from Kitakyushu/Shimonoseki at the western end to Tokyo in the east (see Figure 14–2). In between are scores of smaller cities, such as Hiroshima, Okayama, Oita, Takamatsu, Tsu, and Shizuoka.

The urban concentration is most intense in three huge urban nodes, which are gradually coalescing into what is called the **Tokaido megalopolis** (Figure 15–5), named after an old post road that ran through the region in pre-Meiji times. The three nodes are Tokyo-Yokohama, Nagoya, and Osaka-Kobe-Kyoto. Today, approximately 53 million people, or about 43 percent of Japan's total population, live in those three nodes. The Tokyo metropolitan region has 29 million people; the Nagoya region, 8 million; and the Osaka region, 15.9 million. If migration and natural population growth rates continue, 80 million Japanese will live in the Tokaido megalopolis by the year 2000, making it one of the largest urban concentrations in the world.

The remaining 71 million Japanese people are found predominantly in other cities scattered throughout the core region. The few significant cities outside the core region include Sapporo and Hakodate on Hokkaido; Sendai in northern Honshu; and Toyama, Fukui, and Niigata on the Sea of Japan side of Honshu. But all of those cities are relatively small. Southern Shikoku and southern Kyushu have no major cities.

Fortunately, the growth rate in the central cities of the Tokaido megalopolis has slowed almost to a standstill. In the past two decades the trend has been for the fastest growth to occur in the suburbs and satellite cities of the major metropolitan centers, a pattern analogous to the urbanization in the United States in recent years. Of course, that trend further contributes to urban sprawl, which can create major problems for a land-shy nation.

In Japan, as in most developed countries, industrialization provided the major stimulus for urbanization. In Japan's case, however, an important additional factor was the desire of Japan's business and government leaders to concentrate industry, especially heavy industry, in a few areas, most of them near the coast. Concentration was useful to take advantage of economies of scale, and location near the seashore made it cheaper to handle large quantities of imported raw materials, such as iron ore, coal, and oil. Much of the postwar development of industry occurred on reclaimed land built along the shoreline of the Inland Sea and the Pacific coast of the core region (Figure 15–6).

In addition to their general concentration of industry, the Japanese have developed *kombinats*, which are groups of closely interrelated and integrated factories clustered around one or more large-scale core factories. Those complexes are designed so that the products of one factory can be easily and efficiently used by the others. Most of the *kombinats* produce chemicals and petrochemicals and typically include a petroleum refinery; others specialize in iron and steel or other products. The *kombinats* allow huge amounts of bulky raw materials to move from incoming ships into the production process without expensive land transport. In turn, finished products for export can be loaded back onto outgoing ships. *Kombinats* have made a major contribution to Japan's industrial competitiveness, but they have also tended to become primary causes of air and water pollution near major population centers.

The pattern for light- and small-scale industry in Japan is somewhat different. Because access to overseas sources of raw materials and shipping is not as important for them, those types of industry are more widely distributed in both urban and rural areas. Indeed, the incidence of part-time farming in the agricultural sector was made possible, in part, by the distribution of industry in

Figure 15-5
Urban and industrial patterns of Japan. Much of Japan's industrial activity is concentrated along the southern coast of Honshu, particularly in the three regions of Tokyo-Yokohama, Nagoya, and Osaka-Kobe-Kyoto. Those three conurbations constitute the Tokaido megalopolis.

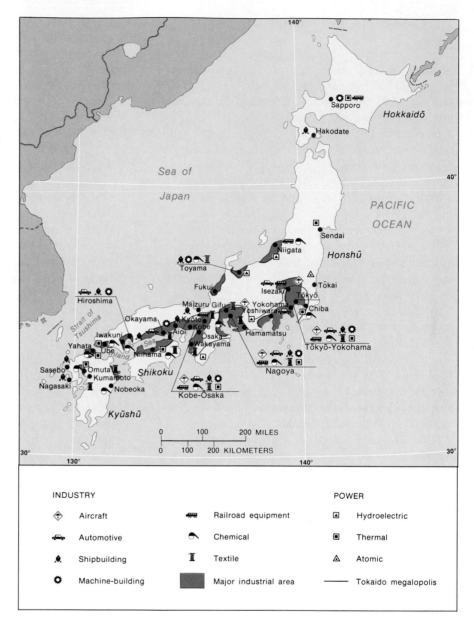

rural areas, where farmers could commute daily between farm home and nonfarm job. As a result, many small towns and nonurban centers around the country have industrial plants that form important bases for local economies. That situation is less prevalent, however, in the northern part of the country, where the environment for industrial development remains less attractive than in the south.

THE CONSEQUENCES OF "JAPAN, INC."

By the 1970s at least, Japan had begun to realize the price it was paying for its development strategy; national attention had been focused on growth in the GNP and on making Japan number one in the world, at the expense of social welfare, the environment, and relations with other nations. Japan had achieved an economic miracle, but the cost was proving to be high.

Figure 15-6
Mazda autos at an export station near Hiroshima on the Inland Sea. Japan's economic system requires the continued import of food, raw materials, and energy resources and the export of manufactured goods. Maintaining markets worldwide is essential to Japan's economic health.

Regional Imbalances

Every country in the world has regional imbalances in its distribution of population and levels of development, but especially sharp contrasts emerged in Japan. The population and modern economy were increasingly concentrated on the outward, or Pacific, side of the nation, at the expense of the inner side, which borders the Sea of Japan. Hokkaido, northern Honshu, the part of Honshu facing the Sea of Japan, southern Shikoku, and southern Kyushu all lost population as massive movement toward the core took place. Then, in the late 1970s and 1980s some industry relocated in underdeveloped parts of the country in an effort to overcome environmental

pollution in the core region. Thus, the gap between the modern, industrialized, urbanized, and densely populated core and "backwoods" Japan has begun to narrow, though the contrast between the two halves of the country is still striking.

Japan's regional imbalance, which has bedeviled the best efforts of the government for several decades, has no easy solution. Some critics contend that part of the solution lies in such measures as decentralizing the Japanese government and making the prefectures larger and more autonomous, especially in taxation and budgeting. That effort might also include moving the national capital, or at least central governmental functions, out of Tokyo to other sites. Frequently mentioned are Sendai (in northern

Honshu), Nagoya, and Kyoto. Others see a **Japan corridor** or **Maglev megalopolis** emerging between Osaka and Tokyo, in which high-tech communications, including a maglev (magnetic levitation) ultra-high speed train system, links together the urban core and diffuses some of the functions now excessively concentrated in the Tokyo region.

Urban Ills

An assortment of urban ills was another by-product of rapid economic growth. One problem began in the 1960s with the advent of the automobile society. Cars have certainly enhanced Japan's prosperity: fully 10 percent of the labor force now works in auto-related jobs. But Japan lacks the space and facilities to adequately accommodate its automobiles, and their impact on the environment, especially the urban environment, has been devastating. Traffic congestion, noise, parking problems, accidents, air pollution—all have escalated rapidly. To deal with those problems, the government has built freeways and elevated roadways and enacted what are probably the world's strictest auto-emission controls, and drivers are tested stringently. Nonetheless, the problems persist. More than 60 million motor vehicles were in use in Japan by 1990. The ratio of cars per person is smaller than that of most major developed countries, especially the United States, but Japan's cars are crammed into a much smaller space with far fewer roads.

To accommodate huge urban populations, the Japanese government has developed some of the finest public transportation systems in the world. In fact, Tokyo functions as well as it does principally because of its superb public transport system which—fortunately—rarely malfunctions. Nonetheless, because demand for public transportation far exceeds capacity during rush hours, commuter trains are crowded to unbelievable levels that would never be tolerated in most developed Western countries.

Other problems have also arisen in the cities. Probably the most critical now is the skyrocketing cost of land and housing. The peculiar policy of taxing farmland in urban areas at very low rates has helped keep that land undeveloped and thus has pushed the price of remaining land even higher. Between 1955 and the late 1980s the cost of land in Japan's major cities increased ninetyfold. Although this speculative bubble burst in the early 1990s, the average middle-class family still can afford only a tiny apartment or a house that is far smaller than the average home in the United States. The average for all of Japan in 1990 was only 869 square feet (80 square meters), compared with an average of 1,744 square feet (162 square meters) in the United States. Affordable, good-quality housing remains a critical social and economic issue (Figure 15–7).

Most foreigners are also struck by the seemingly unplanned, often unaesthetic appearance of Japan's cities, especially Tokyo. Postwar reconstruction

Figure 15-7
Homeless people in a park in Osaka, Japan. Despite its economic success, Japan has not been able to escape such urban ills as homelessness and environmental pollution.

failed to correct the lack of zoning and planning, and the eclectic way in which the Japanese have adopted architectural styles and superficial Westernization sometimes gives their cities a rather bizarre appearance. There is also a relative lack of green space—parks and recreation areas. On the positive side, though, Japan's cities are renowned for their low crime rates and general civility of life.

Pollution of the Environment

Of all of Japan's problems, one of the most infamous has been environmental pollution. Until the late 1960s Japan had done less than any other major industrial nation to protect its natural environment from the effects of uncontrolled industrial development. Traffic police had to breathe pure oxygen periodically while on duty in Tokyo's crowded streets. Factories, intermingled with houses, emitted huge amounts of pollutants, which led to an increase in lung diseases. Organic mercury poisoning was widespread, as were cases of cadmium poisoning. And the reported cases were believed to be merely the tip of the iceberg.

The Japanese government finally recognized the seriousness of the problem and officially declared certain areas to be dangerous to human health. Every city and prefecture in Japan was affected to some degree. Growing public protest forced the government to start taking action in the early 1970s, using a two-pronged attack. One approach was the creation of a national environmental protection agency in 1970, along with the allocation of billions of dollars for fighting pollution. Measures enacted included the emission-control standards for cars already referred to and toughened pollution-control measures for industry. Significant improvements were made by the 1980s; for example, the Sumida River, which flows through Tokyo and used to be known as a stinking sewer, recovered to the point that fish were returning to it. In addition, fishing as an economic activity began to reappear in Tokyo Bay. And Mt. Fuji is visible from Tokyo more than twice as many days a year as it was in 1970. Visitors can also see improvement in the quality of the air and the general cleanliness of the urban environment. The cleanup is far from complete, but the Japanese have certainly made great progress.

The other approach over the years has been to try to shift polluting industries out of congested urban areas, especially the core region. Since the 1960s, Japan has developed four National Comprehensive Development Plans, plus other measures, to promote industri-alization in a regionally planned manner. Those plans have included construction of the *kombinats,* new industrial cities, the **Shinkansen** (a high-speed railway system), tunnels and bridges linking all four main islands, special industrial zones known as **technopolises** for high-tech industry, and more. All of those measures attempted to de-emphasize the Tokaido megalopolis and strengthen the outer areas of Japan, which had been losing population. Unfortunately, even though some of those measures had limited regional success, the net overall effect was that the core area increased its share of urban population and the modern economy. Tokyo increased the most.

Social Problems

Other problems in Japan may be less tangible but are no less important. Many stem from the vast social changes that have spread through Japan since World War II, including the breakdown of the family, the increasing independence of children from parental authority, the rising desire of young married couples to live apart from their parents and relatives, and juvenile delinquency and crime in general (even though those rates remain much below the levels of developed Western countries). Other changes are reflected in the increased freedom of women in a society where women's liberation has been slow to develop; the trend toward pursuit of happiness at the expense of the work ethic; and the neglect of older people, who had always been cared for by the family, not the government. By the year 2040 the over-sixty-five age group is projected to account for 24 percent of Japan's population. Such problems are inseparable aspects of industrialization and urbanization in most countries, but in Japan they have taken on their own special nature.

Social inequality is also considerable in Japan, as a result of the double structure of the economy. Employees in the larger firms, the top 30 percent of the labor force, reaped the greatest benefits from Japan's growth through the 1970s. Those larger businesses fostered a paternalistic relationship between management and workers, and workers tended to stay with a firm for life, identifying with a particular company rather than a particular skill. If a person's skill became obsolete, the company provided retraining with no loss in pay. Thus, unions did not resist new technology; and employers, in turn, had the freedom to shift workers from one job to another and to invest huge sums in training without worrying that workers would leave the company. Not surprisingly, labor mobility was extremely low.

The large companies rewarded their employees' loyalty and hard work with lifelong security, relatively modest salaries, and generous fringe benefits, which brought the level of living for those workers up to the level of workers in the United States. During the high-growth years of the 1950s through the 1970s, the ability of Japanese management to extract such extraordinary hard work and devotion from employees drew foreign admiration and spawned a new field of study—Japanese management techniques.

For the majority of Japanese workers, however, life was not so dependable. Their job security and fringe benefits were much less. Indeed, the high savings rate of the Japanese is sometimes attributed to the lack of a social security system and to the uncertainty of employment for most workers. Thus, many critics have regarded the Japanese system as one that exploits labor.

In the 1980s and 1990s that management/labor system began to show cracks. The general slowdown in the economy forced some companies to resort to layoffs, and unemployment edged up to almost 3 percent by the late 1980s, a historic high for Japan. At the same time, lifetime employment became less certain, even in the large corporations; and labor mobility was on the rise, partly because

of young workers' increasing dissatisfaction with the demands that society was placing on them. Those cracks in the system should not be exaggerated, however. The double structure still exists in the Japanese economy and is likely to remain there for the foreseeable future. Whether the inequality inherent in that system can be corrected is problematic.

Rural Problems

For political and social reasons, farming has been one of the last sectors of the economy to modernize. The farmers' natural conservatism was reinforced in the late 1940s by the land-reform program that awarded tenant farmers the small plots they had tilled for generations. Those smallholders, still farming only an average of 3.5 acres (1.4 hectares) today, have been loyal supporters of the postwar conservative governments. In return, Japan has offered its farmers higher government subsidies and support prices for their rice crop than are offered by any other country in Asia, thereby contributing directly to the high food prices that urban Japanese must pay. A paradoxical situation now exists: Japan has the highest rice yields per unit of land in Asia, but its rice is seven times more expensive to produce than rice that is grown in the United States.

Figure 15-8
The familiar golden arches near Senji Station in Tokyo. The arches provide evidence of the changing diets and tastes among the Japanese people. The many bicycles belong to daily commuters.

Even with all of that assistance, however, farming is still not profitable enough to sustain a Japanese farm family that uses mechanization and large amounts of chemical fertilizers. By the end of the 1980s only 14 percent of Japan's farm families were engaged in full-time farming; 72 percent earned the major portion of their income from nonagricultural activities. And agriculture had now reached the point where further gains in productivity can be achieved only by removing marginal farmers from their land and consolidating landholdings through such measures as cooperative farming or larger private farms. Progress along those lines has been slight, though, because farmers are reluctant to part with their land—unless they are fortunate enough to be in the path of urban-industrial sprawl.

Japan's food situation has been further complicated by changes in diet. As Japanese food habits have become more Westernized, especially in the large cities (Figure 15–8), the Japanese have developed a liking for beef and other meats, dairy products, sugar, and tropical fruits, as well as products made from wheat and soybeans. But the country cannot produce enough of those commodities to meet the demand. As a result, imports of foodstuffs have risen dramatically. By 1990, Japan's self-sufficiency in total food supply had fallen to 47 percent (on caloric basis), with wheat, soybeans, and livestock feed being the principal imported agricultural commodities. Ironically, rice has been produced in surplus until just recently and the government had great problems storing it or even disposing of it. The beginning of rice imports, finally, in 1993 began to change this, as U.S. pressure forced open the domestic market at a time of temporary shortage.

Supporters of agricultural subsidization have argued that the system is essential, at least for rice farmers, for three main reasons: (1) agriculture is not only an economic activity, but is also part of the nation's cultural heritage and must be protected as such; (2) the nation needs to protect its food security, for Japan could not be ensured of adequate supplies of rice at reasonable prices if it began to rely on imports; and (3) paddy land, once converted to other uses, could not be changed back to rice cultivation if the need arose.

On the other hand, critics of subsidization argue that: (1) Japan is predominantly urbanized and industrialized, and the farmers must accept that change; (2) the issue of food security is a false one because Japan's effective exporting will provide the money and ability to buy whatever imported foods are needed; and (3) subsidization is an admission that Japan has lost its comparative advantage in rice production (the same is true with cattle raising and dairying), and the nation should not prop up an inefficient sector of the economy. Incidentally, similar arguments can be heard in other parts of the world, such as in the EU or the United States, where substantial subsidization of agriculture also occurs. The subsidization system in Japan is currently under grave pressure to cave in, but the outlook is not yet clear.

Foreign Trade and Aid: International Ill Will

Another problem that emerged with Japan's success was a rising tide of antagonism toward its foreign trade, aid, and investment policies. In 1991 Japan's total foreign trade came to $552 billion; exports accounted for $315 billion, and imports, $237 billion. That trade surplus of $78 billion was part of a decade-long gap between exports and imports that brought domestic prosperity but international difficulties (Figures 15–9 and 15–10).

Figure 15-9
Japanese balance of trade in U.S. dollars. Japan's imports and exports remained crudely balanced through the 1970s. During the 1980s, however, the value of its exports soared above the value of its imports, creating tension among many of Japan's trading partners. (From *Statistical Handbook of Japan 1990*, Tokyo: Statistics Bureau, Management and Coordination Agency, pp. 82, 84.)

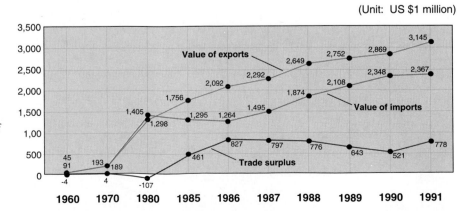

Exports

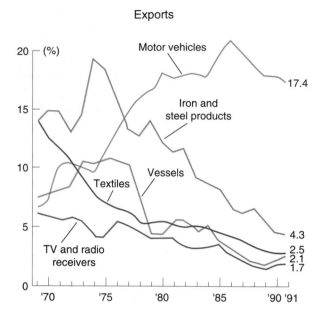

Imports

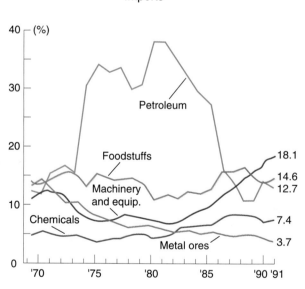

Figure 15-10

Japan's major exports and imports. Japan's dependence on imported foods and raw materials and exported finished products is evident from the structure of trade illustrated on these graphs. (From *Statistical Handbook of Japan 1990,* Tokyo: Statistics Bureau, Management and Coordination Agency, p. 84.)

Those problems are most critical with the United States. In 1991 Japan's trade imbalance with the United States was $38 billion, or 49 percent of the total trade surplus for Japan. While the United States share of the surplus has declined, it remains a problem. Clearly, the U.S. market is essential to the long-range health of the Japanese economy, but protectionist demands in the United States have greatly strained relations between the two countries. Critics sometimes contend that the United States has become an economic colony of Japan; the United States supplies Japan with foodstuffs and raw materials and, in return, buys vast amounts of manufactured goods.

The trade imbalance with Japan is also one of the major contributing factors to the huge budget deficits that plagued the U.S. economy in the 1980s. At the same time Japan has become a major investor in the United States, thereby offsetting some of the budget deficit but also protecting itself against possible protectionist policies.

The European Union has not been happy with Japanese trade either and has used various measures to restrict Japanese imports—with limited success. Similar complaints have been raised by other major trading partners of Japan, particularly in East Asia and Southeast Asia. Japan is the top source of imports for China, South Korea, Indonesia, Taiwan, Thailand, Malaysia, and Singapore (Figure 15–11); and Japan also has a trade surplus with all of those countries except Indonesia. The problem is complicated by memories of wartime atrocities committed by Japanese military forces, memories that have been revived by the sometimes undiplomatic behavior of Japanese tourists and business representatives who have flooded those countries.

In addition, Japan has set up overseas operations in those Asian countries, finding it profitable to move labor-intensive industries, such as assembly plants for electronic goods, where labor costs are much lower than they are in Japan. Although many benefits accrue to those countries, Japanese investments have met with mixed responses. Some critics who espouse the notion of economic nationalism contend that Japan has succeeded in creating economically what it failed to create militarily during World War II: the so-called **Greater East Asia Co-Prosperity Sphere**. In other words, Japan is the headquarters of an Asian economic system that

Figure 15-11
Japan's most important trading partners for exports and imports. The United States is the single largest trading partner of Japan; highly developed countries do normally generate the largest flows in world trade. The largest trading partner of most Southeast Asian countries is Japan, but what may be a dominant trade relationship for those countries may not be particularly significant for Japan. That paradox was noted in our more general discussion of trade in Chapter 3. (From *Statistical Handbook of Japan 1990*, Tokyo: Statistics Bureau, Management and Coordination Agency, p. 85.)

Export Markets

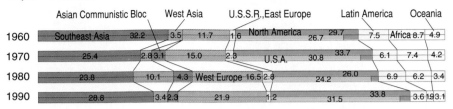

Import Markets

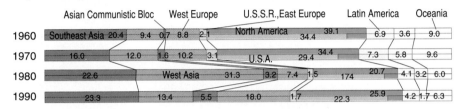

Export Structure

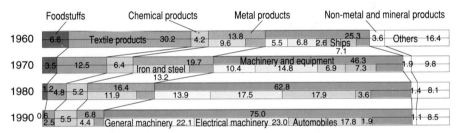

Import Structure

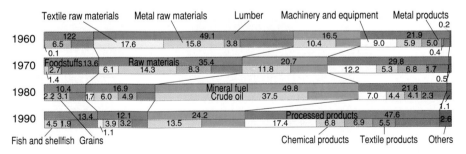

depends on Japanese capital and leadership. The other Asian countries, in a neocolonial relationship, provide the cheap labor, raw materials, and markets for industrial manufactures. Although the Japanese deny that allegation, there is no escaping the fact that the economies of the countries of East Asia and Southeast Asia are increasingly tied to Japan.

Even in the realm of foreign aid, Japan often reaps more criticism than praise. Although Japan has been more generous in recent years than the United States in terms of aid as a percentage of GNP, critics complain that the relatively harsh terms of the aid agreements tie the economies of the recipient countries even more tightly to the economy of Japan.

FROM OTOMOGO TO TOYOTA

No industry better typifies the extraordinary success of Japan's postwar transformation into an economic giant than the motor vehicle industry. Probably few people have heard of the Otomogo, Japan's first mass-produced car from the early 1920s. On the other hand, probably few have *not* heard of Toyota, the General Motors of Japan, the country's largest corporation and the world's fourth-largest. In just the past twenty years Japan has emerged as one of the top two producers of motor vehicles, and as the first in automobiles. That industry illustrates well the principle of comparative advantage and an international division of labor.

Japanese entrepreneurs started experimenting with cars around 1902, about the same time as Henry Ford and others in the United States. The industry had a slow start in Japan, however; domestic cars could not compete with imported ones, especially those from the United States. The Japanese auto industry was not then competitive because the country's machine-building industry was inadequately developed and the domestic market, in terms of purchasing power, was limited. In 1923 the Kanto earthquake destroyed much of Japan's automobile-producing capacity, and the government then began importing Model-T Fords. Ford and General Motors established subsidiary plants in Japan in 1925–1926 to assemble trucks and passenger cars, using parts imported from the United States. Imports into Japan averaged 15,000 to 16,000 cars a year by the 1930s. Japan's domestic auto industry was then diverted, under government direction, to the production of trucks for the military. Modest civilian production continued, mainly by the two major companies, Toyota and Nissan (the latter was one of the *zaibatsu* of that time); and foreign manufacturers were forced to stop production in Japan in 1940.

After World War II, truck production was the first to revive, especially with the stimulation provided by Korean War procurements. In the early 1950s Japanese auto manufacturers developed joint ventures with some European producers and borrowed their technology by buying patent rights, a common tactic in postwar Japanese reindustrialization. Domestic auto production resumed in 1952, although production was small and was limited mainly to taxis. Then, in the mid-1950s the Japanese government, through its **Ministry of International Trade and Industry (MITI)**, targeted automobiles (and motor vehicles as a whole) as an industry with a high growth potential. Consequently, MITI did all it could to help domestic producers, by restricting vehicle imports and foreign investment in Japan and by giving technical advice and financial assistance to auto companies. The whole motor vehicle industry took off in the early 1960s.

The government's **income-doubling plan**, which aimed to make 1970 per capita income twice that of 1960, was hugely successful and led to a surge in domestic demand for autos. Foreign markets also grew rapidly, especially in the United States but also in Europe. By 1970 Japanese car manufacturers, with shrewd foresight, saw the potential for small, well-designed, fuel-efficient cars; and an industrial legend was begun. By the 1990s a mystique had developed around Japanese vehicles, even though the quality gap between American and Japanese cars had significantly narrowed—vanished, some might argue—by then.

The growth in Japanese production of motor vehicles has been phenomenal (Figure A). Automobiles increased from just 20,000 in 1955 to almost 10 million by 1991 (Figure B). Trucks and buses increased from less than 50,000 to almost 3.5 million. Motorcycles peaked at more than 7.4 million in 1981 (because of competition from Taiwan and other lower-cost producers) but stabilized at over 3 million by the early 1990s. More than 90 percent of Japan's motor vehicles were produced by the "big five" auto companies: Toyota, Nissan, Honda, Mazda, and Mitsubishi. By 1988 Japan had surpassed the United

Figure A
Japanese motor-vehicle production (unit: thousands). (From Japan Automobile Manufactures Association, in *Japan Almanac 1993*, Asahi Shimbun, p. 134.)

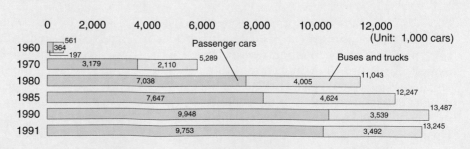

States in automobile production (Table A) and by the 1990s was producing one-third of all the cars produced worldwide. In total exports, however, Japan is far ahead of any other nation, with over 5.7 million vehicles sold abroad in 1991, which, adding in exports of automobile parts, amounted to $65 billion and 23 percent of Japan's total exports.

Over the years the automobile has become a major means of private transportation in Japan. Indeed, cars, along with trucks and buses, contributed to the decline of Japanese railroads, in a pattern reminiscent of that in the postwar United States. Thus, the motor vehicle industry has acquired the same vital role in Japan's economy that it has in the United States.

The industry is not without its problems, though. Japan is beginning to feel the pinch of competitors that are chipping away at the country's comparative advantage, just as the United States has felt it since the early 1970s. Newer and lower-cost producers, such as companies in South Korea, are making some of the smaller Japanese autos increasingly uncompetitive in world markets, forcing Japan to shift to larger and higher-priced cars. The basic problem is that, with the world auto industry currently turning out more than 49 million vehicles a year, there is a surplus production capacity of several million cars. Even with the surplus, however, automobile production is an attractive industry for many countries because of its multiplier effect on other sectors of the economy. Consequently, new auto plants and new companies continue to be created around the world, and autos have become one of the most competitive industries, where comparative advantage is put to the acid test.

Another problem stems from U.S. sensitivity to Japan's auto exports to the United States. Because of that politically explosive issue and because Japan needs the U.S. market to sustain the production capacity of its auto industry, it has been opening up assembly plants in the United States that use parts imported from Japan. The Japanese hope that this approach will offset protectionist trends in the United States and will ensure market access. By 1991, Japanese manufacturers were producing 1.5 million cars and trucks a year in U.S. plants. In addition, Japanese companies are forming cooperative or joint-venture agrrangements with U.S. car manufacturers.

Similar linkages are also being formed with European carmakers. One authoritative prediction is that by 1995 one in three cars in Europe will be wholly or partly of Japanese design or will feature major Japanese components. Japan is also forming joint ventures in a number of other countries, such as South Korea, Taiwan, and China. Such linkages with foreign producers took on new significance in the 1980s, as the auto business became more and more internationalized and decentralized. With an international division of labor, an increasing number of cars are assembled from parts produced in a number of countries and in various locales within countries.

For the rest of this century, at least, Japan is likely to remain at the top of world auto production, certainly of exports. But the country's continued dominance of that vital industry will require the utmost attention to styling, quality, and price in a brutally competitive environment. That attention, in turn, will require the unique strength of the Japanese management and production system operating within the double structure of Japan's economy.

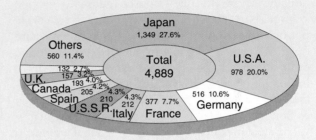

Figure B
Passenger-car production, 1990 (unit: ten thousands). (From Japan Automobile Manufacturers Association, in *Japan Almanac 1993*, Asahi Shimbun, p. 134.)

Table A
Production, exports, and imports of passenger cars, in thousands, 1990 and 1991.

	Production		Exports		Imports
	1990	1991	1990	1991	1991
Japan	9,948	9,753	4,482	4,452	197
U.S.A.	6,078	5,440	548	533	—
Germany	4,661	4,660	2,598	2,185	2,520
France	3,295	3,188	1,882	1,996	1,160
Italy	1,875	1,633	743	639	—
Spain	1,679	1,774	1,066	1,284	—
U.K.	1,296	1,237	414	605	821
Canada	1,076	1,044	799	674	—
World, total 35,787	—	—	—	—	—

Source: JAMA (Japan Automobile Manufactures Association), in *Japan 1993: An International Comparison* (Japan Institute for Social and Economic Affairs), p. 21.

JAPAN'S THIRD TRANSFORMATION: CHARTING A NEW COURSE

As Japan heads toward the twenty-first century, internal and external pressures, as well as the natural evolution of the country's economy and society, are causing the Japanese to seriously reassess their goals and improve their international image. Important structural changes are taking place in the economy that are forcing the nation and its leaders to alter their course. A number of industries that thrived in past decades are now declining, and the government is assisting them to diversify and phase out activities that are no longer competitive internationally. Those so-called **sunset industries** include shipbuilding, textiles, some chemicals (especially petrochemicals), and aluminum smelting. Other industries that are fully mature are also encountering difficulty and are being forced to retrench. The most important of those is iron and steel, which faces increasing pressure from Third World producers such as South Korea. Japan will remain a major force in world steel production and exports, but at a reduced level. The automobile industry, though still strong, has also encountered various problems (see the boxed feature From Otomogo to Toyota).

To maintain their competitiveness, the Japanese are pursuing a number of other strategies. First, to placate U.S. protectionists, they are moving plants to the United States. Second, Japan is making it easier for U.S. manufacturers to invest in Japan and market products there. The decline in the value of the dollar has lowered the price of goods from the United States and is having a definite impact on Japanese imports, which are rising faster than exports. Third, the Japanese government is stimulating industry to move faster into high-tech areas, where Japan can maintain a comparative advantage. Those new areas of high growth potential include microelectronics, biotechnology, new materials, and optoelectronics. For example, the Japanese are already giving the United States competition in the development of so-called supercomputers.

The first, the late-nineteenth-century transformation from a feudal state into an industrial one, culminated in the disastrous experience of World War II. The second transformation was Japan's postwar industrial recovery and expansion into a world economic power. The third transformation is now beginning, as a restructuring of the Japanese economy.

Those three transformations should be viewed as separate phases of a single, ongoing process of development. In fact, the third transformation is simply a recognition by Japan that its modern economy is maturing and can no longer be expected to maintain the phenomenal growth rates of past decades. As heavy industry assumes a naturally decreased importance, the economy will shift increasingly toward a service orientation, just as it has in the United States.

Sentiment is strong within Japan for greater attention to domestic consumption. The government is also being encouraged to spend more money on social welfare, improve housing, develop social security, and take other measures that will enhance the quality of life rather than simply increase the GNP. In other words, some Japanese are now questioning the goal of being number one in the world.

Such processes take time, of course, so Japan's huge trade surplus is not going to turn around overnight. And even when the trend is finally reversed, Japan will remain a formidable economic giant in world affairs. From that position a much greater political and perhaps military role is apt to follow in the next century.

SUMMARY
Japan's Second Century of Economic Development

We have charted Japan's economic development through two major economic transformations.

KEY TERMS

Greater East Asia
    Co-Prosperity Sphere

income-doubling plan

Japan corridor

kombinats

Maglev megalopolis

Meiji Restoration

Ministry of International
    Trade and Industry
    (MITI)

Shinkansen

split technology

sunset industries

technopolises

three transformations

Tokaido megalopolis

zaibatsu

16

Australia and New Zealand: Isolation and Space

Australia

New Zealand

Plateau on the dry Pilbara Coast of western
Australia. The limited water resources translate
into low population density for most of Australia.

The secret of development in Australia and New Zealand lies in the successful transplantation of Western society and economy in undeveloped territories that, by accidents of geography and history, had been largely unknown and untouched by the peoples of Asia. Although Australia and New Zealand differ greatly from each other in size and physical environment, they share many characteristics of historical development and economic circumstances. Both were established in the late eighteenth century as British colonies for white settlers. Both have large land areas in proportion to their populations, high standards of living, and much closer cultural ties with the United Kingdom and the United States than with most Asian countries. In addition, both developed prior to World War II as supermarkets for Britain; that is, they provided many of the foodstuffs that Britain and the British Empire needed. That function is still important today, but it is no longer dominant.

New Zealand remains the more pastoral and agriculturally based of the two countries; its high level of living depends on abundant production of dairy products, meat, wool, and other animal and forest products. Australia's wealth is more diversified, with rich deposits of metals, coal, and natural gas; a bountiful agricultural assortment of meat, diary products, wool, wheat, and sugar; and, increasingly, industrial manufactures.

Australia and New Zealand both depend on trade with industrialized nations to maintain their high standards of living. For many decades that trade was directed primarily toward Great Britain and the British Commonwealth. Because of preferential tariff treatment and other trade privileges, as well as exclusion elsewhere and a lack of real markets in nearby Asia, it was profitable for Australia and New Zealand to market their products thousands of miles away. Since World War II, however, and particularly since Britain entered the European Common Market, the overseas relations of Australia and New Zealand have undergone a metamorphosis. Ties with the British have gradually weakened, whereas those with the United States, Japan, East Asia, and—to a lesser extent—other Asian countries have assumed new importance.

AUSTRALIA

A Vast and Arid Continent

Much of Australia's development experience is related to the continent's physical environment, particularly its isolation, vastness, aridity, and topography. With almost 3 million square miles (7.8 million square kilometers), including the offshore island of Tasmania, Australia extends for 2,400 miles (3,864 kilometers) from Cape York in the north at 11°S latitude to the southern top of Tasmania at 44°S latitude; it also extends about 2,500 miles (4,025 kilometers) from east to west (Figure 16–1). Although that land area is approximately equal to the area of the lower forty-eight states of the United States, Australia's population is far smaller—17.8 million in 1994. On the basis of population, Australia is actually one of the smaller countries of the world. Even though Australia's average density of population is low, however, its people are concentrated in a relatively small part of the continent.

Only 11 percent of Australia gets more than 40 inches (1,015 millimeters) of rain a year; two-thirds of the country receives less than 20 inches (508 millimeters) (Figure 16–2). On the basis of both climate and relief five major natural regions can be distinguished. The core region is the humid highlands, which extend in a belt 400 to 600 miles wide (644 to 966 kilometers) along the east coast. In addition to Tasmania, the narrow and fragmented coastal plains along the base of the highlands are the only part of Australia that is not subject to recurrent drought, and most of the nation's population, major cities, agriculture, and modern industrial economy are concentrated in that coastal fringe. In the southwestern corner of Australia and in a band along the eastern portion of the southern coast, the climate is Mediterranean, or dry summer subtropical. Those two areas have the second major concentration of population, particularly around the cities of Perth and Adelaide, but the total population is still sparse.

The three other natural regions have various disadvantages for human settlement, and land use is confined largely to mining and livestock raising, which results in a very low population density. Along the northern fringe of Australia are the tropical savannas, where the monsoon climate—3 to 4 months of heavy rain followed by 8 to 9 months of

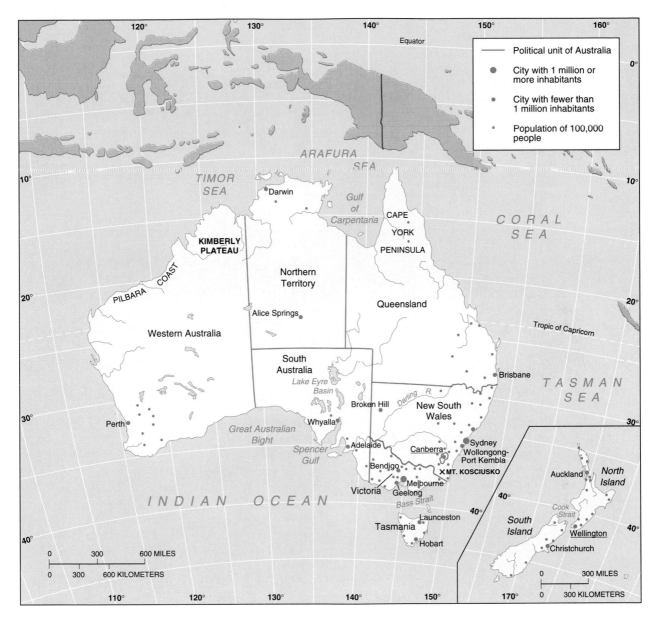

Figure 16-1

Selected cities and population distribution of Australia and New Zealand. Australia
and New Zealand are two outposts of European culture in Asia. Both are sparsely
populated and trade more with European nations than with their Asian neighbors.
Those traditional trade relationships are undergoing change, however.

almost total dryness—makes settlement and agriculture extremely difficult (see the boxed feature Frontiers: Australia's Northwest). The huge interior of Australia is desert surrounded by a broad fringe of semiarid grassland (i.e., steppe), which is transitional to the more humid coastal areas. Again, those two dry areas cover nearly two-thirds of the continent.

The western half of Australia is, in fact, a vast plateau of ancient rocks with a general elevation of only 1,000 to 1,600 feet (305 to 488 meters). The few

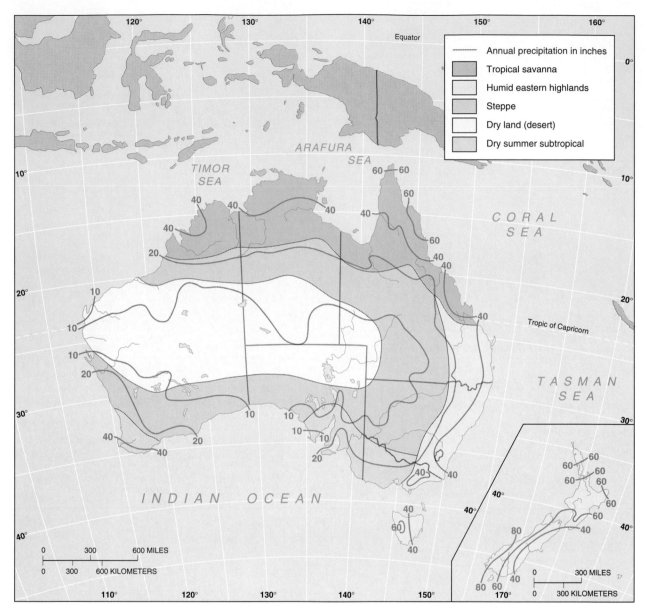

Figure 16-2
Natural regions and precipitation in Australia and New Zealand. Much of Australia is little used because water is scarce; a large area of Australia receives less than 20 inches of precipitation yearly. New Zealand is much better watered.

isolated mountain ranges are too low to influence the climate significantly or to supply perennial streams for irrigation. The continent as a whole was once joined to Antarctica, as the easternmost part of **Gondwana**, which broke up into modern continents about 230 million years ago. Australia moved northward, carrying with it unique wildlife, especially kangaroos and other marsupials.

The Shortage of Arable Land

For such a large landmass Australia has a remarkably small amount of arable land. The arid interior region, which makes up fully one-third of the continent, cannot be used at all for agricultural purposes, even for livestock raising. Another 40 to 42 percent of the continent—to the north, east, and west of the arid interior—receives only enough rain to support cattle and sheep. The remaining land area, about 25 percent of the total, receives sufficient rainfall to support agriculture, but rough terrain and poor soils further reduce the truly arable area to no more than about 8 percent (Figure 16–3). And much of that arable land is already used for sheep and cattle raising and dairy farming. Thus, in reality, less than 2 percent of Australia's total land area is currently devoted to crop cultivation, and only one-twelfth of that crop area is irrigated for intensive farming—indications of the very extensive use of the land resources of the continent.[1] Droughts and other harsh climatic factors cause large seasonal variations in agricultural output.

Settlement and Population Growth

The long delay in the European discovery and settlement of Australia was due to many factors, including the vastness of the Pacific Ocean, the direction of the prevailing winds and currents, and the lack of any sign that the continent possessed resources worth having. Until 1788 Australia was inhabited only by **aborigines**, who numbered perhaps 300,000 (Figure 16–4). Those dark people of complex origin had been in Australia for thousands of years, leading a primitive existence as hunters and gatherers. In 1770 Captain James Cook became the first European known to reach the east coast of Australia, the part of the continent that appeared most suitable for settlement. For initial British settlers, who were primarily convicts, Australia served as a remote penal colony.

Exploration and settlement by adventurers, emancipists (convicts who had served out their sentences), and others continued into the nineteenth century. Immigration was encouraged by Britain through land grants in the developing continent, but the total population remained small. One of the greatest stimuli to development and immigration was a gold rush in the 1850s, which brought large

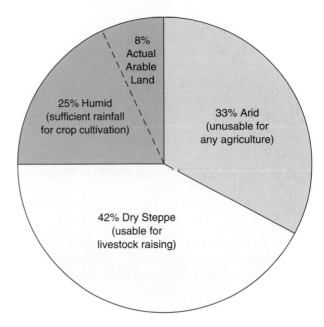

Figure 16-3

Land use in Australia. Aridity, rough terrain, and poor soils reduce the actual proportion of arable land to approximately 8 percent. The majority of arable land is used in extensive activities, such as sheep and cattle raising.

numbers of prospectors and settlers. In 1901 the six Australian colonies—Queensland, New South Wales, Victoria, South Australia, Western Australia, and Tasmania—were federated into the Commonwealth of Australia, with the planned city of Canberra as the national capital.

One of the most important developments of the nineteenth century was the implementation of the **White Australia policy,** officially termed the Restricted Immigration Policy, after the first nonwhite settlers set foot on the continent. Successive Australian governments recognized the vulnerability of a relatively small white population controlling such a large land area so close to overpopulated regions of Asia. Immigration into Australia, thus, was a major concern. In general, government policy can be summarized in three main statements:

1. alternating support for large-scale immigration during periods of domestic prosperity and opposition to immigration during recessions
2. strong preference for people of British origin
3. exclusion of nonwhites, with only a few exceptions, from the late nineteenth century until the 1970s

FRONTIERS: AUSTRALIA'S NORTHWEST

One of the few true frontiers remaining on the earth's overcrowded surface is Australia's northwest, which is composed of the Northern Territory and the Kimberley Plateau and Pilbara Coast regions of Western Australia. That vast area, which covers about one-fourth of Australia, illustrates the problems associated with the development of frontier regions: small population, isolation and poor transportation linkages, harsh physical environment, difficulties in resource exploitation, and neglect by the country's power center (urban-industrial core). Much the same can be said of other frontier regions in the world, such as Brazil's Amazonia.

Australia's northwest region runs in a band roughly between 12°S and 25°S latitude. Tropical wet and dry climate dominates in the north, gradually blending into steppe and eventually becoming desert in the southern part of the region. Most settlement and development has taken place in the wet and dry tropics, or savanna, a torrid region where massive rainfall occurs in the hot, wet summer and temperatures can reach 113°F (45°C). An 8-month dry period follows, with temperatures cooling down only to about 86°F (30° C) in the winter. It is not a climate that Europeans, at least, have found very pleasant, which partly explains why only 300,000 people live in the whole region today. Most of the area's inhabitants live in widely scattered towns and settlements, the largest being Darwin (68,000). Settlers' historical disdain for the region persists today in the attitude of the Australian government—and most of the people—against investing much money or effort in the region.

In addition to climatic difficulties, lack of access to good transportation greatly hinders development (Figure A). There still is no rail connection to the south; the nearest railhead is at Alice Springs in the interior. Darwin's current ties with the rest of Australia are long, straight roads that run south to Alice Springs and east to Queensland, (see Figure 16–1). Air links exist, but Darwin does not have an adequate airport. The lack of good port facilities and regular shipping service out of Darwin is unlikely to be remedied until a railhead is acquired.

Resource development is also difficult. Agriculture is hindered by the harsh environment, distances, and high production costs. The Ord River Dam project, aimed at providing irrigation water to stimulate agriculture, proved to be an expensive white elephant and has discouraged further efforts to develop irrigation. Sugarcane and cotton cultivation have waned, and success in producing specialized crops—such as bananas, sunflowers, vegetables, and melons—has been modest. The region is rich in minerals, however, including diamonds and uranium, and those have contributed the most in recent years to economic growth. But associated activities are isolated and capital-intensive and do little to stimulate long-term settlement. Transportation remains the key, both for agriculture and for mineral exploitation.

The latest development tack has focused on attracting Asian investors to the region, using an approach that China and many other developing countries have had some success with, the special economic zone (SEZ), or as Australians call it, a **trade development zone.** Accordingly, an industrial estate, or park, has been established in Darwin to provide low-cost factory and office space, warehousing, and storage; Darwin is aiming for capital-intensive finishing activities. So far, a few Asian manufacturers have been lured, mostly from Taiwan and Hong Kong.

That modest but growing Asian involvement in the region is a reflection of the proximity of northwest Australia to Asian countries. Asians are also attracted by the familiar tropical climate and by what they see as pioneering opportunities. The northwest historically has been more tolerant of Asians than has the rest of the country. Darwin has even had ethnic Chinese mayors, and intermarriage with Asians is common. Given the poor linkages with the rest of the country and the comparative distances—Darwin is closer to Jakarta in Indonesia than it is to Sydney—it makes sense for the northwest to orient itself more toward Asia than toward the rest of Australia.

About half of Australia's aborigines live in this northwest region, and they constitute about one-fourth of the region's population. Since the passage of the Civil Rights Act of 1967 and the Aboriginal Land Rights Act in the early 1970s, the aborigines have had a much stronger voice in local and national affairs and in development opportunities in the northwest.

Even under the best of circumstances, however, Australia's northwest is likely to remain a marginally populated and marginally developed part of the country. The region's handicaps will continue to outweigh its assets for the foreseeable future.

Figure A
A large ranch, or station, in the outback of the Northern Territory. The isolation and low population density of this region are clearly evident here. The aircraft in the left foreground are used to herd livestock as well as to maintain contact with the outside. The overall vegetation pattern is characteristic of many wet-dry precipitation regimes.

Figure 16-4
Aborigine children at school in Central Reserve Western Australia. These Negroid inhabitants of Australia greatly declined in numbers after white settlement. Today, probably fewer than 50,000 people of pure aborigine ancestry remain, with another 100,000 or so of mixed ancestry. Most live in poverty, either on the fringes of white society or in the remote lands of Australia's far north.

Britons predominated in the immigration pattern until World War II and were aided by the Australian government. After World War II the government changed its policy and accepted other European and Anglo-American settlers as long as they were white. Since then more than 3 million people—almost one-fifth of the present total population—have moved to Australia from various other parts of the world. Those new residents have helped to create an increasingly distinct Australian character, to replace the dominantly British type of Australian society. Australia continues to cultivate immigration at a carefully controlled rate.

The White Australia policy was quietly shelved in 1973, as Australia's focus shifted away from Europe. Instead, the nation now selects immigrants on the basis of education, job skills needed by Australia, and potential for adapting to life in Australia (primarily, an English-language ability), as well as for family reunion. During the 1980s, the proportion of Asian immigrants rose significantly as a result, and by 1990–1991 accounted for nearly 60 percent of all immigrants. Those from Europe and the former Soviet Union dropped from 51 percent to about 27 percent of the total. By 2025, projections estimate that Asian-born migrants will represent about 7 percent of Australia's population, up from the current 2.6 percent.

Australia's Asian minority includes a sizable number of Indochinese refugees, as well as people from Malaysia, Singapore, and Hong Kong. The swelling tide of Asian immigration renewed concern among some Australians in the 1980s, with one camp arguing for immigration being cut back to 50,000–60,000 a year and reduced numbers of family reunions (who tend to put a strain on welfare and social security systems.) The pro-immigration camp argues that Australia can easily absorb at least 160,000 settlers a year (i.e., about 1 percent of the total population). The parallels with immigration debates in the United States are striking.

The other major nonwhite minority remains, of course, the original natives, the aborigines, who total around 150,000, or about 1 percent of Australia's population. Many of the aborigines exhibit problems that are typical of dispossessed cultural groups in other societies around the world. An effort is now under way to revive the aboriginal culture and way of life through a homelands movement that involves deurbanizing the aborigines.

An Urbanized Society

For a country with so much land and so few people, Australia's high degree of urbanization is unusual. About two-thirds of the population lives in cities with more than 100,000 residents. Around 40 percent of the people live in the two great metropolitan areas of Sydney and Melbourne, each with a population of about 3 million (Figure 16–5). One reason for this urban pattern is that Australia's agricultural production is extensive and employs few people. In addition, especially since World War II, Australia has encouraged industrialization to provide more home-produced armaments for defense and to secure greater economic stability through a more diversified and self-sufficient economy.

All five of Australia's largest cities—Sydney, Melbourne, Brisbane, Adelaide, and Perth-Freemantle, in decreasing size—are seaports, and each is the capital of one of the five mainland states of the commonwealth. Much of the country's production is exported by sea, and much internal trade is also conducted by coastal steamers. Before federation in 1901, each state had built its own rail system linking the hinterland to the chief port and thus to international markets. Ultimately, however, the varied railroad gauges that were used hampered national integration.

The Bases of Australia's Economy

Australia's high standard of living can be attributed to its small population and its reasonably well-developed and diversified export economy, which depends on the production of agricultural, mineral, and industrial goods. That production trilogy provides a solid base for a prosperous economy.

From the initial settlement of the country until recent times, agriculture was the mainstay of the economy, generating about 80 percent of the export income in the early post-World War II years. Today, the total value of farm exports has increased, but their relative share of export trade has plunged significantly—to only about 30 percent—mainly because of the dramatic increase in mineral exports.

Agriculture is dominated today by sheep and cattle ranching and by wheat farming—extensive forms

Figure 16-5
Waterfront and opera house in Sydney, Australia. Sydney is Australia's largest city, industrial center, and major seaport. More than 40 percent of Australia's highly urbanized population lives in the two most prominent cities—Sydney and Melbourne. Both are beautiful cities occupying magnificent harbor sites.

of agriculture that are well suited to Australia's environment (Figure 16–6). Sheep and cattle ranches, or **stations**, are usually quite large in Australia, often encompassing thousands of acres and making motor vehicles and airplanes important equipment. For example, Anna Creek cattle station in South Australia encompasses 12,000 square miles (31,080 square kilometers). Sheep ranching became a mainstay of the economy in the nineteenth century, when it provided wool for Britain's textile industry. By 1850 Australia was the world's largest exporter of wool, and it still produces 30 percent of the world's wool, though wool now accounts for only 5 percent of its total exports. In addition, since World War II, mutton and lamb have been exported in increasing quantities.

Generally, cattle have been relegated to areas that are not suitable for sheep, and the cattle industry remains secondary in importance. Dairy farming is largely confined to the eastern and southeastern coastal fringes and to the Murray Valley north of Melbourne but has seen strong growth since World War II. Development of refrigerated shipping after 1880 enabled Australia to supply European markets with both meat and dairy products. In recent years much of the increased demand for wool, beef, and dairy products has come from the countries of East Asia, especially Japan, and Southeast Asia, as well as the Middle East, where rising standards of living are changing consumption habits.

Australia's wheat production has also benefited from modern technology. The introduction of mechanization in the twentieth century permitted it to be extensively cultivated, and some 60 percent of Australia's total cropland is now devoted to wheat. Like Canada and the United States, Australia has become one of the great breadbaskets of the world.

Australia also produces many other crops and is self-sufficient in foodstuffs. Sugarcane, one of the more important crops, is grown along the northeastern coastal fringe (Figure 16–7). Annually, Australia produces more than 3 million tons of sugar, most of which is exported to Japan and other Asian markets. Thus, Australia is one of the largest participants in world sugar trade. Other important crops include a wide variety of temperate and tropical fruits for both domestic consumption and export markets.

Further growth in agricultural exports will be constrained by the tariffs levied by the European Union, which limit the amounts of Australian meat, butter, grain, fruit, and sugar that can be sent to Britain and other European markets. In addition, the EU and the United States send their own agricultural surpluses to other markets in which Australia is competing. Consequently, the growth potential is not as great for Australia's agriculture as it is for its mining.

In terms of mineral resources Australia is a veritable cornucopia (see Figure 16–6); it is among the most favorably endowed of all major world regions. The resource base does not include just one commodity, such as petroleum in the Middle East, which can produce severe limitations. Rather, in Australia the resource base is both varied and large in volume. Australia has enormous reserves of coal, uranium, iron ore, bauxite, natural gas, lead, zinc, and other minerals. The mining sector expanded at remarkable rates through the 1960s and 1970s so that Australia now accounts for about one-fifth of world coal exports, one-third of bauxite, and one-fifth of alumina. Although many countries buy those mineral products, Japan has quickly become Australia's major market, especially for coal and iron ore. In fact, Japanese capital is playing a major role in the development of Australia's mineral wealth; Australia now ranks third (after the United States and Indonesia) in Japanese overseas investment. Petroleum is Australia's only serious mineral deficiency, though production of petroleum did increase significantly in the 1980s, and the country now meets most of its needs. Nonetheless, oil remains a major import commodity.

Industry is the weakest link in Australia's economy. What have developed so far are primarily **import-substitution industries**, which are geared to consumer goods, as well as the partial processing of mineral and agricultural products and the modest beginnings of some heavy industry, such as iron and steel and automobiles. Australian industry, however, is still protected by tariff barriers because the relatively small and scattered domestic market does not yet prompt production that is competitive with foreign imports. In addition, like Great Britain, Australia has been troubled by extreme trade unionism (60 percent of the work force is unionized), which tends to stifle productivity improvements, though that problem seemed to be improving by the late 1980s/early 1990s, particularly through reforms in the wage bargaining system and changing worker attitudes.

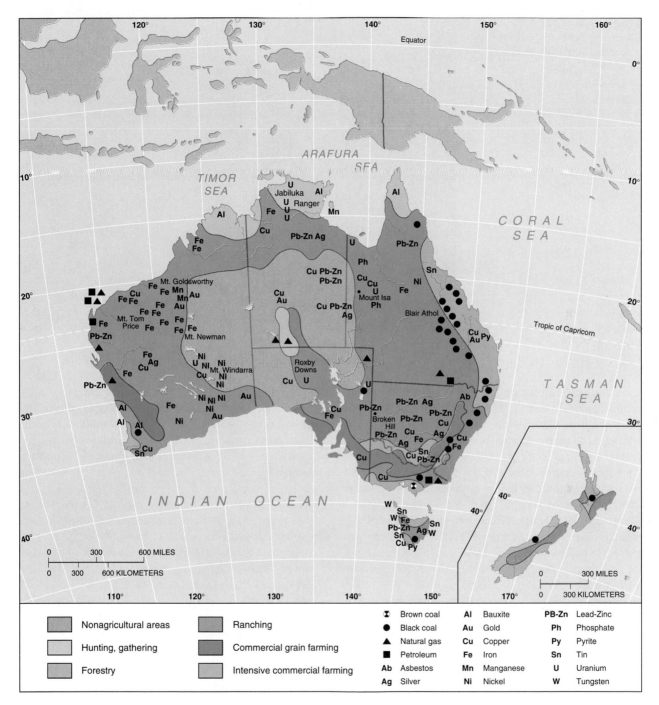

Figure 16-6
Rural land use and mineral resources of Australia and New Zealand. Australia and
New Zealand have extensive forms of agriculture (see chapter endnote); ranching
dominates much of the area of each country. Other extensive activities include
mechanized commercial grain farming in Australia and forestry in New Zealand.

Figure 16-7
Sugarcane fields in Queensland, along the northeastern coast of Australia. A major crop in this region, sugarcane is produced in subtropical and tropical environments on both family-sized and plantation-sized landholdings.

Manufacturing in Australia is concentrated in the state capitals, where three-fourths of all factory workers reside and where industry also has access to available markets, fuel, business and government contracts, and both overseas and internal transportation systems. Much of the remaining industrial activity is located in a few large provincial centers on or near the coast, such as Wollongong and Newcastle. The leading industrial state is New South Wales, centered in Sydney; Victoria is second, focused in Melbourne.

In the late 1980s tourism began to assume new importance as a kind of fourth leg in the Australian economy. Currently, Australia has more than 2 million visitors a year; by the year 2000 that figure is expected to reach 5 million. In addition to traditional attractions such as Sydney and the **outback** (i.e., interior), many tourists are drawn to resort developments that are springing up along the **Gold Coast** in Queensland. There the 1,250-mile-long (2,000-kilometer) **Great Barrier Reef**, one of the world's greatest natural wonders, provides marvelous opportunities for tropical recreation.

Although there have been significant shifts in Australia's economic sectors in recent decades, the country still depends essentially on exporting primary or semiprocessed primary products in exchange for manufactured goods from the more developed world. The United States and Japan together account for about 40 percent of both total imports and total exports; the United States dominates in sales to Australia, but Japan greatly dominates in purchases from Australia. The United Kingdom, Germany, and New Zealand are distant runners-up as trade partners.

Any truly fundamental change in the Australian economy must be tied to a number of future development: further increases in population, greater efficiency in industry, further development of the continent's resources, and greater trading ties with the countries of Asia. Since none of those developments are likely to occur quickly, Australia will probably remain, at least for a while, in the unusual position of being a prosperous nation without a strong industrial base.

NEW ZEALAND

More than 1,000 miles (1,610 kilometers) southeast of Australia, New Zealand consists of two main islands—North Island, with a smaller area but two-thirds of the population, and South Island—as well as a number of lesser islands (see Figure 16–1). The country is located entirely in the temperate zone, from about 34°S to 47°S latitude. Like the Japanese islands, New Zealand was formed from a section of the orogenic zone, or unstable crust belt, rimming the Pacific. The islands are the crest of a giant earth fold that rises sharply from the ocean floor.

Almost three-fourths of South Island is mountainous, dominated by the Southern Alps, which rise to elevations above 12,000 feet (3,658 meters). North Island, which is volcanic, is less rugged, but many peaks still exceed 5,000 feet (1,524 meters). New Zealand has a humid temperate climate, commonly known as marine west coast, with mild summers and winters; but in the highlands of South Island, weather conditions are severe enough for glaciers to form. The country's great north-south extent means that average temperatures in the north are at least 10°F (4.5°C) warmer than those in the south.

A Pastoral Economy

Settlement of New Zealand has been confined largely to the fringe lowlands around the periphery of North Island and along the drier east and south coasts of South Island. A large section of the country is relatively unproductive, though a tourist industry is being developed in the mountains, capitalizing on the attractive scenery.

In 1642 the Dutch explorer Abel Janszoon Tasman became the first European known to have sighted the islands, but it was not until Cook arrived in 1769 that exploration began, and settlement really did not get under way until the 1840s. Hence, the development of New Zealand closely parallels that of Australia in time. Because the climate is ideal for growing grass and raising livestock, New Zealand, like Australia, has specialized in pastoral farming from the very founding of the country. Some 200 years later, New Zealand remains dependent on its **pastoral economy** and the production of livestock and livestock products (see Figure 16–6). Even the 3 percent of the land area that is cropped is devoted in large part to animal feeds. Horticultural crops, wood, and wood products are also of some importance.

New Zealand has one of the world's highest proportions of livestock to human population—a ratio of 23:1 (the ratio for Australia is around 11:1). Pastoral industries completely dominate exports and, because of the country's small population, make New Zealand a world leader in per capita trade. It is among the world's top two or three exporters of mutton, lamb, butter, cheese, preserved milk, wool, and beef. In exchange, New Zealand re-

ceives most of its manufactured goods and considerable quantities of food.

The Need for Industry and Diversification

With such a heavy dependence on trade and a narrow economic base, New Zealand is far more vulnerable to the vagaries of world economic conditions than is Australia. As a result, New Zealand's per capita income is rather consistently only about half that of Australia.

Attempts at diversification, primarily through industrialization, have not been very successful. Although New Zealand has coal and some iron ore, it does not have the rich mineral resources that Australia has. Furthermore, the local market is small and dispersed, thus restraining large-scale production and efficient marketing. The cost of skilled labor is also high, and competition from overseas producers, such as Japan and the United States, can be severe. Most of the current manufacturing industries in New Zealand are high-cost producers that survive because they are protected by tariffs. Overall, manufacturing contributes more than 25 percent of the gross domestic product in New Zealand and employs about the same proportion of the labor force (Figure 16–8).

The economy of New Zealand has benefited from a free-trade agreement known as Closer Economic Relations, which was signed with Australia in 1983. That agreement opened Australia's larger domestic market to New Zealand's products and gave a much-needed stimulus to New Zealand's industry. Nonetheless, both countries are still relatively small trading partners with each other.

In spite of the predominantly agricultural economy, most of New Zealand's 1994 population of just over 3.5 million lives in cities, just as the population does in Australia. However, the cities of New Zealand are generally much smaller; the largest is Auckland, with 800,000 people, on North Island. Other major cities are Wellington, the capital, which is also on North Island, and Christchurch and Dunedin on South Island (see Figure 16–1).

About 10 percent of New Zealanders are Polynesians, mostly descendants of the pre-European **Maori** inhabitants. As with the aborigines in Australia, there have been some problems integrating the Maori into modern society in New Zealand. However, New Zealand has been much more successful in this regard than has been Australia.

Figure 16–8
New Zealand sheep being moved to pasture. Australia and New Zealand have both
been major exporters of meat, dairy products, and wool. New Zealand currently retains the more pastoral economy, whereas Australia is developing a manufacturing
economy in addition to its traditional agricultural sector.

SUMMARY
A Unique Location and New Directions

Australia and New Zealand are unique. Although
far from the Western world in location, they are
Western in culture and in their approach to economic development. Production in both countries
has been oriented toward utilizing agricultural resources (and minerals, in the case of Australia) for
export to the developed world.

Past trade relationships with the United
Kingdom were particularly strong. Both
Australia and New Zealand, however, are now
in the process of reorienting their economic re-
lationships, largely toward the Pacific rim, with
Japan and the United States currently playing

dominant roles. That reorientation also includes
increased attention to diversification of economic activity, a goal that will be more easily
attained by Australia than New Zealand because
of differences in resource endowment. Economic changes, along with the significant change
in immigration policy during the 1970s, signal
that Australia and New Zealand recognize the
realities of their location in the economically
developing world.

KEY TERMS

aborigines   Gondwana

Gold Coast   Great Barrier Reef

import-substitution
industries

Maori

outback

pastoral economy

stations

trade development zone

White Australia policy

NOTES

1. An extensive agricultural activity is one in which limited amounts of labor and/or capital per unit area are expended on a relatively large area, as, for example, in wheat farming. In contrast, an intensive agricultural activity requires large expenditures of labor and/or capital per unit area.

FURTHER READINGS
Part Five

Association of Japanese Geographers, eds. *Geography of Japan*. Tokyo: Teikoku-Shoin, 1980. A collection of writings about Japan's geography by members of the Association of Japanese Geographers; a somewhat specialized but very useful supplement to Trewartha's book (listed separately).

Blainey, G. *The Tyranny of Distance*. New York: St. Martin's Press, 1966. An interesting analysis of Australia's vastness and its effect on development.

Brian, Peter J. *Population, Immigration, and the Australian Economy*. London: Croom Helm, 1979. An examination of the relationship between Australia's economic development and its population growth, particularly the role of immigration.

Burks, Ardath W. *Japan, A Postindustrial Power*. 2d ed. Boulder, CO: Westview Press, 1984. A fine overview of Japan's history, culture, and economic development and problems.

Condliffe, J. B. *The Economic Outlook for New Zealand*. New York: Praeger, 1969. The general economic picture and some possible future trends, as seen by a well-known economist.

Courtney, P. P. *Northern Australia: Patterns and Problems of Tropical Development in an Advanced Country*. Melbourne: Longman Cheshire, 1982. A look at development issues and prospects in Australia's remote and environmentally difficult north, a region with great but largely undeveloped resources.

Hall, Robert B. *Japan: Industrial Power in Asia*. 2d ed. New York: Van Nostrand, 1976. A brief introductory survey emphasizing modernization, industrialization, and urbanization.

Kornhauser, David H. Japan: *Geographical Background to Urban-Industrial Development*. London: Longman, 1982. An interesting account of the formation of the Japanese urban and rural landscapes, viewed from the perspective of both their historical development and their present patterns.

Meinig, D. W. *On the Margins of the Good Earth: The South Australian Wheat Frontier, 1869–1884*. Skokie, IL: Rand McNally, 1962. An important study of the early period of wheat farming and grazing on the frontier of the steppe.

Noh, Toshio, and **Douglas H. Gordon,** eds. *Modern Japan: Land and Man*. Tokyo: Teikoku-Shoin, 1974. A translation of the Japanese edition by Noh and others; although somewhat dated now, still very useful because of its many illustrations, maps, and graphs; especially suitable for the study of the individual regions of Japan.

Okimoto, Daniel I. *Between MITI and the Market: Japanese Industrial Policy for High Technology*. Stanford, CA: Stanford University Press, 1989. An impressive successor to Chalmers Johnson's classic, *MITI and the Japanese Miracle* (Stanford, 1981).

Olsen, Edward A. *Japan: Economic Growth, Resource Scarcity, and Environmental Constraints*. Boulder, CO: Westview Press, 1978. A slim but very useful analysis of the relationship between Japan's economic development and its resource base.

Patrick, Hugh, ed. *Japanese Industrialization and Its Social Consequences*. Berkeley: University of California Press, 1976. A series of articles focusing on Japan's manufacturing labor force from economic, cultural, and political points of view.

Reischauer, Edwin O. *Japan, The Story of a Nation*. New York: Alfred A. Knopf, 1970. A fine analysis of Japan's historical development, written by the dean of Japanologists, all of whose books on Japan are now standard references.

Robinson, K. W. *Australia, New Zealand, and the Southwest Pacific*. 3d ed. London: University of London Press, 1974. A fine overview of the whole region of Oceania, but especially of Australia.

Rowland, D. T. "Theories of Urbanization in Australia." *Geographical Review* 67 (1977): 167–176. A review of several theories that have been offered to explain the dominance of Australia's metropolitan centers.

Schlosstein, Steven. *The End of the American Century.* New York: Congden & Wee, 1989. An impressive, if controversial, analysis of the thesis that the United States is in its sunset years as the dominant world power, and Japan is a rising economic star destined to command the stage in the next century.

Spate, O. H. K. *Australia.* New York: Praeger, 1968. Still a classic general study of Australia.

Trewartha, Glenn T. *Japan: A Geography.* Madison: University of Wisconsin Press, 1965. The basic geography of Japan, still useful, especially for its treatment of the physical environment and resource base.

Williams, D. B., ed. *Agriculture in the Australian Economy.* Sydney: Sydney University Press, 1982. Originally published in 1967, an updated and expanded comprehensive analysis of the agricultural sector; a solid reference for all aspects of rural Australia.

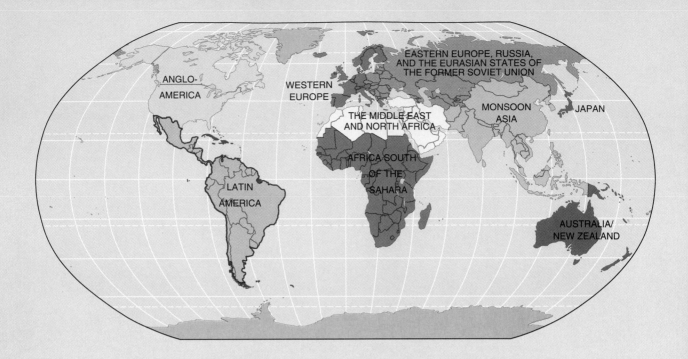

Although Latin America is physically close to the United States and Canada, for many in Anglo-America, it is one of the least understood culture regions in the world. That lack of understanding and familiarity can be traced in part to the historic economic and religious rivalries of colonial England and Spain. And in modern times linguistic, political, and technological differences have often masked many of the common needs and aspirations of Anglo-Americans and Latin Americans.

Many Anglo-Americans think of Latin America as a region of simple peasant farmers living in tiny, isolated villages without benefit of medical care or education. They envision those villagers faithfully attending Catholic mass in a colonial-era church, while corrupt military leaders and politicians carry out a never-ending series of revolutions in the distant cities. In reality, that stereotype may have been reflective of selected settings in the past, but it has never been a totally accurate portrayal and is certainly an inappropriate image for today. Although thousands of agrarian villages do still dot the region, most Latin Americans now live in great cities that are among the largest and fastest growing in the world.

Urbanization has brought to Latin America not only better-paying industrial jobs and the beginnings of a middle class but also increasing pressure for political reform and democratization. And with that political change has come fundamental social reform, including the spread of new religious faiths and practices and dramatic improvement in health care and education.

Latin American development has been financed in part through Anglo-American economic assistance. Consequently, Anglo-Americans have often expected Latin Americans to reciprocate by supporting the political and economic interests of Anglo-America. Thus, when Latin American nations disagree with the positions of the United States, many Anglo-Americans become confused and upset. At the same time many Latin Americans may become disturbed by what they perceive to be unwarranted outside intervention in their internal affairs. When emotions run high, the peoples of both regions may lose sight of any positive interaction and their mutual commitment to freedom and development.

PART 6

David L. Clawson

LATIN AMERICA

It is imperative that both Anglo-Americans and Latin Americans really learn about one another. We begin our study of Latin America by looking first, in Chapter 17, at the historical evolution of Latin American culture and at the challenges and opportunities that face all Latin Americans. We then examine the specific regional characteristics and potentials of Mexico and the Central American and Caribbean countries in Chapter 18 and of the South American nations in Chapter 19. As we proceed, we come to recognize not only the differences between the Anglo-American and Latin American cultures but also the common hopes and needs that are likely to bind them more closely in the years ahead.

17

Latin America's Heritage: Foundations and Processes of Change

The Iberian Heritage

The Colonial Period

The Era of Independence

Modern Latin America

The Incan ruins of Machu Picchu in the Peruvian Andes.
The Incan civilization was one of several civilizations that
thrived in Latin America before European colonization.
The most advanced Indian cultures of South America
evolved in highland environments.

Latin America extends from Mexico's border with the United States to the politically divided island of Tierra del Fuego, which faces Antarctic waters in the far south. Latin America is a region of great contrast and rapid change. It includes Brazil and Argentina, two of the largest and most richly endowed countries on earth, as well as Haiti, Grenada, and other Caribbean island nations that rank among the world's smallest and poorest countries. The physical environments of Latin America range from the Atacama Desert, where years pass without measurable precipitation, to the luxuriant Amazonian rain forest, and from snow-capped volcanoes that watch over cold and barren plateaus to hot, sandy tourist beaches.

In addition to physical contrasts, Latin America is a region of deep social and economic divisions. Vast, mechanized plantations produce export crops of sugarcane and tropical fruits on broad, fertile lowlands, while at the same time traditional farmers work tiny plots of extraordinarily steep land on distant mountain slopes. Every year countless thousands of those subsistence farmers and their families flee the poverty and isolation of the countryside and migrate to the cities, hoping to achieve a better life for themselves and their children. All too often their dreams are crushed by the realities of urban poverty and unemployment. Unable to afford decent accommodations, many find themselves forced to live in crowded and squalid inner-city tenement housing where dozens of families living in one-room "apartments" may be forced to share a single shower and toilet. Others build tiny, flimsy dwellings from discarded lumber, cardboard, or tar paper—ofttimes within sight of the high, guarded outer walls of the great mansions of the elite, where swimming pools, horse stables, and garages for foreign sports cars share space with manicured lawns and tropical flowers.

In the cities, old ways and new have been compressed into almost unimaginable combinations. Chevrolets and donkeys may be double-parked on narrow, cobblestoned streets lined with colonial buildings. Aggressive, well-educated businessmen dressed in Western suits and ties pass barefooted Indian women wearing hats and long, full skirts, while carrying babies wrapped in shawls on their backs. Customers in chic specialty shops pretend to ignore the homeless children and peddlers on the sidewalks and streets. Modern supermarkets often stand within view of traditional open-air market-places, where housewives and servants go daily to haggle over the price of fresh produce.

In a region of great mineral and agricultural resources, it is ironic that the greatest resource of all—human beings—has often been tragically wasted. Limited educational opportunities, rigid social stratification, graft, and corruption retard present-day economic development just as surely as did the colonial exploitation of the past. The Latin American nations' collective burden of wasted development opportunities, both internal and external, has resulted in some of the highest inflation rates and heaviest foreign-debt loads in the world.

As mentioned earlier, many of the long-held perceptions of Latin America are no longer accurate. In a land of supposedly universal allegiance to Roman Catholicism, fundamentalist Protestantism is growing at an explosive rate, while the Catholic Church struggles with politically leftist ideology and widespread apathy, both of which tend to undermine church tradition and authority. In a region often described as a land of revolutions, the great majority of the Latin American and Caribbean nations are now blessed with freely elected governments. The goal of establishing true and complete democracies remains difficult to achieve, however, owing to the continuing dominance of elite families who have resisted substantive change from the colonial era to the present. Pulled primarily by the perception of economic opportunity abroad, millions of Latin Americans attempt to emigrate to the United States or Canada each year, either legally or illegally.

Although Latin America has a troubled past, it is also a region of great progress and even greater potential. Never before have so many Latin Americans been so healthy, so well fed, housed, and educated, and so free to pursue their lives as they choose. Progress has been greater in some places than in others, however. Future development will depend, in large measure, on the continuing reformation of both internal structures and external relationships.

THE IBERIAN HERITAGE

The Roman Influence

The land-use patterns found today throughout Latin America owe much of their existence to practices that were initially instituted by Roman settlers in **Iberia**, the peninsula that encompasses the countries of Spain and Portugal. Ancient Roman society was largely preoccupied with social position and an ostentatious way of life. Wealth and social standing were achieved primarily through ownership of land, the most basic means of economic production. Ironically, however, the Romans' participation in the good life depended on their residing in Rome or in another major urban center rather than at their rural estates, for it was in the cities that the pleasures of Roman civilization were most available. Upper-class Romans met both needs by acquiring huge estates, called *latifundia*, and then practicing absentee ownership; the landowner, or *latifundista*, resided in a distant city and entrusted the day-to-day management of the estate to an overseer.

The effects of the *latifundia* system were significant. As the Roman, and later the Spanish and Latin American, elites flaunted their wealth by refusing to engage in manual labor of any kind, farming acquired a stigma of inferiority. Simultaneously, huge urban bureaucracies developed in the cities, where countless unnecessary jobs were created and staffed with friends and relatives of aristocratic government officials. It did not matter much that these positions offered limited salaries, since they permitted participation in a broad array of bribes and speculative ventures through which bureaucrats enriched themselves at the expense of the poor.

The *latifundia* system also encouraged use of the best lands for grazing animals, which required relatively little human labor and supervision, rather than for growing food crops, which would have been labor-intensive. Land use in Roman Iberia was a frontier version of that in Italy itself. Although some classic Mediterranean crops—such as wheat, barley, grapes, olives, and vegetables—were cultivated, the dominant land-use pattern was one of exploitive animal grazing. Even the fall of the Roman Empire did little to alter the nature of those entrenched patterns.

Roman control also brought a new religion to the Iberian Peninsula. As Roman military conquests had expanded throughout the Mediterranean Basin, Roman society itself had been gradually but steadily transformed by the revolutionary teachings of Christianity. Christianity had first been embraced secretly by the repressed lower-class urban masses but had subsequently gained believers among the ruling elite. It was finally recognized as a state religion in A.D. 313 by Emperor Constantine, whose deathbed conversion in A.D. 337 symbolized the spiritual conquest of the Roman world. Before the end of the fourth century, Christianity became the official state religion of the Roman Empire. By the time Spain and Portugal were colonized by Rome, all upper-class persons were landowning, urban, and Christian.

The Moorish Era

The outward stability of Roman-style life in Iberia was shattered in 711, when North African **Moors**, bent on spreading the Islamic faith throughout Europe, invaded the peninsula. The Moors initially overran the Spaniards, crossed the Pyrenees Mountains into France, and marched on Paris, where they were finally defeated at the Battle of Tours. Following that defeat, the Moors retreated into central and southern Spain and brought a golden age to the peninsula over the next 700 years. The Moors introduced advanced hydrologic engineering and metallurgical technology. They also brought numerous crops—including rice, citrus, coffee, cotton, sugarcane, and bananas—which were subsequently transported by the Spanish and Portuguese to the New World. In short, the Moors made Iberia a center of education and relative enlightenment at the very time that central and northern Europe had largely receded into the isolation and ignorance of the Dark Ages.

The Moorish occupation influenced the local culture in three additional ways. First, it removed any negative bias that the native Romans might have harbored toward people of darker skin color. Rather than associating dark skin color with inferiority, as was later to be the attitude among the Puritan and other northern European settlers of Anglo-America, the Spanish and Portuguese peoples came to view racial mixing as socially and politically advantageous. Their willingness to mix with darker-skinned peoples provided the basis for the subsequent development of Latin American race relationships.

Second, Moorish culture had a tradition of political instability and chaotic transfer of power. As time passed, Iberian politics became increasingly dominated by political fragmentation, charismatic personal leadership, and succession to leadership through violent rather than democratic mechanisms. Those traits were later transferred by the Spaniards to Latin America.

Third, and perhaps the most profound impact of Moorish occupation on Spanish culture, was the unification of church and state. Because the occupying Moors were of a different faith, those Spaniards who resisted the Moors came to perceive ethnic nationalism and religious belief as inseparable. To them, all true Spaniards were Catholic. All non-Catholics were then, by definition, non-Spaniards and were, therefore, unworthy of holding any major office. In fact, regulations were passed that required an applicant for the Christian priesthood to prove the purity of his blood line. Anyone with an ancestor in the previous four generations who had been a Jew, a Muslim, or any type of heretic could not gain high social standing.

Catholicism thus became fanatical and militant among the Roman Spaniards who took refuge in northern Spain after their defeat by the Moors. For them the unification of church and state made religion the overriding issue, which negated earlier racial tolerance.

In the eleventh century the Spaniards began a long series of wars aimed at driving the Moors from the peninsula. The popes in Rome were so grateful to the Spanish monarchs for reclaiming lands in the name of Christianity that they bestowed on the Spanish rulers the title of Defenders of the Faith. The papacy also ceded to the Spanish monarchs two far-reaching privileges, both of which continued in effect during the subsequent conquest and settlement of the Americas. The first was **royal patronage**, which gave Spanish kings the power to appoint all clergy in conquered lands. In colonial Latin America that practice resulted in the politicizing of at least the upper clergy; their decisions and behavior were frequently influenced more by allegiance to the crown than by loyalty to principle. The second privilege was the right of the crown to collect the tithe (theoretically, a tenth of a person's income) on behalf of the church. In colonial Latin America, the tithe came to serve as a government tax. Bound by those two extraordinary powers, church and state became inseparable, first in medieval Spain and later in colonial Latin America.

For young Spaniards, men coming of age during this uncertain time, wealth and prestige were limited to three primary career options. The preferred choice, that of *latifundista,* was available only to the oldest son in each family. It was he who inherited the entire family estate and who, by taking a wife from another prominent family, perpetuated the dominance of the landed aristocracy. The remaining sons were generally forced to choose between a military career, which offered the prospect of glorious conquests and the acquisition of land and an upper class way of life in conquered territories, and the clergy, which promised high social standing and the indirect control of the vast wealth of the church. Those two great forces, the military and the church, stood poised, both filled with crusading fervor, as the Moorish era wound down in Spain and Portugal.

It is historically significant that the Battle of Granada, the final defeat of the Moors, was fought only six months before Christopher Columbus discovered America. Although the great admiral never accepted the idea that he had opened up a New World, his contemporaries viewed his achievement differently. With Iberia now firmly under Christian control, an entire new continent awaited military and spiritual conquest and, with it, the achievement of personal fame and wealth.

THE COLONIAL PERIOD

The Spanish Conquest

News of the discovery of America spread rapidly through Spain and Portugal. Although the Spanish were the first to plant their flag in the New World, the Portuguese had been actively colonizing Africa and Asia for the previous 100 years and were anxious not to be excluded from America. In 1493 the pope, hoping to strengthen his ties with the emerging colonial powers, issued a bull (decree) that was ratified by Spain and Portugal in the **Treaty of Tordesillas** (1494). As the earthly representative of Christ, the pope granted half of the non-Christian world to Spain and half to Portugal. The imaginary line separating the two spheres was drawn 370 leagues (approximately 1,100 miles, or 1,800 kilometers) west of the Cape Verde Islands. As a result, Spain received all of the Americas except the easternmost extension of South America, which eventually became Portuguese Brazil.

Spanish settlement in the New World was dominated by pursuit of the three *G*s: gold, God, and glory. Bernal Díaz del Castillo, the chronicler of Hernando Cortés's conquest of Mexico, wrote, "We came to serve God . . . and to get rich." For the ***conquistadores,*** or conquerors, the two objectives went hand in hand, and both required the presence of large numbers of native peoples. The natives could be quickly converted to Catholicism and then could be forced to labor on behalf of the Spaniards in the fields and mines.

Native Indian Civilizations. At the time of the conquests, it is likely that some 75 to 100 million Indians inhabited the Latin American and the Caribbean island realms. These were divided into thousands of indigenous groups that differed one from another in dialect, levels of social and political organization, and customs, as well as the physical environments which they occupied. The largest population clusters were found among four socially and politically advanced groups situated primarily in the highlands of western Latin America (Figure 17–1). The most urbanized of those groups was the **Aztec** Empire, whose capital of Tenochtitlán was one of the largest and most impressive cities on earth, with a population of over 200,000 residing in the midst of magnificent temples, plazas, and marketplaces, supplied with produce transported from throughout southern Mexico and northern Central America. Tenochtitlán later was razed by the Spanish *conquis-*

tadores, who built Mexico City upon its ruins. Prior to being defeated by the Spaniards, the Aztecs had become a very fatalistic and warlike people, offering on special occasions the hearts of thousands of human sacrificial victims to a god named Huitzilopochtli. At the same time, they were also a sensitive and highly educated people who achieved high levels of philosophy, poetry, and the arts.

Of all the indigenous, pre-Columbian (before arrival of Columbus) high-culture groups that were present at the time of the Iberian Conquest, none was as ancient as the **Maya**, whose civilization emerged at approximately 3000 B.C. in the highlands of Guatemala and neighboring Mexico. By the seventh century B.C., the focus of Mayan civilization had shifted from the highlands onto the surrounding lowlands to the east and north. There a Classic, or golden, age emerged, characterized by the erection of great monumental cities in the midst of rainforests extending from Tabasco to the Copán River Valley of northern Honduras. Although this group achieved levels of mathematics and writing equal or superior to those present in Old World civilizations, the Mayan world was also one of much uncertainty and violence, as dozens of independent states warred against one another in a never-ending series of shifting political alliances. By the ninth century A.D., the cities of the rainforest had been abandoned and the population, now much reduced from previous periods, had reverted to the practice of shifting, slash-and-burn agriculture. This period was followed by a brief reflowering of urban life on the limestone plains of the Yucatán peninsula during the Post-Classic period of the thirteenth to fifteenth centuries. The Spanish Conquest brought an end to Mayan political identity, but not to the people and their culture, both of which continue to form the basis of rural life throughout the region.

The third of the pre-Columbian high-culture groups of the New World was the **Chibcha**, who at the time of the Spanish Conquest lived in agricultural villages scattered through the eastern Andes of Colombia. Although lacking the large cities and sophisticated agricultural technologies of the Aztec, Maya, and Inca peoples, the Chibcha had developed levels of social and political organization superior to those of the lowland forest dwellers residing within the Amazon and Orinoco river valleys to the east of the Andes.

The greatest of the pre-Columbian empires of South America was that of the **Inca**, which arose in

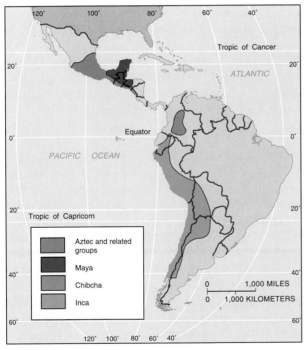

Figure 17–1
Pre-Columbian Indian cultures of Latin America. Most of the pre-Columbian population (i.e., before Columbus arrived) lived in four high-culture clusters, where population density was substantial. Throughout the remainder of Latin America the Indian population was widely scattered and lived by traditional production systems.

the high mountain valleys of southern Peru and Bolivia in the century prior to the Spanish Conquest. The Inca civilization was, in many respects, inferior to that of the Aztec and Maya. Its capital city of Cuzco, for example, never approached Tenochtitlán in size or grandeur, and the Inca never developed a written language. What they did excel at, however, was the imposition of authoritarian social and political control and the construction of remarkable highways and bridges, many of which continue to this day. These characteristics were what enabled the Incas to conquer and subject countless other peoples and to establish an empire that, when the Spaniards arrived, stretched over 2,500 miles (4,000 kilometers), from northern Ecuador to central Chile.

Agriculture formed the livelihood base for all of these four high-culture civilizations, as well as the socially and politically less-developed peoples of Latin America's central and eastern lowlands. Advanced land-management techniques—including land drainage, terracing, fertilization, crop and land rotation, and intercropping—were widely practiced. Among the domesticated crops were maize (corn), beans, squash, chile peppers, tomatoes, manioc (cassava), sweet potatoes, white potatoes, peanuts, pineapples, papayas, avocados, cacao (chocolate), American cotton, and tobacco. As for animals, dogs were everywhere. In addition, the Incas had guinea pigs as pets and as a food source, llamas (a humpless relative of the camel) as beasts of burden, and alpacas and vicunas (relatives of the llama) as sources of fine wool. However, none of those animals was used in farming; the Indians cultivated their land entirely by hand, with the aid of simple digging sticks.

To that agricultural complex the Spaniards added large Old World animals, including pigs, sheep, goats, donkeys, beef and dairy cattle, and horses. They also introduced animal-drawn plows and a wide array of Old World grains, fruits, and vegetables.

European New World Settlement.   The initial focus of Spanish settlement in the New World was the Caribbean island of Hispaniola, which is divided today into the Spanish-speaking Dominican Republic and the French-speaking Haiti. Hispaniola served as a testing ground, where the Spaniards experimented with crops, animals, and cultural notions they had brought from Iberia. The output of the small gold mines on the island soon diminished, however, and in what was to become a tragic and common pattern, great numbers of native Indians died from exposure to European diseases, overwork, and undernourishment. With the discovery of the vast wealth and power of the Aztec and Inca empires of Mexico and Peru, respectively, Hispaniola and the other Caribbean islands soon became settlements of only secondary significance to the Spaniards. Most were eventually lost to British, French, Dutch, and American military conquest.

Spain's conquest of Mexico was accomplished under the leadership of Hernando Cortés. The Spaniards were armed with both sword and cross—as well as guns and horses. In addition, an even more powerful weapon was on their side—the Indian legend of the promised return of a great fair-skinned, bearded god. As Cortés's ragged party of 400 men steadily advanced toward Tenochtitlán, the Aztec chiefs vacillated, initially engaging the intruders in battle but then, at the final hour, bowing and kissing the earth beneath Cortés's feet in a futile attempt at appeasement. Unswayed, Cortés abducted and tortured the Aztec chiefs and took possession of the country in the name of God and the Spanish king.

Meanwhile, in Peru and Bolivia, Francisco Pizarro was conquering the Incan realm in a similar fashion. Within just a few decades, all of Latin America had fallen under European control (Figure 17–2).

Economic Relationships

Following their military conquests, the Spaniards immediately set about restructuring the economic and social life of the natives. One of the first steps was the establishment of the *encomienda* system, in essence a New World version of the medieval European manorial system. The Indians were informed that they had been entrusted to the care of their Spanish masters, who were required to provide them with physical protection and spiritual salvation. In return for the privilege of being at least superficially indoctrinated into the holy faith and exposed to the civilizing influences of the Spanish language, the Indians were told that they owed their Spanish masters tribute in the form of labor or produce or both. Huge *latifundia*-like land grants were given to the Spanish *encomenderos,* who then took up residence in the distant cities, where they could better enjoy the fruits of their Indians' labor.

Figure 17-2
La Paz, Bolivia's capital city, at an elevation of 12,000 feet (3,650 meters) on the *altiplano* (high plain). This high plateau within the Andean Mountain system illustrates the harsh environments to which the early Spanish colonizers adapted in Columbia, Ecuador, Peru, and Bolivia. The mixture of old and new architectural styles reflects the long history of settlement in this area.

Ironically, those Spaniards who were given control of the Indians were themselves subjected to unwanted controls by the Crown, which attempted to regulate for the benefit of the mother country all economic activity in the new colonies. The regulatory vehicle was *mercantilism*, a governing philosophy under which a colony could trade only with its mother country; trade between colonies was severely restricted. Furthermore, all goods shipped between Spain and its colonies had to be carried by Spanish vessels. (Those Spanish ships, often laden with gold and silver, were exposed to such great danger from pirates or buccaneers that the Spanish government erected a series of strategically situated fortresses at key cities—including Havana, Cuba; Veracruz, Mexico; Cartagena, Colombia; San Juan, Puerto Rico; and St. Augustine, Florida—and instructed the ships to travel only in semiannual convoys.) In addition, Spanish mercantile policy curtailed manufacturing-related activities, which meant that even raising sheep and growing wheat, olives, and grapes—all of which competed

with Spain's support of its own textile or food-processing industries—were suppressed. And finally, a tax of 20 percent, called the royal fifth, was levied.

The long-term effects of mercantilism on the economic development of the colonies were extremely negative. Economic initiative, diversification, and self-reliance were discouraged; contraband and smuggling became rampant. Graft and dishonesty among government officials were the norm. Competition, rather than unity, was fostered among colonies with a common cultural heritage, and feelings of resentment toward Spain grew even stronger.

Social Organization

Society in colonial Latin America was highly stratified, largely according to race initially. But, as the Spaniards and the Portuguese intermingled with the darker-skinned natives, they produced mixed European-Indian offspring called *mestizos.* Then, as great numbers of Indians died and as those who remained proved to be poor workers in the hot and humid lowlands, large numbers of black slaves were introduced, especially in the Caribbean basin and northeastern Brazil. The offspring of white-black unions were called **mulattos**, and those of Indian-black unions, **zambos**. Soon, race was an inadequate social standard. How, for example, would one even identify, let alone classify, the offspring of a mestizo-mulatto union?

Because of the widespread racial mixing, a cultural racial classification system came to be adopted that ranked individuals by their occupations, languages, and life-styles. At the top were the Europeans, who held the highest managerial and governmental jobs, spoke Spanish or Portuguese, and lived in cities. Then came the *mestizos* and the *mulattos,* who generally managed the great agricultural estates or performed menial urban tasks. At the bottom were the blacks and the Indians, the latter term becoming synonymous with rural, agricultural laborers. Indians worked with their hands and generally went barefoot or wore sandals. The men wore hats, and the women had long, braided hair and babies in shawls on their backs. Indians spoke in their native tongues and were uneducated in European ways.

The Spanish preoccupation with race and position was a reflection of the social inequalities of colonial society, which, in turn, were transmitted through the educational system. Members of the wealthy European class, wanting to perpetuate their dominance, paid great sums of money to enroll their children in private, usually Catholic-sponsored, schools. Because they then refused to tax themselves to support public education for *mestizo* and Indian youths, the resulting educational system contributed directly to the continued underdevelopment of Latin America. In contrast to the efforts of Spain's and Portugal's northern European rivals, the English and the Dutch, who turned to public education to create a literate and democratic work force in their colonies, Latin American society remained largely illiterate, totalitarian, and technologically backward.

The Spread of Catholicism

While the *conquistadores* were pursuing the military conquest of the New World, the Catholic clergy were undertaking the spiritual conquest of the native peoples. Spanish and Portuguese conversion efforts, however, emphasized outward compliance with sacramental ordinances, such as baptism,

rather than a thorough understanding and implementation of the teachings and beliefs of the Catholic Church. To facilitate that outward conversion of the natives, the clergy related Catholic practices and beliefs to their pagan counterparts and permitted indigenous ceremonies and customs to continue.

Not surprisingly, millions of Indian converts were reported annually in the years immediately following the European arrival. Most of the conversions were doctrinally superficial, however. The vast majority of the Indians did not understand the Spanish language, much less Catholic teachings. What resulted was a fusion, or mixing, of Iberian Catholicism with native American practices.

Four distinct forms of Catholicism evolved in colonial Latin America, and they persist to this day. The first is formal Catholicism, which was practiced by the small, European upper class that resided in the urban centers. Formal Catholicism emphasizes piety, faith, and participation in the Catholic sacraments. Women attend mass regularly, and a heavy emphasis is placed on devotional societies, charities, and social clubs. Membership in a formal Catholic church reinforces a person's upper-class standing within the community.

The second form is nominal Catholicism, which came to include the majority of the rural peasant population as well as almost all of the urban poor. Nominal Catholics make no financial contributions to the church, except for the rare occasions when they pay a priest to perform a sacrament on behalf of a family member. Priests are viewed negatively, an attitude known as anticlericalism. Men are unlikely to enter a church more than twice during their lifetimes: once when their parents carry them in as infants to be baptized and once to be married. When asked whether they consider themselves Catholics, their response may be "in name only" or "yes, but in my own way."

The third form is folk Catholicism, which was developed by isolated tribal peoples. Their beliefs and customs are a mixture of pre-Columbian animistic and medieval Catholic practices, centered in the ancient holy places of mountains and valleys as well as in the local church.

The fourth Catholic form is spiritism, which evolved in the lowland areas of the Caribbean basin and Brazil among the predominantly black and mulatto populations. Its emphasis on close communion with spirit beings is of African derivation; and its doctrines, ceremonies, and celebrations bear only the slightest resemblance to those of the formal Catholic church. Haitian Voodoo, Cuban and Dominican Santería, and Brazilian Candomble are some of the many forms of spiritism currently practiced in Latin America and the Caribbean.

Although the colonial church was highly tolerant of diversity in internal belief and practice, it attempted to shield the people, through the office of the church known as the Inquisition, from what it perceived to be corrupting Protestant theology. The Inquisition was originally established in Catholic Europe to preserve the purity of the faith by screening or censoring literature and works of art. As time passed, however, Spain came to dread England and the other Protestant powers so greatly that any book or publication from northern Europe was automatically banned, whether or not its content was religious. Even books that would have aided the diffusion of technology were suppressed. Thus, as the Industrial Revolution gained momentum in northern Europe and in the Anglo-American colonies, Catholic Latin America fell further and further behind.

THE ERA OF INDEPENDENCE

A major division arose in class-conscious colonial Latin America between those Europeans born in the Iberian peninsula, who were called *peninsulares,* and those born in the American colonies, who were called *criollos,* or creoles. The highest civil and ecclesiastical offices were reserved exclusively for the blue-blood *peninsulares.* In fact, it was so important to be born in Spain that upper-class Spanish women, on finding themselves pregnant, often booked passage for the mother country. Even a child born at sea was classified as a *peninsular* as long as the mother was en route to Spain.

As long as the *penisulares* outnumbered the *criollos,* colonial society remained relatively stable. As the centuries passed, however, the increasingly predominant *criollos* grew ever more resentful of their second-class status. The revolutions that swept the continent in the early 1800s were essentially a class war between the two dominant European subclasses. And although freedom and liberty were proclaimed throughout every land by the victorious *criollos,* little meaningful change took place in the lives of the *mestizo, mulatto,* and Indian masses.

Political independence also failed to resolve the fundamental problem of unequal landholdings in a predominantly rural, agrarian society. Indeed, in many areas, access of the lower classes to land actually worsened under the reign of *criollo* and foreign investors. The great estates, or *latifundia,* took three forms, which have survived in varying degrees to the present. The first was the plantation, established in the hot, lowland zones, usually near a coast. Plantations were, and continue to be, essentially monocultural; **monoculture** identifies agricultural production that centers on one dominant crop, such as sugar cane or bananas. Since the crop is produced primarily for export, plantations are basically commercial ventures aimed at generating cash profits for the owners, typically through the use of mechanized equipment and a historically black or *mulatto* work force.

In contrast, the interior highlands came to be dominated by the *hacienda,* huge areas given over primarily to extensive cattle grazing and the use of Indian labor. The *criollo* owners, though anxious for profits to support their urban way of life, nevertheless viewed their *haciendas* primarily as a source of prestige rather than as a business. The *estancia*, the third form of *latifundia,* designated the great cattle ranches found on the fertile pampas, or prairies, of Argentina and Uruguay.

All three estate forms used inherited debt to enslave their laborers, thus discouraging the development of both democratic institutions and a middle class. The huge *latifundia* supported the privileged few in indolent luxury, while the countless small farmers of the region continued to work isolated, tiny plots that they often had no hope of ever owning. Working under a wide range of local conditions—from steep, forested mountain slopes to high interior volcanic basins—those creative, self-reliant small farmers, like their descendants today, sustained themselves and their families through polyculture.

Polyculture identifies the growing of several crop species at the same time or the cultivation of multiple varieties of each crop species. Today, for example, the Indian farmers of Mexico and Central America raise maize, beans, and squash, sometimes in shared space and sometimes in separate fields. At the same time they cultivate four different-color varieties of maize, as well as seven or eight varieties of beans of differing shape, size, and color (see the boxed feature Multicolored Maize and the Green Revolution). Each variety differs from the others, not only in physical appearance but also in taste and environmental har-

MULTICOLORED MAIZE AND
THE GREEN REVOLUTION

Traditional farmers in Latin America maximize the security of their harvest by using the natural genetic diversity of their principal food crops as fully as possible. For example, the highland farmers of Mexico and Central America cultivate four varieties of maize: yellow, white, blue-purple, and red (Figure A).

For cultural reasons yellow maize is considered unfit for human consumption and suitable only for animal feed. Because most of the farmers are too poor to keep large animals, yellow maize is not widely grown. Of the remaining three varieties, white maize is the most productive and is the principal ingredient of tortillas. It is planted first because it takes the longest to mature. Blue-purple maize is considered to have excellent taste but is less productive than white maize. It is used to replant those portions of fields where white maize has not germinated well. Red maize is considered the worst tasting and least productive of the edible varieties, but it has the advantage of the shortest growing season. It

is used as an emergency survival food and is planted only where both white and blue-purple varieties have failed. Multicolored maize thus functions as crop insurance, giving farmers three opportunities to obtain a complete harvest.

In recent years agricultural development personnel have attempted to persuade traditional peasant farmers to adopt hybrid maize as part of the Green Revolution package of agricultural inputs, which also includes chemical fertilizers and insecticides. The farmers have generally rejected the so-called modern technologies, however, because the single-color hybrid varieties would result in a potentially life-threatening loss of crop diversity. In addition, the new hybrid varieties cost more to grow but fail to produce more grain than the traditional varieties do. Certainly, Latin American small farmers are anxious to increase their productivity, but they will adopt new products only when they are truly superior, both culturally and economically.

diness. The Indian farmers of the high Andes raise twenty to thirty varieties of potatoes, each with distinct physical characteristics and environmental needs. With that genetic security blanket, the traditional farmers of Latin America have been able not only to feed themselves and their families but also to supply the basic needs of distant urban dwellers.

Outdoor markets have functioned historically as the principal interface between the dominant urban culture and the subservient rural culture (Figure 17–3). As housewives and maids haggle daily with peasant vendors and intermediaries over the price of fresh produce and handicrafts, urban dwellers obtain essential food and fuel, and rural folk earn cash with which to purchase commodities that cannot be produced on the farm, such as manufactured appliances and medicines.

MODERN LATIN AMERICA

Latin America today, though strongly linked to the past, is experiencing all the changes and challenges of economic and social modernization. Many of those changes have come so recently and so forcefully that the peoples of the region have had little time to adjust.

Demographic Change

Many parts of Latin America originally supported dense native populations, which were drastically reduced as a consequence of European occupation. Jamaica, for example, had approximately 60,000 Arawak Indians when Columbus arrived; a century later the total Jamaican population was only 1,500, of which only 74 were Arawaks. Other areas expe-

Figure A
An Indian village in Bolivia, not far from La Paz on the *altiplano* (high plain). Maize, the common food grain throughout much of Latin America, is being dried after harvest. Many rural Latin Americans continue to live much as their ancestors did centuries before, including cultivating multiple color-based varieties of the staple food crop.

rienced population declines that were similarly radical, not because of any intentional, systematic destruction of the Indians by the Europeans but as a result of the interplay of three factors.

First, a massive disruption of native food production was brought about by the loss of the best farmlands to Spanish cities and animal grazing. The Indians were forced to flee to the distant hills and mountain slopes to eke out a meager existence. Food shortages became chronic among the native peoples, whose decline in numbers was matched by a corresponding increase in horses and cattle. The second factor that contributed to the great loss of Indian population was the introduction of European diseases—including smallpox, measles, and typhus—to which the natives had no resistance. And third, weakened by both malnutrition and disease, countless Indians died of overwork in the mines and on the plantations. By 1650, the native population of Latin America and the Caribbean was only 5 to 10 percent of what it had been prior to the arrival of the Europeans.

Almost 300 years were to pass before the population of the region would begin to grow rapidly again. Indeed, most parts of Latin America did not regain their preconquest population levels until the mid-twentieth century. The primary cause of such slow population growth was high death rates, especially among infants, which counterbalanced the traditionally high birthrates. The only exception to that overall pattern was some immigration, principally of southern Europeans to Brazil, Uruguay, and Argentina in the late nineteenth and early twentieth centuries. Overall, however, Latin America has attracted comparatively few immigrants.

403

The relatively low population levels of Latin America began to change dramatically in the mid-twentieth century. Improved health care and sanitation, including the introduction of antibiotics and mosquito-controlling chemical compounds, made the traditional population centers healthier and opened up vast lowland regions to colonization and economic development. The result was unprecedented population growth, which continues today at only a slightly slower pace.

Two examples illustrate the magnitude of the change. The population of Nealtican, a peasant village in the central Mexican highlands, grew by over 600 percent between 1950 and 1993 (Table 17–1). That pattern, repeated countless times, also has affected the population of Mexico as a whole. In 1950 the population of Mexico only slightly exceeded its preconquest level in 1519; however, since 1950 Mexico's population has more than tripled, placing unprecedented pressure on the rural land base.

Urbanization

While opportunities for personal advancement have steadily dwindled in the rural areas of Latin America over the past four or five decades, the cities have increasingly assimilated technological advances that have integrated them into the mainstream of world commerce and industry. The result has been an ever-widening gap in living levels between urban residents and newly arrived migrants from the countryside.

Seemingly overnight, Latin America has been transformed from a predominantly rural region to one in which 73 percent of the people now reside in urban areas. Many Latin American cities that were formerly compact, orderly, and pleasant places in which to live have exploded in population and are rapidly taking their places among the largest and most congested urban centers in the world (Table 17–2). Much of that growth is occurring in huge outer rings around the traditional cores of the cities. As the rural migrants pour in, most settle first in old, rundown inner-city housing stock, which they eventually leave in favor of newer, self-built residences erected within vast **shantytowns**, or squatter settlements, found on the outskirts of the city (Figure 17–4). Municipal governments—which are hard pressed to provide basic services such as drinking water, sewerage, electricity, garbage disposal, and police protection to the older, established neighborhoods—find themselves almost totally incapable of servicing the newly settled periphery.

Most of the major urban centers in Latin America are now caught in a self-perpetuating cycle of growth that brings as many problems as benefits. As more and more people flock to the cities, new industries and businesses are established there in response to the growing market. Those industries and businesses, in turn, attract even more migrants. As the accompanying number of automobiles and diesel-powered buses and trucks has also spiraled, traffic has become a nightmare. And levels of air, water, and solid-waste pollution rank among the worst in the world. Crime and corruption run rampant.

Figure 17-3
An Indian market in Chincheru, Peru. The highland population of Ecuador, Peru, and Bolivia is predominantly Indian. Outdoor markets continue to thrive in Latin America, where peasant farmers sell their surplus products to urban dwellers. Produce is fresh and prices negotiable.

Many Latin Americans, dissatisfied with their current economic and political circumstances, attempt either legal or illegal international migration. The crossing of millions of Mexicans into the United States every year has been the most widely publicized of those movements and prompted a stiff new U.S. immigration policy in 1986. Mexico itself, however, is now beset with large numbers of Guatemalan refugees who have crossed into the Mexican state of Chiapas. Similarly, the Greater Antilles—including the Dominican Republic, Puerto Rico, Haiti, and Cuba—have recently sent large numbers of migrants to the United States, yet those islands are viewed as lands of opportunity by the even poorer peoples of the Lesser Antilles. Other significant international migrations affecting Latin America and the Caribbean include blacks from the English-speaking Caribbean to Great Britain, Colombians to oil-rich Venezuela, and Hondurans, Salvadorans, and Guatemalans to the United States. Given the ever-increasing income gaps between the wealthy and the poor in much of Latin America, these migration pressures are likely to continue and possibly worsen.

Social and Religious Change

When political independence was achieved by the liberal *criollos* in the early 1800s, the constitutions of the new nations were invariably modeled after those of the United States or France, both of which had recently established new, democratic governments. The Latin American constitutions provided for democracy in its fullest sense, including the separation of powers among the legislative, judicial, and executive branches of government, as well as extensive guarantees of individual freedoms and rights. The problem, of course, was that the illiterate and socially stratified Latin American societies were inherently incapable of implementing in real life what was prescribed on paper. Totalitarian governments, often associated with military forces, soon rose to power and lasted only until they were replaced by the next generation of colonels and dictators. Little, if any, real power was exercised by the masses, whom the elite did not consider capable of political responsibility.

Table 17-1
Population growth in Mexico in selected years.

	Approximate Population	
	Nealtican	Mexico
1519	2,250	25,000,000
1900	1,264	14,000,000
1950	2,448	27,000,000
1960	3,054	35,000,000
1975	7,000	56,000,000
1993	15,600	87,000,000

Sources: Mexican General Census of Population, 1953, 1964; Robert C. West and John P. Augelli, *Middle America: Its Lands and Peoples*, 3rd ed. (Englewood Cliffs, NJ: Prentice-Hall, 1989; *The Statesman's Year–Book 1993–94* (New York: St. Martin's Press, 1993); World Bank, *World Development Report 1993* (New York: Oxford University Press, 1993).

Table 17-2
Growth of major Latin American urban centers in selected years.

	Estimated Population (in millions)			
	1950	1970	1990	2000
Mexico City, Mexico	2.0	8.6	20.2	27.8
São Paulo, Brazil	2.5	7.8	18.1	25.4
Rio de Janeiro, Brazil	2.9	6.8	11.4	14.2
Buenos Aires, Argentina	4.5	8.4	11.5	12.9
Lima, Peru	1.2	3.3	6.6	9.2
Bogotá, Colombia	.6	2.5	5.7	7.9
Santiago, Chile	1.4	2.9	5.3	6.3

Sources: United Nations, Population Division, *Trends and Prospects in the Populations of Urban Agglomerations, 1950–2000* (New York: United Nations, 1975); Charles S. Sargent, "The Latin American City," pp. 201–249, in *Latin America: An Introductory Survey*, edited by Brian W. Blouet and Olwyn M. Blouet (New York: Wiley, 1982); *The World Almanac and Book of Facts 1993* (New York: Pharos Books, 1992).

Figure 17-4
Slums outside São Paulo, Brazil. Latin America's fast-growing cities commonly exhibit ultramodern and wealthy residential neighborhoods, as well as vast shantytowns with festering poverty. Slums in Latin American cities are often located on the periphery of a city rather than in the inner city.

That totalitarian political tradition finally began to fade in the post–World War II era, as urbanization and industrialization created pressures for a better-trained work force. Then, as an urban middle class gradually developed, democratic political practices began to take root. Today, the political trend in Latin America is clearly toward democratic civilian governments. A significant milestone occurred in 1990 with the fall of Chile's military regime. For the first time in modern history, each South American nation was under the administration of a freely elected civilian government. Although it is probable that individual countries will continue to pass through temporary authoritarian regressions—indeed, military government was reestablished in Suriname during parts of 1990 and 1991, and martial law was declared in Peru in 1992—the forces of economic modernization will likely continue to move the region as a whole toward greater levels of individual freedom.

The same forces that are working to increase the levels of individual participation in political matters are also contributing to a major transformation of the traditional religious landscape. The institutional Catholic Church in Latin America is being challenged today by three powerful movements. The first is secularism, or a pervasive lack of religious interest and involvement by the general membership. This natural outgrowth of nominal Catholicism has been reinforced by the process of urbanization, which disrupts traditional behavior patterns.

The second challenge, **fundamentalist Protestantism**, originated as a spin-off from Chilean Methodist congregations in 1909 and has since diffused extensively throughout the region at the grass-roots level. Appealing first to the repressed masses, its emphasis on literacy, education, and frugality has resulted in the rise of second- and third-generation members into professional-level positions of influence. Pentecostalism and other non-Catholic fundamentalist Christian faiths—including Latter-day Saints (Mormons), Seventh-day Adventists, and Jehovah's Witnesses—have made major inroads in Latin America. All of those faiths are now viewed by the masses as socially upscale, with teachings of benefit not only in the next life but in this one as well. Fundamentalist Protestantism has reached every corner of Latin America today. In many nations, including Brazil, Chile, Haiti, and Guatemala, it is estimated that more worshipers attend Protestant services on any given Sunday than attend Catholic mass.

The third challenge to the institutional Catholic Church is leftist ideology, which takes several forms in Latin America. One is overt Marxism, or communism. Although some people find it appealing, communism is never likely to freely attract great numbers of Latino followers because of its restrictions on freedom of worship, speech, and movement and because of its emphasis on individuals' placing the interests of the party and state ahead of their own personal ambitions. Those ambitions have traditionally been expressed in Latin America through the culturally-cherished values of *machismo* and *dignidad de la persona* (inherent self-worth of the individual). Many Catholic priests, however, have become intellectually converted to a different ideology known as **liberation theology**, which advocates a preferential treatment for the lowest classes. Those priests have organized small self-help study groups, known as basic ecclesial communities (CEBs). CEBs are similar, in organization and methodology, to the small, grass-roots Protestant congregations. Viewed collectively, both fundamentalist Protestantism and liberation theology may represent a rejection of the traditional class structure of Latin society and a movement toward increased levels of individual freedom and participation.

Economic Change

Economic development, in its broadest sense, is associated throughout the world with the processes of industrialization and urbanization. Until recently, manufacturing in Latin America was generally limited to small, family-owned and -operated establishments that focused on food processing, textiles, and other low-technology enterprises. Industrial expansion was hindered by inadequate transportation and communication networks, an untrained work force, small local markets with limited purchasing power, and little accumulation of money or capital.

Latin American nations have made great strides in overcoming many of those obstacles. New highways and freeways are now crowded with trucks carrying industrial components and products. Telephone and

computer communications are common. Literacy rates now average 70 to 75 percent and are even higher among the younger generation. The growth of cities is creating an urban middle class, many of whose members are employed in the growing industrial sector of the economy. One of the most impressive indicators of the modernization of the region's economy is the growth of manufactured products, whose share of Latin America's exports increased from 10.9 percent in 1970 to 33.0 percent in 1990 (Figure 17–5). At the same time, the share of foods and nonfuel mineral ores, formerly the traditional mainstays of the regional economy, fell from 66.0 to 42.2 percent of all exports. These figures suggest that much of Latin America is exhibiting economic traits more similar to those of developed rather than developing regions. Despite such restructuring progress, however, economic problems throughout Latin America caused a marked slowing of the annual rate of growth during the 1980s.

In the minds of many Latin Americans the greatest obstacle to continued industrial expansion is the accumulation of sufficient capital to establish the types of plants and facilities that will be competitive in the international market. In other words, how can the Latin American nations get enough money to make money?

The classic Western capitalist response is that the Latin American nations should reinvest at least 10 percent of their annual gross national product

Figure 17–5
The changing structure of Latin American exports, by product category. The composition of Latin American exports is changing rapidly, with food, animal products, and nonfuel mineral ores decreasing in relative importance and manufactured products becoming more prominent. (From Montague J. Lord, "Latin America's Exports of Manufactured Goods," in *Economic and Social Progress in Latin America*, Washington, DC: Inter-American Development Bank, 1992, pp. 171–279).

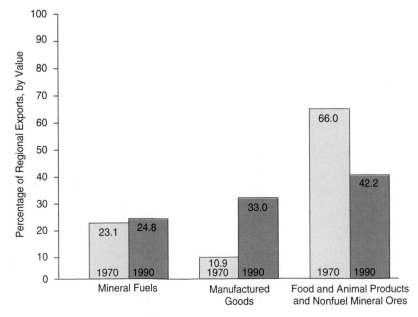

Figure 17–6
A family in the eastern lowlands of Peru. For many families low income, limited education, and poor health care combine to make economic progress a nearly impossible dream.

(GNP) in the industrial infrastructure, including roads and factories. Although that approach is undeniably correct conceptually, it is somewhat like telling the poverty-ridden parents of eight children that all they have to do to become prosperous is to wisely invest 10 percent of their annual gross earnings. Regardless of how much they may want to follow that counsel, doing so would imperil the immediate health and the very lives of that family (Figure 17–6). The poor Latin American nations that are struggling to meet the most basic needs of their people—adequate food, health care, sanitation, and education—are hard pressed to reinvest 10 percent of their economic output in industry.

Funding for industrial development in Latin America, then, must usually be obtained from external sources rather than from internal ones. During the 1950s most external capital came into Latin America through direct foreign investment by multinational corporations. That approach brought much-needed cash into the Latin economies, but it also increased foreign meddling in the internal affairs of those nations. That situation, often described as neocolonialism, was and is politically unacceptable to Latin Americans because it deprives them, to varying degrees, of their collective pride and freedom to chart their own course of development. Consequently, in the 1960s most external funds came through direct foreign-aid grants by so-called friendly nations. But, foreign aid also comes with preconditions and expectations for both donor and recipient nations.

The Latin American Debt Crisis

Since the early 1970s most foreign money flowing into Latin America has come in the form of loans from huge, private international banks and their representatives, including the International Monetary Fund and the World Bank. Although the intentions of both the world banking community and the leaders of the Latin American nations have been honorable, the loans have created such serious problems that many observers, both Latin American and foreign, are now questioning the wisdom of the lending approach.

What has happened, in brief, is that Latin American nations have borrowed huge sums of money for development projects. Neither they nor the lending institutions, however, have paid sufficient attention to the countries' long-term ability to repay the loans. Ironically, those countries that showed the greatest potential for economic modernization—including Brazil, Mexico, and Argentina—borrowed most heavily and now find themselves with the greatest debt loads. The foreign debts of both Brazil and Mexico exceeded $100 billion by 1991, and other Latin nations were also carrying heavy burdens. Ironically, although Latin America's largest nations are presently the most indebted in terms of total amount of money owed to overseas institutions, many of the smaller nations are carrying a greater debt burden in terms of their capacity to repay the loans (Table 17–3). Nicaragua, Jamaica, Panama, Ecuador, and Honduras, for example, each owe more

money than the value of all goods and services produced in a given year. When debt reaches those levels, countries find it difficult to make timely payments of even the interest due on the loans; repayment of the principal is almost entirely out of the question.

In the 1980s the initial response of the international banking community to the debt crisis was simply to arrange for "bridge" loans to the Latin American and other Third World nations to enable them to pay the interest due on the previous loans. That strategy, sometimes referred to as the Baker plan (after then–U.S. Treasury Secretary James Baker), essentially took the questionable position that the solution to unmanageable debt is more debt. Those actions succeeded in buying time for lenders and borrowers alike but failed to address the need for fundamental changes in attitudes and policies among both the international financial community and the debtor nations.

Those long-overdue changes finally began in the late 1980s with the election of new political leadership in the United States and in many key Latin

Table 17-3
Foreign indebtedness of selected Latin American and Caribbean nations, 1980-1991.

	Total External Debt (millions of U.S. dollars)		Total External Debt as a Percentage of GNP	
	1980	1991	1980	1991
Argentina	$27,157	$63,707	48.4	49.2
Bolivia	2,700	4,075	93.3	85.3
Brazil	71,046	116,514	31.3	28.8
Chile	12,081	17,902	45.5	60.7
Colombia	6,941	17,369	20.9	43.5
Costa Rica	2,744	4,043	59.7	74.9
Dominican Republic	2,002	4,492	31.2	65.7
Ecuador	5,997	12,469	53.8	114.5
El Salvador	911	2,172	26.2	37.4
Guatemala	1,166	2,704	14.9	29.5
Haiti	303	747	20.9	28.8
Honduras	1,470	3,177	60.5	113.8
Jamaica	1,904	4,456	78.3	134.9
Mexico	71,046	101,737	30.5	36.9
Nicaragua	2,176	10,446	108.5	153.5
Panama	2,974	6,791	87.5	130.1
Paraguay	954	2,177	20.7	35.0
Peru	9,386	20,709	47.6	44.3
Uruguay	1,660	4,189	17.0	45.3
Venezuela	29,345	34,372	42.1	65.3

Source: The World Bank, *World Development Report 1993* (New York: Oxford University Press, 1993), 278–285.

Table 17-4
Annual variation in the consumer
price index for selected Latin
American nations.

	Percentage of Annual Increase in Consumer Prices		
	1961–1970	1971–1980	1981–1990
Argentina	21.4	141.6	437.7
Bolivia	5.6	20.2	220.0
Brazil	46.2	36.7	337.0
Chile	27.1	174.1	20.3
Dominican Republic	2.1	10.5	24.6
Mexico	2.8	16.8	65.2
Nicaragua	1.7	20.4	618.9
Peru	9.7	31.9	332.0
Uruguay	47.8	63.1	60.3
Venezuela	1.0	8.5	23.3

Sources: Annual Report: 1989 (Washington, DC: Inter-American Development Bank, 1990), p. 127; and *Annual Report: 1992* (Washington, DC: Inter-American Development Bank, 1993), p. 113.

American nations. Faced with the prospect of a collapse of the international financial order, the Bush and, later, the Clinton administrations implemented a new and more realistic set of debt-management proposals, which has been largely accepted by debtor countries. Known originally as the Brady plan, these strategies acknowledge that debtor nations are often financially incapable of repaying all of their loans without severely limiting the domestic investment needed for long-term development. Thus, they propose that a significant part of the debt be forgiven by the commercial banks in exchange for a guarantee by the International Monetary Fund and World Bank of repayment on the remaining debt. The debtor nations are required, in turn, to implement far-reaching internal economic reforms that center on reducing national expenditures.

These reforms, which are currently ongoing in many Latin American countries, can be very painful. They frequently include the reduction or elimination of government subsidies for food, fuel, utilities, health care, and other basic services that the lower economic classes have come to expect. These neo-liberal reforms also entail the privatization of countless enterprises formerly owned and operated by the national governments and the opening of the Latin markets to renewed foreign investment. Most of the old government-controlled companies, characterized by bloated bureaucracies and economic inefficiency, were operating constantly in the red, thereby contributing to deficit spending.

As the reforms are implemented, great hardships may be inflicted on the local citizenry. The costs of

basic commodities and services may increase so dramatically that the social and political stability of the nation is threatened. In August, 1990, for example, the government of newly elected Peruvian President Alberto Fujimori decided, as part of an economic reform package, to remove controls on the national currency, then called the *inti*. Virtually overnight, gasoline prices went from $.07 to more than $2 a gallon (in U.S. dollars). Private bus lines stopped running, and thousands of commuters in Lima fought one another for room in the backs of pickup trucks. Stores and markets were looted by people desperate for basic foodstuffs, which were disappearing in spite of price increases surpassing 300 percent. Similar scenes have occurred recently in Venezuela, and Brazil. Another result of austerity measures, at least in the short term, is increased unemployment as thousands of workers formerly employed by government-owned businesses are discharged and thousands more are laid off by private companies unable to cope with increased business expenses. Many consider those actions, as bitter as they are, to be necessary remedies for decades of unwise fiscal behavior, characterized by excessive government borrowing and spending. Others consider the changes to be an assault on the poor, not worth the internal social and political costs.

Regardless of perspective, one of the consequences of the debt crisis has been the fueling of inflation (Table 17–4). Official inflation rates of 50 to 400 percent per year have become common, with rates of over 1,000 percent occurring occasionally. Among the highest official inflation rates recorded in

Table 17-5
Devaluation of currency in
selected Latin American
countries.

		Local Currency per U.S. Dollar		
	Currency	1982	1987	1991
Argentina	*Austral*[a]	2.6	2,144.0	9,535.5
Chile	*Peso*	50.9	219.5	349.4
Colombia	*Peso*	64.1	242.6	633.1
Costa Rica	*Colón*	37.4	62.8	122.4
Ecuador	*Sucre*	30.0	170.0	1,046.2
Mexico	*Peso*	56.4	1,378.2	3,018.4
Paraguay	*Guaraní*	126.0	550.0	1,325.2
Uruguay	*Peso*	13.9	226.7	2,018.8
Venezuela	*Bolívar*	4.3	14.5	56.8

Source: *Economic and Social Progress in Latin America* (Washington, DC: Inter-American Development Bank, 1992), 331.

[a]In *australes* per thousand dollars through 1988 and per dollar thereafter.

Latin America in recent years are Nicaragua's 14,295 percent in 1988, Peru's 7,482 percent in 1990, Argentina's 3,080 percent in 1989, and Brazil's 2,968 percent in 1990. And along with inflation have come spiraling devaluations of national currencies, thus reducing even further the purchasing power of the citizenry and pushing ever-increasing numbers of people into poverty (Table 17–5). Occasionally, beleaguered national leaders motivated more by a sense of political expediency than by economic wisdom, attempt to solve their problems by ordering that more money be printed, thereby cheapening the value of the national currency. As a last-gasp measure, they may then decide to start all over by removing three to six zeros from the value of the currency and giving it a new name. But, none of those quick-fix solutions are of any real worth in raising the living levels of the masses; they only delay the implementation of substantive reforms.

The tragic truth is that the "lost decade," which some call the 1980s, brought a significant regression, rather than improvement, in the economic circumstances of most Latin Americans (Table 17–6). Living levels throughout much of the region fell back to those of the 1960s and 1970s, and when compared to conditions in developed nations, Latin American life seemed to be getting worse rather than better.

Many hope that the reforms now being implemented will eventually result in renewed economic growth. In addition to eliminating price subsidies and inefficient state-owned enterprises, there are a number of other promising development strategies. None is a panacea, but each is worthy of consider-

ation. One approach that has proven highly beneficial to many Caribbean and Central American nations is the promotion of foreign tourism. Tourism is a major source of foreign exchange and employment in Mexico, Jamaica, Puerto Rico, the Bahamas, the Dominican Republic, and many nations of the Lesser Antilles. Tourism, however, is of relatively minor significance in those countries not favored with tropical beaches, Indian ruins, internal political stability, or proximity to the United States.

Perhaps the most basic way to increase a nation's foreign earnings is through trade. Unfortunately, most Latin American countries are handicapped by their overreliance on two or three major exports, usually agricultural products or minerals (Table 17–7). The world prices of such commodities are extremely volatile, often rising and falling dramatically in just a few months' time. One example is petroleum, the value of which has fluctuated wildly in recent years. The prices of sugar, coffee, bauxite, and other major Latin American exports have also experienced similar oscillations. In addition, the Latin American nations are overly dependent on a single market, usually the United States or the European Union. Such a narrow focus puts the Latin countries at the mercy of the trade policies and economic cycles of their principal trading partner, which may enact trade restrictions to protect local enterprises.

A more creative approach to the debt crisis is the debt-for-equity program. Under that strategy the debtor Latin American nations sell economic assets in exchange for a write-off of part of their debt. Although such a program risks renewed foreign intervention, that risk can be minimized by limiting the foreign in-

Table 17-6
Gross domestic product (GDP) per capita for selected Latin American nations.

	1988 U.S. Dollars			
	1960	1970	1980	1991
Argentina	$2,476	$3,256	$3,535	$2,798
Bolivia	799	1,010	1,159	929
Brazil	937	1,289	2,385	2,210
Chile	1,718	2,086	2,303	2,637
Colombia	737	909	1,253	1,461
Costa Rica	1,087	1,384	1,778	1,671
Dominican Republic	390	470	713	650
Ecuador	660	791	1,377	1,277
El Salvador	986	1,238	1,267	1,077
Guatemala	647	836	1,098	904
Haiti	288	262	352	247
Honduras	537	679	843	758
Jamaica	1,276	1,835	1,365	1,472
Mexico	1,167	1,703	2,439	2,299
Nicaragua	828	1,166	845	522
Panama	1,158	1,850	2,306	2,127
Paraguay	772	910	1,560	1,550
Peru	1,041	1,725	1,877	1,353
Uruguay	2,087	2,200	2,849	2,787
Venezuela	2,912	3,787	4,082	3,682

Source: Annual Report 1992 (Washington, DC: Inter-American Development Bank, 1993), p. 109.

vestors to a minority share of a given enterprise. The advantage of that strategy is its potential to significantly increase long-term investment and development in the host country by the foreign firms.

One final development strategy is the establishment of multinational economic unions, similar to the EU. Such regional associations may be able to reduce trade barriers with neighboring countries and more effectively market member products, thereby increasing the volume of trade both within and outside the group. The success of such groups is totally dependent, however, on high levels of trust and cooperation among member nations. An example of the difficulties associated with the formation of multinational economic unions is the recently approved North American Free Trade Agreement, which provides for free trade among Mexico, the United States, and Canada. Although most Mexicans view the treaty as a means of attracting more and higher-paying industrial jobs, American labor and environmental leaders worry that it will result in reduced employment opportunities in the United States, as well as increased pollution and contamination of the Mexican border region. Economic

unions that already exist on paper in Latin America include the **Latin American Integration Association**, the **Andean Common Market (Ancom)**, the **Central American Common Market**, the **Caribbean Community (Caricom)**, and the **Southern Cone Common Market (Mercosur)**. While expectations are presently growing for the future success of these groups, none succeeded to any meaningful degree in the past because of internal rivalries.

SUMMARY
A Region in Need of Change

Latin America is in a state of ferment: conditions, institutions, and values that prevailed for centuries are being challenged and rapidly modified. The problems facing a new generation of Latin Americans are possibly the greatest ever, but great resources are also available for their solutions. In addition, in this age of international interdependence, we must realize that the challenges of one region are the challenges of us all. The Latin American debt crisis must be resolved because neither the Latin American nations nor the in-

Table 17-7
Principal primary exports and trading partners of selected Latin American countries, 1990.

	Principal Primary Exports	Principal Export Destination
Argentina	wheat, soybeans, beef	European Union
Belize	sugar, citrus	European Union
Bolivia	natural gas, tin, silver	Latin America
Brazil	soybeans, coffee, iron ore	United States
Chilo	copper, fruits, fish	European Union
Colombia	coffee	United States
Costa Rica	bananas, coffee	United States
Cuba	sugar	Russia
Dominican Republic	sugar, coffee	United States
Ecuador	petroleum, bananas, fish	United States
El Salvador	coffee	United States
Guatemala	coffee, sugar	United States
Guyana	bauxite, sugar	European Union
Haiti	coffee	United States
Honduras	bananas, coffee	United States
Jamaica	bauxite	United States
Mexico	petroleum, fruits, silver	United States
Nicaragua	coffee, cotton	United States
Panama	bananas, fish	United States
Paraguay	soybeans, cotton	Latin America
Peru	copper, fish meal	United States
Suriname	bauxite	United States
Uruguay	beef, wool	Latin America
Venezuela	petroleum	United States

Sources: *The Statesman's Year–Book 1991-92* (New York: St. Martin's Press, 1991); Statistical Yearbook 1988/89 (New York: United Nations, 1992); *Trade Yearbook 1990* (Rome: Food and Agriculture Organization of the United Nations, 1991).

dustrialized countries can afford the alternative—the collapse of the world financial system.

As the Latin American nations work to bring about modifications in the international economic order, they should recognize that changes from within are also needed. Additional land reform, meaningful assistance for poor farmers, improved environmental management, and the purging of graft and corruption, are all necessary components of lasting economic development. As its human resources are more fully developed, Latin America will begin to realize its almost unlimited potential.

KEY TERMS

Andean Common
  Market (Ancom)

Aztec

Caribbean Community
  (Caricom)

Central American
  Common Market

Chibcha

conquistadores

criollos

encomienda

estancia

fundamentalist
  Protestantism

hacienda

Iberia

Inca

latifundia

Latin American
  Integration Association

liberation theology

Maya

mercantilism

mestizos

monoculture

Moors

mulattos

penisulares

polyculture

royal patronage

shantytowns

Southern Cone
  Common Market
  (Mercosur)

Treaty of Tordesillas

zambos

18

Latin American Regions: The North

Mexico

Central America

The Caribbean

The Independence Monument on the Paseo de la Reforma in Mexico City. Latin America's cities, among the largest in the world, include ultramodern, wealthy neighborhoods as well as vast areas of poor shantytowns. Mexico City is the largest city in the Western Hemisphere and, because of its high birthrate, may soon surpass the Tokyo-Yokohama agglomeration as the largest in the world.

Ｗe now examine more closely the various regions of Latin America in order to appreciate their differences and understand some of the development challenges and potentials of each nation. For our purposes Latin America is divided into six regions: Mexico, Central America, the Caribbean, Andean South America, southern South America, and Brazil. The focus of this chapter is Middle America: Mexico, Central America, and the Caribbean. (Figure 18–1).

MEXICO

Mexico, by many indicators, should be among the most prosperous nations on earth. It is a large country, occupying some 72 percent of the land of Middle America and containing 58 percent of the population of that area. It has benefited throughout its history from some of the richest mineral deposits on earth—first its silver in the colonial period and now its petroleum in the twentieth century. Mexico's proximity to the technologically advanced and wealthy United States is also a potential economic advantage of significance. So are its varied agricultural landscapes, which range from irrigated deserts in the north to tropical rain forests in parts of the gulf coastal lowlands.

Yet Mexico, though it has achieved much, has fallen far short of its potential. Some observers attribute that underachievement to physical geography, pointing out that most of Mexico's land is either too dry or too mountainous to support modern

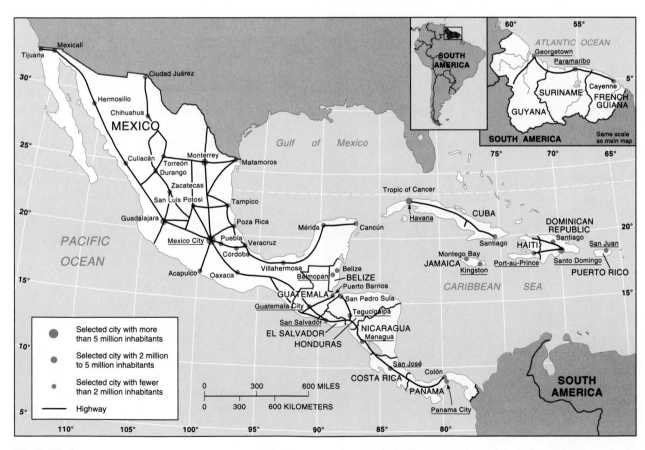

Figure 18–1
The nations, cities and major highways of Middle America. This designation includes three regions: (1) Mexico, (2) Central America, and (3) the Caribbean, which includes the Greater and Lesser Antilles, Belize, Guyana, Suriname, and French Guiana.

agriculture. Other countries, however, including Switzerland and Japan, have demonstrated that well-developed human resources can more than compensate for natural physical limitations. To understand Mexico's limited economic achievement, then, we must first evaluate the treatment of its people. We will begin by reviewing its quest for political stability, one of the fundamental preconditions of national development.

A Land of Revolutions

From the moment Cortés captured Tenochtitlán, Mexico exceeded almost every other Spanish colony in wealth and grandeur. Not only did the central volcanic highlands possess almost inexhaustible numbers of Indian laborers, but silver and other precious ores were also found in great abundance in Zacatecas, San Luis Potosí, and other parts of the western and eastern Sierra Madres. The quest for wealth and converts led the Spanish explorers ever farther northward, until the colony stretched across the southwestern United States from Texas to California. Had the poor been permitted to own their own family farmsteads, as they were in the United States, and had good public education been established, along with the free exchange of goods and ideas with the non-Spanish world, a vigorous and aggressive middle class would likely have developed and would have placed Mexico in the forefront of the Industrial Revolution and economic modernization.

In reality, colonial Mexico was so strangled by the mercantile system, and its social development was so stunted by class stratification that when independence came in the early 1800s, the country lapsed into a century of political chaos and despotism. At the center of the storm, initially, was a flamboyant demagogue named Antonio López de Santa Anna. Described as the curse of his native country, Santa Anna managed almost single-handedly to lose Texas in the 1830s and contributed to the loss of California and the remainder of the southwestern United States in the 1840s.

As Santa Anna was pursuing his own personal interests at the expense of the republic, Mexican society became divided into conservative and liberal factions. The conservatives consisted primarily of upper clergy and landed and monied elements, who favored a return to a European monarchy as the best means of protecting their social and economic privileges. The liberals, though mostly sincere in their Catholic faith, favored a separation of church and state as the best means of achieving democratic reform and economic modernization.

With Santa Anna's final exile in 1855, the liberals rose to power under the leadership of Benito Juárez, an Indian from the southern state of Oaxaca. Almost the opposite of Santa Anna, Juárez ruled until his death in 1872 with a moral rectitude unmatched either before or since in Mexican history.

After that brief flowering of liberalism, Mexico lapsed again into tyranny under the dictator Porfirio Díaz. While paying lip service to the democratic ideals of his predecessor, Díaz proceeded systematically to move the country back to a colonial status. Foreign interests were encouraged to locate in Mexico and, depending on their generosity to the dictator, were given almost unlimited latitude in their operations. Mexico became the mother of foreigners and the stepmother of Mexicans.

By 1910 U.S. investment in Mexico exceeded the total capital owned by the Mexicans themselves. In addition, the English dominated Mexican petroleum, metals, utilities, sugar, and coffee production; the French controlled most of the nation's textile mills; and the Spanish monopolized retail trade and tobacco. The great *hacendados,* or *hacienda* owners, had grown ever more powerful, and land consolidation had proceeded to the extent that approximately half of the country belonged to fewer than 3,000 families, while 95 percent of the millions of rural peasants owned no land at all.

Revolution finally erupted throughout the country in 1910, and for seven years Mexico was effectively without a central government, as various leaders struggled for power. Then a most remarkable change occurred. A new constitution, drafted in 1917, ushered in a period of political stability that has continued to the present. The constitution provided for a single six-year presidency with no possibility of reelection, civilian control of the military, limitations on the ownership of property by churches and foreign corporations, universal suffrage and education, a minimum-wage law, and agrarian reform.

National Unity

The achievement of political stability marked the beginnings of economic and social development in modern Mexico. One of the first and most necessary tasks was the building of a new national consciousness that would cause the Mexican people to place allegiance to the nation ahead of old ties to individual charismatic leaders. That objective has been accomplished to an extraordinary degree through three approaches.

The first approach has been to establish good public education as a national priority. Countless schools have been built —everywhere, from the inner cities to the most remote, poverty-stricken hinterlands—and have been staffed with dedicated, capable teachers. As a result, Mexico's literacy rate has risen from 56 percent in 1950 to 83 percent at present. In addition, trade schools and universities have broadened their roles and are now turning out increased numbers of skilled technicians and agricultural specialists, practical professions that traditionally were viewed as inferior in Latin American societies. Although private, mostly Catholic schools still service the wealthy, public education is functioning as the vehicle for the socioeconomic mobility and democratic values that were so seriously lacking in the colonial era.

The second approach to building national allegiance has been the glorification of Mexico's Indianness. The great Aztec chiefs and other historical Indian figures have become focal points of national pride, to which all Mexicans, regardless of race, can relate. Huge monuments and murals depict the greatness of the Indian forebears, often in exaggerated tones. The veneration of Indianness is also carried out in the schools, where the Indian children of today are taught—in Spanish, ironically—to have pride in their Indian heritage.

The third approach to strengthen national allegiance has been the creation of a single dominant political party, the **Institutional Revolutionary Party, (PRI)**. From its inception, PRI leaders have attempted to portray the party as the embodiment of an ongoing revolution in favor of the poor and repressed. Labor, business, and agriculture are all represented as separate interest groups within the organization. Thus, according to the PRI, Mexico is a one-party democracy. Even though minority parties have existed on both the far left and the extreme right, PRI candidates swept every presidential and almost all state and municipal elections from 1917 to the mid-1980s, generally claiming more than 90 percent of all votes cast. Charges of electoral fraud were occasionally leveled by opposition candidates, but

as long as the majority of the people felt that their living levels were improving, few were willing to openly criticize the PRI.

The collapse in the 1980s of Mexico's oil-driven economy, with the attendant decline in personal living levels, opened the floodgates of political pluralism and, by the 1990s, Mexico appeared to be evolving into a multiparty democracy. The principal opposition to the PRI has come from a leftist coalition claiming to represent the interests of the poor and from a conservative business alliance with historical ties to the institutional Catholic Church. Regardless of whether a true multiparty system emerges at this point, Mexico's three-pronged approach to national unity has certainly been successful in promoting a national consciousness and self-respect.

Agricultural Development

Modern Mexico's agricultural development has also followed a threefold approach. The first facet has been agrarian reform, or land redistribution. Fundamental to that movement has been the reestablishment of the ancient Indian *ejido* system, under which land belongs to villages rather than individuals. Now, when the government expropriates the lands of a *hacienda* or other estate, the original owners are allowed to retain at least 247 acres (100 hectares), and often more. That provision ensures that relatively large, efficient, privately owned farms will continue to operate throughout the country. The remaining lands can then be redistributed, either as private *ejidos* or as collective *ejidos*. Under the former, the land is given to individual farmers to work as they see fit; under the latter, the land is worked as a collective. In both instances the land may be passed on to the descendants of the farmers.

The second thrust of agricultural development in Mexico is the use of Green Revolution, or industrial, technologies on the farm, including irrigation, mechanized farm equipment, chemical insecticides, hybrid seeds, and inorganic fertilizers. Utilization rates have been high among the large private farmers and collective *ejidos* in the northern part of the country, but the technologies have not proven to be economically or culturally compatible with the needs of small Indian farmers in central and southern Mexico.

The third agricultural focus has been lowland colonization, particularly along the southeastern gulf coast, from Veracruz to the Yucatán Peninsula. Beginning with the Papaloapan River Basin Development Project of the late 1940s and continuing on several fronts at the present time, integrated development schemes have done much to improve the quality of life in those traditionally neglected regions.

Today, Mexico's diverse physical environments facilitate the production of a wide variety of crops. Maize, beans, and squash remain the basic crops of the rural peasantry. Commercial agriculture includes: irrigated cotton, vegetable oils, and winter vegetables in the northwest; wheat, dairy products, and vegetables in central Mexico; sugarcane, bananas, and mangoes along the southeastern lowlands; and coffee in the foothills of the eastern Sierra Madre. Parts of the northeastern lowlands and the Yucatán Peninsula also specialize in the production of citrus and henequen, a hard fiber used in the manufacture of bags, carpeting, and twine (Figure 18–2). In addition, extensive grazing of beef cattle and, in the drier and colder regions, goats and sheep continues in the classic Hispanic tradition.

Mining

Foreign control of mining was almost absolute during the Díaz era. An American named William "Big Bill" Green, for instance, owned the Cananea Consolidated Copper Company, which held mining, grazing, and forest rights to almost 1 million acres (404,700 hectares) of land in northwestern Mexico. Prior to the revolution, Big Bill's Mexican workers were paid 2.5 to 3 *pesos* (the equivalent then to slightly more than 1 dollar) per twelve-hour shift in the shafts and pits. But the revolution limited foreign ownership of resources, and in 1938 all U.S. petroleum interests were nationalized.

Today, Mexico's petroleum reserves, found both onshore and offshore, primarily in the southern gulf coast area, are among the greatest in the world (Figure 18–3). Mexico is also of world importance as a producer of silver, copper, lead, zinc, and sulfur. In addition, coal near the city of Sabinas and iron ore deposits from the state of Chihuahua support a growing iron and steel industry centered in Monterrey, Monclova, and Mexico City.

Figure 18-2
Henequen harvesting on the Yucatán Peninsula of Mexico.
The fleshy leaves are pressed to extract long, tough fibers, which are dried and then manufactured into rope and coarse textile products.

Industrialization and Urbanization

Mexican industry in the colonial and early independence eras was based primarily on textiles, milling, and furniture and tile making. It was centered in Puebla, Orizaba, Mexico City, and Monterrey. Although those activities are still important, more technologically sophisticated forms of manufacturing began to appear around 1940 (Figure 18–4).

At present, Mexico is one of the leading industrial nations in Latin America. Its two most important industrial regions have evolved around Mexico City and Monterrey; both produce a great array of consumer and capital, or producer, goods. Automobiles are assembled in Puebla, Cuernavaca, and Hermosillo; agricultural machinery is made in León; and seamless steel pipes are produced in Veracruz.

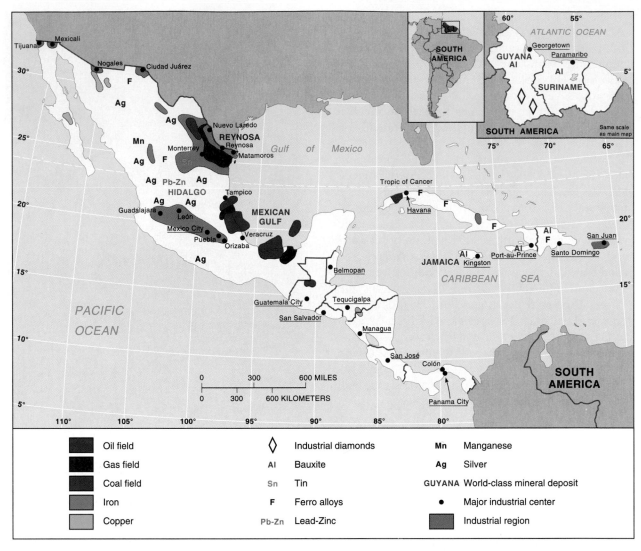

Figure 18-3
Principal mineral-producing areas of Middle America. The major minerals in this region include petroleum and silver in Mexico and bauxite in Jamaica, Guyana, and Suriname. Mexico also contains sufficient coal and iron ore to sustain a steel industry.

Giant petrochemical complexes have been built along the gulf coast, in Poza Rica, Minatitlán, and Villahermosa. Additionally, thousands of factories have sprung up in Ciudad Juárez, Tijuana, and other border cities, where special plants, called *maquiladoras,* are permitted (see the boxed feature Mexico's Border Industrialization Program). *Maquiladoras* are American manufacturing plants that operate in Mexico using American technology and Mexican labor. The American firms benefit from comparatively low labor costs and the absence of import duties or tariffs on the finished goods that are

shipped back to the United States. Mexico benefits from the creation of hundreds of thousands of, by Mexican standards, relatively high-paying jobs.

In recent years tourism has become one of Mexico's leading growth industries. World-class hotels and facilities now abound in Mexico City and Acapulco, and the Mexican government is aggressively developing others north of Acapulco along the Pacific Coast and at Cancún on the Yucatán Peninsula. Those travelers who prefer a more relaxed (and less expensive) exposure to the traditional charms of Mexican society frequently seek

Figure 18-4
Burning residue at a sugar mill.
Mexico has become one of the
most industrialized countries of
Latin America. Once largely a
processor of its own agricultural commodities, it now produces a great variety of consumer and capital goods.

out Mérida with its Mayan culture or Oaxaca, Cuernavaca, and Guadalajara (see Figure 18–1).

Many Mexicos

Mexico can be divided into seven regions, and they are so distinct that the country has been referred to as "many Mexicos."[1] The first contains the border cities, where the economy and culture have been greatly altered by proximity to the United States. The border economy is dominated by *maquiladoras,* import-export businesses (some of which specialize in illegal aliens and drugs), and tourism. Unfortunately, what most tourists see is a Hispanic culture that has been modified—corrupted, some would say—by U.S. influence. Even the language of the region is filled with English words that have been made into Mexican verbs, such as *lunchear* ("to eat lunch") and *typear* ("to type"). The seemingly rampant mix of smuggling, prostitution, gambling, quack medicine, and low-quality tourist shops can easily mislead visitors into believing that all of Mexico is a physical and cultural wasteland.

A second region is northeastern Mexico, dominated by the giant industrial city of Monterrey (3,200,000) and its distant port of Tampico (420,000). Supported by extensive reserves of natural gas, private industrialists have developed five large manufacturing groups that specialize in chemicals, steel, paper, glass, and beer. In addition, vast areas of semiarid land are given over to extensive sheep and cattle grazing on huge ranches dominated by unimproved pasture grasses, mesquite and creosote shrubs, and cacti. In recent years, many of these ranches have been converted to large farms specializing in the production of grain sorghum, which is mixed in poultry feedstocks, whereas others have been transformed into private hunting preserves that cater to foreign tourists.

A third region, one of the most rapidly developing regions of Mexico, is the gulf coast, centering on the states of Veracruz and Tabasco. In addition to its great petrochemical and textile industries, the region is one of the leading agricultural zones in all of tropical Latin America. An almost continuous stream

MEXICO'S BORDER INDUSTRIALIZATION PROGRAM

One of the most rapidly industrializing zones in all of Latin America and the Caribbean is Mexico's border region, which, since the late 1960s, has gained over 2,200 foreign-owned manufacturing plants that employ over half a million Mexican workers. The roots of this unprecedented industrial growth reach back to 1942, when the American and Mexican governments signed an agreement, called the *bracero* program, that allowed Mexican agricultural laborers to work legally in the United States. Although the program initially was designed to be terminated once the Second World War had ended, when returning American GIs would again be available to work the fields, it proved so attractive to both countries that it was extended until 1964. The following year, the Mexican government established the Border Industrialization Program in the hope of promoting the creation of manufacturing jobs for its displaced farm workers.

The basic idea behind the program was to encourage American and other foreign firms to establish branch assembly plants in Mexico, where they could take advantage of inexpensive Mexican labor. In order to entice the so-called *maquiladora* ("to manufacture")

plants to come, Mexico agreed to provide subsidized land, utilities, and tax holidays to the foreign firms, as well as to allow the imported American-made parts and exported Mexican-assembled finished products to be transported duty-free across the border.

Most of the products produced during the early years of the Border Industrialization Program were low-technology items such as textiles and toys. As time passed, however, the region evolved into a center for electronics, communications, and transportation manufacturing. Today, the Mexican border cities are characterized by large industrial parks that house plants owned by such leading multinational corporations as IBM, Honeywell, GE, GM, Nissan, and Zenith, to name but a few.

Although the Border Industrialization Program has proven to be an enormous boon to the Mexican economy, it is not without its problems. The flood of migrants from central and southern Mexico into the border region has led to a rapid population growth that has overwhelmed municipal sewerage treatment facilities. This, in turn, has resulted in increasingly frequent outbreaks of hepatitis, typhoid, cholera, intestinal parasites, and other serious diseases. The presence of large quantities of inadequately disposed industrial wastes—including solvents, acids, and PCBs—is also raising short- and long-term health concerns. Ironically, most of the Mexican factory workers are single women under the age of twenty-five. Job stress is so great that the typical laborer works for less than three years, despite an average hourly wage of U.S. $0.60, which is relatively high in comparison to other Mexican jobs. Notwithstanding its economic success, then, the program has come under increasing criticism for its attendant social and environmental ills.

of cargo trucks laden with sugar, coffee, pineapples, bananas, papayas, cacao, mangoes, citrus, and coconuts passes through Córdoba and Orizaba, as well as the lushly forested escarpment of the eastern Sierra Madre, on its way to markets in Mexico City and other highland population centers (Figure 18–5). The rich volcanic and alluvial soils of the southern gulf coast also support Mexico's largest remaining stands of tropical rain forest. However, those forests, which once covered much of southern Mexico, are being converted at an alarming rate to poor, unimproved pasture. Absentee city-dwelling landowners stock the pastureland with mixed Zebu breeds of cattle that can tolerate the disease and periodic flooding characteristic of the region. The gulf coast also benefits from the city of Veracruz (354,000), the

nation's chief port; the traditionally liberal attitudes of Veracruz residents have made the city's fun-loving culture renowned throughout the republic.

A fourth region is the Yucatán Peninsula, which consists of a low, flat, limestone plateau covered with scrubby savanna forest vegetation that alternates between lush green during the rainy summer months and parched brown during the dry winter season (Figure 18–6). Over time, rainwater has filtered down through the red topsoils into the underlying limestone bedrock, forming carbonic acid that has begun to dissolve the limestone itself. Subsurface caverns have then been formed and have continued to grow until the surface has collapsed from lack of support, producing sinkholes. Much of the drinking water of the Yucatán has traditionally come from ponds created when high water tables have intersected the sinkholes.

Historically one of the poorest regions in Mexico, the Yucatán is now prospering, as irrigated citrus groves are planted on former henequen lands. Tourism focuses on the beaches of Cancún and the Mayan Indian ruins at Chichén-Itzá. In addition, the capital city of Mérida (602,000) is attracting foreign and Mexican investment with a courteous, well-trained work force. Despite foreign influence, the Yucatán has retained a distinctive regional culture characterized by widespread use of the Mayan language, hammocks rather than beds, and colorful clothing.

A fifth region, perhaps the poorest and most isolated of Mexico today, is the south, which includes the states of Guerrero, Oaxaca, and Chiapas and consists mostly of vast, rugged mountain ranges. Shortly after the conquest of the Aztec heartland, Cortés took much of the present-day state of Oaxaca as his personal *encomienda*. On a later occasion, when asked to describe Mexico, Cortés took a piece of paper and crumpled it tightly, forming a misshapen wad. Holding the contorted object in his hands, he replied, "This, sir, is New Spain."

Outside the administrative and tourist centers of Oaxaca (230,000) and Acapulco (640,000), the south continues to be a region of scattered highland

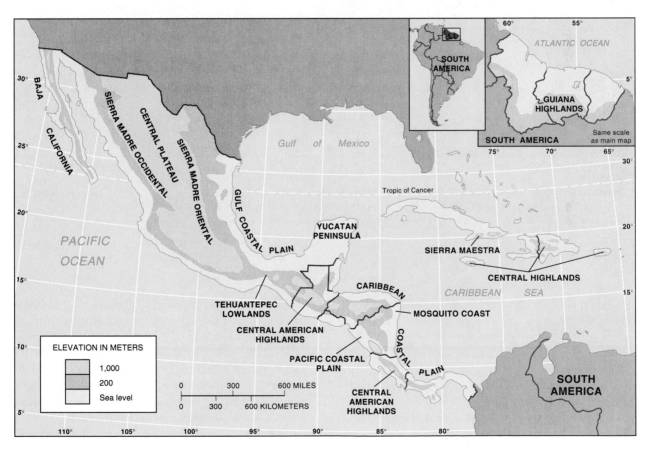

Figure 18-5
Physiographic regions of Middle America. The landscape of much of Middle America reveals mountains or mountain basins. Both Mexico and Central America have a long history of earthquake and volcanic activity; along with Andean America, they are part of the circum-Pacific Ring of Fire. Significant tropical lowlands do exist, however, as evidenced in Mexico's Yucatán Peninsula, Nicaragua's Mosquito Coast, and the lowland of Cuba.

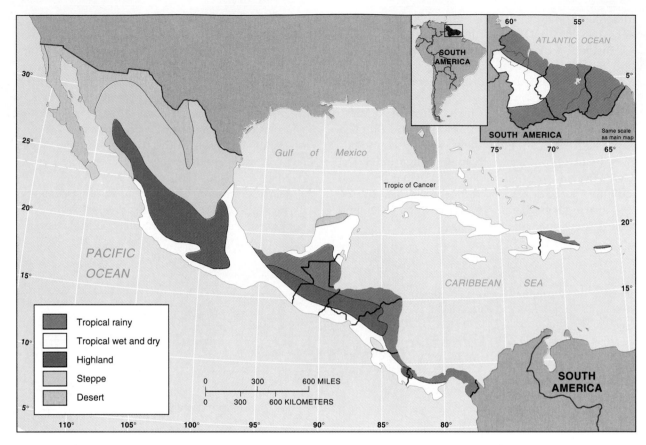

Figure 18-6
Climatic regions of Middle America. The climates of Middle America are largely
tropical rainy and tropical wet and dry, although northern Mexico is subtropical
desert and steppe. Much of Middle America experiences at least one season of
moisture deficiency.

Indian villages with agricultural practices and religious ceremonies that have changed little since preconquest times. Unfortunately, the region is experiencing increasingly severe environmental degradation from a vicious cycle of spiraling rural population growth, deforestation, soil erosion, and agricultural abandonment.

A sixth region—Mexico's core region—consists of a great, interlocking series of snow-capped volcanoes and highland valleys extending east to west along the 19th parallel. The largest of those valleys, the valley of Mexico, lies above 7,000 feet (2,134 meters) in altitude and experiences cool temperatures throughout the year. Virtually uncontrolled population growth there has combined with exten-

sive industry and millions of diesel- and gasoline-powered buses, trucks, and automobiles to make Mexico City not only one of the world's most populous cities with approximately 19.4 million in the metropolitan area, (Figure 18–7), but also one of the world's most polluted. Chronic water shortages, massive traffic congestion, and vast squatter settlements—contrasted with some of the world's greatest museums, finest shopping districts, and most exclusive residential areas—make Mexico City a window to the intense change that is sweeping the nation. Heavy industry and rapid population growth also characterize the other urban centers of the core region—Puebla (1,138,000), Toluca (527,000), Cuernavaca (305,000), and León (942,000). In the

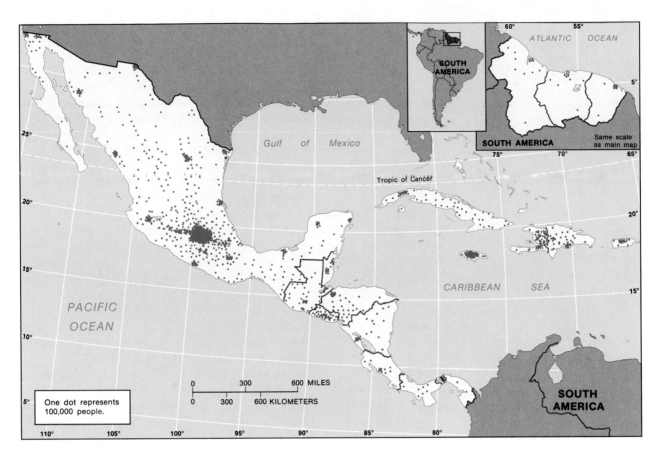

Figure 18-7
Population distribution in Middle America. Mainland Middle America is characterized
by several high-density population clusters separated by areas of lower density.
Extremely high density characterizes many of the islands of the Antilles.

thousands of small peasant villages in the region,
however, life goes on much as it has for hundreds
of years.

Mexico's final region is the west, centering on
Guadalajara (3,640,000) and the oasis cities of
Culiacán (650,000), Ciudad Obregón (336,000), and
Hermosillo (486,000). This semiarid region is developing rapidly through irrigated commercial agriculture and trade with the United States. It is also the
home of the Mexican cowboy tradition.

Mexico has reached Rostow's takeoff stage of economic development; it is a nation of great, yet largely
untapped, potential. If political stability can be maintained and if the government continues to develop
its human resources, Mexico will eventually take its
place among the leading nations of the world.

CENTRAL AMERICA

Central America is a troubled region of six small
countries, each struggling to raise its people's levels
of living in the face of serious economic and political challenges. Unlike Mexico, Central America has
limited mineral wealth. That lack of raw minerals, as
well as physical isolation and poor transportation
networks, has handicapped industrial development.
Also unlike Mexico, which has benefitted from the
complementary nature of its various regions, Central
America has been severely hampered by rivalries
and duplication: more than twenty-five attempts at
regional economic or political union have failed.
Another difference is that Mexico's revolution
brought about agrarian reform and the beginnings

of a middle class. In Central America, however, social relationships and land-tenure patterns have changed little—except in Nicaragua—since the colonial era. Political stability has yet to be achieved in this region, which has been torn apart by leftist guerrilla movements, rightist vigilante death squads, and military intervention by both the former Soviet Union and the United States.

Historical Land Use

Central America was settled simultaneously from two directions. In the south Vasco Núñez de Balboa first occupied Panama on his march to the Pacific Ocean. In 1519 Panama City was founded on the Pacific side of the isthmus, and the area soon established itself as the premier overland, interoceanic transportation route of the Americas, (see Figure 18–1). Then, from Panama, Spanish colonizers traveled northward into the lowland lake country of Nicaragua. There, rivalry between two cities, León and Granada, eventually led to the selection of centrally located Managua as the national capital.

In the 1560s rumors of gold prompted a group of Nicaraguans to move southward to present-day Costa Rica. Neither gold nor Indians were found in significant quantities, but the settlers did find rich farmland in the cool, healthful volcanic basins of the central plateau. What evolved was a nation whose population was composed largely of middle-class, European farmers, whose traditions of universal education and political stability have made Costa Rica an enclave of relative prosperity and tranquility.

Meanwhile, settlers pushed into Guatemala, El Salvador, and Honduras from Mexico. And soon all of Central America, with the exception of portions of Costa Rica and Panama, had fallen into the classical colonial land-use pattern of great grazing estates and scattered mines, a pattern from which some areas have yet to emerge.

The first commercial crop introduced into Central America was coffee, which had earlier become established on the Caribbean islands as an excellent upland complement to lowland sugarcane. The first coffee plants came from Cuba to Costa Rica in 1796, and by 1850 small, family-operated coffee farms, called *fincas* or *cafetales*, dominated the central plateau. From Costa Rica coffee diffused northward, finding ideal growing conditions in the rich soils of the volcanic uplands of western El Salvador and Guatemala (see the boxed feature, Coffee Production in Latin America).

Bananas

Although coffee has had a major impact on the economies of Guatemala, El Salvador, Nicaragua, and Costa Rica, the crop that has most strongly influenced the character and development of Central America as a whole is bananas. The Spaniards introduced the first plants to Hispaniola (present-day Dominican Republic and Haiti) in 1516 and to the floodplains of eastern Central America shortly thereafter. The crop thrived in the hot, moist climate and the fertile, well-drained soils.

Commercial production of such a highly perishable fruit was made possible by the development of refrigerated ships and boxcars in the late nineteenth century. The 1870s brought the first shipments of bananas to Boston and New Orleans, and the fruit quickly assumed a prominent place in American diets. From 1880 to 1930, banana plantations expanded rapidly along the sparsely settled, humid eastern lowlands, using imported West Indian wage laborers. As sales soared in the United States, the Standard and United Fruit companies were formed and achieved positions of inordinate influence in many Central American countries. The boom slowed in the 1920s, however, as soil exhaustion and plant diseases made cultivation of the standard Gros Michel banana unprofitable.

The decline of commercial banana cultivation in the Caribbean lowlands prompted a search for alternative plantation sites, which ultimately were found in the Pacific lowlands. This second production phase, which lasted until the early 1960s, was characterized at times by such great dependence on the crop that the countries of the region came to be called by many people as "banana republics." Unfortunately, the deadly plant diseases ultimately established themselves on the Pacific plantations as well, and further changes were necessary.

The third and current phase of banana production has involved a switch to the Giant Cavendish plant variety. Its resistance to disease has permitted renewed development along both coasts. In addition, because of allegations of political meddling, the multinational fruit companies are increasingly shifting their emphasis from production on company lands to the marketing of fruit purchased from small, individual farmers.

For years to come, scholars will debate the impact of the fruit companies in Central America. On the negative side, many observers are convinced that the companies intervened, often in illegal ways, in the internal affairs of the host countries. The com-

COFFEE PRODUCTION IN LATIN AMERICA

Central American and Colombian coffees, which are renowned throughout the world for their superior quality, are grown under altogether different conditions from those of coffee cultivated in Brazil, the world's leading producer. Brazilian coffee is grown on vast estates in the southern part of the Brazilian plateau; Central American and Colombian coffees are grown on small highland farms, or *fincas*.

The principal distinction, however, between those two dominant coffee regions is that the Brazilian bushes are planted in full sun under monocultural (single-crop) conditions, whereas those of Central America and Colombia are grown largely in the shade in polycultural (multiple-crop) holdings, which may include plantains (cooking bananas), citrus, avocados, mangoes, and the evergreen cinchona, the bark of which is useful for medicinal products, as well as various tropical hardwoods.

The chief advantage of shade-grown coffee is the method by which its berries are picked. Because each berry ripens separately and because the slopes of the small landholdings are steep, mechanized harvesting of the Central American and Colombian coffees is impractical. Instead, each berry is picked by hand at the time of optimum ripeness (Figure A). In contrast, the mechanically harvested Brazilian bushes are picked only once, with both immature and overripe berries being blended into the final product. Thus, Brazilian coffee tends to be more bitter than the "suaves" of Central America and Colombia.

Other advantages of shade-grown coffee include less flower drop, as a result of cooler temperatures; lower fertilizer requirements, because of the nutrients supplied by fallen leaves and other organic debris; and less soil erosion. Also, farmers can grow subsistence or commercial food crops simultaneously. Although well-fertilized sun-grown plants are more productive, the world's finest coffees continue to come from the polycultural highland *fincas* of Central America and Colombia.

Figure A
Kuna Indian coffee harvesters in Central America. The shade-grown coffee berries of Central America and Colombia are commonly harvested by hand.

panies are also criticized for monopolizing huge tracts of fertile farmlands that could be given to poor farmers for the production of badly needed domestic foodstuffs. On the positive side, however, it is recognized that those same companies brought schools, roads, hospitals, and harbors, all of which benefited local residents. Some scholars have also suggested that the banana plantations have contributed to the development of more progressive, open societies which have often supported industrial as well as agricultural modernization.

Economic Development

Agriculture dominates Central American economies and is likely to do so for the foreseeable future. Any serious development plan must take into account the 56 percent of the regional work force that is engaged in agriculture.

Two new agricultural products have recently joined coffee and bananas as important sources of regional revenue. The first is irrigated cotton, which showed rapid expansion from the 1950s into the early 1980s along the dry Pacific lowlands of Guatemala, El Salvador, and Nicaragua. The long-term sustainability of large-scale Central American cotton production is increasingly threatened by its heavy reliance on expensive and highly toxic pesticides and herbicides. The second new product is chilled beef for export. Even though cattle grazing has historically been a major focus of Latin American society, its low output was targeted almost exclusively for local consumption. The past three decades, however, have witnessed the growth of scientific animal husbandry, which places improved animal breeds on imported African pasture grasses. Nonetheless, one of the unfortunate consequences of expanded cattle ranching, both modern and traditional, is an alarming loss of Central America's remaining tropical rain forests.

Commercial fishing, especially for shrimp, is also expanding. Tourism has performed poorly as a rule, with Guatemala and Costa Rica benefiting the most. Political instability, however, has recently hampered promotion efforts in Guatemala.

Guatemala

Guatemala is the largest of the Central American nations in population and is also one of the poorest. The northern half, called the Petén, is sparsely pop-

ulated, lowland rain forest that offers an agricultural frontier. Colonization projects have been established there, and roads have been constructed to connect the region to the rest of the country. However, the highlands that parallel the Pacific Ocean contain the bulk of Guatemala's population. In the western part of the highlands live most of the Indians, who follow traditional ways of life and still maintain many customs of their Mayan ancestors (Figures 18–8 and 18–9). In and around Guatemala City, *mestizos* and whites follow European, or *Ladino,* life-styles. Guatemala City (2,000,000) is the only truly modern city of the nation and is the social, economic, industrial, educational, and political center. Along the southern coast and slopes of the adjacent mountains lies the main commercial agricultural zone. Cotton, sugar, coffee, and cattle are widely produced.

El Salvador

El Salvador is the most densely populated of all Central American nations. The effects of that heavy population pressure are seen in the deforested and eroded hillsides, the flow of rural migrants to shantytowns in the principal cities of San Salvador (the capital; 1,522,000) and Santa Ana (258,000), the migration of Salvadorans to less densely settled areas in neighboring Honduras and Guatemala, and the frequent armed conflicts between government forces and those who demand sweeping changes. In contrast to other Central American nations, El Salvador does not have an agricultural frontier. Thus, increased production must come from higher yields per unit of land rather than from expansion of the area under cultivation. But the traditional landholding patterns have not been broken, and little has been done to improve agricultural efficiency. Rather, the emphasis is on industrialization, even though El Salvador does not possess many of the attributes that are needed for manufacturing. No minerals of significance are known, and power supplies are largely imported. The only local raw materials are those of agriculture, and the labor supply, though abundant and cheap, is not skilled.

Honduras

Honduras, with an area of more than five times that of El Salvador, has a population of only 5.5 mil-

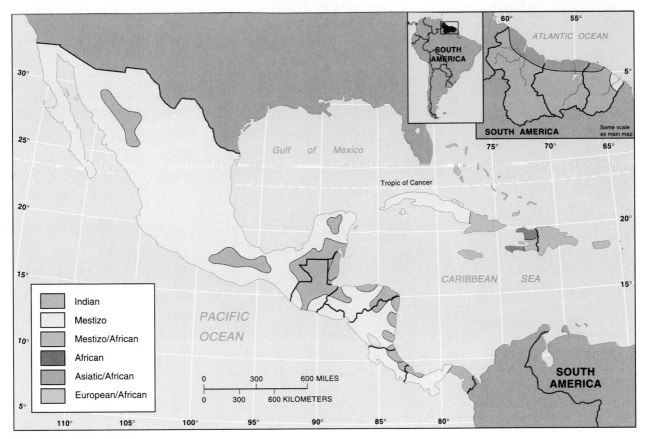

Figure 18-8
Dominant ethnic groups of Middle America. Considerable ethnic and cultural varia-
tion exists in Middle America. Mexico, for example, is dominantly *mestizo,* but
southern Mexico and Guatemala are populated by Indian peoples, and persons of
African descent dominate significant portions of many Caribbean Islands. The pre-
Columbian Indian population of the Antilles was largely decimated early in the
European colonization period.

lion. Thus, many parts of Honduras are sparsely settled. Outside the major cities of Tegucigalpa
(733,000), the capital, and San Pedro Sula (497,000),
where services and limited manufacturing provide
employment opportunities, agriculture is almost the
sole occupation. In the largely deforested highlands,
subsistence farming, traditional livestock raising,
small-scale mining, and commercial coffee growing
are the dominant activities. Social relationships
continue to be highly stratified among the peoples
of the interior cities and villages and the masses
have little opportunity to advance. Along the coast
around San Pedro Sula, foreign-sponsored banana
plantations contribute much of the nation's exports.
The lowland coastal region is more industrialized

and open to change than is the interior highland zone. Attempts to promote foreign tourism
have met with some success on the Bay Islands off
the north coast of the country but have largely
failed elsewhere.

Nicaragua

Nicaragua has a long history of political instability.
For a time in the nineteenth century, the British tried
to control part of its Caribbean coast. Later, an
American adventurer captured the capital briefly.
Then, in the early twentieth century, conflict between conservatives and liberals contributed to internal instability, which prompted U.S. military oc-

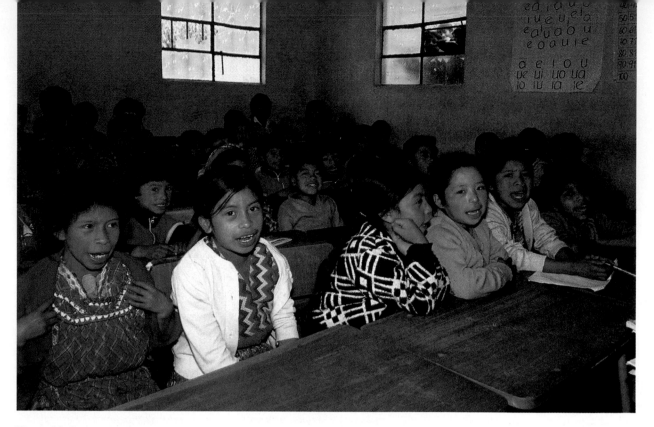

Figure 18–9
School children in the highlands of Guatemala. The children in this bilingual school reflect their Indian heritage in dress and physical features.

cupation from 1912 to 1933. Finally, in 1937 the Somoza family gained control of the government and held power until it was overthrown in 1979 by the leftist Sandinistas. It is estimated that, at the time of their ouster, the Somoza family controlled half the wealth of the impoverished nation. Thereafter, the Sandinistas attempted to reorient the country toward the Soviet bloc and away from close political and economic ties to the United States. In the process they achieved a massive military buildup. Although voted out of office in 1990, the Sandinistas remain a potent force in a poor and deeply divided nation.

Nicaragua is basically an agricultural country, with most of its production coming from the lowland area near Managua (737,000), the capital. Much of eastern Nicaragua is sparsely populated and little developed. The Mosquito Indians, who dominate this Caribbean lowland region, engage in subsistence farming and fishing, and search for gold which can be found in limited quantities within old stream beds that have since been covered by sandy, unproductive soils. Banana plantations, so common along the Caribbean coast of the isthmus, have never been important in Nicaragua.

Costa Rica

Costa Rica differs from the other Central American nations in several respects. More than any of its neighbors, Costa Rica has developed a spirit of national unity. In addition, almost 93 percent of the population is literate, and the infrastructure is well developed. The government is democratic and forward looking, with a history of stability. And large landholdings coexist with small- and medium-sized owner-operated farms, yielding a relatively high productivity. Even though Costa Rica is small in area, it has considerable regional specialization. For example, high-quality coffee, cut flowers, and vegetables are grown in the temperate highlands of the central plateau around San José (312,000) the capital. Large-scale cattle ranching dominates in the northwestern province of Guanacaste and banana plantations are common along the Caribbean coast.

Population growth is rapid in Costa Rica, as it is in other mainland Middle American nations. Many rural people are moving into the rainy tropics and to the San José area. Costa Rica presents a picture of progress, yet high energy costs and a high population growth rate spell the need for continued economic expansion.

Panama

Panama owes its existence and its economic viability to the Panama Canal (Figure 18–10). Built by the United States on land leased from Panama, the canal is now being turned over to the Panamanians under a treaty signed in 1978; they are to assume full control in 1999. The canal divides Panama into two parts: an eastern part, called the Darién, which is a little-developed rain forest; and a western part, which contains numerous banana plantations along the Caribbean coast and beef cattle, rice, and staple food crops in the interior. Tertiary activities in and along the Canal Zone—including retailing, shipping, and banking (some of which is connected to illicit drug trafficking)—contribute more than 55 percent of the total gross national product and represent the most rapidly growing sector of Panama's economy. Panama City (the capital; 619,000) on the Pacific Coast and Colón (149,000) on the Caribbean Sea are the major urban centers. Both cities cater to tourists and transit passengers by offering duty-free goods.

The area in and around the Panama Canal is truly a crossroads of the world. Both English and Spanish are spoken by a majority of the population, and U.S. currency is used everywhere. Since the canal acts as a funnel, finished products and raw materials can be brought together in Panama for transshipment elsewhere, as well as for processing. Manufacturing, however, is only slightly developed. The region's importance to U.S. interests was clearly demonstrated by the U.S. military invasion and ouster of former President Manuel Noriega in 1989.

THE CARIBBEAN

The Caribbean culture realm consists of: (1) the Greater Antilles—Cuba, Hispaniola, Jamaica, and Puerto Rico; (2) the smaller islands of the Lesser Antilles, which are situated in the eastern Caribbean between Puerto Rico and Trinidad; and (3) the rim-

Figure 18-10
The Panama Canal, the major focus of Panama's activities. The canal divides Panama into two parts, of which the western sector is the more developed. A change of control is under way that will remove the Canal Zone and the canal from U.S. jurisdiction.

land nations of Belize, Guyana, Suriname, and French Guiana (Table 18–1). Often portrayed in the popular media as tropical paradises, the Caribbean nations face three common challenges in their quest for economic development.

The first obstacle is their small size and relatively harsh physical environment. By world standards each of the countries is tiny in population, area, or both. Not surprisingly, the island nations with relatively small populations find it difficult to attain industrial self-sufficiency. In addition, those small nations face shortages of farmland, as well as occasional shortages of fresh water. For roughly half

Table 18-1
The Caribbean culture realm in 1993.

Political Entity	Original Dominant European Culture	Current Dominant Culture	Political Status	Date of Independence or Autonomy
Anguilla	Spanish	British	Dependency	
Antigua and Barbuda	Spanish	British	Independent	1981
Aruba	Dutch	Dutch	Autonomous[a]	1986
Bahamas	British	British	Independent	1973
Barbados	British	British	Independent	1966
Belize	British	British	Independent	1981
Cuba	Spanish	Spanish	Independent	1901
Dominica	Spanish	British	Independent	1978
Dominican Republic	Spanish	Spanish	Independent	1844
French Guiana	French	French	FAR[b]	1974
Grenada	French	British	Independent	1974
Guadeloupe	French	French	FAR[b]	1974
Guyana	Dutch	British	Independent	1970
Haiti	Spanish	French	Independent	1804
Jamaica	Spanish	British	Independent	1962
Martinique	French	French	FAR[b]	1974
Montserrat	French	British	Crown colony	
Netherlands Antilles, (Bonaire, Curaçao, St. Eustatius, St. Martin, Saba)	Various	Dutch	Netherlands	
Puerto Rico	Spanish	American/Spanish	Commonwealth	1952
St. Christopher (St. Kitts) and Nevis	British	British	Independent	1983
St. Lucia	Spanish	British	Independent	1979
St. Vincent and the Grenadines	Various	British	Independent	1979
Suriname	Dutch	Dutch	Independent	1975
Trinidad and Tobago (a single country)	Spanish	British	Independent	1962
Virgin Islands	Danish	American/British	Various	

Sources: The Statesman's Year-Book 1993–94 (New York: St. Martin's Press, 1993); and John MacPherson, *Caribbean Lands*, 4th ed. (London: Longman Caribbean, 1980).

[a]Aruba constitutionally separated from the Netherlands Antilles on January 1, 1986. The Netherlands has promised full independence by 1996.

[b]French Administrative Region, considered part of the French nation.

of each year, December through April, almost no rain falls (see Figure 18–6). Then, when the tropical afternoon thunderstorms do begin, they are frequently accompanied by devastating hurricanes.

The second challenge facing the Caribbean nations is the need to overcome a colonial legacy. Although most of the islands are now politically independent, many continue to function as economic colonies, exporting relatively low-value raw materials, such as bananas or bauxite, and importing relatively expensive processed products. The colonial legacy has also left deep social and racial divisions. Following the almost total extermination of native Indians, African slaves were introduced as a labor supply. Their descendants now constitute the principal population of the Lesser Antilles, Jamaica, and Haiti and a significant minority in Trinidad and Tobago (a single country), Cuba, the Dominican Republic, and Puerto Rico. All of the populations, however, have a European culture base—except Haiti, which has a mixture of African and European cultures. And generally speaking, in divided Caribbean societies the lighter a person's skin color is, the higher that person's socioeconomic standing tends to be. That pattern extends even to those islands that are racially almost entirely black; in those settings lighter-skinned *mulattos* dominate.

The third challenge is to preserve both the local ways of life and the environmental balance in the face of an ever-increasing number of foreign visitors. Along with much-needed jobs for local residents, tourism has often brought drug trafficking, organized crime, and vice.

Cuba

Although Cuba contains well over half the level land of the Caribbean islands, throughout the colonial era it was largely ignored by the Spaniards, who found few Indians and little gold there. By the beginning of the twentieth century, when Spain lost Cuba and Puerto Rico to the United States, Cuba's population was only 1.5 million people, most of whom were centered in or near Havana, and only 3 percent of the land was under cultivation.

Status as a U.S. protectorate brought far-reaching changes to the island. Yellow fever was eradicated, thereby opening up the lowlands to human occupancy. Tourism exploded as Havana, the capital, became a mecca of nightclubs and gambling. Sugarcane became the grass of Cuba, as American

interests oversaw its planting throughout almost the entire island in order to profit from the preferential tariffs authorized by the U.S. Congress. Following the granting of independence, Cuba remained almost totally dependent on U.S. sugar purchases and tourism, and average citizens saw little improvement in their levels of living. Corrupt governments continued.

In 1959 a young Marxist revolutionary named Fidel Castro overthrew the government with the promise of major reforms. Castro's first stated objective was to lessen Cuban dependence on foreign nations; his second, to diversify Cuban agriculture; his third, to convert land from private to government ownership; and his fourth, to eliminate the traditional Spanish bias toward farming.

Castro's progress to date in accomplishing his four objectives can be summarized as follows. Cuba's dependence on foreign nations initially shifted from reliance on the United States to subservience to the Soviet Union, whose estimated 5 billion dollars in annual aid compensated partially for the devastating effects of the U.S. economic embargo. The fall of communism and the breakup of the Soviet Union resulted in the loss of Soviet subsidies and a crippling of the Cuban economy, whose output had fallen by 40 percent by 1993. Facing the prospect of even further economic decline, Castro then announced, in a manner reminiscent of former Soviet president Mikhail Gorbachev's actions preceding the fall of Eastern European communism, that temporary compromises would have to be made with the capitalist world in order to save Cuban socialism. These concessions have included legalizing the holding of American dollars by Cuban citizens, which serves to increase the country's foreign currency reserves, and the licensing of foreign petroleum corporations to explore for oil in offshore Cuban waters. Castro also implemented a harsh austerity program, further reducing the already limited quantity of consumer goods available to the Cuban people. Ironically, then, the achievement of economic and political self-sufficiency has been accompanied by a significant deterioration of the living levels of the average Cuban worker. It remains to be seen whether the newfound self-reliance will prove to be temporary or permanent.

Castro's second objective, that of reducing Cuba's dependence on sugar, has yet to be achieved, though nickel mining operations and biomedical-related exports do provide secondary sources of foreign earnings. Castro's third goal, that of eradicating private property, has largely been accomplished. Cuba presently has one of the highest levels of collectivized land in the world. Castro has also succeeded in removing much of the old Hispanic prejudice toward farming and farmers. This goal has been obtained, in part, by allowing a large portion of the country's urban, white-collar professional class, which was centered in the capital city of Havana (2,096,000) to emigrate to the United States. A second tool used by Castro has been the channeling of most of Cuba's resources into rural development projects, including schools, electrification, and health-care clinics. In so doing, Cuba has improved considerably the social and economic conditions of its rural poor, whose continued support of Castro has been instrumental in his retaining control of the country.

Cuba thus stands today as a nation of deep ambiguities. Castro himself continues to rely on police-state tactics to quell internal opposition, yet receives considerable support from the rural masses. The nation is now finally free of foreign dependence, yet its overall economy and material living levels have seldom been worse. Finally, Cuba ranks among Latin America's leading countries in many social indicators, yet it is governed by an aging dictator whose pride seemingly is preventing him from charting a new course in a changing world.

Puerto Rico

For many years after becoming a dependency of the United States, Puerto Rico progressed little. Unlike Cuba, with its large area of level land and excellent soils for sugarcane, Puerto Rico received U.S. corporate attention only along the ribbon of level land that fringes the island. Interior Puerto Rico is hilly and mountainous.

Following World War II, however, Puerto Rico began a period of continuous economic growth through a program called Operation Bootstrap, a three-pronged development plan. The first prong was industrialization. Like other Caribbean islands, Puerto Rico had few raw materials other than those of agriculture, few power sources, a small market, and an inexpensive but unskilled labor supply. Nonetheless, the Puerto Rican government appealed to U.S. industry with attractive tax exemptions, training programs for labor, and a strenuous advertising effort. By 1956 the industrialization

movement was so successful that manufacturing produced more revenue than agriculture. Much of that manufacturing is centered in the capital city of San Juan (1,816,000).

Agricultural improvement was the second prong of the program. Experimental stations were established that used the help of soil conservation agents to introduce better land-management practices. Dairying, truck gardening, and poultry farms—new kinds of land use—competed with the traditional crops of coffee in the highlands and sugarcane in the lowlands. In more recent years rural development has focused on improving housing and bringing water, electricity, and schooling to farm families.

The third prong of the program was expansion of tourism. Again the government played a major role, by sponsoring hotel construction and extensive promotion (Figure 18–11). In addition, tourism benefitted greatly from Castro's takeover of Cuba. In 1953 118,000 persons visited the island; by 1963 tourists numbered almost 500,000; and recently that figure has grown to almost 2,000,000. Much of the tourist trade has come from the United States.

Puerto Rico presently holds the status of an American commonwealth. The people pay no U.S. federal tax and do not vote in federal elections but are otherwise entitled to all federal programs. The population is fairly evenly divided between those who favor statehood and those who wish to remain a commonwealth.

Hispaniola: The Dominican Republic and Haiti

Haiti occupies the western third of the island of Hispaniola; the Dominican Republic, the eastern two-thirds (See Figure 18–1). Even though the two nations have the same physical environment, the contrasts between them are marked.

Haiti, with its Afro-French culture and almost entirely black population, is a country of extreme poverty. Small subsistence farm plots worked with hoes and machetes support almost 80 percent of the population. Decay is seen everywhere: from potholed roads, abandoned irrigation systems, and erratic plumbing and water supply in the capital city of Port-au-Prince (1,144,000), to deforested and eroded hillsides and a deteriorated social organization. After being run by the Duvalier family as an almost feudal kingdom for decades, Haitians elected a leftist Catholic priest named Jean-Bertrand Aristide as president in 1991. Aristide was

Figure 18-11
Tourist hotels in Puerto Rico. Tourism is a major industry in the West Indies, where beautiful beaches, warm temperatures, first-class accommodations, and proximity to the United States result in millions of visitors annually, mostly during the drier months of December through April

soon forced into exile by the military, whose leaders governed ruthlessly until deposed by an occupying American force in 1994. Haiti is presently struggling with the need for massive social and economic reforms.

In contrast, the Dominican Republic has a Hispanic flavor, with areas of subsistence agriculture as well as large, mechanized farms. Road transportation is especially good, and the infrastructure is improving. Tourism is booming, especially along the north coast and in the capital city of Santo Domingo (2,400,000). Although the Dominican Republic remains a poor country, it has achieved one of the highest rates of economic growth in Latin America during the past three decades.

Jamaica

Jamaica consists of a high, rugged core surrounded by a limestone plateau that grades into some of the most beautiful and popular beaches in the Caribbean. Bauxite, or aluminum ore, is abundant in lowland basins and is the nation's leading export (see Figure 18–3). Industry is limited by an almost total lack of domestic energy sources.

Jamaica today is largely British in culture, having been captured from Spain in 1655. It is also an island of contradictions. Neat and orderly in many aspects, with English town clocks and efficient scheduling, the island is also experiencing severe social turmoil. Fostered by a colonial prohibition against slave women marrying, which resulted in many slave "families" without an adult male in residence, a matriarchal society now dominates the island's overwhelmingly black population. Unemployment is chronically high, and crime is increasing, from the shantytowns of Kingston (702,000) to the marijuana vendors in the northern beach resorts. Although mining and tourism are welcome and needed revenue sources, long-term development will come to the island only as Jamaican society is strengthened.

Belize

Considered a rimland nation primarily because of its ethnic makeup, Belize gained its independence from Great Britain in 1981, though Guatemala continues to claim the region (see Figure 18–1). Its population is only slightly more than 200,000, and much of its 8,866 square miles (22,963 square kilometers) is little used. For many years the nation's principal exports were wood and other forest products. Within the past thirty years, however, sugar and citrus have come to dominate the export market. The English influence on the predominantly black population is evidenced in its language and Protestant religion. The city of Belize (47,000) is the principal urban center although a new capital city, Belmopan, has been built inland, where hurricane damage is likely to be less severe.

Guyana, Suriname, and French Guiana

These three little-known, culturally Caribbean nations occupy the northeastern coast of South America (see Figure 18–1). The region was initially settled in the 1600s by Dutch colonists, who established plantations along the banks of the main rivers, all of which flowed northward from their forested headwaters in the Guiana Highlands. Soil exhaustion caused settlements to diffuse eastward and westward along the marshy coasts, and British and French settlers were allowed entry to increase the labor force. Eventually, the areas that today are Guyana and French Guiana were ceded to Britain and France, leaving Suriname a Dutch possession.

The cultivation of sugarcane on the coastal estates of Guyana and Suriname led to the importation of large numbers of slaves. When they were freed in the nineteenth century, thousands of workers from the Indian subcontinent were imported as indentured laborers. After five to seven years of farm service, the so-called East Indians were considered free men. Many of them have remained in the rural areas as independent farmers; most blacks have sought residence in the urban centers.

Collectively, the three nations, for all their physical size, have far fewer people than either Jamaica or Puerto Rico, and the population is clustered along the coast. Bauxite and diamonds are mined in the interior highlands. French Guiana, which the French consider to be an integral part of their nation, serves as a principal European spaceport. Both Guyana and Suriname are experiencing much social turmoil, as East Indians and blacks, Marxists and capitalists, vie for power at the edge of the jungle.

SUMMARY
The Struggle for National Identity

Middle America is a troubled region that comprises one large country, Mexico, and numerous small ones that have been searching for national identity and environmentally balanced economic development. The quest for national identity centered first on political independence from European colonial masters. It has focused subsequently on the need to maintain friendly, yet independent, relationships with the economically and politically powerful United States.

It is ironic that the struggle for national identity has also contributed indirectly to the economic underdevelopment of the region. It is unlikely that a highly fragmented region such as Middle America composed as it is, primarily of ministates with populations smaller than that of the city of Los Angeles, can be economically competitive without some form of regional cooperation. The extent to which the dream of a lasting regional union is achieved in the years ahead will influence to a large degree, the economic and social development of the Middle American peoples.

KEY TERMS

bracero	Institutional Revolutionary
ejido	Party (PRI)
finca	*Ladino*
	maquiladoras

NOTES

1. Lesley Byrd Simpson, *Many Mexicos,* 4th ed., rev. (Berkeley: University of California Press, 1967).

19

Latin American Regions: South America

Andean South America

Southern South America

Brazil

Caracas, Venezuela. Several of Venezuela's major cities are found within the basins located within the Andean mountain system, a feature common to several of the Andean countries.

Three final regions (together with the three regions of Middle America) complete the broad realm of Latin America: Andean South America, southern South America, and Brazil, a single nation with an area larger than any of the other five regions.

ANDEAN SOUTH AMERICA

Andean South America includes Venezuela, Colombia, Ecuador, Peru, and Bolivia (Figure 19–1). Each is dominated by a high mountainous core, which gives way on the eastward side to the humid lowlands of the Amazon and Orinoco river basins. With the exception of Bolivia, each of those countries also has a narrow coastal lowland, which facilitates trade with the outside world. Although the Andean nations have been independent since the early nineteenth century, each continues to struggle to overcome internal physical fragmentation and isolation, colonial social relationships, and regional inequalities.

Venezuela

Venezuela has a rich and diverse resource base, consisting of four regions. The first is the Andean Highlands, which curve eastward from Colombia to run parallel to the Caribbean coastline. Within the mountains are numerous large basins endowed with temperate climates and fertile soils. Finding little gold and few Indians, the Spanish colonists settled in those basins. Today, they house much of the Venezuelan national population in the urban centers of Caracas (the capital), Maracay, Valencia, Barquisimeto, Mérida, and San Cristóbal (see chapter-opening photo).

The northwesternmost part of the Andes divides into two ranges, which almost totally enclose the broad Maracaibo Lowlands (Figure 19–2). Those lowlands are dominated by the brackish Lago de (Lake) Maracaibo, which is 75 by 130 miles (121 by 209 kilometers) in size and opens into the Caribbean Sea. That lake, which has one of the most oppressively hot and humid climates in Latin America, was inhabited at the time of the Spanish conquest by Indians who lived in stilt houses above the shallow water. Those houses inspired the name Venezuela, or "Little Venice." Although largely ignored by the Spaniards in colonial times, the Maracaibo Lowlands have prospered in the twentieth century with the discovery of some of the largest petroleum deposits on earth, and the city of Maracaibo ranks today as the nation's second largest.

In the southeast a second mountainous region, called the Guiana Highlands, has just begun to be developed for its vast iron ore and bauxite reserves. And between the Andes and the Guiana Highlands lies Venezuela's fourth region, the great plain of the Orinoco River known as the llanos. The llanos have one of the most colorful histories of all Latin American regions. Tall, coarse grass grows on the inundated lowlands during the rainy season and dies off during the dry winter months, exposing a baked, rock-hard soil. Hordes of mosquitoes and other noxious insects heighten the human risk of disease. Historically the llanos were used primarily for the grazing of tough criollo cattle, which had to be walked hundreds of miles to the highland market centers, where they arrived as little more than skin and bones. In addition, the llanos produced a series of violent, illiterate dictators, who ruled the country off and on until 1935.

Venezuelan Economy.   Today Venezuela is one of the most stable and progressive nations in Latin America. Much of the turnaround is due to the discovery of petroleum, which has given the country one of the highest per capita GNPs in the Western Hemisphere. Oil and oil products now account for more than 87 percent of the country's exports, for 25 percent of the GNP, and for more than 60 percent of the government's revenue. Petroleum and development are synonymous in Venezuela.

The modern oil industry of Venezuela began in the early part of this century, when the dictator Juan Vincente Gómez encouraged foreign petroleum companies to develop the nation's reserves. The petroleum fields of the Maracaibo Basin—and later, the eastern llanos—became major sources of oil entering international trade. For many years Venezuela exported crude oil to refineries on the nearby Dutch islands of Aruba and Curaçao, to the United States, and to northwestern Europe. Since World War II, however, refineries have been built in Venezuela, and the by-products provide the raw materials for tires, synthetic fibers, medicines, and a host of other industries. In the process the government, in partnership with the petroleum companies, has obtained a greater share of the industry's profits, and

Figure 19-1
The nations, cities, and major highways of South America. Settlement in this region remains somewhat peripheral to the continent.

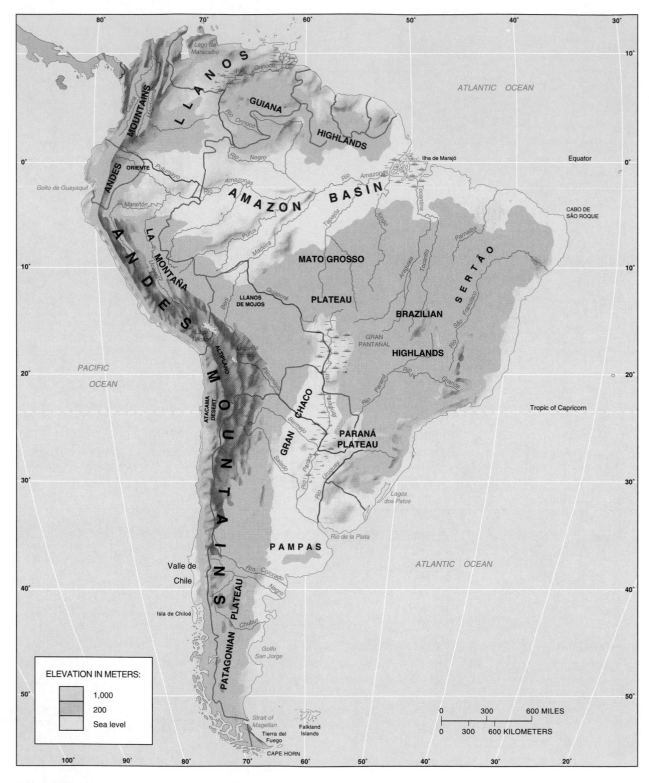

Figure 19-2
Major physiographic regions of South America. South America is composed of many different physiographic regions, each of which possesses a distinctive environment with particular opportunities and challenges for development.

in 1976 Venezuela nationalized the industry. Nationalization was the final step in Venezuela's move to regain control over its single most important economic activity.

Iron ore along the northern fringe of the Guiana Highlands has also contributed substantially to Venezuelan exports (Figure 19–3). The ores are located in what was a little-developed part of Venezuela and required large capital investments and an extensive infrastructure. Originally developed by U.S. corporations, operations in the area received additional investments from the Venezuelan government, with the goal of creating a national center of heavy industry. Those operations were nationalized in 1975. Hydroelectric power and imported coal are now used to make iron, steel, and aluminum. Ciudad Guayana (543,000) and nearby Ciudad Bolívar (267,000) are the centers of that ambitious development program.

For many years the Venezuelan government has reinvested profits derived from petroleum and iron ore to stimulate other sectors of the economy and to provide a better level of living for the population. Funds have been used for highway construction and farm-to-market roads, low-cost housing and education, agricultural improvement and colonization, and industrialization. In that way the wealth produced by mining has been allocated to the population, since the mining industry itself employs only about 3 percent of the labor force.

Urban Centers. Venezuela is one of the most urbanized nations of Latin America: some 85 percent of the population is considered urban. Of the country's 20 million people more than 3.3 million live in the metropolitan area of Caracas; the next four largest centers are Maracaibo (1,363,000), Valencia (1,031,000), Maracay (800,000), and Barquisimeto (745,000) (Figure 19–4). Away from the urban centers traditional agriculture is characteristic.

Colombia

The economic development of Colombia has been restricted by physical and cultural isolation so extreme that the very survival of the nation has been threatened. Western Colombia, where the bulk of the population resides, is divided by three parallel, primarily north-south arms of the Andes, which have severely restricted east-west movement. Until the advent of air transportation, the only feasible way to move goods and people was to follow the valleys of the Cauca and Magdalena rivers, which flow northward between towering volcanic ridges (Figure 19–2).

One consequence of the nation's fractured terrain has been the strengthening of isolated, regional economies and cultures at the expense of national unity. That condition is all the more troublesome in the east, beyond the Andes, where vast expanses of Orinoco *llanos* and the rain forests of the Amazon Basin extend to the distant frontier. Much of those two regions has remained free of effective national control and today harbors not only subsistence agriculture but also illegal drug production and processing operations.

Colombia's Past. The Spanish occupation of Colombia began with the founding of the Caribbean port of Santa Marta in 1525. Searching for gold, the *conquistadores* then pushed up the Magdalena Valley toward the highland basin of Cundinamarca, where they met significant numbers of Chibcha Indians. There they established the capital, Bogotá. Shortly afterward, in 1533, the port of Cartagena was built west of Santa Marta, and a second settlement cluster emerged along the lower Cauca Valley. That region came to be known as Antioquia. Unlike the people of Bogotá, who took advantage of an abundant supply of Indians to establish great highland haciendas, the isolated ***antioqueños*** found that development depended totally on their own labors. They established small, independent farms and businesses and produced a conservative, self-reliant middle-class society, which, fed by an extremely high birthrate, pushed southward up the Cauca.

Colombia was dominated throughout the colonial era by an oligarchy of church, military, and civil officers. Independence did little to change those patterns, which persisted until 1936, when a new land law was enacted. The intent of the framers of the law was to assist the poverty-stricken small farmers, many of whom illegally worked unimproved lands belonging to *latifundistas*. The law declared that if *colonos,* or small squatter farmers, could show that they had brought certain lands into economic utilization through fencing, cultivation, or the pasturing of cattle, they were entitled to receive those lands as their own.

Although well-intentioned, the land law had the unanticipated effect of provoking the complacent land barons into evicting the *colonos* from their sub-

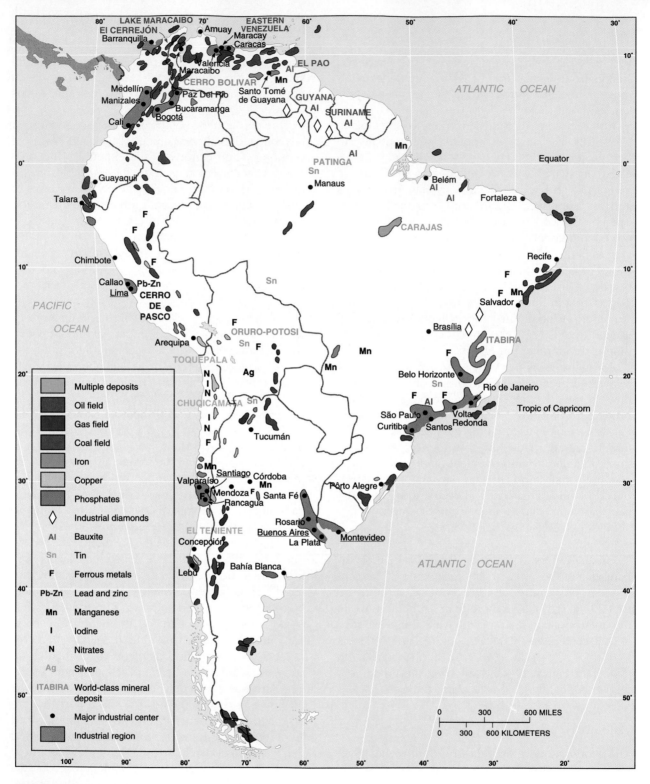

Figure 19-3

Principal mineral-producing areas of South America. Petroleum production in
Venezuela and Ecuador is of world importance, as is iron ore production in Brazil,
coal in Colombia, tin in Bolivia and Brazil, silver in Peru, copper in Chile and Peru,
and bauxite in Venezuela and Brazil.

444

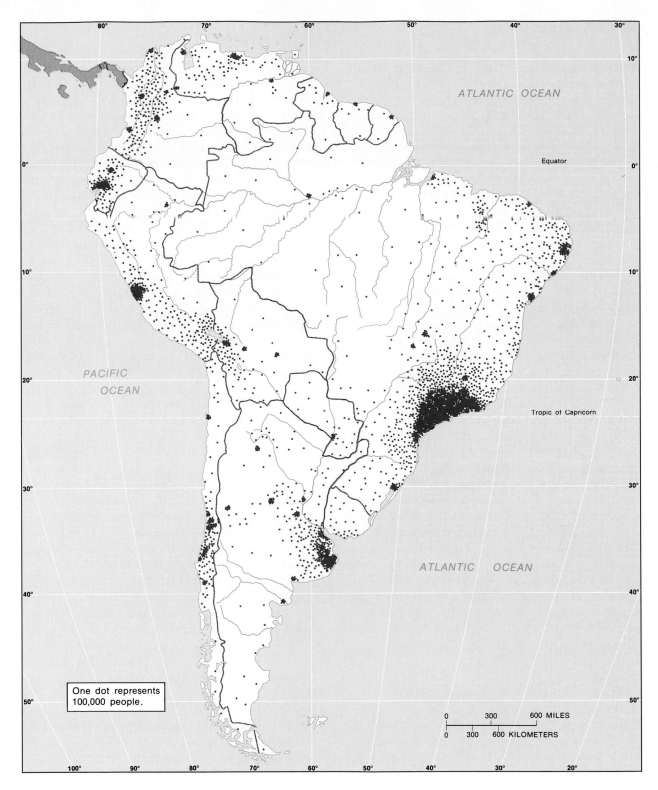

Figure 19-4
Population distribution in South America. The distribution of population in South America is oriented toward the fringes of the land; almost 90 percent of the population is located within 200 miles of the coast. Densely settled areas include the highlands formerly occupied by pre-Colombian cultures, the northeast coast of Brazil, the Rio de Janeiro–São Paulo area, and the Argentine pampas.

445

sistence plots, in order to prevent the breakup of the barons' great estates. Deprived of their livelihood, the *colonos* emerged as a vast, homeless subclass, and Colombia lapsed into an era of almost indiscriminate violence. Outwardly, the violence, which lasted into the 1960s, was a war between the liberals of Bogotá and the conservatives of Antioquia, with its regional capital of Medellín. More fundamentally, however, it was a class conflict between the haves and the have-nots, and it resulted in the migration of great numbers of rural dwellers to the more secure cities. For example, Cali, in the heart of the violence-torn middle Cauca Valley, grew from 27,000 inhabitants in 1912 to 200,000 in 1950 and to approximately 1,700,000 in 1993. Now, 69 percent of all Colombians live in cities.

Hope for domestic tranquillity increased in 1957 when the two dominant political parties, liberal and conservative, agreed to divide national cabinet posts, governorships, and mayoral offices in proportion to the number of votes each obtained. The elections of 1990 marked another historic turning point on the difficult road to national unity when the leadership of the powerful leftist guerrilla April 19 Movement (M19) announced an end to its sixteen-year insurgency and campaigned for national office. Unfortunately, peace is still not at hand, as numerous other groups continue to terrorize the citizenry.

Perhaps the greatest threat to Colombian society in recent times has been organized crime syndicates. Armed with both wealth and weapons, the drug warlords have hired guerrilla bands as private armies and effectively control parts of the hinterlands. When opposed by elected national officials, they have been so bold as to kidnap or assassinate the highest officers of the land, from supreme court justices to cabinet ministers and presidential candidates.

Modern Economy. Colombia's recent economic development is all the more remarkable, then, when viewed in the light of this history of violence and isolation. Bogotá has emerged as one of the leading cities of South America. Its cosmopolitan population of more than 6 million prides itself on its culture and produces a broad array of agricultural and industrial products. Antioquia, built on agriculture, continues to produce much of the world's high-grade coffee, which provides about half of the nation's legal exports. And Barranquilla, with a population of 1,019,000, has become Colombia's leading Carib-

bean port. Textiles, food processing, and banking sustain the economies of Manizales (310,000) and Pereira (302,000), as well as that of Medellín (1,664,000). But perhaps the most rapid growth in recent years has occurred in Cali, where a diversified economy is fueled by both Colombian and foreign interests. In addition, major coal deposits have been worked since the 1970s at El Cerrejón, in the dry Guajira Peninsula northwest of Venezuela's Maracaibo Lowlands (see Figure 19–3).

In recent years major transportation projects have linked formerly isolated areas. Cartagena has been connected by a waterway called El Dique to the Magdalena River and by a superhighway to Medellín and the Cauca Valley. In addition, a railroad now links Santa Marta to Honda on the middle Magdalena and indirectly to Bogotá beyond. Colombia's portion of the new Simon Bolívar Highway, which is an improved roadway intended to eventually link much of northern South America from Caracas to Quito, is also complete. And air transportation has been improved so that it now ranks among the best in Latin America.

Ecuador

Ecuador has long been beset by social and economic problems. During the colonial period it was largely neglected in favor of the wealth and splendor of Peru. The few Spaniards who did settle there gained their livelihood from the sweat of Indian workers on large *haciendas* in the high basins of the Andes. The Spaniards themselves lived in Quito, the capital and former Inca center, and in smaller regional centers. For many of the Indians, European conquest had little impact beyond the introduction of new crops and animals. In the *oriente,* an area east of the Andes, the fierce Amazon Basin Indians and the lack of resources of interest to the Spanish kept the area free from colonial administrative control. To the west the Pacific lowlands were largely neglected, because of the prevalence of malaria and yellow fever in the humid north and the severe aridity in the southern Guayas Basin (see the boxed feature Altitudinal Life Zones in the Andes).

Today, the Pacific lowlands are Ecuador's most dynamic and progressive region. Guayaquil (2,000,000) has surpassed Quito as the nation's largest city and functions as the principal port and manufacturing center. Since 1940 a vigorous road-building program has opened large areas of formerly mosquito-infested lowlands to settlement and the commercial farming of rice and cacao. In addition, Ecuador is the world's leading exporter of bananas produced by smallholder lowland farmers. Fishing in Pacific waters has also contributed substantially to the nation's wealth. Ecuador's claim of control over Pacific waters up to 200 miles (322 kilometers) off its shores is a reflection of the importance of fish products to the nation's exports, as well as of a strong sense of nationalism. Furthermore, natural gas is being developed near Guayaquil.

Unlike the Pacific lowlands, the Andean highlands of Ecuador have changed little since colonial times. Population is concentrated in the Callejón Andino, which consists of a series of intermontane basins and the surrounding hillsides. Quito (1,500,000), the urban center of the region, serves as the national capital, the home of the landed aristocracy, and a regional service center. Agriculture, largely for local consumption, is the major economic activity. The best bottomlands are in large farm units that specialize in dairying and maize. The remaining lands are divided into thousands of minuscule, often incredibly steep Indian subsistence plots (Figure 19–5). Wheat and barley are cultivated on dry lands, potatoes are grown at higher elevations, and sheep are pastured in alpine meadows. The Andes of Ecuador present a classic example of both *minifundia* or small landholdings and *latifundia*.

The *oriente* is a sparsely settled rain forest inhabited largely by Amazon Indian groups, such as the Jívaro, who possess few modern techniques of production. In past times the *oriente* has received temporary influxes of people from the Andes in search of balsa wood, rubber, and cinchona (i.e., quinine used to battle malaria). Each time, however, the gathering of those wild products has lost out to commercial production elsewhere or to synthetic substitutes. Then, in 1967 a major oil field was discovered in the *oriente,* and Ecuador became a leading exporter of unrefined petroleum. Almost 500,000 barrels a day can be shipped by pipeline to a Pacific terminal. Ironically, however, Ecuador must still import some refined oil.

Despite the disparity in their areal distribution, Ecuador's 11.4 million inhabitants are about evenly divided between Andean Indian farmers and the Spaniards and *mestizos* who live in the cities and the Pacific lowlands (Figure 19–6). The two groups differ greatly, and communication between them is

minimal. The Indians, many of whom are illiterate, are oriented toward their local highland communities rather than toward the nation as a whole. They earn a meager existence from manual toil, and their material possessions are few: a one-room hut, a sleeping mat and woolen blanket, and clothing to shelter them from the cold. Their diet consists of tubers—such as potatoes, ulluco, and oca—guinea pigs, and highland grains, including wheat, barley, and quinoa. In contrast, the Westernized urban dwellers are highly nationalistic and mostly literate; they aspire to white-collar employment. Integrating the people of those two cultures is one of Ecuador's most urgent needs.

Bananas, petroleum, and fish products provide Ecuador with valuable exports, but national development is hampered by the cultural dualism as well as by isolation. The Andes are a formidable barrier to internal transport, and few all-weather roads connect the intermontane basins of the highlands or link the highlands with the coast. Roads are almost nonexistent in the *oriente*. Ecuador's economic development has also been hampered by limited access to the markets of eastern Anglo-America and Europe. Since about 1950, however, as Japan has become a major trading nation and the population on the West Coast of the United States has grown, Ecuador's access to markets has improved. Japan, particularly, has become an important trading partner for Ecuador and other west-coast South American nations.

Peru

Like Ecuador, Peru emerged from the Spanish conquest as a nation deeply divided between European and Indian values and economic production systems. The Spanish introduced the concept of privately held property; the Indians were accustomed to working communal lands. The Spanish established large-scale commercial agriculture; the Indians continued to practice semisubsistence farming. The Spanish economy was geared toward mining; the Indians were oriented toward agriculture. Spanish loyalty was directed primarily toward the nation-state; Indians were loyal to their local villages. The Spaniards lived in cities and were Westernized in their culture; the Indians resided in the rural highlands and clung to their traditional languages, dress, and diet.

ALTITUDINAL LIFE ZONES IN THE ANDES

To a great degree the climates of the Latin American tropics are controlled by elevation. Communities located just a few miles from each other often have radically different physical environments as a result of their different altitudes. The temperature of motionless air changes approximately 3.5°F (1.9°C) for every 1,000 feet (305 meters) of altitude. Thus, one could leave the coastal Ecuadorian city of Guayaquil where the afternoon temperature might be a broiling 96°F (36°C) and arrive by airplane a few minutes later in the Andean city of Quito, elevation 9,350 feet (2,850 meters), only to find the temperature a chilly 63°F (17°C).

A trip by automobile or train from Guayaquil to Quito would pass through three altitudinal life zones, where natural vegetation and agriculture reflect the changing climates. The lowest zone is the *tierra caliente,* or hot lands (Figure A). The lightly clothed farmers of that zone, which lies below approximately 3,300 feet (1,000 meters), cultivate heat-loving crops, such as coconuts, cacao, rice, bananas, sugarcane, rubber, papayas, mangoes, and manioc. The second life zone is the *tierra templada,* or temperate land, which extends from the *tierra caliente* to about 8,200 feet (2,500 meters). That zone has year-round mild temperatures, which are conducive to the cultivation of such crops as coffee, citrus, cinchona, cotton, maize, and a variety of vegetables, including beans, tomatoes, and peppers.

Quito itself lies in the third altitudinal life zone, the *tierra fría,* or cold land. The inhabitants of those higher elevations must dress warmly throughout the year and must protect themselves as much as possible from the intense solar radiation (Figure B). Agriculture centers

Figure A
Altitudinal life zones in the Andes.
Differences in elevation strongly influence crop ecology and, therefore, the agricultural options available to the region's inhabitants.

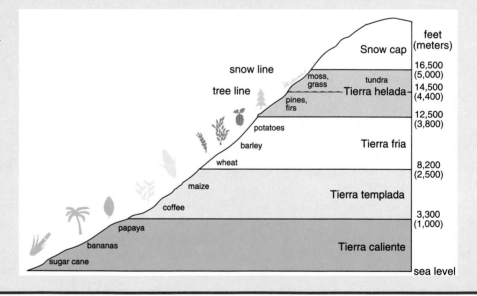

Peru is also similar to Ecuador in physical geography. Each has three major areal units: the coast, the Andes, and the east. Unlike Ecuador, however, Peru has expended much effort in incorporating the Amazon lowlands into the national economy. Peru has also aggressively pursued a policy of national unity, attempting to integrate the Indian societies into a common national culture. And Peru's economy is more diversified than Ecuador's.

Coastal Peru. The Peruvian coast is a narrow ribbon of desert. Its extreme aridity and surprisingly cool temperatures are the result of prevailing westerly winds that blow inland over the cold, offshore Peru

around the cultivation of plums, peaches, apples, and other cold-tolerant fruits, as well as grains and tubers, including wheat, barley, quinoa, and potatoes.

Beyond those zones is a fourth life zone, the *tierra helada,* or frozen land, which begins at around 12,500 feet (3,800 meters) and continues to the glacial snow line, between 16,000 and 17,000 feet (4,880 to 5,180 meters). The *tierra helada* supports agriculture only on its lower slopes; above the tree line only hardy grasses and lichens can survive.

In reality, it is inaccurate to speak of a single tropical climate; because of vertical zonation almost every environment on earth, from rain forest to tundra, can be represented in a single tropical region. Thus, travelers in the tropics should dress according to the altitudes included in their itineraries.

Figure B
A street scene in Quito, Ecuador. Despite its nearness to the equator, Quito's elevation puts it in the *tierra fría.*

Current. As the air is warmed over the coastal plains, it is also dried. When it reaches the lower slopes of the westward-facing Andes, it is forced upward and cooled, producing thick fog that sustains grasses and lichens; at higher elevations it produces rain.

The cold, upwelling Pacific waters have also traditionally supported one of the world's riches fishing grounds, with great harvests of anchovy and tuna. Huge flocks of sea birds feed off the fish; and for years the bird droppings, called guano, constituted Peru's most valuable export, nourishing some of the finest gardens of Anglo-America and Europe. In recent years Peru's coastal fishing industry has suffered from severe overfishing and periodic inva-

449

Figure 19-5
Small farms in the Andean high-lands of Ecuador. The scattered small farmsteads suggest the small acreages available for each peasant family. The high-lands of Ecuador, Peru, and Bolivia are largely occupied by Indians.

sions of a warm equatorial current, called *el niño.* In addition to disrupting the fragile marine ecosystem, *el niño* brings unaccustomed heat, humidity, and flooding to the desert lowlands.

Despite its struggles, the offshore fishing industry remains an important segment of the Peruvian economy, the most prosperous components of which are concentrated along the arid coastal plains. Coastal settlement focuses on the margins of some forty rivers that rise in the Andes and cross the desert to the sea, and most of the nation's commercial crops are grown in the river oases, with sugarcane, cotton, and rice being the most important export crops. Those crops used to be grown on large estates, many of which were owned by foreign corporations. In the late 1960s, however, most of the estates were nationalized and turned into worker cooperatives. The oases near the capital city of Lima and the nearby port of Callao (with a joint population exceeding 7.0 million) are oriented to truck gardening and dairying for the urban market. The southern oases have a subsistence economy, but some grapes and olives are grown for the national market, and assorted food crops for the regional center of Arequipa (635,000). Since 1950 the government has imple-

mented many projects to provide greater amounts of water, in order to expand the irrigated area.

The coast is also endowed with some significant mineral deposits. In the north, petroleum has been pumped since the late nineteenth century. The south features copper and iron ore deposits. The iron ore is shipped north to Chimbote, where it is processed into iron and steel sheets, rods and ingots.

Lima-Callao forms the nation's social, political, and economic focal point. While preserving many of its colonial traditions, Lima has become increasingly industrialized. Historic buildings on narrow streets contrast with modern architecture and broad avenues. Around the city's fringes and on formerly vacant land near the city center are squatter settlements, occupied by the urban poor and migrants from the rural highlands and small towns. The population of the Lima-Callao area is growing at about twice the national rate.

The Peruvian Interior. The coastal area is the home of Europeans and *mestizos;* the Peruvian Andes are inhabited mainly by peasant Indians of **Quechua** and **Aymara** descent (Figure 19–7). The official languages of Peru are Spanish, which is spoken by 68

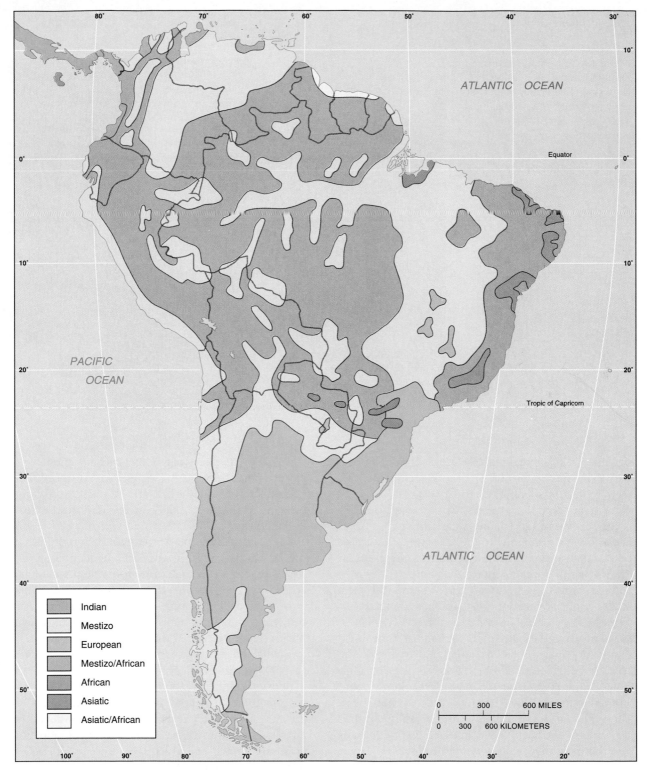

Figure 19-6

Dominant ethnic groups of South America. The most common group in South
America is the *mestizos*, but Indians still predominate in the highlands of Ecuador,
Peru, and Bolivia. Europeans dominate in Chile, Argentina, Uruguay, and southern
Brazil. Africans dominate in many coastal lowland areas of Colombia, Venezuela,
and Brazil.

Legend:
- Indian
- Mestizo
- European
- Mestizo/African
- African
- Asiatic
- Asiatic/African

Figure 19-7
Local Indian children at the Inca fortress at Ollantaytambo in the Peruvian Andes. The Quechua and Aymara Indians of the Peruvian-Bolivian border region are farmers who grow potatoes and hardy grains and raise sheep and llamas.

percent of the population, and Quechua, which is still the dominant tongue of 27 percent of the people. Only 3 percent speak Aymara.

Population in the Andes is dense, levels of technology are low, and many peasants migrate temporarily or permanently to the coast and, to a lesser degree, to the east in search of work. Land tenure in the highlands remains much the same as it was in colonial times. Large *haciendas* control the best lands, while poverty-ridden Indians continue to work tiny, privately or communally owned hillside plots, much as they did in pre-Colombian times. The Peruvian government has attempted to break the aristocracy's hold on the land and the peasants, and some of the large estates have been broken up and allotted to the smallholders who have worked them. Those actions are intended to further a larger policy of national unification by integrating the Indians into the national Spanish-*mestizo* culture.

The mountains of Peru are also noted for their extensive mineral deposits (see Figure 19–3). The most famous mining district is Cerro de Pasco, an old colonial silver center that has been redeveloped to produce copper, silver, gold, lead, zinc, and bismuth. In addition, coal is mined in several locations along the western flank of the Andes.

Peru has made repeated attempts to tame its vast eastern lands in the Amazon Basin. For more than 100 years the nation has sponsored colonization projects in the area, many in the region of transitional border valleys called the ***montaña*** (see Figure 19–2). Those attempts have greatly intensified in the past forty years. Roads have been built across the Andes into the east, and along each road have come highland peasants in search of new economic opportunities. Peru's proposed Marginal Highway is projected to extend along the eastern flank of the Andes (Figure 19–8). At this time, however, much of the east remains sparsely populated. Iquitos (270,000) is the regional urban center and Peru's major port on the Amazon River, which empties into the Atlantic Ocean 2,300 miles (3,700 kilometers) to the east. The existence of petroleum deposits in the area has been known for some time, but production was long limited by inadequate transport. In 1977 a 525-mile (845 kilometer) pipeline connecting the Amazonian fields with Pacific terminals was completed, and Peru became a modest oil exporter in 1985.

Government Policies. In recent years the Peruvian government has been playing an active role

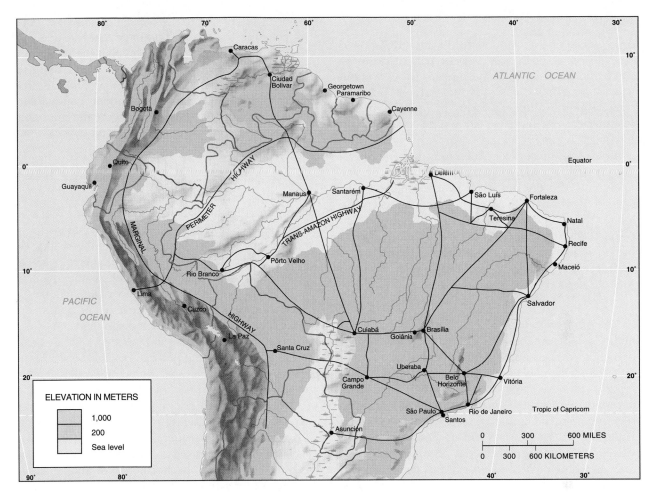

Figure 19-8
Proposed Amazon Basin highway system and connections to other regions. An extensive highway system is being built as part of a major development effort in the Amazon Basin. The northern Andean nations have also proposed the construction of the Marginal Highway, which may, in time, connect to the Trans-Amazon Highway network.

in directing change, both economic and social. Many of Peru's policies mirror those that were instituted much earlier in Mexico: seizure of political power from the landed gentry, unification of society, emphasis on education, and agrarian reform.

Unfortunately, the 1980s and 1990s brought mounting economic and social reversals to the proud nation that once was Spain's greatest colonial prize. In recent years, Peru has had one of Latin America's highest rates of inflation and heaviest foreign debt loads. Living levels have declined dramatically. Much of the economic dislocation is attribut-

able to the expansion of **coca** farming within the *montaña*. Coca leaves are the source of cocaine. The Peruvian drug producers have recently joined forces with a Maoist guerrilla group called *Sendero Luminoso*, or Shining Path, to form a formidable threat to internal peace and order. Alberto Fujimori, an agricultural engineer of Japanese descent who was elected president of Peru in 1990, justified his disbanding of Congress and the Supreme Court and imposition of martial law in 1992 as short-term evils needed to restore economic and political order to the troubled nation.

Bolivia

As a result of the War of the Pacific (1879–1884) Bolivia lost territory that is now part of northern Chile and became the only Andean nation without a coastline. Bolivia also lost the present Brazilian state of Acre in the early 1900s, as well as much of its southeastern territory, known as the *chaco,* to Paraguay in the 1930s.

Bolivia has historically been one of the least politically stable nations in the world. Between the mid-1960s and the mid-1980s, for example, it had sixteen governments, some of which lasted no longer than a few months. This instability now appears finally to have ended, however, and Bolivia has achieved much economic growth over the past decade. It remains, nevertheless, one of Latin America's poorest nations.

The *Altiplano*.

The heart of Bolivia is a series of high mountain basins nestled between two branches of the central Andes. Centered on Lake Titicaca—which, at 12,507 feet (3,812 meters), is the world's highest large freshwater lake—the *altiplano,* or high plain, is a perpetually cold and arid region dominated by hardy, windswept grasses (see Figure 19–2). There, rural Indian farmers in remote villages raise sheep and llamas and cultivate potatoes and other highland tubers and grains. Indian dress is a distinctive blend of medieval European serf and pre-Hispanic American styles, with the men often wearing pants with long, ankle-length skirts. Both sexes wear sandals, woolen ponchos, and hats to help fight the effects of the cold and the intense solar radiation. The dress, language, and customs of the rural Indians stand in stark contrast to those of the Westernized, urban elite living in La Paz (1,100,00), Bolivia's largest city and administrative seat of government.

Within the mountains that tower above the *altiplano* the Spaniards discovered some of the richest mineral deposits of the New World. At their zenith the fabled mining centers of Potosí and Oruro produced more than half of the world's silver. Unfortunately for the country, in the early independence era Bolivian mining interests came to be dominated by three aristocratic families, whose members ran the country as an economic colony while they lived in lavish residences in Paris and other overseas locations. Little regard was given to the Aymara- and Quechua-speaking Indian masses, whose leaders became politically radical over time. As pressure for change mounted, the president of the republic announced in 1939 that the great mining companies, which by then were producing tin primarily, must invest part of their profits in Bolivia itself. Shortly thereafter, the president met a violent death. Not until the early 1950s were the mines expropriated by the government and a sweeping agrarian reform law enacted.

Economic Development. To the extent that Bolivia can emerge from its legacy of social and political turmoil, the prospects for economic development appear bright. The highlands continue to be one of the greatest mining districts in the world. Tin mines at altitudes of 12,000 to 18,000 feet (3,658 to 5,486 meters) account for half of all the minerals mined in Bolivia and for 69 percent of the nation's export value (Figure 19–9). But, extraction from deep-shaft mines is difficult, and transportation is costly. Large petroleum and natural gas deposits have also been developed in the Bolivian *chaco,* and a pipeline has been built to the highland urban centers and beyond to the Chilean port of Arica on the Pacific.

Bolivia is also a nation of great agricultural potential. In the southeastern lowlands around Santa Cruz (529,000), considerable recent development has made the nation self-sufficient in sugar, rice, and cotton. In addition, the northern lowland Amazonian region is a frontier zone of active colonization and is the source of most of Bolivia's coca. For centuries, the highland Indians have chewed the leaves of the coca tree for their mild narcotic effects but, as is true in Peru, the leaves are now processed into cocaine, which is by far Bolivia's most valuable crop. The cocaine warlords appear to have replaced the mining elite as the latest threat to the stability and integrity of the nation.

SOUTHERN SOUTH AMERICA

Southern South America is composed of Chile, Argentina, Uruguay, and Paraguay (see Figure 19–1). Chile, Argentina, and Uruguay share several features that separate them from many of their neighbors. They all have relatively high per capita GDPs (See Table 17–6). In addition, each is highly urbanized, has a well-defined middle class, and has a high literacy rate. In each the nation-state idea is well established, and all three populations are culturally unified. Measured by many standard indicators, Chile, Argentina, and

Figure 19-9
Indian women working at a Bolivian tin mine. The Spanish were first attracted to
these highlands by their gold and silver. From that time on, Indian peasants have
provided the labor to extract Bolivia's rich mineral deposits.

Uruguay appear to be among the world's developed
nations (See Chapter 4). That assessment is further
supported by demographic features. A review of
birthrates, death rates, and growth rates shows that all
three countries have followed the demographic transformation model and are now nearing the final stage.
In addition, each has developed a significant industrial base and has entered the later stages of Rostow's
model of economic development.

Chile

Chile has achieved cultural unity in spite of its unique
long, narrow shape. Extending 2,630 miles (4,234
kilometers) north to south but never more than 250
miles (403 kilometers) east to west, Chile is physically
almost the inverse of the varied environments of the
Pacific Coast of North America, from Baja California to
southeastern Alaska. The heart of the nation is central

Chile, between 30° S and 42° S latitude, where the climate is Mediterranean, with hot, dry summers and
cool, wet winters that are similar to those of central and
southern California (Figure 19–10). Within that area a
cohesive society has formed.

To the north is the bone-dry Atacama Desert,
where decades can pass without measurable rainfall. The Atacama is sparsely populated but possesses nitrates, copper, and iron ore, which constitute most of the nation's mineral exports. The south
has a marine west coast environment, much like that
of coastal Oregon, Washington, and British
Columbia. Occupied by the descendants of nineteenth-century German immigrants, the south is a
cold, mountainous region endowed with abundant
forest and waterpower potential. In the far south
some coal, petroleum, and natural gas are found,
and sheep are raised for wool. Fishing is a growing
industry all along Chile's extensive coastline.

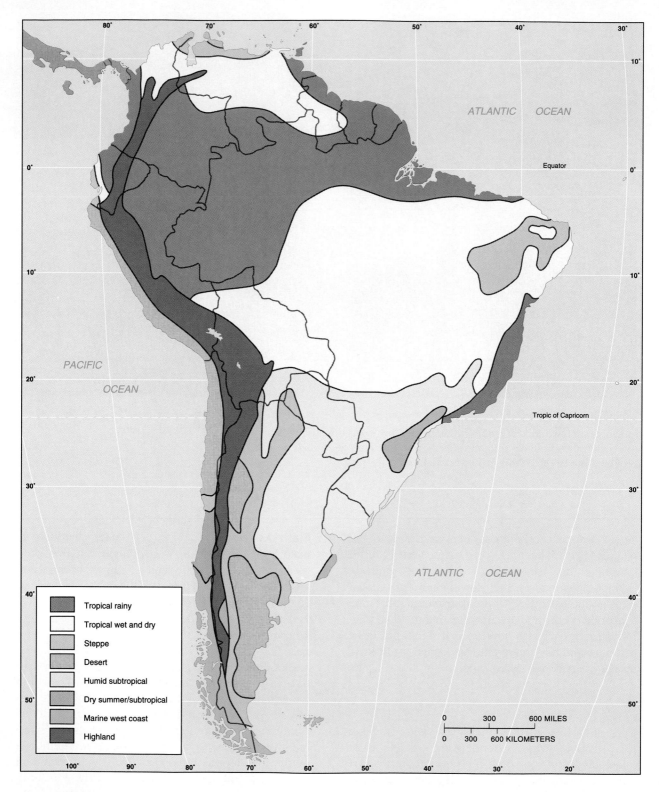

Figure 19-10
South American climates. South America has a great variety of climates, ranging from hot tropical lowlands to polar alpine zones. Each climate offers distinct opportunities for agricultural development.

Central Chile. Most of the population, industry, and commercial agriculture is located in the temperate and fertile lands of central Chile (see Figure 19–4). The country's major cities—including the capital, Santiago (5,800,000); Viña del Mar (316,000); Valparaíso (306,000); and Concepción (338,000)—all lie within that zone, which is also the agricultural heartland of the nation. In addition to the traditional grain and tuber crops, the region is now emerging as a major supplier of high-quality fresh fruits. Table grapes, apples, pears, peaches, plums, and citrus are produced in abundance and have found acceptance overseas, especially in Northern Hemisphere countries, where seasons are the opposite of those in Chile.

Political History. Chile's unified society is of recent vintage. In colonial times the economy revolved around *haciendas*, the owners of which permitted the poor peons to work small subsistence plots. Because of a shortage of workers brought about by a scarcity of Indian laborers, however, the hold of the *hacendados* was not strong. And the Chilean population became united in a common cause during the War of the Pacific, which resulted in their control of the rich nitrate deposits of the northern Atacama Desert. Work in the nitrate mines, and later in copper and iron ore mines, provided Chilean laborers with additional nonagricultural employment options and contributed to the transfer of much of the nation's capital investment from agriculture to industry. That shift was reinforced in the early twentieth century, especially during World War I, when goods from the industrialized world became difficult to obtain and prompted local industrialization.

Cultural unity, national allegiance, valuable export products, a lack of heavy rural population pressure, and diversification of the economy with manufacturing and service largely account for Chile's development. In addition, about 92 percent of the population is literate, and political stability has been characteristic during most of Chile's history. In recent years political power has passed to urban-oriented parties that have campaigned for economic and social reform along two main lines: (1) greater control of foreign investment, especially the mining industries that provide most of the nation's exports, and (2) land redistribution in the rural sector.

In 1970 Salvador Allende became the first self-acknowledged Marxist president of Chile. He was elected by a minority of the electorate, with barely more than one-third of the vote in a three-man race. The Allende government attempted to reorganize Chile's economic and social structure very rapidly, nationalizing the mining industry, accelerating the redistribution of land, and taking over most banks and communications media. A true socialist economy was in the offing.

The restructuring was not without problems and serious opposition, however. Allende almost bankrupted the nation, and he alienated a large part of the population. The Chilean Congress repeatedly attempted to rescind Allende's actions, and strikes of protest were common among workers and in the middle class. In 1973 the protest was brought to a head, and the military revolted, ending forty-six consecutive years of constitutional government, the longest at that time among South American nations. Allende was killed, and a military government, led by General Augusto Pinochet, was formed to rule the country. Pinochet's sixteen-year reign was marked by accusations of massive human rights violations and international isolation. It was also characterized by a return to a market-oriented economy. Pinochet's democratically elected successors have restored respect for civil liberties while maintaining the free-market policies that have sustained Chile's recent economic growth.

Argentina

Argentina has the second largest territory in Latin America and one of the richest agricultural bases in all the world. For the past century it has been second only to the United States as the destination of European emigrants. By Latin American standards Argentina's annual per capita GDP of almost $2,800 is high, but Argentina remains poor in comparison to the economically advanced nations of Europe and Anglo-America. It has failed to achieve its potential primarily because of misguided political and economic policies that have restricted the initiative and energies of its work force throughout much of history.

Argentina's History. During the colonial period Spanish interest in southern South America centered on the silver and gold mines of the high Andes in arid northwestern Argentina, bordering Bolivia. Agricultural communities—such as Salta, Tucumán, and Córdoba—were founded along rivers in the adjacent foothills and lowlands to provide mules and other work animals, hides, and food for the highland mining centers (see figure 19–1). Buenos Aires and other settlements along the humid Atlantic coast languished from Spanish neglect and served primarily to block further Portuguese expansion from Brazil.

The development of Buenos Aires and its rich agricultural hinterland, the *pampas,* began in the eighteenth century (see Figure 19–2). Argentine cowboys, called *gauchos,* roamed the pampas in search of hides and tallow, which they obtained from rangy, wild cattle that had evolved from European animals released on the grassy plains two centuries earlier. By the end of the colonial period, the wild herds were mostly exhausted, and *estancias,* or large cattle ranches, began to be established around the city.

Argentina gained its independence in 1816, but it remained a sparsely settled nation until Great Britain became interested in the country as a potential source of wheat and beef and a market for British industrial products. The turning point in Argentina's economic development came in about 1870, with the invention of refrigerated railroad cars and ships, which made possible the exportation of fresh Argentine beef to Europe. The few remaining Indians were either killed or driven southward into the cold deserts of the Patagonian Plateau, and the *estancias* were fenced, in preparation for British purebred cattle. Unwilling to work on the *estancias* themselves, the landed aristocracy imported between 1860 and 1930 more than 6 million workers from southern Europe, mostly from Italy and Spain, as indentured laborers.

Under the terms of the indenture agreements, passage to South America was provided by the landowners, who also contributed small plots on which the immigrants could have a family garden. In return, the workers were obligated to farm the estate lands for five to seven years. Many of the natural grasslands, formerly used for the inefficient grazing of the scrawny *criollo* cattle, were then planted with wheat. But at the conclusion of the indenture period, much of the land was converted from wheat to improved pasture crops, such as alfalfa. In contrast to the native prairie grasses, those provided a tender pasture suitable for the imported European breeds of cattle.

Once released from the bonds of indenture, the dispossessed farm workers, called *descamisados,* or shirtless ones, gravitated toward Buenos Aires, Rosario, and other urban centers in search of em-

ployment. They eventually formed an urban proletariat, and their poverty made them highly vulnerable to the influence of charismatic political or military leaders.

The worldwide depression of the 1930s severely damaged the fragile Argentine economy, as Great Britain cut back on purchases of Argentine agricultural products. Matters were further aggravated by the fall of the constitutional government and the assumption of power by the military. In 1946 a young army colonel named Juan Perón took control in a coup. Anxious to build a base of political support, Perón nationalized most major industries. Countless *descamisados* were given jobs in state-controlled factories, where inefficiencies were subsidized by heavy taxes on the agricultural sector. Without sufficient investment money for agricultural development, the output of the previously productive pampas dropped, and Argentina's economy nose-dived.

Perón was ousted in 1955, but many of his policies continued. Runaway inflation became chronic. In addition, widespread nepotism in the large industrial firms restricted the opportunities for career advancement among the most capable of the younger generation and led to an out-migration of skilled workers, which further damaged Argentina's chances for recovery.

Frustrated by economic decline, Argentinians experienced political and social polarization. One military regime followed another in the midst of strikes, demonstrations, and urban violence. A nostalgic longing for the stability of the past led to Perón's return from exile in 1973, but he died the following year. He was succeeded by his widow, Eva, who, in turn, was deposed in 1976. Subsequent military and civilian rulers, anxious to shift attention away from the nation's economic problems, engaged in a series of questionable activities. In 1982 they declared war on Great Britain over the Falkland (Malvinas) Islands, which resulted in a humiliating defeat for Argentina. More recently, they announced a plan to transfer the capital from Buenos Aires to the small Patagonian port town of Viedma. In the meantime the effects of the trade deficit were temporarily delayed by foreign borrowing, leaving Argentina with one of the highest per capita levels of indebtedness in the world.

The vicious cycle of waste and mismanagement was finally slowed by the election in 1989 of a reform-minded president named Carlos Menem. Menem sold off hundreds of inefficient state-owned industrial plants, encouraged foreign investment, and brought inflation under control. In so doing, he was criticized by some as neglecting the needs of the poor while others lauded him for having laid the foundation for Argentina's long-awaited emergence as one of the world's leading economic powers.

Argentine Economy.   Argentina thus remains an enigma. Its population is both literate (94 percent) and urban (86 percent). In addition, some 98 per cent of the nation's 33 million people are European; only 2 percent are *mestizo* (see Figure 19–6).

Buenos Aires and the *pampas* form the country's heartland, by far the nation's most important area. Greater Buenos Aires, with a population of approximately 12 million, is one of the largest and most sophisticated cities in the world. A well-integrated road and railway system radiates outward from the city, and goods funnel through the city's port to the world market. From the fertile, subtropical *pampas* come beef, maize, and wheat, which are largely exported to the developed world. Imports are mainly manufactured goods from Western Europe and the United States.

Most of Argentina's manufacturing and service activities are in Buenos Aires, where some 45 percent of the nation's industrial labor force is also located. Most of that force, however, is employed in small, inefficient workshops that specialize in metal fabricating, petrochemicals and plastics, meat packing, milling, and textiles. About 50 percent of all those who hold jobs in the tertiary sector are also found in the capital. Thus, with more than one-third of the population of the entire country residing in greater Buenos Aires, the city constitutes a classic example of a primate city, an urban area that totally dominates the economy, culture, and politics of the nation. Such primate cities are common in the developing nations of the Third World. Although they function as centers of development and change, they also frequently experience the greatest levels of congestion, pollution, and poverty.

Several other Argentine regions provide products that complement the economy of the *pampas*. In the west the old cities of Córdoba (1,167,000), Mendoza (729,000), and Tucumán (626,000) have become important growth centers. The west, a dry region in the rain shadow of the Andes, has an agricultural base. The arid zones are devoted to raising cattle; the irrigated districts, to sugarcane and grapes for the national market. In the Andean highlands of the extreme northwest are a few small mines of asbestos and several metals. In addition, some petroleum is produced from a giant geologic trough just east of the Andes.

To the north of the *pampas* is a low, humid area between the Paraná and Uruguay rivers. Those two rivers are wide and subject to great variation in water flow, so transportation has been difficult. However, the area is already noted for its tea, maize, flax, cattle, and sheep; and the Río de la Plata watershed development program—in which Argentina, Paraguay, Uruguay, and Brazil participate—may make the Argentine "Mesopotamia" even more productive.

In southern Argentina is Patagonia, a sparsely populated, dry, windswept plateau (see Figure 19–2). Most of Patagonia is used for raising sheep; but the lower, well-watered valleys have irrigated alfalfa fields, cattle ranches, vineyards, and mid-latitude fruit orchards. In this century some mineral resources have also been exploited. Small quantities of petroleum have been discovered in the south near Comodoro Rivadavia, and limited amounts of coal and iron ore are shipped to Buenos Aires to be processed into iron and steel. Large phosphate deposits are also under development in the Río Colorado Basin.

Argentina's outlying regions are primarily product suppliers for the *pampas* and its center, Buenos Aires (Figure 19–11). Those regions support much of the population of the *pampas*, and their development is reflected in the improved well-being of the nation's heartland.

Uruguay

Although Uruguay is one of the smallest nations in South America, it has historically enjoyed one of the highest levels of living on the continent. Much of its prosperity can be traced to the unity of Uruguayan society, which has been supported by the country's uniformly rich agricultural base. Geologically, Uruguay is a transition zone. In the north it contains a low-altitude extension of the Brazilian Paraná Plateau; in the south, a continuation of the Argentine *pampas*. The central part of the nation is a region of low, rounded hills. All three of those low-lying landform regions are characterized by a humid subtropical climate and fertile soils. As a result, a higher proportion of land (90 percent) is used for agriculture in Uruguay than in any other Latin American nation.

Figure 19-11
A view of Buenos Aires showing the obelisk. South America's rapid urbanization and sometimes spectacular cities suggest a transition to developed-region status.

The agricultural transformation of Uruguay began in the late 1800s, when high-grade Merino sheep were introduced to the traditional *estancias*. Animal grazing now occupies 90 percent of the nation's agricultural lands, with mutton, wool, and beef as the primary products. The remaining farmlands produce rice, sugarcane, wheat, maize, and fruits. Industry is concentrated in the capital, Montevideo (1,312,000), and focuses on processing the nation's agricultural produce such as meat packing, foodstuffs, leather, and textiles. Most of the factories are small, family-controlled operations.

Uruguay's long tradition of two-party democratic government ended in the 1970s when a military coup followed years of economic stagnation associated with national welfare economics. Civilian rule was restored in 1986, and the nation's economy and government are presently among the most stable in Latin America.

Paraguay

Paraguay is a poor, landlocked nation in the heart of South America. The western two-thirds of the country, known as the **gran chaco,** is a sparsely settled, semiarid region of intermittent streams lined with quebracho trees, a source of tannin (see Figure 19–2). The *chaco* has one of the harshest environments on the continent. During the rainy season, from November to April, the rivers overflow their braided channels and flood vast stretches of land. In May the waterlogged soils begin to dry out and by the end of the dry season they are often caked with thick layers of mineral salts, left by the evaporating waters. Summer temperatures frequently reach a sizzling 110°F (43°C), the highest in South America, and add to the discomfort of the scattered inhabitants. Although considerable oil exploration has taken place in the *chaco,* no significant deposits of petroleum or other minerals have been discovered.

Eastern Paraguay is an extension of the fertile volcanic Paraná Plateau of southern Brazil (see Figure 19–2). Situated between the Paraguay and Paraná rivers, that humid region supports the bulk of the population, including the capital city of Asunción (970,000). The great majority of the people are *mestizos*, of mixed Spanish–Guaraní Indian stock (see Figure 19–6). The Guaraní were taught sedentary agriculture by Jesuit missionaries, who were very influential until they were expelled in 1767. After that and for most of its independence period, the country has been ruled by somewhat moderate, benign dictators, largely content to perpetuate colonial socioeconomic structures. In 1989, however, the aged General Alfredo Stroessner, who had been elected president every five years since 1954, was deposed in a military coup led by General Andrés Rodríguez. Although Rodríguez and his successor, Juan Carlos Wasmosy, have since governed as freely-elected civilian leaders, the nation's military leaders continue to exercise great power behind the scenes.

Much of what little economic development has occurred in Paraguay has come from external sources. Paraguay is a partner with Brazil in the development of Itaipu, the largest hydroelectric dam in the world, which is situated on the Paraná River. Paraguay is also participating with Argentina in the development of a second major hydroelectric project, at Yacyretá. However, the bulk of the power generated from both projects will be routed to Brazil and Argentina.

The limited industry that does exist within Paraguay focuses on the processing of local agricultural products and textiles. Land is abundant, but fewer than 2 percent of the farmers own their own land; the vast majority work subsistence crops of manioc (cassava) on the estates of the aristocracy or on otherwise unused public lands. Attempts to stimulate commercial agriculture have focused on imported Mennonite agricultural colonists around Filadelfia, in the heart of the *chaco,* as well as on Japanese, Korean, and Brazilian settlers and investment in the eastern section. Perhaps the leading source of income is the undocumented smuggling of foreign goods to both Argentina and Brazil.

BRAZIL

Brazil is by far the largest of all Latin American nations, only modestly smaller than the United States. Indeed, it is the fifth largest country in the world in area and the sixth largest in population. Brazil's large area is underlain by a diversity of geologic formations, some of which contain rich and extensive ore deposits. These include gold and diamonds as well as such important industrial minerals as iron ore, bauxite, and ferroalloys. Brazil is also blessed with several different climatic environments, within which a wide array of crops are grown (see Figure 19–10).

Brazil's physical resource base, then, is as abundant as that of any nation on earth. Yet Brazil has yet to fulfill its great potential. While ranking among the world's leading nations in industrial and agricultural output, it also carries the greatest total debt burden and has been ravaged in recent years by some of Latin America's highest inflation rates. Corruption is rampant at all levels of society, and crime has increased to the point where some are suggesting that national discipline can only be restored through the reimposition of military rule. As is the case in Peru, personal living levels have deteriorated rather than improved over recent decades.

Boom and Bust Cycles

One reason for Brazil's limited development thus far has been the exploitative nature of its economy. Since the days when Brazil was a Portuguese colony, emphasis has been placed on deriving maximum wealth in minimal time, without regard for building a stable, long-term economic base. Several cycles of boom-and-bust economic activity have resulted.

Sugarcane along the northeast coast was the basis of Brazil's first economic boom. Planted on large plantations worked by African slaves, sugar yielded great profits during the sixteenth and seventeenth centuries. But the boom eventually collapsed in the face of stiff competition from other parts of Latin America and the Caribbean. Brazil had failed to apply the improved technology that was being used elsewhere.

The second boom cycle occurred within the Brazilian Highlands north of Rio de Janeiro, where deposits of gold and diamonds were discovered. Exploitation of those minerals led to partial settlement of the interior, and the discoveries encouraged other colonists to come to Brazil. Unfortunately, after the many surface ores were removed, there was an exodus from the area.

The third cycle was an Amazonian rubber boom, centered on the inland port city of Manaus (see Figure 19–1). Trappers extracted the latex, smoked it into balls, and sold the balls to traders for shipment to the United States and Europe. Rubber first gained importance with the development of the vulcanization process, but the demand increased greatly in the latter part of the nineteenth century, with the development of the pneumatic bicycle tire and, shortly afterward, the automobile tire. Rubber prices skyrocketed. Such great fortunes were made that many of the wealthy residents of Manaus could afford to send their shirts and dresses out to Europe to be laundered, and a magnificent opera house was constructed of the finest Italian marble. But the boom ended as quickly as it had begun, when some Brazilian rubber seeds were smuggled to England, providing the stock for the great rubber plantations of the Far East and West Africa. Once plantation rubber came on the market and petroleum-based substitutes for rubber were developed, world prices of natural rubber collapsed, and wild-rubber gathering in the Amazon dwindled to almost nothing.

The fourth cycle took place after 1850, with the search for areas that were suitable for coffee cultivation. Coffee production reached its zenith on the famous *terra roxa* soils of São Paulo and southern Brazil. Until early in the twentieth century, coffee commanded such a high price that its cultivation expanded into areas that were environmentally marginal for its growth. Then, when the inevitable fall in prices occurred, the peripheral lands were abandoned.

Nonetheless, coffee production did put Brazil on the map, and for many years Brazil exported more coffee than all other nations combined. By around 1910, however, world production exceeded demand, and prices dropped rapidly. The Brazilian government tried to protect its most important export by buying the harvest and holding it back from the world market until an acceptable price was attained. But other Latin American nations, notably Colombia, undercut Brazil and captured a large part of the market. Since then Brazil has occasionally repeated its attempt to control coffee prices but has lost markets to other countries each time. In recent years other coffee-producing nations have joined Brazil in trying to limit production and control prices. But such endeavors, called valorization, can work only when producing nations cooperate fully.

The production of coffee in Brazil illustrates a method of land development that requires little money and is similar to the tenant-owner agreement used in the Argentine *pampas*. When coffee production began its great expansion, thousands of emigrants from Europe entered Brazil. Most went to the southern half of the country as tenants on large *fazendas* (farms), the owners of which were rich in land but poor in money. Thus, owners and tenants made agreements that involved little or no cash. Tenants leased portions of the *fazendas* (often uncleared land) and planted coffee bushes provided by the owners. For a period of years the tenants tended the young coffee plants and cultivated their own crops, both subsistence and commercial, between the rows of coffee. After five to seven years the coffee bushes began to bear heavily, and the tenants moved on to other plots. In that manner an entire *fazenda* was planted in coffee with little capital outlay. Once harvesting began, cash-wage employment was available to the tenants and their families.

Land of Contrasts

Today, Brazil is a nation of striking contrasts. The western half of the country is sparsely populated, but the east is densely settled. In addition, Brazil is both traditional and modern. Traditional Brazil survives in parts of the agricultural sector, with landowners of European extraction controlling workers of European, African, and Indian stock. The workers are poor and often illiterate; they cultivate their small farms or work on large *fazendas* using hand tools. Modern Brazil is urban and industrialized. Living levels are relatively high, literacy is nearly universal, and machines have replaced muscles. In the south, modern Brazil includes mechanized grain-farming areas.

The Regions of Brazil

Brazil's six regions differ significantly in both population and economic activity (Figure 19–12). Our discussion orders those regions according to a decreasing level of development.

São Paulo.   The state of São Paulo is Brazil's most modern and productive region. Per capita income is far above the national average, and almost one-third of the national GDP is produced there.

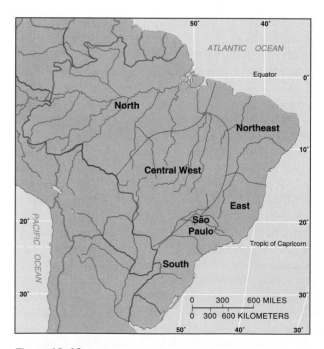

Figure 19–12

Brazil's six regions. Brazil's coastal regions are largely settled, but the interior regions (Central West and North) are part of Brazil's frontier. Ambitious projects are under way to develop those interior regions.

São Paulo state alone accounts for almost two-thirds of the country's industrial output, producing practically all of Brazil's motor vehicles and leading the nation in the manufacture of textiles, cement, shoes, paper products, processed coffee, pharmaceuticals, and electrical goods. Petroleum refining, petrochemicals, and steel production are important there, too.

The state of São Paulo also leads the nation in agricultural production. Coffee, soybeans, beef, sugarcane, cotton, peanuts, truck crops, and rice are grown under scientific conditions on large, mechanized farms.

Urbanization has progressed rapidly in this region. The city of São Paulo has grown from a backland trade center to one of the world's largest urban areas. Growth has been especially rapid in the last half century, with the city's population increasing from 600,000 in 1935 to over 8.0 million in 1970. The metropolitan area now contains approximately 18.4 million residents, making it the fourth largest city in the world. It generates 55 percent of the entire nation's manufacturing, with some 30,000 factories. It is also Brazil's leading financial center, with the largest number of banks and the biggest stock exchange (Figure 19–13).

São Paulo's rapid economic growth has not come without problems, however. Many migrants from the countryside and from other regions have been attracted to the city. Most, illiterate and unskilled, live in great poverty. Only a few have access to the city's water supply and sewage network, and housing, public health, and schools are generally inadequate for them. The city has become so large and its streets are so choked with traffic that many residents spend two to three hours each way commuting to and from work. Air pollution is so severe that the World Health Organization considers breathing the city's air to be dangerous to human health. Water pollution is also severe. Other cities in the region, including the port of Santos (489,000), are experiencing similar problems on a smaller scale.

The South.   Southern Brazil has its own distinctive flavor. In the nineteenth century large numbers of German and Italian farmers settled in the area, and many retained their ethnic identity well into the twentieth century (see Figure 19–6). German and Italian architecture is still noticeable.

Agriculture is the basis of livelihood in the area, but several cities located on or near the coast have

more than 100,000 in population and are growing at rates of about 4 percent per year. Pôrto Alegre (3.2 million) and Curitiba (1.4 million) are the largest. Most of the region is well settled, but the western section is still part of a pioneer fringe. Transport facilities have been greatly expanded and have contributed much to the South's prosperity.

Exploitive agriculture, which focuses on maximum immediate return, is less prevalent in the South, which is characterized by cattle ranching and mechanized wheat and soybean farming. Coffee farming occurs in the northernmost parts of the region but is prevented from reaching farther south by freezing winter temperatures. Rice, maize, and hogs are raised in the traditional manner. Hogs are associated especially with German settlements, whose products include sausage. Many Italian communities are noted for their grapes and wines.

Urban areas in the South are basically regional service centers, but in the larger cities, such as Pôrto Alegre, industrialization based on the processing of farm and ranch products provides employment for a sizable portion of the labor force. Milling, meat packing, tanning, textiles, and breweries are typical manufacturing activities.

The South's mineral resources are limited. Small deposits of low-grade coal are mined to provide energy in the area and to be shipped to São Paulo and the eastern region of Brazil.

The East.   Modern Brazil meets traditional Brazil in the East, where large, modern urban centers stand in stark contrast to nearby rural areas that have changed little in the past 100 years. The East is basically the hinterland of Rio de Janeiro (11.1 million), the former capital and the second city of the nation. The region has experienced several waves of exploitation—first sugarcane, then gold and diamonds, followed by coffee, rice, and, most recently, citrus fruits. After each boom has come a time of population decrease and reversion to a grazing economy.

Rio de Janeiro is the focal point of the East. Nestled around one of the most beautiful and easily defensible harbors of Brazil's Atlantic coast, Rio grew rapidly throughout the colonial era owing to its proximity to the inland gold and diamond fields of Minas Gerais. When Brazil's capital was moved from the Northeast to Rio de Janeiro, the city's functions increased. As long as Brazil was a coastal nation, Rio continued to be the national focal point. Access to the interior was difficult, however, be-

Figure 19-13
São Paulo, Brazil. This view of the central portion of São Paulo illustrates the degree
of urban development that has occurred in some parts of Brazil.

cause a steep escarpment rises just behind the narrow coastal plain. The advent of motor vehicles and
paved roads has partly offset that natural disadvantage, but other cities located inland have taken some
of Rio's former trade area. Rio itself faces a severe
shortage of level land for urban development.

The hinterland of Rio de Janeiro has both an agricultural and a mining base. Most of the land is used
for grazing. Although some of the cropland is devoted to the cash crops of sugarcane, coffee, rice,
and citrus, much of it is used for subsistence crops.
Land rotation is common.

In addition, the east contains one of the most
mineralized areas in the world, the **Mineral Triangle**.
Only within this century, however, has large-scale
mining been developed. Gold, diamonds, and a
number of precious and semiprecious gems have
been mined in this region for centuries. Industrial
minerals—such as manganese, chromium, molybdenum, nickel, and tungsten—are of growing sig-

nificance. But iron ore is the most important mineral. The amount of iron ore reserves is unknown
but is certainly one of the largest in the world. A
conservative estimate is 15 billion tons of easily recoverable high-grade ore.

Volta Redonda is Brazil's iron- and steel-making
center. The site is almost ideal: it is close to iron ore
deposits, limestone, water, and the markets of São
Paulo and Rio de Janeiro (see Figure 19–3). Coal, the
one vital ingredient that is lacking, is brought in
from the South or is imported from the United
States. Since the Volta Redonda plants opened in
1946, their production capacity has increased several times over. Today, Brazil is the leading steel
producer in South America and the ninth largest
steel maker in the world.

The Northeast. The Northeast was once the
center of Brazilian culture, the location of the capital, and the most developed part of the nation. That

status was based on sugarcane cultivation under the plantation system, which used African slaves, and on the region's location as the part of Brazil closest to Portugal. That proximity was advantageous during the days of sailing ships but lost importance with the advent of steamships. In addition, although sugarcane is still grown in the region, that industry is no longer prosperous. Today, much of the Northeast is poverty stricken; per capita income is less than half the national figure, and feudalistic social structures continue to retard the development of human resources. Thousands of people in this region have migrated to other parts of Brazil, adding to the number of unskilled laborers searching for work in the cities farther south and in the new capital of Brasília.

Nonetheless, population pressure remains great in the Northeast, and livelihood is precarious even in the best of times. Over the years, settlement has moved inland, away from the moist coast into a drier environment. In the backlands, hillsides are cultivated with minimum regard for conservation, and pastures are overgrazed. Both practices have resulted in soil destruction and rapid water runoff, causing the naturally semiarid environment to become even more moisture deficient. Prolonged, severe droughts are frequent yet unpredictable. When they occur, large numbers of people move from the interior to the already-overcrowded coast and to other parts of the nation. Yet, so strong is the tie to the Northeast that many of those persons return when they can.

The Northeast has three cities with more than 2 million people each: Recife, Salvador, and Fortaleza. All three are port cities that function as service centers. Manufacturing is limited.

Since about 1960 a number of government-financed projects have been directed to the Northeast, and a regional development corporation has been established. Dams for hydroelectric power and irrigated agriculture are being built, and roads are being improved and extended. In addition, industries that locate in the northeast receive special tax rebates. But none of those efforts have yet been effective in lessening the widespread poverty of the region.

The Central West. The Central West region is part of Brazil's *sertão,* the backlands where a frontier spirit and life prevail. Many parts of the region remain sparsely settled. Brasília (1,596,000) was con-

structed on the eastern edge of the Central West to symbolize and encourage the occupation of the backlands. In addition, the nearby city of Goiânia (921,000) has developed into a second regional center. Roads have been built to connect Brasília with other parts of the nation and to lead westward to new lands. Some commercial agriculture has evolved along the eastern fringe of the region, but elsewhere subsistence agriculture, grazing, small-scale lumbering, and mining are carried on.

The frontier, or pioneer zone, is gradually moving westward, as new lands are opened for agriculture. Like the United States of a century ago, Brazilians believe their country's future lies in the west. Pioneering is at best a risky venture, but the farmers have discovered a relationship between vegetation and the quality of land for cropping. That relationship is especially important because there are few weather stations or soil surveys to provide more scientific data. Six vegetative types are recognized. In descending order of quality for agriculture, they are first-class forest, second-class forest, mixed grassland and woodland, scrub woodland, grassland with scattered trees, and grassland.

Forested land is regarded as good and as suitable for cropping. On the other hand, grasslands and scrub woodlands are generally considered unusable for crops, though mechanized cropping has occasionally been attempted, usually with disappointing long-term results. Most often, however, those types of vegetation are used only for grazing. Use of mixed grasslands and woodlands holds the key to occupation of the Central West, for that vegetative type covers about 75 percent of the region. Unfortunately, its soils lack nutrients and are subject to drought. Extensive mechanized agriculture emphasizing wheat and soybeans has been somewhat successful in the eastern part; alfalfa, a deep-rooted plant, offers another possibility. However, the main use of mixed grasslands and woodlands at this time is for grazing.

The North. In recent years much effort has been exerted to tame the Amazon Basin. But that vast, multilayered tropical rain forest, with its fragile soils and incredible diversity of plant and animal life, has repeatedly turned back attempts at large-scale commercial agriculture and forest development. Although the basin has long been considered a region of great potential—it occupies more than 40 percent of Brazil's area—it supports only 4 percent of the nation's people. Only along the Amazon River itself and its principal tributaries have people of European culture been able to gain a foothold. Manaus (1,011,000) near the center of the basin, and Belém (1,334,000), near the mouth of the Amazon, are the major urban centers. Away from the rivers live an ever-dwindling number of Indians, who still cling to their traditional ways. They support themselves with shifting subsistence agriculture—which emphasizes manioc, maize, and beans—and they supplement their diet by hunting, fishing, and gathering (Figures 19–14 and 19–15).

Although the Amazon Basin remains one of the world's largest wilderness areas, economic development is coming to the region. Commercial agriculture has been stimulated by immigrant Japanese farmers, who cultivate rice, jute (a hard fiber), and black pepper. However, mining, rather than agriculture, may hold the key to the future prosperity of the area. The largest mineral district in the world is under development at Carajás (see Figure 19–3). In addition to an estimated 18 billion tons of hematite, or high-grade iron ore, an abundance of manganese, copper, bauxite, and nickel can be found there. Additional Amazonian mining sites include the Pitanga mine, which has the world's largest known tin ore reserves, and several world-class bauxite and titanium deposits. Other important mineral resources are likely

to be discovered in the future. Taken together, the mineral deposits of the Amazon Basin and the Brazilian Highlands have already made Brazil one of the world's leading mining nations.

Recently, the Brazilian government initiated an industrial development program for the basin that focuses on Manaus. Attracted by tax exemptions and other fiscal incentives, some 400 companies, many of them leading foreign high-tech firms, have established industrial plants under the sponsorship of the Manaus Free Trade Zone Authority. Development is also coming from tourism: more than 250,000 visitors come every year, many of them for jungle safaris and Amazon River cruises.

In 1970 work on the **Trans-Amazon Highway** began (see Figure 19–8), the start of a massive road system throughout the basin and the connection of that region to other parts of the nation (Figure 19–16). With the development of the road system comes the expectation, already partially realized, that migrants from the Northeast and elsewhere will settle the area. Plans call for government-sponsored construction of urban areas and for lumber and pulp plants, hydroelectric plants, and schools. Government officials and most Brazilians look on the Amazon Basin development program as vital to the continued economic growth of the nation and a better life for its citizens.

Figure 19-14
An Auca Indian settlement in Ecuador on the banks of an Amazon tributary. The Amazon Basin is largely the domain of Brazil, but its outer margin is included within the borders of Venezuela, Colombia, Ecuador, Peru, and Bolivia. Settlement and transportation development are rapidly encroaching on this vast tropical forest.

That view has been challenged by some ecologists, however, who maintain that this short-term economic growth may bring disastrous results in the long term. Many ecologists believe that destruction of the tropical forest may substantially change the area's climate, giving way to drier and warmer conditions. The critics also point out that many of the soils of the basin are low in plant nutrients and require careful handling to prevent their destruction. According to some estimates, the forest could be cleared within the next century (see the boxed feature Deforestation in the Amazon).

Figure 19–15
An Auca Indian family inside their dwelling. Numerous small groups of Indian peoples similar to these were scattered in low density throughout the Amazon Basin prior to the arrival of Europeans. Because of isolation their cultures survived for several centuries, but now the groups are declining in numbers as developing societies approach.

Figure 19–16
A segment of the Trans-Amazon highway system between Brasília and Belém. Effective use and settlement of the Amazon Basin has long been a dream of many Brazilians; it is now being realized through costly and ambitious governmental development programs. Some believe that the accompanying destruction of the tropical rain forest will lead to an environmental disaster.

DEFORESTATION IN THE AMAZON

The Amazon River Basin encompasses half of the South American continent, extending from the slopes of the Andes eastward some 4,000 miles (6,500 kilometers) to the Atlantic Ocean. The region was occupied for thousands of years by native American Indian tribes, which sustained life by hunting, fishing, gathering forest produce, and maintaining small polycultural gardens and farms. Those traditional peoples lived in the midst of the world's largest tropical rain forest, where multilayered canopies supported more than one-third of the plant and animal life forms found on the entire earth, each species adapted to a unique microenvironment.

Ever since that early settlement the sheer size of the Amazon rain forest has fascinated all who have come to know it and has evoked a variety of responses. Many Brazilians, awed by the luxuriant vegetation, have been convinced that great fortunes were easily to be made by exploiting the resources of the area. To other Brazilians, especially those residing in cities and farms along the distant Atlantic coast, the Amazon has represented a virtually endless frontier, to be conquered much as early settlers developed the western United States.

European Brazilians did little to occupy Amazonia until the mid-twentieth century, when poverty and accelerated population growth prompted many to seek their fortunes in the region. Spurred by the establishment of the new inland capital of Brasília and the construction of the Trans-Amazon Highway, ever-increasing numbers of settlers have pushed into the basin, cutting and burning the rain forest to create small family farms and large cattle ranches. Most of the settlers are poorly prepared for pioneer life. And they are stunned to learn that the lush forest vegetation is sustained not by fertile soils but by the natural recycling of organic matter, derived from the litter of the very trees they have just destroyed. Within a few years most of the residual soil nutrients are exhausted, and many of the settlers move on to repeat the process, leaving scarred, eroded landscapes in their wake.

So rapid has been the destruction of the rain forest that, according to estimates, an area equivalent in size to the state of Texas has been deforested just since 1978. Alarmed scientists note that if the cutting continues at this rate, the entire rain forest will be lost in less than 100 years. They point out further that the Amazonian rain forest is the most genetically diverse **biome** (major ecosystem) on earth and that thousands of plant species are being lost annually, many with valuable medicinal properties.

Shocked by reports that as many as 6,000 fires are set in Amazonia on a single day, and pressured by worldwide criticism, Brazil announced in 1989 a new environmental protection program call Our Nature. The plan rescinded tax incentives previously provided to large-scale cattle ranchers, created new forest reserves and Indian reservations, and called for the study and mapping of Amazonian environments. Conservative Brazilian business interests reacted angrily, accusing the government of capitulation to foreign "ecological imperialism" and insisting on their right to continue to develop the region. We must hope that all Brazilians will come to understand that it is in the best long-term interest of both Brazil and the world to ensure the survival of the irreplaceable biological resources of the Amazonian rain forest.

SUMMARY
Unfulfilled Resource Potential

South America is one of the most richly endowed regions on earth. Blessed with a wide array of physical environments, it has for centuries provided much of the world's greatest mineral production. It also possesses the largest remaining stand of tropical rain forest and some of the world's most productive agricultural regions. Favored with vast expanses of underutilized land, South America is likely in the decades ahead to strengthen its position as one of the world's leading suppliers of raw materials.

We must recognize, however, that the presence of raw materials, however abundant and valuable, does not constitute an assurance of economic development. The greatest resource of any region will always be its people. South America's steady development of its human resources—as expressed in improved health care and sanitation, housing, literacy and education, and political and social democratization—offers the most compelling evidence of the region's progress. Even though the pace of change has varied from place to place and even though much remains to be done, that one area of progress gives every reason for confidence in the future development of the continent.

KEY TERMS

altiplano	*gran chaco*
antioqueños	*llanos*
Aymara	Mineral Triangle
biome	*minifundia*
chaco	*montaña*
coca	*oriente*
colonos	*pampas*
descamisados	Quechua
el niño	*sertão*
fazenda	*terra roxa*
gauchos	Trans-Amazon Highway

FURTHER READINGS
Part Six

Bastide, Roger. *The African Religions of Brazil,* trans. Helen Sebba. Baltimore: Johns Hopkins University Press, 1978. An outstanding description of Candomblé, Xango, macumba, Umbanda, and other forms of African spiritist faiths in Brazil.

Brenner, Anita. *The Wind That Swept Mexico.* Austin, TX: University of Texas Press, 1971. A powerful pictorial history of the Mexican Revolution.

Butzer, Karl W., ed. "The Americas Before and After 1492: Current Geographical Research." Special thematic issue of *Annals of the Association of American Geographers* 82 (1992). The volume contains a collection of scholarly articles focusing on the geography of Latin America and the Caribbean prior to the European Conquest and the land use and cultural changes that followed.

Clawson, David L. "Changing Religious Patterns in Mexico." In *Latin America: Case Studies,* edited by Richard G. Boehm and Sent Visser, 39–56. Dubuque, IA: Kendall/Hunt, 1984. An analysis of the expansion of non-Catholic Christian faiths in Mexico.

————. "Harvest Security and Intraspecific Diversity in Traditional Tropical Agriculture." *Economic Botany* 39 (1985): 56–67. A study of the creative uses by small-scale peasant farmers of the many varieties of food crops found in the tropics.

Coleman, William J. *Latin American Catholicism: A Self-Evaluation.* Maryknoll, NY: Maryknoll Publications, 1958. An overview of Latin American Catholic subreligions and the beliefs and practices of their practitioners.

Conference of Latin Americanist Geographers Yearbook. Austin, TX: Conference of Latin Americanist Geographers, annual. The principal publication of the Conference of Latin Americanist Geographers, whose membership consists of scholars with an interest in the geography of Latin America and the Caribbean. (Information on membership, publications, and services may be obtained by writing the Executive Secretary, Conference of Latin Americanist Geographers, Department of Geography, University of Texas, Austin, TX 78712).

Crist, Raymond E. "The Latin American Way of Life." *American Journal of Economics and Sociology* 27 (1968): 63–76, 171–183, 297–311. One of the most insightful and interestingly written overviews of Latin American culture and its Iberian antecedents; authored by one of the most knowledgeable and influential teachers of Latin American geography.

Crist, Raymond E., and Charles M. Nissly. *East from the Andes.* Gainesville, FL: University of Florida Press, 1973. The standard reference on the colonization of the Amazon Basin by Andean highlanders.

Dean, Warren. *The Industrialization of São Paulo, 1880–1945.* Austin, TX: University of Texas Press, 1969. An insightful overview of the growth of Latin America's leading industrial city.

Denevan, William M., ed. *The Native Population of the Americas in 1492,* 2nd ed. Madison: University of Wisconsin Press, 1992. The standard reference for estimating the sizes of pre-Conquest Indian populations and the extent and causes of their collapse under the European conquerors.

Fittkau, E. J., et al., eds. *Biogeography and Ecology in South America.* The Hague: Dr. W. Junk N. V., 1968. An excellent scholarly collection of articles addressing different aspects of the physical geography of South America.

Gade, Daniel W. *Plants, Man, and the Land in the Vilcanota Valley of Peru.* The Hague: Dr. W. Junk N. V., 1975. A delightful regional study in the classic cultural ecology tradition.

Gillin, John. "Ethos Components in Modern Latin American Culture." *American Anthropologist* 57 (1955): 488–500. A perceptive description of the values that influence how Latin Americans perceive themselves and their place in society.

Griffin, Ernst, and Larry Ford. "A Model of Latin American City Structure." *The Geographical Review* 70 (1980): 397–422. The standard starting point for the study of Latin American urbanization.

Inter-American Development Bank. *Annual Report* and *Economic and Social Progress in Latin America.* Washington, DC: Inter-American Development Bank, annuals. Contain the most current and dependable statistical information, both economic and social, on Latin America and the Caribbean.

James, Preston E., and C. W. Minkel. *Latin America.* 5th ed. New York: Wiley, 1986. The most complete introductory text on the geography of Latin America.

Klein, Herbert S. *African Slavery in Latin America and the Caribbean.* Oxford: Oxford University Press, 1986. One of the most thorough treatments of slavery in Latin America and the extensive African influences found in many parts of the region.

Lowenthal, David. *West Indian Societies.* London: Oxford University Press, 1972. The most comprehensive synthesis of ethnicity and race relations in the Caribbean Basin.

Macpherson, John. *Caribbean Lands.* 4th ed. Trinidad: Longman Caribbean, 1980. The standard introduction to the lands and peoples of the Caribbean islands.

Martinson, Tom L., ed. *Benchmark 1990.* Auburn, AL: Conference of Latin Americanist Geographers, 1992. A collection of forty-two papers presented by leading Latin Americanist geographers summarizing almost every aspect of geographical research on Latin America in the 1980s with recommendations for research in the 1990s.

Richards, Paul W. *The Tropical Rainforest.* London: Cambridge University Press, 1952. A classic, masterful analysis of the structure, composition, and function of tropical rain forests.

Sauer, Carl O. "Geography of South America." In *Handbook of South American Indians,* edited by Julian H. Steward, 319–344. Bureau of American Ethnology Bulletin, no. 143. Washington, DC: Smithsonian Institution, 1963. Arguably the finest, most concise, single overview of the physical geography of South America; written by the dean of twentieth-century Latin Americanist geographers.

Simpson, Lesley Byrd. *The Encomienda in New Spain.* 3d ed. Berkeley, CA: University of California Press, 1966. A detailed analysis of Spanish-Indian relationships in colonial Latin America and their impact on economic development.

———. *Many Mexicos.* 4th ed., rev. Berkeley, CA: University of California Press, 1967. One of the most entertaining and perceptive analyses of Mexican and, by extension, Latin American subcultures ever published.

Wagley, Charles. *An Introduction to Brazil.* rev. ed. New York: Columbia University Press, 1971. The standard introduction to the peoples and regions of modern Brazil.

Watts, David. *The West Indies: Patterns of Development, Culture and Environmental Change Since 1492.* Cambridge: Cambridge University Press, 1987. A detailed analysis of the cultural and environmental impacts of European conquest on the lands and peoples of the Caribbean island realm.

West, Robert C., ed. *Natural Environments and Early Cultures: Handbook of Middle American Indians.* vol. 1. Austin, TX: University of Texas Press, 1964. Detailed analyses of the cultural and physical geography of Mexico, Central America, and the Caribbean, edited by one of our greatest Middle Americanist scholars.

West, Robert C., and John P. Augelli. *Middle America: Its Lands and Peoples.* 3d ed. Englewood Cliffs, NJ: Prentice-Hall, 1989. The best single reference on the geography of Mexico, Central America, and the Caribbean islands.

Wilken, Gene C. *Good Farmers: Traditional Agricultural Resource Management in Mexico and Central America.* Berkeley, CA: University of California Press, 1987. A detailed analysis of the agricultural strategies and cropping systems of Latin American traditional farmers.

Wilson, E. O. "Threats to Biodiversity." *Scientific American* 261 (3 September 1989): 108–116. An overview of the extent and potential consequences of the loss of the earth's biodiversity.

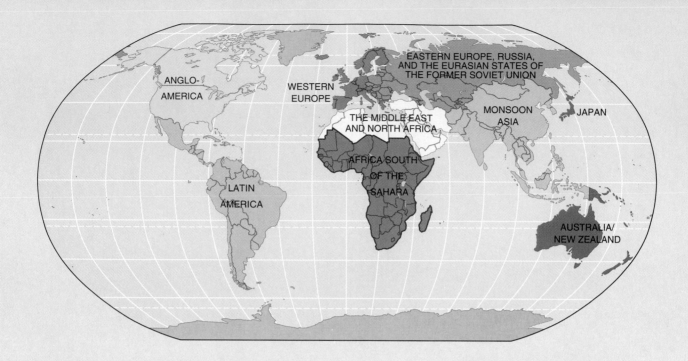

For most people Africa evokes a variety of images: jungles, deserts, drought, famine, wars for independence, and great stores of natural resources. More recently, images of Rwanda and Somalia come to mind. In this part we examine the features that have given rise to those images. Throughout our discussion of Africa, however, we must always remember that much remains hidden, for Africa south of the Sahara is a vast and varied region, home to over 540 million people.

Most black African peoples have achieved self-governance. And even the Republic of South Africa has instituted a multiracial government. Despite Africa's long cultural history, however, most of the region's countries have been independent states for less than thirty years. The boundaries established by the colonial process during the late nineteenth and early twentieth centuries have complicated the effectiveness of those states.

The tremendous variety that is the African continent can be difficult to convey. Some African countries are among the poorest in the world, with inadequate agricultural or industrial resources for economic development. Others are making significant progress and have the resource potential for even greater growth. The two chapters that follow set forth the geographical basis for the development of this diverse part of our world. We look at Africa from an economic development perspective and examine selected national case studies. In these chapters we attempt to provide insight into the progress and problems of black Africa and to illustrate the approaches that are being taken toward national development.

PART 7

Leonard Berry and Douglas L. Johnson

AFRICA SOUTH OF THE SAHARA

20

Africa:
East and West

The Least Developed Nations

Intermediate Nations

Mother and son gathering firewood in the dry Sahel of Africa. Drought and internal warfare combine to create suffering for many people of the Sahel—most recently for those in Sudan, Ethiopia, and Somalia. People in developed countries have difficulty understanding the precious nature of firewood as a marketable commodity in regions such as the Sahel.

Africa south of the Sahara, or **sub-Saharan Africa**, is dominated by black African culture and political systems. But it has also been influenced by European settlement and colonialism. And although political colonialism has ended, its imprint persists in many ways, including the continued dominance of European trading partners and the widespread use of European languages. In addition, Arab culture has long influenced sub-Saharan Africa; black African culture and Arab culture have mixed and fused over a broad transition zone that extends from the middle of the Sahara to the more humid areas along the desert's southern border and along the East African coastal zone. Because of that transition zone, the boundary between Arab North Africa and black sub-Saharan Africa is drawn through the Sahara. Countries to the north of the boundary have a focus on the Mediterranean Sea and are clearly Arab. Countries south of the boundary exhibit both an Arab and a black heritage, and their focus is generally to the south (Figure 20–1).

Sub-Saharan Africa was colonized by Great Britain, France, Belgium, Portugal, Spain, and Germany. At the end of the nineteenth century those European powers divided the continent into formal spheres of influence, and those subdivisions provided the basis for national development throughout the region, except in South Africa. Prior to that division the peoples of the region had been organized in a number of ethnic (tribal) groups, many of which had attained seminational status. But the European subdivisions paid little attention to preexisting political organization, and the new boundaries cut across tribes and clans, in some cases including mutually antagonistic groups within one colonial entity.

Sub-Saharan Africa is one of the poorest parts of the world. Two-thirds of the least developed nations—a United Nations designation for countries with a very low per capita GNP—are found there. But the region is also marked by diversity, especially in mineral wealth, environment, economic well-being, religion and culture, as well as in patterns of colonial and postcolonial change. For example, oil and minerals are important to the economies of the Republic of South Africa, Botswana, Zimbabwe, Nigeria, and Gabon. South Africa is the only country in the region with a fully developed industrial and service sector, though both Zimbabwe and Nigeria have well-diversified economies. The environment ranges from a little-disturbed tropical rain forest, which covers much of central Zaire, to wide expanses of dry desert, which form most of northern Mali and Sudan. The diversity of livelihood systems in the region reflects both the interaction of Arab, African, and European culture systems and the differing environments.

Sub-Saharan Africa makes up about 20 percent of the world's total land area and is divided into forty-seven countries. Rather than cataloging each country's features, we focus on the economic standing of the different nations and use case studies to illustrate characteristics of development. The countries can be categorized in a number of ways; in this book the nations of East and West Africa are separated from those of Central and Southern Africa. The economies of the countries in Central and Southern Africa have tended to revolve around that of the Republic of South Africa; those nations are the subject of the next chapter. In this chapter we examine the diverse states of East and West Africa (Figure 20–2). No sharp dividing line separates east from west, but a range of historical, political, and economic circumstances helps make a convenient division.

The twenty-seven countries of East and West Africa fall into two main groups: (1) the least developed nations, which are very poor and (2) the intermediate nations, which are poor but are economically more diversified, with better prospects for economic advancement (Table 20–1). The seventeen least developed nations have per capita GNPs that are commonly less than $300 (measured in 1985 dollars), economies with less than 10 percent of their value in manufacturing, and literacy rates of 20 percent or less. The other ten countries may have somewhat higher per capita GNPs—though usually less than $500—and higher literacy rates, but very few of them have a substantial manufacturing sector.

THE LEAST DEVELOPED NATIONS

The seventeen least developed nations of East and West Africa are all characterized by small areas or populations, limited wealth, a low percentage of the labor force in manufacturing, a reliance on subsistence agriculture, high rates of illiteracy, significant environmental problems, a colonial heritage, and—in many cases—isolation. Although a lower per capita GNP is clearly a distinctive characteristic of all of these nations, the causes of their limited economic development are varied.

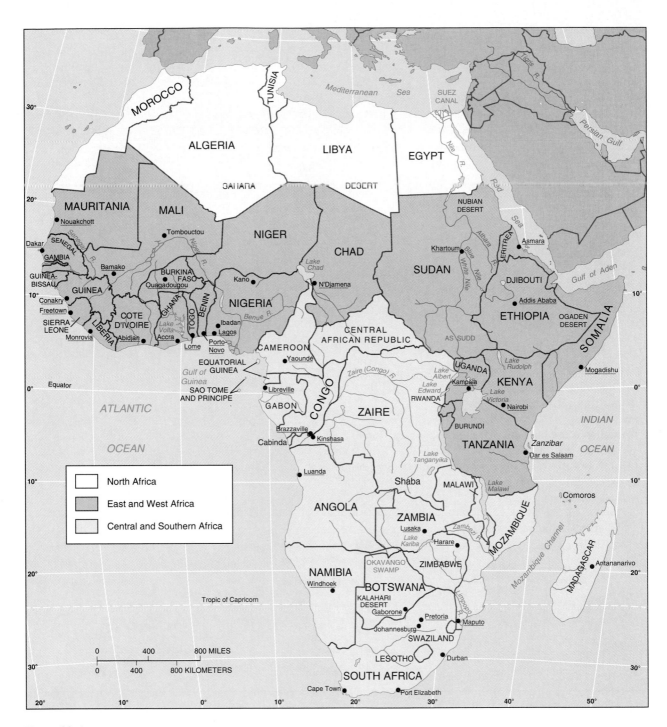

Figure 20-1
Africa south of the Sahara. Many nations with diverse cultures comprise this region. Both traditional and modern cultural and economic systems are often found within a small area.

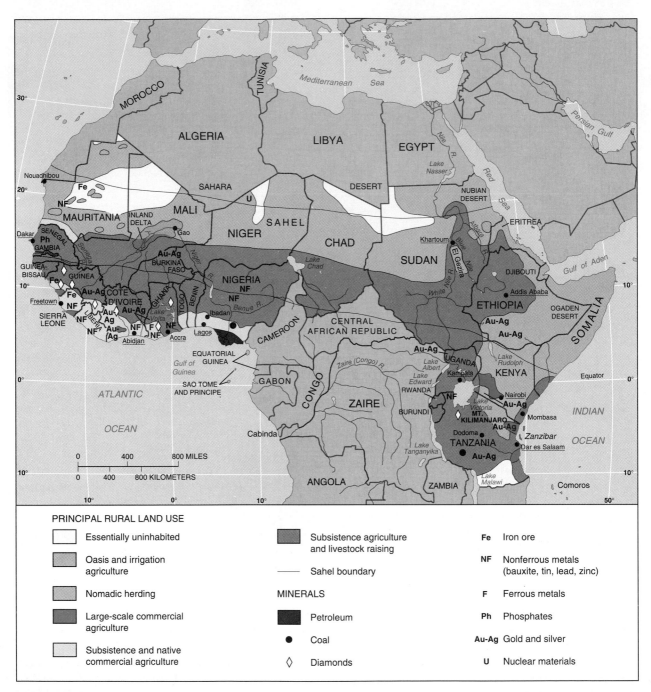

PRINCIPAL RURAL LAND USE

☐	Essentially uninhabited
▨	Oasis and irrigation agriculture
▨	Nomadic herding
▨	Large-scale commercial agriculture
▨	Subsistence and native commercial agriculture

▨	Subsistence agriculture and livestock raising
—	Sahel boundary

MINERALS

▨	Petroleum
●	Coal
◇	Diamonds

Fe	Iron ore
NF	Nonferrous metals (bauxite, tin, lead, zinc)
F	Ferrous metals
Ph	Phosphates
Au-Ag	Gold and silver
U	Nuclear materials

Figure 20–2

Land use and minerals in East and West Africa. The various forms of land use range from traditional nomadic herding to modern plantations. A number of different minerals, such as petroleum in Nigeria, are important exports.

Table 20-1
The twenty-seven countries of East and West Africa, classified by region and
development status.

	West African Sahel	Humid West Africa	East Africa
Least Developed Nations	Burkina Faso Cape Verde Chad Mali Niger	Benin Gambia Guinea-Bissau Sierra Leone Togo	Burundi Djibouti Eritrea Ethiopia Rwanda Somalia Uganda
Intermediate Nations	Mauritania Senegal	Côte d'Ivoire Ghana Guinea Liberia Nigeria	Kenya Sudan Tanzania

These countries fall into three regional group-ings. The first group includes the nations in the West African **Sahel**, the semiarid ecological zone between the Sahara and the savanna lands to the south: Cape Verde (an island nation nearly 400 miles west of the mainland), Mali, Burkina Faso, Niger, and Chad. The second group is in humid West Africa: Gambia, Guinea-Bissau, Sierra Leone, Togo, and Benin. The third is a more diverse East African group: Burundi, Rwanda, Uganda, Ethiopia, Djibouti, and Somalia (Figure 20–3).

Environmental Characteristics

Most of the least developed nations in Africa are characterized by fluctuating weather conditions, es-pecially in rainfall, causing uncertainty in both basic food supplies and export earnings. Because agricul-tural products account for a large proportion of the total economy in these countries, such fluctuations can have a significant impact on the overall national economy. For example, during the Sahelian drought of the 1980s the GNP of Mali, already low, dropped by more than 20 percent.

Problems related to the environment—such as a lack of good drinking water, insect infestation, and disease—also take their toll on the health and vigor of many people. **Malaria** is the most widely known tropical disease, but **yellow fever, cholera, schistoso-miasis** (bilharzia), and **onchocerciasis** (river blind-ness) are the most common diseases in Africa (Figure 20–4). In addition, AIDS, though not directly related to the environment, has become a major killing disease in both eastern and central Africa.

The total combined effect of those diseases on the region is devastating. In addition to the fever associ-ated with them, they leave their victims susceptible to follow-up illnesses, such as measles, which is still a prominent killer of children in Africa. Major strides have been made against onchocerciasis, but malaria and yellow fever have recently increased in severity. In addition, animal-borne diseases, such as east coast fever and infections carried by the **tsetse fly**, cause large areas of land to be removed from certain kinds of economic activities. Despite these continuing health problems, though, life expectancy has in-creased to just over fifty years in most countries (com-pared with seventy plus in Western Europe). And in-fant mortality rates, while still high, have dropped 30 to 40 percent over the last twenty-five years.

The least developed nations are also character-ized by an absence of biome diversity; that is, they are all chiefly arid/semiarid or humid. Each type of biome has its benefits and its costs. However, when a whole country mainly falls within one type, the lack of diversity places severe restraints on the range of agricultural and pastoral life-support systems that can be established economically. Of these least de-veloped countries, only Ethiopia shows such diver-sity. In that country great altitudinal variations result

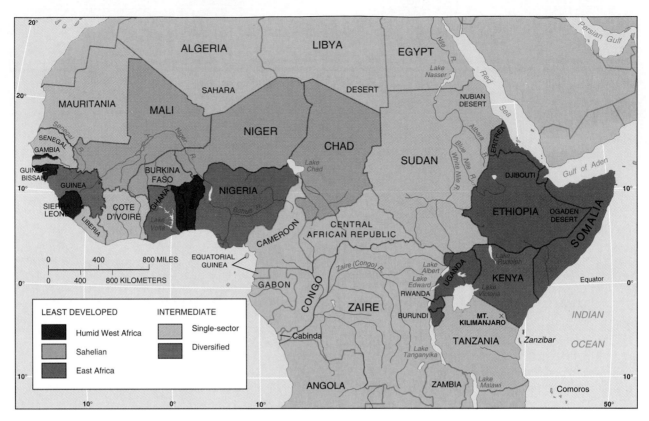

Figure 20-3
Levels of development in East and West Africa. Many East and West African countries are among the poorest in the world, yet others have important actual or potential growth sectors in which development is possible.

in major differences in temperature, precipitation, soils, and vegetation, which in turn permit a considerable range of crops and land use. Unfortunately, Ethiopia's political, social, economic, and ecological problems have kept per capita GNP on a par with the poorest of the least developed nations. With the end of its civil war in the 1990s—and the creation of former-province Eritrea as a new country—there is some hope that Ethiopia's situation may begin to change.

The problems of single-biome countries are dramatically highlighted when those biomes are placed under stress—such as during periods of drought. In the 1970s all of Mali, Niger, and Chad were affected by drought, and international help was essential for the survival of much of the population and the national economies (see the boxed feature, Drought in Africa). But even when external help is available, internal stability and the political environment may determine

how successfully that aid is implemented. In the 1980s drought in Sudan, much external aid could not be delivered because of an ongoing civil war between the northern and southern sections of the country.

Subsistence Activities

Poorly developed nations are marked by low income and simple economic structures, with a sizable component of subsistence farming. Most small farmers in Africa are primarily concerned with producing enough to eat. A typical peasant farm is about 1.25 acres (0.5 hectare), not much larger than many house lots in the United States. That farm, however, would typically include: a field of maize or sorghum, often intercropped with beans; a family garden, with many different vegetables; some oilseeds; cooking bananas (in humid areas); and, always, chickens and goats. Cattle and sheep are also

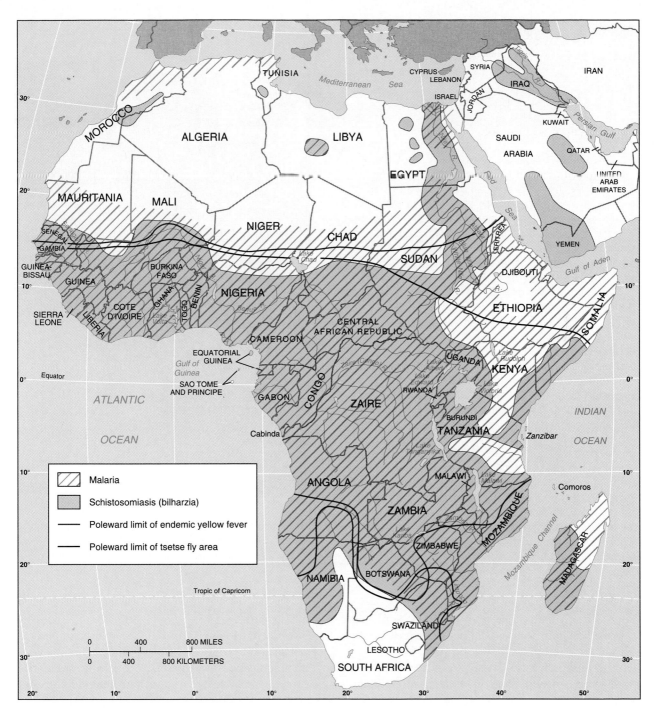

Figure 20–4
Disease-infested areas in Africa. Disease inhibits development in some parts of Africa.
Malaria, schistosomiasis, and yellow fever are endemic throughout much of the area,
and the tsetse fly carries parasites that infect both people (sleeping sickness) and
livestock. (From Ernst Rodenwaldt, *World Atlas of Epidemic Diseases,* Hamburg:
Fale, 1952, p. 61; and *Atlas of Distribution of Disease,* New York: American
Geographical Society, 1950, p. 55.)

DROUGHT IN AFRICA

In the early 1980s large parts of Africa were hit by devastating drought. A change in global rainfall patterns resulted in a shortfall of moisture in crop-producing regions across much of dry Africa. Among the countries most severely affected were Mali, Niger, Chad, Sudan, Ethiopia, and Kenya. In 1984 and 1985, the worst years of the drought, almost no rain fell in any of those countries. In 1986, fortunately, the rains returned to normal over much of dry Africa.

The impact of the drought on individual countries depended on many factors, including the ability of the government and external agencies to assess need and mobilize help. In Sudan and Ethiopia, information on the extent of the shortfall in food production was slow in materializing, and donors were cautious in their reaction until the horrors of starvation were flashed across their television screens. When relief efforts were finally mobilized, food poured in from many countries (Figure A); the United States supplied more than half. Slowly the suffering was eased, but not before many people had died, many more had suffered from severe malnutrition, and still others had been reduced to abject poverty. In Mali, Chad, and Kenya the food-production shortfall was also large. But the people, the governments, and the external donors were able to work together to greatly reduce the worst suffering, even though large quantities of food were needed in each country.

Figure A
Young girl receiving food through a relief effort. Many people on the edge of the Sahara continue to live a marginal existence.

kept in many areas. The farm has to be sufficiently diverse and consistently productive to provide food for the farm family all year long.

Almost every farm family in Africa also needs cash—to pay school fees, buy clothes and fertilizers, and pay taxes, among other things. Sometimes cash is obtained by selling an animal or surplus food crops; women often acquire cash by selling eggs. But typically the farm also has crops that are grown especially for sale—for example, coffee, tea, pyrethrum, cocoa, cotton, and palm oilseeds. Those crops often supply international markets, as well as national and local ones. If the crop is grown specifically for export, government or cooperative marketing arrangements are made for the orderly movement of goods from local to national markets. But peasant farmers who have poor access to good communication systems or are far from population centers have almost as much trouble selling their crops as growing them.

Modern Agricultural Enclaves

The colonial powers encouraged the development of cash crops, mainly to serve overseas markets. Two main methods were utilized. The first was the native smallholder production of such crops as peanuts, cotton, and cacao. The second was the es-

The possibility of drought is ever-present in the dry areas of Africa, and food-production shortages will undoubtedly occur again. The events of the early 1980s showed that drought-prone nations must be prepared with good information systems to provide early warning of production shortfalls, and the rest of the world must have the means to supply food quickly and effectively. It is encouraging that Americans and Europeans, working with African nations, have set up prototype information systems that will give the world early warning of impending problems.

A few years of good rainfall must not promote undue complacency; African governments must also learn how to manage drought. Countries such as Kenya and Botswana have good systems in place, but others—including Sudan and Ethiopia—do not. All African governments in dry areas need to be prepared for drought and ready to deal with internal and external food-relief issues when local resources fail. Drought will return sooner or later, and food will be short—of that we can be sure. But no one need die as a result. The recent history of Somalia shows, conversely, that when national disorder accompanies drought, people die in large numbers.

The situation that developed in Somalia in the early 1990s illustrates the severe problems that occur when internal government breaks down. For some thirty years, Somalia was an important strategic country in the cold war. First, in the 1960s and 1970s, it provided a Soviet foothold in the Horn of Africa, the part of East Africa that contains Somalia and its neighbors. Then, after Ethiopia came under communist control, Somalia became a U.S.-supported state, from the late 1970s through the 1980s.

The end of the cold war coincided with the breakdown of the government of President Mohammed Said Barre in Somalia and also with a period of drought and food shortage. Clans are the main organizing force in Somalia, especially in south and central Somalia. There clan competition for power produced chaos, which led to a near total breakdown of both the economy and the government in 1991 and 1992. Somalians were often unable to plant their crops because of the fighting (often carried out with modern sophisticated weapons), so death from starvation and malnutrition was combined with death from clan warfare. Several hundreds of thousands of people lost their lives. Finally, the United Nations, primarily the United States, sent troops to provide food and, as a necessary accompaniment, to restore order. When the last U.S. troops left Somalia in 1994, the outcome remained in doubt. The clans were still fighting, though there were possibilities of some progression to a more stable government. But such stability seemed years away. Politics, culture, economy and the vagaries of climate all contribute to the uncertainties of Somalia's future.

tablishment of large-scale commercial or plantation enterprises for those same crops, as well as for others—such as rubber, pineapples, and tea—that required a large investment and experienced management. In some countries expatriate farmers—those from the colonial power—were encouraged to set up private plantations. In other countries governments initiated state farms or joint ventures with overseas companies. Many of Africa's least developed countries still contain small enclaves of such agricultural activities; in some cases, as in Kenya, these enclaves are being expanded under the management of international food companies, such as Del Monte.

In semiarid areas attempts have also been made to introduce large-scale ranching, to test possibilities for commercial animal husbandry. But such ranching requires the removal of much land from the traditional pastoral economy; the investment of considerable capital (including imported animal stock), and considerable management skill. As a result, large-scale ranches have generally been less successful than crop or tree (e.g., cacao or oil palm) agriculture.

The Industrial Sector

In the least developed nations the industrial sector is small. Industries are typically concerned with first-stage industrial processing of mineral and agricultural products—such as peanut shelling or cotton ginning. Small-scale, consumer-oriented production of cement, inexpensive household goods, beer, soft drinks, shoes, plastic items, textiles, and heavier industry, including construction materials and products, comprises the bulk of the industrial effort. Because the internal markets of these countries have low purchasing power and many countries in this group are small, such industries are often not very profitable.

The Service Sector

A major change in the national economic balance in these countries is that the service sector has become—statistically, at least—of growing importance. Although agriculture remains important, contributing typically 40 to 50 percent of GDP, industry often contributes 12 to 30 percent and services 30 to 40 percent. Such statistics reveal trends but undervalue the importance of agriculture to most of the people of the country.

Links with the International Trading Network

The pattern of trade for many of these countries shows continuing strong links with the former colonial power; for others, a strong dependence on one or two trading partners (Table 20–2). The total volume of trade in relation to population size is low; these countries still have largely self-sufficient societies. Typically, their exports consist of primary agricultural or mineral products, for which there are often many alternative sources. Consequently, price levels for those exports have generally risen only slowly over the past two

decades, and some commodities have even dropped in value, despite inflation. The small volume of imports, on the other hand, typically includes oil, which is vital for industry and communication. In addition, these countries must import machinery, specialized goods of all kinds, and fertilizers, and the price of most imports has increased sharply since the 1970s. Thus, even if local production has expanded and exports have grown in volume during this period, these countries may still be economically worse off because of the pattern of price changes, which has made producer goods comparatively more expensive. For example, it cost Tanzanians four times as much cotton to buy a tractor in 1986 as it did in 1976.

The Sahelian Least Developed Nations

The Sahelian group of least developed nations—Cape Verde, Mali, Burkina Faso, Niger, and Chad—illustrates the problems of development in arid and semiarid areas. All (except Cape Verde) lie on the southern margin of the Sahara. As a result, a large part of each country is desert, and much of the rest is semiarid rangeland. Although productivity is low, total available grazing resources are immense. Nomadic and seminomadic peoples have utilized those resources quite effectively in flexible systems of land use. Mixed herds of camels, cattle, sheep, and goats are common, with camels becoming less important as nomadism declines.

Nomadism, or the wandering of groups, is associated with a closely knit social and economic system, which, though effective in its use of the environment, is often difficult to fit into the fabric of new nation-states (Figure 20–5). Governments tend to favor the

Table 20-2
Trade patterns of three of Africa's least developed nations.

	Major Import Sources	Percent of Total Import Value	Major Export Destinations	Percent of Total Export Value
Chad	France	45	France	72
	Japan	22	West Germany	7
	West Germany	10	Netherlands	6
Uganda	United States	26	United Kingdom	31
	United Kingdom	23	Japan	16
	Japan	19	West Germany	12
Ethiopia	United States	55	Italy	20
	West Germany	9	United States	18
	Italy	9	Japan	18

Figure 20-5
Nomads at a makeshift well in the Somalian desert. The nomadism of these black Africans reflects their contact with Arabic culture. The nomadic groups of the Saharan margin sustain themselves by raising cattle, sheep, goats, and sometimes camels. But population growth, political pressure, and drought are breaking down the nomadic system and causing a shift to sedentary ways of life.

settlement of nomads, for reasons of taxation, security, ease of administration, and national image. Today, the nomadic system, which provides for some flexibility when confronted with change, has almost entirely broken down because of political and economic pressures and severe droughts (1969–1973 and 1981–1985). The effects of the droughts have been intensified by a variety of other factors: increased numbers of livestock, a reduced amount of land available as a result of increased settled agriculture, new national boundaries, and larger populations.

Because the southern parts of the Sahelian countries receive greater amounts of rainfall, dryland agriculture there complements irrigated agriculture along the rivers. These agropastoral livelihood systems provide a wider range of survival options in times of drought. But the combined production from animal husbandry and crop raising—which account for most of the economy of the Sahelian countries—provides only a modest level of living.

When drought and its attendant problems have reduced production, considerable outside assistance has been needed.

West African Humid Least Developed Nations

The West African humid least developed nations—Gambia, Guinea-Bissau, Sierra Leone, Togo, and Benin—involve a different set of environments. The

natural vegetation, particularly in lowlands, is a thick forest with several layers of vegetation. When the land is cleared, it is good for growing root crops, such as yams or cassava; and it has potential for cash crops, such as palm oil, cacao, and rubber. Clearing is hard work, though, and not all of the soils are fertile. In addition, under continual cultivation, fertility declines quite rapidly, because most of the nutrients of the tropical rain forest are locked in the vegetation mass itself (see the boxed feature Deforestation in the Amazon in Chapter 19). Thus, unless the natural vegetation is replaced with a similar cultivated system—tree crops, for example—the nutrients are lost.

Traditional **shifting cultivation** (slash-and-burn agriculture) provides a mechanism whereby land is allowed to regenerate after a few years' use while a new plot of land is cleared. When land is plentiful, shifting cultivation seems to be a reasonable economic use of labor and land, from the point of view of the traditional cultivator. Clearing can be effected economically by cutting and burning the smaller trees and forest litter. The ash provides a short-lived fertilizer, and the small size of the plots prevents major soil-erosion problems. After a few years, the vegetation is allowed to reestablish itself, and a new nutrient-rich plot is cleared.

But shifting agriculture cannot be sustained when land is in short supply. As population grows, land

485

comes into permanent use, and problems of soil fertility and erosion arise. The small countries of West Africa have yet to evolve productive small-farm systems that can provide alternatives to either shifting cultivation or plantation agriculture. In nearby countries, such as Côte d'Ivoire, plantation-type farms have been successful in preserving soil and maintaining production levels, but only because of capital inputs in the form of fertilizers and machinery that are beyond the capability of small peasant farmers.

A further problem of the humid tropics is that animal husbandry, apart from pigs and chickens, is difficult. Cattle suffer from a variety of diseases in the wetter areas and are more plagued there by the tsetse fly than they are in drier savanna conditions.

Figure 20-6
Workers opening valves on an irrigation dam near Makelle in Ethiopia. With 55 million people, Ethiopia is one of Africa's poorest countries. It has been handicapped both by drought and by serious internal conflict.

The result is a generally lower level of human nutrition in some of the humid areas than in the arid zones, where animal products are used much more.

These conditions result in a generally low level of production in the West African countries. Some diversity is brought about by small-scale mineral development; for example, Sierra Leone has scattered diamond deposits, and 35 percent of Togo's exports are phosphates. But those additional resources have not significantly changed the overall economy of the countries concerned.

East African Least Developed Nations

The East African countries—Burundi, Rwanda, Uganda, Ethiopia, Djibouti, Somalia, and the new country of Eritrea—have less uniform characteristics. Burundi and Rwanda are small, densely populated, isolated countries situated mostly in humid uplands. Ethiopia, in contrast, is a large country with one of the biggest ranges of climate and environmental conditions in Africa, including humid uplands and arid lowland plains (Figure 20–6). Uganda, also, has a humid, fertile plateau and mountain area, with arid conditions prevailing in the east. Somalia, though has only a small zone of rain-fed agriculture, supplemented by irrigated agriculture in the south. Most of the 7 million Somalis are pastoralists, though some commercial banana production takes place under irrigation in the south. The other five East African countries are also predominantly agricultural; all of them grow and export coffee.

With a population of more than 55 million, Ethiopia is one of the largest countries in Africa. But it has not yet been able to translate its size advantage into a productive and growing economy. Addis Ababa, with more than 2 million inhabitants, is one of Africa's largest cities, as well as the headquarters of the Organization of African Unity and other pan-African bodies. But a combination of infrastructure deficiencies, archaic social and political forms, internal separatist movements, and conflicts with Somalia have retarded Ethiopia's economic development. Although the country did not suffer directly the ill effects of colonial occupation, neither did it reap the benefits of the colonial experience, such as improved infrastructure and civil services.

In all of the countries of East Africa, conflict has played a large role in holding back or reversing development. For example, in addition to a protracted war with Somalia, Ethiopia was divided by civil war for decades, until 1991, when a major conflict with rebels in the province of Eritrea was resolved—though only by the creation of a new country. Eritrea came into formal being in 1993, when it became independent of Ethiopia after a thirty-year independence struggle. A nation of 3.5 million people with its capital at Asmara, Eritrea will depend economically on the highland agriculture of the interior including coffee, and the activity of the port of Massawa.

Another example of conflict holding back development is Uganda. It was a prosperous country until the early 1970s, when conditions badly deteriorated under the government of General Idi Amin. And a conflict between Uganda and Tanzania seriously affected Tanzania's development.

Ethnic conflict has particularly plagued both Rwanda and Burundi. The origins of these conflicts are complex, but one underlying factor has been the ethnic and cultural differences within countries, differences that have arisen in part from the way in which the colonial powers divided up East Africa. Since independence Rwanda has experienced power struggles between the Tutsi ethnic group, the traditional rulers of the country, and the Hutu ethnic group, which makes up over 80 percent of the population. This ethnic division—together with power struggles within the Hutus themselves—became a force for the widespread unrest and horrible massacres that erupted in early 1994 after the country's president was killed in a suspicious plane crash. More than a half a million people died in less than two months, and perhaps a million more fled Rwanda for refugee camps in Zaire. It is noteworthy that in neigbhoring Burundi, where more democractic processes had been instituted, much less violence occurred, though the Burundi president was also killed in the same crash.

Like many of the other least developed nations, the East African countries share the characteristic of isolation. The need to move goods through a neighboring country to reach the coast often means not only long distances to be covered but also external controls over national trade routes. For example, Uganda relies completely on Kenya for access to the sea, because routes through Zaire, Sudan, Tanzania, or Ethiopia are so difficult that they are not realistic alternatives. Similarly, landlocked Rwanda and Burundi must use long land routes through Uganda, Kenya, Tanzania, or Zaire. Ethiopia once had a long coastline, though with poor access to the sea; Ethiopia's problems are now complicated by the creation of Eritrea, which in-cludes the major coastal port of Massawa. Thus, the East African least developed nations are plagued not only by low production levels but also by poor trade routes for their exports. Equally damaging are the costs that long and difficult transportation routes add to imports.

INTERMEDIATE NATIONS

The economic development and long-term potential of the least developed countries contrast somewhat with the conditions found in the intermediate nations, though similarities exist, too. These are all poor countries.

Two types of intermediate nations can be identified. The first set—Mauritania, Senegal, Liberia, Côte d'Ivoire (Ivory Coast), Sudan, and Tanzania—includes nations that are dominated by a single economic sector—for the most part, agriculture. Mauritania is somewhat an exception because it also depends on a single mineral resource—iron ore—as well as on ocean fishing. The second set—Guinea, Ghana, Nigeria, and Kenya—has more diversity in individual national economies: one or more mineral resources and an agricultural base.

Countries with Dominant Single-Sector Resources

In some respects nation-states are like biomes: a diversity of biomes provides for more stability. Likewise, nation-states with diverse economies are less vulnerable than are those whose economies depend heavily on only one or two products. Vulnerability increases further when a country must compete with many others in the world market. Thus, states with diverse environments and a number of developed economic components stand a better chance of being able to provide prosperous and stable conditions for their citizens. Countries dependent on a single resource rarely find that resource sufficient to overcome all other difficulties, though that sometimes occurs.

In Mauritania, for example, even though most of the people maintain their precarious existence with agricultural and pastoral activities, mineral exploitation and fishing offer the best hope for future economic growth, though neither employs large numbers of citizens. Côte d'Ivoire, Sudan, and Tanzania, in contrast, are nations that rely almost totally on agriculture, not only as a prime source of daily subsistence but also as a generator of foreign exchange.

In fact, Côte d'Ivoire has used that agricultural base to stimulate economic growth.

Indeed, Côte d'Ivoire, has been something of an economic miracle. Between 1965 and 1980 its economy grew at a rate of about 7 percent per year—a rate higher than that of many European economies. Almost 1.5 million workers from surrounding countries flocked there to share in the boom. Coffee, timber, and cacao account for 80 percent of all Côte d'Ivoire exports, with specialty crops such as pineapples, peanuts, sugarcane, bananas, and rubber comprising most of the remaining earnings. Unlike the small industrial and tourist sectors, where management and ownership are concentrated in French hands, most of the cash crops in Côte d'Ivoire are produced by peasant farmers. The broad base of that growth—as well as the country's political stability—has created a climate that is conducive to foreign investment as a complement to government expenditures on ports, roads, and other infrastructural improvements. Since 1980, however, the growth rate is only 2.5 percent and many of the foreign workers have been displaced. A concern is the current period of political transition. With the death in 1994 of President Houphouet-Boigny, the country's founding father, Côte d'Ivoire is now faced with a difficult political situation at a time of economic difficulty. The peaceful transfer of power that occurred after his death created hope for continued stability.

Nonetheless, dependence on only one sector to stimulate growth can cause serious problems. Internally, concentration on agricultural development often takes the form of cash-crop production for overseas sales. But agricultural developments of that type often place great strain on local socioeconomic systems. For example, capital generated from commercial farming frequently benefits only a small section of the agricultural community. In addition, commercial agriculture may disrupt traditional agricultural patterns by encouraging the removal of land from subsistence food production or encroachment on fallow land or pasture which may be an essential part of a agricultural system.

Concentration on the commercial agricultural sector may also make a country extremely vulnerable to price fluctuations on the world market. Cotton in Sudan, cacao in Côte d'Ivoire, and coffee and cloves in Tanzania are all major foreign exchange earners. As long as commodity prices are high, the economies of these countries prosper. When prices fall, however, major economic setbacks can occur.

The economies of almost all of these single-sector countries have provided a narrow base on which to develop manufacturing. Agricultural-processing industries frequently remain small; most products are either consumed fresh or are shipped in an unprocessed state to overseas markets. Even Mauritania's iron ore is exported overseas after only minimal processing.

Accordingly, the governments of one-resource countries have tried various solutions to foster economic growth. Those alternative strategies may be ideological in nature, such as Tanzania's attempts to instill in its people a spirit of socialist cooperation and a sense of pride. Or they may be attempts to increase diversity by applying technology. Giant irrigation schemes, such as in Sudan, are examples of attempts to create totally new agricultural environments in order to spur increased productivity. Still other strategies call for the creation of new sources of revenue—such as a tourist industry based on a mild climate and an attractive waterfront, as in Côte d'Ivoire, or the development of known mineral resources, as in Mauritania. Each strategy has its good points and its bad, its successes and its failures.

Ujamaa in Tanzania.   Like other countries in the intermediate group, Tanzania derives most of its resources from the agricultural sector. Most of its population is engaged in cropping and animal husbandry. Exports of agricultural commodities—such as coffee, tea, cotton, and cloves—are the country's major foreign-exchange earners. But all of those crops are affected by fluctuations in world market prices. Cloves were especially hard hit by a steady decline in price through the 1980s, though recently there has been partial rebound. The situation sparked efforts to diversify the economy of Zanzibar and nearby islands, where most of the cloves are grown, by introducing cattle ranching and new crops such as rice, cacao, and coffee.

Tanzania is unusual in the overall strategy it selected to deal with its development problems. That country has placed its emphasis on increasing the motivation and aspirations of the people in ways that are authentically Tanzanian and African. *Ujamaa* is the country's focus—a philosophy of pride in self, commitment to self-improvement, and development of the individual, region, and nation along communal and cooperative lines. That type of African socialism is seen by Tanzanians as preserving the best features of the African tribal social sys-

Figure 20–7
Agricultural workers in small communal fields in Tanzania. *Ujamaa* is an attempt by government to incorporate into the development process the best of African-tribal communalism.

tem (Figure 20–7). Involving the people in the development process at a grass-roots level has produced generally good results in creating a sense of national purpose and in improving social welfare, including basic education. But it has not been an economic success.

Originally the Tanzanian government experimented with building new villages with modern amenities to promote rural development. The costs were high, however, and many Tanzanians were reluctant to move to the new settlements. The government then turned to a process of self-help in creating village settlements. The country's president, Julius Nyerere, set forth the policy of *ujamaa,* under which people were to move into close-knit villages and work on individual farms as well as communal projects. Local people were encouraged, exhorted, and sometimes even forced to move into the centralized villages, which were intended to be centers of healthcare delivery, education, and social services. An estimated 15 percent of the rural population shifted into *ujamaa* villages. Some later returned to their original villages, but many remained.

Although Tanzania made major strides in decreasing illiteracy and making health services more widely available, the necessary production increases did not occur, partly because of the lack of incentives in the new system and partly because of drought and other external factors. In the mid-1980s the push for *ujamaa* was replaced by a greater concern for production increases, but the new village structure remains an important feature of the country. With a liberalization of the economy from certain facets of state control, production did grow between 1986 and 1992.

The government's socialist principles affect many aspects of life in Tanzania. Mobility of products and prices for agricultural goods are controlled by the government, but cooperative societies are encouraged. Great efforts have also been made to utilize technology that may be particularly appropriate for a local area—such as providing stronger and more efficient ox plows as well as tractors and other machinery. With foreign exchange reserves at low levels, the policy of improving what already exists also conserves badly needed cash.

Tanzania is still in the throes of change, but the change is toward a less idealistic yet still self-sufficient economy. Tanzania is a country with good resources that may well see significant progress before the end of this century.

The Application of Technology. The diffusion of Western technology throughout the world has made it possible for all countries to use modern approaches to development. For example, common in the arid zones of sub-Saharan Africa have been large-scale agricultural development projects based on large dams and extensive irrigation systems. Sudan has adopted that strategy to promote the growth of agriculture as well as to provide hydro-electric power for the towns and for industries.

Sudan has utilized irrigation technology for a long time. In fact, efficient traditional technology has been used there, as well as in Egypt, for several thousand years. Modern technology and large-scale irrigation arrived in 1925, with the construction of the Sennar Dam on the Blue Nile. The first stage of development brought irrigation to more than 1 million acres (404,700 hectares), much of which lies in the **Gezira**, a triangular area between the White Nile and the Blue Nile. Formerly a semiarid plain used primarily by pastoral nomads, the Gezira has now largely been converted into intensively cultivated and productive agricultural land.

For years the primary product in the Gezira—and the major foreign-exchange commodity for Sudan—was long-staple cotton, which yields a high-quality fiber that produces fine cloth for expensive clothing. Long-staple cotton was first produced for the Lancashire cotton mills in England. The Gezira has now become more diversified, with the addition of short-staple cotton, wheat, sorghum, and other crops. This means the Gezira is an important source of food for domestic consumption; half of the country's wheat is produced there, as well as substantial amounts of other crops.

The early success of this coordinated, integrated irrigation system has led to major expansions. The so-called Manaquil Scheme has extended irrigation to an additional 800,000 acres (324,000 hectares), and the al Rosaires Dam on the Blue Nile has added another 300,000 acres (121,000 hectares). Much of that new cropland is planted in short-staple cotton, both to avoid excessive dependence on the spe-cialty cotton market and to provide an easier-to-process fiber that can meet the competition of artificial fibers. In addition, the Khashm al Qirbah Dam on the Atbara River irrigates 740,000 acres (299,000 hectares) of cotton and food crops. Those projects, which employ relatively simple technology and construction, rely on an efficient and inexpensive gravity-flow water system. In each scheme the tenant farmers participate in the decisions of the local development board.

Irrigation is now a vital part of Sudan's agricultural system. Yet even that huge investment did not prevent Sudan from suffering major setbacks in production in the droughts of 1983 to 1985. Weakened since then by civil war and poor management of its irrigated agriculture, Sudan has not been able to recapture the full benefits of its irrigated lands.

Tourism and Development. All countries in the intermediate group gain some income from tourism. Côte d'Ivoire in particular, though, has placed special emphasis on the tourist industry as a means of accelerating economic growth and reducing the risk of sudden market variations for its agricultural exports. Consequently, large sums of money in that country are being expended to increase the number of hotel rooms, ease access to inland locations with cultural and environmental interest, and improve tourist facilities. More than 10,000 hotel rooms now exist in Côte d'Ivoire, at least half of which are in or near the capital, Abidjan. Lured by long, sandy, palm-lined beaches, luxurious hotels, exotic game parks, and excursion air fares, tourists—especially from France—are expected to spend lavishly in Abidjan and several other target zones along the coast and in the interior.

Realistically, however, tourism is not necessarily a satisfactory approach to economic growth. Tanzania also has important tourist potential but has hesitated until recently to commit resources to that sector, fearing that it would mainly benefit foreign companies and would also encourage servant attitudes among local people. Indeed, a culture conflict is inherent in a tourist industry, which threatens local values and often accounts for the hostility that frequently accompanies a massive tourist influx. Thus, although tourism may help diversify a local economy, it is a mixed blessing. Furthermore, because the tourist's ability to spend is linked directly to the health of the global economy, a tourist-oriented economy may be subject to many of the same fluctuations that affect cash-crops. For example, in the early 1990s, a period of global recession, tourist expenditures in both East and West Africa dropped significantly.

A Mineral Alternative.   Mauritania provides an interesting comparison with other nations in the intermediate group, because the major activities suitable for rapid economic growth are mining and fishing, each nontraditional enterprises. Although most of Mauritania's small population (1.7 million) is actively employed in agriculture, only 1 percent of the country's land is arable, and most of that land is concentrated in the extreme south of the country, in the Senegal River valley. The remainder of the country is dry grassland or desert. Thus, most of Mauritania is suitable only for raising livestock. It is no accident that nomadic pastoralism continues among 70 percent of Mauritania's population.

Mauritania's situation would be truly desperate if it were not for several rich mineral deposits and rich offshore fishing grounds. The existence of extensive iron ore deposits in northern Mauritania—many with a metal content of 60 percent—has been known since 1935. Only since 1960, however, has exploitation of those reserves been possible. Considerable infrastructure had to be built before major exports could be made to Europe and North America. For example, a railroad was built to move the ore to the coast, and port facilities at Nouadhibou were constructed to speed handling. Exports began in 1963 and increased rapidly. Iron ore was the country's largest export until 1983, when stagnating sales were overtaken by a surge in fish exports. Fish has remained the major export since, reaching $23 million in 1992. Copper deposits also promise to generate substantial revenue, and a search for petroleum is under way.

As a result of royalties and taxes generated by the fishing and mining industries, Mauritania's foreign trade balance has improved from one of small deficits to a modest favorable balance. But that improvement has not come without problems, for it has proved difficult to distribute the newly found wealth, modest though it is, equitably among Mauritania's citizens. Today some 15 percent of the population, largely those with managerial and professional skills or with positions in the government bureaucracy, control 65 percent of the country's wage income. Such inequities are likely to have future political and social repercussions.

Countries with Diversified Resources

Guinea, Ghana, Nigeria, and Kenya are blessed with a combination of agricultural, forestry, and mineral resources. Guinea has the world's second-largest bauxite deposits, together with good agricultural potential. Ghana is a major cacao exporter and has used its surplus capital to spur industrialization and diversify its agricultural base. Nigeria and Kenya are examples of countries with diversified resource bases, and a closer examination of those two countries may be instructive.

Nigeria.   Because of oil and gas deposits in the southern part of the country, Nigeria is economically different from all of the other countries of East and West Africa. However, the massive income generated from that resource in the latter part of the 1970s diminished considerably in the early 1980s, and investing the oil income successfully in other parts of the economy has proved to be difficult.

With a population of perhaps 90 million people (a number, derived from a 1991 census, much lower than earlier estimates) and a per capita GNP of $250, Nigeria has the largest economy in sub-Saharan Africa except for the Republic of South Africa. Much of Nigeria's economic growth has occurred since 1968 as a result of the discovery and exploitation of oil in the Niger River delta area. In 1968 total exports were valued at $321 million, with oil accounting for only $58 million. In 1972, before the abrupt rise in oil prices, exports were $2.2 billion, with oil representing $1.8 billion of the total. Oil revenues then jumped to $7 billion in 1974 and soared to $12.9 billion in 1980, only to drop back to $6 billion in 1986. With petroleum and petroleum products accounting for more than 90 percent of the export total, it is not difficult to imagine the impact of that growth and retreat. Initial growth in revenues changed the whole economy, and heavy investments were made in roads, schools, and other aspects of an urban infrastructure. Agriculture was neglected, and corruption was endemic. Then, with the dramatic drops in revenue, the economy went into a crisis, and much investment was halted. An effort has lately been made to reduce the obvious imbalance in the Nigerian economy by reinvesting in agriculture and promoting local industry. In the last few years, oil revenue has increased to $12 billion, helping a slow economic recovery.

Before the oil boom the main staples of Nigeria's export trade were cacao, peanuts, and tin. Today, cattle and peanuts are dominant in the north; palm oil, rubber, timber, and cacao, in the south. But during the oil boom agriculture fell in importance in Nigeria: output in 1971 was only about 36 percent of the 1960 level, though some recovery occurred in the 1980s. Perhaps the major factor accounting for that decline in agriculture has been the social and economic differential between towns and surrounding countryside. Wages, standards of health, and diversity of opportunity have all become greater in the cities, and young people are reluctant to stay on farms. Nonetheless, with all data indicating that the country will maintain a rapid population growth, increased food production is essential. By 1992, agriculture had recovered some of the lost ground, accounting for 35 percent of GDP and employing 55 percent of the labor force.

Oil continues to exert a major influence on internal investment in Nigeria. The country has always placed a priority on higher education: it has twenty-four universities and many technical colleges, as well as a variety of research institutions of national and international stature. Oil money was used to reinforce and broaden some of those institutions, but the economic downturn has made it difficult to maintain that thrust. Oil revenue has also recently been invested in infrastructural improvements, such as paved roads and new railway equipment, as well as in large-scale industrial enterprises. Earlier attention had focused on increasing oil-refinery capacity and beginning an iron and steel industry, but the drop in oil revenues postponed many such plans.

Oil money has also been used to improve Nigeria's status in West Africa. The country has contributed to such humanitarian and prestige-enhancing projects as drought relief in Mali, the 1975 All-Africa Games, and a peacekeeping mission to Liberia in the early 1990s. Efforts to improve regional commercial ties have also emerged. Nigeria has invested heavily in Guinea's iron ore mines, hoping that much of the ore can someday be used in Nigeria's hoped-for iron and steel industry. In addition, transit taxes have been removed on goods crossing some of Nigeria's borders, in an effort to promote regional trade, and further efforts are being made to promote regional development through the Lake Chad Basin Commission. Unfortunately for Nigeria, it was forced

to expel many guest workers from neighboring countries when the Nigerian economy lost momentum in early 1982. And Nigeria's economic power, though still considerable, lessened dramatically when oil prices dropped in the mid-1980s.

Nigeria has long had a varied industrial sector, most of which is composed of thousands of small units working at the craft or local level. The little modern industry that does exist, is concentrated in textiles, food processing, and beverages; the local sector, though, continues to flourish. In years of good oil revenue—when export earnings were growing—imports of food and Western-type machinery and equipment increased phenomenally, as did the importation of manufactured goods. In the early 1990s, Nigeria achieved a surplus in basic import and export trading. But the cost of debt servicing inherited from the 1980s continues to drag down the economy, as well as the government's ability to invest.

Kenya.   Kenya does not fit easily into any simple classification of countries by degree of economic development. In some respects it should be regarded as a least developed nation, because its economy is based on agriculture, and it has a relatively low per capita GNP. In other respects it can be regarded as having more diversified resources, because of its important service-center role in East Africa and in Africa as a whole.

Kenya's relatively small area of humid upland is highly productive, with coffee, tea, and fruit being the major export crops. Flowers, vegetables, and fruit are airfreighted to Europe in a modern production system. Much of the rest of Kenya, however, consists of arid and semiarid areas where grain production and livestock raising are the main enterprises. Although some meat is exported, the arid part of the nation relies heavily on subsistence activities.

In terms of physical resources, Kenya depends very much on its agricultural base, which is coming under the pressure of a rural population that is growing at the rapid rate of 4 percent per year. But two factors have encouraged the evolution of Nairobi, Kenya's capital, as a regional and continental center and as a small industrial center for East Africa: its central location with respect to other East African nations, and its history of foreign capital investment. Tourism has provided another form of investment, and the country's game parks and beaches continue to provide attractive vacation packages (Figure 20–8). And tourism has been

Figure 20-8
The town of Shiela Beach on Lamu Island just off the Kenyan coast. Although our images are often of interior Africa, great beauty also exists along the Indian Ocean coast.

helped by Nairobi's development as a center of the African air-transportation network. In addition, Nairobi has been chosen as the headquarters of a number of regional and international agencies and as an important conference center.

Industry in Kenya includes food processing, particularly dairy products, tea, and coffee. Light manufacturing also exists, including, for example, a company that exports sports equipment. Kenya's major industrial foreign exchange, though, comes from the refinery at Mombasa; in some years refined foreign petroleum is the country's top exchange earner.

verse sets of resources and much greater potential for long-term growth. Notable in West Africa, Côte d'Ivoire and Nigeria are making progress in effectively utilizing their potential to create economic wealth. In East Africa, Kenya has a similar opportunity. For many Africans, however, the path to a reasonable standard of living will be long and difficult. They must continue to surmount debilitating health problems, align population growth and production systems with the capacity of the environment, and develop or maintain enlightened and stable political systems. Only then will significant progress toward economic development become sustainable.

SUMMARY
Regions at Risk

This chapter has outlined a division of Africa south of the Sahara that is based on the relative economic development of the various nations. The least developed countries in Africa are economically the poorest in the world. The specter of drought and starvation is ever-present in several of the Sahelian countries. Other African nations, however, have di-

KEY TERMS

cholera	schistosomiasis
Gezira	shifting cultivation
malaria	sub-Saharan Africa
nomadism	tsetse fly
onchocerciasis	*ujamaa*
Sahel	yellow fever

21

Central and Southern Africa

Fishermen at sunset on Lake Kivu on the boundary between Zaire and Rwanda. Lake Kivu is one of a series of lakes occupying the Great Rift Valley of Eastern Africa.

The second major region of sub-Saharan Africa includes Central and Southern Africa (see Figure 20–1). The range of economic well-being in the region is wide, as it is throughout Africa. Mozambique, Malawi, Lesotho, and Madagascar, like their counterparts in East and West Africa, are among the world's least developed nations. The Republic of South Africa, in contrast, is relatively rich. The other nations are of intermediate economic status. In this chapter we first consider the characteristics of the region as a whole and then turn to each of the subregions—Central Africa, South-central Africa, Southern Africa, and the islands—again using selected countries as case studies.

THE COLONIAL LEGACY

The stamp of Belgian, Portuguese, and British **colonialism**—the maintenance of foreign possessions—is strong in Central and Southern Africa. One reason is the relatively large number of European settlers in many of the countries.

Most of the countries in Central and Southern Africa achieved their independence only recently—many during the 1960s. Some gained their independence even later: Mozambique and Angola in 1975, Zimbabwe in 1980, and Namibia in 1989. Unlike the experience of much of East and West Africa, the transition to independence in central and southern Africa has not always been peaceful. In Zaire, for instance, the rapid exodus of the Belgians in 1960 left a country with few trained local people, except in the lowest levels of government. Not surprisingly, that large and diverse country was plagued by problems in the years that followed: internal strife, the death of a president under suspicious circumstances, UN intervention to halt civil war, and a long period of military rule leading to the current anarchy in that country. In both Mozambique and Angola, independence from Portugal came only after extended revolutionary struggle, and armed dissent against the government in power lasted until recently, a relic of the factionalism of the independence movement. Zimbabwe, once called Rhodesia, won independence and majority rule only after a long war against the white-minority government. In a number of countries the aftermath of independence is continued internal strife between opposing groups of revolutionary forces. In South Africa the battle not for independence but for equal rights for all citizens has only recently been resolved.

THE RESOURCE BASE

The countries of Central and Southern Africa tend to be endowed with a broader range of resources than are found in the countries of East and West Africa (Figure 21–1). Equatorial Guinea, Gabon, the Central African Republic, and Zaire have considerable timber resources. Zaire, Zambia, and Zimbabwe are important for copper production, and Zaire has a number of other mineral resources, including cobalt. Gabon and Angola have oil and gas, plus reserves of several metallic minerals. Botswana, once a country with few apparent mineral resources, has gained economically from the discovery and mining of diamonds and other minerals and is now one of the world's major producers of industrial diamonds. Namibia and Swaziland also have mineral wealth. And the Republic of South Africa is one of the world's major producers of a whole range of minerals, including gold, diamonds, and coal. This great abundance of mineral resources (not shared by Malawi and Lesotho) has helped many of the nations of this region achieve their intermediate economic status.

Despite the importance of mineral production, agriculture remains the backbone of most economies in the region, providing income for a large segment of the population. Mineral production is the main foreign-exchange earner and provides the various governments with much of their revenues. Manufacturing is important for income and employment only in the Republic of South Africa and, to a lesser degree, in Zimbabwe. But agriculture remains basic even in these countries. The economy of Malawi is based almost entirely on agriculture, and most of the people in Botswana rely on cattle and other livestock as a major source of their income. Angola and Mozambique both have diversified and potentially productive agricultural sectors, but are held back by internal disorder. Zaire's once-flourishing agricultural sector is also currently in a moribund state. Zimbabwe, in contrast, has a highly productive agricultural economy, and the Republic of South Africa has one of the world's more diversified farming systems. Zambia, Namibia, and Lesotho have small agricultural economies.

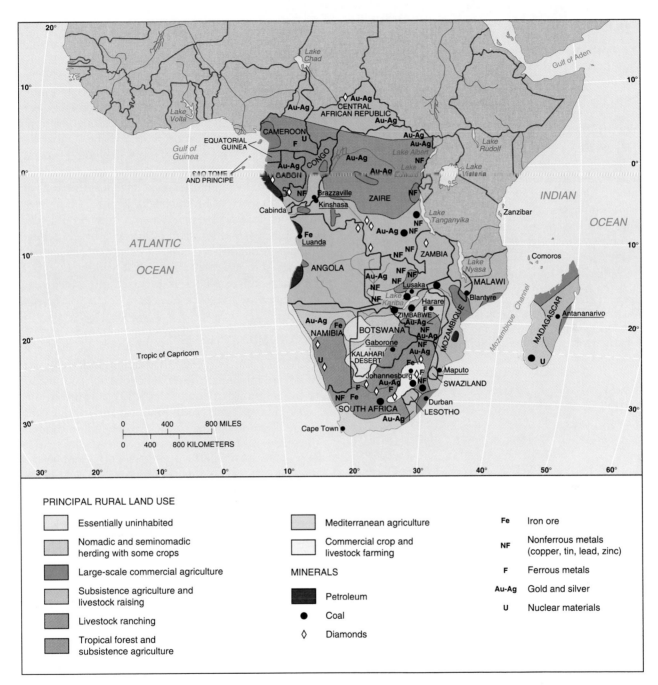

Figure 21-1

Land use and minerals in Central and Southern Africa. Some forms of land use, such as herding, support only a few people per square mile, whereas others are intensive and provide a livelihood for many. The mineral industry supports few people directly but provides valuable foreign exchange, especially in Zaire and South Africa.

THE PHYSICAL ENVIRONMENT

The diversity of Central and Southern Africa is perhaps best expressed in its great range of physical conditions. The basin of the Zaire (Congo) River is the locale of most of Africa's tropical rain forest, nurtured by year-round rainfall. The tropical rainy climate, with no distinct dry season, gives the river a high, regular flow and thus provides Zaire with potential for much hydropower, which is only partially utilized. Cameroon, the Central African Republic, Gabon, Angola, and Mozambique also have large areas of rain forest. Forest depletion—caused by lumbering for export and expansion of agriculture—is becoming a major problem in these countries.

Figure 21–2
The Kalahari Desert landscape. The Kalahari Desert is found in Namibia, Botswana, and South Africa. Rainfall in many parts of this subtropical desert is less than 2 inches per year.

In contrast, Namibia and Botswana are some of the driest parts of the continent, receiving less than 2 inches (51 millimeters) of rain during the year (Figure 21–2). In between the rain forest and the desert lie plateaus with moderate, seasonally distributed rainfall (30 to 45 inches, or 760 to 1,140 millimeters, per year) and with mediocre-to-good potential for agriculture. The moist uplands of Malawi and Zimbabwe are ideal for a wide range of crops, including tea and coffee. The lowland areas of Zambia and Zimbabwe are more suited to maize and animal raising and have varying degrees of productivity.

Other physical zones are found within the Republic of South Africa. Climates there include coastal Mediterranean conditions and inland subhumid to semiarid plateaus with a variety of grain crops, including wheat and maize, and wide areas dominated by livestock raising.

ECONOMIC SYSTEMS

The economic systems of central and southern Africa are oriented in three directions: (1) southward to the Republic of South Africa; (2) outward to the ocean, Europe, and North America; and (3) outward to the countries of the former Soviet Union, though the extent of that orientation is much smaller than it was in the 1970s and early 1980s and continues to decrease. The economies of most of the countries in southern Africa are tied primarily to that of the Republic of South Africa. The sheer economic strength of South Africa and the infrastructural orientation of those southern countries toward serving the economic relationship with South Africa almost ensure that domination. The enclosed or adjacent countries of Botswana, Swaziland, Lesotho, and Namibia have especially close ties to South Africa. In addition, Zimbabwe, Malawi, Mozambique, and—to a lesser degree—Zambia all retain close economic ties to South Africa.

On the other hand, Gabon, Zaire, Angola, Zambia, and Zimbabwe all have export economies—mostly natural resources—that are closely linked to Europe and North America. Angola and Mozambique formerly had strong ties to the Soviet Union, but they have reoriented their trade to link more closely with Europe and North America. The links that Angola, Congo, and Mozambique (among others) had with the Soviet Union were related to cold war politics and, since the dissolution of that power, are fast declining in significance.

CENTRAL AFRICA

Central Africa consists of Cameroon, Equatorial Guinea, Gabon, Congo, the Central African Republic, and Zaire. Two of the countries—Gabon and Zaire—provide a good sample picture of central Africa; both are intermediate in economic status or potential. Gabon is one of Africa's main petroleum-product exporters and also possesses a timber and mining industry. It has a strong economy, shared by a population of 1.1 million, which results in a high per capita GNP of more than $3,500 (albeit somewhat misleading in terms of the wealth of most people in Gabon); this puts Gabon in the same group as Argentina and Chile. Zaire, with its diversified mining industry, is a large country of 38 million people. But Zaire's per capita GNP of only $220 has been declining. Potentially a wealthy country, Zaire is almost bankrupt, as a result of low international prices for its minerals, mismanagement and corruption, and the basic difficulties of leading a country of this type to a more sustained pattern of economic development.

Gabon: Timber, Petroleum, and Mining

Gabon is a small country, best known to many people as the long-time residence of the great German humanitarian Albert Schweitzer. Subsistence agriculture has been replaced in Gabon as the basic form of livelihood, first by the timber industry and then by mining and petroleum production—though two-thirds of the people still work in some form of agriculture. Gabon is now a member of the Organization of Petroleum Exporting Countries (OPEC), and in the past twenty years the country's GNP has increased from $167 million to about $6 billion.

In terms of climate, soils, and general environmental resources, the long-term potential for land productivity in Gabon is moderate, but at present that potential is being realized only in lumbering (Figure 21–3). Less than 2.0 percent of the land is under cultivation, and of that amount two-thirds is used for subsistence crops. The remainder is planted with cacao, coffee, and palm oil for export. The proportion of land under cultivation is slowly declining as urban opportunities encourage people to move to the towns, leaving Gabon with a high import bill for foodstuffs—food imports are 20 percent of all imports.

Forests cover 56 million acres (22.7 million hectares), or 25 percent, of Gabon. Formerly, forest products accounted for more than half of Gabon's total exports, until the surge in oil production in the 1980s reduced that proportion to 20 percent. Gabon's timber is exploited by large European companies and, more and more, by small local enterprises. One great advantage of timber production is that processing industries can be established without massive capital investment. Currently, timber processing accounts for more than 50 percent of Gabon's industry and much local employment.

Since the 1960s mining has become increasingly significant in Gabon. In the 1970s and 1980s petroleum and natural gas became economically dominant; in the late 1980s and 1990s mining gained in importance, with manganese and uranium joining the list of key exports. Iron ore and gold have also helped to provide a diversified and expanding mining economy. Currently, wealth from mining and petroleum is being generated rapidly, yet many rural people still live at low economic levels. Gabon does have great potential, but its human resources may be a major future constraint.

Figure 21-3
Lumbering operations in Gabon. The tropical rain forest contains a variety of valuable trees that can be harvested for export.

Zaire: Minerals and Hydroelectric Power

Zaire is a nation with diverse mineral resources and considerable agricultural potential. It has relied heavily on copper for export earnings; in most years copper accounts for over 60 percent of Zaire's total export value. Cobalt and diamonds also provide important mining income and rank with coffee and palm oil in export value. The Zairian export of cobalt is very important to the industrial economy of the United States; in addition, Zaire is the world's largest producer of industrial diamonds. A range of other mineral resources also exists, including silver, iron ore, manganese, and oil. Most of Zaire's mineral wealth is in the southern part of the country.

Zaire has considerable agricultural potential, too, though agriculture remains a struggling sector. Much of that potential is found in the far east of the country, where upland volcanic soils provide a good base for growing coffee, cacao, and tea. One great problem, however, is the remoteness of those productive areas. Coffee, cacao, tea, cotton, and tobacco have been export crops, but the plantation economy is no longer functioning. Coffee is the only current major agricultural export. And the amount of food imported continues to grow; reasons for that importation include the increasing rate of population growth of urban centers, particularly Kinshasa, the capital, with a population of more than 3.0 million; the relatively high degree of employment in mining; and internal transportation difficulties.

Zaire has the long-term advantage of one of the world's great hydroelectric power sites at Inga, near the mouth of the Zaire River. Initially, 1,300 megawatts has been developed. That energy resource is one key to Zaire's development prospects, and its significance is increased by the rising price of other energy sources. A number of industrial projects have been considered that use hydroelectric power, including a steel complex, a caustic soda factory, a polyvinyl factory, a nitrogen fertilizer factory, and an aluminum smelter. The steel complex was initiated, and the caustic soda and polyvinyl plants advanced to the planning stage. But in the early 1990s chaos reigned in Zaire, placing all these projects on hold.

With a large urban population and major mineral and power resources, Zaire may well build up a major manufacturing sector some time in the distant future. Indeed, manufacturing is one focus of current government development plans. But much of that industry will be capital intensive, and there is a great need for massive training of skilled workers, as well as improvement in the service sector. The country needs a long period of economic modernization in order to become an industrial nation. Unfortunately, the opposite is what has been happening. The government lost control of the country and its economy in 1990, and years of turmoil followed. The growth of Zaire as a modern state has been suspended until that political situation is resolved.

SOUTH-CENTRAL AFRICA

South-central Africa comprises the countries of Angola, Zambia, Malawi, and Mozambique, all of which have strong ties with both the north and the south. Zambia well illustrates some of the development problems of all four countries of this region.

Zambia: The Copper State

With a population of over 8 million and a per capita GNP of $420, Zambia is a moderately prosperous country in comparison with others in Africa. Many of its problems reflect a development base tied almost solely to one resource. Until the sharp decline in copper prices at the end of the 1970s, Zambia had a favorable balance of trade. Today, copper still accounts for more than 90 percent of Zambian foreign-exchange earnings and is directly responsible for 20 percent of government revenues, contributing additional sums indirectly. Cobalt, zinc, and tobacco are minor export commodities. Even though Zambia has considerable agricultural potential, it imports 40 percent of its food. For some years after independence, little investment was made in agriculture, and the proportion of people working on the land has decreased significantly. The higher standard of living in the towns is a major factor in the rural-to-urban migration.

Zambian cities appear to have a standard of living as high as any in Africa, but employment opportunities in the cities are not growing as fast as the cities themselves. And the variation in wealth among working adults is great. Ironically, much wealth remains untapped because there is not yet a sufficient reservoir of trained technical and managerial workers to run the copper mines and other industries that were formerly run by colonial interests. Efforts to solve that problem are under way. Through the University of Zambia and formal technical-education programs, the Zambian government

Figure 21–4
The teaching of young adults in an outdoor setting in Zambia, in south-central Africa.
The establishment of basic and technical education programs remains an essential
part of the development programs of several countries in this region.

is attempting to create a reservoir of skilled laborers (Figure 21–4).

In agriculture the situation is also changing. One success story is sugar: in 1960 all of Zambia's sugar needs were met by imports; by 1974 Zambia had become self-sufficient as the result of just one project. Prospects are good for cattle, too. Zambia has the potential to become a major exporter of meat and maize—for which Zaire is a large potential market—as well as fruit, particularly pineapples and mangoes. But progress has been very slow in those areas. The Zambian economy is still unbalanced, and much needs to be done to use nonmineral resources more effectively.

SOUTHERN AFRICA

Namibia, Botswana, Zimbabwe, Swaziland, and Lesotho have one thing in common: strong economic ties to the Republic of South Africa. Lesotho is physically surrounded by South Africa; and Swaziland, which borders Mozambique on the northeast, is met on three sides by South Africa. Not surprisingly, both countries are economically dependent on the larger country. Namibia has only recently gained its independence from South Africa, following long, drawn-out negotiations and elections. And Botswana and Zimbabwe both have close commercial and infrastructural links with South Africa, though great efforts have been made to change that situation. For all of these countries, the tension between economic concerns and a desire to distance themselves politically from South Africa was long a major and continuing problem, one that may be lessened with the new majority rule in South Africa.

A closer examination of three countries of southern Africa follows. Botswana and Zimbabwe are intermediate in their economic status; South Africa is one of the most developed nations in Africa.

Botswana

With a population of about 1.6 million people, Botswana has few significant towns. The capital, Gaborone, is close to the South African border and is in the wetter part of the country. The mineral industry has led to the establishment of a number of small towns, but the country is essentially one of scattered small villages.

One of the world's poorest countries at independence in 1966, Botswana now boasts a per capita GNP of over $2,500 as result of economic growth at a phenomenal rate—over 12 percent a year for twenty-five years. Male migration to work in the mines of South Africa has long been a facet of economic life for families in Botswana, and a period of work in South Africa is still part of the life experience of many Botswana men. But it has been Botswana's own thriving mineral industry, which is based on diamonds, copper-nickel matte, and coal, that has caused a dramatic rise in the country's GNP. The large increases in internal mining income, as well as political concern for greater economic independence, have greatly reduced the mining linkages with South Africa. Also, the government has encouraged the growth of manufacturing, and over 30,000 people are now employed in textiles, food processing, and other industries.

Before the mineral industry was developed, Botswana was dominated by pastoral activities; only a small part of the southern margin of the country has enough rainfall for sustained agriculture. Cattle were and are the dominant agricultural resource; and beef exports, mostly to South Africa, constitute Botswana's most important agricultural product.

Botswana is a country where rapid economic growth has been accompanied by political stability and strong democratic institutions. For its relatively small population, it is one of the continent's success stories.

Zimbabwe

Zimbabwe, formerly Rhodesia, became independent only in 1980. The country is relatively small, covering an area of approximately 150,804 square miles (390,582 square kilometers)—about the size of Montana. Zimbabwe's population of 11.2 million comprises roughly 200,000 Europeans and more than 10 million Africans.

The economy of Zimbabwe is more diversified than those of most African countries. Mining ac-

counts for more than 50 percent of its foreign-exchange earnings, and manufacturing produces about 25 percent of the GNP. A well-developed commercial agricultural sector not only provides most of the nation's food supply but also contributes to foreign exchange. Zimbabwe is a major exporter of agricultural products, though drought in 1991 and 1992 considerably reduced production and necessitated food imports.

As the second-largest producer of chrome in the world, Zimbabwe also has strategic importance. But its landlocked position and its need to transport goods through South Africa are a disadvantage. In addition, Zimbabwe depends on the South African government for oil-importing facilities.

Mounting oil costs are hindering development in Zimbabwe, and the search for new sources of energy is a high priority of the government. Electric power is being developed through the Zimbabwe-Zambia Kariba Dam on the Zambezi River; and a 1600-Mw hydroelectric project, at a cost of a billion dollars, is planned for the Batoka gorge also on the Zambezi. Thermal power based on local coal deposits is also being developed and will improve Zimbabwe's energy status still further. In addition, there continues to be a search for nonpetroleum fuels—bio-gas and ethanol—as well as efforts to develop wind and solar power.

Although most of Zimbabwe's population depends directly on agriculture for a living, a small minority—which includes some 5,000 European and a growing number of African small farmers (300–400 at present)—is responsible for the highly developed commercial sector (Figure 21–5). A change during the last decade has been the increased importance of production by small African farmers who are newly occupying good-quality land. Most other African farmers are still subsistence oriented and are confined to specific communal land areas.

Communal lands are a consequence of Zimbabwe's colonial history. In 1930 land was divided between the European minority and the African majority. White farmers were allotted approximately half of the land, including the most fertile uplands; the natives' lands, with a communal form of tenure, were created out of the remainder, except for a small area reserved for African freehold farms. The communal lands continue to suffer from heavy population pressure, while the white-owned land is not all used to its potential.

The land issue is central to the reconstruction of the Zimbabwean economy for two important reasons. First, land is the basis of livelihood for most of the population, so farming improvements hold the key to higher standards of living. Second, environmental deterioration is a mounting concern in the areas of peasant farming. In the communal lands cropland has been extended at the expense of both grazing land and woodland, though not all areas have experienced the same severity of soil erosion, deforestation, and overgrazing.

Zimbabwe is a vitally important country in southern Africa. It is significant economically because of its strong mining, manufacturing, and agricultural activities. It is important politically in terms of its relationship with both South Africa and other parts of black Africa.

Republic of South Africa

South Africa is a large country in terms of area (471,000 square miles, or 1,219,890 square kilometers), population (41.2 million), and economy. Its per capita income of approximately $2,500 gives it the highest GNP of any country south of the Sahara except Gabon and Botswana. South Africa is also the only sub-Saharan nation that is not in the tropics. That location, combined with the altitude of much of the South African interior, produces soils and climate that are different from those of most of Africa. And those differences were an important fac-

tor in the large-scale European settlement of South Africa. The economic structure of South Africa is also different from that of most African countries. Almost 50 percent of the South African people live in towns (Figure 21–6). Only 30 percent of the work force is in agriculture; the remainder is in industry and services. Those are the characteristics of a country with a well-developed, integrated economy.

Demography also makes the Republic of South Africa different from other African countries. Nearly 5 million of its people are of European descent, mainly of Dutch or English origin but with a significant German component. Nowhere else in Africa is the European population so sizable. Another 3 million people in South Africa are of mixed background; they are referred to as **colored**. And 1 million people are Asian (mostly Indian), also included in the colored classification. However, the majority of the population—more than 31 million—is of black African origin.

Within South Africa both the white population, which evolved from initial settlements as early as the 1650s, and the majority black population regard the country as their homeland. But the white population long dominated the government and the economy, following a long-established policy of **apartheid**, or racial segregation. That white domination led to major conflict in South Africa and controversy throughout the world. The apartheid system was rapidly dismantled in the early 1990s (see the boxed feature Apartheid and Race Relations in Southern Africa).

Figure 21–5
Commercial vineyards in the Cape region of South Africa. Well-developed commercial agricultural sectors are evident in Zimbabwe, Zambia, and South Africa. Many Africans, however, continue to gain their livelihood from subsistence agricultural systems.

APARTHEID AND RACE RELATIONS
IN SOUTHERN AFRICA

Not only does the Republic of South Africa dominate southern Africa economically, but its former policy of apartheid has also had strong influence on the whole of southern and central Africa. In theory, apartheid meant separate-but-equal treatment of the three major racial groups in the Republic of South Africa: the 5 million or so whites (mostly descendants of English and Dutch settlers), the 3 million coloreds (people of mixed racial origin), and the 26 million Africans. In practice, however, apartheid meant strong discrimination against nonwhites—coloreds as well as Africans.

Several million nonwhites have lived in segregated urban townships with low levels of municipal and educational services. Soweto township, with its grinding poverty and recurring violence, is perhaps most well known to those outside Africa (Figure A). The so-called homelands were another device that contributed to the unique South African system. In those ten rural areas created by the white South African government blacks engaged in limited self-governance, though with a paucity of resources that rendered the homelands little more than Third World islands of abject poverty in an otherwise economically developed country. It is estimated that nearly half of South Africa's black population were forced to live in these homelands.

Under apartheid, nonwhites were not able to move into the senior ranks of many professions in South Africa, except to serve exclusively in nonwhite groups. Perhaps most telling, however, nonwhites were effectively excluded from national political processes.

Many governments around the world, including those of the United States and Canada, condemned apartheid and tried to isolate South Africa in order to force change.

After many diplomatic attempts to dissuade South Africa from its apartheid policies, economic sanctions against the country were applied by many western nations in the 1980s. The restriction on both imports and exports had a depressing effect on the country's economy for much of that period; there were also strong economic and political internal pressures to integrate the country. Finally, in the 1990s, there was a rapid dismantling of the apartheid framework. In 1994 elections brought to power the first-ever truly inter-racial government, with Nelson Mandela as president.

Mandela, the leader of the once-outlawed African National Congress (ANC), had been released from jail in 1990 after more than twenty-seven years of imprisonment. He immediately became the primary African representative in negotiations with the white government for political and economic reform. In 1991 President F. W. de Klerk introduced legislation to repeal all legislative restrictions on landownership and choice of residence, and this was followed by a political transition to majority rule. Sanctions were then lifted by all countries.

Several different scenarios seem to be possible in South Africa. One, unfortunately, includes a major confrontation between different groups of black South Africans. For example, the ANC, composed primarily of Xhosas and other tribal peoples, has had violent confrontations with the Inkatha, led by Chief Buthelezi and composed mostly of Zulus. After the elections in April 1994, this violence subsided. Under the various agreements, the homelands are being reintegrated with South Africa though some homeland leaders have resisted this process because it dilutes their power. The homeland issue is likely to be an important focus in the coming years.

This struggle among Africans has included substantial violence, but the 1994 elections were an important step in the right direction. There is an impressive pattern of change at work in South Africa with the ultimate prospect of an economically strong democratic state.

For effective economic development in Africa a strong natural resource base is a key prerequisite. An educated and trained workforce is important for a modern economy. But the recent history of South Africa (and many other African countries) illustrates the importance of the right political context. Although the transition to a democratic state in South Africa was accompanied by widespread violence, the actual elective process in 1994 was achieved peacefully. An orderly transfer of power took place from a white minority government to a government of shared responsibility, with Nelson Mandela as president and the former President de Klerk serving as one of the vice presidents. Although there may well be difficulties along the way, this political event, achieved peacefully, is vital for South Africa's economic future. Already relations, both economic and political, with the rest of Africa are changing and the "geography" of this region may well be significantly different in ten years time because of this changed political context.

Figure A
South African family, apparently part of the minority of successful black families, in the residential quarter of Soweto township, South Africa. The legacy of apartheid is poor educational services and limited economic opportunity for millions living in such townships and the homelands. The immense task for the new government will be to undo that legacy.

Figure 21–6
Johannesburg, on the South
African Veldt (plateau). With
nearly 4 million people,
Johannesburg is the largest city
and industrial center in South
Africa.

South Africa is the world's leading producer of gold, antimony, platinum, and diamonds and the second leading producer of uranium, chromium, manganese, vermiculite, and vanadium. The country is also noted for its reserves of copper and nickel. In addition, South Africa has more than 90 percent of the continent's known coal deposits, which enables South Africa to meet most of its internal energy needs and still export coal to Zimbabwe and Zambia. The mineral sector provides the leading edge in the economic growth of South Africa (Figure 21–7).

The country's southerly location also provides a strong comparative advantage in the production of fruit and vegetables for Northern Hemisphere markets. Sheep and cattle raising and the production of several mid-latitude crops serve local needs, and also provide some foreign exchange. South Africa is prosperous, certainly, but it is not using a large part of its available human resources effectively. The new political system may allow this to occur.

THE ISLANDS

The Indian Ocean islands can be regarded as either separate from or linked to the African mainland. Of the four main island groups—the Comoros, Madagascar, Mauritius, and the Seychelles—Madagascar is perhaps the most closely tied to the mainland. Mauritius and

the Seychelles lie east and northeast of Madagascar, well out into the Indian Ocean.

Madagascar

Madagascar is a poor nation with a per capita GNP of only $230. It is large in terms of area—almost as big as Texas—and has a population of 13.7 million people, which puts the little-known island republic well into the middle range of African countries.

Madagascar has a wide range of climates; different parts of it come under the influence of moist or dry air streams. Most of the rainfall is brought by northeast winds, so the northern and eastern parts of the island are much wetter than the semiarid southwest. Annual rainfall ranges from 25 to 100 inches (635 to 2,538 millimeters).

Madagascar's economic base is largely agricultural, and its wide variety of environmental conditions is reflected in its many different food crops. Rice is the most important, but there are more than fifty other significant food crops that, together with rice, utilize more than two-thirds of the country's cultivated land. Coffee, beef, and cotton are major exports, though French aid remains an important factor in maintaining Madagascar's economic viability.

Like the other three island countries to the east of southern Africa, Madagascar does not fully regard itself as African. Its historic and ethnic ties also link it to South and Southeast Asia, and its culture reflects that blend.

Figure 21-7
South Africa's agricultural systems and mineral deposits. South Africa is one of the most developed nations in Africa, possessing varied ecosystems and a diversity of minerals, which have contributed to an integrated economy.

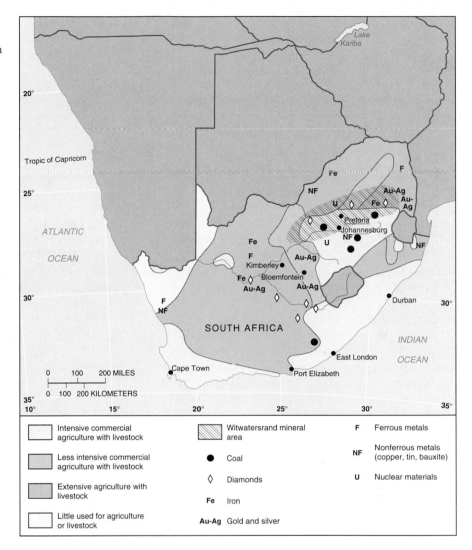

SUMMARY
Unfulfilled Potential

The critical issues in Central and Southern Africa differ substantially from those in the remainder of the continent. Although most of the people in Central and Southern Africa still depend on agriculture, the resource base for food production is much more stable in those countries than it is in the Sahelian nations. Furthermore, the substantial mineral resource base of central and southern Africa offers several countries the prospect of significant development. To date, economic development has evolved around South Africa or around exports to developed regions outside Africa. Most of the independent countries, however, have been attempting to reorganize their economies and communications to become less dependent on South Africa, though the political changes underway in South Africa may diffuse this initiative.

Both Angola and Zimbabwe have potential in terms of economic development, but each has been held back by prolonged internal conflict, which is continuing unabated in several other areas of Africa, also. In South Africa, there is hope in that with the tragic policy of apartheid finally drawing to a close the country will take full advantage of its own substantial mineral, agricultural, technological, and human-resource base.

KEY TERMS

apartheid   colored
colonialism

FURTHER READINGS
Part Seven

Achebe, Chinma. *Things Fall Apart*. London: Heinemann, 1986. A West African novel describing the trauma of colonization and early independence.

Chapman, Graham P. and K. M. Baker. *The Changing Geography of Africa and the Middle East*. London: Routledge, 1992.

Coquery-Vidrositch, Catherine. *Africa: Endurance and Change South of the Sahara*. Translated by D. Maisel. Berkeley, CA: University of California Press, 1988.

Davidson, Basil, ed. *The African Past: Chronicles from Ancient to Modern Times*. Boston: Little, Brown, 1964. A well-written general account that presents many aspects of African civilization.

Grove, A.T. *The Changing Geography of Africa*. New York: Oxford University Press, 1989. A good general treatment of the contemporary geography and development of Africa; an analytical and comprehensive work.

Hance, William A. *The Geography of Modern Africa*. Rev. ed. New York: Columbia University Press, 1975. An excellent and comprehensive introduction to the entire continent.

Monod, Theodore, ed. *Pastoralism in Tropical Africa*. London: International African Institute, Oxford University Press, 1975. One of the few volumes to present the work of both French-speaking and English-speaking researchers.

Ominde, S. H., and C. N. Ejiogu, eds. *Population Growth and Economic Development in Africa*. London: Heinemann; New York: Population Council, 1972. A valuable, comprehensive compendium on African demography.

Pratt, D. J., and M. D. Gwynne, eds. *Rangeland Management and Ecology in East Africa*. Melbourne, FL: Krieger, 1977. The best scholarly statement on this topic that is accessible to the layperson.

Sullivan, Jo, and Jane Martin, eds. *Annual Editions: Africa*. Guilford, CT: Dushkin, 1987. An annual publication reprinting articles treating topics of concern to the developed and developing world; a comprehensive treatment of contemporary events in Africa.

Thiong'o, Ng Ug I Wa. *Petals of Blood*. London: Heinemann, 1986. An excellent novel on the postindependence experience of Kenya.

Udo, K. R. *The Human Geography of Tropical Africa*. London: Heinemann, 1982. One of the first and still the best regional textbook on Africa written by an African scholar.

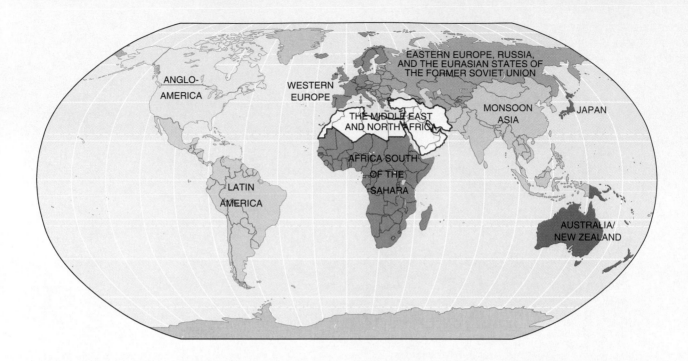

The Middle East and North Africa is a large and distinctive region characterized by internal contrasts and beset by conflicts. The contrasts are evident in levels of development, extent of dependence on oil, cultural differences, religious differences, ethnic diversity, and uneven progress toward stable societies.

The intertwining of those contrasting elements has created tension and conflict within the region. Indeed, recent years have witnessed three major arenas of violent conflict. One is the conflict between Israel and its Arab neighbors over Israel's territorial legitimacy and the displacement of Palestinian Arabs from their traditional homeland. For the first time since the establishment of Israel, these problems have lately been tackled by direct negotiations between the parties concerned rather than by exclusive reliance on hostility and violence. Another arena of conflict has been the civil war in Lebanon, where ethnic, religious, and political contradictions have undermined the integrity of the Lebanese nation-state. These divisive pressures have begun to moderate as regional solutions to the Arab-Israeli conflict emerge. The third arena of conflict involves interstate rivalries, typified by the inconclusive eight-year war fought between Iran and Iraq over resources and regional leadership. That conflict formally ended in 1990, but another soon began that pitted Iraq against not only regional rivals such as Egypt and Syria but also most of the rest of the world in a dispute over Kuwait's oil resources and independent existence.

The geography of this complex region is influenced by various elements of the Middle Eastern and North African physical and cultural environments. First, aridity dominates the region in a way that renders much of it unusable—or at least of low utility—for agriculture. Second, the existence or absence of oil in today's world ensures a difference in direction and extent of development, standards of living, and political influence in international relationships. Third, the Islamic faith remains a powerful force in structuring both society and state. Fourth, the location of the Middle East and North Africa has meant either good fortune or calamity, depending on perspectives of time and place. The area has functioned as a crossroads for Europe, Asia, and Africa, enabling an exchange of goods and ideas throughout history. The colonial influence of the late nineteenth century culminated in an invasion of Western ideas and technology, which remains a significant issue in the politics of many of the region's countries.

PART **8**

Douglas L. Johnson and Leonard Berry

THE MIDDLE EAST AND NORTH AFRICA

The residents of the Middle East and North Africa wish to control their own destiny, at a minimum, and insist that they be treated in the world political arena as a significant and independent force. In addition, increasing numbers of people in the Islamic realm hope intensely for the revival of a fundamentalist Islamic culture that will provide the legal and moral framework for society and state. Iran exemplifies that movement: the prevailing view in that country sees secular societies and states as degrading by-products of Western influence.

For simplicity's sake, we examine the various facets of the Middle Eastern and North African realm within a two-chapter framework. But that division into two subregions—the Mediterranean crescent and the gulf states—should not obscure the common themes and problems that transcend their boundaries.

CHAPTER 22
The Mediterranean Crescent

CHAPTER 23
The Gulf States

22

The Mediterranean Crescent

Regional Themes and Diversity

Overall Features of the Mediterranean Crescent

Large States, Integrated Economies

Small States, Unique Economies

The Wailing Wall in the Old City section of Jerusalem.
Because Jerusalem is a holy city for Jews, Christians,
and Muslims, its status will remain a major issue in the
relationship between Israel and its neighbors. A mosaic
of cultures characterizes this region, which earlier
functioned as one of the world's great culture hearths.

513

The Middle East and North Africa together constitute a distinctive region, within which we recognize two subregions: the Mediterranean crescent and the gulf states (Figure 22–1). We discuss North Africa and the countries along the eastern end of the Mediterranean Sea together because they share a long history of interaction with Europe. The Arabian Peninsula and countries along the shores of the Persian Gulf, in contrast, have had less contact with Europe. Before examining the two subregions, however, we should discuss some of the important similarities and differences found in the region as a whole.

REGIONAL THEMES AND DIVERSITY

Ethnicity, religion, aridity, and the interaction associated with a crossroads location have contributed common elements to the geography of this region over many centuries. Yet significant contrasts are also evident, particularly in the level of development and wealth enjoyed.

Ethnic Complexity

The principal cultural feature of the region is its rich, complex mosaic of ethnic groups. The largest single group is the **Arabs**, who have a common language, a common pattern of cultural and historical development, and a common awareness of being a single people, despite being divided into many political units and dialectal districts. More than 150 million people share the Arab culture and tradition, but almost as many non-Arabic people inhabit the region. Turks, Persians, Kurds, Jews, and Armenians, among others, dominate or are important minorities in several Middle Eastern countries; and Berbers are prominent in some North African nations. All of those groups maintain different cultural and linguistic patterns, but they remain integral components of the region.

Religion

Most of the ethnic groups share a common religion—**Islam**. The spread of that religion, first by the Arabs and later by other Islamized groups, accounts for the dominance of Arabic culture. Because Islam's sacred

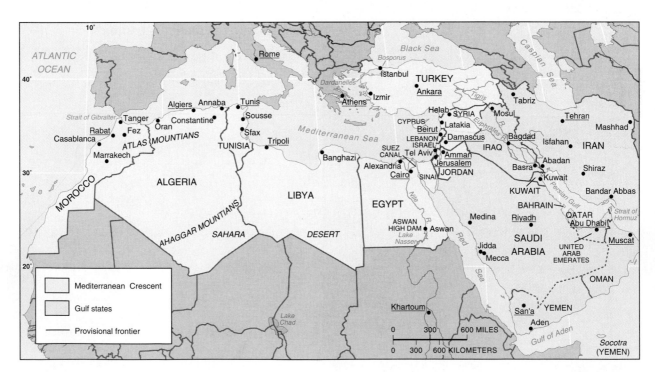

Figure 22–1
Countries and selected cities in North Africa and the Middle East. This distinctive region is strongly Arabic in cultural tradition yet does contain significant non-Arabic ethnic groups.

scripture, the Koran, is recorded in Arabic, that language has acquired a high status. Many people who today consider themselves Arabs are actually the descendants of other ethnic groups, which gradually adopted Arab culture. Of course, many other peoples accepted Islam without abandoning their indigenous culture. And some groups, such as the **Christian Copts** of Egypt and the **Maronite Christians** of Lebanon, adopted Arabic speech and culture without converting to Islam. Still others, such as the Armenians and the Jews, have remained faithful to both their ancestral religions and their cultural traditions.

The spread of Islam south of the Sahara into zones of black African culture resulted in still greater diversity of speech and ethnicity. Islam also spread eastward into Pakistan, Bangladesh, Indonesia, and the Philippines, resulting in a complex mosaic of languages, cultures, and religions. Nonetheless, the core elements of that mosaic remain the Arab people and the religion of Islam.

Aridity

Aridity is another characteristic of the Middle East and North Africa. This arid monotony is relieved only in ribbons of cultivation along the region's few rivers, around the Mediterranean coastal fringe, and in isolated areas where mountain ranges capture more moisture. Few of the region's countries, however, can use more than 50 percent of their land surface for farming, forestry, or pasture. In many, including Libya and Egypt, only 3 percent of the territory can be used for agriculture. The impact of aridity both constrains agricultural possibilities and encourages its intensification.

Crossroads Location

The Middle East and North Africa are also a meeting ground for Europe, Africa, and the Orient. With Europe the region shares many common scientific and literary traditions; much of the ancient culture of Greece and Rome was preserved by Islamic scholars. In addition, there was trade across the Sahara, as well as overland trade between the Mediterranean Sea and the Red Sea or the Persian Gulf that connected European economies with those of the Orient. But European colonization in the nineteenth and twentieth centuries had a disruptive effect on Middle Eastern society. The conflicts sparked by that contact continue to disturb the

region. The decline of Beirut, Lebanon, as a regional banking and commercial center linking Europe and the Middle East is just one illustration of the difficulties associated with a crossroads location, where contrasting cultures meet and often clash.

Contrasts

A region that stretches from the Atlantic Ocean to Afghanistan can be expected to contain a great deal of diversity. In the Middle East and North Africa no contrast is greater than that between countries with and without rich oil resources. Morocco, Jordan, Syria, and Yemen are handicapped in their efforts to modernize and industrialize because they lack petroleum. In contrast, the extremely high per capita incomes of Kuwait, Qatar, and the United Arab Emirates are made possible by oil revenues.

Other elements of diversity include contrasts between: relatively industrialized states (such as Turkey) and largely preindustrial societies (such as Yemen); large, diversified economies (such as Turkey and Egypt) and less developed ones (such as Oman); and large states (such as Algeria and Saudi Arabia) and small states (such as Lebanon, Bahrain, and Qatar). This area also exhibits sectarian fragmentation within Islam, Christianity, and Judaism, as well as traditional value systems in conflict with modernist and secular schools of thought (see the boxed feature The Reassertion of Islamic Values).

Another type of contrast hinges on the distinction between fact and fiction. Of the variety of images and myths that people in the West hold about this region, two are particularly prominent. One is associated with the cities of the coastal crescent that serve as contact points between Middle Eastern and Western cultures. Often they are pictured as sleazy and decadent, a jumble of crowded slums and fortified palaces, in which high life and low life, sophisticated culture and abject poverty, are inextricably linked. The other image is that of the heroic nomadic desert warrior, the practitioner of an austere, simple, openhanded way of life. The elegant simplicity of life in the desert, together with its apparent rejection of crass materialism in favor of such values as freedom, self-reliance, and independence, appealed to Victorian romanticism. That more than half of all Middle Easterners were and are farmers rather than nomads, and live in villages rather than large cities, has done little to dispel the images launched in literature and perpetuated in movies and on television.

THE REASSERTION OF ISLAMIC VALUES

Perhaps the most significant development now taking place in the Middle East is the reassertion of traditional values by fundamentalist Islamic groups. That powerful force, which has only recently come into view in many countries and which the Western public and popular press are just beginning to recognize, has deep roots. The Islamic resurgence represents a reaction to centuries of increasing contact with and pressure from Western European and North American values and institutions.

That contact took many forms, but the initial consequence was to erode the self-confidence of Islamic states and societies and to undermine their ability to defend themselves. The rapid industrialization of Western societies in the eighteenth and nineteenth centuries gave them military superiority over their traditional Middle Eastern rivals. As a result, the Ottoman Empire gradually lost its outlying provinces and tributary states as the **caliphate**—the secular and religious leadership of the Islamic community—proved incapable of defending the House of Islam against the encroachment of Austria, France, and Russia. Christian populations reemerged to form non-Islamic states (i.e., Lebanon, Armenia, Greece); foreign powers asserted themselves as the protectors of Christian minorities within the boundaries of the shrinking empire; missionaries, both Protestant and Catholic, attempted to win converts; and French and Italian colonists arrived to settle the best agricultural lands in Algeria and Libya. Both France and Italy considered those territories to be integral parts of the mother country, rather than colonies, and had limited respect for indigenous Islamic institutions and values.

Where military power led, economic penetration followed. By the twentieth century most of the Middle East was divided into political and economic spheres of influence or control, and the modern sectors of the economy, particularly the oil industry, were dominated by Western interests. Most **Muslims** (believers in Islam) who sought a modern education were forced to find it in schools permeated with Western values, emphasizing individualism, separation of church and state, equality of the sexes, material and technological progress, rationalism, and secular, nonsectarian nationalism. Traditional Islamic knowledge and understanding of state and society were set aside, despite protest and resistance.

Traditional voices were never completely silenced, however. And since the emergence of post–World War II movements for political independence, proponents of more traditional Islamic values have gained increasing influence (Figure A). Successful leaders of that time—such as Muhammad V in Morocco, Habib Bourguiba in Tunisia, or Gamal Abdel Nasser in Egypt—were able to use traditional values in a nationalist context to defy the Western powers. Increasingly, though, fundamentalist Islamic forces now demand a return of the *sharia*, the traditional legal code based on the Koran, in place of legal systems derived from European models. They also demand intensified resistance to Israel and increased support for the Palestine Liberation Organization, the widely-recognized political organization representing Arab Palestinians. The more fundamentalist the Islamic group or nation state, the more likely it is to oppose the prospect of peace and compromise with Israel. For to Islamic purists Israel constitutes an alien entity in the Islamic body politic. Israeli control of Islamic holy places in Jerusalem is a constant source of humiliation and a reminder of past political, technological, and military inferiority.

In each country the particular local situation has determined which forces have dominated the fundamentalist revival. In Iran in the 1970s the Shiite clergy, led by the Ayatollah Ruhollah Khomeini, spearheaded resistance to the secular policies of the shah, or king, and opposed the inequitable distribution of wealth generated by the oil economy. In Egypt a fundamentalist group on the fringes of the Muslim Brotherhood assassinated

OVERALL FEATURES OF THE MEDITERRANEAN CRESCENT

Stretching in a crescent shape from the Atlantic coast of northern Africa around the eastern end of the Mediterranean, the coastal zones of the Middle East are distinctive and distinguishable from the Islamic core areas of the Arabian Peninsula and the Persian Gulf. Several features of this coastal region set it apart: it is a zone of cross-cultural interaction; its uplands contrast sharply with its lowlands; and it has a diversity of resources (Figure 22–2).

President Anwar Sadat in 1981, in part because he signed a peace treaty with Israel. In Tunisia the primary effective opposition to President Bourguiba was confined to religious groups, until an unexpected coup within the ruling elite removed the ailing, aging president. In Syria resistance to the authority of the secular Ba'ath party, which contains a significant proportion of members of the minority Alawite sect among its leaders, is maintained by orthodox Sunni movements. And in Algeria fundamentalist political groupings pose an increasingly powerful challenge to the one-party socialist state.

The influence of the Islamic revival also extends to regions and countries outside those normally regarded as Islamic. Muslim missionaries often have a fundamentalist perspective and increasingly act to radicalize Muslim minorities. Several violent confrontations between radical Muslims and government forces in northern Nigeria are an example of that process. A variant of the theme is the fighting in southern Sudan, where Christian and animist rebels feel threatened by the government in the north, which is influenced by the Muslim Brotherhood.

In short, no country in the Middle East is without the tension generated by an increasingly intense struggle between secular and religious forces. The outcome of that struggle will determine the nature of both internal politics and international relationships.

Figure A
Men praying in a mosque in Riyadh, Saudi Arabia. Islam remains a powerful force throughout the Arab world. Fundamentalists in many countries are seeking the elimination of secular values, especially those associated with the West, and a return to traditional values.

Cross-Cultural Interaction

The coast is a zone of contact between the Middle East and Europe. Indeed, the Mediterranean Sea has more often served as a link among the lands around its shores than as a barrier between them. Greeks settled eastern Libya in the seventh century B.C. And Carthage, in modern Tunisia, began life as a Phoenician trading colony. Later on, the Romans unified all of the Mediterranean Basin into one political unit and, in the process, promoted trade, cultural contact, and population exchanges. In addi-

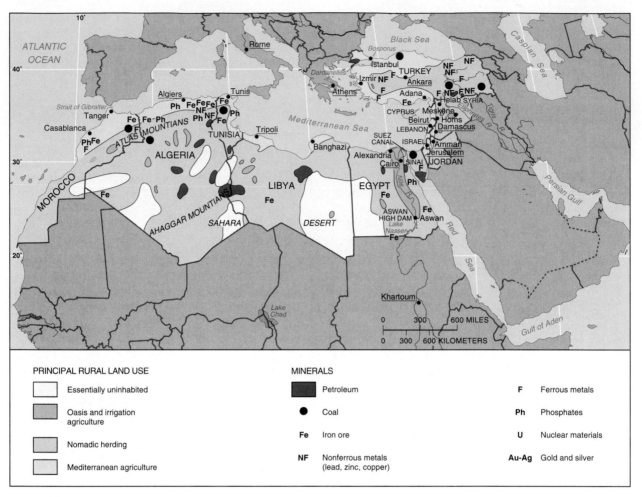

Figure 22–2
Land use in the Mediterranean crescent. Much of the Middle East and North Africa is
too dry to support much economic activity. The region's population is concentrated in
the more humid coastal sections and along the major rivers.

tion, Muslims, Jews, and Christians from all realms look to Jerusalem as a common focus for important parts of their religious experience.

The Mediterranean has also served as a permeable membrane through which have filtered the religious, artistic, literary, and scientific accomplishments of the peoples dwelling on or near its shores. In many instances cultural contact has been associated with political conflict and conquest. Alexander the Great overthrew the Persian Empire and extended Greek culture deep into Southwest Asia. Islamic expansion into Spain and the Balkans also

permanently influenced the culture and political organization of the southern peripheries of Europe. More recently, European colonial expansion in the Middle East and North Africa left a veneer of European culture, countless psychic scars, and a patchwork of political entities that still pose problems for policymakers. As a crossroads of contact between East and West and as a seedbed of cross-cultural contact, the coastal Mediterranean Crescent has acquired a characteristic diversity and complexity—an intricate, small-scale, mosaiclike texture that is both fascinating and perplexing.

A more contemporary pattern of interaction between the Mediterranean Crescent and Europe builds on some of those past experiences. Middle Eastern workers have been migrating in large numbers to overseas jobs, moving to the major metropolitan areas of former colonial rulers, in part because language and cultural problems are minimized. In the process, however, the workers are giving a decidedly Middle Eastern flavor to many of Europe's cities (see Chapter 10). The low or negative birthrates of many European countries have made it difficult for their economies to grow without those migrant workers, some of whom are adopting permanent or quasipermanent residences in Europe. Even in times of economic difficulty in the host countries, migrants have economic opportunities because the jobs they hold are often scorned by native workers. For Middle Eastern workers who have technical skills and whose language is compatible with the rest of the Arab world, the flow today is often away from Europe and toward the opportunities present in the oil economies of the Persian Gulf. But whether in Europe or the gulf states and whether selling skills or labor, the migrants from the coastal states are converting their talents and their crossroads location into economic opportunities that are less available to more isolated parts of the Middle East.

Upland-Lowland Contrast

A second feature of the coastal crescent is its contrasting lowlands, which contain centers of political and economic power, and uplands, where political, ethnic, and religious dissidents have gathered for survival. The eastern Mediterranean coast provides a perfect example of the use of mountainous uplands as refuge areas. Examples are numerous. Alawites, a minor Islamic sect, inhabit the hilly areas along the Syrian coast near Latakia. Maronite Christians dominate the mountainous central portions of Lebanon east and north of Beirut. **Shiites**—an Islamic sect that long ago separated from mainstream, orthodox **Sunni** Muslims in a dispute over religious and secular authority—and Druze (a splinter sect that is nominally Muslim) are scattered across the uplands of south Lebanon, southern Syria, and northeastern Israel. Likewise in the uplands of North Africa, the **Berber**, a non-Arabic speech and culture, survives in western Libya and

southern Tunisia as well as in the Atlas Mountains of Algeria and Morocco (Figure 22–3). All of those mountain peoples have habitually been at odds with their governments, the seats of which are in the coastal cities. Not surprisingly, the continuing presence of such regions markedly complicates the internal unity of the countries in the Mediterranean Crescent.

As physical systems, those mountain massifs also dominate the landscapes of the region. With the exception of Egypt, which derives its annual floodwater supply from the mountains of Ethiopia, the traditional livelihoods of the crescent countries are enormously influenced by their mountain ranges. The precipitation that falls in the highlands once supported the forests, now largely removed, that supplied the fleets of the Mediterranean states. As catchment areas for the perennial rivers of the region, those mountain zones are of critical importance to the agricultural prosperity of the lowlands.

Many parts of the coast and the adjacent interior lands can be used either for nomadic pastoralism or for sedentary agriculture, and at times people have shifted from one livelihood to another in response to political and environmental conditions. The forty years of wilderness existence experienced by the Israelites after their flight from Egypt is just one example of conditions that called for flexibility in livelihood systems. In the past history of the crescent region, farmers moved into drier zones when their security was guaranteed and environmental conditions were suitable, but the power base of the farmers was always the urban-oriented coastal zone. When that power base weakened and settlement retreated, the nomads pressed into potentially cultivatable zones. The fluctuating fortunes of herders and farmers in controlling the land resources of the drier interior margins of the coast has been a recurring theme in the settlement history of the region.

Diverse Resources

One other characteristic of the coastal zone is its diversity of resources. Not only can both pastoralism and widespread agriculture be practiced, but the region's position on the margins of several tectonic plates also makes mineral opportunities available. Although those resources are generally limited and are of greater importance historically and internally than they are internationally, some of the minerals are significant. For example, Morocco is the world's largest producer of internationally traded phosphate; Turkey is a major source of rare but critical minerals, such as molybdenum; and Libya supplies a large amount of high-grade oil to Europe.

Throughout the years the location of minerals and agricultural products close to the coast has made trading easy. The Mediterranean Sea, another very important resource, has facilitated the exchange of products between the crescent and Europe and has favored a mercantile and maritime tradition in the coastal ports. The more cosmopolitan and diversified character of those sites and their outward orientation sets them apart from less diverse parts of the Middle East.

Many of the region's earliest cultural and political traditions emerged in those very habitable coastal settings. Today, population centers on the Nile River, along the Bosporus Strait, in the floodplain of the Orontes River in Syria, and in northern Tunisia provide a depth and a richness in the local scene rarely found elsewhere. Few traditions have died out completely, and many fragments of the past survive to the present, increasing the variety of the coastal zone. Feuds of ancient origin as well as remnants and memories of past glories vie for attention with powerful forces promoting modernization and change.

LARGE STATES, INTEGRATED ECONOMIES

We are now ready to look more closely at three of the largest countries in the Mediterranean crescent—Algeria, Egypt, and Turkey—which have many basic similarities. Thereafter, we examine four of the smaller remaining states—Israel, Lebanon, Jordan, and Syria—as well as the possibility of a future Palestinian state. Morocco, Tunisia, and Libya share numerous similarities with these other crescent states, and they are treated simply as variations of common features.

Features of Similarity

One important common feature of Algeria, Egypt, and Turkey is that they are relatively self-supporting, as a result of three factors: (1) an important industrial sector that processes raw materials, (2) a diversified and productive agricultural base, and (3) a developed service sector. Together with a large population that includes a significant proportion of well-educated individuals, such a diverse natural and human-resource base provides the foundation for a balanced, integrated economy.

A second common feature is that a high proportion of the populace of each country lives in urban areas, the product of a long, rich history of urban life. These three countries contain several of the region's largest cities: Cairo, Egypt (6.4 million); Istanbul, Turkey (6.2 million); and Algiers, Algeria

Figure 22-3
Berber woman with children in the High Atlas Mountains of Morocco. Berbers preceded the Arabs as inhabitants of North Africa and, as highland agropastoralists, have often been at odds with lowland cultures. Berber speech and culture surface today in the highlands of Morocco and Algeria. Many also speak Arabic, and all are Muslims.

(1.5 million). Casablanca, Morocco (2.6 million), also belongs among these primate cities, which dominate their national landscapes. Massive immigration from the countryside has swelled those urban populations far beyond the capacity of urban planners to calculate accurately and beyond the ability of urban systems to absorb satisfactorily. Uncounted, underprivileged people have ballooned Cairo's population to an estimated 12 million inhabitants (though the official population is about 7 million), Casablanca's to more than 4 million. In addition, other urban centers have attained major size and importance: Ankara (2.5 million), Izmir (2.3 million), and Adana (1.7 million) in Turkey; and Alexandria (3.1 million) and Giza (2.1 million) in Egypt.

Because Algeria, Egypt, and Turkey all have large populations—27.3 million, 58.3 million, and 60.7 million, respectively—their cities serve complex functions. They are administrative, industrial, cultural, trading, and often religious centers. Their economic role is enhanced by their countries' large, well-integrated, and relatively powerful economies.

A third common feature is that each country has a rich agricultural base, which is essential both to feed the local population and to earn foreign exchange in overseas markets. Egypt's cotton, Turkey's citrus fruits, and Algeria's wines, dates, and olives are important export commodities; and the domestic food-processing industries are a significant focus of development. Nonetheless, in all three countries (particularly in Egypt, where the pressure of population is especially severe) maintaining and increasing agricultural productivity is a continuous struggle.

A fourth significant common feature is each country's appreciable mineral wealth. Algerian oil and natural gas are important world resources. The coal, iron ore, and chrome of Turkey are less abundant but provide the base for the largest heavy-industry complex in the Middle East. Egypt's oil and phosphates meet internal needs and, together with hydroelectric power from the Aswan Dam, are important bases for economic growth.

Finally, each country is characterized by a large area of semiarid and arid territory of little value to the agricultural economy. Thus, agriculture tends to be concentrated in limited areas and to be more intensive than it is in many other countries of Africa and the Middle East. Egypt—with only the narrow, fertile strip of the Nile Valley and its delta—is the extreme example.

Algeria: A Maturing Economy

More than a century of cultural conflict and discontinuity, terminated by a lengthy struggle for independence, severely interrupted the indigenous patterns of life and development in Algeria. Algeria's major cultural conflict began when the country became a French protectorate in 1830. Large-scale migration of Europeans to Algeria followed, and tremendous pressures were placed on local cultural institutions. Today, despite freedom from French control since 1962, Gallic (French) civilization maintains a very visible presence in Algeria. The resulting French-Arab conflict mirrors the long opposition of the Berber culture, protected by its rugged mountain retreats, to a succession of Phoenician, Roman, and Arab invaders. Ironically, that guerrilla opposition to the French has done much to reduce the differences between Arabs and Berbers in Algeria and to speed the assimilation of Berbers into the mainstream of Arab culture.

In some ways Algeria is similar to other oil states. It has enjoyed a large income from oil exports and has tried to use that wealth as the basis for economic growth. But Algeria has gained a position in the world far above that which might be suggested by its size and economic status. One reason for that position is Algeria's long struggle for independence from French domination. As a result of that struggle, Algeria sympathizes with and is respected by many Third World revolutionary groups. Another reason for Algeria's position is the strong and expanding economy that Algeria is building, made possible by the good mixture of resources available to the nation.

Algeria has the most diverse and integrated economy of the North African countries. With Libya, Algeria shares a wealth of petrochemical resources. And like its near neighbors, Morocco and Tunisia, Algeria possesses rich agricultural resources in the northern and coastal sections of the country. That combination of minerals (i.e., iron ore, phosphates, lead, zinc, and mercury), coupled with petroleum and farming, provides a breadth and richness to the Algerian resource base that is lacking elsewhere in North Africa.

About 80 percent of the country is classified as too dry or too steep to be productive for crops or pasture (Table 22–1). Nevertheless, the desert portions of Algeria are vital to the national economy. Of some importance are the high-quality dates produced in small desert oases for export, but the major resources of the desert are oil and natural gas (Table 22–2). Those two commodities account for most of the value of the country's exports. Algeria has been a pioneer in the production of liquefied natural gas (LNG) for export to industrialized states, with half of its LNG being shipped to the United States. To lessen that dependence on the United States, a pipeline to Italy was completed in 1981. Most of the revenues earned by the sale of oil and natural gas are invested in the northern part of the country, where the bulk of the population and the productive agricultural land is located. However, diminished oil reserves, declining production, lower prices for oil on the world market,

and inefficient parastatal industries have contributed to much slower industrial growth during the last decade and have resulted in economic stagnation.

That northern region of Algeria is relatively fertile and well watered. Because soils are often thin and slopes are steep, it is difficult to farm this potentially fertile area without encountering environmental problems. Once the granary of the Roman Empire, the area today grows wheat and other cereal crops, especially in the drier plateau country between the Saharan Atlas and the coastal mountain ranges. The coastal climate is ideal for citrus fruits, grapes, olives, and other fruits and vegetables, and European markets are close at hand. But penetrating those markets is a problem: the preferential treatment given a colonial area has disappeared, and the entry of Spain and Portugal into the European Union has put Morocco, Algeria, and Tunisia at an increasing disadvantage.

Table 22-1
Land use (in thousand hectares) in Algeria, Egypt, and Turkey.

Land Use	1976	1981	1986	1991
Algeria				
Total land area	238,174	238,174	238,174	238,174
Arable land	7,092	6,885	6,967	7,085[a]
Permanent cropland	654	625	566	568[a]
Permanent pasture	36,275[a]	31,661	31,155	31,000[a]
Forest	4,122	4,384[a]	4,252	4,050[a]
Other	190,031	194,619	195,234	195,471
Egypt				
Total land area	100,145	100,145	100,145	100,145
Arable land	2,596[a]	2,307	2,318	2,267
Permanent cropland	134[a]	161	249	376
Permanent pasture	—	—	—	—
Forest	31[a]	31[a]	31[a]	31[a]
Other	96,784	97,046	96,947	96,871
Turkey				
Total land area	77,945	77,945	77,945	77,945
Arable land	24,862	25,483	24,558	24,666
Permanent cropland	2,841	3,030	2,925	3,023
Permanent pasture	10,200[a]	9,600[a]	8,800[a]	8,500[a]
Forest	20,170	20,199	20,199	20,199
Other	18,890	18,651	20,481	20,575

Source: FAO Production Yearbook, vol. 46 (Rome: United Nations Food and Agriculture Organization, 1993).
[a]Estimate.

Outside the commercial agricultural zone, many peasants till poor soils for a low subsistence level of life. As a result, many people have left those areas to move to the coastal cities, where economic and social opportunities are greater. Also, many Algerians, as well as Moroccans and Tunisians, have migrated to France. Their labor is important to the French economy, and the money they send back home sustains the family members left behind. However, recent restrictions on migration to France place this source of income increasingly at risk.

The basis for industrial growth clearly exists in Algeria. Oil and gas resources are backed by phosphates and major iron ore deposits; and together with lesser quantities of coal, lead, and zinc, those resources form a solid base for industrialization. In addition, worker skills and infrastructure are sufficient to allow the major development initiative to remain firmly in Algerian hands. But in recent years the involvement of the central government in the economy and an excessively large bureaucracy have held back industrial change.

A distinctive feature of Algeria in its immediate postindependence years was the single-minded political strength, intelligence, and insight of its leaders. Those characteristics enabled the government to demand and receive major internal sacrifices in return for the promise of long-term benefits. Accordingly, some 40 percent of Algeria's GNP was

reinvested annually in the development of heavy industry. But the country's yearly industrial growth rate of 7 to 10 percent during the 1970s proved difficult to continue in the 1980s because a world oversupply of both oil and gas reduced prices and diminished the funds available for investment. Moreover, Algeria's oil and gas resources are not unlimited, and concern has developed that they may have only a relatively short life span.

Today, Algeria is finding that its economic growth is insufficient to provide jobs for many of its citizens. The unrest and dissatisfaction that such a situation provokes has promoted simultaneously a fundamentalist Islamic revival, street violence, a decline in the authority of the single-party socialist government, and substantial gains by increasingly powerful opposition forces in Algeria's initial experiments with a more democratic political process. In the early 1990s, when opposition forces won the first free elections in the country's history, the army stepped in to cancel the results of those elections. The consequence of this action has been a heightened level of political violence, an increased scale of repression by the government, and uncertainty and stagnation in the economy.

Traditionally, Algeria has been able to take a leadership role in the Arab League, the **Organization of Petroleum Exporting Countries (OPEC)** (a group of thirteen oil-producing nations), and the Third

Table 22-2
Estimated petroleum production in Mediterranean crescent countries.

	1980	Change from 1979 (%)	1990	Change from 1989 (%)	1992	Change from 1991 (%)
Algeria	1000.0	−10.1	797.0	+11.2	771.3	−3.9
Egypt	585.0	+15.6	873.0	+2.6	870.7	−0.8
Israel	0.7	−98.0	0.3	—	0.2	—
Jordan	—	—	0.4	—	0.1	—
Libya	1780.0	−13.4	1369.0	+21.2	1468.7	−2.7
Morocco	0.2	—	0.3	—	0.3	—
Syria	165.0	+1.2	385.0	+13.2	530.3	+10.9
Tunisia	100.0	—	93.0	−9.7	110.3	+2.5
Turkey	42.0	−25.0	70.0	+25.0	84.6	−0.7

Sources: Oil and Gas Journal, vol. 79, no. 52 (December 29, 1980); vol. 88, no. 52 (December 24, 1990); vol. 90, no. 52 (December 28, 1992).

World in general. That position of influence is accompanied by respect in both capitalist and socialist countries. As a result, Algeria was able to serve as intermediary between the United States and Iran to help settle the hostage crisis that destroyed relations between those two countries in 1979 and 1980. At the same time Algeria supports those revolutions and wars of national liberation that it views as legitimate, a consequence of its own struggle for national independence against French colonialism. Algeria's history also explains its active assistance to the **Palestine Liberation Organization (PLO)**, the Palestinian umbrella organization formed to coordinate opposition to Israel. There is reason to believe that continued international political involvement will be characteristic of Algeria, but that its influence will be directly dependent upon its ability to solve its internal political, social, and economic problems.

Egypt: Gift of the Nile

The richness of Egyptian civilization was a wonder even in Greco-Roman times, and the splendor of its scholarly institutions increased further after the Arab conquest in A.D. 640. At al-Azhar University and other religious centers in Cairo, Arab scholars were largely responsible for preserving the writings of the classical world and transmitting them to the Christian West. When the Dark Ages characterized Western Europe, the acme of scholarship and invention was reached in the universities of the Middle East. Even when political independence was lost in the region, a spirit of national independence survived and fueled the drive for complete independence after World War II.

Today Egypt is a country of contrasts. Cairo and Alexandria are two of the largest cities in Africa, but many peasants in Egypt live under relatively the same conditions that their ancestors experienced a thousand years ago. The Egyptian economy is diversified, with a wide range of basic and processing industries and many large and small consumer-oriented enterprises; but its population is growing at a rate of 2.3 percent per year, so a constant increase in productivity is necessary just to stay abreast of the population. Currently, Egypt has the largest population of any Arab state, yet less than 3 percent of its land surface is arable (see Table 22–1).

Egypt is both a center of Muslim culture and tradition and is a powerful political force, but employment opportunities for college-educated Egyptians

are limited, and many must seek work elsewhere. For example, Egypt manufactures most of the world's Arabic-language films, and its colleges enroll more than 600,000 students, many of whom come from other Arab countries. Yet more than 2 million Egyptians of all skill levels were employed in other Arab countries when the Kuwait crisis forced many to return.

Egypt's employment pattern has increased its influence outside Egyptian borders. But when oil prices decline, causing opportunities for migration to diminish throughout the region, that influence also diminishes, along with the flow of income back to Egypt. In addition, both the decline of the pan-Arab nationalism of the 1950s and 1960s and Egypt's support for the 1979 Camp David agreements, which established peaceful relations with Israel, decreased Egyptian influence by isolating Egypt politically from other Arab states. Recently, though, partly because Egypt is seen as a counterforce to Iran, several countries have reestablished diplomatic ties with Egypt.

Egypt has built its history on a limited resource base. Its agricultural resources, especially, are constrained by a lack of water and suitable soils. Because very little rain falls in Egypt, except over a thin strip of land along the Mediterranean coast, cultivation is concentrated in the valley and delta of the Nile River, where both adequate water and good soils coincide (Figure 22–4). Outside the Nile Valley significant cultivation is possible only in a few small oases. Alfalfa, cotton, rice, maize, and wheat are the main crops in Egypt; cotton is the most valuable export crop and is also the basis for a substantial textile industry. Land use is already intense in Egypt; and without significant changes, major breakthroughs to higher levels of production are unlikely.

Nonetheless, one attempt to achieve such a breakthrough was made when a high dam on the Nile was constructed in the 1960s at Aswan, creating a huge lake. That water represents the flood that previously inundated Egypt each year, providing a natural supply of irrigation water and soil-enriching silt to the fields. The Egyptians expected to increase their agricultural production in two ways. First, releasing the stored water slowly makes it possible to raise two, and sometimes three, crops a year on the same land. In addition, surplus water can be channeled into the desert to develop areas that are without rainfall—an effort called the New Valley Project.

Figure 22-4
Traditional plowing and seeding in the Middle Nile Valley of Egypt. Because of the limited rainfall, crop cultivation must be concentrated in the Nile Valley and Delta, where irrigation is possible. Not surprisingly, those are also the major regions of population concentration.

The economic and ecological effects of the Aswan High Dam have been both good and bad. Desert soils have proven more difficult to manage than was anticipated, and many development areas have been afflicted with **salinization**, an accumulation of salt in the soil that inhibits the growth of crops. In addition, the spread of year-round cropping has expanded the habitat of schistosomiasis, a debilitating parasitic disease with a complicated life cycle that affects a large percentage of the workers engaged in irrigated agriculture. Moreover, even with the water saved by the dam, Egypt faces serious water shortages in the foreseeable future; drought in the 1980s caused a serious depletion of stored water behind the dam. Thus, Egypt's situation calls for conservation efforts and closer political and economic ties with Sudan, Egypt's neighbor to the south, where new water sources might be developed.

On the brighter side, hydroelectricity produced at the Aswan High Dam has promoted industrial growth, and a fertilizer industry has emerged to restore fertility to the soils now deprived of Nile silt. Equally important, the dam has been an important symbol of Egypt's determination to develop. Thus, the dam has had a psychological effect that may be as significant as its economic impact.

Despite efforts to increase agricultural productivity, Egypt's food imports now exceed $1.5 billion annually. That amount is a significant proportion of Egypt's trade deficit and increases Egyptian incentive to achieve agricultural growth. Current efforts are reflected in plans to integrate agricultural, in-dustrial, and urban development in northeastern Egypt. Those plans envision the reconstruction and improvement of areas along the Suez Canal and in the Sinai Peninsula that were regained in the early 1980s from Israeli control. But Egyptian hopes that those areas would play the same role in the 1980s that the Aswan High Dam did in the 1960s and 1970s were not fully realized.

Egyptian industry, which is quite diversified, expanded in the late 1970s and increased its labor force by almost 20 percent. Despite that record of growth, the limited domestic-resource base places major constraints on rapid expansion of manufacturing. These limitations combined with a recession in the international economy to produce economic stagnation in Egypt by the late 1980s. Food processing, textiles, and fabricated metal products remain the major industries—reflecting the important role of agriculture in the overall economy, the central position that cotton occupies with respect to the textile industry, and the significance of imported materials. Not reflected in standard statistics is small-scale manufacturing organized on a traditional, household basis. Frequently engaging too few employees to be included in official statistics, those craft enterprises nonetheless make an important contribution to the national economy.

Turkey: Unrealized Potential

As heirs to the Byzantine (Eastern Roman) Empire, the Ottoman Turks assumed the mantle of power in the eastern Mediterranean during the mid-fifteenth century. Only when it was outstripped by the industrial development of the West did the Ottoman Empire lose its internal cohesion; and even then, Turkey retained enough vitality and creative drive to renew itself and escape colonial rule.

The end of World War I witnessed the demise of Ottoman Turkey and the start of a new, smaller, and more homogeneous Turkish state. After a revolution led by Kemal Atatürk in the 1920s, the forces of modernization cut the ties to the past. Throughout the whole process the army played a crucial role, serving as an integrating institution of national regeneration to replace the discredited Ottoman bureaucracy. In the end many old customs were abandoned, a secular state was created, and great impetus was given to industrial and agricultural development.

Turkey is unusual among Middle Eastern states in two ways. First, it possesses sufficient mineral resources (i.e., coal and iron) to develop its own heavy industry without having to import basic materials (see Figure 22–2). Second, it has a greater percentage of usable land than any other country in the region (see Table 22–1). Those advantages, combined with virtual self-sufficiency in petroleum, have helped to create the most powerful and integrated economy in the region (Figure 22–5).

Much of Turkey's development has been centered on industry, which consumes a large part of the capital invested in overall national development. Until the global economic recession of the early 1980s, Turkey's industrialization program was progressing well. In addition, concentration on basic metallurgy and textiles stimulated the development of the country's primary resource base. Despite the economic slowdown, industrial gains continued into the 1980s (Table 22–3). In 1988 Turkish industry continued to employ 953,400 workers, and manufacturing and mineral extraction generated 30 percent of the country's GNP.

Figure 22–5
Istanbul, on the Bosporus at the entrance to the Black Sea. Turkey is an urbanizing country with the largest and most integrated economy in the Middle East.

Despite economic growth, rapid population increases throughout the 1960s and 1970s outpaced the ability of Turkish industry to absorb new workers. As a result, large numbers of Turks have sought employment abroad, replicating the pattern of labor migration experienced by the North African countries. The bulk of Turkish migrant labor has flowed to West Germany, Turkey's traditional European ally, and the remittances of that labor force have been important for the economy at home.

Even though Turkey has made great industrial progress, most of its industrial products are consumed at home, and only rare minerals—such as chromite, meerschaum, and manganese—enter world trade. Currently, three-fourths of all Turkish exports are agricultural products, with cotton, tobacco, fruit, and nuts being the most important.

Much of Turkey's commercial crop production is concentrated in coastal districts that have a mild, dry summer subtropical climate, rich soils, gentle slopes, adequate moisture, good potential for irrigation, and relatively easy access to good transporta-

tion facilities. Since 1970 agricultural activity has intensified considerably in those coastal districts. Because most of Turkey's farmland is privately owned, continued agricultural growth depends on farmer recognition of the positive economic benefits accompanying a change from subsistence to commercial activities. That change in orientation is being achieved in many areas as dry farm operations are converted to irrigation, more fertilizers are employed, and more high-yielding commercial crops are planted. Such changes are assisted by liberal credit policies, government extension services, and support from cooperative societies, in which Turkish farmers are participating more frequently.

Those progressive trends in the coastal districts have not been matched elsewhere in the country. Although much of interior Turkey is suitable for cereal cultivation and animal husbandry, there are serious constraints. High elevations and steep slopes, cool temperatures, short growing seasons, and semiarid conditions limit the productivity of much of the more traditional agricultural zones. In addition,

Table 22–3
Population (in thousands) employed in manufacturing in Turkey.

Industry	1980	1982	1984	1986	1988
Food and beverage processing	133.0	133.0	131.7	135.3	141.0
Tobacco	52.8	44.4	47.7	41.0	33.5
Textiles	165.0	172.8	180.4	178.3	193.8
Apparel (except footwear)	10.5	18.4	21.9	32.3	61.5
Leather and footwear	8.7	10.9	9.5	10.5	9.3
Wood and cork (except furniture)	13.5	13.5	12.5	12.8	13.7
Furniture and fixtures (nonmetal)	3.2	3.8	3.4	4.3	5.0
Paper and paper products	17.9	18.8	19.8	21.0	21.0
Printing	10.4	11.3	10.9	11.9	13.6
Chemical products	43.5	46.4	48.5	56.2	56.6
Petroleum refining and coal products	10.0	10.6	7.4	8.2	9.2
Rubber and plastics	21.2	26.0	19.4	21.6	26.3
Pottery, glass, and nonmetallic products	58.7	59.9	61.8	70.1	78.8
Iron and steel	53.3	55.1	46.0	57.7	62.5
Nonferrous metals	20.8	21.6	21.6	21.4	21.6
Fabricated metal products (except machinery)	35.8	40.9	37.5	39.2	40.1
Machinery (except electrical)	46.7	52.4	47.6	49.4	54.1
Electrical machinery and appliances	30.2	33.1	35.0	41.7	42.6
Transport equipment	47.5	49.4	52.0	55.4	59.6
Scientific equipment	1.3	2.1	1.9	2.1	3.8
Other manufacturing industries	3.1	4.0	4.4	4.7	4.9
Total	787.1	828.4	820.9	874.9	953.4

Source: Yearbook of Labour Statistics (Geneva: International Labour Office, 1984, 1987, 1988, 1992).

gains in permanent cropland are made at the expense of permanent pastureland and the dry farmland included in arable land (see Table 22–1), the only categories of agricultural land use to decline between 1972 and 1987. That shift results in both overgrazing on the remaining pastureland and encroaching on and degrading remaining forest land.

Although the productivity of Turkish agriculture has kept pace with Turkey's rapid population growth (2.2 percent per year), the government's continued emphasis on commercial and industrial crops such as cotton and tobacco, at the expense of food and livestock production, could result in serious future difficulties. A critical challenge in Turkey's development is to extend the modernization and development that characterize its urban, industrial, and coastal districts into the still largely rural and traditional interior areas.

A tough, hard-working, and disciplined people, a strong military, and a growing agricultural and industrial base have made Turkey a powerful state. Yet that political and economic power is seldom applied outside its own borders for three reasons, all of which relate to issues that were never fully resolved by Atatürk's revolution. First, Western notions of democracy are imperfectly transplanted in Turkey. The nation was founded by a strong military leader, and the military perceives itself as both a guarantor of the ideals of the revolution and a preserver of national unity. As a result, the army has intervened several times in the national government and has consistently maintained an internal focus.

Second, Atatürk created a secular state, even though 98 percent of the population is Muslim. With 35 percent of the population still living in rural areas, the influence of the religious leadership remains strong, but the government remains secular for the time being. Before long, however, Turkey is likely to be affected by the fundamentalist current now surging through the Middle East and appealing to conservative Turks. The country may then be forced to look outside its boundaries.

Third, Turkey's ambivalent location between East and West causes uncertainty over the best foreign policy to follow. Although Turkish leaders remember traditional quarrels with Russia, a vocal minority continued to agitate for closer ties to the Soviet Union. In light of recent changes in East-West relations, it is likely that concerns over past problems will exert less influence on Turkey's future relations with countries of the former Soviet Union. In addi-

tion, even though it was Turkey's strategic location at the outlet of the Black Sea that made it a valuable member of the North Atlantic Treaty Organization (NATO), that military role is less important now. As Europe heads toward greater economic union, attention will inevitably turn to economic concerns. Can Turkey, with a foothold in Europe, claim entry into the European Union? With the bulk of its territory and population rooted in the Middle East, does Turkey want to? Turkey's in-between position is complicated further by a series of historical hostilities and contemporary economic conflicts with its fellow NATO member Greece over the island of Cyprus, control of the Aegean Sea, and offshore mineral- and oil-exploration rights. In addition, a large Kurdish minority exists in eastern Turkey. With aspirations for recognition, autonomy, and independence that go largely ignored by the Turks and the international community—but with an increasingly active underground liberation movement—the Kurdish minority issue is certain to cause future problems for development in the dry and mountainous southeastern portion of Turkey.

Caught between Europe and the Middle East, between modernization and tradition, between freedom and authority, Turkey struggles to establish a sense of identity and purpose. If the country achieves agreement on a course of action, its regional effect could be enormous.

SMALL STATES, UNIQUE ECONOMIES

Four countries on the eastern margin of the Mediterranean Sea, together with one increasingly recognized movement that aspires to full state status, present a different set of issues. In those countries agricultural and mineral resources, basic factors for many countries, are of secondary importance. They are superseded by questions of human resources, service functions, and various kinds of inflowing support for the nations concerned. Israel, Lebanon, Jordan, and Syria are the states in this group, with the PLO representing the national aspirations of the bulk of Palestinians. Syria is significantly larger than the other states (Table 22–4). But its occupation of parts of Lebanon in the 1980s, its similar problems and potentials, and its involvement in the affairs of other eastern Mediterranean states make it reasonable to include in this group.

The eastern end of the Mediterranean has a reputation as a strategic area that controls important

Table 22-4
Land use (in thousand hectares) in Israel, Jordan, Lebanon, and Syria.

Land Use	1976	1981	1986	1991
Israel				
Total land area	2077	2077	2077	2077
Arable land	325	325	346	350[a]
Permanent cropland	87	93	92	86
Permanent pasture	118[a]	120[a]	151	144
Forest	116	116	110	120
Other	1387	1379	1334	1333
Jordan				
Total land area	8921	8921	8921	8921
Arable land	293[a]	300[a]	304[a]	312[a]
Permanent cropland	34[a]	37	58	90[a]
Permanent pasture	790[a]	790[a]	791[a]	791[a]
Forest	60[a]	65[a]	70	70[a]
Other	7716	7701	7670	7630
Lebanon				
Total land area	1040	1040	1040	1040
Arable land	231[a]	210	208[a]	216
Permanent cropland	99[a]	88	90[a]	90
Permanent pasture	10[a]	10[a]	10[a]	10[a]
Forest	90[a]	85[a]	80[a]	80
Other	593	630	635	627
Syria				
Total land area	18,518	18,518	18,518	18,518
Arable land	5260	5275	5013	4870[a]
Permanent cropland	412	484	614	755[a]
Permanent pasture	8541	8356	8293	7750[a]
Forest	457	486	523	730[a]
Other	3748	3804	3963	4287

Source: FAO Production Yearbook, vol. 46 (Rome: United Nations Food and Agriculture Organization, 1993).
[a]Estimate.

nodes of communications and trade. Because routes linking Africa with Asia and the Persian Gulf with Europe pass through the area, control of those routes has long been important. Beirut, for example, was a vital air link between Europe and the East for a time, although jet travel and the political crisis of the late 1970s and early 1980s have encouraged travelers to route their flights through other intermediate points.

The religious significance of this area is also remarkable. It is the seedbed of the Jewish religion, out of which grew the various Christian denominations. In addition, the area is significant to Muslims: Mecca, located in Saudi Arabia near the Red Sea, is the central holy place of Islam; and Jerusalem, the site of the Prophet Muhammad's ascension into heaven, is a major pilgrimage center. Medieval maps show Jerusalem as the center of the world, with Asia, Africa, and Europe all focused toward it. Present power politics have greatly modified but not totally destroyed that view. From a religious and a geopolitical viewpoint, the area is still vital to the world at large.

Israel: Resurrected Homeland

Israel is a major focal point. It is unique among countries in that it became established territorially on the basis of 2,000-year-old claims and in response to Jewish persecution around the world.

That establishment on disputed land long occupied by indigenous peoples unsympathetic to the Israeli national cause was bound to be contested.

The small state of Israel, established in 1948 from the British mandate of Palestine amid considerable conflict, was difficult to defend against surrounding Arab pressures. As a result of the 1967 War, Israel was able to rationalize its frontiers (i.e., make its borders more defensible), but it did so at the territorial expense of Egypt, Jordan, and Syria. At the same time the Palestinians, who had lost part of their lands in the 1948 hostilities, found all of their traditional territory in Israeli hands after the 1967 War (Figure 22–6). That war sparked a new wave of Palestinian migration into neighboring states, and subsequent hostilities culminated in Israel's 1982 invasion of southern Lebanon, which pushed refugees from the 1948 conflict into a new round of forced migration. Thus, Israel's search for a secure and peaceful existence has involved permanent insecurity for Palestinians.

Apart from this continuing struggle to maintain and expand Israeli territory, statistics can provide some clues as to the kind of state Israel is. In an area where per capita GNPs are generally low, Israel's is $11,330, approximately ten times that of its eastern Mediterranean neighbors. Thus, in spite of a high rate of inflation, Israel is a comparatively rich country in a poor part of the world. In addition, Israel is basically an urban country: in 1986, 90 percent of the population lived in urban areas. Industry is an important part of the economy, with diamond cutting, the manufacture of textiles and woolen goods, and many other small industries providing a livelihood for the bulk of the population.

Part of Israel's wealth comes from the industriousness of its people. The farming cooperatives of Israel are especially well known; the **kibbutz** (a collective farm) and the **moshav** (a smallholders' village) are the two main types of production and marketing cooperatives that help Israel maximize production on land that is fertile only in the narrow coastal plain. Water that is moved southward from the Sea of Galilee along the national water carrier assists in the intense cultivation of citrus fruits, vegetables, and some grain crops. High-quality farm exports make a significant contribution to the economy, although only 5.7 percent of the population works on farms.

Extremely efficient use of water is absolutely necessary for Israeli agriculture and urban life.

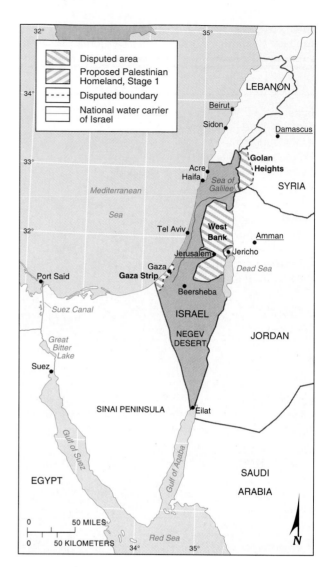

Figure 22-6

Small eastern Mediterranean states. Serious confrontation continues along the eastern coast of the Mediterranean Sea, largely as a result of the Arab-Israeli conflict. But prospects for peace are better than they have been in forty years. Recognition of an autonomous zone of Palestinian authority in the Gaza Strip and around the city of Jericho may be the first step toward a larger Palestinian Arab homeland that incorporates the West Bank. Settlement of the Palestinian issue would make it easier for Arab states around Israel to make peace and for Israel to return the occupied Golan Heights to Syria. A homeland to which Palestinian refugees could return would reduce (but not eliminate) internal conflicts present in Lebanon and reprisal attacks across the Lebanon-Israel border.

Almost all of Israel's available water is currently being exploited, and desalinization of seawater is still too expensive to be a practical alternative. One-third of Israel's area is unusable (essentially, the area of the Negev Desert), and aridity makes much of the permanent pastureland low in productivity. In order to increase agricultural yields, Israelis have become the most efficient managers of water in the world, developing innovative techniques in irrigation, hothouse agriculture, and rainfall and runoff management.

Another striking feature of the country is its high level of education. It has four main universities, and many people who immigrate to Israel from the United States, the countries of the former Soviet Union, and other countries are highly qualified academically and technically. In fact, Israel is one of the few countries that has difficulty because of the high level of its human resources; providing satisfying employment that matches existing skills is not always easy. As a result of those resources, however, the quality of Israel's technical and academic achievement is unsurpassed in some fields. For example, Israel's work on both hydrology and horticulture as well as in some electronic fields is particularly important and has enabled Israel to provide significant aid to developing countries.

With its high standards, technological sophistication, large and well-educated elite, and substantial European-derived population, Israel is actually more European in its values and orientation than it is Middle Eastern. Thus, Israel is doubly at odds with its neighbors; their political conflicts are reinforced by a clash of cultural values. In addition, that cultural conflict is mirrored within Israeli society, as Jews who migrated to Israel from other Middle Eastern countries find themselves at odds with Jews whose origins are European.

Even with such rich human resources, Israel would not be a self-sufficient state without the large flow of capital received from Jews around the world. And that support is augmented by massive assistance from governments that are Israel's allies or friends. Israel receives more foreign aid from the United States than does any other country, and both private and public assistance flows to Israel from Western European countries. The high burden of defense costs is one reason for that capital inflow, but current levels of living would probably be difficult to maintain on internal resources alone, even without the defense costs.

Lebanon: A Crisis of Identity

Lebanon, which shares the eastern Mediterranean coast with Israel, is also small in both area and population, but Lebanon is culturally complex, with a society highly fragmented along religious and ethnic lines. The political parties and armed militias that have proliferated during the past two decades have usually been based on a Christian or Muslim community or sect, many of which were historically attracted as refugees or traders to Lebanon's rugged mountain interior and strategic economic location. But the very mountains that have promised protection also place strict limits on prospects for economic growth in the agricultural sector.

As a result, the Lebanese have for many years moved out from the poor agricultural lands of their own country to become merchants and entrepreneurs in other parts of the world. Until recently, most of the traders in many African capitals were Lebanese, as were the bankers of the Arab world and parts of Africa. Large numbers of Lebanese also moved to South America, and important Lebanese communities can be found in many U.S. cities. Remittances from the overseas Lebanese population have supported many of the country's rural villages at living standards well above their usual subsistence level.

Until the mid-1970s that overseas activity was balanced by the steady growth of Beirut as the financial center of the Arab world, with more and more traders returning to their homeland. Beirut also played a major educational role in the Middle East; at the American University of Beirut, 30 percent of the student population was composed of non-Lebanese Arabs. However, because its curriculum emphasized a liberal arts orientation and because new universities were being founded elsewhere in the Middle East, American University and other Beirut institutions of higher learning lost influence to schools that emphasized engineering, science, and technology. Nonetheless, the Christian and Muslim mixture that characterizes Lebanon, together with a considerable veneer of French culture from the colonial era, made Beirut the most cosmopolitan city of the Middle East, albeit with deep social, cultural, political, and religious antagonisms that eventually flared into serious conflict.

Lebanon has no firm agricultural base, though bananas and citrus fruits grown in the coastal plain and deciduous fruits from the upland area form the basis of an export trade with surrounding Arab states. Industry is only now beginning to expand, with metal goods, processed foods, textiles, and pharmaceuticals the leading components. Before the late 1970s, Lebanon was a major center for Arab services, which accounted for 70 percent of the Lebanese national income and provided jobs for 55 percent of the active population. Moreover, until recently, oil sheikhs, who were reluctant to invest in non-Arab countries, invested in Lebanese real estate much of the capital that could not be employed in development projects at home. Thus, Lebanon was a classic crossroads economy; its location resulted in a good standard of living and a steadily expanding economy as the Arab hinterland grew in wealth.

Unfortunately, the prosperity generated was not evenly distributed. Urban residents with service-sector skills, both Muslim and Christian, gained wealth from the growing economy, but recent migrants from rural areas were less fortunate. Christians who migrated overseas sent money back to benefit their villages; but Muslims, especially Shiites from southern Lebanon, did not have access to similar support. Thus, Lebanon has a relatively low per capita GNP ($1,070 in 1983; since that date, an economy shattered by conflict and the collapse in central-government authority has prevented gathering statistics). That statistic reflects the depressed conditions of large segments of the population and masks the privileged status of other groups.

The status of the entire country changed in 1975, when tensions burst into the open. The pact that ac-companied independence from France in 1943 had guaranteed a dominant political and economic role to Christians, particularly the Maronites, the largest Christian group in Lebanon. In fact, the president of Lebanon was required to be a Maronite, whereas the prime minister had to be a Sunni Muslim. Other important political and administrative posts were also distributed on the basis of religious and ethnic affiliation. Over time, however, the numerical balance between Christian and Muslim populations changed, without any shift in the political structure. In addition, although jobs were distributed according to a community formula, the nation's wealth was not equitably shared. Adding to the unrest was a large Palestinian population that lived in Lebanon but often operated outside state control. In 1975 a civil war erupted in which many were killed, and effective central government collapsed.

Today, while Lebanon's long-term future remains cloudy, its immediate condition is improved. Although conflicting internal pressures remain, a tenuous peace has settled on the country. If a new formula for sharing internal political power can be developed and the Palestinian issue can be resolved, there is a prospect that Lebanon can rebuild its economy and infrastructure and recapture something of its former crossroads function (Figure 22–7). In this way Lebanon, thoroughly Arab, yet neither fully Christian nor fully Muslim, neither fully capitalist nor fully socialist, neither pro- nor anti-Palestinian, may once again turn its internal contradictions into positive advantage.

Figure 22–7
Street scene in Beirut, Lebanon, near the Palace of Martyrs.
Lebanon's mixture of Christians and Muslims is further complicated by fundamentalist Muslims and Palestinian refugees. The underlying antagonisms have generated intense civil conflict since the mid-1970s. The result has been the destruction of much of what was once one of the beautiful cities of the Middle East.

Palestine: A People Struggling for a Home

The **Palestinians**—or, more specifically, the Arab population of the former British mandate of Palestine, represented by the PLO—are unusual: they are a people who view themselves as a nation but have not had a recognized national territory (Figure 22–8). Areas in which Palestinian Arabs are a majority of the population, such as the West Bank and the Gaza Strip, have long been controlled by Israel. But significant numbers of Palestinian refugees also live in other countries, while many Palestinians have become citizens of other nation-states. Until recently, Israel, the United States, and a number of other countries refused to recognize the PLO and Palestinian aspirations.

It was the creation of the state of Israel in 1948 that resulted in the suppression of Palestinian nationalism and the dispersal of Palestinian Arabs among neighboring states. Many fled to the Gaza Strip, which fell under Egyptian control; to the West Bank, which was annexed by Jordan; or to Syria and Lebanon. Grouped into refugee centers, they subsisted on UN relief handouts.

Unabsorbed into the structures and economies of their fellow Arabs and unreconciled to the loss of their homes and property, the Palestinian Arabs developed a distinct national consciousness. At the same time, neighboring governments were unwilling to accept them as full members of their states; only Lebanon has granted citizenship to limited numbers of Christian Palestinians. In many cases Palestinians have refused to be absorbed because they wish only to regain their ancestral land. As a result, they have long been the most volatile element in the politics of the Middle East. Their numbers were swelled by additional refugees after the 1967 war, and the 1982 Israeli invasion of Lebanon further increased the refugee total.

The Palestinian population has never been accurately counted. Although the largest numerical concentration of Palestinians is found in Jordan, where they comprise at least 46 percent of the total Jordanian population, only in the **Gaza Strip**, a small territory on Israel's southwest border, and on the **West Bank**, the territory immediately west of the Jordan River, do Palestinians constitute a distinct majority (Table 22–5).

In late 1993 Israel signed a peace treaty with the PLO that granted autonomy to the Gaza Strip and to the Jericho region of the West Bank. Palestinians expect this to extend sooner rather than later to an expanded state that includes all of the West Bank and at least some part of Jerusalem. When and how this

Figure 22–8
Palestinian Arab children waving the Palestinian flag in East Jerusalem after the Hebron Massacre of 1994. Numerous Palestinians are found in Jordan, Israel, and Lebanon, on the West Bank, and in the Gaza Strip. Generally represented by the PLO, this national group gained its first recognized state territory in the Jericho area of the West Bank and the Gaza Strip.

Table 22-5
Total estimated Palestinian
refugee population in 1992.

	Palestinian Population	Percentage of Total Refugees	Percentage of Host Country Population
Algeria	5,000	0.1	0.1
Egypt	104,400	2.9	0.2
Gaza Strip	560,200	15.4	—
Iraq	70,000	1.9	0.4
Jordan	1,760,700	48.4	46.3
Kuwait	20,000	0.5	1.2
Lebanon	359,400	9.9	9.9
Syria	299,200	8.2	2.2
West Bank	459,100	12.6	—
Total	3,638,000	99.9	

Sources: World Refugee Survey 1993 (Washington, DC: U.S. Committee for Refugees, 1993); Population Reference Bureau, *World Population Data Sheet* (Washington, DC: 1993).

Note: Estimates at best; the sources for these figures can vary widely in the numbers reported.

will happen awaits resolution of major issues, including the status of numerous Jewish settlements on the West Bank and the reconciliation of Israel's security concerns with the Palestinian desire for a fully sovereign state with a modern army. Solving these enormous political difficulties would only be the first step in erecting a viable state with a functioning economy. If such a Palestinian state does emerge to share the space of the former Palestine mandate with Israel, its national profile will show strong similarities to that of Israel, Lebanon, and Jordan.

Jordan: A Precarious Kingdom

Jordan and the future of the Palestinian people are closely linked. Jordan's population comprises three elements: (1) Palestinians, (2) the pre-1948 settled Arab population of the Transjordan (the area east of the Jordan River), and (3) the **Bedouin**, a people who have traditionally been predominantly mobile animal herders. Jordan was originally created after World War I as a British-mandated territory with a member of the Hashemite family as its ruler. It possessed few agricultural and mineral resources and had a sparse population of largely pastoral nomads. Those nomadic herders were loyal supporters of the Hashemite dynasty and today comprise approximately half of the Jordanian army. Between 1948

and 1967, Jordan occupied large sections of the West Bank and attempted to carry out programs of industrial and agricultural development throughout its territory. But these programs were hampered by Jordan's limited resource base (see Figure 22–2 and Table 22–4). Other obstacles to development included significant land-use problems associated with deforestation, overgrazing, and soil erosion, as well as military conflicts with both Israel and supporters of the PLO.

In a sense, Jordan is a homeland in search of a people. Over time, Palestinian refugees and West Bank Arabs with Jordanian citizenship have drifted eastward across the Jordan River. But the loyalty of that Palestinian population to Jordan is uncertain. Numerically they outnumber the Bedouin, who dominate both the government and the army. Israel might prefer to see Jordan designated as the Palestinian homeland, since that solution would undercut PLO demands for a national territory in land now occupied by Israel, but this idea has found no support. However, Jordan's resource-base limitations do place severe constraints on economic development opportunities. Without linkage of some sort to the richer and better-developed West Bank territories, an economically viable Jordanian state is hard to envisage (Figure 22–9). Thus, movement toward settlement of the Palestinian issue presents Jordan with new opportunities for growth and development.

Syria: An Expanding Agriculture

Unlike its smaller neighbors, Syria is endowed with natural resources, primarily agricultural but also including small-scale mineral deposits and sufficient petroleum to meet immediate domestic requirements. Although much of the country lies in the rain shadow of coastal mountain ranges, sufficient rainfall occurs in the central and northern areas to support dry farming. There, cereal grains and Mediterranean tree crops (i.e., olives and grapes) are the important products. To the east, rainfall becomes too small in amount and too variable in occurrence to make cultivation secure or successful.

Historically, the areas east of the cities of Homs and Halab (Aleppo) have been important zones of nomadic animal husbandry, and they continue to be significant producers of animal products for the urban market. Now organized on a cooperative basis, those pastoral districts are being increasingly integrated into the cereal-based agriculture of the fertile semiarid zones along the Homs-Halab axis. Efforts to intensify production and reduce the impact of drought include utilizing mechanization, integrating fodder rotation into grain-farming operations, increasing the use of fertilizers, improving crop varieties in order to increase yields (especially of strategic crops such as cotton and wheat), and protecting and restoring rangeland productivity.

Major capital investments in agricultural intensification are concentrated in irrigation, which is an ancient technology in Syria. Lever-operated buckets, underground water-collection tunnels (*qanat*), and waterwheels have long been used to bring water to agricultural fields. After World War II, however, major efforts were made to develop the irrigation potential of the Orontes River by using modern technology. Recently, more attention has been directed to improving rain-fed farming and pastoral activities, which utilize 80 percent of the country's cultivated area.

The gains from such development projects, though important, have been minor when compared with Syria's total arable area (see Table 22–4). Consequently, attention turned to the Euphrates Valley, which represented the last major source of water available for irrigation. A giant dam, at-Tabqah, completed in 1978 and located 20 miles (32 kilometers) south of Meskene, created an artificial lake, Assad, that is 50 miles (80 kilometers) long and has the potential to provide water to irrigate 1.5 million acres (607,000 hectares). That project, when fully implemented, will more than double Syria's irrigated area, dramatically increase crop yields, and produce more cotton for export. A series of three smaller dams planned for the Khabur River valley in the northeast is intended to increase that region's irrigated acreage tenfold, matching the productive potential of the Euphrates project. Unfortunately, poor management of existing irrigated areas has led to salinization, which has meant that irrigated cropland has increased less rapidly than expected.

The Euphrates Dam could improve Syrian standards of living considerably. Its hydroelectric power

Figure 22-9
A view of Amman, Jordan's capital. Home to non-PLO Jordanians, Palestinians, and Bedouin, Jordan has struggled to develop its economy and preserve its existence in the face of numerous problems.

capacity exceeds that of the Aswan High Dam in Egypt and should help to compensate for Syria's lack of coal and extensive oil resources. But environmental and political problems have made it difficult for the dam to reach its full power potential. Drought, combined with Turkey's withdrawal of Euphrates water for its own irrigation and power projects, reduced power output from the dam by 60 percent in 1984. Thus, the dam has not yet solved Syria's agricultural and power problems in the ways that were originally intended.

In addition, construction of the dam displaced more than 60,000 farmers from floodplain areas that are now inundated by Lake Assad. Relocating those people and establishing new farms and villages have involved serious social costs, which—together with possible ecological side effects of the project—constitute the major hidden costs of this vast, technologically sophisticated scheme. The expectation is that local problems will be compensated by substantial gains at the national level and that potential conflicts with Iraq and Turkey over distribution of Euphrates River water can be avoided.

Syria's major regional significance resides in its role as a front-line state confronting Israel politically and militarily. That role has involved Syria in several unsuccessful military confrontations with Israel, a protracted and costly intervention in Lebanon, and the loss of the Golan Heights (an upland area in Syria's southwest) to Israeli annexation—a loss that Syria does not accept. The high cost of the struggle with Israel also includes a diversion of energy and resources from development, and that struggle also partially masks conflict within Syria itself, between orthodox Muslims and the exponents of pan-Arab socialist nationalism.

SUMMARY
Conflict in the Crescent

The countries of the Mediterranean crescent have attained a significant level of economic develop-

ment; and except for Algeria and Libya, that development has been achieved without the aid of readily available, massive oil revenues. Instead, Egypt, Israel, Turkey, and other Middle Eastern states have made progress by utilizing their agricultural and industrial resources. That feature of development distinguishes the crescent countries from the gulf states, which are discussed in the next chapter.

Despite economic progress, however, the stability and future of the Mediterranean crescent are jeopardized by severe political, ethnic, and religious tensions. The fascinating cultural mosaic that resulted from the interactions of the Middle East, North Africa, and Europe is also a source of conflict and instability. The civil war in Lebanon pitted different religious, ethnic, and political forces against each other and nearly wrecked the Lebanese state and economy. The Israeli-Palestinian dilemma is underlain by historic claims that are fundamentally opposed and require major compromise on both sides if they are to reach a mutually satisfying resolution. In addition, the fundamentalist Islamic revival, which has so far been the greatest in Iran, has also appeared in Algeria, Egypt, and Lebanon and will no doubt influence other Islamic countries as well.

KEY TERMS

Arab
Bedouin
Berber
caliphate
Christian Copts
Gaza Strip
Islam
kibbutz
Maronite Christians
moshav
Muslim
Organization of Petroleum Exporting Countries (OPEC)
Palestine Liberation Organization (PLO)
Palestinians
salinization
Shiite
Sunni
West Bank

23

The Gulf States

Regional Characteristics

Development and the Petroleum Economy

The Impact of Oil

Worshipers before the Kaba (center) in the Great Mosque at Mecca. Islam remains a powerful force throughout the Arab world. Fundamentalists in many countries are seeking the elimination of secular values, especially those associated with the West, and a return to traditional values.

In the minds of most people no region of the world is more intimately associated with oil than the Middle East is. And that image is not unreasonable, for more than one-fourth of the world's known petroleum reserves are found there. But the "black gold" is unevenly distributed within the Middle East; some nations, by the accidents of geology and discovery, have much greater oil reserves than others do (Table 23–1). So abundant are the proven reserves and present output of such oil producers as Iran, Iraq, Kuwait, and Saudi Arabia that they deserve independent treatment as a realm within the larger Middle Eastern region. The oil industry dominates the economies of those states, pouring more money into their national treasuries than the countries can spend, in the short run, on productive internal enterprises. With prosperity so closely tied to one resource, however, these countries must grapple with a complex array of developmental prospects and problems.

The problems are greatest in the countries that surround the Persian Gulf, or the **gulf states** (Figure 23–1). The overwhelming impact of oil has dramatically altered the economies and shaken the social systems of those countries. Nations such as Iran and Iraq, which once had viable agrarian economies and an economic structure that mirrored the diversity and integration of the Mediterranean crescent, were destabilized by the social changes that the expanding oil economy unleashed. Even countries that produce limited amounts of oil—such as Yemen, where oil production is just beginning to reach commercial scale—or that lack the resource entirely—such as several of the sheikhdoms of the United Arab Emirates—have become enmeshed in the oil economy of the region. Often their citizens migrate to neighboring countries in search of employment, thereby seriously disrupting both societies, the labor-exporting and the labor-absorbing.

Thus, all of the countries in or near the gulf have experienced change as a result of the exploitation of petroleum resources. In this chapter we first explore other similarities and differences within the region and then review the uses to which the petroleum-generated wealth has been put. Finally, we look at the impacts and changes that have followed from petroleum-based development.

Table 23-1

Population and estimated petroleum production of the gulf states.

	Population (millions)	Petroleum Production (in thousand barrels per day)					
		1980	Percentage Change from 1979	1990	Percentage Change from 1989	1992	Percentage Change from 1991
Bahrain	0.6	49	−2.0	42	+7.7	36.6	−3.9
Iran	61.2	1,280	−58.8	3,120	+11.4	3,415.3	+1.7
Iraq	19.9	2,600	−24.3	2,083	−28.1	417.3	+47.5
Kuwait	1.3	1,400	−36.6	1,080	−32.2	845.3	+521.5
Neutral Zone[a]	—	550	−3.0	315	−20.7	311.3	+141.3
Oman	1.9	280	−5.1	658	+2.8	729.0	+4.0
Qatar	0.5	470	−5.8	387	—	415.3	+7.6
Saudi Arabia	18.0	9,620	+4.0	6,215	+24.4	8,206.7	+0.6
United Arab Emirates	1.7						
Abu Dhabi		1,380	−5.7	1,587	+12.9	1,891.4	−2.9
Dubai		350	−1.1	469	+12.9	402.0	−7.4
Ras al Khaimah		—	—	10	—	0.8	—
Sharjah		10	−23.1	35	—	43.0	+24.3
Yemen	12.9	—	—	179	+0.5	176.0	−11.0

Sources: Oil and Gas Journal, vol. 79, no. 52 (December 29, 1980); vol. 88, no. 52 (December 24, 1990); vol. 90, no. 52 (December 28, 1992); and Population Reference Bureau, *World Population Data Sheet* (Washington, DC: 1994).

[a]Area of shared authority between Iraq and Saudi Arabia.

Figure 23-1

Land use and mineral resources in the gulf states. Aridity characterizes the Persian Gulf region, and much of the area is sparsely inhabited. The wealth derived from petroleum is being used, in part, to find ways to support the region's population in spite of that dryness. However, many people in the rural areas of large countries, such as Iran, have been unaffected by the oil wealth and remain poor.

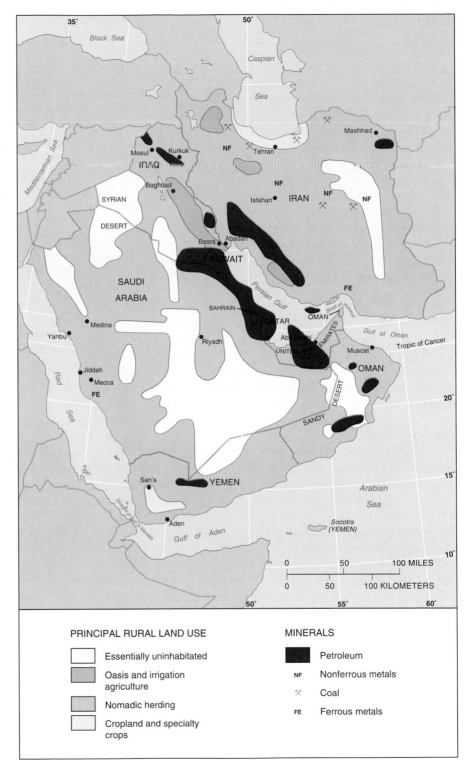

PRINCIPAL RURAL LAND USE

- Essentially uninhabited
- Oasis and irrigation agriculture
- Nomadic herding
- Cropland and specialty crops

MINERALS

- Petroleum
- NF Nonferrous metals
- Coal
- FE Ferrous metals

REGIONAL CHARACTERISTICS

Limited Resource Base

One of the most basic characteristics shared by gulf states is a limited natural-resource base. Only hydrocarbons are available in abundance; other minerals are nonexistent or are found in insufficient quantities to make mining profitable under present conditions. Only Iran possesses enough mineral reserves to support a modern metallurgical industry. However, because much of the gulf region, particularly its more mountainous districts, has yet to be explored by modern methods, some caution is justified in any assessment of the mineral-resource potential of the region. At present only petroleum and natural gas, often found in deposits of staggering amounts, are of great significance to the area.

Limited Agricultural Resources

A second characteristic of most gulf states is that agricultural resources are limited. Most of the gulf states suffer from extremely limited water supplies, which are concentrated either in highland areas, such as those in Yemen or western Saudi Arabia, or in lowland oases, where groundwater is close to the surface. Only in Iraq and Iran are substantial areas suitable for cultivation (Table 23–2). Iraq has both rain-fed agriculture in the north and irrigation potential in its arid south, based on the Tigris and Euphrates rivers. In Iran the mountains and the Caspian seacoast receive appreciable rainfall, but the central core is very arid. And even in Iraq and Iran, less than one-fourth of the total land surface can be cultivated. In other gulf states slopes are too steep or rainfall is too limited for nonirrigated agriculture.

The traditional **qanat** system of tapping deep groundwater and bringing it to the surface by gravity flow originated in Iran. It is an ingenious response to water shortage and is most applicable on **alluvial fans**, areas deposited by rivers at the base of mountains. But the qanat system can also be used to bring water long distances to regions far from the mountain water sources.

Population growth, agricultural intensification through irrigation, and urbanization all place great pressure on local water supplies. Overexploitation of groundwater, waste disposal, the economic limitations of desalting ocean water, and salinization of irrigated soils are all problems that relate to the region's limited water supplies.

Low Population Density

A third characteristic of most gulf states is low population density and small total population (see Table 23–1). Exceptions do exist, however; both Iraq and Iran have large populations that dominate the regional scene, and some of the small states have very high population densities. Moreover, even in countries with low overall population densities, the effective density is much higher because the population is concentrated in small, highly productive zones. Thus, in Abu Dhabi, a part of the United Arab Emirates (UAE), approximately three-fourths of the emirate's total population is concentrated in one large urban area of the same name. The contrast between small nodes of dense population with high levels of economic activity and the vast expanses of essentially uninhabited space characterizes the landscapes of the gulf states.

Weak Urban Traditions

A fourth characteristic is that until oil development created new employment opportunities and sparked massive population movement to a few urban centers, much of the population in the region was engaged in traditional livelihood activities. These primarily included oasis agriculture, rain-fed farming in the more mountainous areas, and pastoral nomadism. Thus, urban traditions are generally weak in the oil-rich states, and the educational and technological sophistication of the bulk of the population is limited. That characteristic stands in sharp contrast to the urban sophistication and historical importance of the main urban centers of the large states in the region—such as Tehran, Isfahan, Shiraz, Mashhad, and Qum in Iran and Baghdad, Basra, and Mosul in Iraq. In the smaller, more traditional states of the Arabian Peninsula, however, skills are almost entirely in the traditional sector of the economy and are unsuited to employment in many aspects of the oil industry.

That shortage of necessary skills has serious political consequences. It encourages the importation of skilled personnel from industrialized countries—as well as from India, Pakistan, and Palestinian areas—to fill specialized job niches. Dissatisfaction with that situation has led most of the oil-producing states to engage in vigorous educational and job-training activities in an effort to replace foreign experts with local personnel (Figure 23–2).

Table 23-2
Land use (in thousand hectares) in selected gulf states.

Land Use	1976	1981	1986	1991
Iran				
Total land area	164,800	164,800	164,800	164,800
Arable land	15,330	13,550[a]	14,100[a]	14,100[a]
Permanent cropland	620	730[a]	880[a]	950[a]
Permanent pasture	44,000[a]	44,000[a]	44,000[a]	44,000[a]
Forest	18,000	18,000[a]	18,020[a]	18,020[a]
Other	85,650	87,320	86,600	86,530
Iraq				
Total land area	43,832	43,832	43,832	43,832
Arable land	5,100[a]	5,250[a]	5,250[a]	5,250[a]
Permanent cropland	185[a]	189[a]	200[a]	200[a]
Permanent pasture	4,000[a]	4,000[a]	4,000[a]	4,000[a]
Forest	1,920[a]	1,910[a]	1,890[a]	1,880[a]
Other	32,532	32,388	32,397	32,407
Kuwait				
Total land area	1,782	1,782	1,782	1,782
Arable land	1	2	4	5[a]
Permanent cropland	—	—	—	—
Permanent pasture	134	134	134	136[a]
Forest	2	2	2	2[a]
Other	1,645	1,644	1,642	1,639
Oman				
Total land area	21,246	21,246	21,246	21,246
Arable land	13[a]	13[a]	15[a]	16[a]
Permanent cropland	25[a]	28[a]	35[a]	45[a]
Permanent pasture	1,000[a]	1,000[a]	1,000[a]	1,000[a]
Forest	—	—	—	—
Other	20,208	20,205	20,196	20,185
Saudi Arabia				
Total land area	214,969	214,969	214,969	214,969
Arable land	1,680[a]	1,940[a]	2,150[a]	2,300[a]
Permanent cropland	70	73	75[a]	75[a]
Permanent pasture	85,000[a]	85,000[a]	85,000[a]	85,000[a]
Forest	1,520[a]	1,200[a]	1,200[a]	1,200[a]
Other	126,699	126,756	126,544	126,394

Source: FAO Production Yearbook, vol. 46 (Rome: United Nations Food and Agriculture Organization, 1993).
[a]Estimate.

International Relationships

A fifth characteristic shared by the gulf states is the overwhelming importance of the oil resource to international relationships. The size of the oil deposits in the area is staggering. More than two-thirds of the known oil reserves outside North America, the countries of the former Soviet Union, and Eastern Europe are found around the Persian Gulf. Saudi Arabia alone may possess more oil reserves than any other nation—perhaps one-third of the world's reserves—and it is already one of the world's top three largest producers. Iran, Iraq, Kuwait, and Oman are also major regional oil producers (see Table 23–1), although both Iraq and Kuwait's output have been adversely affected by the impacts of the Gulf War.

Figure 23-2
Women of Iran in traditional dress learning how to type. Modernization requires new skills and often includes changes in life-style. In Iran such changes may run counter to the fundamentalist movement, which encourages a return to the culture and values associated with traditional Islam.

Beginning with the discovery of oil in Iran in 1908, the pattern of location-and-development has spread southward through the coastal regions of the Arabian Peninsula. Not only have new petroleum deposits been found, but knowledge of the areal extent and extractable quantity of oil in existing deposits has also grown rapidly. In light of improvements in the technology of recovery, coupled with the traditional tendency to understate or otherwise obscure the reserve capacity, the continued dominance of the gulf states in the world petroleum economy seems assured for the foreseeable future.

During the 1980s it appeared that the gulf states' dominance in petroleum production might diminish. A combination of global economic stagnation and energy conservation reduced demand significantly in some industrialized countries. In addition, new petroleum deposits were located in other parts of the world. Moreover, the political turmoil in Iran and the prolonged war between Iran and Iraq damaged the production, refining, and oil-transportation facilities in both countries (see the boxed feature Conflict in the Gulf). At the same time other gulf states were forced to reduce their output in order to maintain high prices and conserve oil reserves for possible development of petrochemical industries.

Despite all of those factors, however, the continued vulnerability of the world economy to any fluctuation in gulf oil output was reflected in the dramatic rise in oil prices that occurred in industrialized countries when the Kuwait crisis occurred in 1990.

The dominance of the world's oil supply, as well as the increasing importance that has accompanied that dominance, has allowed most oil-producing states to participate directly in their own oil operations, thus reversing previous arrangements. In the early years of development, foreign countries, often operating in a consortium such as Aramco (partly owned by several American oil firms), received concession rights to explore defined areas. Most gulf-state revenues were then generated from concession sales, royalties, and taxes paid on the oil that was extracted and exported. Local governments had few skilled administrators, and oil companies had a monopoly on extractive technology and market distribution in industrialized states. In addition, the impoverished and politically weak states of the gulf region lacked the capital to develop their own oil resources.

Gradually, that situation changed. As administrative and technical skills were accumulated and a better understanding of the intricacies of oil economies developed, Middle Eastern countries demanded more favorable agreements with the oil companies. Tough new leaders appeared, and increased percentages of profits were returned to national treasuries. Greater pressure was placed on oil companies either to develop their concessions or to relinquish them to someone who would, and many countries nationalized at least a controlling interest in the firms that were developing their resources. In the world market, demand for oil outstripped the supply. Thus, nationalization and dramatic increases in oil prices took place in tandem, a combination of conditions unlikely to recur in the near future.

Local Impact of Oil Wealth

One final characteristic of the gulf states is the tremendous impact that oil revenues have had on local societies and economies. No state in the region has been able to isolate itself from oil wealth and the stress it places on indigenous social and cultural systems. As a result, controversy has arisen over the role of traditional values in governing contemporary life. The wave of fundamentalist Islamic revival that was responsible for much of the opposition to the oil-rich shah of Iran—who was deposed in 1979—stresses the importance of traditional values and patterns of behavior in opposing Western-style modernization. The more rapid and extreme the pressure for change, the more violent is the reaction from traditional centers of authority and belief. In Iran the response to secular modernization and nationalism has been so strong that it has swept away much of the new in its affirmation of traditional practices.

Dependence on Nonregional Suppliers

One additional characteristic that is not equally shared by all of the gulf states but is an important and disruptive force in most is an increase in dependence on nonregional suppliers for basic necessities. Much of the food consumed in the gulf states today is imported, and in many countries a large part of the labor force is foreign. Iran—by virtue of its size, diverse agrarian resource base, and large population—has been more immune to those pressures. In Iraq, however, large numbers of agricultural workers from Egypt enabled Iraqis to pursue industrial and military employment, until the foreign laborers were forced to leave in the early stages of the Kuwait crisis. Thus, as a consequence of oil development, none of the gulf states have been able to remain isolated.

DEVELOPMENT AND THE PETROLEUM ECONOMY

The discovery and development of vast petroleum deposits have had a drastic impact on the economies and sociopolitical systems of the oil states. Large petroleum outputs and soaring oil prices have moved such former backwaters as Kuwait, Abu Dhabi, and Oman into international prominence. Formerly impoverished, the oil-producing states now face the task of coping rationally with an embarrassment of riches. And although abundance has been the watchword of the recent past, the long-term future is by no means assured. Smaller states, such as Oman, have sufficient revenue for the present but must use their money wisely to prepare for the day when oil revenue is no longer available. Diversification of oil-based economies, development of industrial processes that do not depend on oil, and rejuvenation of often-sluggish agricultural sectors are obviously high-priority items in the gulf region.

The gulf states have dealt with the eventual decline in oil revenues in two ways. Their first approach has been to invest petroleum income internally both in development projects that generate long-term income and employment and in social services that improve material well-being in the short term. The second approach has been to invest in overseas enterprises the capital that cannot be usefully absorbed internally.

Internal Investment of Petroleum Income

Large sums of petrodollars—the wealth gained from oil resources—are currently being expended to improve infrastructures in the gulf states. Ports have been built, such as Doha in Qatar, where none existed before. And investments in airports, highways, sewer systems, water systems, and pipelines have drastically changed the appearance of most oil states. Housing projects are also common. For example, Oman is rebuilding its capital, Muscat, and in the process is destroying much traditional architecture in order to construct modern housing units for its growing urban population. Most citizens see that change as an inevitable and progressive aspect of modernization.

Substantial sums are also being invested in agricultural improvements. In many oil states desalinization plants are now in operation, providing water not only for drinking but also for irrigation of

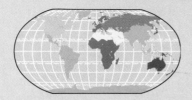

CONFLICT IN THE GULF

The disputes that make the contemporary Persian Gulf area a volatile and unpredictable political setting mirror many of the unsettled issues influencing the entire region of the Middle East and North Africa. Underlying all else is that most Arabs think of themselves as part of one people, whose unity has been artificially disrupted by colonial boundaries. Thus, a threat to one Arab country, particularly when that threat comes from a non-Arab state, is regarded as a hostile act directed at all Arabs. But only about one-third of all Arabs live in countries that possess rich oil resources, and even in those wealthy countries the income from oil revenues is unequally distributed among the citizenry. Consequently, gulf states with great oil incomes are often viewed with hostility and envy by less fortunate and more dependent neighbors, even by fellow Arabs. Disagreements also exist between those with socialist and secular political ideologies and those who advocate a return to fundamental religious structures and controls. In addition, the unsettled conflict between Israel and the Palestinians exerts an important influence on the geopolitical scene. Thus, when nationalism, religion, political ideology, and equity issues are all mixed together, the situation that results is highly explosive.

Those volatile components have produced several notable explosions. Some, such as the struggle of the Kurds for an independent homeland, have remained confined and relatively isolated. Others, like the two major disputes of the last decade, have been broader based and have had more widespread impact.

Throughout most of the 1980s, Iran and Iraq engaged in a deadly struggle for dominance in the gulf. The conflict was initiated by an Iraqi invasion of Iran in 1980, but a long history of disputes between the two countries preceded the outbreak of fighting. The immediate reason for the conflict was disagreement over control of the Shatt al-Arab waterway, which is Iraq's only outlet to the sea and also provides primary access to Iran's oil refinery at Abadan. A 1937 treaty had given control of the vital waterway to Iraq; but in the late 1960s, when Iran felt strong enough militarily, it asserted its right to control the Shatt al-Arab and refused to submit the dispute to arbitration. Iraq was not then strong enough militarily to contest that unilateral decision, especially since it was occupied in fighting the rebellious Kurds, also supported by Iran, in northeastern Iraq.

In 1979, however, when the monarchy of Shah Mohammad Reza Pahlavi collapsed in Iran, undermined by a fundamentalist Islamic revolution, Iraq's secularist government, led by Saddam Hussein and his Ba'th party, tried to capitalize on Iran's internal chaos by invading western Iran. Saddam hoped to regain control of the Shatt al-Arab, end Iranian occupation of disputed islands in the Persian Gulf, suppress the Kurdish independence movement, and stop anticipated Iranian agitation among Iraq's Shiite population. A collapse of the Iranian government and state would have been an additional bonus.

The Iraqis failed to meet any of those objectives. Instead, a revitalized and enraged Iran forced an Iraqi withdrawal from most Iranian territory and followed with a series of costly assaults aimed at blocking Iraq's access to the gulf and capturing the important southern city of Basra. Iran also hoped to drive out a leader, ruling party, and state structure that it regarded as evil and non-Islamic.

The battle raged inconclusively for many years. Iranian "human wave" attacks were met by Iraqi defensive tactics that featured elaborate entrenchments, dug-in tanks and artillery, and the use of chemical weapons. Iraq also employed destructive missile attacks against Iranian cities in an effort to weaken civilian morale. The losses sustained by both sides were huge; some estimates suggest that more than 1 million casualties occurred, with Iran suffering more than half of the total. Eventually, the brutal, grinding conflict culminated in a cease-fire in 1988, with neither country having the will or the resources to gain its objectives.

Less than two years later, Iraq's ambitions prompted another military adventure. On August 2, 1990, after ar-

vegetables to help feed the burgeoning urban populations. That type of agricultural operation, while not economically sound, is one way in which almost unlimited financial resources can help to reduce food imports. In Saudi Arabia vigorous attempts have been made to diversify agricultural output by encouraging cereal and vegetable production. In addition, artesian wells have been drilled there to expand the agricultural area and should result in production increases.

Unfortunately, few of those agricultural development schemes are practical in economic terms, al-

ticulating an escalating series of grievances and demands, Iraq sent its troops into Kuwait and six days later announced its annexation of Kuwait. The response of the international community was immediate; a series of UN resolutions condemned the invasion, applied economic sanctions, and authorized the use of force to evict Iraq if it failed to withdraw. The **Gulf War** followed.

For the next six months both sides assembled troops, moved in supplies, and prepared for a war that no one really wanted. The United States contributed most of the coalition forces, though substantial contingents came from Great Britain, Egypt, Syria, France, and Saudi Arabia, as well as smaller, symbolic units from other countries. Military conflict broke out on January 17, 1991, when coalition air forces began systematically bombing military and infrastructure targets in Kuwait and Iraq. After a short and decisive ground battle, the coalition forces were victorious. United States forces withdrew by mid-1991, yet many loose ends remained unresolved. These included international supervision of

Iraq's military capability, security and autonomy for Iraq's Kurdish minority, and resolution of conflicting border claims between Iraq and Kuwait.

The long-term prospects for stability in the region remain bleak. The ecological consequences of the war will continue for a long time: military vehicles disturbed land surfaces and destroyed vegetation, oil spills and blown-up wells polluted both terrestrial and aquatic ecosystems, and land mines and ordinary refuse pose long-term management problems (Figure A). In addition, changes in both internal governmental structures and state boundaries can be expected. And the original issues—inequitable distribution of oil wealth, disagreement between modern and traditional forces, the status of the Kurdish minority in Iraq and neighboring states, and final settlement of the Arab-Israeli conflict—remain unresolved. When the hostilities from even more recent wars are added to the equation, we can see that a just and lasting peace in the Persian Gulf area is a complex objective.

Figure A
Burned-out oil storage tanks near Kuwait City after the Gulf War. The human and environmental destruction that followed Iraq's annexation of Kuwait demonstrates the intensity of conflict that can be generated in this region.

most all of them result in considerable social disruption, and most require a level of skill that is beyond the experience of local residents. In addition, the technology employed frequently brings with it serious land-management problems. Many of the irrigation schemes in Iraq, for example, have caused serious salinization of the soil as the application and drainage of irrigation water has been mismanaged. Both continued government subsidies and the extensive involvement of expatriate labor and expertise have been required to keep many projects from collapse.

Currently, little effort is being directed toward building on areas of local expertise. Especially neglected is the pastoral sector, where considerable traditional experience still exists and where past use of low-productivity rangeland has been well managed. Today, most gulf states import their meat from industrialized countries, such as Australia, even though the population prefers to consume local sheep, now largely unattainable at a reasonable price.

In Oman the investment of oil revenue in agricultural development is especially crucial because existing oil reserves are expected to be depleted early in the twenty-first century and prospects of additional discoveries are not positive. Because agricultural use of the land in Oman is limited by the country's small and unreliable rainfall, great expansion of farm holdings is not possible. Consequently, Oman aims to achieve food self-sufficiency both by improving the efficiency of existing agricultural systems and by developing underground water resources. Projects now underway include improvement of marketing and transportation facilities, discovery of new and more productive plant strains, control of plant diseases, and use of fertilizers and mechanized equipment wherever they meet the needs of local farming traditions. Investment in the agricultural sector is necessary in the oil-producing states to ensure economic viability in the future, yet it becomes less likely when low-cost food supplies can be imported from abroad.

Industrial development is also taking place in the gulf states. First priority is frequently given to the building of cement factories, in order to support the construction industry. Also common are petrochemical plants that produce fertilizers, chemicals, and plastics, as well as plants that liquefy gas for export. In addition, there are many consumer-oriented enterprises, including soft-drink bottling plants, flour mills, fish-processing establishments, and textile-weaving firms. Craft traditions often give focus to small-scale industrial development that caters to the tourist and export trade. The uniquely designed silver jewelry of Oman is one example. In many oil-rich states carpets, slippers, pottery, brass, copperware, and leather products, such as hassocks, unite productive development and cultural continuity.

Few resources to support heavy industry are known. Mineral exploration, however, is in its infancy, and major discoveries may yet occur. Reports have circulated of major finds of gold, silver, nickel, and copper in mountainous western Saudi Arabia. If those reports are confirmed, Saudi Arabia may be able to translate its oil wealth into a diversified economic base that includes indigenous mineral-based industry.

The gulf states are also attempting to overcome their shortages of skilled workers. Almost every country has invested in modern universities as well as the rapid development of a primary and secondary school system. To staff those systems, numerous foreign teachers have been hired, often recruited from more educationally advanced countries such as Egypt. Large numbers of students, however, also study abroad under governmental contract. When they return home, they are channeled into decision-making positions at all levels of the government. That newly acquired expertise underlies both the rapid replacement of foreign personnel in the larger oil-producing states of Iraq and Saudi Arabia and the tougher and more aggressive posture of gulf-state governments in dealing with the international oil companies.

Petrodollar Investment Overseas

Faced with an inability to absorb all of their oil revenues in internal investment projects, oil-producing states are seeking investment opportunities overseas. In some cases such a transfer of funds represents the actions of wealthy private investors, but most frequently it reflects the actions of the governments. Increasingly those transfers of capital have involved the purchase of property, banks, farmland, or industrial enterprises in industrialized countries. Thus, the governments of oil-producing countries have become active investors in the industrial infrastructure of oil-consuming countries.

THE IMPACT OF OIL

Because of the extraordinary economic importance of the gulf states to the world economy, oil revenue will continue to have a profound impact for at least the next few decades. That impact is most pronounced in three areas: international political relationships, internal social and economic conditions, and internal political structures.

Changing Power Relationships

Oil wealth has altered the world's balance of power in several ways. For one thing, most of the oil states are now able to use their rapidly accumulating wealth to purchase arms with which to modernize their military forces. Possession of sophisticated weaponry made it possible for Iraq to attack Iran in 1980 and prompted other Arab states to purchase arms to counterbalance Iraq's power, as well as that of Israel. The result has been an arms race in the gulf states, in which the industrialized nations supply weapons to various opposing factions. That those weapons can also be used on brother Arabs was demonstrated by Iraq's invasion of Kuwait in 1990.

The region's dominance in OPEC also gives it substantial power on the world political scene. Proposals to raise prices or threats to embargo oil shipments to supporters of Israel have sent tremors through the industrial world. The oil-producing states are clearly aware of their position of influence and are not afraid to use it. The psychological satisfaction derived from such a new and superior political position explains much of the contemporary behavior of these states. They can no longer be ignored or dominated; they must be dealt with as countries of great power and influence.

The gulf states' position of influence makes them important to countries around the world. During the cold war both the Soviet Union and the United States competed for influence in the region, and any change in the internal politics of the region still takes on global significance. The immediacy and near unanimity of international opposition to Iraq's invasion and forced annexation of Kuwait was unprecedented, as was the readiness of both Western and Middle Eastern countries to send troops to defend Saudi Arabia and to force Iraq to disgorge its conquest. That extraordinary level of interest and concern was a measure of the geopolitical significance of the gulf states in world affairs.

The emergence of the **Gulf Cooperation Council**—including Saudi Arabia, Kuwait, Bahrain, Qatar, the United Arab Emirates, and Oman—as a regional organization was a local response to the need for a unified approach to common security concerns. But the council's relative lack of military power means that it must rely on support from other countries.

Changing Social Conditions

Developmental growth fueled by oil wealth has brought massive changes to the societies of the oil states. One important change has been rapid urbanization. Attracted by new job opportunities, social welfare programs, and an atmosphere of excitement and diversity, rural folks have flocked to urban centers. Doha, the capital of Qatar, went from insignificant village status to more than 250,000 inhabitants in a period of twenty-five years. Similar growth has taken place in the capitals of most of the region's states and sheikhdoms: Baghdad, Iraq, now exceeds 4 million; Tehran, Iran, is a metropolis of more than 8.0 million; and Riyadh, Saudi Arabia, has passed the 1.3 million mark. In some of the sheikhdoms much of the population lives in the capital city; overall, nearly one-third of the 1.7 millon inhabitants of the United Arab Emirates reside in Abu Dhabi, the capital. Manama, Bahrain, is an urban center of 150,000, and that, too, represents almost one-third of that state's population. In those instances city and state nearly coincide (Figure 23–3).

Secondary cities have also served as a focus of regional migration in the large gulf states—for example, Mosul and Basra in Iraq; Isfahan, Tabríz, and Mashhad in Iran; and Mecca and Jidda in Saudi Arabia. Much of the growth of those cities has been accompanied by the erection of shantytowns and other temporary housing on the outskirts of the urban areas. The sanitary and health problems that have resulted from excessive crowding are gradually being relieved as oil money is invested in improved housing and infrastructure.

As centers of economic growth and change, the expanding cities are also the scenes of cultural conflict. Many rural migrants have difficulty adjusting to urban life in the gulf states, just as their counterparts do in other parts of the world. Moreover, traditional Islamic and customary values are receiving their strongest challenge in the urban areas. Bombarded by a variety of exotic stimuli—ranging from the material possessions of the industrialized West to the clothes, movies, and behavior patterns of the foreign employees of oil and construction firms—the citizens of the oil-producing states have been forced to adjust to a new social setting (Figure 23–4).

Figure 23-3
The city of Abu Dhabi in the sheikhdom of Abu Dhabi, United Arab Emirates. The oil
boom has led to rapid urbanization. Fast-growing cities exhibit both the modernization supported by oil wealth and the shantytowns of poor migrants. In the countries
with small populations, such as the emirates, the majority of the population may live
in the capital city.

A conflict of values can produce serious social strains. Traditional leaders often react violently to apparent violations of cultural and social norms. In Iran much of the opposition to the shah was guided by religious leaders who objected to the pace and direction of social change. When they gained power, one of their first actions was to make religious law the basis for social relations and the legal system. The resurgence of funda-mentalist Islamic approaches to social organization represents a profound challenge to the secular, modernist, Western-inspired governments of the region.

Equally profound are differences in work habits and social priorities. New urban arrivals seldom ac-cept Western notions of the sanctity of time, and they often apply their financial gains to social needs, such as the price of a bride or the obligations of kin, rather than to savings or job advancement. An inad-equate understanding of respective cultural values easily results in tension between native workers and foreign employees.

Great distinctions in income and status have also appeared as a result of the oil boom. Although some of the newfound wealth has filtered down to lower social levels, much of the income gained is eroded by an inflationary spiral triggered by oil develop-ment and accelerated imports. Individuals close to the import trade, those serving as local representa-tives of foreign firms, and professionals of all sorts have benefited the most from petroleum growth. The unskilled have been left behind. Some states—Kuwait, for example—have instituted a progressive policy of free social services to improve living con-ditions, but others have been less farsighted. Often, the gap between the ruling elite and the bulk of the population is wide, a condition that is particularly evident in states with low population densities and massive oil revenues but a characteristic that is also found in the region's more populous states (Figure 23–5).

Changing Political Allegiances

Social unrest stemming from cultural change and in-come inequities casts shadows over the political fu-tures of many of the oil states. Opposition to the central governments in many of those countries is coming from a variety of sources, including ethnic and religious minorities within the state, traditional leaders who are alarmed at the changes that are tak-ing place, rural people who feel neglected by distant governments, and modernist forces that wish to ac-celerate the pace of change and radically restructure society. In addition, many oil states have large numbers of foreign workers within their jurisdiction who feel no particular loyalty to the existing government. The result is a highly unstable set of conditions that could explode into conflict at any moment.

The **Kurds** are an example of an ethnic minority in Turkey, Iraq, and Iran that has long struggled for greater autonomy, either within the structure of the existing states or through complete independence. In Iraq the Kurdish population of the north was engaged for years in armed rebellion against the Arab-dominated central administration. Although a desire for greater regional autonomy was the apparent motive, increased access to revenue from the northern oil fields in or near Kurdish territory was certainly an underlying motivation.

In addition, revolutionary Iran has many sympathizers in the nonorthodox, Shiite religious minorities in the gulf-state region. Thus, Iran's emergence as a regional religious power has numerous implications. Equally significant are the military and technological capabilities developed by Iraq during the 1980s, which forced its Arab neighbors to ally themselves with outside political and military powers in order to confront Iraqi aggression. Caught between a secular and aggressive Iraq, a religiously zealous Iran, and the economic interests of the Western powers, the traditionalist societies of the gulf states are finding themselves in a perilous situation. Even with the liberation of Kuwait and the present limitations placed on Iraqi military power, the likelihood

Figure 23-4
The stock exchange building in Kuwait City, showing a reflection of the nearby state mosque. Taken prior to the occupation by Iraq, this photo evidences the contrast between modern and traditional influences brought about by oil wealth.

Figure 23-5
A camel caravan resting near an oil derrick in Saudi Arabia. The visual contrast between traditional and modern is often striking in the gulf states.

of confrontation over the political future of the gulf states remains great.

Equally probable are governmental changes as a result of military coups. Young officers in many of the oil states possess nationalistic and pan-Arab ideals. Impatient with the slow rate of economic progress, the pronounced social and economic inequalities in many of the oil states, and the corruption that frequently characterizes a boom economy, they are apt to use their positions to seize power. In addition, concern over excessive social permissiveness and the employment of foreign nationals is likely to spark unrest in the lower levels of the military hierarchy.

SUMMARY
Oil, Development, and Traditional Values

The petroleum economy is changing many features of the political, economic, and social fabric of the gulf states. Prospects for considerable instability—aggravated by interstate rivalries, the uncertainties of the Arab-Israeli conflict, and the aftermath of the Gulf War—are very real. Traditional life-styles are struggling to adjust to the forces of change.

The challenge facing the gulf states is the harnessing of their petroleum wealth to promote the enduring development of their economies. How well they can accommodate development and change without drastic alteration in traditional values will determine the degree of stability and lasting change the region will experience.

KEY TERMS

alluvial fan	Gulf War
Gulf Cooperation Council	Kurds
gulf states	*qanat*

FURTHER READINGS
Part Eight

Allan, J. A. *Libya: The Experience of Oil.* London: Croom Helm; Boulder, CO: Westview Press, 1981. A perceptive study of development without capital constraints and its social and economic impact.

Beaumont, Peter, Gerald H. Blake, and J. Malcolm Wagstaff. *The Middle East: A Geographical Study.* 2nd ed. New York: Halsted Press, 1988. A systematic examination of problem areas and issues blended with country case studies to give a most reliable and readable overview of the contemporary Middle East.

Beaumont, Peter, and Keith McLachlan, eds. *Agricultural Development in the Middle East.* Chichester: Wiley, 1985. A series of sectoral and country studies explore progress and problems in the use of land and water for agriculture.

Beck, Lois. *Nomad: A Year in the Life of a Qashqa'i Tribesman in Iran.* Berkeley, CA: University of California Press, 1991. This study examines the factors impacting and changing the life of Turkish-speaking pastoral nomads in southwestern Iran by following the daily activities and seasonal round of the leader of a tribal group.

Bogary, Hamza. *The Sheltered Quarter: A Tale of a Boyhood in Mecca.* Translated by Olive Kenny and Jeremy Reed. Austin, TX: Center for Middle Eastern Studies, University of Texas at Austin, 1991. The urban culture of Mecca before the discovery of oil is captured in this Saudi Arabian novel.

Burke, Edmund, II, ed. *Struggle and Survival in the Modern Middle East.* Berkeley, CA: University of California Press, 1993. By examining the life histories of two dozen precolonial, colonial, and contemporary individuals, the variable texture of social change is graphically illustrated.

Crystal, Jill. *Oil and Politics in the Gulf: Rulers and Merchants in Kuwait and Qatar.* Cambridge: Cambridge University Press, 1990. Beneath the surface of apparant stability lurk structural problems and dynamic forces that threaten the viability of the oil monarchies.

Drysdale, Alasdair, and Gerald H. Blake. *The Middle East and North Africa: A Political Geography.* Oxford: Oxford University Press, 1985. A combination of case studies and general theory cast an illuminating light on the spatial dimensions of contemporary regional politics and conflicts.

Entelis, John P., and Phillip C. Naylor, eds. *State and Society in Algeria.* Boulder, CO: Westview Press, 1992. Authoritarian and centralizing patterns are contrasted with decentralizing and democratizing forces in a country afflicted by conflicts between modernists and traditionalists and suffering from a stagnant economy.

Fernea, Elizabeth Warnock, ed. *Women and the Family in the Middle East: New Voices of Change.* Austin, TX: University of Texas Press, 1985. Combining literary and scholarly insights by both natives of the region and outside observers, this collection makes available in English many otherwise inaccessible materials on the changing status of women.

Gunter, Michael M. *The Kurds in Turkey: A Political Dilemma*. Boulder, CO: Westview Press, 1990. The political problems encountered by Kurds in Turkey mirror their experience in neighboring states.

Hobbs, Joseph J. *Bedouin Life in the Egyptian Wilderness*. Austin, TX: University of Texas Press, 1989. The conservation ethic of nomadic pastoralists in Egypt's Red Sea Hills is the cornerstone of this satisfying account of Bedouin life.

Hinnebusch, Raymond A. *Peasant and Bureaucracy in Ba'thist Syria. The Political Economy of Rural Development*. Boulder, CO: Westview Press, 1989. Examination of animal husbandry, cooperatives, land reclamation, and irrigation informs this evaluation of the effectiveness of Syrian state socialism.

Mahfouz, Naguib. *Midaq Alley*. Translated by Trevor Le Gassick. Washington, DC: Three Continents, 1981. A powerful novel by Egypt's best-known author and Nobel winner for literature, this is an unforgettable and unsentimental portrait of the everyday lives of a spectrum of Cairo's central city inhabitants.

Peres, Shimon. *The New Middle East*. New York: Henry Holt, 1993. The rush of events has given this insider's vision of an Arab-Israeli peace process prophetic power and concrete reality.

Peters, Emrys. *The Bedouin of Cyrenaica: Studies in Personal and Corporate Power*. Edited by Jack Goody and Emanuel Marx. Cambridge: Cambridge University Press, 1990. Four previously unpublished chapters are combined with six influential journal articles to give an unparalleled insight into Middle Eastern social relations.

Swearingen, Will D. *Moroccan Mirages: Agrarian Dreams and Deceptions, 1912-1986*. Princeton, NJ: Princeton University Press, 1987. What colonial developers hoped to achieve and what their distorted perceptions have meant for present-day Morocco are the subject of this fascinating study.

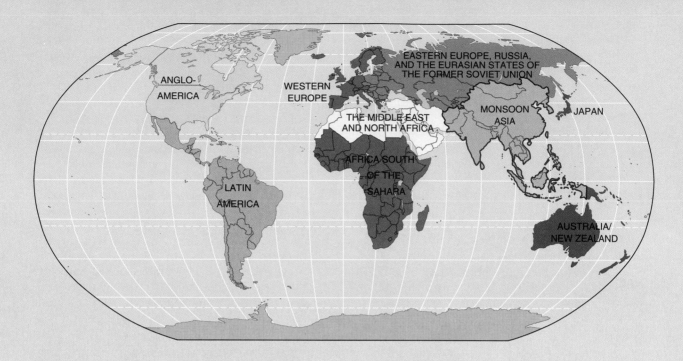

P eople are the most important asset of **Monsoon Asia**, the quarter of Asia strongly affected by monsoon winds. At the same time, the presence of too many people is a serious problem in many parts of the region. This southeastern quadrant of the Eurasian landmass, which accounts for only 7.2 percent of the earth's total land surface (excluding Antarctica and Greenland), supports about 56 percent of the world's population—an estimated 3.392 billion people in 1994. Nowhere is population density greater, and nowhere have humans been using, abusing, and modifying their land and water resources more than in this dynamic but sometimes backward part of the world.

Monsoon Asia has enormous human and physical variety. One of its most enduring and pervasive themes, however, is the closeness of the people to the earth; the rhythm of seasonal farming cycles dominates the lives of most of the people in this vast and ancient realm. Nowhere is this characteristic more apparent than in China and India, where more than 70 percent of the people continue to farm and live in rural areas. Village life, with its traditional values and methods, remains the norm for hundreds of millions in those two countries, and it is there that fundamental change must occur if China and India are to modernize and move their economies forward.

One of the most challenging aspects of development and growth in Monsoon Asia is employment for the rapidly growing populations. China, for example, currently needs to provide off-farm jobs for more than 100 million people, as its economy shifts from agriculture to secondary and tertiary activities. And India must provide more than 15 to 18 million new jobs each year, just to keep pace with its rapidly growing population. The need for adequate employment is a major consequence of rapid population growth; the inability of national economies to absorb new workers leads to poverty, misery, and political and social instability. It also helps explain the forces that drive Asians to migrate to North America and other locations in search of better jobs and opportunities.

Changes are taking place everywhere in Monsoon Asia, and improvements in livelihood as well as an overall change for the better are evident in many parts of the region. Although not treated here as a part of Monsoon Asia, Japan is the most obvious Asian example, with its great wealth, high standard of living, and modern, trendy urban life-

PART **9**

Clifton W. Pannell

MONSOON ASIA

styles. However, conditions of economic takeoff are also occurring in countries in earlier stages of economic development. Thailand, Malaysia, Singapore, Taiwan, and South Korea offer smaller but still valuable and instructive examples of rapid economic growth and development under Asian conditions.

Unfortunately, growth, progress, and wealth are not evenly distributed, and many parts of the realm reveal only poverty, isolation, and economic stagnation—as evidenced by the interior of China and India, Burma, the Philippines, Bangladesh, and Nepal. Such poverty and slow growth have both structural and spatial causes: economic and political systems on the one hand and size and physical attributes on the other.

Conditions may improve in the future for Monsoon Asia. Much of the region faces the Pacific, and the twenty-first century, according to some observers, may be the Pacific Century. New patterns of trade, travel, and transportation are focusing increasingly on the Pacific and the Monsoon Asian countries, and those forces may push the realm faster along the track of economic growth and development.

24

Monsoon Asia: An Overview

Environment: The Basis for Human Occupancy

The Monsoon and the Rhythm of the Seasons

The Cultural Basis

Processes of Development

Women farm laborers from the Santhal tribe, West Bengal, India. Asia contains over half the world's population, and it is difficult for Westerners to fathom the enormousness of human effort that must daily be exerted on the production of food.

More than half of the world's people live in Monsoon Asia, many of them in extreme poverty. And they have lived there since time immemorial. In the valleys of the Indus and Huang He (Hwang Ho, or Yellow)[1] rivers lie the remains of two major primary culture hearths, which influenced much of Monsoon Asia. The result was an immense cultural mosaic, to which the introduction of European habits and practices has added even greater complexity.

A number of cultural and geographical features, which underlie the development processes in Monsoon Asia, suggest a division of that broad area into three regions: South Asia, East Asia, and Southeast Asia (Figure 24–1). South Asia is a physical unit, the Indian subcontinent. It is also a social unit, because it includes similar cultural origins and characteristics. East Asia has less physical unity, but many of the region's cultural characteristics originated in China. For example, Tibet and Inner Mongolia have special administrative identities as autonomous regions within China; they also have close historical and ethnic ties with the Chinese. Southeast Asia, which is composed of many smaller and medium-sized states, has less cultural homogeneity than its two neighbors do. In many ways Southeast Asia is a buffer zone between Indian and Chinese civilizations; it certainly has received significant contributions from both. The unity of Southeast Asia is based on its tropical and maritime character.

India and China are of special importance in Monsoon Asia. Both countries have gigantic populations, and most of their people continue to work in agriculture or other rural activities. Both countries are also important industrial producers and their economies are growing rapidly. While official figures for their average per-capita incomes are low (less than U.S. $400.00), recent studies suggest the methods of measuring the size of the Chinese economy may have grossly underestimated its size.[2] Although there are variations in the rates of economic growth and the approach and policies selected to promote growth in India and China, by virtue of their size the progress in both countries is watched closely by other nations and will have an enormous impact on world patterns of well-being and suffering.

The economic systems of both countries had impressive growth during the 1980s. The World Bank estimated that China's average annual growth in GDP 1980 through 1990 was 9.5 percent, an impressive performance by any standard. India during the same period grew at an annual rate of 5.3 percent, lower but nevertheless quite good. China's average annual growth in agricultural output during the same period was 6.1 percent, whereas India's was 3.1 percent.

Even though Japan is geographically a part of Monsoon Asia—one of several medium-sized states in both population and area—it was discussed separately in Chapters 14 and 15 because its remarkable economic growth in the past 100 years sets it apart from other states in the region. Japan serves as an excellent model of sustained progress and rapid development, highly visible to other Monsoon Asian states.

ENVIRONMENT: THE BASIS FOR HUMAN OCCUPANCY

The distribution of population in Monsoon Asia reflects an ordered relationship between people and particular physical environments (Figure 24–2). For example, the densest population concentrations are in the great alluvial valleys and floodplains of the major rivers. The main clusters are located in the Indo-Gangetic Plain of India; the Chang Jiang (Yangtze) and Xi (Hsi) river basins and the northern plains of China; and the Tonkin Delta of Vietnam, as well as along the Irrawaddy, Chao Phraya, and Mekong rivers in mainland Southeast Asia. Even where there are no great rivers, Asian peasants have clustered in the smaller alluvial basins and plains. The exceptions—peninsular India, the island of Java, and the Loess Plateau of northern China—can be explained by special circumstances and historical events.

Because of geographical proximity, several large arid areas—western and northwestern China and Mongolia—are also included in Monsoon Asia. Sparse populations in those arid areas reflect an environment with limited potential for food production. Many inhabitants are pastoralists because sedentary cultivation is difficult there.

Figure 24-1

Political units and capital cities of Monsoon Asia. More than half of the world's population is found in Monsoon Asia, and most of those people are concentrated in alluvial plains and river basins.

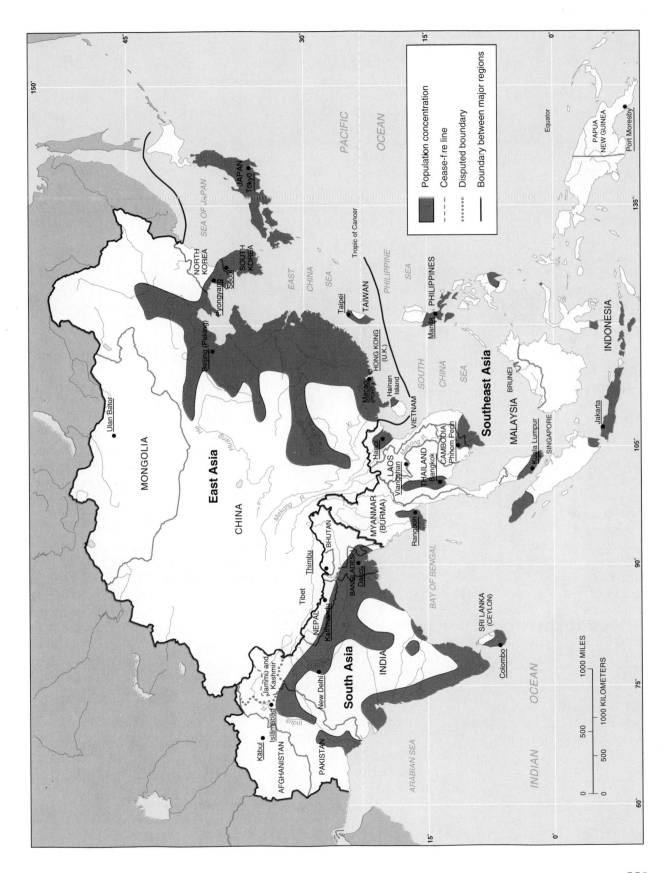

Population concentration

Cease-fire line

Disputed boundary

Boundary between major regions

East Asia

South Asia

Southeast Asia

PACIFIC OCEAN

SEA OF JAPAN

EAST CHINA SEA

PHILIPPINE SEA

SOUTH CHINA SEA

BAY OF BENGAL

ARABIAN SEA

INDIAN OCEAN

Equator

Tropic of Cancer

MONGOLIA
Ulan Bator

CHINA

Tibet

Huang He
Huang

Mekong R.

NORTH KOREA
Pyongyang

SOUTH KOREA
Seoul

JAPAN
Tokyo

Beijing (Peking)

TAIWAN
Taipei

HONG KONG (U.K.)
Macao (Port.)
Hainan Island

VIETNAM
Hanoi

LAOS
Vientiane

MYANMAR (BURMA)
Rangoon

THAILAND
Bangkok

CAMBODIA
Phnom Penh

MALAYSIA
Kuala Lumpur

BRUNEI

SINGAPORE

INDONESIA
Jakarta

PHILIPPINES
Manila

BHUTAN
Thimbu

NEPAL
Kathmandu

BANGLADESH
Dacca

INDIA
New Delhi

Jammu and Kashmir

Islamabad

PAKISTAN

AFGHANISTAN
Kabul

Indus

SRI LANKA (CEYLON)
Colombo

PAPUA NEW GUINEA
Port Moresby

1000 MILES
1000 KILOMETERS
500
500
0
0

45° 30° 15° 0°

150° 135° 105° 90° 75° 60°

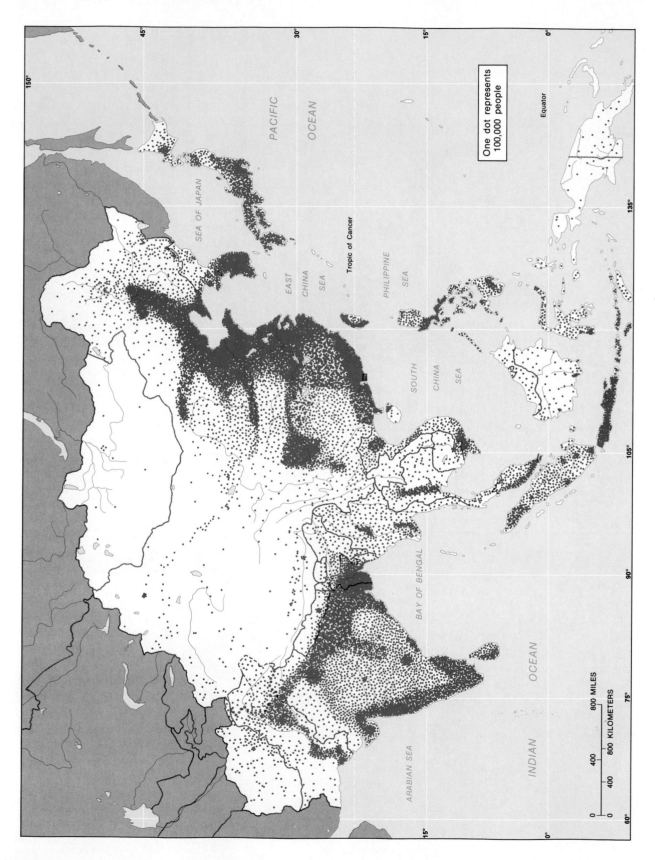

One dot represents
100,000 people

PACIFIC
OCEAN

SEA OF JAPAN

EAST
CHINA
SEA

Tropic of Cancer

PHILIPPINE
SEA

SOUTH
CHINA
SEA

BAY OF BENGAL

ARABIAN SEA

INDIAN
OCEAN

Equator

150°

45°

30°

15°

0°

135°

105°

90°

75°

60°

15°

0°

800 MILES

800 KILOMETERS

400

400

0

0

The point is that in Monsoon Asia people have gathered and proliferated most where the agricultural potential has been the greatest. By contrast, some of the most densely populated regions in the United States are in the Northeast, a region not particularly well suited to agriculture yet the site of original European settlement and eventual centers of commerce and industry. In Monsoon Asia, water has played a key role; where it has been available, agriculture has generally been oriented to wet rice (i.e., paddy), which is grown in many different ways. Although yields vary considerably, rice is the principal food crop in Monsoon Asia (Figure 24–3). Where environmental conditions permit, two crops a year are customary in China. In India, double-cropping is not as widespread, even where the environment is suitable.

Population clustering also reflects accessibility. Perhaps the best example of that principle is seen in the Yangtze Basin of central China. Historically, areas within the basin where navigation was possible prospered and grew in population. Away from navigable streams, the economy stagnated, and population grew only slowly. Even more than 1,000 years ago food grains were transported by water from the Yangtze region to the ancient capitals in the plains of northern China, a pattern that suggests a remarkable degree of economic and spatial integration. Thus, accessibility and the ability to move foodstuffs inexpensively have both been important in determining where people would concentrate.

THE MONSOON AND THE RHYTHM OF THE SEASONS

The term **monsoon**, believed to be of Arabian origin, describes a seasonal reversal in wind direction. That reversal results from the different heating and cooling rates of land and water in the summer and winter months, coupled with latitudinal shifts in major air masses. Southwesterly (onshore) winds dominate during the Northern Hemisphere's summer, whereas northeasterly (offshore) winds are customary during the winter.

Figure 24–2
Population distribution of Monsoon Asia. Great population concentrations are found in the alluvial valleys and floodplains of major rivers.

The Indian monsoon has three distinct seasons, the most important of which is the June-to-September rainy season. The warm, moisture-laden winds blow from the southwest, usually striking the southern coast of Sri Lanka (formerly Ceylon) in late May and moving northward onto the Indian peninsula by June (Figure 24–4).

The rainy season in South Asia is followed by a comparatively mild, dry autumn and winter season. Although its duration varies by location, that period of cooler and drier weather generally extends from October to March. In March the hot-weather season begins, and by May the heat becomes almost unbearable, reaching average daytime temperatures of more than 100°F (38°C) in many places. Northern India, with its dry air and cloudless skies, is the hottest, and relative humidity there is very low. As the landmass heats up, a low-pressure system is created that begins to attract onshore winds, forerunners of the summer, wet-season monsoon. Southwesterly winds usually become well established quite suddenly in June and bring life-renewing precipitation. As the rainy season begins anew, the South Asian monsoon seasons have completed a full cycle.

This southwest monsoon is divided into two branches—one in the Arabian Sea and one in the Bay of Bengal. Winds from the Arabian Sea strike the sharp mountain ridges of the Western Ghats of India, are forced upward, and dump very heavy rains on the windward slopes of the Ghats (Figure 24–5). In the east, winds from the Bay of Bengal move rapidly northward and arrive at Calcutta, India, in early June. Those winds blow north as far as the Khasi Hills, where a piling-up effect forces them northward up the Ganges Plain. By the end of June the winds reach New Delhi, India; and by early July, Lahore and Rawalpindi in Pakistan.

The monsoons determine, in good part, the agricultural calendar of farmers throughout the region. Despite some use of irrigation, it is the arrival of the southwest monsoon that brings the surge in farming operations in South Asia and also directs many of the peasant activities. During the extremely hot, dry season that precedes the arrival of the summer rains, rural life slows. The earth is parched and cracked, and little can be done to prepare for sowing. With rain, human activity resumes at an intense pace. Soil preparation, planting, weeding, and the many tasks associated with the growing season must be compressed into a relatively brief time.

Figure 24–3
Harvesting rice near Yangshuo, Guangxi Province, in southern China. Agricultural and transport technology remains very traditional in remote areas of China. The device shown is a mechanical foot-powered rice thresher now available to some farmers.

In East Asia the monsoon pattern generally yields a similar wet-dry and warm-cool alternation of seasons. In winter the Siberian high-pressure system controls the climate over much of China, especially the area north of the Qinling (Chin-ling) Mountains and the Chang Jiang (Yangtze River). The result is the dominance of cold, dry air flowing east and south from the vicinity of Lake Baikal, just north of the Mongolian border (Figure 24–6). Average winter temperatures in northern China are often 5° to 10°F (3° to 6°C) cooler than they are at comparable latitudes and locations in Anglo-America. As some of the winds flow across the warmer Sea of Japan and the East China and South China seas, great quantities of moisture are added to the air mass. When those winds strike land areas, heavy precipitation can result. More commonly, however, winters are dry and cool. Some winter cropping is possible, but generally the tempo of farming operations relaxes in the winter—it practically ceases on the Loess Plateau and in northeastern China.

During the summer monsoon (May to September) in East Asia and Southeast Asia, the winds move in great counterclockwise arcs toward a center of low pressure situated in central Asia.

Moisture is brought overland, and the pattern of maximum summer rainfall described for South Asia is characteristic, with the monsoon first influencing the Indonesian Archipelago, then mainland Southeast Asia, and finally China (see Figure 24–4). Farming activity picks up in late spring (mid-April to mid-June), and the entire cycle of soil preparation and planting gets under way. Precipitation peaks during the summer months, when it is most needed to nourish the rapidly growing crops. Conditions at that time include high average daily temperatures and longer periods of sunlight, which are essential for photosynthesis and plant growth.

Figure 24–4
Annual rainfall and dominant atmospheric stream lines over Monsoon Asia during the summer. At that time the main wind directions for the South Asian and East Asian monsoons are on shore. Warm, moist, and unstable air masses enter the landmass from adjacent warm waters to the southwest and the southeast, bringing heavy precipitation to the land surface, especially where converging air masses or increased elevation cause lifting.

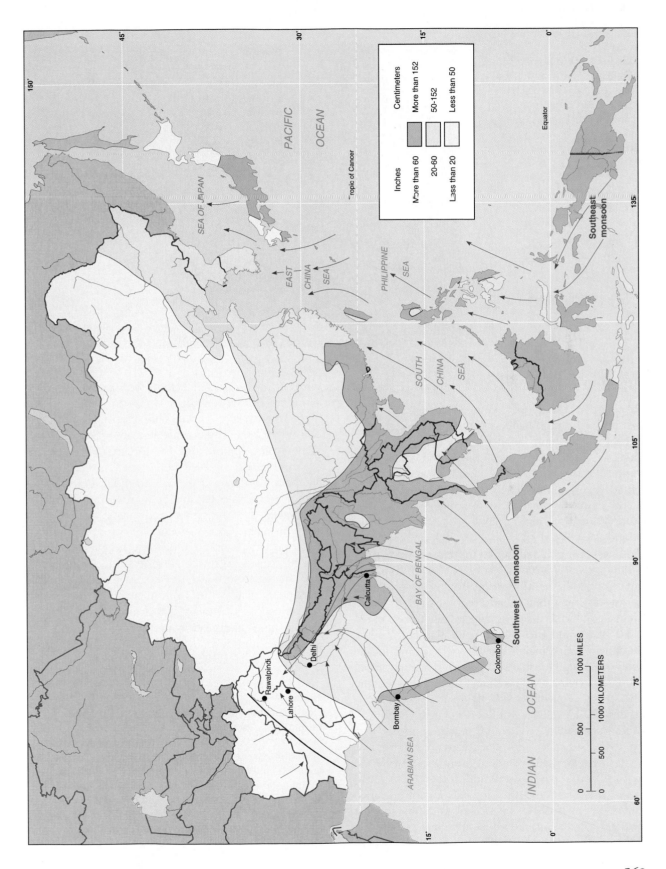

Figure 24–5
Monsoon rains in Bombay, India. The summer monsoon winds are forced to rise over the Western Ghats (mountain chain) on the Indian Peninsula, resulting in heavy precipitation along the coast.

THE CULTURAL BASIS

The cultural variety of Monsoon Asia is well expressed in the multiplicity of ethnic and racial types and the astonishing number of spoken and written languages. The gene pools of several major geographical races are represented by the people of Monsoon Asia, though the Asiatic and Indic types are dominant. And more than 1,000 languages are spoken there; Mandarin Chinese, Japanese, Korean, Bahasa Indonesian, Hindi, Urdu, Bengali, Chinese Wu, Cantonese, and Fukienese are the most widely used.

Religious affiliation is also varied. The dominant Asian religions, including Hinduism and Buddhism, are mystical in character and recognize many gods; but Monsoon Asia also contains largely Christian nations, such as the Philippines (and formerly, Vietnam), and Muslim states, such as Indonesia, Malaysia, Bangladesh, and Pakistan. In addition, China and other Marxist states, including Vietnam, officially deny or discount religion. As old traditions are cast aside, religious influences are declining in some areas—with possible far-reaching effects.

Other distinctive cultural features are present to a greater or lesser degree throughout Monsoon Asia. Architectural styles, agricultural systems and fertilization practices, and the organization of administrative systems have all been used to define specific regions. Political and administrative institutions and land-tenure relationships also provide good measures of similarity or difference among the major regions or cultural realms of Monsoon Asia.

On the basis of cultural characteristics and historical development, we can delineate a Chinese Sinic (East Asian) realm and an Indian (South Asian) realm. For example, Korea, Japan, and northern Vietnam all borrowed heavily from the Chinese cultural system. The use of ideographs in the written language, the religious and value systems of Buddhism and Confucianism, the nature of architecture and city planning, and even the intensive manner of growing wet rice all reflect the common cultural matrix from which those customs and practices derived. Similarly, the South Asian subcontinent can be viewed as an Indian historical and cultural unit, despite its fragmentation along linguistic and religious lines and despite the partitioning that occurred in 1947, when Pakistan broke away from India.

Figure 24-6
Dominant atmospheric stream lines over Monsoon Asia during the winter. Major climate control results from the clockwise direction of the winds emanating from the Siberian high-pressure system centered just southeast of Lake Baikal. Dry, cold air flows mainly east and south, bringing dry, cold winters to most of China. Some Asian archipelagoes receive increased winter precipitation on their windward flanks as a result of the prevailing northeastern winds, which pick up moisture as they blow south.

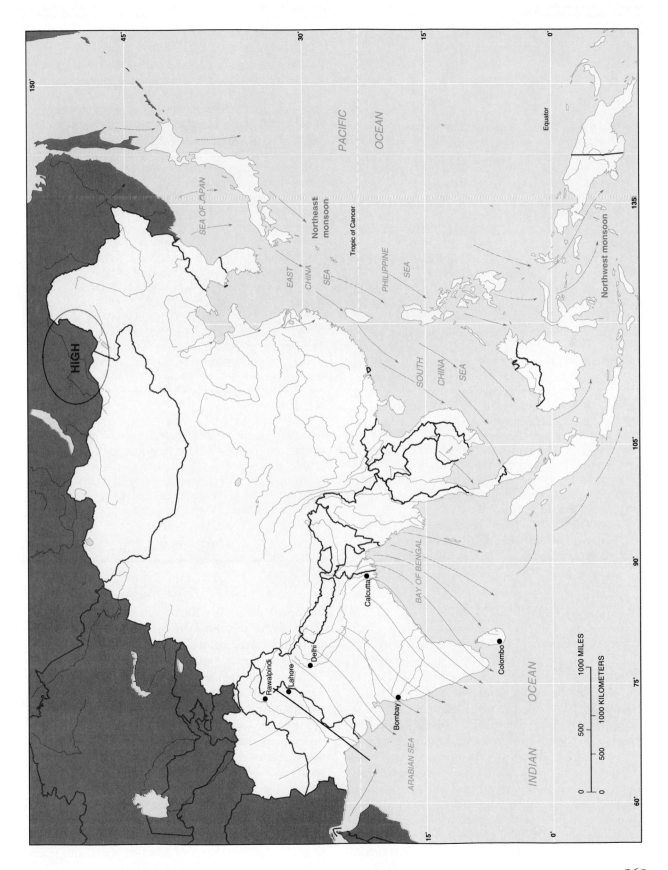

A TALE OF THREE ASIAN CHILDREN

A look at three representative Asian children highlights the significant differences in opportunities that exist for young people in Monsoon Asia (Figure A). The first child, Meihua, is the daughter of a Chinese farmer who lives in a village outside the city of Nanjing, near the Chang Jiang (Yangtze River) in east central China. Meihua, who is six years old, lives with her parents, grandparents, older sister, and younger brother. Meihua's family has a small farm that they lease from their collective unit. Meihua's father also has a job in a nearby factory that is owned by the collective. He works on the farm after he finishes his factory job. Meihua's mother helps with the farm work, as does her older sister. In recent years the family has come to depend less on the farm income. Although not wealthy, Meihua's family has plenty of food for everyone, and Meihua and her sister attend school. When their grandfather had pneumonia last winter, he was taken to the commune hospital and eventually recovered. The family owns a motorcycle, two bicycles, a sewing machine, a TV set, radios, and watches. They also have a savings account in the farm credit union with more than 2000 yuan (1 yuan equals $.11 U.S.).

Across the Taiwan Strait in Taipei lives Xuda, a fourteen-year-old boy who lives in a two-bedroom apartment with his parents and older sister. Xuda's parents are both university graduates, and both work. His father works for an export firm as an accountant; his mother is a high school teacher. Both Xuda and his sister attend school, and both spend most of their time at school or studying. Both must take competitive examinations in order to advance to a good high school and later to a good college or university. Both Xuda and his sister expect to graduate from college and have their own professional careers. Xuda's parents own a small car, and their apartment is air-conditioned and well furnished. It includes a color TV set and a washing machine. During vacations they drive south to visit Xuda's grandparents and aunts, uncles, and cousins, who live near Taichung. Xuda likes Taichung because the air is much cleaner than it is in Taipei, and there are not so many people.

Far away in South Asia lives Mahendra in a small Indian village in the eastern Punjab. Mahendra, who is ten, is one of four children and lives with his parents, siblings, and grandmother. His grandfather died last year. An older sister also died some years earlier, during infancy. Mahendra's father is a farmer, and the family owns about five acres (two hectares) of land. The family is poor, though last year's crop was good and Mahendra's father was able to pay off some debts. Mahendra's mother provides some income by doing knitted piecework for a local purchasing agent. The family lives in a three-room house made of adobe brick. There are no modern water or toilet facilities, but water is available at a nearby pump. Food is adequate, yet Mahendra is sometimes hungry. He and his brothers and sister go to the village school. When his father needs them, however, they stay home to help with the farm work. Mahendra's mother is eager for him to do well in school

PROCESSES OF DEVELOPMENT

Both environment and culture have had far-reaching effects on the path and pace of development in Monsoon Asia, as can be seen in the spatial variation of development in different realms within this vast region. Thus, we can also delineate a Chinese and an Indian realm according to the distinctive approaches to development found within East Asia and South Asia. Southeast Asia, however, is a shatter belt of many political, cultural, and geographical regions, much like Eastern Europe (see Chapter 11). Normally, such instability and fragmentation retard economic progress, but when shattering leads to the easing of political turmoil, it can promote progress over the long term. The net effect of fragmentation

on development is difficult to assess, but a comparison of the development performance of various countries within the different regions can provide instructive data.[3]

Approaches to development in Asia span the distance between communist and free-enterprise economies, and political approaches offer an equally broad set of alternatives, from highly authoritarian systems of control to Western-style democracies. Some of the more obvious possibilities for evaluative comparisons are India/China, North Korea/South Korea, and Myanmar/Thailand. Of course, economic-growth goals may be achieved at some sacrifice of personal and political freedom. As we discussed in Chapter 4, development can proceed in a number of ways, and many

Figure A
School children in Changchun, China. This particular city is located in Manchuria, the northern region colonized by the Chinese in the late nineteenth and early twentieth centuries. China assures its citizens of a sixth-grade education or its equivalent, yet illiteracy remains a problem. Further education is available on a limited and highly competitive basis.

so that he might gain admission to a high school in a nearby town. Eventually she hopes he will be able to migrate to New Delhi, 124 miles (200 kilometers) away, and find something besides farming, which she believes results only in poverty.

What will life be like for these three Asian children in the year 2020? Three alternative paths to progress are seen in these three countries; each has special problems and challenges. The chapters that follow should help the reader better understand the conditions and processes of change and development operating in Asia and better evaluate the prospects for improvement in the lives of the billions who live in Monsoon Asia.

forces can affect it, everything from biophysical and historical influences to ideological and policy-oriented issues.[4]

One of the most notable and challenging issues in the development of Monsoon Asia is the nature of income distribution among the populations of the various countries (see the boxed feature A Tale of Three Asian Children). Even though such data are rarely collected in a consistent manner and are not reported in many countries, enough information is available to raise interesting questions about how development and well-being are proceeding in this vast and diverse part of the world (Table 24–1). Of the five countries included in the table, Japan and South Korea have had the most egalitarian patterns of income distribution; Sri Lanka, the least egalitar-

ian. In addition, the data show that the lowest income groups in all five countries have done poorly.

Political events since World War II have been unsettling in most of Monsoon Asia. Strife, war, famine, and hard times have been common themes running through the recent history of the region. Those same themes have occurred in other developing areas, but cataclysmic events—such as China's civil war, the end of colonialism in South Asia and Southeast Asia, the Vietnam War, the internal ravaging of Cambodia, the forging of Bangladesh, the Philippine revolution, and sectarian conflict in the Punjab and Sri Lanka—have been especially common and frequent in Monsoon Asia. Moreover, such events in Monsoon Asia involve so many lives that they take on special significance.

Table 24-1
Percentage share of total national income available to various groups of households in selected countries.

	Household Groups					
	Lowest (poorest) Quintile	Second Quintile	Third Quintile	Fourth Quintile	Highest (richest) Quintile	Highest 10%
Bangladesh (1985–1986)	10.0	13.7	17.2	21.9	37.2	23.2
Sri Lanka (1985–1986)	4.8	8.5	12.1	18.4	56.1	43.0
Philippines (1985)	5.5	9.7	14.8	22.0	48.0	32.1
Republic of Korea (1976)	5.7	11.2	15.4	22.4	45.3	27.5
Japan (1979)	8.7	13.2	17.5	23.1	37.5	22.4

Source: World Bank, *World Development Report,* 1989 (New York: Oxford University Press, 1989) and 1992.
Note: Because of the difficulty and variation in methods of collecting the income data, they should be treated with caution.

SUMMARY
A Panorama of the Less Developed World

More than one-half of the world's population resides in Monsoon Asia. That population has been building for many centuries and now features some of the world's highest densities. Many of the region's people have seen improvements in well-being in recent decades, but many millions remain in poverty. The approaches to development within Monsoon Asia have differed, as illustrated by the contrast between India and China. Regardless of approach, however, the effectiveness of all development programs will be thoroughly tested in the region in the years to come.

Monsoon Asia's massive population, its distribution pattern along major river systems, and its overwhelming dependence on subsistence agriculture, which follows the seasonal patterns of the monsoon, suggest a certain consistency in the region. But those common elements have not produced a unified Asia. Indeed, the culture and traditions of Monsoon Asia derive from at least two major culture hearths and several of lesser stature. The result has been a cultural mosaic constructed of and reflected in the many religions, languages, and customs of South, East, and Southeast Asia. That cultural pluralism, together with some racial diversity, permeates the entire region.

The whole range of success and failure is evident in the experiences of these developing states, and most of the approaches to development can be found and evaluated within this broad panorama of the less developed world.

KEY TERMS

monsoon   Monsoon Asia

NOTES

1. In the past two decades, pinyin, a system for spelling Chinese names and terms in English, has come into increasingly widespread use. The system follows standardized rules and is being substituted for the older forms of romanization, such as the Wade-Giles system. In order to minimize problems here, this book uses the pinyin spelling and follows it with the Wade-Giles or other conventional spelling in parentheses—Huang He (Hwang Ho), Beijing (Peking), or Xi'an (Sian), for example—unless the pinyin spelling is the same as the conventional one. Certain names—such as Yangtze River, Canton, or Manchuria—that are well known in the West through established usage will continue to be used here, though the pinyin spelling will be given at least once.

2. For analytical comparisons of the two nations, as well as quantitative indexes of growth, see S. Swamy, "Economic Growth in China and India, 1952–1970: A Comparative Appraisal," *Economic Development and Cultural Change* 21 (1973): 1–83; and W. Mandelbaum, "Modern Economic Growth in India and China: The Comparison Revisited, 1950–1980," *Economic Development and Cultural Change* 31 (1982): 45–84. See also "When China Wakes," *The Economist,* 28 Nov. 1992 (Special Survey); and The World Bank, *World Development Report, 1992* (New York: Oxford University Press, 1992).

3. See Stuart Corbridge, ed., *World Economy* (New York: Oxford University Press, 1993), for a look at differential growth rates and performances. Monsoon Asia offers a number of excellent comparative situations.

4. Students who wish to explore conceptual approaches and different models of policy and ideological perspectives on development should read Ronald H. Chilcote, *Theories of Development and Underdevelopment* (Boulder, CO: Westview Press, 1984), 1–12. For a perspective from development economics, see Michael P. Todaro, *Economic Development in the Third World* (New York: Longman, 1989).

25

South Asia:
Past and Present

Srinagar in Kashmir, in northwestern India. This setting
high in the Himalayas provides spectacular beauty.

571

Known to the world as the Indian subcontinent, or South Asia, this region today is composed of three extremely populous countries—India, Pakistan, and Bangladesh—and three smaller nations—Sri Lanka and the Himalayan states of Nepal and Bhutan (Figure 25–1). To the northwest is Afghanistan, a transitional state with historic ties to both South Asia and the Middle East. And in the adjacent Arabian Sea, Indian Ocean, and Bay of Bengal are numerous islands and island groups that are also part of South Asia. The Laccadive, Andaman, and Nicobar islands belong to India.

India dominates the South Asian subcontinent, but several of the bordering countries are themselves large. Bangladesh and Pakistan rank among the ten most populous countries in the world; and Sri Lanka, Afghanistan, and Nepal are among the fifty largest countries in population. Pakistan and Bangladesh are relatively new countries: Pakistan was created in 1947 and Bangladesh in 1971 as the result of special political, religious, and linguistic problems. The status of another divided region— that of Jammu and Kashmir in the northernmost tip of India—is still contested today and further illustrates the political fragmentation of the subcontinent (see the boxed feature South Asian Strife and Conflict). Nepal and Sri Lanka are closely akin to India in cultural makeup, but each has managed to maintain its autonomy and independence. The small Himalayan kingdom of Bhutan is a border state that shares some of the physical characteristics of Nepal, but its origins and ethnic composition, as well as its cultural heritage, are more closely linked to Tibet and Buddhism. Sikkim, formerly a semi-independent nation similar to Bhutan, was incorporated as an Indian state in 1975.

A considerable range in levels of development is represented in the countries of South Asia. All are poor by Western standards, but several have demonstrated substantial capacity to initiate new development programs. Nonetheless, success has been difficult to measure. In most of the South Asian countries—especially Sri Lanka, Bangladesh, Pakistan, and India—political disputes and military conflict have inhibited growth. An examination of the history and cultural origins of South Asia, as well as the region's contemporary situation, will help in understanding the nature of the development processes under way there and the likelihood of their success or failure.

ORIGINS AND CULTURAL DIVERSITY

The origin of the earliest inhabitants of South Asia is still disputed, but it is well established that sedentary cultivators were farming the Indus floodplain more than 5,000 years ago. Indeed, the term *India* is derived from the Sanskrit word for river that was used to describe the Indus. Although little is known of the ancient civilization that emerged in the Indus floodplain, it was focused on the cities of Mohenjo-Daro and Harappa (Figure 25–2). Those cities were well planned and constructed, indicating the presence of an advanced civilization—the equal of contemporary civilizations in lower Egypt and Mesopotamia. Those early inhabitants are sometimes labeled **Dravidians**, referring to a highly mixed linguistic and cultural group that is found today mainly in southern India.

A second distinctive group entered the subcontinent in successive migratory waves from the mountains of Baluchistan and Afghanistan in the northwest. Those invaders were Caucasian people, commonly described as **Indo-Aryans**, and they infiltrated the subcontinent over a long period of time. Other invaders included the army of Alexander the Great, Islamic Moors, and Persians and Afghans; but none had the significance of the earlier blending of the ancient Dravidians and early Indo-Aryans. It was the synthesis of those two groups that produced the Hindu-based civilization that we refer to as Indian.

Religion and the Development of Indian Civilization

The formation of India and Indian civilization is tied closely to the Hindu religion, or **Hinduism**. This formalized set of religious beliefs with both societal and political implications emerged 1,000 to 2,000 years before the Christian era. Local priests established themselves at the apex of the social strata and became a potent political force. So influential was the priestly **Brahmin** group that even today it is looked on as the capstone of modern Hindu-Indian society. Its members, whether rich or poor, continue to wield considerable power at the local level.

The role of Hinduism in the development of Indian civilization and society has been all-pervasive for three millennia. Lacking a formal organizational structure and a single established code of beliefs, Hinduism is based on a set of traditions and values contained in early Sanskrit writings and epic

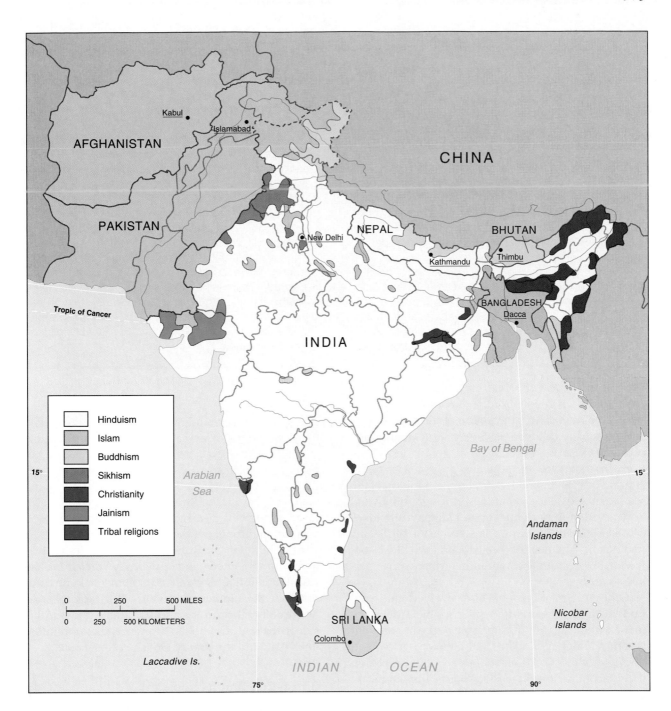

Figure 25–1
Countries, capitals, and major religions of South Asia. India dominates the subcontinent by virtue of its large population and area. Dashed lines indicate disputed
boundaries between China and India and between India and Pakistan.

SOUTH ASIAN STRIFE AND CONFLICT

Conflict and strife—religious, sectarian, ethnic, political, geopolitical—are present almost everywhere in South Asia. Within India today, however the conflict is serious enough to threaten the unity of the Indian nation. The assassination of Prime Minister Rajiv Gandhi in 1991 was a striking example of how serious the threat is.

Major religious conflicts have beset India for hundreds of years. In the middle of this century they caused the subcontinent to be divided into major political units that are predominantly Hindu (India) and Muslim (Pakistan and Bangladesh). More recently, religious and sectarian strife within India led to a major division be-tween Sikhs and Hindus in the states of Punjab and Haryana, and a major Sikh insurgency was put down with force. Nevertheless, Sikh separatists, who want a Sikh homeland called Khalistan within the state of Punjab, continue to find themselves at odds with the Hindu-controlled Indian government.

A major insurgency also raged in Sri Lanka between the majority Sinhalese (i.e., native Sri Lankans), who are Buddhists, and a minority Tamil (i.e., South Indian) population of Hindus who seek their own territory in northern Sri Lanka. In 1987 a settlement was reached with Indian assistance—and perhaps insistence, as well—and the insurgency has died down. But future peace is not assured.

Other problems also continue to fester: the political and geopolitical conflicts related to the Soviet invasion of Afghanistan; the Jammu and Kashmir border dispute between India and Pakistan; and border disputes in the Karakoram Mountains (western) and the Himalayas (eastern) between India and China. Indeed, India has difficulties with most of its neighbors. All of those examples are evidence of the many problems that result from cultural and ethnic fragmentation.

stories. The concept of *dharma,* a kind of duty or fate in society, is found in every individual, along with *karma,* a kind of tallying of good and evil actions that leads to an individual's present status in Hindu society. Embedded within the tradition is the idea that existence continues through time, and reincarnation in both human and animal form takes place repeatedly in an endless cycle of birth, life, and death. Whether good or bad, an individual's behavior in previous existences determines that person's current status.

Other religious groups also evolved in India. **Buddhism**, a religious and philosophical development with ties to Hinduism, appeared early and enjoyed a brief period of dominance. It spread throughout most of Monsoon Asia, but its impact on the subcontinent itself faded. Today, it is significant only in Sri Lanka and some of the northern mountain areas (see Figure 25–1).

The introduction of Islam from the Middle East challenged the dominance of Hinduism in the eighth century A.D. It offered identity and status to those who were excluded from or downtrodden in the well-established Hindu system. Islam came from the northwest, the traditional direction of Aryan invaders, and made itself felt most intensely first in the Indus Basin.

The spread of Islam followed the main drainage systems and did not extend rapidly into peninsular India, a plateau with greater barriers to movement. The period of most intense Muslim influence was perhaps the Mogul period (1526–1739), which saw the culmination of centuries of invasion by Islamic and Persian invaders. However, resistance to the Islamic invasion was strong throughout the centuries.

On the eve of British colonialism India was highly fragmented and politically divided. The British entered as traders and commercial entrepreneurs in the eighteenth century but rapidly organized colonial territory and integrated the various sultanates and kingdoms, a process that continued until 1947 and the end of British colonial rule.

British Rule and Its Impact

By the eighteenth century the commercial activity of foreign colonial powers was well under way in South Asia. The Dutch, Spanish, Portuguese, French, and British all wanted to establish a firm presence in South Asia, and competition among them was keen. Gradually, the **British East India Company** became the dominant commercial force in the South Asian subcontinent and established

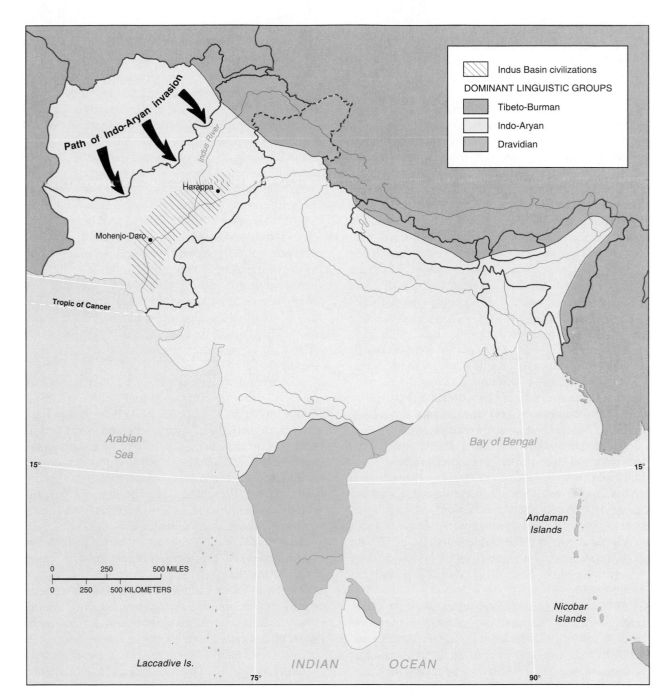

Figure 25–2
Early civilizations and major language groups of South Asia. Although culturally and
politically fragmented today, South Asia had its ancient roots in the Indus Basin.
Indo-Aryan languages prevail throughout most of the subcontinent.

both commercial and political relationships with the many local monarchs, sultans, and princes who controlled the fragmented political territory of South Asia. By the middle of the nineteenth century the East India Company had established itself throughout the region, but it had also created resentment against its activities.

A great uprising—the **Sepoy Rebellion**—took place in 1857. The British government then moved to take control of India and eliminated the East India Company as the manager of the territory. At that point Great Britain formally colonized and took responsibility for governing large parts of the subcontinent; it also established formal relationships with those territories and sultanates that remained outside the scope of its control. Over the next ninety years Great Britain consolidated the territory of South Asia and administered it as a crown colony through a far-flung and generally effective—even if increasingly unpopular—colonial civil administration.

The effects of British colonial rule were far-reaching and enduring. First, the territory of the subcontinent was more or less united. Second, the economic development of India continued to be skewed in favor of Great Britain, the colonizing power. Through this process Britain sought to exploit India as a source of raw materials and a market for manufactured food. Trade under British colonial rule was intended to benefit Britain, the colonizing power. Third, British rule influenced the spatial layout of India's production and circulation systems. Several focal cities grew rapidly, and a railway system was constructed to integrate them with each other and with their regional hinterlands, which were then able to be developed and exploited easily.

All together, the infrastructural work in transportation, cities, harbors, and industry that resulted from British colonialism, though not undertaken unselfishly, was reasonable and left India with a fair but somewhat spatially unbalanced legacy on which to build and modernize. However, British rule was politically very unpopular, and the British preparation for Indian self-rule was neither well conceived nor well executed.

Religion and the Hindu Caste System

Religion has continued to shape the political geography of South Asia. In 1947, religious differences were responsible for the partitioning of the subcontinent into a Hindu component (i.e., India) and a Muslim component (i.e., Pakistan), from which East Pakistan broke off to form the state of Bangladesh in 1971 (see Figure 25–1). Although all three states have significant religious minorities, the Hindu-Muslim split has shaped and influenced political patterns and human activities more than any other.

Other religious groups—for example, the Sikhs, Christians, Jains, and Parsis—exist in relatively modest numbers, and none have been effective in establishing a separate state based on religion. Sikhism and Jainism are two independent religions based on a strong dislike for the traditional Hindu caste system. **Sikhs** have attempted to form a separate political territory and have gained some recognition of the Punjab state in the north as a Sikh administrative subunit of India. Nevertheless, it is likely to remain a part of the Indian union, which is one of the world's largest and most complex countries. The Parsis are an ancient religious group whose mystical belief system entered India from Persia.

The dominant Hindu society is a highly formalized order that determines virtually all facets of life for an individual (Figure 25–3). Despite recent legal proscriptions to the contrary, a person's occupation, diet, spouse, and daily habits have been largely determined at birth. Hindu society is composed of four main groups that are considered clean. Arranged hierarchically, they are the Brahmins (priests), Kshatriyas (warriors), Vaisyas (merchants), and Sudras (laborers and cultivators). Within those four main groups are the myriad of **castes**, which are highly localized groupings of families that marry only among themselves.

Below the four main groups are people who are considered polluted and unclean. They are the untouchables, or scheduled castes and tribes, as the government calls them. Untouchables perform society's unclean tasks, such as the slaughter of animals, leather tanning, sweeping and cleaning, laundry services, and undertaking. Historically, the higher castes have systematically discriminated against the untouchables and have kept them at the bottom of the social spectrum. Although now illegal, such discrimination continues, reflecting the more than 2,000 years of traditions and customs within Hindu society. The caste system cannot be expected to disappear anytime soon, but it may be weakening in urban areas, where opportunities for social mobility exist.

Figure 25-3
Dasaswameda bathing ghat in Varanasi on the Ganges River in northern India.
Thousands of Hindus come to Varanasi each year to bathe in the sacred waters of
the Ganges. Varanasi is also a spiritual center for Buddhists because Buddha formulated his principles in this vicinity around 500 B.C.

Some scholars have concluded that the lighter-skinned Aryans set themselves up as Brahmins and that the darker-skinner Dravidians were forced into the lower castes. But such an ethnic-racial basis for the evolution of castes has never been clearly established. And some degree of mobility among the castes does exist; some vigorous, wealthy caste members have been able to advance in the social hierarchy.

Linguistic Variety

Although four or five languages dominate in South Asia, India has fifteen major regional lan-guages and several hundred dialects (Figure 25–4). The major regional languages are the pri-mary basis for the territorial division of India into states. Overall, the dominant languages are: **Hindi** (India's national language) and its two deriva-tives, Punjabi and **Urdu** (the main language of Pakistan); **Bengali**; and English, the lingua franca of the subcontinent. Hindi and Bengali are Indo-European languages, derived from the Indo-Aryan Sanskrit. In the south, several Dravidian languages, including Tamil and Malayalam, are spoken, which differ in origin from Indo-Aryan languages.

577

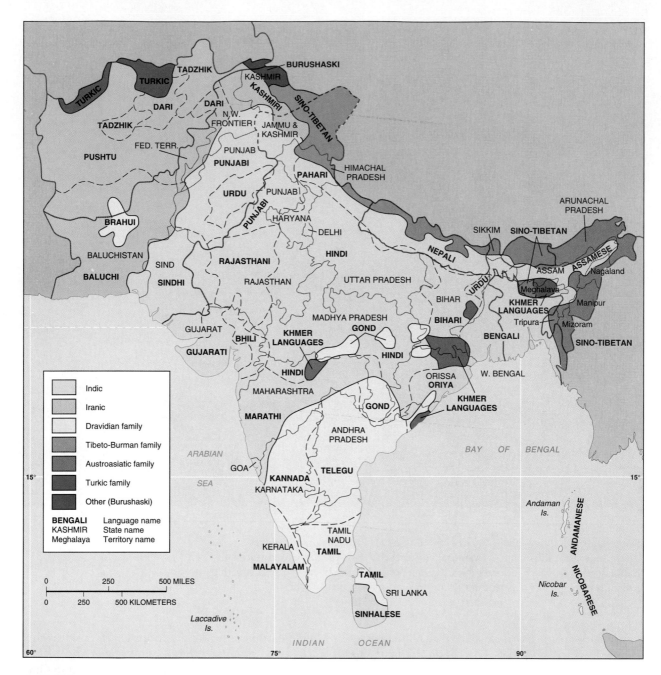

Figure 25-4

Languages of South Asia. The languages of the Indian subcontinent derive from two
major groups: the Indo-European languages, which are dominant in the central and
northern regions, and the Dravidian languages, dominant in the south. The diversity
of language and culture on the subcontinent contributes to the difficulty in forging
unified national states.

The language difference, coupled with other distinctive traditions, is serious enough to give rise to separatist movements among the more than 100 million Dravidians. And certainly the language difference between Pakistan and Bangladesh—their use of Urdu and Bengali, respectively—provided one motive for their political separation, in spite of their common religion, Islam. English, despite its association with former colonialism, continues as the semiofficial language of administration. Inasmuch as it belongs to no South Asian group, it serves as an important integrating element.

The Impact of Diversity on Territory

India is thus a human mosaic of immense variety and complexity. There is no single India, any more than there is one representative Indian. Differences in ethnic group, religion, caste, and language illustrate the enormous diversity, which presents problems for development planners. Yet out of that diversity has emerged a common bond of allegiance to the Indian nation, which represents the essential spirit of modern India.

SOUTH ASIAN ENVIRONMENTS AS A RESOURCE BASE

South Asia, like Russia, China, and the United States, spans a large area and contains great physical variety. Most of the subcontinent is tropical; only at higher elevations in the north and northwest is frost common. Consequently, the main climatic variable is the amount of precipitation and its seasonality.

The landforms of the subcontinent are divided into three major regions: (1) the southern peninsular massif; (2) the northern mountains—the Himalayas, Karakoram, Pamirs, Sulaiman, and Hindu Kush; and (3) the interconnected drainage basins of the Indus, Ganges, and Brahmaputra rivers (Figure 25–5). Considerable variety exists within each of those major units, but they stand apart as significant surface regions.

The Peninsular Massif

Peninsular India is an ancient massif composed of weathered crystalline rock. The peninsula is a plateau, tilted up on the west to elevations that exceed 6,000 feet (1,828 meters) and sloping gently eastward. A narrow lowland fringes the coasts, but abrupt ridges—the Ghats—rise a short distance inland along both the eastern and western flanks. The coastal lowland is wider on the eastern flank, where the main river basins broaden to form extensive alluvial plains. Drainage in the south is generally to the east, but north of Bombay the major rivers flow westward.

The peninsular massif contains most of the mineral wealth of India: copper, iron, gold, lead, manganese, and coal. Soils vary in fertility, but a shortage of water is a more serious problem to agricultural production than is the quality of soil.

The Northern Mountains

Several mountain ranges comprise the northern margins of the subcontinent, forming a mountain wall that is one of the most imposing physical features on earth. The height and magnitude of the mountain system exceed that of all others, and its geology indicates compressional forces and stress at work that are almost unparalleled. Fossil evidence suggests a fairly recent uplifting of gigantic rock waves, which formed the Himalayas. The high ridges are parallel to the margins of the plains farther south.

To the southwest of the Pamirs radiate two major ranges: the Sulaiman of eastern Afghanistan and western Pakistan and the Hindu Kush of Afghanistan. To the east are the Karakoram and the Himalayas, which form the wall that divides the Indian and Chinese cultural realms. Since other mountains have proved to be less of a barrier to movement and communications, India has long exchanged ideas and goods more with the Middle East and Southeast Asia than with East Asian civilizations.

The Indo-Gangetic Plain

Of the three main physical divisions of South Asia, the neighboring plains of the Indus, Ganges, and Brahmaputra rivers are the most significant. They form the heartland of ancient Hindu civilization, the core of India. Together, the drainage systems compose the largest continuous alluvial plain on earth, covering more than 300,000 square miles (777,000 square kilometers).

The plain is a structural depression that was formed at the same time the Himalayas were formed. Because the main drainage of the subcontinent has been oriented to that depression, the re-

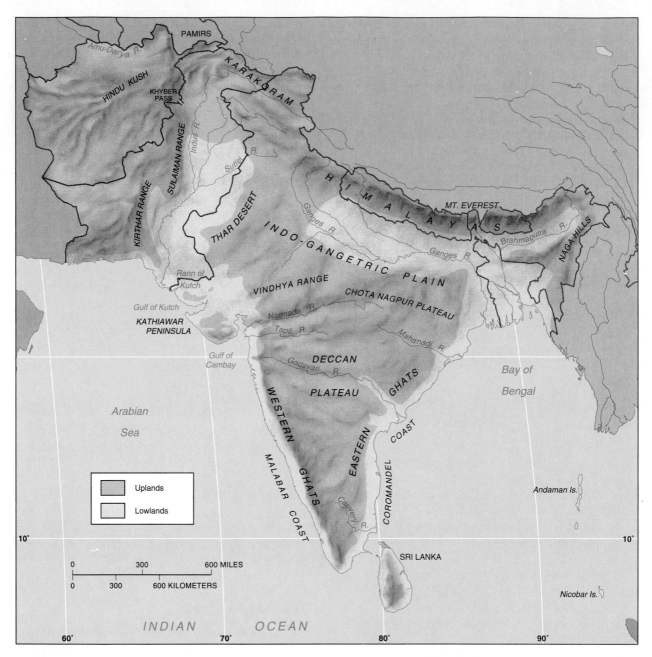

Figure 25–5

Physical regions and drainage patterns of South Asia. Three major physiographic regions comprise the subcontinent: the southern plateau, the northern and western
mountain wall, and the intervening Indo-Gangetic Plain. There are also narrow
coastal plains on the eastern and western coasts.

sultant floodplain has been covered with vast quantities of alluvial material. Today, the Indo-Gangetic Plain supports roughly half of the population of the subcontinent and is the political focal point for the three major states of South Asia. The selection of New Delhi, a city located in a commanding position in the upper Ganges Basin, as the capital of India reflects well the Indian view of the special significance of that region.[1]

Mineral and Land Resources

The resource base of South Asia, and of India in particular, is impressive. Coal, iron ore, manganese, and chromite exist in large quantities; and smaller amounts of other valuable minerals are also present. Perhaps the most serious mineral deficiency that faces the subcontinent is the lack of petroleum; future increases in food production may be tied, in part, to increases in the production of petroleum-derived chemical fertilizers. Currently, India imports more than 60 percent of its petroleum, which represents a serious drain on its scarce foreign-exchange reserves. However, recent offshore discoveries near Bombay have brightened India's prospects for energy self-sufficiency.

The Indo-Gangetic Plain is the largest and one of the most productive alluvial lowlands found anywhere on the globe. The availability of water and the partial renewal of nutrient materials through irrigation and floodwaters have allowed that great floodplain to sustain large numbers of people for several millennia.

Peninsular India contains a high percentage of land that is suitable for farming; the major problem is sufficient water to nourish crops. Only in the dry west—the Thar Desert of Rajasthan, the Sind region, the Rann of Kutch, and the basins and plateaus of Baluchistan in western Pakistan—and in the high mountains of the north is the agricultural environment too harsh to sustain large numbers of people (Figure 25–6).

POPULATION AND POPULATION GROWTH

Second among the world's countries in population, India was estimated to have 911.6 million people in 1994. To that number roughly 18 to 19 million newborn citizens are added each year. Only China matches such huge annual increases in population.

Regionally, India is not alone in its rapid growth. South Asia as a whole has roughly 1.3 billion people, and its annual growth rate is 2.3 percent. Indeed, if the high growth rates continue in India, Bangladesh, and Pakistan, South Asia may soon contain more people than East Asia.

Birthrates, Death Rates, and Growth Rates in India

According to UN estimates, life expectancy for the average Indian is fifty-nine years. The nation is progressing through Stage II of the model of demographic transformation (Figure 25–7; see also Figure 2–4). Despite a considerable effort to control births, the annual birthrate is 3.1 percent. With a death rate of 1.0 percent, India clearly has much to accomplish if the growth rate is to be reduced.

Much public education and many inducements have been directed toward India's peasantry to encourage various forms of birth control. Free transistor radios were given to men who volunteered to have vasectomies, and animated cartoons depicted the disadvantages of having too large a family. Government workers are provided with special incentives for small families or are penalized if they have more than two children. In 1975 and 1976 serious consideration was given to laws and regulations controlling family size, but political reaction to such stringent measures led to their abandonment.

Today, the official policy toward family planning is restrained. The problem appears to lie not so much in India's disapproval of birth control or neglect of family planning programs as in the sheer magnitude of spreading effective family-planning concepts and aids to half a million villages. Family-planning techniques are provided in most cities and many nearby villages, but the main challenge is rural India.

Continuation of the high population growth rate will give India a population of more than 1 billion by the year 2000. Based on what we know of India's cultural values and the high esteem in which Indian peasants hold large families, it is unlikely that rapid reductions in birthrates and growth rates can be achieved in this century.

Population age and sex structures also support the likelihood of continued growth. The population pyramid for India parallels the pattern that is found in most poor countries (Figure 25–8; see also

Figure 25-6
Camel caravan in the Thar Desert near Jaisalmer; an ancient fortress is visible in the background. Despite the monsoonal climate that brings heavy rainfall to many parts of India, the far northwest remains arid.

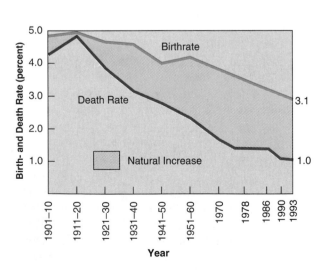

Figure 25-7
Trends in Indian birthrates, and death rates. Although the birthrate in India has been decreasing steadily in recent years, it has been offset by a rapidly declining death rate. Thus, the net growth rate has been high, and India's annual population increase has been sizable.

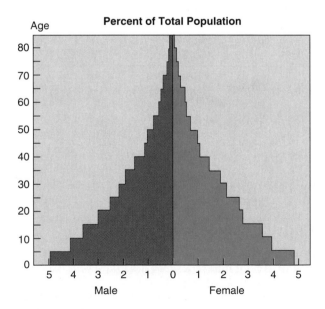

Figure 25-8
Population pyramid for India in the late 1980s. The population pyramid presented here is cone-shaped with a wide base of young people, indicating a youthful population with great potential for future growth.

582

Figure 4–12). The marked concentration of people in the younger age groups provides an ever-enlarging potential for future growth, as more people enter their childbearing years. It is that pattern, as much as anything about India's demography, that suggests little or no letup in population growth in the near future.

Even though India's population growth is not encouraging, hopeful signs do exist. For one thing the pace of change in today's developing countries is much greater than it was for comparable experiences in Western history. New technologies and techniques of communication, education, and public health appear continually, and change in values and traditions has been accelerated. Thus, changes can be quick if they have to be. If the information available from China accurately indicates recent events there, rapid and far-reaching demographic changes are possible even in large developing states. Whether similar events will take place in India is another matter, but population growth is certainly one of the most serious impediments to rapid economic growth and development.

Distribution of the Population

The population of the subcontinent is not evenly distributed (Figure 25–9). The middle and lower Ganges Basin, the lower Brahmaputra Basin, and the coastal lowland along the Eastern and Western Ghats are the most densely inhabited regions. That pattern appears to reflect the attraction of people to the most favorable agricultural environments, for those locations offer concentrated, dependable sources of water and productive alluvial soils. Such environments can be shaped and manipulated into productive farming regions that can support a large number of people and can sustain frequent plantings of intensive food grains, such as wet rice.

The population of peninsular India is large, but it is less dense than the populations of the rice-growing alluvial lowlands of the great river floodplains and the coastal lowland. Because much of the peninsula is dry, it is given over to such crops as wheat and millet; and yields per land unit are lower there than in the rice-growing areas. As a result, peninsular India cannot support as high a population density as the rice areas can. In the drier desert-and-steppe regions of western India and Pakistan (the Thar Desert of Rajasthan and the Rann of Kutch), populations are sparse, reflecting those environments.

AGRICULTURE IN SOUTH ASIA

A salient feature of India's contemporary economy is that most of its employed people work on farms. From their toil and production must come food for the large and growing population, as well as some of the capital needed to finance new investment in other sectors of the economy. Thus, successful development of the agricultural sector is critical for both food supply and growth of the industrial and service sectors.

Arable Land and the Environment for Agriculture

Half of India's land is arable, a much higher proportion than that in most other countries of Monsoon Asia. About 409 million acres (165.4 million hectares) have been under cultivation in recent years.

The ratio of arable land to total area is even higher in Bangladesh than it is in India. A remarkably dense rural population has evolved in that favorable agricultural environment, and the delta regions of the lower Ganges and Brahmaputra are as crowded as any place on earth (Table 25–1).

Pakistan has a smaller percentage of land that is suitable for agriculture. Consequently, the Indus floodplain and other areas where sufficient irrigation water is available are intensively cultivated, and they support a large population. Much of Pakistani territory, however, has limited agricultural potential because of its aridity. Improvements in the irrigation systems may permit some expansion of the agricultural land.

The smaller states of South Asia are even less favorably endowed with arable land than Pakistan is. Much of their surface terrain is too rugged, and significant agricultural development has taken place only in the level river valleys and basins.

The distribution of agricultural systems and crops in South Asia corresponds closely to variations in the environmental setting and, particularly, to water availability (Figure 25–10). In the dry west and the northern mountains, herding is characteristic over much of the area. Herding is a land-extensive enterprise, however, and supports only a modest population. Most of the people in those areas are supported by subsistence agriculture in the irrigated valleys of the west and in the mountain basins of the north. In the humid areas rice and jute are dominant. In the drier areas wheat, millet, corn, cotton,

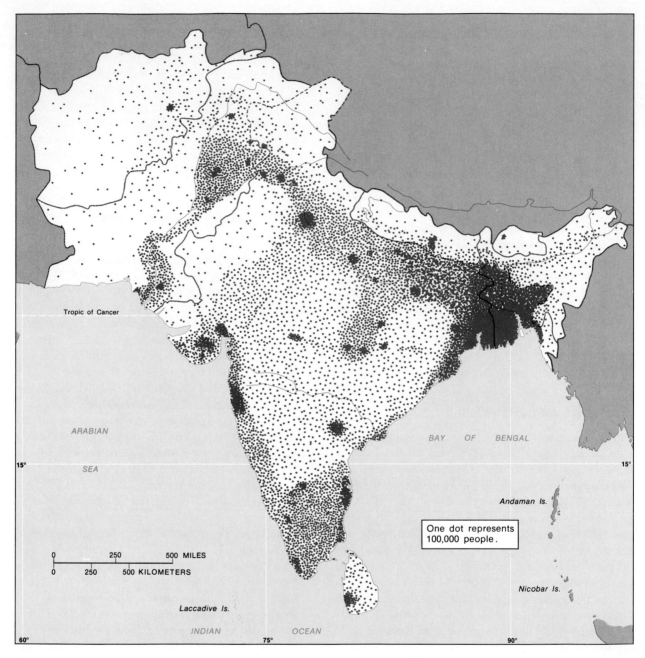

Figure 25-9
Distribution of South Asian population. South Asia has one of the world's greatest
concentrations of people. Yet, as the map indicates, those people are not dispersed
evenly throughout the subcontinent. The densest concentration is in the middle and
lower Ganges Valley, especially in the delta region, which is occupied largely by
Bangladesh. Important clusters, somewhat less dense, are found throughout the
peninsula and the Indus River floodplain.

Table 25-1
Population per land unit in Monsoon Asia, the United States, and Japan.

	Number of People per Unit of Land (1993)		Number of People per Unit of Cultivated Land[a] (1990)	
	Per Square Mile	Per Square Kilometer	Per Square Mile	Per Square Kilometer
South Asia				
Afghanistan	69	27	541	209
Bangladesh	2,266	875	3,411	1,317
Bhutan	43	17	3,080	1,189
India	782	302	1,344	519
Nepal	386	149	1,935	749
Pakistan	411	159	1,497	578
Sri Lanka	715	276	4,878	1,881
East Asia				
China	327	126	3,196	1,234
Hong Kong	15,142	5,846	254,683	98,333
Mongolia	4	2	409	158
North Korea	487	188	3,320	1,282
South Korea	1,170	451	5,726	2,211
Taiwan	1,501	579	6,014	2,322
Southeast Asia				
Cambodia (Kampuchea)	132	52	632	244
Indonesia	266	102	2,937	1,134
Laos	51	20	1,194	461
Malaysia	145	56	4,556	1,759
Myanmar (Burma)	171	66	1,139	440
Philippines	562	217	3,545	1,369
Singapore	11,982	4,626	725,200	280,000
Thailand	290	112	800	309
Vietnam	571	220	3,077	1,188
Other Regions				
United States	73	28	349	135
Japan	858	331	7,780	3,004

Sources: Food and Agriculture Organization, *Production Yearbook 1991* (Rome: United Nations, 1992); and Population Reference Bureau, *World Population Data Sheet* (Washington, DC: 1990, 1993).

[a]Includes cropped area and temporary pasturage but does not include permanent pasture or orchards, or long-term pena tree crops and shrubs such as cocoa, coffee, rubber, and tea.

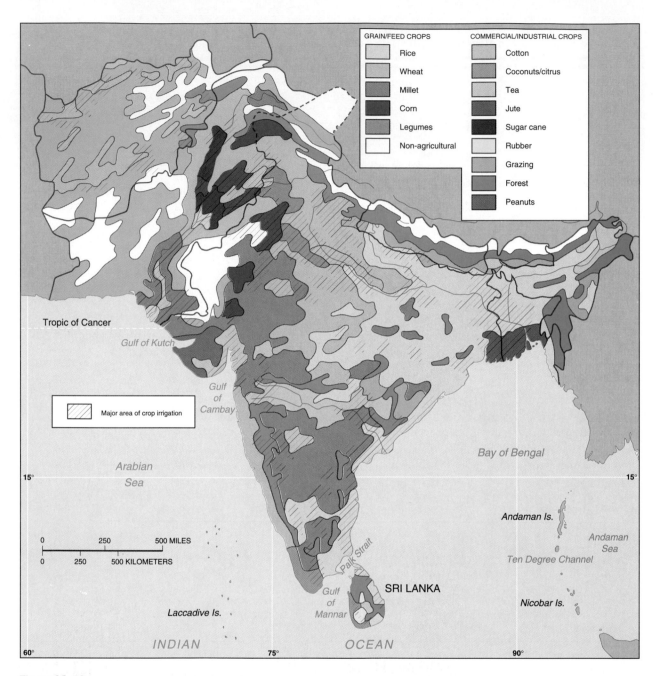

Figure 25-10
Main crops and crop regions of South Asia. Three main crop systems exist in the sub-continent, based largely on the availability of water. Rice, tea, and jute prevail in the most humid areas. Corn, cotton, wheat, sorghum, and millet are found in the drier interior, often associated with irrigation. In the driest and highest areas of the north and west, where sedentary agriculture is marginal, herding and subsistence farming are common.

sorghum, and gram (a type of chick-pea) are characteristic. Estate agriculture (i.e., large-scale commercial production mainly for export) occupies some of the south-facing mountain slopes and nearby hills of northeastern India. Tea in Sri Lanka and coconuts along India's Malabar Coast are also estate crops. Those estate crops, a legacy of British rule, are also grown in humid areas.

Traditional Indian Agriculture and the Village

Throughout India, agricultural life revolves around the local village. More than 500,000 villages pepper India's landscape. These villages and small towns account for roughly 70 percent of the population (Figure 25–11). The economy, society, and politics of the village set the style and tempo of life. Thus, as the primary production and social unit, the village holds the key to the character of modern India and the forces that oppose change and modernization.

For many centuries a high degree of autonomy and self-sufficiency existed at the village level; each village functioned largely as an independent operating and producing unit. Paralleling that economic independence was a social system in which occupation was a major indicator of caste and social rank. And because most castes operated at the village level, the result was a strict and rigid social stratification. The few external contacts that existed were generally with neighboring villages, and any intervillage linkages were formed along kinship lines within equivalent caste groupings. The commonplace image of rural India as conservative, tradition-bound, and slow to change has been a reasonably accurate one, though improved communications networks and technological changes may gradually alter that picture.

Some change in villages did occur with the spread of British control and the improved transportation system associated with the colonial enterprise. Prior to British rule, India had been compartmentalized into a number of social, economic, and political units. But regional and local isolation began to break down with improvement in the transportation and communication networks. As the villages were integrated more into the national framework, powerful social cleavages emerged between villagers and the new elite in the urban centers. Such cleavages are characteristic of societies in transition from traditional to modern status.

INDIAN AGRICULTURAL DEVELOPMENT

Two prominent factors are significant for long-term alteration of the traditional Indian patterns of society and economy. Those changes—rapid population growth and agricultural modernization—are interrelated and in some ways mutually reinforcing.

Figure 25–11
Oxen being used for threshing. India is a heavily populated country with thousands of villages in which technology remains traditional. The day-today task of these villagers is the production of food for survival.

The Boserupian Thesis

Enormous emphasis has been placed on the agricultural sector to continually increase food production. Yields per unit throughout much of India are still low by Western, Japanese, or Chinese standards (Figure 25–12). But production in India has managed to keep pace with the huge population growth. At least one economist, Ester Boserup, has suggested that rapid population growth is a positive factor because the intensified demand on the agricultural sector has opened it to reform and modernization (see Chapter 2).

According to the **Boserupian thesis**, without the stress of increased demand the traditional agricultural system simply continues without basic alteration. Population growth, however, forces an agricultural system to begin a process of transformation and modernization. Boserup's thesis is interesting if for no other reason than that it is contrary to the neo-Malthusian viewpoint of population growth (see Chapter 2). It should be pointed out, however, that Boserup's support of population growth is qualified. She claims that the forced pace of rural modernization brought on by rapid population growth is a short-term proposition. Once the transformation process is well under way, she predicts that population growth will begin to taper off.

One of the problems associated with rapid population growth in India is that labor absorption in rural areas becomes crucial, since so many new hands must be employed each year. In recent years such large numbers of workers have been absorbed in some areas that their marginal productivity (i.e., the additional output per additional unit of input) is zero. In other words, if those workers were removed from the labor force, production would not be affected at all; thus, their contribution is worth nothing. Unless that condition is changed, peasants will remain poor throughout much of India.

India's Green Revolution

The greatest promise for India's rural modernization may well lie in the Green Revolution (see Chapter 4). The new high-yield varieties (HYVs) of grains, including rice, are now widely cultivated in India; and total grain production has increased substantially during the past two decades. The average yearly increase during the 1980s has been 3.1 percent, a figure somewhat above the annual rate of

population growth. And although the area under cultivation has also expanded, much of that increase is attributable to improved yields per land unit. Nonetheless, yields per unit for all food grains are still only half of what they are in China.

The difference in yields between China and India is caused by four factors:

1. China has a much higher proportion of cultivated land under irrigation (51 percent versus India's 26 percent).
2. China uses about four times as much fertilizer per unit of cropped land than India does.

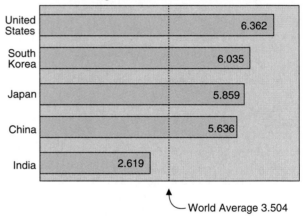

Average Rice Yields, M/Tons/Ha, 1993

United States	6.362
South Korea	6.035
Japan	5.859
China	5.636
India	2.619

World Average 3.504

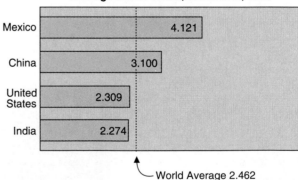

Average Wheat Yields, M/Tons/Ha, 1993

Mexico	4.121
China	3.100
United States	2.309
India	2.274

World Average 2.462

Figure 25–12

Grain yields for selected countries. Despite the expenditure of many hours of work per land unit, rice yields in India are significantly below the world average. South Korea and Japan, on the other hand, have rice yields almost twice that of the world average. (From Food and Agriculture Organization, *Production Yearbook, 1992*, vol. 46, Rome: United Nations, 1993.)

3. China's best land is generally used for grains; but some of India's best land, much of which is irrigated, is used for other crops, such as cotton or jute.
4. China's rate of double-cropping is approximately twice that of India.

Most of those differences—the rate of irrigation, fertilizer usage, and double-cropping—indicate that India has considerable potential to increase grain production. If the use of HYVs is expanded, also, India's agriculture can be made much more productive.

Despite considerable progress, Indian agriculture still has many problems. The Green Revolution has helped improve many of the basic inputs for farming, but institutional problems remain. In many regions serious land-tenancy problems persist; for example, in the northeastern state of Bihar land is unevenly distributed, and many peasants continue to be tied to landlords. In other areas agricultural credit systems are poorly developed or lacking, or landholdings are so small that farmers cannot take advantage of new techniques and technical improvements. Thus, agricultural progress is uneven across India. Some regions, such as the Punjab, have made rapid progress, and yields are high; but others, such as Bihar, show little change.

India's Progress Toward Self-Sufficiency

India's progress toward agricultural transformation will be closely linked to its resolution of a basic conflict. As mentioned earlier, approximately 70 percent of India's population is directly dependent on agriculture for its livelihood, and because of population growth that employment sector must incorporate huge numbers of new workers every year. At the same time, however, agriculture is attempting to modernize and become more efficient by substituting capital for labor to improve yields. Thus, an obvious contradiction exists between the realities of India's current demographic situation, which encourages underemployment of the rural labor force, and the nation's desire and capacity to transform its traditional agricultural system.

The program of rural transformation that has been under way in India has experienced both success and failure. For the most part, India's food production has kept pace with the country's rapid population increase. In fact, despite the frequent importation of foodstuffs, India has stood on the threshold of food self-sufficiency, and great gains are being made. Unfortunately, however, population growth has matched the gains in production, and yields per land unit remain low, suggesting that the agricultural transformation is still in its early stages. The sheer size of India's peasantry makes that transformation a monumental task (Figure 25–13).

At the same time, in certain areas of India, such as the states of Punjab and Haryana, and in scattered locations in Kerala, Karnataka, and other states, advances in agriculture have been rapid and impressive. In those places—as a result of high rates of investment, irrigation, double-cropping, and mechanization—yields per unit have raised farm incomes substantially and have demonstrated the potential for progress and change in Indian agriculture (Figure 25–14). Available capital, farm extension education and other services, and a well-organized and hard-working farm population are essential if such developments are to become more widespread.

Another problem that continues to plague Indian farming is the unreliability of the summer monsoon rains. When those rains fail or are seriously diminished, as they were in 1981 and 1982, farm production throughout much of the country is devastated, and yields fall off sharply.

CENTRALIZED PLANNING AND ECONOMIC GROWTH IN INDIA

Since independence in 1947, India has developed its own form of central planning and government control to promote development. That control has been expressed mainly in a series of five-year plans that have focused on the nationalization of key industries and services: iron and steel making, heavy-machinery manufacturing, fertilizer and chemical production, irrigation systems, and transportation and communication networks. In general, India's planning has attempted to channel large investments into those enterprises. It is important to realize that such plans have been made by a national planning commission within a democratic context in which local, regional, and national interests have been considered. That fact, in itself, is significant since many less developed nations look to the experiences of both India and China for development strategies. And such procedures are not entirely dif-

Figure 25-13
The Bose Road Market in Madras on India's southeastern coast. India's densely populated rural areas and its growing urban population require a major effort to assure a
reliable food supply.

ferent from those that operate in the U.S. political system, even though the United States has no single national commission charged with overall economic planning.

Since 1951, economic controversy in India has centered on one principal issue: the relative attention and investment given to manufacturing and agriculture. An important subissue has been the extent to which the manufacturing sector should be nationalized. During the first three decades of development following independence in 1947, economic planning in India emphasized the Soviet model, which encouraged state-operated heavy industries and the manufacture of producer goods. A small private sector was allowed to continue. By the 1970s the inefficiencies and difficulties of this approach became more clear and India began to allow more incentives and development of the private sector and the growth of consumer oriented manufacturing.

Agricultural Investment Versus Industrial Development

Most Western planners have argued that India should focus more attention and investment on modernizing its agriculture. However, many Indians view an emphasis on agriculture as an extension of the nation's dependence on foreign sources for basic equipment and industrial goods. That approach has therefore been unappealing. Moreover, the Indians believe that an agricultural emphasis would prolong India's political and military impotence in world affairs. That basic disagreement may have been a factor in the misunderstanding and mutual criticism that have often characterized U.S.-Indian relations during the past four decades.

At this time India has largely achieved freedom from reliance on foreign manufacturers, though it has sporadically looked to external sources of foodstuffs to meet internal deficiencies. In recent years,

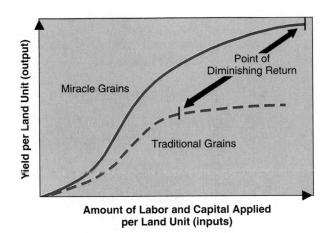

Figure 25-14
Hypothetical difference in yields. High-yield, or miracle, grains offer substantially greater rewards for developing countries. Yields from the miracle grains are much higher per unit of labor and capital input.

however, rapid population growth and periodic droughts have shown that agricultural production must be increased rapidly. Consequently, investments in those industries and services that support agriculture have been intensified. An associated policy—aimed at providing more rural jobs in community development, self-help, and education-related projects—has also received increased attention. It has become obvious that industrial jobs in large cities will not provide sufficient employment for the additional millions who enter the labor force each year.

The real crisis for India's development program continues to lie in the countryside. Some means must be found to satisfy immediate needs for food, clothing, and housing, not to mention long-term aspirations for education and a better life. Indian planners and politicians are coming to realize that drastic solutions are required in rural India if the more sophisticated benefits of industrial growth and national development are to be achieved.

The Industrial Economy

Industrial development and expansion in India evolved from a tradition of cottage manufacturing associated with metal smelting and consumer goods. British plans for India in the nineteenth century neglected those native industries and concentrated instead on new industries that complemented

manufacturing in Great Britain. British interests encouraged labor-intensive industries, such as textiles, or industries that relied on local commodities, such as jute processing, sugar refining, and leather tanning. The British wanted to sell India the more sophisticated manufactured goods, and their colonial rule ensured success for that strategy.

The shortages that accompanied World War I brought some expansion in Indian industries, such as iron and steel, cement, and paper. During World War II those developments intensified as India became a rear supply area for China's theater of war. Despite those improvements, however, on the eve of independence India had few machine-building or chemical industries.

Planned Industrialization, 1947 to the Present

In line with its desire to achieve greater self-sufficiency, India has followed an import-substitution strategy. Planners have targeted industries that supply the entire range of producer and consumer goods, except for highly specialized luxury items. That range extends from the well-established textile, jute, and sugar-processing mills to locomotive, shipbuilding, and aircraft factories; it even includes computer manufacturing and the processing of materials for atomic energy. Industrial growth during the 1980s averaged 6.6 percent annually, whereas manufacturing output grew at an average rate of 7.1 percent.

Production of a wide range of goods has been possible because of the large domestic market and the ability of producers to achieve economies of scale sufficient to keep prices low. India is reasonably well endowed with resources and materials for industrial production.

Industrial Regions

British colonial policy had concentrated industrial production in the three major port cities of Calcutta, Bombay, and Madras. Since independence the Indian government has focused on distributing new industry throughout the nation, locating industries closer to raw materials or markets so that centers of production and growth can be spread out more evenly.

Most prominent among the recently created industrial regions is the cluster of heavy manufacturing in the **Damodar Valley** region west of Calcutta (Figure 25–15). Symbolized by the planned indus-

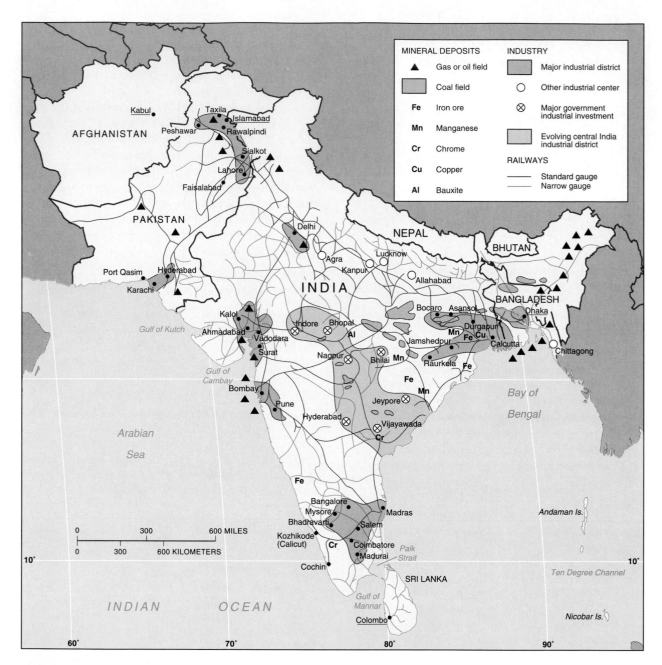

Figure 25-15
Major mineral and industrial regions of South Asia. Although poor, the subcontinent has a well-developed surface transportation network, inherited in part from British colonial investments.

trial city of Jamshedpur, that center of iron and steel production is largely raw-material oriented. Because Jamshedpur is close to the major iron ore deposits and coalfields of the subcontinent, most of the recently established heavy-metal and associated chemical and machining industries are located in that area. With each new project the raw material and assembly factors that have favored the area from the beginning have been reinforced by economies of scale and agglomeration. In fact, the growth and concentration of Indian industry in the Damodar Valley have been impressive enough to make that region one of the major metal- and machinery-production centers not only of Asia but also of the world.

Some industries do not benefit from clustering, however. Many are oriented to local or regional markets or are best associated with agricultural or other raw materials that are dispersed more broadly. Textile mills are common in the cotton-producing region of Rajasthan; and sugar refineries and paper mills, which depend on crushed sugarcane pulp, are situated in peninsular India near the areas of heaviest sugarcane production. In addition, older centers of industry continue to attract new establishments, because the older areas have the advantages of large markets, accessibility and transportation linkages, and large and relatively skilled labor pools.

INDIA'S TRANSPORTATION NETWORKS

Railroads

India has possessed a large and dense railway system for more than a century. It is the longest, densest rail network in Asia, with Japan excluded, and it is one of the longest systems in the world. The usefulness of the railroad system in promoting urban and economic growth is hindered, however, because the system was designed to further colonial aims—that is, to stimulate exports and imports—rather than to foster internal development; some of the routes are not interconnected.

Historically, the railroad system has focused on the four major urban centers of Delhi, Bombay, Calcutta, and Madras. Those cities were linked together by a skeletal framework of broad-gauge lines. Each city, in turn, was tied to its large hinterland by a network of lines of different gauges. Thus, a fully integrated railroad system did not exist; nor was there a means of stimulating growth in smaller

centers in the interior. Such a system typified British colonial practice. Recently, attempts have been made to standardize gauges wherever feasible and not too costly, but a long-term standardization project has yet to be devised.

After independence the rail system was divided into a series of regional railway networks under the direction of the government-owned Indian Railways. Despite problems of administration and operation, railways continue to be the most efficient and least expensive method of hauling goods and carrying people throughout the nation.

The Highway System

In recent years attention has been given to highways as an alternative to railroad transport. Indeed, a long-term plan has been drawn up for construction of an integrated system of all-weather roads, which may provide an effective means of linking the many areas of India. Those roads may also effectively stimulate growth and economic activity in smaller cities.

The long-term plans are designed to integrate most of the settled areas of India through a network of main highways and secondary roads that reflect population densities. In thickly settled agricultural regions a dense network of interlocking roads is to place all villages within 2 miles (3.2 kilometers) of a secondary road and 5 miles (8 kilometers) of a main highway. In sparsely settled nonfarming areas the network is to be thinner but is still to link the areas in a systematic manner.

In addition to new highway construction, recent efforts have concentrated on improving and upgrading existing roads. Important roads carrying much traffic are to be widened to increase capacity. Secondary roads are to have their surfaces improved, and rural roads are also to be upgraded. The Indian system may appear inadequate by Western European standards, but when compared with that of most other developing nations, especially other large countries, India's highway network is extensive.

Air Transportation

Air transportation has developed rapidly in recent decades, as the Indian government has promoted both an international air carrier (Air-India) and a domestic one (Indian Airlines). Most of the major cities and many intermediate ones are now linked through the domestic carrier, and international service is available through major gateway cities, such as Delhi, Calcutta, Madras, and Bombay. Although service is not as frequent as it is in modern, wealthy countries, air transportation in India is well developed when compared with that of most other developing countries.

Transportation and Development

A good transportation system is imperative in a large, developing state. Without access to its own territory and integration of its regions, a state cannot function effectively or promote the kinds of programs that are necessary for proper economic growth. In China, for example, the expansion of transport networks has been critical to economic growth policies and to the political-military goals of national strength and power.

India offers a somewhat contrasting pattern. A fairly dense transportation network was one of the consequences of British colonialism, providing a broad base on which to develop a locational strategy of economic growth. Such a base permitted India to concentrate investment on other problems and simply improve the transport system that already existed.

URBAN INDIA: CONTRASTING POINTS OF VIEW

Although perhaps only one-fourth of India's population resides in cities and towns, that 25 percent includes more than 220 million people. By that standard, then, India must rank as one of the world's leading urban states. Those millions of urban residents are distributed among a variety of different-sized cities and towns, which have given rise to several competing schools of thought regarding future urban growth.

Some planners and scholars believe that India is neglecting to influence urban growth and thus can look forward to huge concentrations in a few great metropolitan areas: Calcutta, Delhi, Bombay, Madras, and Hyderabad. Those scholars also suggest that such concentration is bad because income will be inequitably distributed, and increasing urbanization will destroy the traditional social patterns that are focused on small and more personalized villages. Those experts point to future dense crowding in huge supercities, with attendant social break-downs, and note that political unrest is already being experienced in some of the large cities.

Calcutta and Bombay

Greater Calcutta, with its 12 million people, is probably the most frequently cited example of everything that is wrong with big-city life and activities in a developing state. Its poverty and disease and the congestion in its streets, over which cars speed and sacred cows meander, have been chronicled so frequently that they need little repetition (Figure 25–16). Political confrontation and urban violence are also no strangers to Calcutta's urban scene, and many sympathetic Westerners despair over the hopeless condition of one of India's largest urban centers.

Bombay, by contrast, is sometimes viewed as an example of the positive aspects of urban India. The city (estimated at 13.3 million) is surrounded by a less densely populated and more prosperous agricultural hinterland. Bombay has always seemed to be one of India's most advanced and progressive places. Big, modern factories—staffed by an industrious and relatively well-fed labor force—create a large industrial output, which supports a thriving commerce and growing middle and upper classes of professionals and entrepreneurs. Cultural and educational institutions abound, and the city, with its international orientation and booming economy, is among India's most cosmopolitan centers. Yet Bombay has its problems, too: 40 to 50 percent of its population now resides in slums, and the availability of urban housing has become a serious problem.

Both Calcutta and Bombay have good and bad points; both provide examples of growth and progress, poverty and despair. The two cities, like all of India's cities, will no doubt continue to grow. Despite problems of widespread urban unemployment, the cities are an irresistible lure that continues to attract large numbers of rural people. And unlike China, India has no regulations or other means of restricting rural migrants from moving to cities.

Metropolis Versus Town

Some planners claim that the greatest production efficiencies are achieved in the larger cities, with good transport systems and skilled labor forces. Others assert that towns and cities with a population of 250,000

Figure 25-16
Street scene in Calcutta. Congestion, decaying infrastructure, and rural-to-urban migration that generates slums are problems for all of India's cities, but perhaps none more so than Calcutta.

or less are big enough to provide the economies of scale necessary for efficient production; therefore, India should direct more of its future economic growth to the smaller centers, spreading the wealth more equitably. Such dispersal also appeals to local and regional political interests and satisfies the sectional interests of the Indian political system.

It is too early to predict India's urban future, but already it seems that India's gigantic population will require both styles of urban growth. The great metropolitan centers can be used intensively for the production of specific goods, especially those that are export-oriented. The smaller cities and towns can continue to satisfy local needs and demands, both commercial and industrial, as they always have. To the extent that the economy modernizes, however, those local and regional production cen-

ters will have to become more sophisticated as they contribute increasingly to the national, and even the international, economy.

PAKISTAN

The 1947 partitioning of British India's Muslims and Hindus into two nations has had serious consequences, not the least of which are periodic eruptions of violence. Most outbreaks have involved Indian and Pakistani forces fighting over the control of Kashmir. An outbreak in the early 1970s, however, involved the eastern section of Pakistan, a Bengali-speaking region. And unfortunately for Pakistan, the linguistic and sectional differences between the Bengali- and the Urdu-speaking Muslims overcame whatever religious affinities had existed previously. The result was that East Pakistan, with help from the Indian army, established itself as the independent state of Bangladesh, and Pakistan was left as a single territorial unit focused on the Indus River floodplain.

Although the reasons behind the political breakup of Pakistan are many, the basic difficulty revolved around the position of one group—the West Pakistanis. The Urdu-speaking West Pakistanis had dominated the politics and military affairs of the nation, even though their popular support was a minority position. The numerically dominant, Bengali-speaking East Pakistanis had been to some extent exploited and, in their view, oppressed. Consequently, following the free elections in late 1970 in which the East Pakistani Awami League party won a majority of seats in the Pakistan National Assembly, disagreements broke out. Fighting followed. Ultimately, the state broke into two political entities: Pakistan (the western sector) and Bangladesh (the eastern sector).

The New Pakistan

The Pakistan that emerged from that political division is considerably different—politically as well as economically—from the joint state that existed before 1971. First, the new Pakistani state is patterned politically along British lines, with the addition of an interesting blend of local religious feeling and socialist doctrine. The economy has become increasingly socialistic, with less freedom for the free-enterprise sectors of industry, commerce, and finance. Such a socialist pattern may, to some extent, reflect Pakistan's attraction to China and its policies of state control throughout the economic system.

Although separation from Bangladesh has presumably led to greater political and social coherence in Pakistan, other problems have become more apparent. The large, arid Baluchistan region west of the Indus floodplain, beset by various tribal interests and political groupings, has become an area of major domestic difficulty. And in the northwest, tribal elements that look at Afghanistan or Iran for political support and cultural identity create other problems. Pakistan must somehow knit together those diverse ethnic threads into a strong social fabric. To complicate matters, the 1979 Soviet invasion of Afghanistan led to a large influx of Afghans into Pakistan. Thus, Pakistan found itself embroiled in a conflict against the Soviets, further complicating its

relations with India. When longtime strongman and president of Pakistan Mohammad Zia ul-Haq and several of his leading military supporters died in a 1988 airplane crash, the political tension and instability in this troubled region simply increased and have persisted ever since.

Jammu and Kashmir

No problem in contemporary Pakistan is of greater magnitude than the territorial dispute with India over **Jammu and Kashmir**, an area in the high Himalayas. The cease-fire line drawn in the 1950s has become an effective boundary, leaving India to occupy the most productive and densely populated parts of the region. But territorial claims have not yet been resolved; and given today's political climate, the stalemate over Jammu and Kashmir is not likely to change. After Pakistan was divided into two nations, its economic and military position vis-à-vis India was weakened. India, on the other hand, emerged from that division as the dominant political and military force on the subcontinent and is unlikely to be challenged in the near future.

Growth and Progress

Like its neighbors, Pakistan is poor; and its past political problems have aggravated its impoverished condition. Most of its population, 126.4 million in 1994, is concentrated in the watershed of the Indus, where two main productive regions stand out. One of those regions is focused on Karachi, the early capital and a large port and industrial center at the mouth of the Indus. The upper Indus region—focused on Lahore and the new capital, Islamabad—is the modern political center and the region of greatest concern for contemporary planning.

Agriculture continues to dominate the economy of Pakistan, though its share of output has declined in recent years as industrial output has grown more rapidly. However, even where irrigation is commonly practiced, as in the Indus Basin, weather patterns often play a key role in determining agricultural output and, thus, the size of the GNP.

Pakistan's agriculture is based on three main crops: wheat, rice, and cotton. Sugarcane is also important, as are certain oilseeds from which cooking oils are extracted. Government objectives, as implemented by various rural-development programs, are to increase agricultural production through greater application of chemical fertilizers, better strains of seed, and improved farming techniques. Agricultural imports and exports have generally been balanced, though a modest export surplus has existed recently.

Industry's share of the GDP almost equaled that of agriculture (about 25 percent) in 1990, and it is growing more rapidly. A broad range of industrial facilities exists, but the socialization of industry may alter past patterns of growth by reducing entrepreneurial investment. Traditionally, cotton textiles have been the most important foreign-exchange earner, and a high rate of investment in such activities continues.

The years since separation from Bangladesh have witnessed more rapid economic growth, yet Pakistan continues as an impoverished country with a traditional, agricultural economic system. Nonetheless, its large area and population provide many advantages, and industrial production can be geared to exploit the advantages of scale economies. With help from the Chinese and other external sources of investment capital, Pakistan will now be able to focus more energy on its economy than was possible in past years.

BANGLADESH

The creation of a new country is never simple or easy, and the conditions of South Asian politics and society make it even more difficult to create the permanent loyalties and symbols so necessary for successful statehood. Nevertheless, against a background of political, social, and linguistic discrimination, Bangladesh emerged as a new nation-state. India's military backing was important in forging the new state, but it was the desire for self-determination that led the former eastern sector of Pakistan to wrench itself free from the confinement and pressure imposed by West Pakistan.

The Delta Environment

Bangladesh is an unusual place. Its tropical delta environment, limited territory, large number of people, and language differences present a host of problems. The failure of the former Pakistan government to recognize and cope with those features led Bangladesh to seek its own destiny as an independent state. With almost 117 million people in 55,598 square miles (143,999 square kilometers), Bangla-

desh is one of the most crowded places on earth (see Table 25–1). If we put fifteen New York Cities into an area the size of Illinois or Georgia, we would have about the same population density as that in Bangladesh.

Most of the land area of Bangladesh is low lying, made up of the intricate network of streams and distributaries that form the mouths of the Ganges River and its confluent, the Brahmaputra. The extent of the delta is almost without parallel in the world, and it is that delta environment that has permitted so many people to live on so little land. Almost two-thirds of the land area is farmed, and a productive agricultural system has evolved that is based largely on the cultivation of paddy rice. A variety of other food crops and some specialized cash crops, such as jute, are also produced in large quantity, but rice is the main staple of the great mass of people (Figure 25–17).

The rhythm of alternating wet and dry seasons (described in Chapter 24) governs agricultural life in Bangladesh; 80 to 90 inches (2,030 to 2,284 millimeters) of rain, concentrated in the summer months, provides much of the water that is necessary for rice cultivation. A finely developed system of irrigation supplements the rainwater and provides the controls for the sustained high yields necessary to feed so many people. Unfortunately, tropical storms originating over the adjacent warm Bay of Bengal disrupt life in Bangladesh by causing periodic severe floods in many coastal areas. And because of the extreme crowding on the delta, the destruction and loss of life are great. It is a sad irony that so much productive agricultural land is so vulnerable to natural catastrophes.

Prospects for Economic Growth

Bangladesh entered nationhood in 1971 after considerable suffering and natural disaster. Its war of independence damaged the infrastructure severely; bridges and transportation systems were wrecked, ports were clogged and nonfunctioning, and power facilities were damaged. A great storm had also caused enormous loss of human and animal life, and agricultural production declined sharply. The UN sponsored relief efforts, which were supplemented with additional donations from other foreign nations and private agencies. Bangladesh was not without friends and sympathizers, and those external suppliers saw the nation through the immediate crisis.

Figure 25-17
Land utilization in Bangladesh.
Bangladesh is focused around
the main drainage channels of
the Ganges and Brahmaputra
rivers. Almost the entire country is a large delta plain, much
of which is given over to rice
production to feed the country's large and growing population.

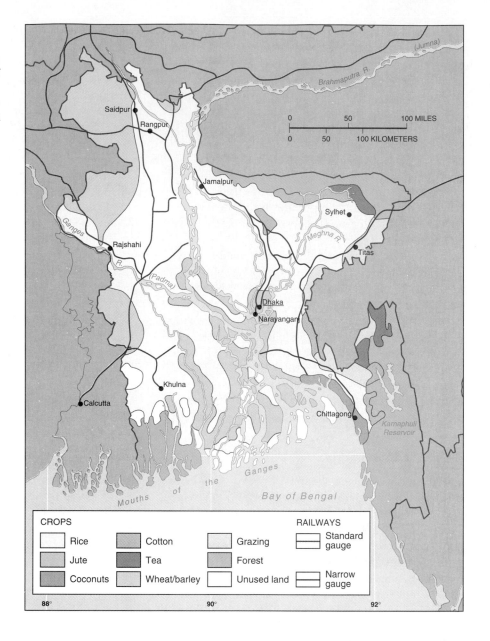

The short-term goal of restoring production to its
preindependence level was set forth in a one-year
plan. Then, in 1973 a five-year development plan
was adopted to promote future growth; it set an annual goal of 5.5 percent for production increases,
primarily in the agricultural sector. In view of the
many natural and human problems, however, that
goal was unrealistic. The principal difficulty was the
high degree of reliance on foreign capital, which is
difficult for such a poor country to obtain; nonetheless, during its first five-year development plan
Bangladesh procured about 60 percent of its invest-

ment capital externally. Unfortunately, the capital
was frequently used to purchase foodstuffs, the
most critical need, with little left for development
projects.

The second five-year plan, launched in 1980,
placed more emphasis on industrial production and
investment by the private sector. Laws were enacted
to encourage private foreign investment in
Bangladesh, and several large joint projects, such as
a major urea fertilizer plant, were developed. In addition, industrial production of such items as sugar,
caustic soda, diesel engines, motor vehicles, and

television sets rose sharply during those years. Nevertheless, agriculture continued to be the mainstay of the economy, accounting for almost 40 percent of the gross domestic product in 1990. Production of rice and wheat, the two most important food grains, increased steadily.

The third five-year plan began in 1986 with a goal of 5.4 percent economic growth annually. That plan also sought food self-sufficiency and a reduction of the population growth rate to 1.8 percent per annum, both by 1990. Unfortunately, none of the goals were met. Two major problems beset the economy of Bangladesh—the persisting unfavorable balance of trade and the poor fiscal position of the country. A substantial national and foreign debt still exists, although the annual service on the debt has been reduced in recent years. If foreign aid continues in sufficient amounts, the outlook for continued economic growth is reasonable. However, population growth, based on a current annual birthrate of 3.7 percent, will undermine that economic progress, unless continuing declines in the rate of increase follow. Agricultural output improved in the early 1990s, and Bangladesh's overall prospects for economic growth show some improvement.

SRI LANKA

Of all the South Asian states, Sri Lanka (which was called Ceylon until 1972) is perhaps the most modern and the most certain of the direction in which its society and economy are moving. Although poor, it has initiated a massive effort to cut its birthrate and to promote improvements in the agricultural economy. Sri Lankan agriculture, with its large plantation sector, has long been commercialized. However, the plantation sector has been plagued with inefficiencies, and certain aspects of the agricultural economy have stagnated in recent years, perpetuating low yields and intensive manual inputs. That economic bottleneck must be overcome before real growth can be achieved.

Despite continuing modest growth in agriculture and industry, Sri Lanka has pursued policies of social development that have improved the well-being of its people. The state invests heavily in basic health care, education, and welfare, and the results have given the average citizen a better quality of life compared with India and other South Asian neighbors. For example, in 1993 average life expectancy was seventy-one in Sri Lanka, compared to fifty-nine in India.

Land and Environment

Sri Lanka is a pear-shaped island state of 25,332 square miles (65,610 square kilometers)—about the size of West Virginia—that lies 12 miles (19 kilometers) southeast of India. The island is tropical, though the hot, humid climate is moderated at higher elevations in the interior mountains. Rainfall follows a seasonal pattern; the southeast monsoon dominates between May and August, bringing heavy rains to the southwestern quarter of the island. From November to early spring the wind direction is reversed, and the eastern flank receives most of the rain. Frost is unknown, and average monthly temperatures vary only slightly from the coldest month to the hottest one.

About 44 percent of Sri Lanka is forested, though much of today's plantation complex was formerly forest land (Figure 25–18). Mineral deposits of graphite, quartz, feldspars, and gemstones are commercially significant, and exploration for additional minerals continues.

Contemporary Patterns of Development

Sri Lanka faces a serious investment dilemma: conflicting concern for immediate consumer interests and for long-term economic development goals has led to inadequate funding of both. Another problem is the serious inflationary spiral that has affected all of the world's economies. The export prices of tea, rubber, and coconuts, the principal cash crops, have boomed; but those prices have been offset by equally large increases in the cost of imports: rice, sugar, flour, and crude oil. The net effect has been to impede the accumulation of capital and thus to restrict the rate of investment to promote economic growth.

Social problems also continue to plague the island. Of the 17.9 million inhabitants 70 percent—known as **Sinhalese**—are of Indo-Aryan origin and are descended from the ancient settlers. About 20 percent are more recently arrived **Tamils**, or south Indian Dravidians (Tamil speakers). The Sinhalese are Buddhists, and the Tamils are Hindus; thus, their division is not only ethnic and linguistic but also religious. Violence between the Sinhalese and the Tamils has been characteristic for several centuries. More recently, newly arrived Tamil plantation work-

Figure 25-18
Sri Lanka, a large tropical island. Sri Lanka's substantial agricultural economy is based on both estate (cash) crops and subsistence farming. Much of the island's interior remains underdeveloped, supporting either shifting cultivation or forest vegetation.

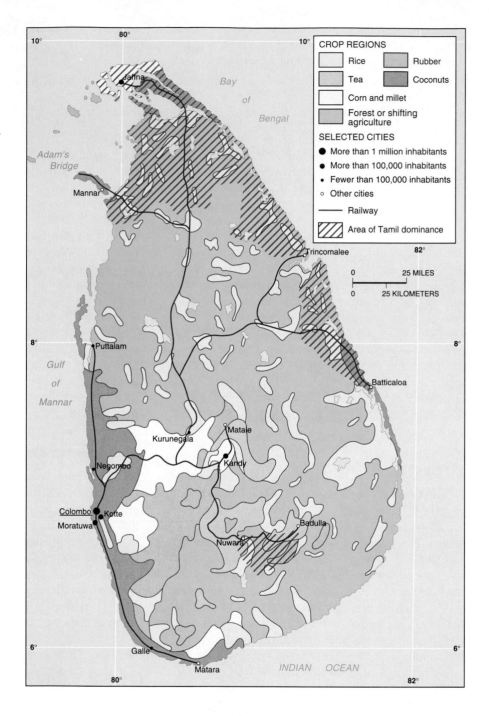

ers have created additional stress, and the government has worked to repatriate some of those people to India. In July 1983 more than 200 persons were reported killed in a week of violent clashes between the two groups. In 1987, after increasingly violent clashes, Indian troops were invited in, and a truce with the Tamil separatists was achieved. Sporadic fighting has continued nevertheless (Figure 25–19).

Overall, the government of Sri Lanka has followed relatively enlightened economic and social policies and has confronted and, in most cases, resolved political and social problems and unrest. But because of its limited resource base, Sri Lanka is economically vulnerable. Another small island state in Asia, Taiwan, has been in a similar situation, and Sri Lanka may draw some inspiration from the remarkable economic growth and progress of Taiwan. The lesson learned is that such achievement requires disciplined effort by the people, in addition to investment capital. If those two criteria can be met, Sri Lanka may have the same kind of success that Taiwan has had. In that case its small-island accessibility, high level of administrative control, and integrated economic system can become advantages that outweigh the liabilities of a limited resource base.

AFGHANISTAN

Strictly speaking, Afghanistan is not in Monsoon Asia, but it has long figured prominently in the political and military history of the Indian subconti-

Figure 25-19
Aftermath of violence between Sinhalese and Tamils. The two groups are distinctive in ethnicity, language, and religion; their clashes have been one of the social-political problems the government has had to confront in recent years.

nent. For more than twenty-three centuries (since the time of Alexander the Great) the strategic location of Afghanistan—with its command of the mountain passes that link eastern, southern, southwestern, and central Asia—has attracted conquerors and rulers. The recent history of the country reflects a continuation of that competition, between British and Russian interests in the nineteenth and early twentieth centuries and more recently among the Russians, Indians, Pakistanis, and Chinese.

The Physical Basis of Livelihood

Most of Afghanistan is high and enclosed, rather like the Basin-and-Range region of the western United States. With the exception of the Kabul River and its tributaries, which flow eastward into the Indus system, all other drainage is internal, that is, without an outlet to the sea (Figure 25–20). Afghanistan is a landlocked nation.

The dominant landforms of Afghanistan are the Hindu Kush Mountains, which separate the plains of northern Afghanistan from the rest of the country. Despite that division, the country has managed to maintain a strong political cohesiveness. South of the Hindu Kush are a great desert plateau-and-basin region in the southwest and south and a large alluvial basin, centered on Kabul, in the east. The Kabul Basin is the most densely settled part of the country and forms the heartland of Afghanistan.

Most of Afghanistan is dry; annual precipitation averages 20 inches (508 millimeters) or less and is concentrated in the winter and early spring, much of it falling as snow. Thus, the seasonal distribution is the reverse of the monsoonal pattern found farther south and east. Temperatures differ from the monsoonal pattern also; both daily temperature variations and seasonal ranges are great.

Isolation and a rugged land surface have impeded both the introduction of technological innovations and the speed of economic change and growth (Figure 25–21). Afghanistan has no railroads, and its primary roads serve only the major urban centers. Even though a great deal of investment has focused on transportation improvement recently, large sections of the country still have no modern means of transportation. Thus, in view of the impediments to internal movement of goods, people, and ideas, the poverty and extremely low level of economic development are not surprising.

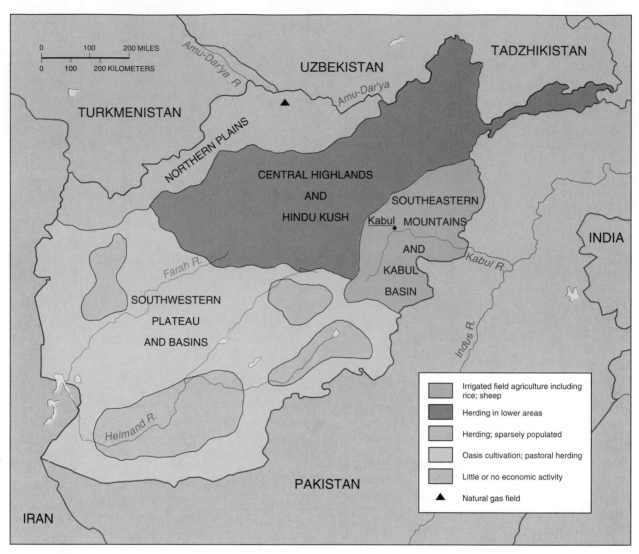

Figure 25–20
Physical and agricultural regions of Afghanistan. Afghanistan exhibits many Middle Eastern features, such as aridity and adherence to the Muslim religion. However, the country's contact with the outside world has occurred through South Asia. The Afghan population is generally conservative, and regional loyalties are often more important than allegiance to the nation as a whole.

Afghan Society

Afghanistan is composed of a number of tribal groupings and is dominated by the largest of them, the Pashto-speaking **Pathans**, who are concentrated in the Kabul Basin. Of the almost 18 million Afghans, probably 90 percent are of Caucasian stock, and the remaining 10 percent are Mongoloid. Although strong dialectal differences exist among the major tribal groups, a common religion, Islam,

provides a cultural cement that holds that traditional society together.

One of the most striking features of Afghanistan is its demography. The country possesses one of the highest annual birthrates and death rates in the world: 4.9 percent and 2.2 percent, respectively. Such a pattern suggests that Afghanistan is still in the initial stage of the demographic transformation. With an average life expectancy of only forty-two years and an estimated illiteracy rate of 71 percent

Figure 25-21
A view across the Bamiyan Valley in Afghanistan. Although a statue of Buddha is visible in the background, Afghanistan is predominantly Muslim. This dry land of mountains, plateaus, and basins has served as a crossroads for eastern, southern, southwestern, and central Asia. Even though isolated and poor, Afghanistan has also attracted numerous invaders over the centuries, the Soviet invasion during the 1980s being the most recent example.

of the population, Afghanistan emerges as one of the poorest and least developed states in the world.

The Changing Economy

Subsistence farming of grains, fruit, and a few specialty crops, along with animal herding, is the traditional mainstay of the Afghan economy. More than 80 percent of the population is employed in such activities. In the Kabul Basin, the most productive region in Afghanistan, irrigation is commonly practiced in an intensive agricultural system that includes paddy rice. Recent agricultural innovations, such as new seed strains and better techniques of cultivation, are expected to increase agricultural productivity and meet the future demands of the growing population. Although Afghanistan possesses reserves of several important minerals, only the production of natural gas is significantly developed. The Soviet Union assisted with the production of that gas, and most natural gas produced is sold to the countries that composed that nation.

Economic Development and the Five-Year Plans

Since 1957 Afghanistan has followed a series of government-formulated five-year plans, designed to bring the country into the age of economic development. Initially, the major focus was on capital im-

provements: roads, bridges, irrigation systems, and power production and transmission. Since 1968, however, when the third five-year plan began, more attention has been focused on social and educational problems. Funds have recently been channeled into the improvement of literacy levels and into the commodity-producing sectors of the economy. Annual economic growth rates of 4 percent or better are the goal, but military and political situations have been so unstable that the economy has suffered greatly.

The five-year plans have relied heavily on foreign financing, most of which has come from the United States and Germany, as well as, previously, the Soviet Union. Those countries and the World Bank have assisted in arranging foreign trade and special external purchases. In addition, Afghanistan has helped pay for some of its modernization programs by exporting cotton, wool, rugs, fruit, and natural gas. It seems likely, however, that the country will continue to rely on outside aid to finance its economic development for some years to come.

The Soviet Invasion and Recent Political Problems

Afghanistan is an extremely poor, landlocked buffer state that has only recently begun its push toward modernization. That process has come under increasing stress, in part as a result of pressure by the former Soviet Union.

Since 1973, when its monarchy was overthrown, Afghanistan has experienced severe political upheaval. The republic proclaimed in that year was superseded in 1979 by the Soviet-backed, communist government of President Babrak Karmal. And in order to ensure the tenure of that government, the Soviet Union invaded Afghanistan later that year, expecting to suppress the Afghan insurgents in short order. The insurgents, however, were supported by neighboring Pakistan and China and also received some assistance from other foreign governments. A bloody war ensued, and the Soviets found themselves unable to stabilize Afghanistan into a client state. Political events in central Asia since then have led to the breakup of the former Soviet Union and the emergence of very unstable independent Islamic states in Central Asia. A fundamentalist Islamic insurgency in Tadzhikistan has led to the return of Russian troops to that republic and shelling and fighting along the Tadzikistan/Afghanistan border. The continuing political instability and fighting provide a very poor prospect for economic growth and development in the near term.

SUMMARY
Prospects for Development

In Chapter 4 we defined *development* as broad improvements in economic and social patterns and in people's life-styles. From the perspective of Rostow's stages of economic growth, most of the countries of South Asia appear to be in either the second stage, preconditions for takeoff, with production increasing only modestly but changes in traditional outlook and attitude beginning to take hold, or the third stage, takeoff, with new technologies and capital being applied to production processes and agricultural and manufacturing output beginning to increase rapidly. One problem is that those changes and improvements are unevenly distributed within the large South Asian realm and each country's wealth is unevenly distributed among the various strata of its society, as discussed in Chapter 24 (see Table 24–1).

Another problem, which may be viewed as a criticism of the Rostow model, is that population growth is so rapid in South Asia that the urban and industrial economies cannot generate enough jobs and sufficiently high wages to meet the demands

of the enormous and growing pools of surplus labor. Consequently, growth processes that occurred in the industrializing West a century ago and that Rostow assumed would occur in all countries fail to take place in South Asia. Prospects for takeoff will be dim until population growth is moderated.

Development economics offers a better approach to analyze and understand the condition and problems of the impoverished countries of South Asia. As Todaro had noted, development economics is concerned far more than traditional economics with cultural, political, and economic requirements, "for affecting rapid structural and institutional transformation of entire societies in a manner that will most efficiently bring the fruits of economic progress to the broadest segments of their populations."[2] In other words, old and generalized assumptions about how to stimulate economic growth in poor Third World countries do not suffice. It is necessary to look at the structure of individual societies, polities, and economies to begin to develop approaches and methods to explain the conditions and processes of development in these countries.

KEY TERMS

Bengali	Hinduism
Boserupian thesis	Indo-Aryan
Brahmin	Jammu and Kashmir
British East India Company	*karma*
Buddhism	Muslim
caste	Pathans
Damodar Valley	Sepoy Rebellion
dharma	Sikhs
Dravidian	Sinhalese
growth poles	Tamils
Hindi	Urdu

NOTES

1. The city of Delhi is the historic capital of India and the primary site of several early dynasties. New Delhi, which is adjacent to the older city, was designated as the capital in 1931.

2. See Michael P. Todaro, *Economic Development in the Third World,* 4th ed. White Plains, NY: Longman, 1989.

26

The Origin and Development of Chinese Civilization

The Great Wall of China. The 1500-mile-long wall, built during the third century A.D., reflects China's concern with barbarian invaders from the north, a problem throughout China's early history. To the south, mountainous southern China, the Tibetan Highlands, and the Himalayan Mountains served as effective natural barriers.

According to the earliest written records, Chinese civilization dates back almost 4,000 years. Extensive archeological evidence, however, indicates the presence of proto-Chinese cultural groups in many different regions of China much earlier, between 5000 B.C. and 2000 B.C. That archeological record establishes through the uniqueness and age of artifacts and other materials that Chinese civilization developed independently of other major cultures. In North China that society evolved out of late Stone Age culture and developed techniques of sedentary agriculture; writing; formal religious, social, and political systems; and distinctive technological, industrial, and architectural practices.

THE NORTH CHINA CULTURE HEARTH

Chinese culture and civilization developed on the Loess Plateau and the western flank of the North China Plain, along the middle reaches of the Huang He (Hwang Ho, or Yellow River) and the Wei River (Figure 26–1). The nature of some important late Stone Age discoveries made in that same area strengthens the idea that Chinese civilization emerged independent of South Asian or Western cultures.

Ancient China

Scholars have traditionally traced the origins of the Chinese state to the Shang dynasty (ca. 1766–1122 B.C.). Shang culture possessed a language with written characters, the forerunner of modern Chinese script. Largely discovered on ancient bones (known as the Oracle bones), that writing has told us much about the formation of Chinese institutions and civilization and has enabled us to construct a picture of ancient China.

Shang civilization contained most of the cultural attributes assigned to China, attributes that distinguish China from other cultural systems of equivalent age. Shang priests, scholars, administrators, and artisans developed a society and culture that rivaled other contemporary civilizations. Settled agriculture; formalized religious, administrative, and legal systems; writing and literature; the tradition of a dynastic ruling house; sophisticated fabrics, ceramics, and metallurgy; and a great city—Anyang, in the western part of the North China Plain—all existed in Shang times. In addition, the regional roots of the evolution of East Asia into a broader cultural realm

with common historical antecedents and traditions may lie in the Shang era, making it a key to understanding all other East Asian cultures and societies, both historical and contemporary.

One of the most interesting aspects of China's cultural development was the creation of a dynastic system, with Shang as the first dynasty (see the boxed feature The Dynastic Cycle in China). Shang was followed by Zhou (Chou), which extended from 1122 to 221 B.C. and is sometimes called the classical period of Chinese civilization (Table 26–1). Many of China's early great philosophers and thinkers, including Confucius, lived and wrote during the Zhou dynasty; it was a powerful, formative age of literature, philosophy, and history. In 221 B.C. the great unifier of China, Qin Shi Huangdi—the first emperor of the Qin (Ch'in) dynasty—seized power and forged the territorial integration of the country, which focused on the eastern core region of China proper (Figure 26–2).

Qin Shi Huangdi also standardized the written language, promoted the building of the Great Wall and many canals, and worked vigorously to develop an administrative and imperial system that could govern China for a long time. So effective was that dynastic system—a national bureaucracy—that it lasted until A.D. 1911, despite numerous changes in individual dynasties.

Loess Land and the Physical Environment

In order to better understand some of the issues and problems in China's historical evolution and spatial expansion, it is useful to examine the nature of environmental and ecological conditions in the source area from which Chinese civilization and culture grew. Much of North China is covered by a mantle of fine, windblown, dustlike soil material, or **loess**—called *huang-tu* ("yellow earth") by the Chinese (see Figure 26–1). Common not only in China but also in parts of Anglo-America and Europe, loess is usually associated with past glacial activity. In North China the glacial deposition was so extensive that

Figure 26-1
The Huang He and other major rivers of China. Although not China's largest river, the Huang He was the focus of much of China's ancient history. The map also indicates areas of loessial soil as well as major shifts in the bed of the river.

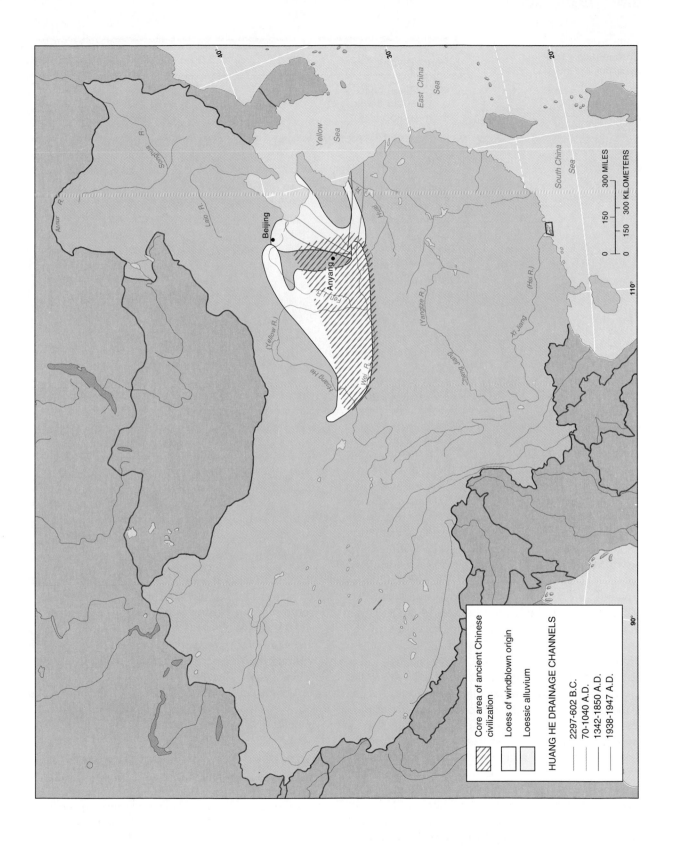

East China
Sea

Yellow
Sea

South China
Sea

Amur R.

Songhua R.

Liao R.

Beijing

Anyang

(Yellow R.)

Huang He

Fen R.

Wei R.

Huai R.

(Yangtze R.)

Chang Jiang

Xi Jiang

(Hsi R.)

300 MILES

0   150   300 KILOMETERS

0   150

40°

30°

20°

110°

90°

Core area of ancient Chinese
civilization

Loess of windblown origin

Loessic alluvium

HUANG HE DRAINAGE CHANNELS

2297-602 B.C.

70-1040 A.D.

1342-1850 A.D.

1938-1947 A.D.

609

Table 26-1
Chronological table of
dynasties in China.

Period/Dynasty	Dates
Yangshao culture	ca. 5000–3200 B.C. (?)
Longshanoid culture	ca. 3200–1850 B.C. (?)
Xia (mythological?)	ca. 1994–1766 B.C.
Shang	1766–1122 B.C.
Zhou (Chou)	1122–221 B.C.
Qin (Ch'in)	221–207 B.C.
Han	207 B.C.–A.D. 200
The Three Kingdoms	220–280
The southern dynasties	280–589
The northern dynasties	386–581
Sui	581–618
Tang	618–907
The Five Dynasties	907–960
Liao (Khitan Tartars)	916–1125
Song	960–1279
Jin	1125–1234
Yuan (Mongol)	1279–1368
Ming	1368–1644
Qing (Ch'ing or Manchu)	1644–1911
Republic	1912–1949 on mainland
	1949–present on Taiwan
People's Republic	1949–present

the loess is as much as 500 feet (152 meters) deep in places. Over time, however, the Huang He has carried much of it off the Loess Plateau and redeposited it as alluvium on the North China Plain.

The climate of North China is characterized by dry, cold winters and hot summers. During the cooler months dry winds of Siberian origin sweep down from the north and west, and sandstorms are common in spring. On the Loess Plateau annual precipitation is between 10 and 20 inches (254 and 508 millimeters). On the North China Plain precipitation is greater: between 16 and 30 inches (406 and 761 millimeters) annually. South of the 30-inch isohyet, or equal rainfall line, loessial soil dissipates and is not found in the Chang Jiang (Yangtze River) Basin. Throughout North China, rain is concentrated in summer; and although that concentration is good for farming, the evapotranspiration rate is high enough to make the Loess Plateau and much of the North China Plain marginal for many crops unless irrigation is used.

It is interesting that such an area was the birthplace of Chinese agriculture. According to the historian P'ing-ti Ho, Chinese agriculture first developed on the Loess Plateau because the loessial soils were fertile, porous, and easy to work.[1] The early Chinese, who had only primitive wooden digging tools, could operate much more effectively on such soils than they could on the dense, more compact alluvial soils of the low-lying North China Plain farther east.

The Huang He and Loess

The Huang He has affected the Chinese in many ways and through many centuries. The difficulty of controlling and using it has been a long and not-always-happy chapter in Chinese history. The epithet **China's sorrow** gained currency long ago in describing the devastation brought on by that powerful and unusual river.

The Huang He rises among the swamps and lakes in the eastern part of the Tibetan Plateau. It initially flows east and north and, after 1,000 miles

Figure 26-2
Major regions of China, including principal lowlands. The line identifying China proper separates roughly the eastern third of the country from the remainder. China proper is occupied predominantly by Han Chinese and is viewed as distinct from the outlying non-Han regions.

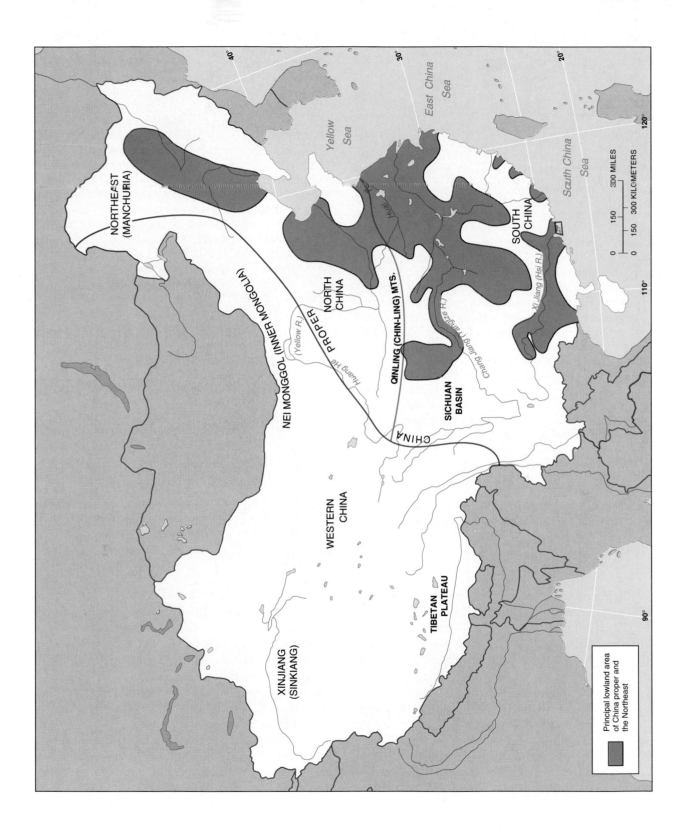

NORTHEAST (MANCHURIA)

NEI MONGGOL (INNER MONGOLIA)

NORTH CHINA

CHINA PROPER

Huang He (Yellow R.)

QINLING (CHIN-LING) MTS.

SICHUAN BASIN

Chang Jiang (Yangtze R.)

SOUTH CHINA

Xi Jiang (Hsi R.)

WESTERN CHINA

XINJIANG (SINKIANG)

TIBETAN PLATEAU

Yellow Sea

East China Sea

South China Sea

40°

30°

20°

120°

110°

90°

300 MILES

300 KILOMETERS

0   150

0   150

Principal lowland area of China proper and the Northeast

THE DYNASTIC CYCLE IN CHINA

The evolution of Chinese civilization and the history of China have characteristically been interpreted as a series of cycles.* Dynasties rose and were vigorous in their early stages; then they matured, began to decline, and eventually ended. The end was usually abrupt; the emperor and his court were incompetent to rule and unable to administer, so they lost the right—the mandate of heaven—to reign. Administrative and economic factors were probably more important than individual factors, that is, than the personages of the emperor and his chief advisors. The key determinants in the rise and decline of dynasties were the fiscal soundness and the administrative and military efficiency of the dynasty.

Young dynasties were typically effective in building walls, canals, and a great capital. Gradually, however, the bureaucracy would expand, and expenditures would increase. Court living would become lavish and wasteful, and revenues would be siphoned off for frivolous rather than fiscally sound purposes. As things began to deteriorate, reforms would often be attempted.

Sometimes they would succeed, at least for a while; but eventually spending would increase again, deficits would rise, and the quality and effectiveness of administration and military security would decline. Canals and dikes would not be maintained properly, and crop failures would become more common. The resulting famines would lead to peasant uprisings, and soldiers would begin to desert and defect. Insurrection would result, and soon the dynasty would collapse. When that happened, a new and effective sovereign would gain control and would implement a wholesale turnover of the court personnel. In that way a new dynasty was established, and the cycle continued.

Such an interpretation is appealing in its simplicity and common theme and is no doubt useful as a means of explaining the changing political leadership throughout China's long history. However, as Fairbank, Reischauer, and Craig have indicated, even though there is validity to the concept of dynastic cycles, such a view is far from complete and obscures a series of significant changes taking place from Shang times all the way through Chinese history. In other words, changes within Chinese civilization have sometimes been given less attention because of the concentration on the ebb and flow of dynastic change. Examples of overlooked accomplishments include (1) the agricultural changes and commercial development that began in the Song dynasty (A.D. 960–1279) as a consequence of widespread use of early ripening rice in the eleventh century and (2) improvements in the cultivation and irrigation of wet rice. Increases in commercial exchange and the growth of commercial cities signaled a period of extensive economic development during that era. Thus, the regularity of China's dynastic cycles does not explain and should not detract from China's long history of achievement.

---

*John K. Fairbank, Edwin O. Reischauer, and Albert M. Craig, *East Asia, Tradition and Transformation* (Boston: Houghton Mifflin, 1973).

(1,610 kilometers), reaches the vicinity of the modern city of Lanzhou (Lanchou). By then the river, with its steep gradient, has cut its way down to the western Loess Plateau, a drop of some 10,000 feet (3,048 meters). Once on the plateau, where its gradient and velocity are suddenly reduced, the river broadens, meanders, and becomes shallow. As considerable volume is lost to irrigation and evaporation, the Huang He turns into a sluggish, undramatic stream. At the top of the Great Loop (see Figure 26–1), the river shifts direction abruptly and begins to flow south. It then turns almost due east and within a short distance drops sharply off the Loess Plateau and enters the North China Plain (see Figure 26–2) near the city of Luoyang (Loyang).

As the Huang He turns southward in the Great Loop, its character changes. It begins to flow through poorly consolidated and easily eroded loess lands. Numerous tributary streams, some of them large, join the main channel; and they, too, flow through the easily eroded loess and contribute enormous quantities of silt to the main stream. As the river descends more rapidly, its capacity to carry silt increases. Because rainfall also increases, more water enters the Huang He, bringing greater quantities of silt from the tributary network.

At that point the stream is much larger and carries a heavy silt burden. But the seasonality of rainfall, which is concentrated in the summer months of July and August, complicates matters further. Such a concentration of rainfall results in great changes in the river's volume of flow. In addition, the absence of heavy vegetative cover and the nearness of a number of important tributaries combine to further increase the speed with which rainwater is funneled into the main stream. During one nineteenth-century flood the Chinese claim that the Huang had a discharge rate 250 times greater than that of its lowest flow, a record for the world's major rivers.

After the Huang He enters the North China Plain, the mechanics of stream flow change once more. Gradient and velocity are reduced suddenly, so the river cannot carry its heavy silt load. When the concentrated seasonal rainfall is added, the result is the legendary annual floods.

Most rivers overflow periodically, but the floods on the Huang He are spectacular. The character of that river, coupled with agricultural abuse of the loess lands and the progressive degradation of local vegetation, has led to increased flooding over time. And because the river is continually building up its bed by dropping its heavy sediment load, the streambed has become elevated for much of its path across the North China Plain. The Chinese have responded by building levees, which must continue to be raised as the river bed is elevated, but it is impossible to build a dike high enough to protect against every flood. Such a vicious spiral of progressively higher levees has resulted in the elevation of the bed high above the surrounding floodplain. Consequently, when major floods have occurred, the river has broken out of its bed and has inundated enormous areas of the North China Plain.

Since 602 B.C. the Huang He has changed its course fifteen times, ultimately flowing to the sea through different channels. Some of those channels have entered the sea as much as 500 miles (805 kilometers) south of the present mouth (see Figure 26–1). At one time the flow was actually channeled south into the Huai River and eventually into the Yangtze. That situation would be comparable to a Mississippi River flood that altered the river channel so much that the river flowed to the Gulf of Mexico through the Rio Grande.

The Huang He floods are truly monumental, and the results are catastrophic. For example, in 1938 the Chinese Nationalist government destroyed the dikes on the south side of the river in an effort to slow the advance of the invading Japanese army. More than 6 million acres (2.4 million hectares) were flooded, and an estimated 6 million refugees had to be relocated. As many as 500,000 people may have died in that induced flood. Nine years passed before the river was rechanneled to resume its flow north of the Shandong (Shantung) Peninsula.

DIFFUSION OUT OF THE NORTH CHINA HEARTH

The Chinese have long struggled with an environment over which they could exercise little control or direction. The ecological conditions they confronted as they developed sedentary agricultural practices in northern and northwestern China were unusual and were probably not dependable. However, through their various activities of cultivation and forest removal, they may have made their environment even more unmanageable and uncertain. Whatever the reasons, the Chinese began to migrate southward, away from the ecological rigors of the Loess Plateau and the North China Plain. In so doing, they met a substantially different environmental setting, one that offered new opportunities for agriculture and more dependable physical conditions for human sustenance. Migration southward also extended the influence of their cultural practices, as tribal peoples who inhabited South China were acculturated and absorbed by the more advanced Chinese.

The Landscapes and Environments of South China

The surface geography of southeastern China is complex. The major rivers and their tributary networks dissect the uplands into a system of river valleys separated by rugged and sometimes high ridges. With the exception of the Yangtze and Xi (Hsi) drainage basins, there are no extensive low-lying floodplains. The consequences of such diverse and rugged landscape are restricted movement and communication, isolation of local areas, and sectionalism.

The Chinese adapted easily to the alluvial lowlands and floodplains and began specialized rice growing (Figure 26–3). Native peoples who were not absorbed were forced into the rugged uplands, where some of them isolated themselves and preserved a certain degree of ethnic and cultural independence and integrity. Some of that ethnic separateness has continued even to the present. Wherever tribal peoples remained in the lowlands, however, they were converted to Chinese thought, speech, and practice.

Thus, the environments of South China, too, played a role in shaping historical and social patterns. On the one hand, the Chinese were drawn to the environment because it proved more tractable and dependable and could support more people

Figure 26-3
Rice harvesting near Zunyi in Guizhou, China. Rice is the staple crop of this region in South China, whereas wheat is more common in North China.

through rice cultivation and water control. Sustained food production could feed large numbers of people and also provide a backup when agricultural conditions became bad in the traditional North China area. On the other hand, the ruggedness and diversity of landscapes in the south promoted political fragmentation and regional interests. China, like the United States, has old and powerfully established sectional interests, which even a communist government, with its emphasis on centralization, cannot dissipate.

The Outer, Non-Chinese Regions

Several distinct areas lie inside China's boundaries but outside what is commonly referred to as China proper; they include Tibet, Xinjiang (Sinkiang), Nei Monggol (Inner Mongolia), and Dongbei (Manchuria) (see Figure 26–2). Those regions, with the exception of the Manchurian Plain, all have some common physical characteristics. For the most part they are high and dry, with great seasonal temperature extremes. Much of their mountain and basin area is characterized by internal drainage, salt marshes, and desert; and the environment has never

supported a dense, productive agricultural system. Most livelihood is derived from herding, oasis cultivation, and subsistence farming. Traditionally peopled by non-Chinese, those areas have long been divided politically and culturally between China and neighboring countries and peoples. Today those non-Chinese regions, except for Outer Mongolia, have once again been attached to China, but their physical and human features serve to distinguish them from China proper.

During the twentieth century, and especially since 1949, there has been extensive migration of ethnic Chinese—sometimes called Han people or **Han Chinese** to distinguish them from non-Han minority nationalities—to the traditionally non-Chinese outer regions of Manchuria, Mongolia, Xinjiang, and Tibet. That movement has resulted in a substantial increase in the Han Chinese share of the population in traditionally non-Chinese areas. Consequently, the Chinese have been accused of trying to make those often sparsely populated outlying areas integral parts of China by overwhelming their populations with ethnic Han Chinese migrants.

614

THE THREE CHINAS

Based on broad environmental and ecological factors, at least three distinct Chinas exist. To some extent those areas may be identified with human populations, but occupancy styles and activities are a better way of describing them. The first region is western China—the high, dry China with its greatly specialized, adaptive styles of livelihood that are closely attuned to the physical environment. The people in that area were originally Turkic, Tibetan, and Mongol.

The other two parts of China lie in the east and can be divided between north and south. South China begins south of the Qinling (Chin-ling) Mountains–Huai River line and includes the main agricultural lands of the Yangtze and Xi (Hsi) drainage systems. The area's climate is mild and wet, much like the climate of the southeastern United States; its agriculture is mainly wet rice. Although included in China proper and typically inhabited by Chinese, it entered the Chinese orbit during the late formative period of the Qin (Ch'in) dynasty (221–207 B.C.), and that late entry is reflected in the diversity of the area's regional languages and people.

The third ecological region is North China, the source area from which China grew. North China, which includes the middle and lower Huang He drainage basin and Manchuria, is a cold, dry region in winter, but its summers are hot and humid and support intensive Chinese-style agriculture. The people are largely **Mandarin** speakers; and although there are ethnic infusions of Manchu, Mongol, and other tribal elements, it was here that early Chinese culture emerged.

Those three broad regions still distinguish the main areal parts of the Chinese state, despite strong government efforts to counter diversity. Environmental and geographical features, as much as politics, continue to shape modern China.

SOCIAL AND POLITICAL UNITY

One of the most interesting and unusual facts about China is its permanence and long political tenure. Despite changes in dynasties, occasional disruption by outside groups, and the sometimes short terms of ruling factions, China has managed to persist and maintain control over essentially the same territory for some 2,000 years. A similar scenario in Europe would have had the Roman Empire remaining virtually intact right up to the present, with its government institutions surviving, though with certain modifications.

The Administrative Structure

One reason for China's long-term cohesiveness has been a powerful and effective central political apparatus that prevented fragmentation. Even early governance was based on a large and centralized bureaucracy, which operated with surprising efficiency on a modest budget. And the constant circulation of bureaucrats from one post to another reduced the growth of powerful local interests. Through such practices the central administration was able to maintain a remarkable degree of control, even without modern means of communication and transportation. When times were bad or a dynasty was overthrown, a new dynasty emerged, yet the political system persisted and remained effective. In the absence of an integrating economic system, that centralized bureaucracy provided some of the glue that held the diverse parts of the empire together.

The Chinese Language

The people of early China spoke a variety of different dialects and languages, many of which were mutually unintelligible. In contrast, written Chinese based on ideographs (i.e., picture symbols that represent ideas, objects, and actions) was used in all parts of China. It was the language of government and provided the primary means of communication among the various language groups—another aspect of Chinese culture that promoted the integration of its territories.

That the written language was known only to a small fraction of the total population was not a great disadvantage. The literate group—scholars, government functionaries, and the wealthy landed gentry—formed the leadership group at the local level. They were the decision makers, with whom the central government communicated and to whom it addressed calls for taxes, laborers, and military conscripts. Both the central government apparatus and the common written language became national symbols for the Chinese, important components of the emerging cultural system of the Chinese state.

Confucian Social Order

Another key integrating element was the **Confucian tradition**. Confucius and his many disciples and interpreters established a Chinese social order that has been pervasive for more than 2,000 years. For ancient Chinese society Confucius outlined a set of social and behavioral patterns, which were transmitted through an important segment of China's rich literature. Over time those views became embedded both within the social system—which governed most, if not all, relationships among individuals and families—and within the political system. In general, the Confucian precepts emphasized stability, discouraging any fundamental change in the existing order of social, economic, and political relations. Consequently, Confucianism has often been viewed as rigid and conservative.

It is not surprising, therefore, that Confucius has been blamed frequently in recent years for disallowing innovation and technical change and preventing China's economic modernization. Such criticism oversimplifies the nature of traditional China; Confucianism was only one of many underpinnings of traditional Chinese society. Nevertheless, recent communist leaders in China have occasionally waged vigorous campaigns to exorcise the ghost of Confucius, in an attempt to change attitudes on such matters as the number of children a family should have or the nature of social stratification. Communist planners want a new order as they seek economic modernization and growth; thus, Confucian ideas have an ambivalent place in their revolutionary society. At this point it seems likely that the status of Confucius as a great man of Chinese history and literature will continue to be challenged.

THE IMPACT OF THE WEST

In the early part of the nineteenth century, new influences entered China along its coasts and rivers to challenge the traditional system of government. For example, British foreign policy, supported by the British Navy, forced China to accept the superiority of Western power in the Opium War (1839–1842).

The British wanted to trade with China; but in order to pay for the valuable goods they wanted—such as silk, fine porcelains, and tea—the British needed something to sell to China. Opium was the answer. The problem was that opium was illegal, and the Chinese began to confiscate and destroy contraband opium in 1839. Unhappy with that, the British forced the issue and created a small war, which their superior naval force officially ended by defeating the Chinese garrison around Canton. The Treaty of Nanking became the first of what the Chinese perceived as unequal treaties, because of their favorable bias toward British or European interests. As a result of that treaty, five ports were opened to foreign trade, the tightly controlled Chinese trading system was eliminated, and the British were permitted to trade with any local Chinese they wished.

Those new privileges were soon extended to other foreign countries, such as the United States; and the five ports became **treaty ports**, where foreigners could not only trade but could also enjoy the privileges of home without being subject to Chinese laws. The treaty ports became, in fact, the colonial enclaves of foreign powers; and eventually there were about 100 of them, mainly on the coast and along the Yangtze River (Figure 26–4).

The inroads of foreign powers were only one of the several forces at work in China during the nineteenth century that indicated the demise of the old dynastic order. Peasant rebellions were also occurring whenever times were bad in the countryside. Population had grown steadily after 1600, less farmland was available, and periodic famine and landlessness became more common. The combination of domestic hard times and foreign pressure led to increasing social and political instability.

In the middle of the nineteenth century one of the great Chinese domestic upheavals took place. The **Taiping Rebellion** (1850–1864) was an odd mixture of religious zeal and traditional thought, focused around a political fanaticism aimed at overthrowing the Qing (Manchu) dynasty. The rebellion, based on ideals of community property and the brotherhood of man, was stronger in areas where economic conditions were bad, in part as a result of the outcome of the Opium War. Although it spread throughout most of China and the peasant armies did defeat imperial forces in several major battles, the uprising was increasingly opposed by the gentry class and eventually dissipated. Nonetheless, it clearly signaled the weakness and difficulties of the imperial Manchu government.

The Taiping Rebellion was followed at the turn of the century by the **Boxer Rebellion**. The Boxers

Figure 26-4
The Shenzhen shipyard in Shanghai. Shanghai was one of the original five treaty ports and, as such, experienced substantial nineteenth and early twentieth century growth in response to trade with the West. With the renewed economic growth of China, Shanghai is once again experiencing a rise in economic power.

were a secret society devoted to ridding China of the foreign influences introduced by commercial interests and missionaries. Eventually foreign troops arrived to quell the disturbances and protect foreigners who had sought refuge in Peking and Tientsin. A settlement was reached in 1901 (the Boxer Protocol), whereby the Chinese government had to pay an enormous indemnity, and foreign troops were stationed in North China. That outcome was one more indication of the weakness and ineffectiveness of China's imperial government. In 1911, when the old dynastic order could stand no longer, fledgling revolutionary forces succeeded in establishing the Chinese Republic.

Through those years of foreign intrusion, China was increasingly set upon by people who were not susceptible to acculturation and who introduced modern weapons and industrial technologies that were superior to China's indigenous techniques. For the first time China was confronted with an external force that asserted and promoted its own racial and cultural superiority and supported that position with power, money, and technology.

CHINA'S REVOLUTION AND THE RISE OF CHINESE COMMUNISM

Among the ideas and innovations introduced into China in the nineteenth and twentieth centuries were the concepts and views of Western democracy and Marxism. After the overthrow of the Qing dynasty in 1911 and a brief period of near anarchy, the Chinese Republic was established under the guidance of the revolutionary patriot Sun Yat-sen. His party, the Chinese **Nationalists**, announced the Three Principles of the People, which were to reform politics, society, and the economy. That reform looked toward the enfranchisement of individuals and their improved status and economic well-being within the state.

Upon Sun's death in 1925, Chiang Kai-shek took over the Nationalist party and government. Except for brief periods, he ruled the Nationalists and their exiles in Taiwan until his death in 1975. Chiang had a more conservative political outlook than Sun did, and he soon aligned himself with urban commercial interests and the large landholders in the rural areas.

In the meantime a number of young Chinese had been sent to study in Europe and the United States. Among the ideas they were exposed to was Marxism, a political philosophy of great interest in light of the communist revolutionary movements in Europe and Russia. With the success of the Russian Revolution and the establishment of the Soviet Union, a base of support existed, and Marxist ideas gained currency in China as a competing approach toward achieving the goals of reform and modernization. The various Marxist groups in China fought bitterly among themselves, however, especially over whether the Communist party revolutionary strategy should focus on converting urban workers or rural

Figure 26-5
Guarding the photo of Mao Tse-Tung in Beijing. Mao was the leader of the movement that, after a long struggle, brought the Communist party to power in 1949.

peasants. Among those who supported the rural-peasant focus was a young librarian in Beijing (Peking) named Mao Zedong (Tse-tung) (Figure 26–5).

After a short period of unsuccessful competition with the Nationalists, the Communist urban strategy failed, and the Communists turned to the peasantry for support. In the 1930s, however, Chiang Kai-shek attacked the rural Communists and drove them out of southern and central China to a remote location in the Loess Plateau. That retreat of the Communists from the south to the isolated Great Loop of the Huang He, referred to as the **Long March**, is now an epic in Chinese revolutionary literature.

In hiding the Communists regrouped. Then, when the Japanese invaded China in 1937, the Nationalists were preoccupied with fighting them and were no longer able to campaign vigorously against the Communists. In a short time the Nationalists managed to lose both the political and the military initiative, and by the war's end in 1945 the Communists had gained formidable military and political arms. The Chinese Communist party offered itself as a new and energetic answer to the plight of the poor, landless peasants, and the peasants responded.

Increasingly, the Communists established their power in North China, and the Nationalists were no longer able to compete for popular support. The results are well known: Chiang Kai-shek and the remnants of his army retreated to Taiwan, and Mao Tse-tung and his followers established a new, revolutionary government. Those actions were the culmination of events that had begun early in the nineteenth century, when the West first challenged the traditional Chinese system. The ascendancy of a Communist government with the founding of the People's Republic of China in 1949 was the final outcome in a century of turmoil for China. The Communists, now firmly in power, are carrying on the processes of change as rapidly as possible.

SUMMARY
Tradition and Progress in Conflict

Much of China's progress and development is based on its almost 4,000 years of culture, tradition, and knowledge. Not all of that impressive legacy has been beneficial, however. Some of China's traditions hardened into outmoded rules and behavior; and when coupled with the extended use and even abuse of China's enormous environment, those rigid patterns seriously impeded progress. As a result, China found itself weak, vulnerable to foreign pressure, and lagging behind the outside world. The Chinese Communist revolution sought to break with the past and propel the country along a path of modernization.

In the past fifty years conditions in China have changed, and fresh challenges have appeared. New methods and policies for economic, social, and political development have evolved or are being tried experimentally. The following chapter explores some of those efforts. The geography of China remains important to the process of change that is under way there; it presents both challenges and opportunities for the development and modernization of that vast land and its people.

KEY TERMS

Boxer Rebellion	Confucian tradition
China's sorrow	Han Chinese
loess	Nationalists
Long March	Taiping Rebellion
Mandarin	treaty ports

NOTES

1. P'ing-ti Ho, "The Loess and the Origin of Chinese Agriculture," *American Historical Review* 75 (1969): 1–36.

27

China and Its Neighbors: Changing Societies and Economies

China's Population

China's Changing Social Patterns

China's Changing Socialist Economy

Agriculture

Industrialization and Economic Growth

China's Rimland

Da Yunhe (Grand Canal) connecting the Yangtze Delta of South China with the North China Plain and the Huang He of North China. The canal was built during the late sixth and early seventh centuries to enable tribute grains to be transported from the rice-growing south northward to the capital.

The objective of China's Communist government was to completely make over the country. The political system had been replaced during the revolution, but the new government sought also to modernize the economy and the society. Indeed, since 1949 radical new economic and social programs and policies have been proclaimed. These revolutionary proposals and the events associated with them constitute the modern phase of China's development and are the subject of this chapter. In 1978 far reaching economic reforms were introduced in China, and these modified the centrally controlled economy in favor of a more market-oriented system. Growth since then has been remarkable (see the boxed feature China's Changing Socialist Economy: Reform and Rapid Growth).

We also look briefly at some of China's East Asian neighbors: Hong Kong, Taiwan, and the two Koreas. Hong Kong, Taiwan, and South Korea have free-market economies and offer interesting comparisons with the reforming economic system of China and the continuing command economy of North Korea.

CHINA'S POPULATION

China is believed to have had a population of 60 to 70 million people as long ago as A.D. 2. Although the population may have fluctuated by more than 20 million during certain periods, ten centuries later it was still around 60 million. Such a demographic history suggests that early China achieved a crude balance between the number of people living in the area and the ability of the agricultural system to support them. Without innovations or technical changes, that population did not grow.

Population Growth

By 1400 the population had begun to increase, and by 1751 it had reached 207 million. A century later China's population had grown to about 420 million. Better farming techniques, technical innovations, and greater internal movement of large amounts of food grains had led to substantial growth in the population.

The outbreak of the Taiping Rebellion in 1850 began a century of turmoil, war, and demographic change. The consequences were a high death rate and a decrease in the rate of population growth.

After the Communists assumed power, however, they reported a 1949 population of 542 million people, an increase of almost 25 percent since the mid-1800s. Since 1949, population growth has been great. For example, 1982 official Chinese census figures indicated that 1.008 billion Chinese were living on the mainland. The mid-1990 census reported a population of 1.133 billion, with another 26 million Chinese residing in Taiwan, Hong Kong, and Macao. In 1994, the population on the mainland was estimated at 1.192 billion.

Communist Policies

One of the most significant things the Communist government did when it took over in 1949 was to institute a comprehensive program of state-assisted public health. That program led to a rapid decline in the death rate; but because the birthrate remained high, the annual population growth rate increased. Only after 1960 did it begin to subside. In 1986 the rate of net natural increase had declined to 14.08 per thousand, yet that amounted to almost 15 million new mouths to feed and support each year. That enormous annual increment in China's population is challenging the ability of the economic system to provide a better future for all Chinese.

Family planning has been increasingly stressed in China in recent years. Much effort has gone into changing social attitudes about the value of female children, in order to persuade Chinese families not to keep having children until they have one or more sons. In addition, in 1979 China implemented a policy to promote one-child families, using economic incentives and advantages for families with one child and penalizing women who give birth to more than two children (Figure 27–1). The program reduced the birthrate dramatically, especially in urban precincts in Shanghai and other large cities. The policy was not applied uniformly, however, and by 1986 the one-child-family campaign had been somewhat relaxed in rural areas, where peasants disregarded it and paid fines in order to have two or three children. In 1987, despite the one-child policy, more than 40 percent of rural women had as many as three children, and the number of second births was up more than 1.37 million over 1986. This demographic reality has continued into the 1990s, and the one-child policy has been only partially effective.

Different factors are at work in the Chinese countryside, where roughly 70 percent of China's people

CHINA'S CHANGING SOCIALIST ECONOMY: REFORM AND RAPID GROWTH

Chinese communism has undergone remarkable and sporadic shifts and changes during the more than four decades since the founding of the People's Republic in 1949. There have been radical phases such as the Great Leap Forward (1958–61) and the Cultural Revolution (1966–71). Paralleling these have been periods of economic growth and stagnation. Perhaps the most momentous shift has been the far-reaching **economic reform** intitiated in 1978 which has largely abandoned the strong central control of the economy and in the process ignored the Marxist precepts for directing economic growth in favor of a market-driven process. China has evolved into a hybridized form of a Marxist/socialist state in which the Communist party is still in charge of administration but is moving away from central control of the economy; the new form permits individual ownership and allows incentives and market-driven demand-and-supply relationships to determine price and allocate resources. The net effect of this has been remarkably rapid growth during the 1980s and the early 1990s. The adjusted real growth in GDP during 1992 was 12.8 percent, a remarkable achievement for such a large economic system. The government projects average growth rates of 8 to 9 percent throughout the mid-1990s. Such sustained growth rates over the next two decades could give China the world's largest economy early in the twenty-first century.

There have also been problems that have accompanied this growth. Perhaps the most serious has been the rise of serious corruption among the Communist party administrators at all levels, as they take advantage of their administrative role to secure bribes for approving commercial and other deals. In addition, both inflation and price distortions between production costs and sales prices have created serious disparities among different groups and regions. Perhaps the most serious manifestations of this unhappiness were the demonstrations and subsequent massacre in Tiananmen Square. Although allegedly a "pro-democracy" movement, as reported in the Western media, the root causes of those demonstrations were in fact (1) the growing inequities in income among groups and (2) the egregious corruption that allowed officials to benefit from the reforms while denying many professionals and workers the benefits of the fast economic growth.

live. The perceived need for more farm workers in the family production systems is especially critical because the income of rural families is apportioned according to the total output achieved by the production units. Even in the face of a large surplus of rural labor, peasants think of their own family situations. Thus, the economic policy of production responsibility seems to conflict with the family-planning goal of one child per family. Farm families do make logical and rational decisions about the number of children they desire; if more children increase production and thus family income, farm families are likely to have more children. For now, at least, China seems to be in a posture of promoting greater social harmony by allowing families, especially peasant families, to have more than one child. How long that modification of the family-planning policy will be allowed is difficult to gauge, but after years of severe control, farm families are indeed having more children.

At present the annual birthrate in China is estimated at 1.8 percent, a significant decline from the traditional birthrates of 4.5 to 5.0 percent. But offsetting the decline in birthrates is a continued decline in death rates, to an estimated 0.7 percent (Figure 27–2). Thus, the annual growth rate of 1.1 or 1.2 percent, if the figure is accurate, indicates that China is more than midway in its course of demographic transformation (see Figure 2–4). This is a remarkable achievement for a large, poor country still in the throes of its drive for economic development.

Most claims about China's birthrates and death rates are difficult to evaluate because the country is so large; family-planning programs that have been implemented in Shanghai and other large, modern cities may not have diffused to many rural areas. Nevertheless, enough information on rural areas has been made available to suggest that family-planning policies and programs are now being extended to them. Teams of **barefoot doctors** (i.e., paramedics), for example, functioned in part to disseminate birth control knowledge and aids. The monthly periods of all women in China are monitored to determine who is pregnant. The Chinese have clearly demonstrated the powerful role of central-government direction in producing rapid demographic results.

Even the current moderate growth rate has not been achieved easily, however. Traditionalists believed that large families were good—the natural order of things in Confucian terms. And as in agrarian societies throughout the world, children, especially sons, were seen as economic assets because they would look after their parents in the parents' declining years. Although the Communist government was initially skeptical about birth control, it appears that after 1960, family planning was viewed with increasing favor as a necessary prerequisite for rapid economic progress. From then on, except for the period of the **Cultural Revolution** (1966–1971), when Mao Tse-tung attempted to purify China's communist movement, China seems to have promoted family planning vigorously. The country's extensive public health and welfare system has been an effective agent in promoting birth control; pills are the most commonly used method, though a variety of other means, including sterilization (especially of females) and abortion, are also practiced.

China seems to be making considerable progress in altering the value systems of its citizens. With improvements in medicine and greatly reduced death rates, parents can now expect their children to reach adulthood. And today the state or collective unit cares for those who are too old to work but have no descendants to look after them. Against those improved conditions the new ideal of a small family with one child has been proclaimed and, if we can believe the available information, is being accepted, though not always happily. At the same time, sex ratios indicate female infanticide continues to be a problem in rural areas.

Where the People Are

The Chinese are concentrated today where they have been concentrated for many centuries; more than 1 billion people reside within the eighteen provinces of China's traditional settled, or core, area. Only one large area, Manchuria, has become densely populated for the first time within the last century. If a line were drawn connecting Qiqihar (Tsitsihar) in northwestern Manchuria with Kunming in southern

Figure 27-1
A one-child-only poster in Xiamen, on the island of Gulangyu in the Formosa Strait. Posters throughout China promote the one-child family as the model family size.

Yunnan (Yunan) Province, more than 93 percent of China's people would be found east of that line (Figure 27–3). Not surprisingly, the eastern part of China contains most of the well-watered, productive agricultural land. Thus, there exists in China a correlation between arable land and population. With the heavy settlement of the central part of the Manchurian Plain during this century, however, China's last major region able to support a dense population was occupied. Future development of other agricultural lands will depend on expensive and difficult irrigation and reclamation projects if population densities similar to those in the core region are to be supported. To better comprehend those densities, a comparison with the United States is helpful: China, which is just slightly larger than the United States in area, concentrates a population more than four times that of the United States within approximately 40 percent of China's territory.

West of the **Qiqihar-Kunming line**, rainfall decreases to the point that settled agriculture is marginal. Perhaps for that reason most of the region has traditionally been the domain of pastoralists and

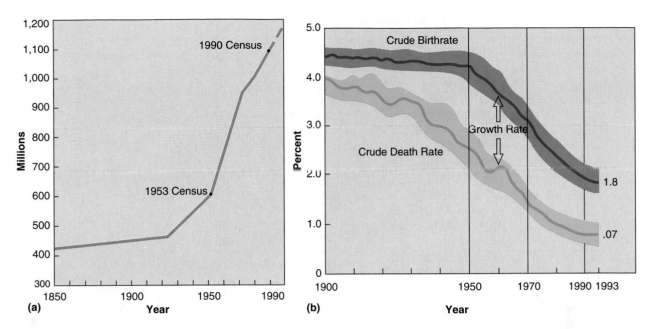

Figure 27-2
**Chinese population trends: (a) estimated population growth and (b) birthrates and
death rates.** China's rapid population growth is explained by the fact that the death
rate has dropped more rapidly than the birthrate. (From: "China: Population in the
People's Republic," *Population Bulletin* 27, 1971, and Population Reference Bureau,
World Population Data Sheet, Washington, DC: 1994.)

specialized oasis farmers. Although 60 percent of
China's territory lies west of the line, only about 83
million people live there, many of whom are members of China's minority nationalities. Such relatively
empty areas would appear to invite migrants from
crowded eastern China, but the nature of the environment with its paucity of rainfall is alien to the traditional methods of intensive farming that are common in eastern China. Perhaps new technologies,
such as mechanized agriculture and improved irrigation techniques, will open more of that region to
denser settlement, but it seems unlikely that Han
people will live in western China in the concentrations that are so common in the more humid east.

CHINA'S CHANGING SOCIAL PATTERNS

Chinese society has been altered dramatically in recent years. Some of the changes are those that
would be expected in any society transforming itself
from traditional to modern, from rural to urban, and
from agricultural to industrial. But China has an
added element—Marxism—which seeks to trans-

form the basic value system rapidly and thereby
speed up modernization. In China's case the
Marxism has been modified to fit local conditions,
and more recently far-reaching reforms have altered
the Marxist character of China's economy.

The Traditional Pattern

Society in traditional China focused, for the most
part, on family relationships at the village level. For
more than 2,000 years a family-oriented social system existed, based on the ethical norms and values
outlined by Confucius as early as 436 B.C. In that
system, order depended on the primacy of the head
of the household, and his desires prevailed over the
younger generation living in the same household.
Male heirs, who could carry on the family name and
line, dominated the system. Women were important
for the work they performed but had little participation in formal decision making and no proprietary
rights. Thus, they were excluded from a full role in
the affairs of the family and the village.

Beyond the family there were common-surname
associations, or clans, which frequently acted to

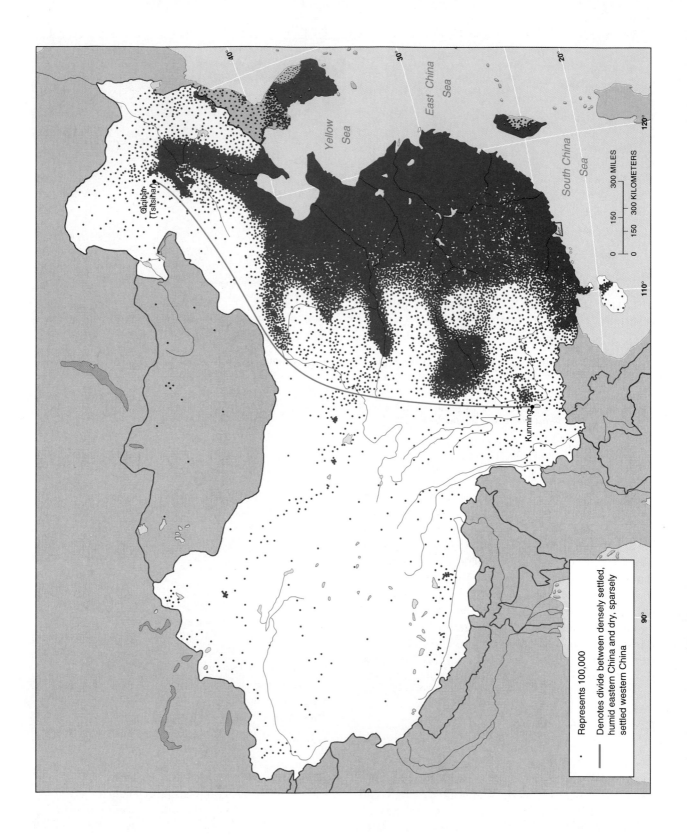

satisfy larger mutual interests by temporarily siding with other clans when some joint purpose could be served. In addition to clans, other voluntary associations and groups emerged, often focused around a religious objective or some common commercial or special-activity interest.

Such was traditional society. It centered on the village, and most of the relationships that grew up were village-oriented, based on kinship ties. To a considerable extent, villages were self-sufficient, with an economic system tied to the inward-looking social system. Social links with the outside did exist, but for most peasants they were not well established and were rarely used. It was the political system, as much as anything, that linked the village with the rest of China.

Society in the New China

Social revolution is as much a part of the Maoist and post-Maoist remaking of China as is change in the political and economic systems. In fact, social reform and land redistribution have followed wherever communists have been able to establish themselves. Among the most important consequences of the social revolution has been the shift in family dominance. Authority has shifted from the traditional head, the oldest male member of the family, to a younger man, usually the oldest son, who is also the most productive member of the family. That shift is a reversal of the established Confucian norm and an indicator that social changes in China are fundamental and far-reaching.

Another abrupt change from established practice has been the creation of new roles and rights for women. Women have been freed from their traditional subservience and lower status and have been encouraged to spend time away from home, often as salaried members of the labor force. At the same time men have been encouraged to view their wives as equals and to share in the household chores. Men also have had to recognize the right of their wives to join in political activities and associations that promote the group interests of women. Thus, with that new set of relationships, another basic alteration in the established Confucian order has been set in motion.

The central government believes that the special approach to and reform of China's traditional villages has played a key role in revolutionizing China in less than a generation. Such an accomplishment is believed to be a unique contribution of the Chinese to the theory and process of development and modernization.

AGRICULTURE AND THE CHANGING SOCIALIST ECONOMY

The economy of China has always been rooted in and dependent on agriculture. Even after four decades of Communist rule, China remains an agricultural country, with approximately 60 percent of its people engaged in farming and related activities. The economic reforms initiated in 1978 began with agriculture, and progress in agriculture remains something of a bellwether for the overall health of China's economy.

Crop Regions and Crop Types

Food grains, including rice, are China's leading crops. As a general rule, rice is grown wherever environmental conditions permit. In the southeast, where frost is uncommon, double-cropping of rice is customary. Rice tends to produce the largest quantity of edible grain on a given unit of land, provided the supply of labor, nutrient materials, and water is sufficient. Thus, the alluvial valleys and basins of southeastern and central China, where rice can be grown, are among the most productive (and the most densely inhabited) parts of the country (Figure 27–4).

Dry cereals, wheat, millet, and gaoliang (a type of sorghum) tend to dominate the foodstuffs in the drier, cooler north, although cash crops, such as cotton, are also common. In the south the more common cash crops are tea, fruits, sugarcane, and oilseeds. The most striking contrast of Chinese agriculture is the transition from wet rice in the south to dry cereals north of the Qinling Mountains–Huai River divide. Some rice is also grown in northern Manchuria, however.

Figure 27–3
Distribution of population in China and neighboring states. China's population is heavily clustered east of a line connecting Qiqihar (Tsitsihar) and Kunming. In that area approximately 93 percent of the Chinese people reside, a reflection of geographic accessibility and farming opportunities.

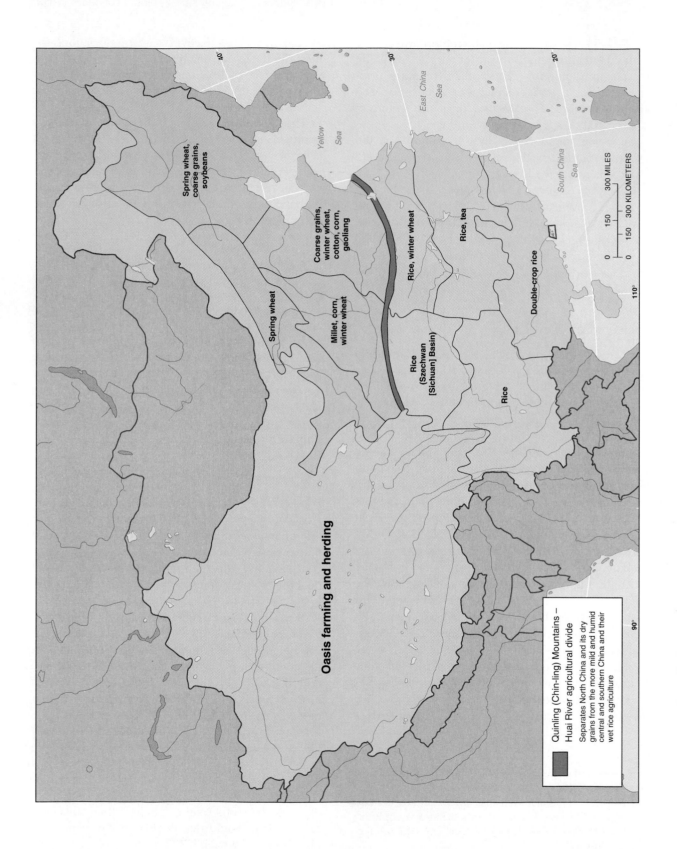

Spring wheat, coarse grains, soybeans

Coarse grains, winter wheat, cotton, corn, gaoliang

Spring wheat

Millet, corn, winter wheat

Rice, winter wheat

Rice, tea

Double-crop rice

Rice (Szechwan [Sichuan] Basin)

Rice

Oasis farming and herding

Yellow Sea

East China Sea

South China Sea

40°

30°

20°

110°

90°

| | 0 | 150 | 300 MILES |
| | 0 | 150 | 300 KILOMETERS |

Quinling (Chin-ling) Mountains – Huai River agricultural divide

Separates North China and its dry grains from the more mild and humid central and southern China and their wet rice agriculture

Traditional Agriculture

The nature of the rural economy has changed greatly; nonetheless, some of the old cropping practices and farming techniques still linger. One traditional means whereby China increased its agricultural production was through expansion of its cropland. That process reached its zenith in the rice-growing environment of the south, as the frontiers of Chinese settlement expanded over the centuries. But now that Manchuria has been settled, no more attractive agricultural frontiers remain. Thus, greater agricultural output in the future must come primarily from increased per-unit yields.

Other traditional techniques of increasing crop output in China were simple: add more labor; add organic manures, such as night soil (decomposed human excrement); and intensify multiple-cropping. More people were then supported from the increased crop outputs, and the larger population reinforced the cycle by providing more laborers and more human waste. Since gains in production were always countered by an increased population, many people existed at only a subsistence level.

That self-reinforcing chain reaction provided few stimulants for technical breakthroughs or innovations, which might have lessened the traditional demand for labor and thus reduced the incentive for large families. Instead, the population continued to swell, in step with the expanded commodity output. Per capita wealth and demand remained stagnant and may even have decreased after the sixteenth century. That "high-level equilibrium trap" resulted in increasing poverty and created great stress in the traditional Chinese economy and society.[1] It has been argued that that stress was the main precondition for the demands for reform and modernization of China.

Thus, peasant life in traditional China was frequently difficult. Several levels of peasants existed—landlords, middle peasants who farmed their own land, and poor peasants—and even the major landlords were hardly wealthy by Western standards. The poor peasants frequently hired themselves out to the wealthier peasants or otherwise became indentured or tenanted. But the pressure for land among the landlords and middle peasants became more urgent with increasing population, for the effect of more sons was to fragment more and more the existing cropland and thus to continuously reduce the amount of farmland available to most peasant families.

When coupled with the natural catastrophes of drought, flood, earthquake, and locust plagues, such a situation yields an unpleasant picture of traditional peasant life. Indeed, the picture was especially bleak in North China, where those natural events were more erratic and less subject to control. Floods and drought led to food shortages, and many families fled to the south in search of a better situation. Remaining landlords demanded even more of poor families, often leading to local violence. In some cases that violence may have been widespread enough to crystallize into larger movements that eventually led to political change.[2]

The Modernization of Agriculture

Communes (Rural Townships). From the late 1950s to the early 1980s, probably the most important economic unit in modern China was the **commune**. Although at one time the term was used to refer to urban neighborhoods and districts, it is in rural areas that communes have functioned best as operating units. Now called rural townships, they continue today, mainly as units of administrative organization. Organized hierarchically, the current township is large in area (an average of 60 square miles, or 155 square kilometers), usually including the territory and fields of a number of small hamlets and villages. A central office conducts administrative affairs and maintains ties with other political, social, and economic units.

Communes first appeared in China in 1958, about a decade after the Communists came to power. They were organized to support the new efforts to modernize, but they were built on an established pattern of village production and social, political, and economic self-sufficiency. Not only were the communes to grow their own food, but they were also encouraged to build local industries to produce clothing, tools, and other necessities—local produc-

Figure 27-4
Agricultural regions of China. China is a large, middle-latitude land with a variety of environments and, as a result, many different cropping systems. The most significant agricultural regions are the humid rice-growing south and center; the cooler north and northeast, where coarse grains and wheat are grown; and the dry west, with its oasis and herding complex.

tion for local consumption. At the same time, any surplus could be sold and shipped to other regions.

Rural Economic Reform: The Production Responsibility System. In the late 1970s a new rural production system was introduced in China—family **production responsibility**. Under that system farm families lease for long periods a certain amount of land to farm; ownership of the land theoretically remains with the collective unit. The family agrees to a production quota and can keep whatever is produced beyond the quota after expenses and taxes are paid. Any surplus can be used by the family or sold in private markets. Thus, the system fixes much of the farm decision making in the farm family itself. That system has increased production, improved efficiency, raised rural incomes substantially, and resulted in better crop selection (Table 27–1).

The responsibility system must be judged a major improvement for Chinese farmers. Production is up substantially, especially for such cash crops as sugarcane, oilseeds, vegetables, and fruits. In addition, many farm families are specializing in sideline production of chickens, ducks, or other specialty products that are in great demand, often in nearby urban markets. Rural incomes are up sharply, too, as reflected in the many signs of growing prosperity in rural areas—new housing, more power equipment, and more consumer products. Many peasants also have jobs in nearby factories. In areas such as southern Jiangsu (Kiangsu) Province off-farm employment

patterns near larger cities suggest that a rapid shift in the economic structure is under way as the economy converts to a more industrial/commercial type. Other areas lag, however, and rural incomes and prosperity vary substantially from region to region.

How much better off is a family in one of China's villages today than a peasant family was fifty years ago? Most members of each family must still work long and hard, but today there is generally enough food for everyone, even if the government must import it. In addition, an educational opportunity through primary school is provided for everyone at no cost, and health service provides basic, if modest, care to all at very low cost. Along with those benefits, however, goes a certain amount of political indoctrination and social control; the state expects everyone to comply with its directives without question.

Increased Production. In the early 1950s the new government was fortunate to have several years of good weather, and agricultural output increased. The **Great Leap Forward** (1958–1961), however, coincided with several years of poor weather, and crop production fell. Since then, except for some uncertainty during the years of the Cultural Revolution, output of food grains has increased gradually if sporadically, in step with the growing population. As early as 1984 China first produced more than 400 million metric tons of food grain. The 1992 production was estimated at 446 million metric tons, easily the world's largest output.

Table 27-1
Output of selected Chinese agricultural and industrial products, 1981 and 1991.

Agricultural Product	Metric Tons (millions) 1981	1991	Industrial Product	Metric Tons (millions) 1981	1991
All grains	325.0	435.3	Coal	620.0	1,087.0
Rice	143.0	183.8	Crude oil	101.0	144.9
Wheat	58.0	95.9	Crude steel	36.0	71.0
Soybeans	9.2	9.7	Cement	84.0	252.6
Cotton	2.9	5.7	Chemical fertilizer	12.4	19.8
Oilseed	10.2	16.4			

Sources: Beijing Review 25 (1982); and China Statistical Yearbook, 1992.

Nonetheless, despite increased crop production, China has frequently purchased grain (usually wheat) from several Western countries, chiefly Australia, Canada, and the United States. Such sales suggest that periodic large fluctuations in grain output along with rapidly growing demand for animal feed may prevent China from producing enough food to support its huge population. At the same time, however, the country exports a considerable amount of high-cost foodstuffs (e.g., vegetables, pork, condiments, and specialty foods) to Hong Kong, Southeast Asia, and Chinese communities all over the world. Thus, China may well be a net exporter of foodstuffs, despite its large grain purchases. It has claimed self-sufficiency in food production since 1971 (Figure 27–5).

Food exports notwithstanding, China's foreign grain purchases suggest a weakness in agriculture that makes modernization and increased productivity ever more pressing. One major problem is that little good land is available for agricultural expansion, at least under present technologies. By way of comparison, the United States, with less than one-fourth the population of China, has 153 million more acres (61 million more hectares) of arable land. Thus, with only dry or marshy lands available for future expansion, China faces a difficult situation, given the growing population. Statistics on rural land use show that cropland has actually decreased in recent years, to about 245 million acres (99 million hectares). This equals less than a quarter of an acre (less than a tenth of a hectare) of arable land per person in China, a figure that declines each year. Yet China depends on the agricultural economy to help form capital to finance development projects. If that pattern is to continue and if living standards are to improve simultaneously, per capita yields must be increased rapidly. This becomes increasingly difficult as yields rise towards a point of diminishing returns.

An associated and equally urgent problem is that as the economy modernizes, it will increasingly urbanize, and China's cities commonly occupy the best agricultural land. Thus, as the urban areas grow and spread out, they will encroach on the farmland—a built-in conflict. Without a dramatic shift, modernization and economic-development programs will probably result in the loss of a significant amount of good agricultural land.

INDUSTRIALIZATION AND ECONOMIC GROWTH

One of the important—and fortunate—consequences of China's great size and particular location is a rich and diverse resource base, which has helped to promote industrialization and economic growth. That base includes not only a wide variety of environments for the production of food and cash crops,

Figure 27-5
Rice harvesting with a small-scale combine. Despite some substitution of capital for labor, the main input into Chinese agriculture continues to be human labor.

some of which are closely associated with industrial processing (e.g., cotton, tobacco, soybeans, oilseeds, and tung nuts), but also substantial reserves of fossil fuels (i.e., coal and petroleum) and minerals (e.g., iron ore, tin, manganese, copper, and molybdenum). Even though access to those resources has sometimes been difficult, their presence ensures the country a degree of economic self-sufficiency and less dependence on external sources. As a result, China does not need to spend scarce capital on imported raw materials and may gain foreign exchange through the sale of some of those resources. Recently, for example, China has financed the purchase of sophisticated machinery and technology from Japan through the sale of crude oil. However, imports are now beginning to be financed more through long-term credit arrangements, and exports of a range of manufactured goods have risen sharply.

Accessibility to resources is difficult to assess, for in much of China the landscape is rough, and transportation has traditionally been slow and expensive (Figure 27–6). Water transportation increasingly links China with the outside world, but new emphasis has been placed during this century on other forms of surface travel and on air transportation to tie together the far-flung parts of China's vast territory.

Contemporary Patterns of Industrialization

After seizing power, the Communist leaders and planners established a basic goal of industrializing the state as rapidly as possible. That policy and its implementation appear to have been based on the Soviet model of investing primarily in heavy industry (i.e., producer goods), to the relative neglect of consumer goods and agriculture. Initially, the Soviet Union provided China with a great deal of technical assistance in the construction of new plants and, for a price, supplied much of the needed equipment and machinery.

Things went well in the beginning. Good weather meant large agricultural yields, and the Soviets helped China complete a number of important industrial and construction projects. But relations between the two states soon became strained, and in the late 1950s the Soviets withdrew their assistance. Soviet engineers even abandoned some projects in the middle of construction. At that point the Chinese changed the direction of their central planning and established their own design for industrialization and economic growth.

Paths to Modernization

At the time of the Great Leap Forward in 1958, it was difficult to gauge the full nature of the changes under way in industry; however, subsequent events have permitted a better understanding of the new policies that were in operation. An established objective was to develop the interior parts of China and eradicate the evil influence of the treaty ports and colonial cities as centers of industry and innovation. The new approach, according to the planners, was to develop backward areas, take industry to the raw materials, reduce transportation costs, and provide better protection for the centers of production. A conflict existed, though, because the treaty ports, as great industrial centers, were easily accessible, were well supplied with skilled labor, had already established industrial and power facilities, and were low-cost centers for industrial production. In addition, all of the amenities and advantages of large cities already existed in them. As the Chinese planners knew, such assets are difficult and expensive to create anew.

During the exuberance of the Great Leap Forward, a new experiment was undertaken to shortcut the process of industrialization. That experiment focused on local small units of industrial production; the backyard iron furnace was one example. Communist planners sought to reduce dependence on the great industrial centers by promoting local industries designed to produce the goods required at the local level. The new policy was not wholly successful, however. Products from local industry were often inferior or useless and sometimes expensive. But the principle of local production for local consumption apparently survived; much of the rapid growth of collective industries in the last decade has been of smaller production units often making consumer goods for both local consumption and export.

China has now moved to a policy called the **Four Modernizations**. That polity seeks to modernize four broad sectors—agriculture, industry, science, and national defense—by the end of the century. The frequently stated goal is for China to become a modern, socialist, industrial state by the year 2000, ready to enter a new stage of economic growth and able to compete with major world powers such as the United States. In carrying out that modernization, China has indicated a willingness to borrow or purchase Western technology and scientific knowledge. Industrial

Figure 27-6
Trucks crossing a river by ferry. Chinese transportation systems remain woefully inadequate, despite government modernization programs.

growth has been especially rapid during the last two decades and by 1990 accounted for 53 percent of GDP and 21 percent of labor share (see Table 27–1).

Oil: A Case of Rapid Development

Oil is one industry that has been developed very rapidly under Chinese socialism. Before 1949 less than 3 million metric tons of oil had been produced in half a century. After the establishment of the People's Republic in 1949, the Soviets provided both equipment and personnel for oil production. By 1955, annual crude oil production totaled almost 1 million tons. By 1970, production had increased to 33 million tons, and 1992 production was reported at 142 million tons. Much of that new production has been associated with the development of the Daqing (Taching) oil field in Manchuria. On the basis of that one field China achieved self-sufficiency in petroleum production and initiated oil exports to Japan.

Estimates based on proven and probable reserves suggest that China has between 1 and 2 billion tons of oil in the ground. Increased production, however, especially offshore, will require large capital invest-

ments and sophisticated equipment, both in short supply at the present time. The future of Chinese oil production, then, may be closely tied to political events, for the Chinese will need assistance and capital from Japan, the United States, or other advanced economies.

Industry, Cities, and Transportation

Despite the early aim of China's new planners to shift the centers of production to the interior, the well-established industrial cities—such as Shanghai, Tianjin (Tientsin), Shenyang, Anshan, Guangzhou (Canton), Nanjing, Wuhan, and Beijing (Peking)—continue to dominate (Figures 27–7 and 27–8). A few new centers have been developed, such as the Inner Mongolian city of Baotou (Paotou), with its new steel mills. And many older cities in the interior—such as Urumqi (Urumchi), Chengdu, Lanzhou, Kunming, Xi'an (Sian), Zhengzhou (Chengchou), and Changsha—have been given new industries. Nevertheless, the major centers of industry continue to be the cities of the coast, the Yangtze ports, and the great Manchurian cities—a testimony to the validity of their initial selection.

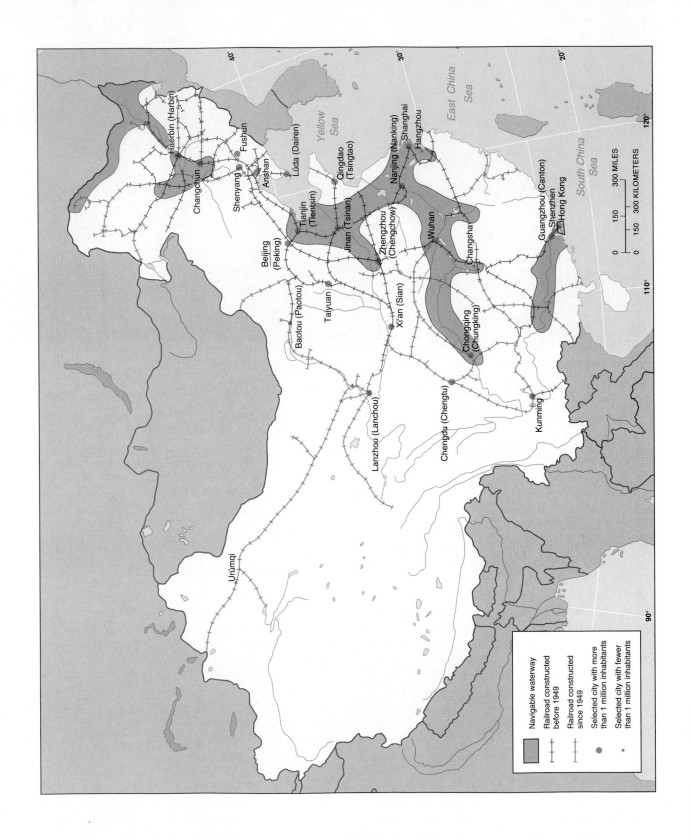

East China
Sea

Yellow
Sea

South China
Sea

Haerbin (Harbin)

Fushun

Changchun

Shenyang

Anshan

Lüda (Dairen)

Qingdao (Tsingtao)

Nanjing (Nanking)

Shanghai

Hangzhou

Tianjin (Tientsin)

Jinan (Tsinan)

Zhengzhou (Chengchow)

Wuhan

Changsha

Guangzhou (Canton)

Shenzhen

Hong Kong

Beijing (Peking)

Baotou (Paotou)

Taiyuan

Xi'an (Sian)

Chongqing (Chungking)

Chengdu (Chengtu)

Kunming

Lanzhou (Lanchou)

Ürümqi

300 MILES

300 KILOMETERS

150

150

0

0

	Navigable waterway
	Railroad constructed before 1949
	Railroad constructed since 1949
	Selected city with more than 1 million inhabitants
	Selected city with fewer than 1 million inhabitants

40°

30°

20°

120°

110°

90°

Figure 27-8
Beijing, China. The walled Forbidden City and the Imperial Palace reveal traditional
Chinese architecture in contrast with contemporary structures.

China's situation is neither startling nor illogical considering the available transportation (see Figure 27–7). The great industrial cities are, for the most part, those that are best served by railroads and are the most accessible by water. By virtue of their large populations and established industries, they are also the sites of the greatest consumption of goods, fuel, and raw materials. Those factors have a tendency to feed each other, reinforcing the growth that is already well established. Moreover, the economic reforms have focused on advancing economic growth most rapidly in the coastal regions where many of these great cities are located.

One plan to counter the influence of the treaty ports involved the construction of new railroad links all through inland China. Accordingly, the Chinese have

Figure 27-7
Railways, waterways, and selected cities of China. China has a modest network of railroads, although many new lines have been constructed in recent years. The rail system is supplemented by an extensive network of rivers and canals, which are especially important in central China.

built and continue to expand an impressive, if not dense, rail network throughout the interior. Nevertheless, the new growth centers will be hard pressed to rival the advantages of international trade linkages and sea transportation shared by the former treaty ports especially as coastal areas benefit from the liberalized rules on investment and export manufacturing.

China's industrial and transportation geography can be usefully compared with India's. India possesses a dense network of railroads focused on the major industrial and commercial centers, all of which were inherited from British colonial days. China, in contrast, contains two patterns: the interior water transport network using China's great rivers and canals, now supplemented with a modest but expanding rail system, and the coastal water transport system, also supplemented now by rail. The main industrial areas are associated with the second pattern, though in recent years the two patterns have been increasingly integrated.

Both China and India have incorporated preexisting networks of transportation into their recent development strategies. Both have also developed new industrial centers; it is difficult to say whether Baotou is

635

more important to China's economy than Jamshedpur is to India's. In addition, both countries have sought to develop other new areas in the interior and redistribute wealth away from coastal areas associated with a colonial past. Neither, however, is likely to follow such a locational policy too closely if it impedes the rate of economic growth and progress. At present in both countries pro-growth policies seem to be more important than those policies that stress equity.

Regional Inequality: A Continuing Problem

One of China's most serious problems is the inequality between the interior region and the coastal region. China's interior, especially that portion away from the Yangtze River, has remained impoverished, whereas Manchuria and coastal areas with better accessibility and rapid industrial development have become more prosperous. That trend has led to increasing income disparity among different parts of China, with sharp regional differences between the lower Yangtze Delta and interior locations, such as the Loess Plateau. Policy statements have emphasized the need to reduce such inequality and improve the regional distribution of industrial production. In fact, during the first twenty-five years of communism in China, net revenue transfers were used to develop interior industries and transportation linkages.[3] Since 1978, however, the new policies associated with economic reform and restructuring have redirected attention and investment to the coastal provinces, indicating more concern today with increasing economic growth than with reducing regional inequality.

Future Trends

Today, China produces a full and growing array of industrial and scientific goods in significant quantities: automobiles, airplanes, locomotives, computers, and atomic bombs. Its production of iron and steel, cement, and electricity exceeds the level of most European countries. In addition, its fossil-fuel production is large and is climbing rapidly, based on new coal and petroleum discoveries. Total industrial production is large, even by U.S., Japanese, or Russian standards. Given China's great population, however, per capita output remains small.

In terms of employment, China's economy remains rural and agrarian, but that situation is changing rapidly. In the Rostow model (outlined in Chapter 4), China would appear to be well into the stage of economic takeoff, though that model may be inadequate to explain China's economic growth. It is conceivable that the recent shift in foreign policy and efforts to buy new technologies will accelerate economic development; both Japan and the former Soviet Union industrialized quickly. However, special conditions and traditions, coupled with a huge population, suggest that China's economic development will proceed somewhat differently, though the pace of the last ten years has been remarkably rapid.

China's future development is also linked to the events of early June, 1989, when, after several weeks of political demonstrations in Beijing, Chinese army troops entered Tiananmen Square and killed more than 1,000 demonstrators (Figure 27–9). That **Tiananmen incident** ended the open popular movement for political reform in China and also signaled continuing uncertainty and instability in the top leadership circles regarding the nature of recent changes in the country. That uncertainty and instability raise questions about the long-term direction and viability of Chinese economic reforms and therefore about the ability of the country to modernize and participate effectively within the community of nations. Yet despite the political uncertainties consequent upon the Tiananmen incident, China's economic growth appears to have accelerated. Clearly economic growth continues apace in China in the context of a highly autocratic and bureaucratic central administration.

CHINA'S RIMLAND

Several nations and colonies on China's eastern and northern flanks have been linked to it either directly or through ancient cultural and historical ties (Figure 27–10). In Korea physical isolation and a degree of political autonomy have promoted a separate and distinctive culture. In other cases—Hong Kong, Macao, and Taiwan, for example—Chinese territory and Chinese-speaking populations are involved. Thus, the Chinese government considers those three areas integral parts of the Chinese state. Hong Kong and Macao, through recently concluded agreements, are actually scheduled to become Chinese territory in 1997 and 1999, respectively.

Mongolia, too, although independent, is considered Chinese territory, but of a somewhat different nature. Its status, in the Chinese view, is analogous to that of Tibet, Xinjiang (Sinkiang), and Nei Monggol (Inner Mongolia). Mongolia's inhabitants are recognized as non-Chinese, but their history and

Figure 27-9
Demonstrators at Tiananmen Square in Beijing. Though economic reforms are in progress, political reforms in significant measure have not been forthcoming.

destiny are so closely linked to China that they are proper subjects for political integration into the People's Republic. If it were not for Soviet and now Russian opposition and power, the Chinese would probably have forced the incorporation of the Democratic Republic of Mongolia into their state. Since the breakup of the Soviet Union, China's economic and political relations with Mongolia have intensified.

Hong Kong

At the mouth of the Xijiang (Hsi) estuary, just within the tropics along China's southeastern coast, is the British Crown Colony of Hong Kong. Hong Kong includes 415 square miles (1,076 square kilometers) of territory, within which 5.9 million people live. Its main resource is its hardworking population, whose efforts have brought prosperity to the colony. The traditional functions of Hong Kong were trade and commerce; from its beginning the British colony was an **entrepôt**

(i.e., a center for trade and transshipment) for South China, and it served that function for a century.

The harbor of Hong Kong is deep and spacious (Figure 27–11). Thus, the development of steam-driven ocean vessels with increasingly deep drafts gave Hong Kong an advantage over neighboring Macao. Although financed and controlled by Great Britain, Hong Kong functioned as an appendage of China's foreign trade structure, accounting for a substantial part of that trade. But after the ascendancy of the Communist government in mainland China, Hong Kong's future appeared bleak; military defense of the colony against China is not feasible. Yet somehow the colony has survived, and indeed prospered, though there have been periods of great uncertainty.

With the interruption in 1949 of its traditional functions of trade and transshipment, Hong Kong of necessity turned to new enterprises. By 1970 more than 40 percent of the labor force worked in manufacturing, with textiles and garments accounting for almost 45 percent of that employment and 60 percent of the

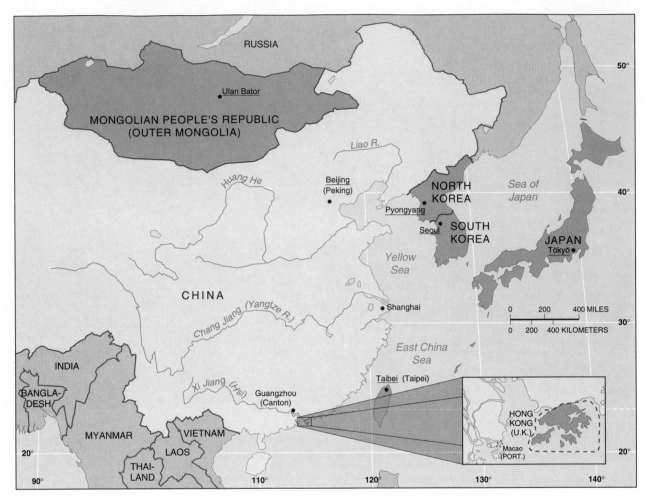

Figure 27–10
Primary political units of East Asia. China dominates East Asia not only because of its size but also in terms of its political geography.

colony's exports. Other important industries have been plastics (e.g., toys, recreational goods, and sundries), wigs, electronic components, and machine tools. By 1992 the employment share of manufacturing had declined to 24 percent, as Hong Kong's traditional functions of service, trade, and transport had resumed their previous importance.

Banking, insurance, and other forms of commerce continue as important activities and make up Hong Kong's other major employment field. The colony continues to serve as an entrepôt, with goods worth approximately $89 billion transshipped in 1992. That transshipment trade—consisting of manufactures such as garments, textiles, footware, electronics, and machinery—is increas-

ing rapidly. China, Japan, Taiwan, and the United States are the main sources of origin and destination. Much of this re-export activity reflects the rapid growth of China's trade and highlights the significance of China as Hong Kong's largest trading partner.

Tourism is also extremely important to the economic health of the colony; more than 7 million tourists arrived in Hong Kong in 1992. The earnings derived from the tourist trade and re-exports—as well as from other less visible sources of foreign exchange, such as banking and insurance—more than offset a small trade deficit that amounted to $4 billion in 1992. Earnings from tourism alone were estimated at $6.1 billion in 1992.

Figure 27-11
Hong Kong Island off China's southeast coast. The view of Kowloon and Victoria Harbor is from Victoria Peak. Hong Kong remains a British territory but will return to Chinese sovereignty in 1997. Overwhelmingly Chinese in population, this city-state flourishes as a financial, trade, manufacturing, and tourist center.

Based on language and place of origin, some 98.5 percent of Hong Kong's citizens are described as Chinese. In fact, about 40 percent of the colony's citizens were born elsewhere, mostly in China. At the end of World War II, Hong Kong had approximately 600,000 people. By 1960 that number had swollen to 3.1 million. At present the colony's population is 5.9 million. Immigration has accounted for much of that remarkable growth— more than 500,000 immigrants since 1977—and events in China provide an explanation. Political activities on the mainland, such as the Great Leap Forward and the Cultural Revolution, apparently spurred emigration. At times the Chinese government has allowed some of its citizens to leave, but others have left illegally.

With such a large population and so modest a land area, Hong Kong is really a city-state. It is one of the most crowded places on earth, with a population density of 14,478 people per square mile (approximately 5,590 per square kilometer). Despite that dense population, 75 percent of the land area is either under cultivation or in rugged uplands and scrub vegetation. Only 25 percent of the area is urbanized. One urban district has about 430,000 people per square mile (166,000 per square kilometer), placing it among the world's densest urban concentrations.

Hong Kong's future political status has been decided. In 1985 the British and Chinese governments ratified an agreement whereby Hong Kong would return to Chinese sovereignty in 1997, after the expiration of the current treaty and lease agreement. Hong Kong will then be granted status as a special administrative region of China, with a high degree of autonomy in all matters except foreign affairs and defense. For example, Hong Kong will have its own freely convertible currency, laws, political freedoms, and local government, and it will be allowed to maintain its capitalist economic system and its status as a free port for another fifty years. It will also be permitted to issue its own travel documents and maintain a local police force.

Many people are skeptical about that agreement. They do not believe that the Chinese will allow Hong Kong that much autonomy and independence, and they think that the vigorous free-market economic system will be stifled. But the Chinese have much to gain by allowing Hong Kong to continue to develop and prosper, even if somewhat independently. First, China gains much economically by trading with and through Hong Kong; China is easily Hong Kong's major trading partner, with a total trade in 1992 of over $81 billion. This provided a surplus of more than $10 billion to China. In addition, what happens to Hong Kong may well serve as a model for the future of Taiwan. If China wishes to peacefully reunite Taiwan with the motherland, the treatment of Hong Kong as a part of China, but with special autonomy and privileges and a much higher standard of living, is a crucial illustration. Thus, the stakes are high for China to maintain Hong Kong's special status and to ensure that its current life-style and high standard of living are preserved.

Taiwan

Within the last two decades certain political events involving China have shocked Taiwan. First of all, in 1971 the People's Republic of China (PRC) took over China's seat at the United Nations, a position that had been held since 1945 by the Nationalist government. But perhaps the most devastating blow came when Taiwan's long-time ally, the United States, withdrew recognition in 1979 in favor of the PRC. Only twenty-three countries continued to recognize Taiwan at that time, and the number has declined since then. Even though Taiwan's economic growth and progress have been impressive in recent years, its political future remains uncertain. The island state is occupied by three major language groups and a variety of political factions. All are related in one way or another to the island's past as a frontier territory of China, and all have opinions on China's pressing desire to reintegrate Taiwan into China. For decades Taiwan was a one-party state,

but far reaching political reforms have occurred since 1987 and today Taiwan is a true democracy with free elections.

China has had ties with Taiwan for more than a thousand years and, since the sixteenth century, has sent a steady stream of immigrant farmers and adventurers, first to the Penghu (Pescadore) Islands and then on to Taiwan. At various times that stream has been interrupted by foreign occupation of the island—Dutch, Spanish, French, and Japanese. Nonetheless, ever since Chinese farmers began to cultivate the productive alluvial plains and basins along the western coast, the island has been Chinese in ethnic and linguistic composition.

In 1885 the Chinese Ch'ing (Qing) imperial government made Taiwan a province, two centuries after it had been absorbed by the empire. The new governor then set about modernizing and developing the island as a showpiece province. Ten years later, after the Sino-Japanese War of 1895, the Japanese took over the island as a colony and accelerated the pace of investment and growth. The combined efforts of China and Japan to modernize Taiwan—through the construction of roads, dams, irrigation systems, bridges, a railway system, new cities, and ports—laid the groundwork for a transformation of its traditional economic system.

Fifty years of Japanese colonialism also brought improved standards of public health, a decline in the death rate, and rapid population growth. Approximately 2 million people lived on the island at the beginning of the twentieth century; by 1920 the population had climbed to 3.65 million. In 1949, when the Nationalist Chinese government was exiled on Taiwan, the inhabitants numbered more than 6 million. To those were added more than 1 million soldiers, functionaries, and refugees from the mainland, and that rapid population growth has continued. There are now 21.1 million inhabitants, an incredible number of people for an island of only 13,892 square miles (35,980 square kilometers), roughly the size of Maryland and Delaware together.

Taiwan lies astride the Tropic of Cancer, 100 miles (161 kilometers) east of the China mainland. Its climate is monsoonal, with most of its precipitation occurring in the summer. In the northeast quadrant, however, the pattern is reversed, with heavy winter rains coming with the prevailing northeasterlies. Summer and autumn typhoons are an annual threat and often cause great damage and flooding. Frost is unknown at lower elevations.

The eastern two-thirds of Taiwan is high and rough. Except for a narrow valley and a small alluvial basin in the northeast, that portion of the island contains little land suitable for intensive farming. The western third of the island, however, is composed of a series of alluvial plains and basins, separated by broad, cobble-strewn riverbeds. A dense network of roads and railroad lines covers those plains and basins, integrating well the densely inhabited parts of the island.

A significant consequence of the Chinese Nationalist rule of Taiwan was land reform. A comprehensive and profound land reform program was instituted in the 1950s, giving land to those who tilled it and providing financial support through government-supported, low-interest loans. Land redistribution was accomplished, and output climbed steadily (Table 27–2).

Taiwan's combination of climate and alluvial lowlands has resulted in a productive paddy-rice agricultural environment, much like that of southeastern China. Other crops include sugarcane, tropical fruits, tea, and a rich variety of vegetables. Intensive cropping of the alluvial area—even a double-cropping of rice—has given Taiwan one of the world's most productive agricultural systems. Thus, despite Taiwan's high ratio of people to arable land, the island has been basically self-sufficient in food. During the past decade it has exported sugar, rice, mushrooms, pineapples, and pork—items of relatively high cost in relation to Taiwan's less expensive imports of food grains. That balance has permitted the island to remain close to agricultural self-sufficiency. Growth in overall agricultural production has stagnated, however, as economic emphasis has shifted to manufacturing and service activities (see Table 27–2).

Taiwan's remarkable recent economic growth has come from its success in industrialization (Table 27–3). Today, that component includes, especially, textiles, garments, plastics, chemicals, steel, ships machinery, and electronics. The United States helped early, during the 1950s and 1960s, with foreign aid contributions that were both large and well targeted. Growth since then has been rapid and sustained, as indicated by industrial output and the dramatic annual increases in per capita GDP: from $260 in 1969 to $500 in 1975, more than $3,700 in 1983, $5,000 in 1987, and $10,000 in 1992. Along with that remarkable economic progress has come a shift in the structure of the economy to an urban orientation.

The Two Koreas

Korea might have been part of China and, indeed, owes China a profound cultural debt. For much of its history Korea has existed as a loose political appendage of *Zhongguo,* the **Middle Kingdom,** which is the term the Chinese use to identify their own country as the center of the known universe. And much of what is considered traditionally Korean actually began as Chinese: its religion, art forms, architecture, part of its written language, political and social institutions, agricultural practices, and land-tenure relationships.

But despite the many cultural links to China, Korea emerged as an independent and separate entity. Modern Koreans—with their own distinctive culture, language, and history—see their country as

Table 27-2
Agricultural production in Taiwan.

	Percent of Base Year (1991 = 100)	
	All Agricultural Products	Rice
1968	96.3	137.9
1971	96.7	126.6
1975	101.1	136.6
1977	109.7	145.2
1981	103.6	130.3
1985	102.8	119.4
1989	102.4	102.3
1991	100.0	100.0
1992	96.4	89.5

Source: Industry of Free China 81 (March 1994): 201.

Table 27-3
Growth of industrial production in Taiwan.

	Percent of Base Year (1986 = 100)		
	All Industries	Consumer Goods	Capital Goods
1981	65.7	67.5	63.7
1986	100.0	100.0	100.0
1989	119.3	105.4	119.3
1992	131.2	101.2	144.3

Source: Industry of Free China 81 (March 1994): 101.

an individual East Asian civilization. They have worked, fought, and suffered to establish that cultural integrity, and they are proud of it. Despite the nation's political division into North Korea and South Korea after World War II, Koreans have maintained a sense of nationhood. And in recent years the two countries have discussed reunification, though no definitive actions have been initiated, leaving reunification unlikely. For now, large military forces continue to confront one another across the **demilitarized zone** that splits the country into northern and southern halves and causes the peninsula to remain a place of great political tension and volatility.

As a peninsula jutting off the Asian mainland toward Japan, Korea has become a sensitive and strategic bridge, and it has been so used by various warring groups for centuries. Traditionally, however, it was under China's protection and influence. Then, in 1905, after the Russo-Japanese War, Korea became a Japanese protectorate. Five years later it was annexed and became a part of the Japanese Empire. Although that colonial rule lasted only until 1945, its impact was far-reaching, for Japanese investment and development projects initiated the transformation of Korea's traditional economy and society. Without the Japanese contributions of roads, railroads, ports, mines, factories, and irrigation systems, Korea's later growth and progress would probably not have been possible. However, Japanese rule also left a legacy of distrust and dislike that continues to sour relations, especially between South Korea and Japan.

Korea's 84,565 square miles (219,023 square kilometers) make it roughly the size of Minnesota. It lies in the mid-latitudes, and its climatic patterns largely reflect its peninsular location and position. Summers are warm and moist; winters are dry and cold, the result of the dominant air mass (the Siberian high) that controls much of the winter climate of eastern Asia. In North Korea, especially at higher elevations, winters are very cold and harsh. Farther south the influence of the adjacent water bodies moderates the temperature and provides a better opportunity for moisture to accumulate in the air. Thus, the southern part of the peninsula has a much greater potential for agricultural production (Figure 27–12). Its less severe winter, longer growing season, and higher average daily temperatures make a cool-season second crop possible, thus providing support for a dense population dependent on agriculture.

Landforms in Korea reinforce the agricultural pattern; the largest alluvial plains are in the south. Most of the peninsula is part of a north-south mountain system with peaks rising 9,000 feet (2,743 meters) above sea level; in fact, only about one-fifth of North Korea is suitable for cultivation. Despite that serious obstacle, however, the mountains offer other types of resources and economic opportunities. Hydroelectric power production, lumbering, and mining are major activities in the mountainous regions; and North Korea, especially, is well endowed with coal, iron ore, tungsten, graphite, magnesite, and a variety of other minerals.

During colonial rule (1905–1945) the Japanese focused on the north in making their investments and constructing cities, factories, and transport lines. Thus, over time, much of the industrial output of the state became concentrated in the northern half of the peninsula. The south, with its more intensive wet-rice agriculture, supported twice as many people and was looked on as a breadbasket. And so developed two apparently complementary halves of one country, an industrial north and an agricultural south.

Yet such a regional characterization has never been entirely fair or correct, for large cities in the south—such as Seoul, Pusan, and Taegu—have long had important industrial functions. And the north has traditionally been an agricultural land, also. In fact, the North Korean government has recently claimed further progress in agricultural investment, great improvements in farm production, and the successful socialization of its agriculture.

Since the division of the country into two halves—a Soviet-oriented north (with a population of 23.1 million) and a Western-oriented south (with a population of 44.5 million)—and also since the Korean War, which hardened that division, new economic patterns have emerged. Each half has pursued policies to round out its economic structure in order to achieve greater self-sufficiency and reduce reliance on external sources of supply. And to some extent both have succeeded in promoting economic growth and providing more of the manufactured goods necessary for their own economies.

Both North Korea and South Korea have prospered, and both are looking to convert their economies from traditional, agrarian patterns into industrial, service-oriented systems. The growth of per capita GDP has been impressive in recent years. South Korea, especially, has had substantial success

Figure 27-12
Cultivated area of Korea. The Korean peninsula is divided politically between north and south, with the southern part having considerably more cultivated land area than the north.

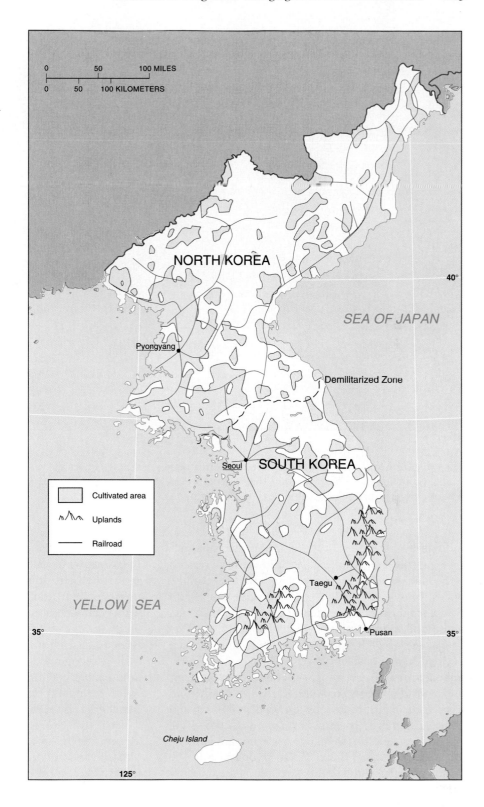

Figure 27–13
The City Hall area (foreground) of Seoul, South Korea. Seoul, the capital of South
Korea, is continuing to grow rapidly. That growth is evident here in the numerous
modern urban structures, which increasingly dwarf traditional Korean architecture.

in exporting textiles, apparel, footwear, automobiles, and electronics to consumer-oriented economies, such as those of Japan and the United States. Heavy industry, a new component of South Korea's industrial base, includes steel, shipbuilding, automobiles, refining, and petrochemicals.

In keeping with their plans for economic growth, both countries have invested heavily in new roads, railroads, mines, irrigation systems, power sources, and ports. For example, South Korea has constructed a four-lane expressway between Seoul and Pusan and is about to begin construction on a high-speed rail system between the two cities. And cities are growing at prodigious rates; the capitals—Pyongyang in the north and Seoul in the south—are among the most impressive. Indeed, Seoul, with 11.3 million inhabitants, is one of the world's largest cities (Figure 27–13).

North Korea was led by the hard-line, intransigent, and Stalinesque leader Kim Il Sung until his

death in 1994. Political reform and truly improved relations with South Korea are perhaps more likely now that he is gone. South Korea, meanwhile, has experienced remarkable economic growth and progress. The South has also followed an increasingly pragmatic foreign policy. In 1992, for instance, despite problems with North Korea, South Korea recognized the People's Republic of China and exchanged ambassadors with Beijing. Its trade with China is expanding rapidly, and in 1992 reached approximately 9 billion dollars.

For both Koreas and especially the booming South, the rate of economic expansion in the industrial and agricultural sectors—resulting from an adequate resource base and an industrious, educated, and disciplined labor force—has created a paradox of economic success in the midst of political and military insecurity. Indeed, the political systems of both countries have recently displayed that instability and immaturity. Animosity between North and South continues, but in 1990 the prime ministers of the two countries met for the first time to discuss improving relations. With the collapse of the Soviet Union and improved South Korean–Chinese relations, North Korea has found itself increasingly isolated. Such realities may lead the two Koreas toward a more peaceful future.

SUMMARY
The New Era

China and its East Asian neighbors are changing rapidly. Economic growth in Hong Kong, Taiwan, and South Korea has been remarkable during the past decade; those three countries have emerged as world leaders in economic transformation and development. China, too, has entered a new era since 1978; it is attempting to accelerate its economic growth by restructuring its economy and using the methods of a market economy to increase agricultural and industrial productivity. Output and productivity there have risen rapidly, but problems have also arisen. Among the more serious are price inflation and the need to maintain incentives in order to ensure continued increases in the production of food grains. Another serious problem is the growing disparity in income among both industrial and service workers; such disparity creates the potential for social and political unrest. Despite their problems, however, China and its neighbors are making impressive gains, and the outlook is very positive for further improvement in economic conditions and the well-being of the people.

KEY TERMS

barefoot doctors	Great Leap Forward
commune	Middle Kingdom
Cultural Revolution	production responsibility
demilitarized zone	Qiqihar-Kunming line
entrepôt	Tiananmen incident
Four Modernizations	

NOTES

1. Mark Elvin, *The Pattern of the Chinese Past* (Stanford, CA: Stanford University Press, 1973), 203–219.

2. A chronicle of such events on the eve of Communist takeover appears in William Hinton, *Fanshen: A Documentary of Revolution in a Chinese Village* (New York: Vintage Books, 1966).

3. Nicholas R. Lardy, *Economic Growth and Distribution in China* (Cambridge, England: Cambridge University Press, 1978).

28

Southeast Asia: Mainland and Islands

Geographical Outlines and Patterns

Tropical Environments and Their Utilization

Mineral Resources

Rapid Population Growth

Regional Disunity

Stagnation, Transformation, and Growth

Terraced fields on the island of Bali, Indonesia. Tropical
environments in conjunction with fertile soils of volcanic
origin provide favorable conditions for food production.
Nevertheless, Indonesia's development problems are
considerable, as it approaches a population of 200
million.

Westerners knew little about Southeast Asia until European powers occupied most of it during the nineteenth century. The region has traditionally been a zone of contact and interaction between India on the west, from which it drew much of its early culture, and China to the north. For many centuries the Chinese have been interested in Southeast Asia and at various times have extended their culture and influence to what is now known as Vietnam. In addition, many Chinese have migrated southward during the past 150 years, giving several Asian countries large and significant Chinese minorities. However, during the nineteenth century and the first half of the twentieth—the era of colonialism for Southeast Asia—many other divisive and heterogeneous forces fragmented the region.

World War II and invasion by Japan brought a political awakening and changes in traditional values to this corner of Asia. More importantly, World War II signaled the decline of European colonialism in Asia because the war exposed the weaknesses of European control. After the war the British, French, and Dutch colonies all emerged as independent nations, though the transfer of power was not always easy. Local groups often fought among themselves for political power, and the polarization between Marxist-oriented movements and other approaches to government was especially bitter. Political democracy has been challenged everywhere and has been under serious stress even in places as modern and Western as Singapore and the Philippines. In southern Vietnam democracy has never really been taken seriously, and nowhere in the Southeast Asian region does it thrive.

With the emergence of Asian nationalism, the traditional view of the region as a cultural interface between India and China is declining. The future is likely to focus more and more on indigenous views and patterns that demonstrate national pride; however, India and China are geopolitical realities that all Southeast Asian states recognize and must consider in designing their own futures.

GEOGRAPHICAL OUTLINES AND PATTERNS

Even though Southeast Asia forms a distinctive region, it is marked by both cultural and physical contrasts and diversity. Perhaps the most obvious division is between the mainland—Myanmar (Burma),

Thailand, and Indochina (Laos, Kampuchea, and Vietnam)—and the insular and archipelagic component—the Philippines, Malaysia, Singapore, Indonesia, and Brunei. Between those two parts are shallow waters that lie over the **Sunda Shelf** (Figure 28–1).

Southeast Asia extends for more than 3,000 miles (4,830 kilometers), from Burma in the west to West Irian in the east. The region contains about 1.7 million square miles (4.5 million square kilometers), including 807,000 square miles (2.1 million square kilometers) of mainland and 915,000 square miles (2.4 million square kilometers) of insular territory. Although the region lies near the equator, it stretches to almost 30°N in northern Burma, and a considerable part extends as far as 20°N.

Areal Organization

One of the most conspicuous features of human activity in mainland Southeast Asia is the formation of national corelands around the major river basins: the Irrawaddy in Burma; the Chao Phraya in Thailand; the Mekong in Laos, Kampuchea, and southern Vietnam; and the Red River in northern Vietnam. These great rivers provide soil-enriching floodwaters, water supplies for irrigation systems, and the primary corridors of transportation and access to the broad alluvial floodplains. The large river basins contain the most productive agricultural environments and the densest concentrations of people (see Figure 24–2).

In contrast, **archipelagic** Southeast Asia, the region's chain of islands, shows no single clear pattern of areal organization or formation of national territories. In that area European colonial policies were especially prominent in shaping the patterns of development and political evolution. To a great extent the political boundaries that form the outlines of the modern states are the result of the activities of several Western powers—Spain and the United States in the Philippines; France in Indochina; Great Britain in Myanmar, Malaya, and northern Borneo; and the Netherlands in Indonesia. Malaysia today comprises peninsular Malaya (Western Malaysia) and the former British-administered territories of northern Borneo, Sarawak, and Sabah (Eastern Malaysia) (see Figure 28–1). Indonesia comprises Sumatra, Java, southern Borneo, and essentially all of the islands eastward, to and including the western half of New Guinea.

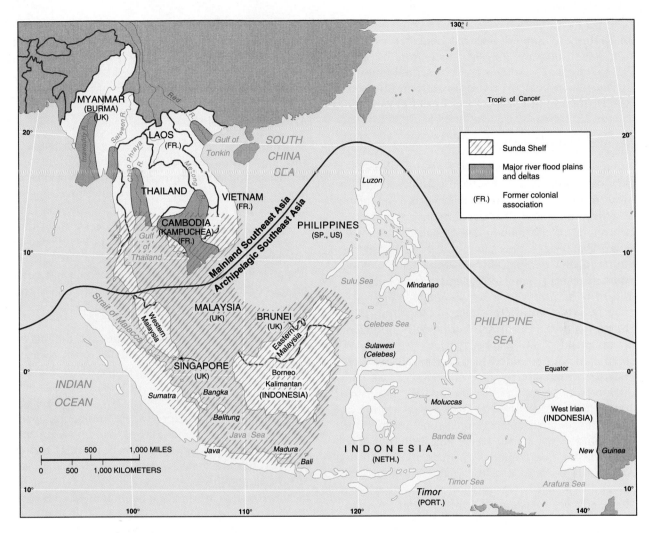

Figure 28-1
Mainland and archipelagic realms of Southeast Asia. Southeast Asia can be divided
between the mainland countries and the islands, with the Malay Peninsula included
with the islands. This map identifies national political units as well as former colonial associations.

Marine Location and Accessibility

Among the most significant features of the geographical setting of Southeast Asia are its maritime
orientation and location. The region is composed of
a series of islands and peninsulas; and except for
Laos, no country is without a shoreline and adequate anchorage for oceangoing ships. In fact, the
Strait of Malacca, which separates Sumatra from the
Malay Peninsula, is one of the world's great shipping corridors, and most maritime traffic between
Europe and eastern Asia passes through it. Thus, ac-

cessibility ranks high among the assets of Southeast
Asia, and the seas that separate the various countries
and islands are much more a link than a barrier.

That maritime accessibility can best be illustrated
through the example of Singapore, the region's most
important entrepôt. British colonials created that
great city in the mid-nineteenth century from a tropical island and mangrove swamp. Singapore's carefully selected location, at the southeastern end of
the Malacca Strait, gives it control over access to and
through that part of the world. Thus, location was
the basis of Singapore's past growth and will be the

basis for its future, which is likely to be prosperous. Like Europe, Southeast Asia has benefited as much from its location and accessibility as from its physical resources. The difference is that utilization of that access developed more recently in Southeast Asia than it did in Europe.

Mainland Southeast Asia

For most of mainland Southeast Asia the dominant physical features are the rugged cordilleras (mountains) that splay out from the Himalayas to the north and arc to the south. Those mountains are underlain by an ancient crystalline mass of stable granite material. That mass and its subterranean extension, the Sunda Shelf, geologically tie together much of Southeast Asia's mainland, islands, and peninsulas as a physical unit.

Although physically related to the taller Himalayas to the north, the north-south mountains of mainland Southeast Asia have been heavily weathered and rounded in the tropical, rainy climate. Consequently, they are much lower than their counterparts in southern Tibet; few rise more than 10,000 feet (3,048 meters) above sea level. The ranges in Southeast Asia parallel one another and separate the major river basins that form the corelands of the five countries of mainland Southeast Asia. From west to east the main ranges are the Arakan Yoma of western Myanmar; the Shan Highlands of eastern Myanmar and western Thailand, which extend the length of the Malay Peninsula; and the Annamite chain of Vietnam. Active seismic forces, such as faulting, are not associated with the mainland highlands and the Sunda Shelf but are common along the archipelagic southern flank of the shelf, as well as from the Philippines to New Guinea.

Although the mainland accounts for less than half of the total land area of Southeast Asia, it probably contains the greatest cultural fragmentation. For example, the groups that inhabit the mainland highlands are composed of diverse tribes with cultural orientations and linguistic systems different from those of their more advanced, less isolated, lowland cousins. Most of those highland people, by virtue of the territory they occupy, have found themselves part of a state with political, social, and religious ideals they may not share. Long ago, the stage was set for conflicts between the politically dominant majorities that inhabit the major river basins and the

groups that occupy interior highland locations; and that problem is serious in almost every country of mainland Southeast Asia. The **Karen** of northern Thailand and Myanmar represent just one of many such minority groups.

Archipelagic Southeast Asia

A string of volcanic islands stretches from Sumatra and Java east to Celebes (Sulawesi) and the Moluccas and north to the Philippines. Not only is that area one of the most geologically active regions on earth, but it also presents a highly diverse land surface that reflects the newer processes of landscape formation. As part of the circum-Pacific belt of volcanism known as the **Pacific Ring of Fire**, the influence of volcanic materials on local soils has been profound enough to affect both fertility levels and cropping patterns, thereby adding to the complexity of the region's physical makeup.

The islands of Southeast Asia and the Malay Peninsula have been called the Malay realm because of the dominance of the Malay people. But the presence of large numbers of Chinese and other significant minorities, such as South Asian Indians, makes that label somewhat inappropriate. Indigenous peoples of ancient Australoid (i.e., native Australian) stock are also present in certain locations; and in New Guinea the native people are predominantly Melanesian. Religion adds some additional diversity; most Malays are Muslim, but the Filipinos are largely Christian. Those religious differences inhibit both understanding and interchange between otherwise closely related peoples.

TROPICAL ENVIRONMENTS AND THEIR UTILIZATION

Despite the diversity of landforms, the shared marine orientation and tropical climate give Southeast Asia a common set of environmental characteristics, which promote similar economic patterns and provide the basis for a unified approach to economic growth and development.

Effects of Equatorial and Tropical Location

High average temperatures and humidity are common within five or six degrees of the equator. With little seasonal variation in rainfall or temperature, Singapore (2°N) is a typical equatorial climatic station. Similar climatic regimes are found throughout much of the Indonesian and Malaysian archipelagoes, though local landforms and prevailing winds may alter the typical pattern somewhat.

Farther away from the equator, seasonal rainfall produces distinct wet and dry seasons. In general, those seasons follow the alternations of the monsoon wind system. During the Northern Hemisphere's summer, essentially from April through September, the monsoon takes the form of a southerly wind; during winter, from October through March, it becomes a northerly wind. Although most rainfall is concentrated in the summer months, surface relief creates some variations. Examples of unusual and unexpected patterns are found in the autumn maximum rainfall along Vietnam's central coast and in the summer dry areas in the rain shadow of Myanmar's southeastern mountains.

A Fragile Environment. The uniformly high temperatures and heavy rainfall of the tropical environment produce a fragile ecological condition that requires careful management to prevent serious and perhaps irreversible damage to the natural resource base. Tropical rain forests, the original vegetative cover of much of Southeast Asia, are characteristic of most of the humid tropics of the world (Figure 28–2).

Because rain forests appear luxuriant and prolific, the uninformed often assume that a rich soil supports the thick forest cover. In reality, however, the soil is not rich; it has been heavily leached of plant nutrients. The lush growth is supported in large part by the sparse accumulation and rapid decomposition of its own litter on the forest floor. Thus, the growing forest, through a rapid recycling of nutrients, produces much of its own food supply. The process involves a great many species of trees, plants, and vines and produces an ecological system that is extremely sensitive to any alteration.

One exception to that pattern is the fertile alluvial soils of the floodplains and deltas, where flooding periodically adds plant nutrients to the soils. Another exception occurs wherever volcanic action has produced soil of great fertility, as it has in parts of Sumatra and Java. Both types of exceptional areas are densely settled and provide the basis of livelihood for most of the people of Southeast Asia.

Of the resources that are associated with the tropical environment, one—timber—is especially prominent. Tropical hardwoods include such valuable species as teak, ebony, and mahogany, which are exported for furniture, veneer, and plywood. Other tropical trees, including the rattan palm, are used for carvings or for household accessories.

Forest Loss and Grassland Invasion

One of the most serious problems in the Southeast Asian rain forests has been the replacement of the forest by tough, fire-resistant, fibrous grasses of the genus *Imperata,* which are known locally by a va-

Figure 28–2
Primary rain forest in Sarawak, Malaysia. These tropical rain forests have been heavily cut in recent years because of demand for their exotic woods. In addition to the loss of tropical forest, severe erosion often accompanies the widespread cutting.

riety of names, such as cogonales, cogon, or just plain elephant grass. Wherever a large area of the forest has been cleared and improperly maintained, or wherever small plots are continuously cultivated, those grasses invade the fields and, once established, are difficult to eradicate. *Imperata* grasses cannot be controlled by indigenous farming methods; instead, their removal requires heavy equipment and machinery, which the people of the region do not have and cannot get. The grasses have already taken over large areas in Thailand, Indochina, and the Philippines.

In Southeast Asia, where the population growth rate is high and agriculture is an important means of livelihood, loss of land to *Imperata* is a serious problem. Interestingly, *Imperata* grasses have not been a significant problem wherever land is farmed strictly in the traditional shifting manner and a stable population is maintained. Because those small forest clearings are cultivated for only a few years and are then abandoned, forests around the edges of the clearings gradually encroach on the cleared areas and shade out the *Imperata*.

Shifting Cultivation

Over large areas of the humid tropics, including Southeast Asia, shifting agriculture is widespread (Figure 28–3). It is a low-yield system, with the use of hand tools still characteristic. The cycle of clearing, burning, cultivating, and fallowing enables the soil to store up plant nutrients between cropping periods and then release them over the short period that the land is cropped. In some cases the forest is allowed to grow back to maturity, but more commonly the slash-and-burn phase is repeated after a dozen years or so. The objective is to use the land only until yields decline and to stop cultivation before any serious soil destruction takes place.

Shifting cultivation is an adaptive, perhaps primitive, farming method that attempts to simulate natural conditions. A great number of different crops, vines, cover crops, tubers, and legumes are intertilled, replicating, in part, the natural characteristics of the tropical ecosystem. Their diversity adds strength to the crop system by providing a more balanced output and a more assured food supply, as well as by protecting the soil. The ability to grow things quickly and get the land surface covered protects the soil from rain and sun and retards the process of leaching.

Those techniques indicate that where populations are sparse and the land is given sufficient time to lie fallow, shifting cultivation can conserve rather than destroy; and the system can support a sparse population indefinitely. However, if the population grows or too-frequent cropping takes place, the end result may be degradation of the tropical rain forest and a rapid decline of soil nutrients. If the overall balance is disturbed, large areas may be lost to elephant grasses, making the land useless both to shifting cultivators and to other sedentary users who might want it for more intensive exploitation.

Paddy-Rice Agriculture

The most common form of agricultural cultivation in Southeast Asia is that of **paddy rice**, which provides the primary food grain for most of the population (see Figure 27–5). Rice has also long been a major export commodity of Myanmar, Thailand, Cambodia, and Vietnam. However, recent conflict and unrest have disrupted agricultural production; populations have grown rapidly and traditional exports have declined.

In Southeast Asia paddy rice is grown in several ways, all of which depend on water to sustain plant growth. The main difference in the methods is the source and control of the water. In some cases, as in the Irrawaddy Delta of Myanmar and parts of the Philippines, rainwater is the source. More common, however, is the use of supplementary water. In the floodplain of the Chao Phraya in Thailand and along the lower Mekong in Cambodia and Vietnam, the irrigation of wet rice depends on the annual flooding of the rivers. In other locations, as in Java, water is provided and controlled through irrigation systems. Irrigation is the most sophisticated approach and gives the highest yield per land unit.

Commercial Agriculture

Estate, or plantation, agriculture in Southeast Asia is commercialized and involves the use of considerable capital. Because of its association with money and international trade, this form of agriculture can be a dynamic force for modernization and economic progress in the region. It is not, however, without its problems.

A number of different crops have been utilized in estate cropping, and some have succeeded better than others. Sugar has dominated in Java and the Philippines, but until recently special marketing arrangements and guaranteed prices for certain quantities resulted in stagnation. In contrast, rubber trees, which are concentrated mainly in Malaysia and Sumatra and are grown on estates and smallholdings, have been very successful and now account for more than half of the estate crop area in Southeast Asia (Figure 28–4). Other important cash crops include coconuts, coffee, and recent, vast plantings of oil palm. All of those crops are remarkably well suited to local environments, though the rubber tree, imported in the late nineteenth century from the New World by way of England, is probably the most adaptable to a great variety of conditions.

Costs of cultivation, harvesting, processing, and transportation to market affect the success of commercial crop ventures. Because rubber can be cultivated and harvested inexpensively and is relatively easy to process and transport, natural rubber producers have managed to remain competitive with synthetic producers. Because other crops, such as coconuts or oil palm, may require more sophisticated forms of processing, often only an estate or firm large enough to produce in great quantity can be financially successful.

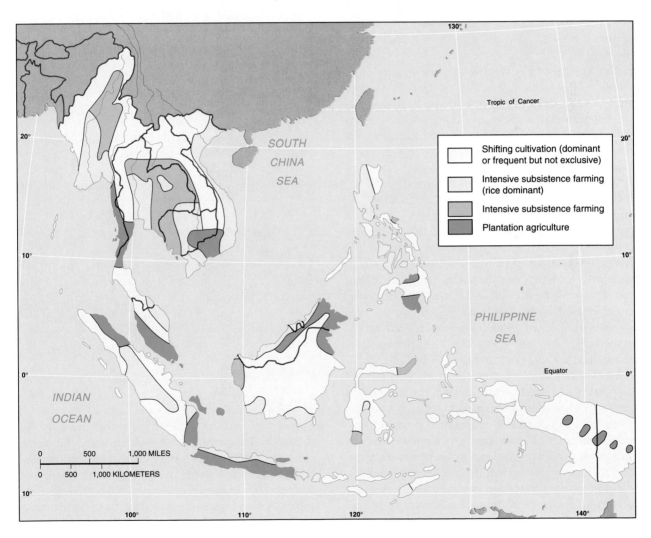

Figure 28–3
Major agricultural systems of Southeast Asia. The three main agricultural systems are identified here by location and approximate areal extent: shifting cultivation, intensive subsistence farming, and plantation agriculture. Although intensive rice cultivation supports a high percentage of the population, shifting cultivation and plantation agriculture occupy the majority of the available land.

Figure 28-4
Firestone rubber fields in Sumatra, Indonesia. The commercial production of rubber on large plantations has been very successful in Southeast Asia, particularly in Malaysia and Indonesia.

The foreign-owned estate, with its greater capitalization, has distinct advantages. Yet, as Donald Fryer has pointed out, despite its many advantages and its potential success as both a money-maker and a development device in Southeast Asia, the foreign-owned estate has a political problem.[1] Many Southeast Asians resent such vestiges of the colonial period, and disapprove of their continuation.

Cash cropping accounts for less than half of the estimated cultivated area in Southeast Asia (20 million acres, or 8 million hectares). But the contributions of those crops are much greater than is evident from the area or the number of people employed in cultivating them. Not only does the estate-crop sector earn capital through the sale of crops, but the operations fundamental to large-estate cropping can also be powerful models of modern techniques in cultivation, processing, transportation, and marketing, thereby promoting economic growth and change.

Alternative points of view regarding estate cropping are not so optimistic. Some authorities assert that estates, especially when they are controlled by foreign investors, impede rather than promote economic growth. Their argument is that a dual economy is created that can lead to friction within the producing area and a maldistribution of wealth. In addition, estate production is characteristically limited to one or two crops that are sold to only a small number of nations.

MINERAL RESOURCES

Southeast Asia possesses some important mineral resources, among which are metallic minerals and fossil fuels—some in large concentrations. Of the various resources tin is probably the best known, with a major tin-producing belt located in granitic ore and placer deposits (i.e., superficial deposits in stream gravels) on the Malay Peninsula and adjacent islands (Figure 28–5). Those deposits are among the most productive and accessible in the world. Other important minerals found in large quantities include iron ore (in the Philippines and on the Malay Peninsula), manganese (in the Philippines and Indonesia), and tungsten (in Myanmar and Thailand). Significant minerals in lesser quantities include gold, bauxite, copper, zinc, and chromium. Tin, which leads all minerals in the value of its production, has played an important role in the development and economic growth of the Malay Peninsula and the Indonesian islands of Bangka and Belitung.

Of greater importance than those minerals, however, are the extensive fossil fuel resources, especially oil. Coal is found in exploitable quantities in several states (namely, Thailand, Vietnam, the Philippines, and Indonesia), but only the deposits of Tonkin (in northern Vietnam) are ample enough for industrial requirements. Petroleum, on the other hand, exists in great quantities in the Indonesian archipelago and along the coasts of Malaysia and Borneo. The existence of that resource is particularly fortunate, for Indonesia is among the poorest states of the region and greatly needs the foreign exchange from the sale of crude oil and natural gas. Currently, Indonesia exports billions of dollars' worth of petroleum products every year, largely to Japan. The sultanate of Brunei, on the coast of north Borneo, is quite small but is also rich in oil. With a modest pop-

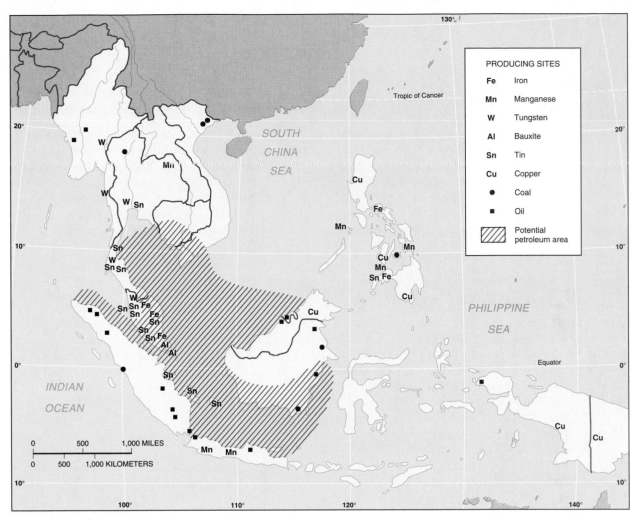

Figure 28-5
Mineral production in Southeast Asia. Although several significant minerals are found in Southeast Asia, tin and oil are clearly the most important. The major producer of tin is Malaysia, followed by Indonesia and Thailand. Indonesia is the region's major producer of oil and ranks as one of the world's major exporters.

ulation and a large resource of oil, Brunei resembles the tiny oil sheikhdoms of the Persian Gulf (see Chapter 23). It stayed out of the federation of Malaysia in order not to have its wealth diluted.

Since 1970 almost every country in Southeast Asia has been involved in the search for oil. On the mainland several large sedimentary basins appear to be potential sources, but the major hope seems to lie offshore. The Sunda Shelf, which underlies the Gulf of Thailand, the Java Sea, and much of the South China Sea, has an average depth of only about 150 feet (46 meters) and thus makes offshore drilling rel-

atively simple. Although questions of political control and ownership of the offshore deposits remain, those reserves may be a means of generating capital and assisting economic development throughout the region.

POPULATION GROWTH: RAPID BUT SLOWING

Compared with other parts of Monsoon Asia, Southeast Asia as a whole is not densely populated (see Table 25–1). The exceptions—parts of the islands of Java, Madura, and Luzon; the lower delta regions of the Irrawaddy, the Chao Phraya, the Mekong, and the Red rivers; and the city-state of Singapore—achieve densities equal to those along the lower Yangtze and Ganges rivers (Figure 28–6). The densely populated areas of Southeast Asia are the core regions of their respective countries.

The total population of Southeast Asia is estimated at slightly more than 460 million people. With a regional annual growth rate of 1.9 percent, many Southeast Asian countries have begun to slow their growth rates and to show evidence of a significant reduction in the demographic surge of the last half century. Thus, Southeast Asia has a great opportu-nity for economic growth and development; its slowing population growth is an important signal that far reaching social change is underway in parallel with economic growth and change.

The Primate City: A Southeast Asian Dilemma

Nowhere in Southeast Asia are the problems of income inequality so conspicuous as they are in the great primate cities of the region. There the largest concentrations of wealth are juxtaposed with the densest clusters of poverty. The most modern commercial, political, administrative, educational, and medical institutions are located near the largest

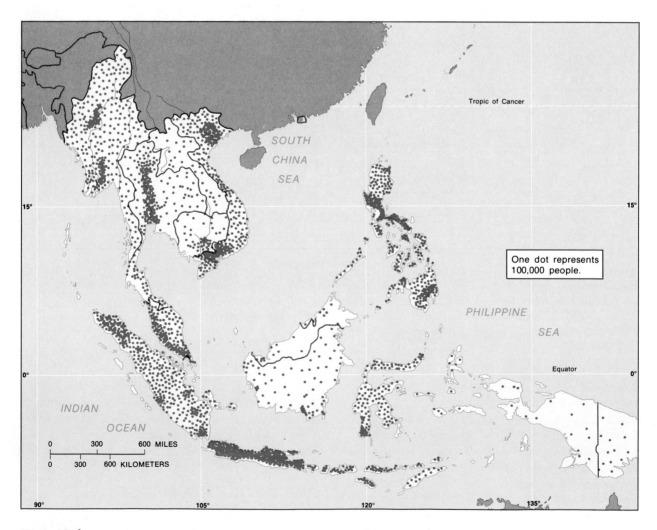

Figure 28–6
Population distribution in Southeast Asia. The large and rapidly growing population is dispersed unevenly throughout the region.

squatter settlements, the most vocal and often radical politicians, and the largest numbers of itinerant peddlers and vendors. Indeed, the term *primate* was coined to describe just that disproportionately large concentration of people, activities, and wealth.

The great capitals of Southeast Asia—Rangoon, Myanmar; Bangkok, Thailand; Jakarta, Indonesia; and Manila, Philippines—are primate cities (Figure 28–7). They are the largest cities of their countries, as well as the greatest ports and commercial trade centers. Each contains the major international airport and accounts for a major share of the nation's industrial output. In each are found the best universities, hospitals, research centers, newspapers, and other cultural institutions. In some of the Southeast Asian countries—such as Thailand and Myanmar—few other cities in the nation have more than 100,000 inhabitants.

Primate Cities and Modernization. Primate cities dominate the political and economic life of their countries; whether the consequences are positive or negative is not at all clear. It has been suggested that the division between city and countryside is also a division between a modernizing economy and society and a traditional economy and folk society. Some authorities argue that the dominance of primate cities is temporary and self-adjusting and that

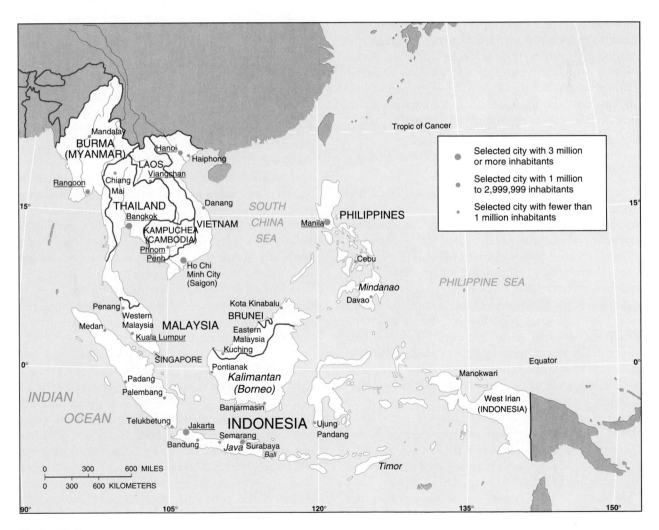

Figure 28–7

Major Southeast Asian cities. Many of Southeast Asia's large cities are primate cities, which grew rapidly during the colonial era. Rangoon, Manila, and Bangkok are good examples.

the situation requires no special corrective strategy. Others claim that primate cities control and exploit the rest of the country and that strategies are needed to interrupt their growth and decentralize wealth and benefits.

One thing is clear: if an economic gulf exists between the primate city and the rest of the nation, the stage is set for the emergence of two distinct and antagonistic political camps—one of which is urban-oriented, modern, and sometimes foreign-associated; the other of which is rural-based, traditional, and native.

REGIONAL DISUNITY

In some ways the contemporary map of Southeast Asia resembles the map of Europe; the region is fragmented into a number of independent states, most of which are relatively small in area, if not in population. In Southeast Asia, though, political instability and conflict have been commonplace and represent a serious challenge to the viability of sovereign states throughout the region.

Insurgency in Southeast Asia

One of the most serious issues facing Southeast Asia is the political legitimacy of various groups and governments. World War II and the end of European colonialism were followed by the rise to power of popular native governments, which have represented several different political perspectives. Of the political movements operating in Southeast Asia, the Communist party was one of the best organized. Its emphasis on sound and effective organization and discipline among party members was a clear strength. However, most of the colonial powers did not want to see communist governments in control and worked vigorously to install political regimes acceptable to the West as they prepared to grant independence to their colonies. After independence the challenge of well-organized insurgency movements, inspired and supported by Marxists, became a serious threat to the political survival of several states and to the stability of the entire region.

Virtually every country in Southeast Asia has been affected by insurgent political-military efforts. Malaysia had a serious insurgency problem in the 1950s, but sharp military and political reactions, coupled with improved social conditions and popular support of the government, appear to have curbed the movement. In Indonesia the Communist party was legalized and was the third largest in the world in the early 1960s. After a bloody overthrow of the government, however, the party was outlawed and remains illegal today.

In the late 1940s the Philippines had a violent communist insurgency, the Huk movement, which was crushed, but it has been revived from time to time. In addition, a Muslim-inspired separatist movement has plagued the southern Philippine island of Mindanao. Civil rights were suspended by then-President Ferdinand Marcos in 1971; but chronic unemployment, poor distribution of income, rapid population growth, stagnant economic growth, and political disenfranchisement for many continued, leading to the ouster of Marcos in 1986. Despite substantial popular support for the six-year term of President Corazon Aquino, followed in 1992 by the election of new President Fidel Ramos, the problems of poverty and insurgency continue.

Indochina—the peninsula mainland of Southeast Asia—has experienced more military trauma over the issue of communist governments than any other part of the larger region (Figure 28–8). After full-scale wars with the Vietnamese insurgents that involved both France and the United States, the enlarged Vietnamese state sought to establish its dominance over both Laos and Cambodia (Kampuchea) and thus to control the entire Indochinese peninsula. Relations between Laos and Vietnam remain close. But Vietnam and warring Cambodian factions fought for a dozen years, finally agreeing to a U.N.-sponsored peace agreement. Free elections followed in Cambodia. Given the continuing conflict among the various Cambodian factions, however, true peace remains an elusive goal.

Until political stability is attained, little real opportunity for economic growth and progress is likely in Southeast Asia. Only in those states that have achieved at least a credible level of peace and stability and an outward-looking government (e.g., Malaysia, Singapore, Thailand, and Indonesia) has economic progress been significant. But Indonesia still depends heavily on oil exports; it needs to continue to diversify its agricultural and manufacturing sectors if the country is to achieve real economic growth. The Philippines are now making progress in efforts to attract foreign and especially Asian investment, but much uncertainty remains on the ability of the Philippines to accelerate real economic growth.

Figure 28-8
A pro-democracy rally in Rangoon, Burma, during the late 1980s. Repressive regimes, political instability, and insurgency, frequently accompanied by warfare, have been common throughout Southeast Asia since World War II.

Efforts to Forge Regional Unity

The problems created by insurgent movements, revolutions, and military actions in Southeast Asia have been counterbalanced by various efforts to forge regional unity. The Southeast Asia Treaty Organization (SEATO), formed in 1954, was primarily a political-military arrangement aimed at containing Asian communism. However, the Vietnam War rendered SEATO ineffective and resulted in its dissolution.

Other important agencies that are working to support regional economic growth include the Asian Development Bank, headquartered in Manila, and the **Association of Southeast Asian Nations (ASEAN)** (see boxed feature ASEAN: The Association of Southeast Asian Nations). Similar in concept and operation to the World Bank and to other regional financial institutions that promote development, the Asian Development Bank is financed through the deposits of wealthy states and lends money for specific projects in the participating states, primarily in Monsoon Asia. Those projects range from irrigation and agricultural-growth schemes to major transportation and industrial efforts.

Cultural Pluralism

Society and politics are closely related in Southeast Asia; many of the region's political problems stem from the pressures of multiethnic societies. Cultural pluralism is evident in the close association between specific occupations and particular ethnic groups. As a result, certain ethnic groups are heavily concentrated in urban locations, whereas others are centered in rural areas or around mining sites. Pluralism and separatism, rather than integration, have characterized the economies, societies, and politics of most states in this region.

Large Chinese and Indian minorities are found in most of Southeast Asia, though their numbers vary considerably from country to country (Figure 28–9). In some cases—for example, Malaysia—the Chinese comprise about 35 percent of the population; Indians, another 10 percent. In the Philippines and Indonesia, however, the Chinese represent only 2 to 3 percent of the total population, and the number of Indians is too small to be of any consequence.

ASEAN: THE ASSOCIATION OF SOUTHEAST ASIAN NATIONS

The Association of Southeast Asian Nations (ASEAN), formed in 1967, is a regional organization of six Southeast Asian states. Thailand, Malaysia, Singapore, Indonesia, and the Philippines were the original members; Brunei joined in 1984. ASEAN is headquartered in Jakarta, Indonesia (see Figure 28–7), and is led by a secretary-general, a post that rotates among the six member states every 2 years. According to the *Statesman's Yearbook, 1993–94,* the goals of ASEAN are "to accelerate economic growth, social progress, and cultural development, to promote active

collaboration and mutual assistance in matters of common interest, to ensure the stability of the Southeast Asian region and to maintain close cooperation with existing international and regional organizations with similar aims."*

The main projects and accomplishments of ASEAN to date have focused on the promotion of economic cooperation and better trade relations and exchanges among its members. Cooperation and sharing in the development of transportation, communications, tourism, science, and education have also been achieved. ASEAN has been effective in advancing common goals and programs for development and growth in the noncommunist and nonsocialist states of Southeast Asia. Together the six member countries have a combined population of more than 300 million and considerable production of food, fiber, natural resources, and industrial goods.

Speaking with a common voice in support of shared common interests and objectives has permitted the members to be more effective in promoting their views throughout their region and the world. The organization has also served as a powerful counterweight to the military force of Vietnam in Southeast Asia and to the growing political and economic power of China and Japan within the Monsoon Asian realm.

*Brian Hunter, ed., *Statesman's Yearbook, 1993–94,* 130th ed. (New York: St. Martin's Press, 1993).

Some Chinese migrants have been integrated and absorbed into the native populations, having been urged or forced to assume local identities, use the local language, and take local names. Integration has been reasonably successful in Thailand, where the Chinese have been present in large numbers for a long time. Much intermarriage has taken place, resulting in cultural assimilation; yet a range of problems inherent in a multiethnic society remains, and no approach has proved entirely satisfactory in coping with them. Racial and ethnic divisions persist and occasionally result in violent political outbursts and activities.

The Chinese in Southeast Asia. The Chinese have been involved in Southeast Asia for many centuries. The history of Vietnam, for example, is in part a history of Chinese attempts to extend their influence southward. In the nineteenth century, extensive Chinese migration to the region took place, partly associated with British colonialism. The British were interested in developing an obedient and industrious labor force to exploit tin deposits in the Malay

Peninsula and to assist in agricultural development programs in northern Borneo. Because the British held the native Malays in low regard, they sought workers from the outside, encouraging the immigration of Chinese from southern China and Tamils from southern India.

Over the years, large numbers of Chinese migrated to Malaysia and other parts of Southeast Asia. Ties between China and those migrants were fundamentally social and cultural in the beginning but were rapidly extended to trade, production, and shipping. The Chinese in Malaysia quickly acquired land and began to produce coconuts, sugar, spices, rubber, and other cash crops. They also established small tin mines with modest capital requirements. Their social system provided the linkages to assure a constant supply of inexpensive labor and ready access to markets, both local and international.

Over time, the Chinese carved out a large niche in the economy, not just of Malaysia but of every state in Southeast Asia. They were seldom involved in primary production; instead, they concentrated

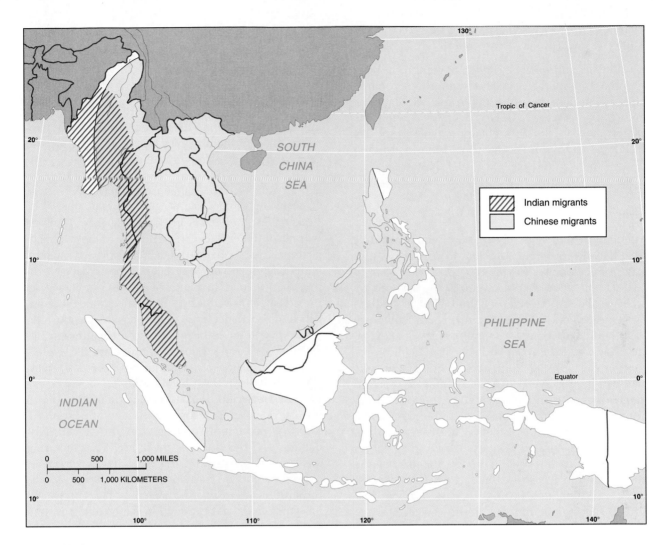

Figure 28–9
Nonnative ethnic groups of Southeast Asia. Two main nonnative ethnic groups are
found in Southeast Asia—the Indians and the Chinese—and their areas of principal
concentration are shown.

in cities and specialized in trade, shipping, and finance. In some cases they gained control of the
rice-milling industry, a key element in most of the
agricultural economies of Southeast Asia. In other
cases they dominated virtually all forms of local
commerce. Because the European colonials were
unwilling to perform those business functions and
the native population had no acquaintance with
the particular skills of commercial entrepreneur-
ship, the Chinese filled a vacuum and, in the
process, established themselves in a position of
privilege and wealth in the various Southeast Asian
societies.

The Chinese in this region gradually expanded
their economic role until their position was too
powerful to be controlled by local non-Chinese
forces. And the more concentrated the Chinese
were, the more vigorously they resisted acculturation and integration. As a result, the customs and traditions of old China have been better preserved in
some Southeast Asian communities than in China itself. But that cultural distinctiveness, coupled with a
privileged economic position, has led to enormous
resentment; their clannishness has made them an
easy and convenient target for the frustration and
anger of impoverished masses of Southeast Asians.

STAGNATION, TRANSFORMATION, AND GROWTH

A variety of approaches to development have been attempted in Southeast Asia, ranging from communism to socialism to free enterprise. No one approach has succeeded. However, evaluating the achievements of the different approaches in specific countries may permit some conclusions as to their relative merit in the context of the Southeast Asian region.

Myanmar (Burma)

Although Myanmar is a large state with a resource base that is more than sufficient to support its present population, its growth record has been poor. In fact, its per capita output of goods and services actually declined between 1939 and 1969, a situation that speaks poorly of Myanmar's particular approach to development—a kind of authoritarian isolationism and locally derived socialism.

After years of stagnation and declining economic well-being, however, Myanmar's military government softened its policies slightly in 1973. In addition to declaring a new constitution, the government relaxed its support of isolation and began to encourage more foreign contacts. Since then, things have begun to improve. Through the rest of the 1970s and into the early 1980s, the GNP increased substantially, though declines occurred in the mid-1980s. The agricultural sector showed an average annual increase in production of 5.4 percent between 1980 and 1985, reflecting increased use of Green Revolution seeds, fertilizers, and insecticides. And the growth in industrial production during that same period averaged 7.0 percent annually. Free-market activities were allowed in late 1988, and overall economic growth has picked up a bit from the poor years of 1986 and 1987; nevertheless, agricultural productivity has declined and the overall economic outlook is poor.

By the 1980s years of authoritarian military rule had led to a growing gap between the small ruling elite, who controlled the government and military, and the bulk of the country's people, most of whom are farmers and workers. In the summer of 1988 a popular revolution, sparked by student dislike of that authoritarian rule, broke out and led to the overthrow of the government. But the law-and-order military rulers who seized power that year did not change the basic power structure of the coun-

try, despite changing the country's name from Burma to Myanmar. The name change was apparently an effort to appeal to all ethnic groups in the country, not just the dominant ethnic Burmese. Although it is difficult to know exactly who is in charge, the authoritarian military group that has controlled the country for more than thirty years appears to be continuing its rule, and no Burmese democracy seems likely in the near future.

Thailand

Unlike the other states in Southeast Asia, Thailand was never under direct colonial rule. In the twentieth century it has generally been ruled by a monarchy with declining power, but recently the actual government has been in the hands of a series of military figures. That situation has resulted in centralized political control of the country, which has frequently been somewhat unstable because of conflicts among different cliques and groups seeking power.

With its extensive land and water resources, Thailand is potentially wealthy. Its economy, however, has reflected fluctuations in commodity prices for its rice, estate crops, and natural resources. About 57 percent of Thailand's labor force is in agriculture, and this share is declining. Manufacturing has grown rapidly, and the export of a variety of consumer goods (garments, shoes, canned goods, furniture, and frozen chickens) has propelled growth. Oil and gas production is increasing in spite of the decline in world petroleum prices.

Despite the recent recession and the lower rate of return for resources and farm commodities, Thailand's generally open-market economic system has done well when compared with that of other Third World and Southeast Asian countries. Per capita income in 1991 stood at $1,580, and the average annual increase in GNP was 10.4 percent between 1987 and 1991. Thailand's healthy agricultural production and extensive resource and land base relative to its population indicate a good long-term prospect for continued economic growth.

Cambodia (Kampuchea)

Cambodia, which was known for a time as Kampuchea, has had an extremely difficult recent past. The country—all that remains of the powerful and extensive Khmer kingdom, which flourished from the tenth to the fourteenth century—has long suffered from attacks by neighboring Thailand and Vietnam. Ruled by the French from 1863 until World War II, Cambodia has been unstable ever since and has experienced much foreign interference. The wars in Vietnam created especially serious problems.

In 1976, a year after the U.S. withdrawal from the area, Cambodian leader Pol Pot established a government led by the communist **Khmer Rouge**. Great chaos and isolation followed in Cambodia, now called Kampuchea. The cities were emptied of their people, social relations changed abruptly, religion was forbidden, and education was suspended. In essence, a purging of almost all educated and upper-class citizens took place, and more than 1 million people died of starvation, exhaustion, disease, or punishment. Some who fled the country wound up in Thailand as refugees.

Tension with Vietnam then led to a Vietnamese invasion in 1978, and in 1979 the Vietnamese created a puppet Kampuchean democratic government and installed Heng Samrin as its head. Civil war then raged among the Khmer Rouge, various nationalist factions, and Vietnamese-backed government forces. The government controlled most of the country's territory because of the presence of more than 100,000 Vietnamese army troops; but the Khmer Rouge and other allied rebel groups, with help from China and Thailand, maintained an active guerrilla presence in western rural areas.

In 1988 the Vietnamese began to withdraw their main army units. The United Nations entered the country in a peace keeping role with the goal of guaranteeing free elections, which were finally held in 1993. Kampuchea once again became Cambodia, with an elected government. From years of war and instability, the Cambodian economy has stagnated. UN relief agencies and various nations have stepped in to provide aid in order to stabilize the economy. Certain countries have also pledged more than $1 billion for reconstruction now that a political solution seems to have been achieved.

Vietnam

The 1954 Geneva accords divided Indochina into separate national entities and also created a North and a South Vietnam. After 1954, however, the bitterness among the Vietnamese people over which group would guide the political destiny of the country sharpened; the Vietnam War of the 1960s and 1970s was a painful expression of that bitterness. The 1973 Paris Peace Agreement provided for an end to direct U.S. participation in the fighting in Vietnam, but fighting erupted again a year later. Many observers were astonished to see how quickly South Vietnam collapsed, and in 1975 the country was united under the control of a communist government.

The dispute between the two Vietnams stemmed, in part, from the desire of the northern half to incorporate the southern half and forge one unified Vietnam. The two halves complement each other economically: the north is more industrial but is a food-deficient region, whereas the south has traditionally been a rice-surplus area. The argument for separating the two halves was the existence of the Annamite Mountains, Indochina's most prominent physical feature, which touch the sea midway down the coast very near the former demilitarized zone. Historically, the two parts have rarely been politically integrated.

The heartland of northern Vietnam is focused on the Red River drainage basin and the Tonkin Delta. In many ways that region, with its dense population and intensive double-cropped rice complex, resembles Chinese occupancy patterns farther north. However, the northern Vietnamese have not been able to replicate the agricultural achievements and yields of the Chinese, and northern Vietnam has long suffered from food shortages. In 1981 a 4-million-ton deficit in rice was reported.

To some extent those shortages have been offset by the presence of metallic minerals and coal, which prompted the former French colonial regime to initiate a number of industrial development projects. The communist government in North Vietnam later expanded those earlier industries, but the war, especially the heavy bombing, left much of the industrial complex in ruins. Vietnam thereafter embarked on a crash program to rebuild it, depending heavily on the Soviets for direct assistance.

Early in 1979 a new conflict erupted in Indochina: China staged a limited, three-week invasion of Vietnam's northern border areas. China justified that action on the basis of Vietnam's mistreatment of Chinese persons living in Vietnam, many of whom had been driven out of that country. Another factor was Vietnam's earlier invasion of Kampuchea (Cambodia), an ally of China. Negotiations followed, but much bitterness remains between China and Vietnam, and the border is still tense.

The traditional rice surpluses of southern Vietnam disappeared during the war of the 1960s. The problem of peasant insurgency and rural insecurity became so great that much productive land was simply abandoned or was little cultivated. In addition, the war had many other consequences for southern Vietnam, some of which accelerated the pace of economic growth. For example, U.S. aid provided training programs for Vietnamese civilians, made huge investments in capital improvements (e.g., roads, harbors, cities, power grids, and irrigation systems), and drew large numbers of people into urban centers to contribute to the industrial and commercial sectors of the economy. But the abrupt withdrawal of U.S. soldiers and civilians in 1971 and 1972 and the cutbacks in U.S. military and economic aid created problems of unemployment, inflation, and economic instability. When coupled with insecurity in rural areas, those problems created an atmosphere of uncertainty about the future of South Vietnam, which may have played a part in the quick demise of the government in early 1975.

Southern Vietnam has great potential for economic growth. Most promising is its enormous potential for increased agricultural production. Restoring abandoned land to cultivation and opening new land in the Mekong Delta marshlands have stimulated greater output. Equally promising are improved irrigation, new seed strains, and more chemical fertilizer and insecticides on lands already cropped. Grain production reached record levels in 1992, and more than 1 million tons of rice was exported. For ten years, however, the Vietnamese government had done a poor job of organizing the economy for production. Since 1987 there has been improvement, as the government has liberalized its economic policies in agriculture and commerce and has allowed some private production and marketing to take place. In addition, new regulations have permitted joint ventures with Western firms. Those new market-oriented initiations have stimulated economic growth and have increased contacts and trade with foreign countries.

Vietnam in 1993 was at a watershed. Almost twenty years after the formal end of the Vietnam War, the United States and Vietnam reached agreement to end the political separation between the two countries. While a number of other Asian countries, such as Japan and Singapore, have already begun to trade with and invest in Vietnam, the United States had continued a trade embargo of Vietnam since 1975. Ending this embargo and extending normal diplomatic relations with its former chief antagonist was a crucial step forward, one that no doubt will have positive economic consequences for Vietnam.

Malaysia and Singapore

The two richest countries in Southeast Asia may well be the progressive neighbors Malaysia and Singapore. The two were politically integrated when they gained their independence in 1963, but the Malay-Chinese dichotomy was severe enough to disrupt the political alliance. Now, despite their political separation, both the federation of Malaysia and the city-state of Singapore continue to thrive economically and stand as solid examples of prosperity in Southeast Asia. Despite the partially authoritarian nature of politics in the two countries, both have vigorous and growing private sectors, which, when coupled with an outward-looking attitude, may account for the steady economic growth.

Malaysia's growth rate has been more modest than Singapore's, but the federation has progressed steadily in recent years. Its 1991 per capita income was estimated at $2,500, and average annual economic growth rates of 8.3 percent were recorded between 1987 and 1991. Malaysia has been especially fortunate in the exploitation of its natural and agricultural resources; tin, rubber, timber, coconuts, palm oil, and—more recently—crude oil are its main products. But whether the level of demand and the world prices for those commodities will remain high is difficult to predict.

Malaysia. One of the most serious problems in Malaysia's history is the difficulty of reconciling the position of the main ethnic groups—the Malays (Bumiputras) and the Chinese, who have been immigrating to Malaysia over the last century. The Chinese have accumulated considerable wealth and hold great economic power, whereas the Malays dominate the politics and control the country's civil administration, police, and military. To equalize the economic position of the Malays, a New Economic Policy (NEP) was created in 1970. This policy, now in place for more than twenty years, seeks to guarantee business participation and ownership for Malays as well as labor participation in all firms. Beyond that, Malays get easier school and university admission, and a broader goal of creating a Malay culture and society is implicit in the policy.

Although poverty has been reduced, especially among Malays, during the two decades of implementation, the policy is frankly discriminatory against the Chinese. The overall impact may have been to retard growth and progress in Malaysia, as Chinese and other foreign investors seek alternative locations. Whatever the case, the NEP poses a major challenge to the goal of a prosperous and happy multiethnic, pluralistic modern Malaysia (Figure 28–10).

Singapore. Singapore, with a 1991 per capita GNP of roughly almost $13,000, stands next to Japan as the most prosperous place in Monsoon Asia. Despite the physical constraints and problems of its small area, Singapore has made good use of its location and traditional economic functions of trade, shipping, and service (Figure 28–11). Building on that base, it has recently turned to sophisticated manufacturing, in which the skills and industry of its talented and disciplined labor force are employed. Cameras, watches, and electronic components are some of its products. Oil refining, which depends on crude oil from Indonesia and the Persian Gulf, is also a major industry for Singapore.

Singapore is successful in many ways. The island republic demonstrates, as does Japan, that even under conditions of limited natural resources, Asians can achieve rapid economic growth and high standards of living—and they can do it in a relatively short time. However, economic growth and successful industrialization also bring certain problems; for as standards of living rise, so, too, do the costs of labor. As a result, a continuing process of educational and technological upgrading is necessary to maintain competitiveness if the standard of living and per capita income are to continue to rise.

Indonesia

After gaining independence from the Netherlands in 1949, Indonesia emerged as an important voice among the nonaligned states of the world. Led by the charismatic but troubled Sukarno, the island republic attempted to portray itself during the 1950s and early 1960s as a leader among those states following a new and independent socialism. But the political rhetoric and ambitions of Indonesia's leaders far outdistanced the nation's economic performance. Their claim that Indonesia was the best model for other less developed areas could not be supported, and the situation led to severe social and political stress, which finally resulted in a 1965 uprising and the overthrow of Sukarno.

Since 1966 the Indonesian military regime has set its sights on repairing the economic neglect and damage of the Sukarno days. One aspect of the new policy has been to seek assistance from Japan, the

Figure 28-10
A night view of the Sultan Abdul Samad (High Court) Building in Kuala Lumpur, Malaysia's capital city. The architecture shows the influence of Islamic culture, as introduced by Arab traders centuries ago.

United States, the World Bank, and other outside sources. The performance of the military government has not been dramatic, nor has the economic growth rate been spectacular; but despite the vagaries of world oil prices on which Indonesia became dependent during the 1970s and early 1980s, overall economic growth has been generally encouraging. And Indonesia has worked to diversify its exports during the last decade.

The completion of the nation's first five-year development plan in 1974 was one such achievement, and annual economic growth averaged about 7 percent. The goals of the second five-year plan were more ambitious, focusing on faster rates of growth in the agricultural sector. The third five-year plan (1979–1984) looked for growth in earnings from petroleum sales to finance development. The fourth five-year plan was plagued by a decline in petroleum prices. As a result, the income side of Indonesia's national budget, which depended very heavily on the export of crude oil, was undercut; and the government has had to revise its spending goals and rethink its approach to development along more conservative lines. Real economic growth slowed, but began to recover in the early 1990s with diversification of the mix of exports and a surge of export sales of goods with a high labor content, such as footware, textiles, and garments.

Even though Indonesia is still poor, it illustrates that economic conditions can change and improve. Indonesia is justified in pointing with pride to the recent growth of its GNP as it diversifies and strengthens its economy.

The Philippines

The most dramatic development in the Philippines in many years was the ouster of former President Ferdinand Marcos in 1986 and his replacement by the popularly supported Aquino government. That change and the succeeding election of Fidel Ramos in 1992 has strengthened the forces of democracy and increased the political and social stability of the

Figure 28-11
Singapore, a prosperous city-state at the southern tip of the Malay Peninsula.
Singapore's prosperity is based on its role as a major Asian trade center. In recent years it has also added manufacturing to its economic base.

Philippines. Although the Aquino government had serious problems, it nevertheless was strongly committed to broadening the economic base in the Philippines and ensuring that the economic wealth of the country is shared more equitably among the Filipino people. Real economic growth since 1987 has been around 3.8 percent annually, and conditions are continuing to improve, though the early 1990s were years of slow growth. Overall, though, the country remains poor; population growth is rapid, thereby placing more strain on available resources and the economy, and the political situation remains volatile. Serious political threats to democracy remain on both the left (a continuing but declining communist insurrection) and the right (residual Marcos supporters and extreme nationalists within the military). Thus, despite the promise and idealism of the popularly elected governments since 1986, the prospects for the Philippines have not improved much, given the economic and political realities.

SUMMARY
Implications for Growth

No single path to rapid economic growth and social change exists in Southeast Asia, though some lessons can be learned from past experiences. Those states that have become preoccupied with their own problems or ambitions and have isolated themselves from a community of states have performed poorly. Only after they have reshaped their policies has their performance improved. Indonesia is a good example.

The potential for growth and progress in Southeast Asia is enormous. Moderate policies that emphasize growth and take advantage of international assistance appear to be the most successful. For example, the shift in Indonesian policies and political and economic behavior after Sukarno's ouster suggests the desirability of a moderate policy. And that country's turnabout is an excellent indication of the effect that political shifts can have on an economy. The Indonesian experience also illustrates how quickly things can change for the better, offering a beacon of hope to many other less developed, impoverished areas of the world.

KEY TERMS

archipelagic

Association of Southeast Asian Nations (ASEAN)

Imperata

Indochina

Karen

Khmer Rouge

Pacific Ring of Fire

paddy rice

Sunda Shelf

NOTES

1. Donald Fryer, *Emerging Southeast Asia: A Study in Growth and Stagnation,* 2d ed. (New York: Wiley, 1979), 66–78.

FURTHER READINGS
Part Nine

Asia Yearbook. Hong Kong: Far Eastern Economic Review, 1993 and annually. Up-to-date coverage of political, economic, and social patterns in all countries of the region.

Bouton, Marshall M., and **Philip Oldenburg.** *India Briefing, 1990.* Boulder, CO: Westview Press, 1990 and annually. Like *China Briefing,* a good collection of timely essays on the changing economy and politics of contemporary India.

Dernberger, Robert, K. J. Dwoskin, S. M. Goldstein, Rhoads Murphey, and M. K. Whyte, eds. *The Chinese: Adapting the Past, Building the Future.* Ann Arbor, MI: Center for Chinese Studies, University of Michigan, 1986. A useful collection of articles on all aspects of China.

Dutt, Ashok, and **Margaret Geib.** *Atlas of South Asia.* Boulder CO: Westview Press, 1987. A good cartographic and explanatory survey of the geography of South Asia.

Fisher, Charles A. *Southeast Asia: A Social, Economic and Political Geography.* 2d ed. London: Metheun, 1966. Still the major standard geography text on Southeast Asia, despite its age.

Fryer, Donald W. *Emerging South-East Asia: A Study in Growth and Stagnation.* 2d ed. New York: Wiley, 1979. Oriented toward economic topics and focused on the contrast between stagnant and progressive economic systems in the region.

Ginsburg, Norton, Bruce Koppel, and T. G. McGee, eds. *The Extended Metropolis: Settlement Transition in Asia.* Honolulu, HI: University of Hawaii Press, 1991. A collection of papers that introduces a new paradigm and model for metropolitan growth and development in Monsoon Asia.

Joseph, W. A., ed. *China Briefing, 1991.* Boulder, CO: Westview Press, 1991 and annually. A good collection of essays by specialists on China's culture, politics, economics, and military and foreign affairs.

MacDonald, Donald S. *The Koreans, Contemporary Politics and Society.* rev. ed. Boulder, CO: Westview Press, 1990. A well-conceived survey of the society and politics of the Korean peninsula.

Noble, Allen, and **Ashok Dutt, eds.** *India: Cultural Patterns and Processes.* Boulder, CO: Westview Press, 1982. A series of essays focusing on the diversity and unity of India's culture, with emphasis on the spatial distribution of cultural forms.

Pannell, Clifton W., ed. *East Asia: Geographical and Historical Approaches to Foreign Area Studies.* Dubuque, IA: Kendall-Hunt, 1983. Analysis by geographers and historians of cultural differences and development in East Asia.

Pannell, Clifton W., and **Laurence J. C. Ma.** *China: The Geography of Development and Modernization.* New York: Halsted Press, 1983. A geography of China's development efforts, placed in the context of its large area, population, and resource base.

Rigg, Jonathan. *Southeast Asia: A Region in Transition.* London: Unwin Hyman, 1991. An up-to-date thematic human geography that focuses on the six ASEAN countries and their recent changes and developments.

Schwartzberg, Joseph E. *A Historical Atlas of South Asia.* Chicago: University of Chicago Press, 1978. A definitive historical atlas of India; a major contribution to geographical knowledge of South Asia.

Spate, Oscar H. K., and **A. T. A. Learmonth.** *India and Pakistan: A General and Regional Geography.* 3d ed. London: Methuen, 1967. The closest thing to a standard geography of the subcontinent.

Spencer, Joseph, and **William Thomas.** *Asia, East by South: A Cultural Geography.* 2d ed. New York: John Wiley & Sons, 1971. A major work on Monsoon Asia with a cultural approach.

Ulack, Richard, and **Gyula Pauer.** *Atlas of Southeast Asia.* New York: Macmillan, 1989. An excellent general atlas of Southeast Asia with good textual descriptions of all the countries of the realm.

U.S. Congress. Joint Economic Committee. *China's Economy Looks Toward the Year 2000.* Vols. 1 and 2. Washington, DC: Government Printing Office, 1986. An excellent collection of recent papers that covers economic policy, manufacturing and extractive industries, population and labor utilization, agriculture, and foreign economic relations.

APPENDIX A

Phillip C. Muehrcke

Map Scale and Projections

Unaided, our human senses provide a limited view of our surroundings. To overcome those limitations, humankind has developed powerful vehicles of thought and communication, such as language, mathematics, and graphics. Each of those tools is based on elaborate rules, each has an information bias, and each may distort its message, often in subtle ways. Consequently, to use those aids effectively, we must understand their rules, biases, and distortions. The same is true for the special form of graphics we call maps: we must master the logic behind the mapping process before we can use maps effectively.

A fundamental issue in cartography, the science and art of making maps, is the vast difference between the size and geometry of what is being mapped—the real world, we will call it—and that of the map itself. Scale and projection are the basic cartographic concepts that help us understand that difference and its effects.

MAP SCALE

Our senses are dwarfed by the immensity of our planet; we can sense directly only our local surroundings. Thus, we cannot possibly look at our whole state or country at one time, even though we may be able to see the entire street where we live. Cartography helps us expand what we can see at one time by letting us view the scene from some distant vantage point. The greater the imaginary distance between that position and the object of our observation, the larger the area the map can cover but the smaller the features will appear on the map. That reduction is defined by the *map scale,* the ratio of the distance on the map to the distance on the earth. Map users need to know about map scale for two reasons: (1) so that they can convert measurements on a map into meaningful real-world measures and (2) so that they can know how abstract the cartographic representation is.

Real-World Measures

A map can provide a useful substitute for the real world for many analytical purposes. With the scale of a map, for instance, we can compute the actual size of its features (length, area, and volume). Such calculations are helped by three expressions of a map scale: a word statement, a graphic scale, and a representative fraction.

A *word statement* of a map scale compares X units on the map to Y units on the earth, often abbreviated "X unit to Y units." For example, the expression "1 inch to 10 miles" means that 1 inch on the map represents 10 miles on the earth (Figure A–1). Because the map is always smaller than the area that has been mapped, the ground unit is always the larger number. Both units are expressed in meaningful terms, such as inches or centimeters and miles or kilometers. Word statements are not intended for precise calculations but give the map user a rough idea of size and distance.

A *graphic scale,* such as a bar graph, is concrete and therefore overcomes the need to visualize inches and miles that is associated with a word statement of scale (see Figure A–1). A graphic scale permits direct visual comparison of feature sizes and the distances between features. No ruler is required; any measuring aid will do. It needs only to be compared with the scaled bar; if the length of 1 toothpick is equal to 2 miles on the ground and the map distance equals the length of 4 toothpicks, then the ground distance is 4 times 2, or 8 miles. Graphic scales are especially convenient in this age of copying machines, when we are more likely to be working with a copy than with the original map. If a map is reduced or enlarged as it is copied, the graphic scale will change in proportion to the change in the size of the map and thus will remain accurate.

The third form of a map scale is the *representative fraction* (RF). An RF defines the ratio between the distance on the map and the distance on the earth in fractional terms, such as $1/_{633,600}$ (also written $1/_{633,600}$ or 1 : 633,600). The numerator of the fraction always refers to the distance on the map, and the denominator always refers to the distance on the earth. No units of measurement are given, but both numbers must be expressed in the same units. Because map distances are extremely small relative to the size of the earth, it makes sense to use small units, such as inches or centimeters. Thus, the RF 1 : 633,600 might be read as "1 inch on the map to 633,600 inches on the earth."

Herein lies a problem with the RF. Meaningful map-distance units imply a denominator so large that it is impossible to visualize. Thus, in practice, reading the map scale involves an additional step of converting the denominator to a meaningful ground measure, such as miles or kilometers. The unwieldy 633,600 becomes the more manageable 10 miles when divided by the number of inches in a mile (63,360).

On the plus side, the RF is good for calculations. In particular, the ground distance between points can be easily determined from a map with an RF. One simply multiplies the distance between the points on the map by the denominator of the RF. Thus, a distance of 5 inches on a map with an RF of 1/126,720 would signify a ground distance of

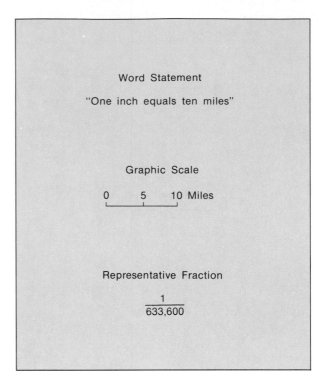

Figure A-1
Common expressions of map scale.

5 × 126,720, which equals 633,600. Because all units are inches and there are 63,360 inches in a mile, the ground distance is 633,600 ÷ 63,360, or 10 miles. Computation of area is equally straightforward with an RF. Computer manipulation and analysis of maps is based on the RF form of map scale.

Guides to Generalization

Scales also help map users visualize the nature of the symbolic relation between the map and the real world. It is convenient here to think of maps as falling into three broad scale categories (Figure A–2). (Do not be confused by the use of the words *large* and *small* in this context; just remember that the larger the denominator, the smaller the scale ratio and the larger the area that is shown on the map.) Scale ratios greater than 1 : 100,000, such as the 1 : 24,000 scale of U.S. Geological Survey topographic quadrangles, are large-scale maps. Although those maps can cover only a local area, they can be drawn to rather rigid standards of accuracy. Thus, they are useful for a wide range of applications that require detailed and accurate maps, including zoning, navigation, and construction.

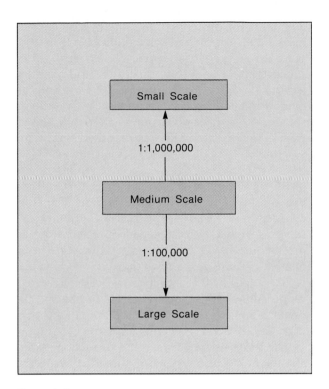

Figure A-2
The scale gradient can be divided into three broad categories.

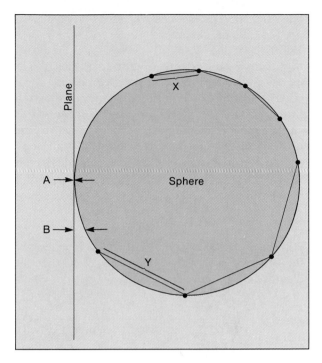

Figure A-3
Relationships between surfaces on the round earth and a flat map.

At the other extreme are maps with scale ratios of less than 1 : 1,000,000, such as maps of the world that are found in atlases. Those are small-scale maps. Because they cover large areas, the symbols on them must be highly abstract. They are therefore best suited to general reference or planning, when detail is not important. Medium- or intermediate-scale maps have scales between 1 : 100,000 and 1 : 1,000,000. They are good for regional reference and planning purposes.

Another important aspect of map scale is to give us some notion of geometric accuracy; the greater the expanse of the real world shown on a map, the less accurate the geometry of that map is. Figure A–3 shows why. If a curve is represented by straight line segments, short segments (X) are more similar to the curve than are long segments (Y). Similarly, if a plane is placed in contact with a sphere, the difference between the two surfaces is slight where they touch (A) but grows rapidly with increasing distance from the point of contact (B). In view of the large diameter and slight local curvature of the earth, distances will be well represented on large-

scale maps (those with small denominators) but will be increasingly poorly represented at smaller scales. This close relationship between map scale and map geometry brings us to the topic of map projections.

MAP PROJECTIONS

The spherical surface of the earth is shown on flat maps by means of map projections. The process of "flattening" the earth is essentially a problem in geometry that has captured the attention of the best mathematical minds for centuries. Yet no one has ever found a perfect solution; there is no known way to avoid spatial distortion of one kind or another. Many map projections have been devised, but only a few have become standard. Because a single, flat map cannot preserve all aspects of the earth's surface geometry, a mapmaker must be careful to match the projection with the task at hand. To map something that involves distance, for example, a projection should be used in which distance is not distorted. In addition, a map user should be able to recognize which aspects of a map's geometry are accurate and which are distortions caused by a particular projection process. Fortunately, that objective is not too difficult to achieve.

It is helpful to think of the creation of a projection as a two-step process (Figure A–4). First, the immense earth is reduced to a small globe with a scale equal to that of the desired flat map. All spatial properties on the globe are true to those on the earth. Second, the globe is flattened. Since that cannot be done without distortion, it is accomplished in such a way that the resulting map exhibits certain desirable spatial properties.

Perspective Models

Early map projections were sometimes created with the aid of perspective methods, but that has changed. In the modern electronic age, projections are normally developed by strictly mathematical means and are plotted out or displayed on computer-driven graphics devices. The concept of perspective is still useful in visualizing what map projections do, however. Thus, projection methods are often illustrated by using strategically located light sources to cast shadows on a projection surface from a latitude/longitude net inscribed on a transparent globe.

The success of the perspective approach depends on finding a projection surface that is flat or that can be flattened without distortion. The cone, cylinder, and plane possess those attributes and serve as models for three general classes of map projections: *conic, cylindrical,* and *planar* (or azimuthal). Figure A–5 shows those three classes, as well as a fourth, a false cylindrical class with an oval shape. Although the oval class is not of perspective origin, it appears to combine properties of the cylindrical and planar classes (Figure A–6).

The relationship between the projection surface and the model at the point or line of contact is critical because distortion of spatial properties on the projection is symmetrical about, and increases with distance from, that point or line. That condition is illustrated for the cylindrical and planar classes of projections in Figure A–7. If the point or line of contact is changed to some other position on the globe, the distortion pattern will be recentered on the new position but will retain the same symmetrical form. Thus, centering a projection on the area of interest on the earth's surface can minimize the effects of projection distortion. And recognizing the general projection shape, associating it with a perspective model, and recalling the characteristic distortion pattern will provide the information necessary to compensate for projection distortion.

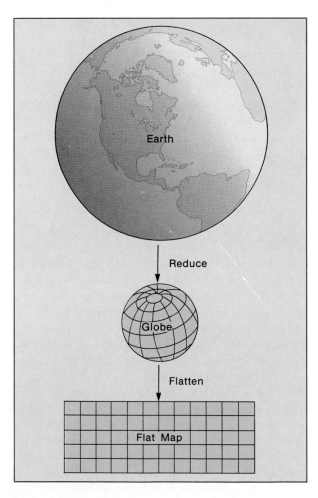

Figure A–4
The two-step process of creating a projection.

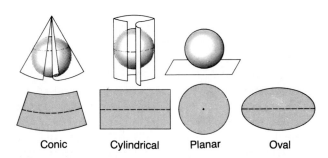

Conic   Cylindrical   Planar   Oval

Figure A–5
General classes of map projections. (Courtesy of ACSM)

Cylindrical

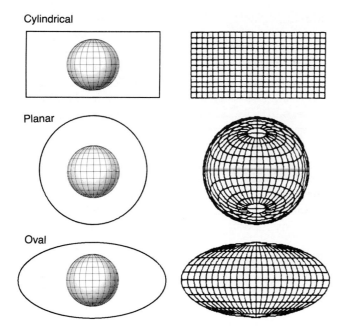

Planar

Oval

Figure A-6
The visual properties of cylindrical and planar projections combined in oval projections. (Courtesy of ACSM)

Cylindrical   **Planar**

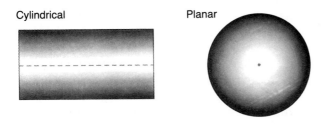

Figure A-7
Characteristic patterns of distortion for two projection classes. Here, darker shading implies greater distortion. (Courtesy of ACSM)

Preserved Properties

For a map projection to truthfully depict the geometry of the earth's surface, it would have to preserve the spatial attributes of *distance, direction, area, shape,* and *proximity.* That task can be readily accomplished on a globe, but it is not possible on a flat map. To preserve area, for example, a mapmaker must stretch or shear shapes; thus, area and shape cannot be preserved on the same map. To depict both direction and distance from a point, area must be distorted. Similarly, to preserve area as well as direction from a point, distance has to be

distorted. Because the earth's surface is continuous in all directions from every point, discontinuities that violate proximity relationships must occur on all map projections. The trick is to place those discontinuities where they will have the least impact on the spatial relationships in which the map user is interested.

We must be careful when we use spatial terms because the properties they refer to can be confusing. The geometry of the familiar plane is very different from that of a sphere; yet when we refer to a flap map, we are in fact making reference to the spherical earth that was mapped. A shape-preserving projection, for example, is truthful to local shapes—such as the right-angle crossing of latitude and longitude lines—but does not preserve shapes at continental or global levels. A distance-preserving projection can preserve that property from one point on the map in all directions or from a number of points in several directions, but distance cannot be preserved in the general sense that area can be preserved. Direction can also be generally preserved from a single point or in several directions from a number of points but not from all points simultaneously. Thus, a shape-, distance-, or direction-preserving projection is truthful to those properties only in part.

Partial truths are not the only consequence of transforming a sphere into a flat surface. Some projections exploit that transformation by expressing traits that are of considerable value for specific applications. One of those is the famous shape-preserving *Mercator projection* (Figure A–8). That cylindrical projection was derived mathematically in the 1500s so that compass bearing (called rhumb lines) between any two points on the earth would plot as straight lines on the map. That trait let navigators plan, plot, and follow courses between origin and destination, but it was achieved at the expense of extreme areal distortion toward the margins of the projection (see Antarctica in Figure A–8). Although the Mercator projection is admirably suited for its intended purpose, its widespread but inappropriate use for nonnavigational purposes has drawn a great deal of criticism.

The *gnomonic projection* is also useful for navigation. It is a planar projection with the valuable characteristic of showing the shortest (or great circle) route between any two points on the earth as straight lines. Long-distance navigators first plot the great circle course between origin and destina-

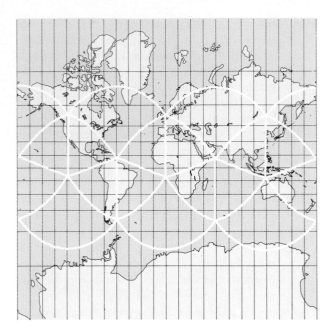

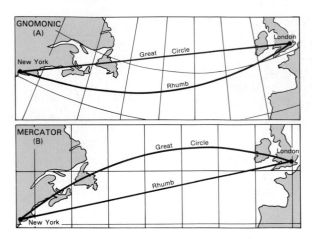

Figure A-9
A gnomonic projection (A) and a Mercator projection (B), both of value to long-distance navigators.

Figure A-8
The useful Mercator projection, showing extreme area distortion in the higher latitudes. (Courtesy of ACSM)

tion on a gnomonic projection (Figure A–9, top). Next they transfer the straight line to a Mercator projection, where it normally appears as a curve (Figure A–9, bottom). Finally, using straight-line segments, they construct an approximation of that course on the Mercator projection. Navigating the shortest course between origin and destination then involves following the straight segments of the course and making directional corrections between segments. Like the Mercator projection, the specialized gnomonic projection distorts other spatial properties so severely that it should not be used for any purpose other than navigation or communications.

Projections Used in Textbooks

Although a map projection cannot be free of distortion, it can represent one or several spatial properties of the earth's surface accurately if other properties are sacrificed. The two projections used for world maps throughout this textbook illustrate that point well. Goode's homolosine projection, shown in Figure A–10, belongs to the oval category and shows area accurately, although it gives the impression that the earth's surface has been torn, peeled, and flattened. The interruptions in Figure A–10 have

been placed in the major oceans, giving continuity to the land masses. Ocean areas could be featured instead by placing the interruptions in the continents. Obviously, that type of interrupted projection severely distorts proximity relationships. Consequently, in different locations the properties of distance, direction, and shape are also distorted to varying degrees. The distortion pattern mimics that of cylindrical projections, with the equatorial zone the most faithfully represented (Figure A–11).

An alternative to special-property projections such as the equal-area Goode's homolosine is the compromise projection. In that case no special property is achieved at the expense of others, and distortion is rather evenly distributed among the various properties, instead of being focused on one or several properties. The *Robinson projection,* which is also used in this textbook, falls into that category (Figure A–12). Its oval projection has a global feel, somewhat like that of Goode's homolosine. But the Robinson projection shows the North Pole and the South Pole as lines that are slightly more than half the length of the equator, thus exaggerating distances and areas near the poles. Areas look larger than they really are in the high latitudes (near the poles) and smaller than they really are in the low latitudes (near the equator). In addition, not all latitude and longitude lines intersect at right angles, as they do on the earth, so we know that the Robinson projection does not preserve direction or shape either. However, it has fewer interruptions than the Goode's homolosine does, so it

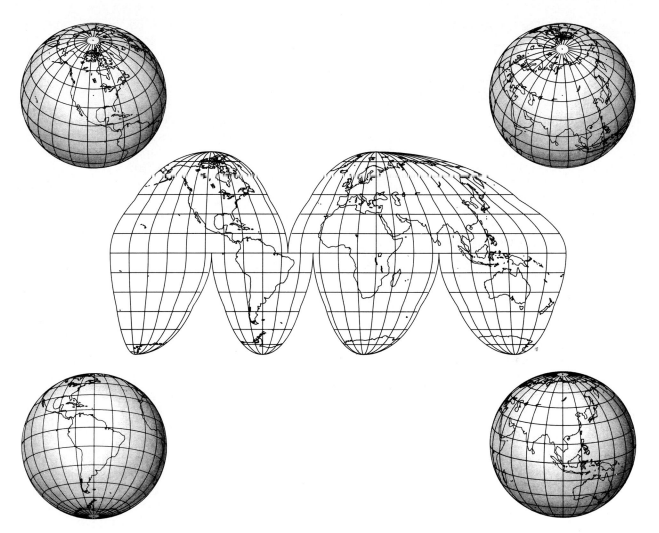

Figure A–10
An interrupted Goode's homolosine, an equal-area projection. (Courtesy of ACSM)

preserves proximity better. Overall, the Robinson projection does a good job of representing spatial relationships, especially in the low to middle latitudes and along the central meridian.

SCALE AND PROJECTIONS IN MODERN GEOGRAPHY

Computers have drastically changed the way in which maps are made and used. In the preelectronic age, maps were so laborious, time-consuming, and expensive to make that relatively few were created. Frustrated, geographers and other scientists often found themselves trying to use maps for purposes not intended by the map designers. But today anyone with access to computer mapping facilities can create projections in a flash. Thus, projections will be increasingly tailored to specific needs, and more and more scientists will do their own mapping rather than have someone else guess what they want in a map.

Computer mapping creates opportunities that go far beyond the construction of projections, of course. Once maps and related geographical data are entered into computers, many types of analyses can be carried out involving map scales and projections. Distances, areas, and volumes can be computed; searches can be conducted; information from

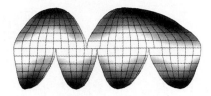

Figure A–11
The distortion pattern of the interrupted Goode's homolosine projection, which mimics that of cylindrical projections. (Courtesy of ACSM)

different maps can be combined; optimal routes can be selected; facilities can be allocated to the most suitable sites; and so on. The term used to describe such processes is *geographical information system,* or GIS (Figure A–13). Within a GIS, projections provide the mechanism for linking data from different sources, and scale provides the basis for size calculations of all sorts. Mastery of both projection and scale becomes the user's responsibility because the map user is also the map maker. Now more than ever, effective geography depends on knowledge of the close association between scale and projection.

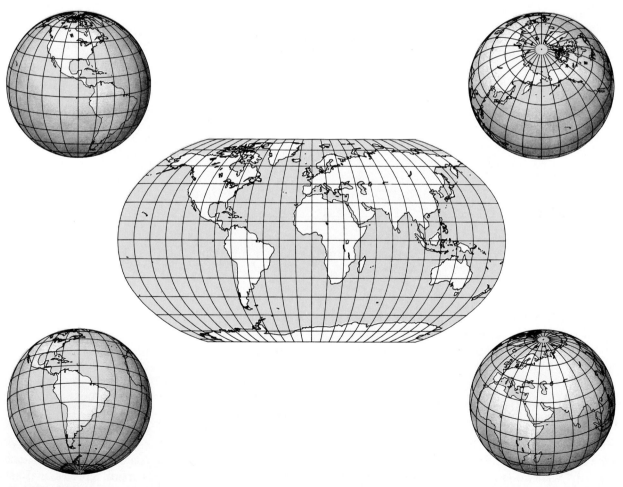

Figure A–12
The compromise Robinson projection, which avoids the interruptions of Goode's homolosine but preserves no special properties. (Courtesy of ACSM)

Figure A-13
Within a GIS, environmental data attached to a common terrestrial reference system, such as latitude/longitude, can be stacked in layers for spatial comparison and analysis.

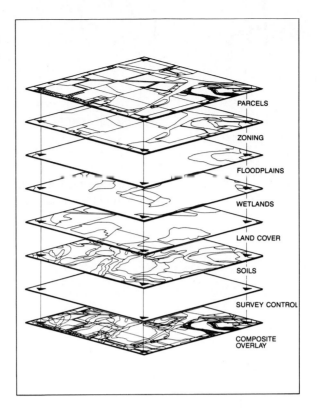

	Population (millions)	Area		Birthrate (%)	Death Rate (%)	Infant Mortality (less than age 1) (%)
		Square Miles (thousands)	Square Kilometers (thousands)			
Anglo-America						
Canada	29.1	3,831	9,976	1.4	0.7	0.7
United States	260.8	3,679	9,363	1.6	0.9	0.8
Western Europe						
Austria	8.0	32	84	1.2	1.0	0.7
Belgium	10.1	12	31	1.2	1.0	0.8
Denmark	5.2	17	43	1.3	1.2	0.7
Finland	5.1	130	337	1.3	1.0	0.4
France	58.0	211	547	1.3	0.9	0.7
Germany	81.2	96	249	1.0	1.1	0.6
Greece	10.4	51	132	1.0	1.0	0.8
Iceland	0.3	40	103	1.8	0.7	0.4
Ireland	3.6	27	70	1.4	0.9	0.6
Italy	57.2	116	301	1.0	1.0	0.8
Liechtenstein	0.03	0.06	0.16	1.4	0.6	0.3
Luxembourg	0.4	1	3	1.3	1.0	0.9
Malta	0.4	0.1	0.3	1.5	0.8	0.8
Netherlands	15.4	16	41	1.3	0.9	0.6
Norway	4.3	125	324	1.4	1.0	0.6
Portugal	9.9	34	92	1.2	1.0	0.9
San Marino	0.02	0.02	0.06	1.0	0.7	0.9
Spain	39.2	195	505	1.0	0.9	0.8

Selected National Statistics

all based on 1994 Pop. Data Sheet.

Population under Age 15 (%)	Life Expectancy at Birth	Annual Growth Rate (%)	Per Capita GNP (U.S. dollars)	Daily Food Supply (calories)	Annual per Capita Energy Consumption (kilograms of oil)	Portion of Labor Force in Agriculture (%)
21	77	0.7	20,320	3,242	10,009	3
22	76	0.7	23,120	3,642	7,822	2
18	76	0.2	22,110	3,486	3,503	6
18	76	0.2	20,880	3,925	2,807	2
17	75	0.1	25,930	3,639	3,618	5
19	75	0.3	22,980	3,066	5,650	8
20	77	0.4	22,300	3,593	3,845	5
16	76	−0.1	23,030	3,591	3,491	4
19	77	0.1	7,180	3,775	2,092	24
25	78	1.1	23,760	3,473	3,730	7
27	74	0.6	12,100	3,692	2,653	13
16	77	0.0	20,510	3,498	2,754	7
19	—	0.8	—	—	—	—
17	76	0.3	35,260	3,925	7,796	3
23	75	0.7	7,300	3,169	1,246	4
18	77	0.4	20,590	3,078	5,123	4
19	77	0.4	25,800	3,221	9,083	5
17	74	0.2	7,450	3,342	1,507	16
16	76	0.4	1,920	3,574	—	—
19	77	0.1	14,020	3,472	2,201	10

	Population (millions)	Area Square Miles (thousands)	Area Square Kilometers (thousands)	Birthrate (%)	Death Rate (%)	Infant Mortality (less than age 1) (%)
Sweden	8.8	174	450	1.4	1.1	0.5
Switzerland	7.0	16	41	1.2	0.9	0.6
United Kingdom	58.4	94	245	1.3	1.1	0.7
Eastern Europe						
Albania	3.4	11	29	2.3	0.6	3.3
Bosnia-Hercegovina	4.6	20	51	1.4	0.7	1.5
Bulgaria	8.4	43	111	1.1	1.3	1.6
Croatia	4.8	22	57	1.0	1.1	1.1
Czech Republic	10.3	30	79	1.2	1.1	0.9
Hungary	10.3	36	93	1.1	1.4	1.3
Macedonia	2.1	10	26	1.6	0.7	2.4
Poland	38.6	121	313	1.3	1.0	1.4
Romania	22.7	92	238	1.1	1.1	2.3
Slovakia	5.3	19	49	1.4	1.0	1.6
Slovenia	2.0	8	20	1.0	1.0	0.7
Yugoslavia	10.5	39	102	1.4	1.0	1.7
Eurasian States of the former Soviet Union						
Armenia	3.7	12	30	2.1	0.7	1.8
Azerbaidzhan	7.4	34	87	2.6	0.6	2.5
Belarus	10.3	80	208	1.2	1.1	1.2
Estonia	1.5	17	45	1.0	1.4	1.3
Georgia	5.5	27	70	1.7	0.9	1.6
Kazakhstan	17.1	1,049	2,717	2.0	0.8	2.7
Kyrgyzstan	4.5	77	199	2.9	0.7	5.2
Latvia	2.5	25	65	1.2	1.3	1.7
Lithuania	3.7	25	65	1.4	1.1	1.7
Moldova	4.4	13	34	1.6	1.0	1.9
Russia	147.8	6,592	17,075	1.1	1.2	1.8
Tadzhikistan	5.9	55	143	3.5	0.6	4.0
Turkmenistan	4.1	188	488	3.3	0.7	4.5
Ukraine	51.5	233	604	1.2	1.3	1.4
Uzbekistan	22.1	173	447	3.3	0.6	3.5
Japan and Australia/ New Zealand						
Japan	125.0	146	372	1.0	0.7	0.4
Australia	17.8	2,968	7,687	1.5	0.7	0.7
New Zealand	3.5	104	269	1.7	0.8	0.7
Latin America						
Argentina	33.9	1,068	2,767	2.1	0.8	2.6
Bahamas	0.3	5	14	2.0	0.5	2.4
Barbados	0.3	0.2	1	1.6	0.9	0.9
Belize	0.2	9	23	3.8	0.5	2.3
Bolivia	8.2	424	1,098	3.7	1.0	7.5
Brazil	155.3	3,286	8,512	2.5	0.8	6.6

Population under Age 15 (%)	Life Expectancy at Birth	Annual Growth Rate (%)	Per Capita GNP (U.S. dollars)	Daily Food Supply (calories)	Annual per Capita Energy Consumption (kilograms of oil)	Portion of Labor Force in Agriculture (%)
18	78	0.3	26,780	2,978	6,447	4
16	78	0.3	36,230	3,508	3,902	4
19	76	0.2	17,760	3,270	3,646	2
33	72	1.8	—	—	1,152	48
23	72	0.7	—	—	—	—
20	72	−0.2	1,330	3,695	4,945	12
19	71	−0.1	—	—	—	—
21	72	0.0	2,440	3,574	5,081	9
19	69	−0.3	3,010	3,608	3,211	11
26	72	0.3	1,960	3,426	3,416	20
25	71	−0.1	1,090	3,081	3,623	19
22	70	0.3	—	—	—	—
25	71	0.1	6,330	—	—	—
20	73	0.4	—	3,545	2,409	21
23	72	—	—	—	—	—
31	70	1.4	780	—	—	—
33	71	1.9	870	—	—	—
23	71	0.1	2,910	—	—	—
22	70	−0.4	2,750	—	—	—
25	73	0.8	850	—	—	—
31	69	1.2	1,680	—	—	—
38	69	2.1	810	—	—	—
21	69	−0.1	1,930	—	—	—
22	71	0.3	1,310	—	—	—
28	69	0.6	1,260	—	—	—
22	68	−0.2	2,680	—	—	—
43	69	2.9	480	—	—	—
40	66	2.6	1,270	—	—	—
21	69	−0.2	1,670	—	—	—
41	69	2.7	860	—	—	—
17	79	0.3	28,220	2,921	3,563	6
22	77	0.8	17,070	3,302	5,041	5
23	75	0.9	12,060	3,461	4,971	9
30	71	1.3	6,050	3,068	1,801	10
30	72	1.5	12,020	2,777	1,390	6
25	75	0.7	6,530	3,217	992	6
44	68	3.3	2,210	2,575	339	—
42	61	2.7	680	2,013	257	41
35	67	1.7	2,770	2,730	915	24

	Population (millions)	Area Square Miles (thousands)	Area Square Kilometers (thousands)	Birthrate (%)	Death Rate (%)	Infant Mortality (less than age 1) (%)
Chile	14.0	292	757	2.2	0.6	1.5
Colombia	35.6	440	1,139	2.5	0.5	3.3
Costa Rica	3.2	20	51	2.6	0.4	1.4
Cuba	11.1	44	115	1.5	0.7	1.0
Dominica	0.1	0.3	1	2.0	0.7	1.8
Dominican Republic	7.8	19	49	2.8	0.6	4.3
Ecuador	10.6	109	284	3.1	0.6	5.3
El Salvador	5.2	8	21	3.3	0.7	4.5
Grenada	0.1	0.1	0.3	3.1	0.7	1.3
Guatemala	10.3	42	109	3.9	0.7	5.7
Guyana	0.8	83	215	2.5	0.7	4.8
Haiti	7.0	11	28	4.2	1.9	11.1
Honduras	5.3	43	112	3.8	0.7	5.0
Jamaica	2.5	4	11	2.4	0.5	1.3
Mexico	91.8	762	1,973	2.8	0.6	3.5
Nicaragua	4.3	50	130	3.7	0.7	5.7
Panama	2.5	30	78	2.3	0.5	2.1
Paraguay	4.8	157	407	3.4	0.6	4.8
Peru	22.9	496	1,285	2.8	0.8	8.1
Puerto Rico	3.6	3	9	1.8	0.8	1.3
St. Lucia	0.1	0.2	1	2.7	0.6	1.9
St. Vincent and the Grenadines	0.1	0.2	1	2.3	0.6	2.1
Suriname	0.4	63	163	2.3	0.6	2.7
Trinidad and Tobago	1.3	2	5	1.8	0.7	1.7
Uruguay	3.2	68	176	1.8	1.0	2.1
Venezuela	21.3	352	912	3.0	0.5	2.0
Sub-Saharan Africa						
Angola	11.2	481	1,247	4.7	2.0	13.7
Benin	5.3	43	113	4.9	1.8	8.7
Botswana	1.4	232	600	3.6	0.9	4.3
Burkina Faso	10.1	106	274	5.0	1.8	2.3
Burundi	6.0	11	28	4.6	1.7	10.5
Cameroon	13.1	184	475	4.1	1.2	8.1
Cape Verde	0.4	2	4	3.6	0.7	4.0
Central African Republic	3.1	241	623	4.4	2.0	14.2
Chad	6.5	496	1,284	4.4	1.8	12.2
Comoros	0.5	1	3	4.7	1.2	8.6
Congo	2.4	132	342	4.2	1.6	11.6
Côte d' Ivoire	13.9	124	321	5.0	1.5	9.1
Djibouti	0.6	9	23	4.7	1.7	11.2
Equatorial Guinea	0.4	11	28	4.2	1.6	11.0
Eritrea	3.5	48	124	4.2	1.6	—
Ethiopia	55.2	424	1,098	4.6	1.5	11.0
Gabon	1.1	103	268	4.3	1.6	9.4
Gambia	1.1	4	11	4.8	2.1	9.0

Population under Age 15 (%)	Life Expectancy at Birth	Annual Growth Rate (%)	Per Capita GNP (U.S. dollars)	Daily Food Supply (calories)	Annual per Capita Energy Consumption (kilograms of oil)	Portion of Labor Force in Agriculture (%)
31	72	1.7	2,730	2,484	887	12
34	68	2.0	1,290	2.453	811	27
36	76	2.3	2,000	2,711	622	23
23	77	0.8		3,120	1,000	10
31	76	1.3	2,520	2,911	190	—
38	68	2.2	1,040	2,310	336	36
39	69	2.5	1,070	2,399	678	30
44	66	2.7	1,170	—	233	36
43	70	2.5	2,310	2,400	230	—
45	65	3.1	980	2,254	171	51
33	65	1.8	330	2,495	336	22
40	46	2.3	380	2,005	53	63
47	66	3.1	580	2,210	198	55
33	74	1.8	1,340	2,558	931	27
38	70	2.2	3,470	3,062	1,300	29
46	63	2.9	410	—	261	38
35	72	1.8	2,440	2,269	1,694	24
40	67	2.7	1,340	2,684	232	46
38	65	2.0	950	2,037	509	34
27	74	1.0	6,610	2,460	1,745	3
44	72	2.0	2,900	2,424	318	—
37	71	1.7	1,990	2,460	150	—
41	69	1.6	3,700	2,436	891	16
32	71	1.2	3,940	2,770	5,940	7
26	73	0.8	3,340	2,668	821	13
38	70	2.6	2,900	2,443	2,582	11
45	46	2.7	—	—	203	69
47	46	3.1	410	2,383	46	60
48	62	2.7	2,790	2,260	425	62
48	48	3.1	290	2,219	17	84
46	48	2.9	210	1,948	21	91
45	56	2.9	820	2,208	147	60
44	68	2.9	850	2,778	32	42
43	44	2.4	410	1,846	30	62
41	48	2.6	220	—	17	74
48	56	3.5	510	1,760	36	79
44	49	2.9	1,030	2,295	213	59
47	52	3.5	670	2,568	173	55
41	49	3.0	—	—	233	—
43	51	2.6	330	—	58	54
—	—	2.6	—	—	—	—
49	52	3.1	110	—	20	74
33	54	2.7	4,450	—	1,158	67
45	45	2.7	390	2,290	77	81

	Population (millions)	Area Square Miles (thousands)	Area Square Kilometers (thousands)	Birthrate (%)	Death Rate (%)	Infant Mortality (less than age 1) (%)
Ghana	16.9	92	239	4.2	1.2	8.1
Guinea	6.4	95	246	4.6	2.1	14.7
Guinea-Bissau	1.1	14	36	4.3	2.1	14.0
Kenya	27.0	225	583	4.4	1.0	6.6
Lesotho	1.9	12	30	3.1	1.2	7.9
Liberia	2.9	43	111	4.7	1.4	12.6
Madagascar	13.7	227	587	4.6	1.3	9.3
Malawi	9.5	46	118	4.7	2.0	13.4
Mali	9.1	479	1,240	5.2	2.1	11.0
Mauritania	2.3	398	1,031	4.6	1.8	11.7
Mauritius	1.1	1	3	2.1	0.7	18.5
Mozambique	15.8	302	782	4.5	1.8	14.7
Namibia	1.6	318	823	4.1	0.8	6.6
Niger	8.8	489	1,267	5.3	1.9	12.3
Nigeria	98.1	357	925	4.4	1.3	8.7
Réunion	0.6	1	3	2.3	0.6	0.7
Rwanda	7.7	10	26	4.0	1.7	11.7
Sao Tomé and Principe	0.1	0.4	1	3.5	1.0	7.2
Senegal	8.2	76	197	4.3	1.6	8.0
Seychelles	0.1	0.2	1	2.3	0.7	1.2
Sierra Leone	4.6	28	72	4.8	2.2	14.3
Somalia	9.8	246	638	5.0	1.9	12.2
South Africa	41.2	471	1,220	3.4	0.8	4.9
Sudan	28.2	968	2,506	4.4	1.3	8.5
Swaziland	0.8	7	17	4.4	1.2	9.8
Tanzania	29.8	365	945	4.8	1.5	10.2
Togo	4.3	22	56	4.9	1.2	9.4
Uganda	19.8	91	236	5.1	2.1	10.4
Zaire	42.5	906	2,345	4.8	1.5	9.3
Zambia	9.1	291	753	4.6	1.8	10.7
Zimbabwe	11.2	151	391	4.1	1.1	5.9
North Africa and the Middle East						
Algeria	27.9	920	2,382	3.2	0.7	6.5
Bahrain	0.6	0.3	1	2.9	0.5	2.5
Cyprus	0.7	4	10	2.0	0.9	1.0
Egypt	58.9	387	1,002	3.0	0.8	6.2
Gaza Strip	0.7	0.1	0.4	5.6	0.6	4.3
Iran	61.2	636	1,648	4.4	0.9	6.6
Iraq	19.9	168	435	4.5	0.8	7.9
Israel	5.4	8	21	2.1	0.6	0.8
Jordan	4.2	38	98	3.8	0.5	3.4
Kuwait	1.3	7	17	3.5	0.2	1.6
Lebanon	3.6	4	10	2.5	0.5	2.8
Libya	5.1	679	1,760	4.2	0.8	6.8

Population under Age 15 (%)	Life Expectancy at Birth	Annual Growth Rate (%)	Per Capita GNP (U.S. dollars)	Daily Food Supply (calories)	Annual per Capita Energy Consumption (kilograms of oil)	Portion of Labor Force in Agriculture (%)
45	54	3.0	450	2,144	68	49
44	43	2.5	510	2,242	73	73
43	44	2.1	210	—	43	78
40	50	3.3	330	2,064	100	77
41	61	1.9	590	2,121	—	79
45	55	3.3	—	2,259	169	69
45	56	3.3	230	2,156	40	76
48	44	2.7	210	2,049	41	75
46	45	3.0	300	2,259	24	80
44	48	2.9	530	2,447	114	64
30	69	1.5	2,700	2,897	394	22
44	45	2.7	60	1,805	85	81
45	59	3.3	1,610	—	—	34
49	47	3.4	300	2,239	40	87
45	54	3.1	320	2,200	138	64
30	74	1.8	—	3,082	509	11
48	46	2.3	250	1,913	41	91
41	63	2.5	370	2,153	115	—
47	49	2.7	780	2,322	156	78
35	69	1.5	5,480	2,356	554	—
45	43	2.7	170	1,899	77	62
47	47	3.2	—	1,874	64	70
39	65	2.6	2,670	3,133	2,447	13
46	53	3.1	—	2,043	58	59
47	56	3.2	1,080	2,634	—	66
47	51	3.4	110	2,195	38	80
49	56	3.6	400	2,269	51	69
47	42	3.0	170	2,178	27	80
45	52	3.3	—	2,130	71	65
48	44	2.8	290	2,016	379	69
48	56	3.0	570	2,256	525	68
42	62	2.5	1,830	2,944	1,956	24
32	71	2.4	7,150	—	10,275	2
26	76	1.1	9,820	—	702	20
40	62	2.3	630	3,310	598	40
60	66	5.0	—	—	—	—
47	65	3.6	2,190	—	1,026	29
48	64	3.7	—	—	774	22
31	76	1.5	13,230	3,220	2,050	4
41	67	3.3	1,120	—	994	6
43	76	3.3	—	3,043	6,414	2
33	75	2.0	—	—	968	18
47	63	3.4	—	3,293	3,399	13

	Population (millions)	Area Square Miles (thousands)	Square Kilometers (thousands)	Birthrate (%)	Death Rate (%)	Infant Mortality (less than age 1) (%)
Morocco	28.6	275	713	3.0	0.7	5.7
Oman	1.9	82	212	5.3	0.4	2.4
Qatar	0.5	4	10	1.4	0.4	2.0
Saudi Arabia	18.0	830	2,150	3.6	0.5	2.4
Syria	14.0	71	185	4.4	0.6	4.4
Tunisia	8.7	63	164	2.5	0.6	4.3
Turkey	61.8	301	781	2.9	0.7	5.7
United Arab Emirates	1.7	32	84	2.3	0.4	2.3
West Bank	1.4	2	6	4.6	0.7	4.0
Western Sahara	0.2	103	267	4.8	2.0	—
Yemen	12.9	204	529	4.8	1.4	11.5
South Asia						
Afghanistan	17.8	250	648	4.9	2.2	16.8
Bangladesh	116.6	56	144	3.7	1.3	11.6
Bhutan	0.8	18	47	4.0	1.7	13.0
India	911.6	1,237	3,204	2.9	1.0	7.9
Maldives	0.2	0.1	0.3	3.8	0.6	3.8
Nepal	22.1	54	141	3.9	1.5	9.0
Pakistan	126.4	320	829	4.0	1.2	10.9
Sri Lanka	17.9	25	66	2.1	0.6	1.9
East Asia						
China	1,192.0	3,692	9,561	1.8	0.7	3.1
Hong Kong	5.8	0.4	1	1.2	0.5	0.6
Korea, North	23.1	47	121	2.4	0.6	3.0
Korea, South	44.5	38	98	1.6	0.6	1.5
Macao	0.4	0.006	0.02	1.9	0.4	0.8
Mongolia	2.4	604	1,565	3.4	0.7	4.8
Taiwan	21.1	14	36	1.6	0.5	0.6
Southeast Asia						
Brunei	0.3	2	5	2.9	0.3	0.9
Cambodia	10.3	70	181	4.6	1.7	11.2
Indonesia	199.7	753	1,950	2.5	0.9	6.8
Laos	4.7	91	237	4.4	1.6	10.7
Malaysia	19.5	128	333	2.8	0.5	1.4
Myanmar (Burma)	45.4	261	676	2.8	0.9	9.8
Papua-New Guinea	4.0	178.7	462.8	3.5	1.2	7.2
Philippines	68.7	116	300	3.0	0.7	4.0
Singapore	2.9	0.2	1	1.7	0.5	0.5
Thailand	59.4	198	513	2.0	0.6	4.0
Vietnam	73.1	127	329	3.0	0.7	3.6

Sources: Population Reference Bureau, *World Population Data Sheet* (Washington, DC: 1994); supplemented by other international statistical sources.

Population under Age 15 (%)	Life Expectancy at Birth	Annual Growth Rate (%)	Per Capita GNP (U.S. dollars)	Daily Food Supply (calories)	Annual per Capita Energy Consumption (kilograms of oil)	Portion of Labor Force in Agriculture (%)
40	67	2.3	1,040	3,031	247	36
36	71	4.9	6,490	—	2,648	62
23	73	1.0	16,240	—	15,318	39
43	70	3.2	7,940	2,929	5,033	3
48	66	3.7	1,170	3,122	913	24
37	68	1.9	1,740	3,122	520	23
35	67	2.2	1,950	3,196	857	47
32	72	2.9	22,220	3,285	10,874	3
50	69	4.0	—	—	—	—
—	—	—	—	—	—	—
51	54	3.4	520	—	234	55
46	42	2.8	—	—	90	54
44	53	2.4	220	2,037	57	68
39	49	2.3	180	—	13	91
36	57	1.9	310	2,229	231	66
47	61	3.2	500	—	138	—
44	51	2.4	170	2,205	25	92
44	60	2.8	410	2,280	233	49
35	73	1.5	540	2,246	179	52
28	70	1.1	380	2,641	598	67
21	78	0.7	15,380	2,860	1,717	1
29	69	1.9	—	2,843	1,896	33
24	71	1.0	6,790	2,826	1,898	24
25	79	1.6	—	2,294	751	—
44	65	2.7	—	2,361	1,277	30
26	74	1.0	—	—	—	37
36	71	2.6	—	2,858	6,992	—
44	49	2.9	200	—	59	70
37	60	1.6	670	2,605	272	48
45	51	2.9	250	—	39	71
36	71	2.3	2,790	2,671	974	31
36	59	1.9	—	2,454	82	46
40	55	2.3	950	—	233	72
39	64	2.4	770	2,341	215	48
23	74	1.2	15,750	3,121	5,685	1
29	69	1.4	1,840	2,280	352	64
39	65	2.3	—	—	100	60

APPENDIX C

Conversion Factors

Conversion factors for some widely used measures

From	To	Factor
Inches	Centimeters	Multiply inches by 2.54
Centimeters	Inches	Multiply centimeters by 0.3937
Feet	Meters	Multiply feet by 0.3048
Meters	Feet	Multiply meters by 3.2808
Cubic feet	Cubic meters	Multiply cubic feet by 0.0283
Cubic meters	Cubic feet	Multiply cubic meters by 35.3145
Miles	Kilometers	Multiply miles by 1.6093
Kilometers	Miles	Multiply kilometers by 0.6214
Square miles	Square kilometers	Multiply square miles by 2.59
Square kilometers	Square miles	Multiply square kilometers by 0.3861
Acres	Hectares	Multiply acres by 0.4047
Hectares	Acres	Multiply hectares by 2.4710
Gallons (U.S.)	Liters	Multiply gallons by 3.7853
Liters	Gallons	Multiply liters by 0.2642
Pounds	Kilograms	Multiply pounds by 0.4536
Kilograms	Pounds	Multiply kilograms by 2.2046

Glossary

aborigines Descendants of the Negroid inhabitants occupying Australia at the time of European settlement.

acculturation The cultural modification of a group because of contact with other cultures; the merging of cultures through prolonged contact.

acid rain Rainwater with a higher-than-average acid content, caused by the burning of fossil fuels and the release of sulfur and nitrogen oxides into the atmosphere; damaging to plant and marine life.

African National Congress (ANC) A black political group in South Africa, committed to majority rule and abolition of apartheid; victorious in 1994 national elections, the first in which blacks could participate.

agrarian society A society in which the majority of the population and the economic activity is agriculturally based.

agricultural calendar The chronological sequence of farming operations throughout the year, including the period of land preparation, sowing, cultivation, and harvesting.

Agricultural Revolution A period beginning 7,000 to 10,000 years ago and characterized by the domestication of plants and animals and the development of farming.

Ainu The proto-Caucasian population of ancient northern Japan; still found in small numbers on the island of Hokkaido.

alluvial fans Alluvium deposited at the base of mountains by streams flowing from mountains to plains.

alluvium Material, often very fertile, that has been transported and deposited by water.

altiplano A high plateau or plain; the high plateau of Bolivia, which contains most of the Bolivian population.

Andean Common Market (ANCOM) A free-market organization formed by Venezuela, Colombia, Ecuador, Peru, and Bolivia.

antioqueños Residents of Antioquia, or the area around Medellín in Colombia; considered economically aggressive people.

apartheid The former policy of the South African government that maintained strict white-nonwhite segregation.

Appalachia That part of the Appalachian Highlands of the United States designated as a poverty area.

Appalachian corridor Another form of reference to the Appalachian Highlands, particularly that segment where economic lag has been an ongoing problem.

aquaculture The cultivation of fish or aquatic plants for food or other uses.

Arabs The more than 150 million Semitic people of the Middle East and North Africa who share a common language, cultural history, and religion (Islam).

Arabic Referring to the language and culture of the Arabs.

archipelagic Describing a group or chain of islands.

area studies tradition A geographic perspective that emphasizes the study of specific regions and an understanding of the varied aspects of those regions.

Association of Southeast Asian Nations (ASEAN) A political-economic organization formed in 1967 to promote cooperation among member nations.

Atatürk, Kemal   The found of modern Turkey after World War I and the demise of the Ottoman Empire; strove to create a Westernized, secular state.

autonomous region   The highest-level political unit in China by which ethnic minorities are theoretically allowed some local self-rule and preservation of customs.

average annual precipitation   The average total precipitation during the year, expressed in inches or centimeters. Precipitation figures are presented in rainfall equivalents but include all forms of precipitation.

Aymara   One of two Indian ethnic and linguistic groups of Peru and Bolivia.

Aztec   One of the four high civilizations of pre-Colombian Latin America, centered on the area around present-day Mexico City.

baby boom   The immediate post–World War II period of comparatively high birthrates in the United States, when birthrates attained a high of 2.7 percent before declining during the mid-1960s.

Balkanization   The breakup or fragmentation of a large political unit into several smaller units, such as that which occurred in the Ottoman and Austro-Hungarian empires during the nineteenth and twentieth centuries.

band   A small society of a few dozen people occupying a loosely defined territory.

Bantu   The family of Negroid peoples occupying Central, Eastern, and Southern Africa.

barefoot doctors   Chinese paramedics used in rural areas to provide medical service and disseminate birth control information and supplies.

Bedouin   Arabs who live by nomadic herding in the deserts of North Africa and the Middle East.

Benelux   The nations of Belgium, the Netherlands, and Luxembourg, considered as a group.

Bengali   The Indo-European language dominant in Bangladesh.

Berber   A pre-Arabic culture group of Morocco and Algeria, many of whom now speak Arabic and all of whom are Muslims.

Berlin Wall   The physical wall established between East and West Berlin to prevent movement from one sector of the city to the other; symbolized the tension between east and west during the cold war era; removed in 1989.

biome   The particular assemblage of plants and animal life associated with a given large environment; a major ecosystem.

birth dearth   The record-low birthrates in the United States during the 1970s and 1980s, immediately following the baby boom.

birthrate   The number of births occurring in a given year per 1,000 units of population.

Black Death   The bubonic plague that devastated Europe's population during the late Middle Ages.

black migration   The movement of blacks in the United States from rural to urban areas.

Boers   Literally, Dutch farmers; specifically, persons of Dutch heritage living in the Republic of South Africa.

Bolsheviks   A Russian word meaning "majority," now taken to mean a communist, or adherent of communism.

Boserupian thesis   The theory developed by Ester Boserup that rapid population growth can speed economic development.

Boxer Rebellion   A political uprising (1899–1900) promoted by a secret Chinese society and directed, in part, against the intrusion of foreign interests and foreign missionaries into China.

bracero   Mexican agricultural worker legally working in the United States between 1942 and 1964 through an agreement between the U.S. and Mexican governments.

Brahmin   The highest group in the hierarchy of the Hindu caste system, composed basically of Aryans who are teachers and religious leaders.

British East India Company   The dominant commercial enterprise on the Indian subcontinent during the eighteenth and nineteenth centuries, prior to full incorporation of India into the British Empire.

Buddhism   A religion founded in India during the sixth century B.C.; currently found in South, Southeast, and East Asia.

buffer zone   A small, relatively weak area or country between two large groups or nations; serves to reduce conflict between the larger areas.

Bulgarize   A contemporary effort to diminish the appearance of a Turkic ethnic makeup in Bulgaria; encourages the changing of last names that reflect a Turkish heritage.

burakumin   A social minority in Japan occupying the bottom of the social and economic ladder.

by-product   A secondary or incidental material obtained in the mining or manufacturing process; for example, in the refining of petroleum for gasoline, heavy hydrocarbons might also be obtained that can be used in the chemical industry.

calcification   A process occurring in dry regions where limited precipitation results in less leaching of soluble materials and thus the accumulation of calcium carbonates in the soil.

caliphate   In Islam, the office of the caliph, which was the head of the theocratic organization; the first caliph was established after the death of Mohammed; title used by the Ottoman Empire until the rulers of Turkey abandoned it in 1924.

canton   The small political division or state that makes up the confederation of Switzerland.

capital   Any form of wealth that can be used to produce more wealth; resources.

capital goods   Items produced that can be used to create wealth or other goods; for example, a home washing machine is a consumer good, but the machines used to manufacture that washing machine are capital goods.

cardinal temperatures   The temperature range within which a specific plant can grow; the upper and lower temperature limits for plant growth.

Caribbean Community   A grouping of British and former British colonies in and around the Caribbean Sea; formed to reduce trade barriers among member states.

carrying capacity   The maximum number of animals or people an area can support; with population, depends on many variables, such as nutrition level, level of living, and trade.

caste   A rigid system of social stratification based on occupation, with a person's position passed on by inheritance; derived from the Hindu culture.

Central American Common Market   A group of five Central American nations—Guatemala, El Salvador, Honduras, Nicaragua, and Costa Rica, currently ineffective as a common market.

central city   The central business district, plus surrounding warehouse, manufacturing, and residential areas within a metropolis; also referred to as the inner city.

centrally planned economies   Productive systems controlled by a national government; based on communist and socialist principles.

chaco   Lowland plain; specifically, the *gran chaco* of Argentina, Paraguay, and Bolivia.

chernozem   A Russian term referring to the fertile black soils of the steppe or semiarid zone of Russia, Ukraine, and Kazakhstan.

Chibcha   One of the four high civilizations of pre-Colombian Latin America, centered on the area around present-day Bogota, Colombia.

China's sorrow   The Huang He (Yellow River) of China, which has so frequently flooded and changed its course over the centuries, often with great destruction and loss of life.

Ch'ing dynasty   See *Qing dynasty.*

cholera   An acute infectious disease caused by bacteria transmitted by polluted food or water; causes severe intestinal problems and death; frequently occurs in less developed areas.

chorologic   Referring to place.

Christian Copts   Persons of the Middle East and North Africa who are Arabic in speech and culture but who have not adopted Islam.

chronological   Referring to time.

circular causation   A development theory based on an upward or downward spiraling effect.

city-state   A sovereign country consisting of a dominant urban unit and surrounding tributary areas.

climate   The average temperature, precipitation, and wind conditions expressed for an extended period of years; prevailing conditions over time.

climatic classification   Temperature and precipitation conditions reduced to meaningful generalities for a segment of the earth.

climatic divide   A natural barrier that serves as a divide between climate types; for example, the Alps of Europe, which separate the temperate marine regions of central and western Europe from the dry summer subtropical climate of Mediterranean Europe.

climax vegetation   The concept that an area without human interference for a long enough period will exhibit plants that reflect soil and moisture conditions.

coca   South American shrub, the leaves of which are the source of cocaine.

coke   Coal that has undergone partial combustion and is almost pure carbon; used for smelting iron ore.

cold war   The period of hostility, just short of open warfare, between the Soviet Union and the United States and its allies, essentially from 1945 to the mid-1960s, though its end is often dated as 1989 with the fall of the Berlin Wall.

collective farm   One of two forms of government-organized and -supervised large-scale agricultural organizations in the former Soviet Union and Eastern Europe; a collective leases land from the government, and workers receive a share of net returns to the organization.

collectivization   The process of forming collective or communal farms, especially in communist countries; nationalization of private landholdings.

colonialism   The system by which several powers maintained foreign possessions, usually for economic exploitation; most prevalent from the sixteenth through the mid-twentieth centuries; essential to understanding contemporary development in many developing regions.

colonos   Small squatter farms of Colombia, subsistence in nature.

colored   A South African term used to refer to persons of mixed racial ancestry; any person of mixed European, African, or Asian ancestry.

command economy   A centrally controlled and planned livelihood system; for example, the socialist and communist systems.

commercialism   A system of interchange of goods; the activities that lead to sale and exchange of products.

Common Market   A customs union among a group of nations, with no or reduced tariff walls among members and a uniform tariff system with the outside world; specifically, the Common Market of Europe, also previously called the European Economic Community (EEC) or the European Community (EC), but now officially known as the European Union.

Commonwealth of Independent States (CIS)   A loose confederation of eleven former republics of the Soviet Union created in 1991 to work out solutions to their common economic, political, and defense problems.

commune   The basic socioeconomic unit of present-day China; the rural Chinese collective community; currently functioning as more of an administrative unit than an operational agricultural unit.

communism   An age-old concept with several variants in meaning; used here to refer to Marxist communism, the political ideology established in the Soviet Union and China as well as in the countries of Eastern Europe.

comparative advantage   The idea that a given area gains by specializing in one or more products for which it has particular advantages; leads to trade to obtain other needed commodities.

Confucian tradition   The thinking of Confucius, upon which a social order in China was based for 2,000 years; may have prevented innovation and change, thus inhibiting China's modernization.

coniferous (boreal) forest   The large, mostly evergreen forest extending across Canada and part of the northern United States.

conquistadores   The Spanish conquerors of America, particularly sixteenth-century Mexico and Peru.

consumer goods   Commodities produced for use by an individual or family, such as a car, radio, and clothing; designed for consumption rather than the creation of additional wealth.

continental architecture   The arrangement of plains, uplands, and mountains that provides the physical framework of a region, specifically Europe.

conurbation   A network of urban centers that have grown together.

cooperatives   As used in the former Soviet Union, teams of small farmers who cooperate in producing and marketing food products.

core area   An area of dense population that forms the urban-industrial heart of a nation; also the cultural, economic, and political center of a nation or group of people.

cottage industry   A system of manufacture in which raw materials are processed in the worker's home.

Council for Mutual Economic Assistance (CMEA, or Comecon)   The organization formed in 1949 to regulate economic relations between the Soviet Union and Eastern Europe.

criollos   Persons of Spanish descent born in Spanish America.

crop rotation   The practice of using the same parcel of land for a succession of different crops in order to maintain or improve yields.

cultural convergence   The idea that the way in which people live tends to become more similar as development occurs around the world.

cultural determinism   The theory that a person's range of action—food preference, desirable occupation, rules of behavior—is limited largely by the society within which he or she lives.

cultural imprints   Those aspects of culture within a region that are identifiable as coming from particular source areas.

cultural landscape   The mankind-modified environment, including fields, houses, highways, planted forests, and mines, as well as weeds, pollution, and garbage dumps.

cultural norm   A standard of conduct sanctioned by a society.

cultural pluralism   The presence of two or more groups that follow different ways of life within the same area.

Cultural Revolution   The upheaval in China during the 1960s when old cultural patterns were condemned and new Maoist patterns were strongly enforced.

culture   The ways of life of a population that are transmitted from one generation to another.

culture complex   A group of culture traits that are activated together; for example, how clothing is made and distributed to consumers.

culture hearth   The source area for particular traits and complexes.

culture realm   An area within which the population possesses similar traits and complexes; for example, the Chinese realm or Western society.

culture trait   A single element or characteristic of a group's culture—for example, dress style.

Cyrillic alphabet   The alphabet used for Russian and some other Slavic languages.

Damodar Valley   The principal heavy-industrial region of India, located west of Calcutta, with Jamshedpur serving as the region's focus.

Dark Ages   The period from about A.D. 500 to 1000, during which Europe was in political, economic, and cultural decline.

death rate   The number of deaths occurring per 1,000 persons in a given area.

debt peonage   A system formerly used in Latin America to hold the labor force in bondage; debts accumulated by one generation were passed on to the next.

deciduous forest   A forest composed of trees that lose their leaves annually during either cold or dry seasons.

demilitarized zone   The "neutral" border zone that separates North and South Korea.

demographic transformation   A theory of the relationship between birthrates and death rates and urbanization and industrialization; based on Western European experience.

demokratizatsiya   Democratization, which—along with *glasnost* and *perestroika*—is used to define the 1980s reform in government and economy in the Soviet Union.

dependency ratio   The ratio of dependent persons, both young and old, to those in the economically productive age groups.

dependency theory   The notion that a lag in economic development is perpetuated by trade patterns that leave developing areas dependent on or vulnerable to developed realms.

descamisados   The "shirtless ones"; late nineteenth and early twentieth century immigrants from southern Europe who settled in Argentina and Uruguay.

desertification   The process by which desert conditions are expanded; occurs in response to naturally changing environments and the destruction of soils and vegetation brought on by human overuse; takes place on the margins of desert regions.

detente   Improved relations between countries or blocs; referring specifically to East-West political relations.

developed   Used in this book to identify nations or regions with a high level of economic production per person; synonymous with rich, advanced, and modern.

development   A process of continuous change for the better; economically, a progressive improvement in livelihood for an area, country, or people; usually measured on a per capita basis for comparative purposes.

dharma   A Hindu concept that a duty or fate exists for every individual.

diffused culture   Culture traits and complexes that are diffused, or spread, from one region or source to another area.

diffusion   The spread of an idea or material object over space.

double-cropping   The raising of two crops in succession in the same field during one growing season.

Dravidian   One of the earliest inhabitants of India; referring to dark-skinned Caucasoids of peninsular India; also, a family of languages that includes Tamil, Kannada, and Telugu.

drought   A sequence of months or years in which precipitation is significantly below normal.

dual economy   The existence of two separate economic systems within one region; common in the less developed world, where one system is geared to local needs and another to the export market.

Dutch miracle   The massive reclamation of land from below sea level in the Netherlands.

earth science tradition   A geographic perspective in which emphasis is on understanding the natural environment and the processes shaping that environment.

economic base   The set of economic activities from which a region can derive income.

economic imperialism   Domination of another country's economy through trade or competitive imbalance.

economic integration   The evolution of interrelated economies within two or more countries; for example, within the United States and Canada or within the various countries of Europe.

economies of scale   The decrease in production costs brought about by high-volume production; commonly the result of mass production techniques.

ecosystem   The assemblage of interdependent plants and animals in a particular environment.

ejido   A form of land tenure in Mexico by which land is given to a farming community, which may allocate parcels of land to individuals but retains title to the land; a derivative of indigenous Indian land tenure systems, brought back into use after the Mexican Revolution.

el niño   The warm equatorial current of the South Pacific.

encomienda   A grant of authority and responsibility from the Spanish crown to Europeans in Latin America; included control over large parcels of land and became a mechanism by which Europeans and their descendants gained and maintained control over land and Indian villages.

English Canada   That portion of Canada where the English language and culture are dominant.

entrepôt   A center, usually a port, where goods are collected for redistribution; often a transshipment point.

entrepreneur   A person who organizes economic activities.

environment   That which surrounds; the setting, both natural and cultural, within which a group lives.

environmental determinism   A general geographical theory, now largely discredited, according to which the physical environment controls, directs, or influences what humankind does; contends that variations in the physical environment are associated with different levels of economic well-being.

environmental maintenance   The care of physical surroundings that is necessary for sustained productivity.

erosion   The wearing away and transporting of earth materials by moving water and other natural agents.

estancia   A Spanish term used in Latin America to describe a large rural landholding, usually devoted to stock raising, especially of horses and cattle; similar to a ranch.

estate   The term characteristically used in parts of Africa and Asia for a large export-oriented agricultural enterprise, usually owned by a foreign company but using local labor; a plantation.

ethnic group   A group of people who share a common and distinctive culture.

ethnic religion   A religion associated with a particular group and area, such as Shintoism, Taoism, and Hinduism.

ethnocentrism   The attitude that one's own ethnic or racial group is superior; fosters social, political, and economic exclusivity.

European Coal and Steel Community (ECSC)   A common-market-type organization set up after World War II to facilitate movement of coal and iron ore among the Benelux nations, France, and West Germany.

European explosion   The spread of Western culture traits and complexes worldwide; the Europeanization of the world.

European Free Trade Association (EFTA) A group of seven European nations (Austria, Finland, Iceland, Liechtenstein, Norway, Sweden, and Switzerland) that seeks the reduction of tariffs among member nations.

Europeanization Diffusion, throughout the world, of European ways of doing things; began with the Age of Discovery but accelerated with the Industrial Revolution.

Europeanness The set of traits that define European culture, many of which have diffused elsewhere.

European Economic Area (EEA) The integrated European market formed in 1993 by the joining of the seven EFTA members with the twelve EU members into a trade region.

European Parliament An elected body of representatives chosen from the various European Union nations; exercises democratic control over the executive and administrative units of the Common Market.

European Union The common market structure of twelve European countries with a goal of complete economic integration.

evapotranspiration rate The combined loss of water from direct evaporation and transpiration by plants.

expatriate One who no longer resides in his or her homeland.

exploitive agriculture Farming that maximizes short-term income with no consideration of long-term effects.

extensive agriculture A farming system characterized by small inputs of labor or capital per land unit.

factory A manufacturing unit based on quantity production, a distinct division of labor, and use of machinery driven by inanimate power.

fazenda A Portuguese term used in Brazil to describe a large rural landholding; may be devoted to crop or animal production or both.

feed grains Cereals such as maize (corn), oats, and sorghum used as food for poultry and livestock.

ferroalloy A mineral, such as manganese, that is mixed with iron to make steel; gives steel a variety of properties such as rust resistance or strength.

fertile triangle The area of the former Soviet Union containing most of the region's agriculture; corresponds roughly with the humid continental and steppe climates; extends from the western border of the Baltic states, Russia, Belarus, and Ukraine eastward to Novokuznetsk.

field rotation The movement of cropping from one parcel of land to another; a practice common in tropical areas of low population density.

finca Family-size, or small, farm in Central America.

fjord A glacially eroded valley that has subsequently been invaded by the sea.

Flemish Referring to Belgians who speak a Dutch dialect and occupy northern Belgium; one of the nation's two principal national groups.

floodplain The low-lying area adjacent to a river that is subject to recurrent flooding; often provides exceptionally fertile soils because of the covering of alluvial materials.

flow resources Renewable resources, such as trees, grass, rivers, and animals.

food grains Cereals—such as wheat, rye, rice, and maize (corn)—used for human consumption.

form utility The change in shape, constitution, or character of a material to increase its usefulness and hence its value; for example, the smelting of iron ore or the processing of cloth into clothing.

fossil fuels Organic energy sources formed in past geologic times, such as coal, petroleum, and natural gas.

Four Modernizations Development policy and program that China's leaders designed in the late 1970s to promote the country's modernization until the end of the twentieth century; includes four broad sectors for development—agriculture, industry, science, and national defense.

fragmented modernization Development in selected areas of a country that leaves other areas economically lagging; produces regional disparity.

free trade The unrestricted movement of goods among independent nations.

French Canada That portion of Canada where the French language and culture are dominant—that is, Quebec.

frost-free period The period during each year when frost is not expected to occur, based on average conditions.

fundamentalist Islamic culture A culture that bases all social, economic, and political structures on Islam; a movement gaining strength in the Islamic world that reflects a desire to eliminate the Western influences of the colonial era.

fundamentalist Protestantism Includes those Protestant religions in Latin America that are growing rapidly at the expense of nominal Catholicism; emphasizes a literal interpretation of the Bible as the basis for Christian life.

fund resources Nonrenewable resources, such as minerals.

Gaelic A language of Celtic origin; the Irish form is currently encouraged by the Irish government, in addition to English.

gauchos Cowboys of the Argentine pampas.

Gaza Strip A small territory on the southeast coast of the Mediterranean Sea; occupied by Israel since the 1967 war; contains 400,000 Palestinians.

General Agreement on Tariffs and Trade (GATT) A multinational agreement of the mid-1960s by which signatory nations agreed to reduce tariffs and, in general, improve international trade.

geography A branch of knowledge concerned with the study of how and why things are distributed over the earth; includes four traditional emphases: (1) the study of distributions, (2) the study of the relationship between people and their environment, (3) the study of regions, and (4) the study of the physical earth.

geopolitical Characterized by the use of geopolitics.

geopolitics The use of geography, economics, and ethnicity to rationalize politics, especially foreign policy.

Gezira The triangular area, or "island," between the Blue and White Nile in the Sudan; the site of large-scale commercial agriculture, carried on with irrigation water from several large dam projects.

Ghana Empire A West African trading state that flourished from the ninth to the thirteenth centuries but dates from even earlier times; source of the name of the modern nation of Ghana.

ghetto A segment of a city in which minority groups are forced to live because of economic, social, or political constraints.

Gibraltar The British-controlled territory at the southern tip of Spain; serves as a gateway to the Mediterranean Sea.

glaciation The process by which alpine or continental ice and snow accumulations move over and modify landforms; shaped much of the land surface of middle and high latitudes of North America and Europe.

glasnost A Russian term meaning "openness"; refers to a more open policy in social, economic, and political matters that was introduced in the Soviet Union in the 1980s.

global interdependence Increasing economic integration on a worldwide scale, as reflected in the growth of multinationals, joint international economic ventures, and world trade.

GNP gap The difference in GNP between well developed and less developed countries.

Gold Coast The coast of Queensland in Australia, which is attracting great numbers of international tourists.

gold horseshoe An industrial district in Canada extending from Toronto to Hamilton, on the western end of Lake Ontario.

Gondwana An ancient continent that included what is now Australia, Antarctica, Africa, America, and a segment of South Asia.

Gosplan The Soviet Union's state agency charged with making national development plans; usually outlined five-year goals.

gran chaco The vast lowland plain of western Paraguay, northern Argentina, and the adjacent portion of Bolivia.

Great Barrier Reef The 1200-mile (1931-kilometer) coral reef forming a natural breakwater off the coast of Queensland, Australia; site of exotic marine life.

great circle Any line that divides the earth into equal halves; the shortest distance between any two points on the surface of the earth; usually used by ships and planes whenever possible, especially if a great distance is to be covered.

Great Leap Forward China's 1958–1961 attempt to socialize agriculture and increase production in both farming and industry.

Greater East Asia Co-Prosperity Sphere The perception of an East Asian economic system for which Japan functions as the headquarters and provides leadership, capital, and control.

Green Revolution The use of new, high-yielding hybrid plants—mainly rice, corn, and wheat—to increase food supplies; includes the development of the infrastructure necessary for greater production and better distribution to the consumer.

gross domestic product (GDP) The total value of all domestic goods and services output during a single year within one country.

gross national product (GNP) The total value of all goods and services output during a single year within one country (inclusive of GDP and income generated from abroad).

growing season The period during the year that crops can be grown without artificial heat.

growth poles Selected sites, usually urban, where development efforts are concentrated, with the expectation that improvements will spread outward from those sites.

growth rate The rate at which population is added to a region; expressed in percentages or a number per 1,000 persons.

guest workers Workers from other countries who seek employment in the urban industrial centers of Europe's coreland.

Gulf Cooperation Council A regional organization to deal with common problems in a unified manner; consists of Bahrain, Kuwait, Oman, Qatar, Saudi Arabia, and the United Arab Emirates—countries with large oil reserves, small populations, and a location along the Persian Gulf.

gulf states The states surrounding the Persian Gulf.

habitat An environment; the place where an organism lives.

hacienda A Spanish term used in Latin America for a large rural landholding, usually devoted to crop and animal production; formerly had a high degree of internal self-sufficiency and operated under the patron system.

Han Chinese the name used by the Chinese to refer to themselves, to distinguish "cultured" Chinese from others; most of the population of China proper.

hardwood Referring to angiosperm trees, commonly called broadleaf and usually deciduous.

heavy industry Manufacturing that uses large amounts of raw materials—such as coal, iron ore, and sand—and that has relatively low value per unit of weight.

high-level equilibrium trap   Increasing population growth tied to increasing production, so that levels of living remain constant; a situation that apparently existed in traditional China.

Hindi   The national language of India; one of India's several Indo-Aryan languages of Indo-European origin.

Hindu   A person of Indian ancestry who speaks Hindi and adheres at least nominally to the religious beliefs of Hinduism.

Hinduism   A formalized set of religious beliefs with social and political ramifications; the dominant religion of Indian society.

hinterland   The tributary area of a port or city; its size and productivity are usually reflected in the size and wealth of the port or city.

Hispanic   Persons in the United States of Puerto Rican, Cuban, Central or South American, or other Spanish culture or origin, regardless of race; the fastest growing governmentally recognized minority in the United States.

Hispanic-American Borderland   The region in the southwestern United States in which Hispanic influence is particularly strong.

homelands   An outgrowth of apartheid policy in South Africa; ten states that were formed within the country for settlement of nonwhite Africans; intended to function as economically independent units.

human geography   The study of various aspects of human life that create the distinctive landscapes and regions of our world.

humid regions   Those regions that receive precipitation in excess of the amount needed for evaporation and transpiration; normally more than 20 inches (50 centimeters) per year.

humus   Partially decayed organic material that is an important constituent of soils; improves water-holding capacity, provides some plant nutrients, and makes soils easier to cultivate.

hybridization   The selective crossing of different varieties of species of plants or animals to produce offspring with certain desired characteristics.

Iberia   The peninsula of southwest Europe comprising Spain and Portugal; Iberians are persons of either country.

immigration   The legal or illegal movement of people into a country of which they are not native residents.

Imperata   A Southeast Asian grass that invades cleared areas and is difficult to control; elephant grass.

imperialist theory   The idea that colonial-type trade relationships are deliberately perpetuated by more developed countries to maintain less developed countries in a dependent status.

import-substitution industries   Manufacturing concerns that produce needed goods locally rather than relying on importation; often supported by subsidies, loans, and protective tariff regulations.

Inca   One of the four high civilizations of pre-Colombian Latin America, centered on the city of Cuzco, Peru, in the Andes and extending from southern Colombia to central Chile.

income disparity   Significant differences in income between specified groups of people or regions.

income-doubling plan   A plan of the Japanese government to double per capita income during the 1960s and thereby greatly enhance not only the standard of living in Japan but also the market strength of the domestic economy.

Indo-Aryan   Referring to some of the earliest inhabitants of India, who came from the northwest and spoke a Sanskrit language; a light-skinned Caucasoid of northern India.

Indochina   The mainland or peninsular portion of Southeast Asia inclusive of Malaysia, Thailand, Myanmar, Laos, Cambodia, and Vietnam; French Indochina, that portion which was a possession in the French colonial empire, was restricted to Vietnam, Laos, and Cambodia.

Industrial Revolution   The period of rapid technological change and innovation that began in England in the mid-eighteenth century and subsequently spread worldwide; accompanied by the development of inexpensive, massive amounts of controlled inanimate energy.

industrial structure   The mix or set of industries constituting the industrial makeup of a region.

infrastructure   The services and supporting activities necessary for a commercial economy to function, such as roads, banking, schools, hospitals, and government.

inherited culture   Culture traits and complexes that are passed on from one generation to another.

initial advantage   Early factors that propel the development and expansion of particular activities.

Inland Sea   A body of water enclosed by Japanese islands of Honshu, Shikoku, and Kyushu; the small alluvial plains adjacent to the Inland Sea served as an early culture hearth for Japan.

inquisition   A right granted by papal power to the Spanish monarchy during the sixteenth century; allowed authorities to punish non-Christian groups.

Institutional Revolutionary Party (PRI)   The ruling party of Mexican politics, which has held power since the revolution and claims to be carrying on the goals of the revolution; now being seriously challenged by alternative political forces.

intensive agriculture   A farming system characterized by large inputs of labor or capital per land unit.

intercropping   The raising of two or more crops in the same field at the same time.

iron curtain   A popular expression for the boundary between Eastern and Western Europe during the cold war, signifying the difficulty of moving people and information across the border.

irredenta   An area ethnically and historically related to one political unit but controlled by another.

irredentism   Policies or actions aimed at retrieving irredentas from the control of other political units; often leads to tensions between countries.

Islam   The monotheistic Muslim religion that worships the deity Allah; includes principally two groups, the Sunni and Shiite Muslims.

isohyet   A line along which all points have the same precipitation value; usually designated in average yearly amounts.

Jammu   One of two territories disputed by India and Pakistan, located in the high Himalayas and largely under the de facto jurisdiction of India.

Japan corridor   The megalopolitan concentration emerging in Japan between Osaka and Tokyo.

Japan, Inc.   A term used by some of Japan's competitors, acknowledging the aggressiveness of Japanese businesses and government in attaining a favorable position in the global economy.

jihad   A holy war, traditionally declared against unbelievers by the spiritual and secular leader (caliph) of Islam.

job out   To subcontract with a specialized firm or person for production of a specific item or component.

jute   A hard fiber used in the manufacture of bags and cordage, obtained from a species of *Corchorus* and produced primarily in Bangladesh and adjacent parts of India.

Kanto Plain   The alluvial lowland that became a focal point of Japanese culture and politics during the Tokugawa period (1615–1867); locus of growth for the Tokyo-Yokohama conurbation.

Karen   An ethnic minority in northern Thailand.

karma   The Hindu concept of accounting for one's acts, either good or evil, in society; determines status, or destiny, in this life and the next.

Kashmir   One of two territories disputed by India and Pakistan, located in the high Himalayas and currently under the jurisdiction of India.

Khmer Rouge   The communist party of Cambodia, overthrown by the Vietnamese but of continuing importance as an insurgent group and a political force.

kibbutz   An Israeli collective farming community, often located near the frontier; serves defense functions as well.

kombinats   Functionally linked small and large manufacturing enterprises in proximity; usually coastal in location and dependent on imported materials.

Koryo dynasty   The dynasty lasting from A.D. 918 to 1392, during which Korean culture matured.

Kurds   An ethnic minority of Turkey, Iraq, and Iran.

Lacostian view   The notion that rapid population growth alone is not an adequate explanation for development lag; suggests that several underlying factors work in concert to create such a lag.

Ladino   One of two principal culture groups in Guatemala; particularly a person who speaks Spanish and exhibits Spanish culture traits; most often of mixed blood or Caucasian ancestry, but occasionally of Indian ancestry.

Land Hemisphere   That half of the earth that contains roughly 80 percent of the world's total land area; centers on Northwestern Europe, with the Water Hemisphere centering on New Zealand.

landscape modification   The constant change that landscapes undergo in response to natural and human-induced processes.

laterization   A process of soil formation in the tropics; the leaching of soluble minerals from soils because of copious rainfall, thereby leaving residual oxides of iron and aluminum.

latifundia   Literally, large landholdings; more generally, control of most of the land by a small percentage of landowners.

Latin America   That part of the New World south of the United States; a cultural region largely, but not totally, composed of former Spanish or Portuguese colonies.

Latin American Free Trade Association (LAFTA)   A loosely organized multinational grouping of Latin American nations, joined together for economic integration; became defunct in 1980.

Latin American Integration Association   The free-trade organization that includes nearly all Latin American countries; functions as a successor to the Latin American Free Trade Association, which became defunct in 1980.

legumes   Plants of the family *Leguminosae,* especially those used agriculturally, such as beans, peas, alfalfa, and soybeans, with underground nodules that enable bacteria to remove nitrogen from the air and fix it in a form that is usable by plants.

less developed countries   Those countries with low levels of human well-being, as measured by economic, social, and biologic indicators.

level of living   The actual material well-being of a person or family, as measured by diet, housing, and clothing.

liberation theology   A theology based on biblical interpretation granting preferential treatment to the poor or lower classes; gaining acceptance in the Latin American realm.

life-style   The mode or manner of behavior of an individual or group; a way of life evidenced in dress, material possessions, and diet.

light industry   Manufacturing that uses small amounts of raw materials and employs small or light machines.

lingua franca   An auxiliary language used by peoples of different speech; commonly used for trading and political purposes.

llanos   The open, flat grasslands of Colombia and Venezuela, drained by the Orinoco River and its tributaries.

local relief   The difference in elevation between the highest and the lowest points of an area.

loess   Deposits of wind-transported, fine-grained material; usually easily tilled and quite fertile.

Long March   The retreat of the Chinese Communists from southern China to the Great Loop of the Huang He during the 1930s, the result of pressure from the Nationalist forces; an important part of Chinese revolutionary lore.

Maglev megalopolis   See *Japan corridor.*

Magyar   The dominant ethnic group of Hungary, whose language is of the Ugric family.

malaria   A widely known tropical disease that is infectious and recurrent; caused by protozoans and transmitted by mosquitoes; a serious health hazard in the tropics.

Malthusian theory   A theory advanced by Thomas Malthus that human populations tend to increase more rapidly than the means to care for the population.

Mandarin   The principal dialect of the Chinese.

mangoes   Yellowish-red tropical fruit.

manioc (cassava)   A woody plant of the genus *Manihot,* having tuberous roots that are used extensively as a food source in tropical areas; the source of tapioca.

man-land tradition   A geographic perspective that emphasizes the relationship between people and the physical environment used for their sustenance.

Maoism   The philosophy and behavior patterns extolled by the Chinese Communist leader Mao Zedong (Mao Tse-tung).

Maori   The pre-European Polynesian inhabitants of New Zealand, who have been more successfully integrated into modern society than the aborigines of Australia.

maquiladora   From the Spanish verb maquilar, meaning "to mill or to process"; in this instance used to denote foreign-owned (largely U.S.) manufacturing firms that locate just across the border in Mexico to realize the advantage of low-cost labor.

marginal land   An area in which production costs are almost equal to income and little or no profit is possible.

market economies   Nations with a productive system based on capitalistic principles.

Maronites   A Christian sect in Lebanon; Arabic in speech and culture but not in adherence to Islam.

Marxism   The economic-political ideologic system based on the views of Karl Marx.

materialism   Devotion to tangible objects, as opposed to spiritual needs and thoughts.

Maya   One of the four high civilizations of pre-Colombian Latin America, situated in southern Mexico and northern Central America.

mechanization   The substitution of capital for labor in agriculture and other primary economic activities.

megalopolis   Originally the continuous urban zone between Boston and Washington, DC; now used to describe any region where urban areas have coalesced to form a single massive urban zone.

Meiji Restoration   Marked the end of Tokugawa rule in 1868 and the beginning of the period when Japanese society and its economy were transformed from feudal to modern; *Meiji* means "enlightened rule," which in this case meant adopting selected Western traits, particularly education and technology.

mercantilism   The philosophy by which most colonizing nations controlled the economic activities of their colonies; held that the colony existed for the benefit of the mother country.

mestizos   Persons in Latin American of mixed European and Indian blood.

Mezzogiorno   The largely rural and poor region of southern Italy that has been the focus of considerable planning and effort for economic development.

microstate   A political unit of tiny proportions in population and territory; exemplified by Liechtenstein.

Middle Ages   The period in European history from about A.D. 500 to 1350; includes the Dark Ages.

Middle Kingdom   A reference to China, reflecting the traditional Chinese view of China as the center of the known universe.

millet (dura)   A widely cultivated cereal grass, used as both a feed and food grain particularly in parts of Africa and Asia.

mineral deposit   A naturally occurring concentration of one or more earth materials.

Mineral Triangle   The highly mineralized area of eastern Brazil around Belo Horizonte.

minifundia   Literally, small landholdings; more generally, control of only a small percentage of the total farm area by most of the landowners.

Ministry of International Trade and Industry (MITI)   The Japanese government agency responsible for guiding and directing the development of the Japanese economy.

miracle grains   New hybrid varieties of maize, wheat, and rice that produce a greater quantity of useful calories than do traditional varieties.

mixed forest   Woods composed of both deciduous and evergreen trees; a transitional woodland.

modern commercial economy An economic system based on the use of current technology, specialization, and production for exchange.

Mogul period The period (1526–1739) in which Muslim power was consolidated and reached its zenith, controlling most of the Indian subcontinent.

monoculture The growth or cultivation of a single crop.

Mongoloid The major racial stock native to Asia.

monsoon The seasonal reversal in surface wind direction over the southeast quadrant of Asia.

Monsoon Asia That quarter of Asia strongly impacted by the seasonal monsoon winds; contains the bulk of the Asian population.

montaña The eastern slopes of the Andean Mountains in Peru.

Moors People of northwest Africa who invaded and inhabited Spain during the eighth century, thereby diffusing racial and cultural traits to the Iberian Peninsula.

more developed countries Those countries with high levels of well-being, as measured by economic, social, and biologic indicators.

moshav The smallholders' agricultural village in Israel; also functions as an agricultural cooperative.

mulattos Persons in Latin America of mixed European and African blood.

multinational alliance A grouping of several countries into a single alliance for economic, political, or military reasons.

multinational corporation A company with operations in several countries; may exert considerable economic and political influence in the countries within which it operates.

multiplier effect The idea that for each new worker employed in an industry, other jobs are created to support and service that worker.

Muslim One who surrenders to the will of God (Allah) as revealed by the prophet Muhammad; a follower of Islam.

nationalism The emotional attachment of an individual or group to a country or region.

Nationalists The political party of the Chinese Republic, which followed the overthrow of the Qing dynasty in 1911; lost political control to the Communist party in 1949.

nationalization The expropriation and operation of an enterprise by the government.

nation-state A political grouping of people occupying a definite area and sharing a common set of beliefs and values.

natural region An environmental realm with a climate, vegetation, and soil association that is related and interdependent.

natural vegetation The plant life that can be expected in a particular environment if free of human impact.

Neolithic period The later part of the Old World Stone Age; characterized by well-developed stone implements and some food raising.

neo-Malthusian Referring to contemporary adherents of the notions of Thomas Malthus regarding population growth and production capacity.

net migration The net increase or decrease in population that results from a combination of in-migration and out-migration.

New South The urban-industrial South advocated by many progressive thinkers of the late nineteenth and early twentieth centuries who considered agrarianism to be holding back southern development.

New World The American continents of North and South America.

night soil Human excrement used as a fertilizer; a practice common in parts of Monsoon Asia.

nomadism The wandering of a band or tribe over vaguely defined territory, normally gaining sustenance from the raising of livestock; a common economic system used by traditional societies in deserts or semiarid environments.

nomenklatura The old-line communist functionaries throughout Eastern Europe.

North American Free Trade Agreement (NAFTA) Trade agreement signed by Canada, Mexico, and the United States in 1993 and intended to foster trade and economic growth for all parties.

North Atlantic Drift The warm ocean current, an extension of the Gulf Stream, that passes Northwest Europe and modifies the air masses that determine European weather patterns.

North Atlantic Treaty Organization (NATO) A multinational military alliance of Western nations, founded in 1949.

Okinawans Residents of the Ryukyu Islands south of Japan; share a common racial descent with other Japanese but are often treated as second-class citizens.

Old World The continents of Europe, Asia, and Africa.

onchocerciasis A tropical disease that results in blindness; caused by a parasite transmitted by flies; a particular scourge in the savanna lands of Africa immediately south of the Sahara; also called river blindness because of the locales where it is most common.

Operation Bootstraps Puerto Rico's post–World War II development plan emphasizing manufacturing, agricultural reform, and tourism.

Opium War A British-initiated war (1839–1842) designed to protect British commercial interests in China; started when the Chinese refused to cooperate in opium trade; ended in Chinese defeat and treaties that provided the British with access to several coastal ports for trade.

ore   A mineral deposit that is economically profitable to mine; the material mined.

Organization for African Unity   A group of African states concerned with the political and economic relations among African nations and between Africa and other parts of the world.

Organization for Economic Cooperation and Development   Originally established to assist the Marshall Plan fund distribution; reorganized in 1961 and now striving for expanded international trade and development in the poor world.

Organization of Petroleum Exporting Countries (OPEC)   A thirteen-nation group of oil-producing countries that controls 85 percent of all the petroleum entering international trade; a valorization scheme to regulate oil production and prices.

oriente   The eastern lowlands of Ecuador.

orogenic zone   An area where folding and faulting of the earth's crust result in mountain building.

Ottoman Empire   A Turkish sultanate that controlled a large area from southern Eastern Europe through the Middle East and into North Africa; survived for about six centuries until it collapsed after World War I.

outback   The interior and isolated backlands of Australia, particularly those areas beyond intense settlement.

Pacific Rim   Includes those countries rimming the Pacific Ocean in both East Asia and the western Americas; sometimes refers more exclusively to the East Asian rimland countries.

Pacific Ring of Fire   The circum-Pacific zone of earthquake and volcanic activity.

paddy rice   A term used in Monsoon Asia to refer to the rice plant, also to rice grown in flooded fields.

Paleolithic Age   The earlier part of the Old World Stone Age, during which time the human race lived by hunting, fishing, and gathering.

Palestine Liberation Organization (PLO)   An umbrella organization created by the Arab states in 1964 to control and coordinate Palestinian opposition to Israel; originally subservient to the wishes of the Arab states, now dominated by the independent, nationalist ideology of El-Fatah, the largest and most moderate of the Palestinian resistance groups.

Palestinians   The Arabs who claim Palestine as their rightful homeland; some 5 million Palestinian Arabs residing in various Middle Eastern states.

pampas   A Spanish term for grasslands; also used as a proper noun to identify the most important region of Argentina.

pastoral economy   An economic system dependent on the raising of livestock—sheep, cattle, or dairy animals.

Pathans   A Muslim and Pashto-speaking ethnic group of northwest Pakistan and Afghanistan.

patron system   The economic and social interaction of the large landowner in Latin America and his workers; a paternalistic relationship.

peninsulares   An alternate term for Iberians, used in colonial Latin America.

people's democracies   The fifteen republics of the former USSR that were theoretically autonomous; these ethnically based, though not necessarily homogenous republics, are now independent.

people's republics   See *people's democracies*.

perestroika   The "restructuring" of the Soviet economy instituted in the 1980s; entailed changes in management, application of incentives, and sensitivity to market forces in economic decision making.

permafrost   Permanently frozen ground common in high latitudes.

permanent crisis   The continual problem of low productivity in the agriculture of the old Soviet Union; generally attributed to harsh environments, poor management, and undercapitalization.

petrochemical industries   Manufacturing that uses raw materials derived from petroleum or coal; for example, industries producing fertilizers, synthetic rubber and fibers, medicines, and plastics.

photoperiod   Length of daylight, or the active period of photosynthesis.

physical geography   That component of geography that focuses on the natural aspects of the earth, such as climate, landforms, soils, or vegetation.

physiologic density   Population density expressed as the number of people per unit of arable land.

pine barrens   Sandy pine lands of the southeastern United States; considered infertile and not favored in early settlement.

placer deposits   A concentration of one or more minerals in alluvial materials.

place utility   The change in location of a product, usually to increase its value; for example, the movement of oil from the Arctic to the eastern United States.

plantation   A large agricultural unit emphasizing one or two crops that are sold and having distinct labor and management groups.

plural society   See *cultural pluralism*.

podzolization   A process in humid regions whereby soluble materials are leached from upper soil layers, leaving residual soils that are frequently infertile and acidic.

polder   A tract of land reclaimed from the sea and protected by dikes; includes about 40 percent of the Netherlands.

polyculture   The growing or cultivating of several crops for subsistence or commercial purpose, as opposed to dependence on a single crop (see also *monoculture*).

population density   The number of people per unit of area.

population distribution   The placement or arrangement of people within a region.

population explosion   A rapid natural increase in human numbers within a short time period, generally within the last 100 years.

population pressure   The strain or demands placed on an area's resources by a population; the ratio of the number of animals or people to carrying capacity.

population pyramid   A graph that depicts the population of a region by the proportion of individuals in various age groups.

postindustrial society   The evolving society in the United States and other selected countries in which traditional manufacturing activity gives way to the growth of high-technology industry and an employment emphasis on services, government, and management-information activities.

poverty   Material deprivation that affects biologic and social well-being; the lack of income or its equivalent necessary to provide an adequate level of living.

prairie   A grassland area with little or no forest vegetation; normally occurs in response to moisture limitations.

primary activity   An economic pursuit involving production of natural or culturally improved resources, such as agriculture, livestock raising, forestry, fishing, and mining.

primary processing   Manufacturing that uses the products of primary activities, such as wheat, iron ore, fish, and trees; produces goods that may be sold to consumers (e.g., fish) or used as a raw material for further processing (e.g., steel bars).

primate city   An urban center more than twice the size of the next largest city in the country; has a high proportion of its nation's economic activity; most obvious in the less developed world.

private plots   The small plots of an acre or less allowed the workers on collectives and state farms for private production; essential to food production in the former Soviet Union.

privatization   The shifting of government-controlled enterprises to the private sector.

producer goods   A product used to create income, such as a tractor, newspaper press, or processing machine.

production responsibility   Ability of individual farm families in China to lease land from collective units, contract for production quotas, and retain any surplus after quotas are met.

productive capacity   The total amount of resources that can be marshaled in an area with a given level of technology; cannot be accurately measured.

proven reserves   The amount of a given mineral known to exist and to be economically feasible to retrieve.

push-pull migration   A theory used to explain the movement of people from rural areas to urban centers where they are forced out of one area by limited opportunity and attracted to cities by perceived advantages.

qanat   An underground tunnel, sometimes several miles long, tapping a water source; water flow accomplished by gravity; common in several Middle Eastern countries, where they are used to tap groundwater found in alluvial fans.

Qing (Ch'ing) dynasty   The last imperial dynasty of China (A.D. 1644–1911); founded by the Manchus.

Qiqihar-Kunming line   A line of demarcation extending from Qiqihar in western Manchuria to Kunming in southwest China, leaving approximately 90 percent of the Chinese population in the humid eastern third of the country.

quaternary activity   Information-oriented economic activity, such as research units, think tanks, and management-information services.

Quechua   An ethnic and linguistic Indian group of Peru and Bolivia.

region   A portion of the earth that has some internal feature of cohesion or uniformity; for example, the trade area of a city or an area of similar climate.

regional disparity   Distinctive differences in well-being among the inhabitants of the several regions of a given country; most likely to be seen in economic, social, and biologic conditions.

regional geography   That component of geography that focuses on a particular region and the geographic aspects of the economic, social, and political systems of that region.

regional specialization   Division of production among areas, with each area producing those goods or providing those services for which it has some advantage and trading for goods that can be produced more cheaply elsewhere.

Renaissance   The reawakening of the arts, letters, and learning in Europe from the fourteenth to the sixteenth centuries; the transition period between medieval and modern Europe.

resource concept   A focus on anything that can be used to satisfy a need.

restructuring   A shift in emphasis in economic sectors; within the United States and selected other countries, a contemporary shift to the service sector; in less developed countries, a shift from primary to any other sector.

royal patronage   The privilege granted by the popes of Rome to the Spanish crown to appoint all clergy in conquered lands; politicized the upper level of clergy in colonial Latin America and resulted in a close church and state relationship.

Russification   A policy of cultural and economic integration practiced in the former USSR that required all other Slavic and non-Slavic groups to learn the Russian language.

Sahel   The semiarid grassland along the southern margin of the Sahara in Western and Central Africa.

salinization   The accumulation of salts in the upper part of the soil, often rendering the land useless; commonly occurs in moisture-deficient areas when insufficient or salt-laden water is used for irrigation.

Sandinistas   Nicaraguan rebels who overthrew the Somoza regime in 1979 and formed the post-Somoza government of Nicaragua; took their name from an early Nicaraguan revolutionary.

schistosomiasis (bilharzia)   A debilitating tropical disease caused by a parasite and transmitted by snails; may not be fatal but often leaves victims vulnerable to other serious health problems; a particular scourge in tropical Africa where major irrigation projects have been introduced.

secondary activity   The processing of materials to add form utility; manufacturing.

secondary processing   Manufacturing that uses the products of primary processing, such as flour and steel bars, to produce a commodity that is more valuable, such as bread and automobiles.

sedentary agriculture   A farming system based on continual cropping or use of the same fields.

Sepoy Rebellion   A rebellion in India against the British East India Company in 1857; resulted in the British government's extended control over much of the subcontinent.

sertão   A Portuguese term used in Brazil to refer to the frontier spirit and life; the backlands.

Shang dynasty   The period from about 1766 to 1122 B.C., during which most of the cultural attributes of modern China were established.

shantytowns   Urban areas of low socioeconomic characteristics; common in most cities in the less developed world; often inhabited by squatters.

sharia   An Arabic legal code based on the Koran.

shatter belt   A politically unstable region where differing cultural elements come into contact and conflict; especially, Eastern Europe.

shifting cultivation   A farming system of land rotation, based on periodic change of cultivated area; allows soils with declining productivity to recover; an effective adaptation to tropical environments when population density remains low.

Shiite   One of two main branches in Islam, predominant in Iran and in parts of Iraq and Yemen.

Shinkansen   The high-speed railway system of Japan.

Sikhs   A religious minority group of India that has actively sought a separate political territory in the state of Punjab.

Sinhalese   The dominant ethnic group of Sri Lanka; Indo-Aryan in origin and Buddhist in religion.

sleeping giant   A reference to Brazil as a country with enormous potential that has long gone unrealized.

softwood   Referring to gymnosperm trees, commonly called needle-leaved and usually evergreen.

Songhai Empire   A West African trading state that flourished in the fifteenth and sixteenth centuries and centered along the middle Niger River.

Soviet   A Russian word meaning "council"; one of the councils that governed the former Soviet Union through the Communist party.

Soviet bloc   The former Soviet Union and those countries of Eastern Europe that were under strong Soviet influence.

Soviet Socialist Republic (SSR)   The highest-level political-territorial division of the former USSR, in which major ethnic groups are permitted some semblance of self-identity. The SSRs emerged as independent countries after the breakup of the USSR.

spatial organization   The structures and linkages of human activities in an area.

spatial tradition   A geographic perspective that emphasizes how things are organized in space, especially spatial distributions, associations, and interactions.

split technology   The presence of two forms of production, one characterized by modern methods of production and the other by traditional production practices, common in Japan.

stages of economic growth   A theory developed by Walt Rostow in which five stages of economic organization are recognized: traditional society, preconditions for takeoff, takeoff, drive to maturity, and high mass consumption.

standard of living   The material well-being judged to be adequate by a society or societal subgroup; measured by diet, housing, and clothing.

state farm   One of two large agricultural systems controlled and managed by the government in the old Soviet Union; workers were paid wages.

stations   The very large sheep or cattle ranches associated with Australia.

steppe   A large grassland in southwestern Russia; any area of short grass; also, an arid climate more moist than a desert but still water-deficient.

sub-Saharan Africa   That portion of Africa located south of the Sahara.

subsistence agriculture   A farming system in which the farmer's family consumes most or all of the production; noncommercial.

suburbanization   The spread of cities into surrounding nonurban or rural regions.

Sunda Shelf   The area of shallow seas between the Malay Peninsula, Sumatra, Java, and Borneo.

Sunni   The second and majority branch of Islam; predominant throughout most Middle Eastern countries, with the exception of Iran.

sunset industries   Industries in Japan that the government considers no longer competitive and therefore appropriate to be phased out.

systematic geography   An approach to geographic study in which the emphasis is on specified subjects; for example, economic geography, urban geography, climatology, water resources, or population geography.

taconite   A low-grade iron ore formerly considered worthless but now, because of technological advances, an important resource.

taiga The large coniferous forest extending across northern Russia.

Taiping Rebellion One of China's major uprisings (1850–1864), which proved almost fatal to the Manchu dynasty; arose out of local conflicts but quickly grew and spread throughout most of the country, embracing vague principles of equality and religion; failed but demonstrated the weakness of Manchu control.

Tamils The largest minority group of Sri Lanka; south Indian Dravidian in origin and Hindu in religion.

tariff The system of duties or customs imposed by a nation on imports and exports.

technocratic theory The belief that technology increases at a rate greater than that of the population.

technopolises Special industrial zones in Japan, established for the higher technology industries.

tectonic plate One of many sections of the continental portions of the earth, which "float" on a denser mass; at its boundaries with other plates produces zones of instability in which volcanism, earthquakes, and mountain building occur.

Tennessee Valley Authority (TVA) A U.S. regional-development commission charged with the planning and execution of development projects in the Tennessee River Valley; the first major regional development project by the federal government, begun in the 1930s.

terra roxa A soil found in Brazil and other tropical areas that is especially suitable for coffee cultivation.

tertiary activity An economic pursuit in which a service is performed, such as retailing, wholesaling, government, teaching, medicine, repair, and recreation.

Third World Another designation for less developed countries, especially those not included in the former Soviet bloc.

three transformations The three major directional changes enhancing Japanese development, the first after the Meiji Restoration, the second after the devastation of World War II, and the third under way now as a possible economic restructuring.

Tiananmen incident The violent suppression of political demonstrators in Beijing's Tiananmen Square in the summer of 1989.

tierra caliente, templada, fria, and *helada* The altitudinal life zones of the Andean Mountains, which mean, respectively, the hot lands, temperate lands, cold lands, and frozen lands; an altitudinal determination of differences in environment.

Tokaido megalopolis A large, multinuclei urbanized region in Japan extending from Tokyo to Osaka.

Tokugawa period The period (1615–1868) during which the focus of power in Japan shifted to the Kanto Plain area and many of the modern Japanese characteristics were firmly fixed in the culture.

topographic regions Physiographic regions with similarity in surface landforms, such as plains, mountains, or hills.

township A black residential area in or near a South African city; normally offers poor housing and municipal services.

trade development zones Australia's version of the special economic zones used by China and other developing nations.

traditional subsistence economy An economic system, either pastoral or agricultural, in which there is little or no commercial exchange.

Trans-Amazon Highway An east-west highway intended to run the length of the Brazilian Amazon; part of an ambitious project to develop the Amazon Basin.

transhumance The practice of moving animals seasonally between summer alpine and winter lowland pastures.

Treaty of Rome The agreement signed in 1957 by the Benelux nations, France, West Germany, and Italy, creating the European Economic Community.

Treaty of Tordesillas A treaty negotiated between Spain and Portugal in 1494 that divided the New World between those two countries at roughly the 50th meridian, giving Portugal the rights to areas to the east and Spain, areas to the west; this treaty followed a papal bull from the previous year, which had declared the New World as belonging to Spain and Africa and India to Portugal.

treaty ports Those cities in China that were opened to foreign trade after the Opium War and through which foreign influence in China increased.

tribalism Allegiance primarily to the local group and continued observance of the group's customs and life-style.

tribe A group of families or clans with common kinship or ancestry; may occupy a definable territory but lacks modern state organization.

tsetse fly A member of the genus *Glossina*, common in parts of Africa; transmits a number of diseases harmful to humans and domestic animals, thus inhibiting the development of livestock herds in tropical lowland Africa.

tubers Food plants with edible roots or other subterranean parts, such as the white potato, sweet potato, manioc, and yams.

tundra Originally a vast treeless plain in Russia; now the treeless area poleward of the forest limit and equatorward of the polar ice cap; also, the climate of that type of region.

typhoons The equivalent of hurricanes or tropical cyclones; occur in the Pacific, especially in the area of the China seas.

ujamaa A Swahili word meaning "familyhood," expressing a feeling of community and cooperative activity; a term used by the Tanzanian government to indicate a commitment to rapid economic development according to principles of socialism and communal solidarity.

Ulster   The traditional name for Northern Ireland, the six counties that remain part of the United Kingdom and the three northernmost counties of the Republic of Ireland.

underdeveloped   Used in this book to identify the nations or regions with a low level of economic production per person; also designated as less developed, poor, undeveloped, emerging, backward, and developing.

underemployment   The incomplete use of labor, either because a person works only part-time or seasonally or because individuals are employed inefficiently; for example, the use of five people to perform a task that two could do, or a person working below his or her skill level.

Union of Soviet Socialist Republics (USSR)   The former federal state that, as the largest state in the world, stretched from the Baltic to the Pacific. The fifteen former member Soviet Republics are now each recognized as independent states.

United State of Europe   A hope of some for Europe as a unified political system as an outgrowth of the European Economic Community and the European Union.

universalizing religions   Religions considered by their adherents to be appropriate for all humanity; often characterized by proselytizing.

untouchables   The lowest group in the hierarchy of the Hindu caste system; comprised basically of Dravidian people with the most menial occupations.

urban-industrial district   A single region that features both a significant urban population and a distinctive mix of industrial activities.

urban-industrial society   A society in which people reside predominantly in urban settings and work in secondary or tertiary occupations, as opposed to agrarian societies.

urbanism   The social-cultural aspects of city living; the way of life of those who live in cities.

urbanization   The agglomeration of people in cities; a pervasive process throughout the contemporary world.

Urdu   A derivative of Hindi; the dominant language of Pakistan.

valorization   The attempt by a nation or a group of nations to control the price of an item that it produces.

virgin and idle land program   The attempt by the former USSR to expand agriculture to the east, into Siberia and central Asia.

volcanism   The process by which volcanic materials are ejected from inside the earth to form plains, hills, or mountains.

Walloons   French-speaking Belgians concentrated in southern Belgium; one of the nation's two principal national groups.

West Bank   The territory occupied by Israel since 1967 that lies immediately west of the Jordan River and the Dead Sea; claimed by Palestinians.

White Australia Policy   The policy formerly used by Australia in an attempt to exclude nonwhites from migrating permanently to Australia and to encourage whites, especially the British, to settle in Australia; officially termed the restricted immigration policy.

workers' self-management councils   A less-centralized planning approach used by the communist government of the former Yugoslavia from the 1950s.

Yamato people   The Japanese of the Yamato Plain (Kyoto), which served as the focal point of Japanese culture for many centuries, prior to the ascendancy of Tokyo.

Yamato Plain   The alluvial lowland at the eastern end of the Inland Sea; served as the culture hearth for the Yamato people.

Yayoi   The culture group located in Kyushu, from which many Japanese traits and complexes evolved.

yellow fever   A viral disease transmitted by mosquitoes; a severe problem in the wet tropics of Africa.

zaibatsu   A large Japanese financial enterprise, similar to a conglomerate in the United States but generally more integrated horizontally and vertically.

zambos   Persons in Latin America of Indian and Negro blood.

zero population growth   The maintenance of a stable population in which births and in-migration are balanced by deaths and out-migration.

Zulu   A large African tribe of relatively high cultural attainment, located along the southeastern coast of the continent.

Credits

Chapter 1

Opening photo by Wolfgang Kaehler

Figure 1-1	Historical Picture Service
Figure 1–2	Du Boiberranger/Gamma Liaison
Figure 1–4	Jim Lukoski/Black Star
Figure 1–5	John Chiasson/Gamma Liaison
Figure 1–6	Ron Sanford
Figure 1–7	Nicholas Devore III/Photographers Aspen

Chapter 2

Opening photo by Michael Nichols/Magnum Photos

Figure 2–3	Joe Viesti/Viesti Associates
Figure 2–7	Wolfgang Kaehler
Figure 2–13	John Paul Kay/Peter Arnold, Inc.

Chapter 3

Opening photo by Noboru Komine/Photo Researchers

Figure 3–2	Christian Simon Pietri/Sygma
Figure 3–5	Ferry/Gamma Liaison
Figure 3–6	Betty Crowell
Figure 3–8	Jacques Jangoux/Peter Arnold, Inc.
Figure 3–10	Guido Alberto Rossi/The Image Bank

Chapter 4

Opening photo by Eric L. Wheater/The Image Bank

Figure 4–6	Wolfgang Kaehler
Figure 4–12	Jack Novak/Superstock
Figure 4–15	Wolfgang Kaehler

Chapter 5

Opening photo by James Blank/The Stock Market

Figure 5–2	Bob Llewellyn
Figure 5–4	Nicholas Devore III/Photographers Aspen
Figure 5–7	Nicholas Devore III/Photographers Aspen
Figure 5–9	Maxwell Mackenzie/Tony Stone Worldwide
Figure 5–15	Spencer Grant/Gamma Liaison

Chapter 6

Opening photo by Kunio Owaki/The Stock Market

Figure 6–2	Sandra Appel
Figure 6–3	Robert Frerck/Odyssey/Chicago
Figure 6–6A	Jim Stratford/Black Star
Figure 6–6B	Peter Patz/The Image Bank

Figure 6–9   Randy G. Taylor/Gamma Liaison
Figure 6–10   Ken Ross/Viesti Associates

Chapter 7

Opening photo by Alan S. Weiner/Gamma Liaison

Figure 7–1   John T. Barr/Gamma Liaison
Figure 7–5   Randy Taylor/Gamma Liaison
Figure 7–8   Barry W. Barker/Odyssey/Chicago
Figure 7–10   Gerard Champlong/The Image Bank

Chapter 8

Opening photo by Photri

Figure 8–4   Photri
Figure 8–6   Jean-Marc Giboux/Gamma Liaison
Figure 8–7   Hiroshi Higuchi/Tony Stone Worldwide
Figure 8–9   Alain Le Garsmeur/Tony Stone
               Worldwide
Figure 8–10   Robert Frerck/Odyssey/Chicago

Chapter 9

Opening photo by David Barnes/The Stock Market

Figure 9–2   Wolfgang Kaehler
Figure 9–7   Roland Falkenstein/The Stock Market
Figure 9–9   J. Barry O'Rourke/The Stock Market
Figure 9–10   Tony Craddock/Tony Stone Worldwide
Figure 9–11   Paul Chesley/Photographers Aspen
Figure 9–13   Eberhard Shreichan/Superstock

Chapter 10

Opening photo by WITT/Sipa Press

Figure 10–2   Bruno Widen/Tony Stone Worldwide
Figure 10–4   Jill Passmore/Tony Stone Worldwide
Figure 10–5   Kenneth Rappalee/Root Resources
Figure 10–6   Larry Hamill
Figure 10–8   Wolfgang Volz/The Stock Market
Figure 10–9   Robert Frerck/Odyssey/Chicago
Figure 10–10   Paul Chesley/Photographers Aspen

Chapter 11

Opening photo by Blaine Harrington/The Stock Market

Figure 11–4   Eastcott/Momatiuk/The Image Works
Figure 11–6   Linda Bartlett/Photo Researchers, Inc.
Figure 11–7   D. Aubert/Sygma
Figure 11–9   Dr. Kramarz/Root Resources

Chapter 12

Opening photo by Robert Wallis/Sipa Press

Figure A   Fred Mayer/Magnum Photos
Figure 12–4   Erik Sampers/Gamma Liaison
Figure 12–5   Joan Baron/The Stock Market
Figure 12–7   Johannes/Sipa Press

Chapter 13

Opening photo by Laski/Sipa Press

Figure 13–3   Nickelsberg/Gamma Liaison
Figure 13–5   Stein P. Aasheim/Gamma Liaison
Figure 13–6   Wolfgang Kaehler
Figure 13–7   Peter Turnley/Black Star

Chapter 14

Opening photo by Shizuo Iijima/Tony Stone Worldwide

Figure 14–6   Tony Stone Worldwide
Figure 14–7   Mamoru Muto/Tony Stone Worldwide
Figure 14–9   Paul Chesley/Photographers Aspen

Chapter 15

Opening photo by Noboru Komine/Photo Researchers, Inc.

Figure 15–2   Steve Vidler/Leo de Wys, Inc.
Figure 15–6   Brian Brake/Photo Researchers, Inc.
Figure 15–7   Noboru Hashimoto/Sygma
Figure 15–8   Jean Paul Nacivet/Leo de Wys, Inc.

Chapter 16

Opening photo by Australian Overseas Information Service

Figure 16–4   Robert Garvey/Black Star
Figure A   Robin Smith/Tony Stone Worldwide
Figure 16–5   Fritz Prenzel/Tony Stone Worldwide
Figure 16–7   Gunther Deichmann/Auscape
Figure 16–8   Paul Chesley/Photographers Aspen

Chapter 17

Opening photo by Mary Altier

Figure 17–2   Robert Frerck/Tony Stone Worldwide
Figure 17–3   Wolfgang Kaehler
Figure A   Jacques Jangoux/Peter Arnold, Inc.
Figure 17–4   Anthony Suau/Gamma Liaison
Figure 17–6   Sean Sprague/Panos Pictures

Chapter 18

Opening photo by Russell Cheyne/Tony Stone Worldwide

Figure 18–2   Karl Kummels/Superstock
Figure 18–4   C. Allan Morgan/Peter Arnold, Inc.
Figure A   Sarah Stone/Tony Stone Images
Figure 18–9   Fred Chase/Impact Visuals
Figure 18–10   Joe Viesti/Viesti Associates
Figure 18–11   Joseph Lawton/DOT

Chapter 19

Opening photo by Georges de Steinheil/Superstock

Figure 19–5   Klaus D. Francke/Peter Arnold, Inc.
Figure B   Larry Hamill

Figure 19–7   Wolfgang Kaehler
Figure 19–9   Elizabeth Harris/Tony Stone Worldwide
Figure 19–11   O. Franken/Sygma
Figure 19–13   Ricardo Beliel/Gamma Liaison
Figure 19–14   David Perry
Figure 19–15   David Perry
Figure 19–16   T. Linck/Superstock

Chapter 20

Opening photo by Steve McCurry/Magnum Photos

Figure A   P. Frilet/Sipa Press
Figure 20–5   Michael Yamashita
Figure 20–6   Sean Sprague/Panos Pictures
Figure 20–7   Wolfgang Kaehler
Figure 20–8   Wendy Stone/Odyssey Productions

Chapter 21

Opening photo by Daniel J. Cox/Gamma Liaison

Figure 21–2   Alain Degre/Gamma Liaison
Figure 21–3   Superstock
Figure 21–4   Jana Schneider/The Image Bank
Figure 21–5   Wendy Stone/Odyssey Productions
Figure 21–6   M.C. Price/Viesti Associates
Figure A   P. Habans/Sygma

Chapter 22

Opening photo by Sarah Stone/Tony Stone Worldwide

Figure A   Don Smetzer/Tony Stone Worldwide
Figure 22–3   Robert Frerck/Odyssey Productions
Figure 22–4   Barry Durand/Odyssey Productions
Figure 22–5   Kurt Scholz/Superstock
Figure 22–7   Axel Saxe/Sygma
Figure 22–8   Rula Halawani/Sygma
Figure 22–9   Don Smetzer/Tony Stone Worldwide

Chapter 23

Opening photo by Nabeel Turner/Tony Stone
Worldwide

Figure 23–2   Hari Shourie/Superstock
Figure A   S. Compoint/Sygma
Figure 23–3   Kurt Scholz/Superstock
Figure 23–4   James Willis/Tony Stone Worldwide
Figure 23–5   W. Eastep/The Stock Market

Chapter 24

Opening photo by Cheryl Sheridan/Odyssey Productions

Figure 24–3   Lee Day/Black Star
Figure 24–5   Naren Drashab/Superstock
Figure A   Ric Ergenbright

Chapter 25

Opening photo by Neil Beer/Tony Stone Worldwide

Figure 25–3   David Sutherland/Tony Stone
                 Worldwide
Figure 25–6   Nicholas Devore III/Photographers
                 Aspen
Figure 25–11   N. Durrell McKenna/Panos Pictures
Figure 25–13   P & G Bowater/The Image Bank
Figure 25–16   Joe Viesti
Figure 25–19   Sam Wilson/Sipa Press
Figure 25–21   George Hunter/Superstock

Chapter 26

Opening photo by Dallas & John Heaton/After Image

Figure 26–3   Michael Yamashita
Figure 26–4   Alistair Berg/FSP/Gamma Liaison
Figure 26–5   Averswald/Photri

Chapter 27

Opening photo by Michael Yamashita

Figure 27–1   Wolfgang Kaehler
Figure 27–5   Gregory Veeck
Figure 27–6   Michael Yamashita
Figure 27–8   D. E. Cox/Tony Stone Worldwide
Figure 27–10   Doug Armand/Tony Stone Worldwide
Figure 27–12   Brian Payne/Black Star

Chapter 28

Opening photo by Hilarie Kavanaugh/Tony Stone
Worldwide

Figure 28–2   Nigel Dickenson/Tony Stone
                 Worldwide
Figure 28–4   Sergio Dorantes/Sygma
Figure 28–8   Alain Evrard/Gamma Liaison
Figure 28–10   Hugh Sitton/Tony Stone Worldwide
Figure 28–11   Steve Vidler/Leo de Wys, Inc.

Index